THE AMERICAN NEPTUNE

A QUARTERLY JOURNAL OF MARITIME HISTORY

1941
JANUARY

Columbus and Polaris, by Samuel Eliot Morison, *p.* 6.

American Naval Policy, 1775-1776, by William Bell Clark, *p.* 26.

Inspection Comments on American Ships and Barks, by Robert G. Albion, *p.* 42.

Auxiliary Steamships and R. B. Forbes, by Cedric Ridgely-Nevitt, *p.* 51.

A Boy's First Day at Sea - 1886, by William B. Sturtevant, *p.* 58.

The Historic American Merchant Marine Survey, by Frank A. Taylor, *p.* 63.

PUBLISHED BY THE AMERICAN NEPTUNE, INCORPORATED
SALEM, MASSACHUSETTS

$5.00 a year $1.25 a copy

The American Neptune
Fifty-Year Index

Volumes I–L, 1941–1990

Copyright 1997 by the Peabody Essex Museum
Salem, Massachusetts, USA

Co-Published By

THE PEABODY ESSEX MUSEUM
Salem, Massachusetts
and
THE GEORGICA PRESS
Wainscott, New York

Produced in cooperation with TenBroeck Consulting Company
Salem, Massachusetts, USA

ISBN 0-87577-162-9
Printed in the United States of America

Acknowledgments

We deeply appreciate the participation of Donald A. Petrie in the development of this major aid to maritime history research. It was Donald's idea. His enthusiasm and generosity made the fulfillment of this work possible. His concern with making the product of maximum use to scholars led us to broader and more helpful contents and format.

Most particularly, we thank our Managing Editor, Mrs. Geraldine "Jerry" Ayers, for having developed the annual and five-year indices — in addition to all her other tasks — for more years than we can count. She is in so many ways the heart of *The American Neptune*.

Nancy TenBroeck carried out the task of entering some 40,000 lines of information from the ten earlier five-year indices, then supervised proofreading of the entries, followed by the more difficult task of correcting earlier differences and errors. Her associates in this task included the late Thomas T. Howarth. Subsequently, she reworked the entire product to insert the new topical reference material. We are indebted to her for her effective and dedicated pursuit of accuracy and clarity.

John Koza contributed his knowledge of how to organize entries according to the Library of Congress classifications. He put in order the entries of our first fifty volumes of *The American Neptune* to incorporate the topical inventory of materials in the principal articles of the *Neptune*. This was an enormous task and a major contribution to the final product.

John Arrison, librarian of the Penobscot Marine Museum, initiated the first steps in evolving a topical inventory of the material in the *Neptune*'s articles. He broke the way through our untried efforts to distill useful data for the Fifty-Year Index.

The Neptune Staff

Foreword

This index provides a unified alphabetized listing of the entries in the first ten *American Neptune* five-year indices, encompassing the first fifty volumes (I through L). Those indices were themselves integrated from annual indices. The fifty volumes involved were published between 1941 and 1990. Subsequently, the list of topical index entries for the fifty years has been inserted.

The *Neptune* Index is particularly suited for research in maritime history, since it includes the names of captains, masters, and some of the crew and passengers of many of the vessels that are referred to in the quarterly issues. The Index also includes the names of authors and their articles published in *The Neptune*. In addition to the ship's name (shown in *italics*), the specific volume (in Roman numerals), and page number reference in which they appear, most ship entries provide the category of vessel (bark, schooner, steamer/steamboat, etc.), together with the year in which the vessel was constructed (in regular type) or the year to which the vessel is referred in the narrative (in italics).

Because the entry name of the ship is usually cited in full (where known) in its alphabetical order, we have also included a separate table listing the last name of most compound names, inasmuch as some references in articles may cite that vessel only by its last name. Because there may be cumulative references to the same ship over time in several volumes — references which may contain slightly varied data — some sequences of vessels with the same or similar names appear in the Index. Some listings are quite extended, especially when the same name is used for different vessels. The standard entry for an individual or organization is shown either in full or, in some cases, by initials in which the last name of the individual is often listed first. Although Roman numerals are used to identify *Neptune* volume numbers, sometimes they are used to refer to illustrative plates.

The Index also includes the titles of many books which have been reviewed, with references to the *Neptune* volume and page number where the review is located. The small letters "f" or "ff," following a page number, indicate that data relative to the topic continues on the following page or pages. Some geographical features are cited (*e.g.*, Abaco Island, Bermuda). A ship's name with the preceding "ex-" indicates a former name of the same vessel. The letter "n" is used to denote a short note, rather than the usual article presentation.

Changes in the index format and style over the past fifty years have resulted in some variation of index entries; hence, the users of this volume may encounter certain idiosyncracies in the listings. We have tried to minimize oversights, and present a volume that is as all-inclusive as permitted by the information we have.

Readers of the *American Neptune* know that this journal has always had some level of indexing. Annual indices usually appear in the fourth issue of each year. At five-year intervals, these annual indices were combined and published as part of the last issue of each five-year period. In compiling this Fifty-Year Index, the first task performed was combining all the five-year indices into a single unit. During this process, it became clear that, despite the great level of detail already included in the index, there was a bare minimum of subject indexing. A book or periodical index that includes subjects typically traces the subject ideas on every page of the publication. To go back and perform this level of subject indexing on fifty years of *The American Neptune* would be a gargantuan and costly task. Therefore, a decision was made to provide a broad level of subject analysis for the articles, using the *Library of Congress Subject Headings* as a guide.

The *Library of Congress Subject Headings* have become the *de facto* standard list of subject headings for books in academic libraries in the United States. Based on the Library of Congress' collection, the *Library of Congress Subject Headings* provides a uniform list of headings to be applied to all works. One consistent term is selected for each subject so that all works about a subject are located in the same place. For example, a reader could choose from a number of terms to search for information on cars, such as motor vehicles, autos, or automobiles. The Library of Congress has designated the term "Automobile" as the one heading under which all works about cars will be located. References pointing to this heading are supplied throughout the index (*e.g.*, Cars — see Automobiles"). One example from *The American Neptune* Fifty-Year Index is "Seafaring Life," which is used for such terms as "life at sea," "sea life," or "sailor's life at sea." Terms are created by subject specialist cataloguers at the Library of Congress.

The method employed in the creation of this Fifty-Year Index is to treat each article as if it were a separate book, and choose appropriate headings from the *Library of Congress Subject Headings* that represent the major subjects represented in each article. These headings are, by necessity, broad. They do not trace every instance of a subject throughout the journal. Because these headings were created independently from the five-year indices, there is some minor duplication between the original work and the new subject headings. Many of these apparent duplications were retained because a minor variation helps to bring out an additional aspect of the subject.

Whole books have been written on the application of the *Library of Congress Subject Headings*, so the few words which follow, while not a complete guide, will help the reader to work with the headings as they are found in this index. Within each broad heading there can be subheadings, or subdivisions, which help to further specify the subject represented in an article. For example, "Arctic Regions" contains three subdivisions: "Description and Travel," "Discovery and Exploration," and "Fiction." Subdivisions can help the reader home in on specific areas of interest, or sometimes rule out areas which are not pertinent to their research. Subdivisions breaking down periods of time are very common, particularly under the names of countries (*e.g.*, "United States — History — " followed by the various periods in US history in chronological order). Names of countries can serve as subdivisions, as can be seen under "Shipbuilding," and "Privateering." When specific government departments are the subject of an article, they are found under the name of the country, followed by the name of the government department (*e.g.*, "Argentina. Navy").

While the subject index items will be useful for finding items specific to a reader's work, they can also be used effectively by browsing.

Some practical notes:

1. **Boldface** type is used to indicate the subject headings.
2. An indent and a long dash separate the minor subject index headings from major components.
3. Alphabetizing is arranged by putting the subject entries before the ships of the same name, which in turn precede other entries starting with the same words.

A

A. A. Bandel, schooner *(1861),* XV, 103, 122/
A. B., steamship *(1862),* XII, 52
A. B. Howlett, schooner *(1861),* VIII, 215
A. B. Johnson, schooner *(1917),* XXXVI, 268 f.
A. B. Noyes, steamship *(1863),* XII, 154
A. B. Valentine, steamship, XVIII, 230
A. Bently and Sons Co., XXII, 162
A. C. Shelton, sloop *(1862),* XII, 52
A. C. Totten, schooner *(1855),* XXIV, 142
A. Crandal (1861), XI, 279
A. D. Bordes, ship (1884), IX, 298
A. D. Vance, steamship *(1863),* VIII, 228, 233
A. E. Sonyrk, brig *(1861),* VIII, 215
A. F. Beach, steamship *(1884),* XVIII, 233, plate 16
A. G. Ropes, ship (1884), XXVIII, plate XXIV
A. H. Bull and Co., XXII, 177, 178; XXIV, 28
A. H. Partridge, schooner *(1862),* VIII, 222
A. Heard & Co., XXII, 10, 13
A. J. Child, schooner *(1861),* VIII, 215
A. J. De Rosset, schooner *(1861),* VIII, 215
A. J. Fuller, ship (1881), II, plate 26
A. J. Hodge, schooner, XXI, 86, 89; *(1863),* XII, 154
A. J. Ingersoll, steamship (1866), XVI, 243, 256
A. J. Lane, steamship (1885), VII, 148
A. J. View, schooner, XXI, 87, 95; *(1861),* XI, 279
A. J. Whitmore, steamship, XXI, 100
A. Marx and Sons Co., Inc., XXII, 167
A. R. Tilby & Co., XLIII, 297
A. Sewall & Co., XXIII, 15
A. W. Perry (ex-*Beverly*) (1899), XXXVII, 238
A. W. Thompson, schooner *(1861),* VIII, 216
A. Z., packet ship (1847), I, 47
A and A, bark *(1861),* VIII, 215
Aaron L. Reid, ship (1860), V, 148
Aaron Manby, steamship (1821 or 1822), VIII, 133; X, 165–166; XIII, 157 ff.
Aaron Ward, U.S. destroyer (1944), XXV, 227–228
Abaco Island, Bahamas, XXV, 195, 198, 200–201
Abaelino, brig *(1814),* XXVIII, 38
Abarantes, Marquis d', XV, 291 ff.
Abato, Chilean ship *(1864),* XXXIX, 276
Abbans, Marquis Claude de Jouffroy d', XVI, 102
Abbey, Captain David, Jr., VI, 279 ff.
Abbie Bradford, schooner *(1882),* XXXIX, 11
Abbie C. Stubbs, schooner *(1882),* V, 286–287, plate 17
Abbie Carver, bark *(1889),* XLIV, 153
Abbie S. Walker, schooner (1883), Pictorial Supplement, XXXVI, plate XVIII
Abbot, Captain Joel, XXXVIII, 33
Abbotsford, steamship (1870), XVII, 54; XVIII, 68

Abbott, Edwin A., XL, 43
Abbott, Henry, XXXVI, 239, 240, 246
Abbott, The Reverend Jacob, XXVI, 81–95
Abbott, Captain R. H., XVIII, 82
Abbott Lawrence, brig (1849), Pictorial Supplement, XXXIII, plate VI
Abbott Lawrence, ship (1856), XIX, plate X
Abbottsford, steamship *(1870),* XLIX, 24
Abdul Hamid, Sultan, XXV, 173
Abeel, David, XLVIII, 275 ff.
Abeel, Reverend David, XXXIX, 54
Abelia, H.M. escort ship *(1943),* XLIV, 52
Abell, Sir Westcott, *The Shipwright's Trade,* reviewed, IX, 232
Abercrombie, Rev. Doctor James, L, 245 ff.
Abercrombie, General Robert, XLVI, 21
Aberdeen White Star Line, XXXV, 33
Aberenda, supply ship, XXXVII, 138 n.
Abigail, schooner (1815), XXIV, 270
Abigail, schooner (1837), XXIV, 58
Abigail, schooner (1930), XXIV, 58
Abigail, ship, XIV, 7; *(1795),* X, 53; *(1796),* XXXIV, 250; *(1836),* XII, 102, 103, 105
Abigail, whaler, XXV, 105
Abner Coburn, ship *(1897),* XLIV, 153
Aboard the U.S.S. Monitor: 1862, Robert W. Daly, Editor, reviewed, XXIV, 219–221
Aboriginal Watercraft on the Pacific Coast of South America, by Clinton R. Edwards, reviewed, XXVI, 224
Aboukir, H.M. cruiser, XXXVI, 43 n.
Abraham Rydberg, XXX, 219
Abraham Rydberg, bark (1892), II, 289–298, plates 37–42
Abraham Rydberg, bark (1936), XVI, 134
Abrantes, British ship *(1814),* XLII, 106
Abrolhus, ship (1855), IV, 239
Acacia, U.S.S. *(1863),* XIX, 58
Acadia, screw steamship, automobile-carrying liner (1932), XXXIII, 93, 94, plate 4
Acadia, steamship *(1932),* XXXIV, 184
Acantha, steamship (1868), XVII, 138, 312; XVIII, 68
Acapulco, steamship (1873), X, 132
Acapulco, Mexico, VII, 35, 37, plate 4
Acasta, H.M. frigate *(1813),* XLII, 107 ff.; *(1814),* XXIV, 174, 177, 181
Accidence or The Pathway to Experience, Necessary for All Young Sea-Men, or Those That Are Desirous to Goe to Sea, XXX, 40
Accidents. See Disasters; also individual subjects, e.g., Collisions at Sea; Fire at Sea; Ships (Collisions, Fires); Shipwrecks
"Account of the Advantage of Virginia for Building Ships Communicated by an Observing Gentleman, An," Note by Phillip Drennon Thomas, XXXIV, 65
Account of the Construction, and Embellishment of Old Time Ships, An, by John R. Stevens, reviewed, X, 236

"Account of the Scuttling of His Majesty's Armed Sloop *Liberty*, An," by Constance D. Sherman, XX, 243–249

Acerra, Martin and Jean Meyer, *La Grande époque de la Marine à voile,* reviewed, XLVIII, 207

Acevedo, Rafael, XXX, 267

Achilles (1861), XI, 279

Achilles, steamship (1839), XXVI, 12–15, 17, 202–204, 208

Achusnet, whaler *(1851),* XXXII, 35

Ackerman, Edward A., editorial comment, XL, 4; *New England's Fishing Industry,* reviewed, II, 261

Ackermann, XXX, 219

Acme, bark (1855), III, 73

Acme, bark (1901), VII, 319; VIII, 279–288, plates 25–26; XVI, 5, 114; XVII, 65

"*Acme,*" by Harold D. Huycke, VII, 319

Acorn, H.M. brig *(1845),* XXXVI, 128–130

Acorn, schooner, XXI, 92; (1861), VIII, 215, 222

Acorn, steam packet, XXIV, 135, 140 ff.

Acteon, H.M. frigate *(1831),* VII, 191

"Act for the Increase and Encouragement of Seamen, An," 1696, XXXI, 193

Actie, bark *(1875),* II, 333

"Acting Master Samuel B. Gregory: The Trials of an Unexperienced Captain on the South Atlantic Blockading Squadron," by Mark Roman Schulz, L, 89–93

Active (1801), XXII, 217

Active, brig *(1778),* VII, 203; *(1793),* XXII, 87 n., 88; *(1814),* XII, 28; XIII, 279 ff.

Active, brigantine *(1779),* XXXVII, 293

Active, coast survey steamship *(1861),* XXXIII, 46

Active, French ship *(1800),* XXXI, 174

Active, gunboat *(1782),* XXXIX, 216

Active, schooner *(1777),* V, 187; *(1790),* XVIII, 137; *(1862),* 222

Active, ship *(1801),* XXV, 181; *(1802),* XLVIII, 246 ff.; *(1805),* XLI, 285; *(1811),* X, 54; *(1860),* XXVII, 235

Actor, schooner *(1862),* VIII, 222

Acts of Trade and Navigation, XXXI, 19

"Act to prevent Damage by Fire in the Towns of *Salem* and *Marblehead,* An," document contributed by Russell W. Knight, XXV, 146

Acuna, Don Diego Sarmiento de, XXVIII, 252–255, 258, 259

Acushnet, steamship *(1873),* XXXIX, 100

Adam, Edouard, XXVII, plates V, XVII, XIX; XXVIII, plate XI

Adamant, ship *(1777),* XLVII, 8

Adamas, Greek merchant ship *(1943),* XLIV, 57 ff.

Adams, brig *(1806),* XLIII, 250

Adams, frigate *(1814),* XLIV, 172

Adams, ship *(1813),* XLIX, 42; *(1842),* XLVII, 92

Adams, U.S.S. *(1799),* XXXI, 173; XXXV, 238; *(1802),* XIV, 209; *(1806),* XVIII, 183; *(1812),* XXXVI, 207, 215

Adams, U.S.S. (1873), XX, 138, 141

Adams, Abigail, XXXVI, 58

Adams, Captain Abraham, XXI, 41

Adams, Alexander, IX, 65

Adams, Arthur C., III, 357; illustrator of *American Paddle Steamboats,* IV, 175

Adams, Charles Francis, XXXI, 127; XXXIII, 6; XXXVII, 6, 201; XLIX, 119

Adams, Honorable Charles Francis, XXVI, 279

Adams, Daniel, XXXVII, 11

Adams, Captain Edward H., I, 68; II, 129, 209–222, plates 29–32

Adams, Frank P., Sr., "Notes on the Maritime History of Lubec, Maine," XXIV, 38–60

Adams, George, XL, 43

Adams, Captain H. A., U.S.N., IV, 312

Adams, Henry, XXX, 154; XXXIX, 23

Adams, Henry Brooks, *Tahiti, Memoirs of Arii Taimai,* reviewed, XXIX, 148–149

Adams, James L., XVII, 114

Adams, John, I, 297–300; XXVI, 177, 178, 183–188, 231 ff.; XXX, 117–132, 141; XXXVI, 54 ff., 84 ff., 169 ff.; XL, 30 ff., 270

Adams, John E., "Maritime Industry of the St. Vincent Grenadines, West Indies," XXXII, 180–194

Adams, John Quincy, I, 324; XIII, 239; XXVI, 258, 259; XXX, 283, 297; XLVI, 148; XLVII, 27

Adams, John Quincy, Secretary of State, XXXII, 265; XLI, 209; XLII, 26, 169 ff.

Adams, President John Quincy, XXI, 211; XXII, 264, 266, 267, 274, 275; XXIII, 183; XXV, 33, 35–45, 60, 141–142

Adams, Josiah, L, 213 ff.

Adams, Moses, L, 211 ff.

Adams, Captain R. J., VII, 136, 160

Adams, Samuel, XXXVI, 80

Adams, Dr. Samuel, XXIII, 22 ff.

Adams, Thomas, XXXVII, 12; XLVII, 90

Adams, Thomas Boylston, XXX, 283

Adams, William, XIII, 8; XXI, 9

Adam Scott and Co., XXXIV, 48

Adams & Hitchcock Shipyard, 1872–1884, XXVII, plate XXII

Adamson, James, XXXVI, 242

Adario, bark *(1847),* XXX, 237

Adderly, George, XX, 16, 23

Addie Branford, coasting sloop (1898), XXXVII, 165

Addie M. Anderson, schooner (1890), XXVIII, plate XXV

Addie M. Lawrence, schooner (1902), IV, 325

Addie Ryarson, schooner (1865), XXIV, 44, 58

Addie S. Riggin, schooner (1898), VII, 243

Addingham, ship *(1840),* XXXV, 261

Addison, ship *(1856),* XXVII, 73–74; XXXVIII, 205 ff.

Addison Gallery (Andover, MA), I, 196; III, 356; XIV, 14; XVII, 87

"Additional Data on the Dismal Swamp Canal," by Alexander Crosby Brown, VII, 240–242

"Additional Note on *Margaret and Jessie*," by Marcus W. Price, XI, 221–223

"Additional Note on Paddle Box Decorations, An," by Alexander Crosby Brown, VI, 136–137

"Additional Notes on *Ella and Annie*," by Marcus W. Price, XIV, 61–63

"Additional Notes on Later History of American Sailing Ships 'Sold Foreign,'" by John Lyman, III, 264–265; IV, 244; V, 241–242, 327

"Additional Notes on *Star of Lapland* ex *Atlas*," Harold Huycke, XVII, 65

"Address by King Neptune, An," document contributed by John Lyman, III, 85

Addy, Captain John H., XXII, 239, 245, 249

Adee, Alvey A., Secretary of State, XL, 103

Adelaide, bark (1847), I, 49

Adelaide, brig *(1862)*, VIII, 222; XXI, 102

Adelaide, schooner *(1861)*, XV, 122; *(1862)*, VIII, 222

Adelaide, ship (1854), III, 263; XIX, plate VIII

Adelaide, steamship (1830), VI, 210, 211; *(1840)*, XX, 80, 263

Adelaide, steamship (1852), XXVI, 194, 196, 204, 208

Adelaide, transport *(1861)*, XXXVI, 190

Adelaide, U.S. steamship (1854), XXXIII, 86, 94, plate 1

Adelaide, whaler *(1833)*, XLI, 289

Adelaide Baker, ship (1865), III, 65

Adela S. Hills, bark (1874), III, 66, 265

Adele, schooner *(1861)*, VIII, 215

Adelia, tug (1864), XXVII, plate VIII

Adelia Chase, schooner (1875), Pictorial Supplement, XXXIII, plate III

Adelia Chase, ship, XIII, 121

Adeline, schooner, XXI, 101; *(1861)*, XV, 103, 116, 122; *(1863)*, VIII, 228

Adeline Townsend, schooner *(1861)*, VIII, 215

Adelso, schooner, XXI, 95; *(1861)*, VIII, 215

Aden, steamship (1856), XXVI, 23, 24, 26, 29, 203, 208

Adirondack, steamship, XVIII, 224

Adirondack, U.S.S. *(1864)*, XXVII, 43

Adirondack guideboat, XXVI, plates 3–8

Adirondack Guideboat, The, by Kenneth and Helen Durant, reviewed, XLIII, 306–307

Adirondack ice punt, XXVI, 48, plate 6

Adirondack Museum, The (Blue Mountain Lake, NY), XXIV, 231–232; XXVI, plate 3

"Adirondack Museum Boat Building, The," by Robert Bruce Inverarity, XXVI, plates 3–8

Adirondack river-driving boats, XXVI, 48, plate 4

Adjutant Dorme, auxiliary (1917), XXXII, 8, 9, 30

Adkins, Captain J. M., XXI, 105

Administrator, steamship (1842), XX, 250

Admiral, ship *(1861)*, XV, 109, 122

Admiral, steamship (1843), XX, 262; *(1863)*, XII, 288, 293; *(1840)*, XXVIII, 124; *(1847)*, XXXIII, 84, 94

Admiral, The, by Laurin Hall Healy and Luis Kutner, reviewed, IV, 337

"Admiral Bell and the New Asiatic Squadron 1865–1868," by E. Mowbray Tate, XXXII, 123–135

Admiral Blake, schooner *(1861)*, VIII, 215

Admiral Bradley A. Fiske and the American Navy, by Paolo E. Coletta, reviewed, XLI, 233–234

Admiral Dewey, schooner (1898), XXVI, plate XIV

Admiral Dewey and the Manila Campaign, by Commander Nathan Sargent, U.S.N., reviewed, VIII, 157–158; mentioned, IX, 237

Admiral DuPont, U.S. iron sidewheeler *(1847)*, XXXIII, 88, 94

"Admiral George Dewey after Manila Bay: Years of Ambition, Accomplishment, and Public Obscurity," by Philip Y. Nicholson, XXXVII, 26–39

Admiral Halstead, steamship (1943), X, 143

Admiral Harold R. Stark: Architect of Victory 1939–1945, by B. Mitchell Simpson, III, reviewed, L, 146

Admiral Line, XXVII, 151

Admiral Nulton, steamship *(1943)*, X, 143

Admiral of the Ocean Sea: A Life of Christopher Columbus, by Samuel Eliot Morison, reviewed, II, 178–181

Admiral P. Jordenskjold, bark *(1861)*, VIII, 215

Admiral Rodney, by Captain Donald Macintyre, reviewed, XXIII, 288–289

"Admiral Rodney Warns of Invasion, 1776–1777," by William B. Willcox, IV, 193–198

Admirals, Biography, XXXV, 97; XXXVII, 26; XLIV, 179

Admiral Scheer, German cruiser *(1940)*, XIV, 130

Admiral Sims and the Modern American Navy, by Elting E. Morison, reviewed, III, 93

"Admiral Sir Peter Parker's First Ship of the Line," by Marshall Smelser, III, 266

Admiralty, British, I, 304–306

Admiralty Board, XXX, 210, 215

Admiralty Chart: British Naval Hydrography in the Nineteenth Century, The, by G. S. Ritchie, reviewed, XXVIII, 151

Admiralty Court Records, Jamaica, XX, 44–48

Admiralty Courts:
  Jamaica, II, 203
  Tortola, IV, 18

Admiralty Hydrographic Service 1795–1919, The, by Vice-Admiral Sir Archibald Day, reviewed, XXXV, 67

"Admiral Wilkes at the Bermudas," by W. Salisbury, XXV, 140

"Admiral Wilkes Visits Bermuda during the Civil War," by S. W. Jackman, XXIV, 208–211

"Admiral William S. Sims and United States Naval Policy in World War I," by Dean C. Allard, XXXV, 97–110

Admittance, brigantine *(1802)*, XIV, 39

Admittance, ship *(1810)*, XIV, 39; (1834), XIV, 39; XXII, 216

Adney, Edwin Tappan, and Howard I. Chapelle, *The Bark Canoes and Skin Boats of North America,* reviewed, XXV, 295–297
Adolph Obrig, bark (1881), XVIII, 177–180
Adolph Vinnen, ship *(1927),* XVIII, 217
Adonis, brig *(1814),* VII, 169
Adriadne, steamship (1824), XXIV, plate XIX
Adriana, ship, XXII, 266
Adriana, ship *(1798),* XXXIX, 31
Adrianna, schooner *(1861),* XXXIII, 48
Adriatic, steamship *(1849),* XLVIII, 113
Adrien Badin, auxiliary schooner (1917), XXXII, 32
Adrienne, schooner *(1883),* XXX, Pictorial Supplement, plate II
Adroit, minesweeper *(1941)* XXXVIII, 274
Advance, schooner *(1864),* XII, 229
Advance, ship, XXI, 88
Advance, ship *(1850),* XX, 105
Advance, ship (1852), IV, 242; *(1861),* XI, 266, 279
Ad-Vance, steamship, XXI, 91, 92, 104, 106, plate I
Advance, steamship *(1864),* VIII, 233
Advantage, ship *(1590),* XIV, 10
Adventure, bark (1847), V, 147
Adventure, British ship *(1776),* XLVIII, 16; *(1825),* L, 32
Adventure, H.M.S. *(1674),* XXV, 282
Adventure, ketch (1970), XXX, 79, 81–85
Adventure, ship, XXII, 224
Adventure, ship *(1582),* XIV, 269; *(1627),* XIV, 10, 11, 15, 16
Adventure, ship *(1776),* XX, 46; XXVIII, 146; *(1789),* XXXIV, 7
Adventure, ship (1796), Pictorial Supplement, XXXII, plate I
Adventure, sloop *(1770),* XXXV, 299; *(1776),* XXX, 220
Adventure, steamship (1843), XVII, 102; XX, 262
"*Adventure,* A Seventeenth-Century Ketch," by William A. Baker, XXX, 81–85
Adventurer, schooner *(1862),* XII, 52
Adventures (merchant seamen). *See* Ventures
"Adventures of the ketch *John,* The," by James Duncan Phillips, IV, 18–30
"Adventures of Two Women Whalers, The," by Suzanne J. Stark, XLIV, 22–24
Advice, ship, XXI, 90; *(1861),* XI, 279
Advocate, sloop, XXI, 90; *(1861),* XI, 279
Aegean, steamship (1870), XVII, 141; XVIII, 68
Aegger, Norwegian destroyer *(1939),* XXXII, 111
Aeolus, bark, *(1861),* XI, 279
Aeolus, barque, XXI, 94
Aeolus, H.M. Frigate *(1813),* XXVIII, 37
Aeolus, H.M.S. *(1914),* XXVIII, 107
Aeolus, ship *(1805),* X, 54
Aeolus, steamship (1899), IX, 221
Aerial, French ship *(1800),* XXXI, 175
Aeronaut, whaleship *(1837),* XXVII, 99
Aeronautics, History, L, 249
Aetna, British ship *(1738),* XLVIII, 23
Aetna, steamship *(1814),* VI, 266
Aetna, steamship (1815), XVI, 33, 34 n.
Aetos, ship (1854), XV, 188
Af Chapman, ship, XXX, 219
"Affidavit Regarding *Ann and Hope,*" document contributed by Robert H. I. Goddard, Jr., XXI, 73–75
Affondatore, Italian warship (1865), XV, 201
Africa, ship *(1861),* XI, 279
Africa. *See* Confederate States of America; Niger River; Pirates; Shipping (Africa); Slave Trade; South Africa; United States (Foreign Relations); Whaling; World War (1939–1945)
African, ship *(1805),* XLI, 285
African American or African-American: Seamen, XXIII, 192; XXXV, 197
See also Black-owned shipping; Negro Pilots
African Inland Commercial Co., XXXV, 81
African Steam Navigation Co., Ltd., XLVIII, 55
African Steam Ship Co., The, XLVI, 108
African trade, XXX, 174–186, 229–248
African Trading Co., XXXV, 204
Afrika, merchant ship *(1943),* XLIV, 54
Against Wind and Weather, The History of Towboating in British Columbia, by Ken Drushka, reviewed, XLIII, 58–59
Agamenticus, U.S. monitor (1862), X, 18, 31
Agassiz, Alexander, V, 11 ff.
Agassiz, Louis, XLV, 81 ff.; XLVI, 60; XLIX, 36
Agawam, U.S. gunboat (1863), XXV, 113
Agenoria, brig *(1832),* XXXV, 83
Agenoria, schooner *(1808),* XVI, 197
Agero, Charles, XXXVI, 13, 25
Aggie, schooner yacht (1880), V, 86
Agnes, cartel *(1814),* XXVIII, 190
Agnes, schooner, XXI, 96; *(1863),* XII, 154, 229; XV, 125
Agnes Barton, brig, XXVIII, 148
Agnes C. Frey, steamship *(1864),* VIII, 232, 236
Agnes E. Fry, steamship *(1864),* VIII, 232, 237
Agnes Fry, steamship, XXI, 105
Agnes G. Donahoe, Canadian schooner *(1902),* XLIX, 280
Agnes H. Ward, schooner, XXI, 88; *(1861),* VIII, 215, 222
Agnes Louisa, steamship *(1862),* VIII, 222, 232
Agnes Manning, schooner *(1892),* XIV, 122
Agra, ship (1863), III, 69
"Agricultural Roots of Maritime History," by Gaddis Smith, XLIV, 5–10
Agrippina, coal-ship *(1862),* XXXIII, 9
Agrippina, ship *(1863),* XV, 291, 294
Aguinaldo, Emilio, XXXV, 184
Agulia, Mexican ship *(1845),* XXX, 53
Agwilines, Inc., XXII, 176, 177, 178
Aid, schooner *(1861),* VIII, 215, 236; XI, 279
Aigburth, schooner, XXI, 91; *(1861),* VIII, 215; XV, 122
Aigle, French ship *(1800),* XXXI, 174

Aigum, ship *(1762),* XXI, 9
Aikoku, steamship *(1918),* XXIII, 272
Ailsa Craig, Scotland, 1835, XXIX, plate XXVI
Air Line, steamship (1857), XVIII, 233
Ajax, carrier *(1924),* XXXVII, 115
Ajax, H.M. cruiser *(1947),* VIII, 131
Ajax, U.S. monitor (1862), X, 19, 32
Akbar, H.C.S.S. *(1842),* XXVI, 6 n.
Akbar, ship, XXII, 149; (1839), XLV, 181; *(1876),* VI, 108–111
Akin, James (engraver), XXV, 48
Akveld, L. M., Ph. M. Bosscher, J. R. Bruijn, and Kltz F. C. van Oosten, Editors, *Vier Eeuwen Varen — kapiteins, kapers, kooplieden en geleerden,* reviewed, XXXIV, 282
Alabama, bark (1841), II, 324; *(1861),* VIII, 215
Alabama, battleship *(1900),* XXXVIII, 130
Alabama, C.S.S., XXVI, 96–108; XXVII, 39, 265–268, 271, 276–278; XXIX, 5, 14, 102, 167–173; *(1862),* XV, 291 ff.; *(1863),* I, 46, 241; III, 132–133; XXII, 45, 239; XXIII, 262, 268; XXV, 18–28, 105, 110; *(1864),* XIX, 126–128; XXXII, 198; XXXIII, 5, 52 ff.; XXXIV, 63, 82 ff.; XLVII, 118; XLIX, 117
Alabama, sailing packet, XXXVII, 141 n.
Alabama, schooner, XXI, 89, 98; *(1863),* XII, 154, 229
Alabama, ship *(1883),* XL, 123
Alabama, steamship, XXI, 87, 88, 93
Alabama, steamship *(1861),* XI, 263, 279; XII, 154
Alabama, steamship *(1914),* XXXVIII, 191 ff.
Alabama, U.S. revenue cutter *(1831),* VII, 18
Alabama, U.S.S. (1818), XX, 137
Alabama, warship *(1863),* XLII, 98 ff.; XLV, 193
"*Alabama* at the Cape, 1863," by Alan R. Booth, XXVI, 96–108
Alabamas, clipper *(1873),* XXXVIII, 239
"*Alabama* Versus *Kearsarge*: A Diplomatic View," by William M. Leary, Jr., XXIX, 167–173
Alameda, ship (1876), II, 335
Alamo, bark (1855), V, 154
Alandske Segelsjöfartens Historia, Den, by Georg Kahre, reviewed, II, 351–352
Alar, oceangoing tug *(1863),* XLV, 191
Alarm, H.M.S *(1763),* I, 304–306
Alarm, schooner yacht *(1861),* XXVII, 250
Alaska, P.M.S.S. ship *(1869),* XLV, 238
Alaska, schooner, XXIII, plate 1
Alaska, scow schooner, I, 88
Alaska, steamship (1867), X, 130; *(1868),* II, 20, 23, 35, plate 8; *(1871),* VII, 108, 112, 113, plate 11
Alaska Packers, XXII, 214
Alaska Packers Association, I, 336–339; II, 172, 294–295; IV, 200 ff.; VII, 288, 290–293; VIII, 120 ff.; X, 115 ff.; XVI, 119 ff.; XVIII, 210–222
Alaska Steamship Co., I, 80
Albano, steamship *(1887),* XIV, 121
Albany, grain elevator *(1883),* XXXVIII, 141

Albany, H.M. sloop *(1775),* XXXVII, 291; *(1776),* XLII, 11 ff.; *(1778),* VII, 204, 209
Albany, steamship *(1880),* XIV, 280 ff.
Albany, U.S. sloop of war *(1848),* XXX, 264 ff.
Albany (II), steamship, XVIII, 223, 226, 231
Albany and Rensselaer Iron & Steel Co., XLVIII, 129
Albany Iron Works, XLVIII, 107 ff.
Albany Nail Factory, XLVIII, 107 ff.
Alba Smith, schooner *(1862),* XII, 52
Albatross, capture of, in 1848; XXV, 144
Albatross, ship *(1816),* XXIX, 89
Albatross, ship *(1853),* XV, 252; *(1860),* XXVII, 235
Albatross, steamship *(1873),* XXXIX, 105
Albatross, two-sail bateau (1899), IV, 291, 301
Albatross, U.S. Fish Commission steamship (1882), V, 5–26, plates 1, 2
Albatross, U.S.S., XXXII, 3, 53
Albatross, yacht *(1975),* XXXVI, 235
Albay, steamship (1872), XVII, 56; XVIII, 60, 68
Albee, Dr. Fred H., VII, 318
Albee, Parker B., Jr., XLVI, 111; editorial mention, XLIII, 164
Albemarle, Confederate ironclad *(1864),* XVIII, 148; XXV, 73; XLII, 85 ff.; *(1865),* XLVIII, 104; XLIX, 122
Albemarle, H.M.S. *(1782),* XI, 239 ff.
Albemarle, schooner *(1862),* VIII, 222
Albemarle, ship *(1683),* XI, 14
Albemarle, sloop or shallop *(1670),* XXX, 82
Albemarle, steamship (1844), V, 302; *(1862),* VIII, 222
Albemarle-Chesapeake Canal, VI, 52–54
Alberg, C. A., review by, I, 408–409
Albert, H.M.S. *(1844),* XXX, 231
Albert, schooner, XXI, 87, 95; *(1861),* VIII, 215, 222; *(1863),* XII, 154
Albert Edward, bark (1860), III, 70
Albert Edward, schooner, XXI, 98; *(1863),* XII, 154, 229
Albert F. Paul, schooner (1917), III, 60, 163–166, plates 19, 20
Albert Fearing, brig (1845), XXIV, 57
Albert Galatin, ship *(1853),* XVII, 21
Albert Gallatin, ship (1849), III, 262; (1850), III, 66
Albert H. Willis, schooner (1914), II, 243–245; III, 163
Albertine, bark *(1861),* XI, 153
Albert Jeffers, steamship (ex-*Eastern Importer*), XXIII, 276
Albert Kahn, concrete ship (1944), XXII, 179
Albert L. Ellsworth, tanker *(1942),* L, 46
Albert Perkins, brig *(1845),* XVI, 64
Albert Russell, bark *(1888),* XLIV, 153
Albert T. Spears, ship (1883), XVII, 118
Albia, steamship *(1895),* XI, 259 ff.
Albion, bark (1815), I, 45, 49
Albion, fishing schooner *(1853),* XLIV, 83
Albion, schooner, XXI, 88, 97, 101, 102; *(1861),* VIII, 215; XV, 122
Albion, ship *(1814),* XLII, 111 ff.

Albion, ship (1855), VI, 81; (before 1864), V, 151
Albion, steamship (1840), XX, 85
Albion, steamship (1845), XXIV, plate XXII
Albion, Robert G., XII, 4; "Recent Writings in Maritime History," XVI, 66–76, 139–152, 214–228, 286–296; XVII, 157–168, 231–243, 315–325; XVIII, 86–99, 253–267, 325–332; "Writings in Maritime History," XII, 64–94, 163–172, 241–248, 297–304; XIII, 68–76, 141–152, 215–230, 282–301; XIV, 66–78, 142–156, 218–232, 300–317; XV, 83–92, 157–168, 233–244, 311–320; *Seaports South of Sahara,* reviewed, XIX, 309
Albion, Robert G., William A. Baker, Benjamin W. Labaree, Marion V. Brewington, *New England and The Sea,* reviewed, XXXIII, 63–64
Albion, Robert G. K.; "An Appreciation," by Archibald R. Lewis, XLIV, 61–62; XLII, 244; XLIV, 66 ff.; mention, XLV, 41 ff.
Albion, Robert G. K., Jack Bauer and Paolo E. Coletta, *American Secretaries of the Navy (2 Volumes),* reviewed, XLI, 142
Albion, Robert Greenhalgh, XLVI, 221; XLVII, 92; review by, I, 93; "Inspection Comments on American Ships and Barks," I, 42–50
Albion, Robert Greenhalgh and Jennie Barnes Pope, *Sea Lanes in Wartime; the American Experience, 1775–1942,* reviewed, III, 91
Alborough, H.M.S. (1706), XXI, 260–278; *(1763),* XXIII, 175
Albright, Alan B., XXXVII, 81
Album of American Battle Art, reviewed, VIII, 258–259
Albuquerque, L. de, L, 281
Alburkah, side-wheel steamship *(1831),* XXXV, 81
Alcade, Senor Manuel, XXXIX, 272 ff.
Alcaea, schooner *(1892),* XXX, Pictorial Supplement, plates VI, VII
Alceste, British frigate (1819), XXXI, 180
Alciope, schooner XXI, 91; *(1861),* XI, 279
Alciope, steamship (1828), VI, 209; VII, 48
Alcoa Pilot, steamship *(1942),* IV, 174; VI, 134
Alcock, Rutherford, XXX, 158–160, 163–166
"Alcohol Cargoes," query by Charles Edey Fay, IV, 251
"Alcohol Rocks," shipwreck on, allegorical view, XXV, plate V
Alcyone, schooner (1870), XXIV, 44, 45, 58
Alden, John, XIII, 119
Alden, John D., "Born Forty Years Too Soon," XXII, 252–263
Alden, John G., XLVIII, 182
Aldham, Alfred Robert, XXVI, 203
Aldrich, Thomas Bailey, XXV, 65
Aldrich, William T., I, 82
Aldridge, Alfred O., XXXIV, 126 ff.
Aldworth, Robert, XX, 10; XXXVII, 11
Aldworth, Thomas, XXXVII, 11
Alecto, H.M.S. *(1845),* XXXVI, 138, 140–142
Alert (1800), XXIII, 216

Alert, bark *(1856),* XL, 121; *(1862),* XXVII, 265
Alert, brig, XXII, 212; *(1798),* XXXIII, 160 ff.; *(1835),* XXIX, 87
Alert, H.M.S. *(1897),* XXVIII, 89, 98
Alert, lighthouse tender *(1861),* XL, 298; XLVIII, 87
Alert, sailing cutter, XXIV, 14
Alert, Salem-built brigantine *(1798),* XLIX, 272
Alert, schooner, XXI, 93, 94, 100, 102; *(1861),* VIII, 215, 223; XV, 125
Alert, ship *(1800),* XL, 48; *(1804),* XLI, 228, 301; XLV, 110; *(1828),* XII, 177, 181–185; XIII, 172–176; *(1862),* XXXIII, 52 ff.; *(1864),* XLVII, 121, 165; L, 32; *(1967),* XXXIX, 182
Alert, sloop *(1814),* XXIX, 195
Alert, steamship *(1860),* XXI, 143
Alert, U.S.S. (1873), XX, 139
Alexander, schooner, XXI, 86; *(1862),* VIII, 223; XII, 52
Alexander, ship *(1799),* XVIII, 122; *(1800),* XL, 47; *(1801),* XXIII, 211; *(1827),* VI, 10
Alexander, steam bark *(1894),* XXXVIII, 85
Alexander, steamship (1865), XVIII, 68
Alexander (II), steamship, XVII, 304 ff.
Alexander, Arthur J., "A Footnote on Massachusetts' Deserters who went to Sea during the American Revolution," X, 43–51
Alexander, R. H. XXXVI, 232
Alexander I, Emperor, XXX, 287
Alexander II, Czar, coronation of, XXV, 223
Alexander Cooper, schooner *(1863),* VIII, 228; XVIII, 145
"Alexander Dalrymple, Hydrographer," by W. A. Spray, XXX, 200–216
Alexander Denny and Bros., XXVI, 191, 207
Alexander Duncan, tanker *(1875),* XXXVIII, 176 ff.
Alexander Gordon & Co., XLVII, 90
Alexander Hall and Co., XXII, 44
Alexander Hamilton, steamship *(1956),* XVIII, 234
Alexander Hamilton, U.S.C.G. (1921), XX, 142
Alexander Hogsdon, ship *(1802),* XXII, 208; XXIV, 264
Alexander LaValley, steam crane boat (1887), XXIV, 198, 199
Alexander Mansfield, ship *(1811),* XII, 105
Alexander McNeil, bark (1860), III, 264
Alexander Nevsky, Russian warship *(1863),* XX, 52, 53, 55, 56, 58, 59
Alexander Stephen and Sons, XXVI, 132, 208; XLIII, 124 ff.
"Alexander Stuart," query by M. V. Brewington, VI, 153
Alexander the Great, VII, 261–263
Alexandra, XXIX, 19, 21, 22
Alexandra, bark (1828), III, 73
Alexandra, bark (1836), III, 68
Alexandra, H.M.S. (1884), XXVIII, 65
Alexandra, sloop yacht *(1907),* XXXVI, 243–246, plate 6
Alexandria, British ship *(1810),* XLII, 115
Alexine, bark (1862), V, 327
Alfonseau, schooner, XXI, 97

Alfonso V, King of Portugal, XXXIX, 251, 253
Alfonso XII, Spanish ship *(1898),* XLI, 100
Alfred, brig *(1812),* XXII, 216; *(1813),* XXVIII, 188
Alfred, Continental Navy ship *(1776),* XXV, 193, 195, 200, 204, 209, 211, 213–215
Alfred, schooner *(1850),* XLV, 125
Alfred, ship *(1766),* XXVIII, 49–52, plate 2; XLVIII, 158; *(1778),* XLIII, 27; *(1779),* XXXVII, 293
Alfred, ship (1800), II, 283; *(1812),* XXI, 18; *(1814),* I, 120
Alfred, steamship *(1864),* VIII, 233; XVII, 259
Alfred, U.S.S. *(1775),* XVIII, 303; *(1777),* XIV, 49, 56
Alfred, warship *(1775),* XL, 13
Alfred Allen, schooner *(1811),* XXXIV, 245
Alfred D. Snow, ship *(1888),* IX, 68
Alfred Gibbs, bark (1851), II, 330
Alfred Holt & Co., XXVI, 148
Alfred Jones, launch *(1930),* XXXIX, 180
Alger, Russell A., Secretary of War, XL, 169 ff.
Algiers, 1815, view of; III, plate 6
Algiers, 1828, view of; XXIX, 56, plate XV
Alhambra, schooner *(1940),* III, 163
Alhambra, ship *(1846–1857),* XLII, 122
Alhambra, ship (1859), III, 171; *(1861),* XI, 279
Alhambra, steamship *(1864),* XXXVII, 234
Alice, British brig *(1889),* XXVI, 174; XXXVII, 88
Alice, schooner *(1861),* XI, 279; XII, 133
Alice, ship *(1795),* XII, 162
Alice, sloop *(1791),* XLI, 168
Alice, sloop yacht *(1866),* XXX, 199
Alice, steamship, XXI, 81, 88–90, 101–102, 106; *(1863),* VIII, 228, 232; IX, 39, 40; *(1864),* XI, 276; XII, 52, 154, 229
Alice, vessel *(1864),* XXXVI, 204
Alice Ball, ship XXI, 93; *(1861),* XI, 279
Alice Brown, schooner (1819), XXIV, 58
Alice C. Wentworth, schooner (1905), IX, 179
Alice Counce, ship (1853), II, 246
Alice D. Cooper, ship (1874), III, 63
Alice Dollar, merchant ship *(1937),* L, 260 ff.
Alice Gertrude, Canadian schooner *(1902),* XLIX, 280
Alice Ida, schooner *(1861),* VIII, 215
Alice Knowles, whaling bark, inboard profile, Pictorial Supplement, XXXI, plate XXIX
Alice Lee, schooner *(1861),* XI, 279; XV, 114, 122
Alice M. Jacobs, steamship *(1902),* XLIV, 116
Alice M. Lawrence, schooner (1906), IV, 325; XXIII, plate XXIII
Alice M. Moran, steam tug (1946), XXIV, 137
Alice May Davenport, schooner, XXIV, 25
Alice Royce, schooner (1890), I, 75
Alice S. Wentworth, schooner (1905), Pictorial Supplement, XXXVI, plate XXIX
Alice Vivian, steamship, XXI, 86; *(1863),* XII, 154
Alicia, schooner *(1862),* XV, 125
Alicia B. Crosby, schooner, XXIII, plate I; *(1902),* XXIV, 51

Alicia Haviside, barkentine (1920), V, 82
Alida, steamship *(1855),* XIV, 163
Alien and Sedition Acts, XXX, 119
Alijador del lago, Lake Albufera (Valencia), I, 357–359
Ali Saib Pasha, steamship *(1886),* XI, 258 ff.
Al Jones, schooner *(1861),* XI, 279; XII, 52
Allaire, James P., XII, 148
Allaire Iron Works, XLVIII, 119
Allan, Captain George W., XXIV, 39, 59
Allan, John, XLVI, 261
Allan, Colonel John, XLII, 17
Allan A. Chapman, brig, XXI, 95; *(1861),* XI, 279
Allan Line, XXXVII, 236
Allanwilde, barkentine, XXXV, plate 4
Allard, Dean C., "Admiral William S. Sims and United States Naval Policy in World War I," XXXV, 97–110; "Naval Technology During the American Civil War," XLIX, 114–122
Allard, Dean Conrad, Jr., *Spencer Fullerton Baird and the U. S. Fish Commission: A Study in the History of American Science,* reviewed, XLII, 306–307
Allardyce, Governor William Lamond, XLIX, 282
Allas Straits, XXX, 208
Allcard, Edward C., *Single-handed Passage,* reviewed, X, 235–236
Allefonsce, Jean, XI, 99
Allegator, steamship *(1865),* XLIII, 212
Alleghany, iron steam frigate (1843), XXIV, 8 ff., plate 2
Alleghany, schooner (1804), VII, 317
Alleghany, U.S.S. *(1848),* XIX, 244
Allegheny, tanker (1890), XXXVIII, 178 ff.
Allen, wooden steamship *(1917),* XXXV, 279
Allen, Captain Benjamin, XXIII, 24
Allen, Captain Charles H., Jr., XLVII, 121
Allen, E. B., VII, 61
Allen, Captain Edward, XIII, 42
Allen, Edward W., *The Vanishing Frenchman: The Mysterious Disappearance of LaPérouse,* reviewed, XX, 71
Allen, Gardner W., XXXIX, 209; XL, 10
Allen, George, XXIX, 134, 137
Allen, Captain George, VII, 119, 121, 122
Allen, George F., XIV, 237 ff.
Allen, George H., XLVII, 119
Allen, Henry, XXXVIII, 206 ff.
Allen, Horatio, XLVIII, 112
Allen, Jay, I, 101, 103; III, 357
Allen, Jeremiah, XXI, 213
Allen, John, XXXIV, 210
Allen, Captain Joseph, XIV, 43
Allen, Captain L., XX, 89 n.
Allen, Malachi, XXXIV, 200
Allen, Mrs., XXX, 62–67
Allen, Nellie, XXXVIII, 206 ff.
Allen, Seth, VII, 112
Allen, Solomon III, XIII, 269; XLVI, 214
Allen, Timothy Henry, XXXV, 297

Allen, Captain Thomas, XVI, 245; XVIII, 82
Allen, William, XLVII, 122
Allen, Captain William W., XVIII, 82
Allen, Rev. Young J., *A Diary of a Voyage to China, 1859–1860,* reviewed, IV, 256
Allen: Family, chart of, XLVII, 122
Allen & Co., XLIII, 215
Allerton, ship, XXXVI, 3; *(1748),* I, 297
Alley, Captain Perry W., IX, 172–173
"All Hands Aboard Scrimshawing," by Marius Barbeau, XII, 99–122
All Hands Aloft! An Account of the Voyage of the Square-Rigger Arapahoe *to Manila in 1918,* by Lou A. Schmitt, reviewed, XXVI, 224–225
"All Hands Reef Topsails," Pictorial Supplement, XXXI, plate XXI
Alliance, American frigate *(1777),* XXXI, 244
Alliance, blockade ship, XXI, 89
Alliance, Continental frigate *(1781),* XXVI, 63, 141–144, 210–214; XXVIII, 200, 203; *(1785),* XXXVI, 55; XXXIX, 30, 165
Alliance, ship, XXV, 182
Alliance, steamship *(1837),* VII, 305; VIII, 38; *(1840),* XX, 80; *(1861),* VIII, 215; *(1863),* XXI, plate XIX; *(1864),* XV, 128
Alliance, steamship (1857), III, 138
Alliance, U.S. frigate (1777), XXII, 271; XXV, 255 ff.
Alliance, U.S.S. *(1781),* XIII, 65; XLI, 282; XLIV, 169
Alliance, U.S.S. (1873), XX, 138
"*Alliance,* The Voyage of." See "Voyage of the Alliance."
Allied Maritime Transport Council, XLI, 266
Alligator, gunboat *(1814),* XLII, 105; XLIV, 172
Alligator, schooner, XXI, 90; *(1821),* XXXII, 266 ff.; *(1862),* VIII, 223; XV, 116, 125
Alligator, steamship (1888), VII, 159
Alligator, submarine *(1863),* XLIX, 122
Allin, Lawrence C., "The First Cubic War—The *Virginius* Affair," XXXVIII, 233–248; "Ill-Timed Initiative: The Ship Purchase Bill of 1915," XXXIII, 178–198; "S.S. *Bangor*: Harbinger of Destiny," XXXIX, 218–224; "*Telos,* the Last American Brig and Bangor River's Class of '83," XLIX, 29–33
Allis, Frederick S., Jr. and Philip Chadwick Foster Smith (editors), *Seafaring in Colonial Massachusets,* reviewed, XLII, 69–71
Allison, James, Editor, "Five Dana Letters," XIII, 162–176; Editor, "Journal of a Voyage from Boston to the Coast of California," by Richard Henry Dana, Jr., XII, 177–185
Alloway, N. J., XXXVI, 252 ff.
"All Souls Saved," by Freeman Cleaves, XXVII, 61–65
Allyn, Edwin, XXXIV, 91
Allyn, Captain Gurdon, XLI, 289
Alma (l'Alma), steamship (1855), XXVI, 25, 28, 118
Alma, bark (1854), XXX, 294
Alma, schooner, XXI, 105; *(1864),* XII, 229

Almaz, Russian warship *(1863),* XX, 53, 55, 56, 57
Almeida, bark (1848), I, 49
Almira, schooner *(1804),* XLIII, 43
Almirantazgo de Castilla, El, by Florencio Pérez Embid, reviewed, VII, 250
Almirante Cochrane, Chilean ironclad (1874), XXXIX, 275
Almira Robinson, ship (1874), II, 335
"Almost Down East," by John C. Bower, Jr., XLV, 253
Almy, Commander J., XVII, 256
Almy, William, XXXVIII, 209
Alodia, sloop, XXII, 95
Aloha, bark-yacht (1910), XXXIII, 63
Aloha, yacht *(1908),* XXXVI, 245, 246
Along the Waterfront, by Lieutenant Commander H. M. Delanty, U.S.N.R. (ret.), reviewed, IV, 340
Alpha, steamship *(1858),* IX, 74
Alpha, steamship *(1884),* XXXIV, 177
Alphen, Dutch frigate *(1778),* XXXVI, 165 n.
Alphonsine, schooner *(1861),* XI, 279; XII, 52
Alpine, brig, XXI, 95. *(1861),* XI, 279
Alsace, auxiliary schooner *(1917),* XXXII, 32
Alsberg, Libby, review by, XLVI, 129
Alta, barkentine (1900), I, 397
Altair, schooner *(1901),* XXXVIII, 88
Altamaha, brig *(1862),* XXVII, 265
Althea, bark (1847), III, 68
Althea, schooner *(1861),* XI, 279
Altmark Affair, XXV, 140
Altobelli, Richard J., "Captain Nicholas Thorndike, Mariner and Merchant," XXIV, 247–271
Altona, steamship (1872), XVIII, 68
Alva, yacht *(1892),* XLVII, 127
Alvarado, bark *(1861),* XI, 151
Alvarado, prize brig *(1861),* XV, 122
Alvarado, Juan, XXXII, 119
Alvarez, General Don Fermin Jaudenes y, XXXV, 184
Alvena, four-masted schooner, XXXIV, 147
Alvord, Colonel Benjamin, XXXIV, 271
Always Ready! The Story of the United States Coast Guard, by Kensil Bell, reviewed, IV, 176
Amanda, bark (1852), XLV, 183
Amanda, schooner *(1864),* XII, 229
Amaranth, schooner *(1863),* XII, 154
Amarapoora, steamship (1871), XVII, 138
A Maritime History of Bath, Maine and the Kennebec River Region, reviewed, XXXIV, 285
Amazon, bark *(1861),* XV, 108; XXI, 256
Amazon, brig *(1813),* XV, 60
Amazon, ship *(1814),* I, 122
Amazon, ship (1854), I, 47
Amazon, steamship (1865), XV, 131
Amazonas, Chilean transport (1864), XXXIX, 275
Amazon Explorations, 1851–1852, XXXI, 8
Ambassador, ship, XXVIII, 124
Amberman, Captain John C., XVI, 14, 107 ff.; XVII, 65
Ambition, sloop *(1864),* XV, 112, 128

Ambra, submarine *(1942),* XXVII, 201
Ambres, steamship *(1863),* XX, 179
Ambriz, British steam ship *(1893),* XXXIX, 175
Ambrose, ship *(1630),* XXIII, 63, 65
Ambuscade, warship, XLI, 85
Amelia (1799), XXVII, 144 n., 145
Amelia, schooner, XXI, 88; *(1861),* VII, 19; VIII, 215, 228
Amelia, whaling schooner, inboard profile, Pictorial Supplement, XXXI, plate XXIX
Amelia Ann, schooner *(1863),* XII, 154
Amelia F. Cobb, schooner, XXVIII, 148
America, bark *(1849),* IV, 331
America, brig *(1803),* Pictorial Supplement, XXXII, plate IV
America, brig *(1824),* XIX, 16
America, British ship *(1749),* XLVIII, 26
America, grain elevator *(1949),* XXXVIII, 139
America, liner *(1936),* XXXVI, 8
America, schooner *(1777),* V, 187
America, schooner *(1850),* XV, 125; *(1851),* XI, 245 ff.; XII, 154, 239–240
America, schooner yacht *(1855),* XXXVI, 172; *(1860),* XXVII, 233 ff.
America, schooner yacht (1890), XXX, Pictorial Supplement, plate I
America, ship *(1774),* XLII, 302; *(1795),* XVIII, 137–141; XLI, 174; XLIV, 23
America, ship (1804), Pictorial Supplement, XXXVIII, plate XIII; *(1804),* XIII, 247
America, ship (1846), IV, 73
America, ship *(1861),* XXI, 242, 258
America, ship (1864), II, 333
America, ship of the line, XXVIII, 196
America, sloop *(1856),* X, 231 ff.; *(1862),* VIII, 223
America, steamship, XVIII, 230
America, steamship *(1831),* VII, 42
America, steamship (1840), XX, 85; *(1850),* XXXVII, 233; *(1853),* XXXIV, 98
America, steamship (1868), X, 130, 131, 134; (1869), II, 8, 36–37, plates 6, 7
America, steamship (1934), XXIX, 233, 235
America, steamship (1940), I, 188
America, steamship (Pacific Mail) (1868), XXV, 231
America, steamship (U.S. Lines) (1940), XXV, 224
America, twin-engine seaplane (1917), XLVII, 249
America, U.S. aircraft carrier (1964), XXV, 224
America (ex-*Pompey*), ship *(1789),* Pictorial Supplement, XXXII, plates II, III, V; *(1800),* XXIII, 216
America (former French frigate *Blonde*), Pictorial Supplement, XXXII, plate IV
America:
  Discovery and exploration, XI, 95
  —, Early accounts (to 1600), XLV, 249
  See also Central America; Shipping; United States (History)
American, bark *(1861),* XV, 108 n.; XXI, 256
American, ship *(1847),* XXXVII, 250
American, yacht *(1892),* XXXVI, 235, 236
Americana, schooner, XXVIII, 224
Americana, topsail schooner (1892), II, 326, plate 45; III, 261
American Activities in the Central Pacific 1790–1870, R. Gerard Ward, Editor, reviewed. Vol. 1, XXVII, 285–286; Vol. 2, XXVIII, 293–294; Vols. 3 and 4, XXIX, 69–70; Vols. 5, 6, and 7, XXIX, 291
American Agricultural Chemical Co., XXIV, 27, 37
"American and British Naval Historians and the American Revolutionary War, 1875–1980," by David Syrett, XLII, 179–192
"American and Canadian Fishing Schooners," by A. M. Barnes, XXVI, plates I-VIII, 64; plates IX-XVI, 140; plates XVII-XXXIV, 200; plates XXV-XXXII, 242
American and West African Steamship Co., XXXV, 204
American Association of Museums, The; mentioned, XL, 163
American Battleships, 1886–1923, by John C. Reilly, Jr. and Robert L. Scheina, reviewed, XLI, 231–233
American Bethel Society, XXXIX, 47
American Board of Customs Commissioners, XXVII, 218, 219; XXXI, 193
"American-built Vessels Owned in the Bristol Channel," by Grahame E. Farr, VI, 80–83
American Bureau of Shipping, XXII, 173; XXX, 24, 31, 32
American Civil War, XXIX, 6
American Coast Pilot, XXX, 41; XXI, 5–15; XXV, 46–49, plate 2
American Colonization Society, XXXII, 264
American Colonization Society, Baltimore, XXXV, 83; XXXVIII, 52
"American Commodore in the Argentine Navy, An," by Phyllis DeKay Wheelock, VI, 5–18
"American Concrete Steamers of the First and Second World Wars," by Jean Haviland, XXII, 157–183
American Congress, packet ship (1849), I, 44, 47
American Express, XXXIV, 246
American Figureheads and their Carvers, by Pauline A. Pinckney, reviewed, I, 178–181
American Fishermen, by Albert Cook Church and James B. Connolly, reviewed, I, 181–182
American Fishing Schooners 1825–1935, The, by Howard I. Chapelle, reviewed, XXXIV, 142–144
"American Four Mast Bark *Star of Poland,* ex-*Acme,* The," by Harold D. Huycke, VIII, 279–288
American Fuel Oil and Transportation Co., XXII, 170, 171
American Fur Co., XXVIII, 132
American Geographical and Statistical Society, 1851, XXXI, 8
American Girl, schooner (1875), V, 86
American Hampton Roads Line, XXIX, 233
American-Hawaiian Steamship Co., II, 326; XLIV, 154
American Hawaiian Steamship Co., XXIX, 231

"American Invasion of Nassau in the Bahamas, The," by John J. McCusker, Jr., XXV, 188–217, plates 21, 22

American Iron and Steel Institute, XXXV, 278

"American Ketches," by John Lyman, XI, 291

"American Ketches," query by John Lyman, III, 177

American "Little Men": (Williams-Thaxter, Boston and Marblehead), XXXIV, "B" plate 10; (unidentified, New York State Historical Assoc., Cooperstown, N. Y.), XXXIV, "C" plate 10; (James Fales, New Bedford), XXXIV, "D" plate 10; (Riggs & Brother, Philadelphia), XXXIV, "E" plate 10

American Lloyd's Register of American and Foreign Shipping, XXX, 21

American Lloyd's Universal Register of Shipping, XXX, 21, 34

American Lloyd's Universal Standard Record of Shipping, XXX, 22

American Marines in the Revolutionary War, by Rowland P. Gill and Henry I. Shaw, Jr., XXXI, 4

American Maritime Industries and Public Policy, 1789–1914, The, by John G. B. Hutchins, reviewed, II, 260–261

American Maritime Prints, reviewed, XLVI, 120

"American Maritime Prisoners of War, 1812–1815," NASOH paper given by Captain Ira Dye, XXXVII, 81

American Merchant, steamship *(1933)*, XIV, 127

"American Merchant and Naval Contacts with China, 1784–1850," by E. Mowbray Tate, XXXI, 177–191

"American Merchant Marine Library Association: The First Decade of Its Development, 1921–1930, The," by James G. Neal, XLI, 5–24

American Merchant Sailing Vessels of the Nineteenth Century, Mariners' Museum, reviewed, XI, 234

American Museum of Natural History, VI, 233.

"American Naval Guns, 1775–1785," by M. V. Brewington, III, 11–18, 148–158

"American Naval Policy, 1775–1776," by William Bell Clark, I, 26–41

"American Naval Prints at the Grolier Club," by Charles D. Childs, III, 5–10

American Naval Revolution, The, by Walter R. Herrick, Jr., reviewed, XXVII, 286–287

American Navigation Co., XXXVIII, 196 ff.

American Navy, XXVI, 177–188; birthplace of, XXX, 87. *See also* U.S. Navy

"American Navy, 1817–1822: Comments of Richard Rush, The," by Anthony M. Brescia, XXXI, 217–225

"American Navy at Work on the Brazil Station, 1827–1860, The," by Donald W. Giffin, XIX, 239–256

American Neptune, *List of Maritime Titles in Print by Member Organizations of the Council of American Maritime Museums*, compiled by Philip Chadwick Foster Smith, XXXIX, 58–77

AMERICAN NEPTUNE, THE
MICROFILM, XX, 3–4
PICTORIAL SUPPLEMENTS, XXXV, 72

—, XXVI, Photographs of American and Canadian Fishing Schooners

—, XXVII, Photographs of Shipbuilding in Bath (ME)

—, XXVIII, Selections from the Penobscot Marine Museum, Searsport (ME)

—, XXIX, Selection of Marine Paintings by Robert Salmon

—, XXX, Photographs of Yachting by Henry G. Peabody and Willard B. Jackson

—, XXXI, Life Between Decks Under Sail

—, XXXII, Marine Paintings by Michele Felice Cornè

—, XXXIII, Photographs of Whaling Vessels

—, XXXIV, Steamship Paintings of Antonio Niccolo Gasparo Jacobsen (1850–1921)

—, XXXV, Instruments of Navigation

—, XXXVI, Marine Paintings of John Faunce Leavitt, [Part I] 32–33; [Part II] 138–139; [Part III] 198–199; [Part IV] 250–251

—, XXXVII, The Art of the Shipcarver at the Peabody Museum of Salem, [Part I] 32–33, [Part II] 124–125, [Part III] 200–201, [Part IV] 242–243

STATEMENT OF EDITORIAL POLICY, I, 3–5

STATEMENT OF POLICY REGARDING BOOK REVIEWS, I, 91–92

American Paddle Steamboats, by Carl D. Lane, reviewed, IV, 175–176

American Passenger Ships: The Ocean Lines and Liners, 1873–1983, by Frederick E. Emmons, reviewed, XLVII, 55

American Philosophical Society, XXXV, 112

American Polynesia: Coral Islands of the Central Pacific, by Edwin H. Bryan, Jr., reviewed, I, 407

American Practical Navigator, by Nathaniel Bowditch, reviewed by Captain John F. Campbell, XIX, 141–146

American President Lines, XXVII, 151

American President Lines and its Forebears, 1848–1984, by John Niven, reviewed, XLVIII, 201

"American Prisoners of the French Privateers, 1707," by Margaret K. Ritchie and Carson I. A. Ritchie, XX, 112–117

"American Privateering in America's War for Independence, 1775–1783," by William James Morgan, XXXVI, 79–87

"American Privateers in the Leeward Islands, 1776–1778," by Alan G. Jamieson, XLIII, 20–30

American Revolution, XXVI, 72–73

American Revolution 1775–1783, An Atlas of 18th Centuy Maps and Charts, The, by Naval History Division, Department of the Navy, reviewed, XXXIV, 281

American Sailing Education Association, The, XXXIV, 79

"American Saint, The," by Captain Edgar K. Thompson, U.S.N. (ret.), XXV, 122

"Americans and American Trade in India, 1784–1814," by G. Bhagat, XLVI, 6–15
American Seaman's Vocabulary of Technical Terms, and Sea Phrases, XXX, 40
American Seamen's Friend Society, XXXVII, 182 ff.; XXXIX, 45 ff.
"American Seamen's Friend Society and the American Sailor, 1828–1838, The," by Hugh H. Davis, XXXIX, 45–57
American Sea Songs and Chanteys, by Frank Shay, reviewed, IX, 77
American Secretaries of the Navy (2 Volumes), reviewed, XLI, 142
American Shipbuilding Co., XXII, 160; XXXVIII, 196
American Ship Building Company and Predecessors, 1867–1920, Institute for Great Lakes Research, reviewed, L, 139
American Shipmasters' Association, XXX, 22, 23
American Ship Models and How to Build Them, by V. R. Grimwood, reviewed, III, 357–358
"American Shipping Promoters and the Shipping Crisis of 1914–1916; The Pacific & Eastern Steamship Company," by Noel H. Pugach, XXXV, 166–182
American Ships, by Alexander Laing, reviewed, XXXII, 294
Americans in Polynesia, 1783–1842, by W. Patrick Strauss, reviewed, XXIV, 225–226
American Society of Marine Artists, XLI, 84
"American Steam Navigation in China, 1845–1878," by Edward Kenneth Haviland, XVI, 157–179, 243–269; XVII, 38–64, 134–151, 212–230, 298–314; XVIII, 59–85; XLIX, 21–28
American Steamships on the Atlantic, by Cedric Ridgely-Nevitt, reviewed, XLIII, 227–231
American Steel Barge Co., XXXVIII, 195
American Sugar Transit Co., XXXVIII, 183
Americans Who have Contributed to the History and Traditions of the United States Merchant Marine, reviewed, III, 358
American Tartar, ship *(1777),* V, 187
"American Threat to the Newfoundland Fisheries, 1776–1777, The," by Olaf Uwe Janzen, XLVIII, 154–164
American Traders in European Ports, by John Swain Carter, museum exhibit, mention, editorial, XLII, 4; reviewed, XLII, 310–311
"American Trade to China, 1800–1802," by Lawrence H. Leder, XXIII, 212–218
"American Trade with Mauritius in the Age of the French Revolution and Napoleon," by Alfred W. Crosby, Jr., XXV, 5–17
American Union, ship *(1861),* XI, 279
American Whaling on the Chathams Grounds, viewed from an antipodean perspective, by Rhys Richards, reviewed, XXXII, 226
American Windlass Co., XXII, 213

America, Russia, Hemp, and Napoleon: America's Trade with Russia and the Baltic, 1783–1812, by Alfred W. Crosby, Jr., reviewed, XXVI, 222–223
America's Cup, yacht races, XXV, 60
America's Cup Races, XI, 245
"America's First Contacts With India, 1784–1785," by G. Bhagat, XXXI, 38–48
America's Maritime Legacy: A History of the U.S. Merchant Marine and Shipbuilding Industry Since Colonial Times, by Robert A. Kilmarx, reviewed, XL, 142
"Americus Vespucius Symmes and the North Greenland Expeditions of Robert E. Peary, 1891–1895," by George H. Curtis, XXXVIII, 41–51
Amerigo Vespucci, Pilot Major, by Frederick J. Pohl, reviewed, VI, 87
Ames, Edgar, XXXVI, 247
Ames, Fisher, XLVI, 12
Amethyst, British screw-corvette *(1874),* XXXIII, 285
Amethyst, H.M.S., British frigate *(1949),* XLIX, 209 ff.; L, 291
Amethyst, ship *(1807),* X, 54; *(1822),* XV, 136–139
Amherst, Lord, XLVIII, 237
Amherst, Lord Jeffrey, VII, 95
Amiens, auxiliary *(1917),* XXXII, 9, 30
Amiens, Peace of, 1803, XXV, 13
Amity, New York packet *(1816),* XXIII, 142
Amity, schooner, 1802, VII, 317
Amity, ship *(1816),* XV, 306–310
Ammen, Captain Daniel, portrait of, XLIII, 177–185 and plate 7
Ammen, Lieutenant Daniel, XXXI, 9
Ammen, Ulysses Grant, XLIII, 184 ff., plate 5
Ammidon, Otis, XXX, 279
Ammonoosuc, U.S.S. *(1864),* XXVII, 36 n., 39 n., 43
Amory, J., XIII, 122
Amory, Thomas C., XIII, 58
Amory Sibley, steamship *(1847),* XLVII, 34
Amos Lawrence, brig *(1855),* XXIV, 143
Amour de la Patrie, French ship *(1799),* XXXI, 173, 175
Amoy, steamship *(1863),* XLIII, 294 ff.
Amphibious boats, IV, 224
Amphibious Campaign for West Florida and Louisiana, 1814–1815; a Critical Review of Strategy and Tactics at New Orleans, The, by Wilburt S. Brown, reviewed, XXIX, 284
"Amphibious Operations in the Gulf of California, 1847–1848: A Contemporary Account," edited by John Haskell Kemble, V, 121–136
Amphion, schooner *(1778),* VI, 166
Amphirite, H.M.S. *(1776),* XIII, 35
Amphitheatre, ship *(1799),* XLVI, 162
Amphitrite, French ship (1800), XXXI, 174
Amphitrite, U.S. monitor (1862), X, 18, 31; *(1918),* VII, 72
Amphrite, armed merchant schooner *(1798),* L, 270
Ampoletta, I, 211

Amsterdam, Dutch East India ship *(1748),* XXX, 154; XLVII, 279
Amulet, ship *(1850),* XLV, 125
Amundsen, Roald, XXVI, 155; L, 35
Amundsen, Captain Roald, XII, 7–21
Amur Co., XLIII, 91 ff.
Amy A. Lane, barkentine *(1867),* IV, 243
Amytis, schooner *(1861),* VIII, 215
Anacortes, Washington, XXXVI, 231 ff.
Anáhuac, Mexican schooner *(1845),* XXX, 46
Ana Julia, schooner *(1853),* XXX, 275
Analostan, brig (1810), XXVIII, 178–180, 184, 186–190
Anamba Islands, XXX, 201
"Anatomy of a Mutiny," by Philip F. Purrington, XXVII, 98–100
Anatomy of the Ship: The Type VII U-Boat, by David Westwood, reviewed, XLVII, 55
Anatoyn, Captain Joseph D., XVIII, 82
Anchorage, Shanghai, China, XLIII, plate 2
"Anchor Hoy," query by W. B. Yarnall, V, 164; answered by M. V. Brewington, V, 246
Anchoria, steamship (1874), XXXIV, plate XI
Anchor Line, ship of, Pictorial Supplement, XXXIV, plate XI
"Anchor Man," by Captain Edgar K. Thompson, U.S.N. (ret.), XXVI, 62
Anchors, II, 79–80, 285; XI, 77–78; XV, 150–151
Anchor to Windward, by Edward Valentine Mitchell, reviewed, I, 101
"Anchor to Windward: Manuals for Young Americans in the Days of Sail, An," by Hardin Craig, Jr., XXX, 40–45
Ancient Mariners, The, by Lionel Casson, reviewed, XIX, 147
Ancon, steamship *(1914),* XXIV, 186, 187, 207, plate 22
Andaluza, ship *(1869),* XXXVIII, 233
Andersen, Herluf, "Art for Everyday Use," XXIV, 183–185
Andersen, Captain Magnus, XIV, 110
Anderson, Commander A. B., XXXIX, 119
Anderson, A. P., Seaman, U.S.N., XXV, 50
Anderson, Absalom E., XIV, 179 ff.
Anderson, Absalom L., XIV, 161 ff., plate 21
Anderson, Admiral Bern, "A Note on the Banks Baton," XVII, 67
Anderson, Charles L. G., *Life and Letters of Vasco Nunez de Balboa,* reviewed, I, 411
Anderson, Charles R., XLII, 59
Anderson, Edward C., XXXVIII, 117
Anderson, Edward Clifford, XXVII, 239–247, 249–252
Anderson, Midshipman Edwin Maffit, C.S.N., XXV, 20, 21
Anderson, Elizabeth Stanton, *Towboats and Tugs,* reviewed, L, 139
Anderson, Florence Bennett, *A Grandfather for Benjamin Franklin; The True Story of a Nantucket Pioneer and His Mates,* reviewed, I, 409–410

Anderson, Captain Fred, XXV, 289
Anderson, I. (artist), drawing by, XXV, 126, plate 9
Anderson, Captain J. W., XXI, 105
Anderson, Jansen, XIV, 168 ff.
Anderson, Captain Nathan, XIV, 162
Anderson, Colonel P. M., XXII, 179
Anderson, R. C., VI, 3; X, 8; XIV, 13, 14, 15; XVII, 152, 154; answered query, IX, 302; "Captain McGiffin and the Battle of the Yalu," IX, 301; *"Defense* and *Hinchinbrook,"* XIII, 212; *A Memoir of James Trevenen,* reviewed, XX, 276; "La Musee de la Marine," XVII, 65–66; XVIII, 181; *Oared Fighting Ships, From Classical Times to the Coming of Steam,* reviewed, XXIII, 146–147; "The Origin of the Marconi Rig," XX, 64; "Remarks on Seventeenth-Century Ship Design," XV, 151–152; *The Rigging of Ships in the Days of the Spritsail Topmast, 1600–1720,* reviewed, XLIII, 146–147; "Square Sails and Fore-and-aft Sails," XIII, 212; "The Trinity House Ship Models," V, 146
Anderson, R. Wayne, "Naming a Generation of Cunarders," XLII, 295–300
Anderson, Major Robert, XXXVI, 186 ff.; XXXVII, 278
Anderson, Robert Earle, *Merchant Marine and World Frontiers, The,* reviewed, VI, 157
Anderson, Roger Charles, contributed document, XXIV, 126
Anderson, Romer and Co., XIV, 163
Anderson, Taylor and Co., XIV, 162
Anderson, William, VII, 312
Anderson, William G., "John Adams, the Navy, and the Quasi-War with France," XXX, 117–132
Anderson, Commander William R., XX, 174
"And *Oregon* Rushed Home," by Richard H. Bradford, XXXVI, 257–265
Andover Theological Seminary, Andover, MA, XLVI, 35
Andrea Bianco, XXX, 251
Andrea Doria, steamship, XXXVI, 20
Andrea Doria – Dive to An Era, by Gary Gentile, reviewed, L, 144
Andreila, schooner *(1861),* XI, 279; XII, 52
Andrew Doria, Continental Navy brigantine (1776), XXV, 193, 198 n., 202 n., 202 n., 211, 212, 214; XXX, 220; XXXVI, 158 ff.; XXXIX, 29, 198; *(1779),* XXXV, 141
Andrew Foster, ship *(1853),* XVII, 21
Andrew Furuseth Act, 1915, XXIX, 232
Andrew Hicks, bark *(1888),* XXXIX, 8; XLIV, 16; *(1913),* VII, 221
Andrew Jackson, clipper ship (1855), I, 45; III, 72; XXV, 106
Andrew Jackson, ship *(1854),* VII, 318; VIII, 325–330; IX, 148–150
Andrew Ring, brig (1840), XXIV, 57
Andrews, Charles MacLean, XL, 249
Andrews, Captain George W., XVIII, 82

Andrews, Kenneth R., *Elizabethan Privateering, English Privateering During the Spanish War 1585–1603,* reviewed, XXV, 148–149; Editor, *English Privateering Voyages to the West Indies, 1588–1595,* reviewed, XX, 275; Editor, *The Last Voyage of Drake and Hawkins,* reviewed, XXXIV, 284; *The Spanish Caribbean: Trade and Plunder, 1530–1630,* reviewed, XXXIX, 150

Andrews, P. (engraver), XXV, 126
Andrews, Captain Thomas, XV, 178
Andrew Welch, ship, XXXIII, 146
Andromeda, schooner, XXI, 86
Andromeda, schooner *(1861),* XI, 279; XII, 52
Andromeda, schooner (1918), V, 141; IX, 68
Andromeda, ship *(1861),* XI, 266, 279
Anemone, H.M. corvette *(1943),* XLIV, 49 ff.
Angela, brig, XXI, 91
Angela, brig *(1861),* XI, 279
Angelina, sloop, XXI, 93; *(1863),* VIII, 228
Angelique, ship (1833), XIX, plate I
Angell, William, XXXI, 87 ff.
Angler, schooner (1844), XIV, 39; XXII, 216
Anglia, steamship (1847), III, 133; *(1862),* VIII, 223
Anglo-American, packet ship (1847), XLV, 181; *(1850),* XV, 140
"Anglo-American Maritime Relations during the Two World Wars: A Comparative Analysis," by Jeffrey J. Safford, XLI, 262–279
"Anglo-American Naval Diplomacy and the British Pacific Fleet, 1942–1945," by Merrill Bartlett and Robert Williams Love, Jr., XLII, 203–216
Anglo-American Oil Co., XVI, 5 ff.; XVIII, 8; XXXVIII, 175 ff.; XLVII, 47
Anglo-American Steamship Rivalry in China: 1862–1874, by Kwang-Ching Liu, reviewed, XXII, 225–227
Anglo-Saxon, ship *(1846–1857),* XV, 140; XLII, 121 ff.
"Anglo-Spanish Rivalry in the Spitsberg Whale Fishery, 1612–1616," by Calvin F. Senning, XXVIII, 239–260
Angola, brig *(1832),* XIV, 39
Angostura, XXX, 260
Angus, Anne W., XL, 36
Angus, Samuel, XL, 23 ff.
Angus, Lieutenant Samuel, XLII, 109
Angus, Master Commandant Samuel, XLVII, 27
"An Interesting Scene on Board an East Indiaman," Pictorial Supplement, XXXI, plate XX
Anita, schooner *(1862),* XII, 52, 154
Ann, schooner *(1717),* XXV, 82; *(1796),* XXII, 58–61; *(1863),* XII, 154; XV, 127
Ann, ship (1798), XLV, 171; (1805), X, 54, 55; XXI, 20; *(1858),* XXXIV, 21
Ann, sloop *(1862),* XII, 52; XV, 125, 127
Ann, steamship *(1854),* XXII, 19, 21, 22, 32, 37, 42, 43; *(1862),* XII, 52; XXI, 97, plate 21
Ann, steamship (ex-*Maria*) *(1860),* XLIX, 26
Anna, brig *(1808),* L, 103
Anna, merchant ship *(1776),* XLIV, 158 ff.
Anna, schooner, XXI, 93; *(1863),* XII, 154; XV, 114, 122
Anna, ship *(1801),* XXV, 180
Anna, sloop *(1863),* XV, 111, 127
Anna, steamship, XVIII, 230; (1859), XVII, 148 ff.; XVIII, 68; *(1861),* XI, 279; *(1862),* XLIII, 110 ff.; *(1863),* VIII, 228, 232
Anna, victualer, XXII, 108, 109
Anna Bell, schooner, XXI, 102
Anna Belle, schooner *(1861),* XI, 279; XII, 52
Anna Camp, ship (1864), II, 333
Anna Dale, schooner *(1865),* XII, 234
Anna Davis, schooner *(1861),* VIII, 215
Anna Deans, schooner, XXI, 93, 97; *(1861),* VIII, 215, 223; *(1862),* XV, 116, 125
Anna F. Schmidt, ship *(1863):* Capture and Burning of by *Alabama,* XXV, 18–28
Anna G. Lord, schooner (1919), XXVII, plate XXIX
Anna Gibson, schooner *(1864),* XII, 229
Anna Helen, ship *(1862),* VIII, 223
Anna J. Morse, schooner *(1886),* XII, plate 31
Annales Techniques de la Marine Marchande, No. 12, reviewed, IX, 156
Ann Alexander, ship *(1850),* I, 394
Anna M. Frome, oyster schooner (1904), I, 70
Anna Maria, schooner *(1863),* XII, 154
Annan, Edward, XXXVIII, 133
Ann & Hope, ship *(1798),* XLI, 171; *(1799),* XXXIV, 254; *(1800),* L, 270; *(1801),* XXIII, 217
Ann and Hope, ship (1798), V, 90; X, 53, 56; XVIII, 105–136, plates 5, 6; *(1806),* XXI, 73–75
Ann and Sarah, steamship, XXIV, 116
Ann and Susan, ship, XXII, 95
Anna Pendleton, schooner (1890), XXVIII, plate XXV
Annapolis, ship (1851), III, 349
Annapolis, U.S.S. (1897), XX, 142
"Annapolis, Appointment in," by Captain Edgar K. Thompson, U.S.N. (ret.), XXV, 224–226
Annapolis Co., The, XXXIII, 83
Annapolis – Gangway to the Quarterdeck, by Captain W. D. Puleston, reviewed, II, 263
Anna R. Heidritter, schooner (1903), III, 59–61, 163; XXI, 23–27; XXX, 187–193
"Anna R. Heidritter," by Robert H. I. Goddard, Jr., III, 59–61; XXI, 23–27
Ann Arbor No. 6, steamship, XXIII, 70
Anna Shepard, schooner *(1864),* XII, 229
Anna Smith, schooner *(1861),* XI, 279; XII, 52
Anna Smith, steam barge (1872), I, 76
Anna Sophia, schooner *(1862),* XII, 52, 234
Anna Taylor, schooner, XXI, 93, 94; *(1861),* XI, 279; XII, 52
Anna Thompson, sloop *(1863),* XV, 127
Ann C. Davenport, schooner *(1864),* XII, 229
Ann C. Leverett, schooner, XXI, 102; *(1861),* XI, 279
Anne, ship *(1626),* XXXVII, 10
Anne Comyn, barkentine (1920), V, 82
Ann Eliza, brigantine *(1854),* XIV, 257

Anne Lord, schooner *(1894)*, XLII, 265
Annesley, bark (1819), XXXIV, 188 ff.
Annesley, ship *(1896)*, XVIII, 9
Annesley, William, XXXIV, 188 ff.
Annette, iron screw clipper *(1861)*, XLIII, 198 ff.
Annex, steamship, XVIII, 223
Ann F. Lee, schooner *(1863)*, XII, 154
Ann Gillerson, schooner *(1864)*, XII, 229
Annie, schooner, XXVIII, 123; *(1863)*, VIII, 228
Annie, sloop, XXI, 98; *(1862)*, XII, 52, 234
Annie, steamship (1863), III, 137–138; XXI, 100; *(1864)*, VIII, 232, 233
Annie and Jane, schooner *(1829)*, VI, 210
Annie & Reuben, schooner (1891), Pictorial Supplement, XXXVI, plate XX
Annie B., schooner *(1863)*, XII, 154
Annie C. Perry, schooner (1903), XXVI, plate XIX
Annie C. Ross, schooner *(1942)*, III, 60
Annie Childs, steamship (1861), III, 135; XXI, 93, 98; *(1862)*, VIII, 223, 228
Annie Clapp, schooner *(1863)*, XII, 154
Annie E. Larder, Canadian schooner *(1902)*, XLIX, 280
Annie Fish, ship (1868), V, 153
Annie Gee, schooner (1874), V, 86
Annie Gillise, schooner (1868), XXIV, 43, 58
Annie Gus, schooner (1871), XXIV, 45, 58
Annie H. Smith, ship (1877), XV, 182
Annie J. Pardee, schooner (1882), XXVII, plate XX
Annie K. Eaton, schooner (1874), XV, 183
Annie Kimball, bark (1856), IV, 239
Annie L. Henderson, schooner, XXXV, plate 1
Annie Larsen, XX, 218
Annie Lord, schooner *(1883)*, XLIX, 30
Annie Lyle, schooner (1875), V, 86
Annie M. Peterson, schooner (1874), IX, 229–230
Annie M. Small, ship (1868), III, 72
Annie Sophia, schooner *(1865)*, XII, 234
Annie Taylor, schooner, XXI, 94
Annie Thompson, sloop *(1864)*, XV, 112, 128
Annie Torrey, bark (1869), II, 245
Annie Verden, schooner *(1864)*, XII, 229
Annik, Norwegian ship *(1943)*, XLIV, 49 ff.
Ann Louisa, schooner *(1864)*, XII, 229
Ann Maria, bark (1847), Pictorial Supplement, XXXVIII, plate I
Ann Maria, schooner *(1862)*, VIII, 223
Ann McKenzie, ship *(1849)*, XVIII, 310
Ann McKim, clipper ship (1832), XXII, 235; XXIII, 142
Ann McKim, ship (1833), III, 31–34; *(1846–1857)*, XLII, 125
Annotated Bibliography of U.S. Marine Corps History, An, by Paolo E. Coletta, reviewed, XLVII, 215
Ann Parry, bark (1845), XXXII, 34 ff.
Ann Ryan, schooner *(1861)*, XI, 279
Ann S. Deas, schooner *(1861)*, VIII, 215
Ann Walker, hermaphrodite brig (1849), XXIV, 58
Ann Wilson, bark (1854), VI, 81

Anola, schooner, XXI, 92, 94; *(1861)*, XI, 279
Anonimo, barque, XXI, 98; *(1861)*, XI, 279
Anonyma, lorcha, XXII, 34
"Another *Mayflower*?" by William A. Baker, XXV, 218–223
"Another Navy Rodgers," by Commander R. W. Mindte, XIX, 213–226
Ansdell, bark (1854), VI, 81
Ansel, Willits D., review by, XL, 66; *Restoration of the Smack* Emma C. Berry *at Mystic Seaport, 1969–1971*, reviewed, XXXIV, 148–149; *The Whaleboat: A Study of Design, Construction, and Use from 1850 to 1970*, reviewed, XXXIX, 151–153
Anson, H.M.S., XXII, 113; *(1894)*, XX, 191
Anson, Commodore George, XXII, 106–115; XLIV, 155 ff.
Anson, Lord, XXX, 207
Answer, ship *(1590)*, XIV, 10
Antarctic, ship *(1830)*, XXXIV, 255; *(1854)*, XLII, 121 ff.; XLV, 28
Antarctic Ocean, The, by Russell Owen, reviewed, II, 185–187
Antarctic Pilot, The, reviewed, IX, 155
"Antebellum Canton Tea Trade: Recent Perspectives, The," by Robert Gardella, XLVIII, 261–270
"Antebellum Maine Fishing Schooner and the Factors Influencing Its Design and Construction, The," by Wayne M. O'Leary, XLIV, 82–95
"Ante-bellum Steamship Propulsion Machinery," documents contributed by Alexander Crosby Brown, VI, 151–152
Antelope, auxiliary bark (1855), I, 55–57, plate facing 56, 166–167; XVI, 167; XVIII, 68
Antelope, brig *(1863)*, XXV, plate XXIX
Antelope, British ship *(1862)*, XLIX, 21
Antelope, schooner *(1807)*, XVI, 194; *(1809)*, X, 150; *(1863)*, VIII, 228
Antelope, ship (1852), III, 263
Antelope, steamship (1832), VII, 47 n.; *(1860)*, II, 303
Antelope, steam demi bark *(1855)*, XXII, 39; XXV, plate XXIV
"*Antelope* located, The," by Eldon Griffin, I, 166–167
Antequera, Juan Baptista, XV, 52
Anthoensen, Fred, mentioned, XI, 4; XV, 248; XXI, 3; XXVIII, 238; XXXVII, 156; XXXVIII, 79
Anthoensen Press, The (Portland, ME), XXV, 4; XXVIII, 238; XXIX, 229; XXXI, 3; XXXVII, 156; XL, 166
Anthonioz, Pierre, "Postscript to the Voyage of La Pérouse," XXI, 196–206
Anthony, Captain James, XXIII, 27
Anthony, Joseph B., XXXV, 83 ff.
Anti-George, privateer *(1793)*, XXII, 81, 83, 97
Antilla, XXX, 249 ff.
"Antinavalists, The Opponents of Naval Expansion in the Early National Period, The," by Craig Symonds, XXXIX, 22–28

Antioch, ship *(1835),* XLVII, 90 ff.
Antoinette, schooner *(1863),* XV, 127
Antona, steamship *(1863),* XII, 154
Antonia (renamed *Carlotta*) steamship *(1867),* XXXVII, 235
Antonica, schooner *(1862),* XII, 52
Antonica, steamship, XXI, 81, 86, 102, 105; *(1862),* VIII, 223, 228; IX, 44; *(1863),* XII, 154
Antonieta, bark *(1861),* XI, 266, 280
Antonio, barque, XXI, 97; *(1861),* XI, 266, 279
Antonio, schooner *(1861),* XI, 280
Antonio, steamship, XXI, 104
Antonio Lopez, Spanish merchantman *(1898),* XXXIII, 277
Antram, Lieutenant Jose M., XXXVIII, 242
Antrobus, Captain Charles, XXIII, 181
Antwerp, grain elevator *(1883),* XXXVIII, 141
Aomon Island, VI, 71–72
Apache (ex-*White Heather*), steam bark (1809), XXX, plate XXVIII
Apcar and Co., XXVI, 5, 118, 119, 123–126, 201
Aphis, H.M. gunboat *(1930),* L, 188
Apollo, sloop (1807), XXII, 216
"Apologetic English," by Captain Edgar K. Thompson, U.S.N. (ret.), XXIX, 64
Appam, British passenger liner *(1916),* XXXII, 106; XLVIII, 50 ff.; photo of, XLVIII, 53
"*Appam* and American Neutrality, The," by Phyllis A. Hall, XLVIII, 50–58
Appendix 1: Vessels with Letters of Marque, 1625–30, XLIX, 261
Applebee, R. B., XXX, 32
Applebee, Robert B., XIX, 121; "Notes on the Palmer Schooners," V, 79–81
Appleby, Captain Gilman, VII, 302; XVIII, 294, 297
Appleby, John, "A Pathway Out of Debt: The Privateering Activities of Sir John Hippisley During the Early Stuart Wars with Spain and France, 1625–30," XLIX, 251–261
Appleby, John C., "The Charter Party of the *Triall:* An Unsuccessful Virginia Venture, 1606–1607," XLVII, 77–82
Appleton, Ebenezer, XV, 138
Appleton, Dr. John S., XLIX, 34
Appleton, Thomas E., *Usque Ad Mare,* reviewed, XXX, 221–222
Appleton, William, XIII, 122; XV, 134, 138
"Appointment in Annapolis," by Captain Edgar K. Thompson, U.S.N. (ret.), XXV, 224–226
Appollo, bateau (1914), IV, 289
Appomattox, C.S. ship *(1862),* VI, 51
Apprentices, XXIII, 192
"Apprentice's First Voyage, The," Pictorial Supplement, XXXI, plate XXV
Apthorp, Charles, XXXI, 21; XXXIII, 96 ff.
Apurimac, Peruvian ship *(1881),* XXXIX, 287
Aquidaban, Brazilian flagship *(1893),* XLI, 253

Aquidneck, bark *(1887),* XVIII, 191
Aquila, ship *(1861),* XI, 280
Aquilla, schooner, XXI, 103; *(1862),* VIII, 223
Aquitania, steamship, XLII, 295 ff.
Arab (1801), XXIII, 217
Arab, brig *(1840),* XXXV, 261
Arab, H.M.S. *(1814),* XXIV, 174, 180, 181
Arab, ship *(1835),* XLI, 288; XLV, 112
Arab Dhows, XI, 161–202, plates 17–23
"Arab Dhows of Eastern Arabia," by Richard LeBaron Bowen, Jr., IX, 87–132, plates 9–16; reprint reviewed, IX, 306
Arabella, ship (1841), XV, 249–258
Arabia, boats of, XII, 186–221; XIII, 82 ff., 185 ff.; XV, 5–48
Arabia, ship (1882), IV, 46, 47–48, 51, 52; (1863), IV, 241
Arabian, bark (1852), XV, 180
Arabian, steamship *(1863),* VIII, 228
Arabic, steamship *(1924),* IX, 29
Arab Seafaring in the Indian Ocean, by George Fadlo Hourani, reviewed, XI, 292–294
Arago (1861), XXXI, 257
Arago, steam packet *(1840),* XLVIII, 114
Araminta, schooner (1861), XI, 280
Äran, ship (1784), VI, 170
Aranmore, British freighter *(1917),* XXXIV, 182
Arapahoe, bark *(1917),* XVIII, 167–176, 201–213
Arapahoe, knockabout yawl (1893), XXX, 197
Arapahoe, ship *(1922),* XVI, 130
Arapiles, Spanish cruiser *(1873),* XXXVIII, 240
Araujo, Alvaro A., II, 170
Arbella, ship *(1630),* XXIII, 63, 65, 66; XXV, 240
Arbella (II), ship [replica] (1930), IX, 174; XIV, 107, 108
Arbuthnot, Lieutenant-governor Mariot, XLII, 18
Arbuthnot, Admiral Marriot, XXXIX, 160; XLVII, 11
Arbutus, yacht *(1905),* XXXVI, 241
Arc, schooner *(1861),* XI, 280
Arcade, schooner *(1855),* XXXIV, 99
Arcadia, ship *(1868),* IV, 51, 52
Archaeology:
    Excavations, Ireland, XLIX, 14
    Underwater archaeology, XLIII, 5; L, 275
Archaeology of the Boat: A New Introductory Study, by Basil Greenhill, reviewed, XXXVIII, 144
Archangel, ship *(1605),* L, 13
Archangel, XXX, 292
Archangelsk, steamship *(1943),* XIV, 132, 135
Archer, H.M. escort carrier *(1943),* XLV, 59
Archer, ship *(1861),* XV, 108 n.; XXI, 239, 256; *(1873),* XXXIII, 60
Archer, Gabriel, XXV, 237–238, 243; XXXIII, 132 ff.; XXXIV, 240
Archer, Captain George, Jr., XXV, 185
Archer, William S., XXXVIII, 105
Archimedes, steamship, XXVII, 72
Arcola, schooner *(1861),* VIII, 215

Arctic, bark (1852), II, 245; *(1865),* XIX, plate XIII; *(1871),* XIV, 46; (1875), I, 111, 114
Arctic, liner, XXVI, 82; *(1854),* XXXVI, 20, 32
Arctic, schooner *(1861),* VIII, 215; *(1863),* XII, 154
Arctic, steamship *(1849),* XLVIII, 113; (1850), III, 264; XIV, 237–261; *(1854),* XIX, 128–132; XX, 177, 180–183; XXII, 72, 73; XXIV, plate V; XXV, 79, 80
Arctic, steamship *(1923),* X, 120; *(1925),* IV, 202, 204; XVI, 131, 132; XVIII, 214, 215, 220, 221
Arctic, whaleship *(1853),* XXXIV, 248
Arctic, Garlington Expedition to, 1883, XXXVI, 108–124
Arctic exploration, XII, 7–21
Arctic regions:
    Description and travel, XXXVII, 95; L, 35
    Discovery and exploration, XII, 7; XX, 104; XXXVI, 108; XXXVIII, 81; XLIX, 151
    Fiction, XX, 174
    See also Whaling
Arctic Transport Co., XXV, 292
Arctic voyages, Sir John Franklin, XX, 104–111
Arctic Whalers, Icy Seas, by W. Gillies Ross, reviewed, XLVII, 62
"Arctic Whalers," XXII, plate XXVII
"Arctic Whaling," XXII, plate XXVI
Arctic Whaling Diary: The Journal of Captain George Comer in Hudson Bay 1903–1905, An, edited by W. Gillies Ross, reviewed, XLV, 210
Ardent, schooner (1815), XIV, 39
Ardman, Harvey, Normandie: *Her Life and Times,* reviewed, XLVII, 141
Ardrey, yacht, XXXVI, 248
Arethusa, British cruiser *(1939),* XXXII, 111
Arethusa, H.M.S. *(1772),* XXIII, 177
Arethusa, schooner-yacht *(1886),* XLIX, 37
Arey, ship (1856), V, 327
Arey, Captain Ernest L., XXXV, 6
Arey, Captain Seth C., XXXV, 6
Argall, Sir Samuel, XIV, 64–65
Argenteau, before 1674, photo of engraving of, L, 175
Argentina:
    Description and travel, XXIII, 186
    Foreign relations, United States, XXIX, 174; XLVI, 230
    History, 1817–1868, XXIX, 174
    Navy, VI, 5
    See also Atacama
Argentine Central Railroad, XXXV, 6
Argo, Continental sloop (1779), XXV, 109
Argo, gasoline yawl *(1909),* XXXVIII, 91
Argo, schooner *(1753),* I, 89; *(1798),* V, 90
Argo, ship *(1798),* X, 53; *(1843),* XXX, 185
Argo, ship (1856), II, 331; VI, 81
Argo, steam ferry *(1831),* VII, 43, 61
Argo Merchant, tanker *(1880),* XXXVIII, 175 ff.
Argonaut, ship (1849), XIX, 27, 28, 33, 34
Argus, brig *(1813),* XVII, 69–72; *(1814),* XLIV, 174 ff.

Argus, schooner *(1850),* XLV, 122
Argus, sloop of war (1813), XL, 39 ff.
Argus, U.S.S. *(1803),* XXI, 135, 136
Argus, wooden steamship *(1840),* XLIII, 90 ff.
Argyle, H.M.S. *(1740),* XXVI, 38
Argyle, schooner, XXI, 89, 97; *(1862),* VIII, 223, 228
Argyll, oil tanker *(1902),* XLII, 249 ff.
Argyll, steamship (1892), XXVIII, 186
Ariadne, British frigate *(1777),* XLIII, 22 ff.
Ariadne, H.M.S. *(1902),* XXVIII, 98
Ariadne, liner (1951), XXXVI, 28
Ariadne, yawl yacht *(1895),* XXXVI, 238–242, plate 8
Aribe, Lieutenant Luis, XXXIX, 280
Ariel, brig, XXI, 102; *(1861),* VIII, 215, 216
Ariel, H.M.S. *(1778),* XIV, 60
Ariel, schooner, XXI, 88; *(1862),* VIII, 223; XII, 52
Ariel, ship, XXI, 89; *(1787),* L, 245 ff.; *(1849),* XXX, 244; *(1855),* XXXV, 32 ff., 213, plate 5; *(1861),* XI, 280
Ariel, sloop (1832), XXXVI, 255
Ariel, steamship (1855), XVIII, 68; *(1856),* IV, 313; (1858), II, 226; *(1871),* II, 18; XVII, 311 ff.; *(1873),* X, 134
Ariel, Union ship *(1862),* XLVIII, 90
Ariel, yacht *(1892),* XXXVI, 235, 236
Aries, steamship, XXI, 100, plate XXV; *(1862),* VIII, 223, 229
Arismendi-Brion, XXX, 260
Aristides, schooner *(1861),* VIII, 216
Aristomene, ship *(1901),* XVI, 11
Aristotle, on diving bells, VII, 261
Arizona, bark (1857), IV, 240; VI, 82; V, 153
Arizona, Pacific Mail steamship *(1866),* XLVIII, 127
Arizona, steamship, XXI, 91, 101; *(1861),* XI, 280; XII, 52; (1865), II, 20; X, 130; XVIII, 68; *(1895),* XIV, 121
Arizona, transport *(1899),* XXXV, 185
Arizona, U.S.S. *(1864),* XI, 275
Arizona (ex-*City of Chester*), Pictorial Supplement, XXXIV, plate X
Arizona (AZ), Arizona Territory. *See* Steamboats, Steam Navigation
"Arizona Fleet, The," by Hazel Emery Mills, I, 255–274
"Ark, The Stability of the," by J. Frederick Douty, XXV, 261
Arkansas, C.S. ironclad (1862), XXV, 135; XIX, 267
Ark (II), ship [replica] *(1934),* XIV, 108
Arkona, Prussian corvette, XXIX, 26
Arletta, bark (1864), IV, 243
Arletta, schooner *(1864),* XV, 128
Arlington, bark (1863), IV, 241
Arlington, Lord, XXV, 279
Arlington, schooner *(1861),* XI, 280
Armada (1588), XLV, 25; XLIX, 5. *See also* Spain
Armand Considère, concrete ship (1944), XXII, 177, 179
Armbruster, Eugene L., *Brooklyn's Eastern District,* reviewed, II, 352

"Armed Merchantmen and Privateers: Another Perspective on America's Quasi-War With France," by John D. Pelzer, L, 270

Armed Transport Bounty, The, by John McKay, reviewed, L, 72

Armenia, ship *(1877),* IV, 48, 51, 52, plate 10

Armenian, steamship *(1857),* XXVI, 125, 126, 204, 209

Armes, Frank H., journal of, XXV, 110

Armide, brig *(1814),* XLII, 116

Arming and Fitting of English Ships of War, 1600–1815, The, by Brian Lavery, reviewed, XLIX, 306

"Arming the Fleet: Early Cannon Founders to the United States Navy," by Spencer C. Tucker, XLV, 35–40

Arming the Fleet: U.S. Navy Ordnance in the Muzzle-Loading Era, by Spencer Tucker, reviewed, L, 145

Arminius, Prussian ironclad *(1863),* XXIX, 25

Armistead, Elizabeth Mosely, L, 245 ff.

Armored vessels, XXIX, 5; XLII, 193. *See also* Ironclads; Ram; Shipbuilding (Materials); Turret Ships

Arms, Frank H., XXIX, 102

"Arms and Seals of John Paul Jones, The," by Samuel Eliot Morrison, XVIII, 301–305

Armsden, Douglas, XXVIII, plate I

Armstrong, steamship *(1864),* VIII, 233

Armstrong, James, XXVII, 162, 164

Armstrong, James, Flag Officer, XXXII, 123 ff.

Armstrong, General John, XXX, 283

Armstrong, Lieutenant Richard F., C.S.N., XXV, 20, 22

Armstrong, Mitchell and Co., XXXIX, 130

Armstrong, Captain P., XVIII, 82

Armstrong, Pleasant, XXVIII, 135, 140

Arnau, Paul, XV, 119

Arndt, John Penn, boatbuilder, III, 253–254

Arne, Thomas Augustine, XXII, 106, 115

Arniston, ship *(1794),* XIV, 102

Arnold, Allan A., "Merchants in the Forecastle: The Private Ventures of New England Mariners," XLI, 165–187

Arnold, Benedict, XXVIII, 114; XXX, 114, 115

Arnold, Brigadier General Benedict, XLIII, 135 ff.

Arnold, Cheney & Co., XXV, 105–106

Arnold, Craig, editor, *"Euterpe," Diaries, Letters and Logs of the Star of India as a British Emigrant Ship,* reviewed, L, 151

Arnold, David, XVIII, 107

Arnold, J. Barto III, review by, XLIX, 313

Arnold, J. Barto III and David McDonald, *Documentary Sources for the Wreck of the New Spain Fleet of 1554,* reviewed, XL, 139

Arnold, John, VII, 303

Arnold, Julean, XXXV, 175

Arnold, Richard, VII, 303

Arnold, Richard James, XXXV, 83, plate 7

Arnoldus Vinnen, bark *(1917),* XVIII, 162, 165, 170

Arnon, schooner *(1857),* XXIV, 45, 58

Aroostook, tender *(1919),* XLVII, 253

Aroostook, U.S.S. *(1862),* XX, 161, 162; *(1867),* XXXII, 132 ff.

Around the Horn, by Edward Rowland Sill, reviewed, IV, 255

"Around the Horn in *Tam O'Shanter*," document contributed by Worrall D. Prescott, XIV, 136–139, plate 16

"Around the World for Seals: The Voyage of the Two Masted Schooner *Sarah W. Hunt* from New Bedford to Campbell Island, 1883–1884," by E. Lee Dorsett, M.D., XI, 115–133

Arracan, bark *(1858),* XXVI, 193; (1860), III, 171

Aragon, steamship *(1871),* XI, 252 ff.

Arran, ship *(1855),* IV, 238; V, 327

"Arrangement and Construction of Early Seventeenth-Century Ships, The," by William A. Baker, XV, 259–286

Arras, auxiliary schooner (1918), XXXII, 31

Arratoon Apcar, brig *(1853),* XXII, 17

Arratoon Apcar, steamship *(1861),* XXVI, 204, 209

"Arrival of the First Permanent Settlers off Jamestown, Virginia, 13 May 1607," by Griffith Baily Coale, X, 5–14

Arrow, lorcha, XXII, 32; *(1856),* XXXVIII, 36

Arrow, schooner, XXI, 89; *(1862),* XV, 117, 125

Arrow, steamship, XXI, 101; *(1864),* VIII, 233

Arrowsmith, Captain Thomas, XLVIII, 34

Art. *See* specific types of art, i.e., Islamic Art; Marine Art; Prints; Scrimshaw; Ships in art; Whales in art; etc.; also Marine Artists; Marine Museums

Art and the Seafarer, by Hans Jurgen Hansen, Editor, reviewed, XXIX, 68–69

Artesien, French warship [model] *(1765),* XVI, 102

"Artetu thwart," document contributed by Carl W. Mitman, V, 87

"Art for Everyday Use," by Herluf Andersen, XXIV, 183–185

Artful Roux: Marine Painters of Marseille, The, Philip Chadwick Foster Smith, reviewed, XXXIX, 144

Art Gallery & Museum, Glasgow, XXX, 153

Arthur, bark *(1869),* XXX, 294–296

Arthur, ship, XXIII, 252; *(1802),* X, 53; *(1861),* XI, 280

Arthur, snow *(1794),* XLI, 224

Arthur, U.S.S. *(1810),* XXX, 292 n.

Arthur, Charles B., *The Remaking of the English Navy by Admiral St. Vincent — Key to the Victory Over Napoleon,* reviewed, XLVIII, 190

Arthur, Sir George, VII, 308–309

Arthur Benks, schooner *(1863),* XII, 154

Arthur Brooks, schooner *(1863),* XII, 154

Arthur C. Robb, sloop *(1933),* XXXVII, 225

Arthur J. Baldwin, refrigerator ship *(1927),* XXV, 292

Arthur Newell Talbot, concrete ship (1943), XXII, 175, 176

Arthur Pickering, bark (1847), IV, 242

Arthur Sewell, bark *(1899),* XVIII, 177–180

"Articles of Agreement for the Galley *Conqueror*, 1779," by William D. Hoyt, Jr., VI, 101–107
Artificial Horizon, Pictorial Supplement, XXXV, plate VIII
Artist, schooner *(1863)*, XII, 154
Artizan, ship *(1855)*, IV, 240
Artizan, The, XXX, 15
"Art of Cook's Voyages, The," query, XL, 64
Art of Navigation in England in Elizabethan and Early Stuart Times, The, by David W. Waters, reviewed, XX, 274
AR VAG, by Bernard Cadoret, reviewed, XLVII, 142
Asa Eldridge, ship *(1856)*, V, 147; X, 235
Ascension, schooner *(1863)*, XII, 154
Ascension, ship *(1582)*, XIV, 8, 10, 11
Ashanti, H.M.S. *(1942)*, L, 49
Ashby, George, IV, 313 ff.
Ashby, Henry, XXV, 106–107
Ashcraft, Allan C., "Civil War Naval Weapons that Might Have Been," XXII, 280–289
Ashe, Captain, XXXVI, 248
Asheville, gunboat *(1921)*, XXXV, 121
Ashford, Captain J. G., XXX, 199
Ashland, ship *(1843)*, XXV, 18 n.
Ashley, Clifford W., IX, 29; XXII, plates XXV, XXVI; painting by, IX, plate 1; *The Ashley Book of Knots*, reviewed, IV, 338–339; 336
Ashley, Edward R., XIII, 119
"Ashley Bowen Outwits a British Press Gang," document contributed by Russell W. Knight, XXIII, 143–145
Ashley Cooper, Lord Anthony, XXX, 82
Ashmun, Jehudi, XXXII, 269; XXXVIII, 54
Ash Point, ME, II, 307–323
Ashuelot, ship *(1871)*, XLV, 238
Ashuelot, side-wheel gunboat *(1867)*, XXXII, 130; XXXV, 29
Ashuelot, steamship (1863), XVII, 62; XVIII, 68; *(1869)*, XLIX, 25; *(1870)*, XXV, 73, 118
Ashuelot, U.S.S., XXVIII, 143; XXIX, 113
Asia, ship *(1795)*, XII, 162; *(1799)*, XLV, 86 ff.; *(1804)*, XVIII, 135; XXIV, 265
Asia, ship (1854), II, 331
Asia, steamship (1850), XXIV, plate VI; *(1906)*, X, 138
Asia, U.S.S. *(1810)*, XXX, 292 n.
Asiatic, ship *(1866)*, XXXII, 124
Asiatic Petroleum and Butterfield & Swire, L, 260 ff.
"Asiatic Squadron: 1835–1907, The," by James M. Merrill, XXIX, 106–117
Askalad, motor ship *(1917)*, XXII, 158
Askew, Roy, XXXVI, 248
Askold, Russian cruiser *(1915)*, XXXVII, 39, 41
Asp, schooner *(1813)*, XLII, 110 ff.; XLIII, 6 ff.
Aspasia, ship, (1801), XXIII, 217; XXXIII, 166; *(1800)*, XIV, 209
Asphodel, steamship *(1900)*, II, 140
Aspinall, Butler, XXXV, 48 ff.
Aspinwall, Captain John, XLVIII, 33
Aspinwall, Mark D., "Passenger Ships in the Coastwise Trade: American Public Policy Since 1789," XLVIII, 173–177
Aspinwall, William H., X, 125, 129; XX, 127; XLVIII, 114
Assam Valley, ship *(1854)*, III, 64
Assistance, hospital ship *(1859)*, XXVII, 171, 172
"Assistant Charles O. Boutelle, of the United States Coast Survey, with the South Atlantic Blockading Squadron, 1861–1863," by Darwin H. Stapleton, XXXI, 253–267
Associated Lake Underwriters, XXX, 25
Associated Oil Co., XXII, 172
Association des Descendants de Corsairs, XXV, 232
Association for Asian Studies, Raleigh, NC, XLVIII, 224
Asta, schooner *(1917)*, V, 138
Astatula, steamship *(1881)*, VII, 119, 142, 143, 146 n., 150, 152, 153, 155, 158, 159, 164, 165, 225, 226, 234, 238, 239, plates 17, 19, 30, 31
Astell, ship *(1810)*, XIV, 102
Asthore, yacht *(1908)*, XXXVI, 245
Astice, Lieutenant Commander R. W., L, 49
Astor, John Jacob, mention, XLII, 4; XLVI, 32; XLVIII, 246
Astor, William, III, 162–163; V, 146
Astoria, schooner *(1851)*, XLIV, 88
Astoria, ship *(1875)*, II, 335
Astral, bark *(1900)*, VIII, 279–281, 283; XVI, 5, 110
Astrea, British frigate *(1782)*, XXXIX, 169
Astrea, schooner *(1822)*, XXIV, 58
Astrea, ship *(1789)*, XLI, 173; *(1796)*, V, 102; XXV, 180; XLVII, 124
Astrée, ship *(1778)*, XIII, 212
Astria, whaler *(1802)*, XLI, 285
Astro, Richard, XLIV, 110
Astrolabe, French warship *(1788)*, XXI, 196 ff.
Astrolabe, ship *(1837)*, XXVII, 3
Astronomer's Astrolabe, Pictorial Supplement, XXXV, plate II
Astronomical Clock, Pictorial Supplement, XXXV, plate XVIII
Astronomy, I, 6, 123, 209. *See also* Navigation, Navigational Instruments, etc.
Asturian Prince, steamship *(1895)*, XLII, 273
Asuncion de Jesucristo, pinnace *(1609)*, XVII, 181–194
Asunçion, tanker *(1903)*, XXXVIII, 178 ff.
Atacama (Chile and Argentina), XXXIX, 271
Atahualpa, Peruvian ironclad *(1866)*, XXXIX, 275
Atahualpa, ship *(1805)*, XIX, 12
Atalanta, French ship *(1799)*, XXXI, 173
Atalanta, ship *(1857)*, IV, 243
Atalanta, U.S. steam launch *(1871)*, VII, 112
Atalante, British ship *(1858)*, XLIII, 274 ff.
Atalayador, brig *(1861)*, XI, 280
Atchafayla, brig (1845), XXIV, 45, 57

Athena, schooner *(1908),* XXVI, plate XXII
Athena, ship *(1857),* V, 152
Athenia, liner *(1939),* XXXII, 101
Athenian, vessel *(1801),* XXX, 212
Atjeh, steamship *(1880),* XVII, 54
Atkin, William, *Of Yachts and Men,* reviewed, X, 157
Atkins, Captain E., XIII, 58
Atkinson, Samuel, VII, 269
Atkinson, schooner *(1861),* VIII, 216
Atkinson, Theodore, 271
Atlanta, brig *(1864),* XL, 108 ff.
Atlanta, Confederate gunboat *(1862),* X, 25, 26; XLII, 199 ff. and plate 3; *(1863),* XV, 111; XLIX, 116
Atlanta, cruiser, XXXIII, 274; *(1883),* XXXIX, 129 ff.
Atlanta, H.M.S. *(1776),* XX, 45
Atlanta, ship *(1876),* XXXVIII, 123 ff.; *(1903),* XXXVII, 260
Atlanta, sloop *(1862),* XII, 52
Atlanta, steamship *(1864),* VIII, 233
Atlante, brig sloop *(1813),* XLII, 107 ff.
Atlantic, brig *(1863),* XII, 155
Atlantic, hermaphrodite brig, XXI, 96
Atlantic, schooner, XXI, 96; *(1861),* VIII, 216; *(1862),* XII, 52, 154
Atlantic, ship *(1846),* I, 115; *(1848),* XLIV, 8 ff.; *(1858),* V, 153
Atlantic, steamship, XXI, 96, 101; *(1849),* XLVIII, 113; *(1853),* XVII, 18; *(1862),* XII, 52, 155; *(1863),* VIII, 229
Atlantic, transport *(1861),* XXXI, 259; XXXIII, 87
Atlantic, wreck, XXII, 235
Atlantic Coast Fisheries Co., XLIV, 126
Atlantic Coast Steamship Co., XXXV, 172
"Atlantic Crossing of the Seventeenth Century, An," by George Carrington Mason, XI, 35–41
Atlantic Four-Master: The Story of the Schooner Herbert L. Rawding, *1919–1947,* reviewed, XLVIII, 193
Atlantic Islands: Madeira, the Azores and the Cape Verdes in Seventeenth-Century Commerce and Navigation, by T. Bentley Duncan, reviewed, XXXIII, 225
Atlantic Line, XIV, 121
Atlantic Mutual, XXX, 22
Atlantic Mutual Insurance Co., New York, I, 42–45
Atlantic Neptune (marine atlas of charts), I, 145; VIII, 4; XXV, 241; XLVI, 173–178
Atlantic Ocean. See Fisheries; Pirates; Sealing; Shipping; Shipwrecks; Steam navigation
Atlantic Ocean chart of C. H. Townsend, L, 121
Atlantic Refining Co., XXII, 169, 171
Atlantic Steam Packet Company of the Confederate States, IX, 44, 46–47
Atlantic Transport Co., XXXV, 175 ff.
Atlantic Transport Line, XXXII, 156; ship of, Pictorial Supplement, XXXIV, plate XXV
Atlantus, concrete steamship *(1918),* XXII, 160, 161, 164, 167, plate 6, 182
Atlas, auxiliary schooner (1911), I, 78–79
Atlas, bark (1901), VIII, 279–280, 283; (1902), XVI, 5–27, 107–136; XVII, 65; XVIII, 177–180
Atlas, H.M.S. *(1782),* XXXVI, 68
Atlas, ship (1792), VI, 83; *(1818),* L, 213
Atlas, ship *(1908),* X, 200
Atlas, steamship *(1873),* XXXVI, 91
Atlas, steamship (1898), XXXVIII, 178 ff., plate 6
Atlas, topsail schooner (1829), XXII, 235
Atlas, vessel *(1863),* XXVI, 102, 104
Atlas, whaler *(1848),* XLI, 291
Atlas of Lake Champlain, 1779–1780, by Captain William Chambers, R.N., reviewed, XLVII, 211
Atlas to Cook's Voyages, copy of engraving, Pictorial Supplement, XXXII, plate XXXI
Atmosphere, ship (1856), IV, 72
Atokan, steamship, XXIII, 272
At Sea and By Land: The Reminiscences of William Balfour Macdonald R.N., edited by S. W. Jackman, reviewed, XLIV, 278
"Attacking a Sperm Whale," XXII, plate XII
"Attack on the Marquis, The," by James Duncan Phillips, IX, 239–248
"Attacks on vessels by enraged whales," by Alexander Crosby Brown, I, 393–394
Attack Transport, by Lieutenant Lawrence A. Marsden, U.S.N.R., reviewed, VI, 310
"Attack with a Shoulder Gun," XXII, plate XIX
"At the Sign of the Quadrant: The Navigational Instrument Business in America to the Civil War," by Deborah Jean Warner, XLVI, 258–263
Attress, ship *(1804),* XLIII, 43 ff.
Attwaye, Captain John, XLI, 298
Atwood, Captain T. T., XX, 89 n., 90 n.
Atwood, Thomas, XXV, 16
Auckland, Lord, British, 1844, XXXII, 236
Audacity, H.M.S. *(1941),* XLV, 58
Audaz, torpedo boat *(1850),* XLI, 95
Audrey, brigantine *(1757),* XLVIII, 38 ff.
August, Freidrich, II, King of Saxony, XLIX, 226–229 ff.
Augusta, brig *(1799),* XLVI, 161 ff.
Augusta, schooner *(1822),* XXXII, 273
Augusta, schooner *(1849),* XXIV, 45, 58; *(1865),* XII, 234
Augusta, schooner, XXI, 95
Augusta, ship, XIII, 121; *(1807),* IX, 12
Augusta, slaver *(1821),* XXXVIII, 53
Augusta, steamship (1867), XVII, 222
Augusta, steamship *(1919),* XXXII, 11
Augusta, steamship (1848), XXX, 266
Augusta, U.S.S. *(1800),* XXXI, 174; *(1862),* XVI, 55; *(1863),* XLIV, 266 ff.
Augusta W. Snow, brig *(1905),* XLIX, 31
Augusta W. Snow, schooner, XXIV, 34
Augustine Heard and Co., XVIII, 42–64, 137; XVII, 66; XLIII, 91 ff.; XLIX, 21 ff.; ship of, XXXIV, 17 ff., plate 3
Augustine Kobbe, bark (1866), XXVIII, plate XI

Augustus, bark (1857), II, 332. Augustus, George, XXXVII, 87
Augustus, scow schooner (1897), I, plate facing 72
Augustus, ship, XXV, 186; *(1805),* II, 282
Augustus Heard and Co., XXII, 225
Augustus Hunt, schooner (1882), XXIII, 12
Augustus Palmer, schooner (1894), V, 80; XX, 238–239, 241
Aukland, bark (1843), XIX, 27
Aulick, Commandant John H., XXXIV, 192 ff.; XXXVIII, 28
Aulick, John B., XXXV, 22
Aurelia, schooner *(1861),* XI, 280
Aurelia, sloop, XXI, 103; *(1863),* VIII, 229; XV, 111, 127
Auroa, XXV, 28
Aurora, brig, XXII, 82; *(1855),* XXIV, 143
Aurora, frigate *(1778),* XLIII, 28
Aurora, Russian frigate *(1854),* XXXI, 268 ff.
Aurora, schooner (1831), XXIII, 7
Aurora, ship *(1807),* XVI, 1921; *(1810),* X, 54, 55; XVII, 68
Aurora, ship *(1860),* XXVII, 235
Aurousseau, M., Collector and Translator, *The Letters of F. W. Ludwig Leichhardt,* reviewed, XXX, 304
Austen, Captain Francis, XXXVI, 138
Austin, steamship, XXI, 91, 101; *(1861),* XI, 280; XII, 53, 299; XIV, 61, 62; *(1863),* VIII, 229
Austin, Texas sloop, XXX, 49
Austin, Texas warship *(1843),* XXI, 221 ff.
Austin, Bert, XXXVI, 242, 243
Austin, Calvin, XXXIV, 182
Austin, Captain, XLVIII, 240
Austin, Hall & Co., Newcastle, ME, XXXIV, 70
Austin, James T., XV, 138
Austin, S., Jr., XV, 135
Austin, Chaplain William, XLVI, 163
Australasian Steam Navigation Co., XXXIV, 24; XLIII, 127 ff.
Austral continent, XXX, 205 ff.
Australia, Australian cruiser *(1914),* XXIV, 275
Australia, steamship *(1875),* X, 133; *(1879),* XLIII, 188 ff.
Australia. See Shipping
Australia, XII, 258–270; XVIII, 109–117; early voyages to, X, 52–64
"Australia and New England," by Thomas Dunbabin, XV, 153–154
Australia in the Antartic: Interest, Activity and Endeavour, by R. A. Swan, reviewed, XXIII, 150
Australian, steamship *(1863),* XXVI, 196
Australian grain trade, II, 296–297
Australian Royal Mail Steam Navigation Co., XXVI, 194–196
Australia Station: A History of the Royal Navy in the South West Pacific, 1821–1913, The, by John Bach, reviewed, XLIX, 307
Australis, steamship (ex-*America*) (1940), XXV, 224
Austria (1817–1818), XXXI, Pictorial Supplement, plate II
Austria, ship (1870), IV, 48, 51, 52
"Austrian View of the United States Navy: 1867, An," by Armin Mruck and Arnold Blumberg, XXXIV, 59–64
Austro-Italian War (1866), XV, 199
Autran, Lieutenant, XXXVI, 90
"Auxiliary Steamships and R. B. Forbes," by Cedric Ridgely-Nevitt, I, 51–57
Ava, ship *(1833),* XV, 175, 185
Ava, steamship (1855), XXVI, 118, 203, 204, 208
Avalon, steam schooner *(1913),* XXIX, 263
Avarucho, ship *(1833),* XXIX, 90
Aveline, James O., XXVII, 271
Avenger, H.M.S. *(1943),* XLV, 59
Avenger, sloop *(1863),* XV, 126
"Average Sailing Vessel Passages to San Francisco," by John Lyman, III, 56
Averell, Jonathan, XIV, 52
Averill, Albert E., "A Maine Boy at Sea in the Eighties," X, 203–219
Averill, Captain Cyrus B., X, 215
Averill, James, VII, 57; XVII, 101
Avery, Abigail, XXXIX, 191
Avery, Fred, VII, 243
Avery, John, VIII, 13
Avery, Reverend Joseph, XXV, 244–245
Avery, William, VII, 43, 44, 50, 54
Avery his Fall (reef), XXV, 244–245
Aviateur de Terlines, auxiliary (1918), XXXII, 10, 30
Avila, hermaphrodite brig *(1848),* XXX, 266
Avoca, H.M.S. *(1917),* XXXVI, 268 n.
Avon, American brig *(1834),* XXXII, 120
Avon, brig *(1834),* XII, 182; *(1848),* XLVII, 93
Avon, ship *(1814),* XLIV, 171
Avonmore, ship (1863), I, 110, 114; V, 151
Awkright, British frigate *(1840),* XXXV, 260
Axilda, schooner, XXI, 93
Ayacucho, brig *(1834),* XII, 180–183
Ayala, Pedro de, XXX, 255; XXXVII, 158
Ayde, ship *(1569),* XLIV, 26 ff.
Ayer, Robert McCormick, reviews by, XL, 139, 151
Ayers, Geraldine M., XXXV, 225; XXXVII, 155
Ayrault, Daniel, XII, 226
Ayres, Dr. Eli, XXXII, 266 ff.
Ayrshire Lass, steamship *(1861),* XLIII, 186 ff.
Ayscoghe, Henry, VII, 269
AZ. *See* Arizona
Azalea, schooner *(1928),* XVIII, 219
Azara, auxiliary three-masted schooner (1904), XXX, plate XIX
Azimuth Compasses: American, circa 1823, Pictorial Supplement, XXXV, plate XV; English, circa 1793, Pictorial Supplement, XXXV, plate XIV; Russian, 1809, Pictorial Supplement, XXXV, plate XIV
Azof, steamship (1855), XXVI, 26, 203, 204, 208

Azor, bark *(1851)*, XV, 222
Azor, bark (1878), XXXV, 202
Azores, brig (1847), VI, 80
Aztec, steamship *(1895)*, X, 137
Aztec, steamship *(1930)*, IV, 64
Aztec, transport *(1899)*, XXXV, 189
Azuma. See *Stonewall*, C.S.S

B

B. Aymar, ship *(1840)*, XXVIII, plates II, III
B. B. B., sloop, XXVIII, 123
B. D. Metcalf, ship (1856), IV, 240; V, 327
B. D. Pitts, schooner *(1861)*, VIII, 216
B. F. Carver, ship (1863), III, 65
B. F. Jones, stern paddle steamship (1945), XXXIII, 155 ff.
B. F. Martin, brig *(1861)*, VIII, 216
B. F. Reeves, schooner *(1861)*, XI, 280
B. Hilton, bark (1874), III, 106 ff.
B. R. Woodside, schooner (1883), XXVII, plate XXII
B. Shephard's Sketchbook of the H.M.S. Challenger Expedition 1872–1874, by Harris B. Stewart, Jr. and J. Welles Henderson, Editors, reviewed, XXXIII, 307
Baahlam, William, XIV, 243 ff.; XX, 183
Babbage, Charles, XLVII, 177
"Babbidge, Captain E. S.," query by John E. Tyler, I, 310
Babbidge, Lieutenant James, British Army, XXV, 214
Babbitt, U.S. destroyer *(1943)*, XLIV, 52
Babcock, Adam, VII, 211–212
Babcock, Elias, XLI, 181 ff.
Babcock, George, XXVII, 99, 101
Babson, John J., *History of the Town of Gloucester, Cape Ann including the Town of Rockport*, reviewed, XXXIII, 224
Bach, John, *The Australia Station: A History of the Royal Navy in the South West Pacific, 1821–1913*, reviewed, XLIX, 307; "The Imperial Defense of the Pacific Ocean in the Mid-Nineteenth Century: Ships and Bases," XXXII, 233–246; *A Maritime History of Australia*, reviewed, XLV, 204
Bachante, H.M.S. *(1879)*, XVII, 156
Bache, A. D., XXV, 95
Bache, Alexander Dallas, XXXI, 254; XXXII, 50; XLVII, 177; XLVIII, 44 ff.
Bache, Colonel, U.S. Coast and Geodetic Survey, XXV, 262
Bache, Lieutenant Richard, XXVIII, 47; XLVII, 175
Bachman, J. F., XX, 119
Backstaff, XXI, 107
"Back Staff, The," by M. V. Brewington, XXI, 107–109
Backus, Elijah, L, 201 ff.
Bacon, Captain Daniel, XLI, 172

Bacon, Francis, VII, 265–266
Bacon, Sir Francis, XXXI, 101
Bacon, Lieutenant Commander George, XII, 271–281
Bacon, Jacob, XIV, 59
Bacon, Major Robert, XXXIV, 271
Bacon, Roger, VII, 263
Bactria, ship, XXXVI, 3
Baden-Powell, Canadian schooner *(1902)*, XLIX, 280
Badger, brig *(1778)*, XIII, 183
Badger, cruiser *(1898)*, XLI, 103
Badger, S.F.M., XXVII, plate XXVIII
Badger, schooner, XXI, 88, 103; *(1863)*, XII, 155, 229
Badger, steamship (1864), XII, 234, 308; *(1864)*, VIII, 233; XXI, plate IV, 87
Badger, steam scow (1837), VII, 64
Badger, Senator, XXX, 144
Baehr, Harry W., Jr., answered query, I, 173–174
Baffin, whale ship, XXV, plate 8
Baffin, William, L, 35
Baga tribe, West Africa, XXX, 179
Baghdad Packet, steamship (1863), III, 138
Bagot, Charles, British Minister in Washington, 1816, XXXIII, 252 ff.
Bahama, C.S.S. *(1862)*, XXV, 21
Bahama, steamship (1861), III, 133; *(1862)*, XXVII, 265
"Bahamas, The American Invasion of Nassau in the," by John J. McCusker, Jr., XXV, 189–217, plates 21, 22
Bahamas, History, 18th century, XXV, 189
Bahama Star, steamship *(1965)*, XXXVI, 10, 12, 18–22, 25–28, plates 3, 4
Bahia, XXX, 239
Bahiana, steamship (1854), XXVI, 192–194, 204, 208
Baigorry, schooner, XXI, 100
Baigory, schooner *(1862)*, XII, 53
Baikal, Russian transport *(1855)*, XXXI, 272
Bailey, U.S. torpedo boat (1897), XXII, 142
Bailey, Charles Kingsley, III, 88
Bailey, Thomas A. and Paul B. Ryan, *The Lusitania Disaster: An Episode in Modern Warfare and Diplomacy*, reviewed, XXXVI, 300
Bai Ling, Governor-General, XLVIII, 240
Baily, George, XIV, 245
Bain, Captain A., XVIII, 82
Bainbridge, schooner *(1844)*, XXIX, 177; XLVI, 234
Bainbridge, U.S.S. *(1860)*, XIX, 256
Bainbridge, Lieutenant James, XXI, 134
Bainbridge, Master Commandant Joseph, XLIV, 175
Bainbridge, William, XXXI, 287; XLVII, 20; L, 245 ff.
Bainbridge, Captain William, U.S.N., XXV, 159; XXVI, 248; XLII, 285; XLIV, 245
Bainbridge, Commodore William, U.S.N., VII, 168; XXXVII, 131, XXXVIII, 66; XL, 39 ff., 215
Baird, Captain E. M., XXXII, 22
Baird, Dr. Spencer F., XLV, 81 ff.; XLIX, 34 ff.
Baird, Spencer Fullerton, V, 5 ff.

"Baiting trawls at night in the hold of a haddock schooner," Pictorial Supplement, XXXI, plate XXVII
Baker, schooner *(1862),* XII, 53
Baker, Captain Arch, Jr., XII, 103
Baker, Mrs. B. C., "Reminiscences of a Voyage in the Bark *William H. Besse,"* edited by Harold Bowditch, VI, 121–131
Baker, Bernard N., XXXII, 156
Baker, Charles H., U.S.N., XXXIX, 120
Baker, Colonel, XXV, 67
Baker, Daniel Walker, XLV, 180
Baker, E. (artist), XXII, plate XIII
Baker, Captain Edward, XLV, 180; XXI, 260
Baker, Commander Francis H., XXXII, 132
Baker, Captain Lorenzo Dow, XXV, 106
Baker, Marcus, XXXIX, 11
Baker, Mathew, XIV, 8, 11, 17, 266 ff.; XV, 275, 284; XVII, 175
Baker, Newton D., XXXIV, 268 ff.
Baker, Captain Otis, XX, 62
Baker, Robert Benjamin, XXVI, 203
Baker, Captain Robert E., XLIII, 108 ff.
Baker, Robert H., XXXVIII, 170; "The Sakonnet River Boat," XVI, 61–62, plate.
Baker, Sarah, XXXVIII, 206
Baker, W. A., and Tre Tryckare, *The Engine Powered Vessel: From Paddle-Wheeler to Nuclear Ship,* reviewed, XXVI, 150–151
Baker, Captain William, XIII, 26
Baker, William A., IX, 159; XIV, 4; XV, 151–152; XXXVII, 81; XLI, 147–148, 231–233, 306–312; XLII, 66–67; XLV, 45; mentioned, XXX, 79; note by, XL, 226; document contributed by, XXXI, 289; editorial comment, XXXVIII, 3–4
"*Adventure,* A Seventeenth-Century Ketch," XXX, 81–85; "Another *Mayflower?"* XXV, 218–223; "The Arrangement and Construction of Early Seventeenth-Century Ships," XV, 259–286; *"Colonial Vessels: Some Seventeenth-Century Sailing Craft,"* reviewed, XXII, 290–291; "Deck Heights in the Early Seventeenth Century," XXII, 99–105; "Early Seventeenth-Century Ship Design," XIV, 262–277; "Garret Archaeology," XXXVIII, 170–174; "The Gjøa," XII, 7–12; "Gosnold's *Concord* and Her Shallop," XXXIV, 231–242; *A History of the Boston Marine Society, 1742–1967,* reviewed, XXIX, 141–142; *The Lore of Sail,* reviewed, XLVII, 142; "The *Mayflower* Problem," XIV, 5–17; XVI, 79–80; *The New Mayflower,* reviewed, XIX, 149; XXV, 231; "Notes on a shallop," XVII, 105–113; review by, XXXII, 70; *Sloops and Shallops,* reviewed, XXVI, 284–285; *Steam Whaling in the Western Arctic,* contribution to, reviewed, XXXVIII, 72; "U.S. Light-Vessel No. 50 *Columbia River,"* IX, 273–277, plate 29, folding plan, 274

Baker, William A., Robert G. Albion, Benjamin W. Labaree, Marion V. Brewington, *New England and the Sea,* reviewed, XXXIII, 63–64
Baker, William and Co., VII, 50
Baker Library (Harvard University), XXXIV, 57
Library resources, XIII, 118
Baker Library, Harvard University,
Baker Palmer, schooner (1901), V, 80
Bakewell, Henry P., Jr., "U.S.S. *Sabine,"* XXIII, 261–263
Bakhuysen, L., XXII, plate XXVIII
Balaena, steam bark (1883), Pictorial Supplement, XXXIII, plate XVI; *(1892),* XXXVIII, 84 ff.; XLIV, 16 ff.
Balambangan, XXX, 202, 203, 204
Balboa, Vasco Nuñez de, I, 411
Balch, Daniel, XXVIII, 145
Balch, Lieutenant G. B., XXI, 242
Balch, Mr., XXX, 62–67
Balch, Thomas H., XXVIII, 145
Balch Brothers (shipbuilders), XXIV, 40, 57
Balchen, Captain George, XVIII, 82
Balchen, Vice-Admiral John, XXVI, 38
Balclutha, ship (1886), IV, 199–206; XV, 171; XXII, 212 ff.; XXIV, 4; mentioned, XL, 164
Baldridge, Captain H. A., U.S.N., query by, IV, 335; *A Catalogue of the Rosenbach Collection of Memorable Documents Depicting the Rise and Development of the American Navy,* reviewed, VI, 158
Baldwin, Rear Admiral C. A., U.S.N., XXV, 223
Baldwin, Captain C. H., XXVI, 103–105
Baldwin, Leland D., *The Keelboat Age on Western Waters,* reviewed, II, 343–344
Baldwin, Colonel Loammi, XXX, 56
Baldwin, M. W., XXXIV, 90
Baldwin, Samuel, XXX, 132
Baldwin, Captain Samuel, XLI, 177
Baldwin, Mrs. William P., XXX, 82
Balear, bark *(1861),* XI, 280
Baleares, schooner, XXI, 90; *(1861),* XI, 266, 280
Balena, ship *(1819),* XIV, 43
Balestier, Joseph, U.S. consul, XLVII, 172
Balfour, Arthur J., British Secretary of State, XXXIV, 159 ff.
Balfour, Williamson & Co., VII, 288
Bali, boats of, XIII, 96 ff.
Ball, Sarah B., query by, XI, 291
Ball, XXV, 260
Ballacitta, Bulgarian ship *(1944),* XLIII, 35 ff.
Ballarat, steamship *(1863),* XLIII, 294 ff.
Ballard, Lieutenant G. A., XXIII, 69
Ballard, Captain H. A., XVIII, 82; XLIII, 115 ff.
Ballatt, Samuel, XXX, 57, 60
Ballentine, Captain James, VII, 298
Ballin, wooden steamship *(1917),* XXXV, 279
Balsa (boat), XXI, 157. *See also* Rafts
"Balsa and Dugout Navigation in Ecuador," by Emilio Estrada, XV, 142–149

Balsa-wood raft, II, plate 20
Baltic, brig (1821), XIV, 39; XXII, 216
Baltic, ocean liner *(1917),* XXXIV, 263 ff.
Baltic, schooner, XXI, 96; *(1862),* XII, 53; *(1888),* X, 193
Baltic, ship (1854), IV, 51
Baltic, steamship, XXVII, 259; (1850), XIV, 240; XXI, 241; XXIV, plate IV
Baltic, transport *(1861),* XXXVI, 186 ff.; XXXVII, 279
Baltick, schooner *(1763),* XXX, plate 3; *(1765): rigging plan of,* XLIX, 201
Baltick, topsail schooner (1765), XXV, 89; sail plan, XXV, 88
Baltimore, American sloop of war *(1798),* XLV, 94
Baltimore, brigantine *(1777),* XXXIX, 29 ff.
Baltimore, cruiser *(1886),* XXXVIII, 127, 291; XXXIX, 136; *(1919),* XLVII, 252
Baltimore, galley (1780), XXXIX, 30 ff.
Baltimore, schooner *(1783),* XXXIX, 30 ff.; *(1861),* VIII, 216
Baltimore, ship *(1760),* IX, 144; *(1799),* XXX, 128
Baltimore, submarine (1978), XXXIX, 29 ff.
Baltimore, U.S. cruiser *(1896),* XXIX, 116
Baltimore, U.S. flagship (1890), XXXIV, 212; XXXV, 184 ff.
Baltimore, U.S.S. *(1798),* XXII, 264 ff.; XXXI, 173
Baltimore, Maryland, ca. 1850, XXV, plate XVIII
Baltimore City, steamship (1888), XXIV, plate XIV
Baltimore Co., VI, 301 ff.
Baltimore customs records, IX, 72
Baltimore Hero, sloop (1776), XXXVI, 160
Baltimore Hero, sloop (1977), XLIII, 24
Baltimore in World Trade, 1729–1947, by Wilbur Harvey Hunter, Jr., reviewed, IX, 78
Baltimore on the Chesapeake, by Hamilton Owens, reviewed, II, 89–90
"Baltimore Painter, A," query by J. Hall Pleasants, II, 339
Baltimore Steam Packet Co., I, 96; XXII, 150
Bamberg, ship (1856), V, 327
Bamford, Roger, XXXI, 88
Banbury, Philip, *Shipbuilders of the Thames and Medway,* reviewed, XXXII, 72
Banca, coolie ship, XXII, 32
Banca (boat), XIX, 257
  Plans, XIX, 250
Bancroft, U.S.S. (1883), XX, 143
Bancroft, Andrew, XV, 256
Bancroft, George, XXV, 273
Bancroft, George, Secretary of the Navy, XLI, 28; XLVII, 172; L, 109
Bancroft, Hubert H., XXIX, 85 n., 86 n., 89, 90, 91 n.
"Band of Brothers," by Captain Edgar K. Thompson, U.S.N. (ret.), XXVIII, 286
Baneberry, ship (1858), IV, 242; V, 327
Bangor, American steamship *(1840),* XXVIII, 124; *(1842),* XXXIII, 83; *(1846),* XXXVII, 250; XXXIX, 218 ff.

Bangor, schooner *(1863),* XII, 155
Bangor Navigation Co., XXXIX, 218
Banka Straits, XXX, 208
Bankhead, Commander J. P., XXXII, 125
Bank Notes, XV, 213–216, plate 11
Bank notes, Maine, XV, 213
Banks, Sir Joseph, XII, 253–270; XIV, 216–217; XVI, 62; XVII, 67; XXX, 205; XLIX, 151
Banks, Nathaniel P., XXXI, 62
Bank sail, VII, 243
Banning, Kendall, *The Fleet Today,* reviewed, I, 187
Banning, Phineas, XXV, 262
Banning, William, XXXI, 90
Bannister, John, XLII, 45 ff.
Bannockburn, ship *(1861),* XV, 122
Banri Maru, steamship (ex-*Banri,* ex-*Cosmopolite*), XXVI, 113
Banryu Maru, steamship (ex-*Emperor*) *(1858),* XLIX, 26
Banshee, steamship, XXI, 102, 105, plates XII, XVI
Banshee, steamship *(1862),* II, 134; *(1863),* VIII, 205–206, 229
Banshee, steamship (1864), III, 134–135; *(1865),* XII, 234
Banshee, yacht *(1900),* XXXVI, 240
Banshee (II), steamship *(1864),* VIII, 233, 236
Bant, William, XLII, 27
Banta, Jacob, VII, 64
Banta & Bidwell, VII, 63
Banterer, British ship *(1858),* XLIII, 274 ff.; *(1859),* XXVII, 168
Banton, ship *(1667),* XIII, 7
Baptiste, Pierre Maisonnat, XXXV, 154
Baranov, Aleksandr A., XLI, 227
Barb, ship *(1944),* XXXIX, 123
Barbados, bark (1845), I, 50
Barbados Naval Office records, XXX, 97 ff., plates 1, 2
Barbara, schooner *(1916),* XLI, 45
Barbarie, John, XXXVII, 271
Barbary War. See United States History (Tripolitain War)
Barbeau, Marius, "All Hands Aboard Scrimshawing," XII, 99–122
Barber, Commander Francis M., XLI, 102
Barber, Henry, XLI, 224–230
Barber, Ira Wilson, Jr., XXIX, 155
Barberel, A. J., XXXVI, 275
Barberie, Peter, XXXVII, 57
Barbour, Captain Charles H., XLIX, 29
Barbour, Philip L., Editor, *The Jamestown Voyages Under the First Charter 1606–1609,* reviewed, XXX, 302
Barbour, Thomas, IV, 15–16
Barcelona, steamship (1836), VII, 62, 305–306
Barcelona (ex-*Erie*), steamship (1855), XXVI, 31
Barcham, Captain R., XVIII, 82
Barck, Dorothy C., VII, 316
Barclay (1801), XXIII, 216
Barclay, President Arthur, XXXIX, 176

Barclay, Captain (British Commander), XLIV, 178
Barclay, Edwin J., XXXIX, 180 ff.
Barclay, Captain H. A., XVI, 177; XVIII, 82
Barclay, Captain H. W., XIV, 124
Barclay, James, XXII, 9, 44
Barclay, John, XXXVII, 271
Barclay, Thomas, British Consul, XLI, 212; XLIII, 43
"Bard, J. & J., Picture Painters," by A. J. Peluso, XXXVI, 170–173
"Bard, James," query by Harold S. Sniffen, II, 81
Bard, James, XXXVI, 170–173
Bard, James (painter), II, 81, 94; III, 163, plate 22; VI, plate 33
Bard, John, XXXVI, 170–173
Bard, John & James, XI, 300
Barents, Willem, XXVIII, 240
Barge No. 81, XXXVIII, 179 ff.
Barham, H.M.S. *(1917)*, XL, 60 ff.; *(1940)*, XXVII, 186
Baring, Thomas, M. P., XXXIV, 9 ff.
Baring Brothers, XXIII, 136, 137
Baring-Gould, Sabine, XXX, 250. (Move to Bs)
Bark Canoes and Skin Boats of North America, The, by Edwin Tappan Adney and Howard I. Chapelle, reviewed, XXV, 295–297
"Barkentine *Leighton*, 1852," query by John Lyman, I, 171; answers by John Lyman, I, 311; IV, 77
Barkentines: I, 396–397, plate facing 397; V, 81–82, plate 8, 85; VII, 315–316, plate 39
Barkentines, XXV, 112. See also Masts and Rigging
Barker, A. R., XXXIX, 104
Barker, Captain Albert S., XLI, 98
Barker, Rear Admiral Albert S., U.S.N., XXXVII, n. 138 ff.
Barker, Edwin, XXX, 184, 185
Barker, Captain Frederick A., XXXIX, 9
Barker, Jacob, VII, 181, 185
Barker, John, XIII, 22; XXXVII, 11
Barker, Roland, *Tusitala: The Story of a Voyage in the Last of America's Square Riggers,* reviewed, XX, 70
Barkhausen, Henry N., contributed document, IX, 229–230
Barkin, Mr. and Mrs. Nathan, XXXVI, 21 ff.
"Bark *Kaiulani*, The," by John Lyman, II, 172
Barkley, M. M., XLI, 15
Bark of Boulogne, ship *(1569)*, XLIV, 26 ff.
Barks, II, 289–290; VIII, 152–153, 279 ff.
"Bark *Vernon*," by Alexander Crosby Brown, IX, 150
Barleux, auxiliary schooner (1917), XXXII, 31
Barley, Captain Jack, XXI, 201 ff.
Barley, Commander Frederick, "A British Sailor Looks at the United States Navy of the Early Nineteenth Century," XXI, 57–69
Barling, Henry, XXXIII, 54
Barlow, Joel, XXV, 64; XXVI, 241, 243; XXX, 290
Barlow, Moses, XX, 45
Barlowe, Rev. William, XXXVII, 175
Barnard, Reverend John, XXVIII, 265–266

Barnard, Major John G., XXXI, 256; XXXII, 50
Barnard, Lyman G., VII, 47 n.
Barnes, Albert M., in memory of, XLVIII, 66
Barnes, Captain Corbin, XXXIX, 203
Barnes, Elenor & James A., Editors, Samuel P. Boyer, *Naval Surgeon: Blockading the South, 1862–1866; Naval Surgeon: Revolt in Japan, 1868–1869,* reviewed, XXV, 72–73
Barnes, J. B., XXII, 172
Barneson, John, XXXVI, 237
Barnes, Surgeon General Joseph K., XXV, 67
Barnes, Captain S. W., IV, 236–237
Barnett, steamship *(1861)*, VIII, 216
Barnett, Richard C., "The View from Below Deck: The British Navy, 1777–1781," XXXVIII, 92–100
Barnette, Captain W. J., XXIX, 43 ff.
Barney, Joshua, I, 317
Barney, Captain Joshua, XXXVI, 221; XXXIX, 166
Barney, Commodore Joshua, XLIII, 5 ff.
Barney, Lieutenant Joseph N., XXXVI, 202, 203, 205
Barney, Lieutenant Joshua, XXXIV, 138
Barnley, Captain Henry, XXV, 240–243
Barns, A. M., "American and Canadian Fishing Schooners," XXVI, plates I-VIII, 64; plates IX-XVI, 140; plates XVII-XXIV, 200; plates XXV-XXXII, 242
Barnum, Phineas T., XIII, 53
Barnum Museum (Bridgeport, CT), XXX, 170
Barometers, American, Instruments of Navigation, Pictorial Supplement, XXXV, plate XXXII
Baron, J. S., XVII, 60
Baron And. von Höpken, cat (1759), VI, 166
Baron Douglas, steamship *(1942)*, XXVII, 190
Baron of Renfrew, steamship *(1825)*, XLVIII, 77 ff.; illustration of stranding, XLVIII, 84
Barons, Benjamin, XL, 245 ff.
Barr, Henry, XXVI, 278
Barr, Captain Henry, XXI, 292
Barracouta, H.M.S., XXII, 34; *(1895)*, XXIV, 185
Barracouta, ship *(1855)*, XXXI, 273
Barracouta, steamship *(1890)*, X, 137
Barralet, John James, II, plate 22
Barranca, tug *(1920)*, XXII, 169
Barraud chronometer, London, Pictorial Supplement, XXXV, plate XX
Barrell, George, II, 174; "The Journal of Voyages of the Brig *Venus* and the Schooner *Louisiana* in 1806," III, 222–238
Barrell, John, XLVIII, 26
Barrell, Joseph, XLII, 27
Barrell, N., XIII, 122
Barrett, Andrew, XIV, 177
Barrett, Elizabeth G. Barber, XXXVII, 203
Barrett, Ensign, British Army, XXV, 209
Barrett Manufacturing Co., XXXVIII, 183 ff.
Barriè, Jean, VII, 267
Barrington, Colonel John, VI, 291 ff.

Barrington, Major General John, VII, 24–32, 34
Barrington, Rear Admiral the Hon. Samuel, R.N., VII, 89, 92, 103
Barrin Island, map of, XLIX, 16
Barrios, General Gerardo, XXXII, 282 ff.
Barron, James, XXX, 74; XXXVI, 209
Barron, Captain James, XLII, 286 ff.; XXI, 131, 133 ff.
Barron, Commodore James, XX, 167; XXXI, 58; XLVII, 20; L, 245 ff.
Barron, Captain Samuel, XXXVII, 282; XXXIX, 33; XLIII, 130 ff.
Barron, Commodore Samuel, XXIX, 24, 169; XXX, 74, 136
Barrosa, British ship *(1894),* XXXIX, 175
Barrosa, frigate *(1813),* XLII, 109 ff.
Barrows, Ebeneazar, XXXIX, 89
Barrows, Nat. A., II, 84
Barry, Commander E. M., XXXV, 194
Barry, John, VI, 301; XXXI, 248; "Defence of frigate *Raleigh,*" I, 168–170
Barry, Captain John, U.S.N., XXI, 293–295; XXV, 35
Barry, Captain John, XVIII, 304; XXVI, 63; XXX, 75
Barry, Commodore John, XLVI, 159 ff.
Barry, Mrs. Lillian, X, 111
Barry, Paul James, review by, II, 344–345
Barslow, Thomas, XLVI, 9 ff.
Barstow, Caleb, XXXIX, 83 ff.
Barstow, John B., XXV, 222
Barstow, William P., XXXIX, 90
Bart, J. & J., XXIV, plates IV, V
Bart, Rear-Admiral Sir Michael Seymour, L, 32
Bartell, Joyce C., editor, *The Yankee Mariner & Sea Power, America's Challenge of Ocean Space,* reviewed, XLIV, 66–68
Barthelmess, Klaus, "Legacy of a Saxon King: Royal Prints of Whale Strandings in the Peabody Museum," XLIX, 226–229
Bartholomew, Captain Riley, XXVII, 19, 24–27
Bartholomew Gosnold: Discoverer and Planter, by Warner F. Gookin, reviewed, XXIV, 144–145
Bartlett, Bailey, XLVI, 143
Bartlett, Captain David H., XII, 104
Bartlett, Major Henry A., XLIX, 298 ff.
Bartlett, Captain J. F., XXII, 245
Bartlett, Commander John R., U.S.N., XXXIII, 275
Bartlett, Jonathan, XXVIII, 121, 124
Bartlett, Josiah, VIII, 13, 17
Bartlett, Merrill, and Robert William Love, Jr., "Anglo-American Naval Diplomacy and the British Pacific Fleet, 1942–1945," XLII, 203–216
Bartlett, Merrill L., "Commodore James Biddle and the First Naval Mission to Japan, 1845–1846," XLI, 25–35
Bartlett, Captain Nicholas, XXX, plate 4
Bartlett, Captain Robert A., III, 88
Bartlett, William, XXX, 111

Barton, Captain John, Pictorial Supplement, XXXII, plate VI
Barton, Harvey W., XXXVI, 21
Barton, William S., XLIII, 129 ff.
Basch, Jal (writer), L, 193
Basch, Lucien, *Le Museé imaginaire de la marine antique,* reviewed, L, 63
Basco, ship *(1899),* XXXV, 192
Bascobel, tug, XXII, 172
Basilide, schooner, XXI, 97; *(1861),* XI, 280; XII, 53
Baskerville, steamship *(1946),* XIV, 133, 135
Basoco, Richard M., "A British View of the Union Navy, 1864: A Report Addressed to Her Majesty's Minister at Washington," XXVII, 30–45
Bason, John, XI, 35 ff.
Bass, Captain, XXIX, 63
Bass, Captain Nathaniel, XXXVII, 13
Bass, George, mention, XLVII, 281
Bass, George F., Frederick E. van Doornick, Jr. *et al., Yassi Ada, Vol. 1: A Seventh Century Byzantine Shipwreck,* reviewed, XLIII, 58–59
Basse Terre, Guadeloupe, VII, 21–22, 24–27, plate 3
Bassett, Captain Thomas, XVIII, 82
Baston, T., XXX, 219
Bat, steamship, XXI, 94, plate XV; *(1864),* VIII, 233
Bataan, carrier *(1944),* XXXIX, 43
Batchelder, Charles F., reviews by, XXVI, 149; XXVII, 73–74, 226–227, 285–286; XXVIII, 72–73, 74, 293–294; XXIX, 69–70, 291; "Corrections on Whaleships," XXVI, 217; *Steam Whaling in the Western Arctic,* contribution to, reviewed, XXXVIII, 72
Batchelder, Charles F., and John R. Bockstoce, "A Chronological List of Commercial Wintering Voyages to the Bering Strait Region and Western Arctic of North America: 1850–1910," XXXVIII, 81–91
Batchelder, Charles F., Jr., XX, 184
Batchelder, Captain J. M., XXXIV, 51
Batchelder, Joseph M., XVII, 225–226
Batchelder, Captain Nathan A., XX, 121
Batchelor, sloop *(1746),* XLVIII, 33
Bateau, IV, 270 ff.; two-sail built at Taylors Island (1902–3), IV, 290, 298
Bateaux, Colonial, XXVI, 48, plate 4
Bates, Commodore, XL, 52 ff.
Bates, James L., XXII, 173
Bates, John, XXXV, 292; XLVI, 175
Bates, Rebecca and Abigail, XLV, 7
Bath (ME), shipbuilding, IV, 45–52; V, 79–81
Bath City, steamship *(1880),* XIV, 116, 118, 134
Bath City, steamship *(1899),* XIV, 124, 134
Bathe, Greville, *Ship of Destiny,* reviewed, XI, 233
Bath Iron Works, XXV, 156; XXXII, 166; XXXVIII, 181 ff.; XLIII, 3
Bath Iron Works Shipyard, XXVII, plate XXXI

Bath Marine Museum (Bath, ME); XXV, 156, 231; XXVII, plate I; editorial comment, XXXIX, 158; *Maritime Titles in Print,* XXXIX, 59

Bathurst, Lord, XII, 268; XXX, 66, 177 ff., 230 ff.

Batten, Sir William, XI, 5 ff.

Battick, John F., "The Searsport 'Thirty-Six': Seafaring Wives of a Maine Community in 1880," XLIV, 149–154

Battista Beccario, XXX, 251

Battle at sea, early fourteenth century, XLVI, 98

Battle for Convoy TM 1, January 1943, The," by David Syrett, L, 42–50

Battle for Leyte Gulf, The, by C. Vann Woodward, reviewed, VII, 247–248

Battle of Camden, VI, 52

"Battle of Campeche, The," by Commander Tom Henderson Wells, XXI, 216–221

Battle of Muddy Flat, XXX, 155–166

"Battle of Orleans, Massachusetts (1814) and Associated Events, The," by Richard K. Murdoch, XXIV, 172–182

"Battle of Plattsburg, 1814—The Losers, The" by Waldo H. Heinrichs, Jr., XXI, 42–56

"Battle of Porto Praya, 1781, The," by William B. Willcox, V, 64–78

"Battle of Priest's Cove, The," by Llewellyn Howland, X, 243–248

"Battle of the Atlantic: 1943, The Year of Decision, The," by David Syrett, XLV, 46–64

Battle of the Atlantic, The, 1939–1943, by Samuel Eliot Morison, reviewed, VIII, 155–157

"Battle of the Rams, The," by Lee Nathaniel Newcomer, XXV, 128–139

Battleships: Allied Battleships in World War II, by William H. Garzke, Jr. and Robert O. Dulin, Jr., reviewed, XLII, 147–148

Battleships in Transition: The Creation of the Steam Battlefleet, 1815–1860, by Andrew Lambert, reviewed, XLVI, 129

Batty, Robert, XXXVI, 269

Bauer, K. Jack, *"General Gates,"* X, 155

Bauer, K. Jack, Robert G. Albion and Paolo E. Coletta, *American Secretaries of the Navy,* reviewed, XLI, 142; "The *Sancala* Affair: Captain Voorhees Seizes an Argentine Squadron," XXIX, 174–186; *Surfboats and Horse Marines: U.S. Naval Operations in the Mexican War, 1846–48,* reviewed, XXXII, 147–148

Bauer, K. Jack and Paolo E. Coletta, *United States Navy and Marine Corps Bases: Domestic,* and *United States Navy and Marine Corps Bases: Foreign,* reviewed, XLIX, 59

Baugh, Daniel A., *British Naval Administration in the Age of Walpole,* reviewed, XXVII, 74–75

Baury, Midshipman Frederick, XLVII, 16

Bavaria, ship (1846), III, 262

Baxter, Captain Andrew, III, 88

Baxter, Captain, XXV, 113, 114

Baxter, James Phinney, XXIX, 6 n.; XLIX, 115

Baxter, Professor James Phinney, III, XXII, 261

Baxter, W. T., *The House of Hancock, Business in Boston, 1724–1775,* reviewed, V, 249

"Bay and River of Delaware, The," chart, XXV, 46–49, plate 2

Bayard, Senator James A., XL, 30

Bayard, Senator Richard H., XXIV, 12

Bayard, Thomas F., XLI, 258

Bayard, William, portrait of, XLVI, 154

Bayless, G. A. and M. S. Kline, *Ferryboats: A Legend on Puget Sound,* reviewed, XLIV, 205

Bayne, Peter, XXXIX, 14

Baynham, Henry, *From the Lower Deck, The Royal Navy 1780–1840,* reviewed, XXX, 299

Baynton, Wharton & Morgan, XXV, 106

Bay of Bengal, XXX, 207, 208

"Bay of Gibraltar and surrounding area," XXVII, plate 5

Bay of Naples, steamship (1906), XXIV, 239, 241, plates 27, 28

Bayonnaise, warship, XLI, 85

Bayonne, tanker (1889), XXXVIII, 175 ff.

Bayou City, C.S.A. (1861), XI, 272

Bayou City, gunboat (1862), XXXVI, 200–201

Bayou City, steamship (1862), XLVIII, 92

Bayside (ME), IX, 169 ff.

Bay State, steamship (1853), XIV, 202

Bay State, U.S.S. (1941), XX, 140

Bay State, U.S. steamship (1894), III, plate 13; (1895), XXXIII, 92, 94; XXVIII, 124

Bay State Fishing Co., XLIV, 114 ff.

Bazaar, ship (1834), XIX, 27, 28

Bazan, ship (1873), XXXVIII, 242

"B*Browne Math(l) Inst(t) Maker &c Bristol," Pictorial Supplement, XXXV, plate XIII

BC. British Columbia; *See* Canada

Bêche-de-mer trade, in South Pacific, XXV, 274–277

Beach boat, Riviera, I, 369–371, plates facing 367, 370

Beach Scene, 1830, XXIX, 198, plate XVIII

Beacon, steamship (1837), XXXIV, 48

Beacon Fisheries Co., XLIV, 131

Beacon Oil Co., XLVII, 47

Beadle, Charles, XLVII, 122

Beadle, Lieutenant Colonel Elias, XXXV, 129

Beagle, H.M.S. (1825), L, 32

Beagle, ship, XXVIII, 151

Beagle, steamship (1826), XXXVII, 246

Beaglehole, J. C., Editor, *The Journals of Captain James Cook on his Voyages of Discovery: Volume II, The Voyage of the* Resolution *and* Adventure *1772–1775,* reviewed, XXII, 224–225; *The Journals of Captain James Cook on his Voyages of Discovery: Volume III, The Voyage of the* Resolution *and* Discovery *1776–1780,* reviewed, XXVIII, 146–148; mentioned, XXX, 222

Beaglehole, John C., XVI, 282–285; *The Life of Captain James Cook,* reviewed, XXXV, 70–72
Beal, Captain Jack, X, 214–215
Beale, U.S.S. *(1918),* XLIV, 180 ff.
Beale, Henry, XXXVII, 15 ff.
Beale, Howard K., XXXII, 259
Beale, Mrs. Truxtun, V, 156
Beall, John Yates, XXXII, 208; XXXIII, 199
Beals, Herbert K., editor, *For Honor and Country: the Diary of Bruno de Hezeta,* reviewed, XLVIII, 197
Beaman, Louis A., XXXIV, 266
Bean, Tarleton H., XXXIX, 11
Bean, Dr. Tarleton N., XLV, 81
Bear, barkentine *(1874),* XXIII, 156
Bear, U.S. Revenue Cutter *(1888),* XXXIX, 9
Bear, U.S.S. (1873), XXVIII, 71–72
Beardslee, Lieutenant Commander L. A., XXXII, 132
Beardslee, Rear Admiral L. A., U.S.N., XXII, 49, 50; XXV, 50
Beary, Ensign Donald B., U.S.N., VII, 36
Beasso, Captain Pierre, XXIII, 279
Beatrice, British schooner *(1893),* XXXIX, 175
Beatrice, ship *(1849),* XIX, 27
Beatrice, steamship, XXI, 105; *(1864),* VIII, 233
Beatrice L. Corkum, Canadian ship *(1902),* XLIX, 279
Beattie, William, XXIV, 17
Beatty, Admiral Sir David, XL, 51
Beatty, Sir David, XXXVII, 105
Beatty, Rear Admiral Frank E., XLIII, 270
Beaufort, C.S.S. *(1862),* XX, 158
Beaufort, ship *(1774),* IX, 183; XXVI, 47; *(1777),* XIII, 44
Beaufort, Captain F., XXX, 212
Beaufort, Rear Admiral Sir Francis, XXVIII, 151
Beaufort, South Carolina, VII, 316
Beaufoy, Colonel Mark, XXVII, 10, 28
Beauharnois Canal, VIII, 58
Beaumont, I. C., XXIII, 55
Beauregard, C.S. ironclad *(1862),* XXV, 138
Beauregard, schooner *(1861),* VIII, 216
Beauregard, sloop *(1862),* XII, 53
Beauregard, General Pierre G. T., XLII, 196 ff.; XLIV, 259 ff.
Beaver, brig (1772), XXV, 218–219
Beaver, ship *(1791),* XII, 23, 100; *(1803),* VII, 178
Beaver, steamship *(1836),* IX, 64–65; XXXV, 249
Beaverton, Great Lakes freighter *(1933),* L, 35
Beavis, L. R. W., *Passage from Sail to Steam,* reviewed, XLIX, 63
Beck, Horace P., "A Maritime Heritage," XXV, 51–67; reviewed book, XXIII, 148–149; "Tales of Banks Fishermen," XIII, 125–130
Becket, brig *(1820),* XIII, 242
Becket, John (shipbuilder), II, 279 ff.
Beckley, John, XXVI, 178, 181 n.
Beckwith, David (shipbuilder, of New London, CT), XXV, 102
Beckwith, G. C., XXI, 304
Beckwith, James (shipbuilder, of New London, CT), XXV, 102
Beckwith, Captain N. W., XVIII, 82
Bedford, ship (1772), XXV, 218–219; *(1812),* XLVI, 168
Bedford, Vice-Admiral Sir Frederick G., XXVIII, 112
Bedini, Silvio, XLVI, 260; *Thinkers and Tinkers: Early American Men of Science,* reviewed, XXXVIII, 69
Bedini, Silvio A., *Early American Scientific Instruments and Their Makers,* reviewed, XXV, 71–72
Bedouin, cutter *(1882),* XXX, plate IX
Bedwell, Thomas, XXXVII, 177
Bedwell, Rev. William, XXXVII, 177
Bedwill, Benjamin, V, 28
Bee, brig *(1835),* XLI, 297
Bee, H.M. gunboat *(1930),* L, 188
Bee, George E., XXXVI, 255
Bee, William C., IX, 36–40, 43–44, 56–57, 59
Beebe, Anna Maria, XVI, 234
Beebe, Edward, VII, 178
Beebe, William, VII, 281
Beebe, Captain William, XVI, 234
Beebe, William M., Jr., XXXVI, 109, 110
Beecher, Laban S., figurehead attributed to, Pictorial Supplement, XXXVII, plate XV, 124–125
Beest, A. van, XXII, plate XXIII
Beetle, Captain James, III, 350–352
"Beetle's Boat Shop," query by H. G. Purcell, IV, 251
"Beetle Whale Boats," document contributed by Carl W. Mitman, III, 350–352
"Before the *Nautilus,*" by Robert C. Fox, XX, 174–176
Begent, Louis, XXVIII, 57
"Beginnings of Trade between the United States and Russia, The," by Alfred W. Crosby, Jr., XXI, 207–215
Behaim, Martin, XIV, 187; XXX, 252, 254, 256
Behar (ex-*Erie,* ex-*Barcelona*), steamship *(1855),* XXVI, 31, 203, 204, 209
Beinecke, Walter, XXXIV, 258
Beiner, fishing vessel *(1963),* XLI, 59
Belanger, Robert, XXVII, plates IX, XXVI
Belcher, Chief Justice, XXXI, 35
Belcher, Captain Edward, XXVIII, 151
Belcher, Governor Jonathan, XXXVII, 268
Belcher, Jonathan, Jr., XXXI, 29
Belden, Charles, XLI, 9
Belfort, auxiliary *(1917),* XXXII, 10, 30
Belgian King, steamship, XV, 225
Belgic, ship *(1884),* XXXI, 126
Belisarius, brig *(1823),* VIII, 173
Belisarius, ship, XXV, 181; *(1794),* II, 281; XIII, 235; Pictorial Supplement, XXXII, plate V; *(1795),* XVIII, 137, 138
Belize, steamship *(1878),* XI, 255
Belknap, Commander George, XXXII, 131
Belknap, Henry W., IV, 252; "The Ship *Crusoe,*" IV, 235–236; query by, III, 353
Belknap, Jeremy, XXXIII, 132 ff.

Belknap, Joseph, XVII, 60
Bell, steamship *(1861),* XI, 280
Bell, Commander Bankhead, XXXII, 125
Bell, Charles, XXXV, 295
Bell, Admiral Charles H., XXXII, 283 ff.
Bell, Rear Admiral H. H., U.S.N., VII, 20
Bell, Henry H., XXXVI, 202
Bell, Rear Admiral Henry H., XXIX, 113; XXXII, 123 ff.; XXXV, 28
Bell, Captain Henry H., XII, 272
Bell, Hugh F., "'Melancholy Affair' — James Otis and the Pirates," XXXI, 19–37
Bell, Major General J. Franklin, XXXIV, 263
Bell, John, XXXVII, 276
Bell, Kensil, *Always Ready! The Story of the United States Coast Guard,* reviewed, IV, 176
Bell, Thomas, XLVI, 8 ff.
Bell, Captain Thomas, XXXI, 40 ff.
Bell, William, Jr., L, 203
Bellairs, Lieutenant W. T., XXVI, 11
Bellamy, John, eagle carving by, Pictorial Supplement, XXXVII, plate XXIII
Bellarosa, James M., "The Tragic Slaving Voyage of *St. John,*" XL, 293–297
Bellatty, Captain Wellington C., IX, 172–173
Belle, schooner (1856), I, 74; *(1862),* XII, 53, 155, 229; XV, 127
Belle, sloop, XXI, 87, 92, 97; *(1861),* VIII, 216, 223; XI, 280
Belleau Wood, carrier *(1944),* XXXIX, 43
Belle Brown, steamship, XXVIII, 125
Bellefont, sloop *(1862),* XII, 53
Belle Hoxie, ship (1874), I, 45
Belle Italia, sloop *(1862),* XII, 53
Belle Morse, ship (1867), XXVII, plate VII
Belle of Bath, ship (1877), VI, 125; XXVIII, plate XVII
Belle of Oregon, bark (1876), I, 59–62, plates facing 58, 176; VI, 73–76
Belle of the Bay, brig *(1861),* XI, 280
Belle of the West, ship (1853), XXII, 239, 240
Bellerephon, H.M.S. *(1864),* XXVIII, 14, 15–17, 87
Bellerophon 74, ship *(1803),* XLV, 97
Belle S. Neal, schooner (1885), XXVI, plate VII
Belle Sauvage, ship *(1799),* X, 53; (1800), V, 90
Bellew, Captain Henry, XL, 17
Bellinger, Patrick N. L., L, 54
Bellingham, Washington, XXXVI, 231 ff.
Bellinghausen, Thaddeus, VII, 83
Belliqueux, vessel *(1801),* XXX, 212
Bell-Irving, Henry, XXXVI, 232
Bellomont, Lord, XVII, 292
Bellona, brig *(1813),* XIX, 218
Bellona, Dutch warship [model] (1780), XVI, 102
Bellona, frigate (1782), VI, 170
Bellona, ship *(1803),* XLI, 285
Bellona, sloop (1832), XXXVI, 255
Bellona, steamship (1872), XVIII, 68

Bellona Furnace Co., XLV, 39
Bell-Wallace Shipbuilding Co., XLI, 189
Belmont, ship *(1861),* XI, 266, 280
Belona, steamship *(1817),* XVI, 278
Beloved Little Admiral: Admiral of the Fleet the Hon. Sir Henry Keppel, G.G.B, O.M., The, by Vivian Stuart, reviewed, XXVIII, 73–74
Beluche, Commodore Renato, XXX, 270
Beluga, steam bark (1894), XXXVIII, 85 ff.; XXXIX, 8
Beluga, steamship *(1883),* XLIV, 17 ff.
Belvedere, steam bark *(1895),* XXXVIII, 86
Belvedere, steamship *(1880),* XLIV, 15 ff.
Belvedere, warship *(1814),* XLII, 112 ff.
Bemis, Seth, XXXI, 135
Ben, schooner *(1863),* XII, 115
Benares, ship *(1857),* XXV, 108
Benches, sailmaker's, IX, 291–292
Bendall, Captain, XIII, 20
Ben Deford, transport *(1862),* XXXI, 262
Bender, Bert, "Jack London in the Tradition of American Sea Fiction," XLVI, 188–199
Bendigo, steamship *(1863),* VIII, 229, 233
Benetor, sloop *(1864),* XV, 111, 128
Ben Franklin, steamship (1842), XX, 250
Bengal, steamship (1853), XVII, 62; XVIII, 68
Benham, Admiral Andrew E. K., XLI, 245
Benicia, U.S. steam sloop (1869), VII, 108, 111, 113, plate 11
Benin, steamship *(1898),* XLVI, 105
Benjamin, schooner *(1776),* XX, 45
Benjamin, schooner (1851), XXIV, 58
Benjamin, ship (1792), II, 281
Benjamin, Judah, XIX, 53
Benjamin, Judah P., XXXIII, 205
Benjamin, Lyman, XXXV, 87
Benjamin, Park, XXXVII, 112
Benjamin B. Odell, steamship (1911), XIV, 283
Benjamin Bangs, ship (1860), V, 149
Benjamin F. Packard, ship (1883), XXVIII, plate XXIII; XXXIX, plate 5; XLVII, 131
Benjamin Franklin Isherwood, Naval Engineer: The Years as Engineer in Chief, 1861–1869, by Edward William Sloan, III, reviewed, XXVI, 286–287
"Benjamin King, Instrument Maker," document contributed by Charles H. P. Copeland, XV, 232
Benjamin Russell, schooner (1901), XXVIII, 123
Benjamin Sewall, ship (1874), I, 113, plates facing 114, 115
"Benjamin Stoddert, Politics, and the Navy," by Robert L. Scheina, XXXVI, 54–68
Benjamin Thompson, schooner (1923), XXVI, plate XXX
Benjamin Tucker, ship (1839), X, 298–300; Pictorial Supplement, XXXIII, plate IX
Benjamin Tucker, ship (1850), XIV, 45; *(1862),* XXVII, 265
Benmore, ship (1871), VII, 289

Bennestvet, ship *(1922),* XVIII, 211
Bennet, Captain Lewis L., XII, 36
Bennet and Henderson, VII, 48
Bennett, Daniel, XLI, 285
Bennett, Frank M., XL, 128
Bennett, Frederick D., XII, 106
Bennett, Captain J. C., XVIII, 82
Bennett, Captain P., XVIII, 82
Benning, Captain A. A., XVIII, 82; XLIII, 95
Bennington, ship *(1892),* XXXVIII, 297; *(1899),* XXXV, 189
Benson, Captain Joseph, XXI, 105
Benson, William S., XXXVII, 113
Benson, Admiral William S., XLI, 267; XLVII, 255; L, 56
Benson, Rear Admiral William S., XXXV, 286
Bent, Judge Silas, XXV, 94
Bent, Lieutenant Silas, U.S.N., XXV, 93–98; XXVI, 215
Bentinck, steamship (1843), XXVI, 9, 30, 203, 204, 209
Bentley, Christopher, XVIII, 107, 108, 132
Bentley, Captain Christopher, XXXIV, 254
Bentley, Reverend Mr. William (of Salem), XIII, 236 ff.; XXIII, 143, 144, 145; XXVI, 274–276; XXXIII, 168
Benton, U.S.S. (1861), XIX, 266, 267, 269 ff.; *(1862),* XXV, 134–136, 138
Benton, Senator Thomas Hart, XLIX, 109
Ben Willis, schooner *(1865),* XII, 234
Benzon, Otto, X, 230
Bequia and Outlying Islands, Map III, XXXII, 185
Berceau, U.S. torpedo boat (1896), VI, 66
Berckman, Evelyn, *Nelson's Dear Lord: A Portrait of St. Vincent,* reviewed, XXIII, 73–74
Bereau, Captain William, XXXVIII, 44
Berçeau, French ship *(1800),* XXXI, 175
Berengaria, S.S., XXIX, 234; XXXIV, 260
Berenson, B., answered query, III, 270
Berg, Lieutenant Hans, XLVIII, 50 ff.
Bergen, Julia, Margery Walton, Janet Paul, *John Cawte Beaglehole: A Bibliography,* reviewed, XXXIII, 222–223
Bergh, Christian, VII, 179
Bering, steamship *(1923),* X, 120; *(1925),* XVI, 131; XVIII, 215
Berings's Voyages: Whither and Why, by Raymond H. Fisher, reviewed, XXXVIII, 302
Bering Strait, Discovery and exploration, XXXVIII, 81
Berkeley, Edmund, Jr., "The Naval Office in Virginia, 1776–1789," XXXIII, 20–33; document by, XXVIII, 68–69
Berkshire, steamship (ex–*Eastern Tempest*), XXIII, 276
Berlin, ship (1841), XIX, 27
Berlin Decree of 1806, XXIII, 157 ff.; XXX, 281
Berlin Mills Co., XXXV, 9
Bermuda, H.M.S. *(1796),* XVIII, 140
Bermuda, steamship, XXI, 102; (1861), III, 132–133; *(1861),* XV, 104, 105, 106, 122, 125
Bermuda, History, XXIV, 208

"Bermudas, Admiral Wilkes at the," by W. Salisbury, XXV, 140
Bermuda sloop, XIII, 177. *See also* Sloops
Bermudian, ship *(1915),* XLIII, 273
Bernabé, Admiral Jose Polo de, XXXVIII, 246
Bernard, Captain Alexandre, XXIII, 279, 280
Bernard, Andrew, XXXIX, 34
Bernard, Governor Francis, XL, 250 ff.
Bernard, Isaac, XXVI, 203
Bernardiston, ship *(1679),* XIII, 20, 26
Bernard Steamship Co., XXXVIII, 187 ff.
Bernie, schooner *(1916),* XLI, 45
Bernina, steamship (1876), XI, 255
Bernsdorff, Count, XLIII, 272
Bernstrosse, Danish ship *(1798),* L, 270 ff.
Berry, Captain Gordon C., XVIII, 82
Berry, Robert Elton, *Yankee Stargazer — The Life of Nathaniel Bowditch,* reviewed, II, 257–258
Berry-Hill, Henry and Sidney, *Chinnery and China Coast Paintings,* reviewed, XXXI, 149–150
Bertha, bark *(1877),* Pictorial Supplement, XXXIII, plates XXII, XXXII
Bertha, schooner *(1863),* XV, 111, 127
Bertha A. Walker, schooner *(1889),* XXXVII, 86
Bertha Ann, ship *(1803),* X, 53. See also *Wertha Ann.*
Bertha D. Nickerson, schooner (1883), Pictorial Supplement, XXXIII, plates V, XXXII
Bertha Deane, schooner, XIII, 121
Bertolino, Andrew, XLV, 84
Bertonccini, Captain John, VII, 294
Bertram, John, house flag of, Pictorial Supplement, XXXVIII, plate XX
Bertram, Kate and Richard, *Caribbean Cruise,* reviewed, VIII, 260–261
Berwick, H.M.S., XXVIII, 107, 108 n.
Berwickshire, ship, XIV, 102
Berwick Walls, steamship *(1862),* XLIII, 106 ff.
Berwind, steamship *(1904),* XIV, 134
Berwind, J. E., XIV, 123
Bessarabia, Rumanian-flag vessel *(1944),* XLIII, 33 ff.
Besse, Captain W. H., VIII, 152–153
Besse, Sumner B., II, 252
Bessemer, steamship (1874), XXIV, Plate IX
Bessemer Steel Co., XLVIII, 129
Bessie, schooner *(1916),* XLI, 45
Bessie A. Anderson, schooner (1901), XXVI, plate XVII
Best, Elsdon, XXIII, 126
Best on the Bay: Fifty Years of Racing, The, by Jane Carter Webb and George Randolph Webb, reviewed, XLV, 135
Bethania, German liner, XXVIII, 108
Bethel, Lieutenant Colonel Walter A., XXXIV, 265 ff.
Bethel, Captain William H., XXXVIII, 269
Bethia (Bethiah) Thayer, ship (1856), IV, 244; VI, 82
Bethlehem Iron Co., XXXIX, 137
Bethlehem Shipbuilding Corp., XXII, 182

Bethlehem Steel Co., XXXIX, 42; XLIV, 123; Shipbuilding Division, VIII, 76; IX, plate 29
Bethlehem Steel Corp., XXXII, 165
Bethulia, Lawley steam yacht *(1893),* XLIV, 121
Bethume, Donald, XX, 83, 268
Betsey, brig *(1784),* XXVI, 234; (1785), III, 19–25, 252–253; (1796), VI, 136; (1811), IV, 46; *(1824),* VIII, 173–174
Betsey, brigantine, XXV, 109; (1775), XIII, 29; *(1808),* X, 149
Betsey, schooner *(1762),* XXI, 9; *(1775),* XXXI 115, 116; *(1777),* II, 208
Betsey, schooner (1783), II, 278; (1795), VI, 136; (1805), VII, 317
Betsey, ship *(1784),* XLI, 210; XLIII, 24
Betsey, ship (1795), II, 278
Betsey, sloop, XXII, 85; (1792), VI, 136
Betsey Ames, brig *(1861),* VIII, 216
Betsey & Polly, schooner *(1804),* XLI, 180
Betsey and Sophia, whaler *(1831),* XLI, 289
Betsey Ann, sloop *(1807),* XVI, 196
Betsey Jane, schooner *(1815),* XV, 214
Betsey Ross, steam auxiliary (1917), V, 140
Betsy, schooner *(1797),* XL, 193; *(1814),* XXIV, 177, 178, 180
Betsy, ship (1801), XL, 47; *(1800),* XXIII, 216; XXIX, 85; *(1801),* XXIII, 216, 217
Bett, James, XIII, 27
Bettencourt, Antonio, XXXIX, 19
Bettie Cratzer, schooner *(1863),* VIII, 229
Betts, Guernsey B., XIV, 169 ff.
Betts, Harlan and Hollingsworth, Marine Ironworks, XXXIX, 219
"Between Decks in an Emigrant Ship," Pictorial Supplement, XXXI, plate XV
Between the Devil and the Deep Blue Sea, by Marcus Rediker, reviewed, XLVIII, 61
Between Wind and Water, by Gerald Warner Brace, reviewed, XXVI, 287
Beulah, schooner (1811), VII, 317
Beveridge, Senator Albert J., XXII, 192
Beverley, H.M. destroyer *(1943),* XLIV, 49 ff.
Beverly, schooner *(1861),* VIII, 216
Beverly, steamship *(1899),* XXXVII, 238
Beverly (MA), XXX, 86 ff.; view of Beverly Harbor, XXV, plate XXV
"Beyond Cape Horn: The Voyage of the Ship *Minerva* October 1799-September 1802," by Norman E. Muller, XXXIII, 160–173
Beyond the Capes: Pacific Exploration from Captain Cook to the Challenger 1776–1877, by Ernest S. Dodge, reviewed, XXXII, 138–139
Bhagat, G., "Americans and American Trade in India, 1784–1814," XLVI, 6–15; "America's First Contacts With India, 1784–1785," XXXI, 38–48
Black Joker, steamship, XXI, 101
Bianca, auxiliary schooner (1919) V, 140

Bibb, ship *(1861),* XXXI, 259
Bibb, U.S. Coast Guard Cutter *(1943),* XLIV, 49 ff.
Bibliography. *See* individual subjects, e.g., Maritime history
Bibliography: maritime articles in periodical publications, 1941, II, 264–266
Bibliography: "Recent Writings in Maritime History," by Robert G. Albion, XVI, 66–76, 139–152, 214–228, 286–296; XVII, 74–84, 157–168, 231–243, 315–325; XVIII, 86–99, 253–267, 326–332
Bibliography: XII, 64–94, 163–172, 241–248, 297–304; XIII, 68–76, 141–152, 215–230, 282–301; XIV, 66–78, 142–156, 218–232, 300–317; XV, 83–92, 157–168, 233–244, 311–320
"Bibliography of Richard LeBaron Bowen, Jr., A," XX, 272–273
Biblioteca Maritima Magallanes-Elcano, I, 316
Bicaise, John N., XXX, 178, 184, 185, 232 ff.
Bicker, Captain Martin, XLII, 50
Bicker, Lieutenant Victor, XXXVIII, 25
Bickett, Governor Thomas, XLI, 190
Bickford, Robert, XXVIII, 68–69
Bickford, Ward, III, 141
Bickham, Martin, U.S. Consul, XXV, 15
Bicon, schooner (1797), VI, 136
Biddeford, brig *(1777),* VI, 83
Biddeford, H.M.S. *(1719),* XXI, 262, 263
Biddeford, sloop *(1749),* XX, 242
Biddle, Charles, XX, 45
Biddle, Commodore James, U.S.N., XXV, 94; XXXI, 187; XLI, 25 ff.; XLII, 166 ff.; XLIII, 180; XLIV, 245; XLVII, 28; XLIX, 112
Biddle, Master Commandant, XL, 27, 40
Biddle, Captain Nicholas, Continental Navy, XXV, 193
Biddle, Captain Nicholas, IX, 303; XXX, 220
Biddle, Owen, XL, 12
Bidleman, J. B., XX, 119, 120
Bien Aimé, British ship *(1747),* XLVIII, 28
Bienfaisant, H.M.S. *(1777),* XIII, 212; (1778), VII, 95
Bienville, merchant steamship, XXXII, 48; *(1872),* X, 134
Biersdorf, M., XXXVI, 236
Bierstadt, Albert (artist), XXV, 59
Big Bonanza, ship (1874), XVII, 117
Bigelow, Henry B., and W. T. Edmonson, *Wind Waves at Sea, Breakers and Surf,* reviewed, IX, 304
Bigelow, Dr. Jacob, XLVI, 213
Bigelow, John, XXIX, 10, 10 n.
Bigelow, William Sturgis, XLVI, 56 ff.
Biggs, Thomas, XLVI, 260
Big Gun Monitors, by Ian Buxton, reviewed, XLI, 147–148
Big Mick, sandbagger *(1898),* XI, 93
Big Ship: The Story of the S.S. United States, *The,* by Frank O. Braynard, reviewed, XLII, 72–74
Bijou, steamship, XXI, 103; *(1864),* VIII, 233

"Bikini, Atom Atoll," note contributed by Captain Edgar K. Thompson, U.S.N. (ret.), XXIII, 222–224
Bilboa, brig, XXIII, 144
Biles, Professor J. H., III, 188
Biles, Professor John H., XLVII, 198
Bill, Jacob, XXXV, 292
Billard, Rear Admiral, U.S.C.G., XLI, 20
Billetheads, Pictorial Supplement, XXXVII, plate XXX
Bill for construction of steamship, May 1790, photo of, L, 203
Billias, George A., contributed document, XVIII, 323–324; *General John Glover and his Marblehead Mariners,* reviewed, XX, 146; "Misadventures of a Maine Slaver," XIX, 114–119; "Nathaniel T. Palmer's Fleet of Great Schooners," XX, 237–242
Billias, George Athan, *George Washington's Opponents: British Generals and Admirals in the American Revolution,* reviewed, XXIX, 285
Billings, Noyes and William W. (whalers of Stonington, CT), XXV, 103
Billop, Captain Thomas, XXI, 267
Billow, steamship (1887), VII, 235
Billow, trawler (1913), XLIV, 121
Billy Butts, schooner *(1870),* XXXVIII, 241
Biloxi shrimp fishing schooners, I, 71–72
"Binding Strake. Landing Strake," query by Baron R. de Kerchove, II, 81
Bingham, ship *(1806),* XLVIII, 248 ff.
Bingham, Rev. Hiram, XLVI, 46
Bingham, Rev. and Mrs. Hiram, IV, 111–112
Bingham, William, XIV, 54–56; XXXIII, 17; XLIII, 21 ff.
Bingham, Senator William, XXX, 142
Bingley, Sir Ralph, XXXI, 85 ff.; XLVII, 77 ff.
"Binnacle List," by Captain Edgar K. Thompson, U.S.N. (ret.), XXV, 217
Biography. See names of professions, e.g., Admirals; Commodores; Ship captains; Shipowners
Biography: National Maritime Museum Catalogue of the Library, Volume Two, reviewed, XXXI, 76
Biography of a Business, 1792–1942, by Marquis James, reviewed, IV, 176–177
"Biography of the *List of Merchant Vessels of the United States,*" by Forrest R. Holdcamper, XXIV, 119–123
Birch, Captain C., XVIII, 82
Birch, Thomas, II, plate 21; XXV, 59
Birchall, William, XXIV, plates XIII, XVI
Bird, Ann P., XXX, 62–67
Bird, Caroline, XXXVII, 206
Bird, Lieutenant Colonel Charles, XL, 172 ff.
Bird, Henry, XXVI, 37
Bird, Mrs. Isaac, XXX, 62–67
Bird carving from unidentified vessel, Pictorial Supplement, XXXVII, plate XXII
Bird head from unidentified vessel, Pictorial Supplement, XXXVII, plate XIX
Birdseye, Clarence, XLVII, 268

Bird's-eye View of Tynemouth, 1673, L, 20, 22
Birkbeck, Sir Edward, XXXIV, 10
Birkner, Michael, "The 'Foxardo Affair' Revisited: Porter, Pirates and the Problem of Civilian Authority in the Early Republic," XLII, 165–178
Birmingham, ship (1836), IV, 329–334
Birmingham, ship (1860), III, 62; *(1861),* XI, 280
Birmingham, U.S.S. (1908), XXII, 142, 146
Birmingham City, steamship *(1950),* XIV, 133, 135
Birth of the Steamboat, The, by H. Philip Spratt, reviewed, XIX, 148
"Birthplace of the American Navy," XXX, 87
Bishop, Captain Charles, XIII, 213; XXVIII, 227–228
Bishop, Daniel H., XIV, 169 ff.
Bishop, Captain Thomas, XXIII, 178
Bishop & Clerks, light-vessel *(1862),* V, 245
Bishop Museum, Honolulu, XXIV, 3; XXVIII, 163
Bishop of Oporto, XXX, 249, 252
"Bishop Synesius' Voyage to Cyrene," by Lionel Casson, XII, 294–296
Bismark, German battleship *(1941),* L, 131
Bismark Archipelago, boats of, XIII, 111
Bissau, XXX, 178, 180, 181, 238
Bissell, Commander Simon B., XXXIII, 44
Biter, H.M. escort carrier *(1943),* XLV, 59
Bittern, British sloop of war *(1795),* XLIX, 45
Bittern, ship *(1855),* XXXI, 272
Bittle, William, XXXV, 198
Bixby, William, *Track of the Bear, 1875–1963,* reviewed, XXVIII, 71–72
Bixley, Valentine & Co., XIX, 17–20
Black, Hugo, XLI, 118
Black, Jeannette D., "Disaster in the South Seas: The Wreck of the Brigantine *Eliza* and the Subsequent Adventures of Captain Corey," XXIII, 233–254
Black, Jeremy and Philip Woodfine, *The British Navy and the Use of Naval Power in the Eighteenth Century,* reviewed, XLIX, 314
Black, John, VII, 177
Black, John H., XXVIII, 69
Black, Thomas, XXVI, 203
Black, William L., XXXII, 209
Black Ball Line, I, 85–87; XV, 133; XVI, 60–61
Blackbeard (pirate), XXX, 137
Blackbeard Island, Georgia, map of, XXXV, 229
Blackbirders in Pacific, IV, 112–113
Blackbraes, ship (1891), XVIII, 5
Black Cloud, sloop *(1887),* XXX, plate X
Black Dog, ship *(1588),* XLIV, 31 ff.
Blackey, Thomas, XXX, 299
Black Fish, brig (1861), XV, 103, 122
Blackford, wooden steamship *(1917),* XXXV, 283
Black Hawk, schooner *(1847),* XLIV, 89
Black Hawk, ship (1856), III, 263; XIX, plate XI; (1857), XXVIII, plate X; (1861), XIV, 46
Blackhawk, steamship (1833), VII, 50
Black Hawk, U.S.S. *(1936),* XLIV, 185

Black Joker, steamship *(1861),* XI, 280; XII, 53
Blackledge, Richard, XLIX, 84 ff.
Blackledge, Singleton & Co., XLIX, 84
Blackler, Captain William G., XXXII, 210
"Black List," by Captain Edgar K. Thompson, U.S.N. (ret.), XXV, 127
"Black-Owned Shipping Before Marcus Garvey," by Rodney Carlisle, XXXV, 197–206
Black Prince, brigantine *(1776),* XLII, 9 ff.
Black Prince, ship *(1866),* XXXV, 32 ff.
Black River (1742), XXVI, 49
Black Ships off Japan, by Arthur C. Walworth, Jr., reviewed, VI, 234
Black Snake, galley *(1813),* XLIII, 6 ff., 26
Black Squall, schooner, XXI, 103; *(1861),* XI, 280
Black Star Line, XXXV, 205
Blackstone, Edward H., *Farewell Old Mount Washington: The Story of the Steamboat Era on Lake Winnipesaukee,* reviewed, XXIX, 286
Black Swan, British cruiser *(1949),* XLIX, 221; L, 291 ff.
Black Walnut, brig (1805), VII, 317
Black Warrior, schooner *(1862),* VIII, 223
Black Warrior, ship (1853), III, 62
Blackwood, John G., XLVIII, 89
Blaes, Adriaen, XL, 294
Blain, Tate & Co., XLIII, 195 ff.
Blain, William, *Home is the Sailor: the Sea Life of William Brown, Master Mariner and Penang Pilot,* reviewed, I, 186–187
Blaine, James G., XXXIX, 290; XXXV, 54
Blair, Montgomery, XXXVII, 279
Blair, Victor, Jr., XXV, 181
Blaisdell, Paul H., *The New S.S.* Mount Washington ... *for Lake Winnipesaukee,* reviewed, I, 411
Blake, Captain Chesley, XX, 89 n.
Blake, Captain Chesly, VII, 49
Blake, Captain Daniel, XLIV, 151
Blake, Edward, XIII, 39, 43
Blake, Captain G. S., XXIII, 55
Blake, Captain George S., U.S.N., XXV, 224–225
Blake, Commander H. C., U.S.N., VII, 110, 111, 113, plate 9
Blake, Commander Homer C., XV, 301; XXIX, 108
Blake, Lieutenant Commander Homer C., XLII, 96
Blake, Joshua, XV, 138
Blake, Lieutenant Joshua, XXI, 130–141
Blakely, Captain Johnston, U.S.N., VII, 168
Blanch, John, XIV, 59
Blanchard, Captain A., XVIII, 82
Blanchard, C. P., XXXVI, 236
Blanchard, Clara E. Pendleton, XLIV, 151 ff.
Blanchard, Captain Hollis H., XXVIII, plate XXXI
Blanchard, N. M., XXXVI, 245
Blanchard, Norman, XXXVI, 245, 248
Blanchard, Captain P. Banning, XXVIII, plate III
Blanchard, Samuel, XLI, 177
Blanchard, Thomas, XXXIV, 92

Blanchard, Captain William, II, 194
Blanchard, William H., XLIV, 151 ff.
Blanche, steamship, XXI, 101; *(1862),* XII, 53
Blanche Moore, ship (1854), V, 147
Blanche Ring, trawler *(1921),* XLIV, 128
Blanchette, Paul O., review by, XXVIII, 151–152
Blanco, General, XXXVI, 90
Blanco Encalada, Chilean ironclad (1874), XXXIX, 275
Bland, Schuyler, XLI, 116
Blankenese, Schleswig-Holstein, Germany, XXX, 70
Blankett, Commodore John, XXX, 211
Blazer, sloop, XXI, 89; *(1863),* XII, 155
Blegen, Theodore C., *John Quincy Adams and the Sloop* Restoration, reviewed, I, 324
Blencathea, ship (1847), V, 151, 242
Blenheim, English steamship *(1878),* XXIV, 44
Blenheim, steamship, XXI, 105; *(1864),* VIII, 233, 236
Blethen, C. P., XVII, 140
Blethen, Captain W., XVII, 141; XVIII, 82
Blewer, Captain Joseph, XXXII, 249
Bligh, Admiral William, XI, 146–147; XII, 253, 270; XIII, 213, 281
Bligh, Captain William, XXVI, 215; XXVIII, 146; XXX, 211; *The Log of H.M.S.* Bounty, *1787–1789;* and *The Log of H.M.S.* Bounty, *1791–1793,* reviewed, XXXVIII, 71
Bligh, Lieutenant William, R.N., IV, 53–54
Blinn, James, XXI, 22
Bliss, E. Jared, contributed document, XVI, 211
Bliss, Hezekiah, XLVIII, 112
Bliss, John, XVII, 126
Bliss, General Tasker H., XXXII, 262; XXXIV, 268
Bliss, William, XXX, 277
Bloch, Claude C., XXXVII, 121
Block, Captain W. F., XVII, 251
Blockade. See United States History (Civil War)
Blockade, Civil War, XVI, 49–59; XVII, 249–261; XVIII, 142–148
Blockade runners, III, 131–140, 265; XXI, 81–107, plates I–XXXII; XXV, 113
Blockade running, VIII, 196–241, 259–260; IX, 31–62; XI, 262–290; XII, 52–59, 154–161, 229–238, 276–281; XIV, 61–63; XV, 97–132; XXVI, 134–137; in Florida, VII, 121 ff.
"Blockade Running as a Business in South Carolina during the War between the States, 1861–1865," by Marcus W. Price, IX, 31–62
"Blockade-Running Charter: Spring 1862, A," edited by Peter Payne and Frank J. Merli, XXVI, 134–137
"Blockading the New England Coast: The Journal of Lt. Henry Napier," by Philip K. McLaughlin, XLV, 5–9
Block Island boat, XII, 137–141, Plate 12
Blogg, Henry, British coxswain, XXXIV, 7 ff.
Blok, Dutch ship *(1783),* XLVII, 245
Blom, Baron, XXX, 284
Blonde, H.M. frigate *(1778),* VII, 207, 209
Blonde, H.M.S. *(1873),* XXIX, 261

Blonde, ship *(1779),* XXXVII, 296
Blondel, Maurice L., XXXII, 19
Blood, Hiram, XXXIX, 97
Blood, James, XVII, 115
Bloodhound, H.M.S. *(1847),* XIII, 259
"Blood is Thicker than Water," by Edith Roelker Curtis, XXVII, 157–176
Bloomer, schooner (1855), IX, 175, plate 24; *(1855),* Pictorial Supplement, XXXVI, plate IX; (1874), XXIV, 45, 60
Bloomfield, Meyer, XXXII, 163
Blooming Youth, schooner (1861), XV, 122
Blount Marine Corp., XXXVIII, 139
Bludworth, J. Z., XXII, 169
"Blue, A Shot into the," by Captain Edgar K. Thompson, U.S.N. (ret.), XXV, 140–141
"Blue" and "Black" Fleet, XXXII, 259 ff.
Blue Bell, sloop *(1863),* XII, 155
Bluebird, sail (ex-*Ypres*) *(1923),* XXXII, 32
Bluebird, yacht *(1892),* XXXVI, 236
Blue Book of American Shipping, XXX, 31
Blue Jacket, ship (1854), V, 148
Blue Jay, yacht *(1890),* XXXVI, 235
Bluenose, MV ferry (1971), XXXIV, 186
Bluenose, schooner, XXIV, 4; XXVI, plate XXIX; XXXIV, 142
Bluenose, schooner [replica], XXX, 80
Blue Star, British shipping line, XLVI, 108
Bluett, E. J., XXIX, 133, 135
Blue Water Coaster, by Francis E. Bowker, reviewed, XXXIV, 146–147
Blumberg, Arnold and Armin Mruck, "An Austrian View of the United States Navy: 1867," XXXIV, 59–64
Blume, Kenneth J., review by, L, 139, 233
Blume, Kenneth John, "The Hairy Ape Reconsidered: The American Merchant Seaman and the Transition from Sail to Steam in the late Nineteenth Century," XLIV, 33–47
Blumer and Co., XIV, 122
Blundeville, Thomas, XXXVII, 175
Blunt, E. and G. W., XXX, 21
Blunt, Edmund B., XLVI, 260
Blunt, Edmund M., V, 102–103; XXX, 41, 42
Blunt, Edmund March, XXI, 5–15; XXV, 3, 46 ff.; *American Coast Pilot,* quoted, XXV, 233, 235; chart by, XXV, 241
Blunt, Eliza Carlton, XXV, 49
Blunt, George W., II, 100, 102; XXX, 42
Blunt, George William, XXV, 47
Blythewoode, steamship (1870), XVI, 54, 59; XVIII, 68; XLIX, 24
Boadicea, H.M.S. *(1803),* XXXV, 110
Boardman, sidewheeler *(1863),* XLII, 193 ff.
Boardman, Francis, XXX, 220
Boardman, James, XX, 45
Boardman, Thomas H., XVII, 119

Boardman, W. B., XVII, 116
Board of Trade and Plantations, XXXI, 131
Boatbuilding:
   Chesapeake Bay Region (MD/VA), IV, 269
   Chile, XXVI, 33
   Maine, II, 307; III, 141
   Marshall Islands, VI, 71
   Massachusetts, XI, 83
   Middle East, IX, 87; XII, 186
   New England, XII, 123
   New York, 19th century, IV, 224
Boatbuilding, A complete Handbook of Wooden Boat Construction, by Howard I. Chapelle, reviewed, II, 181–182
Boatbuilding, Classical, XXIV, 84–94
Boats:
   Andes Region, II, 107
   Archives, XLVIII, 182
   Chile, XXVI, 33
   Ecuador, XV, 142
   Mediterranean Sea, I, 352; II, 56
   New Brunswick, XVII, 5
   Nile River, XII, 45
   Oceania, XXIII, 41
   Philippines, XIX, 257
   Piscataqua River (NH), II, 127, 209
   Seal fishery, III, 327
   South America, XXI, 157
   West Indies, XXIV, 95
See also Indians of North America; Indians of South America
Boats: Arabian, XII, 186–221; XV, 5–48; Dories, XIII, 78–80; Double-enders, XIV, 123–141; Indonesian, XIII, 81–117, 185–211; XV, 5–48; Mediterranean, XII, 240; XV, 5–48; New England, XIII, 123–141; Oceania, XII, 306–308; XIII, 81–117, 185–211; Philippine Islands, XIX, 257–264; Sakonnet River boat, XVI, 61–62; Shallop, XVII, 105–113; South America, XIII, 81–117, 185–211; Whaleboat, XX, 63–64
"Boats of Ash Point, Maine, The," by Alfred A. Brooks, II, 307–323
Boat types. *See* names of individual types, e.g., Dhow; Schooner
Boat yard at Ancud, Chiloé (province of Chile), 1958, XXVI, plate 2
Bob, power yacht *(1924),* IX, 17–18, 21, 24
Bobtail Nag, brigantine (1870), XXIX, 290
Bockstoce, John, XLIV, 18
Bockstoce, John R., *Steam Whaling in the Western Arctic,* reviewed, XXXVIII, 72
Bockstoce, John R., and Charles F. Batchelder, "A Chronological List of Commercial Wintering Voyages to the Bering Strait Region and Western Arctic of North America: 1850–1910," XXXVIII, 81–91
Bocock, Senator Thomas S., XXX, 145

Bode, Carl, XXXIX, 114
Boden, Mrs. Sarah, XXXI, 286 ff.
"Boden, William, A Vignette of the Naval Career of," document, XXXI, 286–288
Bodfish, Captain Hartson, XLIV, 19 ff.
Bodleian Library (Oxford University, England), **Library resources**, XXIX, 244
Boelen, Jacobus, *A Merchant's Perspective: Captain Jacobus Boelen's Narrative of his Visit to Hawai'i in 1828*, reviewed, XLIX, 135
Boerchel, P., App., U.S.N., XXV, 50
Boerner, C. G., mention, XLIX, 226
Boer War, XXVIII, 93, 99
Boggs, S. Whittemore, IV, 99
Bogotà, steamship *(1851)*, XXXV, 272
Bogota, ship *(1861)*, XXI, 258
Bogue, U.S. escort carrier *(1941)*, XLV, 59
Bohemia, schooner (1884), IX, 70–71, plate 7; X, 155
Bohemia, ship (1875), IV, 46, 51, 52; XVI, 122; XVIII, 213
"*Bohemia*, Last of the Chesapeake Schooners," by A. L. van Name, Jr., IX, 70–71, plate 7
Bohlen & Co., V, 255 ff.
Boiseé Anchorage, Korea, VII, 112, 113
Boit, Captain John, Jr., XXV, 8
Boké (Debucca), XXX, 182
Bolander, Louis H., I, 316; "The C.S.S. *Stonewall*; Ship of Many Names and Many Flags," I, 241–254
Bold Hunter, ship *(1863)*, XLV, 197
Bolero, MV ferry *(1971)*, XXXIV, 187
Bolimke, George, XXIX, 135
Bolina, ship (1857), II, 79–80
Bolinder Oil Engines, XXV, 288
Bolivar, steamship *(1853)*, XXX, 274
Bolivar, steamship (1866), II, 76
Bolivia, grain elevator *(1883)*, XXXVIII, 141
Bolivia, iron paddle steamship *(1849)*, XXXV, 272
Boliviana, Venezuelan schooner *(1848)*, XXX, 266
Bolster, Jeffrey, review by, XLI, 145–146
Bolt, Daniel R., II, 252; VI, 240; "The Later History of American Sailing Ships 'Sold Foreign,'" II, 245–246, 330–335; III, 62–73, 169–173, 261–264, 349; IV, 72–73, 238–244, 326; V, 147–155
Bolton, brig (1819), IV, 46, 51
Bolton, ship (1858), IV, 51
Bolton, Charles Knowles, I, 316; IV, 252; "John Adams of Pitcairn's Island," I, 297–300; contributed document, IV, 245–246
Bolton, Rebecca, XXXV, 245
Bolton, Robert, XXXV, 245
Bolton, Stephen, XXXVII, 17
Bolton, Commodore William C., XLIII, 173 ff.
Bolton, Captain William Compton, XIII, 272
Bolívar, Simon, XXX, 261
Bomani, Jamshedi, XL, 284
Bombard, Allen, XXIII, 116
Bombay, ship (1847), IV, 73

Bombay, steamship (1852), XXVI, 17, 18, 23, 24, 116, 202–204, 209
Bombay, XXX, 204
Bombay Castle, steamship (1857), XXVI, 110, 112, 204, 209
"Bombay Marine, The," by Keith A. Parker, XL, 280–292
Bombay Mercantile S.N. Co., XXVI, 201
Bombay Steam Co., XXII, 16; XXXIV, 18
"Bomb Guns and Bomb Lances," by Reginald A. Hagerty, XXVII, 279–280
Bombshell, steamship *(1864)*, VIII, 233
Bomford, Colonel, XLVII, 117
Bona, schooner *(1825)*, XXXVIII, 55
Bonanza, schooner *(1890)*, XXXIX, 14
Bonaparte, Prince Charles, XXXIX, 116
Bonaparte, Jerome, XVII, 196
Bonaparte, Napoleon, XXIII, 157, 160
"Bonaparte Toscan and the Cuban Pirates," by Kenneth Scott, VI, 93–100
Bond, George, XV, 138
Bond, Sir Francis, VII, 301
Bonetta, H.M.S., XXVI, 54
Bonetta, pink *(1718)*, IX, 133–141
Bonham, Sir George, XXX, 158, 166; XXXIV, 103
Bonham, Julia C., "Feminist and Victorian: The Paradox of the American Seafaring Woman of the Nineteenth Century," XXXVII, 203–218
Bonhomme Richard, French ship (ex-*Duc de Duras*) (1765), XXVIII, 197–204; XLVI, 184 ff. See also *Bon Homme Richard*.
Bon Homme Richard, frigate (1775), XLIV, 104, 169 ff.; (1779), XXXIX, 162 ff.
Bon Homme Richard, U.S.S. *(1778)*, XIII, 65; *(1779)*, XVIII, 304
Bon Homme Richard, U.S.S. (1864), XXVII, 43
Bonita, brig *(1860)*, XXI, 40
Bonita, Mexican gunboat *(1846)*, XXX, 55
Bonita, schooner yacht *(1900)*, XXXVI, 240
Bonita, steamship *(1862)*, VIII, 223
Bonita, steamship (1881), II, 75
Bonne Amitie, French ship *(1800)*, XXXI, 174
Bonneau, Captain F. N., XIV, 62
Bonner, Captain John, XX, 45
Bonnet, Stede, XXXVII, 46
Bonnin, Henry, XII, 227
Bonomo, Captain Emile, XXXII, 16; XXXIII, 51
Bon Pere, French ship *(1799)*, XXXI, 173
Bonus, Nathaniel, XIII, 22
"Book Smuggling in Mexican California," by William F. Strobridge, XXXII, 117–122
Books Received: XXIII, 76, 152, 228, 291; XXIV, 75–76, 150–151, 227–228; XXV, 76, 151, 299–301
Books Reviewed: XIX, 141, 307; XX, 68, 146, 224, 274; XXI, 147–151, 223–228; XXII, 71–75, 145–152, 222–227; XXIII, 70–76, 146–152, 228, 285–290; XXIV, 74–75, 144–150, 217–227; XXV, 71–75,

147–151, 227–228, 295–299; XXVI, 72–76, 145–152, 220–225, 284–287; XXVII, 66–75, 150–151, 221–227, 281–289; XXVIII, 70–75, 146–153, 225–234, 287–298; XXIX, 65–75, 139–149, 282–291; XXX, 68–75, 217–224, 297–304; XXXI, 73–77, 148–150, 226–229, 291–292; XXXII, 69–76, 136–150, 224–226, 287–296; XXXIII, 63–69, 146–150, 212–225, 304–308; XXXIV, 142–149, 278–286; XXXV, 67–72, 211–222; XXXVI, 144–149, 296–302; XXXVII, 70–75, 223–225; XXXVIII, 68–74, 144–150, 225–228, 301–304; XXXIX, 144–153, 302–304; XL, 65–75, 139–151, 229–236; XLI, 70, 142, 231, 306; XLII, 66, 138, 221, 305; XLIII, 56, 142, 224, 303; XLIV, 66, 132, 199, 276; XLVI, 120, 200, 269; XLVII, 54, 141, 211, 286; XLVIII, 61, 131, 186; XLIX, 59, 133, 232, 305; L, 63, 138

Books to Build an Empire: A Bibliographical History of English Overseas Interests to 1620, by John Parker, reviewed, XXVII, 75

Book Trade, in California, XXXII, 117

Boone, Governor, XXV, 124

Booth, Alan R., "*Alabama* at the Cape, 1863," XXVI, 96–108

Booth, John Wilkes, XXV, 67

Booth, Mordecai, XXX, 136

Bo Peep, steamship *(1860),* XXXIV, 28; *(1861),* XLIII, 99 ff.

Borah, Senator William E., XXXIV, 163

Borden, Gilbert Bennett, XXXIX, 10

Borden, Norman E., Jr., *Dear Sarah: New England ice to the Orient and other incidents from the Journals of Captain Charles Edward Barry to his wife,* reviewed, XXVII, 72

Borden, Simeon, XXXI, 254

Borden, William, XXXI, 131

Bordes fleet, XXX, 209 f.

Boreham Wood, Hertfordshire, XXXIV, 12 ff.

Borelli, Joseph, VII, 266

Borghese, Commander Junio Valerio, XXVII, 185–201

Borgia, schooner, XXI, 98; *(1862),* XII, 53

Borinquen, liner *(1931),* XXXVI, 12

Borland, Senator Solon, XXX, 144 n.

Borneo, IV, 217–223; XXX, 201, 202

"Born Forty Years Too Soon," by John D. Alden, XXII, 252–263

Borough, William, XIV, 10, 11

Bosanquet, Vice-Admiral Sir Day H., XXVIII, 112

Boscawen, three-decker ship *(1748),* XLVII, 243 ff.

Bosch, Justus, XXXVII, 57

Bosforo, steamship *(1882),* XIV, 134

Bosscher, Ph. M., L. M. Akveld, J. R. Bruijn, and Kltz F. C. van Oosten, Editors, *Vier Eeuwen Varen — kapiteins, kapers, kooplieden en geleerden,* reviewed, XXXIV, 282

Bostock, cartel *(1814),* XXVIII, 190

Boston, American whaler *(1824),* XXXIV, 254

Boston, barque *(1849),* XLV, 124

Boston, British frigate *(1804),* XLII, 278; XLIII, 42

Boston, frigate *(1776),* VIII, 11, 13, 17, 21–24; X, 46; XLII, 27; *(1777),* V, 187; XLVIII, 160; oil painting of, XLVIII, 161; *(1778),* XXXVII, 73

Boston, frigate *(1799),* XLVI, 151 ff.

Boston, gondola *(1776),* VIII, 256; XXXV, 142

Boston, packet ship *(1830),* XXV, plate I

Boston, ship *(1748),* XLVIII, 25; *(1777),* XIV, 49 n.; *(1828),* XV, 139

Boston, ship *(1832),* XV, 139; *(1883),* XXXVII, 254; XXXVIII, 297; XXXIX, 41, 129, 140

Boston, sloop of war *(1842),* XXIX, 110; XXXI, 184

Boston, steamship *(1850),* XXXVI, 171; *(1864),* VIII, 233; *(1890),* XXXIV, 180 ff.; XXXV, 184 ff.

Boston, trawler (ex-*Ripple*) *(1916),* XLIV, 129

Boston, U.S. cruiser *(1942),* XXII, 148

Boston, U.S.S. *(1776),* XXI, 76; *(1799),* XXVII, 144; XXXI, 173; *(1805),* L, 60; *(1806),* XVIII, 183; *(1826),* XXI, 64, 65; XXIII, 58 n.

Boston, John, XV, 102 ff.

Boston (MA). History, Revolution (1775–1788), XLII, 25. *See also* Ship chandlers; Shipping; Smuggling

Boston (MA), XXV, plates IV, VII, XXII, XXVII; Old State House, ca. 1832, XXIX, 198, plate XIX; stone redoubt projected for Beacon Hill, 1774, I, plate facing 146; wharves of, 1829, XXIX, plate XVII

Boston (A History of the Boston Yacht Club) 1866–1979, The, by Paul E. Shanabrook, reviewed, XLIV, 199

Boston and Bangor Steamship Co., ship of, Pictorial Supplement, XXXIV, plate XXVI

Boston & Colonial Steamship Co., XXXVII, 234

Boston and Gloucester Steamboat Co., XII, 288–291

Boston and Hingham Steamboat Co., XII, 288

Boston and Liverpool Packet Co., XV, 133 ff.

Boston and Yarmouth Steamship Co., XXXVII, 238

Boston Athenaeum, VI, 155, 162; VIII, 154; XXV, 29, 32, 33, plate I

"Boston: A Topographical History," by Walter M. Whitehill, XX, 3–4

Boston City, steamship *(1893),* XIV, 122, 123, 125, 134; *(1916),* XIV, 125, 130, 135; *(1920),* XIV, 126, 128, 130, 132, 135

Boston Fish Pier Co., XLIV, 125

Boston from Pemberton Hill, 1829, XXIX, 124, plate XVI

"Boston-Halifax Steamship Lines, The," by Arthur L. Johnson, XXXVII, 231–238

Boston Harbor from Constitution Wharf, ca. 1829, XXIX, 198, plate XVII

Bostonian Society, The, XVII, 3; comment in Editorial, *The American Neptune,* XXXVIII, 3–4

Boston Importing Co., The, XV, 133; XXVIII, 32; XXX, 285

Boston Lighthouse, 1729, mezzotint of, IX, 237–238

Boston Long Wharf Co., XIII, 120

Boston Marine Society, XXVIII, 32, 35, 39

"Boston Merchant Fleet of 1753, The," by Murray G. Lawson, IX, 207–215

Boston National Historical Park: comment in Editorial, *The American Neptune,* XXXVIII, 3–4

Boston Naval Shipyard, XXV, 33

"Boston Navy Yard, 1840," document contributed by Vernon D. Tate, VII, 67–69, plates 7–8

Boston Navy Yard, XXV, 28; XXX, 56

Boston News-Letter, XXV, 61, 82, 83

Boston Packet, ship *(1748),* XLVIII, 34

"Boston Packet, A," query by Thomas Hornsby, II, 81; query answered by Arthur C. Wardle, II, 176

"Boston Packets, The," by Henry C. Kittredge, XXIV, 127–137

Boston Port Act, XXVII, 220

"Boston: Portrait of a Harbor," lecture series, comment in Editorial, *The American Neptune,* XXXVIII, 3–4

Boston Sail Cloth Manufactory, XXXI, 135

"Boston Shipbuilding Contract of 1747, A," document contributed by M. V. Brewington, V, 328

"Boston's Little-Known Packet Lines," by Dana M. Hastings, XV, 133–141

"Boston Smuggling, 1807–1815," by John D. Forbes, X, 144–154

Boston Tea Party, The, by Benjamin Woods Labaree, reviewed, XXV, 149–151

Boston Towboat Co., III, 195–196

Boston Tow Boat Co., XLII, 255; XLVII, 126

"'Boston': Two 'New' Texts of an Old Favorite Sea Song," by Stuart M. Frank, XLV, 175–179

Bosworth, Nathaniel, XXX, 96 n.

Botany Bay, by James Norman Hall and Charles Nordhoff, reviewed, II, 354

Boucaline, Charles, XXX, 184

Bougainville, barge (1863), VIII, 114–126

Bougainville, XXV, 252–254, 258, 260

Boulton, Dallett & Boulton, XXX, 272

Boulton, Dallett & Co., XXX, 267

Boulton, Henry Lord, XXX, 277

Boulton, John, XXX, 273

Boulton and Watt, XXVII, 5–8, 12–14, 21, 22, 27, 28

Boulware, L. R., XXXVIII, 280

Bouncer, British ship *(1858),* XLIII, 274 ff.

Bouncer, ship, XXXIV, 118

Boundary, sailing packet, XXVIII, 121

Bounding Billow, bark *(1888),* XXXIX, 8

Bounty, H.M.S. *(1789),* IV, 53–56; XI, 146–147; XII, 253

Bounty, H.M.S., XXVI, 215; XXVIII, 146

Bounty, H.M.S. [replica], XXX, 80; *(1935),* XVI, 137–138

Bounty, ship (1809), XXXIII, 163

Bounty Mutiny (1789), Manuscripts, XII, 253

Bouquet, Michael, *South Eastern Sail: from the Medway to the Solent 1840–1940,* reviewed, XXXIII, 213; *Westcounty Sail: Merchant Shipping 1840–1960,* reviewed, XXXIII, 213–214

Bourboulon, M. de, XXX, 158

Bourn, Melatiah, XL, 248

Bourn and Co., XIII, 121

Bourne, Jonathan, XXV, 103

Bourne, William, VII, 264–265; XXXI, 27, 37

Bourne Whaling Museum, New Bedford (MA), IX, 29, 296

Boussole, French warship *(1788),* XXI, 196 ff.

Boutelle, Charles Otis, XXXI, 254 ff.

Boutilier, James A., editor, *RCN in Retrospect 1910–1968,* reviewed, XLIII, 150–151

Boutwell, Commander Edward, XXXV, 26

Boutwell, George A., Secretary of the Treasury, XXXVIII, 240

Bouvet, French warship [model] (1866), XVI, 103

Bouvier, Pierre, XXI, 201 ff.

Bowden, K. M., *Captain James Kelly of Hobart Town,* reviewed, XXVI, 75–76

Bowden, William Hammond, reviews by, XXXIII, 305–307; XXXVII, 72–73

Bowditch, Habakkuk, V, 99–100

Bowditch, Harold, IV, 252; V, 165; "Nathaniel Bowditch," V, 99–110; query by, V, 89; VI, 155; edited "Reminiscences of a Voyage in the Bark *William H. Besse,*" by Mrs. B. C. Baker, VI, 121–131; reviewed book, XXIV, 221–223

Bowditch, N. Ingersoll, clock of, Pictorial Supplement, XXXV, plate XVII

Bowditch, Nathaniel, II, 257–258; V, 99–110; XIII, 247; XXIII, 132; XXV, 3, 58, 179–181, 183, 187, plate 18; XXVI, 277; XXXIX, 116; XLVI, 263; instrument by, Pictorial Supplement, XXXV, plate I; *American Practical Navigator,* reviewed, XIX, 141

Bowdoin, schooner *(1969),* XXIX, 154

Bowdoin, James, XXXIII, 111 ff.

Bowen, steamship (1874), XXIV, plate V

Bowen, Ashley, XXIII, 143–145; XXX, 95–111; XXXIII, 305–307

Bowen, Dana Thomas, *Lore of the Lakes,* reviewed, I, 187

Bowen, Captain Francis, XXXVI, 90; XXXVIII, 242

Bowen, Sir George, XXXII, 245

Bowen, John, XXVI, 203; reviews by, XXX, 69, 75, 223–224, 304

Bowen, Drs. Pardon and William, XL, 193 ff.

Bowen, Richard LeBaron, Jr., IX, 82; "Arab Dhows of Eastern Arabia," IX, 87–132, plates 9–16; bibliography, 272–273; "The Dhow Sailor," XI, 161–202; "The Dipping Lug," XX, 273; "Eastern Sail Affinities," XIII, 81–117, 185–211; *Marine Industries of Eastern Arabia,* reviewed, XI, 300; "Maritime Superstitions of the Arabs," XV, 5–48, plates 1, 2; A Melanesian Outrigger," XXIII, 255–260; "Origin and Diffusion of Oculi," XVII, 262–291; XVIII, 25–58, 235–252; "The Origins of Fore and Aft Rigs," XIX, 155–199, 274–306; XXIII, 115; *Pearl Fisheries of the Persian Gulf,* reviewed, XI, 300; "Primitive Watercraft of Arabia," XIII, 186–221, plates 17–19;

reprint mentioned, IX, 306; XX, 64–66; "River Craft of the Lower Nile," XIII, 45–51; "Twentieth-Century Parallelisms of the Double Canoe and the Double Outrigger," XIII, 306–308

Bower, John C., Jr., mentioned, XXXVII, 156; note by, XXXIV, 69–70; reviews by: XXXI, 77, 148, 228; XXXII, 136, 143, 293; XXXIII, 65, 149, 216, 223; XXXIV, 280; XXXV, 214; XXXVI, 146, 149, 298–300; XXXVII 224–225; XXXVIII, 69, 72, 149; XXXIX, 302–304; XL, 71, 72, 73, 139, 143, 149; XLI, 73, 312; XLII, 67, 146; XLIII, 224, 226; XLIV, 132, 133; "Almost Down East," XLV, 253; "Firing a Western River-type Firetube Boiler," XXXIII, 155–159; "My One Trip Playing Boatswain," XXXVI, 101–107; "The Standing Lug," XX, 271–272

Bowers, Captain Henry, XLIV, 6
Bowers, Sylvester, VIII, 13, 19, 20
Bowhead, steam bark *(1900),* XXXVIII, 88
Bowhead (II) (ex-*Haardraada*) *(1917),* XLIV, 21
Bowker, Francis E., *Blue Water Coaster,* reviewed, XXXIV, 146–147
Bowker, Captain Francis E., *Atlantic Four-Master: The Story of the Schooner* Herbert L. Rawding, *1919–1947,* reviewed, XLVIII, 193
Bowles, Rear Admiral Francis T., XXXV, 280
Bowles, Admiral Francis Tiffany, XLIV, 116
Bowles, Commodore William, L, 30
Bowman, James, XXX, 159
Bowring, Sir John, XXX, 166
Bowring, Thomas B., XIV, 121
Boxer, British brig *(1814),* XXVIII, 118
Boxer, H.M.S. *(1870),* XXXVI, 232; *(1879),* XXVIII, 24
Boxer, schooner *(1832),* XXXII, 275; XXXIV, 189 f.
Boxer, ship *(1814),* XLIV, 171
Boxer, U.S.S. (1904), XX, 144
Boxer, U.S.S. *(1834),* VII, 18; *(1837),* XXI, 303–304; XXIII, 58 n.
Boxer, Professor C. R., XIII, 11
Boxer, C. R., Editor, *Further Selections from the Tragic History of the Sea, 1559–1565,* reviewed, XXIX, 75; *The Tragic History of the Sea, 1589–1622,* reviewed, XX, 275
Boxwood schooner, Pictorial Supplement, XXXVI, plate XXIV
Boyd, Captain, XXV, 260
Boyd, Norman, *Discovering Ship Models,* reviewed, XXXII, 287; *The Discovery of Ship Models,* reviewed, XLVII, 59
Boyd, Robert, XXV, 125
Boyd, Sir Robert, VII, 95
Boyd, William V., VII, 123
Boyd and Hanson Co., XIII, 120
Boyer, Samuel P., Elenor & James A. Barnes, Editors, *Naval Surgeon: Blockading the South 1862–1866; Naval Surgeon: Revolt in Japan 1868–1869,* reviewed, XXV, 72–73

"Boyhood Under Sail: 1874–1881. Letters to his son by Joseph C. Hilton," edited by Joanna C. Colcord, III, 106–130
Boyle, John, XXXVIII, 108
Boyle, Commander R. C., L, 44
Boyle, Thomas, XXXVI, 211, 220
Boylston, Nicholas and Thomas, XL, 267
Boynton, steamship (1837), VII, 64, 65
Boynton, E. Moody, X, 252
Boynton, P., VII, 51
Boynton, T. H., XXXVI, 235
"Boy's First Day at Sea in the Bark *Belle of Oregon* – 1886, A," by William B. Sturtevant, I, 58–62
Br. Barnett, steamship *(1861),* XV , 99, 118, 122
Brabant, Rev. J. A., IV, 318–323
Brace, Gerald Warner, *Between Wind and Water,* reviewed, XXVI, 287
Brace's Rock, Eastern Point, Gloucester (MA), XXV, plate XXVIII
"Brace Winches," comment by W. J. Grubb, VII, 78
Bradbury, Captain, XXXI, 126
Bradbury, George H., XXXI, 123
Bradford, Captain Alfred, XLIV, 115
Braddock, Captain, XIII, 50
Bradford (ex-*Ewing*), gunboat *(1862),* XLVIII, 87 ff.
Bradford, Captain and Mrs. Daniel, VIII, 163–164, 242–245
Bradford, Rear Admiral Edward, XXVIII, 107, 112
Bradford, Gershom, VIII, 163–164; contributed note, XXIV, 212–213; "Cushing of Shokokon," XVIII, 142–148; "The Ezra Westons, Ship-builders of Duxbury," XIV, 29–41, plates 5, 6; "For Better or for Worse," VIII, 242–245; "Further Notes on Weston Vessels," XXII, 216; *A Glossary of Sea Terms,* reviewed, II, 345–346; *In With the Sea,* reviewed, XXII, 291; "*Mary Celeste.* No, Not Again!" X, 191–202; "The *Mayflower*'s Jones," XVII, 128–133; "Nelson in Boston Bay," XI, 239–244; "On a Lee Shore," XII, 282–287; "Sea Serpents? No or Maybe," XIII, 268–274, plates 15, 16; *The Secret of Mary Celeste,* reviewed, XXVIII, 74–75; "The *Speedwell*—Another Look," XXII, 136–141; "The Trials of an Unarmed Brig," IX, 11–16; *Yonder is the Sea,* reviewed, XIX, 308
Bradford, Captain Gershom, IX, 11 ff.
Bradford, James C., XXXVIII, 232; review by, XLIX, 59; *Captains of the Old Steam Navy: Makers of the American Naval Tradition, 1840–1880,* reviewed, XLIX, 61; editor, *Command Under Sail: Makers of the American Naval Tradition,* reviewed, XLVI, 122
Bradford, John, XIV, 49, 51, 53; XXXI, 238
Bradford, Captain John, XIV, 35 ff.
"Bradford, John," query by William Bell Clark, I, 310; "John Bradford to William Ellery," document contributed by William Bell Clark, II, 247
Bradford, Lawrence, XVIII, 145, 148

Bradford, Richard H., "And *Oregon* Rushed Home," XXXVI, 257–265; "That Prodigal Son: Philo McGiffin and the Chinese Navy," XXXVIII, 157–169
Bradford, William, XIII, 52; XVII, 128 ff.
Bradford, William (artist), XXII, plate XVII; painting by, XLIV, 13
Bradford, Governor William, XXII, 136, 140; XXV, 61
"Bradford and Palfrey to Bradford and Palfrey," document contributed by George McKee Elsey, I, 395–396
Bradford C. French, schooner (1884), XXIII, 11, 12
Bradford E. Jones, schooner *(1930)*, IV, plate 13
Bradley, A. Day, and H. Armour Smith, "George Watson's *Diagram of Navigation*," XI, 147–148
Bradlee, Francis B. C., XXXIII, 82
Bradley, James, XXXVII, 50 ff.
Bradley, Thomas Frederick, XXIX, 136
Bradshaw, Ephrian, XXXII, 36
Bradshaw, John, XXXII, 200
Bradstreet, Captain Peter, XXXIV, 98
Brady, Cyrus T., Jr., *Commerce and Conquest in East Africa*, reviewed, XI, 232–233
Brady, Brigadier General Hugh, VII, 305
Brady, William, XXX, 40, 43
Brady Collection, National Archives, VI, 138–139, plate 20; IX, plate 20
"Brady Photographs," query by Vernon D. Tate, I, 309; answer by George F. Gilmore, I, 399. See also I, 410
Braeside, barkentine *(1921)*, V, 82
Braganza, ship (1833), IV, 51
Braganza, steamship (1836), XXVI, 10, 11, 13, 14, 202–204, 209
Bragozzi, II, 56–57
Braine, John C., XIX, 51–72
Braine, John Clibbon, XXXII, 200; XXXIII, 199 ff.
Braisted, William R., review by, L, 150
Braisted, William Reynolds, *The United States Navy in the Pacific, 1909–1922*, reviewed, XXXII, 224–225
Bralia, steamship *(1883)*, XIV, 134
Bram, Thomas, XVI, 183–184
Bramin, ship (1816), XIV, 39
Branch, W. J. V., and E. Brook-Williams, *A Short History of Navigation*, reviewed, IV, 177
Brand, C. C., XXVII, 279
Brandt, fishing vessel *(1964)*, XLI, 61
Brandt, Karl, *Whale Oil: an Economic Analysis*, reviewed, I, 101
Brandywine, flagship *(1845)*, XLI, 29
Brandywine, frigate *(1844)*, XXXI, 185
Brandywine, U.S. frigate *(1824)*, XXVI, 258–261, plates 21, 22; XXVII, 29; *(1825)*, XL, 218; *(1826)*, XXI, 64; XXIII, 58 n., 261; XXIV, 223; XXV, 159
Brandywine, U.S.S. *(1863)*, XVIII, 143
Brannock, Samuel, XXIX, 92
Brant, schooner *(1814)*, XLII, 114 ff.
Brattle, James, XL, 13
Brattle, William, XXXIII, 97 ff.

Brave, schooner *(1863)*, XII, 155
Brave, sloop, XXI, 91; *(1862)*, VIII, 223
Brave Ship Brave Men, by Arnold S. Lott, reviewed, XXV, 227–228
Bray, John, XXVI, 37
Bray, Maynard, *Mystic Seaport Watercraft*, reviewed, XL, 66–67
Braynard, Francis O., "The First American Steam Passenger Line to South America," IV, 137–163
Braynard, Frank O., note by, XLIII, 302; reviews by, L, 139, 140, 145; *The Big Ship: The Story of the S.S. United States*, reviewed, XLII, 72–74; *Leviathan, "The World's Greatest Ship," Volume I*, reviewed, XXXIII, 218–221; XXXV, 76; *"Leviathan, The World's Greatest Ship," Volume II*, reviewed, XXXVI, 299–300; "A Tale of Two Pictures," XXVII, 254–262, plate 11
Brazil, schooner *(1861)*, XI, 280
Brazil:
   Foreign relations, Confederate States of America, XV, 287
   —, **United States,** XIX, 239; XXII, 45; XLI, 245
   History, Naval Revolt (1893–94), XLI, 245
Brazil, boats of, XIII, 91
Brazileira, U.S.S. *(1862)*, XVI, 51, 53, 55
Brazilian, steamship (ex-*New York*, ex-*Mersey*, ex-*Adelaide*), XXVI, 196
"Brazilian Students of Naval Construction," by Richard G. Wood, XII, 162
Brazil Line, IV, 137 ff.
Brazonia, sloop *(1862)*, XII, 53
Brazos, schooner *(1861)*, XI, 280
"'Breadfruit Bligh': Bligh Papers in the Banks Collection," by Richard H. Dillon, XII, 253–270
Breaker, schooner *(1862)*, XII, 53
Breaker, trawler *(1913)*, XLIV, 121 ff.
"Breakfast," Pictorial Supplement, XXXI, plate XIX
Break O'Day, schooner *(1861)*, XI, 280; XII, 53, 155
Break o" Day, schooner, XXI, 91, 97, 100
Break O'Day, ship (1853), III, 63; XV, 179
Breakwaters: Port of Los Angeles, California, XXV, 264 ff.; San Pedro, California, XXV, 268
Breame, H.M S. *(1814)*, XXVIII, 118
Breckinridge, John C., XXXVII, 276
Breese, Commander Samuel, XL, 42
Breese, Senator, XXX, 144
Bremen, ship (1777), III, 62; *(1861)*, XI, 280
Bremen cog, ca. 1350, photograph of, XLVI, 94, 95
Bremener, Roberto, XXX, 49
Bremerton, yacht *(1893)*, XXXVI, 237
Brems, L. C., XXXVII, 85
Brendan Voyage, The, by Tim Severin, reviewed, XXXVIII, 303
Brent, H. M., XX, 62
Brent, Theodore, XXXII, 157
Brent, Captain Thomas W., XLVIII, 94
Brent, William, Jr., Chargé d'Affaires, XLVI, 235

Brenton, E. P., VII, 88

Brereton, John, XXXIII, 140 ff.; XXXIV, 240

Brescia, Anthony M., "The American Navy, 1817–1822: Comments of Richard Rush," XXXI, 217–225

Breshwood, Captain John G., XL, 303; XLVIII, 87

Breslau, warship *(1914)*, XXXVI, 34

Brettle, Robert E., *The* Cutty Sark, *Her Designer and Builder Hercules Linton, 1836–1900,* reviewed, XXX, 223–224

Brew, Richard, XXXV, 295

Brewer, David, XLVI, 220

Brewer, John N. M., XV, 175 ff.

Brewington, Dorothy E. R., I, 68; XXVIII, 83; XXXV, 4; mentioned, XLI, 4; XLII, 83; XLV, 41; contributed documents, I, 304–306; III, 74–85; query by, I, 309; answered query, I, 399; *Marine Paintings and Drawings in Mystic Seaport Museum,* reviewed, XLII, 312

Brewington, Dorothy and Marion Vernon Brewington, XXV, 4; editorial comment, XXXIX, 81; *Kendall Whaling Museum Prints,* reviewed, XXX, 218, 219; "The Marine Museums of Italy, Southern France and Spain," XX, 231–236; *The Marine Paintings and Drawings in the Peabody Museum,* reviewed, XXVIII, 289–290

Brewington, Marion Vernon, I, 68, 82, 177, 400; III, 89, 178; IV, 280; IX, 161 ff.; XI, 4; XV, 3–4; XVI, 3; XVII, 3, 248; XXI, 76, 143; answered queries, III, 86, 269–270; V, 245–246; VII, 170–171; contributed document, I, 85–87; II, 247; V, 243–244, 328; VI, 138; XIV, 215, 215–216; XVII, 72–73; queries by: I, 89, 172, 398; II, 248; III, 177, 353; VI, 153; reviews by: I, 94–95, 178–181, 402–404; II, 89–90, 91, 260–261, 341, 343–344; XXII, 73–74, 148–149, 151–152; XXIII, 289–290; XXIV, 149; XXV, 71–72; XXIX, 71–72; XIX, 146; XX, 147, 148, 225, 274; "American Naval Guns, 1775–1785," III, 11–18, 148–158; "The Back Staff," XXI, 107–109; "The Broad Pendant," XI, 72–73; *Chesapeake Bay Bugeyes,* reviewed, II, 86–88; *Chesapeake Bay Log Canoes and Bugeyes,* reviewed, XXIII, 286–287; "The *Constitution's* 1812 Guns," VII, 240–241; "Correction concerning *Guerriere's* Guns," VII, 316; "The Designs of Our First Frigates," VIII, 11–25; "The Dolphin Striker," XIII, 65–66; "Durham Boat Migration, A," III, 253–255; "Four American Cross-Staves," XIX, 138–140; "Gunnery Practice, 1807," IV, 324; "Navy Allowance Tables," V, 326–327; "Notes from Baltimore Customs Records," IX, 72; "Notes on the Cross Staff," XIV, 187–191, plates 23, 24; XXXV, 4; XLIX, 46 ff.; "Potomac Long-Boat, The," I, 159–163; "The Sailmaker's Gear," IX, 278–296, plate 30; *Shipcarvers of North America,* reviewed, XXIII, 72–73; "Signal Systems and Ship Identification," III, 205–221; "Tonnage Rules in 1799," I, 295–296; "Two Revolutionary Naval Inventories," XXVI, 63–71, 138–144, 210–214; XXVIII, 83, 238; "Washington's Boat at the Delaware Crossing," II, 167–170; "Who Built the *Enterprize* ?" IV, 233–235

Brewington, Marion Vernon and Dorothy Brewington, XXV, 4; editorial comment, XXXIX, 81; *Kendall Whaling Museum Prints,* reviewed, XXX, 218, 219; "The Marine Museums of Italy, Southern France and Spain," XX, 231–236; *The Marine Paintings and Drawings in the Peabody Museum,* reviewed, XXVIII, 289–290

Brewington, Marion Vernon, Robert G. Albion, William A. Baker, Benjamin W. Labaree, *New England and The Sea,* reviewed, XXXIII, 63–64

Brewster, ship (1885), III, 70

Brewster, André W., XXXIV, 265

Brewster, Mary (Mrs. William E.), XXV, 104

Brewster, Phineas, XIII, 20

Brewster, Captain William E., XXV, 104

Briceño, General Justo, XXX, 271

Brickdale, Lieutenant C., XXXVI, 136

Bricole, schooner *(1780),* XXXV, 141

Bride, XXII, 235

Bridge, Lieutenant Thomas, XXI, 262

Bridgeport, steamship *(1861–1865),* VI, plate 20

Bridger, Jim, XXVIII, 131, 132

Bridger, John, XIII, 22, 26, 27

Bridges, ship *(1814),* I, 122

Bridges, Robert, XLVIII, 252

Bridges, Thomas, XXX, 186

Bridgewater, ship *(1863),* XXV, 107

Bridgman, Elijah Coleman, XLVI, 34 ff.; XLVIII, 274 ff.

Bridgman, Captain H. T., XVIII, 6–8

"Bridgman in China in the Early Nineteenth Century," by Frederick W. Drake, XLVI, 34–42

Bridgtown Galley, ship *(1732),* VI, 179–193

Brief Account of the Yacht America, *A,* by State Street Trust Co. of Boston, reviewed, XI, 300

"Brief Description of an Actual Episode that Occurred when the English Clipper *Torrens* was Getting Under Way for London, A," note contributed by J. F. Mann, XXIII, 140–141

Brief History of Richmond, Fredericksburg, and Potomac Railroad, A, by John B. Mordecai, reviewed, II, 91–92

Brierly, Sir Oswald, XXII, plate VII

"Brig *Betsey* of Norwich, The," by David C. Duniway, III, 252–253

Briggs, Adam, XXXVIII, 212 ff.

Briggs, Alden, XXV, 222

Briggs, Daniel W., XLII, 246 ff.

Briggs, Enos (Shipbuilder), II, 280 ff.; IV, 18; V, 43

Briggs, Captain George, XVI, 251; XVII, 134; XVIII, 82; XLIII, 188 ff.

Briggs, Henry, XXXVII, 178

Briggs, Captain J. C., XL, 47

Briggs, James (shipbuilder, of Pembroke, Massachusetts), XXV, 218–221

Briggs, Captain Jeremiah, XXV, 184

Briggs, Captain John, XXV, 82

Briggs, Mate Johnson, XXV, plate 17
Briggs, Joshua, XV, 173 ff.
Briggs, Lieutenant Commander, XXXIX, 41
Briggs, Luther (shipbuilder), XXV, 221–222
Briggs, Thomas, II, 287
Brigham, Reverend Hiram, XIII, 243 ff.
Bright, schooner, XXI, 99; *(1926–1940)*, IV, 61–62, plate 15
Bright, sloop (1861), XI, 280; XII, 155
Bright, Captain Francis, XLV, 95
"Bright Light on *Flying Cloud* vs. *Andrew Jackson*," by John Lyman, IX, 148–150
Brighton, Ray, *Clippers of the Port of Portsmouth and the Men Who Built Them*, reviewed, XLVIII, 197
"Brig *Sarah Bentley:* An Unlucky Ship," by E. Lee Dorsett, M.D., XVI, 63–65
Brigs: VIII, 171; IX, 11–16
Brillante, French ship *(1800)*, XXXI, 175
Brillante Jeunesse, French ship *(1800)*, XXXI, 174
Brilliant, H.M.S. *(1907)*, XXVIII, 105; XXIX, 129
Brilliant, ship *(1860)*, XXVII, 235; *(1862)*, XXXIII, 57
Brilliante, schooner, XXI, 90, 101; *(1861)*, XI, 280
Brinckerhoff, Captain John H., XIV, 182, 185
Brind, Admiral, L, 291 ff.
Brine, J. E., XXX, 162
Brink, Captain Andrew, XXVII, 16, 17
Brinkerhoff, Fox, and Polhemus, XXXI, 137
Brinkerhoff, Turner & Co., XXXI, plate 1
Brinkman, Captain Thomas, XXI, 105
Brinton, Daniel, VII, 115, 116, 118, 119, 129, 132, 160
Brion (Venezuelan naval officer), XXX, 260
Brisbane, Sir Thomas, XXI, 51
Bristol, H.M.S. *(1914)*, XXXIII, 35 ff.; XXVIII, 107
Bristol, ship, XXXVI, 176
Bristol, steamship (1867), III, 43, plate 12; IV, 175; *(1887)*, XI, 256 ff.; *(1897)*, XI, 258 ff.
Bristol, Captain R. C., VII, 63; XVIII, 285
Bristol Bay, fishing boat, XXXVIII, plate 8
Bristol Channel, Flat Holm, XX, 5–43
Bristol City, steamship (1879), XIV, 116, 117, 134; (1899), XIV, 124, 125, 134; (1920), XIV, 126, 127, 129, 135; *(1946)*, XIV, 132, 135
"Bristol City Line of Bristol, England, The," by Grahame E. Farr, XIV, 115–135, plates 13–15
Britain's Glory: or Ship-Building Unvail'd, XXX, 83
Britannia, schooner *(1775)*, XXXIX, 194; *(1776)*, XLII, 16 ff.; *(1815)*, XXIV, 270
Britannia, ship (1759), VI, 85
Britannia, ship (1792), XXXIV, 250
Britannia, steamship, XXVI, 270; (1833), VII, 50, 51; VIII, 53; (1840), XXIV, plate I; XXV, plate XXX; *(1840)*, XX, 87; XXXVII, 232
Britannia, steamship (ca. 1861), XXI, 89; *(1863)*, VIII, 229
Britannia, yacht *(1898)*, XXXVI, 239, 244, 245
Britannia (or "Steam and the Sea"), painting by Fitz Hugh Lane, XLIV, 63
Britannic, steamship *(1840)*, XXXV, 254
Britannic, steamship (1874), Pictorial Supplement, XXXIV, plate XII
British Admiralty, The, by Leslie Gardiner, reviewed, XXXII, 150
British and Japanese Ships Entering Chinese Ports, Table I, L, 190
British Battleships "Warrior" 1860 to "Vanguard" 1950: A History of Design, Construction and Armament, by Oscar Parkes, reviewed, XXVII, 281–284
British Coasting Vessel, Table I, XLVIII, 6
British Colonial Policy, XXVII, 211–220
British Columbia, yacht racing in, XXXVI, 231–250
British Columbia Fisheries, The, by W. A. Carothers, reviewed, II, 353
British Corporation Register, XXX, 18 ff.
British Destroyers: A History of Development, 1892–1953, by Edgar J. March, reviewed, XXVII, 281–284
British Dominion, tanker *(1942)*, L, 48
British East India Co., The, XIV, 101 ff.; XXXI, 183 ff.; XLVIII, 244 ff.
British East Indiaman (1812), XXIX, 48, plate IV
British Empire, schooner, XXI, 99; *(1861)*, XV, 117, 120, 122, 125
British Fleet off Algiers, 1829, XXIX, 124, plate XVI
British Indian Ocean Territory, History, XXXI, 104. *See also* Shipping (Indian Ocean); Chagos Islands
British Indian Ocean Territory, XXXI, 118
British India S.N. Co., XXVI, 196
British India Steam Navigation Co., XXXI, 118
British Isles, ship *(1912)*, XVIII, 153
British Lake Ontario squadron, sketch of, XLIX, 265
British "Little Men": (William Heather, London), XXXIV, "F" plate 11; (unidentified – National Maritime Museum, Greenwich, XXXIV), "G" plate 11; (Henry Hughes, London), XXXIV, "H" plate 11; (Charles Frodsham, London), XXXIV, "I" plate 11; (David Stalker, Leith), XXXIV, "J" plate 12; (unidentified – State Street Bank, Boston), XXXIV, "K" plate 12; (Harrison, Kingston-upon-Hull), XXXIV, "L" plate 12; (unidentified – English origin, used at Hamburg, Germany), XXXIV, "M" plate 12
British Maps of Colonial America, by William P. Cumming, reviewed, XXXVIII, 73
British Mariner's Vocabulary of Technical Terms and Phrases, XXX, 40
British Marquis, steamship *(1920)*, X, 193–194
British Merchant Vessels Lost or Damaged by Enemy Action, 1939–1945, reviewed, VIII, 74–75
British Museum Newspaper Library, Colindale, England, XXXIV, 57
British Naval Administration in the Age of Walpole, by Daniel A. Baugh, reviewed, XXVII, 74–75
British Navy and the American Revolution, The, by John A. Tilley, reviewed, XLIX, 317

British Navy and the Use of Naval Power in the Eighteenth Century, The, by Jeremy Black and Philip Woodfine, reviewed, XLIX, 314
"British Navy in the Delaware, 1775 to 1777, The," by George Comtois, XL, 7–22
British Navy: XXVII, 31; XXVIII, 5–30, 118, 151, 229–232
British Order in Council of 1807, XXIII, 157 ff.
British patent specifications for a water-driven hopper mill, 1790 drawing of, L, 205
British Queen, S.S., XXVII, 258; *(1902),* XXXVIII, 195 ff.
British Queen, schooner *(1861),* VIII, 216, 223
British Queen, steamship (1838), IX, 267–268; *(1862),* XII, 53
"British Sailor Looks at the United States Navy of the Early Nineteenth Century, A," by Commander Frederick Barley, XXI, 57–69
British Sail Training Association, The, XXXV, 76
British Sea Power, XXV, 39 ff.
British Shipbuilding Industry, 1870–1914, The, by Sidney Pollard and Paul Robertson, reviewed, XLII, 67–68
"British Ship Names," by Captain Edgar K. Thompson, U.S.N. (ret.), XXVIII, 224
"British Ship Names," by R. C. Anderson, XXVI, 261
"British Ship Names," document contributed by R. C. Anderson, XXIV, 126
British Shipping, by R. H. Thornton, reviewed, XX, 225
British Viceroy, grain elevator *(1871),* XXXVIII, 135
"British View of the Union Navy, 1864: A Report Addressed to Her Majesty's Minister at Washington, A," edited by Richard M. Basoco, William E. Geoghegan, and Frank J. Merli, XXVII, 30–45
British Vigilance, tanker *(1942),* L, 44
British Warship Names, by T. D. Manning and C. F. Walker, reviewed, XIX, 310
Brittania, British ship *(1776),* XLVIII, 16
Brittania, schooner *(1814),* I, 122
Brittania, steamship (1840), IX, 270–272
Brixham Museum (Gt. Britain), XXX, 154
Brizé-Fradin, M., VII, 280
Broadbay, schooner *(1775),* XXX, 115, 116
Broadley, Captain Housman, XLIX, 264 ff.
"Broad Pendant, The," by M. V. Brewington, XI, 72–73
Broadwater, John D., review by, XLIV, 136
"Brockbanks' London," Pictorial Supplement, XXXV, plate XIX
Brockenbrough, John W., XL, 300
Brock monument demonstration, 1840, VIII, 52–53
Brockville, steamship (1833), VII, 50
Broderick, John Joyce, XXXIV, 164
Broderick, Captain Thomas, XXVI, 48
Brodie, Bernard, *A Guide to Naval Strategy,* reviewed, V, 93; *A Layman's Guide to Naval Strategy,* reviewed, III, 92–93
Broeze, Frank, XXXIX, 4; review by, L, 70
Broke, Philip Bowes Vere, XXIX, 67–68

Broke and the Shannon, by Peter Padfield, reviewed, XXIX, 67–68
"Broken Anchors," document contributed by Samuel W. Lewis, II, 79–80
Brombeck, Tallock, XVII, 122
Brookbank, Gloucester (MA), XXV, plate XXXI
Brooke, Field Marshal Sir Alan, XLII, 215
Brooke, George M., Jr., "The Role of the United States Navy in the Suppression of the African Slave Trade," XXI, 28–41; "The Voyage of *Kanrin Maru,* 1860; an Episode in American Naval Diplomacy," XX, 198–208
Brooke, Lieutenant John M., XX, 198–208
Brooke, Rajah of Sarawak, IV, 221, 223
Brookes, Captain, XLIV, 6
Brooking, Charles, XXX, 219; *(1754),* XXII, plate IV
Brookline, ship *(1829),* XXIX, 89
Brooklyn, cruiser *(1898),* XLI, 97
Brooklyn, ship *(1846),* XXIX, 92; *(1847),* IX, 228
Brooklyn, U.S.S. *(1860),* XXXI, 256; XXXIII, 281; (1861), XI, 265 ff.; XIX, 265; *(1861),* XXXVI, 192, 202; *(1864),* XXVII, 43
Brooklyn, U.S. flagship *(1905),* XXXVIII, 27, 150
Brooklyn City, steamship (1881), XIV, 116, 117, 124, 134
Brooklyn's Eastern District, by Eugene L. Armbruster, reviewed, I, 352
Brooks, Alfred A., II, 340; "The Boats of Ash Point, Maine," II, 307–323
Brooks, Captain Anthony, XXVIII, 115, 118
Brooks, Charles Wolcott, XXIII, 125, 126
Brooks, Captain G. S., XXVI, 29, 203
Brooks, George E., and Frances K. Talbot, "The Providence Exploring and Trading Company's Expedition to the Niger River in 1832–1833," XXXV, 77–96
Brooks, George E., Jr., "Enoch Richmond Ware, African Trader; 1839–1850: Years of Apprenticeship," (Part I), XXX, 174–186; (Part II), 229–248
Brooks, Captain N. C., VIII, 179
Brooks, Noah, XXVI, 262 ff.
Brooks-Williams, E., and W. J. V. Branch, *A Short History of Navigation,* reviewed, IV, 177
Brook Watson, whaler *(1804),* XLI, 285
Brother Barnett. See *Bro. Barnett.*
Brother Jonathan, steamship (1850), XIV, 200
Brothers, bark (1848), V, 147, 241
Brothers, schooner, XXI, 97
Brothers, ship *(1805),* X, 54
Brothers, steamship (1839), XVIII, 295, 299
Brother Whale, A Pacific Whalewatchers Log, Roy Nickerson, reviewed, XVIII, 301
Broughton, Nicholson, I, 30; XXX, 88–116
Broughton, William, XXVIII, 151
Broughton & Girdler, XXX, 112, 113
Broughty Castle Museum, XXX, 153
Brouillan, Jacques Francois de, XXXV, 156

Brouncker, Sir Henry, XXXI, 99

Broussard, Edwin Sidney, XXXVII, 120 ff.

Brouwer, Norman J., *International Register of Historic Ships,* reviewed, XLVII, 216

Brower, Charles, XXXIX, 13

Brower, John H., papers, XXV, 105–106

Brown, Alexander, XXX, 302

Brown, Alexander Crosby, I, 177, 400; III, 89, 159; IV, 175; V, 165, 247; VI, 235; VII, 127 n; VIII, 4, 265; IX, 233; X, 35, 242; XI, 4; XIII, 4; XV, 3, 95–96, 172; XVII, 171–172; XXIV, 5 n.; XXV, 79; XL, 3; contributed documents: I, 396–397; VI, 151–152; VIII, 153; XII, 63; XIX, 128–132; contributed notes: XXIII, 141; XXV, 224; editorial coment, XL, 3; query by, II, 339; VII, 321–322; XXIV, 137; reviews by, I, 185, 187, 401; II, 91–92, 92, 346–347; XXIV, 145–146, 219–221; XXVIII, 295–296; XXX, 71–72; XLV, 135; XXVI, 76, 152, 225–226, 287–288; XXVII, 76, 227–228; XXVIII, 75–76, 152–153, 234, 296–298; XXIX, 75–76, 149–150, 291–294; XXX, 147–150; XXXI, 77–80, 151–154, 292–294; XXXII, 297–299; XXXIII, 69–73; XXXIV, 71–76, 222–225; XXXV, 144–148; XXXVI, 69–74, 222–225; XXXVII, 145–151; XXXVIII, 75–76, 150–151, 225–228; XXXIX, 225–229; XL, 152–155; XLVII, 138–140; XLVIII, 59

"Additional Data on the Dismal Swamp Canal," VII, 240–242; "An Additional Note on Paddle Box Decorations," VI, 136–137; "Attack on vessels by enraged whales," I, 393–394; "Bark *Vernon,*" IX, 150; "Contemporary Half-model of the Yacht *America,*" XI, 245–250; *Dilemma,* reviewed, II, 94; "Dismal Swamp Canal, The," V, 203–222, 297–310; VI, 51–70; "An Early American *Neptune,*" XII, 148–153, plates 13–15; "The 'Elegant' Steamboat *Commonwealth,*" VIII, 246–254

"The Elizabeth Islands Jingle," X, 71–73; "Enchanted Voyage," VII, 213–223; *"Exodus 1947: An Interim Report on the Career of the Steamer President Warfield,"* VIII, 127–131; *The Good Ships of Newport News,* reviewed, XXXVII, 74–75; "Hornet Journals, The," I, 164–165; *James and John Bard,* reviewed, XI, 300; *Juniper Waterway: A History of the Albemarle and Chesapeake Canal,* reviewed, XLIII, 303; "The *Lady of the Lake* in Dismal Swamp," VII, 66; *The Mariners' Museum,* reviewed, XI, 226–228; "Mr. Hardy Lee," XI, 291

The Old Bay Line, reviewed, I, 96; "Paddle Box Decorations of American Sound Steamboats," III, 35–47; "Reminiscences of the Last Voyage of the Bark *Wanderer,*" IX, 17–30; "Rollo On The Atlantic, by Jacob Abbott," XXVI, 81–95; XXVIII, 238; "A Roster of American Steam Vessels Equipped with the Hunter Wheel," XXIV, 8–9; "The Sheet Iron Steamboat *Codorus,*" X, 163–190, plates 21–24; "Shipwreck in the Mountains: The Loss of the Canal Boat *Clinton* and the Heroism of Boatman Frank Paget," XVI, 41–48; "Some Replicas of Historic Ships," XIV, 105–114, plates 11, 12; "Steamboat *Pocahontas,* 1893–1939, The," II, 223–228; "The Steamer *Vesta,* Neglected Partner in a Fatal Collision," XX, 177–184, plates 5, 6; *Steam Packets on the Chesapeake,* reviewed, XXII, 150; "Tow-boat *Seth Low,* The," III, 161–163; *The United States Frigate* Constitution, *A Sesquicentennial Exhibition,* reviewed, VIII, 75; *Women and Children Last,* reviewed, XXII, 72–73; "Women and Children Last: The Tragic Loss of the Steamship *Arctic,*" XIV, 237–261; "The *Yarmouth Castle* Inferno," XXXVI, 5–32

Brown, Lieutenant Commander Allen D., XXXIX, 121

Brown, Andrew, XVII, 121

Brown, C. Donald, "Eastport: A Maritime History," XXVIII, 113–127

"Brown, Capt. Nathaniel, Documents from the Letter-Book of," edited by Lawrence Waters Jenkins, VI, 19–50

Brown, Captain, XXX, 239

Brown, Captain Carl R., XXXVI, 18–21, 26, 31

Brown, Charles, XXXVI, 272

Brown, Captain George, XXXVII, 85

Brown, Rear Admiral George, XXXVIII, 291

Brown, George Loring (artist), XXV, 59

Brown, Giles T., *Ships That Sail No More: Marine Transportation fom San Diego to Puget Sound 1910–1940,* reviewed, XXVII, 150–151

Brown, Captain Henry, XVIII, 82

Brown, Captain J. F., XVIII, 82

Brown, Lieutenant J. H., R.N., Registrar General, XXX, 14

Brown, J. R., XXXVI, 248

Brown, J. R. (artist), Pictorial Supplement, XXXI, plate XXII

Brown, James, XIV, 237 ff.; XIX, 128–132; XXXII, 172

Brown, John, XXIII, 240; XXIX, 5 n.; XLII, 45

Brown, John Carter, Library. See John Carter Brown Library.

Brown, Joseph, XXXI, 250; XXXII, 172 ff.

Brown, Karl, I, 400; "Materials of Maritime Interest in the New York Public Library," I, 381–390

Brown, Lloyd A., I, 177; review by, II, 351; *Early Maps of the Ohio Valley,* reviewed, XX, 148; *Jean Domenique Cassini and His World Map of 1696,* reviewed, II, 94; "Manuscript Maps in the William L. Clements Library," I, 141–148; *The Story of Maps,* reviewed, IX, 305

Brown, Mary Elizabeth, XIV, 237

Brown, Moses, XXIX, 205; XXXII, 172 ff.

Brown, Captain Moses, XXI, 12

Brown, Nicholas, XVIII, 105, 134; XXXII, 172 ff.

Brown, Noah, XXI, 47, 50

Brown, Orlando, XXI, 284

Brown, Peleg, XLII, 45

Brown, Captain Peleg, XXV, 70

Brown, Dr. R. H., XL, 43
Brown, Ralph H., *Mirror for Americans, Likeness of the Eastern Seaboard, 1810,* reviewed, III, 355
Brown, Richard Edwin, reviewed book, XXVII, 150–151
Brown, Robert, XXVII, 279
Brown, Captain Robert, XVIII, 119
Brown, Samuel, XXX, 94
Brown, Dr. Thomas, XXX, 83
Brown, Captain W., XX, 89 n.
Brown, Captain W. N., XVIII, 275–276
Brown, Wilburt S., *The Amphibious Campaign for West Florida and Louisiana, 1814–1815; a Critical Review of Strategy and Tactics at New Orleans,* reviewed, XXIX, 284
Brown, William, XXV, 166; XXXVI, 126–128, 131
Brown, Captain William, I, 186–187
Brown, William H., XIV, 237 ff.
Brown, Captain Zephry, XL, 196
Brown and Ives, XXIII, 233 ff.; XXX, 292
Brown Brothers, ship (1876), III, 72
Brown Brothers & Co., XLVIII, 115
Browne, E. P. G., XXVI, 203
Browne, James, XXVI, 203
Browne, Governor Montfort, of Nassau, XXV, 196 ff.
Browne, Richard, XIII, 22
Brown Hall, ship (1775), XLVII, 7
Browning, John, XIII, 67
Browning, Lieutenant Robert L., XXIX, 177 ff.
Browning, Spencer, XLVI, 261
Brownlee, Edward G., I, 160–161; II, 169; III, 98; VII, 3; reviews by, XLVI, 130; XLVII, 57; XLVIII, 198; XLIX, 317
Brownlee, Walter, *The First Ships Round the World,* reviewed, XLVI, 125
Brownne, Charles, XXIV, 159, 161, 162 n., 170; XXVII, 5, 9–12, 19, 20, 26, 28; XXXII, 220
"Brown's Ferry Boat: An Archeological Discovery, The," NASOH paper by Alan B. Albright, XXXVII, 82
Browns of Providence and the Slaving Voyage of the Brig *Sally,* 1764–1765, The," by Darold D. Wax, XXXII, 171–179
Brown's Wharf, Portland (ME), XXXV, plate 1
Brownville, steamship (1830), VI, 210; VII, 42, 43
Browson, Captain William H., XXXIII, 278
Bruce (Ambassador to China, 1859), XXVII, 164, 166, 167
Bruce, Captain John, XXVI, 38
Bruce, Frederick (British Minister in China), L, 178
Bruce, Sir Frederick, XXXIV, 114
Bruce, Lieutenant J. A., XXIX, 270
Bruce, Peter Henry, XXV, 202
Bruce, Rear Admiral William, XXXI, 272
Bruce and Co., VIII, 12
Bruïjn, J. R., L. M. Akveld, Ph. M. Bosscher, and Kltz F. C. van Oosten, Editors, *Vier Eeuwen Varen — kapiteins, kapers, kooplieden en geleerden,* reviewed, XXXIV, 282
Bruïjn, J. R. and I. Schöffer, *Dutch Asiatic Shipping in the 17th and 18th Centuries,* reviewed, XLVIII, 206
Bruïjn, Jaap R., "The Dutch East India Company as Shipowner, 1602–1796," XLVII, 240–248
Bruiser, sloop (1892), X, 244 ff.
Bruno, Joanna Colcord, XLIV, 149
Brunswick, cartel (1815), XXVIII, 176
Brunswick, whaler (1865), XXVII, 275
Brunts, G. J., XXXI, 139
Bruster, Thomas, XXXV, 292
Brutus, brig (1812), XIII, 280
Brutus, ship (1811), XII, 162
Brutus, sloop of war, XXIV, 70
Bruun, Dr. Anton, XLVI, 220
Bruyns, Willem F. J. Mörzer, "Matthew Fontaine Maury and the Introduction of Oceanography to the Netherlands in the Second Half of the Nineteenth Century," XLVIII, 44–49
Bryan, Edwin H., Jr., *American Polynesia: Coral Islands of the Central Pacific,* reviewed, I, 407
Bryan, George S., *Mystery Ship: The* Mary Celeste *in Fancy and Fact,* reviewed, II, 256
Bryan, William Jennings, XXXIII, 193; XXXV, 193; XXXVII, 30
Bryant, John, XIII, 122, 242; XIV, 139
Bryant, Joseph, XXXIX, 218
Bryant, Samuel W., "Details of the Late Yankee Victory off Labrador — 1782," XXIX, 211–223
Bryant, William, IV, 54–56
Bryant, William Cullen, VII, 146 n.; quoted, 127
Bryant & Lee, XLVII, 100
Brynhilda, pojama-type vessel [model], VI, plate 23
Bryson, Leslie, XLIV, 9
Bryson, Thomas A., *Tars, Turks, and Tankers,* reviewed, XLI, 73
Buache, XXV, 254, 260
Buccanneer, barkentine (1918), IV, 60, 68
Buchanan, Captain Franklin, U.S.N., XXV, 225
Buchanan, James, L, 115
Buchanan, James, Secretary of State, XXXI, 11; XLI, 28
Buchanan, President James, XXXVI, 178 ff.; XL, 37
Buchanan, Thomas, XXXII, 270; XXXVIII, 58
Buck, brig (1827), XXI, 292
Buckeye, bark (1852), VII, 318
Buckeye State, steamship (1921), X, 141
Buckhart, schooner (1863), XII, 155
Buckingham, Lieutenant Benjamin H., XXXIX, 140
Buckland, Captain Thomas, XLIII, 127 ff.
Buckland Abbey, XXX, 153
Buckler's Hard Maritime Museum (England), XXX, 154
Buckley, Rowland, XXXI, 90
Bucknam, Captain Ransford D., XXV, 173
Buckram, schooner (1777), V, 187
Buckridge, H., XXVIII, 58, 59
Budd, Lieutenant George, XLIV, 172

Buena Vista, steamship *(1840),* XXXVII, 233
Buenos Aires, cruiser *(1850),* XLI, 95
Buenos Ayres, steamship (1854), XXXI, 13
Buffalo, gunboat *(1898),* XXXVI, 262, 263
Buffalo, ship, XXXVII, 40 n.
Buffalo, sloop, XXI, 103; *(1813),* XLII, 108 ff.; *(1864),* XV, 112, 128
Buffalo, steamship (1814), XVI, 34; (1837), VII, 64; *(1838),* XVIII, 279, 280, 283, 285, 289, 291; XX, 89 n., 266
Buffalo, wooden scow (1899), XXXVIII, 134
Buffalo Historical Society, VII, 303, plate 37
Buffington, Captain Nehemiah, XXI, 214
Bugler, Arthur, O.B.E., *H.M.S. Victory — Building, Restoration & Repair,* reviewed, XXVII, 287–289
Building of a Wooden Ship, The, by Dana A. Story and John M. Clayton, reviewed, XXXII, 70–71
Building the Blackfish, by Dana Story, reviewed, L, 151
Building the Wooden Fighting Ship, by James Dodds and James Moore, reviewed, XLVI, 202
Buker, Commander George E., "Captain's Mast: Conservatism vs. Liberalism," XXX, 139–146; "The Seven Cities: The Role of a Myth on the Exploration of the Atlantic," XXX, 249–259
Bukley, Thomas, XXVII, 51, 52
Bulah, ship *(1807),* XVI, 194
Bulbil, Bulgarian ship *(1944),* XLIII, 35 ff.
Bulfinch, Charles, XXXVIII, 103
Bulkeley, Colonel Charles S., XXXVI, 50
Bulkeley, Richard, XLII, 11
Bulko Steamship Corp., XXXVIII, 185
Bulldog, H.M.S. *(1941),* XLV, 54
Bullen, Frank T., *The Men of the Merchant Service,* reviewed, XLI, 145–146
Bullen, W. F., XXXVI, 239
Bullitt, William C., XXXII, 109
Bulloch, Archibald Stobo, XXXV, 237
Bulloch, Captain James D., I, 241–243
Bulloch, Commander James D., XIX, 126
Bulloch, James Dunwoody, XXIX, 8–29
Bullock, galley *(1779),* XXXV, 141
Bullock, Archibald, XIII, 35
Bullock, Captain Jabez, XL, 196
Bulward, H.M.S. *(1812),* XLV, 7
Bulwark of Empire: Bermuda's Fortified Naval Base, 1860–1920, by Roger Willcock, reviewed, XXIII, 75–76
"Bumboat Bonbon," by Captain Edgar K. Thompson, U.S.N. (ret.), XXVI, 176
Bunau-Varilla, Philippe, *From Panama to Verdun: My Fight for France,* reviewed, I, 411
Bunker, Captain Charles G., XVIII, 82
Bunker, David, XXXIII, 163
Bunker, Captain Elihu S., XXVII, 24–26
Bunker, John Gorley, *Liberty Ships,* reviewed, XXXIII, 223–224

Bunker, Captain Matthew, XXIII, 27; letters of, XXV, 110
Bunker Hill, privateer (1812), XLII, 106 ff.
Bunker Hill, ship (1857), V, 150
Bunker Hill, steamship (1837), VII, 65; *(1843),* XVII, 103; XX, 82 n., 86, 89 n.; (1861), XVII, 60, 307; XVIII, 68
Bunker Hill, tug *(1861),* XLIII, 96 ff.
Bunting, W. H., *Portrait of a Port — Boston, 1852–1914,* reviewed, XXXIII, 215; *Steamers, Schooners, Cutters & Sloops: Marine Photographs of N. L. Stebbins Taken 1884 to 1907,* reviewed, XXXV, 215
Bunting, William, document contributed by, XXXVII, 219–220
Buonaparte, French ship *(1799),* XXXI, 173
Burchmore, George, XXIII, 132
Burden, Dr. Charles, mention, XLI, 164
Burden, Henry, VII, 54
Burdett, Captain H. W., XVIII, 82
Burdette, Richard C., XVIII, 191, 197
Burdick, Charles, *The Frustrated Raider: The Story of the German Cuiser* Cormoran *in World War I,* reviewed, XL, 72–73
Burdick, Charles B., "The Frustrated Raider," XXIV, 272–279
Bureau of Steam Engineering, The, XXXVII, 111 ff.
Bureau Veritas, XXX, 25, 26, 27, 37
Burg, B. R., "Legitimacy and Authority: A Case Study of Pirate Commanders in the Seventeenth and Eighteenth Centuries," XXXVII, 40–49
Burges, Sir James Bland, XXIX, 244 ff.
Burgess, Charles P., query by, IX, 74
Burgess, Edward G., XXXVIII, 133
Burgess, Hannah, XXXVII, 204
Burgess, P. Douglas, review by, XLIV, 133
Burgess, Robert H., VII, 243; XXXI, 84; query by, VII, 77; answered query, II, 251; review by, XLIV, 204; *Chesapeake Circle,* reviewed, XXVI, 222; Editor, *Coasting Captain — Journals of Captain Leonard S. Tawes,* reviewed, XXVIII, 148–149; "Schooner Bohemia," X, 155, 230; Editor, *The Sea Serpent Journal: Hugh McCulloch Gregory's Voyage around the World in a Clipper Ship, 1854–55,* reviewed, XXXV, 213; *Steamboats out of Baltimore,* reviewed, XXX, 71–72
Burgess, Captain Samuel, XXXVII, 46
Burgess and Paine, designers, VII, 171
Burgevine, General, XLIII, 289
Burgis, William, IX, 237
Burgis, William (artist), XXV, 59
Burgoyne, General John, XXXIX, 201
Burhill, steamship *(1951),* XIV, 133, 135
Burke, Captain Edmund, XV, 222
Burke, John, *Pete Culler's Boats,* reviewed, XLV, 212
Burke, Lieutenant, British Army, XXV, 206–208
Burke, Captain W. J., XXI, 105
Burke, Captain William, XIV, 58 ff.

Burlingame, Anson C., XXXII, 128
Burlington, steamship (1837), VII, 64, 65; VIII, 51, 53; *(1840),* XX, 86
Burmah, XXII, 242
Burman Steam Tug Co., XLIII, 297
Burn, Randolph Seaton, XXVI, 203
Burnard, Thomas, XXIX, 63
Burne, George Charles, XXVI, 203
Burnell, Samuel, XXXIII, 163
Burnett, Edmund Cody, *The Continental Congress,* reviewed, II, 350
Burnett, Captain John, XVIII, 233
Burney, Captain Jonathan, XXIII, 27
Burnham, Mark, XXX, 96 n.
Burning of the ship *Anna F. Schmidt,* XXV, 22
Burns, Cornelius, XXI, 115, 116, 119, 120
Burns, George, XIV, 242 ff.
Burnside, barkentine *(1921),* V, 82
"Burnt Wine," query by Sarah B. Ball, XI, 291
Burpo, Robert S., Jr., "Notes on the First Fleet Engagement in the Civil War," XIX, 265–273
Burr, Aaron, XXXVI, 63
Burr, Captain George H., XXVIII, 223
Burr, Captain T. F., XVIII, 82
Burrell, Colonel Isaac S., XXXVI, 199–200
Burrell, Juan M., XXXVIII, 245
Burridge, George Nau, IX, 229
Burriel, Brigadier General D. Juan, XXXVI, 95–98
Burrill, John, XVII, 115
Burrill, Samuel, XXXV, 84
Burroughs, Alan, *John Greenwood in America 1745–1752,* reviewed, III, 356
Burroughs, Captain Thomas, XXI, 105
Burrows, Captain Ambrose H., "My Last Voyage on the Coast of Peru," VII, 282–287
Burrows, Captain Brutus, VII, 282, 285
Burrows, Captain Samuel, XXI, 105
Burrows, Silas E., VII, 282; XLVI, 232
Burrows, Captain Sylvester, Jr., XXI, 105
Burruss, Captain E. T., XXI, 105
Burruss, Captain George W., XXI, 105
Burruss, Captain J. N., XXI, 105
Burruss, Captain T. J., XXI, 105
Burruss, Captain Thomas, XXI, 105
Bursley, Captain Ira, XV, 140
Burstyn, Harold L., XXI, 7, 14, 15; XXX, 41, 42
Burtis, John, VII, 43
Burton, Alfred, XLI, 16
Burton, Brigadier General Henry S., XXXIV, 62
Burton, Humphrey, *Westward Crossing,* reviewed, XI, 231–232
Burton, John, XLIII, 11 ff.
Burutu, British merchantman *(1918),* XXXIX, 179
Bury, Captain Frank, VII, 57
Busch, Briton Cooper, reviews by, XLIV, 204; XLIX, 136; L, 70; Editor, *Alta California 1840–1842: The Journal and Observations of William Dane Phelps, Master of the Ship* Alert, reviewed, XLIII, 226–227; "Cape Verdeans in the American Whaling and Sealing Industry, 1850–1900," XLV, 104–116; "Elephants and Whales: New London and Desolation, 1840–1900," XL, 117–126; *The War against the seals: A History of the North American seal fishery,* reviewed, XLVIII, 131
Bush, F. T., XXII, 13
Bush, William S., Marine Lieutenant, XLVII, 18
Bush and Co., XXII, 13
Bushnell, Cornelius S., XXXV, 60
Bushnell, David, XXIII, 205
Bushnell, Edward, XIV, 265
"Business of War: Boston as a Navy Base, 1776–1783, The," by William Fowler, XLII, 25–35
Buss, ship *(1578),* XLIX, 15
Bussell, Stephen, XXX, 58
Bussen, Norwegian ship (ca. AD 995), XLIV, 99 ff.
Buster, R.N. tug *(1897),* XXVIII, 90
Busy, British brig *(1805),* XLIII, 45
Bute, Earl of, XX, 7, 14 n.
Butland, John, Jr., XIV, 217
Butledge (?), sloop *(1777),* XLIII, 24
Butler, Benjamin, XXVII, 243
Butler, General Benjamin, XXXI, 262
Butler, General Benjamin F., U.S.A., XXI, 123, 124, 125
Butler, Captain Francis, XXX, 109
Butler, Captain John, XLVIII, 32
Butler, General, XXXVI, 189 ff.
Butler, Martin J., "Steamers to the Whalemen's Port: The New Bedford-New York Lines, 1853–1880," XXXIX, 83–108
Butler, Senator, XXX, 143
Butler, Stuart, XXXIX, 254
Butman, Francis C. (Boston merchant), XXV, 107
Butt, Marshall W., XXII, 232
Buttersworth, J. E., 19th Century Marine Painter, by Rudolph J. Schaefer, reviewed, XXXVI 146–147
Butterworth, William John, XLVII, 172
Buxton, Ian, *Big Gun Monitors,* reviewed, XLI, 147–148
Buzzard, H.M.S., XXVIII, 17, 18
By, John, VII, 47
By Chance, brig *(1825),* XII, 104, 114, 115
Byers, Edward, *The Nation of Nantucket,* reviewed, XLVIII, 188
By George, schooner *(1862),* XV, 125
"Bygrave, W.," query by M. V. Brewington, I, 309–310
Bygrave, William (Artist), *Bark* Vernon *of New York leaving Messina Harbor,* reviewed, VII, 249; IX, 150
Byng, John, British Admiral, XXXIV, 140
Byran, George, XXXI, 236
Byrd, Admiral Richard E., U.S.N., XXVIII, 71–72
Byrd, Rear Admiral Richard E., XXIII, 156
Byrd, Richard Evelyn, photo of, L, 56
Byrd, Colonel William II, V, 204 ff.
Byrne, ship (1740), I, 297
Byron, Admiral, XXXVIII, 93

Byron, Captain John, R.N., XXV, 252, 297
Byron, Commodore John, R.N., IV, 91–92
Byron's [Captain John] *Journal of his Circumnavigation 1764–1766,* edited by Robert E. Gallagher, reviewed, XXV, 297–298
Bythesea, Captain, XXXIV, 62
Bytown, steamship (1836), VII, 62, 65
Byvanck, John, XXXVII, 65
Bywater, Charles E., XXXII, 29
"Byzantine and Moslem Shipping in the Mediterranean, 500–1250," by Archibald R. Lewis, XLVII, 157–160

CA. *See* California
C.A.A.M. *See* Council of American Maritime Museums.
C. A. Heckscher, schooner *(1861),* VIII, 216
C. A. L. Lamar, schooner *(1861),* XV, 114, 122
C. A. Thayer, ship, XLVII, 131
C. A. White, schooner, XIII, 121
C. B. Glover, schooner *(1861),* VIII, 216
C. B. Paine, schooner, XXVIII, 123
C. Baker, brig, XXXVI, 176
C. C. Trowbridge, steamship (1838), XVIII, 282
C. D. Bryant, bark (1878), XXVIII, plate XX
C. E. Jayne, bark (1859), III, 72, 265
C. E. Williams, steamship, XXIV, plate II
C. F. Sargent, ship (1874), I, 111, 113
C. G. Matthews, schooner *(1851),* XLIV, 89
C. H. Ingalls (ex-*Oriole*), schooner *(1871),* XXIV, 44
C. H. Prior, schooner *(1861),* VIII, 216
C. H. Soule, ship (1863), IV, 241
C. I. R. M. (International Radio-Medical Centre, Rome), XXVI, 230
C. J. Mare and Co., XXVI, 23, 24, 190, 207
C. M. Davis, bark (1863), IV, 241
C. M. Lamson & Co., XLIX, 281 ff.
C. P. Gerrish, schooner (1871), XXIV, 44, 58
C. P. Knapp, schooner, XXI, 95; *(1861),* XI, 281
C. Ronterean, sloop *(1863),* VIII, 229
C. Routereau, sloop, XXI, 93
C.S.S. Florida: Her Building and Operations, by Frank Lawrence Owsley, Jr., reviewed, XXV, 298–299.; re-reviewed, XLIX, 236
"C.S.S. *Georgia:* Memory and History," by Hawley Stevens, XLV, 191–198
C.S.S. No. 61. See Danmark.
"C.S.S. *Stonewall,* The; Ship of Many Names and Many Flags," by Louis H. Bolander, I, 241–254
C. Vanderbilt, schooner *(1846),* XXXVI, 170
C. Vanderbilt, steamship, XXI, 101; *(1861),* XI, 280, 281; XII, 54
C. W. Lawrence, revenue cutter *(1848),* XLV, 119 ff.

C. W. Morse, steamship, XVIII, 224
C. W. Morse, tug (1889), XXVII, plate VIII
C. W. Pasley, concrete ship (1944), XXII, 178
C. W. Pettit, steamship (1895), VI, 67, plate 4
C. W. Ring, brig (1855), XXIV, 57
C. W. Teagle, lifeboat (1935), XLVII, 51
C. W. Wetmore, tanker *(1894),* XXXVIII, 195 ff.
Cabell, S. G., VII, 123
Cabinet, schooner, XXIV, 135
"Cabin Interior, A," document contributed by Dean A. Fales, Jr., XXI, 222
"Cabin of an unidentified merchant vessel, circa 1880," Pictorial Supplement, XXXI, plate XXIII
"Cabin of the ship *Josephus,*" Pictorial Supplement, XXXI, plate XXIII
"Cabin of the ship *William H. Connor,*" Pictorial Supplement, XXXI, plate XXIV
"Cabin Plan of the Pacific Mail Steamer *Japan,*" by John Haskell Kemble, II, 243
Cabins of sailing vessels, II, 193 ff., plates 25–27; V, 200–201
Cable, Boyd, "The World's First Clipper," *The Mariner's Mirror,* XXIX (1943), reviewed, III, 273–274
Cables, submarine, VIII, 179
Cabo da Roca, schooner (1919), V, 141
Cabot, Continental Navy brigantine *(1776),* XXV, 193, 204, 211
Cabot, ship (1775), XXXIX, 29; *(1776),* XLVIII, 158
Cabot, David, "The New England Double Enders," XII, 123–141
Cabot, George, XXII, 265; XXIX, 204; XXX, 120
Cabot, Lieutenant Godfrey L., XXXVII, 113
Cabot, Harriet Ropes, "The Early Years of William Ropes & Co. in St. Petersburg," XXIII, 131–139
Cabot, John, XXXIII, 174 ff.; XLV, 249 ff.
Cabot, John (Explorer), XXIX, 276; XXX, 251, 255, 258
Cabot, Merle and Co., XIII, 277
Cabot, Samuel, XIII, 272
Cabot, Sebastian, XLV, 249 ff.
"Cabotian Conjectures: Did a Cabot Reach Maine in 1498?" by John H. Gilchrist, XLV, 249–252
Cabot Voyages and Bristol Discovery under Henry VII, The, by James A. Williamson, reviewed, XXIII, 148
Cabrillo, Juan Rodriguez, II, 258–259
Cacheu River, XXX, 178 ff.
Cacique, brig *(1827),* VI, 12–17
Cadet, brig, XXII, 91; *(1850),* XXV, plate XIV
Cadiz, steamship (1853), XVII, 138, 139; XVIII, 68; XXVI, 19, 21, 22, 23, 25, 27, 28, 202–204, 209
Cadmus, British warship *(1863),* XLIV, 268 ff.
Cadmus, ship *(1842),* XXVII, 109 n.
Cadmus, steamship *(1824),* XXXVII, 244
Cadoret, Bernard, *AR VAG,* reviewed, XLVII, 142
Cady, Kenneth G., review by, XLIX, 62
Caesar, ship *(1678),* XIII, 16; *(1776),* XIII, 44
Caesar, steamship *(1910),* XIV, 134
Cahawba, steamship *(1861),* XI, 280

Cahawba, transport *(1860),* XXXVII, 281
Cahawba, U.S.S. *(1861),* XXI, 240, 241, 243
Cahoon, B. P., XX, 85
Cahoon, Captain W., VII, 43
Cai, Professor Hongsheng, XLVI, 26 ff.
Caille, D'Audibert, American Consul, XLI, 209
Caird, XXIII, 117
Caird and Co., XXVI, 13, 207
Cairngorm, ship *(1858),* XXXIV, 21
Cairo, ironclad gunboat *(1861),* XLIX, 116
Cairo, ship *(1843),* XV, 140
Cairo, U.S.S. (1861), XIX, 266; *(1862),* XXV, 134
Cairo, Lieutenant Robert F., U.S.N., reviewed books, XXVII, 67–71, 281–284; XXVIII, 229–232
Calahan, Harold Augustin, *Rigging,* reviewed, I, 189
Calais (ME), XV, 173–190
Calais Steamboat Co., XXXIII, 86
Calawii, steamship (1893), IX, 223, 226, 227
Calchas, steamship *(1941),* XXVI, 148
Caldbeck, John Browne, XXVI, 203
Calder, George, XXXIX, 31
Calder, Sir Robert, XVII, 203
Calder, Senator William M., XXXV, 284
Calderhead, William L., "Naval Innovation in Crisis: War in the Chesapeake, 1813," XXXVI, 206–221
Caldwell, schooner *(1838),* XXXVIII, 57
Caldwell, Andrew, XXXII, 249
Caldwell, Lieutenant C. H. B., XII, 273; XXXV, 27
Caldwell, Eben, XIII, 134–139
Caldwell, Mr., XXX, 296
Caldwell H. Colt, schooner (1887), II, 230
Caleb Curtis, pilot schooner (1859), I, 78
Caleb Cushing, U.S.S. *(1863),* XIX, 54
Caledonia, bark *(1845),* XXXVI, 142
Caledonia, brig (1828), IV, 51; XXVII, plate II
Caledonia, ship *(1812),* XLIV, 171
Caledonia, ship (1860), IV, 51
Caledonia, steamship, XXVI, 269; (1818), VIII, 133; *(1863),* XXI, plate V; *(1864),* VIII, 233
Calef, John, IV, 207 ff.
Calesta Haws, ship, XXI, 93; *(1861),* XI, 280
Caley, Samuel, XXX, 94
Calhoon, Mathew, XXIX, 277
Calhoun, steamship *(1861),* XI, 280; XII, 53
Calhoun, John C., XXX, 137; XXXIV, 96
Calhoun, John C., President, XLII, 169 ff.
Calhoun, Scott, XXXVI, 246, 248
Calhoun, Captain Walter C., XXXIX, 43
California, American ship *(1840),* XXIX, 90
California, bark *(1855),* XXIV, 142; *(1905),* XLIV, 18 ff.
California, ship *(1834),* XII, 181, 183
California, ship (1864), V, 148; *(1903),* Pictorial Supplement, XXXIII, plates X, XXVII, XXVIII, XXIX (upper).
California, steamship, XXI, 93, 98, 99; (1848), X, 125–126, 130, plate 17; *(1861),* XI, 267, 280; *(1875),* XIV, 213

California (CA). *See* Book trade; Emigration and Immigration; Shipping; Smuggling; Steamboats; Steam Navigation
California-Alaskan Contacts, XXIX, 83
Californian, ship under sail *(1984),* photo, XLV, 131
Californian, steamship *(1900),* II, 140; *(1902),* XXIV, 49
California Pacific Railroad Co., XXXI, 121
California Shipbuilding Corp., Wilmington, Cal., VIII, 76
California Steam Navigation Co., II, 299 ff.; XVI, 168, 169; XXXIV, 18
California Steamship Co., XXXI, 120
Calista, schooner (1845), XXIV, 45, 58
"Calking Iron, Making Iron," query by Baron R. de Kerchove, II, 81; answer by Inman Sealby, II, 175–176
Callao, gunboat *(1899),* XXXV, 184
Calliope, British corvetter *(1889),* XLVI, 115
Calliope, H.M.S., XXVIII, 17; XXIX, 270, 271
Calliope, schooner *(1861),* VIII, 216
Callisthenes, VII, 262–263
Callwell, Major General Charles E., XXXVI, 44
Calmer, steamship (ex-*Albert Jeffers,* ex-*Eastern Importer*), XXIII, 276
Calpe, steamship (1825), IX, 257
Calumet, sardine carrier (1921), XXVIII, 126
Calumet, ship *(1807),* XVI, 195
Calvert, Reverend James, XXV, 274
Calvert Marine Museum, Maritime Titles in Print, XXXIX, 60
Calvin, John, XXXVII, 48
Calvin Austin, screw steamship (1903), XXXIII, 92, 94, plate 3; XXXIV, 182; XXVIII, 124
Calvin F. Baker, schooner *(1850),* XXXVII, 92 (footnote).
Calypso, H.M.S. *(1902),* XXVIII, 98, 107
Calypso, ship (1841), XV, 81
Calypso, steamship, XXI, 87, 94, 106; *(1862),* XVII, 249 ff.; *(1863),* VIII, 229; IX, 35–36
Calypso, U.S.S. *(1863),* XVII, 252
Camajee, D. J., XXII, 13
Camajee, P. and D. N., XXII, 13; XXXIV, 19
Camanche, U.S. monitor (1862), X, 17, 31
Cámara, Rear Admiral Manuel de la, XLI, 93 ff.
Cambay, bark (1857), VI, 82
Cambria, steamship, XXVI, 270; *(1854),* XIV, 252; *(1862),* VIII, 223
Cambrian, British frigate *(1804),* XLIII, 42 ff.
Cambrian, H.M.S. *(1859),* XXVII, 173
Cambridge, ship *(1847),* XVI, 65
Cambridge, steamship (1889), XI, 259 ff.
Cambridge, U.S.S. *(1864),* XXIII, 225
Cambronne, French bark *(1917),* XXXVI, 268
Cambuston, Henri, XXXIII, 121
Camden, privateer *(1776),* XXXVIII, 25
Camden, sloop, XXII, 60 n.

Camden, steamship (1907), XXVIII, 124; XXXIII, 92, 94; Pictorial Supplement, XXXIV, plate XXXI
Camden Hills (ME), XXV, plate IX
Camel, sloop *(1813),* XLII, 108; *(1814),* XXIV, 175, 176, 179, 180
Camella, British ship *(1777),* XL, 21 ff.
Cameo, schooner (1878), Pictorial Supplement, XXXIII, plates V, XXXII
Cameron, Captain, XXV, 260
Cameron, John, VIII, 185 ff.
Cameron-Genoa Mills Shipbuilders, Ltd., Victoria, British Columbia, XXXII, 32
Camilla (1800), XXIII, 216
Camilla, bark (1862), IV, 243; V, 327
Camilla, frigate (1784), VI, 170
Camilla, H.M. frigate *(1778),* VII, 207; *(1779),* XXXV, 142
Camilla, schooner *(1863),* XII, 155, 229; XV, 117, 122
Camilla, schooner yacht (ex-*America*) *(1860),* XXVII, 233 ff.
Camilla, sloop *(1779),* XXXVII, 300
Camillus, ship (1811), XIV, 39; XXII, 216
Cammillieri, Nicolas (artist), mention, editorial comment, XLII, 3
Campania, steamship (1893), XXIV, plate XIII; XXVII, 66
Campanula, H.M.S. *(1943),* XLIV, 55 ff.
Campbell, revenue cutter *(1832),* XXXVIII, 58
Campbell, schooner cutter *(1839),* XXXV, 199
Campbell, Lady Amelia, XLVI, 19 ff.
Campbell, Archibald, XXII, 13
Campbell, Sir Archibald, XLVI, 19 ff.
Campbell, Benjamin, XXX, 178, 184, 185, 237
Campbell, Colin, XV, 175
Campbell, David, XL, 8 ff.
Campbell, Edward H., XXXVII, 123
Campbell, George Duncan, "The Sailors' Home," XXXVII, 179–184
Campbell, George W., XXV, 26
Campbell, Hugh, XXXIII, 236
Campbell, Captain Hugh, XXI, 133
Campbell, Captain Hugh G., XLVII, 27
Campbell, Commodore Hugh G., XLII, 112
Campbell, Captain James, XXI, 105
Campbell, John, XXXVII, 269
Campbell, Captain John, XVIII, 188; XX, 184; reviewed book, XIX, 141; "Marine Intelligence from the *Panama Star* and *Star and Herald,*" XX, 118–133; "A Voyage for Health," XIX, 200–212
Campbell, Sir John, VII, 100 n.
Campbell, Captain John F., XXV, 3, 4; contributed note, XXIII, 219–221; "Captain 'John,' The Panama Canal's First Pilot," XXIV, 186–207; "Captain Lawrence Furlong (1734–1806), Author and/or Compiler of Blunt's *American Coast Pilot,*" XXI, 5–15; "A Cartographical Study of a Blunt Chart," XXV, 46–50; "The Havana Incident," XXII, 264–276; "A Marine Note of Protest," XXIII, 46–55; "Pepper, Pirates and Grapeshot," XXI, 292–302
Campbell, Judge Lewis D., XXXIV, 62
Campbell, Miles W., "An Inquiry into the Troop Strength of King Harald Hardrada's Invasion Fleet of 1066," XLIV, 96–102
Campbell, Mrs. Peter Scarlett, XXXV, 252
Campbell, Robert B., XXII, 248
Campbell, Stafford, *The Yachtsman's Guide to Celestial Navigation,* reviewed, XL, 139
Campbell, W. S., XXIX, 119 ff.
Campbell, Walter, XXXVI, 239
Campbell, Lord William, XIII, 29
Campeador V, H.M.S., II, 342
Campeche, Battle of (Mexico, 1843), XXI, 216
Campecheano, Mexican warship *(1843),* XXI, 222 ff.
"Campeche Days," by Fred Hunt, II, 229–242
Campello, steamship (1922), XXXIII, 51
Campobello (ex-*General Leavitt,* ex-*Spray*), steamship (1901), XXIV, 54, 55
Canada, H.M.S. *(1880),* XXVIII, 17, 88
Canada, ship *(1802),* XXXIV, 251; *(1846),* XXXVIII, 210
Canada, steamship *(1826),* VI, 204, 206–208, plate 29
Canada, steamship (1835), VII, 56, 57, 65; (1841), XX, 88; *(1850),* XXXVII, 233
Canada:
  History, to 1763 (New France), XLIX, 262
  See also Cartography; Fishers; Fishing; Louisbourg; Newfoundland; Nootka Sound (BC); Shipbuilding; Shipping; Steam navigation; Yacht racing
"Canada and China: Early Trading Links by Sea," NASOH paper by Professor Barry M. Gough, XXXVII, 81
Canada Atlantic & Plant S.S. Co., XXXVII, 237
Canada Atlantic Steamship Co., XXXVII, 237
Canada West Coast Navigation Co., XXXII, 33
Canadian, steamship *(1885),* X, 113; *(1926),* XXXIV, 171
Canadian Coastal and Inland Steam Vessels, 1809–1930, by John M. Mills, reviewed, XL, 145
Canadian Coast Guard, XXX, 221
Canadian Department of Transport, XXX, 221
Canadian Pacific: The Story of a Famous Shipping Line, by George Musk, reviewed, XLII, 223
Canadian Steam Navigation Co., XXVI, 23, 191
Canal, 2nd Lieutenant Francisco, XXX, 54
Canal Museum. *See* Erie Canal Museum (Syracuse, NY)
Canals:
  Maine, XXIV, 233
  North Carolina, V, 203, 297; VI, 51
  Virginia, V, 203, 297; VI, 51; XVI, 41
Canals, VIII, 56–59: Albemarle-Chesapeake, VI, 52–54; Beauharnois, VIII, 58; Cornwall, VIII, 58; Cumberland and Oxford, VIII, 175; Dismal Swamp, V, 203–222, 297–310; VI, 51–70, plates 3–8; VII, 66, 240–242; Erie, VI, 203–204; VIII, 58, 175; Florida,

proposed, VII, 130–131; Rideau, VIII, 56; Welland, VIII, 57
Canan, John, XXVIII, 135
Canandaigua, screw sloop, XXXII, 49
"Canaries as Ports of Call, The," by Walter E. Minchinton, XLVI, 100–110
Canary Islands, History, XLVI, 91. See also Shipping
"Canary Islands and the Question of the Prime Meridian: The Search for Precision in the Measurement of the Earth, The," by Wilcomb E. Washburn, XLIV, 77–81
Canathina, bark *(1861),* XI, 280
Canberra, British cruise ship *(1980),* XLVI, 109
Canby, R. S., XXII, 285 n.
Canceaux, H.M.S., XXVII, 222; *(1775),* XXXI, 215
Candia, steamship, XXVI, 31
Candidate, British steamship *(1915),* XXXV, 41
Candler, Captain Benjamin, XXI, 262
Canell, Adam, XXI, 120
Cannenburg, Dr. Willem Voorbeijtel, VI, 3; "Quarter Wagener," VII, 316–317
"Cannenburg, Dr. Willem Voorbeijtel," by Vernon D. Tate, V, 240
Cannibalism, XVI, 180
Canning, George, Secretary of State, L, 29 ff.
Canning, Stratford, IV, 327–329
Cannon, destroyer escort *(1943),* XXXVIII, 283
Cannon, naval, XXXVI, 276–295
"Canoe from the Penobscot River, A," by Wendell S. Hadlock and Ernest S. Dodge, VIII, 289–300
Canoes, I, 374; VIII, 91, 289; IX, 185; XXVIII, 53
  Marshall Islands, VI, 71
  Melanesia, XXIII, 255
Canoes: Bark, North American, XXV, 295–297; early, XXVI, 48, plate 6; Indian, VIII, 91–98, 289–300; IX, 185–206; Indian, of Northwest Coast, I, plates facing 376, 377; Melanesian [model], XXIII, plate 13; Oceania, XII, 306–308; Outrigger, XXIII, 255–260; Polynesian, X, 40–41, plate 9. *See also* Boats.
Canonicus, U.S. monitor *(1862),* X, 19, 26, 27, 32; *(1864),* XXVII, 42
Canopus, H.M.S., XXXI, Pictorial Supplement, plate VIII; XXXIII, 35 ff.
Canot, Theodore, XXXV, 199
Canova, ship *(1823),* XLVII, 90
Cantania, tanker *(1881),* XXXVIII, 202
Cantino map, XXX, 258
Canton, Confederate ship, XXIX, 15, 23
Canton, steamship, XXII, 11, 13–18, 20–24, 30–31, 33, 38, 42, 43; *(1851),* XXVI, 14, 116, 203; *(1858),* XXXIV, 19 ff.
Canton & Macao Steam Boat Co., XLIII, 196 ff.; XXXIV, 41
Canton Captain, by James B. Connolly, reviewed, II, 349
Cantonese rebels, XXX, 155 f.
Canton Factories, map of, XLVIII, 263

"Canton Factories," query by Walter Muir Whitehill, II, 248
"Canton Packet *Cohota,* The," by Michael Costagliola, VII, 5–8
Canton River (China). See Steam Navigation
Canton River, Map of, XXII, plate 1
Canute, ship *(1869),* I, 114
Canvas, XXXI, 130
Cao, Cliff, XXXVI, 245, 247 n.
Cape Ann, steamship *(1895),* XII, 290, 293, plate 28
Cape Ann (MA):
  Discovery and exploration, XXV, 233
  in fiction, XXV, 233
Cape Ann (MA), XXV, 233 ff., plate XXXII
Cape Ann: Cape America, by Herbert A. Kenny, reviewed, XXXI, 291
"Cape Ann Visits of the Great Sea-Serpent (1639–1886)," by Ralph W. Dexter, XLVI, 213–220
Cape Breton Ships and Men, by Captain John P. Parker, M.B.E., reviewed, XXVIII, 287–289
Cape Chignecto, XXXI, 23
"Cape Cod Northeaster, A," by Commander Francis E. Clark, U.S.N. (ret.), XXIV, 138–143
Cape Cod shipbuilding, XXII, 233–251
Cape Fear, concrete steamship *(1919),* XXII, 161, 165, 168, 182
Cape Fear Shipbuilding Co., XLI, 193
Cape François, XXX, 126
Cape Henlopen, XXXII, 248
Cape Henlopen Lighthouse, VIII, 33, plate 8
Cape Henry Lighthouse, VIII, 26–36, plate 8
Cape Horn, VII, 39–41
"Cape Horn," query by H. C. Palmer, I, 398; answer by John Lyman, II, 83
Cape Horn Pigeon, bark *(1888),* XLIV, 16
Capella, brig *(1861),* XI, 280
Capels, merchant ships, XLV, 227
Cape Maranguing, XXXI, 24
Cape May, steamship (ex-*State of Maine,* ex-*Edgemont*), Pictorial Supplement, XXXIV, plate XVI
Capes, William VII, 44
Cape Sierra Leone, XXX, 235
Cape Smythe Whaling Co., XXXIX, 13 ff.
Capetown, South Africa, Fireboard by Cornè, 1804, Pictorial Supplement, XXXII, plate XXIX
Cape Verde Islands. See Sealers, Whalers
Cape Verdeans in the American Whaling and Sealing Industry, 1850–1900," by Briton Cooper Busch, XLV, 104–116
Cap Finisterre, auxiliary schooner *(1918),* IX, 68; XXXII, 33
Cap Horn, auxiliary schooner *(1918),* IX, 68; XXXII, 33
Capistran, schooner *(1861),* XI, 280
Capitaine de Beauchamp, auxiliary *(1917),* XXXII, 10 ff.
Capitaine Guynemer, auxiliary *(1917),* XXXII, 11, 30
Capitaine Rémy, auxiliary *(1917),* XXXII, 11, 30
Capital City, steamship *(1867),* II, 303

Capitol, ship (1847), XLV, 183
Cap'n Bill III, ship *(1961),* XLI, 51
Cap'n Fatso, by Daniel V. Gallery, reviewed, XXX, 75
Cap Nord, auxiliary schooner (1918), V, 141; XXXII, 33; IX, 67–68
Cap Palos, auxiliary schooner (1918), XXXII, 33
Cappon, Lester J., and Stella F. Duffy, *Virginia Gazette Index,* reviewed, XI, 229–230
Capps, Washington L., XXXIX, 131
Capps, Rear Admiral Washington Lee, XXXII, 160; XXXV, 278
Capron, steamship, XVII, 306; XVIII, 68
Cap Trafalgar, German ship, XXVIII, 108 n.
Captain, H.M.S., XXII, 262
Captain A. F. Lucas, tanker *(1903),* XXXVIII, 192 ff.
Captain A. H. Bowman, steamship *(1861),* XXXIX, 94
Captain Cook, snow *(1786),* XI, 155–156
Capt. Gray's, ship *(1672),* L, 21
Captain Greene, schooner *(1795),* XXXVIII, 255
Captain Prat, cruiser *(1891),* XXXVIII, 298
Captain (or Capt.) Spedden, schooner, XXI, 97; *(1861),* XI, 281
Capt. Vicar's, ship *(1672),* L, 21
"Captain Arthur H. Clark in his cabin, 1876," Pictorial Supplement, XXXI, plate XXII
"Captain Basi Ivanković, Painter of Mediterranean Sailing Vessels," by Josip Luetić, XXIV, 124–126
"Captain Benjamin F. Simmons in Australia," by Ida Leeson, IV, 324–325
Captain Charles Hervey Townshend: Self-Portrait of an American Packet Ship Sailor, edited by Carl C. Culter, reviewed, I, 95
"Captain Codman on the Mutiny in Dorchester Church, and the Seamanship of Saint Paul," by Samuel Eliot Morison, II, 99–106
"Captain Codman on Yankee Traders and Elephants," II, 271–277
"Captain Cook's First Voyage," by Ernest S. Dodge, XVI, 281–285
"Captain Crowninshield Brings Home an Elephant," by Robert and Gale McClung, XVIII, 137–141
Captain Dauntless: The Story of Nicholas Biddle of the Continental Navy, by William Bell Clark, reviewed, IX, 303
"Captain Frankland's *Rose,*" by W. E. May, XXVI, 37–62
Captain From Connecticut: The Life and Naval Times of Isaac Hull, by Linda M. Maloney, reviewed, XLIX, 238
"Captain James A. Whipple: Marine Salvor, Engineer, and Inventor," by Howard L. Dickman, XXXIV, 89–102
Captain James Cook and His Voyages of Discovery in the Pacific, by Norman J. W. Thrower, reviewed, XXXI, 74–75
Captain James Cook – After Two Hundred Years: A commemorative address delivered before the Hakluyt Society, by R. A. Skelton, reviewed, XXX, 222
Captain James Kelly of Hobart Town, by K. M. Bowden, reviewed, XXVI, 75–76
"Captain Jared Fisher and the Loss of the Steamship *Independence,*" document contributed by E. Jared Bliss, Jr., XVI, 211
"Captain John," broadside, XXIV, plate 21
"Captain John Henry," query by E. Lee Dorsett, IV, 77
"Captain 'John;' The Panama Canal's First Pilot," by John F. Campbell, Master Mariner, XXIV, 186–207
"Captain Joseph Fry, of S.S. *Virginius,*" by Jim Dan Hill, XXXVI, 88–100
Captain Joshua Slocum, by Victor Slocum, reviewed, X, 156–157
Captain Kidd and the War against the Pirates, by Robert C. Ritchies, reviewed, XLVII, 282
"Captain Lawrence Furlong (1734–1806), Author and/or Compiler of Blunt's *American Coast Pilot,*" by Captain John F. Campbell, XXI, 5–15
"Captain Leroy Dow and *Clarissa B. Carver,*" by John R. Richardson, XL, 108–116
"Captain Marryat Surveys the American Maritime Scene," by S. W. Jackman, XXIII, 56–61
"Captain McGiffin, and the Battle of the Yalu," by R. C. Anderson, IX, 301
Captain Moses Rich Colman, edited by Addie Cushing Colman, reviewed, X, 235
Captain Nat Herreshoff, by L. Francis Herreshoff, reviewed, XLVIII, 186
"Captain Nicholas Thorndike, Mariner," by Richard J. Altobelli, XXII, 194–211
"Captain Nicholas Thorndike, Mariner and Merchant," by Richard J. Altobelli, XXIV, 247–271
Captain of the Phantom, *The Story of Henry Jackson Sargent, Jr., 1834–1862, The,* reviewed, XXVIII, 152
"Captain Paul Pinkham, Nantucket Hydrographer," by Peter J. Guthorn, XLIII, 51–55
"Captain Philo McGiffin at the Battle of the Yalu," by Earle R. Forrest, VIII, 267–278
"Captain Richard H. Gayle of Alabama and the Voyage of the *Rodmond,* 1856," by W. Stanley Hoole, XI, 42–58
"Captain Richard Maples, Early Mariner and Adventurer in the East," by Sir Charles Fawcett, XIII, 5–26, plates 1, 2
Captain Robert Bennet Forbes House, Milton (MA), XXV, 156
"Captain Robert Niles, Connecticut State Navy," by Sheldon S. Cohen, XXXIX, 190–208
Captains. *See* Ship captains
Captain Samuel Tucker (1747–1833), Continental Navy, by Philip Chadwick Foster Smith, reviewed, XXXVII, 72–73

"Captains and Diplomats: Americans in the Río de la Plata, 1843–1846," by Robert W. Randall, XLVI, 230–239

"Captain Sands' Locust Tree," query by S. B. Detwiler, I, 90; answer by Robert F. Livingston, II, 250

Captain's Best Mate: the Journal of Mary Chipman Lawrence on the whaler Addison *1856–1860, The,* by Mary Chipman Lawrence, edited by Stanton Garner, reviewed, XXVII, 73–74; XLVIII, 201

"Captains' Children: Life in the Adult World of Whaling, 1852–1907, The," by Margaret S. Creighton, XXXVIII, 203–216

"Captain's Mast: Conservatism vs. Liberalism," by Commander George E. Buker, XXX, 139–146

Captains of the Old Steam Navy: Makers of the American Naval Tradition, 1840–1880, by James C. Bradford, reviewed, XLIX, 61

Captain's Papers, a Log of Whaling and Other Sea Experiences, by Ellsworth Luce West, reviewed, XXVI, 149

Captains to the Northward, by William J. Morgan, reviewed, XX, 148

"Captain Thomas Petersen, Marine Artist," by Lawrence W. Jenkins, XV, 154

"Captain W. J. Logan," query by W. John Logan, IX, 74

"Captain William Robert Stewart," query by Charles H. P. Copeland, XI, 291

"Capture and Burning of the Ship *Anna F. Schmidt* by *Alabama*," by Robert R. Newell, XXV, 18–28

"Capture of the CSS *Florida,* The," by F. L. Owsley, Jr., XXII, 45–54

"Capture of the Mellish, 1776, The," XXVIII, plate 1

"Capture of William C. Clark, The," note by Dee Herbrandson, XXXV, 139–141

Cap Vert, auxiliary schooner (1918), IX, 68; XXXII, 33

Cap Vincent, schooner (1918), IX, 68; XXXII, 33

Carabobo, XXX, 260

Caracas, brig *(1842),* XXX, 261

Caravel, Portuguese vessel, XLV, 225

Carbon, barkentine (1851), XV, 178

Card, U.S. escort carrier *(1943),* XLV, 63

Cardenas, bark (1867), XV, 186

Cardinal Cisneros, Spanish ship *(1898),* XLI, 100

Cardwell, Samuel, XIV, 52, 56, 57, 59

Careless, Captain Edward, XXXVII, 174

Caress II, fishing vessel *(1963),* XLI, 59

Carey, George C., "The Tradition of the St. Elmo's Fire," XXIII, 29–38

Carey, George G., "Enchanted-Island Traditions of the Sixteenth and Seventeenth Centuries," XXIX, 275–281

Carey, Captain I., XXI, 105

Carey, Captain J. J. XIV, 125

Carey, Mathew, Title pages of two naval histories printed for, XXVI, 177–188, plate 20; XXX, 42

Cargoes of the East, by Esmond Bradley Martin and Chryssee Perry Martin, reviewed, XL, 231

"Caribbean Catastrophe: The Earthquake and Fire at Kingston, Jamaica, B.W.I., 17–19 January 1907," by Colonel Roger Willock, USMCR, XXIX, 118

Caribbean Cruise Lines, Inc., XXXVI, 10

Caribbee, bark (1852), XV, 180

Carioca, ship (1850), I, 48

Carisbrooke Castle, ship (1814), XVII, 69

Carl, ship, XXI, 96; *(1861),* XI, 281

Carl D. Lothrop, schooner (1873), XXIV, 44, 58

Carlin, Captain James, XXI, 81

Carlisle, Rodney, "Black-Owned Shipping Before Marcus Garvey," XXXV, 197–206

Carlotta, bark *(1856),* XVIII, 318–319

Carlotta (ex-*Antonia,* ex-U.S.S. *Antonia*), steamship *(1863),* XXXVII, 235

Carlowitz and Co., XL, 90

Carlson, Captain Carl H., L, 260 ff.

Carlson, W., XXXVI, 242

Carlton, bark (1863), XV, 186

Carlton, Captain John, XXI, 292

Carmagnole, privateer *(1793),* XXI, 81, 93 ff.

Carman, Esekiel, XXXI, 144

Carmania, R.M.S., XXVIII, 108 n.

Carmania, steamship, XLII, 295 ff.

Carmarthenshire, steamship *(1921),* XXII, 169

Carmichael, C. Ed., VII, 234–235

Carmichael, J. W., XXIV, plate XXVIII

Carmichael, William, XLI, 212

Carmick, Captain, U.S.M.C., XXV, 31, 32

Carmita, schooner *(1863),* XII, 155

Carnarvon, British ship *(1914),* XXXIII, 35 ff.

Carnatic, 74, British ship *(1798),* XXII, 264, 270, 271, 272; XXIV, 250; XXXIX, 32; XLV, 96

Carnes, Captain Jonathan, XXI, 292; XXV, 178

Car of Concordia. See *Cleopatra's Barge.*

Car of Neptune, steamship *(1807),* XVIII, 317; (1809), XXVII, 9, 12, 19, 20, 22–25, 27, 28

Carolina, H.M.S., XXVI, 46

Carolina, ship (1670), XXX, 82

Carolina, steamship (1896), XXVI, 85; Pictorial Supplement, XXXIV, plate XXII

Carolina, steamship, XXI, 81, 88, 96; (1849), XVII, 143 ff.; XVIII, 68; XXII, 28, 42; *(1859),* VII, 119; *(1861),* VIII, 216, 223; *(1862),* XII, 53; XV, 99, 115, 120, 122, 125

Carolina, vessel, XXVI, 47

Carolina Packet, ship (1740), XXVI, 38

Caroline, boat *(1953),* XIII, 126

Caroline, schooner *(1801),* X, 53; *(1815),* XLIV, 172; *(1850),* X, 269; *(1861),* XI, 281; XII, 155

Caroline, sloop, XXI, 96; *(1807),* XVI, 197; *(1862),* XII, 53; XV, 111, 127, 128

Caroline, steamship, XXI, 91, 99; (1823, 1824 or 1825), VI, 199, 203; XIII, 160; IX, 255–256; *(1834, 1837),* VII, 54, 65, 298–314, plate 37; VIII, 51 n., 54; *(1861),* XI, 154, 280, 281; XII, 53, 155, 229; *(1864),* VIII, 233, 236; IX, 39, 44

Caroline Brutus, schooner *(1834),* XXXVIII, 270
Caroline Gertrude, schooner *(1863),* XII, 155
Caroline H. Kennedy, brig (1853), XXIV, 57
Caroline Islands, boats of, XIII, 93 ff.
Caroline Read, bark (1848), I, 49
Caroline Virginia, schooner *(1862),* VIII, 223
Carolus Magnus, ship (1852), III, 62
Carondelet, U.S. ironclad (1861), XIX, 266, 269 ff.; *(1862),* XXV, 129, 131, 134, 136, 139
Caronia, steamship, XLII, 295
Carpenter, Lieutenant Commander C. C., XXXII, 128; XXXIV, 213
Carpenter, Rear Admiral Charles C., XL, 101
Carpenter, Francis R., comment, Editorial, The American Neptune, XXXVIII, 3–4
Carpenter, John, XIII, 14, 23
"Carpenter's Measurement," note contributed by John Lyman, XXIII, 141–142
Carr, Frank G. G., *Sailing Barges,* reviewed, XXXII, 144–145
Carr, J. Revell, XXXVIII, 231
Carr, James A., "John Adams and the Barbary Problem: The Myth and the Record," XXVI, 231–257
Carr, William C., and Harold C. Wilson, "Gosnold's Elizabeth's Isle: Cuttyhunk or Naushon?" XXXIII, 131–145
Carrack, fifteenth century vessel, XLV, 225
Carriages and carts, XLIV, 245
Carribean Cruise, by Kate and Richard Bertram, reviewed, VIII, 260–261
Carrick and Bidwell, VII, 57
Carrie, schooner, XXI, 98
Carrie E. Phillips, schooner (1887), XXVI, plate IX
Carrie Hoth, schooner *(1864),* XII, 229
Carrie M. Clark, ship (1874), III, 66
Carrie Mears, bateau (1902), IV, 289
Carrie Muir, schooner *(1864),* XII, 229
Carrier Dove, schooner (1890), V, 144
Carrie Reed, ship (1870), III, 62
Carrie Sanford, schooner, XXI, 93; *(1861),* VIII, 216, 223; XI, 281; XV, 117, 125
Carrie W., schooner, XXVIII, 123
Carrillo, Dona Josefa, XXXII, 119
Carrington, Edward, XVII, 72–73; XXIX, 209; XLVII, 248
Carrington, Hugh, ed., *The Discovery of Tahiti,* reviewed, IX, 154
Carroll, steamship *(1871),* XXXVII, 235
Carroll, Lieutenant Michael B., XXI, 133
Carroll, Richard, XLVII, 52
Carroll, Reverend Thomas J., XXV, 243
Carroll A. Deering, schooner (1919), V, 139; X, 200
Carroll-Maccubbin Papers, Maryland Historical Society, VI, 302–303
Carrollton, ship (1872), XXVII, plate XI
Carrolton, Fireman Herman, XXXVII, 89
Carronades, XXXVI, 276–295

Carrosso, Vincent, XXXVII, 50
Carrothers, W. A., *The British Columbia Fisheries,* reviewed, II, 353
Carry-away boat, XII, 123
Carson, Sir Edward, XXXV, 43
Carson, Kit, XXVIII, 130–133
Cartago, steamship *(1908),* XXIV, 200
Cartegena, gunboat *(1903),* XXXVII, 260
Cartels, XXVIII, 163–194
Cartel ships, XXVIII, 165
Carter, Benjamin, XXXIV, 254
Carter, Doctor Benjamin B., XVIII, 107, 108, 123–127, 134–136, Plate 6
Carter, Charles, XXX, 49
Carter, Edward C., II, "Mathew Carey, Advocate of American Naval Power, 1785–1814," XXVI, 177–188
Carter, Edwin, XXXV, 292
Carter, John, XXXV, 291
Carter, Commander John C., XLVIII, 97 ff.
Carter, John Swain (Curator of Maritime History, Peabody Museum of Salem; Managing Editor, *The American Neptune*), XXXIX, 233; editorials by, XL, 3–6, 83–84, 163–166, 243–244; editorial comment by, XLI, 3, 83, 163, 243; XLII, 3, 83, 163, 243; XLIII, 3, 83, 163, 243; reviews by, XL, 145, 146, 147, 234, 235; *American Traders in European Ports,* reviewed, XLII, 310
Carter, Robert, *A Summer Cruise on the Coast of New England,* reviewed, XXXI, 77
Carter, Commander S. P. mentioned in 1867, XXXII, 130
Carteret, Sir George, XXV, 286
Carteret, Captain Philip, R.N., XXV, 252–254, 260, 297–298
Carteret's [Captain Philip] *Voyage Round the World 1766–1769,* edited by Helen Wallis, reviewed, XXV, 297–298
Cartha, Richard, XXI, 112 ff.
Carthage, steamship (1857), XXVI, 25, 111 n., 126–128, 205, 209; painting of, XXVI, plate 16; XLIII, 96 ff.
Cartographers, Biography, XLIII, 51
Cartography:
   America, XLVI, 173
   Canada, XLIV, 186
   History of, VIII, 302; XXI, 260; XXV, 46, 176; XXX, 200; XXXI, 253; XLIV, 77
   United States, —, **18th century,** I, 141; XLIII, 51
   —, **Massachusetts,** XXV, 233
   —, **New York, 19th century,** XXIV, 280
   —, **20th century,** IV, 119
   See also Fuller Projection; Nautical charts
Cartography, XI, 95–107; XVII, 28–37; XIX, 44–50; XXX, 200
Cartwright, Captain, XL, 47
Cartwright, George, L, 36
Caruthers, J. Wade, "Influence of Maritime Trade in Early American Development: 1750–1830," XXIX,

199–210; "The Seaborne Frontier to California 1796–1850," XXIX, 81–101
Carver, George A., XL, 108
Carver, Captain Jesse T., XXVIII, plate XXII
Carver, Captain Nathaniel, XI, 240 ff.
Carvill, J. F., XXVII, plates XXVIII, XXX, XXXII
Carving (decorative arts), III, 35; VII, 255; XXXIV, 197. *See also* Art; Figureheads; Ship decoration
Carysfort, British *(1843),* XXXII, 243
Casasy, XXX, 182, 184
Cascade, brig *(1850),* painting of, XLVII, 94
Casdorp, John, VI, 302–303
Case, Rear Admiral A. Ludlow, XXXIII, 280
Case, Calvin, VII, 42
Case, Phillips N., *To the Rescue: a true story,* reviewed, II, 263
Caselli, Aldo, "The San Martino Museum," XXI, 143–144
"Case-oil and Canned Salmon: *Star of Lapland,* ex *Atlas,*" by Harold Huycke, XVI, 5–27, 107–135, plates 1–8, 11, 12
Case oil trade. *See* Oil trade
Cashman, Jeremiah, XVII, 118
Cashmere, bark (1885), XXIV, 72
Cas Navires, Martinique, VI, 294 ff.
Cass, Lewis, XXVII, 164
Cassader Garding, ship *(1756),* XXXV, 294
Cassidy, Arthur B., XXVII, plate XXXII
Cassie F. Bronson, schooner *(1901),* XXIII, plate VII
Cassie Hayward, schooner (1875), V, 86
Cassie Holt, sloop *(1864),* XII, 229
Cassini, Jean Domenique, II, 94
Cassius, supply ship, XXXVII, 138 n.
Casson, Lionel, reviewed book, XXIII, 146–147; XXIX, 72–73; XLIV, 281; XLVI, 121; XLVIII, 200; *The Ancient Mariners,* reviewed, XIX, 147; "Bishop Synesius' Voyage to Cyrene," XII, 294–296; "Greek and Roman Shipbuilding: New Findings," XLV, 10–19; "New Light on Ancient Rigging and Boatbuilding," XXIV, 81–94; "The Origin of the Lateen," XXXI, 49–51; "Rome's Maritime Trade with the Far East," XLVIII, 149–153; "A Sea Drama in Stone," XV, 217–219, plate 12; *Ships and Seamanship in the Ancient World,* reviewed, XLVIII, 63
Cassou, Berten E., XXXIV, 274
Castelar, Emilio, XXXVI, 99
Castel Del Rey, ship (1703), XVII, 292–297
"*Castel del Rey,* an Early New York Privateer," by James G. Lydon, XVII, 292–297
Castellano, ship *(1899),* XXXV, 191
Castelli, General, XXX, 265
Castilla, Captain H., XXII, 18
Castillo, de, Joaquin Manuel, XXX, 47
Castillo, del, 2nd Lieutenant Esteban, XXX, 53
Castine, ship (1857), IV, 326; *(1903),* XXXVII, 140 n., 260

Castine (ME), VII, 200 ff.; bank notes of, XV, 213–216; view in 1855, XXV, plate XXIII
Castle, William, XI, 13
Castle of Patrick Stewart, photo of, L, 128
Castlereagh, British Foreign Secretary, XXXIII, 252 ff.
Castor, ship *(1863),* XV, 293 ff.
Castro, bark (1847), IV, 73
Castro, João de, L, 281
Castro, Jose, XXXII, 119
Castro, President Cipriano, XXVIII, 97–99
"Cast Your Money on the Waters," by Captain Edgar K. Thompson, U.S.N. (ret.), XXIX, 198
Caswell, state ship *(1779),* XXXV, 141
Casualties at sea. *See under* types of casualties, individual subjects, e.g., Ships (Collisions; Fires.) *See also* Collisions at Sea, Fire at Sea, Shipwrecks, etc.
Catalan, sloop *(1861),* XI, 281
Catalina, brig *(1834),* XII, 181–182
Catalina Island, California, XXV, 262
Catalogue of a selection of water color drawings ... and related items of early and modern Shipping of the Great Lakes, reviewed, IV, 81–82
Catalogue of the Robert L. Hague Collection, reviewed, II, 93
Catalogue of the Rosenbach Collection of Memorable Documents Depicting the Rise and Development of the American Navy, A, by Captain H. A. Baldridge, U.S.N., reviewed, VI, 158
Catalonian fishing boat, I, 359–360, plate facing 360
Catania, steamship *(1902),* XXXVIII, 181 ff.
Cataract, fire boat (1889), I, 77
Cataraqui, steamship *(1836, 1839),* VII, 62; VIII, 51; *(1839),* XVIII, 299; XX, 86
Catarina, brig *(1861),* XI, 281
Catawaba, monitor *(1869),* XXXVIII, 233; XXXIX, 275
Catawamteak, schooner (1864), Pictorial Supplement, XXXVI, plate X
Catawba, Confederate steamship *(1861),* XLIV, 258
Catawba, steamship, XXI, 87; *(1826),* VIII, 223
Catawba, U.S. monitor (1862), X, 19, 29, 32
Cate, Mrs. Margaret Davis, XXIII, 79, 80; "Gascoigne Bluff," XXIII, 81–94
Cates, Captain G. W., IX, 69
Catharina, schooner, XXI, 94
Catharine, whaler *(1865),* XXVII, 275
Cathcart, James, XXVI, 248; XLI, 216
Cathcart, James Leander, III, 239 ff.
"Cathcart's Journal and the Search for Naval Timbers," by Bess Glenn, III, 239–249
Cathedral, ship *(1857),* XV, 141
Cather, Willa, XXV, 65
Catherina, schooner *(1862),* VIII, 223
Catherine, privateer *(1744),* XLII, 49
Catherine, Royal Yacht *(1740),* XXVI, 38
Catherine, schooner (1826), XXXVIII, 55; *(1850),* XLV, 123; *(1861),* XXXVI, 188

Catherine, ship *(1800),* XL, 48; *(1805),* X, 54; *(1824),* XXV, 185
Catherine Apcar, sailing vessel *(1857),* XXVI, 125
Catherine C., fishing vessel *(1964),* XLI, 61
Catherine Sudden, barkentine (1878), V, 86
Catherine T. Dix, schooner *(1862),* XX, 159
Catherine the Great, XXXI, 133
Catherine Whitting, ship *(1870),* XXXVIII, 237
Catskill, steamship, XVIII, 229; (1864), XII, 289, 293
Catskill, U.S. monitor (1862), X, 17, 23, 24, 31; XLVIII, 122; *(1863),* XLII, 196 ff.; XLIV, 268
Catskill Evening Line, XVIII, 225, 228, 229
Catton, Bruce, XXIX, 6 n.
Caulfield, Captain Robert, XXXIX, 30
Cavalier, ship *(1861),* XI, 281
Cavally, Baltimore clipper (1846), XXXVIII, 60
Cavanagh, Captain Daniel, XVII, 60; XVIII, 82; XLIII, 296
Cavell, Edith, XLIII, 272
Cavendish, Henry, Earle of Ogle, L, 24
Cavendish, Thomas, The Last Voyage Of, 1591–1592, edited by David Beers Quinn, reviewed, XXXVI, 298
Cawley, Robert Ralston, *Unpathed Waters: Studies in the Influence of the Voyagers on Elizabethan Literature,* reviewed, I, 321–322
Cayuga, grain boat *(1871),* XXXVIII, 135
Caziarc, Lieutenant Louis, XXXVI, 113
Cecelia D. (1863), XII, 155
Cecil, George, VII, 156
Cecil, Sir William, XLIV, 25
Cecile, steamship, XXI, 81, 88; (1857), VIII, 198, 216, 223; IX, 36–37; *(1861),* XV, 99, 114, 115, 120, 122, 126
Cecilia, schooner *(1861),* XI, 281; XII, 229
Cecil Powney, steam launch *(1907),* XXXIX, 177
Cedar, U.S.C.G. *(1928),* XVIII, 220, 221
Cederlund, Carl Olof, *The Old Wrecks of the Baltic Sea: Archaeological Recording of the Wrecks of Carvel-built Ships,* reviewed, XLIV, 210
Celarayn, Mariano, XXX, 53
"Celebrating the Capture of a Large Whale," XXII, plate XXXII
Celestial, ship (1850), I, 45
Celestina, schooner, XXI, 100; *(1862),* VIII, 223
Celia F., schooner (1890), XII, plate 31
Celis, Captain José, XXX, 263
Celt, steamship, XXI, 93; *(1864),* VIII, 233, 236; IX, 35
Celtic, supply ship, XXXVII, 138 n.
Celtic, U.S.S. *(1907),* XXIX, 125
Cemeteries, Micronesia, XXV, 157
"Cemetery, A Long-Forgotten American Naval," by James M. Maps, XXV, 157–167, plates 11–14
Centaur, H.M.S. *(1858),* XLIII, 274 ff.; *(1861),* XXXIV, 118
Centaur, lorcha, XXII, 33
Centaurus, ship *(1945),* XXXIX, 262

Centenary of the Ostend-Dover Line, The, by A. de B. de Wesenbeek, reviewed, VIII, 261
Centennial, barkentine *(1923),* XVIII, 213, 214
Centennial, schooner (1876), XXIV, 60
Centennial Celebration of Portland, Connecticut – 1841–1941, reviewed, II, 263
Centennial Exhibition, 1876, illustration of, XLVII, 180
Centenniel, schooner (1876), XXIV, 58
Centipede, launch *(1813),* XLII, 110 ff.
Central America, steamship (1852), IV, 312–317
Central America, Foreign relations, United States, XXXII, 277
Central America Transit Co., X, 128
Central and Union Pacific Railroad, XXXI, 122
Central Hudson Steamboat Co., XIV, 283
Central Pacific, XXXI, 121 ff.
Central Rail Road and Banking Co. of Georgia, XLVII, 34
Central Rail Road and Canal Co., XLVII, 34
Central Wharf Co., XIII, 120
Centurion, British steamship *(1915),* XXXV, 41
Centurion, English naval ship *(1742),* XXII, 106, 108, 109, 111, 112; *(1744),* XLIV, 158 ff.
Centurion, H.M.S. *(1859),* XXVIII, 286
Century, schooner(?) *(1775),* XXX, 115
Century Association, I, 314
"Century of Fishery Biology at Cape Ann, Massachusetts, A," by Ralph W. Dexter, XLV, 81–85
"Century of Pacific Steamers, A," by John Haskell Kemble, I, 83
Century of Progress, sloop (1931), I, 73
Century of Ship Agency and Brokerage, A, reviewed, VII, 323–324
Cerebus, H.M.S. *(1776),* XXXIX, 196; XLIII, 12 ff.
Ceres, brig (1828), XIV, 39
Ceres, grain elevator *(1883),* XXXVIII, 141
Ceres, H.M. eighteen-gun sloop *(1778),* XLIII, 29
Ceres, steamship, XXI, 94; *(1863),* VIII, 229
Ceres, towboat *(1882),* VI, 286
"Certain Considerations on the Origin and Diffusion of Oculi," by Carroll Quigley, XV, 191–198
Cervin, G. B. Rubin de, "A 26-foot American Cutter in the Naval Museum of Venice," XV, 199–204, plates 9, 10, plan.
Cesarwich, ship (1852), XXIV, 56
Cespedes, General Pedro, XXXVI, 91
Ceylon, bark *(1841),* XXIII, 138; *(1885),* X, 193
Ceylon, boats of, XIII, 85 ff., 186 ff.
Chacabuco, Argentine ship (1867), XXXVI, 137; XXXIX, 276
Chadade Steamship Co., XXXVI, 6, 9, 23
Chadwick, French Ensor (Captain, then U.S. Naval Attaché), XXXVII, 31; XXXVIII, 126; XXXIX, 126 ff.; XL, 130
Chadwick, Lieutenant Commander French E., XLIX, 295
Chadwick & Pritchard, XXXVI, 3

Chafee, General A. R., XXXV, 194
Chagos Archipelago, XXXI, 107
Chagos Islands. *See* British Indian Ocean Territory; Shipping (Indian Ocean)
Chalco, Peruvian ship *(1879),* XXXIX, 278
Chaleur, H.M.S. *(1764),* XXIII, 179
Challenge, clipper ship *(1850),* XLV, 127
Challenge, schooner (1849), XXIV, 58; *(1908),* XXXVIII, 90
Challenge, ship (1850 or 1851), I, 45; III, 262; XIX, plate XXIV
Challenge, XXII, 242
Challenger, H.M.S. *(1872–1876),* V, 5, 7, 9–10
Challenger, ship, XXII, 239; XXVIII, 151; *(1883),* XXXVII, 205, 214; XL, 122
Challenger, whaler *(1859),* XLI, 304
Challons, Henry, XXXI, 95, XXXIV, 233
Chalmers, M., XXXVI, 242
Chamberlain, Austen, British Secretary of State, XXXIV, 162
Chamberlain, Sir Austen, L, 188
Chamberlain, John, XVII, 116
Chamberlain, Paul M., *It's About Time,* reviewed, II, 354
Chamberlain, Robert S., VI, 307; "The Spanish Treasure Fleet of 1551," VI, 241–252
Chamberlain, Samuel, *Martha's Vineyard: A Camera Impression,* reviewed, I, 403–404; *Old Marblehead: A Camera Impression,* reviewed, I, 320–321
Chamberlain, Silas, XVII, 116
Chambers, Arthur, XXXI, 88; XLVII, 77
Chambers, George, XXXI, 88; XLVII, 77
Chambers, J. A., I, 315
Chambers, Captain John S., XXXIV, 274
Chambers, Thomas, XXVIII, plate IV
Chambers, Captain William, XXV, 203–204, 210; *Atlas of Lake Champlain, 1779–1780,* reviewed, XLVII, 211
Chambers, William Bell, London, XXXIV, 209
Chamblett, Captain, XIII, 6
Chameleon, steamship *(1864),* VIII, 233
Chamorro, General Emiliano, XXXV, 126
Champion, galley *(1779),* XXXV, 141
Champion, H.M.S., XXXVII, 127 n.
Champion, schooner *(1861),* VIII, 216; *(1862),* XII, 53
Champion, snow *(1775),* XXX, 99–101
Champion of Sail: R. W. Leyland and his Shipping Line, by David Walker, reviewed, XLVII, 213
Champion of the Seas, ship (1854 or 1855), III, 170; XIX, plate XII; *(1846–1857),* XXVI, 159, 161, 170; XLII, 121 ff.
Champlain, steamship, XXXII, 33; *(1838),* VIII, 47; *(1840),* XX, 80; *(1843),* XX, 261, 266, 267
Champlain, Lake, XXI, 42–56
Champlain, Samuel de, XI, 105; XXV, 238–239, 243
Champlin, Christopher, XIII, 120; XXXV, 298
Champlin, George, XIV, 52, 56; XXXV, 298
Champlin, Robert, XXXV, 298

Chance, schooner *(1810),* L, 104 ff.; *(1862),* VIII, 223; *(1863),* XII, 155; XV, 126
Chance, schooner yacht (1925), II, 339
Chancellor, ship (1856), IV, 242; VI, 81
Chancellor, Richard, XXVIII, 240
Chancellor Livingston, steamship *(1815),* XXIV, 163 n.; *(1820),* I, 414
Chancey, Samuel, XXXVI, 180–181
Chandler, Charles R., XXI, 123
Chandler, Daniel Hicks, XXXIII, 5 ff.
Chandler, Mary Stark, XXXIII, 5 ff.
Chandler, Porter R., "How My Grandfather Nearly Lost the Civil War," XXXIII, 5–15
Chandler, Ralph, XXXIII, 5 ff.
Chandler, Rear Admiral Ralph, XXIX, 114
Chandler, William E., XXXIX, 127
Chandler, William E., Secretary of the Navy, XLIX, 302
Chandos, ship (1869), III, 66
Change and Adaptation in Maritime History: The North Atlantic Fleets in the Nineteenth Century, by Lewis R. Fischer and Gerald E. Panting, reviewed, XLVII, 64
"Changed Meaning of *Cargar,* The," by John Lyman, XIX, 234
"Changing Times," contribution by Captain Edgar K. Thompson, U.S.N. (ret.), XXXVI, 250
Chang Sz, XXIX, 271
Changyon, steamship *(1895),* 102 ff.
Channing, John, XLII, 42 ff.
"Chanteying Aboard American Ships," by Frederick Pease Harlow, VIII, 81–89
Chanteying Aboard American Ships, by Frederick Pease Harlow, reviewed, XXII, 149–150
Chanteys, "The Oxford," I, 61–62
Chanteys, VIII, 81–89, 175; IX, 77
"Chant for Timing Salutes," query by Robert C. Tracy, II, 81; answer by C. M. Blackman, II, 175
Chanticleer, steamship *(1863),* XLIII, 109 ff.; *(1865),* XLIX, 22
Chanticleer, vessel *(1828),* XXX, 209
Chanties. *See* Sea songs
Chaos, schooner *(1865),* XII, 234
Chapel, Robert B., "The Word Against the Cat: Melville's Influence on Seamen's Rights," XLII, 57–65
Chapelle, Howard I., I, 66–72, 102, IV, 336; VII, 3; XI, 247; XIV, 61; XV, 3; XXI, 76; XXII, 83; XXV, 81 n., 83, 84, 85, 91; XXXV, 226; XLVI, 152; XLIX, 39 ff.; XLII, 118, 220; XLIV, 86 ff.; XLV, 45; answered queries, I, 311–312; II, 249–250; III, 353; VII, 170–171; *The American Fishing Schooners 1825–1935,* reviewed, XXXIV, 142–144; *Boat-building, A Complete Handbook of Wooden Boat Construction,* reviewed, II, 181–182; "The Colonial Sloop *Mediator,*" XIII, 177–184; "The Design of the American Frigates of the Revolution and Joshua Humphreys," IX, 161–168, plates 17–19; drawings: of two-sail bateau *Ellsworth,* V, 88; and of Log Canoe

Monkey and Bugeye *Norah E. Lawson*, IV; page 250; *The History of the American Sailing Navy*, reviewed, X, 74–76; "Lines of *Spray*," XIX, 232; *The National Watercraft Collection* (Second Edition), reviewed, XXXVII, 73–74; "Notes on Chesapeake Bay Skipjacks," IV, 269–292; "The Origin of the Marconi Rig," XX, 64–66; "Reply to Mr. Ferguson's Comments," X, 66–68; "Revenue Cutter designed by Samuel Humphreys, A," I, 80–81; *The Search for Speed Under Sail, 1700–1855*, reviewed, XXVIII, 225–227; *Yacht Designing and Planning for Yachtsmen, Students & Amateurs*, reviewed, XXXIII, 65–66

Chapelle, Howard I., with E. Tappan Adney, *The Bark Canoes and Skin Boats of North America*, reviewed, XXV, 295–297

Chapelle, Howard I. and Leon D. Polland, *The Constellation Question*, XXXII, reviewed, 71–72

Chaplin, Ruth, XV, 248; XXV, 4; XXVIII, 238

Chaplin, Lieutenant William Craig, U.S.N., IV, 181, 217–223

Chaplin, Captain W. R., IV, 336; V, 115; contributed documents, VI, 228–231, 304–306; XV, 303–306; reviewed book, XX, 68; "The History of Flat Holm Lighthouse," XX, 5–43, plates 1–4; "History of Harwich Lights and Their Owners," XI, 5–34; "A Seventeenth Century Chart Publisher," VIII, 302–324; "Sir Samuel Argall, Kt. of East Sutton, an Elder Brother of Trinity House and Sometime Governor of Virginia," XIV, 64–65; "Spencer, Browning and Rust: Nautical Opticians," XIII, 66–67; "The Trinity House Ship Models," IV, 261–268; VI, 307; IX, 159–160; "A West Indian Trader," XIV, 83–104, plates 9, 10; "William Mountaine, F.R.S., Mathematician," XX, 185–190, plates 8, 9

Chapman, Captain George, XXVI, 276

Chapman, Frederik Hendrik, XXV, 82, 83, 85

Chapman, Fredrik Hendrik af, XIII, 177 ff.; VI, 163–178, plates 21–28

Chapman, Isaac N., IV, 22 ff.

Chapman, King, and Co., XVI, 170; XLIII, 124 ff.

Chapman, R., XIV, 11, 17

Chapman, William, XXV, 108

Chapman and Flint, II, 324–326; VII, plate 21

Chappell, R., XXIV, plate XXV

Chappell, Richard, XXI, 235, 236

Chapultepec, ship *(1861)*, XI, 281

Chard, Donald F., "The Impact of French Privateering on New England, 1689–1713," XXXV, 153–165

Chariot, ship *(1851)*, XIV, 44

Chariot of Fame, ship (1853), III, 169; *(1846–1857)*, XLII, 123; XV, 141

Charity, schooner, XXI, 103; *(1861)*, VIII, 216

Charles, galley (1676), XXIII, 108–112

Charles, schooner *(1807)*, XVI, 194

Charles, ship *(1630)*, XXIII, 63; *(1705)*, XVII, 294; *(1803)*, X, 53

Charles, steamship (1906), IX, 217

Charles II, King of England, XXV, 278

Charles XII, yacht *(1876)*, XXXVI, 233

Charles, Robert, XXI, 201 ff.

Charles, W. B., XXXVI, 232

Charles A. Briggs, schooner *(1879)*, XXIII, 10

Charles A. Campbell, schooner (1890), XXIII, plate X

Charles A. Farwell, ship *(1861)*, XI, 281

Charles A. Ropes, schooner (1868), XXIV, 44, 58

Charles A. Warren, tug *(1896)*, XXXV, 11

Charles & Jane, ship (1852), XXVIII, plate VI

Charles C. Stratton, schooner *(1854)*, XVII, 23–25

Charles Cammell and Co., XXXIX, 130

Charles Carroll, ship *(1847)*, XLI, 280

Charles Carroll, steamship *(1831)*, VII, 42–43

Charles Colgate, schooner *(1871)*, XLV, 108; *(1883)*, XL, 122

Charles Cooper, ship *(1861)*, XI, 266, 281

Charles Davenport (1856), V, 154

Charles Doggett, brig, XXV, 186 *(1840)*, XXXV, 24

Charles E. Sears, schooner (1874), XXIV, 39, 40, 41, 47, 53, 58

Charles E. Wilbur, schooner *(1904)*, III, 290

"Charles Ellet, Naval Architect: A Study in Nineteenth-Century Professionalism," by John D. Milligan, XXXI, 52–72

Charles F. Crocker, barkentine *(1916)*, XVI, 126

Charles F. Gordon, schooner (1919), V, 296

Charles Forbes, sailing ship *(1851)*, XXVI, 14

Charles Frodsham & Co., Ltd. (watchmakers), XXXIV, 207

Charles G. Rice, bark (1879), III, 63

Charles Grant, East Indiaman *(1812)*, XXV, 110

Charles H. Klinck, schooner (1901), V, 287–288, plates 17, 21, 22

Charles H. Lord, ship (1860), IV, 24

Charles H. Lunt, ship (1859), V, 151; model for the figurehead, Pictorial Supplement, XXXVII, plate XX

Charles H. Marshall, ship (1869), III, 263

Charles H. Roan, U.S. destroyer *(1960)*, XXV, 166

Charles Hanson, gasoline schooner *(1905)*, XXXVIII, 89

Charles Heddle and Co., XXX, 233 ff.

Charles Henry, sloop *(1861)*, XI, 281; XII, 53

Charles Houghton, steamship, XXVIII, 125; (1863), XII, 288, 293

Charles Humberton, ship (1838), XV, 185

Charles Lüling, bark (1865), V, 152.

Charles Martel, steamship (1856), XXVI, 189, 190

Charles Morgan, steamship XXI, 95; *(1861)*, XI, 281. See also *Charles W. Morgan.*

"Charles Morris as a Commodore," by John Lyman, XXVII, 29

Charles Northcote, bark *(1861)*, VIII, 216

Charles R. Lewis, bark *(1877)*, XXXV, 11

Charles R. Wilson, schooner *(1928),* XVIII, 219
Charles Russell, schooner *(1864),* XII, 230, 234
Charles S. Pennell, ship *(1861),* XI, 281
"Charles Swaine," query by Howard N. Eavenson, VI, 232–233
Charles T. Smythe, schooner *(1861),* VIII, 216
Charles Thompson, ship (1871), IV, 241
Charleston, Confederate steamship *(1861),* XLIV, 258 ff.
Charleston, cruiser *(1888),* XXXVIII, 127, 291 ff.; XXXIX, 136; *(1894),* XXXIV, 213; XXXV, 184; *(1896),* XXIX, 116
Charleston, galley, XXVI, 46
Charleston, gunboat *(1937),* XXXV, 136
Charleston, schooner, XXI, 93; *(1862),* VIII, 223–229
Charleston, steamship, XXI, 95, 102; *(1863),* VIII, 229, 233; XV, 111, 127
Charleston, U.S. cruiser (1901), XXII, 146
Charleston (SC), History, XLIV, 257
Charleston Bethel Union, XXIV, 111, 112
Charleston Importing and Exporting Co., IX, 44–46
Charleston's Navy Yard: A Picture History, by Jim McNeil, reviewed, XLVIII, 206
Charlestown, galley, XXVI, 47
Charlestown (MA), XXX, 56–60
Charles Townsend, steamship (1835), VII, 57
Charles Vickery, schooner *(1863),* XX, 166
Charles W. Brooks & Co., XLIII, 208
Charles W. Morgan, bark (1841), I, 391–393; III, 340; VII, 221; IX, 18, 77; Pictorial Supplement, XXXIII, plate XXVI; XXXIV, 145; *(1888),* XLIV, 16 ff.; XLV, 114; *(1916),* XXXVIII, 207 ff., XL, 125; *(1958),* XX, 63
Charles W. Morgan, whaleship (1841), XXII, 212, plates XXV, XXVI; XXV, 100, 102, 103, 104; XXVII, 226–227; interior views of, Pictorial Supplement, XXXI, plates XXX, XXXI
Charles W. Morgan, The, by John F. Leavitt, reviewed, XXXIV, 145
Charles W. Morgan, *The Last Wooden Whaleship, The,* by Edward A. Stackpole, reviewed, XXVII, 226–227
Charles W. Waterbury, schooner *(1857),* XV, 232
Charles W. Wetmore, whaleback steamship *(1891),* XXV, 171–173
"Charles Ware, Sail-maker," III, 267–268
"Charles Ware's Sail Plans of U.S. Brigs *Spark* and *Prometheus,*" V, 79
Charlie Morton, schooner (1873), XXIV, 58
Charlie York, Maine Coast Fisherman, by Harold B. Clifford, reviewed, XXXVIII, 144
Charlot, Royal Yacht *(1740),* XXVI, 38
Charlotte (1801), XXIII, 217
Charlotte, H.M.S. *(1813),* XVII, 210
Charlotte, schooner, XXI, 100; *(1861),* VIII, 216; *(1862),* XII, 53
Charlotte, ship *(1787–1788),* IV, 93–96
Charlotte, sloop *(1769),* XXXIII, 296
Charlotte, steamship *(1864),* XXI, plate X; *(1865),* VIII, 237
Charlotte A. Littlefield, bark (1864), IV, 238; *(1882),* XLVI, 111
Charlotte Amalia, Danish frigate, XXVIII, 70
Charlotte Ann, schooner, XXI, 91; *(1861),* XV, 122
Charlotte Dundas, steamship [model of William Symington's 1802 vessel], photo of, L, 208
Charlotte of Oswego, schooner *(1838),* VIII, 39 ff.
Charlotte of Toronto, schooner *(1838),* VIII, 39 ff.
Charlotte Read, ship (1845), IV, 51, plate 9
Charlton, ship (1739), I, 167
Charm, schooner *(1863),* XV, 127
Charmer, schooner, XXV, 107; *(1863),* XV, 127
Charmer, ship (1854), III, 70; (1869), III, 173; (1881), XXVIII, plate XXI
Charming Betsey, XXII, 93 n.
Charming Betsy, British ship *(1776),* XLVIII, 19
Charming Betty, brig *(1728),* XII, 222
Charming Betty, privateer sloop *(1744),* XLII, 42
Charming Betty, ship *(1730),* VI, 180–181
Charming Lydia, brigantine *(1742),* XLI, 178
Charming Molley, schooner *(1752),* XX, 236
Charming Peggy, schooner *(1756)* (ex-*Margaret*), XXIII, 277 ff.
Charming Polly, brig *(1784),* XLIV, 6 ff.
Charming Sally, ship *(1729),* XXI, 265
Charry M., schooner (1866), I, 72
Charter Oak, steamship *(1845),* XXXIX, 222
"Charter Party of the *Triall:* An Unsuccessful Virginia Venture, 1606–1607, The," by John C. Appleby, XLVII, 77–82
Charters, Professor Alexander N., XXXIX, 125
Charting, XXX, 200–216
Chart of the Marquesas, by A. Arrowsmith, 1798, XXXIII, plate 9
Chart publishing, VIII, 302–324
Charts. See Cartography; Nautical charts
Charts: "Delaware, The Bay and River of The," XXV, 36–49, plate 2; Mariner's, XXV, 177, 241–242; New England, XXV, 241–242; New York Harbor, XIX, 44–50
Charts and Coastal Views of Captain Cook's Voyages: The Voyage of the Endeavor, *1768–1771, The* (The Hakluyt Society Extra Series No. 43), edited by Andrew David, Rudiger Joppien and Bernard Smith, reviewed, XLIX, 319
Charybdis, H.M.S. *(1902),* XXVIII, 98
Chasca, bark (1861), III, 171
Chase, schooner, XXI, 86, 93; *(1862),* VIII, 223, 233, 236
Chase, sharpie schooner (1903), I, 71
Chase, steamship *(1867),* XXXVII, 235
Chase, Fannie S., *Wiscasset in Pownalborough,* reviewed, II, 262–263
Chase, Captain Judah, XXXIX, 222
Chase, Captain Nathan, XXI, 222
Chase, Captain Peter, XIII, 279

Chase, Philip P., "St. Lucia Dugouts," II, 71–73; "Schooner *William Jewell,* 1853–1947," XIX, 120–122, plate 5
Chase, Salmon P., XX, 157; XXXIII, 50
Chase, Samuel, VIII, 14; XLV, 244
Chasseur, privateer (1812), XXIX, 195, 198
Chasseur, schooner (1825), IX, 72
Chatard, Ferdinand E., "An Early Description of Birchbark Canoes," VIII, 91–98
Chatard, Captain Frederick, XLIII, 133
Chateaubriant, ship (1901), I, 77
Chatfield Joliff, vessel, XXVI, 59
Chatham, H.M.S. *(1738),* XXVI, 37; *(1792),* XIII, 212–213
Chatham, ship *(1794),* XLI, 225
Chatham, ship (1834), XIX, 27; XV, 139, 140
Chatham, steamship *(1847),* XLVII, 34; *(1863),* XV, 111, 112, 115, 127
Chaumont, U.S.S. *(1923),* XLIV, 180
Chauncey, Commodore, XXXI, 219
Chauncey, Isaac, XLVII, 27
Chauncey, Captain Isaac, XLII, 174 ff.
Chauncey, Commodore Isaac, XL, 26, 215
Chauncey, Commandant Wolcott, XL, 41
Chauncey Vibbard, steamship (1864), XVIII, 223, plate 15; *(1868),* XIV, 177, 178, 280, 282
Chautauque, steamship *(1839),* XVIII, 299; XX, 86, 90 n., 97, 254, 259
Chave, Captain Thomas, XXI, 105
Chazel, René, XXXVI, 275
Chebacco boat, XII, 133–135
Chebacco Parish, XXXVI, 77
Checklist of Narratives of Shipwrecks and Disasters at Sea to 1860, A, by Keith Huntress, reviewed, XLIII, 142–143
"Checkmate," contribution by Captain Edgar K. Thompson, U.S.N. (ret.), XXXVI, 87
Cheemaun, sand-bagger sloop (1872), I, 72
Cheeseman, Joseph J., XXXIX, 174
Cheever, Lawrence Oakley, *Edward A. Wilson, Book Illustrator,* reviewed, II, 353
Chekiang, steamship (1862), XVI, 248, 262; XVIII, 68; XLIII, 119 ff.
Cheltenham, ship (1861), III, 62
Chenery, Lieutenant Commander Leonard, XXXIII, 258
Cheney, Robert K., "Industries Allied to Shipbuilding in Newburyport," XVII, 114–127, plates 9–12
Chenny, William, XIV, 52, 59
Chen Tuen, Chinese battleship (1882), VIII, 267–275; IX, 301
Chen Yuen, Chinese battleship *(1876),* XXXVIII, 164 ff.
Chepman, steamship (1944), XIV, 135
Cherokee, bark *(1861),* XI, 281
Cherokee, brig (1829), IV, 240
Cherokee, H.M.S. *(1775),* XIII, 29 ff.

Cherokee, H.M.S. (1842 or 1843), VIII, 138–139, 144–145; XX, 262
Cherokee, steamship, XXI, 98, 103; *(1847),* XLVII, 34; *(1863),* VIII, 229, 233; *(1886),* VII, 137
Cherpak, Evelyn M., "Remembering Days in Old China: A Navy Bride Recalls Life on the Asiatic Station in the 1920's," XLIV, 179–185
Cherub, H.M. sloop *(1814),* XXXVI, 288; XLIV, 174 ff.
Cherub, whale ship, XXV, plate 8
Cheruco, Spanish ship *(1873),* XXXVIII, 242
Chesapeake (1861), XV, 103 n.
Chesapeake, American frigate *(1825),* XXXI, 217
Chesapeake, frigate *(1790),* XLIX, 41 ff.; L, 60; *(1799),* XLIII, 257 ff.; XLV, 36
Chesapeake, H.M.S. *(1859),* XXVII, 173
Chesapeake, ship *(1807),* XXXIV, 125
Chesapeake, steamship *(1813),* XXX, 72; *(1838),* XVIII, 282, 297; XX, 79, 80, 86, 89 n., 92, 101, 251, 252; *(1863),* XIV, 62; XIX, 51–72; XXXIII, 89, 201 ff.
Chesapeake, steamship (1883), IX, 299
Chesapeake, U.S. frigate, XXVI, 277; XXVIII, 30, 116, 295–296; XXIX, 67–68; XXXVI, 209, 293; *(1799),* VII, 253; XXII, 264.; *(1808),* XVI, 206; XVIII, 183; *(1813),* III, 90; XIII, 237
Chesapeake, U.S.S. (1899), XX, 142
Chesapeake: *A Biography of a Ship, The,* by Charles B. Cross, Jr., reviewed, XXVIII, 295–296
Chesapeake Affair, XXX, 73
Chesapeake Bay Region (MD & VA):
  Discovery and exploration, XVII, 181
  History, XXXVI, 206
  –, **Colonial period (ca. 1600–1775),** XXX, 133
  See also Shipbuilding; Shipping; Yachting
Chesapeake and Delaware Bay, map of 1781, I, plate facing 142
Chesapeake and Delaware Canal, The, reviewed, II, 94
Chesapeake and Delaware Canal Co., XLVIII, 112
Chesapeake Bay: IV, 269–292; IX, 142–147, 180–184; early shipping, XXX, 133–138; Naval Action in, XXXVI, 206 ff.; piracy, XXX, 133 ff.
Chesapeake Bay Bugeye, XX, 66
Chesapeake Bay Bugeyes, by M. V. Brewington, reviewed, II, 86–88
Chesapeake Bay Log Canoes and Bugeyes, by M. V. Brewington, reviewed, XXIII, 286–287
Chesapeake Bay Maritime Museum, St. Michaels, Maryland, XXV, 232; Maritime Titles in Print, XXXIX, 60
"Chesapeake Bay Schooner," query by Naomi Yarnall, VII, 171; answers by John Lyman and Robert H. Burgess, VII, 243
Chesapeake Circle, by Robert H. Burgess, reviewed, XXVI, 222
Chesapeake's Revenge, boat *(1813),* XXXVI, 217
Chesapeake Steamship Co., XXX, 72
Cheshire, ship, XXI, 89; *(1861),* XV, 109, 122
Chester, bark *(1861),* XI, 281

Chester, cruiser *(1909),* XXXVII, 111 ff.; XXXIX, 178; *(1921),* L, 54
Chester, George, XXXV, 21
Chester, H.M.S. *(1707),* XX, 112
Chester, schooner *(1862),* XII, 53
Chester (ex-*City of Chester*), Pictorial Supplement, XXXIV, plate X
Chesterfield, ship *(1792),* XLI, 282; *(1795),* XXV, 182
Chesterfield, steamship *(1861),* VIII, 216
Chesterfield, steam tender *(1863),* XLIV, 264
Chester W. Chapin, steamship *(1929),* XXXIX, 107
Chevalier, Haakon, *The Last Voyage of the Schooner Rosamond,* XXXII, reviewed, 291
Chew, Captain Samuel, XIV, 48 ff.
Chew, Purser Thomas, XLVII, 15
Chiang Kai-shek, XLVIII, 283
Chicago, cruiser *(1883),* XXXVIII, 297; XXXIX, 129
Chicago, steamship (1835), VII, 57; (1842), XVII, 99, 103; XX, 250, 255, 256, 259, 264, 268
Chicago, U.S. cruiser (1885), XXII, plate 15
Chicago, Illinois, land boom headquarters, VII, 58
Chicago City, steamship (1892), XIV, 122, 125, 126, 134
Chicago Historical Society, VI, 194 n., plates 29–30; VII, 43 n., 298 n., plates 5, 6; VIII, 134 n., plate 15
Chicago Lighterage Co., XXXII, 157
Chicago Line, XVIII, 273–300
Chichester, ship *(1740),* XXXII, 84
Chichester, Sir Arthur, XXXI, 93; XLVII, 77 ff.
Chickamauga, privateer *(1873),* XXXVIII, 234 ff.
Chickamauga, ship *(1874),* XXXIII, 60
Chickasaw, U.S. monitor (1862), X, 18, 31
Chicora, Confederate ironclad (1862), XLIV, 259
Chicora, ship, XXIII, 139
Chicora, steamship, XXI, 88, 102, 105; *(1864),* XII, 308–310; *(1864),* VIII, 233, 236; IX, 44
Chicora Importing and Exporting Co. of South Carolina, IX, 44–45
"Chicora (Let Her B)," by Marcus W. Price, XII, 308–310
Chief, bark *(1837),* XXXII, 66
Chief, schooner (1861), VIII, 216; XV, 122
Chief Justice Robinson, steamship (1840), VIII, 135 ff., plate 15; (1842), XX, 250
Chief's Fan from Marquesas, 1801, XXXIII, plate 11 (left).
Chieftain, steamship (1859), XVII, 216; XVIII, 68
Chieftan, ship (1865), V, 148
Chi-er-hang-a, XXX, 160, 161, 163–165
Chihli, steamship (1867), XVI, 256, 261; XVIII, 68; (1871), XVII, 39; XVIII, 68
Chih Yuen, Chinese cruiser (1886), IX, 301
Chikiang, steamship (1862), XVII, 146
Chi Kiang, steamship (1862), XVIII, 68
Chikuma, Japanese warship *(1917),* XXXVI, 274
Chilberg, J. E., XXXV, 177
Chilcomb, brig, XXII, 94
Child, Jacob I., XL, 100

Childe Harold, schooner (1886), XXIII, plate VII
Childers, H. C. E., XXXII, 239 ff.
Childs, Charles D., I, 102; III, 89; review by, XXIX, 139–141; XXXIX, 144; "American Naval Prints at the Grolier Club," III, 5–10
Chile, Chilean warship *(1843),* XXXIX, 272
Chile, steamship (1840), XXXV, 248 ff.
Chile:
Foreign relations, United States, XXXVIII, 291
History, 1891–1892, XXXVIII, 291
"Chilean Crisis of 1891–1892, The," by Francis X. Holbrook and John Nikol, XXXVIII, 291–300
"*Chile* and *Peru:* The First Successful Steamers in the Pacific," by Roland E. Duncan, XXXV, 248–274
Chilean Reefer, steamship *(1939),* XXVI, 148
Chili, whaleship *(1811),* XLIV, 104 ff.
Chillicothe, bark *(1918),* XVIII, 170
Chilmark boat, XII, 135
Chiloé, South America (Province, Chile), XXVI, 33–36, plate 2
Chimborazo, ship (1851), IV, 72, 244
Chimo, ship, XXXV, 60
Chimu pots, II, plates 17, 19
China, ship (1866), IV, 51
China, ship *(1915),* XXXV, 175
China, steamship *(1863),* XLIII, 294 ff.; (1866), XVII, 227
China (ex-*Alma*), steamship (1855), XXVI, 28–30, 203, 205, 209, plate 1
China, steamship (1866 or 1867), II, 8, 25, plates 2, 3, folding plan facing 8; X, 130, 131; (1889), X, 137, 139, plate 19
China:
Archives, XLVIII, 283
Description and travel, XLIV, 179; XLVI, 34
Foreign relations, XLVIII, 225, 230
—, **Gt. Britain,** XXVII, 135; XXXIV, 103; XLIX, 208; L, 178
—, **United States,** XX, 209; XXV, 116; XXXI, 177; XXXIV, 103; XXXV, 166; XXXVII, 185
History:
—, **1795–1861,** XLVIII, 237
—, **Taiping Rebellion (1850–1864),** XXX, 155; XXXVIII, 28
—, **1854,** XXX, 155
—, **Shanghai Invasion (1932),** XXXVII, 185
—, **Civil War (1945–1949),** XLIX, 208
—, **1949,** L, 291
Naval, XLVIII, 230
Periodicals, XLVIII, 271
Politics and government, XLVIII, 283.
See also China trade porcelain; Coolies; Marine Photography; Merchants; Missionaries; Opium War; Pirates; Shipping; Steamboats; Steam navigation; Tea trade; Yalu River; Yangtze River
China & Japan Steam Navigation Co., XLIII, 297
China, boats of, XIII, 185 ff.

China Bird, The, by David MacGregor, reviewed, XXII, 71–72
China Coast steamships, XVI, 157–179, 243–269; XVII, 38–64, 134–151, 212–230, 298–314; XVIII, 59–87
China Coast Steam Navigation Co., XXII, 226; XVII, 39, 40; XVIII, 63
China Mail, XXII, 11, 16, 21, 22, 23, 39
China Mail, The, XXX, 166
China Mail Steamship Co., XXXV, 174
China Mercantile Steam Navigation Co., XVII, 53, 54; XXVI, 201
China Merchants Steam Navigation Co., XVI, 247, 248, 252, 254, 259, 260, 261, 262, 265, 267; XVII, 40; XVIII, 60, 61, 63, 64, 66; XXII, 226
China Navigation Co., XVI, 176, 267; XVII, 39, 40, 137; XVIII, 61, 63; XXII, 226
China Navigator, ship *(1942),* XXXVIII, 196 ff.
China Overland Trade Report, XXXIV, 50
China Sea, Saigon, and Straits Steamship Co., XVII, 57
China's New Historical Archives," by Frederic Wakeman, Jr., XLVIII, 283–285
"China Sojourn: A Brief Account of Commander Bushrod B. Taylor's Tour of Duty [with the Asiatic Squadron, 1869–1871, Together with Some of His Purchases]," by John Quentin Feller, XLV, 237–243
China Steamship and Labuan Coal Co., XVII, 52
China trade, XXIII, 212–218
"China Trade," query by Dorothy R. Brewington, I, 309
"China Trade," query by Lawrence Schwab, VI, 153
"China Trade, The," lecture by Francis R. Carpenter, Museum of the American China Trade, comment, Editorial, The American Neptune, XXXVIII, 3–4
China Trade and Its Influences, The, reviewed, I, 324
China Trade Museum, Milton (MA), XLVI, 32
China trade porcelain, XLIII, 177; XLV, 237. *See also* Shipping (China)
China Trans-Pacific Steamship Co., XVII, 61
Chinese American Products Exchange Co. (CAPEC), XXXV, 175 ff.
"Chinese Charts," query by R. W. Leopold, III, 177
Chinese Compass, circa 1800, Pictorial Supplement, XXXV, plate XII
Chinese-Japanese War. *See* Sino-Japanese War
Chinese Military guard post on Grand Canal, 1793–94, photo of engraving, XLVIII, 232
Chinese Repository (Christian publication), XLVI, 38 ff.; XLVIII, 217 ff.
"Chinese Ship Portraits," query by Henry Darnell, Jr., IV, 77
Chinese text of Petition of Consequa, Canton, 1814, photo of, XLVIII, 255
Ching Yuen, Chinese cruiser (1886), IX, 301
Chinnery, George, portrait of Benjamin Chew Wilcocks (photo of), XLVIII, 248
Chinnery and China Coast Paintings, by Henry and Sidney Berry-Hill, reviewed, XXXI, 149–150
Chinsi, steamship (1862), XVII, 39; *(1877),* XVI, 249

Chinting, steamship (1870), XVII, 39; *(1877),* XVI, 260
Chipman, Zechariah, XV, 186
Chippewa, steamship (1824), VI, 199, 202; *(1859),* XXIII, 285
Chiquita, cutter (1888), XXX, plate XI
Chirikoff, steamship *(1923),* X, 120; *(1928),* XVI, 131
Chiri Maru, steamship *(1871),* XVI, 256
Chishima, Japanese warship *(1895),* XX, 191
Chisholm, Messrs., and Co., VII, 47
Chitty, XXX, 260
Choate, George W., XLVI, 261
Choice Yacht Designs, Richard Henderson, reviewed, XL, 147
Cholera, Great Lakes epidemic, VII, 44–45
Cholmley, Nathaniel, XIII, 12, 18, 19, 24, 26, 27
Chomley, The Hon. F., XXXIV, 37
Chona, tanker *(1942),* L, 44
Choptank Steamboat Co., XXX, 72
Chou Chou, French ship *(1800),* XXXI, 174
Chowan, barge (1829), V, 301
Chown, Thomas A., XXX, 230
Christensen, Captain, XXIX, 262
Christian, Edward, XXVI, 203
Christian IV, King of Denmark, XXVIII, 257–259
Christian Radich, training ship *(1964),* XXIV, 79
Christie, John, reviews by, XLII, 72–74; XLVII, 141
Christina, bark *(1840),* XXXV, 261
Christina, bark (1857), XV, 185
Christine and Dan, fishing vessel *(1963),* XLI, 60
Christopher, ship *(1479),* XXXVII, 159
Christopher, ship *(1602),* XXXVII, 11
Christopher Columbus, whaleback steamship (1893), XXV, 170
Christopher Hall, ship, XXII, 245, 247, 248
Christopher Mitchell, ship (1849), XXXIII, 19
Christy, Lowe, and Heyworth, XXXV, 281
"Chronological List of Commercial Wintering Voyages to the Bering Strait Region and Western Arctic of North America: 1850–1910, A," by John R. Bockstoce and Charles F. Batchelder, XXXVIII, 81–91
Chronometers: XXX, 211, 212; English, Pictorial Supplement, XXXV, plates XIX, XX
"*Chrysopolis:* the Queen of the Golden River," by John Haskell Kemble, II, 299–306, plates 43–44
Chubb, Percy, 2nd, document by, XXXVII, 66–69
Church, Albert Cook, and James B. Connolly, *American Fishermen,* reviewed, I, 181–182
Church, Thomas, XXXV, 87
Churchill, Joseph, XIV, 217
Churchill, Winston, Prime Minister, XLII, 204
Churchill Barriers, Scapa Bay, photos of, L, 130–131
Chusan, steamship (1852), XVIII, 68; XXVI, 21, 22, 24, 32, 116, 202, 203, 205, 209; XLIII, 100 ff.; (1866), XVI, 259, 262; XVIII, 68; (1874), XVI, 263, 265; XVIII, 68
Chydenius, Anders, VIII, 91–98

Cíbola (Antilles), XXX, 250
Cicero, English letter-of-marque *(1799),* XXVII, 142
Cicero, ship *(1856),* XII, 103
Cimmerone, ship *(1863),* XLV, 237
Cincinnati, steamship (1836), VII, 62; *(1841),* XX, 93, 94
Cincinnati, U.S. ironclad, (1861), XIX, 266, 269 ff.; *(1862),* XXV, 130, 139
Cincinnatus (1801), XXIV, 262
Cincinnatus, brig (1817), VII, 317
Cinco de Marzo, see under *Five (5) de Marzo.*
Cinta, launch *(1930),* XXXIX, 180
Cipango, Japan, XXX, 254
Cipolla, Carlo M., *Guns, Sails and Empires: Technological Innovation and the Early Phases of European Expansion, 1400–1700,* reviewed, XXVI, 225
Circassian, ship *(1872),* XXXVIII, 238
Circe, steamship *(1891),* XI, 219
Circle (English navigating instrument), Pictorial Supplement, XXXV, plates VII, VIII
Circumnavigation. *See* Voyages around the world
Ciscar, Gabriel de, XV, 54
"Citadel," Korean Fort, VII, 109, 111, plate 12
Citizen Genet, schooner *(1793),* XXII, 81 ff.
Citizen's Line, XVIII, 224
Citnalta, schooner *(1942),* III, 163
Citoyen, French ship *(1800),* XXXI, 175
Citta de Monreale, steamship *(1949),* XIV, 132, 135
City of Adelaide, bark (1864), IV, 238
City of Alberni, schooner (1920), V, 141; *(1942),* VII, 294
City of Atlanta, steamship *(1920),* XXII, 165, 168
City of Austin, barkentine (1918), V, 82
City of Austin, steamship *(1877),* VII, 136
City of Baltimore, schooner *(1884),* XXVIII, 148
City of Beaumont, barkentine (1918), IV, 68; V, 82
City of Boston, steamship (1861), XLVIII, 119
City of Brooklyn, ship (1854), III, 263
City of Buenos Ayres, steamship *(1867),* XXIV, plate XI
City of Catskill, steamship (1880), VI, 284–285
City of Chester, steamship (1873), Pictorial Supplement, XXXIV, plate X
City of Chicago, steamship *(1885),* XIV, 121
City of Dallas, barkentine (1918), V, 82
City of Dallas, steamship *(1877),* VII, 136
City of Dublin Steam Packet Co., XXVI, 10
City of Dundee, steamship *(1863),* VIII, 229
City of Everett, tanker *(1903),* XXXVIII, 195 ff.
City of Everett, whaleback steamship (1894), XXV, 173–174, plate 15
City of Exeter, steamship (1870), XVII, 38; XVIII, 68
City of Fitchburg, steamship *(1874),* XXXIX, 101, plate 4
City of Flint, American freighter *(1939),* XXXII, 100 ff., plates 7, 8
City of Flint 32, steamship *(1930),* XXIII, 71
City of Galveston, barkentine (1919), V, 82, plate 8
City of Gloucester, steamship (1883), XII, 289, 293, plate 27
City of Grand Haven, schooner (1872), I, 75
City of Green Bay, schooner (1872), IX, 229
City of Guatamala, steamship (1873), X, 132, 134
City of Gulfport, barkentine (1918), V, 82
City of Hankow (1862), XXXIV, 32
City of Haverhill, steamship (1902), XII, 290, 293, plate 28; XIII, 214
City of Honolulu, steamship (1896), IX, 220–221; (1900), IX, 224
City of Houston, barkentine (1917), V, 82
City of Hudson, steamship, XVIII, 231, 232; (1864), XII, 289, 293
City of Jackson, barkentine (1919), V, 82
City of Jacksonville, steamship *(1869),* VII, 133
City of Kingston, steamship, XVIII, 224; (1843), XX, 262
City of Lafayette, barkentine (1919), V, 82
City of Los Angeles, steamship (1899), IX, 220–221 ff., 226, 227
City of Lowell, steamship, XXXIV, 259
City of Madras, ship, XXII, 213, 231
City of Merida, steamship *(1869),* XLVIII, 127
City of Mobile, barkentine (1918), V, 82
City of Mobile, ship (1855), III, 263
City of Nantes, steamship *(1856),* XLIII, 189 ff.
City of Natchez, barkentine (1920), V, 82
City of New Bedford, steamship *(1874),* XXXIX, 101, plate 4
City of New York, ship *(1854),* XLV, 29
City of New York, steamship (1862), XLVIII, 119; (1875), X, 132, 138; (1889), XXIV, 126
City of Ocala, steamship (1912), VII, 234–237
City of Orange, barkentine (1917), V, 82
City of Orleans, barkentine (1919), V, 82
City of Palaces, bark *(1858),* IV, 33
City of Panama, steamship (1873 or 1874), V, 82; X, 132
City of Panama, steamship (1925), X, 142, 143
City of Papeete, schooner *(1928),* XVIII, 219
City of Para, steamship *(1881),* X, 13; *(1895),* XXIV, 197
City of Paris, steamship (1889), XXIV, 126; Pictorial Supplement, XXXIV, plate XX
City of Pascagoula, barkentine (1919), V, 82
City of Peking, steamship (1873 or 1874), X, 132, plate 19; XLVI, 62; (1875), II, 21, 76
City of Petersburg, steamship, XXI, 91, 105; *(1863),* VIII, 229, 233, 236
City of Portland, auxiliary schooner (1916), V, 140
City of Portland, steamship *(1840),* XXVIII, 124
City of Portland (ex-*New England*), steamship *(1872),* XXXIII, 90
City of Richmond, ship *(1861),* XLIII, 130 ff.
City of Richmond, steamship, XXVIII, 124; (1864), I, 249–250
City of Rio de Janeiro, steamship *(1881),* X, 137
City of Rio de Janeiro, steamship *(1887),* XL, 116
City of Rockland, steamship (1901), Pictorial Supplement, XXXIV, plate XXVI; *(1902),* XXIV, 52
City of Saint John, sidewheeler *(1885),* XXXIV, 178

City of San Antonio, barge *(1905)*, XXXVIII, 191 ff.
City of San Francisco, steamship (1875), X, 132, 134; (1925), X, 142, 143
City of Santiago, steamship (1875), XI, 256 ff.
City of Savannah, steamship (ex-*Carolina*), Pictorial Supplement, XXXIV, plate XXII
City of Seattle, sloop yacht *(1880)*, XXXVI, 233
City of St. Helens, auxiliary schooner (1917), V, 140
City of Sydney, steamship (1875), IV, 326, plate 52; V, 82; X, 132; *(1891)*, XXIV, 197
City of Tokio, steamship (1874), X, 132, 138; *(1875)*, II, 21, 76; *(1877)*, XLVI, 61; painting of, XLVI, 62
City of Topeka, steamship (1884), IX, 219
City of Toronto, steamship *(1840)*, XX, 83, 84, 89, plate 3
City of Troy, steamship, XVIII, 224, 225
City of Valparaiso, steamship (1875), XI, 256 ff.
City of Vicksburg, barkentine (1919), V, 82
City of Waco, barkentine (1919), V, 82
City of Worcester, steamship (1881), III, plate 9
City Point, steamship *(1871)*, VII, 132, 137
Civilian, bark (1851), I, 49
Civilian, brig *(1855)*, XXIV, 140, 142
Civility, schooner, XXI, 103; *(1861)*, XI, 281
Civil War: I, 183–184; XXVI, 96 ff., 134–137, 224; XXVII, 30, 52, 174–175, 233–253, 263–278
Civil War: Its Photographic History, The reviewed, I, 410
"Civil War Legend Examined, A," by Howard P. Nash, Jr., XXIII, 197–203
"Civil War Letters of Lieutenant Commander George Bacon, The," by John K. Mahon, XII, 271–281
"Civil War Naval Weapons that Might Have Been," by Allan C. Ashcraft, XXII, 280–289
"Civil War Riverside Shipyard, A," document contributed by Vernon D. Tate, VI, 138–139, plate 20
Cixi, Empress Dowager of China, XLVIII, 284
Claiborne, Governor W. C. C., XVI, 28 ff.
Claims (International Law), III, 48; XXXII, 257
Clam bake at Pasque Island, VII, plate 28
Clampitt, Captain Edward, IX, 135 ff.
Clan MacTavish, British ship (#1916), XLVIII, 50 ff.
Clapham, Sir John, XLVIII, 11
Clapp, Captain William, XXXVI, 113, 123, 124
Clapperton, Hugh, XXXV, 79 ff.
Clara, schooner, XXI, 94, 96, 100; *(1861)*, VIII, 216; XI, 281; XII, 53, 155
Clara A. Donnell, schooner (1889), XXVII, plate XXIV
Clara Ann, ship (1850), IV, 51
Clara Bell, whaling bark (1855), XXV, 104, plate 6
Clara Dinsmore, schooner (1876), XXIV, 45, 58
Clara E. McGilvery, barkentine (1873), photo of, XLVI, 112
Clara J. Adams, brig (1869), XXIV, 44, 57
Clara Jane, schooner (1864), XXIV, 58
Clara Louisa, sloop, XXI, 101
Clara Louise, sloop *(1863)*, XV, 127
Clara Morse, ship *(1866)*, XI, 281

Clara W. Benbury, schooner, XXI, 97; *(1861)*, XI, 281
Clarence, brig *(1863)*, XV, 293
Clarence, C. S. prize *(1863)*, XXV, 298
Clarence, ship *(1873)*, XXXIII, 60
Clarence & Richmond River Steam Navigation Co., XLIII, 111 ff.
Clarence L. Evans, destroyer escort *(1944)*, XXXVIII, 283
Clarendon, Earl of [b. 1641], XXV, 281
Clarinda, schooner *(1861)*, XI, 281; XII, 53
Clarion, propeller-driven ship *(1840)*, XLVIII, 117
Clarion, steam bark, XXXVII, n. 140 ff.
Clarion, steamship (1841), XVII, 93 n.
Clarissa Ann, bark (1824), IV, 51, plate 9
Clarissa B. Carver, ship (1876), XXVIII, plate XVI; XL, 108 ff.
Clarissa Claiborne, schooner (1807), VII, 317
Clarissa Vera, bark (1858), III, 349
Clarita, schooner *(1863)*, XII, 155
Clark, A. Howard, XL, 117
Clark, Admont G., "They Built Clipper Ships in Their Back Yard," XXII, 233–251
Clark, Captain Arthur H., XIV, 33; XXX, 199; XLII, 126; XLV, 81; in his cabin, Pictorial Supplement, XXXI, plate XXII; XXXV, 32
Clark, Captain Arthur Hamilton, XVI, 256; XVII, 50 ff., 58; XVIII, 82
Clark, Bennett Champ, XLI, 118
Clark, Captain Charles E., XXXVI, 257 ff.
Clark, David, XXIII, 12, plate VII
Clark, Edward Strong, I, 102, 204, 307–308, 316; plates facing 88, 296, 297, 312, 313, 334, 338, 339
Clark, Ephraim, XXVII, 46 ff.
Clark, Commander Francis E., U.S.N. (ret.), contributed notes, XXIV, 216; XXV, 112–115; "A Cape Cod Northeaster," XXIV, 138–143; "The Last Days of the Sail Navy," XX, 134–145
Clark, Commander Frank, XXVII, 260, 261
Clark, Huntington, XXXII, 158
Clark, J. H., XXX, 219
Clark, Captain Jabez, XVII, 57; XVIII, 82
Clark, John, I, 301–302; III, 20–25; XVII, 128
Clark, John Innes, XXX, 280
Clark, Rear Admiral Joseph J., XXXIX, 43
Clark, Governor Robert, of Nassau, XXV, 200
Clark, Thomas, XXVI, 183–188
Clark, W., XXIV, plate XXI
Clark, William, XIV, 117
Clark, William B., *George Washington's Navy*, reviewed, XX, 224
Clark, William Bell, I, 177; XXII, 3; contributed documents, I, 168–170; II, 247; VI, 301–302; XIV, 298–299; mentioned, XXIX, 80; XXX, 80; query by, I, 310; review by, II, 350; "American Naval Policy, 1775–1776," I, 26–41; *Captain Dauntless: The Story of Nicholas Biddle of the Continental Navy*, reviewed, IX, 303; "The Continental Brigantine *General*

Gates," X, 280–287; "The Continental Brigantine *Resistance,"* XIV, 47–60; Editor, "Journal of the Ship *Empress of China,"* X, 83–107, 220–229, 288–297; XI, 59–71, 134–144; Editor, *Naval Documents of the American Revolution,* reviewed, Vol. I, XXVI, 72–73; Vol. II, XXVII, 221–222; Vol. III, XXIX, 287; Vol. IV, XXX, 220–221; "Officers who served under John Paul Jones, The," III, 55–56

Clark, Captain William H., XV, 300

Clarke, A. Howard, XLI, 40

Clarke, Captain Jeremiah, XXXI, 250

Clarke, Captain Peleg, XXXV, 299

Clarke, Dr. William, VII, 169

Clarkson, Captain James, XXX, 115

Clarkson, Mathew, XXXVII, 59

Clary, Captain A. G., XIX, 58, 59

"Classical Caper," by Captain Edgar K. Thompson, U.S.N. (ret.), XXVII, 45

"Classification Society Registers from the Point of View of a Marine Historian," by E. K. Haviland, XXX, 9–39

Claudia, schooner *(1861),* XI, 281

Clausen, Charles, XXX, 187

Claussen, Martin P., and Friis, Hermon R., *Descriptive Catalog of Maps Published by Congress, 1817–1834,* reviewed, II, 351

Clavell, Walter, XIII, 21

Claver, Captain Adrian, XVII, 292–297

Clavering, Brigadier General John, VII, 27, 28, 32

Clavering, Sir John, VII, 95

Claxton, Alexander, XXVIII, 69

Claxton, Commodore Alexander, XLVI, 231

Clay, ship, XXV, 186

Clay, Henry, XLII, 172 ff.; XLVIII, 27

Clay, Henry, Secretary of State, XL, 218

Clay, John Randolph, XXXV, 274

Clayton, Gary, XLIV, 112

Clayton, John M., XLIV, 23; answered query, IX, 73–74

Clayton, John M. and Dana A. Story, *The Building of a Wooden Ship,* reviewed, XXXII, 70–71

Clearwater, sloop (1969), XXIX, 153

Clearwater, steamship (1894), Pictorial Supplement, XXXIV, plate XXI

Clearwater Steamship Co., ship of, Pictorial Supplement, XXXIV, plate XXI

Cleaves, Freeman, "All Souls Saved," XXVII, 61–65

Cleeves, Robert, XX, 269

"Clement Drew, Ship Portrait Painter," note contributed by Ralph L. Drew, XXIII, 68

Clementine, schooner, XXI, 100

Clements, Captain Nehemiah K., XXXIV, 175

Clements (William L.) Library, University of Michigan (Ann Arbor, MI), I, 141–148, 304–306; IV, 194; V, 68, n. 6; VII, 88; Clinton Papers at, XXV, 125

Clements Line, The, XXXIV, 176

Clemmons, Captain James, Pictorial Supplement, XXXII, plate XII

Clemson, Professor Thomas G., XXXIX, 116

Clenched Lap or Clinker: An Appreciation of a Boatbuilding Technique, by Eric McKee, reviewed, XXXIII, 147–148

Cleone, bark *(1859),* XXXVIII, 83

Cleopatra, H.M.S. *(1796),* XVIII, 140; *(1894),* XXVIII, 88, 92

Cleopatra, ship (1867), III, 263

Cleopatra, steamship *(1845),* XII, 151; (1852), XXVI, 190–192, 205, 209; *(1883),* XXXIV, 177

Cleopatra's Barge, hermaphrodite brig/yacht (1816), II, 280; XIII, 156, 235–251, plates 9–11; XV, 83; L, 214; cabin ornament from, Pictorial Supplement, XXXVII, plate XXI (lower).

Cleopatra's Barge (II), schooner (1917), XIII, 246

"Cleopatra's Barge, Navy Style," by Captain Edgar K. Thompson, XV, 83

Cleremont, steamship *(1807),* XXXII, 211 ff. See also *Clermont.*

Clerke, Captain Charles, XXVIII, 146, 147

Clerke, Captain James, XVII, 67

Clermont, sidewheel yacht (1892), XXX, plate XXIX

Clermont, steamship XXVI, 74; XXVII, 11, 13, 24, 27; XVIII, 224; (1809), XXIV, 161 ff. See also *Cleremont.*

Clermont (II), steamship [replica] (1909), XIV, 112 ff.; photo of, XIV, plate 12

Cleveland, brigantine (1743), I, 297

Cleveland, cruiser *(1921),* XXXV, 122

Cleveland, German steamship *(1919),* XLVIII, 175

Cleveland, H.M. yacht *(1674),* XXV, 279

Cleveland, ship (1873), I, 115

Cleveland, steamship (1837), VII, 64; *(1838),* XVIII, 280, 283, 291, 297; XX, 89 n., 91

Cleveland, Benjamin D., XL, 125

Cleveland, President Grover, XXVII, 55 n., 57, 58; XXXIX, 10; XL, 167; XLI, 246

Cleveland, Captain Richard, XIX, 137; Pictorial Supplement, XXXII, plate XVII

Cleveland, Richard J., XXIX, 85

Cleveland, William, XLVI, 53

Cleveland Forwarding Co., XXXIV, 246

Cleveland Tankers, Inc., XXV, 174

Clew, John, XXVII, 46–48, 53

Clifford, Harold B., *Charlie York Maine Coast Fisherman,* reviewed, XXXVIII, 144

Clifford, John Garry, "Odyssey of *City of Flint,"* XXXII, 100–116

Clifford, Judge, XXVII, 50

Clifford, Nathaniel, XXI, 124

Clifford, Robert L., "The Unexpected End to *Seeadler,"* XXXVI, 266–275

"Clifford Day Mallory, 1881–1941," by Carl C. Cutler, I, 205–208

Clifford Wayne, ship *(1844),* XII, 111

Clift, Ira H., XXV, 103

Clifton, gunboat (1862), XXXVI, 196, 198

Clifton, schooner *(1862),* VIII, 223; *(1864),* XII, 230
Clifton, ship *(1861),* XI, 281
Clifton, Union Island, XXXII, 189 ff.
Cline, Walter, XXXVI, 247 n.
Clinker Boatbuilding, by John Leather, XXXV, 216
Clinton, bark (1840), IV, 51
Clinton, beam trawler *(1956),* XLV, 84
Clinton, brig (1838), V, 154
Clinton, canal boat *(1854),* XVI, 41–48
Clinton, De Witt, XXV, 155; XXXVI, 66; XLIII, 43
Clinton, De Witt, Jr., XVIII, 315–316
Clinton, General Henry, XXXVII, 291; XXXVIII, 26; XXXIX, 160; XL, 17
Clinton, General Sir Henry, I, plates facing 142, 145–146
Clinton, Sir Henry, VII, 87–106, 200; XLVI, 23
Clinton, Lord Admiral, XLIV, 27
"Clinton, Sir Henry, Letters of Captain Sir John Jervis to, 1774–1782," edited by Marie Martel Hatch, VII, 87–106
Clintonia, bark (1846), I, 49
Clinton Papers. *See* Clements Library, University of Michigan
"Clinton Roosevelt's Invulnerable Steam Battery, 1835," by Marshall Smelser, XX, 167–173, plate 5
Clio, brig *(1811),* XLIV, 105
Clio, British sloop of war *(1833),* L, 31
Clio, steamship, XXII, 220
"Cliometrics: Its Application to Nautical Research," by Norman N. Rubin, XLVI, 179–187
Clipper, schooner *(1864),* XII, 230
Clipper City, schooner (1854), I, 74
Clippers, De, by Anno Teenstra, reviewed, VII, 324
Clipper-schooner, IX, 142
Clipper-schooners, Chesapeake, IX, 142–147, 184
Clipper ships, XXIII, 264; XLII, 118
Clipper ships: I, 44–47, 85; VII, 318, 324; VIII, 151–152, 325–330; IX, 148–150; XXII, 233–251
"Clipper Ships," query by Daniel F. MacNeil, VI, 232; answered by M. V. Brewington, VII, 170
Clippers of the Port of Portsmouth and the Men Who Built Them, by Ray Brighton, reviewed, XLVIII, 197
Clocks and Watches of Captain James Cook, 1769–1969, The, by Derek Howse and Beresford Hutchinson, reviewed, XXXI, 74–75
Cloete, William D., XXVI, 203
Clorinde, British frigate *(1810),* XLV, 159 ff.
Closson, Captain Albert E., IX, 171
Closson, Freeman, IX, 179
Clothier, ship *(1801),* XXIII, 216
Clothing and dress, XVII, 195
Clothing, sailor's, XVII, 195–201; XX, 62
Clotilda, sloop *(1863),* XV, 127
Cloud, Reverend Fred, XLVI, 25
Clough, Benjamin, XXVII, 98, 99, 102–110
Clown, gunboat *(1858),* XXXIV, 20 ff.

Clowse, Converse G., "Shipowning and Shipbuilding in Colonial South Carolina: An Overview," XLIV, 221–244
Cluff, Dohn A., "Killicks," XV, 150–151; "Lobster Fishing on the Maine Coast Past and Present," XIV, 203–208; "A New England Seafaring Family," XIX, 140
"Clump-built," query by H. J., I, 90
Clyde, schooner *(1863),* XII, 155
Clyde, tug *(1894),* XLII, 267 ff.
Clyde, Thomas, XXXVI, 253
Clyde, View Down the, 1820, XXIX, 48, plate VIII, 124, plate XI
Clyde Pilot Boat, 1824, XXIX, 124, Plate XI
Clyde ram, XXIX, 17, 21, 23
Clyde S.S. Co., XXII, 167
Clyde steamships, reference to, XLVIII, 77
Clytie, brig *(1879),* XL, 108 ff.
CN. *See* Connecticut
Coal, Transportation, XXX, 187; XXXIII, 155; XLII, 245
Coale, Griffith B., XI, 220–221; XIV, 106
Coale, Commander Griffith B., XVII, 173
Coale, Griffith Bailey, X, 3–4, 239 ff.; "Arrival of the First Permanent Settlers off Jamestown, Virginia, 13 May 1607," X, 5–14; *North Atlantic Patrol,* reviewed, II, 343
Coalinga, ship (1868), VII, 290–292; X, 115
Coal trade, XXI, 23:
    Philippines, II, 140
Coastal Trade, United States, XXI, 23–27
Coast defenses, United States, XLIV, 257
Coast Defense Society, VI, 259, 261
Coast Guard Museum. *See* U.S. Coast Guard Museum
Coasting Captain—Journals of Captain Leonard S. Tawes, Robert H. Burgess, Editor, reviewed, XXVIII, 148–149
Coasting Passage, by Frederick Sturgis Laurence, reviewed, X, 235
Coasting Schooner, The Four-Masted, by Albert F. Paul and Robert H. Burgess, reviewed, XXXIX, 149–150
Coasting Schooners, New England, XXIII, 5–21, plates I–XXXII
"Coasting Voyage, A," document contributed by Richard B. Philbrick, XXIII, 145
Coast of England and Wales in Pictures, The, by J. A. Steers, reviewed, XX, 277
Coastwise Transportation Co., V, 138
Coast Wrecking Co., XXV, 108
Coates, John and Sean McGrail, editors, *The Greek Trireme of the 5th Century B.C.: Discussion of a Projected Reconstruction,* reviewed, XLVI, 121
Coats, Warwick, VIII, 12
Cobb, Albert, XIV, 212–214
Cobb, Butler & Co., XXIII, plates XVII, XXVIII
Cobb, Charles K., "An Explanatory Note to 'The Jakey Boats,'" XIX, 73

Cobb, David (artist), XXII, plate IX
Cobb, Elijah, XLI, 176
Cobb, Howell, XXXVI, 178, 184
Cobb, Captain Sylvanus, XX, 43
Cobb, Captain W. B., XVIII, 82
"Cobblestone Trade," query by Ernest S. Dodge, I, 398; answers by S. E. Morison, Mary C. Wheelwright, and James Otis Porter, II, 82
Cobbs, Captain William H., XV, 249–258
Cobourg, steamship (1833), VII, 50, 65; VIII, 37, 44, 46, 53
Cochet, Captain John, XLV, 96
Cochin China, XXV, 184–185; XXX, 203
Cochran, Robert, XV, 65, 72, 73
Cochrane, Chilean ship *(1891),* XXXVIII, 299
Cochrane, ironclad *(1873),* XXXIX, 273
Cochrane, Admiral Sir Alexander, XLIII, 140
Cochrane, Vice Admiral Sir Alexander, XXIX, 188
Cochrane, Vice Admiral E. L., XXXII, 213, 244
Cochrane, Vice Admiral Edward L., XXXVII, 288
Cochrane, Admiral Lord George, XL, 41
Cochrane, Lord Thomas, XXXV, 248
Cochrane, Vice-Admiral Thomas, XXVIII, 87
Cockburn, Admiral, XXX, 137
Cockburn, Rear Admiral George, XXXVI, 207, 213, 217
Cockburn, Rear-Admiral Sir George, XLIII, 5 ff.
Cockchafer, H.M. frigate *(1926),* L, 187
Cocke, Elizabeth, XXXVIII, 118
Cocke, John Hartwell, XXXVIII, 118
Cock of the Walk, vessel *(1863),* XXVI, 102
Cock Robin, sloop (1904), XXX, plate XX
Cocks, Richard, XXXI, 100
Cocopah, steamship (1859), I, 260–261, plate between 272–273
Cocopah (II), steamship *(1867),* I, 261, 269
"Coda," document contributed by Captain Edgar K. Thompson, U.S.N. (ret.), XXIV, 70
Coddington, Nathaniel, XLII, 45
Coddrington, Benjamin, XXXIX, 213
Codman, John, XIII, 122; XXIII, 135
Codman, Captain John, II, 99–106, 271–277
Codman, Mary Ann, XXIII, 135
Codorus, iron steamship (1825), VIII, 133, 163–190, plates 21, 22; X; XXIV, 23
Cod schooner, Old-style Grand Bank, XXVI, plate VI
Coeur de Lion, ship (1854), III, 67
Coffee, imports from Mauritius, XXV, 9, 16, 17
Coffin, Captain Alexander, XLIII, 52
Coffin, Captain Bartlett, XLI, 282
Coffin, Captain George, XX, 46
Coffin, Captain Hector, XV, 137
Coffin, Admiral Sir Isaac, XLIV, 105
Coffin, Captain Micajah, XXIII, 26, 27
Coffin, Peleg, Jr., XLIII, 52
Coffin, Robert, II, 184
Coffin, W. S., XVII, 126
Coffin, William E., XVI, 172

Coggeshall, George, XLI, 172
Coghlan, Admiral John, XXXVII, 259 ff.
Coghlan, Captain Richard T., XXII, 167
Cogolin, Joseph-Bernard Chabert de, XLIV, 186 ff.
Cohen, Captain David M., XXXII, 205
Cohen, Sheldon S., "Captain Robert Niles, Connecticut State Navy," XXXIX, 190–208
Cohn, Michael B., review by, XLVI, 124
Cohoes, monitor *(1864),* XLVIII, 123
Co-Hong, XXXI, 177 ff.
Cohota, ship (1843), III, 320; VII, 4–8, plates 1, 2, plans facing 8
Coit, Captain W. W., XII, 289
Coke, Vice Admiral C. H., XXXV, 40 ff.
Coker, Stephen, XVII, 116
Col. *See* Colonel.
Colbert, French warship *(1854),* XXX, 160
Colbert, Jean-Baptiste, XVI, 98
Colborne, Sir John, VII, 299
Colby, Bainbridge, Secretary of State, XXXIV, 160
Colby, Charles, XXV, 172
Colby, Captain Charles, XXVI, 55
Colby, Everett, XXV, 172
Colchis, ship (1836), XIX, 27, 28, 29–32
Colcord, Captain Andrew D., X, 273–274
Colcord, Captain and Mrs. B. F., II, plate 28; XXVIII, plate XIX
Colcord, F. W., XXVIII, plate XXII
Colcord, Joanna C., II, 252; III, 178; IV, 336; V, 98; VI, 92, 153–154; VII, 39 n., 282; VIII, 79, 163; XXV, 55; XLVI, 111 ff.; query by, IX, 302; "Boyhood under Sail 1874–1881: Letters to his son by Joseph C. Hilton," III, 106–130; "Correction to 'Domestic Life on American Sailing Ships,'" II, 327; "Domestic Life on American Sailing Ships," II, 193–203; "Loss of the *Malleville,*" IV, 318–323; "Salving the Ship *Crystal Palace:* The Private Journals (1857–1858) of Captain Benjamin F. Simmons and Second Officer Joshua N. Rowe," III, 314–326; IV, 31–44; *Sea Language Comes Ashore,* reviewed, V, 166–169; *Songs of American Sailormen,* reviewed, III, 356–357; "Two American Vessels Wrecked on the Irish Coast," IX, 68
Colcord, Lincoln Alden, I, 102, 177, 315; II, 252; IV, 167; V, 166; XI, 82; XII, 305; XLVI, 111; editorial mention, XLII, 121; XLIII, 164; XLIV, 82 ff.; XXVIII, 237; editorial tribute to, by Walter Muir Whitehill, VIII, 3–6; contributed documents, I, 87–88, 306–308; reviews by, II, 178–181, 254–256, 256; "Eastern Names," IX, 83–86; "A Jury Rudder for the Bark *Guy C. Goss,*" II, 65–70; introductory note to "The Last Voyage of the Ship *Vigilant,*" by Thomas A. Stevens, II, 140–153; "Notes on Chapman and Flint," II, 324–326; "A Tidal Wave at Huanillos, Chile in 1877," I, 108–115
Colcord, Captain Lincoln A., XXVIII, plate XXXI
Colcord, Lincoln and Joanna Colcord, XXXIII, 4
Colcord, Captain and Mrs. Theodore P., II, 26

Colden, Cadwallader, XXVII, 15, 24, 26
Colden, Cadwallader D., XXII, 129; XXIV, 161 ff.; XXV, 123–124, plate 9
Colden, Cadwallader David, XXXII, 215
Cole, Allan B., "The *Mount Vernon's* Voyage from Batavia to Nagasaki in 1807," V, 255–265; *With Perry in Japan: the Diary of Edward Yorke McCauley,* reviewed, III, 356–357; Editor, *Yankee Surveyors in the Shogun's Seas,* reviewed, VIII, 72–73
Cole, Arthur H., XIII, 118
Cole, Charles H., Confederate Captain, XLVIII, 101
Cole, Captain G. W., XIV, 44
Cole, Captain George A., XLVII, 43
Cole, Merle T., "Tankers in the Patuxent: The ESSO Fleet Lay-up Site in the 1930's," XLVII, 45–53
Cole, Rear Admiral, XXXV, 122
Colebrook, vessel *(1770's),* XXX, 207
Colefield, John K., XLI, 132
Coleman, Bennett D., XXX, 188–191
Coleman, Captain Bennett D., XXI, 23–27
Coleman, Captain Joseph, XXIII, 27
Coleman, Captain Timothy, XXIII, 27
Coler, Captain Cowper Phipps, XXII, 253
Coles, Adlard, *North Atlantic,* reviewed, XI, 296
Coles, Captain Cowper, R.N., X, 17; XXIX, 11, 25; XLIX, 115
Coles Turret, XXII, fig. 1, 254
Colesworthy, Captain Jonathan, XLIII, 54
Coletta, Paolo E.; *An Annotated Bibliography of U.S. Marine Corps History,* reviewed, XLVII, 214; "The Court-Martial of Bowman Hendry McCalla," XL, 127–134; "Creating the U.S. Bureau of Aeronautics," L, 51–59; "French Ensor Chadwick: The First American Naval Attaché, 1882–1889," XXXIX, 126–141; "The 'Nerves' of the New Navy," XXXVIII, 122–130; "Pat Bellinger and the May 1919 Transatlantic Flight," XLVII, 249–256; "The Perils of Invention: Bradley A. Fiske and the Torpedo Plane," XXXVII, 111–127
Coletta, Paolo E. and K. Jack Bauer, *United States Navy and Marine Corps Bases: Domestic;* and *United States Navy and Marine Corps Bases: Foreign,* reviewed, XLIX, 59
Coletta, Paolo E., Jack Bauer, and Robert G. Albion, *Admiral Bradley A. Fiske and the American Navy,* reviewed, XLI, 233–234; *American Secretaries of the Navy,* reviewed, XLI, 142
Colfar, Captain Eleazer, XX, 46
Colgate Hoyt, whaleback steamship (1889), XXV, 170
Colima, steamship (1873), X, 132, 138
Collamore, Gilman, XXV, 222
Collamore, Horace, XXV, 222
Collector, schooner (1818), XIV, 39
Collectors Stamp, Freidrich August II (Saxony), photo of, XLIX, 226
Colledge, Caroline Shillaber, XLVI, 37
Collie, Lieutenant A. M., RNVR, XLIV, 52
Collier, Lieutenant C. Myles, XL, 301
Collier, Rear Admiral F. A., XXVI, 13
Collier, Admiral Sir George, XXXVII, 291 ff.
Collier, Sir George, Commander, XLII, 12 ff.
Collier, Colonel James, XLV, 119
Collier, Judge John, XXXI, 27
Collimore, Francis, XXV, 64
Collin C. McNeil, bark (1865), V, 153
Collingwood, British line ship *(1845),* XXXII, 237
Collingwood, Admiral, XLVI, 222
Collingwood, Lord, XXX, 212
Collingwood, Trevor, XXXIII, 34
Collins, Captain, XXXVI, 240
Collins, Charles, XIV, 59
Collins, Miss Clema, XXXII, 22
Collins, Edward K., XIV, 237–261, plate 30
Collins, Edward Knight, XLVII, 39; XLVIII, 114
Collins, Lieutenant Frederick, XXXIX, 125
Collins, Greenville, VIII, 307–309
Collins, Commander Harry E., XXXIV, 171
Collins, Isaac, XIV, 59
Collins, James P., XLVI, 216
Collins, Captain Jason, "Loss of the Steamship *Independence,*" with introduction by John Richards, XIV, 192–202
Collins, John, XXXI, 236, 239
Collins, Captain John, XXX, 89, 90; XL, 11; XLVII, 39
Collins, Captain Joseph, XLIV, 115; XLV, 82
Collins, Captain Joseph W., XIV, 13, 14
Collins, Captain Napoleon, XV, 297 ff.
Collins, Commander Napoleon, XXII, 45–54
Collins, Commander Napolion, XXXIX, 38
Collins, Nathan, XVII, 116
Collins, Pilot, U.S.N., XXV, 138
Collins, W. N., XVII, 116
Collins Line, IV, 139–140; XIV, 237–261; XXII, 72–73; XXVI, 82 ff.
Collinson, Peter, XXXV, 115
Collis, tug *(1913),* XXIX, 265
Collision, between M.V. *Sierra* and S.S. *Wilhelmina,* XXV, 289–290
Collisions at sea, XX, 191; XL, 108; XLVII, 119
Collmar, barge *(1861),* XI, 281
Collmar, bark, XXI, 95
Collmar, schooner *(1863),* XII, 155
Collyer, Robert M., XIII, 214
Collyer, Thomas, XIII, 214; XXXVI, 172
Collyer & Lambert (shipbuilders), XLIII, 88 ff.
Colman, Addie Cushing, query by, VIII, 71; *Captain Moses Rich Colman,* reviewed, X, 235
Colón, Fernando, XXX, 252
Colnett, Captain H. James, XV, 83
Colnett, Captain James, I, 97–98
Colomb, Vice Admiral J. C. R., XXXIX, 126
Colomba, steamship [model] (1878), XVI, 104
Colombo, ship *(1861),* VIII, 216
Colon, steamship (1873), X, 132; *(1875),* XIV, 213

Colonel Abert, U.S. revenue cutter (1843 or 1844), VIII, 143; XXIV, 8 ff.
Colonel Adams, ship (1860), IV, 244
Colonel Albert, steamship (1843), XX, 261
Colonel Ariza (ex-*General Sherman*), ship *(1872),* XXXVIII, 238
Colonel (Col.) Bliss, schooner, XXI, 100; *(1862),* XII, 53
Colonel Driant, auxiliary (1918), XXXII, 12, 30
Colonel E. L. Drake, tanker *(1903),* XXXVIII, 191 ff.
Colonel Fremont, ship *(1850),* XLV, 128
Colonel J. Whitmore, steamship *(1862),* XII, 53
"Colonel John Stevens," by Stanton M. Smith, XII, 239, plates 20–22
Colonel (Col.) Lamb, steamship, XXI, 96, 106, plate III; (1861), III, 135–136; *(1864),* VIII, 233; *(1865),* XII, 234
Colonel Long, schooner *(1861),* VIII, 216; XV, 122
Colonel Lovell, C.S.S. (1862), XIX, 268, 270 ff.
Colonel McRae, schooner *(1862),* VIII, 223
Colonial bateaux, XXVI, plate 4
Colonial ketches, descriptions, XXX, 81–85
Colonial Limited Liability Ordinance, XXXIV, 42
Colonial Navy, The, 1821–1847, XXXVIII, 53 ff.
Colonial shipbuilding, II, 338; IX, 142–147
"Colonial Sloop *Mediator,* The," by Howard I. Chapelle, XIII, 177–184
Colonial Society of Massachusetts, XIV, 81
Colonial Steamships Co. Ltd., XXXI, 118
"Colonial Trader to Museum Ship; The Bark *Star of India,*" by Harold D. Huycke, X, 108–122
Colonial Vessels: Some Seventeenth-Century Sailing Craft, by William A. Baker, reviewed, XXII, 290–291
Colorado, Pacific Mail steamship *(1867),* XXXII, 130
Colorado, schooner, XXII, 244
Colorado, screw frigate *(1850),* XLIX, 112
Colorado, steamship (1855), I, 260; (1863 or 1864), II, 15–17, 21–23, plates 4, 6; X, 130, 131, plate 18
Colorado, steam side-wheeler *(1867),* XLVI, 61
Colorado, U.S. steam frigate (1856), XXI, 144; XXII, 252; XXV, 116–122; *(1871),* VII, 19, 108–109, 111–113, plate 9
Colorado (II) steamship (1862), I, 261, plate facing 264
Colorado African Colonization Co., XXXV, 204
Colorado River steamships, I, 255–274, 405–406
Colshill, Thomas, XLIV, 28
Colson, Captain Albert M., II, plate 28; XXVIII, plate XIX
Colson, John, VIII, 306
Colson, Lancelot, VIII, 305
Colston, William, XXXVII, 11
Colt, John, XXXI, 136
Colt, Samuel, XXXI, 137
Colton, David, XXXI, 121 ff.
Colt's Clipper Duck, XXXI, 137
Columbia, bark *(1860–1862),* I, 406–407
Columbia, barkentine *(1906),* IV, 326
Columbia, C.S.S gunboat *(1864),* XLIV, 273 ff.
Columbia, cruiser *(1888),* XXXIX, 136
Columbia, frigate *(1837),* XLVII, 29; *(1839),* XXXI, 183
Columbia, Lightship, XXVI, 3
Columbia, schooner (1923), VII, 171, 243; IX, 73, 74; XXV, 147
Columbia, schooner, XXI, 89, 92; *(1861),* XI, 281; XII, 53
Columbia, ship (1773), XXV, 218–219
Columbia, ship (1783), XXXIII, 161 ff.; *(1792),* XIII, 65, 212–213; XV, 205–212; XXVI, 3; XLIX, 272 ff.; *(1838),* XL, 119
Columbia, ship (1871), IV, 51, 52
Columbia, sloop (1799), XIV, 39
Columbia, steamship (1850), X, 130; XVII, 305; XVIII, 68; XLIII, 196 ff.
Columbia, steamship (re-named *Otori*/*Taiho Maru*) *(1850),* XLIX, 27
Columbia, steamship (1891), X, 137, 138; *(1916),* X, 140, 142, 143
Columbia, steamship (ex-*Methuen Castle*) *(1897),* XXXVIII, 194 ff.
Columbia, U.S. frigate (1825), XXI, 292, 298–302; XXIII, 261; *(1838),* XXIX, 82, 107
Columbia, U.S.S. *(1894),* XXVIII, 92
Columbia, U.S.S. (ex-*H. F. Alexander,* ex-*Great Northern*), XXVII, 151; *(1922),* XLVII, 203
Columbia, U.S.S. *(1842),* VII, 18, 19; *(1846),* XIX, 247
Columbia, whaler *(1842),* XLI, 289
Columbia, *Voyages of, to the Northwest Coast 1787–1790 and 1790–1793,* reviewed, II, 253
Columbia College, VII, 186
Columbian, steamship (1855), XXVI, 30, 31, 118, 203, 205, 209
"Columbian Coooperage," query by Samuel Eliot Morison, I, 89; answer by Frank Schoonmaker, I, 173
Columbian Iron Works and Dry Dock Co., XXXVIII, 177 ff.
Columbian Steamship Co., XLI, 114
Columbia River, auxiliary schooner (1916), V, 140–145
Columbia River, schooner, XXXVII, 224
Columbia River, U.S. Light-Vessel No. 50 (1891–1892), IX, 273–277, plate 29; XI, 78
Columbia River, XXV, 218; XXX, 298
Columbia River Maritime Museum (Astoria, OR), XXVI, 3
Columbine, brig *(1831),* XXXV, 81
Columbine, H.M.S., XXII, 14; *(1897),* XXVIII, 89, 98
Columbine, U.S. gunboat *(1863),* VII, 124
Columbine, Captain G. H., XXX, 213
Columbus, Continental/U.S. Navy Ship *(1775),* XL, 13; *(1812),* XLI, 29; XLII, 290; *(1776),* XXV, 193, 208, 211; XLVIII, 158; *(1779),* XXXV, 141
Columbus, ship (1862), III, 62; (1870), III, 63
Columbus, steamship (1835), VII, 57, 60; *(1836),* XVIII, 275, 285; XX, 83 n., 89 n., 268
Columbus, steamship *(1825),* XLVIII, 77 ff.; illustrations of, XLVIII, 79, 81, 82, 83

Columbus, steamship (1847), XXXVI, 253; XXXVIII, 130
Columbus, U.S. receiving ship *(1841),* VII, 18
Columbus, U.S.S., III, plate 44
Columbus, U.S. ship-of-the-line (1819), XXIII, 58; XXIV, 37; XXV, 94; *(1820),* XXXI, 288
Columbus, Bartholomew, XXXVII, 160
Columbus, Christopher, I, 6, 123, 209
Columbus, Christopher, II, 178–181; XIV, 187, XIX, 79–113; XXV, 75; XXX, 250 ff.; first voyage of, I, 209–240
"Columbus and Polaris," by Samuel Eliot Morison, I, 6–25, 123–127
"Columbus Landed on Watlings Island," by Captain E. Roukema, XIX, 79–113
Columbus' Ships, by Jose Maria Martinez-Hidalgo, reviewed, XXVII, 67–71
Colusa, steamship *(1917),* X, 140
Colvill, Rear Admiral Alexander, XXIII, 175 ff.
Colville, ship *(1860),* XXVII, 235
Colvocoresses, Lieutenant, XXVIII, 135
Colwell, Lieutenant J. C., XXXVI, 114 ff.
Colwell, James H., XXXVII, 117
Colwell, Lieutenant John C., XLI, 96
Comanche, monitor *(1892),* XXXVIII, 298
Combine, packet, XXIV, 131, 132
Combs, Captain John, XXI, 12
Comedy, ship *(1850),* XIV, 45
Comet, bark *(1852),* XXVIII, 122
Comet, brig *(1863),* XII, 155
Comet, brigantine, XXI, 94; *(1776),* XIII, 36 ff.
Comet, ketch *(1857),* XI, 291
Comet, privateer *(1813),* XXXVI, 211, 219, 220
Comet, schooner *(1862),* VIII, 223
Comet, ship (1851), III, 262; XIX, plate II
Comet, ship (1869), III, 173; *(1871),* XIV, 46
Comet, ship, XXIV, 132
Comet, steamship *(1811),* XLVIII, 77; *(1812),* XIII, 158; (1813), XVI, 35
Comet, steamship (1832), VII, 47 n.
Comet, steamship (1883), VII, 159
Comete, French man-of-war *(1894),* XXIII, 69; *(1895),* XL, 102 ff.
Commager, Henry Steele, mention, XLVIII, 181
Commandant Challes, auxiliary (1917), XXXII, 21, 30, plate 2
Commandant de Rose, auxiliary (1917), XXXII, 13, 30, plate 3
Commandant Roisin, auxiliary (1917), XXXII, 13, 30
Command at Sea, by Harley F. Cope, reviewed, XI, 299
"Commander Otto Hersing and the Dardanelles Cruise of S.M. U-21," by Karl D. Hoover, XXXVI, 33–44
"Command Performance," document contributed by Captain Edgar K. Thompson, U.S.N. (ret.), XXV, 68–69

Command Under Sail: Makers of the American Naval Tradition, by James C. Bradford, reviewed, XLVI, 122
"Comments on "Boston's Little-Known Packet Lines," by Dana M. Hastings, in April 1955 Issue of ***The American Neptune,***" by H. H. Holly, XVI, 60–61
"Comments on the Coale Painting," by D. W. Waters, XI, 220–221
"Comments on 'The Design of the American Frigates of the Revolution and Joshua Humphreys,'" by Eugene S. Ferguson, X, 65–66
Commerce, schooner (1901), I, 77
Commerce, schooner, XXI, 89; *(1861),* XI, 281
Commerce, ship *(1792),* XIX, 10; *(1798),* XXXI, 175; *(1799),* XLV, 92
Commerce, ship (1801), II, 282; *(1801),* XXIV, 262
Commerce, sloop *(1775),* XIII, 29
Commerce, steamship (1837), VII, 65; *(1842),* XX, 259; (1843), XX, 262; *(1864),* XXXVII, 234; *(1871),* XXXIV, 177
Commerce:
   Italy, 12th century, L, 229
   United States, XLIV, 5
   History, XXIX, 199
   See also Shipping (U.S.)
Commerce and Conquest in East Africa, by Cyrus Townsend Brady, Jr., reviewed, XI, 232–233
"Commerce, Crisis, Coercion: The Role of Piracy in Late Eighteenth and Early Nineteenth Century Sino-Western Relations," by Dian Murray, XLVIII, 237–242
Commerce and Culture: The Maritime Communities of Colonial Massachusetts, 1690–1750, by Christine Leigh Heyrman, reviewed, XLVI, 128
Commerce de Paris, steamship (1823), XIII, 160
"Commerce of a Southern Port: New Bern, North Carolina, 1783 to 1789, The," by William Stuart Morgan, III, XLIX, 77–90
Commercial Exporting Co., IX, 34
Commercial law, XLVIII, 243
"Commercial Sail in the Leeward Islands," by Edwin Doran, Jr., XXIV, 95–108
Commercial Wharf, XXXIX, plates 1, 3
Commerell, Vice-Admiral Sir John E., XXVIII, 112
Commissioners and Commodores, The East India Squadron and American Diplomacy in China, by Curtis T. Henson, Jr., reviewed, XLIII, 145–146
Commissions of George Coleman DeKay, VI, plates 1–2
Committee on Maritime Preservation, editorial comment, XXXVII, 3–4
Commodore, schooner *(1941),* VII, 294
Commodore, U.S. steamship *(1848),* XXXIII, 85, 94
Commodore Barrie, steamship (1834), VII, 55, 65; *(1840),* XX, 86, 252
Commodore Blake, steamship (1842), XX, 254
Commodore Hull, schooner *(1830),* XXIV, 130, 132
Commodore Jones, river gunboat *(1864),* XLIX, 121

Commodore McDonnough, U.S.S. *(1862),* XII, 276–281
Commodore Perry, ship (1855), III, 170; *(1846–1857),* XLII, 121 ff.; *(1862),* VI, 51
Commodore Perry, steamship (1834), VII, 55, 57, 62; *(1838),* XVIII, 283
Commodore Preble, freighter *(1840),* XXXIII, 84
"Commodore George DeKay and the Voyage of *Macedonian* to Ireland," by Phyllis DeKay Wheelock, XIII, 252–267, plates 13, 14
"Commodore James Biddle and the First Naval Mission to Japan, 1845–1846," by Merrill L. Bartlett, XLI, 25–35
Commodore John Rodgers, Captain, Commodore, and Senior Officer of the American Navy, 1773–1838, by Charles Oscar Paullin, reviewed, XXVIII, 294–295
"Commodore John Rodgers Goldsborough, U.S.N., Summary of Service of," prepared by Office of Naval Records and Library, Navy Department, VII, 18–20
"Commodore Perry's Landing in Japan – 1853," contributed by John Goldsborough, VII, 9–20
"Commodore Robert W. Shufeldt and America's South African Strategy," by Thomas J. Noer, XXXIV, 81–88
Commodores, Biography, L, 245
Commodores, The, by Leonard F. Guttridge and Jay D. Smith, reviewed, XXX, 73–75
Commonwealth, steamship (1854), III, 37, 41; V, 165; VIII, 246–254, plates 21–24
Commonwealth, steamship (1908), III, 46; Pictorial Supplement, XXXIV, 259, plate XXXII
Communication, Triservice History planned, XXV, 139
Compagnia Italiana Transporto Olii Minerali, XXXVIII, 181 ff.
Compagnie Havraise, XXXI, 118
Compass, XXV, 93. *See also* Nautical instruments
Compass variation: I, 11–13; device to eliminate, XXV, 93–98, plate 4
Compeer, ship (1858), V, 147
Competitor, bark (1853), III, 68
"Complete Modellist of Thomas Miller, 1667, The," by Vernon D. Tate, XVII, 152–155
"Composed for the Editor—E.S.D.," document by Francis Whiting Hatch, XXIV, 279
Comstock, Captain William, XII, 151
Comstock Brothers, XIII, 122
Comtois, George, "The British Navy in the Delaware, 1775 to 1777," XL, 7–22
Comus, H.M.S. *(1880),* XXVIII, 17, 88
Comus, H.M. sloop *(1845),* XXXVI, 129, 133–136
Comus, schooner, XXI, 93; *(1865),* XII, 234
Comyn, W. Leslie, XXII, 159
Conant, Roger, XXXVII, 9
Conard, William, VII, 162
Conception, French ship, XXVI, 56, 57, 59, 60
Concettina, bark *(1861),* XI, 281
Conchita, schooner *(1862),* XII, 53

Concise Catalogue of Paintings, book reviewed by Marion V. Brewington, XIX, 146–147
Concord, English bark *(1602),* XXIV, 145; XXV, 238; XXXIII, 131–145; XXXIV, 232 ff.; sketch of, 34, 239; *(1615),* XIII, 10 n.
Concord, gunboat *(1863),* XXXIV, 212
Concord, ship *(1777),* XXXI, 134
Concord, ship (1798), XXXIII, 161 ff.; *(1802),* XXIII, 217
Concord, ship *(1898),* XXXV, 184; *(1903),* XXXVII, 254; XXXVIII, 298; XXXIX, 41
Concord, U.S. gunboat *(1896),* XXIX, 116
Concord, U.S.S. *(1842),* XIX, 242
Concord, U.S. cruiser *(1926),* XLVI, 240 ff.; L, 291 ff.
Concorde, French frigate, XXII, 95 ff.
Concordia, bark (1867), Pictorial Supplement, XXXIII, plate XV
Concordia, schooner, XXI, 103; *(1863),* XII, 155
Concordia, ship (1784), XI, 61
Concord's shallop, sketch of, XXXIV, 235
Concrete, motor ship *(1917),* XXII, 158
"Concrete Brigantine, A," note contributed by F. E. Clark, XXIV, 216
Concrete ships. *See* Shipbuilding (Materials)
Conde de Palmella, steamship (1820), IX, 252–253
Condell de la Haza, Captain Carlos, XXXIX, 281
Condor, steamship, XXI, 93, 100, 105
Condore, ship *(1676),* XIII, 13
Condy, Benjamin, XLVI, 259
Conestoga, U.S.S. *(1861),* XIX, 266
Coney, Captain Lawrence, XLIX, 31
Confederacy, American frigate *(1777),* XXXI, 244
Confederacy, Continental frigate *(1767),* XLI, 216; XLIV, 169
Confederacy, frigate *(1790),* XLIX, 41 ff.
Confederacy, schooner, XXI, 98; *(1863),* VIII, 229
Confederacy, U.S.S. (1776), XVIII, 133
Confederate Blockade Running Through Bermuda, edited by Frank E. Vandiver, reviewed, VIII, 259–260
Confederate James River Squadron, XLII, 87
Confederate Naval History, XXII, 232
"Confederate Naval Squadron at Charleston and the Failure of Naval Harbor Defense, The," by Paul D. Lockhart, XLIV, 257–275
Confederate Navy: I, 183–184, 241–254; XXVI, 96 ff.; XXVII, 39 n., 174–175, 233–253, 263–278
Confederate Navy in Europe, The, by Warren F. Spencer, reviewed, XLIV, 206
Confederate Ports, Blockade of, 1861–1865, XXI, 81–107
Confederate privateers, XI, 150–155
Confederate River Defense Fleet, XXV, 129 ff.
Confederate States, steamship, XXI, 99; *(1864),* VIII, 233
Confederate States of America:
 Foreign relations, Brazil, XV, 287
 —, **Gt. Britain,** XIX, 51
 —, **South Africa,** XXVI, 96

History, Naval, I, 241
Navy, XV, 287; XXVII, 263; XXXIII, 52, 79; XLIII, 129; XLIV, 257; XLVIII, 87
—, **Ships**, XXIX, 5; XLV, 191
Revenue Marine, XL, 298.
See also Privateering; United States history (Civil War)
Confederate States Government, XXV, 21
"Confederate Warships off Brazil," by Benjamin Franklin Gilbert, XV, 287–302
Conference, ship (1858), I, 114
Confiance, H.M.S. (1814), XXI, 46, 50 ff.; XXXVI, 290
Confidence, ship *(1618)*, XXXVII, 10
Confidence, vessel *(1850)*, XXXVI, 172
Confucius, steamship (1853), XVI, 163; XVIII, 68; *(1853)*, XXII, 17; XLIX, 21; *(1856)*, XLIII, 201
Congalton, Captain W., XLIII, 107 ff.
Congo, British bark *(1844)*, XXXVIII, 59
Congreso (ex-*Widgeon*), brig *(1848)*, XXX, 267 ff.
Congress, American privateer, XXII, 268
Congress, brig-of-war *(1834)*, XXXVII, 247
Congress, C.S.S. *(1862)*, XXIII, 203
Congress, frigate (1776), VIII, 11, 14, 21, 24; *(1813)*, XLVI, 165, 233; XLIX, 49; L, 60; *(1814)*, XLII, 105 ff.; XLV, 5, 36; *(1818)*, XXXI, 179 ff.; XXXV, 141
Congress, ship *(1776)*, XXXVIII, 24
Congress, ship *(1857)*, XII, 102; *(1861)*, XI, 281
Congress, steamship, XXVII, 150; *(1876)*, XXXVIII, 123
Congress, U.S. frigate (1799), VII, 253; XXI, 61; XXIV, 180 n.; *(1817)*, XXVIII, 112; (1841), XXII, 253; XXV, 161; *(1842)*, XXIX, 176
Congress, U.S. galley *(1776)*, VIII, 256; XXI, 76
Congress, U.S.S. *(1801)*, XXVII, 147; *(1806)*, XVIII, 183; *(1846)*, XIX, 247; *(1862)*, XX, 160
Congress, whaler *(1844)*, XLI, 290; *(1865)*, XXVII, 275
Congress Founds the Navy, The, by Marshall Smelser, reviewed, XX, 149
Congressional Gold Life Saving Medal, XXXVII, 92–93, plate 4
Conklin, Lieutenant Augustus, XLIV, 176
Conley and Scott, XXII, 44
Connaroe, Thomas, XXXII, 251
Connecticut, gondola *(1776)*, VIII, 256
Connecticut, ship *(1863)*, XLV, 237
Connecticut, side-wheeler *(1864)*, XXXII, 54
Connecticut, steamship, painting of, XLIV, 64; *(1850)*, XLVIII, 119
Connecticut, U.S.S. *(1799)*, XXXI, 173; *(1801)*, XXIII, 217; *(1863)*, XXI, plate XXVI; *(1864)*, XVII, 256
Connecticut. *See* Shipping
Connecticut Assembly, XXXI, 131
Conner, Commodore David, XXX, 47
Conner, Fox, XXXIV, 265
Connolly, James B., XXV, 62, 65, 234; *Canton Captain*, reviewed, II, 349
Connolly, James B., and Albert Cook Church, *American Fishermen*, reviewed, I, 181–182

Connor, Master Commandant David, XLVII, 29
Conover, Commander Thomas A., XLVI, 252; XLVII, 30
Conqueror, bark (1866), I, 114
Conqueror, barkentine *(1942)*, VII, 296
Conqueror, galley *(1779)*, VI, 101–107
Conqueror, steamship *(1864)*, VIII, 233
Conquest, schooner (1804), VII, 317
Conrad, bark *(1863)*, XV, 295
Conrad, clipper ship *(1863)*, XXVI, 98
Conrad, Joseph: The Making of a Novelist, by John Dozier Gordan, reviewed, I, 411
Conro, Isaac, XXV, 125
Conroy, Edward, XXX, 276
Consequa Pan Zhangyao (P'an Chang-yao), Chinese merchant, XLVIII, 243 ff.; list of loans to Americans, XLVIII, 259; portrait of, XLVIII, 244
Consequa's letter to Peter Dobell, 1812, photo of, XLVIII, 253
Conshohoken, steamship *(1921)*, XXXV, 121
"Consistent Captain," by Captain Edgar K. Thompson, U.S.N.R. (ret.), XXVII, 110
Consolation, steamship (1873), XVII, 141; XVIII, 68
Consolidated Steamship Co. of Charleston, IX, 44, 47
Consort, H.M. destroyer *(1949)*, XLIX, 208 ff.; L, 291 ff.
Constable, Lieutenant D. C., XX, 161–163
Constance, Danish caster (1723), XXXIII, 16
Constance, steamship *(1864)*, VIII, 233
Constance, yacht *(1892)*, XXXVI, 236
Constance Chandler, steamship *(1929)*, IX, 226
Constantia, brig *(1827)*, VI, 17
Constantine, pilot launch, XXIV, 189 n.
Constantine, C. P., XXXVI, 248
Constantine, Captain John A., XXIV, 186 ff., plate 21
Constantine, Grand Duke, Vice Admiral, XXXI, 55
Constant Warwick, ship *(1648)*, XI, 6
Constellation, sailing yacht *(1964)*, XXIV, 231
Constellation, schooner *(1889)*, XXX, Pictorial Supplement, plate VI
Constellation, ship *(1815)*, XL, 39 ff.; *(1853)*, XVII, 21
Constellation, steamship *(1836)*, XVIII, 275, 289, 290, 296; XX, 86, 89 n., 102; *(1837)*, VII, 65
Constellation, U.S. frigate (1797), VII, 253–260; VIII, 8, 75; XVIII, 183; XX, 140; XXXVI, 207 ff., 276 ff.; XXXIX, 30, 235 ff., plates 9, 10, 11, 12; XL, 23 ff.; *(1798)*, XXXI, 173, 184; XXXIII, 64
Constellation, U.S. frigate (1799), XXII, 267, 268; XXIII, 58; XXIV, 246; XXV, 29; *(1799)*, III, plate 2; V, 156; *(1812)*, XLVI, 114, 147; XLVII, 28; XLIX, 43; L, 60 ff.; *(1813)*, XLI, 85; XLII, 109, 284; XLV, 36, 94
Constellation, U.S.S., XXVII, 36 n., 142, 147, 148, 158, 175; XXIX, 70, 110; XXX, 124, 128
Constellation Question, The, by Howard I. Chapelle and Leon D. Polland, reviewed, XXXII, 71–72
Constitución, Venezuelan schooner *(1842)*, XXX, 261 ff.
Constitucion, steamship *(1861)*, XI, 281

Constitution, billethead attributed to, Pictorial Supplement, XXXVII, plate XXXI
Constitution, gunboat *(1812),* XLIII, 264; XLIV, 171; XLV, 5, 175
Constitution, Pacific Mail steamship *(1861),* XLVIII, 120
Constitution, schooner, XXI, 100; *(1877),* XVIII, 193, 194
Constitution, ship (1850), III, 262
Constitution, sloop, XXI, 104
Constitution, steamship (1832), VII, 47, 57; (1837), VII, 65; *(1839),* XVIII, 294; XX, 80, 89 n., 268
Constitution, steamship *(1817),* XVI, 36
Constitution, steamship (1861), X, 130
Constitution, U.S. frigate *("Old Ironsides")* (1797), III, 227; IV, 8, 217–223; VII, 167–168, 240–241, 253, 316; VIII, 75; XXI, 70, 131, 134 ff.; XXII, 155–156, 269, 270; XXIII, 38, 58, 73, 83; XXIV, 174 n., 176, 180 n., 181, 182; XXV, 29–33, 60, 110, 159, 161, 167; *(1798),* XLVI, 147 ff.; XLVII, 14, 169 ff.; photo of Cornè painting of, XLVI, 160; XXXVI, 187, 219, 257 ff., Pictorial Supplement, plate III; XXXVII, 28 ff.; XXXVIII, 61 ff.; XXXIX, 30; XL, 212; *(1799),* XV, 264; XVII, 73; XVIII, 183; XX, 135; *(1812),* Pictorial Supplement, XXXI, plate VII; XXXII, plates XXI-XXVI; XXXIII, 77; XXXIV, 127; XXXV, 228
Constitution, U.S. frigate, trailboards from, Pictorial Supplement, XXXVII, plate XXXII
Constitution, U.S.S., XXVI, plate 19; XXVII, 29, 41 n., 135–149, 288–289; XXVIII, 69; XXIX, 70, 187; XXX, 56, 121, 124, 125; boats of *(1800),* XXV, 30, 31, plate 1
Constitution, U.S.S. [replica] *(1926),* XV, 95
Constitution and *Guerriere,* sketch of action, XLVII, 15
"*Constitution* in the Quasi-War with France: The Letters of John Roche, Jr., 1798–1801," Edited by Christopher McKee, XXVII, 135–149
"*Constitution's* 1812 Guns, The," by M. V. Brewington, VII, 240–241, 316
"*Constitution's* Not So Tattered Ensign," by Dr. Whitney Smith, XXXVII, 128–137
Constitution Wharf, Boston (MA), XXV, plate IV
Consul, brig, XXV, 186
Consul, ship *(1861),* XI, 281; XV, 122
"Consular Privateers: an account of French Privateering in American waters, The," by Melvin H. Jackson, XXII, 81–98
Contarini, G. M., XXX, 258
Conte di Savoia, Italian lifeboat *(1934),* XLVII, 51
"Contemporary Half-model of the Yacht *America,* A," by Alexander Crosby Brown, XI, 245–250
"Contemporary Reports of Confederate Privateers in *The Charleston Mercury,* 1861," document contributed by George F. Haugh, XI, 150–155
Content, sloop, XXII, 142
Contest, British brig *(1813),* XLII, 110 ff.
Contest, clipper ship (1852), I, 46
Contest, ship (1852), XIX, plate IV; *(1869),* XXII, plate XI
Contest, steamship (1859), XVI, 247; XVIII, 68; *(1864),* XLIII, 117
Continental, grain elevator *(1883),* XXXVIII, 141
"Continental Brigantine *General Gates,* The," by William Bell Clark, X, 280–287
"Continental Brigantine *Resistance,* The," by William Bell Clark, XIV, 47–60
Continental Congress, American Revolution, XXV, 35, 36, 191–193
Continental Congress, The, by Edmund Cody Burnett, reviewed, II, 350
Continental frigates, XXX, 220
Continental Iron Works, XLVIII, 119
Continental Marine Committee, XXXI, 133
Continental Navy, American Revolution, XXV, 36, 42, 189–217; XXVIII, 49–52
Continental Trading Co., VII, 77
"Contingency Planning and the Defeat of the Spanish Armada," by Ronald Pollitt, XLIV, 25–32
Contoocook, U.S.S. *(1864),* XXVII, 36 n., 39 n., 43–45
Contraband trade, XXXI, 19; XLVII, 162
Contra Costa, tanker *(1907),* XXXVIII, 198 ff.
"Contract for a Vessel Built at Kennebunk, 1773," document contributed by Kenneth Roberts, XIV, 217
"Contract for building a Bark, 1880," document contributed by John Lyman, VIII, 152–153
"Contract for building a Bark," by Basil Greenhill, XXIX, 62–63
"Contract for Building a Schooner at Annapolis, Maryland, A," document contributed by William D. Hoyt, Jr., VI, 302–304
"Contract to Build a Brigantine," document contributed by Lawrence W. Jenkins, XXI, 15
"Contract to build a Sloop in 1694, A," document contributed by George A. Nelson, II, 338
"Contributions for Robert Fulton's Heirs," document contributed by Alexander Crosby Brown, XI, 63
"Contributions to Exploration of the Salem East India Marine Society, The," by Ernest S. Dodge, XXV, 176–188, plates 17–20
Convict ships, XXX, 10, 11
Convoy, brig *(1834),* XII, 182
Convoy, schooner *(1862),* VIII, 223
Convoy SC 130, L, 219 ff.
Convoy T.M. 1, map of, L, 43
Convoys. See Naval convoys; World War: 1939–1945
Conway, G. R. G., VI, 91–92; contributed document, VI, 139–151
Conway Castle, ship (1866), I, 114
Cook, Alfred, XXXVI, 188
Cook, Frederick Albert, L, 35
Cook, Harold J., V, 165
Cook, Captain James, R.N., XXII, 224–225; XXIII, 125, 129, 143; XXIV, 225–226; XXV, 181, 186, 254, 297;

XVI, 281–285; XXVIII, 146–148, 151; XXX, 153, 205, 206, 211, 222; XXXVIII, 217 ff.; XLI, 123 ff.; XLVI, 28; XLIX, 151; L, 28; Pictorial Supplement, XXXII, plates XVII, XVIII, XXXII; Mentioned, XXXV, 226. *See also* Captain Cook, Captain James Cook.
Cook, James P., XVII, 46
Cook, John A., XLIV, 19 ff.
Cook, Colonel Joseph J., XXXVI, 198
Cook, Philip H., answered query, V, 24; "Salvors versus Sea," VIII, 61–69; "Some Missionary Ships in the Pacific," X, 264–279; "Surgery and Shipbuilding," VII, 318
Cook, Captain William W., XV, 232
Cooke, Captain Augustus P., XXXIII, 263
Cooke, Rear Admiral Charles M., XLII, 209
Cooke, Elisha, Jr., XXXIII, 102 ff.
Cooke, Jay, XXXIX, 103
"Cooking for the Conquistadors," query by Samuel Eliot Morison, I, 89
Cooley, Samuel J., VI, 138–139
Cooley, William Desborough, VII, 83–85
Coolidge, Calvin, XLI, 13
Coolidge, Joseph, XVII, 42
Coolidge, Joseph, Jr., XXXVIII, 102
Coolidge, Lee, XXXVI, 247
Coolies (Chinese laborers), XIX, 227; XX, 209; XXVI, 189. *See also* China
"Coolies in the Ship *Rhine*," by Captain P. W. Robertson, XIX, 227–231
Coolie Steamers, XXVI, 189–192
Coolie trade, XIX, 227–231; XX, 211–216
Cooling, Benjamin Franklin, *Gray Steel and Blue Water Navy: The Formative Years of America's Military-Industrial Complex 1881-1917*, reviewed, XLII, 67–68
Coombe Dingle, steamship *(1920)*, XIV, 126, 135
Coombs, William, XLVI, 155
Cooney, Jerry W., "Doing Business in the Smuggling Way: Yankee Contraband in the Río de la Plata," XLVII, 162–168; "Trials of a Yankee Sailor: Robert Gray in the Río de la Plata, 1798–1802," XLIX, 272–277
Coonley, Howard, XXXII, 170
Coons, James, VII, 159
Coontz, Admiral R. E., XXXV, 119
Coontz, Robert E., L, 53 ff.
Cooper, British ship *(1858)*, XLIII, 274 ff.
Cooper, Lord Anthony Ashley, XXX, 82
Cooper, Benjamin, XL, 30
Cooper, Captain Edward, XXVI, 9, 11, 203
Cooper, Captain George H., U.S.N., VII, plate 9
Cooper, Ms. Grace R., XXXVII, 130
Cooper, James Fenimore, XXV, 61–63; XXXIX, 116; XLVI, 188 ff.; L, 60, 212
Cooper, Paul Fenimore, Jr., review by, XXVI, 73–74
Cooper, Peter, L, 204
Cooper, Reed, XXXVIII, 61

Cooper, Adjutant General Samuel, XLVIII, 91; XL, 299
Cooper, William, XL, 248
Coorong, bark *(1869)*, IV, 73
Coos Bay, wooden steamship *(1917)*, XXXV, 283
Coote, Colonel, XXXI, 46
Coote, Sir Eyre, VII, 95
Copack, schooner *(1813)*, XXII, 216
Cope, Admiral Harley F., *Command at Sea*, reviewed, XI, 299
Cope, Sir Walter, XXXI, 86
Copeland, Charles, XLV, 41 ff.
Copeland, Charles H. P., VI, 307; XI, 291; XIII, 216; XV, 248; XVII, 153, 248; XXI, 3; XXVIII, 238; contributed document, XIV, 139; XV, 232; "Jacob Spin, Ship Portraitist," XV, 81; "A Figurehead of *Talma*," IX, 72
Copeland, Charles W., V, 5; XXXVI, 177
Copeland, Royal, XLI, 117
Copeland, W., XXII, plate XX
Coppering of ships, 1763, I, 304–306
Copper sheathing, VI, 171
Coppin, Robert, XVII, 128
Coptic, steamship *(1906)*, X, 138
Coquette, schooner, XXI, 99; *(1846)*, XLVII, 121; *(1861)*, VIII, 216, 233, 236
Coquette, sloop, XXI, 97; *(1862)*, VIII, 223
Coquette, steamship, XXI, 89, 105, plate VII; *(1863)*, III, 138; *(1863)*, VIII, 207–210, 233, 236
Coquette, vessel, XXXVI, 140
Coquille, French ship *(1824)*, XXXIV, 255
Cora, bark *(1860)*, XXI, 40
Cora, schooner, XXI, 87, 92, 97; *(1862)*, VIII, 223; XII, 53, 155, 230
Cora, ship *(1869)*, III, 66
Cora, steamship *(1865)*, XII, 234
Cora A., schooner *(1889)*, I, 74–75
Cora F. Cressey, schooner *(1902)*, IV, 66–67, 68, plate 16; Pictorial Supplement, XXXVI, plate XXVII
Cora Green, hermaphrodite brig *(1875)*, XXVIII, plate XVI
Corah, schooner, XXI, 98
Coral, bark *(1861)*, XXXVIII, 83
Coral, ship *(1819)*, Pictorial Supplement, XXXIII, plate IX
Coral Sea, Midway and Submarine Actions, May 1942-August 1942, by Samuel Eliot Morison, reviewed, X, 76–77
Cora Smyser, schooner *(1864)*, XII, 230
Corbet, Michael, XXXI, 36
Corbett, Sir Julian, XLVIII, 12; XLIX, 5
Corbett, Sir Julian Stafford, XXXI, 275 ff.
Cordage manufacture, VII, 68–69
Cordelia, bark (1841), XXXVI, 255; (1849), II, 330
Cordelia, brig (1810), VIII, 169
Cordelia, H.M.S. *(1897)*, XXVIII, 88
Cordie S., two-sail bateau *(1943)*, IV, 291, 303
Cordiner, Rev. Mr., XX, 112–117

Cordova, ship (1832), IV, 51
Cordova, General, XXXVI, 91
Core, U.S. escort carrier *(1943),* XLV, 63
Corea, ship *(1861),* XV, 108 n.; XXI, 238, 256
Corea, steamship *(1865),* XLIX, 22
Corelia, schooner *(1862),* XII, 53
Corey, Ebenezer H., XXIII, 234 ff.
Corinthian, ship, XXVII, 73; (1856), XL, 120; XLI, 281
Corinthian war vessel (ca. 575), photo of, L, 197
Corinto, steamship *(1922),* X, 142, 143
Coriolanus, ship *(1861),* XI, 266, 281
Corlett, Ewan, *The Iron Ship: The Story of Brunel's SS Great Britain,* reviewed, L, 230
Corlis, Captain John, XLVI, 215
Cormoran, German raider *(1914),* XXIV, 272 ff.
Cormorant, H.M.S. (1842), IX, 63–65, plate 5; (1859), XXVII, 168, 169–172
Cormorant, ship *(1882),* XXIX, 270
Cornè, Michel Felice (artist), I, 163–164; XIII, 247; XVI, 282; XXV, 54; mentioned, XXXII, 3. Reproductions of paintings by, XLVI, 160; XLVII, 15; Pictorial Supplement, XXXII, Part I, 48–49; Part II, 124–125; Part III, 198–199; Part IV, 274–275
Cornelia, schooner, XXI, 91
Cornelisz, Jan, L, 285
Cornelius, brig, XXII, 95
Cornelius Grinnell, ship *(1846–1857),* XLII, 121 ff.
Cornelius H. Delamater Iron Works, XLVIII, 117
Cornell, Major Thomas, VI, 278 ff.; XIV, 176 ff.
Cornell, William H., VI, 280; XIV, 177, 182
Cornell's Sea Packet, edited by W. M. Williamson, reviewed, II, 188
Cornevilie, Norwegian merchantman *(1962),* XXXIX, 181
Corning, Howard, XIII, 118
Corning, Howard McKinley, *Willamette Landings,* reviewed, VIII, 159–160
Cornish, Dudley Taylor and Virginia Jeans Laas, *Lincoln's Lee: The Life of Samuel Phillips Lee, United States Navy, 1812–1897,* reviewed, XLVIII, 192
Cornubia, paddle steamship (1858), XXI, 88, 92, 106; XXV, 113; *(1862),* VIII, 223, 229
Cornwall, British ship *(1914),* XXXIII, 35 ff.
Cornwall, steamship XXII, 219; (1872), XI, 254 ff.
Cornwall Canal, VIII, 58
Cornwallis, brigantine, XXII, 90
Cornwallis, 1st Marquis, XLVI, 18 ff.
Cornwallis, Sir Charles, XXXI, 102
Cornwallis, Adm. Sir William, XLV, 97
Cornwallis, Governor, XLVIII, 28
Cornwallis, Lord, VII, 103–106; XXXVI, 68
"Cornwallis in India and the American Experience," by Franklin B. Wickwire, XLVI, 18–24
Coromandel, H.M.S., XXII, 23, 36, 37; *(1859),* XXVII, 165, 168, 171; *(1862),* XLIII, 193
Coromandel, ship *(1802),* XXXIV, 255
Coronado, XXX, 251, 259

Coronation, ship (1863), III, 67
Coronet, ship (1838), XV, 185
Coronet, sloop *(1863),* XV, 111, 127
Coronet [model], XXXVII, 172
Corporation of Shipwrights, XIII, 123
"Correction concerning *Guerriere's* Guns," by M. V. Brewington, VII, 316
"Correction of Captain Thompson's 'Haitian Harlequinade,' A," by Samuel Eliot Morison, Rear Admiral, U.S.N.R. (ret.), XXVIII, 283
"Correction on *Hero* in the Pacific," by Thomas Dunbabin, XI, 145–146
"Correction on *Pacific Queen,*" by Arthur M. Rudd, XVI, 137–138
"Corrections on Whaleships," by Charles F. Batchelder, XXVI, 217
"Correction to 'Domestic Life on American Sailing Ships,'" by Joanna C. Colcord, II, 327
Corry, H. T. L., XXXII, 240
Corry, J. P., VII, 292
Corsair, paddle steamship (1827), XXII, 8–11, 26, 42, 43
Corsair, steamship *(1844),* XVI, 160
Corsair, yacht (1930), XXVII, plate XXXII; XLIII, 3 ff.
Corse, French warship [model] (1342), XVI, 103
Corsica, steamship *(1863),* VIII, 229
Cortes, ship *(1834),* XII, 180
Cortes, steamship (1852), XIV, 200; XVII, 44, 45; XVIII, 69
Cortes, Martin, XV, 54
Cortesão, Armando, XXX, 251; Editor, *The Suma Oriental of Tomé Pires and the Book of Francisco Rodrigues,* reviewed, VI, 308–309
Corvaía, Fortunato, XXX, 267
Corwin, U.S. Revenue Cutter *(1884),* XXXIX, 7
Corwin, John A., *A Study of the Customs Service and its History,* reviewed, I, 325
Corwin, Wilbur, IV, 225 ff.
Corwith Cramer, ship *(1971),* XLVII, 206
Cory Brothers, XLVI, 105
Corypheus, yacht *(1862),* XXXVI, 200
Cosmopolite, French steamship, (1859), XXVI, 113; *(1861),* XLIII, 88 ff.
Cosmopolite, sloop *(1812),* XXI, 21
Cossack, bark *(1853),* XII, 103; *(1861),* XV, 108 n.; XXI, 239, 256
Cossack, H.M. cruiser *(1949),* L, 291 ff.
Costagliola, Michael, VII, 4; "The Canton Packet *Cohota,*" VII, 5–8, plates 1–2
Costa Rica, steamship (1863), II, 18, 76; XVII, 311, 313; X, 131, 132; XVIII, 69; *(1872),* X, 132; *(1887),* XI, 258 ff.
Costa Rica, steamship (1891), X, 137
Coste, Captain Napoleon L., XLVIII, 89
Costs of shipbuilding, IV, 50; IX, 73–74, 229–230
Cotesworth-Pinckney, privateer (1777), XIII, 47
Cottage, schooner (1831), XXIV, 58

Cotter, Charles H., *A History of Nautical Astronomy,* reviewed, XXIX, 71–72
Cotter, R. B., XLI, 190
Cottle, Jethro, XLIV, 24
Cotton, Captain C. S., U.S.N., XXV, 50
Cotton, John, VIII, 14, 20
Cotton, Captain Lester, XVIII, 275; XX, 94
Cotton Plant, schooner *(1861),* XV, 122
Cotton Plant, steamship *(1865),* VIII, 237
Couch, Lieutenant John, XIV, 216–217
Coulter, Captain Jack L. S., XLII, 186
Coulter, W. R., XXVII, plate XIII
Council for New England, XXXVII, 7 ff.
Council of American Maritime Museums (CAMM), XXXIX, 3, 58; XL, 163
Countess of Scarborough, ship, XXVIII, 196, 197, 204
Countess of Sussex Mine, photo of rock slices on Baffin Island, XLIX, 18
"Country Galley," query by Maine State Library, V, 164
County of Caithness, bark *(1902),* XVIII, 11
County of Edinburgh, ship (1885), IX, 298
County of Linlithgow, ship (1887), IV, 325; IX, 297
County of Peebles, ship (1875), IX, 297
Courier, schooner, XXI, 89; *(1862),* VIII, 223; XII, 53
Courier, ship *(1830),* XXIII, 133; *(1861),* XV, 108 n.; XXI, 256
Courier, steamship (1866), XVII, 221; XVIII, 69
Course, schooner *(1862),* XII, 54
Courser, schooner *(1862),* XXVII, 265; *(1863),* XXXIII, 53
Courser, schooner (1876), V, 86
"Court-Martial of Bowman Hendry McCalla, The," by Paolo E. Coletta, XL, 127–134
Courtney, brig *(1814),* XXI, 22
Courtney, Captain Charles, XII, 103
Courtney, E. S., XL, 43
Courtney C. Houck, schooner (1913), IV, 63, 68, plates 13, 14
Courts-martial and Courts of Inquiry, XXI, 130; XXIX, 211; XL, 127
Courts of Inquiry. *See* Courts Martial and Courts of Inquiry
Coutance, Captain R., XIII, 277
Coutts and Parkinson, XXVI, 129, 207
Cova, de la, Victor, XXX, 267
Covadonga, Chilean warship *(1866),* XXXIX, 276
Covell, William King, I, 102, 400; *A Short History of the Fall River Line,* reviewed, VII, 248–249; mentioned, VIII, 247
Coventry, H.M.S. *(1765),* XXIII, 177, 179, 180
Coventry, Henry, XXV, 286
Coventry, Sir William, XXV, 282–283
Covill, Admiral Lord, XXVII, 215, 216
Covington, whaler *(1865),* XXVII, 275
Coward, Captain Thomas, XXXI, 97

Cowden, James E. and John O'C. Duffy, *The Elder Dempster Fleet History, 1852–1985,* reviewed, XLVIII, 193
Cowhorn (boat), XII, 123
Cowie & Co., XLIII, 208
Cowley, Richard, XXIX, 59, 60
Cowper, British steamship *(1860),* XLIII, 195 ff.
Cowper, H.M.S. (ex-*Fei Seen*), XXXIV, 26
Cowper, J. C., XXII, 30, 31, 44; XXXIV, 19
Cowper, Master Commandant William, XXXIX, 34
Cox, Edward Hyde, Foreword by, *Paintings and Drawings by Fitz Hugh Lane at the Cape Ann Historical Association,* reviewed, XXXIV, 283
Cox, J. G., XXXVI, 232
Cox, James M., XV, 178
Cox, Captain Joseph, XX, 242
Cox, Midshipman William, XLIV, 172 ff.
Cox, William G., XXXII, 166
Cox & Green, schooner *(1889),* XXXVII, 86
Cox & Stevens, XXXII, plate 1
Coxe, Tench, XXVI, 178, 180, 181, 183 n.
Coxhoorn, Dutch ship *(1731),* XLVII, 245
Coxsackie, steamship (1878), XVIII, 233
Coyngham, Gustavus, XLIII, 20 ff.
Cozzins, Fred S. (artist), XXV, 59
Crabtree, Captain Agreen, XLII, 5–24
Crabtree, Eleazer, XLII, 7 ff.
Cracker State Mariner, steamship, XXXVII, 75
Craddock, George, XL, 249
Cradock, Rear Admiral Sir Christopher, XXVIII, 106 n., 107, 108, 110, 112
Craig, Captain Charles W., XXI, 105
Craig, Hardin, Jr., "Anchor to Windward: Manuals for Young Americans in the Days of Sail, An," XXX, 40–45; "Notes on the Action between *Hornet* and *Peacock*," XI, 73–77
Craig, J. E., XXXIX, 120
Craig, Captain J. W., XXI, 105
Craig, Robert, Editor, *Maritime History, Volume 1, 1971,* reviewed, XXXIII, 216–218
Craig, Captain T. W., XXI, 105
Craig, Taylor & Co., XXXVIII, 178 ff.
Craigforth, steamship (1869), XVII, 138; XVIII, 69
Craighill Board, U.S. Army Engineers, XXV, 266
Cram, R. Jackson, Jr., I, 176
Crammer, Clarkson A., "A Letter to the Editors," X, 68–71
Cramp, William, XXX, 272
Cramp, William, shipbuilder, I, 189
Cramp, William & Sons, XXXVI, 5; XXXVIII, 180 ff.
Cramp Shipbuilding Co. (Philadelphia, PA), VIII, 76
Crane, ship *(1590),* XIV, 10, 11, 17
Crane, Clinton, XXVI, plate 8
Crane, Hart, XXV, 65
Crane, Stephen, XXV, 65; XLVI, 188
Crane, Commodore W. M., XL, 41
Crane, Captain William, XLIX, 106

Crane, William Bowers, and John Philips Cranwell, *Men of Marque,* reviewed, I, 94–95
Crane, Captain William M., U.S.N., XXV, 217
Cranmer, Clarkson A., contributed document, III, 174–176; XLIX, 49 ff.
Cranwell, John Philips, I, 116 n.; VIII, 4; review by, I, 317; *Destiny of Sea Power, The,* reviewed, II, 187–188; *Spoilers of the Sea,* reviewed, I, 401
Cranwell, John Philips, and William Bowers Crane, *Men of Marque,* reviewed, I, 94–95
Crapeau, sloop *(1708),* IX, 145
Crapo, Captain Thomas, XXXVII, 207
Crapo, William W., congressman, XXV, 25, 28
Craton, Michael, XXV, 201
Craven, brig *(1789),* XLIX, 89
Craven, U.S. destroyer *(1918),* VII, 72
Craven, Lieutenant T. A. M., U.S.N., V, 121–136
Craven, Captain Thomas T., XXXVI, 192, 193; L, 51; photo of, L, 53
Craven, Midshipman Thomas T., U.S.N., XXV, 225–226
Crawford, ship *(1961),* XLI, 49
Crawford, U.S. revenue cutter *(1861),* XLVIII, 91; XLIV, 257
Crawford, Michael J., "The Navy's Campaign against the Licensed Trade in the War of 1812," XLVI, 165–172
Crawford, William H., XXXII, 265
Crawford, William H., Secretary of the Treasury, XLII, 171 ff.
Cray, Miss Elizabeth, XXXII, 4
Crazy Jane, schooner *(1863),* XII, 155
Creasey, William, XXI, 284
"Creating the U.S. Bureau of Aeronautics," by Paolo E. Coletta, L, 51–59
"Creation of the Venezuelan Naval Squadron, 1848–1860, The," by Francis James Dallett, XXX, 260–278
Creighton, Commander J. B., XXXII, 132
Creighton, Commodore John Orde, U.S.N., XXII, 70
Creighton, Margaret S.: mentioned, XLI, 164; XLIII, 83; review by, XL, 150; "The Captains' Children: Life in the Adult World of Whaling, 1852–1907," XXXVIII, 203–216
Crenks, Captain Montague E., XIV, 125
Crenshaw, schooner, XXI, 104
Creole, brig, XXI, 100; *(1861),* XI, 281
Creole, H.M.S., XXVIII, 108 n.
Creole, U.S. sidewheeler *(1841),* XXXIII, 94
Creole State, steamship *(1921),* X, 141, 142
Cresap, Logan, VIII, 62
Crescent, frigate *(1798),* XXVI, 242, 244
Crescent, H.M.S. *(1899),* XXVIII, 88, 93, 96, 97
Crescent, schooner (1904), V, 137–138, 142–144, plate 11
Crescent, ship (1826), V, 246
Crescent City, ship (1859), IV, 51
Crescent Shipyards, XXXII, 166
Crespo, President Joaquin, XXVIII, 87, 88
Cressy, H.M. cruiser, XXXVI, 43
Crest, trawler *(1910),* XLIV, 120
Crew, Randolph, XXIII, 65
Crew and Its Organization, 17th Century, XXVII, 111–114
Cricket, steamship (1861), XVII, 146; *(1862),* XLIII, 293 ff.
Cricket, steamship (ex-*Ly-ee-moon*) *(1861),* XLIX, 26
Cricket, steamship (ex-*Meelee*) (1859), XXXIV, 57
Crighton, Captain, XLV, 27 ff.
Crighton, Richard E., "The Wreck of *San Francisco,*" XLV, 20–34
Crime and Punishment at Sea, 17th Century, XXVII, 122–125
Crimean war (1853–1856), XIV, 161
    Naval operations, XXXI, 268
Crimean War, XXII, 253; XXVI, 21, 22
Criminal trial of *Neptune* sailors, Canton, 1807, photo of painting, XLVIII, 244
Crispe, William, XX, 6–13
Cristobal, steamship *(1924),* XXIV, 203
Cristobal Colon, Italian ship *(1898),* XLI, 94
Cristobal Colon, Spanish warship *(1898),* XXXVI, 264
Cristobal Colon, steamship (ex-*Bahiana*) *(1863),* XXVI, 194
Criterion, ship *(1805),* XIII, 278 ff.; X, 54, 55
Critique, schooner, XXI, 91, 97; *(1861),* XI, 281
Crittenden, Charles, XXXVII, 53
Crittenden, Charles Christopher, XXIX, 155
Crocker, Charles F., XXXI, 124
Crocker, S. Sturgis, XLVIII, 182 ff.
Crocker, U. Haskell, XXX, 93 n.
Crocker Archives, XXX, 93–101
Crocodile, H.M.S. *(1847),* XIII, 259
Crocombe, R. G. and Marjorie Crocombe, *The Works of Ta'unga: Records of a Polynesian Traveller in the South Seas, 1833–1896,* reviewed, XXIX, 290
Croft, Thomas, XXXVII, 159 ff.
Crommeline, Charles, XXXVII, 56
Crommelin & Sons, XXX, 286
Crompton, Sir Thomas, XXXI, 95
Cromwell, bark (1848), III, 68
Cromwell, Charles, XV, 62, 80
Cronan, Lieutenant Commander W. P., XXII, 260
Crone, G. R., VII, 85
Cronstadt, steamship, XXI, 94; *(1863),* VIII, 229
Crooke, Ralph, XIII, 23
Crooker, Captain Peleg, XXIII, 27
Crosby, Alexander, *The Dismal Swamp Canal,* XXXII, reviewed, 75–76
Crosby, Alfred W., Jr., "American Trade with Mauritius in the Age of the French Revolution and Napoleon," XXV, 5–17; *America, Russia, Hemp, and Napoleon: America's Trade with Russia and the Baltic, 1783–1812,* reviewed, XXVI, 222–223; "The Beginnings of Trade between the United States and Russia," XXI, 207–215
Crosby, Georgianna Livingston Smith, XXX, 294–296

Crosby, Captain John, XXX, 294–296
Crosby, Leander, XIII, 53, 55
Crosby, Commander Pierce, XVIII, 147
Cross, Austin & Ireland, XXX, 187
Cross, Charles B., Jr., *The Chesapeake: A Biography of a Ship,* reviewed, XXVIII, 295–296
Cross, Francis E., "Nootka Sound: Winter, 1788–89," XV, 205–212; "*St. Paul-Gladiator* Collision: A Personal Narrative," XX, 191–197, plates 10, 11
Cross, Captain George, XLVII, 24 ff.
Cross, Harmon S., and Florence G. Thurston, *Three Centuries of Freeport, Maine,* reviewed, I, 100
Cross, Robert, XXXVI, 258–263, 265
Cross, Stephen and Ralph, VIII, 13, 17, 20, 22–23
Cross, Reverend Wilton E., XIII, 120
Crosse, John, "Peabody Negative No. 864," XXXV, 32–35
Crossing The Equator: Sailors' Baptism and Other Initiation Rites, reviewed, XXIII, 148–149
Crossing the Line ceremony, XXIII, 148–149; XXV, 69
Crossman, Carl L., reviews by, XXXII, 69, 70; XXXIV, 202
Cross-Rip Lightship, XXXIV, 261
Cross staff, XIV, 187
Cross-Staff, XIV, 187–191, plates 23, 24; XIX, 138–140; Pictorial Supplement, XXXV, plate III
Crowe, William, XXXI, 92
Crowell, Benjamin C., XXXIII, 54
Crowell, Clement W., *Novascotiaman,* reviewed, XL, 150
Crowell, Captain J. T., XVII, 53; XVIII, 82
Crowell, Jeremiah, XXII, 234
Crowell, Captain Prince F., XXII, 241
Crowell, Prince S., XXII, 236, 241, 244, 246
Crowell, Captain Seth, XXII, 237, 241
Crowell and Thurlow fleet, IV, plate 13; V, 138
Crowell and Thurlow Steamship Co., XIII, 121
Crowley, barkentine (1873), V, 82
Crowley, Captain Arthur H., V, 138
Crown, ship *(1679),* L, 129
Crownhart-Vaughan, E. A. P., and Basil Dmytryshyn, Editors, *The End of Russian America, Captain P. N. Golovin's Last Report, 1862,* reviewed, XLI, 142–144
Crowninshield, Rear Admiral A. S., XLI, 103
Crowninshield, B. B., V, 81; *Fore-and-Afters,* reviewed, I, 181–182; XXIII, 15, plate XXVII
Crowninshield, B. W., XXXI, 287; B. W., XXXVII, 84 ff.
Crowninshield, Benjamin, XLVI, 11 ff.
Crowninshield, Captain Benjamin, XIII, 238 ff.
Crowninshield, Benjamin, Jr., XIII, 239 ff.
Crowninshield, Benjamin Williams, XIII, 236 ff.
Crowninshield, Clifford (in 1802), XXXIII, 170
Crowninshield, Francis B., XIII, 235 n., 245 ff.
Crowninshield, Mrs. Francis B., XIII, 156, 246 ff.
Crowninshield, Captain George, XIII, 235–237
Crowninshield, Captain George, Jr., XIII, 156, 235–251, plate 12; XXVI, 277

Crowninshield, Jacob (Salem merchant), XIII, 236; XXV, 8, 13, 14; XLVI, 11
Crowninshield, Captain Jacob, XVIII, 137–141; XLI, 174
Crowninshield, Captain John, XLVI, 12, 142
'Crowninshield' or 'India Wharf,' view of, XLVI, 17
Crowninshields of Salem, XXX, 292. *See also* Kronenshelt, Doctor John Kaspar Richter von.
Crowther, J. G. and R. Whiddington, *Science at War,* reviewed, IX, 156
Croyable, French ship *(1798),* XXXI, 159 ff.
Cruger, brig (1788), Pictorial Supplement, XXXII, plate VI
Cruger, John H., XXXVII, 62
Cruikshank, George (1841), Pictorial Supplement, XXXI, plates IV, XVII, XX; sketch by, XXXII, plate 6
"Cruise in the U.S.S. *Lancaster,* A," by Robert E. Johnson, XXXIII, 280–293
Cruise of C.S.S. Sumter, *The,* by Charles Grayson Summersell, reviewed, XXVI, 221
"Cruise of *Charming Peggy,* The," by James G. Lydon, XXIII, 277–284
Cruise of the Lanikai: Incitement to War, by Kemp Tolley, reviewed, XXXIV, 278
"Cruise of the Whaler *Nightingale* in 1768, The," by Kenneth Scott, XXIII, 22–28
"Cruise on the U.S.S. *Sabine,* A," by James N. J. Henwood, XXIX, 102–105
Cruiser, H.M.S. *(1740),* XXVI, 38
Cruiser, ship, XXXIV, 113
Cruiser's Manual, The, by Carl D. Lane, reviewed, IX, 306
Cruising Cookbook, The, by C. McKim Norton and Russell K. Jones, reviewed, IX, 306
Cruizer, H.M.S. (1732), XIII, 179
Cruizer, sloop, XXVI, 47
Crul, Rear Admiral W., XXXVI, 166–168
Crumlin-Pedersen, Ole and Max Vinner, *Sailing into the Past,* reviewed, XLVIII, 205
Crummell, Alexander, XXXV, 200
Crump, H., XXXVI, 235
Crusader, bark *(1860),* XXXVI, 185
Crusader, ship *(1840),* XXXV, 261
Crusades, XLVI, 77
First (1090–1099), XXXVI, 88
Crusoe, ship (1828), IV, 235–236
Cruzier, H.M.S. *(1730),* XXI, 266, 267, 268
Crystal Palace, ship (1854), III, 314–326; IV, 31–44, 324–325, plate 7; V, 175; VIII, 61; *(1864),* XXVIII, 122
Cuba, schooner, XXI, 99; *(1862),* XII, 54; *(1874),* IX, 229
Cuba, ship (1872), IV, 243
Cuba, steamship, XXI, 90, 93, 96; *(1861),* XI, 280, 281; XII, 54, 155; XIII, 293; *(1920),* X, 142

Cuba, History, Insurrection (1865–1878), XXXVIII, 233. *See also* Shipping
Cuddalore, vessel *(1759),* XXX, 201
Cuffe, Paul, XXXV, 198
Cuffe, Captain Paul, XXIII, 192 ff.
Cufic, steamship *(1900),* XIV, 123
Cuillouette, David, IV, 307–308
Cull, Captain H., XLIII, 91 ff.
Cullie, French ship *(1800),* XXXI, 174
Culpepper, schooner *(1861),* VIII, 216
Cumberland, bark (1852), III, 73
Cumberland, H.M.S., XXVI, 37
Cumberland, ship *(1819),* XLI, 286
Cumberland, ship *(1861),* XI, 266, 281
Cumberland, steamship *(1864),* XII, 230
Cumberland, steamship (1884), XXVIII, 124; XXXIII, plate 2, 90, 94; Pictorial Supplement, XXXIV, plate XVIII
Cumberland, U.S.N. training ship (1904), XXXIII, 63
Cumberland, U.S.S. *(1860),* XXXVI, 490; XXXVII, 283; *(1861),* XLIX, 114 ff.; *(1862),* XX, 160
Cumberland, U.S.S. (1903), XX, 143
Cumberland, U.S. Sloop-of-war *(1862),* XXII, 253; XXIII, 203, 261; song about, XXV, 57
Cumberland and Oxford Canal, VIII, 175
Cumberland Blaze, British ship *(1738),* XLVIII, 23
Cum Fá or Cum Fa, steamship (1856), XVII, 144; XXII, 32, 33, 39, 42, plate 2; *(1858),* XXXIV, 18 ff.
Cumloden Castle, ship *(1861),* XI, 281
Cumming, William P., *British Maps of Colonial America,* reviewed, XXXVIII, 73
Cummings, Captain, XXIX, 263
Cummins, J. S., Editor, *The Travels and Controversies of Friar Domingo Navarrete 1618–1686,* reviewed, XXIII, 290
Cunard, Samuel, XXXVII, 231 ff.
"Cunard Cocktails in 1847," by Walter M. Whitehill, XVII, 68
Cunard Line, I, 80
Cunard Steamship Co., XLII, 295
Cunard Steamship Line, ship of, Pictorial Supplement, XXXIV, plate XXXII
Cunha, George M., query by, VII, 319
Cunningham, schooner *(1777),* XLIII, 24
Cunningham, A. and C., II, 271 ff.
Cunningham, Admiral Arthur B., XLII, 208
Cunningham, Consul General, XXXVII, 200
Cunningham, Edward, XVI, 169, 244, 245, 247, 249; XXX, 158; XXXIV, 49
Cunningham, Edwin S., XXXVII, 193
Cunningham, Captain John A., XVI, 172; XVIII, 82
Cunningham, P., XXVII, 280
Cunningham, Captain Robert B., XXI, 143
Cunningham, Stanley, II, 271; "The *Great Eastern* Temporary Steering Gear," IV, 69–71
Cunningham, Captain T., XVII, 227 ff.; XVIII, 82
Cunningham, T. B., XVI, 244

Cuppage, G. V., XXXVI, 241
Curaçao, steamship (1825), IX, 256–258, plate 25
Curityba, steamship (1887), XXXV, 205
Curlew, H.M.S., XXII, 45; *(1833),* XXXV, 92
Curlew, schooner *(1838),* XIV, 192; *(1862),* XII, 54
Curlew, steamship *(1862),* VIII, 223
Curling, Captain Robert, XXVI, 32
Curling, William,, XXVI, 203
Curling, Young & Co., XXXV, 251
Curragh or coracle, Irish vessel, XLV, 225
Currency. *See* Bank notes
Currents. *See* Ocean currents
Currier, tanker (1910), XXXVIII, 199 ff.
Currier, Albert C., XVII, 115
Currier, Charles, XVII, 119
Currier, Captain Charles, XVII, 125
Currier, John, Jr., XVII, 114
Currier, N., XXVII, 260, plate 10
Currier, Nathaniel, XVII, 120
Currier and Ives (lithographers), XXV, 59; XXX, 219
Curry, Captain William, XVI, 169; XVIII, 82
"Curtall," query by Edwin C. Rich, II, 174
Curtis, Edith Roelker, "Blood is Thicker than Water," XXVII, 157–176
Curtis, Edward G., query by, V, 246
Curtis, George H., "Americus Vespucius Symmes and the North Greenland Expeditions of Robert E. Peary, 1891–1895," XXXVIII, 41–51
Curtis-Dunn Marine Industries, Inc., XVII, 172, 175
Curtiss, Glenn, XXXVII, 112 ff.
Curwen, John Christian, XXIX, 57
Curwin, Captain Samuel R., XVIII, 82
Curzon, Lord (British Secretary of State), XXXIV, 160 ff.
Cusacke, Captain, XXIX, 277
Cushing, Caleb, XLI, 28; XLVI, 37
Cushing, Honorable Caleb, XXXI, 185
Cushing, John G., XVI, 173
Cushing, John P., XLVI, 216
Cushing, Pyam, XIII, 120
Cushing, Thomas, VIII, 13, 17, 20, 22–23; XL, 267 ff.
Cushing, Lieutenant William B., XVIII, 142–148
"Cushing on Shokokon," by Gershom Bradford, XVIII, 142–148
Cushman, Mrs. Danièle, XXXVII, 156
Cushman, Captain Frederick, XXXIX, 86
Cushman, Robert, XIV, 7
Custis, Daniel Parke, L, 18
Custis, Edmund, VII, 268; L, 18 ff.
Custis, Major General John, II, L, 18
Custis, Thomas, L, 24
Customs administration, United States, XX, 243
    California (San Francisco), XXXIII, 258
    Massachusetts, Colonial period (ca. 1600–1775), XL, 245
    New Jersey, XXXVII, 262

Customs records, I, 165–166, 167, 188, 275–294, 325, 410; II, 93
Cuthbert, Captain Albert, XXXV, 233
Cuthbertson, G. A., IV, 81
Cutler, Carl C., I, 102; III, 354; V, 286, 327; VII, 282 n., 318; IX, 148; XXV, 100; Editor, *Captain Charles Hervey Townsend: Self-Portrait of an American Packet Ship Sailor,* reviewed, I, 95; "Clifford Day Mallory, 1881–1941," I, 205–208; "Deering and Yeaton, Ship-Riggers," III, 279–291; *"Flying Cloud* versus *Andrew Jackson,"* VIII, 325–326; *Greyhounds of the Sea,* reviewed, XXII, 73–74; "The last whale-ship *Charles W. Morgan,"* I, 391–393; "Old Light on the New Light," VIII, 328–330; *Queens of the Western Ocean,* reviewed, XXII, 73–74
Cutler, Mrs. Carl C., VII, 39 n., 282
Cutler, Captain Charles B., XLII, 65
Cutler, Major Enos, IX, 186, 205
Cutler, John, Jr., XXX, 58, 60
Cutler, Thomas H., XVII, 115
Cutter, schooner *(1779),* XXXIX, 214
Cutts, Captain Oliver, XVI, 64
Cutty Sark, ship, XXII, 212; XXX, 223; XXXV, 33; *(1913),* XLI, 130; *(1955),* XV, 171
Cutty Sark, *Her Designer and Builder Hercules Linton, 1836–1900, The,* by Robert E. Brettle, reviewed, XXX, 223–224
"Cutty Sark: *The Ship and the Model, The,* by C. Nepean Longridge, reviewed, XLIV, 280
Cutwater, ship (1861), III, 69
Cuyahoga, steamship (1854), XVIII, 69
Cuyamaca, tanker (1920), XXII, plate 8, 162, 170, 182
Cuyler, U.S.S. *(1861),* XXXVI, 187
Cuyler, Henry, XXXVII, 60
Cwm Donkin, bark *(1881),* XIV, 118
Cyane, frigate *(1821),* XLVII, 28; XLIX, 43 ff.
Cyane, H.M.S. (1796), Tables of armament, XLIX, 56, 57
Cyane, ship *(1815),* XLIV, 171
Cyane, sloop of war *(1823),* XXXII, 272 ff.; XXXIII, 42 ff.
Cyane, U.S.S. *(1820),* XXI, 28; *(1825),* XIX, 240; XXXVIII, 54 ff.; XL, 216
Cybelle, French frigate *(1804),* XLIII, 42
Cyclones, VII, 35
"Cyclone which seemed to have no center, A," by Captain J. M., Ellicott, U.S.N. (Ret.), VII, 35–38
Cyclops, sloop, XXI, 98, 100
Cyclops, U.S.S. (1910), XVI, 136–137
Cygne, French ship *(1800),* XXXI, 174
Cygnet, H.M.S. *(1765),* XXVII, 218; *(1766),* XXIII, 177, 179, 180, 181
Cygnet, schooner *(1823),* XXXVII, 241; *(1862),* XII, 54
Cynthia, steamship *(1838),* XVIII, 283, 294
Cyprian Prince, steamship *(1936),* XIV, 127, 135
Cyttie, James, XXXVII, 13
Cyypromene, ship (1878), I, 397

Czarina, bark (1859), IV, 240
Czarina, ship, XXIII, 139

D. & E. Kelley, schooner *(1874),* XV, 227–228
D. B. Warner, schooner *(1861),* VIII, 216
D. C. Hulse, schooner *(1861),* VIII, 216
D. Cavanagh, steamship (1864), XVII, 308
D. F. Keeling, schooner, XXI, 100; *(1861),* XI, 267, 282
D. H. Rivers, schooner (1890), XXIII, plates XVIII, XIX; *(1897),* XXXV, plates 3, 10
D. M. Hall, bark *(1855),* XX, 130–131
D. Rutonjee and Co., XXXIV, 46
D. Sargent, sloop *(1863),* XII, 155
D. W. Eldridge, schooner *(1861),* VIII, 217
Dabney, John B., consul, XXV, 122
Dabney, Ralph Pomeroy, XXVIII, 284–286
Dabney, Samuel Wyllys, XXVIII, 284
Dacia, freighter (1915), XXXIII, 191
Da Costa, Didio Iratim Alfonso, ed., *Subsidios para a História Marítima do Brasil,* reviewed, I, 325
DaCosta, Fans, XXXVI, 279
Dacotah, ship *(1861),* XLIII, 276
Dacotah, U.S. warship (1862), XXXII, 130; XXXIII, 202; XXXIV, 119; *(1863),* XIX, 56, 58, 59; XX, 161
Dacres, James Richard, XXX, 74
Dacres, Captain James Richard, XXII, 156; XLVII, 16 ff.
Daedalus, H.M.S. *(1848),* XIII, 272
Daghild, tanker *(1943),* XLIV, 54
Dagmar, bark *(1920),* XVIII, 208
Dahlgren, Commander John, XLVII, 112; XLIX, 111
Dahlgren, Rear Admiral John A., U.S.N., IX, 49–51; XXII, 262, 284 n.; XXXI, 267; XXXII, 52; XXXVIII, 107; XLII, 198 ff.
Dahlgren gun carriage, ordnance instructions, illustration, XLVII, 118
Dahlia, brig (1846), XXIV, 45, 57
Dahlia, ship *(1849),* XVIII, 311
Dahomey and the Slave Trade, An Analysis of an Archaic Economy, by Karl Polanyi, in collaboration with Abraham Rotstein, reviewed, XXVIII, 70–71
Dai Ching, steamship (1862), XVII, 147; XVIII, 69
Dailey, Daniel D., XXX, 241
Daily Life at Sea, 17th century, XXVII, 125–132
Daily United States Mail Steam Packet Line, XLVII, 35
Daintry, Michael, XXXI, 286
Dainty Kate, pinnace *(1628),* XLIX, 258
Daiquiri, Cuba, XL, plate 6
Dairy Maid, British ship *(1776),* XLVIII, 19
Dairy Maid, XXII, 95

Daisy, hermaphrodite brig *(1911)*, XXVIII, 72–73; *(1912)*, X, 77; XLV, 114
Daisy, steamship, XXIII, 88
Daisy Bell, yacht *(1896)*, XXXVI, 239
Daisy Boynton, brig, XXVIII, 123
Dakota, ship (1881), II, 335; XXVII, plate XVII
Dakota, steamship *(1873)*, X, 132
Dakota, steamship (1904), III, 187 ff., plate 26; XLVII, 199
Dakotah, ship (1851), III, 63
Daland, Tucker, XXI, 296
Dalbek, bark *(1917)*, XVIII, 162, 163, 165, 170
Dale, U.S.S. *(1844)*, XVI, 235; XX, 137; *(1851)*, XXXVIII, 61; *(1864)*, XXVII, 36
Dale, U.S. sloop-of-war *(1847–1848)*, V, 121–136; *(1861)*, XXXI, 261
Dale, John B., XLVII, 173
Dale, Mate Richard, XXV, 255 ff.
Dale, Commodore Richard, XXVI, 252; L, 245 ff.
Dalgren, John A., XXXVI, 100
Dalhousie, steamship (1819), VI, 196
Dall, Captain Christopher C., XVII, 45; XVIII, 82; XLIII, 93 ff.
Dall, William Healy, XXXIX, 11
Dallas, U.S. revenue cutter (1845), VIII, 148; XXIV, 8 ff.
Dallas, Alexander, XXXIII, 232
Dallas, Barnes, XLIII, 111 ff.
Dallas, Commodore A. J., XL, 42
Dallas, Pearson & Co., XLIII, 111 ff.
Dallett, Francis James, "The Creation of the Venezuelan Naval Squadron, 1848–1860," XXX, 260–278
Dallett, Francis James, Jr., "William A. K. Martin: Philadelphia Marine Artist," XVI, 233–242
Dallett, John, and Co., XVI, 241
Dallett & Bliss, XXX, 277
Dalmas, Louis, VII, 276
Dalrymple, Alexander, XXII, 224; XXV, 177, 254, 258–259; XXVIII, 151; XXX, 200–216
Dalrymple-Hay, Lieutenant Colonel, D.S.O., XXIX, 123
Dalton, General A. C., XLI, 13
Dalton, Adj. General Samuel, XXXIII, 268
Dalton, Tristram, XXIX, 204
Dalzell, George W., *The Flight From the Flag*, reviewed, I, 183–184
Dampier, Captain William, VII, 84; XXI, 159; XXV, 252, 254; XXVII, 227; XXX, 300
Dan, barge (1828), V, 301
Dan, steamship *(1862)*, XII, 54
Dana, Amos Dwight, XXX, 298
Dana, Charles A., XXXV, 63
Dana, Francis, VII, 200; XXI, 211
Dana, James Dwight, XLIX, 151
Dana, Captain Luther, I, 163–164; query by Richard W. Hale, I, 171

Dana, Richard Henry (1815–1882). *See: Two Years Before the Mast*
Dana, Richard Henry, XVII, 196; XXV, 62; XXX, 43, 300; XXXV, 58; XXXVII, 179; XXXVIII, 104; XLII, 57; XLIV, 5; "Journal of a Voyage from Boston to the Coast of California," edited by James Allison, XII, 177–185; and XIII, 54, 162–176
Dana, Wheeler and Bartlett, XXVIII, 121
Dana & Co., XLVII, 106
Dandolo, Austrian warship *(1866)*, XXXIV, 59
Dane, Dana, and Co., XIII, 122
Danells, XXX, 260
Danenhower, Charles, XXVI, 105
"Dangerous Sport: A Boston Boy's Life at Sea, 1820–1837, A," by Alan Rogers, L, 211–218
Dang Wee, steamship (1861), XVII, 306; XVIII, 69
Daniel Barnes, ship *(1870)*, XXXVIII, 211
Daniel Drew, steamship (1860), XIV, 164, 177, 178, 280, 282
Daniel Elliott, bark (1854), IV, 239
Daniel Grant, ship *(1849)*, XLV, 124
Daniel Marcy, ship (1863), III, 288–289
Daniel Ripley and Co., XXII, 168
Daniel S. Grice, sloop *(1863)*, XII, 155
Daniel S. Miller, steamship, XVIII, 225
Daniel S. Williams, Jr., schooner (1877), I, 70
Daniels, Captain E. T., XXI, 105
Daniels, Josephus, XXX, 138
Daniels, Josephus, Secretary of the Navy, XXXII, 161; XXXV, 288; XXXVII, 32, 112; XXXVIII, 7 ff.; XL, 62; XLIII, 273; XLVII, 255; L, 51
Daniel Townsend, schooner *(1861)*, XI, 281
Daniel Webster, schooner (1834), XXIV, 58
Daniel Webster, ship *(1846–1857)*, XLII, 121 ff.; *(1851)*, XXVII, 63
Daniel Webster, ship (1850), III, 169; XV, 141
Daniel Webster, steamship (1833), VII, 52, 55, 57, 62; VIII, 37; *(1840)*, XX, 82 n., 92
Daniel Webster, steamship (1851), XIV, 201
Daniel Wood, ship *(1852)*, XXI, 114
Danish Settlements in West Africa, 1658–1850, by Georg Nørregård, reviewed, XXVIII, 70–71
Danmark, training ship *(1964)*, XXIV, 79
Danmark, U.S.C.G. *(1943)*, XX, 143 n.
Danmark (ex-*No. 61*, ex-*C.S.S. No. 61*), Danish armored frigate (1864), XXIX, 8, 27, 28; deck plan and profile, XXIX, plate 4
Dann, John C., editor, *The Nagle Journal: A Diary of the Life of Jacob Nagle, Sailor, from the Year 1775 to 1841*, reviewed, L, 65
Dannemarie, auxiliary (1917), XXXII, 14 ff.
Dannoura, Battle of, XXVIII, 206–221
Danskammer Point, VI, 285 ff.
Danske bådtyper (Wooden Boat Designs), by Christian Nielsen, reviewed, XLII, 307
Darby, Vice-Admiral George, R.N., VII, 99, 102 n., 103
Darby, John, XXI, 131

Dardanelles, Cruise of S.M. U-21, XXXVI, 33–44
Darden, Genevieve M., *My Dear Husband*, reviewed, XLI, 70
Dare [The], steamship (1863), III, 137; *(1864)*, VIII, 233
Dare, William, XIII, 17
Daredevil, log canoe (about 1880), IV, 249
Daring, ship (1855), III, 70
Darley, James M., and Melville Bell Grosvenor, *National Geographic Atlas of the World*, reviewed, XXIII, 288
Darling, Jeremiah (insurance inspector), I, 43
Darlington, concrete tanker (1920), XXII, 172, 182
Darlington, steamship *(1859)*, VII, 119; *(1862)*, XV, 116, 126
Darmstaedler Bank, barque, XXI, 98; *(1861)*, XI, 281
Darnell, Henry, Jr., queries by, I, 171–172; IV, 77
Dart, schooner *(1787)*, XXXIII, 31; *(1861)*, XI, 281; XII, 54, 155
Dart, yacht, XXI, 95, 101
Darter, Lewis J., Jr., I, 177; "Federal Archives Relating to Matthew Fontaine Maury," I, 149–158; review by, II, 349
Darwin, Charles, XXXVII, 246; XLVI, 61; XXVIII, 151
Darwin, Thomas L., XXXVIII, 237
Dash, schooner (1813), VI, 226
Dasher, H.M.S. *(1943)*, XLV, 59
Dashiell, Lieutenant, XXXVIII, 53
Dashing Wave, brig *(1863)*, XII, 155
Dashing Wave, ship (1853), XIX, plates XII, XXV
Datetree, Algerine ship (1678), XXIII, 109
Dauntless, schooner *(1887)*, XXVI, 165
Dauntless, schooner (1898 or 1899), XII, 142–147, plate 13; XXVI, plate XIV
Dauntless, ship *(1874)*, VII, 39–41
Dauphin, ship *(1785)*, XLI, 215
Dauphine, galley [model], XVI, 101
Davenport, Reverend Addington, XVI, 88
Davenport, Grindrod & Patrick, XXVI, 207
Davenport, Captain Henry Kollack, XXXII, 205
Davenport, Louis, VII, 43
Davenport, W. S., query by, VIII, 154
Davenport, William, XLVI, 261
Davenport, William (of Philadelphia), Pictorial Supplement, XXXV, plate XVI
Davenport & Co., XXVI, 207
David, Andrew, Rudiger Joppien and Bernard Smith, *Charts and Coastal Views of Captain Cook's Voyages: The Voyage of the* Endeavor, *1768–1771* (The Hakluyt Society Extra Series No. 43), reviewed, XLIX, 318
David, Dr. Charles W., XXV, 99, 100
"David Bates Douglass' journal: . . ." edited by S. W. Jackman, XXIV, 280–293; correctional note to, XXV, 111
David Brown, ship (1874), XXXIII, 285
David Cohen & Co., XXXII, 27
David Crockett, schooner, XXI, 93, 102, 106; *(1862)*, VIII, 223
David Crockett, steamship (1834), VII, 53
David Dollar, ship *(1927)*, XVIII, 216
David Dows, barkentine (1881), I, 75; V, 137
David Faust, schooner *(1861)*, XI, 282
David G. Floyd, schooner, XXII, 149
David Kimball, bark (1853), IV, 243
David O. Saylor, concrete ship (1943), XXII, 175, 176
David Porter, packet schooner (1821), XXII, 234, 236
David Porter, schooner, XXIV, 131, 134, 141
David R. Greene & Co., XXI, 111
David Sassoon, Sons and Co., XXXIV, 18 ff.; XLIII, 100 ff.
Davidson, David, V, 28
Davidson, James, VIII, 303, 320–321
Davidson, Smith and Venner, VIII, 303, 321
David Torrey, schooner (1873), I, 65
Davie, William, XXXVI, 60
Davies, Captain David, XXXIV, 43
Davies, P. N., *The Trade Makers*, reviewed, XXXV, 218
Davis, Abner C., XXXIII, 54
Davis, Benjamin P., XVII, 119, 120
Davis, Captain, XXXI, 97
Davis, Commander C. H., XV, 102
Davis, Charles G., *How to make Ship Block Models*, reviewed, VII, 172
Davis, Charles H., U.S.N., XXIX, 125; XXXVI, 197
Davis, Captain Charles H., XIX, 267; XXI, 240
Davis, Commander Charles H., XXXI, 256; XXXII, 50; XXXV, 61
Davis, Rear Admiral Charles H., U.S.N., XXV, 130, 131, 133, 134, 136, 139
Davis, Lieutenant Commander Cleveland, XXXVII, 120 ff.
Davis, Captain Cornelius, XXIII, 13
Davis, Senator Cushman K., XXV, 264
Davis, Dennis J., *The Thames Sailing Barge, Her Gear and Rigging*, reviewed, XXXII, 144–145
Davis, Francis, VII, 207
Davis, G. H., XXXII, plate 8
Davis, Gartner & Webb, VIII, 133
Davis, George, XXVIII, 135; XXX, 74
Davis, Harold, "Shipbuilding on the St. Croix," XV, 173–190.
Davis, Henry Winter, XXXV, 58
Davis, Hugh H., "The American Seamen's Friend Society and the American Sailor, 1828–1838," XXXIX, 45–57
Davis, Isaac P., XXV, 32, 33
Davis, Captain J. L., XLVII, 181 ff.
Davis, Jefferson, XXVII, 237–239; XXIX, 5; XXXVI, 254
Davis, John, XIII, 22, 25; XIV, 190; XXXV, 21
Davis, Judge John, XXV, 29, 32, 33
Davis, Captain John, XVII, 28, 29; XXI, 107–109
Davis, Senator John, XLVII, 87
Davis, Hon. John A., XXXI, 188
Davis, Rear Admiral John L., XXIX, 114

Davis, Karel A., "Finding Longitude at Sea by Magnetic Declination on Dutch East Indiamen," L, 281–290
Davis, Phineas, X, 172–173, plate 22
Davis, Rear Admiral, XXVIII, 104
Davis, Richard Harding, XXXVIII, 157 ff.
Davis, Samuel, XL, 248
Davis, Captain Soloman, XIX, 138
Davis & Lewis, XXVIII, 38
Davis-Douglas Co., XXXVII, 115 ff.
Davison, Captain Elias, II, 276–277
Davison, Captain John, v. 255 ff.
Davis Palmer, schooner (1905), V, 80
Davis Quadrants: (made by James Halsey), Pictorial Supplement, XXXV, plate III; (made by John Gilbert), Pictorial Supplement, XXXV, plate IV
Davisson, William, XXXVII, 50
Davisson, William I., and Marshall Smelser, "The Longevity of Colonial Ships," XXXIII, 16–19
Dawes, Senator Henry L., XXV, 264
Dawkins, Henry (engraver), XXV, 126
Dawn, steamship (1858), XXXIX, 92 ff., plate 1
Dawpool, ship (1880), VIII, 330
Dawsett, Captain Samuel J., XIV, 44
Dawson, Edward G., associate editor, and Roger J. Spiller, editor, *Dictionary of American Military Biography, Volumes I–III,* reviewed by Colonel Roger Willcock, XLV, 257–267
Dawson, Georgina, "Edward Wright, Mathematician and Hydrographer," XXXVII, 174–178
Dawson, Robert, XIV, 52
Day, Vice-Admiral Sir Archibald, *The Admiralty Hydrographic Service 1795–1919,* reviewed, XXXV, 67
Day, Johan, XXXVII, 157
Day, John, XXX, 258; XXXIII, 174
Day, Ramdollay, XXII, 197, 203
Daybreak, steamship (1872), XVII, 218
Daydream, steamship (1891), XI, 219
Dayes, Mr. *See* Davis, (Judge) John, XXV, 32
"Day in Port, A," by Captain Edgar K. Thompson, U.S.N. (ret.), XXV, 50
Daylight, bark (1902), IV, 326
Daylight, barkentine (1942), VII, 294
Daylight, steamship (1860), XXXIX, 93 ff., plate 1
Daylight, tanker (1943), XLIV, 51 ff.
"Days' Runs of American-Built Ships and Their Commentators, The," by D. L. Dennis, XXVI, 157–170
Dayton, Lieutenant Henry, Continental Marines, XXV, 213
Dayton, William L., XXIX, 167 ff.
DC. *See* Washington (DC); District of Columbia (US)
Deacon, Richard, XVII, 47, 50; XXXIV, 44
Deadeye: How it Was Made in Nova Scotia, The, by John M. Kochiss, reviewed, XXXII, 74–75
Dead Sea, U.S. Naval Expedition to, IV, 71–72

Dead Whale or a Stove Boat, A, by Robert Cushman Murphy, reviewed, XXVIII, 72–73
Deal, Captain James, XLVI, 53
Dean, Nicholas, reviews by: XLIII, 313; XLV, 136; XLVI, 201; XLIX, 236
Dean Brothers, XLVII, 93
Deane, American frigate (1777), XXXI, 244
Deane, French frigate (1778), XLIV, 169
Deane, frigate (1778), VII, 212; X, 285; (1779), XXXVII, 303
Deane, Sir Anthony, XIV, 265 ff.
Deane, Barnabas, VIII, 14; XXXI, 134
Deane, Charles, XIII, 58
Deane, E. B., XXXVI, 241 ff.
Deane, Jimmy, XXXVI, 244 ff.
Deane, Silas, VIII, 14, 19; XXX, 220; XXXI, 134, 241; XXXVI, 81, 161
Dean Emery, tanker (1940), XLVII, 52
Deane's Doctrine of Naval Architecture, 1670, by Brian Lavery, reviewed, XLII, 66–67; reviewed again, XLVIII, 198
De Angelis, Captain Pascal, VI, 78–79, 136
Dean Richard, steamship, (1901), XIV, 287
Dean Richmond, steamship, XVIII, 224, 225
Dearborn, Henry, XXVIII, 35, 36, 37, 39; XXX, 282; XXXVI, 64
Dearborn, Major General Henry, VI, 257 ff.
Dearborn, Captain Henry C., XVIII, 83
Dearborn, Captain Thomas, XVI, 163, 253; XVII, 298; XVIII, 83
Dearborn, Captain Thomas W., XXII, 17
Dear Sarah: New England ice to the Orient and other incidents from the Journals of Captain Charles Edward Barry to his wife, by Norman E. Borden, Jr., reviewed, XXVII, 72
Death at Sea, 17th century, XXVII, 121–122
Death of Captain James Cook, oil on copper, Pictorial Supplement, XXXII, plate XXXI
de Avilés, Pedo Menéndez, XXIII, 81
De Bary Line, VII, 133, 156
Debbie and Jo-Ann, fishing vessel (1963), XLI, 58
de Beaumarchais, Caron, XXV, 191
De Berenger, G. (1818), XXXI, Pictorial Supplement, plate V
de Bisschops, Eric, XXIII, 118, 127
Deblois, Gilbert and Lewis, XL, 267
Deborah Jones, schooner (1861), VIII, 216
de Bouille, Marquis, XXXIV, 230
De Bruls, Michael (engraver), XXV, 126
Debucca (Boké), XXX, 182
de Bussche, E. M., XVII, 48, 56, 58, 61, 62
de Bussy, Marquis, XXXI, 44
Decade, French ship (1800), XXXI, 174
DeCamp, Commander J., XXXVI, 48
Decatur, ship (1815), XL, 39 ff.
Decatur, sloop of war (1859), XXXII, 277 ff.
Decatur, steamship (1864), XXXIX, 96

Decatur, Lieutenant James, XXI, 134
Decatur, Stephen, XXVI, 253, 254; XXVIII, 38, 116; XXIX, 191; XXXVII, 131; XXXIX, 111; XL, 39, 215; XLIII, 252; XLIV, 172 ff.; XLVI, 156 ff.; XLVII, 20; L, 245 ff.
Decatur, Commodore Stephen, XXXI, 179; L, 245 ff.
Decatur, Captain Stephen, Jr., U.S.N., XXI, 133; XXV, 159
Deccan, steamship *(1886)*, XL, 115
Deceada, schooner, XXI, 90; *(1861)*, XI, 282
Decie, Henry Edward, XXVII, 233 ff.
"Deck and interior plan of the New Bedford whaling bark *Alice Knowles*," Pictorial Supplement, XXXI, plate XXIX
"Deck and interior plan of the New Bedford whaling schooner *Amelia*," Pictorial Supplement, XXXI, plate XXIX
Decker, Robert Owen, *Whaling Industry of New London, The*, reviewed, XXXVI, 144
"Deck Heights in the Early Seventeenth Century," by William A. Baker, XXII, 99–105
Deck Seamanship, by Colin Jarman, reviewed, XL, 234
"Decline of the Overseas Station Fleets: The United States Asiatic Fleet and Shanghai Crisis, 1932, The," by Stephen S. Roberts, XXXVII, 185–202
"Decline of the Port of Boston," lecture by Stewart Frank, Mystic Seaport, comment, Editorial, The American Neptune, 3–4
Decoration of ships. *See* Ship Decoration
DeCosta, Benjamin F., L, 9 ff.
Decree of Rambouillet, 1810, XXX, 285
Dedatus, ship (1792), XXXIII, 168
Dee, C.S.S. *(1863)*, XXIII, 225 ff.
Dee, steamship, XXI, 86, 87; (1832), IX, 262; *(1863)*, VIII, 229, 233
Deepwater Family, by Fred B. Duncan, reviewed, XXX, 222–223
Deer, steamship *(1865)*, VIII, 236
Deerhound, steam yacht *(1864)*, XIX, 127; XXVII, 267, 268
Deering, Clement, XX, 249
Deering, G. G., V, 138
"Deering and Yeaton, Ship-Riggers," by Carl C. Cutler, III, 279–291
Deering-Donnell Shipyard, XXVII, plate XVI
Deering Shipyard, XXVII, plate XXXI
Deer Island, schooner, XXI, 97; (1861), XI, 282; XII, 54
Defence, brig (1776), XXXIX, 196
Defence, Navy ship *(1776)*, XXIX, 288; XXXIV, 136
Defence, sloop (1744), XXXI, 133
"*Defence* and *Hichinbrook*," by R. C. Anderson, XIII, 212
"*Defence*, A Vessel of the Navy of South Carolina," by Harold A. Mouzon, XIII, 29–50
Defender, yacht *(1914)*, XXXVI, 247, 248
"*Defense*, A Historic Time Capsule," note by Dean R. Mayhew, XXXV, 142
Defense, schooner *(1775)*, XIII, 29–50, 212
Defense Creek, Shanghai, XXX, 157 ff.
Deffaudis, Baron, XXXVI, 127
Defiance, brig (1824), XXIX, 124, plate IX
Defiance, brigantine *(1777)*, XXXIX, 212
Defiance, H.M.S. *(1807)*, XIV, 91
Defiance, schooner *(1862)*, XV, 126
Defiance, schooner (1884), XXIV, 60
Defiance, ship (1590) XXII, 101
Defiance, sloop (1765), XXIX, 159, 160
Defiance, steamship *(1865)*, XXXIV, 38 ff.
Defiance, yacht *(1895)*, XXXVI, 238
Defiant, ship (1875), IV, 241
Defince [sic.], brig *(1778)*, VII, 205
Defoe, Daniel, XXX, 300; XXXVII, 41
DeFontaine, W. H., and Ernest A. Ratsey, *Yacht Sails*, reviewed, VIII, 260
Defy, schooner, XXI, 100; *(1864)*, XV, 129
De Genouilly, Admiral Girault, XXVII, 163
DeGraaff, Johannes, XXXVI, 157–160
de Grasse, Admiral Comte, VII, 105
de Guichen, Admiral Comte, VII, 99
Deguid, Captain James Alexander, XXI, 90
Dehnkamp, Burgermeister Willy, XXVII, 261, 262, plate 12
Dei Gratia, brigantine *(1872)*, I, 310; II, 250, 255, 256; X, 191, 195 ff.
Deitsch, Alan, XVIII, 3
de Jong, Cornelis, Frederick P. Schmitt, and Frank H. Winter, *Thomas Welcome Roys: America's Pioneer of Modern Whaling*, reviewed, XLI, 144–145
de Jong, Nicholas J. and Marven E. Moore, *Launched from Prince Edward Island: A Pictorial Review of Sail*, reviewed, XLII, 222
De Kalb, steamship *(1861)*, VIII, 216
DeKalb, U.S.S. (1861), XIX, 266
DeKalb, U.S.S. (ex-*Prinz Eitel Friedrich*), XXVIII, 108 n.
DeKay, Commodore George, XIII, 252–267, plate 13
DeKay, Commodore George Coleman, VI, 6–18, 84–85; VII, 175–176, 189 ff.
DeKay, James Ellsworth, VII, 182, 189 ff.
de Kerguelen, Y. J., XLI, 281
de Labourdonnais, Mahé, XXXI, 108
Delage, Peter, XXXVII, 59
Delamater, C. H., & Co. XXXIX, 101
Delamater Iron Works, I, 53; XLVIII, 116
de la Motte, Comte Picquet, VII, 99
DeLancey, Stephen, XXXVII, 56
Delaney Forge and Iron Co., XLVIII, 109 ff.
Delano, Captain Amasa, XXV, 61
Delano, B. F., XXXIX, 244 ff.
Delano, Paul, XXIX, 208
Delano, Samuel, XIV, 29, 30
Delano, Warren, VII, 249
Delano, Warren, American Vice-Consul at Canton, XXXI, 184
Delano, Warren, Jr., XVI, 244; XXXIV, 49

Delanoy, William C., XXXIII, 184
Delanty, Lieutenant Commander H. M., U.S.N.R. (ret.), *Along the Waterfront,* reviewed, IV, 340
Delap, Captain, XXXI, 36
de la Piedra, Captain Philipe, XXIII, 281
Delarof, steamship *(1929),* XVI, 131
de la Roncière, Charles, XXXI, 280
Delaware, brigantine *(1777),* XX, 47
Delaware, frigate (1817), XXXV, 240
Delaware, schooner *(1821),* L, 211 ff.
Delaware, steamship (1833), VII, 52, 62
Delaware, U.S. frigate (1776), VIII, 11, 12, 21, 25; XXI, 76
Delaware, U.S.S. *(1798),* XXXI, 173; XXXIV, 137
Delaware, U.S. ship-of-the-line (1820), XXI, 144–145; XXV, 161
Delaware, U.S. warship *(1833),* XXX, 56
Delaware, warship *(1917),* XL, 51 ff.
Delaware (I) and *Delaware* (II) *(1959),* XLV, 84
Delaware (DL), History, Colonial period (ca. 1600–1775), XL, 7
Delaware, Lackawanna & Western Railroad, XLVII, 193 ff.
"Delaware, The Bay and River of," chart, XXV, 46–49, plate 2
Delaware, University of, XIV, 4
Delaware and Hudson Canal, The, by Edwin D. LeRoy, reviewed, XI, 230–231
Delaware and Hudson Canal Co., XIV, 162
Delaware and Hudson Coal Co., XLVIII, 112
Delaware and Raritan Canal Co., XLVIII, 118
Delaware & Raritan Canal: A Pictorial History, The, by William J. McKelvey, Jr., reviewed, XXXVII, 70–71
Delaware Bay and the Chesapeake, Map of 1781, I, plate facing 142
Delaware River Iron Shipbuilding & Engine Works, XXXVIII, 176 ff.
DeLeon, Jose Rams, XXXVI, 12, 15
Delesdernier, schooner *(1800),* XXVIII, 115, 118
Delgado, James P., "In the Midst of a Great Excitement: The Argosy of the Revenue Cutter *C. W. Lawrence,*" XLV, 119–131; "Steamers to Savannah: The Origins and Establishment of the New-York and Savannah Steam Navigation Company," XLVII, 33–44
Delia, schooner *(1865),* XII, 234
Delia Hodgkins, schooner *(1879),* XI, 116
Delight, schooner, XXVIII, 114; *(1861),* XI, 282
Delight, ship *(1632),* XXIII, 64
Delilah, by Marcus Goodrich, reviewed, I, 189
Del Norte, schooner, XXIV, 58
Delphina, schooner *(1865),* XII, 234
Delphin group of U-boats *(1942),* L, 45
Delta, half brig *(1861),* XI, 282
Delta Queen, steamship, XXXVI, 8
Delucena, Abraham, XXXVII, 56
Delure Co., Paris, ring dial by, Pictorial Supplement, XXXV, plate XVII

Democracía, Venezuelan schooner *(1848),* XXX, 266
Democratie, auxiliary (1918), XXXII, 14, 30
Demologos, U.S. steam frigate (1814), IV, 327–328; VI, 239, 253–274; (1815), XX, 167
Denbigh, steamship, XXI, 92, 95, 96; *(1861),* XI, 271; XII, 230, 234
Denby, Charles, XXXIV, 216; XL, 102
Denby, Edwin, Secretary of the Navy, XXXVII, 118 ff.
Denis, Nicolas, VIII, 290–291
Denman, Admiral, XXXII, 246
Denman, William, XXXII, 156 ff.; XXXV, 276 ff.
Denmark, bark (1835), V, 147
Denn, Job, XXXVI, 255
Dennet, Captain, XXXII, 36
Dennet, Jeremiah, XLVI, 169
Dennett, Joseph Millard, XV, 213
Denning, William, VII, 206–207
Dennis, D. L., contributed note, XXIV, 212; "The Days' Runs of American-Built Ships and Their Commentators," XXVI, 157–170
Dennison, Joseph, VII, 42
Denny & Co., XXVI, 24; XLIII, 187 ff.
Dennys, Captain John, XXIII, 64
Dent, Captain Digby, XXI, 262
Dent, Lieutenant E. F., XXII, 36
Dent, Julia, XLIII, 179
Dent and Co., XVI, 164, 254; XVII, 298–301; XXII, 11, 13, 225; XXVI, 13, 118, 119, 194; XXXIV, 37; XLIII, 87 ff.; chronometer by, XXXV, plate XX
D'Entrecasteaux, Rear Admiral B., XXX, 214
d'Entrecasteaux, Chevalier, XXI, 197; XXV, 260
D'Entrecasteaux lslands, boats of, XIII, 96
Denver, cruiser *(1921),* XXXV, 121 ff.
DePauw, Linda Grant, XLIV, 149
Dependant, bark (1847), VI, 80
De Pere, steamship (1873), I, plate facing 73
dePeyster, Abraham, XXXVII, 56
"Deposition of Nelson Tefft and Others of the Whale-Ship *Brooklyn,* 1847," document contributed by E. Lee Dorsett, IX, 228–229
Deptford Dockyard, XI, 14; XLVII, 8 ff.
Derby, ship *(1805),* XXV, 183
Derby, ship (1855), III, 170; IV, 37; XIX, plate XXXI
Derby, Elias Hasket (Salem merchant), IV, 18 ff.; V, 43 ff., 278 ff.; XIII, 235; XXI, 214; XXII, 197; XXV, 7, 8; XLI, 168; XLV, 153 ff.; XLVI, 9 ff.; XXIX, 205
Derby, Captain Elias Hasket, Pictorial Supplement, XXXII, plates XIII-XV
Derby, John (of Salem), XXXIII, 161 ff.
Derby, Jonathan, IV, 19 ff.
Derby, Richard, XLVI, 9 ff.
Derby, Captain Richard, XXI, 9, 10
Derby, Captain Samuel, XXV, 184
Derby, Captain Samuel G., XLVI, 53
Derelict ships, X, 191

"Derelict *William and Jane* of Wiscasset, The," document contributed by Grahame Farr, XXXI, 288–289

Der Grosse Adler, ship, XV, 273

D'Erneville, Pierre, XXX, 184

DeRochemont, C. H., XVII, 115

DeRochemont, G. W., XVII, 115

DeRoos, Lieutenant Frederick Fitzgerald, R.N., XXI, 57–69

Derrick, Captain J., XVIII, 83

Des Barres, J. F. W.; mentioned, XL, 5

Des Barres, Joseph F. W., XXV, 241

Descelier map, XXX, 259

Descriptions of Many Northern and Southern Lands and Seas in the Indies, Specifically of the Discovery of the Kingdom of California (1632). By Nicolas de Cadona, by W. Michael Mathes, reviewed, XXXV, 215

Deserters, X, 43–51

Deshon, John, XIV, 51; XX, 46; XXXI, 239; XLII, 28

"Design of the American Frigates of the Revolution and Joshua Humphreys, The," by Howard I. Chapelle, IX, 161–168, plates 17–19

"Designs of Our First Frigates, The," by M. V. Brewington, VIII, 11–25

Desire, schooner, XXI, 99

Desiree, schooner *(1861),* XI, 282

Des Moines, cruiser *(1921),* XXXV, 122

Desolation Island (Indian Ocean), Discovery and exploration, XLI, 280

DeSoto, merchant steamship, XXXII, 48

De Soto, ship (1858), II, 332

Despatch, pilot schooner *(1814),* XLII, 105 ff.

Despatch, steamship, XXI, 94; *(1862),* VIII, 202, 229; *(1873),* XXXVIII, 239 ff.

Despatch, U.S. steam-yacht *(1875),* XXXIII, 293

Desperate, H.M.S. *(1862),* XXIV, 209, plate 24

Despite, minesweeper *(1942),* XXXVIII, 274

d'Estaing, Comte, VII, 96 n., 98 n., 99 n., 100 n.

d'Estaing, Admiral Comte, XXV, 189

Destiny of Sea Power, The, by John Philips Cranwell, reviewed, II, 187–188

D'Estrees, French cruiser *(1907),* XXIX, 129

Destroyer, torpedo boat *(1869),* XLVIII, 127

Destroyer (ship type), XLVI, 240

Destroyer from America, by John Fernald, reviewed, II, 342–343

"Details of the Late Yankee Victory off Labrador – 1782," by Samuel W. Bryant, XXIX, 211–223

de Ternay, Admiral, XXXI, 244

Detiene, Diego, XXX, 253

DeTousard, Louis, XXXVI, 279, 286

Detroit, barge *(1919),* XXXII, 11

Detroit, ship *(1812),* XLIV, 171

Detroit, ship (1855), III, 63; *(1874),* XXXIII, 285

Detroit, steamship (1833), VII, 52

Detroit, U.S. cruiser (1895), XL, 106; *(1896),* XXIX, 116

Detroit, U.S.S. *(1862),* XX, 165

Detroit Public Library, II, 335

Detwiler, S. B., query by, I, 90

Deutschland, German battleship *(1939),* XXXII, 100 ff., plate 8

Deutschland, German submarine *(1916),* XLVIII, 57

Devaney, Francis, XXXV, 200

Devany, F., XXXVII, 57

Devastation, H.M. ocean-going ironclad (1873), XLIX, 117

Deveaux, Colonel Andrew, British Army, XXV, 203

"Development of the Port of Los Angeles," by John H. Krenkel, XXV, 262–273

Devereaux, Captain James, XLVI, 51

Devereux, Captain James, XXV, 180

Devil Himself: The Mutiny of 1800, The, by Dudley Pope, reviewed, XLIX, 235

Deville, Captain W. U., XVIII, 83

de Villiers, Sir John A. J., VII, 85

Devlin, Jones F., Jr., "A Look at the American Merchant Marine of the Last Fifty Years," XXIX, 231–243

Devon, steamship, XXII, 219; (1878), XI, 256 ff.

Devonshire, ship *(1869),* XLIV, 9 ff.

de Wesenbeck, A. de B., *The Centenary of the Ostend-Dover Line,* reviewed, VIII, 261

Dewey, Admiral, XXIX, 39 ff.; XXXII, 262

Dewey, Charles, XXXVII, 26

Dewey, Edward, XXXVII, 38

Dewey, Admiral George, U.S.N., II, 140, 152–153; IV, 337

Dewey, Commdore George, XXXV, 183; XXXVI, 262; XXXVII, 26 ff., XL, 171 ff.

Dewey, Rear Admiral George, XLI, 93 ff.

Dewey, Susan G., XXXVII, 38

Dewhurst, Henry, XXXIV, 67

De Windt, Heyliger, X, 72

DeWindt, J., Jr., XXXVI, 157

De Witt, Clinton F., III, 253; V, 165

De Witt, Richard V., XXVII, 13, 15, 19, 21, 23

De Witt Clinton, steamship, XXVI, 74; (1836), VII, 61; *(1836),* XVIII, 275, 282, 298; XX, 86, 89 n., 96, 97

DeWolf, James, XXI, 16

DeWolf, Captain John, XIX, 13, 14, 39

DeWolfe, sloop, XXIV, 134

De Wolfe, Captain Samuel, XLI, 125

Dexburgh, James R., XXXVI, 190

Dexter, ship (1867), V, 152

Dexter, Ralph A., "A Century of Fishery Biology at Cape Ann, Massachusetts," XLV, 81–85

Dexter, Ralph W., "Cape Ann Visits of the Great Sea-Serpent (1639–1886)," XLVI, 213–220; "Essex County and the Development of American Marine Biology, XLIX, 34–38; review by, XLIX, 318

Dexter, Samuel, XLVI, 217

Dexter, Captain Samuel F., XXI, 90

Dexter, Thomas A., XXIII, 46 ff.

Dey, Ramdoolal, Calcutta, XXXI, 39; XLVI, 15
Dhow (boat), IX, 87; XI, 161
Dhow (Indian vessel type), XLV, 226
"Dhow Sailor, The," by Richard LeBaron Bowen, Jr., XI, 161–202
Dhows of Eastern Arabia, IX, 87–132
Dialogue, John, billethead copy, XXXVI, 53; Pictorial Supplement, XXXVII, plate XXXII
Diamond, H.M.S., XXVIII, 103
Diamond, ship *(1805)*, XLI, 285
Diamond, sloop (1817), XXII, 216
Diamond, steamship *(1863)*, XV, 127
Diamond, Sigmond, "Norumbega: New England Xanadu," XI, 95–107
Diamond Cement, steamship (1920) (ex-*Eastern Coast*), XXIII, 276
Diamond Cove, West Highlands, 1839, XXIX, plate XXX
Diamond Head, steamship *(1927)*, IX, 224
Diamont, sailing vessel (ex-*St. Patrick*, ex-*John Bell*) *(1875)*, XXVI, 133
Diana, brig *(1823)*, XXVII, plate IX; *(1834)*, XII, 182
Diana, frigate (1783), VI, 170; *(1854)*, XXXI, 268 ff.
Diana, H.M. paddle steamship (1823), XXII, 5, 6, 42
Diana, hermaphrodite brig *(1848)*, XXX, 266
Diana, schooner, XXI, 93; *(1802)*, XIII, 277; *(1862)*, XII, 54
Diana, ship *(1799)*, XV, 153; XXIII, 217; *(1800)*, X, 53; XVII, 66; XIX, 133; *(1802)*, XXIII, 217; *(1804)*, XLIII, 43
Diana, sloop *(1791)*, XXVIII, 32
Diana, steamship *(1821)*, XVI, 159; XVIII, 69; *(1863)*, XII, 155
Diana, whaler *(1847)*, XLI, 291
Diane, French ship *(1800)*, XXXI, 175
Diane, paddle steamship *(1829)*, XL, 289
Diantha, bark (1834), XXV, 18 n.
Diary of a Voyage to China, A, 1859–1860, by Rev. Young J. Allen, reviewed, IV, 256
"Diary of Our Trip to the U.S.A., July 1913," document contributed by The Reverend Lionel R. Lawrence, Sr., XXVI, 280–282
"Diary of S. H. Brown[e] Aboard the Blockade Runner S.S. *Dee*," document contributed by Forrest R. Holdcamper, XXIII, 225–227
Dias, Joseph, XIII, 119
Diaz-Torrens, Dr. Kisardo, XXXVI, 11
Dibblee, Albert, XIII, 122
Dicatator, steamship *(1871)*, VII, 132, 137
Dick, Colonel Samuel, XXXIX, 212
Dick, Captain Thomas, XX, 84, 262
Dickens, Charles, VII, 84
Dickenson, Thomas, XII, 223
Dickerson, Mahlon, XXXI, 138
"Dickie Brothers of San Francisco in 1881," document contributed by John Lyman, II, 74–76

Dickinson, A. B., "Southern Hemisphere Fur Sealing from Atlantic Canada," XLIX, 278–290
Dickinson, Caleb, XX, 12–16, 21
Dickinson, Emily, XXV, 63
Dickinson, John, XXXI, 236
Dickinson, William, XX, 19 ff., 31–32
Dickison, Captain J. J., VII, 124
Dickman, Howard L., "Captain James A. Whipple: Marine Salvor, Engineer, and Inventor," XXXIV, 89–102
Dickson, Captain E. B., XLIX, 32
Dictator, clipper *(1863)*, XLV, 192
Dictator, ship (1854), XV, 178; *(1865)*, XXVIII, 122
Dictator, U.S. monitor (1862), X, 19, 27, 29, 32; *(1864)*, XVI, 54; XXVII, 37, 42, 44; XLVIII, 123
Dictionary of American Fighting Ships, Volume III, by Naval History Dir., Office of the Chief of Naval Operations; foreword by Paul H. Nitze, preface by Rear Admiral E. M. Eller, reviewed, XXIX, 74–75; Vol. 4, XXX, 224
Dictionary of American Military Biography, Volumes I–III, Edward G. Dawson, associate editor, and Roger J. Spiller, editor, reviewed by Colonel Roger Willcock, XLV, 257–267
Dictionary of American Naval Fighting Ships, by U.S. Navy Department, reviewed, XXIV, 149
Dictionary of American Naval Fighting Vessels, reviewed, XX, 147
Didon, French frigate *(1804)*, XLIII, 42
Diehl, Hugh, XXXVI, 241–243, 245
Diericks, Captain Charles, XXI, 90
Dies, John, XXV, 123
Dieskau, Baron Ludwig von, XXII, 122, 125, 127
Dietz, Anthony G., "The Use of Cartel Vessels During the War of 1812," XXVIII, 163–194
Diez de Junio. See as *10 (Ten) de Junio*.
Diez y ocho de Julio. See as *18 (Eighteenth) de Julio*.
Digby, Sir John, XXVIII, 249, 250, 251, 252
Digby, Sir Kellam, XXIII, 65, 66
Digby, Rear Admiral Robert, R.N., VII, 99
Dignon, John, XIV, 244
Dilemma, sloop yacht (1891), I, 400; II, 94
Dilemma, by Clifford D. Mallory, Alexander C. Brown, and others, reviewed, II, 94
Diligence, brigantine *(1776)*, XX, 45
Diligent, brig *(1778)*, VII, 203
Diligent, sloop *(1779)*, XXXVII, 293
Diligente, French ship *(1799)*, XXXI, 173
Dill, A. T., Jr., query by, II, 174
Dill, Joseph H., XXVIII, 179, 180 n., 183 n.
Dillend, Captain Nathaniel, XXIII, 27
Dillingham, John, XXII, 241
Dillion, Sidney, XXXI, 124
Dillon, Captain Peter, XXI, 179 ff.
Dillon, Richard H., contributed documents, XI, 155–156; XIV, 216–217; XIX, 126–128; "'Breadfruit Bligh': Bligh Papers in the Banks Collection," XII,

253–270; *Embarcadero*, reviewed, XX, 72; "Two Drawings by Bligh of *Bounty*," XI, 146–147
"Dimensions of our First Frigates," document contributed by William Bell Clark, XXI, 76
"Diminutive Side-wheelers," query by Charles P. Burgess, IX, 74
Dinant, 1870, photo of, L, 169
"Dinner Hour on Board a Ship at Gravesend," XXXI, Pictorial Supplement, plate VI
Dinsmore, tanker (1920), XXII, 162, 171, 172, 182
Diomede, British frigate *(1782)*, XXXIX, 169
Diomede, H.M.S. *(1863)*, XXV, 23
Dione, yacht *(1900)*, XXXVI, 240, 241, 244–246
Dione, yacht (S. Crocker) (1964), XLVIII, 184
Diplomats, United States, XLII, 301
"Dipping Lug, The," by Richard LeBaron Bowen, Jr., XX, 273
Dipsey, fictitious submarine *(1947)*, XX, 174–176
Direct, minesweeper *(1942)*, XXXVIII, 274
Director, Canadian ship *(1894)*, XLIX, 278
Director, schooner, XXI, 94; *(1862)*, XII, 54, 155
Dirego, schooner *(1857)*, XXXVI, 256
Dirigo, four-mast bark (1894), XXVII, plate XII
Dirigo, ship *(1912)*, photo of, XLVI, 189
"Disappearance of U.S.S. *Cyclops*," by J. W. McElroy, XVI, 136–137
"Disaster in the South Seas: The Wreck of the Brigantine *Eliza* and the Subsequent Adventures of Captain Corey," by James B. Hedges and Jeannette D. Black, XXIII, 233–254
Disasters: I, 108–115, 138–140, 393–394; II, 36–38, 44–55, 79–80, 243–245, 251; IV, 318–323; V, 40–41, 157–162, 286 ff.; VI, 218–222, 223–227, 247–251, 271, 285–287; VIII, 61–69, 163–164, 173–174, 184–190, 242–245, 288, plate 20; IX, 68–70, plate 6; X, 134, 138, 142, 191–202. Burning of packet ship *Boston*, XXV, plate I; Shipwreck on "Alcohol Rocks," XXV, plate V; Sinking of steamship *Arctic*, XXV, 79–80; Wreck of the Brigantine *Eliza*, XXIII, 233–254
Discipline. *See* Punishment
Discombe, Reece, XXI, 201 ff.
Discoverer, ship *(1602)*, L, 9; *(1603)*, XXXIV, 233
Discovering a Historic Wreck, by Keith Muckleroy, reviewed, XLII, 227
Discovering Ship Models, by Norman Boyd, reviewed, XXXII, 287
Discovery, Captain Cook's ship *(1870)*, L, 128
Discovery, H.M.S. *(1776)* XXVIII, 146, 147; XXXV, 71; *(1778)*, XXXVIII, 217 ff.
Discovery, light-vessel *(1821)*, V, 246
Discovery, pinnace (1603), XXXIV, 233; *(1607)*, X, 5–14, plates 1–3, 5; XIV, 106; XVII, 173–180
Discovery, pinnace [replica] (1956), XVII, 179 ff., plates 15, 18, plans, 176
Discovery, ship *(1622)*, XVII, 132
Discovery, ship *(1793)*, XVII, 67; *(1794)*, XLI, 225
Discovery, XXX, 302

Discovery of Ship Models, The, by Norman Boyd, reviewed, XLVII, 59
Discovery of Tahiti, The, edited by Hugh Carrington, reviewed, IX, 154
"Discovery of the Solomon Islands, 1568," document contributed by G. R. G. Conway, VI, 139–151
Disease and Sickness at Sea, 17th Century, XXVII, 117–122
Diseases, tropical, XXX, 175
Dismal Swamp Canal, VII, 66, 240–242. *See also* Canals.
"Dismal Swamp Canal, The," by Alexander Crosby Brown, V, 203–222, 297–310; VI, 51–70, plates 3–8
Dismal Swamp Canal, The, by Alexander Crosby Brown, reviewed, XXXII, 75–76
Dismal Swamp Steam Transportation Co., VI, 61–62, plate 3
"Dismission of Captain Isaac Phillips, The," by Michael A. Palmer, XLV, 94–104
"Disorderly Voyage of the Brig *Betsey*, The," III, 19–25
Dispatch *(1801)*, XXIII, 217; *(1802)*, XXIII, 217
Dispatch, brig (1815), XIV, 39; (1818), XIV, 39
Dispatch, brig, Pictorial Supplement, XXXII, plate VI
Dispatch, British sloop *(1746)*, XLVIII, 26
Dispatch, ship *(1778)*, XXXIX, 202
Dispatch, steamship (1883), VII, 147, 148 n.
Dispatch, steamship *(1814)*, XVI, 36
Dispatch, steamship (1842), XX, 250; (1847), XXIV, plate XXIII
Disraeli, Benjamin, XXXIX, 291
Distant Dominion: Britain and the Northwest Coast of North America, 1579–1809, by Barry M. Gough, reviewed, XLII, 144–146
Distant Water: The Fate of the North Atlantic Fisherman, by William W. Warner, reviewed, XLIV, 139–140
Ditchburn and Mare, XXVI, 18, 207
Divers, Biography, XXXIV, 89
Divine, A. D., *In the Wake of the Raiders and The Merchant Navy Fights*, reviewed, I, 101
Divine service, XXV, 28
Diving Bell, VII, 261
Diving, History, VII, 261; XXXIV, 89
Dix, John A., XLVIII, 89
Dixie, auxiliary cruiser *(1898)*, XXXIII, 277; XLI, 98
Dixie, schooner *(1861)*, VIII, 216, 223; XI, 152; XLIV, 258
Dixie, ship *(1903)*, XXXVII, 254
Dixie, steamship, XXI, 96; *(1861)*, VIII, 217; XV, 99, 115, 117, 122
Dixie, yacht *(1906)*, XXXVI, 244, 246
Dixmude, auxiliary schooner (1917), XXXII, 31
Dixon, George, XXXVIII, 223
Dixon, Rear Admiral Sir Manley, L, 30 ff.
Dixon, Robert B., XXXIV, 70
Dixon, Roland, XXIII, 114
Dixon, William, XIII, 22, 27
DL. *See* Delaware

Dmytryshyn, Basil and E. A. P. Crownhart-Vaughan, Editors, *The End of Russian America: Captain P. N. Golovin's Last Report, 1862,* reviewed, XLI, 142–144

Doña Janauria, Brazilian warship *(1863),* XV, 296 ff.

Doña Januaria, corvette, XXII, 50, 51

Doane, Bishop, XXV, 246–247

Doane, John, XXXIX, 221

Doars, schooner *(1862),* VIII, 224

Dobbin, U.S.C.G. *(1876),* XX, 143 n.; *(1926),* XLVI, 240 ff.

Dobbin, J. C., Secretary of the Navy, XXXIX, 247

Dobbin, James C., XXXI, 59

Dobbins, James C., Secretary of the Navy, L, 109

Dobell, Peter, XLVIII, 253 ff.

Dobson, Captain Man, XLV, 96

Dock, Karlskrona Navy Yard, VI, plate 25

Doctor, British ship *(1778),* XLV, 248

Doctor, coaster *(1840),* XXXVIII, 60

Doctor Bunting, bark (1856), VI, 82

Doctor Kane of the Arctic Seas, by George W. Corner, reviewed, XXXIII, 304–305

Documents, XXI, 73–76, 303–304; XXII, 142–144, 219–221; XXIII, 143–145, 225–227; XXIV, 70–72; XXV, 68–70, 144–146; XXVI, 63–71, 138–144, 210–214, 280–283; XXVIII, 66–69, 284–286; XXIX, 62–64, 133–138; XXX, 62–67, 294–296; XXXI, 186–290; XXXII, 64–68, 211–223; XXXV, 207–210; XXXVII, 66–69, 219–222

Dod, Daniel, IX, 250; XVI, 275, 277

Dod, John W., XIV, 117

Dodd, J., VII, 42

Dodds, Captain, XXXIII, 31

Dodds, James and James Moore, *Building the Wooden Fighting Ship,* reviewed, XLVI, 202

Dodge, schooner, XXI, 90; *(1864),* XII, 230

Dodge, Captain Asa, XL, 47

Dodge, Bertha S., *Marooned,* reviewed, XL, 143

Dodge, Ernest Stanley: contributed document, XV, 155; query by, I, 398; mentioned, XXIX, 3; XXX, 6; XXXIII, 4; XLIII, 244; XLV, 41; editorial comment concerning: XXXVIII, 3–4, 79–80; XXXIX, 233; XL, 83

    Editorials in *The American Neptune*: XII, 3–6, 97–98, 175–176, 251–252; XIII, 3–4, 79–80, 155–156, 233–234; XIV, 3–4, 81–82, 159–160, 235–236; XV, 3–4, 95–96, 171–172, 247–248; XVI, 3–4, 79–80, 155–156, 231–232; XVII, 3–4, 87–88, 171–172, 247–248; XVIII, 3–4, 103–104, 187–188, 271–272; XIX, 3–6, 77–78, 153–154, 237–238; XXI, 3–4, 79–80, 155–156, 231–232; XXII, 79–80, 155–156, 231–232; XXIII, 3–4, 155–156, 231–232; XXIV, 3–4, 79–80, 155–156, 231–232; XXV, 3–4, 79–80, 155–156, 231–232; XXVI, 3–4, 79–80, 155–156, 229–230; XXVII, 3–4, 79–80, 155–156, 231–232; XXVIII, 3–4, 83–84, 163–164, 237–238;

    Reviews by: I, 182–183, 404–405, 407; II, 184, 350; XIX, 307; XX, 146, 147, 275; XXII, 74–75, 151, 224–225; XXIII, 74–75, 148, 150, 151–152, 288, 290; XXIV, 149, 225–226, 226–227; XXV, 73–74, 75, 297–298, 299; XXVI, 220–221, 224, 285; XXVII, 75, 227; XXVIII, 72, 73, 146–148, 151; XXIX, 71, 75, 145, 282, 287, 291; XXX, 73, 222, 297–298, 300–301, 302, 304; XXXI, 74, 226, 291; XXXII, 148; XXXII, 137, 141, 146, 149, 150, 225, 226; XXXIII, 214, 218, 221, 222, 224, 225, 304, 307; XXXIV, 281, 284; XXXV, 67, 70, 211, 215, 217; XXXVIII, 144, 147, 149, 302, 303; XXXIX, 149, 150

Beyond the Capes: Pacific Exploration from Captain Cook to the Challenger, 1776–1877, reviewed, XXXII, 138–139; "Captain Cook's First Voyage," XVI, 281–285; "The Contributions to Exploration of the Salem East India Marine Society," XXV, 176–188, 296; "Folklore and Anthropological Literature as a Source for Maritime Historians," VIII, 150–151; *Islands and Empires: Western Impact on the Pacific and Asia, Europe and the World in the Age of Expansion,* reviewed, XXXVII, 223; "The Last Days of Coasting on Union River Bay," IX, 169–179, plates 23–24; *New England and the South Seas,* reviewed, XXVI, 147–148; *Peabody Museum of Salem Report of the Director,* reviewed, XI, 234; "Two Marine Articles in Anthropological Journals," XI, 223–224; "Two Photographs of American Naval Vessels?" XV, 81, plate 8

Dodge, Ernest Stanley, with William N. Fenton, "An Elm Bark Canoe in the Peabody Museum of Salem," IX, 185–206, plates 21–22

Dodge, Ernest Stanley, with Wendell S. Hadlock, "A Canoe from the Penobscot River," VIII, 289–300, plates 27–28

Dodge, J. T., XXVIII, plate IX

Dodge, John, XIII, 251

Dodge, Katherine M., contributed document, XVII, 69–72

Dodson, James, L, 288

Doenitz, Admiral Karl, German Commander, XLV, 50

Dogwatch and Liberty Days, exhibit at Peabody Museum, mention, XLII, 244; XLIII, 83

Doherty, Captain J. M., XXI, 90

Dohna-Schlodien, Captain, XLVIII, 50 ff.

"Doing Business in the Smuggling Way: Yankee Contraband in the Río de la Plata," by Jerry W. Cooney, XLVII, 162–168

Dolan, Charles A., XLIX, 31

Dole, George W., XVIII, 274

Dolesh, Richard, XLIII, 11 ff.

Dolland, Peter, of London, variation compass by, Pictorial Supplement, XXXV, plate XV

Dollar, J. Harold, XXXV, 175

Dollar, Robert, XXXV, 167; L, 260 ff.

Dollar Steamship Co., XXVII, 151; XLI, 114

Dollar Steamship Lines, X, 142

Dolle, Captain A. R., XVIII, 83

Dolley, Brian H., editorial comment, XXXIX, 158

Dolliver, Peter E., XIII, 54 ff.
Dolliver's Neck (MA), XXV, plate XXV
Dolly, steamship *(1862),* VI, 55; *(1865),* VIII, 237
Dolly, U.S.S. *(1800),* XXXI, 175
Dolphin, brig *(1775),* XXX, 109; *(1807),* XVI, 193; *(1821),* VIII, 173; *(1848),* XXXI, 188; XXXII, 273
Dolphin, dispatch boat *(1883),* XXXIX, 129; *(1920),* XXXV, 120
Dolphin, French ship *(1800),* XXXI, 174
Dolphin, H.M. brigantine *(1845),* XXXVI, 128 ff.
Dolphin, H.M.S. *(1764),* IV, 91–92; *(1766),* IX, 154; XXV, 297
Dolphin, mackerel clipper *(1851),* XLIV, 89
Dolphin, schooner *(1759),* IX, 144; *(1776),* XLII, 10 ff.; *(1814),* XXVIII, 118; *(1861),* VIII, 217
Dolphin, ship *(1725),* XXXVII, 266; *(1767),* XXIX, 42, 43, 148
Dolphin, ship (1846), XIX, 27
Dolphin, sloop, XXVIII, 123; *(1776),* XVIII, 132; XXXIX, 200 ff.
Dolphin, steamship (1833), VII, 50, 60; VIII, 57; *(1863),* VIII, 229
Dolphin, U.S.S. *(1826),* XLVI, 45; *(1860),* XIX, 256
Dolphin, woodboat (1838), XVII, 12
"Dolphin Striker, The," by Marion V. Brewington, XIII, 65–66
"Domestic Life on American Sailing Ships," by Joanna C. Colcord, II, 193–202, 327
Domingo Santa Maria, ship (ex-*Chancellor*) (1856), VI, 81
Dominion, H.M.S., XXVIII, 103
Dominion, steamship *(1872),* XXXIII, 89; XXXIV, 177
Dominion Atlantic Railway Co., ship of, Pictorial Supplement, XXXIV, plate XXIII
Dominion Bridge Company, Montreal, XXXII, 31
Dominion Line, XXXVII, 236
Dominion Steamship Line, ship of, Pictorial Supplement, XXXIV, plate XIX
Don, steamship, XXI, 89, 93, 100, 106; *(1863),* VIII, 229, 233
Donald, barge (1883), VI, 289
Donald, steamship (1869), XVI, 173
Donald, A. B. Ltd., XXXVI, 275
Donald, David, XXIX, 8 n.
Donald, John A., XXXII, 156; XXXV, 284
Donald Currie's Castle Line to the Cape, XXXVIII, 194
Donald McKay, ship *(1846),* XLII, 121
Donald McKay, ship (1855), III, 170
Donaldson, refrigerator ship *(1927),* XXV, 292
Donaldson, Arthur, XXXII, 250
Donaldson, Elizabeth, XXXVIII, 119
Don Antonio de Ulloa, Spanish ship *(1898),* XXXIX, 41
Donegal, steamship, XXI, 101; *(1861),* XI, 280, 282; XII, 54, 230; XIV, 62
Donitz, Karl, Grand Admiral and Commander-in-Chief of German Navy, L, 219 ff.
Don Jose, schooner, XXI, 96; *(1863),* XII, 155

Don Justo, bark (1869), IV, 240
Don Luigi Re di Portogallo, Italian warship (1864), XV, 199 ff.
Donna Forester, bateau (1911), IV, 289
Donnell, Captain Benjamin, XX, 117
Donnell Shipyard, XXVII, plate XXIV
Donnelly, Ralph W., "Gadfly on the Potomac, CSS *George Page,*" XLIII, 129–134; "Officers of the Revenue Marine Service in the Confederacy," XL, 298–304; "Revenue Marine Service: The Nucleus of the Confederate Navy," XLVIII, 87–95
Donner, Ed, XXVIII, 58
Donovan, Kenneth, "The Marquis de Chabert and the Louisbourg Observatory in the 1750's," XLIV, 186–197
Don Quijote, yacht *(1958),* XXI, 201
Don Quixote, ship (1853), XIX, 27, 28, 35, 36, plate 2
Don Quixote, ship (1868), V, 150; XIX, 39
Don Quixote, steamship (1836), VII, 61
Don't Give Up the Ship – The Eugene H. Pool Collection of Captain James Lawrence, reviewed, III, 90; III, 3–4
Doolittle, Sylvester, XVII, 93, 100
Dora, sloop (1898), XI, 92
Dorade, French ship *(1800),* XXXI, 174
Doran, Professor Edwin, XXXVII, 81
Doran, Edwin, Jr., "Commercial Sail in the Leeward Islands," XXIV, 95–108; *Wangka: Austronesian Canoe Origins,* reviewed, XLIV, 134
Dora Nelson, schooner *(1839),* VIII, 51
Dorchester, ship *(1844),* XIII, 134–139; XV, 140
Dordin, Captain Peter, XXXV, 296
Dorian, Francis, XX, 183
Dorian, Mate, XIV, 248 ff.
Doric, steamship *(1906),* X, 138
Doride, brigantine, XXIV, 216
Dories, II, 310 ff.
"Do Right and Fear No Man Dont Write and Become a Naval Officer," by Rear Admiral J. W. McElroy, U.S.N.R. (ret.), XXVI, 217–218
Doris, H.M.S. *(1814),* XXIX, 197
Doris Hamlin, schooner (1919), II, 174, 251; III, 163; *(1936),* XXVIII, 148
Doris Susan, schooner (1949), XXVI, plate XXXII
Dorothea Reeves, fishing vessel *(1961),* XLI, 53
Dorothy, yacht *(1900),* XXXVI, 240
Dorothy G. Snow, schooner (1911), XXVI, plate XXIV
Dorothy O., schooner (1922), XXVI, plate XXIX
Dorothy Palmer, schooner (1903), V, 80; XXIII, plate XVII
Dorr, Ebenezer, XIX, 133
Dorr, Captain Ebenezer, XXIX, 83
Dorr, John, XIX, 133
Dorr, Sullivan, XXIII, 212 ff.; XXXIII, 170 ff.
Dorr, Captain William, XXIII, 239 ff.
Dorrance, Judge John, XL, 196
Dorset, steamship *(1881),* XI, 257 ff.

Dorsett, E. Lee, III, 271; contributed documents, IV, 245–246; IX, 228–229; X, 298–300; XV, 232; queries by, II, 174; IV, 77; *Around the World for Seals: The Voyage of the Two Masted Schooner Sarah W. Hunt from New Bedford to Campbell Island,"* XI, 115–133; Editor, "The Journal of Voyages of the Brig *Venus* and the Schooner *Louisiana* in 1806," by George Barrell, III, 222–238; "The Killick," IX, 299–300

Dorsett, E. Lee, M. D., contributed document, XVI, 211–213; "Brig *Sarah Bentley:* An Unlucky Ship," XVI, 63–65; "Hawaiian Whaling Days," XIV, 42–46, plates 7, 8; "Letter of Marque. The Brig *Quantibaycook* of Boston, 1799," XI, 224–225; "'This Day Comes in Fine': The Log of the Brig *Selma*," XIV, 212–214; "'Two men at the Wheel,'The bark *Carlotta*, Magune, Master," XVIII, 318–319

Dorsett, Captain George, XXV, 201

Dorsey, U.S. destroyer *(1918),* VII, 72

Dorsey, Florence L., *Master of the Mississippi: The Story of Henry Shreve,* reviewed, II, 346–347

Dorsey, Lieutenant Colonel, XLIII, 129 ff.

d'Orvilliers, Comte Louis, VII, 99

Dorwart, Jeffery M., "The United States Navy and the Sino-Japanese War of 1894–1895," XXXIV, 211–218

Dosher, Captain Julius, XXI, 105

Dosher, Captain Richard, XXI, 105

Dos Reis, Manuel Jose, XXVII, 98, 102–104, 108, 109

Dotson, John E., review by, XLVII, 216; "Naval Strategy in the First Genoese-Venetian War, 1257–1270," XLVI, 84–90

Douaumont, auxiliary schooner *(1917),* XXXII, 31

Double-ender (boat), XII, 123

Double-enders, II, 311 ff.

"Double Gaff Rigs," by John Lyman, VI, 73–77

"Double National Salute, A," document contributed by Captain Edgar K. Thompson, U.S.N. (ret.), XXI, 75

Double topsail rig, I, 53

"Double Trouble: Shipwreck and Enemy Action in the Chesapeake," document contributed by William D. Hoyt, Jr., XII, 60–63

Doucey, Captain F., XXI, 90

Dougherty, wooden steamship *(1917),* XXXV, 279

Dougherty, Captain John, XXI, 90

Doughty, William, IX, 162, 167–168; X, 66; XXX, 74; XXXIV, 192 ff., XXXV, 240; XL, 211

Douglas, steamship, XXI, 104; *(1862),* VIII, 204–205, 229; *(1863),* III, 139

Douglas, Vice-Admiral Sir Archibald L., XXVIII, 98, 112

Douglas, C. L., query by, I, 310

Douglas, Captain, XXXII, 203

Douglas, Carvill, XXVII, plates IX, XIII

Douglas, James, XV, 175; XLVI, 51

Douglas, Captain James, XVI, 88

Douglas, Sir James, VII, 30

Douglas, Lewis W., XLI, 268

Douglas, Senator Stephen A., XXXVII, 276

Douglas, William, XV, 206

Douglas, Commander William, XXI, 264, 266

Douglass, David Bates, XXIV, 280 ff.

Douglass, Dr. William, XXII, 68

Douglas Steamship Co., XVII, 39, 40; XVIII, 60

Doulos, ship (ex-*Franca C.,* ex-*Roma,* ex-*Medina*) *(1914),* XXXIX, 143

Dourabeis, Anargyros, XXXVI, 17

Douro, steamship, XXI, 96; *(1853),* XXVI, 19, 20, 21, 117, 202, 203, 205, 209; *(1863),* VIII, 229

Douty, F. S., XXXI, 124

Douty, J. Frederick, "The Stability of the Ark," XXV, 261

Down Easter (boat), IV, 45

Dove, bark *(1861),* XXI, 258

Dove, French ship *(1800),* XXXI, 174

Dove, schooner *(1832),* XXXIV, 113; XXXV, 83

Dove, sloop, XXI, 89, 96; *(1862),* XII, 54

Dove (II), ship [replica] *(1934),* XIV, 108

Dover, British warship *(1760),* XLVIII, 39 ff.

Dover, H.M.S. *(1707),* XX, 112

Dover, ship *(1827),* XV, 139

Dovrefjeld, schooner *(1918),* VII, 77

Dow, Charles H., *History of Steam Navigation between New York and Providence (1877),* reviewed, II, 340

Dow, George Francis, *Whale Ships and Whaling: A Pictorial History,* reviewed, L, 138

Dow, Captain George W., XXIX, 133–138

Dow, Captain John M., XXXII, 206

Dow, Captain Leroy, XL, 108 ff.

Dow & Co., XLIII, 189 ff.

Dowes, Mowjee Huny, XXII, 241

Down-Easters, XXX, 222

"Down East Merchant Fleet, A," by Raymond H. Trott, IV, 45–52

Downes, Commodore, XXXV, 21 ff.

Downes, Captain John, XLVI, 114; XLVII, 172

Downes, Commodore John, U.S.N., XXI, 293–295; XXXI, 182.

Downie, Captain George, XXI, 50 ff.

Downie, Commodore George, XXXVI, 290

Downing, Bob, XXXIX, 255

Downing, Hon. Thomas N., XXV, 80

Down on T. Wharf, by Andrew W. German, reviewed, XLIII, 310

Downs, Arthur Channing, Jr., XXXVII, 140 ff.; "Reeve & Brothers, New Jersey Saw-Millers and Ship Builders, 1821–1859," XXXVI, 251–257

Drafting Tools, English, Instruments of Navigation, Pictorial Supplement, XXXV, plate XXVII

Draggermen Fishing on Georges Bank, by George Matteson, reviewed, XXXIX, 303

Dragnet boats, Connecticut River, I, 69

Dragon, brig *(1814),* XLII, 111 ff.

Dragon, British ship *(1606),* XLVII, 77 ff.

Dragon, H.M.S., XXVI, 59, 61

Dragon, Salem bark (1850), part of figurehead from, Pictorial Supplement, XXXVII, plate XIX; Pictorial Supplement, XXXVIII, plate XVI
Dragon, tug *(1865),* XXXIV, 38
Dragoon, ship, XXI, 97; *(1861),* XI, 282
Drake, British ship *(1778),* XLV, 248
Drake, ship, XXVIII, 196
Drake, Albert B., XXX, 24
Drake, Sir Francis, XXVII, 183–184; XXXII, 153; XXXVII, 174; XLIX, 5
Drake, Frederick C., *The Empire of the Seas: a Biography of Rear Admiral Robert Wilson Shufeldt, USN,* reviewed, XLVI, 123
Drake, Frederick W., "Bridgman in China in the Early Nineteenth Century," XLVI, 34–42
Drake, Kirby, XLVI, 165
Dravo, Francis Rouaud, XXXVIII, 272 ff.
Dravo Corp., XXXVIII, 272 ff.
Dray, schooner (1825), XIV, 39
Dray, Captain Henry, XXI, 90
Drayton, Doctor Charles, XIII, 30
Drayton, Captain Percival, XXXI, 261
Drayton, William H., XIII, 30 ff.
Dreadnaught, bark (1904), VI, 77; *(1917),* XVIII, 165, 170
Dreadnaught, Liverpool packet *(1812),* XLV, 175
Dreadnaught, packet ship (1853), I, 47; XIX, Plate V
Dreadnot, schooner *(1862),* XII, 54
Dreadnought, British battleship *(1837),* L, 33
Dreadnought, H.M. Battleship (1906), XXII, 190
Dreadnought, H.M.S. *(1904),* XXVIII, 90, 101
Dresden, German cruiser, XXVIII, 107 n., 108; XXX, 301; *(1914),* XXXIII, 36 ff.; *(1915),* XLV, 199 ff.
"Dress Ship Rainbow Fashion," by Captain Edgar K. Thompson, U.S.N. (ret.), XXX, 216
Drew, steamship, XVIII, 224, 225; (1867), III, 43
Drew, Commander Andrew, R.N., VII, 302–304, 306
Drew, Clement, XXIII, 68
Drew, Edwin C., IV, 329–334
Drew, F. Sheldon, contributed document, IV, 329–334
Drew, Ralph L., contributed note, XXIII, 68
Drewry, wooden gunboat *(1865),* XLII, 92 ff.
Dreyfus, Captain Alfred, XXVIII, 91
"Drift Voyages in the Pacific," by J. G. Nelson, XXIII, 113–130
Driggs, Dr. John, XXXIX, 19
Drinkwater, Charles, XIII, 12
Drink-Water Iron Works, XLV, 36 ff.
Drisko, Jeremiah (shipbuilder), XXIV, 38
Dristigheten, ship (1785), VI, 170
Driver, sloop *(1803),* XLIII, 42
Driver, Captain Michael, XXI, 9, 10
Driver, Captain William, XXXVII, 129
Dromo, ship *(1807),* XVI, 195
Drot, Norwegian bark *(1899),* XXXI, 146–147
Drowne, John B., XXVIII, 145
Drowne, Richard W., XXVIII, 145

Drowne, Deacon Shem, XXXIV, 200
Druid, steamship, XXI, 103, 105, plate XIII; *(1864),* VIII, 233; IX, 35, 44
Drum, Hugh A., XXXIV, 265
Drumburton, ship (1881), IX, 298
Drumcliff, bark (1887), IX, 298
Drumcraig, bark *(1896),* XVIII, 9
Drummond, B. McKillan, XXIV, plate XX
Drummond, Lieutenant Edgar, XIII, 273
Drummond, Jacob, XXXIX, 218
Drummond, Joseph T., V, 165
Drummond Castle, steamship, XXIV, plate XIII
Drunks in Gilbert Islands, IV, 115–116
Drushka, Ken, *Against Wind and Weather: The History of Towboating in British Columbia,* reviewed, XLIII, 58–59
Drusilla, sloop (1892), XXX, plate XIV
Dry, William, XXXI, 207
Dryden, Captain David M., U.S.N., XXV, 138
Dry docks, XI, 108, plates 15, 16; XXX, 56
Dry-Land "Dry-Land Terminology," query by Eldon Griffin, VIII, 154
"Dry Retort, A," document contributed by Captain Edgar K. Thompson, U.S.N. (ret.), XXII, 211
"Dry Salvages and the Thacher Shipwreck, The," by Samuel Eliot Morison, XXV, 233–247, plates, 23–26
Drysdale, Winton Roy, XXXVI, 22
Duane, James, XL, 13
Duane, William, XLVI, 7 ff.
Dublin, British ship *(1927),* XXXIX, 179
Dublin, frigate *(1833),* L, 32
DuBois, W. E. B., XXXII, 267
Dubuque, gunboat *(1894),* XXXIV, 221
Duc de Braganza, brig, XXXVI, 176
Duc de Duras, ship, XXVIII, 199
Ducey, Captain F., XXI, 90
du Chaffalt de Besné, Comte Louis, VII, 99
Duchesne, Captain, XIV, 256 ff.
Duchesne, Captain Alphonse, XX, 177–184, plate 7
Duck, brig *(1813),* XIX, 218
Duck manufactories in Salem, II, 284–285
Duddell, M. George, XXXIV, 19
Dudgeon Shoal light-vessel (1736), IV, 265, plate 46
Dudley, sloop *(1862),* XII, 54
Dudley, Governor Joseph, XXXV, 157 ff.
Dudley, Captain O'Brien, XXVI, 61
Dudley, Paul, XX, 63
Dudley, Robert, XVII, 34
Dudley, William S., and Michael A. Palmer, Dudley, William S., *The Naval War of 1812: A Documentary History, Volume I,* reviewed, XLVII, 214; review by, L, 229
Dueling, in the U.S. Navy, XXV, 141
"Duel in the Moonlight," note by Captain Edgar K. Thompson, U.S.N. (ret), XXIX, 281
Duer, William, XLVI, 28

"Duet," document contributed by Captain E. K. Thompson, U.S.N. (ret.), XXII, 220
Duff, ship *(1796),* X, 265; XXII, 74
Duff, Hugh, XXI, 113, 119
Duffie, Peter, XXX, 45
Duffield, Captain Henry, XXXI, 97
Duff Post, sloop *(1863),* XII, 155
Duffy, John O'C. and James E. Cowden, *The Elder Dempster Fleet History, 1852–1985,* reviewed, XLVIII, 193
Duffy, Stella F. and Lester J. Cappon, *Virginia Gazette Index,* reviewed, XI, 229–230
Duguid, Captain James Alexander, XXI, 90
Duhamel du Monceau, Henri-Louis, L, 132 ff.; portrait of, L, 133
"Duhamel du Monceau: *Savant* and Naval Architect," by Victor A. Lewinson, L, 132–137
DuJourdin, Michel Mollat, and Jacques Habert, *Giovanni et Girolamo Verrazano, navigateurs de François I*er*,* reviewed, XLIV, 281
Duke, frigate, XXIII, 71
Duke (The), bark *(1861),* XI, 288
Duke, Captain James, XXI, 90
Duke of Cumberland, privateer *(1744),* XLII, 46
Duke of Manchester, ship *(1837),* XXXII, 67
Duke of Newcastle, woodboat *(1879),* XVII, 13
Duke of Northumberland, steam lifeboat *(1890),* XXXIV, 10 ff.
Duke of Portland, ship *(1826),* XLI, 286
Duke of Sussex, ship, XIV, 103
Duke of York, ship *(1817),* XIV, 102, 103
Dulcino, tanker *(1920),* XXXVIII, 183 ff.
Dull, Jonathan R., mentioned, XLV, 244 ff.; reviews by, XLVIII, 195; XLIX, 315; L, 143; "Was the Continental Navy a Mistake?" XLIV, 167–170
Dulmo, Fernam, XXX, 255
Dumaru, wooden steamship *(1917),* XXXV, 283
Dummer, Jeremy, XXXV, 164 ff.
Dun, Alexander, XXXI, 202 ff.
Duna, steamship (1871), XVII, 54; XVIII, 69
Dunbabin, Thomas, "Australia and New England," XV, 153–154; "Correction on *Hero* in the Pacific," XI, 145–146; "The First Salem Vessel in Sydney and Fiji," XIII, 275–281; "Forgotten American Visitors to Australia," XII, 162; "King George and the *Flying Dutchman,*" XVII, 156; "The Leap Year that Wasn't," XIX, 133–138; "Maori Heads at Nantucket," XVII, 66–67; "Mystery of Banks's Baton," XVI, 62; "New Light on the Earliest American Voyages to Australia," X, 52–64; "Sea Otters, North and South," XVII, 66; "Southern Sea Otters and the Ship *Hope,*" XV, 81–82; "Voyage of *Jenny* of Bristol," XIII, 212–213; "Who Found Foveaux Straits?" XVII, 68
Dunbaugh, Edwin L., *The Era of the Joy Line,* reviewed, XLIII, 307
Dunboyne, ship, XXX, 219

Duncan, H.M. Destroyer *(1943),* L, 219 ff.
Duncan, Captain A. A., XXXV, 12
Duncan, Fred B., *Deepwater Family,* reviewed, XXX, 222–223
Duncan, Commissioner Henry, XLVI, 223
Duncan, Captain Peter, IX, 63; XXVI, 172
Duncan, Roger F., *Friendship Sloops,* reviewed, XLIX, 237
Duncan, Roland E., "*Chile* and *Peru*: The First Successful Steamers in the Pacific," XXXV, 248–274
Duncan, Commander Silas, XLVI, 230
Duncan, T. Bentley, *Atlantic Islands: Madeira, the Azores and the Cape Verdes in Seventeenth-Century Commerce and Navigation,* reviewed, XXXIII, 225
Duncan Hoyle, steamship *(1859),* XXXIV, 24 ff.
Duncombe, John, XXVI, 215
Dundas, Captain A. A. D., XVI, 178
Dundas, Captain Adam Alexander Duncan, XLIII, 107 ff.
Dundas, Captain Henry, R.N., XXV, 143
Dundas, Captain Robert Thomas, XXVI, 24, 203
Dundee, bark (1882), V, 141; XII, plate 31
Dundee, whale ship, XXV, plate 8
Dundee, Perth & London Shipping Co., XLIII, 191
Dunderberg, U.S. ram (1862), X, 19, 29
Dunderberg, U.S. armored cruiser (1865), XXII, 263; XXVII, 37, 42, 44; XLIX, 117; *(1867),* XXXIV, 60
Dunham, Charlotte Corday, XXXVII, 216
Dunham, Captain David A., VII, 128, 130, 139, 147, 148, 150, 152, 154, 155, 157, 158, 160, 165
Dunham Wheeler, schooner (1917), IV, 64, 68; XXIV, 25, plate 4
Duniway, David C., "The Brig *Betsy* of Norwich," III, 252–253
Dunkerque, auxiliary (1917), XXXII, 15, 28, 30
Dunkerque, French warship [model] (1935), XVI, 103
Dunkin, Michael, XIII, 24
Dunlap, Maurice P., XXXII, 112
Dunleavy, T., C.P.O., U.S.N., XXV, 50
Dunlin, Robert O., Jr. and William H. Garzke, *Battleships: Allied Battleships in World War II,* reviewed, XLII, 147–148
Dunmore, John Murray, Fourth Earl of, XXV, 193–195
Dunn, Captain Henry William Frater, XLIII, 197
Dunn, Samuel, *New Directory for the East Indies,* cited, XXV, 178
Dunn & Elliott, XXIII, plates X, XXX
Dunne, Finley Peter, XXXVII, 36
Dunne, William M. P., review by, XLIX, 310; XLVIII, 196; "An Inquiry into H. I. Chapelle's Research in Naval History," XLIX, 39–55; "Pistols and Honor: The James Barron-Stephen Decatur Conflict, 1798–1807," L, 245 ff.; "The South Carolina Frigate: A History of the U.S. Ship *John Adams,*" XLVII, 22–32
Dunsmuir, James, XXXVI, 243
Dunsyre, ship, XXX, 219; (1891), XVIII, 5, 216

Dunway, John A., XXXIX, 180
Dupee, John, instrument maker, Pictorial Supplement, XXXV, plate IV
Duperrey, Captain Louis I., IV, 99–100
Duperrey, Louis Isidor, XXXIV, 255
du Ponceau, Peter S., XXV, 184–185
Dupont, Captain S. F., U.S.N., XXI, 239
Du Pont, Rear Admiral S. F., U.S.N., IX, 49–50
DuPont, Admiral Samuel F., XII, 276; XV, 102 ff.
DuPont, Rear Admiral Samuel F., XLIX, 116; L, 89; XLII, 196 ff.
Dupont, Samuel Francis, XXXI, 254; XXXII, 50; XXXV, 54
DuPont, Midshipman Samuel Francis, XXXVI, 193; XXXVII, 277; XL, 211 ff.
DuPont, Victor Marie, XL, 211
Dupouy, Vice Admiral, XXIX, 169 ff.
Duque, J. G., XX, 120
Durand, H., XLVI, 254 ff.
Durand-Brager, Jean-Baptiste Henri, XLVI, 255
Durant, Kenneth, and Helen Durant, *The Adirondack Guideboat,* reviewed, XLIII, 306–307
Durbridge, ship *(1891),* XVIII, 5–24, plates 1, 3, 4
Durell, Captain Thomas, XXVI, 37
Durfee, Amos, VII, 303–304
Durga (Indian Goddess), statue of, XLVI, 18
Durham, concrete tanker *(1920),* XXII, 172, 182
Durham, Earl of, VII, 311–312
Durham, William, VII, 268
Durham Boat, Delaware River, II, 167–170, plates 21–22; III, 253–255
"Durham Boat Migration, A," by M. V. Brewington, III, 253–255
Durik, destroyer escort *(1944),* XXXVIII, 284
Durkin, Joseph T., XXIX, 7 n.
Duro, Fernandez, XIV, 109
Durrell, Captain Philip, XXIII, 181
Dursley Galley, vessel, XXVI, 61
D'Urville, Dumont, XXI, 197 ff.; XXV, 260
Dutch Asiatic Shipping in the 17th and 18th Centuries, by J. R. Bruijn and I. Schöffer, reviewed, XLVIII, 206
Dutch East India Co., XLVIII, 261 ff.; XLVII, 240–248
Dutch East India Company, L, 275
"Dutch East India Company as Shipowner, 1602–1796, The," by Jaap R. Bruijn, XLVII, 240–248
Dutchess, frigate, XXIII, 71
Dutch Royal Inter Ocean Lines, XXXI, 118
Dutch shallops, sketches of, XLIX, 202
Dutch West India Co., XVII, 292–297
Dutch West Indies, XXXVI, 155–169
Duthie, Archibald, XX, 45
du Treil, Governor Nadau, VII, 29, 33
Dutton, T. G., XXIV, plate XXVI
Dvina, Russian transport *(1855),* XXXI, 272
Dwight, Theodore, XXXIX, 47
Dwight, Timothy, XLVIII, 272
Dwyer, Gunner, U.S.N., XXV, 138

Dye, Captain Ira, U.S.N. (ret.), XXXVII, 81
Dye, Job E., XXVIII, 129
Dyer, Captain Frank A., XX, 239
Dyer, Captain N. Mayo, XXXIX, 41
Dyer, Captain Thomas, XXI, 105
Dyett, Captain Charles Nathaniel, XXI, 90
Dygden, ship *(1784),* VI, 170
Dyke, Charles, XVI, 31, 32
Dykes, barge *(1919),* V, 139
Dymaxion Projection, World Map on, by Richard Buckminster Fuller, IV, between 118–119
Dynamic, minesweeper *(1942),* XXXVIII, 274
Dyson, George W., answered query, IV, 77
"No Mistake About It: A Response to Jonathan R. Dull," XLV, 244–248

E

E. A. Shores, Jr., steam barge *(1892),* I, 76
E. A. Stevens, U.S.R.S. *(1861),* XX, 155–166
E. & I. Oakley, schooner *(1871),* IX, 170–171
E. Ant, schooner *(1861),* XV, 122
E. B. Conwell, schooner *(1859),* Pictorial Supplement, XXXIII, plate II
E. B. Hale, U.S.S. *(1863),* XXI, plate XXIX
E. B. Marvin, Canadian schooner *(1902),* XLIX, 280
E. B. Walters, schooner *(1913),* XXVI, plate XXVI
E. C. Gates, schooner, XXVIII, 123
E. Creighton, ship *(1860),* II, 246
E. Dent & Co., London, Pictorial Supplement, XXXV, plate XX
E. Drummomd, brig *(1857),* XX, 129 n.
E. F. Gabain, ship *(1861),* XI, 282
E. F. Prindel, schooner *(1861),* XI, 282
E. F. Thompson, bark *(1869),* III, 349
E. F. Zwicker, schooner *(1934),* XXVI, plate XXXI
E. H. Atwood, schooner *(1861),* XI, 282
E. H. Blum, steamship *(1943),* XXXVI, 101 ff.
E. H. Green, steamship (ex-*Unicorn*) *(1857),* XVII, 145; *(1858),* XLIX, 26
E. H. Kingman, bark *(1874),* XXXIII, 284
E. J. Roye, yacht *(1952),* XXXIX, 180
E. J. Waterman, schooner *(1861),* VIII, 217; XV, 122
E. L. Frost, schooner *(1849),* XLI, 281
E. Nickerson, whaleship *(1856),* L, 123
E. O. Painter Fertilizer Co., XXIV, 28
E. P. Collier, bateau *(1910),* IV, 289
E. P. Theriault, three-masted schooner, XXXIV, 147
E. R. Sterling, barkentine *(1883 or 1884),* I, 397; IV, 326; V, 81; IX, 297–298
E. R. Ware & Co., XXX, 167, 247
E. S. Brady, schooner, XXVIII, 148
E. S. Janes (or E. S. Jones), schooner *(1861),* XI, 282

E. S. Ritchie & Sons, Inc., Boston, Pictorial Supplement, XXXV, plate XI
E. Stannard and Co., XXII, 260
E. Starr Jones, schooner (1904), XXIII, plate X
E. Tenbrook, schooner *(1861),* XV, 114, 123
E. W. Bliss Co., XXXVII, 113
Eads, James B., X, 18; XIX, 266, 267; XX, 54
Eagan, Captain James, XXI, 90
Eagle, bark (*c.*1852), VI, 81
Eagle, brig *(1798),* XLI, 283; XLII, 27, 42, 108; XLIV, 172; *(1805),* XIII, 276; XIV, 44
Eagle, British ship *(1777),* XL, 20 ff.
Eagle, Mexican warship *(1843),* XXI, 222 ff.
Eagle, revenue cutter *(1799),* XXXIX, 34
Eagle, schooner (?) *(1775),* XXX, 115, 116
Eagle, schooner, XXI, 87; XXII, 83; (1777), V, 187; *(1813),* XXIX, 83, 188; *(1861),* XI, 282; XII, 54; XIV, 39
Eagle, ship *(1629),* XXIII, 65
Eagle, ship (1859), IV, 244; VI, 82; *(1867),* XII, 107; XIII, 17, 27
Eagle, sloop *(1863),* XV, 111, 127
Eagle, Spanish steamship *(1838),* XLVIII, 112
Eagle, steamship, XXI, 88; XXVIII, 124; *(1815),* XXX, 72
Eagle, steamship *(1863),* VIII, 229
Eagle, U.S.C.G. *(1946),* XX, 143 n.
Eagle, U.S. Coast Guard training bark *(1964),* XXIV, 79; *(1971),* XXXI, 157–158; XXXV, 76
Eagle, U.S.S. (1813), XXI, 50, 53, 54; *(1799),* XXXI, 173
Eagle Flight, packet, XXIV, 130
Eagle Foundry, XLV, 37
Eagle Insurance Co., XIII, 121
Eagles, carved: attributed to Samuel McIntire, Pictorial Supplement, XXXVII, plate XXI (upper); from Penobscot steamboat, XXVIII, plate XXXII; by John Bellamy, Pictorial Supplement, XXXVII, plate XXIII; Pictorial Supplement, XXXVII, plate XXII (lower).
Eagleston, Captain James, XXV, 187
Eagleston, Captain John H., XII, 36
Eaglet, steamship (1854), XXII, 24, 25, 37, 42, 43
Eakins, Thomas (artist), XXV, 59
Earl, William, XXXII, 173; XXXV, 294
Earle, Augustus (1806–1838), XXXI, Pictorial Supplement, plate III
Earle, Jamie, XXXVIII, 207 ff.
Earle, John G., review by, II, 86–88
Earle, Ralph, XXXVII, 123
Earle's Ship-Building Co., England, XXXIX, 275
Earling, A. J., XXXV, 171
Earl of Eglington, ship *(1854),* XLI, 298
Earl of Egmont (1767), XXVIII, 226
Earl of Mar and Kellie, ship *(1858),* XXXIV, 21
Earl of Mar and Kelly, coaster *(1863),* XXVI, 102
Earl of Shaftesbury (Lord Anthony Ashley Cooper), XXX, 82

Early, General Jubal, C.S.A., XXII, 258
Early American-Australian Relations, by Gordon Greenwood, reviewed, V, 329; V, 90
"Early American *Neptune,* An," by Alexander Crosby Brown, XII, 148–153, plates 13–15
Early American Scientific Instruments and Their Makers, by Silvio A. Bedini, reviewed, XXV, 71
"Early American Tankers," by Jean Haviland, XXXVIII, 175–202
"Early American Trade with India: Taking an Observation," by Glenn S. Gordinier, XLV, 153–166
"Early Barkentine Illustrations," by John Lyman, VII, 315–316, plate 39
"Early Description of Birch-Bark Canoes, An," by Ferdinand E. Chatard, VIII, 91–98
"Early Florida Salvage Industry, The," by Michael G. Schene, XXXVIII, 262–271
"Early Four-Masted Barkentine, An," by Commander Francis E. Clark, U.S.N. (ret.), XXV, 112–115
Early Great Lakes Steamboats: articles by H. A. Musham. "The *Ontario* and the *Frontenac,*" III, 333–344; "The *Walk-in-the-Water,*" V, 27–42; "1816 to 1830," VI, 194–211, plates 29–30; [Part I] "The First Propellers, 1841–1843," XVII, 89–104, plates 7, 8; [Part II] "The Chicago Line, 1838–1839," XVIII, 273–300; [Part III] "Hard Times and the *Erie* Disaster, 1840–1841," XX, 79–103; [Part IV] "The Last Years of Hard Times, 1842–1843," XX, 250–269; "The Battle of the Windmill and Afterward, 1838–1842," VIII, 37–60; "The *Caroline* Affair, 1837–1838," VII, 298–314, plates 37–38; "Warships and Iron Hulls, 1841–1846," VIII, 132–149, plates 15–16; "Westward Ho! and Flush Times, 1831–1837," VII, 42–65, plates 5–6
"Early History of Midway Island, The," by Lyle S. Shelmidine, VIII, 179–195
Early History of Transportation in Oregon, The, by Henry Villard, reviewed, V, 170–171
Early Maps of the Ohio Valley, by Lloyd A. Brown, reviewed, XX, 148
Early nineteenth century Chinese conract for sale of Minbei tea, photo of, XLVIII, 266, 267
"Early Paintings," query by M. V. Brewington, I, 398
"Early Reform in the Navy Department," by Edward K. Eckert, XXXIII, 231–245
"Early Schooners," query by M. V. Brewington, II, 248
Early Sea Charts, by Robert Putnam, reviewed, XLV, 132
"Early Seventeenth-Century Ship Design," by William A. Baker, XIV, 262–277, plates 31, 32
"Early Shipping Between England and Chesapeake Bay," by Parke Rouse, Jr., XXX, 133–138
"Early Steam Navigation in China," by E. K. Haviland, XXII, 5–44
"Early Steam Navigation in China: Hongkong and the Canton River, 1858–1867," by E. K. Haviland, XXXIV, 17–58; "Overseas Services to 1861," XXVI,

Part I, 5–32; Part II, 109–133; Part III, 189–209; "The Yangtsze River, 1861–1867 [Part I]," XLIII, 85–128; XLIII, 186–221

"Early Visits to Australia," query by Walter Muir Whitehill, V, 89–90

Early Yachting Photographs of H. G. Peabody & W. B. Jackson, Pictorial Supplement, XXX (1970)

"Early Years of William Ropes & Company in St. Petersburg, The," by Harriet Ropes Cabot, XXIII, 131–139

Earthquakes, Jamaica, XXIX, 118

Easby, Captain William, photograph of, XLV, 120

Eason, Captain Robert, VII, 72–76

East, brig *(1861),* XI, 282

East, Harry, X, 244 ff.

East Boston Dry Dock Co., XIII, 120

East Coast Fishing Co. of New York, XLIV, 125

East Coast Sail: Working Sail 1850–1970, by Robert Simper, reviewed, XXXIII, 213–214

"East Coast Steam Schooners," by J. W. Somerville, IX, 71, plate 8

Easter Island, boats of, XIII, 108

Eastern Admiral, steamship, XXIII, 276, plate 17

Eastern Argus, steamship *(1854),* XXXIII, 87

Eastern Belle, ship (1863), V, 150

Eastern Belle, steamship, XXIII, 276

Eastern Breeze, steamship, XXIII, 276

Eastern City, steamship *(1840),* XXVIII, 124; *(1852),* XXXIII, 86, 94

Eastern Cloud, steamship, XXIII, 276

Eastern Coast, steamship, XXIII, 276

Eastern Crag, steamship, XXIII, 276

Eastern Cross, steamship, XXIII, 276

Eastern Crown, steamship, XXIII, 276

Eastern Dawn, steamship, XXIII, 276

Eastern Exporter, steamship, XXIII, 276

Eastern Gale, steamship, XXIII, 276

Eastern Glade, steamship, XXIII, 276

Eastern Glen, steamship, XXIII, 276

Eastern Guide, steamship, XXIII, 276

Eastern Importer, steamship, XXIII, 276

Eastern Knight, steamship, XXIII, 276

Eastern Leader, steamship, XXIII, 276

Eastern Light, steamship, XXIII, 276

Eastern Mail, steamship, XXIII, 276

Eastern Mariner, steamship, XXIII, 276

Eastern Merchant, steamship, XXIII, 276

Eastern Moon, steamship, XXIII, 276

"Eastern Names," by Lincoln Colcord, IX, 83–86

Eastern Ocean, steamship, XXIII, 276

Eastern Passages, chart, II, opposite 148

Eastern Pilot, steamship, XXIII, 276

Eastern Planet, steamship, XXIII, 276

Eastern Point: A Nautial, Rustial, and Social Chronicle of Gloucester's Outer Shield and Inner Sanctum, 1606–1950, by Joseph E. Garland, reviewed, XXXII, 149–150

Eastern Queen, steamship (1857), XIV, 192

Eastern Railway Co. of Minnesota, XLVII, 193 ff.

"Eastern Sail Affinities," by Richard LeBaron Bowen, Jr., XIII, 81–117, 185–211

Eastern Sailor, steamship, XXIII, 276

Eastern Shore, steamship, XXIII, 276

Eastern State, ferry (1971), XXXIV, 187

Eastern State, schooner-rigged steamship *(1855),* XXXIV, 174 ff.

Eastern State, steamship *(1843),* XXXVII, 233

Eastern Steamboat Mail Line, XXXIII, 80 ff.

Eastern Steam Co., XXVI, 8, 9; XXVIII, 124

Eastern Steamship Corp., XXVIII, 124; XXXVII, 238; ship of, Pictorial Supplement, XXXIV, plates XXX, XXXI

Eastern Steamship Line, XXIX, 231

Eastern Steamship Lines, Inc., XXVIII, 124–126; XXXVI, 6, 8, 12

Eastern Sword, steamship, XXIII, 276

Eastern Tempest, steamship, XXIII, 276

Eastern Temple, steamship, XXIII, 276

Eastern Trader, steamship, XXIII, 276

Eastern Visitor, steamship, XXIII, 276

Eastern Yacht Club: A History from 1870–1985, The, by Joseph E. Garland, reviewed, L, 66

East India Co., XIII, 5–28; XXVI, 6, 7, 9, 16, 18, 19; XXX, 10, 200 ff.; XXXIV, 252; XXXVIII, 222; XLVI, 18 ff.; XLVII, 6 ff.; XLVIII, 24

East India Co., British, XXIII, 72; XXV, 177

East India Co., Dutch, XXV, 177

East India Marine Hall, Salem, IV, 5–17; V, 266–285; Pictorial Supplement, XXXII, plate XXVII; XXXVII, plate II, 32–33

East India Marine Society, mention, XLVI, 17; XXVI, 229; XXX, 3; Pictorial Supplement, XXXII, plates XXIX, XXX; XXXIII, 169; XLV, 117

East India Marine Society, Salem, VIII, 289; X, 33–42; XXIII, 255; XXV, 176 ff.

East India Packet, snow *(1778),* I, 309

Eastland, steamship, XXXVI, 20, 32

Eastland Trade and the Commonweal in the Seventeenth Century, by R. W. K. Hinton, reviewed, XIX, 148

Eastman, David, XV, 181

Eastman, Zebina, XVII, 249, 251, 256, 259

East Pilot, steamship, XXIII, 276

Eastport, steamship (1901), XXIV, 54, 55

Eastport (ME), XV, 178

Eastport (ME), History, XXVIII, 113

"Eastport: A Maritime History," by C. Donald Brown, XXVIII, 113–127

Eastport Salt Works, XLVII, 87

Eastwind, schooner (1876), XXIV, 60

East Wind, steamship, XXIII, 276

Eaton, William, XXVI, 246, 256

Eaton, General William, V, 329–330

Eauripik Island, XXXIV, 250

Eavenson, Howard N., query by, VI, 232–233; *Two Early Works on Arctic Exploration,* reviewed, VI, 310

Ebbets, John, XLVI, 46

Ebbs, Samuel and Henry, VIII, 322

Eben, bateau (1911), IV, 289

Eben Dodge, whaler (1863), XXII, Plate VIII

"Eben Caldwell to his Cousin, William Titcomb," contributed by Dana J. Pratt, XIII, 134–139

Ebens, Jonathan, XII, 223

Eberhardt, Charles C., XXXV, 129

Ebner, Harry, XXXVI, 23

Ebner, Sylvana, XXXVI, 23

Ebon Island, XXXIV, 254

Echagüe, brig *(1845),* XXXVI, 127

Echo, brig *(1861),* VIII, 196, 217

Echo, schooner *(1863),* XII, 155

Echo, schooner yacht (1861), XXVII, 248

Echo, sloop *(1861),* XI, 282

Echols, Captain Edward, XVI, 43–48

Eckert, Edward K., "Early Reform in the Navy Department," XXXIII, 231–245

Eckford, Henry, shipbuilder, I, 51; III, 267; V, 115–120

Eckford, Henry, VI, 84–85; VII, 3, 175–195, plate 21; VIII, 7–10; XIII, 263; XIV, 209–210

Eckford Webb, schooner (1855), XXIII, plate III

Eckstorm, Fanny Hardy, XII, 305

Eclair, paddle sloop *(1845),* XXXVI, 130

Eclipse, British brig *(1814),* XXIX, 198

Eclipse, ship *(1838),* XXI, 296 ff.; XLVII, 29; *(1908),* X, 194

Eclipse, steamship *(1860),* II, 300–301

Eclipse, Venezuelan schooner *(1848),* XXX, 267

Eclipse, yacht (1915), XLIII, 267 ff.; plates 9 and 10, between 272–273

Eco, brig *(1865),* XII, 234

Ecola, schooner (1920), V, 140, plate 10

Economist, steamship, XXI, 88; *(1862),* VIII, 224

Economy, Liberian coaster *(1845),* XXXVIII, 59

Economy, schooner (1812), VII, 317

Ecuador, iron paddle steamship *(1845),* XXXV, 270

Ecuador, steamship *(1916),* X, 140, 142, 143

Ed. *See* Edward.

Edan, Benoit, XXX, 160

Eddy, Captain, XXXVIII, 250 ff.

Eddystone light-vessel (1755), IV, 265

Edelstein, J. M., "The Way of a Book," XIX, 123–125

Edes, Captain, XLI, 174

Edgar, W., XXVII, plate XII

Edgar W. Murdock, schooner *(1912),* XXXV, 13 ff., plate 2

Edgecomb, Captain I., XXI, 105

Edgecomb, Captain John, XXIII, 64

Edgecomb, Noah, XXVIII, 117

Edgemont (ex-*State of Maine*), steamship (1881), XXXIII, 92; Pictorial Supplement, XXXIV, plates XVI, IX

Edgerton, Lucile Selk, *Pillars of Gold,* reviewed, I, 405–406

Edisto, bark *(1855),* XXIV, 142

Edisto, ketch, XXX, 82

Edisto, sloop *(1861),* VIII, 217, 224

Edisto, steamship *(1861),* VIII, 217

Edith, auxiliary steam bark (1845), I, 53–54, plates between 56–57, 167

Edith, ship *(1844),* XLIX, 21

Edith, ship (1864), III, 71; XXXIII, 207

Edith, steamship (1844), XVIII, 69; *(1864),* VIII, 233; (1883), VII, 228

Edith Emery, schooner (1883), XXVI, plate V

Edith L. Allen, schooner *(1890),* XXXV, 9 fn.

Edith R. Balcom, Canadian schooner *(1902),* XLIX, 280

Edmond, O. C., XXVI, 14

Edmonds, George W., XXXV, 281

Edmonds, Captain J. L., XVIII, 277

Edmonds, John W., XVIII, 191, 193–195, 196

Edmonsdson, W. T., and Henry B. Bigelow, *Wind Waves at Sea, Breakers and Surf,* reviewed, IX, 304

"Edmund Custis and his 'Wreck-Fishing' Invention," by James B. Lynch, Jr., L, 18–25

"Edmund Fanning and Henry Eckford," by Phyllis DeKay Wheelock, XIV, 209–210

Edmunds, George F., XXXIX, 290

Edna, yacht *(1892),* XXXVI, 237

Edna Christenson, steam schooner (1917), I, 77

Edna Hoyt, schooner (1920), IV, 64–66, 68; V, 138; XXIII, 14; XXIV, 25, plate 3

Edna Jones, schooner, XXI, 96

Edson, Merritt A., Jr., "The Schooner Rig, A Hypothesis," XXV, 81–92, plate 3; "The Schooner Rig, Its First Appearance and Development," XLIX, 198–207

"Education Department at the Peabody Museum of Salem, The," by Gail P. Hercher, XLV, 117–118

Edward, armed sloop *(1776),* VI, 301 ff.

Edward, bark *(1861),* XXI, 258

Edward, schooner (1829), XIX, 23; *(1863),* XII, 156

Edward VIII, Prince of Wales, XXXIV, 11 ff.

Edward A. Horton, schooner (1870), XXVI, plate III

Edward Albert, Prince of Wales, XXXVI, 183 ff.

Edward B. Winslow, schooner (1908), IV, 325; V, 139; XXIII, plate XXIV; XXIV, 34

Ed. Barnard, schooner, XXI, 103; *(1861),* XI, 282

Edward Bonaventure, ship *(1571),* XLIV, 29 ff.

Edward D. Stanley, schooner *(1861),* VIII, 217

Edwardes, A. D., contributed document, XXIII, 284

Edward Everett, ship (1860), III, 171

Edward Hill, schooner (1855), XXIII, plate III

Edward J. Lawrence, schooner, XXIII, 14; (1908), IV, 325

Edward Johnston, British ship *(1853),* XLVII, 101

Edward Kidder, bark (1874), III, 71

Edward Koppisch, bark *(1845),* Pictorial Supplement, XXXVIII, plate IX

Edward L. Swan (ex-*M. Vivian Peirce*), schooner, XXIV, 25, plate 4
Edward O'Brien, ship *(1878),* II, 332; (1883), VIII, 330
Edward Preble, sailing packet, XXVIII, 121
"Edward Preble's Report of the Frigates, 1806," document contributed by Christopher McKee, XVIII, 182
Edward R. Smith, schooner (1911), V, 288, plates 18, 24; Pictorial Supplement, XXXVI, plate XXXI
Edward R. West, schooner (1902), V, 144
Edward Roy, Canadian ship *(1902),* XLIX, 279
Edwards, Captain A., XX, 90 n.
Edwards, Captain A. N., VII, 147, 148, 150
Edwards, Consul Amory, XLVI, 238
Edwards, Clinton R., "The Lancha Velera of Chiloe," XXVI, 33–36; *Aboriginal Watercraft on the Pacific Coast of South America,* reviewed (Vol. XXVI/XXX), 224
Edwards, Edward, explorer, XXV, 260
Edwards, Samuel Hopkins, XLVIII, 272
Edwards, Vere B., XXXVIII, 275
Edward Sewall, four-mast bark, XXXIII, 147; *(1922),* XVI, 130; XVIII, 212, 213; *(1923),* X, 120
Edward Stewart, schooner *(1883),* XLIX, 30 ff.
Edward Vincent, brig *(1840),* XXIV, 215
"Edward Wright, Mathematician and Hydrographer," by Georgina Dawson, XXXVII, 174–178
Edwin, brig, XXV, 186
Edwin, schooner, XXI, 91, 98; *(1861),* VIII, 217, 224; IX, 37
Edwin and Samuel, schooner *(1861),* VIII, 217
Edwin Barclay, launch *(1930),* XXXIX, 180
Edwin Clarence Eckel, concrete ship (1944), XXII, 180
Edwin Reed, bark (1874), XXVIII, plate XV
Edwin Thacher, concrete ship (1944), XXII, 178
Edye Manning & Partners, XLIII, 203
Effective, minesweeper *(1942),* XXXVIII, 274
Effingham, frigate (1776), VIII, 11, 12, 21, 24; XXXIV, 137; XXXV, 141
Effort, sloop *(1903),* XXX, 195
"Efforts Made Before 1825 to Ameliorate the Lot of the American Seaman: With Emphasis on His Moral Regeneration," by Eugene T. Jackman, XXIV, 109–118
Egalité, five-masted schooner (1918), XXXII, 15, 27, 30; XXXIII, 51. See also *Reliance.*
Egan, Captain James, XXI, 90
Eggbasket, schooner (1874), XXIV, 39
Eggleston, Lieutenant E. T., XLII, 89 ff.
Egmont, H.M. storeship *(1874),* XXXIII, 285
Egmont, Lord, XXX, 207
Egypt, bark *(1861),* XI, 282
Egypt, grain elevator *(1883),* XXXVIII, 141
Egypt, steamship (1871), Pictorial Supplement, XXXIV, plate VII
Egypt, boats of, XII, 45–51
Egypt Conquise, French ship *(1799),* XXXI, 173

Egypt, History (640–1250), XLVI, 77. *See also* Fatimites; Nile River
Egypt Mills, steamship *(1865)* VIII, 237
"1856 Proposal for an Inflatable Rubber Life Raft or Lifeboat, An," document contributed by E. L. Towle, XXV, 69–70
"1849 Statement on the Habits of Right Whales by Captain Daniel McKenzie of New Bedford, An," document contibuted by John P. Harrison, XIV, 139–141
18 de Julio, Uruguayan gunboat *(1906),* II, 170–171, plate 23
"Eight Regulations," Imperial Act, 1860, XXXI, 179
Eihei Maru, iron screw steamship (ex-*Fiery Cross*) *(1862),* XXVI, 122
Ellery, William, XIV, 51
Eire, gunboat *(1937),* XXXV, 136
Eiserman, Captain J. J., XXVIII, plate X
Eizabeth, bark *(1854),* XII, 102
Ekston, Captain George, XXI, 90
Elberta, bark (1854), XXVIII, plate VIII
Elbridge, Giles, XX, 10
Elbridge, John, XX, 6–12
Elcano, ship (1864), III, 71
Elder-Dempster, British shipping line, XLVI, 108
Elder Dempster Fleet History, 1852–1985, The, by James E. Cowden and John O'C. Duffy, reviewed, XLVIII, 193
Elderkin, Bela, XXIII, 238 ff.
El Dorado, schooner *(1857),* IV, 315
El Dorado, ship, XXXVI, 174
Eldredge, grain elevator *(1883),* XXXVIII, 141
Eldredge, Elam and George (salvors), XXV, 108
Eldredge, Elwin M., II, 84, 93, 177; XIII, 214; XXX, 15; review by, II, 262; "*Emeline* and *City of Haverhill.*"
Eldridge, Captain George, XLIII, 55
Eldredge, Captain George (cartographer), XXV, 187, 242
Eldridge, Captain Isaiah, XXIII, 27
Eldridge, Captain Joseph, XXI, 19
Eldridge, Captain Salathiel, XXIII, 27
Eldridge, Captain W. J., XXI, 90
Eldredge Collection, The Elwin M., reviewed, II, 93
Eleanor, Baltimore letter of marque *(1812),* XLVI, 168
Eleanor, bark-rigged steam yacht (1894), XXVII, plate XXXII
Eleanor A. Percy, schooner (1900), I, 396; IV, 325; XXIII, 14, 20, plate XXIII
Eleanora, ship *(1792),* XLI, 282
Eleanor B. Conwell. See *E. B. Conwell.*
Electra, British warship *(1848),* XXX, 268
Electric Boat Division, General Dynamics Corp., XXXIX, 29 ff.
Electric Light, schooner *(1889),* XXXV, 12
Electric lighting, V, 9
Elefanten, ship (1554), XV, 273, 274

"'Elegant' Steamboat *Commonwealth*, The," by Alexander Crosby Brown, VIII, 246–254, plates 21–24
Elements of Seamanship, The, by Roger C. Taylor, reviewed, XLIII, 224
Elemka, schooner (1918), IX, 68
Elephant, II, 271; XVIII, 137
Elephants, importation of, II, 275–277; Captain Crowninshield's, XVIII, 137–141
"Elephants and Whales: New London and Desolation, 1840–1900," by Briton Cooper Busch, XL, 117–126
Elezar W. Clark, schooner, XXIV, 46
Elf, bark (1856), V, 242
Elfin, steamship (wooden screw) (1862), XVIII, 69; XXXIV, 41; XLIII, 211; *(1871),* XLIII, 89 ff.
Elfin, steamship (1875), XVIII, 69
Elford, James M., III, 211 ff.
Elgar, John, X, 163 ff., plate 24
Elgin, Lord, XXXIV, 109 ff.; XXXVIII, 38
Elias, schooner (1918), I, facing 73
Elias Beckwith (or *Elisha Beckwith*), sloop, XXI, 92; *(1863),* XII, 156
Elias Reed, schooner, XXI, 87
Eliot, Reverend Andrew, XXV, 234, 246–247
Eliot, Henry, XXV, 234, 236
Eliot, T. S., XXV, 65
Eliot, Mrs. T. S., XXVI, 79
Eliot, Thomas S., *The Dry Salvages,* cited, XXV, 233 ff.
Eliot, William, XXV, 234, 245
Eliot, William Graeme, XXV, 234
Eliot Beckwith, sloop *(1863),* XII, 156
Eliphalet Greely, ship (1856), II, 331
Elisabeth A., steamship *(1968),* XXXVI, 31
Elisha Beckwith, sloop, XXI, 92
Elisha Dunbar, bark *(1862),* XXVII, 265; XXXIII, 56 ff.
Elisha Walker, tanker *(1940),* XLVII, 52
Elite, schooner *(1861),* XV, 116, 123
Eliza (1802), XXIII, 217; *(1806),* XV, 153–154
Eliza, 4-masted schooner (ex-U.S.S. *Osceola*) (1863), XXV, 113
Eliza, bark (1823), Pictorial Supplement, XXXVIII, plate XVII
Eliza, bark *(1888),* XXXIX, 8 ff.
Eliza, barque *(1849),* XLV, 124
Eliza, brig, XXIV, 70; *(1807),* X, 54; XVI, 195; *(1818),* XXX, 186
Eliza, brigantine *(1801),* XXIII, 233 ff., plate 11
Eliza, ketch (1794), II, 281; IV, 18, plate 6; *(1795),* XLI, 169
Eliza, schooner, XXI, 101; *(1775),* XXX, 103, 110; *(1862),* VIII, 224; *(1864),* XV, 129
Eliza, ship (1796 or 1797), XIII, 275 ff.; XLVI, 50 ff.; L, 270 ff.; Chinese painting of, XLVI, 52; *(1805),* X, 54
Eliza, ship, XXV, 186
Eliza Adams, ship, XXII, plate XXII; *(1872),* XXXVIII, 212
Eliza and Catherine, schooner (1861), VIII, 217
Eliza Ann, brig, XXVIII, 120
Eliza Ann, schooner (1850), XXIV, 58; *(1851),* XXXVII, 143; *(1862),* VIII, 224
Eliza Ann, ship *(1812),* XXI, 19
Elizabeth, XXIII, 243, 244
Elizabeth, Austrian warship *(1866),* XXXIV, 59
Elizabeth, barge (1829), V, 301
Elizabeth, bark (1603), XXXIV, 233
Elizabeth, bark *(1849),* IV, 334
Elizabeth, brig (1863), XXXIV, 70
Elizabeth, privateer *(1744),* XLII, 49
Elizabeth, schooner, XXI, 102; *(1799),* XLVI, 161; *(1821),* L, 105; *(1861),* VIII, 217, 224, 229; *(1863),* XII, 156
Elizabeth, ship *(1798),* XXXIX, 32
Elizabeth, ship (1882), XXVIII, plate XXII
Elizabeth, sloop *(1748),* IX, 144; *(1861),* XI, 282; XII, 54; XV, 127
Elizabeth, steamship, XXI, 92, 96, 100, 103; *(1862),* VIII, 224, 229; XII, 54; *(1888),* VII, 159
Elizabeth, steam launch *(1920),* XXXIX, 179
Elizabeth, whale ship, XXV, 184; XXVI, 217
Elizabeth II, Queen of England, XXVII, 32
Elizabethan Privateering, English Privateering During the Spanish War 1585–1603, by Kenneth R. Andrews, reviewed, XXV, 148–149
Elizabeth Bonaventure, ship *(1588),* XXVII, 183; *(1593),* XXXVII, 175
Elizabeth City, steamship (1868), VI, 61, plate 3; VII, 242
Elizabeth City Shipyard, XLI, 190
Elizabeth Hamilton, ship (1847), XXV, 102
Elizabeth Howard, schooner, XXVI, plate XXVIII
Elizabeth Islands (MA), Discovery and exploration, XXXIII, 131
Elizabeth Islands, VII, 214; X, 71–73; U.S.C. & G.S. chart of, XXXIII, plate 5
"Elizabeth Islands Jingle, The," by Alexander C. Brown, X, 71–73
Elizabeth Jonas, ship (1596), XIV, 274, 275
Elizabeth Morse, schooner, XXI, 88, 97; *(1861),* XI, 282; XII, 156
Elizabeth Palmer, schooner, XXIII, plate XVI; (1903), V, 80
Elizabeth Silsbee, schooner (1905), XXVI, plate XX
Elizabeth Swift, bark *(1846),* XXXVIII, 210
Eliza Campbell, bark (1873), I, 114
Eliza Catherine, schooner *(1864),* XII, 230
Eliza Fisk, schooner, XXI, 103. See also *Eliza M. Fisk.*
Eliza Frances, bark (1809), VI, 80
Eliza M. Fisk, schooner *(1861),* XI, 282; XII, 54
Eliza McNeil, ship (1871), II, 246
"*Eliza*'s Treasure," document contributed by C. C. Legge, XXIV, 70
Eliza Warrick, ship (1836), VI, 80; XIV, 32, 39
Elkins, Harry, XXV, 181
Elko Victory, steamship, XXXVII, 75
Ella, brig, XXI, 88; *(1862),* VIII, 224

Ella, schooner *(1861),* VIII, 217–229; XI, 282; XII, 234
Ella, ship (1858), II, 332
Ella, steamship, XXI, 86, 106, plates VI, XIV. *(1863),* VIII, 229, 233; IX, 39, 40, 44
Ella and Annie, gunboat (1862), XXXIII, 202
Ella and Annie, steamship, XXI, 81, 82, 83, 87, 88, 94, 101, 105, plate XXIV; *(1860),* XIV, 61–63; *(1863),* VIII, 229; IX, 39, 40
Ella and Annie, U.S.S. *(1863),* XIX, 56, 57, 58, 61
Ella D., brig *(1862),* VIII, 224
Ella E. Badger, ship (1856), IV, 73
Ella Fleming, brig, XXI, 90, 96; (1848), VI, 80; VIII, 224
El Lagarto, Hydroplane, XXVI, plate 7
Ella M. Willey, schooner *(1897),* XXXV, 16
Ella Norton, ship (1864), III, 66
Ella Warley, steamship *(1861),* VIII, 217, 224; XXI, 100, 102, 105, 242
Ellen, bark *(1857),* IV, 315–316
Ellen, gunboat *(1862),* XXXI, 263
Ellen, schooner, XXI, 95, 103; *(1863),* XII, 156, 230
Ellen, ship *(1834),* XXIII, 137; *(1860),* XXVII, 235
Ellen, sloop *(1862),* XV, 126, 127
Ellen A. Swift, ship *(1902),* XLV, 115
Ellen Goodspeed, ship (1868), II, 334
Ellen J. McKinnon, schooner (1874), V, 86
Ellen Sears, ship (1862), XXII, 245, 246
Ellen Southard, bark (1848), II, 330
Ellen Stewart, ship (1857), III, 73; VI, 82
Eller, Rear Admiral E. M., XVIII, 187
Eller, Rear Admiral Ernest M., U.S.N. (ret.), XXII, 3, 4
Eller, Rear Admiral Ernest McNeill, mentioned, XXIX, 80, 287; XLIX, 9, 43; reviews by, XLIV, 279; XLV, 133; XLIX, 133; L, 230; preface, *Dictionary of American Fighting Ships,* Vol. 3; reviewed, XXIX, 74–75
Ellery, Epes, XLVI, 214
Ellery, William, II, 247; XXXI, 235–252; XXXIV, 140
Ellet, Captain Alfred W., U.S.A., XXV, 133
Ellet, Charles, Jr., XXXI, 52 ff.
Ellet, Colonel Charles, Jr., U.S.A., civil engineer, XXV, 132–134, 139
Ellet, Cadet Charles Rivers, U.S.A., XXV, 133
Ellet, Sharpshooter Eddie, U.S.A., XXV, 133
Ellet Rams, U.S.N. *(1862),* XXV, 131 ff.
Ellice Islands, IV, 99
Ellicott, Captain J. M., U.S.N. (Ret.), "A Cyclone which seemed to have no center," VII, 35–38, plate 4
Ellide, cat yawl *(1895),* XXX, 197
Ellie Knight, steamship (1863), XII, 289, 293
Ellinger, Werner B., and Herbert Rosinski, *Sea Power in the Pacific 1936–1941, A Bibliography,* reviewed, II, 352
Elliot, C., XXI, 109
Elliot, Captain Charles, XLVIII, 281
Elliot, Captain George, XXI, 90
Elliot, Major George, XLVII, 178
Elliot, Captain Jesse, XIX, 240–242
Elliot, Joseph, XXXI, 134
Elliott, Charles G., XXXI, 183, 272
Elliott, Clark, XLVI, 258
Elliott, Captain E. G., XXXVII, 251
Elliott, Captain Edmund, XXI, 90
Elliott, Captain George F., XXXIV, 214
Elliott, H. W. (artist), Pictorial Supplement, XXXI, plates XXVI, XXVII
Elliott, Captain Jesse D., XXXIV, 194
Elliott, Commodore Jesse Duncan, XXXVIII, 67 ff.; XL, 39
Elliott, Master Commandant Jesse Duncan, XLIV, 178
Elliott, Joseph, XXXVI, 279
Elliott, Richard V., *Last of the Steamboats: The Saga of the Wilson Line,* reviewed, XXXI, 76–77
Elliott, William Henry Fletcher, XXXIV, 48
Elliott B. Church, schooner (1882), XXIII, 12
Elliott Richie (ex-*Harriet Lane*), XXXVI, 205
Ellis, C.S.S. *(1862),* VIII, 224; XLVIII, 95
Ellis, snow (1751), I, 297
Ellis, Captain Alma G., U.S.N. (ret.), XXXVII, 81
Ellis, Captain C. B., XVIII, 83
Ellis, Captain, XIII, 50
Ellis, R. Y., XXXVI, 233
Ellis, William, XXIX, 63
Ellis, William A. (insurance inspector), I, 43
Ellis, Lieutenant William B., XXXVII, 97 ff.
Ellis and Brook, British ship *(1776),* XLVIII, 18
Ellissen & Co., XLIII, 203 ff.
Ellsworth, brig *(1834),* L, 217
Ellsworth, Oliver, XXXVI, 60
Ellwood Walter, ship (1855), III, 264
Ellyoff, Captain William, XXIII, 64
Elma, schooner *(1861),* XI, 282
Elma Franklin, schooner *(1862),* XII, 54
"Elm Bark Canoe in the Peabody Museum of Salem, An," by William N. Fenton and Ernest S. Dodge, IX, 185–206, plates 21–22
Elmer, Captain Jacob, Jr., XXI, 90
Elmina, schooner (1905), XXX, plate XXI
Elmiranda, bark *(1901),* XV, 225
Elmore, H. M., *The British Mariner's Directory,* cited, XXV, 178
Elodia A. Kennedy, bark (1866), V, 153
Eloise, bateau (1911), IV, 289
Elphinstone, George Keith, VII, 102
Elsa C., fishing boat *(1961),* XLI, 52
Else, ship (1875), VI, 83
Elsey, George M., XLII, 214
Elsey, George McKee, contributed document, I, 395–396
Elsie, schooner, XXXVI, 77; (1910), XXVI, plate XXIV
Elsie, scow sloop (1874), I, 78
Elsie, steamship *(1864),* VIII, 233; XXI, plate VIII
Elsie, tug *(1887),* XLVII, 116
Elsie M. Reichert, oyster schooner (1898), I, 70
Elsinore, ship, XLVI, 195 ff.

El Sol, lugger, XXI, 104; *(1861)*, XI, 282
Elson, James, XXX, 58, 60
Elsworth, two-sail bateau (1901), V, 88
Elton, Lieutenant John, XLVI, 169
Elvira, hermaphrodite brig (1848), XXIV, 58
Elvira, ship *(1794)*, XLI, 169
Elvira, sloop, XXI, 104; *(1865)*, VIII, 237
Elvira Ball, schooner (1907), V, 327; XXIII, plate XIII
Elvira Eager, schooner *(1861)*, XI, 282; XII, 156
Elvira Egar, schooner, XXI, 99
Elvira Owen, ship (1861), XI, 282
El Virgin del Rosario y El Sancto Christo de Buen Viage, schooner *(1757)*, XXIII, 282–284
Elwin M. Eldredge Collection, The, reviewed, II, 93
Elwood Cooper, bark (1865), IV, 326
Emanuel, ship *(1578)*, XLIX, 14 ff.
Emanuell, ship, XXII, 102, 103
"*Emanuel* of Bridgewater and Discovery of Martin Frobisher's 'Black Ore' in Ireland, The," by Donald D. Hogarth, XLIX, 14–20
Embarcadero, by Richard H. Dillon, reviewed, XX, 72
Embargo, Jefferson's, 1807–1809, X, 144 ff.; XVI, 189–210; XXV, 14
Embargo (United states, 1807–1809), XVI, 189; XLIII, 245
Embuscade, frigate *(1793)*, XXII, 82–84, 88 ff.
Emden, German cruiser *(1914)*, XXIV, 273; *(1915)*, XLV, 199 ff.; *(1917)*, XLVIII, 53
Emelia, ship *(1789)*, XII, 23
Emelie, ship *(1824)*, XLI, 289
Emelie F. Birdsall, schooner (1874), I, 70
Emeline, schooner *(1843)*, XLV, 106
Emeline, ship *(1804)*, XLIII, 43 ff.
Emeline, sloop, XXI, 90; *(1863)*, VIII, 229
Emeline, steamship (1857), XIII, 214; *(1870)*, XII, 288, 293; *(1892)*, XVIII, 232
"*Emeline* and *City of Haverhill*," by Elwin M. Eldredge, XIII, 214
Emerald, bark *(1861)*, XXI, 258
Emerald, H.M.S., XXVIII, 16, 17
Emerald, H.M. cruiser *(1927)*, L, 187
Emerald, H.M.S. *(1778)*, XXXIV, 139
Emerald, schooner (1924), XXVI, plate XXX
Emerald, ship, XXV, 186; *(1823)*, XII, 36; XV, 136, 137
Emerald, sloop, XXIV, 130, 132
Emergence of the Modern Capital Ship, The, by Stanley Sandler, reviewed, XL, 71
Emergency Fleet Corp., The, XXXII, 157; XLI, 264
Emergency Fleet Corp., U.S., XXII, 160; XXIII, 274
Emerson, Albert, XXXIX, 218
Emerson, Charles P., answered query, I, 173
Emerson, Mr., XXX, 62–67
Emerson, Ralph, XXXVI, 241
Emerson, Ralph Waldo, XXV, 59, 64
Emerson, Mrs. Raymond, X, 72
Emerton, Ephraim, XIII, 121
Emerton, James, XIII, 121

Emery, schooner *(1861)*, XV, 123
Emery, John S. & Co., IX, 69
Emery, Samuel (of Salem), Pictorial Supplement, XXXV, plate XIV
Emery Rice, U.S.S. *(1942)*, XX, 140
Emeu, steamship (1852), XXVI, 28–32, 203, 205, 209
Emigrant, steamship (1843), XVII, 103; XX, 261
"Emigrants at Dinner," XXXI, Pictorial Supplement, plate IX
"Emigrants Dancing Between Decks," XXXI, Pictorial Supplement, plate XII
"Emigrant Ship – Between Decks," XXXI, Pictorial Supplement, plate XIV
Emigrant ships, XVIII, 306–314
"Emigrant Ship to Copra Hulk: the Iron Bark *Bougainville*," by Harold D. Huycke, VIII, 114–126, plates 9–12
"Emigrants Tracing a Vessel's Progress," XXXI, Pictorial Supplement, plate X
Emigration and immigration. *See* Liberia, Palestine, United States
Emil, brigantine *(1884)*, XIV, 120
Emile N. Vidal, concrete ship (1944), XXII, 180
Emilia, brig *(1829)*, XXIII, 186 ff.
Emilie, schooner *(1863)*, XII, 156
Emilie, steamship, XXI, 103; *(1861)*, VIII, 217, 224
Emilie and Jessie, ship *(1861)*, XV, 114, 123
Emily, schooner (1845), XXX, 232; *(1862)*, VIII, 224; *(1863)*, XII, 156, 230
Emily, ship *(1806)*, XIV, 91
Emily, steamship, XXI, 106; *(1864)*, VIII, 233; IX, 39–40, 44
Emily Augusta, ship (1857), II, 332
Emily B. Louder, schooner (1846)), XXIV, 44, 58
Emily B. Souder, bark (1864), XXIV, 57
Emily C. Starr, bark, XXVIII, 152
Emily F. Whitney, ship (1879), I, 77; cabin plan, II, 196
Emily Farnum, ship *(1862)*, XXXIII, 57
Emily Fowler, schooner (1854), XXIV, 58
Emily Marshall, yawl *(1947)*, VIII, 6
Emily St. Pierre, ship, XXI, 104; *(1862)*, VIII, 224
Emily Taylor, ship (1832), XIX, 27
Emlen, George, XLVIII, 247 ff.
Emma, bark (1866), III, 66
Emma, brig *(1823)*, VI, 94
Emma, brig (1865), VIII, 178
Emma, schooner, XXI, 100; *(1862)*, XII, 54, 156; XV, 127
Emma, ship *(1839)*, XLI, 297
Emma, sloop *(1863)*, XII, 156
Emma, steamship, XXI, 95; *(1863)*, VIII, 229; *(1864)*, XII, 230
Emma Alexander, steamship (ex-*Congress*), XXVII, 150
Emma Amelia, schooner, XXI, 87; *(1863)*, XII, 156; XV, 127
Emma and Alice, bark (1874), IV, 240
Emma C. Berry, smack, XXXIV, 148–149

Emma C. Latham, schooner, XXV, 107
Emma Clifton, ship *(1884),* XLI, 40
Emma D. Russie, schooner, XXI, 98; *(1861),* XI, 282
Emma Eger, brig *(1861),* VIII, 217
Emma F. Angell, schooner, XIII, 120
Emma Henry, steamship, XXI, 100; *(1864),* VIII, 233
Emma Julia, schooner *(1861),* XV, 123; *(1862),* VIII, 224
Emma K. Smalley, schooner (1874), XXIV, 58
Emmanuel, French polacre *(1800),* XXXI, 174; XXXIX, 35
Emma Tuttle, schooner *(1862),* VIII, 224, 229
Emma Utter, schooner (1875), V, 86
Emma White, steamship *(1863),* VII, 124, 142
Emmerson, George S., *The Greatest Iron Ship, SS* Great Eastern, reviewed, XLIII, 60–61
Emmerson, John C., Jr., *Steam Navigation in Virginia and Northeastern North Carolina Waters, 1826–1836,* reviewed, X, 157–158; *The Steam-Boat Comes to Norfolk Harbor,* reviewed, IX, 78, 234
Emmerton, Ephraim, XVII, 72
Emmet, Thomas Addis, XVI, 271 ff.
Emmigrant, ship *(1849),* IV, 332
Emmons, Frederick E., *American Passenger Ships: The Ocean Lines and Liners, 1873–1983,* reviewed, XLVII, 55
Emmy, Liberian schooner *(1874),* XXXVIII, 63; XXXIX, 173 ff.
Emory, Lieutenant Commander William Hensley, XXXIV, 215; XL, 101
Emperator Carlos V., Spanish warship *(1850),* XLI, 94
Emperor, British brig *(1814),* XLII, 112 ff.
Emperor, side-wheeler (1860), XXXIV, 32, 177
Emperor, steamship *(1854),* XLIII, 95 ff.
Emperor Frederick II, XLVI, 88
Emperor Guangxu, XLVIII, 284
Emperor Kangxi, XLVIII, 233
Emperor Maximilian of Mexico, XXXIV, 59
Emperor of Japan, brig *(1800),* XLVI, 52
Empire, ketch (1854), VI, 81
Empire, ship *(1854),* XVIII, 321; *(1860),* XXVII, 236
Empire Camp, steamship *(1943),* XIV, 133, 135
Empire City, steamship *(1861),* XXI, 241
Empire City Line, X, 126–127
Empire Grey, steamship (1944), XIV, 135
Empire Lytton, tanker *(1924),* L, 44
Empire Mariner, steamship *(1939),* XIV, 132, 135
Empire Nigel, steamship *(1943),* XIV, 132, 135
Empire of the Seas: a Biography of Rear Admiral Robert Wilson Shufeldt, USN, The, by Frederick C. Drake, reviewed, XLVI, 123
Empire Snipe, steamship *(1942),* XXVII, 190
Empire State, steamship *(1921),* X, 141
Empire State, U.S.S. *(1931),* XX, 142
Empress, barque, XXI, 94; *(1861),* XI, 282
Empress, ship (1856), V, 147
Empress, steamship, XXVIII, 124
Empress, yacht *(1903),* XXXVI, 240
Empress (II), yacht *(1905),* XXXVI, 241
Empress Charlotte of Mexico, XXXIV, 59
Empress of Canada, steamship (1922), XXV, 175
Empress of China, ship *(1784),* X, 83–107, 220–229, 288–297; XI, 59–71, 134–144; XIV, 298–299; XXIII, 212; XXXI, 39, 177, 179; XLIII, 178 ff.; XLV, 153 ff.; *(1785),* XLVI, 6 ff.
Empress of China, *The,* by Philip Chadwick Foster Smith, reviewed, XLIV, 205
"*Empress of China*'s Voyage, 1784–1785, The," by Philip Chadwick Foster Smith, XLVI, 25–33
Empress of India, British man-of-war, XXIV, 126
Empress of India, liner, XXXVI, 242
Empress of the Seas, ship *(1846–1857),* XLII, 121 ff.
"Empty the Brig," document contributed by Captain Edgar K. Thompson, U.S.N. (ret.), XXIV, 37
"Enchanted-Island Traditions of the Sixteenth and Seventeenth Centuries," by George G. Carey, XXIX, 275–281
"Enchanted Voyage," by Alexander Crosby Brown, VII, 213–223, plates 25–28
Encounter, cruiser *(1914),* XXIV, 275
Encounter, H.M.S. *(1854),* XXX, 159, 160
Endeavor, British ship *(1776),* XLVIII, 16
Endeavor, ship (1803), II, 283
Endeavor, sloop *(1776),* XXV, 214
Endeavour, bark *(1768),* XXXV, 70; *(1772),* XXII, 224
Endeavour, ship, XIII, 121; *(1770),* XXX, 205, 206; *(1821),* XXV, 183–184
Endeavour, sloop *(1740),* XII, 227
Ender, Thomas (1793–1875), XXXI, Pictorial Supplement, plate II
Enderby, Samuel, XLI, 284
Endicott, Captain Charles, XXI, 293
Endicott, Captain Charles M., XXXI, 182
Endicott, Francis, X, 73
Endicott, H. B., XVIII, 63
Endicott, H. C., XXII, 32
Endicott, Captain J. B., XLIII, 94 ff.
Endicott, James B., XVI, 162 ff.; XVII, 46, 47, 142 ff.; XVIII, 83
Endicott, Captain James B., XXII, 15, 30; XXXIV, 21 ff.; XLIX, 21
Endicott, Captain John, XXV, 185
Endicott, Captain Moses, XXV, 183
Endicott, William, XVII, 43, 46, 60, 63, 143
End of Russian America, Captain P. N. Golvin's Last Report, 1862, The, edited by Basil Dmytryshyn and E. A. P. Crownhart-Vaughan, reviewed, XLI, 142–144
Endurance, ship, XXIX, 143; (1916), XXVIII, 3, 59
Endymion, H.M. frigate *(1812),* XXII, 143, 215; *(1815),* III, plate 5; XLIV, 171
Endymion, ship (1856), III, 170–171
Enea, schooner, XXI, 102; *(1861),* XI, 282
Enemy Sighted, by Alec Hudson, reviewed, I, 410
Engadine, steamship, XXVII, 66
Engage, minesweeper *(1942),* XXXVIII, 274

Engineer, schooner (1832), IX, 72
Engine Powered Vessel: From Paddle-Wheeler to Nuclear Ship, The, by W. A. Baker and Tre Tryckare, reviewed, XXVI, 150–151
Engines, marine steam; back action, VI, 152; inclined, VI, 152; oscillating, VI, 151; side lever, VI, 151
Engines, steamship, IV, 77
England, steamship (1856), XXVI, 130
England, steamship (ex-*Princess Charlotte*) *(1861),* XXVI, 197
England and the Discovery of America 1481–1620, by David Beers Quinn, reviewed, XXXIV, 280
Engle, Commodore Frederick, XXXVIII, 40; XLIII, 165 ff.
Englert, Father Sebastian, XXX, 73
Englis, John, XXXVI, 172
English, Rear Admiral Earl, U.S.N., III, 85
English Navigation Laws: A Seventeenth-Century Experiment in Social Engineering, The, by Lawrence A. Harper, reviewed, I, 93
English New England Voyages, 1602–1608, The, edited by David B. Quinn and Alison M. Quinn, reviewed, XLIV, 137–138
English Privateering Voyages to the West Indies, 1588–1595, Kenneth R. Andrews, editor, reviewed, XX, 275
Engs, Captain Madet, XIII, 46, 47
Engstrand, Iris H. W., *Spanish Scientists in the New World: The Eighteenth-Century Expeditions,* reviewed, XLIV, 278
Ennis, barkentine (1870), IV, 242
"Enoch Richmond Ware, African Trader; 1839–1850 Years of Apprenticeship," Part I, by George E. Brooks, Jr., XXX, 174–186; Part II, XXX, 229–248
"Enoch Richmond Ware: Impressions by His Grandson," by Edward Richmond Ware, M.D., XXX, 167–173
Enoch Train, ship (1854), III, 170
"'...En Otros Tiempos...' Did the Men of Bristol Discover Newfoundland in 1481?" by J. T. W. Hubbard, XXXVII, 157–163
Enrique, Infante Don, XXX, 252
Ensigns. *See* flags
Enstire, Captain R. H., XXI, 90
Enterprise, XXVIII, 118
Enterprise (1801), XXIII, 216
Enterprise, brig *(1817),* XXIV, 287, 288, 292
Enterprise, grain elevator *(1883),* XXXVIII, 141
Enterprise, gunboat *(1782),* XXXIX, 216
Enterprise, schooner *(1805),* XXXIX, 111; XL, 24
Enterprise, screw sloop *(1887),* XL, 127 ff.
Enterprise, ship *(1833),* XIV, plate 7
Enterprise, snow (1740), I, 167
Enterprise, steamship (1824), VI, 199, 210
Enterprise, steamship (1879), VI, 62; VII, 242
Enterprise, steamship, XXI, 99; (1814), XVI, 35 ff.
Enterprise, steamship (1861), XVII, 148; XVIII, 69; *(1862),* XII, 54; XLIII, 209
Enterprise, U.S. atomic aircraft carrier (1961), XXV, 224
Enterprise, U.S.S. *(1800),* XXXI, 174; XXXIV, 189 ff., 245; XXXV, 248; *(1808),* XVI, 206
Enterprise, U.S.S. (1873), XX, 138–139
Enterprise, U.S. schooner (1799), IV, 233–235
Enterprising Colonials, The, by W. Sachs and A. Hoogenboom, reviewed, XXVI, 152
Enterprize (1801), XXIII, 217
Enterprize, H.M.S. *(1781),* VII, 103
Enterprize, schooner *(1803),* XLVII, 27; L, 245 ff.
Enterprize, ship *(1813),* XLIV, 171
Enterprize, sloop *(1776),* VIII, 256; *(1779),* XXXV, 142
Enterprize, steamship *(1825),* XXXI, 114
Envieux, French vessel *(1691),* XXXV, 154
Envoy, bark (1867), V, 152
Eothen, schooner *(1862),* VIII, 224
Eothus, schooner *(1863),* XII, 156
Epaminondas, ship (1861), XI, 266, 282
Epervier, H.M.S. *(1813),* XIX, 215–216; *(1814),* XLIV, 171; *(1815),* XL, 39 ff.
Epidemics, L, 89
— , **Rhode Island,** XL, 192
"Epilogue," by Captain Edgar K. Thompson, U.S.N. (ret.), XXV, 67
"Epitaph on a Sailor," by Captain Edgar K. Thompson, U.S.N. (ret.), XXVIII, 69
Eppes, John W., XLIII, 259
Eppleworth, ship *(1813),* XIV, 98
Epworth, Captain, XLV, 5
Equator, schooner, XXVIII, 84; *(1889),* IV, 114 ff.
Equator, ship *(1819),* XIV, 43; *(1861),* XI, 282
Equity, schooner *(1861),* XI, 282
Era, schooner *(1900),* XLV, 115; *(1904),* XII, 104
Era, whaling schooner, interior view of, Pictorial Supplement, XXXI, plate XXXII; XXXIII, plate IV
Era of the Joy Line, The, by Edwin L. Dunbaugh, reviewed, XLIII, 307
Eratt, Captain George Layton, XXI, 90
Erauso, Captain Juan de, XXVIII, 253, 254
Erben, Admiral Horace, XXXIII, 276
Erebus, British warship *(1814),* XLII, 114 ff.
Erebus, H.M.S. *(1845),* XX, 104
Erebus, ship (1845), L, 128
Erherzog Ferdinand Maximillian, Austrian warship *(1865),* XV, 201
Erickson, Captain Gilbert, XXI, 90
Erickson, Captain H. F., XXI, 90
Ericsson, ship (1853), XXIII, 201
Ericsson, torpedo boat (1861), XXXIV, 221
Ericsson, U.S.S. *(18?1),* XXI, 240
Ericsson, John, I, 53, 54; VI, 212 ff.; X, 15 ff.; XVI, 161; XVII, 93; XXII, 254; XXIII, 197 ff.; XXIV, 5; XXXI, 66; XXXV, 60; XLIX, 96 ff.
Ericsson, Captain John, XXXVI, 253, XXXVIII, 238; XXXIX, 39

Ericsson Line, XXX, 72
Ericsson Turret, fig. 2, XXII, 255
Erie, ship *(1860),* XXI, 40
Erie, sloop *(1813),* XLIX, 41 ff.; *(1835),* XXXII, 275
Erie, sloop of war (1813), XXXVIII, 115; XL, 39 ff., 216; *(1823),* XLII, 283 ff.
Erie, steamship XXXII, 33; (1837), VII, 64; *(1838),* XVIII, 279, 280, 293, 299; XX, 82, 85, 89 n., 95–99, 254, 263
Erie, steamship (1855), XXVI, 31; (1866), IV, 157–159
Erie, U.S. revenue cutter (1832), VII, 306–307; VIII, 139
Erie, U.S.S. *(1824),* XXII, 70; *(1836),* VII, 18
Erie Basin Dock Co., XIII, 120
Erie Canal, VI, 203–204; VIII, 58–59
Erie Canal Museum, Syracuse, New York, XXV, 155
Erika, steamship *(1903),* XIV, 122
Erikson, Gustaf, XXX, 220
Erikson, Captain Gustaf, II, 290
Erin, steamship (1846), XXVI, 17, 18, 21–23, 114, 115, 117, 202, 203, 205, 209; Pictorial Supplement, XXXIV, plate VI
Erkkila, Barbara H., *Hammers on Stone: A History of Cape Ann Granite,* reviewed, XLII, 221
Erlanger, Emile, XXIX, 15, 17, 25
Erl King, steamship (1865), XVII, 52; XVIII, 69
Erl King, steam yacht (1894), XXX, plate XXX
Ernestine, bark (1854), III, 64, 265
Ernestine Giddings, bark (1854), III, 265
Ernst Merck, steamship *(1861),* XI, 282
Eros, yacht *(1876),* XXXIX, 177
Erskine, David, XXIII, 168
Erskine, Vice-Admiral Sir James Elphinstone, XXVIII, 112
Erving, Captain James, XLI, 212
Erving, John, XL, 248
Escadre Estaing, French Navy, 1778, XXV, 126, plate 10
"Escape from Internment on the Yacht *Eclipse:* 1915," by William G. Wing, XLIII, 267–273
Escort, steamship (1862), XII, 289, 293
Eshelman, Dr. Ralph, Calvert Marine Museum of Solomons, Maryland, XLIII, 9 ff.
Esherick, Joseph, Jr., XLVIII, 284
Eshing (silk merchant of Canton), portrait of, XLVI, 29
Esk, whale ship, XXV, plate 8
Eskimos, steamship (ex-*Eastern Belle*), XXIII, 276
"Eskimos in the after cabin of the whaling schooner *Era,* Hudson Bay, 1903," Pictorial Supplement, XXXI, plate XXXII
Esmeralda, Chilean warship *(1843),* XXXVIII, 299; XXXIX, 272
Esmeralda, ship *(1964),* XXIV, 79
Esmeralda, steamship *(1864),* I, 261
Esmond, Captain James, XXI, 90
Esperance, French warship *(1791),* XXI, 197; *(1799),* XXXI, 173
Esperance, sloop *(1856),* X, 231 ff.
Espino, José Manuel, XXX, 49

Espoir, French ship *(1800),* XXXI, 174
Esquimalt, auxiliary schooner (1917), XXXII, 32
Essayons, schooner, XXI, 97; *(1862),* XII, 54
Essays in Modern English History in Honor of Wilbur Cortez Abbott, reviewed, II, 188
Esseiance, schooner, XXI, 94, 97; *(1862),* XII, 54
Essex, brig *(1814),* XVII, 69
Essex, frigate *(1806),* XXXVI, 288; XL, 25
Essex, H.M.S., XXVIII, 107, 108
Essex, ship, XXX, 74; *(1802),* XXV, 181–182, plate 18; *(1820),* I, 393–394
Essex, U.S. frigate (1799), II, 282, 285, 287; III, 269–270; V, 157, 329; VIII, 19; XVIII, 183; XXXI, 179; XXXII, Pictorial Supplement, plate XXV; XXXIV, 154; XXXV, 68; XLVI, 151 ff,; L, 245 ff.; *(1799),* XXIV, 250; XXV, 162
Essex, U.S.S. (1862), XIX, 267; XX, 138
Essex, U.S.S. *(1944),* XXXIX, 43
Essex, whaleship, XXVI, 217; (1796), XXV, 219
Essex (MA), XXV, 147–148; shipbuilding in, XXXVI, 77
Essex County (MA), XXVIII, 261–274
Essex Cruiser, The, XXX, 111
Essex Fire and Marine Insurance Co., V, 106, 108
Essex Gazette, The, XXX, 96, 99, 101; XXXIII, 160
Essex Institute. After 1992, see Peabody Essex Museum
Essex Institute (Salem, MA), I, 196; XXXIV, 57.
"Essex Junto, The," XXIX, 204
Essex Lance, merchant ship *(1943),* L, 220 ff.
Essex Prize, H.M.S. *(1700),* XXX, 135
ESSO (oil company), XLVII, 45 ff.; illustrations of, XLVII, 50
Esso Tokyo, tanker *(1976),* XXXVIII, 101 ff.
Estedio, Algerian brig *(1815),* XL, 40
Esther, bark (1858), III, 264
Esther, brig (1797), VI, 83
Esther, French ship *(1800),* XXXI, 174; *(1799),* XLVI, 162
Esther Eliza, schooner (1835), XXIV, 58
Esther W., bateau (1914), IV, 289
Estrada, Emilio, "Balsa and Dugout Navigation in Ecuador," XV, 142–149
Estrella, Venezuelan schooner *(1848),* XXX, 266
Ethan Allen, bark (1865), V, 149
Ethel Zane, schooner *(1918),* XVIII, 175
Ethyl, S.S. *(1938),* XLVII, 49
Etiwan, barque, XXI, 102; *(1861),* VIII, 217, 224
Etiwan, steamship *(1861),* VIII, 217; *(1863),* XLIV, 264
Etna, ketch *(1814),* XLII, 114 ff.
Etna, schooner *(1897),* XXXVIII, 87
Etna Furnace Co., XLV, 39
Etta, schooner *(1862),* VIII, 224; *(1864),* XII, 230
Eudora, steamship (1843), Pictorial Supplement, XXXIV, plate II
Eugene Hale, hermaphrodite brig, XXVIII, 123
"Eugene Hale and the American Navy," by Martin Meadows, XXII, 187–193

Eugenia, bark *(1839),* Pictorial Supplement, XXXIII, plates XX, XXI
Eugenia, brig *(1840),* XXIV, 215
Eugenia, schooner, XXI, 92, 99; *(1861),* XI, 282; XII, 54; *(1862),* VIII, 224
Eugenia, ship *(1804),* XLIII, 42
Eugenia, steamship, XXI, 106
Eugenie, bark (1864), IV, 242
Eugenie, blockade runner *(1873),* XXXVIII, 243
Eugenie, French ship *(1799),* XXXI, 173
Eugenie, schooner *(1863),* VIII, 229
Eugenie, steamship, XXI, 93. *(1863),* XII, 156
Eugenie Smith, schooner *(1862),* XII, 54
Euler, Leonhard, XXXVIII, 42
Eunice, schooner, XXII, 85
Eunice Nicholas, ship (1856), VI, 81
Euphan, British ship *(1776),* XLVIII, 18
Euphemia, schooner *(1847),* XXX, 236
Euphrates, clipper *(1838),* XXXVIII, 58
Euphrates, whaler *(1865),* XXVII, 269, 275
Eureka, Confederate blockade-runner *(1863),* XXXII, 196
Eureka, schooner *(1863),* XII, 156
Eureka, steamship (1890), VII, 165, plate 17
Euroclydon, ship (1853), III, 73
Europa, bark (1849), V, 85; VI, 19–50
Europa, ship (1859), IV, 51, 52, plate 12
Europa, ship (1898), VII, 324
Europa, steamship *(1850),* XXXVII, 233; *(1854),* XIV, 256
Europa, whaleship *(1868),* XLV, 177
Europa *Ahoy!,* by A. C. Metzelaar, reviewed, VII, 324
"*Europa's* Misfortunes, The. Documents from the Letter-Book of Captain Nathaniel Brown," edited by Lawrence Waters Jenkins, VI, 19–50
Europe, bark (1835), II, 330
European, steamship, XXVI, 30
European and Australian Royal Mail Co., XXVI, 29, 31
European and Eastern S. N. Co., XXVI, 29
European Discovery of America: The Northern Voyages, A.D. 500–1600, The, by Samuel Eliot Morison, reviewed, XXXI, 226–227
European Discovery of America: The Southern Voyages, A.D. 1492–1616, The, by Samuel Eliot Morison, reviewed, XXXV, 211
European Naval and Maritime History, 300–1500, by Archibald R. Lewis and Timothy J. Runyan, reviewed, XLVI, 200
Eurydice, frigate (1785), VI, 170
Eusebia, brig (1852), IV, 244
Eusebia N. Roya, barkentine (1852), IV, 72, 244
Eustace, Captain Richard H., XXI, 90
Eustis, F. A., XXXII, 158; XXXV, 277
Eustis, Captain Richard H., XXI, 90
Eutaw, gunboat *(1865),* XLII, 96 ff.
Euterpe, ship, XXII, 213; (1863), VII, 288; X, 109 ff., plate 15; *(1869),* XXXVIII, 237

"*Euterpe,*" *Diaries, Letters and Logs of the* Star of India *as a British Emigrant Ship,* edited by Craig Arnold, reviewed, L, 151."
Eva, three-sail bateau *(1890),* IV, 288, 292
Eva Bell, schooner *(1862),* VIII, 224
Eva Bramble, schooner (1881), XXXVII, 166
Evance, Sir Stephen, VII, 269
Evangeline, steamship/liner (1927) (renamed *Yarmouth Castle*), XXXIII, 93, 94; XXXIV, 183; XXXVI, 6, plate 1; XXXVII, 238
Evans, Amos A. (Surgeon), XLVII, 16
Evans, Charles, XXVI, 203
Evans, D. T., VII, 290
Evans, Captain David, VII, 288–290
Evans, Frank B., "A Grounding in the Bahamas in 1851," XLIX, 123–125; "A Voyage to Java in 1799–1800," XLV, 86–93
Evans, John, XXXVII, 47
Evans, Captain Richard, XL, 301
Evans, Commander Robley, XXXVIII, 297
Evans, Rear Admiral Robley D., U.S.N., XXIX, 113, 125
Evans, Samuel, XLVII, 27
Evans, Captain Samuel, XL, 32 ff.
Evans, Vaughan, Australia, XXXIX, 4
Evans and Co., John, XLIII, 13
Evarts, William M., XXXIX, 290
Evelina, schooner *(1855),* XXIV, 142
Evelina Rutter, brig *(1861),* XI, 282
Evelyn, schooner *(1861),* VIII, 217, 224, 229
Evelyn, steamship *(1864),* VIII, 233; *(1865),* XI, 277; XII, 234
Evelyn, John, XXV, 284
Evelyn W. Hinkly, schooner (1905), XXVII, plate XXVII
Evening Star, bark (1859), IV, 241; (1863), IV, 239
Evening Star, schooner *(1863),* XV, 127
Evening Star, steamship (1862), XXXIII, 203; *(1866),* IV, 151
Everett, Alexander H., XLI, 28
Everett, J. H., XVII, 47, 50
Everett, Otis, XVII, 47
Everett, Percival L., XVII, 43, 45, 47, 49, 50, 61
Everett, Washington, XXV, 172–174; XXXVI, 231 ff.
Everett G. Griggs, barkentine (1883), IV, 326; V, 81
Everglade, steamship *(1859),* VII, 119; *(1861),* XXVII, 242
Everhard Delius, bark *(1861),* XI, 282
Everingham, John, XV, 59 ff.
Evons, Captain J., XXI, 90
Ewen, Theodore, XXVII, 260, plate 11
Ewer, Peter F., XXXV, 83
Ewer, Robert, XXXI, 27
Ewer vs. Faneuil, XXXI, 28
Ewing, U.S. revenue cutter *(1862),* XLVIII, 94
Excavations. *See* Archaeology
Excel, schooner, XXI, 103
Excellent, fishing vessel *(1964),* XLI, 61
Excellent, H.M.S., XXX, 299

Excelsior, grain elevator *(1900)*, XXXVIII, 134
Excelsior, schooner (1848), Pictorial Supplement, XXXVIII, plates XXVIII, XXIX; *(1861)*, VIII, 217; *(1863)*, XII, 156
Excelsior, ship *(1845)*, XXV, 18 n.
Excelsior, steamship (1882), Pictorial Supplement, XXXIV, plate XVII
"Excerpts from Logbook of Schooner *Yarmouth*, Peleg Brown, master, on a passage from Stonington, Connecticut to West Indian Island with full cargo of horses, bullocks, sheep, etc.," document contributed by Rear Admiral J. W. McElroy, U.S.N.R. (ret.), XXV, 70
Exchange, brig (1806), VII, 317
Exchange, schooner (1816), XIV, 39; *(1820)*, XLVII, 28; *(1863)*, XII, 156
Exchange, sloop *(1861)*, VIII, 217
"Exchanging Signals," XXII, plate X
Exeter, cruiser *(1942)*, XLII, 203
Exeter, ship *(1807)*, XVI, 195
Exeter City, steamship (1887), XIV, 121, 122, 126, 127, 134; *(1933)*, XIV, 126, 135
Exeter Maritime Museum, XXX, 153
Exilda, schooner, XXI, 93
Exile, bark (1863), V, 153
Exmouth, Viscount, XXVI, 254
"*Exodus 1947:* An Interim Report on the Career of the Steamer *President Warfield*," by Alexander Crosby Brown, VIII, 127–131, plates 13–14
Exodus 1947, steamship (of Jewish state), XXII, 150; (1928), VIII, 127–131, plate 14; IX, 300–301. See also *President Warfield.*
"*Exodus 1947* Takes on her Cargo," by H. C. Timewell, IX, 300–301
"Exodus," document contributed by Captain Edgar K. Thompson, U.S.N. (ret.), XXIV, 143
Expedition, packet, XXVIII, 118
Expedition to Explore and Survey the Rio de la Plata, and its Tributaries, 1853–1856, XXXI, 8
Expéditive, French transport *(1845)*, XXXVI, 129, 130, 133, 135, 137
Experiment, barge *(1829)*, V, 301
Experiment, British brig *(1814)*, XLII, 112 ff.
Experiment, H.M.S., XXVI, 54; *(1778)*, I, 168–170; *(1838)*, VIII, 42, 44
Experiment, schooner, XXI, 98; XXXVII, 143 n.; *(1799)*, XLVI, 161 ff.
Experiment, schooner (1832), XXXIV, 188 ff.; *(1862)*, VIII, 224; *(1864)*, XII, 230
Experiment, ship *(1670)*, XIII, 15, 17
Experiment, snow *(1786)*, XI, 155–156
Experiment, steamship (1788), X, 165; *(1825)*, XLVIII, 84
Experiment, steamship (1837), VII, 64, 308–309, 313
Experiment, U.S.S. *(1800)*, XXXI, 174; XXXV, 208
Experimento, warship *(1863)*, XXXII, 279 ff.

"Explanatory Note to 'The Jakey Boats,' An," by Charles K. Cobb, XIX, 73
Exploration of Americas, XIX, 79–113
Explorations, 1696–1697, of Australia by Willem de Vlamingh, The, by William C. H. Robert, reviewed, XXXIII, 218
Explorer's Maps, by R. A. Shelton, reviewed, XIX, 307
Explosion of the "Peace-Maker" aboard U.S. Steam Frigate *Princeton*, photo of, XLIX, 108
Exporter, ship (1874), V, 152
"Exports to the Cape of Good Hope," document contributed by Charles H. P. Copeland, XIV, 139
Express, iron paddle steamship (1861), XXXI, 257; XXXIV, 30, 46; XLIII, 97 ff.; XLIX, 123
Express, schooner, XIV, 39; *(1863)*, XII, 156
Express, ship, XXI, 91; *(1861)*, XI, 282; *(1863)*, XXV, 23, 24
Express, sloop, XXI, 88, 102; *(1861)*, XI, 282; *(1863)*, VIII, 229
Express, steamship, XXVIII, 124; *(1839)*, XVIII, 299; (1861), XVI, 179; XVIII, 69
Exquemelin, Alexander, XXXVII, 42
Exton, Captain George, XXI, 90
"Extracts from the diary of William Saunders, Mariner, 1848 to 1863," with introduction by A. Fred Saunders, XVII, 17–27, plate 4
Eyre, Benjamin, XXXII, 249
Eyre, Manuel, Jehu and Benjamin (shipbuilders, Philadelphia), VIII, 12
Ezekiel Hersey Derby Farm, South Salem, ca. 1800, Pictorial Supplement, XXXII, plate XXVII
Ezilda, schooner *(1861)*, XI, 282
Ezra Ames, frigate *(1799)*, XLVI, 154
Ezra and Daniel, brig (1805), XIV, 39
Ezra Moses & Co., XLIII, 125 ff.
"Ezra Westons, Shipbuilders of Duxbury, The" by Gershom Bradford, XIV, 29–41, plates 5, 6

F. A. Johnson, sloop *(1860)*, XXVIII, 223
F. B. Jones, steamship *(1907)*, XXXVIII, 180 ff.
F. D. Asche, steamship (1918), VIII, 68–69
F. Mertens & Sons, XXXV, 171
F. S. Means, bark (1854), IV, 326; VI, 81
F. W. Cochran, barkentine (1854), III, 64
F. W. Johnson, schooner, XXI, 102
F. W. Lincoln, Jr. & Co., Boston, Pictorial Supplement, XXXV, plate X
F. W. Nickerson Co., XXXVII, 234
Fabens, Captain Samuel Augustus, I, 82–83
Fabia, diesel trawler (1920), XLIV, 127
Fabian, Captain John, XXI, 90

Fabius, ship (1784), XI, 61
Factor, ship *(1824),* XXV, 185
Fäderneslandet, ship (1782), VI, 170
Faerøyvik, Barnhard and Øystein, *Inshore Craft of Norway,* reviewed, XLII, 308–309
Fagatau, boats of, XIII, 93 ff.
Fah Kee, steamship (1862), XVII, 224; XVIII, 69
Faibisy, John D., "The Greening of A. Crabtree: The Downeast Adventures of a Revolutionary Privateersman," XLII, 5–24
"Failure of the Li-ch'uan Hong: Litigation as a Hazard of Nineteenth Century Foreign Trade, The," by Frederic D. Grant, Jr., XLVIII, 243–260
Fair American (1804), XIII, 278
Fair American, cartel *(1814),* XXVIII, 168, 190
Fair American, schooner *(1796),* XLI, 227; *(1805),* XLIX, 86
Fair American, ship, XXII, 92; *(1804),* X, 53
Fairbanks, Douglas, Sr., XXXVIII, 7
Fairchild, Byron, XLV, 42 ff.; "A Sea of Troubles: the Voyage of *Bonetta,* 1718," IX, 133–141
Fairchild, Flora, XXXVIII, 232
Faire et Fraissenet, French shipping line, XLVI, 108
Fairfield, grain elevator *(1883),* XXXVIII, 141
Fairfield, sloop, XXI, 98; *(1861),* XI, 283
Fairfield, U.S.S. *(1841),* XXVII, 160
Fairfowl, James, XXIX, 198
Fairmorse, schooner (1935), XXVI, plate XXXII
Fairmount Park, steamship *(1946),* XIV, 131, 135
Fairplay, schooner (1862), VIII, 224
Fairplay, steamship (1831), VII, 46 n.
Fairport, steamship *(1841),* XX, 90 n.
Fair Wind, ship (1855), III, 170
Fairy, schooner *(1863),* XII, 156
Fairy, ship *(1793),* X, 53
Fairy, steamship *(1864),* XXI, plate IV
Fairy, steamship (1870), XVII, 308, 309; XVIII, 69
Fairy Queen, iron steamship *(1831),* XXII, 157
Faith, concrete ship *(1917),* XXII, 159, 161, 162, 164, 165, 166, 167, plate 5, 173, 175, 182
Faith, steamship *(1918),* XLI, 195
Falaba, ship *(1915),* XXXV, 44
Falcon, bark *(1893),* XXXVIII, 51
Falcon, H.M. Sloop *(1776),* XXX, 220
Falcon, sailing vessel, XXII, 17
Falcon, schooner, XXI, 101; *(1861),* XI, 283
Falcon, ship *(1854),* XLV, 33
Falcon, steamship, XXI, 102; *(1848),* IV, 307; *(1864),* VIII, 233
Falcon, yacht *(1896),* XXXVI, 239
Falcón, José (Paraguayan Foreign Minister), XXXI, 12
Falconer, ship *(1834),* XXIII, 137
Falconer, Lieutenant Commander A. F., XXXVII, 177
Falconer, William, XXV, 82, 85; XXX, 40; XLVI, 223
Fales, Captain A. N., XXXVII, 85
Fales, Dean A., Jr., contributed document, XXI, 222
Fales, James, XXVI, 175

Fales, James, Sr., XXXIV, 205
Fales, Martha G., note by, XXVIII, 144–145
Falkland, British warship *(1695),* XLVIII, 23
Falkland Islands. See World War: 1914–1918
Falkland Islands, XXX, 204; map of, XLIX, 279
Falkus, Hugh, *Master of Cape Horn: The Story of a Square-rigger Captain and his World: William Andrew Nelson, 1839–1929,* reviewed, XLIII, 311–313
"Fall Guy, The," document contributed by Charles S. Morgan, XXXI, 288
Fall River Line, A Short History of the, by William King Covell, reviewed, VII, 248–249
Fall River Line, III, 43–46; XXX, 72; XXXIV, 259
Fall River-Providence Line, XIII, 120
Falls Line, XXX, 220
Falls of Clyde, four-masted ship (1878), IX, 297; XXIV, 3; XXVIII, 163–164
Falls of Clyde, ship, mentioned, XL, 164; *(1941),* XXXVII, 98
Falls of Ettrick, ship (1894), IX, 297
Falmouth, H.M.S., XXVI, 55; *(1817),* XXXIX, 142 ff.
Falmouth, ship *(1851),* XXXV, 26
Falmouth, side-wheel steamship (1872), XXXIII, 89, plate 1, 94; Pictorial Supplement, XXXIV, plate VIII; XXXVII, 236
Falmouth, sloop *(1750),* XX, 242
Falmouth and Harwich Packets, XXX, 10
Falscher, Captain N. C., XXI, 90
Falshar, Captain N. C., XXI, 90
Fame (1800), XXIII, 216
Fame, bark (1854), III, 349
Fame, brig *(1799),* XLV, 92
Fame, schooner, XXII, 60 n.
Fame, ship (or *Belisarius*?), *(1802),* II, 279; Pictorial Supplement, XXXII, plate VII; *(1803),* XXV, 184
Fame, ship (1854), XXII, Plate VII
Fame, sloop (1803), XXII, 216; *(1824),* XXIV, 132
Fame, steamship (1857), XXXIV, 36
Fame, Venezuelan schooner *(1848),* XXX, 266
Fame, whale ship, XXV, plates 7, 8
Families at sea. See Seafaring life
"Famous Chinese Navigator Hee-Li, The," by Francis P. Farquhar, III, 57–59
Fancy (Fancy Xmas), gunboat *(1782),* XXXIX, 216
Fandino, Captain Juan de Leon, XXVI, 43, 54
Fane, Henry, XX, 14
Fane, Thomas, XX, 12
Fanestrand, auxiliary schooner (1918), V, 140
Fannie, steamship, XXI, 87, 97, 105; *(1863),* VIII, 229, 233; IX, 39–40
Fannie Crenshaw, bark (1861), III, 349
Fannie G., water boat *(1896),* XXXIV, 10
Fannie J. Bartlett, schooner *(1893),* XXXV, 12
Fannie Laurie, bark (1862), VIII, 224
Fannie Lewis, brig, *(1861),* VIII, 217
Fannie Paine, schooner, XXI, 97; *(1862),* VIII, 224
Fannie Palmer, schooner (1900), V, 80; (1907), V, 80

Fannie Skolfield, bark *(1873),* III, 66
Fanning, Captain Edmund, XIV, 209–210; XXX, 297
Fanning, Captain Horace B., XXI, 90
Fanning, John, XXXIX, 30
Fanning & Coles, New York, XLVIII, 255
Fanny, bark *(1850),* XV, 181, 185
Fanny, bark (ex-ship) *(1822),* Pictorial Supplement, XXXIII, plates XX, XXI
Fanny, brig, XXII, 85; *(1777),* XLIII, 24
Fanny, H.M. tender *(1845),* XXXVI, 128 ff.
Fanny, schooner, XXI, 101, 103; *(1777),* II, 204–205; *(1861),* XI, 267, 283; XII, 230; XV, 126
Fanny, ship *(1770),* XXXV, 298; *(1786),* XLIX, 83; *(1802),* X, 53; XV, 153
Fanny, steamship *(1862),* VIII, 224; *(1863),* XI, 263; XII, 156; *(1872),* XII, 289, 293
Fanny, transport (1862), XXXVII, 284
Fanny and Jenny, steamship, XXI, 81, 87, 89, 90, 95; *(1863),* VIII, 229, 234; *(1864),* XVIII, 147
Fanny Buck, bark (1853), III, 64
Fanny Dutard, schooner *(1928),* XVIII, 219
Fanny Fern, schooner *(1861),* XI, 283
Fanny Flint, schooner (1872), XXIV, 58
Fanny Lee, schooner, XXI, 91; *(1861),* XV, 114, 123
Fanny Lewis, brig, XXI, 103; *(1862),* VIII, 224
Fanny Lowery, bark *(1862),* VIII, 224
Fanny M., gundalow (1883), I, 68; II, 129, 209–222, plate 30
Fanny Mason, boat *(1848),* IV, 71
Fanny Mason, metallic lifeboat *(1848),* XXIII, 141
Fanny McHenry, ship (1854), III, 170
Fanny McRae, schooner *(1865),* XII, 234
Fanny Skinner, boat *(1848),* IV, 71
Fanny Skinner, metallic lifeboat *(1848),* XXIII, 141
Fanshawe, Captain Charles, XXVI, 40
Fanshawe, Vice-Admiral Sir Edward G., XXVIII, 111
Fantome, H.M.S. *(1902),* XXVIII, 98
Faraday, Michael, XLVII, 177
Far East, steamship *(1861),* XLIII, 186 ff.
Farewell Old Mount Washington: The Story of the Steamboat Era on Lake Winnipesaukee, by Edward H. Blackstone, reviewed, XXIX, 286
Farewell to Steam, by David Plowden, reviewed, XXVII, 151
Farley, Captain James, XLVIII, 42
Farley, Postmaster General James A., XLI, 113
Farly, M. Foster, "John E. Ward and the Chinese Coolie Trade," XX, 209–216
Farmer, schooner *(1777),* II, 206–207
Farmer, Weston, *From My Old Boat Shop,* reviewed, XL, 235
Farn, British ship *(1915),* XLVIII, 55
Farnham, Albert A., insurance inspector, I, 43
Farnham, C. S., and Co., XVII, 140, 150, 151
Farquhar, Alexander, XXVI, 203
Farquar, Rear Admiral Sir Arthur M., XXVIII, 112
Farquhar, Francis P., "The Famous Chinese Navigator Hee-Li," III, 57–59
Farr, Grahame, documents contributed by, XXII, 219–220; XXXI, 288–289; XXXII, 194; "Prize to Privateer Yankee, 1812," XXII, 216–217; *The Steamship Great Britain,* reviewed, XXV, 228
Farr, Grahame and Cyril Noall, *Wreck and Rescue Round the Cornish Coast,* Volume I, reviewed, XXVI, 75
Farr, Grahame E., VI, 3–4; VIII, 199; contributed document, XV, 153; "American-built Vessels in the Bristol Channel," VI, 80–83; "The Bristol City Line of Bristol, England," XIV, 115–135, plates 13–15; *"The Five-Masted Schooner Cap Nord,* and Others," IX, 67–68, plate 6; *"General Gates,* ex-*Industrious Bee,"* X, 230; "The Second Great Western Steamship Company, of Bristol, England," XI, 251–261; "S.S. Great Western – A Correction," XII, 310
Farragut, iron ferry *(1880),* XLVIII, 128
Farragut, Admiral David G., XII, 272–276; XXXVI, 193 ff.
Farragut, Vice Admiral David G., XLII, 95 ff.
Farragut, Mrs. David G., XXXV, 63
Farragut, David Glasgow, XXXII, 51; XXXIV, 63; XXXV, 61 ff.; XXXVIII, 112
Farragut, Admiral David Glasgow, U.S.N., XXII, 283 n.; XXV, 159, 162–163
Farragut, Jorge, XXV, 162
Farralones, auxiliary steam packet (1845), I, 55
Farrand, Commander Ebenezer, XL, 42
Farrar, Frank R., *A Ship's Logbook,* reviewed, XLIX, 306
Farrell, Mrs. Margaret, XXXVI, 21
Farrell, Captain O. R., XXIII, 12
Farrell, Patrick, L, 203
Farris, Thomas, XXXI, 98
Farwell, Robert D., "'Notes,' William Eldridge's memorandum: Interpersonal Conflict in the Whaling Industry," XLII, 217–219
Far West, bark (1846), V, 151; VI, 80
Far West, steamship *(1876),* XXIII, 286
Fashion, schooner, XXI, 97; *(1861),* XI, 283; XII, 156
Fashion, sloop, XXI, 96; *(1862),* XII, 54, 156
Fast Sailing Ships: Their Design and Construction, 1775–1875, by David R. MacGregor, reviewed, XLIX, 315
Fatherland, ship (1854), III, 170
Father's Good Will, British transport *(1777),* XL, 21 ff.
"Fatimid Navy During the Early Crusades: 1099–1124, The," by William Hamblin, XLVI, 77–83
Fatimids, XLVI, 77 ff.
Fatimites, History, naval, XLVI, 77
Fatted Calf, sloop, XXIV, 53
Faucitt, Sir William, XLVI, 19
Faun, brig, XXV, 186
Faunce, Captain John, XXXVI, 177 ff.
Fauria, Captain Juan, XXI, 90

Faust, steamship *(1866),* XLIII, 299
Fausta, steamship (1922), XIV, 135
Favorita, schooner *(1856),* X, 231 ff.
Favorite, French ship *(1800),* XXXI, 174
Favorite, schooner, XXII, 60 n.; *(1812),* XLII, 106
Favorite, ship *(1860),* XLVII, 100; (1863), IV, 72, 244
Favorite, whaler *(1865),* XXVII, 275
Favorite, woodboat (1816), XVII, 12
Favourite, brig *(1808),* XXIII, 253 n.
Favourite, ship *(1805),* X, 54, 55, 56, 62; *(1807),* XIII, 280; *(1819),* XLI, 286
Fawcett, Sir Charles, "Captain Richard Maples, Early Mariner and Adventurer in the East," XIII, 5–28, plates 1, 2
Fawcett, Preston & Co., XXVI, 207
Fawcett, William, XVI, 103
Fawkener, W., XXIII, 173
Fawn, steamship (1847), XXIV, 235, 236
Faxon, William, XXXV, 57
Fay, Arthur D., reviews by, XXII, 72–73, 145–147, 150, 222–223; XXIII, 70–71, 228, 286; XXIV, 74–75, plate I; XXV, 75; XXVI, 74, 145–146, 150–151, 221, 224, 286–287; XXVII, 66–67, 151, 223–224, 286–287, 289; XXVIII, 294–295, 296; XXIX, 74–75, 144–145, 147–148, 286, 290; XXX, 224; XXXI, 77
Fay, Charles Edey, X, 194–195; queries by, I, 310; IV, 251; answered query, II, 250–251; Mary Celeste, *The Odyssey of an Abandoned Ship,* announced, II, 84; reviewed, II, 254–256
Fazio, brig *(1824),* XII, 180–181
Fazl Kereem, Arab dhow *(1853),* XXVI, 18
Fearing, Thatcher & Whiton, XV, 220
Fearless, ship, XXII, 239; (1853), III, 169
Fearless, steam bark *(1894),* XXXVIII, 85
Fearless, steamship (1897), VII, 228, 229, 231
Fearless, steam tug *(1919),* XXV, 290–291
Fearon, C. A., XVII, 47, 50
Febar, Juan Muños, XXX, 273
Febiger, Commander John, XXXV, 29
Febvrier-Despointes, Rear Admiral, XXXI, 269
"Federal Archives Relating to Matthew Fontaine Maury," by Lewis J. Darter, Jr., I, 149–158
Federal Eagle, brig (1800), XIV, 39
Federal George, brig *(1808),* XVI, 202
Federalist, ship *(1812),* XLV, 6
Federal Jack, schooner *(1813),* XXVIII, 36, 37
Federal Trade Commission, 1915, XXXII, 160; XXXV, 278 ff.
Fedhala, French Morocco, III, 99 ff.
Fee, Robert G. C., XIV, 106; model by, VIII, plate 16; "The 1957 Jamestown fleet," XVII, 173–180, plates 15–18, plans.
Fee Yuen, steamship *(1866),* XVII, 214, 308
Fei-Má, ship *(1858),* XXXIV, 17 ff.
Fei Má, Fei Mà or *Feima,* steamship (1856), XXII, 31, 35, 38, 42, 43; XLIII, 125 ff.; XVIII, 59, 69
Feingold, Henry, XLIII, 31 ff.

Fei Pang (ex-*Monitor,* ex-*Union Star*), XXXIV, 47
Fei Seen (*Fei Sun*), steamship (1860), XXXIV, 25 ff.; XLIII, 195 ff.
Fei-wan, steamship (1862), XVI, 163
Fei Yuen, tugboat *(1864),* XLIII, 298
Feland, General, XXXV, 129
Felch, Cheever, XLVI, 218
Felch, Chaplain Cheever, XIII, 271
Felice Adventurer (1788), XV, 206, 207, 211
Felicia, ship (1855), II, 331
Felix, French ship *(1800),* XXXI, 174
Felix, Bishop of Oporto, XXX, 252
Feller, John Quentin, review by, XL, 65–66; XLIII, 149–150; "China Sojourn: A Brief Account of Commander Bushrod B. Taylor's Tour of Duty [with the Asiatic Squadron, 1869–1871, Together with Some of His Purchases], XLV, 237–243; "The White House 'Rose Medallion:' Daniel Ammen and the Ulysses S. Grant Porcelain," XLIII, 157–185
Fe loong, steam ferry *(1867),* XXXIV, 52
Felton, Senator Charles, XXV, 265
Felton Bent, schooner, XXV, 148
"Female Emigrants," XXXI, Pictorial Supplement, plate XVI
"Feminist and Victorian: The Paradox of the American Seafaring Woman of the Nineteenth Century," by Julia A. Bonham, XXXVII, 203–218
Fenella, steamship *(1846),* XLIII, 111 ff.; *(1850),* XVII, 228; XVIII, 69
Fenelon, bark (1849), I, 68
Fenelon, schooner (1806), XIV, 39
Fenger, Frederic, "The Rake of Bugeye Masts," XX, 66
Fenimore Cooper, warship *(1854),* XXXVIII, 33
Fennel, H.M.C.S., British vessel *(1943),* XLIV, 49 ff.
Fennell, A. M., XXVI, 21
Fennell, Captain J. L., XXI, 91
Fenton, Captain Edward, XXVII, 182
Fenton, William N., review by, XXV, 295–297
Fenton, William N., and Ernest Stanley Dodge, "An Elm Bark Canoe in the Peabody Museum of Salem," IX, 185–206
Ferdinanda, U.S.S. *(1862),* XXV, 72
Ferdinando Gorges, ferry, XXVI, 262
Fergus, steamship (1863), III, 137
Ferguson, sloop (ex-*Polly*) *(1776),* XXXIX, 201
Ferguson, E. James, *The Papers of Robert Morris, 1781–1784,* reviewed, XLVII, 54
Ferguson, Eugene F., XLIX, 49 ff.
Ferguson, Eugene S., VII, 254; query by, VII, 322; "Comments on 'The Design of the American Frigates of the Revolution and Joshua Humpreys,'" X, 65–66; "The Figurehead of the United States Frigate *Constellation,*" VII, 255–260; "Mr. Jefferson's Dry Docks," XI, 108–114
Ferguson, Henry, I, 100, 164–165, 185
Ferguson, Homer, XLI, 193
Ferguson, Homer L., XVII, 174; XXXII, 164

Ferguson, James, XV, 95
Ferguson, Major Patrick, XLVI, 21
Ferguson, Robert, XIX, 232–234
Ferguson, Samuel, I, 100, 164–165, 185
Fern, steamship *(1869),* XLVIII, 127
Fern, U.S.S. *(1900),* XX, 136
Fernald, Daniel, XV, 251
Fernald, John, *Destroyer from America,* reviewed, II, 342–343
Fernamdez, Guomcallo, XXX, 253
Fernandes, steamship *(1858),* XVI, 167; *(1861),* XLIII, 124 ff.
Fernandez, Juan, XXVII, 97
Fernandina, U.S.S. (1862), XXXI, 18; XXXII, 48, 55
Fernandina and Cedar Keys Railroad, VII, 122
Fernandina Line, VII, 136
Fernando de Norzagarey, steamship (1858), XVIII, 59, 69
Ferne, Sir John, XXXVII, 10; XLVII, 77
Ferree, Professor Walter L., XXXI, 84
Ferrer, 2nd Lieutenant Francisco, XXX, 54
Ferrer, Captain Joseph, XXI, 91
Ferret, H.M.S. *(1711),* XIII, 177 ff.
Ferris, Theodore, XXXV, 279 ff.
Ferris, Theodore E., XII, 239–240; XXXVI, 5, 6; XLI, 191
Ferris design wooden steamer hull, V, plate 8
Fessenden, Captain B. L., "The Yankee Clipper & the Cape Cod Boy," XXIII, 264–269
Fessenden, Captain Benjamin C., XVIII, 83
Fetchko, Peter J., note by, L, 4; review by, XLIV, 134; "Salem Trading Voyages to Japan During the Early Nineteenth Century," XLVI, 50–54
Fettyplace, Edward, XXX, 103
Fickett, Francis, IX, 249
Fiction. See individual topics, e.g., Arctic regions; Cape Ann; Language, Marine; Navigation in literature; Sailors; Sea in literature; Sea poetry; Ships in literature; Shipwrecks in fiction; Whaling in literature
Fidelio Navigation Corp. of New York, XXXII, 14
Fids, sailmaker's, IX, 283–285
Field, Charles, XXI, 303–304
Field, Earle, "Neutral Trade and the Order in Council of 7 January 1807," XXIII, 157–173
Field, James A., Jr., *The Japanese at Leyte Gulf,* reviewed, VII, 247–248
Field, James Seward, XXVI, 203
Field, Maunsell B., XXXV, 63
Field, Peter, XIII, 17
Fields, Captain James S., XXI, 91
Fiery Brass, schooner *(1864),* XII, 230
Fiery Cross, ship *(1868),* XXII, 241; *(1886),* XXXV, 32 ff.
Fiery Cross, steamship (1855), XXVI, 120–122, 124, 126, 127, 205, 209
Fife, William, XXXVI, 243
Fifield, Charles, XXI, 115, 124

15 Modern Yacht Designs, by Henry A. Scheel, reviewed, XLIV, 201
53 Boats You Can Build, by Richard Henderson, commentator, reviewed, XLVI, 130
"Fifty Years of Sail: The Bark *Abraham Rydberg,*" by John Lyman, II, 289–298
Fifty Years of Shipbuilding, reviewed, I, 325
Fighting Fleets, by Critchell Rimington, reviewed, II, 352; 1944 revised edition, reviewed, IV, 340
"Figurehead of *San Fermin,* The," by Captain Edgar K. Thompson, U.S.N. (ret.), XXII, 217–218
"Figurehead of *Talma,* A," by Charles H. P. Copeland, IX, 72
"Figurehead of *Talma,* A," by Walter Muir Whitehill, I, 82–83
"Figurehead of the United States Frigate *Constellation,* The," by Eugene S. Ferguson, VII, 255–260
Figureheads, VII, 255. See also Carving; Ship decoration
Figureheads: VII, 255–260, 297, 303, plates 36–37; VIII, 125, 138, plate 12; IX, 72. Carving of, IV, 263; XXV, 53, 54; Review of Pauline A. Pinckney, *American Figureheads and their Carvers,* I, 178–181; Unidentified bust head, Pictorial Supplement, XXXVII, plates XVII, XVIII; Unidentified ship, figurehead Britannia from, Pictorial Supplement, XXXVII, plate XIII; Unidentified ship, figurehead from, Pictorial Supplement, XXXVII, plates XI, XII, XIV; Unidentified sternboard carving, Pictorial Supplement, XXXVII, plate XXI
Figureheads of: *Abraham Rydberg,* bark (1892), II, plate 40; *Belle of Oregon,* bark (1876), I, 59, 176; of *General Armstrong,* XXV, 122; *Paul Jones,* ship (1886), I, 59; *Star of Alaska,* ex-*Balclutha,* IV, plate 35; Talma as Nero, I, 82–83, plate facing 82; of a Woman, XXVIII, plate XXXII
Fiji, Foreign relations, United States, XXXV, 20. See also Oceania; Shipping; Shipwrecks
Fijians, XXV, 274
Fiji Islands, South Pacific, XIII, 275–281; XXV, 274 ff., 186–187; map of, XXIII, plate 12; boats of, XIII, 95 ff.
Filleul, Captain J. T., XVIII, 83
Fillmore, President Millard, XXVII, 161; XLI, 32
Filzow, Nick, XXXIX, 255
Finch, Master Commandant William B., XXXI, 181
Finch, Captain William C. B., XLVI, 45
Fincham, John, *A History of Naval Architecture,* reviewed, XLII, 309–310
"Finding Longitude at Sea by Magnetic Declination on Dutch East Indiamen, 1596–1795," by Karel A. Davids, L, 281–290
Findsburg, bark *(1861),* XV, 123
"Fine Forests for the Navy," by M. W. Jacobus, XVIII, 315–316
Fingal, blockade runner *(1861),* XLII, 199 ff.
Fingal, ship *(1814),* XV, 306

Fingal, steamship, XXI, 86; *(1861),* XV, 106, 107, 111, 123
Fink, Captain, C. K., XXXIX, 44
Finker, Captain Edward, XX, 245
Finland, bark *(1840),* XXV, 18 n.
Finland, ship (1844), I, 48; *(1861),* XI, 283
Finlayson, C., XXXVI, 235
Finnpulp, freighter *(1965),* XXXVI, 12, 15–20, 26, 27, plate 4
Fire at sea, XVII, 17; XX, 79; XXXVI, 5; XXXIX, 218. *See also* Steamships (Fires)
Firebrand, British ship *(1738),* XLVIII, 23
Firebrand, H.M. frigate *(1845),* XXXVI, 127 ff.; *(1895),* XL, 102 ff.
Fire Cracker (1862), XVII, 302 ff.; XVIII, 69; XXXIV, 32; XLIII, 201, plate 4; *(1864),* XXXIX, 143
Fire Dart, steamship (1860), XVII, 43, 47, 48; XVIII, 69; photo of, XXXIV, plate 3; XLIII, 93 ff., plate 3; XLIX, 23
Fired by Manley Zeal: A Naval Fiasco of the American Revolution, by Philip Chadwick Foster Smith, reviewed, XXXVIII, 70
Fire Flash, steamship *(1864),* XLIII, 202 ff.
Fire Fly, brig, XXIX, 197
Firefly, ship *(1815),* XL, 39 ff.; *(1860),* XXVII, 235
Fire Fly, steamship (1812), XVIII, 317; XXVII, 25, 27
Firefly, steamship (1846), XVI, 161; *(1846),* XXII, 9, 42
Fire Queen, steamship (1843) XXVI, 8, 9, 205, 209; XXXIV, 49; XLIII, 94 ff.; *(1862),* XXXIX, 143; *(1863),* XLIII, 202 ff.; (1864), XVI, 252; XVII, 38, 304; XVIII, 69
Fire ship, XVII, 21–22, 26–27
"Firing a Western River-type Firetube Boiler," by John C. Bower, Jr., XXXIII, 155–159
Firm, H.M. gunboat *(1868),* XXXIV, 47
First Aid for Marine Finds, by Wendy Robinson, XLII, 227
"First American Hostages in Moslem Nations, 1784–1789, The," by Gary E. Wilson, XLI, 208–223
First Americans in North Africa, The, by Louis B. Wright and Julia H. MacLeod, reviewed, V, 329–330
"First American Steam Passenger Line to South America, The," by Francis O. Braynard, IV, 137–163
First Battle of Modern Naval History, The, by Garland Evans Hopkins, reviewed, VI, 87
"First Cruise of the Privateer *Harpy,* The," by George A. Nelson, I, 116–122
"First Cubic War—The *Virginius* Affair, The," by Lawrence Carroll Allin, XXXVIII, 233–248
"First Flight," document contributed by Captain Edgar K. Thompson, U.S.N. (ret.), XXII, 142
"First Four-masted Schooner," by John Lyman, I, 163
"First Four-masted Ship, query by John Lyman, I, 310; query answered by R. C. Anderson and others, II, 82
First International Congress of Maritime Museums of the Atlantic Basin, XXXII, 229

"First Iron Steamer, The," by H. Philip Spratt, XIII, 157–161
"First Officer Morton's Cabin aboard the clipper ship *Nightingale,*" Pictorial Supplement, XXXI, plate XXII
"First Salem Vessel in Sydney and Fiji, The," by Thomas Dunbabin, XIII, 275–281
First Ships Round the World, The, by Walter Brownlee, reviewed, XLVI, 125
"First Steamboat to Albany," by Donald C. Ringwald, XXIV, 157–171
"First Successful Marine Railway," document contributed by Marion V. Brewington, XIV, 215
"First Use of the Sail by the Indians of the Northwest Coast, The," by F. W. Howay, I, 374–380
"First Word from *Kearsarge,*" document contributed by Richard H. Dillon, XIX, 126–128
Firth of Forth, 1832, XXIX, 198, plate XXII
Fisbay, Joseph, VII, 50
Fischer, Anton Otto, *Focs'le Days,* reviewed, XLIX, 310
Fischer, Lawrence J., "Horse Soldiers in the Arctic: The Garlington Expedition of 1883," XXXVI 108–124
Fischer, Lewis R. and Gerald E. Panting, *Change and Adaptation in Maritime History: The North Atlantic Fleets in the Nineteenth Century,* reviewed, XLVII, 64
Fish, Captain Ansel C., XXXIX, 101
Fish, Hamilton, Secretary of State, XXXVI, 97 ff.; XXXVIII, 238
Fish, Nicholas, XXXVI, 56
Fish, Preserved, XXXIX, 83
Fisher, steamship *(1865),* VIII, 237
Fisher, Carl G., XXII, 168
Fisher, Charles R., "Gun Drill in the Sailing Navy, 1797–1840," XLI, 85–92; "The Great Guns of the Navy, 1797–1843," XXXVI, 276–295
Fisher, Commodore Frederick W., XXVIII, 104, 106 n.
Fisher, Captain Jared, XVI, 211
Fisher, John (Salem Tax Collector), XXXI, 196
Fisher, Rear Admiral John Arbuthnot, XXVIII, 16, 20, 86–93, 100–102, 104, 106 n., 100, 112
"Fisher, Mount and Page, Seventeenth- and Eighteenth-Century Book and Chart Publishers," note contributed by Captain John F. Campbell, XXIII, 219–221
Fisher, Raymond H., *Bering's Voyages: Whither and Why,* reviewed, XXXVIII, 302
Fisher, Redwood, XLVIII, 250
Fisher, Susan Fogle, XXXVII, 213
Fisher, William, VIII, 303–305, 308; XXIII, 219
Fisheries:
   Gulf of Mexico, II, 229
   Newfoundland, XLVIII, 154
   North Atlantic Ocean, XXXIII, 246
   United States, XLVIII, 165
   —, **Massachusetts,** X, 243; XIII, 125; XXVI, 202
Fisheries management, XLV, 81
Fisheries Research, V, 5

"Fisherman's Luck," by Captain Edgar K. Thompson, U.S.N. (ret.), XXVI, 215–216

Fishermen. *See* Fishers

Fishermen, American, by Albert Cook Church and James B. Connolly, reviewed, I, 181–182

Fishers, Nova Scotia, XIII, 125

Fishery, The, oil by Cornè, Pictorial Supplement, XXXII, plate XXVI

Fishery law and legislation, XXXIX, 289

Fishing:
  Nova Scotia, XXXIX, 289
  United States, XLIV, 114

Fishing, IX, 73–74; in Nova Scotia, XIII, 125–130; in Pensacola, Florida, II, 229–242; for lobsters in Maine: XIV, 203–208

Fishing boats, United States, XLIV, 114
  Florida, II, 229

"Fishing Craft of Manfredonia," by Beaumont Newhall, XII, 240, plates 23, 24

Fishing Industry, XXVIII, 261–274

Fishing in Many Waters, by James Hornell, reviewed, XI, 295–296

Fishing Schooners, American and Canadian, XXVI, plates I-VIII, 64; plates IX-XVI, 140; plates XVII-XXIV, 200; plates XXV-XXXII, 242

Fishmongers Co. of London, XXXI, 85 ff.; XLVII, 77

Fishwick's Colonial Express, XXXVII, 235

Fiske, Augustus H., "Wrecks of Civil War Blockade-runners," III, 265; *Five Centuries of Marine Painting,* by W. R. Valentiner, reviewed, II, 353

Fiske, Bradley A., XXXVII, 111–127; XXXVIII, 122

Fiske, Rear Admiral Bradley A., photo of, L, 54

Fister, Lieutenant Thomas D., XL, 303; XLVIII, 89

Fitch, Henry D., XXXII, 119

Fitch, John, XXIII, 204 ff.; L, 201

Fitch, Captain Peter, XXIII, 26

Fitton, Commodore Juan, XXIX, 179

Fitts, George, XVII, 126

Fitzgerald, John, XXXIII, 17

Fitzhugh, Henry, VII, 61

FitzHugh, William, XXX, 135

Fitz Hugh Lane, by John Wilmerding, reviewed, XXXII, 69

Fitz Hugh Lane, American Marine Painter, by John Wilmerding, XXV, plates, I–VIII

Fitzroy, Captain, XXXII, 243

FitzRoy, Captain Robert, L, 32

Fitzsimmons, Thomas, XLVI, 155

Five Brothers, schooner *(1863),* XV, 127

Five Brothers, steamship *(1858),* XXVI, 199, 200, 205, 209

"Five Dana Letters," edited by James Allison, XIII, 162–176

5 de Marzo, schooner (1859), XXX, 276

"Five-Masted Barkentines," by John Lyman, V, 81–82

"Five-Masted Schooner *Cap Nord,* and Others, The," by Grahame Farr, IX, 67–68, plate 6

"Five-masted Schooner *Elvira Ball,* The," by John Lyman, V, 327

"Five-masted Schooners," by John Lyman, V, 137–141

"Five-masted Square-riggers," by John Lyman, VI, 135–136, plate 18

Five-Power Naval Treaty, The, XXXVII, 115

Five Sea Captains, by Walter Teller, cited, XXV, 61

"Five Thousand Miles in a Fifty-Footer," by John Gordon, XIV, 18–29, plates 1–4

Fi Wan (Fei Wan), steamship (1862), XXXIV, 34 ff.; XLIX, 21

FL. *See* Florida

Flag, U.S.S. *(1862),* XVI, 52

Flagg, Horatio C., query by, VII, 77–78

Flag Heritage Foundation, XXXVII, 133

Flagler, tanker *(1943),* XLIV, 51 ff.

Flags, United States, XXXVII, 128. *See also* Signals and Signaling

Flagstaff, schooner (1916), V, 81

Flambeau, French ship *(1800),* XXXI, 174

Flambeau, ship *(1815),* XL, 39 ff.

Flambeau, steamship (1861), XVI, 172; XVIII, 69

Flambo, brig, XXIX, 197

Flamborough, H.M.S. *(1742),* XXVI, 44, 46, 47, 53, 54, 59, 60

Flamingo, steamship *(1864),* XXI, plate XVIII; *(1865),* XI, 277; XII, 234

Flamsteed, John, XXI, 108

Flanders, schooner, XXXII, plate 12

Flanders, Reverend Charles, XXV, 274

Flash, schooner *(1813),* XVII, 71; *(1861),* VIII, 217, 224; *(1863),* XII, 156, 230

Flash, schooner, XXI, 101, 103

Flat Holm Island, XX, 5–43

Flaurence E. Ward, ship *(1908),* VIII, 194

Flavit, Captain Juan, XXI, 91

Flavius, ship *(1851),* XLV, 128

Flayderman, E. Norman, *Scrimshaw and Scrimshanders, Whales and Whalemen,* reviewed, XXXIII, 66–67

Flayhart, William H. III and John H. Shaum, Jr., *Majesty at Sea — The Four Stackers,* reviewed, XLIII, 303

"Fleet, The" by Sidney G. Morse, V, 177–193

Fleet Distribution Table, XXVIII, 102

Fleetford, ship (1864), V, 148

"Fleet That Never Was: Commodore John Crittenden Watson and the Eastern Squadron, The," by William J. Hourihan, XLI, 93–109

Fleet Today, The, by Kendall Banning, reviewed, I, 187

Fleetwing, bark (1854), V, 150; *(1888),* XXXIX, 8

Fleetwood, Captain James M., XXI, 105

Fletcher, Andrew, XXXVI, 172

Fletcher, Captain, XLV, 36

Fletcher, Senator Duncan U., XXXV, 172

Fletcher, Rear Admiral W. B., XXXV, 106

Fletcher and Co., XVI, 251; XVII, 304–305; XLIII, 186 ff.

Fleur de la Mer, French schooner *(1798),* L, 270 ff.

Fleurieu, Comte de, Charles Pierre Claret (1738–1810), XXV, 260
Fleuron, French warship, XXVI, 55
Flexner, James Thomas, *Steamboats Come True,* reviewed, V, 92–93; re-reviewed, XL, 232
Flight From The Flag, The, by George W. Dalzell, reviewed, I, 183–184
Flinders, Matthew, XXVIII, 151; XXX, 212
Flinders, Sir Matthew, XXIII, 119, 120
Flirt, ship *(1863),* VIII, 229, 234
Floating Bulwark, The, by Douglas G. Browne, reviewed, XXIV, 75
"Floating Grain Elevators in New York Harbor, 1848–1959," by Joanne Fuerst, XXXVIII, 138–141
Flogging, XXX, 142 ff.
"Flogging in the Navy," by Captain Edgar K. Thompson, U.S.N. (ret.), XXI, 72
"Flogging through the Squadron," by Captain Edgar K. Thompson, U.S.N. (ret.), XXI, 144–145
Flora, bark (1859), VI, 82; (1895), VI, 135
Flora, British frigate *(1778),* L, 206; oil painting of, XLVIII, 161
Flora, schooner (1810), XIV, 39; *(1861),* XI, 283
Flora, steamship, XXI, 92, 94, 102, 103, plates X, XIX; (1863), III, 137; (1874), VII, 153–154; *(1863),* VIII, 230, 234; XVII, 256
Flora, yacht *(1898),* XXXVI, 239
Flora A. Price, bateau (1910), IV, 289
Florabelle [model], XXXVII, 172
Flora L. Oliver, schooner (1912), XXVI, plate XXV
Flora Temple, ship *(1859),* XX, 215
Flor da Verdade, brig *(1827),* VI, 10–11
Florence, bark (1856), III, 171
Florence, ship *(1887),* XXX, 222
Florence A. Harnden, sloop (1892), Pictorial Supplement, XXXVI, plate XXI
Florence and Anne, bark *(1859),* VI, 82
Florence Louise, bateau (1924), IV, 289
Florence M. Munsie, Canadian schooner *(1902),* XLIX, 280
Florence M. Smith, Canadian schooner *(1902),* XLIX, 280
Florence Treat, bark (1865), IV, 239
Florida, armed schooner *(1861),* XLVIII, 94
Florida, C.S. raider (1862), XXII, 45–54, plate 3; XXIII, 268; XXV, 140, 298–299; *(1862),* XV, 287 ff.; *(1863),* I, 46, 241, 249, 251, 314; III, 132, 136; IV, 255; *(1863–1865),* XXVII, 277; XXXII, 55; XXXIII, 60; XXXV, 139; XXVIII, 122; XXIX, 5, 11, 168; XXXIX, 38
Florida, liner (1931), XXXVI, 28
Florida, schooner, XXI, 94; *(1861),* XI, 283; XII, 54, 156
Florida, ship, XXXVII, 212; (1844), I, 48; (1851), IV, 242
Florida, sloop, XXI, 93; *(1862),* XII, 54, 156, 230, 234
Florida, steamship, XXI, 93, 98; *(1861),* XI, 283; XII, 54; XV, 103
Florida, tanker *(1887),* XXXVIII, 188 ff., 239

Florida, U.S.S. *(1861),* VII, 19; XVI, 50; XVIII, 147
Florida, warship *(1917),* XL, 51 ff.
Florida (FL). *See* Fishing boats; Pensacola Navy Yard; Salvage; Steamboats; Steam Navigation
Florida, proposed canal across, VII, 130–131
Floride, ship *(1915),* XLV, 201
Floridian, container ship, XXXVI, 19
Florie, schooner *(1863),* XII, 156
Florie, steamship, XXI, 90, 96; *(1864),* VIII, 234
Flounder, sloop, XXII, 60 n.
Flow, diesel trawler (1929), XLIV, 128
Flower of Yarrow, vessel *(1863),* XXVI, 102
Floyd, schooner *(1862),* XII, 54
Floyd, Prof. Arva Colbert, ed., *A Diary of a Voyage to China, 1859–1860,* by Rev. Young J. Allen, reviewed, IV, 256
Floyd, William, XXXI, 236
"Fluid Geography," by Richard Buckminster Fuller, IV, 119–136
"Flukes," XXII, plate XXIV
Flummer, Daniel J., XXXV, 203
Flushing, steamship, XXI, 99; *(1863),* XII, 156, 230
Fly, Continental Navy schooner *(1776),* XXV, 193, 198, 200
Fly, French ship *(1800),* XXXI, 175
Fly, H.M.S. (1839), XII, 286
Fly, schooner *(1779),* XXXV, 141; *(1864),* XV, 129
Fly, sloop *(1776),* XXXIX, 211; *(1777),* II, 208
Fly, William, XXXVII, 47
Flyaway, ship (1853), III, 263
Flying Childers, clipper ship (1852), I, 46
Flying Cloud, bark *(1917),* XVIII, 165, 170
Flying Cloud, clipper ship (1851), I, 44, 46; III, plate 28; VII, 318; VIII, 325–330; IX, 148–150; XXII, 240; song about, XXV, 57
Flying Cloud, ship, XXXIII, 64; (1850) XIX, plate II; XX, 131; *(1851),* XXVI, 167 n., XXX, 218
Flying Cloud, sloop *(1862),* XII, 54
Flying Cloud, sloop yawl *(1896),* XXX, 197
"*Flying Cloud* versus *Andrew Jackson,*" by Carl C. Cutler, VIII, 325–326
"*Flying Cloud* versus *Andrew Jackson,*" by John Lyman, VII, 318
Flying Dutchman, ship, XVII, 156
Flying Fish, clipper ship (1851), I, 44, 46
Flying Fish, French ship *(1799),* XXXI, 173
Flying Fish, pilot boat (1838), IV, 105 ff.; *(1838),* XXX, 298; XLIX, 152 ff.; photo of model, XLIX, 161, 164, 165
Flying Fish, schooner (1806), XIII, 183
Flying Fish, ship *(1846–1857),* XLII, 121 ff.
Flying Fish, sloop, XXI, 96; *(1862),* XII, 54
Flying-Fish, sloop, XXIII, 278
Flying Fish, tender *(1814),* XLII, 105 ff.
Flying Fish, U.S.S. *(1799),* XXXI, 175
Flying Horse, steamship, XXII, 31
Flying "P" Liners, XXX, 219

Flying Scud, schooner *(1863),* XII, 156
Flying Scud, ship, XXVI, 169
Flying Serpent, tug *(1900),* XIV, 124
Flying Spur, ship *(1866),* XXXV, 33 ff.
Foam, schooner *(1862),* XII, 54, 156, 234
Foam, steamship, XXI, 96
Foam, steam trawler *(1919),* XLIV, 122
Focs'le Days, by Anton Otto Fischer, reviewed, XLIX, 310
Fogarty, Captain E. C., XXI, 91
Fogg, John M., XXXIII, 135
Fogg, W. H., XVII, 147
Fogg Museum of Art, Cambridge, Mass, III, 88
Fohkien, steamship *(1863),* XVI, 250; XVIII, 69; XVII, 308, 309; XVIII, 69
Fokelin, tugboat *(1864),* XLIII, 298
Folger, Captain Elisha, XIV, 43
Folger, Mayhew, XXXIII, 163
Folger, Captain Seth, XXIII, 22 ff.
Folgier, Captain Abijah, XXIII, 27
Folgier, Captain George, XXIII, 27
Folgier, Captain Nathan, XXIII, 28
Folklore, fishermen, XIII, 125–130
Folklore, Marine, XXIII, 29–38
"Folklore and Anthropological Literature as a source for Maritime Historians," by Ernest Stanley Dodge, VIII, 150–151
Folklore and the sea, XIII, 131; XV, 191; XXIII, 29; XXIV, 172; XXIX, 275; XXX, 249
   Middle East, XV, 5, 191; XVII, 262; XVIII, 25
Folkstone, British ship *(1743),* XLVIII, 23
Follinsbee, ship (1801), X, 53; *(1801),* XIII, 276
Folsom, Nathaniel, XXXI, 239
Folster, George T., XIV, 19 ff., plates 1, 4
Fontain, H.M.S. *(1814),* XXVIII, 118
Food at sea, 17th century, XXVII, 114–117
"Food and Drink on Shipboard 1800," document contributed by Peter Oliver, II, 77–79
Food on Shipboard, II, 77–79, 197–198, 235–236, 238–239; X, 207–208
Food relief, XIII, 252
Foong Shuey, steamship *(1864),* XVI, 253
Foong Suey, steamship (ex-*Plymouth Rock*) (1863), XXXIV, plate 3
Foot, Midshipman Henry D., U.S.N., XXV, 225–226
"Foot and Note Disease," XXXV, 151
Foote, Commander A. H., XXXII, 124; XXXIV, 82 ff.
Foote, Admiral Andrew H., XLII, 198 ff.
Foote, Captain Andrew H., XIX, 267
Foote, Flag Officer Andrew H., U.S.N., XXV, 128–129
Foote, Rear Admiral Andrew Hull, XXXVII, 144; XXXVIII, 36
Foote, Colonel Henry R., XXVI, 282
Foote, Kenneth A., V, 165
Foote, M. R., XXXVI, 236
Footner, Hulbert, *Sailor of Fortune, The Life and Adventures of Joshua Barney,* reviewed, I, 317

"Footnote on Massachusetts Deserters who went to Sea during the American Revolution, A," by Arthur J. Alexander, X, 43–51
"Footnote to the Loss of *Arctic,* A," document contributed by Alexander Crosby Brown, XIX, 128–132
Forbes, paddle steamship (1829), XVI, 159, 160; XVIII, 69; XXII, 6, 42; XXVI, 5, 6
Forbes, Allan, XI, 83 ff.
Forbes, Esther, *Paul Revere and the World He Lived In,* reviewed, II, 348
Forbes, Frank Blackwell, XXXIV, 50
Forbes, H. A. Crosby, XXV, 156
Forbes, Sir Hugh, Sir Maurice Laing, Lieutenant Colonel James Myatt *et al., 1979 Fastnet Race Inquiry,* reviewed, XL, 149
Forbes, James, XXXI, 236
Forbes, John D., "Boston Smuggling, 1807–1815," X, 144–154
Forbes, John M., XXX, 293
Forbes, John Murray, XIII, 122; XVI, 160 ff., 243 ff.; XXII, 8
Forbes, Paul, XXXI, 186
Forbes, Paul Sieman, XVI, 167 ff., 243, 244, 246, 248
Forbes, Paul Siemen, XIII, 122
Forbes, Captain Robert B., XI, 84; XIII, 53, 122, 252–267, plate 13; XIV, 259 ff.
Forbes, Robert Bennet, I, 51–57, plate facing 54; II, 349; VII, 175; X, 231–234; XVI, 160 ff.; XX, 141
Forbes, Captain Robert Bennet, XXII, 8, 9, 15; XXV, 69, 156
Forbes, Captain T., XXI, 91
Forbes, Thomas T., XIII, 122
Forbes, W. H., XVI, 243, 257
Forbes, Captain William H., XXI, 91
Forbes Collection of Whaling Prints at the Francis Russell Hart Nautical Museum, reviewed, I, 410
Forbes rig, I, 53, 56
"For Better or for Worse," by Gershom Bradford, VIII, 242–245, plate 20
Ford, Colin M., XL, 103
Ford, Francis Clare, XXXIX, 291
Ford, Frederick D., XXXIX, 96
Ford, Laurence A., XLIV, 116
Ford, Governor Thomas, Illinois, VII, 58 n.
Ford, Captain W. G., XXI, 91
Fordene 2, schooner *(1864),* XII, 230
Fore-and-Afters, by B. B. Crowninshield, reviewed, I, 181–182
Fore and aft rig, XIX, 155, 274. *See also* Masts and Rigging
Fore-and-aft rig, XIX, 155–199, 274–306
Fore-and-Aft sail, illustration of, XXV, plate XXVI
Foreign Factories at Canton, China; fireboard by Cornè, 1804, Pictorial Supplement, XXXII, plate XXX
"Foreign Fleet, The," by Captain Edgar K. Thompson, U.S.N. (ret.), XXVIII, 143–144

Fore River Shipbuilding Co., XXXVIII, 199 ff.; XXXIX, 42; XLIV, 116
Fore River Shipyard, Quincy (MA), III, 271; XXIII, 14; XXXII, 166
Foresight, ship, XXII, 102; *(1570),* XIV, 266
Forest Belle, bark *(1877),* Pictorial Supplement, XXXVII, plate V, 32–33
Forest City, steamship, XXVII, 260; *(1854),* XXXIII, 88, 94; Pictorial Supplement, XXXIV, plate III
Forest Dream, barkentine (1919), V, 82
Forester, steamship (1871), VII, 141
Forest Friend, barkentine (1919), V, 82
Forest King, brig *(1861),* XI, 283
Forest Oak, warship *(1867),* XXXVIII, 63
Forest Pride, barkentine (1919), V, 82
Forest State, ship *(1855),* XLVII, 89
Forey, General, XXXIII, 11
Forfarshire, steamship *(1838),* XXXIV, 8
"Forgotten American Visitors to Australia," by Thomas Dunbabin, XII, 162
"Forgotten Dry Dock in Colonial Charlestown, A," by Joseph Goldenberg, XXX, 56–60
"Forgotten Fleet: The Mexican Navy on the Eve of War, 1845, The," by Robert L. Scheina, XXX, 46–55
"Forgotten Naval War in the Pacific, A," by Donald W. Mitchell, XXXI, 268–274
Forgotten Wars, The, by Howard P. Nash, Jr., reviewed, XXIX, 70–71
For Honor and Country: The Diary of Bruno de Hezeta, Herbert K. Beals, editor, reviewed, XLVIII, 197
Formidable, H.M.S. *(1942),* XXVII, 199, 200
Formosa, steamship (1852), XXVI, 17, 18, 22, 23, 116, 202, 203, 205; (1885), XVII, 40
Formosa, boats of, XIII, 105
For National Defense, Newport News Shipbuilding and Dry Dock Co., reviewed, II, 94
Forrest, steamship *(1862),* VIII, 224
Forrest, Earle R., IX, 301; "Captain Philo McGiffin at the Battle of the Yalu," VIII, 267–278
Forrest, Stoddert and Murdock, XXXVI, 54
Forrestal, U.S.S. *(1955),* XV, 96
Forrestal, James V. (Secretary of the Navy), XXXVIII, 285
Forrest Box & Lumber Co., XXX, 187
Forrest Sherman, U.S. destroyer *(1960),* XXV, 166
Forsberg, Johanes, XXI, 16, 17, 21
Försigtigheten, ship (1784), VI, 170
Forster, John, VII, 84
Forster, Sir William, VII, 83–85
Forsyth J., XXV, 255
Fort Algernon, XXX, 137
Fort Beausejour, XXXI, 23
Fort Calhoun, XXX, 137
Fort de France, Martinique, XXXIII, 5 ff.
Fort Donaldson, U.S. warship *(1865),* XXXII, 135
Fortescue, Sir John, XXV, 35
Fort George, bark (1884), IX, 298
Fort George, XXX, 137
Fortifications, I, plates facing 143 and 146
Fortitude, sloop *(1813),* XIX, 217
Fort Jackson, merchant steamship, XXXII, 48
Fort Jackson, steamship *(1864),* IV, 143–144, plate 26
Fort Laramie, schooner (1919), IV, 325
Fort Lawrence, XXXI, 23
Fort Malate, XXXV, 185
Fort McHenry, Baltimore, bombardment of, 1814, III, plate 4
Fort Mechanic, XLVII, 23
Fort Monroe, XXX, 133, 137
Fort Montague, New Providence Island, Bahamas, XXV, 203 ff., plate 22
Fort Morgan, steamship (1863), XII, 293
Fort Nassau, New Providence Island, Bahamas, XXV, 202 ff., plate 22
Fort of Itapirú, XXXI, 15
Fort Pillow (TN), XXV, 129, 131, 133–135
Fort Pillow (TN), Battle of (1862), XIX, 265
Fort Pinckney, XLVII, 23
Fort Pitt, XXX, 140
Fortress of Louisbourg, XLIV, 189, 191
Fort Royal, schooner *(1777),* XLIII, 24
Fort Sumter, XXIX, 5
Fortuna, brig *(1861),* XI, 283
Fortunate, sloop *(1864),* XV, 129
Fortune, bark *(1861),* XV, 108 n,; XXI, 256
Fortune, bark (1868), V, 148
Fortune, brigantine (1730), VI, 181
Fortune, French ship *(1800),* XXXI, 174
Fortune, schooner, XXI, 100; *(1826),* XXIV, 58
Fortune, ship *(1621),* XIII, 58; *(1629),* XLIX, 259
"Fortune Bay Affair, 1878–1881: Massachusetts Fishermen Versus The British Crown, The," by Gary Pennanen, XXXIX, 289–301
Fortune of War, privateer *(1814),* XLII, 113
Fort Western, XXX, 115
Forty-four Ship Portraits at The Penobscot Marine Museum, with introduction by Walter Muir Whitehill, reviewed, XXIII, 289–290
Forward, cutter *(1939),* XXXVII, 93
Forward, H.B.M. sloop *(1889),* XXVI, 173
Forward, H.M.S., XXVIII, 18
Forzosa, Venezuelan schooner *(1848),* XXX, 267
Fosdick, Captain Benjamin, XXIII, 27
Foss, Captain E., XXXIX, 221
Foss, Captain Harold G., I, 102; "From Shipmaster to Guano Merchant," XXIV, 25–37
Foster, Dwight, XXXIX, 292
Foster, Ebenezer, XXX, 106, 107, 112, 113
Foster, Elisha, Jr., XXV, 222
Foster, Fred, XXXVI, 245
Foster, Captain H., XXX, 209
Foster, Hannah, XXXVI, 252 n.
Foster, Josiah, XXXVI, 252 n.
Foster, Stephen C., XXIV, 58

Foster, Thomas S., XXVI, 173–175
Foster, W. H., Jr., XVI, 244
Foster, William, XL, 281
Foster, William H., XLVI, 214
Foudroyant, H.M.S. *(1775),* VII, 87 ff.
Fougner, Hermann, XXII, 158
Fougner, N. K., XXII, 157, 158
Fougner Concrete Shipbuilding Co., XXII, 160, 182
Fougueuse, French ship *(1800),* XXXI, 173
Fouliaz, Captain Juan Sarex, XXX, 52
Foundation Co., XXXII, 6
"Founding of the Newport Naval Training Station, 1878–1883: An Exercise in Naval Politics, The," by Anthony S. Nicolosi, XLIX, 291–304
Foundries, United States, XLV, 35
Fountaine, frigate, XXIII, 99
"Four American Cross-Staves," by Marion V. Brewington, XIX, 138–140
Four Brothers, sloop, XXII, 82
"Four from Bristol," by Marcus W. Price, XVII, 249–261
"Four-masted Schooner *Anna R. Heidritter,* The," by Robert H. I. Goddard, Jr., XXX, 187–193
"Four-masted Ships," by John Lyman, IX, 297–298, plate 31
"Four-Masted Topsail Schooners," by John Lyman, II, 326–327
Fournier, George, XIV, 265
Four Sons, brig *(1851),* XXIV, 45, 57
4 steps to longitude (Bicentenary Exhibition, 19th January to 30th September, 1962, catalog reviewed, XXII, 151–152
Fourteenth Conference of the International Commission for Maritime History, XXXIV, 229
Fourth Naval History Symposium; mentioned, XL, 5
4 Years A-whaling: Charles S. Raleigh, Illustrator, by Philip F. Purrington, reviewed, XXXIII, 307
Fowle, Isaac, figurehead attributed to, Pictorial Supplement, XXXVII, plate III, 32–33; plate XIII, 124–125
Fowler, Gene, *The* Jervis Bay *Goes Down,* reviewed, I, 411
Fowler, Captain R., XXI, 91
Fowler, William, review by, XLVII, 214; mentioned, XLVIII, 178; XXV, 292 n.; "The Business of War: Boston as a Navy Base, 1776–1783," XLII, 25–35
Fowler, William M., Jr., reviews by, XLI, 142, 233; XLIII, 164; XLIV, 140; XLIX, 237, 238; *Jack Tars and Commodores: The American Navy, 1783–1815,* reviewed, XLV, 133; "James Nicholson and the Continental Frigate *Virginia,*" XXXIV, 135–141; "The New York Frigates," XXXVIII, 15–27; "William Ellery: An American Lord of Admiralty," XXXI, 235–252
Fowler, William M., Jr. and Jay R. Kaufman, "Into the Ocean World," XLIV, 110–113
Fox, Liberian coaster *(1845),* XXXVIII, 59
Fox, privateer *(1813),* XLII, 110 ff.; *(1814),* XXIX, 197

Fox, ship *(1646),* XI, 35 ff.
Fox, ship *(1777),* oil painting of, XLVIII, 161
Fox, steamship *(1862),* XII, 54, 156, 234; *(1864),* VIII, 234, 237; XXI, 87, plate XI
Fox, Frank, *Great Ships: The Battlefleet of King Charles II,* reviewed, XLII, 143–144
Fox, Gustavus V., XXI, 235; XXII, 256; XXIX, 9, 10 n.; XXXII, 50; XXXV, 53 ff.
Fox, Gustavus V., Secretary of the Navy, XLII, 87 ff.
Fox, Captain Gustavus V., XXXVI, 186; XXXVII, 279; XLVIII, 124
Fox, Lieutenant Gustavus V., U.S.N., IV, 311–313
Fox, Josiah, IX, 162; X, 65 ff.; XXIV, 266; XXVI, 63–71; XXXV, 240; papers of, XXXIX, 236 ff.
Fox, Josiah, Assistant Naval Constructor, XLVII, 24; XLIX, 46
Fox, Reinard Cornelius, XI, 35 ff.
Fox, Robert C., "Before the *Nautilus,*" XX, 174–176
Foxall, Henry, XLV, 37
"'Foxardo Affair' Revisited: Porter, Pirates and the Problem of Civilian Authority in the Early Republic, The," by Michael Birkner, XLII, 165–178
Foz Do Douro, XXX, 219
Fragata, Captain Edward, XLI, 49
Fram, Arctic exploration vessel, XXVI, 156
Frame Up! The Story of Essex, Its Shipyards and Its People, by Dana Story, reviewed, XXV, 147–148
"Framing," query by John R. Stevens, VII, 77; answered by Howard I. Chapelle, VII, 170
Framjee, Pallanjee, XXXIV, 44
France, bark *(1890),* VI, 135; *(1912),* VI, 135
France:
  Foreign relations
  —, **Gt. Britain,** XXIII, 157
  —, **United States,** XXIV, 61; XXIX, 167
  See also Prisoners; Privateering
France and Canada Oil Transport Co., XXII, 170, 172
Frances (1800), XXIII, 216
Frances, schooner *(1862),* XII, 54
Frances, ship *(1807),* VII, 317.
Frances, steamship, XXI, 101; *(1864),* XII, 230, 234
Frances A. Barstow, brig *(1877),* Pictorial Supplement, XXXIII, plate VII
Frances Arthemus, brig *(1861),* VIII, 217
Francesco Cilento, bark *(1870),* XII, plate 30
Frances Henrietta, bark *(1861),* XV, 108 n.; XXI, 238, 256
Frances M. Parker, sloop *(1891),* XXVI, plate XI
France West India S.S. Co., XXII, 166 n.
Franchise, pirate schooner *(1811),* XLII, 115
Francis, ship *(1807),* II, 282; *(1812),* XXI, 20, 21; *(1815),* XVII, 72
Francis, steamship *(1864),* XI, 276
Francis, A. D., *The Methuens and Portugal,* reviewed, XXVII, 224–226
Francis, Captain Richard, XXI, 91
Francis Allyn, schooner *(1887),* XL, 125

Francis Amy, schooner *(1837),* XXV, 107
Francis B. Ogden, screw steamship *(1837),* XLIX, 96
Francis C. Yarnall, schooner (1881), XXIII, 12
Francisca, sloop *(1864),* XII, 230, 234
Francisco de Borja, Spanish warship, XXXVI, 97
Francisco Reyes, transport *(1899),* XXXV, 189
Francis Drake, Privateer, edited by John Hampden, reviewed, XXXIV, 284
Francis Lee Higginson, Jr., Collection of Steamships, The, XXIV, 64–65, 140–141, 216–217, 292–293
Francis Russell Hart Nautical Museum at Massachusetts Institute of Technology (Cambridge, MA), XIV, 13, 14; XXXV, 32; XXXVIII, 170
Franco, Salvador G., *Instruments Nautico En El Museo Naval,* reviewed, XX, 225
Francois I, steamship (1856), XXVI, 189, 190
François Hennebique, concrete ship (1944), XXII, 179
"Franconesia, A Little Known Quarter of the Indian Ocean," by Auguste Toussaint, XXXI, 104–119
Franconia, ship (1872), III, 71
Franconia, steamship, XLII, 295 ff.
Frango, whaling factory ship, XXVIII, plate XXVIII
Frank, schooner (1854), XXIV, 58; *(1874),* XLI, 304
Frank, Stewart, comment, Editorial, *The American Neptune,* XXXVIII, 3–4
Frank, Stuart M., review by, XLIII, 56–58; "'Boston': Two 'New' Texts of an Old Favorite Sea Song," XLV, 175–179; *Herman Melville's Picture Gallery,* reviewed, XLIX, 60; "Moby-Dick: The Two 'Missing' prints by 'H. Durand,'" XLVI, 252–257
Frank A. Morey, schooner, XXIII, plate XXVIII; (1917), III, 163; V, 290, plate 19
Frank A. Palmer, schooner (1897), V, 80; XX, 239, 240, 241; XXIII, 13, plate XI
Frank Boult, ship (1858), II, 332
Frank Brainard, schooner (1908), IX, 178
Frank Brainerd, schooner, XXIV, 34; (1908), V, 288–289, plate 19
Frank C. Munson Institute of Maritime Studies (at Mystic Seaport), XLV, 41
"Frank C. Munson Institute of American Maritime Studies, The," by Benjamin W. Labaree, XLV, 41–45
Frank Flint, ship (1857), II, 246; IV, 244
Frank Foster, schooner (1882) XXVI, plate IV
Frank Herbert, schooner *(1883),* XLIX, 29
Frank Jones, steamship *(1902),* XXIV, 49
Frankland, Henry, XXVI, 37
Frankland, Captain Thomas, XXVI, 37–62
Frankland, Sir Thomas (Lord of Admiralty, 1733–1746), XXVI, 37
Franklin, American Warship *(1817),* XXXI, 218; XXXIII, 280
Franklin, armed schooner *(1775),* XXX, 102–104, 107, 110, 111, 114
Franklin, brig *(1819),* IX, 240, 245–247; XXV, 184
Franklin, schooner (1819), XXII, 216
Franklin, schooner (1849), XXIV, 58; *(1862),* XII, 55
Franklin, ship *(1777),* XIII, 46; *(1798),* XXV, 180; *(1799),* XLVI, 51
Franklin, ship (1826), XIV, 40; *(1829),* XLI, 289; XLV, 110
Franklin, ship (1859), V, 148
Franklin, steam packet *(1840),* XLVIII, 114
Franklin, U.S.S., XXVII, 222; *(1900),* XX, 136
Franklin, U.S. ship *(1823),* VII, 284
Franklin, U.S. ship-of-the-line (1826), XXI, 65; XXIII, 58
Franklin, Benjamin, XXV, 37; XXVI, 179, 232; XXXI, 241; XXXV, 111; XXXVI, 161 ff.; XLI, 209
Franklin, Captain Charles N., XXI, 91; XXIII, 18
Franklin, James, XXV, 237
Franklin, Sir John, XXIX, 65–67; L, 35
Franklin, Sir John (English explorer of Arctic), XX, 104–111
Franklin, Sir John, Expedition of, XXV, 51
Franklin, Governor William, XXXVII, 268
Franklin Allyn, schooner *(1867),* XLV, 111
Franklin and *Eliza,* Japanese painting of, XLVI, 53
Franklin Muzzy and Co. of Bangor, XXXIX, 222
Frank Marion, bark (1865), XXVII, plate X
Frank N. Thayer, ship (1869), III, 62
Frank Pendleton, ship (1874), XXVIII, plate XV
Frank Rockefeller, whaleback steamship (1896), XXV, 174
Franquelin, Jean Baptiste Louis, XXX, 59
Fraser, Captain Alexander, XXXVI, 175, 177; XLV, 119
Fraser, Captain Alexander V., XXIV, 14 ff.
Fraser, Admiral Sir Bruce, XLII, 215
Fraser, John and Co., IX, 32 ff.
Fraser, Trenholm and Co., IX, 32 ff.
Fraser-Trenholm, XXIX, 16, 17
Fratelli, brig *(1861),* XI, 283
Fraternité, auxiliary (1918), XXXII, 16, 27, 30
Frazar and Co., XVII, 308
Frazer, J. M., XXXVI, 48
Frazer, James M., IV, 313 ff.
Frazier, Lieutenant Solomon, XLIII, 8 ff.
Frazier, William, Collector of the Port of Salem, XXXVII, 268
Fred B. Balano, schooner (1890), XXIV, 40, 58
Freddie L. Bennett, coasting sloop (1899), XXXVII, 165
Frederick, schooner *(1855),* XXIV, 143
Fred'k De Bary, steamship *(1869),* VII, 133
Frederick Enoch, brig *(1823),* VII, 282–287
Frederick (Nagasaki Maru), ship (1801), XLVI, 53
Fredericksburg, C.S. Ironclad *(1864),* XXII, 282 n.
Fredericksburg, ironclad ram *(1862),* XLII, 85 ff.
Frederick Tudor, ship (1866), III, 172
Frederick W. Carlon, bark (1875), IV, 243
Frederic the Second, schooner *(1863),* XII, 156, 230
Fred'k. See Frederick.
Fredonia, receiving ship *(1861),* XXXIII, 42 ff.
Fredonia, schooner (1889), XXVI, plate X; XXXIV, 144

"Fredrik Henrik af Chapman," by Gustaf Halldin, VI, 163–178, plates 21–28
Fred T. Ley and Co., Inc., XXII, 161, 182
Fred Warren, ship *(1863),* III, 172
Frederica River (GA), XXIII, 62
Freebody, Samuel, XLII, 42 ff.
Freeborn, ship *(1861),* XLIII, 130 ff.
Freeborn, Captain James, XXI, 91
Freedom, schooner *(1777),* V, 187
Freeman, Captain, XLVIII, 34 ff.
Freeman, Mary Wilkins, XXV, 65
Freeman, Phillip, XXV, 64
Freeman, Robert, XIII, 14, 18, 19, 23, 27, 28
Freeman, S. S. Co., XXV, 292
Freeman Clark, ship (1865), XXVII, plate XI
Freeport (ME), I, 100
Freeport & Tampico Fuel Oil Transportation Co., XXXVIII, 185
Frees, Martin d', XVII, 292
"Free Tow, A," XXII, plate XXIII
Freetown, Sierra Leone, XXX, 177 ff., 230 ff.
Free Trade, ship (1854), V, 151
Freitas, Captain Antonio, XXI, 91
Freja, steamship *(1881),* XIV, 119
Frelinghuysen, Frederick, Secretary of State, XXXIV, 86
Fremantle, Captain, XXXII, 244
Fremont, barkentine (1850–1861), I, 296–297, plate facing 296
Fremont, John C., XLIX, 112
Fremont, General John C., XXXI, 62
Fremont, Lieutenant, XLV, 21 ff.
French, Benjamin, XXI, 109
French, Daniel, XVI, 25
French, Howard B., XXIV, plate XVI
French, James, XLVI, 258
French, Captain Rodney, XXI, 237, 238
French, Brigadier General Samuel G., XLIII, 133
French, Thomas, *The Missionary Whaleship,* reviewed, XXII, 151
French, W. W., XXXVI, 233, 241
French (London instrument maker), chronometer by, Pictorial Supplement, XXXV, plate XIX
French-American S. S. Lines, XXII, 166
French East India Co., The, XXXI, 109
"French Ensor Chadwick: The First American Naval Attaché, 1882–1889," by Paolo E. Coletta, XXXIX, 126–141
French Lake Ontario squadron, sketch of, XLIX, 263; maps, XLIX, 269
French Reconaissance: Baudin in Australia, 1801–1803, The, by Frank Horner, reviewed, L, 70
French settlement of Mascarenes, XXV, 5, 6
"French Siege of Oswego in 1756: Inland Naval Warfare in North America, The," by D. Peter MacLeod, XLIX, 262–271
French spoliation claims, I, 275–276

Freneau, Andrew, XXXVII, 55
Freneau, B. Funnell, XXXVII, 56
Freneau, Philip, VI, 115–120
Frese, Joseph R., "Henry Hulton and the Greenwich Hospital Tax," XXXI, 192–216
Fresia, Chilean torpedo boat *(1880),* XXXIX, 286
Fresnel lens, illustration of, XLVII, 185
Fresno City, steamship *(1940),* XIV, 130
Frieda, ship (1885), IX, 298
Friedlander, ship (1872), III, 63
Friedrich der Grosse, steamship (1896), IX, 220–221
Friend, sloop *(1832),* XXXVIII, 266
Friend, Captain Alphonso F., XVIII, 83
Friendly Emma, brig *(1807),* VI, 83
Friends Goodwill, British ship *(1776),* XLVIII, 16
Friendship, XXVII, 98
Friendship, American ship *(1831),* XXXI, 182; XXXV, 20
Friendship, brig (1792), XV, 175
Friendship, brigantine (1794), II, 281
Friendship, British ship *(1776),* XLVIII, 16
Friendship, schooner *(1776),* XI, 224; *(1778),* X, 284; *(1787),* XLIX, 88; *(1863),* XII, 156
Friendship, ship *(1797),* XXV, 181, plate 19; *(1798),* XXXIX, 32, 215; *(1801),* XXIV, 262; *(1831),* XXI, 293 ff.; *(1832),* XLVI, 114
Friendship, sloop, XXII, 60 n.
Friendship Bay, Bequia, XXXII, plate 10
Friendship Rose, schooner *(1971),* XXXII, 190
Friendship Sloops, by Roger F. Duncan, reviewed, XLIX, 237
Frietchie, Barbara, XXXVII, 128
Frigate Bird, bark (1853), III, 73
Frigate Essex *Papers: Building the Salem Frigate 1798–1799, The,* by Philip Chadwick Foster Smith, reviewed, XXXV, 68–70
"Frigate *Hancock,*" query by Laurence Schwab, VI, 153
Frigates, United States, XXXVIII, 15
Frigates: *No. 61,* longitudinal section of, XXIX, 8, plate 2; bow design of, XXIX, plate 3
Friis, Herman R., review by, I, 322–324; Editor, *The Pacific Basin: A History of its Geographical Exploration,* reviewed, XXVIII, 72
Friis, Herman R., and Martin P. Claussen, *Descriptive Catalog of Maps Published by Congress 1817–1834,* reviewed, II, 351
Frippone, French ship *(1799),* XXXI, 173
Frisco, tanker *(1925),* XXXVIII, 198 ff.
Frisk, Captain Charles, XXI, 91
Fritzinger, Captain J. G., XXI, 91
Frobel, Lieutenant Bushrod W., XL, 301
Frobisher, Martin (Captain) (ca. 1535–1594), XLIX, 14
Frobisher, Martin, XXVII, 182
Frobisher, Sir Martin, L, 35
Frohman, Colonel Louis H., XXVIII, plate I
Fröja, frigate (1784), VI, 170

Frolic, British sloop of war *(1812),* VII, 167, 169; XLI, 28; XLIV, 175 ff.; *(1820),* L, 27 ff.; lithograph of, L, 28
Frolic, schooner *(1851),* XLV, 129; *(1863),* XII, 156
Frolic, ship (1869), IV, 72; *(1901),* XXXV, 195
Frolic, sloop *(1863),* XII, 156
"From Cask to Conquest," note by Captain Edgar K. Thompson, U.S.N. (ret.), XXIX, 186
"From *Eastern State* to *Evangeline*: A History of the Boston-Yarmouth, Nova Scotia Steamship Services," by Arthur L. Johnson, XXXIV, 174–187
"From 'Leg of Mutton' to 'Brigantine,' Nautical ABC's for a Cruising Chaperone," by Francis W. Hatch, XXII, 184–186
From My Old Boat Shop, by Weston Farmer, reviewed, XL, 235
From Panama to Verdun: My Fight for France, by Philippe Bunau-Varilla, reviewed, I, 411
From Sail to Saratoga: A Naval Autobiogaphy, by Rufus Fairchild Zogbaum, Rear Admiral, U.S.N., reviewed, XXII, 145–147
"From Shipmaster to Guano Merchant," by Captain Harold G. Foss, XXIV, 25–37
From the Dreadnought to Scapa Flow: The Royal Navy in the Fisher Era, 1904–1919, Volume I, *The Road to War, 1904–1914,* by Arthur J. Marder, reviewed, XXII, 222–223
From the Dreadnought to Scapa Flow: The Royal Navy in the Fisher Era, 1904–1919: Volume III, *Jutland and After: May 1916-December 1916,* by Arthur J. Marder, reviewed, XXVII, 66–67
From the Lower Deck, The Royal Navy 1780–1840, by Henry Baynham, reviewed, XXX, 299
From the Potomac to the Thames, being the progress of one James Rumsey (1743–1792), by Thompson King, reviewed, III, 357
"From the River Clyde to Unimak Pass: *Star of Falkland,*" by Harold Huycke, XVIII, 5–24, 149–176, 201–222, plates 1–4
"From Warship to School Ship: The History of U.S.S. *Ontario,* America's First Floating School," by Fred Hopkins, XL, 38–45
"From Whence or Where Bound — The Role of the Customs and Naval Officers at Colonial New Jersey's Ports," by James H. Levitt, XXXVII, 262–275
Frontenac, schooner, XXIII, 20
Frontenac, steamship (1816), III, 333–334, plate 42; V, 28; VI, 194, 209, 211; VII, 42, 43 n., 50; (1841), XX, 88, 89
Frontier, American, XXV, 52
Front Street, New Bedford, Pictorial Supplement, XXXIII, plate XXIII
Frost, A., XXIV, 58
Frost, Captain, XXV, 23, 24
Frost, Captain Ferdinand, XIV, 176
Frost, John, IX, 134
Frost, Robert, XXV, 65

Frothingham, Richard, Jr., XXX, 58
Frothingham, Captain Thomas G., XXII, 261
Frou Frou, yacht *(1896),* XXXVI, 239
Frozen Ships: The Arctic Diary of Johann Miertsching, 1850–1854, by L. H. Neatby, reviewed, XXIX, 65–67
"Frustrated Raider, The," by Charles B. Burdick, XXIV, 272–279
Frustrated Raider: The Story of the German Cruiser Cormoran *in World War I, The,* by Charles Burdick, reviewed, XL, 72
"Frustration," by Captain Edgar K. Thompson, U.S.N. (ret), XXVIII, 69
Fry, Agnes Evelina Sands, XXXVI, 88
Fry, Edward Gaynor, XXV, 163, 167
Fry, Captain Joseph, XXXVIII, 243
Frye, Peter (of Salem), XXXI, 198
Frye, Senator, XXV, 264–267
Fubbs, Royal Yacht *(1740),* XXVI, 38
Fuchsia, U.S.S. (1862), XVI, 173
Fuerst, Joanne, "Floating Grain Elevators in New York Harbor, 1848–1959," XXXVIII, 131–141
Fuhle, steamship (1870), XVII, 308, 309; XVIII, 69
Fuimefreddo, Captain Giuseppi, XXI, 91
Fukienese rebels, XXX, 157
Fukuzawa Yukichi, XX, 202 ff.
Fulbe traders, XXX, 178 f.
Fulgor, Italian tanker *(1942),* XXVII, 188, 190, 197
Fullam, George T., XXXIII, 53
Fuller, Captain David S., XVIII, 83
Fuller, Captain F. W., XXI, 91
Fuller, George, XIX, 16, 23
Fuller, Captain Joseph, XL, 120 ff.
Fuller, Richard Buckminster, IV, 85–86; "Fluid Geography," IV, 119–136
Fuller, Thomas, XXV, 237
Fuller Palmer, schooner (1900), V, 80
Fuller Projection (Cartography), IV, 119
Fullerton, barge *(1903),* XXXVIII, 178 ff., 193 ff.
Fullerton, bark *(1907),* XVI, 111
Fullerton, A., XV, 103
Fulop, Ladislav, XLIII, 37 ff.
Fulton, Dr. George, XLVII, 207
Fulton, French steamship *(1845),* XXXVI, 127, 129, 133, 134, 137, 138, 141
Fulton, iron ferry *(1880),* XLVIII, 128
Fulton, steamship (1814), XXVII, 10, 26–28; Pictorial Supplement, XXXIV, plate I. See also *Fulton the First.*
Fulton, U.S. Catamaran steam frigate (1815), XXI, 65
Fulton, U.S.S. *(1864),* XXVII, 44
Fulton, vessel *(1858),* XXXVI, 181
Fulton (II), U.S. sidewheel steamship (1837), XX, 171; XXIV, 6; XLIX, 98
Fulton, Robert, VI, 239, 253–274; VII, 179–180; painting by, VII, 179 n., plate 21; XII, 63; XVI, 28–40, 270–280; XVIII, 316–317; XXIV, 157 ff.; XXVII, 5–29; XXXII, 211 ff.; XXXVI, 216; XLVIII, 112

Fulton Iron Works, XXXVIII, 176 ff.
"Fulton's Steam Frigate," by David B. Tyler, VI, 253–274
Fulton T. Mister, bateau (1910), IV, 289
Fulton the First, U.S. steam frigate (1814), IV, 327–328; VI, 239, 253–274
Fulwood, ship, XXXVI, 3; *(1896),* XVIII, 9
Funch, Edye and Co., Inc., VII, 323–324
Fung Shuey, steamship (1864), XVII, 52, 55, 56, 135; XVIII, 69
Funston, Colonel Frederick C., XXXV, 193
Funter, Captain Robert, XV, 206
Furber, Holden, *Rival Empires of Trade in the Orient, 1600–1800: Europe and the World in the Age of Expansion,* reviewed, XXXVII, 223–224
Furber, Captain W. G., XVIII, 83
Furer, Rear Admiral Julius A., L, 59
Furious, H.M.S. *(1942),* XXVII, 199, 200
Furious, paddle wheel frigate, XXXIV, 112
Furlong, Captain Lawrence, XXI, 5–15
Furneaux, Rupert, note by, XXIX, 132
Furneaux, Captain Tobias, XXII, 224
Furness Abbey, bark (1879), III, 63
Furrow, Captain, XLVIII, 36 ff.
"Fur Seal Hunting in the South Atlantic," by A. Alfred Mattsson, II, 154–166
Fur Sealing, Fur Seals. *See* Sealing; Fur Trade
"Further Note on Reed Boats in the Pacific, A," note contributed by J. G. Nelson, 221–222
"Further Notes on Weston Vessels," note by Gershom Bradford, XXII, 216
Further Selections from the Tragic History of the Sea, 1559–1565, edited by C. R. Boxer, reviewed, XXIX, 75
Fur trade, Northwest Coast of North America, XXIX, 81; XXXVIII, 217; XL, 46; XLI, 224. *See also* Sealing
Furttenbach, Joseph, XIV, 265
Fury, H.M.S. *(1849),* XXVI, 13, 14
Fusiyama, steamship (1863), XVI, 253; XVII, 38, 58, 300; XVIII, 69; *(1863),* XLIII, 88 ff.; *(1865),* XXXIV, 49
Fuson, Robert H., *The Log of Christopher Columbus,* reviewed, XLVIII, 61
Futa Jalon, XXX, 178–180
Fuyi, steamship, XVI, 261
Fychow, steamship (ex-*Nautilus*) *(1864),* XLIX, 23; *(1866),* XVI, 261; XVII, 39; XVIII, 70

G. A. Bigelow, schooner, XXI, 101; *(1863),* VIII, 230
G. B. Cumming, schooner *(1861),* XV, 114, 123
G. C. Trufant, ship (1874), V, 152
G. D. and R. F. Shannon, schooner *(1861),* VIII, 217
G. F. Von Beer, steamship *(1874),* XV, 227
G. Garibaldi, sloop *(1864),* XV, 129
G. H. Smoot, schooner *(1862),* VIII, 224
G. Harper & Co., Hongkong, XXXIV, 58
G. Hunt Wilson, vessel *(1849),* XXXVI, 171
G. J. Boyce, schooner (1884), II, plate 48
G. L. Brockenborough, sloop *(1862),* XII, 55
G. M. Brainard, schooner (1873), X, 203
G. M. Partridge, schooner *(1850),* XLIV, 91
G. Machridachis (ex-*Général Serret*), auxiliary *(1927),* XXXII, 18, 30
G. S. Warner, ship (1859), IX, 68
G. S. Weeks, schooner *(1839),* VIII, 49
G. Taylor (1863), XII, 157
G. W. Baxter, brig *(1861),* XV, 114, 123
G. W. Behm, schooner *(1862),* XII, 55, 157
G. W. Blunt White Library. *See* Mystic Seaport
G. W. Price, schooner *(1861),* VIII, 217
GA. *See* Georgia
Gäa, German submarine tender *(1915),* XXXVI, 38
Gabriel, ship *(1576),* XLIX, 14; *(1635),* XXIII, 64
Gaby, John D., XXVI, 203
"Gadfly on the Potomac, CSS *George Page,*" by Ralph W. Donnelly, XLIII, 129–134
Gadsden, Christopher, XXXIX, 160
Gaelic, ship *(1884),* XXXI, 126
Gaffney, Daniel, XIII, 269; XLVI, 214
Gaffney, Matthew, XIII, 269
Gaff rig, XIX, 155, 274. *See also* Masts and Rigging
Gaff Rig, by John Leather, reviewed, XXXII, 292
Gage, British sloop *(1777),* XLII, 14 ff.
Gage, Alva, XIX, 40
Gage, Captain Henry, XXI, 91
Gage, Captain James, XXI, 91
Gage, General Thomas, I, 141–142; XXXVI, 80, 81
Gager, Captain C. L., XVIII, 275
Gainard, Captain Joseph A., XXXII, 100 ff.
Gainer, Rosemary (Mrs. Patrick A.), XXV, 80
Gainst, John, XXVII, 179, 180
Gainy, William, XXXVII, 14
Galatea, British frigate, XXII, 259; *(1776),* XXXIX, 198; *(1778),* VII, 207, 209
Galatea, ship *(1860),* XXV, 108
Galathé, frigate (1785), VI, 170
Galdy, Louis, XXIX, 53
Gale, Hannah, XXX, 96
Gale, John, XXX, 97–110
Gale, Joseph Goff, XXVIII, 128–141
Galena, ship, XXI, 95; *(1861),* XI, 283
Galena, U.S. gunboat (1861 or 1862), X, 16, 21, 31; XXII, 255; *(1862),* XX, 161–163; XLVIII, 121; *(1889),* XXVI, 173–175, plate 17
Galgorm Castle, bark (1897), XVIII, 9
Galiano, Alfred A., XXXVII, 87
Galiano, Joseph T., XXXVII, 87
Galiano, Louis F., XXXVII, 87

Galibi, steamship *(1823),* IX, 256
Galilah, Zim liner, XXVI, 74
Galileo, steamship *(1895),* XIV, 119
Gallagher, Robert E., editor, *Byron's Journal of His Circumnavigation 1764–1766,* reviewed, XXV, 297–298
Gallagher, William, XLIX, 123
Gallagher, Captain William Bennett, XLV, 86
Gallant Little Campeador, *The,* by Cecil Hunt, reviewed, II, 342–343
Gallatea, sloop *(1779),* XXXVII, 300
Gallatin, Albert, XXVI, 243, 247; XXVIII, 33–36; XXX, 280; XXXIX, 23; XL, 30; XLIII, 247 ff.; XLVI, 148
Gallatin, Albert (U.S. Minister to France, 1818), XXXIII, 255 ff.
Gallaudet, Elisha (engraver), XXV, 126
Gallery, Daniel V., *Cap'n Fatso,* reviewed, XXX, 75
Gallery, Captain Daniel V., XXXVIII, 272
Gallicia, Spanish ship, XXXII, 92
Gallinas estuary, XXX, 230
Gallinger, Senator Jacob H., XXXV, 281
Gallion Leicester, ship (ex-*Gallion Oughtred*) *(1581),* XXVII, 183
Gallion Oughtred, ship *(1581),* XXVII, 182
Galloway, Herman Y., XXXVII, 122 ff.
Galvão, Antonio, XXX, 253
Galveston, cruiser *(1921),* XXXV, 122 ff.
Galveston, steamship, XXI, 94; *(1861),* XI, 283
Gamage, Harvey, XXIX, 4
Gambeau, French ship *(1800),* XXXI, 174
Gambia, bark *(1859),* VIII, 179
Gambia, XXX, 230
Gambia River, XXX, 177 ff.
Gambier, Commodore James, XXIII, 183
Gambier, Governor John, XXV, 203, 216 n.
Gambier, Lord, XXX, 212
Gambier, Samuel, XXV, 203
Gamble, Captain Henry, XXI, 19
Gamble, Lieutenant Peter, XXI, 54
Gambrell, Captain N. C., XXI, 91
Gambrill, Captain N. C., XXI, 91
Gamecock, bark *(1917),* XVIII, 165, 170
Gamecock, ship, XXII, 239; *(1850),* XLV, 128
Gamma, schooner, XXVIII, 148
Gamma Commercial Co., XXII, 167
Gammel, Captain William, XXI, 18
Gammon, William, XXXIV, 13
Gamwell, Arthur, XXXVI, 236
Gamwell, Frederick Robison, XLIII, 216
Ganges, brig *(1826),* XIV, 40
Ganges, ship *(1799),* XXXIX, 34; *(1802),* XXIII, 217; *(1805),* XLI, 285; *(1807),* XVI, 193; *(1816),* XLVIII, 250 ff.; L, 245 ff.
Ganges, ship *(1855),* XXV, 108
Ganges, steamship *(1850),* XVIII, 70; *(1852),* XXVI, 15–17, 19, 21, 23, 25, 27, 30, 116, 202
Ganges, U.S.S., XXII, 275; *(1799),* XXXI, 173

Gangway boards, unidentified vessel, Pictorial Supplement, XXXVII, plate XXIX
Ganong, William Francis, L, 5
Gansevoort, Captain Guert, XXII, 257, 258
García, José Hermengildo, XXX, 269
Garcia De Palacio, Diego, XIV, 265; *Instrucion Nauthica* (1587), reviewed, I, 191–195; Reprint reviewed, VIII, 261
Gardella, Robert, "The Antebellum Canton Tea Trade: Recent Perspectives," XLVIII, 261–270
Gardener, Captain Charles L., XLVI, 63
Gardiner, Captain C. L., XVI, 179; XVIII, 83
Gardiner, Captain Edward, XXI, 91
Gardiner, Leslie, *The British Admiralty,* reviewed, XXXII, 150
Gardner, steamship *(1890),* XXXVIII, 63; XXXIX, 174 ff.
Gardner, Caleb, XXXV, 294
Gardner, Captain Edmund, XIV, 43; XXI, 91
Gardner, Captain Edward, XXXVIII, 255
Gardner, G. Peabody, XIII, 156
Gardner, Captain George H., VII, 66
Gardner, John, *Building Classic Small Craft,* reviewed, XXXIX, 146–147; plans and commentary by, in *The Adirondack Guideboat,* reviewed, XLIII, 306–307
Gardner, John, Jr., IX, 241, 244
Gardner, Peabody, XXV, 247
Gardner, R. S., VIII, 62 ff.
Gardner, Richard, IX, 241, 244
Gardner, Samuel, XXXIII, 163
Gardner, Will, *Three Bricks and Three Brothers,* reviewed, VI, 234–235
Gardner, Captain William H., XXXIII, 47
Gardner, Commander William H., U.S.N., V, 243–244
Gardner C. Deering, schooner *(1916),* VII, plate 24
Gardner W. Tarr, schooner *(1875),* XXVI, plate IV
Gardoqui, ship *(1899),* XXXV, 192
Garibaldi, bark *(1842),* III, 63, 264
Garibaldi, schooner, XXI, 87; *(1862),* VIII, 224; XII, 55; XV, 117, 119, 120, 123, 126
Garibaldi, ship *(1860),* IV, 72
Garibaldi, Giuseppi, XXXVI, 128
Garland, bark *(1861),* XXI, 238, 256
Garland, barkentine *(1847),* IV, 240
Garland, hermaphrodite brig *(1847),* Pictorial Supplement, XXXVIII, plates XXIII, XXIV
Garland, yacht *(1894),* XXXVI, 237, 238, 240, 241
Garland, George, XXVIII, 276, 282
Garland, Joseph E., *Eastern Point: A Nautical, Rustical, and Social Chronicle of Gloucester's Outer Shield and Inner Sanctum, 1606–1950,* reviewed, XXXII, 149–150; *The Eastern Yacht Club: A History from 1870–1985,* reviewed, L, 66
Garland, O. E., XXXVI, 236, 237
Garlington, Lieutenant Ernest A., XXXVI, 111 ff.
Garlington Expedition, 1883, XXXVI, 108 ff.
Garmatz, Edward A., XXXVI, 29, 30

Garner, Stanton, editor, *The Captain's Best Mate, the Journal of Mary Chipman Lawrence on the whaler* Addison *1856–1860,* by Mary Chipman Lawrence, reviewed, XXVII, 73–74
Garneray, XXX, 218
Garneray, Ambroise Louis, XLVI, 252 ff.
Garneray, Ambroise Louis (artist), XXII, plate III
Garonne, schooner, XXI, 91
Garoone, schooner *(1861),* XI, 283
Garrason, Captain T. B., XXI, 105
"Garret Archaeology," by William A. Baker, XXXVIII, 170–174
Garrick, packet ship *(1840),* XXIV, 215
Garrison, Cornelius Kingsland, IV, 141 ff., 149 ff.
Garrison, Nathan, XXI, 282
Garrison, William R., IV, 150
Garrison and Allen, IV, 151
Garst, Lieutenant Perry, XL, 131
Garvey, Marcus, XXXV, 197 ff.
Garvey, Stanton, *The Captain's Best Mate: The Journal of Mary Chipman Lawrence on the Whaler* Addison, *1856–1860,* reviewed, XLVIII, 201
Garzke, William H., Jr. and Robert O. Dunlin, Jr., *Battleships: Allied Battleships in World War II,* reviewed, XLII, 147–148
Gaschen, ship *(1861),* XI, 283
Gascoigne, Captain James, XXI, 260, 263; XXIII, 82
Gascoigne, Captain John R.N., XXI, 260–278
"Gascoigne Bluff," by Margaret Davis Cate, XXIII, 81–94
Gaspee, bark (1858), III, 70
Gaspee, H.M.S. *(1764),* XXIII, 177
Gassendi, French steamship *(1845),* XXXVI, 140
Gaston, Benjamin, XXXV, 203
Gates, schooner *(1779),* XXXV, 142
Gates, Colonel, XLV, 20 ff.
Gathorne, steamship *(1873),* XIV, 116
Gatty, Harold, *The Raft Book,* reviewed, IV, 253
Gauss, bark *(1861),* VIII, 217
Gauthiod, ship (1869), I, 115
Gautier, Lieutenant Thomas N., XV, 66 ff.
Gay, Edwin F., XIII, 118
Gay Head, bark *(1892),* XXII, plate IX
Gay Head, steamship, XXXIV, 261; *(1913),* VII, 221
Gayle, Captain R. H., XXI, 92
Gayle, Captain Richard H., XI, 42 ff.
Gayoso, brig, XXII, 94, 95
Gazeka, yawl yacht *(1908),* XXXVI, 245
Gazelle, schooner *(1842),* XXXII, 273; XXXIII, 82 ff.
Gazelle, ship *(1860),* XXVII, 235; *(1865),* XXXVII, 217
Gazelle, steamship *(1888),* VII, 228
Gêba River, XXX, 178 ff.
Geanakoplos, Professor Deno J., review by, XLIX, 311
Geary, Ted, XXXVI, 241–249
Geddes, Andrew, XXXI, 103
Gee, Joshua, IV, 79
Gee Whiz, yacht *(1896),* XXXVI, 239

Geib, George W., "The Restoration of the Port of Philadelphia, 1783–1789," XXXII, 247–256
Geib, John L., XIV, 256
Geis, Gilbert, XXXV, 198
Geisinger, Commodore David, XXXI, 188
Gelden, George, XL, 43
Geldermalsen, Dutch East India Co. ship *(1752),* XLVII, 275–281
Gellibrand, Henry, VIII, 306
Gellibrand, William, XXIII, 135, 136, 137, 139
Gelm, Captain George E., XLI, 16
Gelpe, Captain Jemme, XXI, 92
Gelston, Captain Roland, XXXVII, 182
Gem, steamship *(1863),* VIII, 230; XXI, plate XV
Gem of the Sea, bark, XXXII, 48
General-Admiral, Russian warship *(1863),* XX, 51
General Armstrong, brig *(1813),* XVII, 71
General Armstrong, privateer *(1814),* XXV, 122
General Armstrong, ship *(1812),* XV, 59–80
General Bailey, brig *(1857),* XXV, 107
General Banks, steamship, XXI, 90, 95; *(1863),* VIII, 230; *(1864),* VIII, 234
General Banks, U.S. iron sidewheeler *(1847),* XXXIII, 88, 94
Général Baratier, auxiliary (1918), XXXII, 16, 30
General Beauregard, C.S.S. *(1862),* XIX, 268, 270 ff.
General Beauregard, steamship, XXI, 81, 89, 96, 106; *(1861),* XV, 99, 123, 127; *(1863),* III, 265; VIII, 230; IX, 44
General Berry, ship (1863), II, 246
General Board of the Navy, XXXVII, 30 ff.
General Bolivar, warship *(1810),* XLII, 115 ff.
General Boves, S.M.C. brig *(1822),* XXIX, 64
General Brady, steamship *(1832),* VII, 48; *(1838),* XVIII, 283
General Bragg, C.S.S. *(1862),* XIX, 268, 270 ff.; *(1862),* XXV, 130
General Brandzen, brig *(1827),* VI, 9 ff.; VII, 175
General Bravo, Mexican ship *(1835),* XXX, 47
General Buckner, steamship, XXI, 100; *(1863),* XII, 156
General Burrows, schooner *(1862),* XII, 55
General Butler, ship (1804), VII, 317
General C. C. Pinckney, schooner, XXI, 95; *(1861),* VIII, 217, 224
General Chartering Corp., XXXII, 24
General Clinch, Confederate ship *(1861),* XLIV, 258
General Clinch, steamship, XXI, 90; *(1861),* VIII, 217, 234
General Cos, Mexican ship *(1835),* XXX, 47
General Crespo, gunboat, XXVIII, 99
General DeKlerk, ship *(1784),* XI, 137 ff.
General Earl Van Dorn, C.S.S. *(1862),* XIX, 268, 270 ff.
General Falcon, schooner *(1855),* XXX, 275
General Finnegan, sloop *(1864),* XII, 230
General Foods Corp., XLIV, 130
General Frank Pierce, schooner *(1862),* XII, 55
General G. W. Goethals, steamship *(1920),* XXXV, 205

General Gates, brigantine (1777), X, 155, 230, 280–287; XX, 46
"General Gates," by K. Jack Bauer, X, 155
"General Gates, ex-*Industrious Bee,*" by Grahame Farr, X, 230
General George S. Simonds, ship (ex-*Great Northern,* ex-*Columbia,* ex-*H. F. Alexander*) (1942), XLVII, 203; XXVII, 151
"General Glover Stows Some Fish," document contributed by George Billias, XVIII, 323–324
General Gratiot, steamship *(1831),* VII, 43, 313
General Greene, U.S.S. *(1799),* XXVII, 144; XXX, 127; XXXI, 173; XLVI, 160 ff.
Gen'l Greene, barque, XXI, 86
General H. M. Sherman, steamship *(1929),* IX, 226
General Hamilton, U.S. ship *(1810),* XXX, 292 n.
General Hancock, wrecking schooner *(1894),* XLII, 265
General Harrison, steamship *(1839),* XVIII, 299; XX, 84, 85, 90 n.
General Jackson, iron steamship *(1848),* XXX, 270 ff.
General Jeff Thompson, C.S.S. (1862), XIX, 268, 270
General Jessup, steamship (1854), I, 260
General John Glover and his Marblehead Mariners, by George A. Billias, reviewed, XX, 146
General Leavitt (ex-*Spray*), steamship *(1883),* XXIV, 54, 55
General Leon Jurado (ex-*Alice May Davenport*), schooner, XXIV, 25, 34
General Leslie, schooner *(1779),* X, 284–285
General Macomb, steamship *(1837),* VII, 305
Général Manoury, auxiliary (1918), XXXII, 17 ff.
General Massena, French ship *(1800),* XXXI, 174
General McDonald, steamship, XVIII, 230
General Meade (ex-*Del Norte*), schooner (1863), XXIV, 44, 58
General Mifflin, ship *(1777),* V, 187
General Mifflin, state Sloop *(1779),* XXXV, 141
General Miramon, steamship, XXI, 94, 96, 100, 103; *(1861),* XI, 283; XII, 55; *(1862),* VIII, 224
General Moultrie, steamship, XXI, 94; *(1863),* VIII, 230
"General Nuisance," by Captain Edgar K. Thompson, U.S.N. (ret.), XXV, 223
General Ogelthorpe, ship (1801), II, 44–45, plate 9
General Parkhill, ship *(1861),* VIII, 217
General Peavy (1st), schooner (1846), XXIV, 58
General Peavy (2nd), schooner (1848), XXIV, 58
General Pike, U.S.S. XXXI, 219; (1813), III, 267, plate 35..
General Pike, whaler *(1865),* XXVII, 98, 275
General Polk, C.S.S. (1862), XIX, 267
General Porter, steamship (1833), VII, 52, 57, 62; VIII, 37; XVII, 102
General Porter, steamship *(1831),* XLVIII, 109
General Price, C.S.S. (1862), XIX, 268, 270 ff.
General Prim, schooner *(1863),* XII, 157
General Prim, steamship, XXI, 94
General Putnam, brig (1807), VII, 317

General Putnam, ship (1862), V, 148
General Ripley, schooner, XXI, 99; *(1861),* VIII, 217
General Rivera, Uruguayan gunboat *(1903),* II, 170
General Rush, steamship *(1862),* XII, 55
General Rusk, steamship, XXI, 89, 101
General Schuyler, state sloop *(1779),* XXXV, 141
General Scott, ship, XXVII, 73; (1806), VII, 317
General Scott, steamship *(1839),* XVIII, 299; XX, 257
General Seafood Corp., XLIV, 130
General Serret (ex-*G. Machridachis*), auxiliary (1918), XXXII, 17, 18, 30
General Sherman, ship *(1866),* VII, 107; XXV, 117; *(1867),* XXXII, 128; XXXV, 28; *(1873),* XXXVIII, 243
General Shipowners Society, XXX, 11
General Siegel, schooner (1886), VIII, 184 ff.
General Slocum, excursion boat *(1904),* XXXVI, 20, 32
General Sumpter, C.S.S. (1862), XIX, 268, 270 ff.
General Sumter, steamship *(1863),* VII, 123, 124
General Surprise, schooner, XXI, 92; *(1861),* XI, 267, 283
General Taylor, bark *(1861),* XI, 283
General Urrea, Mexican ship *(1835),* XXX, 47
General Ward, steamship (1863), XVII, 309; XVIII, 70
General Warren, freighter *(1840),* XXXIII, 84
General Washington, brigantine *(1778),* XLIII, 27
General Washington, gunboat *(1782),* XXXIX, 216
General Washington, ship *(1787),* XLVI, 9 ff.
General Washington, ship (privateer), XXV, 109
General Wayne, steamship (1837), VII, 65; *(1841),* XX, 89 n., 259, 265
General Wellesley, ship *(1812),* XXI, 22
General Whiting, steamship, XXI, 86; *(1864),* VIII, 234
General Whitney, steamship (1873), Pictorial Supplement, XXXIV, plates X, XIX
General Williams, ship, XXI, 93; *(1861),* XI, 283
General Williams, steamship *(1858),* XXVI, 199
General Williams, whaler *(1865),* XXVII, 275
General Worth, sloop *(1862),* XII, 55, 157
Genereaux, Captain E. C., XXXII, 13
Genereaux, Miss Pauline, XXXII, 13
Genereux, French ship *(1799),* XXXI, 175
Genesee, U.S. gunboat (1862), IV, 238; *(1863),* XXV, 113
Geneva, ship (1874), I, 110–113; IV, 48, 51, 62
Geneva May, two-sail bateau (1908), IV, 289–290, 297
Genevie M. Tucker, bark (1870), IV, 242
Genevieve Strickland, ship (1869), II, 334
Gengor, Captain John, XXI, 99
Genkai Maru, steamship (ex-*Hein Maru*) *(1866),* XLIX, 22; *(1875),* XVII, 313, 314
Genko Maru, steamship (ex-*Thames*) *(1870),* XLIX, 26
"Genoese Shipowners and Their Ships in the Twelfth Century," by Hilmar C. Krueger, XLVIII, 229–239
Genovia, ship *(1861),* XV, 114, 123
Genêt, Citizen, XXV, 10
Genêt, Edmund, Minister, XXII, 81, 82, 88
Genêt, Edmond Charles, XXX, 303

Genoa, History, naval, XLVI, 84
Gentile, Gary, *Andrea Doria — Dive to An Era,* reviewed, L, 144
Gentoo, ship *(1850),* XIX, 27
Geo. *See* George.
"Geography of the Balsa, The," by J. G. Nelson, XXI, 157–195
Geoghegan, William E., "A British View of the Union Navy, 1864: A Report Addressed to Her Majesty's Minister at Washington," XXVII, 30–45; "The South's Scottish Sea Monster," XXIX, 5–29
Geographique (ex-*Vaderland*), Pictorial Supplement, XXXIV, plate XI
"Geography, Fluid," by Richard Buckminster Fuller, IV, 119–136
"Geopolitical Reality and the Disappearance of the Maritime Frontier in Quing Times," by Jane Kate Leonard, XLVIII, 230–236
Georg, ship *(1861),* XI, 266, 283
George, balinger *(1481),* XXXVI, 161
George, brigantine (1742), I, 297
George, schooner *(1755),* XLIX, 264 ff.
George, schooner (1831), Pictorial Supplement, XXXVIII, Plate VI
George, ship *(1669),* XIII, 17
George, ship (1814), II, 284; *(1870),* XXII, plate XIII
George, sloop *(1776),* XIII, 42
George, snow *(1744),* XXVI, 52
George V (King of Elgland), XL, 61 ff.
George, Alice C., "A Grain Race of 1891," VIII, 330
George, David Lloyd, L, 186
George, Earl of London, XXXVII, 176
George, Captain William, XXI, 92
George A. Chaffee, steamship (1870), XII, 289, 293
George A. Fuller Co., XLI, 194
George A. Philips, bark (1849), VI, 80
George Albert, grain elevator *(1883),* XXXVIII, 141
George and Hare, ship *(1572),* XLIV, 28
George and Pauline, trawler *(1961),* XLI, 50
George B. Upton, steamship *(1869),* XXXVIII, 237
George Barclay (1800), XXIII, 216
George Barnet & Co., XLIII, 219
George Bentley, hermaphrodite brig (1857), XXIV, 58
George Burkhart, bark *(1865),* XII, 234
George C. Ackerly, brig (1852), IV, 244
"George Barrell," query by E. Lee Dorset, II, 174
Geo. Chisholm, schooner *(1861),* VIII, 217, 224
George Clinton, steamship (1841), XX, 88
"George Crowninshield's Yacht *Cleopatra's Barge,*" by Walter M. Whitehill, XIII, 235–251, plates 9–12
"George DeKay Writes from Constantinople — 1831," document contributed by Phyllis DeKay Wheelock, VI, 84–85
George D. Bolster, bugeye schooner (1905), XXXVII, 166
George Douthwaite, barque, XXI, 89; *(1865),* XII, 234
George E. Billings, schooner (1903), V, 137
George E. Klinck, schooner *(1941),* III, 163; V, 290–291, plates 21, 22
George F. Patten, ship (1848), XXVII, plate XV
Geo. G. Baker, schooner *(1861),* XI, 283
George Gilroy, bark (1862), III, 69, 265
George Griswold, clipper *(1863),* XLV, 194
George H. Power, steamship (1869), XVIII, 233
George H. Warren, ship (1864), III, 172
George Langtry and Co., XXII, 9
George Law, mail ship *(1854),* XLV, 33
George Law, steamship (1852), IV, 304–317, 2 folding plates; VII, 3
George Lawley & Son, shipbuilders, XXXVII, 84
George Laws, ship *(1864),* XLVII, 123
George Loomis, tanker *(1896),* XXXVIII, 178 ff.
George Lyall and Co., XXII, 13, 14, 16
Geo. M. Adams, ship (1868), II, 334
George M. Bibb, U.S. revenue steamship (1843), XXIV, 8 ff.
George M. Case, schooner (1874), I, 74
George M. Stevens & Co., XLVII, 184 ff.
George Peabody, transport *(1861),* XXXVI, 190, 191
"George Peabody and the search for Sir John Franklin," by Franklin Parker, XX, 104–111
George Pollock, ship *(1850),* XLV, 125
George Raynes, ship *(1850),* XX, 121
"George Scott, Slave Trader of Newport," by Kenneth Scott, XII, 222–228
George Shattuck, steam packet, XXIV, 135
Georgetown, bark *(1805),* XXV, 182
George V. Jordan, schooner (1874), XXIII, 9; *(1885),* XXXV, 7, 11, plate 1
George W. Collins, schooner (1876), Pictorial Supplement, XXXVI, plate XVI
George W. Dole, schooner (1836), XVIII, 275, 284, 286; XX, 79, 82, 252, 266
George W. Grice, schooner *(1861),* VIII, 217
George W. Orr, sloop, XXI, 102; *(1862),* XII, 55
Geo. W. Sloat, schooner *(1861),* XI, 283
George W. Wells, schooner (1900), IV, 325, plate 51; XXIII, 14, 17; plate XXII; Pictorial Supplement, XXXVI, plate XXVI
George Washington, brig *(1806),* III, 237
George Washington, brig (1826), XXIV, 38
George Washington, frigate *(1798),* XLV, 36; *(1800),* XXVI, 248, 249; XXIII, 24; *(1802),* XXIII, 217; L, 245 ff.
George Washington, schooner, XXI, 100; (1812), XXII, 216; *(1862),* VIII, 224
George Washington, ship (1861), XI, 283; *(1917),* XLVII, 203
George Washington, steamship, XXIX, 233; (1833), VII, 52; *(1838),* XVIII, 275–276, 291; (1865), VI, 61
George Washington, U.S.S. (1961), XXI, 4
George Washington, U.S. transport *(1918),* VII, 69–72
George Washington's Navy, by William Bell Clark, reviewed, XX, 224

George Washington's Navy, XXX, 86–116
George Washington's Opponents: British Generals and Admirals in the American Revolution, by George Athan Billias, reviewed, XXIX, 285
"George Watson's *Diagram of Navigation,*" by H. Armour Smith and A. Day Bradley, XI, 147–148
"George Wythe Randolph, Midshipman, United States Navy," by George Green Shackelford, XXXVIII, 101–121
Georgia, bark *(1862),* XII, 55
Georgia, C.S.S., XXVIII, 122; XXIX, 168; *(1863),* XV, 178, 293 ff.; XLV, 191–198
Georgia, schooner, XXI, 100; *(1864),* XII, 230
Georgia, ship (1855), II, 331; *(1857),* XXXI, 191
Georgia, steamship (1848), IV, 307; *(1863),* VIII, 230; *(1878),* X, 134
Georgia, tanker (1908), XXXVIII, 199 ff.
Georgia (GA), History, XXII, 81; XXIII, 62. See also Frederica River; Shipping
Georgiana, bark (1857), XIX, 27
Georgiana, steamship *(1863),* VIII, 230
Georgiana McCaw, steamship, XXI, 89; *(1864),* VIII, 234
Georgia Todd, schooner (1868), XXIV, 58
Georgie, schooner *(1863),* XII, 157
Georgio, tanker *(1926),* XXXVIII, 198 ff.
Gerard, steamship *(1861),* XLIII, 211 ff.
Gerberviller, auxiliary (1918), XXXII, 11 ff., plate 2
Gerbeviller, schooner (1918), IV, 62, 68
Germ, U.S. experimental steamship (1841), XVII, 91; XXIV, 7–11
Germain, Lord George, VII, 200; XXV, 199 n.; XXXVII, 289; XLII, 11 ff.; XLVII, 6
German, Andrew W., notes by, XLI, 139, 144; *Down on T. Wharf,* reviewed, XLIII, 310; "Otter Trawling Comes to America: The Bay State Fishing Company, 1905–1938," XLIV, 114–131; XLII, 219
German Africa (German shipping line), XLVI, 108
Germania, packet ship (1850), I, 47
Germanischer Lloyd, XXX, 29, 39
Germantown, brig, XXXI, 15
Germantown, ship *(1857),* XXXVIII, 37
"German U-Boat Attacks on Convoy SC 118: 4 February to 14 February 1943," by David Syrett, XLIV, 48–60
Germany:
  Foreign relations, United States, XXXII, 257; XLVIII, 50
  Navy, Submarines, XXXVI, 33
  See also Shipping
Gerrevinck, Abram van, XLVI, 174
Gerrevinck, Isaac van, XLVI, 174
Gerrevinck, Lubertus van, XLVI, 174
Gerrish, Joseph, XLVIII, 26
Gerry, Elbridge, XXV, 36; XXXVI, 59, 80; XLV, 8; XLVI, 141
Gerry, Samuel Russell, XXX, 100
Gershom, brig (1806), XIV, 40

Gerson, Levi ben. *See* Levi ben Gerson.
Gertrude, steamship, XXI, 99; *(1863),* VIII, 230
Gertrude A. Somerville, schooner (1917), VI, 133–134
Gertrude Abbott, schooner *(1889),* XXXVII, 86
Gertrude D., fishing vessel *(1962),* XLI, 54
Gertrude L. Thebaud, schooner, XXXIV, 142; XXXVI, 77; (1930), XXV, 147
Gertrude L. Trundy, schooner (1883), XXIV, 59
Gertrude Wands, sloop (1899), XXXVII, 165
Gertrude Wands, two-sail bateau (1899), IV, 288–289, 295
Gessler, Clifford, *The Port of Honolulu,* reviewed, II, 350
"Getting Up," Pictorial Supplement, XXXI, plate XIX
Gettysburg, bark (1864), II, 245
Gettysburg, U.S.S. *(1863),* VIII, 205; *(1864),* XI, 223
Geziena Hilligonda, brig *(1864),* XII, 230
Ghent, H.M.S. *(1775),* VII, 89–90
Gherardi, Admiral Bancroft, XXXVIII, 298
Gherardi, Captain Bancroft, U.S.N., XXV, 223
Gherardi, Rear Admiral Bancroft, U.S.N., XXVI, 173
Gherardi, Lieutenant Walter R., XXIX, 125
Ghost of riveter in *Great Eastern,* I, 140
Gibaut, Captain John, V, 101–102, 106
Gibaut, Commander John, XLVI, 10 ff.
Gibb, Livingston and Co., XXXIV, 38 ff.; XLIII, 103 ff.
Gibbon, Lardner, XXXI, 8
Gibbons, Thomas, XVI, 278
Gibbs, Charles E., XXIV, 237, 238
Gibbs, J. S., XXXVI, 232, 246
Gibbs, James A., Jr., *Pacific Graveyard,* reviewed, XI, 231
Gibbs, William Francis, XXXVIII, 275
Gibilterra, steamship (1881), XIV, 134
Gibraltar, H.M.S. *(1781),* XXXVI, 167; *(1782),* XXXIX, 216
Gibraltar, schooner, XXI, 91
Gibraltar, steamship, XXI, 100, plate XVII; *(1863),* VIII, 230
Gibraltar: description of, 1806, III, 226 ff.; Bay of, and surrounding area, XXVII, 192, plate 5
Gibson, Charles Dana, "History of the Swordfishery of the Northwestern Atlantic," XLI, 36–65
Gibson, G. W., Secretary of State, XXXVIII, 63
Gibson, N., and Baxter, Boston, XXV, 113–114
Gideon Howland, bark (1831), V, 242
Gideon Howland, ship *(1835),* XII, 108
"Gideon Welles and Naval Administration During the Civil War," by John Niven, XXXV, 53–66
Gideon Wells—Lincoln's Navy Department, by Richard S. West, Jr., reviewed, IV, 254–255
Gidley, John, XLII, 41 ff.
Giffard, Ann, and Basil Greenhill, *Victorian and Edwardian Sailing Ships from Old Photographs,* reviewed, XXXIX, 304; *Westcountymen in Prince Edward's Isle,* reviewed, XXVIII, 232–233
Giffin, Donald W., "The American Navy at Work on the Brazil Station, 1827–1860," XIX, 239–256

Gifford, Robert, XXXIII, 166
Gift, ship *(1630),* XXIII, 63
Gift, Captain George W., XXI, 92
Gila, steamship (1872), I, 261, plates between 272–273
Gilberd, Dr. William, XXXVII, 177
Gilbert, Captain Bartholomew, XXXIV, 233
Gilbert, Benjamin Franklin, "Confederate Warships off Brazil," XV, 287–302
Gilbert, Captain Frederick W., XLIX, 278
Gilbert, John (instrument maker), Pictorial Supplement, XXXV, plate IV
Gilbert, Martin, *Winston S. Churchill: Finest Hour, 1939–1941,* reviewed, XLVII, 143
Gilbert, Thomas, XXXV, 154
Gilbert, Captain Thomas, IV, 93–96, plate 17
Gilbert, W. W., XIV, 260
Gilbert Islands, IV, 87–118; boats of, XIII, 94 ff.
Gilchrist, David T., Editor, *The Growth of the Seaport Cities, 1790–1825,* reviewed, XXVIII, 149–150
Gilchrist, Captain James, XXV, 182
Gilchrist, John H., "Cabotian Conjectures: Did a Cabot Reach Maine in 1498?" XLV, 249; "Latitude Errors and the New England Voyages of Pring and Waymouth," L, 5–17
Gilder, William H., XXXIX, 10
Gildersleeve, steamship *(1839),* XVIII, 299; *(1840),* VIII, 53
Gildersleeve Shipbuilding Co. (Stonington, CT), XXV, 102
Giles, W. E., *A Cruize in a Queensland Labour Vessel to the South Seas,* reviewed, XXIX, 290
Giles, William Branch, XXXIX, 25 ff.
Gilkison, David and Robert (shipmasters), XLVIII, 77 ff.
Gilkison, Robert, VII, 56; XVIII, 273, 280–281, 284; XX, 83
Gill, E. H., XVII, 226
Gill, Phillip H., XXXVIII, 133
Gill, Rowland P., and Henry I. Shaw, Jr., *American Marines in the Revolutionary War,* XXXI, 4
Gillespie, Lieutenant A. H., U.S.M.C., XXIX, 97
Gillespie, Norton and Co., VII, 64
Gilliam, Henry, XLVII, 16
Gillis, Captain James D., XXV, 184
Gillis, Commander John P., XXXVI, 188 ff.; XXXVII, 276 ff.
Gillis, Seaman William, U.S.N., XXV, 161
Gillmer, T. C., I, 400; II, 84; review by, II, 187–188; "Present-Day Craft and Rigs of the Mediterranean, I, 352–373; II, 56–64
Gillmore, Lieutenant J. C., XXXV, 187
Gillon, Alexander, XXXIX, 159 ff.
Gillon, Captain Alexander, XIII, 36
Gillon, Sartine, XXXIX, 161
Gills, Solomon, XXXIV, 197 ff.
Gillson, Captain W., XLIII, 103 ff.
Gillson, W. M., XXVI, 203

Gilman, Captain Thomas F., XVIII, 83
Gilman, Smull and Co., XXX, 181, 183, 229
Gilman & Co., XLIII, 86 ff.
Gilmer, Major General J. F., XV, 101
Gilmer, Thomas, Secretary of the Navy, XLIX, 109
Gilmore, George F., answered query, I, 399
Gilmore, Captain R. M., XVIII, 83
Gilpin, Vincent, XVIII, 191, 198
Gilt Dragon, ship *(1656),* XXIV, 80
Gim, Consul General Wever, XLVI, 27
Gino, schooner, XXI, 91, 103; *(1861),* XI, 283; XII, 55
Gino Colorado, schooner *(1861),* XI, 283
Gipsey, British ship *(1853),* XLVII, 101
Gipsey, schooner *(1861),* XI, 283
Gipsey, schooner yacht, XXI, 96
Giraffe, steamship, XXI, 90, 103, 104, 105, plate XXXI; *(1862),* VIII, 202–203, 224, 230
Girard, Captain Augustus P., XXI, 92
Girard, Stephen, III, 74–85; IV, 253–254; XIV, 215; XX, 45
Gish, Captain John, XXI, 92
Giuchard, Hubert, XII, 225
Givenchy, auxiliary (1918), XXXII, 18, 19, 30
Givens, Stuart, XXXV, 231
Gjøa, sloop (1872), I, 79; XII, 7–21, plates 1–4
Gjoa Foundation, *An Account of the Perilous Voyage of the Ship* Gjoa, reviewed, X, 158
"Gjøa, The," by William A. Baker, XII, 7–21
Glacier, ship *(1932),* XXXIX, 184 ff., plate 6
Glacier, XXV, 175
Gladiator, bark (1835), III, 261
Gladiator, H.M.S. *(1908),* XX, 192–197, plate 10
Gladiator, steamship, XXI, 87, 94; *(1863),* VIII, 230
Gladstanes, ship *(1837),* VIII, 179
Gladstone, ship (1860), VI, 82
Glad Tidings, pinkie *(1937),* XII, 135
Glamorganshire, steamship *(1885),* XXVIII, plate XVI; XL, 109 ff.
Glanydon (ex-*Pechiney*) (1922), XXXII, 32
Glasgow, British bark *(1832),* XXXVIII, 266
Glasgow, British ship *(1914),* XXXIII, 35 ff.
Glasgow, H.M. frigate *(1776),* XLVIII, 157; XL, 19 ff.; *(1777),* XX, 46
Glasgow, Tom Jr., "Sixteenth-Century English Seamen Meet a New Enemy – The Shipworm," XXVII, 177–184
Glasgow and Liverpool Steam Shipping Co., XXVI, 13
Glashoff, Captain R., XVIII, 83
Glass, Rear Admiral Henry, XXXVII, 254
Glasspoole, Richard, XLVIII, 240
Glatton, H.M.S. *(1803),* XV, 83
Glaucus, steamship *(1871),* XXXVII, 235
Glaucus, steamship (1921), XXIV, plate XVI
Gleaner, brig *(1816),* XLIV, 7
Gleason, Madeline, note by, XL, 137
Glen, bark *(1861),* VIII, 217; XI, 153
Glen Cove, steamship *(1854),* II, 226

Glendarroch, steamship (1871), XVII, 54; XVIII, 70
Glendower, schooner *(1854),* XLIV, 83
Glendower, ship (1860), III, 70
Glendy, William, XL, 43
Glenesslin, British ship *(1913),* XLI, 122 ff.; plates 5, 6
Glengyle, steamship (1864), XVI, 267; XVII, 136, 137; XVIII, 70; *(1865),* XLIII, 98 ff.
Glenn, Bess, III, 271; "Cathcart's Journal and the Search for Naval Timbers," III, 239–249
Glenogle, bark *(1896),* XVIII, 9
Glenside, steamship (1920), XIV, 126, 135
Glenullen, schooner *(1902),* XXIV, 49
Glick, Bill, The Meriden Gravure Co., XXXIX, 234
Glide, log canoe (about 1880), IV, 249
Glide, schooner, XXI, 105; *(1863),* XV, 111, 127
Glide, ship, XXV, 186; (1811), II, 282; *(1829),* XII, 27, plate 5; *(1831),* X, 41
Glide, sloop (1821), XXII, 216
Glimpse, bark (1856), III, 263
Glitra, British steamship *(1914),* XXXVI, 35
Globe, bark *(1869),* XII, 102, 114
Globe, brig (1822), XIV, 40
Globe, ship *(1804),* XLI, 228; *(1824),* IV, 99
Gloire, French warship, XXII, 114; *(1863),* XLIX, 117
Gloire, French warship [model] (1859), XVI, 103
Gloria (ex-*Fjeltind,* ex-*Astri I*), auxiliary (1917), XXXII, 18
Gloria Colita, ship (1939), XXXII, 187
Gloriana, ship *(1860),* XXVII, 235
Glorianna, schooner *(1891),* XXX, Pictorial Supplement, plate VIII
Glory Anna II, schooner (1948), XII, 140, plate 12
Glory of the Seas, ship (1869), XIX, plates XV, XVI; XXVIII, plate XIII; *(1872),* VII, 289
Glory of the Seas, by Michael Jay Mjelde, reviewed, XXX, 217–218
Glossary of Sea Terms, A, by Gershom Bradford, reviewed, II, 345–346
Gloucester, H.M.S. *(1915),* XXXVII, 105
Gloucester, ship, XXII, 108, 109
Gloucester, steamship *(1886),* XI, 258 ff.
Gloucester, warship *(1776),* XLIV, 158 ff.
Gloucester (MA), XXV, plates I–V, VIII, X–XIII, XVII, XXI, XXIII, XXVI, XXVII, XXX, XXXI
Gloucester City, steamship (1881), XIV, 117, 119, 134; (1889), XIV, 122; *(1936),* XIV, 127, 129, 130, 132, 135
Gloucester Committee of Safety, XXX, 88, 89, 109
"Gloucester Steamboats, The," by Charles Rodney Pittee, XII, 288–293
Gloucester trade, XXVIII, 261–274
Glover, Abigail, XXX, 93
Glover, Hannah, XXX, 96
Glover, John, XXX, 86–116
Glover, General John, XVIII, 323–324
Glover, Jonathan, XXX, 86–116
Glover, Mary, XXX, 93

Glover, Captain Mathew, XXI, 18
Glover, Russell E., XXXVII, 141 n.
Glover, Stephen, XIX, 23
Glover, Stephen E., XXXVII, 141 n.
Glover, W. A., XIX, 121
Glover and Co., XVII, 136, 140; XLIII, 220
Glückauf, German tanker *(1886),* XXXVIII, 175
Glyde, steamship *(1861),* XV, 106, 114, 123
Glynn, Commander James, XLI, 32
Glynn, Comander James, U.S.N., XXV, 93–98
Gneisenau, cruiser (1914), XXXIII, 36 ff.
Gneisenau, German battle cruiser (1939), XXVI, 148; XXVIII, 108
"Goals and Enforcement of British Colonial Policy, 1763–1775," by Neil R. Stout, XXVII, 211–220
Goddard, David, XXXIII, 78
Goddard, Robert H. I., Jr., III, 178; "*Anna R. Heidritter,*" III, 59–61; "The Four-masted Schooner *Anna R. Heidritter,*" XXX, 187–193; "Loss of the Schooner *Albert H. Willis,*" II, 243–245; "Notes on Some New England Three-Masters," V, 285–296; "Passing of the Five-Masters," IV, 58–67; "A Recent Problem in Ship Handling," IV, 236–237; "The Schooner *Albert F. Paul,*" III, 163–166; "The Schooner *Lillian E. Kerr,*" IV, 172–174; "The Schooner *Lucy Evelyn,*" II, 327–330; "The Schooner *Rebecca R. Douglas,*" III, 255–258; query by, II, 174
Goddess, ship (1855), II, 174; V, 150; VI, 153
Goderich, steamship *(1839),* XVIII, 299
Godetia, H.M.S. *(1942),* L, 44
Godfrey, Thomas, XXXV, 11 ff.; XLVI, 258
Godine, schooner *(1787),* XLIX, 88
Godolad, Captain John, XXIII, 65
Godspeed, ship (1607), X, 5–14, plates 1–4; XVII, 173–180; plan, XVII, 176; *(1607),* XXXIV, 233
Godspeed, XXX, 302
Godspeed II, ship [replica] (1956), XVII, 178 ff., plates 15, 17; plans, XVII, 176
Godwinson, King Harold, XLIV, 96
Goeben, warship *(1914),* XXXVI, 34 n.
Goethals, Colonel George W., XXIV, 187; XXXII, 158 ff.; XXXV, 277 ff.
Goethals, Major General George, XLI, 197
Goffe, Captain Edward, XXV, 265
Goforth, Captain Zachariah, XX, 45
Gokstadt ships (ca. A.D. 800), XLIV, 98 ff.
Golconda, ship *(1852),* XXI, 114
Golconda, ship (1853), III, 64
Goldberg, Mitchell S., "Naval Operations of the United States Pacific Squadron in 1861," XXXIII, 41–51
Golden Age, steamship (1853), II, 19; XVII, 311, 313; X, 131; XVIII, 70; *(1853),* photo of, XLIX, 22, 27; (1856), XX, 126–129
Goldenberg, Joseph, "Names and Numbers: Statistical Notes on Some Port Records of Colonial North Carolina," XXIX, 155–166; "A Forgotten Dry Dock in Colonial Charlestown," XXX, 56–60

Golden City, ship *(1862),* III, 262; XIX, plate XXIV
Golden City, steamship (1863), X, 130, 134; *(1864),* XXXII, 202
Golden Cross Line, XIV, 126
Golden Cloud, two masted schooner *(1853),* XLIV, 85
Golden Eagle, schooner, XXI, 96
Golden Eagle, ship (1852), I, 83; XIX, plate XXVIII
Golden Eagle, ship *(1959),* XLI, 49
Golden Fleece, American steamship *(1870),* XLV, 241
Golden Fleece, bark (1863), IV, 72
Golden Gate, bark *(1865),* XXXVI, 50; *(1922),* XVIII, 212
Golden Gate, steamship (1851), X, 130, 133, 134; *(1855),* XLVIII, 113; *(1864),* XXXII, 200
Golden Gate, The Story of San Francisco Harbor, by Felix Riesenberg, Jr., reviewed, I, 402
Golden Goose, brig (1813), XXII, 216
Golden Grove, brig (1815), XIV, 40
Golden Hind [replica], XXXII, 153
Golden Horn, ship (1854), III, 64
Golden Lead, brig *(1862),* XXXIII, 57
Golden Liner, schooner *(1863),* VIII, 230
Golden Lyon, ship *(1627),* XXXVII, 12
Golden Phoenix, ship *(1620),* XIV, 64
Golden Rod, sloop *(1861),* XV, 123
Golden Rule, ship (1855), IV, 240
Golden State, ship (1852), XIX, Plate XIV
Golden State, steamship (1921), X, 141, plate 20
Golden West, schooner *(1865),* XXVI, 283; *(1868),* XLV, 111
Golden West, ship (1852), XIX, Plate XXVI
Goldfinch, Harry, XXXVI, 245
Gold Hunter, bark (1849), IV, 238.
Gold Hunter, schooner *(1861),* VIII, 217
Golding, Captain D., XXI, 92
Goldowsky, Seebert J., *Yankee Surgeon: The Life and Times of Usher Parsons, 1788–1868,* reviewed, L, 74
Gold Rush, XX, 118–133
Gold Rush by Sea, by Garrett W. Low, reviewed, I, 406–407
Goldsborough, Charles W., XXXIII, 233 ff.
Goldsborough, John, "Commodore Perry's Landing in Japan – 1853," VII, 9–20
Goldsborough, Captain John R., XXXII, 130
Goldsborough, Commodore John Rodgers, VII, 9–20
Goldsborough, Flag Officer, L. M., U.S.N., VI, 52–54
Goldsborough, Commodore Louis, XXXI, 68; XXXII, 51
Goldsborough, Rear Admiral Luis M., U.S.N., XXI, 234, 235; XXII, 259, 262
Gold shipments, California (1849 & 1850), XX, 125
Gold, Transportation, XX, 118
Goldstein, A., C.P., U.S.N., XXV, 50
Goldstein, Jonathan, "Introduction to Fresh Perspectives on Qing Dynasty Maritime Relations," XLVIII, 221–224

Golladay, V. Dennis, "The United States and British North American Fisheries, 1815–1818," XXXIII, 246–257
Gomez, Estevan, XI, 97
Gomez, Joaquim da Silva, XV, 296 ff.
Gompers, Samuel, XXVII, 47, 55, 56, 57, 58, 59
Gondar, ship, XXI, 92, 94; *(1861),* VIII, 217
Gondomar, Señor de, XXVIII, 252–255, 258, 259
"Gone by the Board," contributed by Captain Edgar K. Thompson, U.S.N. (ret.), XXX, 138
Gonson, William, XXVII, 179
Gooch, Governor William, VIII, 28 ff.
Good Boats, by Roger C. Taylor, reviewed, XXXVII, 225
Goode, G. Brown, XLV, 81
Goodell, bark (1866), III, 66
Goodenough, Captain James Graham, XXVII, 31 ff.
Goodenough Island, boats of, XIII, 96
Good Fortune, schooner *(1760),* XXIII, 145
Good Hope, bark *(1863),* XXVI, 105; XLV, 194
Good Hope, brigantine *(1795),* XXII, 195, 196, 197, 205
Good Hope, British flagship *(1914),* XXXIII, 40
Good Hope, H.M.S., XXVIII, 108
Good Hope, schooner *(1864),* XII, 230
Good Hope, ship *(1795),* XXIV, 254–257
Good Hope, ship (1855), III, 64, 265
Goodhue, Benjamin, XXX, 142
Goodhue, Senator Benjamin, XLVI, 145; L, 270 ff.
Goodhue & Co., XXIII, 134, 136
Gooding, Captain Mathew Robert, XXI, 92
Good Intent, brig, XXII, 90
Good Intent, British ship *(1776),* XLVIII, 16
Good Luck, sloop, XXI, 89; *(1863),* XV, 127
Goodnough, Ezra, XXXII, 34
Goodrich, Caspar F., XXXIV, 215
Goodrich, Lieutenant Commander Caspar F., XXXIX, 122
Goodrich, Marcus, *Delilah,* reviewed, I, 189
Goodridge, steamship (1913), XXIV, 238, 239, 241, 244, plates 26, 28
Goodridge, Charles L., XXIV, 238 ff.
Good Ships of Newport News, The, by Alexander Crosby Brown, reviewed, XXXVII, 74–75
Goodspeed, ship *(1607),* XIV, 106
Goodspeed, Charles E., VI, 136, 239; VII, 316; "Nathaniel Hawthorne and the Museum of the East India Marine Society," V, 266–285; "Quarter Wagener," VI, 78–79
Goodspeed & Co., L. B., XLIV, 116
Goodwin, Charles A., I, 69
Goodwin, Eben P., XVII, 119, 120
Goodwin, Ensign Kenneth R., XXXVII, 98 ff.
Goodwin, Captain N., XVIII, 83
Goodwin, Thomas, XVII, 126
Goodwin Sands, light-vessel (1796), IV, 266, plate 47
Gookin, Rev. Warner F., *A Voyage of Discovery to the Southern Parts of Norumbega,* reviewed, X, 236

Gopher, U.S.S. (1905), XX, 136
Gorch Fock, training bark *(1964),* XXIV, 79
Gordan, John Dozier, *Joseph Conrad: The Making of a Novelist,* reviewed, I, 411
Gordinier, Glenn S., note by, XLIV, 166; "Early American Trade with India: Taking an Observation," XLV, 153–166
Gordon, sidewheel packet *(1861),* XLIV, 258
Gordon, steamship, XXI, 95, 96; *(1861),* VIII, 197, 217, 224; XI, 154
Gordon, Captain Alexander, XXIII, 26
Gordon, Arthur, XXXVI, 22, 23
Gordon, Sir Arthur Hamilton, XXXI, 115
Gordon, Charles, XXX, 73
Gordon, Captain Charles, XXXVI, 209 ff.
Gordon, Charles George, XXIX, 268
Gordon, Eleanora C., M.D., review by, L, 74; "Scurvy and Anson's Voyage Round the World: 1740–1744; An Analysis of the Royal Navy's Worst Outbreak," XLIV, 155–156
Gordon, General, XXXI, 115
Gordon, James, VII, 66
Gordon, Captain James, XXI, 92
Gordon, John, "Five Thousand Miles in a Fifty-Footer," XIV, 18–29, plates 1–4
Gordon, Captain John, VII, 65
Gordon, Captain Nathaniel, XXI, 40
Gordon, Sir Robert, VII, 187
Gordon, Captain W. L., XL, 42
Gordon, Captain William, XX, 262
Gore, steamship (1839), XVIII, 284; XX, 86, 87; *(1840),* VIII, 53
"Gore, Christopher," query by Helen Reisinger, I, 90
Gore, John, XV, 133
Gore, Lieutenant John, XXVIII, 146, 147
Gore, W. S., XXXVI, 240
Goree (island off Senegal), XXX, 177 ff.
Gorges, Sir Ferdinando, XXXVII, 7; L, 16
Gorget, from Marquesas, 1801, XXXIII, plate 11 (right).
Gorgon, H.M. frigate *(1845),* XXXVI, 128–130, 133–137, 140, 141
Gorham, Captain Josiah, XXII, 241
Gorilla, steamship *(1863),* XLIII, 96; *(1865),* XVII, 60
Gorronama, revenue vessel *(1892),* XXXVIII, 64; XXXIX, 174 ff.
Gorton-Pew Fisheries Co., XLIV, 124 ff.
Goshawk, barge, XXV, 168
Goshawk, H.M.S. (1886), XXVIII, 26
Gosnell, H. A., "The Navy in Korea, 1871," VII, 107–114, plates 9–12
Gosnell, H. Allen, answered query, V, 163
Gosnold, Bartholomew, L, 9
Gosnold, Captain Bartholomew, XVII, 173; XXIV, 144–145; XXV, 237–238, 243; XXXIII, 131; XXXIV, 231 ff.

"Gosnold's *Concord* and Her Shallop," by William A. Baker, XXXIV, 231–242
"Gosnold's Elizabeth's Isle: Cuttyhunk or Naushon?" by Harold C. Wilson and William C. Carr, XXXIII, 131–145
Gosport, H.M.S., XXVI, 51
Gosport Navy Yard, Norfolk, VA, XXIV, 7, 11; XXXIV, 61
Goss, R. O., *Studies in Maritime Economics,* reviewed, XXIX, 145–147
Goss, Sawyer and Packard, VIII, 152–153
Goss, Sawyer (& Packard) Shipyard, XXVII, plate XIX
Goss & Sawyer, XXIII, 12
Gossoon, cutter (1890), XXX, plate XIV
Gossypium, brig (1811), VI, 93–100
Gotsche, Frank, XXXIX, 14
Gott, Lemuel, XXV, 245
Gott's Island (ME), XXV, 242
Goudie, James, IX, 259
Gough, Barry M.; mentioned, XXXVII, 81; reviews by, XLIV, 279; L, 150; *Distant Dominion: Britain and the Northwest Coast of North America, 1579–1809,* reviewed, XLII, 144–146; *Gunboat Frontier: British Maritime Authority and the Northwest Coast Indians, 1846–1890,* reviewed, XLIV, 207; "James Cook and the Origins of the Maritime Fur Trade," XXXVIII, 217–224; *The Royal Navy and the Northwest Coast of North America, 1810–1914: A Study of British Maritime Ascendancy,* reviewed, XXXII, 141–142; "Sea Power and South America: The 'Brazils' or South American Station of the Royal Navy, 1808–1837," L, 26–34
Gough, Captain Richard S., XLIX, 24
Gould, Albert T., II, 177, 252
Gould, Alicia B., *Nueva Lista Documentada de los Tribulantes de Colon en 1492,* reviewed, XLVI, 126
Gould, Dr. Augusta A., XLIX, 34
Gould, Captain Charles, XXI, 92
Gould, Jay, XXXI, 124
Gould, R. T., XIX, 79–113
Gould, Richard A., editor, *Shipwreck Anthropology,* reviewed, XLIV, 134
Goulden Lyon, ship *(1593),* XXXVII, 175
Goulds [Chester] (Boston instrument maker), mechanical log, Pictorial Supplement, XXXV, plate XXIII
Gould's patent log, XXV, 180
Goullett, Charles, XLV, 8
Gourde du Pelican, French ship *(1799),* XXXI, 173
Gourlay, Robert J., XIV, 243 ff.; XIX, 129
Gourlay Brothers, Dundee, VII, 288
Govan Steam Packet Co., XLIII, 187 ff.
"Government Owned and Operated Coastwise Mail Service of the Eighteenth Century," by Arthur Hecht, XXII, 55–64
"Government Publications Useful to Model Builders," by Albert E. Parsons, XI, 215–218

Governolo, Italian warship *(1865)*, XV, 202
Governor, steam transport, XXIII, 262
Governor, U.S. sidewheeler (1846), XXXIII, 94
Governor A. Moulton, steamship *(1862)*, XII, 55
Governor Aiken, lighthouse tender *(1861)*, XLIV, 257
Governor Aiken, schooner *(1861)*, VIII, 217
Governor Ames, schooner (1888), IV, 58; V, 138; XXIII, 13, plate XII; *(1889)*, XXXV, 13
Governor Bligh, schooner *(1811)*, XII, 162
Governor Brooks, schooner (1907), XXVII, plate XXVIII
Governor Brown, schooner *(1864)*, XV, 113, 129
Governor Cobb, screw steamship (1906), XXXIII, plate 4, 92, 94; XXXIV, 182
Governor Davis, ship *(1843)*, XV, 140
Governor de Graff, ship *(1780)*, XXXVI, 160
Governor Dingley, U.S. steel screw steamship (1899), XXVIII, 124, 126; XXXIII, plate 3, 92, 94; Pictorial Supplement, XXXIV, plate XXIV, 182
Governor Dudley, steamship *(1862)*, VIII, 225
Governor Endicott, brig *(1823)*, VI, 99
Governor Forbes, steamship *(1922)*, X, 142
Governor General, steamship (1848), XVII, 300; XVIII, 70
Governor General (ex-*New Orleans*), steamship *(1861)*, XXXIV, 121; XLIII, 87 ff.
Governor Langdon, ship (1854), III, 67
Governor Marcy, steamship (1833), VII, 52, 313; *(1840)*, XX, 83 n.
Governor Mason, steamship (1837), VII, 65; *(1840)*, XX, 80
Governor Morton, ship *(1860)*, XX, 215
Governor of Jamaica, schooner *(1864)*, XII, 230
Governor Prence, steamship (1917), XII, 291, 293
Governor Strong, ship *(1807)*, XVI, 195
Governor Tilley, ship (1875), I, 114
Govin, Dr. Manuel, XXXVI, 91
Gowlland, Gladys M. O., *Master of the Moving Seas*, reviewed, XIX, 309
Gozan-Pinder, Ines, XXXVI, 15
Grace, sloop *(1791)*, XLI, 26; XLVI, 51
Grace, W. R., and Co., X, 140, 143
Grace A. Martin, schooner (1904), V, 138
Grace and Co., XVIII, 16
Grace Bradley, schooner *(1889)*, XXXV, 16
Gracedieu, ship (1416), XV, 270
Grace E. Baker, schooner *(1862)*, XII, 55
Grace Lynwood, barkentine *(1898)*, IX, 69
Gracemere, bark (1871), XV, 188
Grace Steamship Co., XLI, 114
Gracie, bugeye schooner (1890), XXXVII, 166
Gracie, sloop *(1868)*, XXX, Pictorial Supplement, Plate IV
Gracie Felitz, yacht *(1893)*, XXXVI, 237, 238
Gracie S., pilot schooner (1893), I, 78
Graf, Herman, XXI, 119
Graf Spee, German battleship *(1939)*, XXXII, 115

Grafton, British warship (1771), XXXVIII, 92 ff.
Grafton, schooner, XXII, 235
Grafton, R. E., XXXVI, 239
Graf von Spee, Vice Admiral, L, 185
Graham, Gerald S., *Great Britain in the Indian Ocean: A Study of Maritime Enterprise 1810–1850*, reviewed, XXIX, 282; *Sea Power and British North America, 1783–1820: A Study in British Colonial Policy*, reviewed, II, 259–260
Graham, Henry, XL, 8 ff.
Graham, James, XX, 45
Graham, James Lorrimer, Jr., XLV, 22
Graham, Captain Thomas, XLII, 109
Graham, Walter, XXVI, 100
Graham, William, XLVI, 168
Graham, William A., Secretary of the Navy, XXXIX, 243 ff.
Grain elevators, XXXVIII, 131
Grainger, Captain G. A., XXVI, 27, 203
"Grain Race of 1891, A," by Alice C. George, VIII, 330
Grampian, schooner (1894), I, 74
Grampus, barkentine *(1890)*, XXXVIII, 84
Grampus, schooner, XXIX, 197; *(1737)*, XXV, 82; *(1839)*, XXXII, 274; *(1885)*, XLIV, 18; XLV, 82
Grampus, U.S.S., XXIII, 58 n.
Granada, schooner *(1861)*, VIII, 217
Granada, ship *(1854)*, XXV, 108
Granada, steamship *(1856)*, XI, 43 ff.; (1857), XXVI, 26, 118, 203, 205, 209
Granada, steamship (1873), X, 132, 138
Grand Bank cod schooner, XXVI, plate VI
Grandbourg, French ship *(1785)*, XLI, 212
Grand Canal south of the Yangtsze River, photo of, XLVIII, 233
Grand Canary Coaling Co., XLVI, 105
Grand Congloué wreck, XXIV, plate 12
Grandee, ship (1873), figurehead of, Pictorial Supplement, XXXVII, plate IX
Grande River, XXX, 178 ff.
Grandes Rivaux, French ship *(1800)*, XXXI, 175
Grandfather for Benjamin Franklin; The True Story of a Nantucket pioneer and His Mates, by Florence Bennett Anderson, reviewed, I, 409–410
Grand Francois, ship, XV, 273
Grandin, Eugene (painter), XXV, 112–115
Grand Sachem, ship *(1807)*, X, 54
Grand Scuttle: The Sinking of the German Fleet at Scapa Flow in 1919, The, by Dan van der Vat, reviewed, XLIV, 132
Grands Voiliers Français 1880–1930, by Jean Randier, reviewed, XXXV, 212
Grand Trunk Railway of Canada, XXXIII, 87
Grand Turk, brig, XXIV, 212; *(1844)*, XXXI, 191
Grand Turk, ship (1780), XLVI, 9 ff.; *(1785)*, XXV, 7, 8; *(1792)*, XLI, 171
Grand Turk, ship (1791), II, 280–281
Grand Turk, ship (1795), XIII, 275; *(1796)*, X, 53

Grand Turk, ship *(1835),* XII, 104, 116
Grand Turk (II), ship *(1793),* XLVI, 11 ff.
Grand Union Flag of United Colonies, 1776, XXV, 212
Grange, ship, XXII, 88
Granite City, steamship, XXI, 92, 104; *(1863),* VIII, 230; *(1865),* XII, 234
Granite State, steamship *(1921),* X, 141
Granite State, U.S.S. *(1904),* XX, 137
Grann, Captain Paul F., XIV, 248 ff.
Grant, Charles, XLVI, 13
Grant, Frederic D., Jr., "The Failure of the Li-ch'uan Hong: Litigation as a Hazard of Nineteenth Century Foreign Trade," XLVIII, 243–260
Grant, Frederick Dent, XLIII, 183 ff.
Grant, Gordon (artist), IV, 202; XXII, 213, 231
Grant, Ira M., IX, 170, 171
Grant, Jesse Root, XLIII, 183 ff.
Grant, Samuel B., query by, II, 174
Grant, Sueton, XLII, 41 ff.
Grant, Thomas, XXX, 110
Grant, Ulysses S., VII, 144; XLIII, 177 ff.; portrait of, XLIII, plate 5
Grant, General Ulysses S., XLII, 87 ff.; XLVIII, 105
Grant, President Ulysses S., XXVII, 53, 54; XXXVI, 97 ff.; XXXVIII, 235
Grant, Lieutenant William, R.N., XXV, 201
Grantham, Captain C. R., XXI, 92
Granville, H.M.S. *(1778),* XIV, 55
Granville R. Bacon, schooner (1911), V, 291–292, plate 20
Grapeshot, schooner *(1869),* XXXVIII, 236
Grapeshot, steamship *(1862),* VIII, 225, 234
Graph of British Imports of Great Masts, 1764–1785, XLVI, 228
Graph of latitude errors, L, 7, 8
Grass, Captain, VII, 51
Grasshopper (ex-*Irene*), brig-of-war (1806), XXX, 301
Grasty, Charles H., XXXIV, 271
Gratitude, fishing smack (1920), XXXII, 12
Grausers, Gustav, XVIII, 219, 220
Graveley, Walter, XXXVI, 233 ff.
Graves, Captain John, XXXI, 22, 37
Graves, Admiral Samuel, XXIII, 184; XL, 9 ff.
Graves, Vice Admiral Samuel, XXX, 89; XXXVI, 82
Graves, Admiral Sir Thomas, R.N., VII, 101, 105
Graves at Bristol Bay, XXXIX, plate 8
Grave stones, Mahon Cemetery, Minorca, Balearic Islands, XXV, 157 ff., plates 11–14
Gray, Alan, *Sailmaking Simplified,* reviewed, I, 101
Gray, Alexander, XXVI, 15 n.
Gray, Asa, XXX, 298
Gray, G. G., XVII, 47, 50
Gray, Harrison, XL, 254
Gray, Henry, XIII, 122
Gray, Captain Henry A., VII, 119, 124, 142, 150, 151, 157, 158
Gray, Captain Horatio, XXXVII, 207
Gray, Captain Horatio N., XVII, 47, 50; XVIII, 83
Gray, Jack L., XXIV, plate XVII
Gray, James, XXVI, 105
Gray, John, XXVI, 118, 207
Gray, Captain Joseph, XXI, 92
Gray, Ralph D., *The National Waterway: A History of the Chesapeake and Delaware Canal, 1769–1985,* reviewed, L, 147
Gray, Robert, XXXIII, 161 ff.
Gray, Captain Robert, XIII, 212–213; XV, 205–212; XXV, 218; XXVI, 3; XLVII, 165; XLIX, 272 ff.
Gray, Captain Samuel, XXIII, 27
Gray, William, XXII, 267; Pictorial Supplement, XXXII, plates IX, X
Grayling, schooner *(1883),* XXX, Pictorial Supplement, plate II
Grays Harbor, wooden steamship *(1917),* XXXV, 279
Gray Steel and Blue Water Navy: The Formative Years of America's Military-Industrial Complex, 1881–1917, by Benjamin Franklin Cooling, reviewed, XLII, 67–68
Great Admiral, ship (1869), XXVIII, plate XIV
Great Age of Sail, The, Joseph Jobé, Editor, reviewed, XXVIII, 233–234
Great Alexander, sloop yacht *(1890),* XXXVI, 235
Great Britain, ship (1843), IV, 325
Great Britain, steamship, XXVII, 72; (1830), VI, 203, 211, plate 30; VII, 42, 44, 48, 50, 56, 57, 60
Great Britain, steamship (1843), XXV, 228; (1840), XX, 83, 86, 268
Great Britain, Foreign relations:
    China, XXVII, 135; XXXIV, 103; XLIX, 208; L, 178
    Confederate States of America, XIX, 51
    France, XXIII, 157
    India, XLVI, 18
    United States, XXIII, 157; XXIV, 61; XXXIX, 289; XLI, 262
Great Britain, History:
    Tudors (1485–1603), XLIV, 25
    Early Stuarts (1603–1649), XLIX, 251
    1740–1750, XXVI, 37
    Naval, XXXI, 275
    —, **18th century,** VI, 290; VII, 21
    —, **19th century,** XXVII, 135
    See also Hastings, Battle of; Historic Ships; Privateering
Great Britain. Admiralty, Impressment Protection Registers, XLVIII, 5
Great Britain. Navy, VII, 87
    Administration, XXIX, 244
    Foreign stations:
    —, **Brazils Station,** L, 26
    —, **China Station,** L, 178
    —, **North American Squadron,** XXVII, 211; XXVIII, 5, 85
    —, **Pacific Ocean,** XXXII, 233
    —, **South East Coast of America Station,** XXXVI, 125

—, **Tangier Galleys,** XXIII, 95
—, **West Indies Squadron,** XXVIII, 5, 85
—, **Yangtze River,** L, 291
Navy Board, XLVII, 5
Recruitment, XXIII, 174
Sea life, XXI, 57; XXXVIII, 92; XLV, 5
Ships, XXVI, 37; XXXIX, 235; XLVIII, 22; XLIX, 91
Training administrators, XVI, 81
Transportation, XLVII, 5

Great Britain in the Indian Ocean: A Study of Maritime Enterprise 1810–1850, by Gerald S. Graham, reviewed, XXIX, 282

Great Circle, The, journal of the Australian Association for Maritime History, XXXIX, 4

Great Coal Schooners of New England, 1870–1909, The, by W. J. Lewis Parker, reviewed, IX, 231–232

Great Eastern, British steamship *(1847),* XLVIII, 114

Great Eastern, iron steamship (1854), XXIV, plate III

Great Eastern, steamship (1859), I, 138–140; IV, 69–71, 325

Great Eastern Fisheries Co. of Rockland, XLIV, 125

"*Great Eastern* in Long Island Sound, The," by David B. Tyler, I, 138–140

"*Great Eastern* Temporary Steering Gear, The," by Stanley Cunningham, IV, 69–71

Greatest Iron Ship, SS. Great Eastern, The, by George S. Emmerson, reviewed, XLIII, 60–61

"Great Experiment: Hunter's Horizontal Wheel, The," by Clark G. Reynolds, XXIV, 5–24

"Great General and Small General," by John Lyman, XXV, 226

"Great Guns of the Navy, 1797–1843, The," by Charles R. Fisher, XXXVI, 276–295

Greathead, Henry (boatbuilder), XXXIV, 7

Great Lakes (US/Canada). *See* Shipping, Steamboats, Steam navigation, etc.

Great Lakes Car Ferries, The, by George W. Hilton, reviewed, XXIII, 70–71

Great Lakes Department of the American Bureau of Shipping, XXX, 25, 36

Great Lakes Historical Society, IV, 252; V, 171–172

Great Lakes: III, 333–334; IV, 81–82, 183–192; V, 27–42, 171–172

Great Lakes maritime exhibition, III, 354

Great Lakes Naval actions, 1813, XVII, 203–211

Great Lakes Register, XXX, 25, 36

Great Lakes schooners, IX, 229–230

Great Lakes steamships: III, 333–344; V, 27–42; XVII, 89–104; XVIII, 273–300

Great Lakes steamships (early): VI, 194–211; VII, 42–65, 298–314; VIII, 37–60, 132–149

Great Lakes Whalebacks, XXV, 168–175

Great Liverpool, steamship *(1845),* XXVI, 9

"Great *Lusitania* Whitewash, The," by Paul B. Ryan, XXXV, 36–52

Great Michael, ship, XV, 273

Great Northern, steamship, XXVII, 150, 151; *(1913),* III, 186; *(1914),* XLVII, 202

Great Northern Railway, XLVII, 193 ff.

Great Northern Steamship Co., III, 185–204; XLVII, 193 ff.; sailing poster of, XLVII, 204

"Great Northern Steamship Co.," query by W. Kaye Lamb, I, 171

Great Republic, bark *(1853),* XVII, 20; XIX, plates VI, IX, XXX

Great Republic, bark (1893), XIII, 234–235

Great Republic, bark [model] (1853), XVI, 103

Great Republic, Pacific Mail steamship *(1866),* XLVIII, 127

Great Republic, ship (1853), I, 85; II, 335–336; III, 169–170; VI, 73; XXV, 231; *(1854),* XXXV, 213

Great Republic, ship, XXVI, 163

Great Republic, steamship *(1846),* XLII, 121 ff.; XLIII, 183 ff.

Great Republic, steamship (1866), II, 8, 23–25, 34–35, plates 1, 2; X, 130, 131

Great Ships: The Battlefleet of King Charles II, by Frank Fox, reviewed, XLII, 143–144

"Great South Bay Scooters," by David B. Tyler, IV, 224–232

"Great Steamboat Monopolies, The," by David Whittet Thomson: [Part I] The Mississippi, XVI, 28–40; [Part II] The Hudson, XVI, 270–280

"Great Stone of Sardis, The," short story by Frank R. Stockton, XX, 174–176

Great Storms and Famous Shipwrecks of the New England Coast, by Edward Rowe Snow, reviewed, IV, 337–338

Great T(asmania), ship *(1846–1857),* XLII, 121 ff.

Great United States Exploring Expedition of 1838–1842, The, by William Stanton, reviewed, XXXVIII, 148

Great Western, packet ship (1851), I, 47

Great Western, sidewheeler *(1839),* XII, 149

Great Western, steamship (1837), IX, 264–265; (1838), XVIII, 282, 286–288, 290, 292, 295, 296; XX, 87, 89 n., 91, 92, 98, 99, 101, 253, 254, 265, 268; XXIV, 149–150, plate II; XXV, 228; *(1839),* XLIX, 104; *(1840),* XXXV, 254

Great Western (II), steamship (1872), XI, 253 ff.; XII, 310

Great Western Steamship Co. (1871), XI, 261–271

Great Western Steam Ship Co., XXXVIII, 185

Great White Fleet, The, by John H. Melville, reviewed, XLII, 149–150

Great White Fleet: Its Voyage Around the World, 1907–1909, The, by Robert A. Hart, reviewed, XXVI, 145–146

Grecian, H.M.S. *(1854),* XXX, 159

"Greek and Roman Shipbuilding: New Findings," by Lionel Casson, XLV, 10–19

Greek Oared Ships 900–322 B. C., by J. S. Morrison and R. T. Williams, reviewed, XXIX, 72–73

Greek Trireme of the 5th Century B.C.: Discussion of a Projected Reconstruction, The, John Coates and Sean McGrail, editors, reviewed, XLVI, 121
Greely, General Adolphus W., XXXVI, 108 ff.; XXXVIII, 45 ff.; XXXIX, 11
Green, Albert Gallatin, V, 111
Green, Captain Alfred J., *Jottings from a Cruise,* reviewed, V, 249–250
Green, Charles, XXVII, 237
Green, Ezra, XII, 282–287
Green, Captain Henry, XXV, 104–105
Green, Captain Henry J., XVII, 53; XVIII, 83
Green, Jacob, XXVIII, 135
Green, Captain John, X, 83–107, 220–229, 288–297; XIV, 298–299; XV, 211; XXXI, 39; XLVI, 8 ff.; XLVII, 31
Green, Captain Lewis, XXI, 92
Green, Captain Michael, XLIV, 118 ff.
Green, Thomas W., "The South's Scottish Sea Monster," XXIX, 5–29, 10 n.
Green, Captain W. R., XXI, 92
Greenall, Captain Thomas, XLII, 50
Green and Wigrams, XXX, 49
Green Bird, sloop *(1862),* XII, 55
Green Book, XXX, 10, 11, 12
Greene, Dana, XXXIII, 274
Greene, Daniel, XXXV, 83
Greene, Brigadier General Francis, XXXV, 183; XLI, 97
Greene, Governor, XXXI, 250
Greene, Griffin, L, 201 ff.; lithograph of, L, 202; photo of model steamboat machinery, L, 207
Greene, General Nathanael, XXXIX, 171
Greene, Richard "Toby," XXXIV, 247
Greene, S. Dana, XXXIX, 120
"'Green Flash,'" query by Alexander Crosby Brown, II, 339; answered by Gladys M. Wrigley, III, 86–87
Greenhill, Basil, mentioned, XXXVIII, 231; editorial mention, XLIII, 83; *Archaeology of the Boat: A New Introductory Study,* reviewed, XXXVIII, 144; *James Cook: The Opening of the Pacific,* reviewed, XXXI, 73–74; XXXII, 229; *Schooners,* reviewed, XL, 232
Greenhill, Basil, and Ann Giffard, document by, XXIX, 62–63; *Westcountrymen in Prince Edward's Isle,* reviewed, XXVIII, 232–233; "The Schooner *Peggy:* An Eighteenth-Century Survival," XXIX, 54–61
Greenhill, Basil and John Hackman, *The Grain Races: the Baltic Background,* reviewed, XLVIII, 62
"Greening of A. Crabtree: The Downeast Adventures of a Revolutionary Privateersman, The," by John D. Faibisy, XLII, 5–24
Greenland, Discovery and Exploration, XXXVIII, 41. See also Canada
"Greenland Whale Fishery," XXII, plates IV, XXXI
"Greenland Whaling," XXII, plates XXIX, XXX
Greenlaw, Captain Elmer, XIX, 120–122
Greenleaf, Jonathan, VIII, 13, 17, 20, 22, 23

Greenleaf, Reverend Jonathan, XXXIX, 47
Greenman, Geo. (shipbuilder, of Mystic, CT), XXV, 102
Greenman, George, XII, 288, 289
Greenock, N. C., XVII, 126
Greenock, Scotland, ca. 1812, XXIX, 48, plate IV; View of, 1836, XXIX, Pictorial Supplement, Part IV, plate XXVIII
Greenock Foundry Co., XXVI, 207
Greenough, Horatio, XXV, 59
Greenough, Captain John, XXI, 92
Greenough, Thomas, XXI, 109; XLVI, 258
Greenough, Walter, XXX, 62–67
Greenport, steamship (1866), XIV, 192 n.
Green's Directory, XXX, 31
Greenwich, H.M.S. XXVI, 54
Greenwich Hospital Tax, XXXI, 192 ff.
Greenwood, steamship (1887), XXIV, 54
Greenwood, Gordon, V, 90; *Early American-Australian Relations,* reviewed, V, 329
Greenwood, John, III, 356
Greer, U.S.S. *(1941),* XLV, 53
Gregory, Captain E., XXI, 262
Gregory, Commodore Francis H., XXI, 33–35
Gregory, Rear Admiral Francis H., XLVIII, 124
Gregory, George F. (artist), XLVII, 130
Gregory, Hugh McCullouch, XXXI, 83
Gregory, Midshipman James, XXI, 265
Gregory, Captain Josiah D. B., XXI, 92
Gregory, Samuel B., L, 90 ff.
Greland, John H., III, 79–85
Grennell, Thomas, XXXVIII, 22
Grenville, George, XXVII, 212–214
Grenville, Lord, XXVI, 253
Gresham, Walter Q., XLI, 248
Gresham, Walter Q., Secretary of State, XXXIV, 212
Greta, Russian brig *(1855),* XXXI, 273
Greta, ship *(1913),* II, 334
Grete, tug *(1866),* XLIII, 299
Gretton, Royal Navy Commander Peter, L, 219 ff.
Grew, Henry Sturgis, XXXIV, 50
Grey, Major General Charles, VII, 96, 104–106
Grey, Sir Edward, XXIX, 130; XXXIV, 156 ff.
Grey, G. Griswold, XVI, 163
Grey, Sir George, XXXII, 245
Grey Eagle, schooner (1851), XXIV, 45, 59
Grey Eagle, ship *(1848),* XVI, 238
Grey Feather, ship (1850), XXVIII, 121, 122; (1851), XV, 178
Greyhound (32), British frigate *(1778),* VII, 207; *(1798),* XXXIX, 32; XLV, 96
Greyhound, British ship (1606), XLVII, 777
Greyhound, C.S.S. *(1864),* XXIII, 225
Greyhound, H.M.S. *(1676),* XXV, 279; *(1728),* XXI, 260, 261, 263
Greyhound, schooner, XXII, 96
Greyhound, snow (1745), I, 297
Greyhound, steamship *(1864),* VIII, 234

Greyhound, U.S. gunboat *(1782)*, XXXIX, 217
Greyhounds of the Sea, by Carl C. Cutler, reviewed, XXII, 73–74
Grey Jacket, steamship, XXI, 97; *(1863)*, XII, 157
Gribble, Captain Joseph G., XXVI, 25, 203
Grice, Francis, XXIV, 11; XXXVI, 177
Gridley, destroyer *(1919)*, XLVII, 254
Griffin, bark *(1861)*, XV, 114, 123
Griffin, Great Lakes boat (1679), XXV, 168
Griffin, steamship (1866), VII, 126, 128–130, 132, 133, 136, 141, 231
Griffin, Captain S. P., XX, 106
Griffin, Eldon, I, 177; query by, VIII, 154; review by, I, 319–320; "The *Antelope* located," I, 166–167
Griffin, William B., XL, 43
Griffith, Captain, XL, 20 ff.
Griffith, Percy, XXXVII, 15
Griffith, W., XXXVI, 67
Griffith & Co., D., VII, 42
Griffiths, Endymion, XIII, 17
Griffiths, John W., VII, 181, 315; VIII, 247–251; XXVII, 11, 13, 15
Griffiths, John Willis, shipbuilder, letter from Donald McKay, I, 85
Griggs, Alexander P., I, 116
Grimes, Senator, XXX, 146
Grimwood, V. R., *American Ship Models and How To Build Them*, reviewed, III, 357–358
Grinnell, Henry, XX, 104–111; XXV, 69
Grinnell, Joseph, XXXIX, 83
Grinnell Arctic Expedition, XX, 104–111
Grissom, Captain Rob. S., XXI, 105
Grissom, Captain Thomas, XXI, 105
Grissom, Captain W. J., XXI, 105
Griswold, G., XVII, 47
Griswold, J. N. A., XVI, 173
Griswold, N. L. and G., VII, 5, 8
Griswold, Captain William, XXXIX, 194
Grob, T. (artist), Pictorial Supplement, XXXI, plate XXII
Groener, Miss Erna, XXXVI, 16
"Grog in the U.S. Navy," by Captain Edgar K. Thompson, U.S.N. (ret.), XXV, 141–143
Grolier Club, New York, exhibition of Naval prints, III, 3, 5–10
Grönwall, Adolf, XXVII, 47 n.
Gropallo, Tomaso, *Ultima Vela – The Last Sail*, reviewed, XXX, 219–220
Gros, Baron, XXXIV, 107 ff.
Grosser Kurfurst, steamship (1899), IX, 221
Grosvenor, Melville Bell, Editor-in-Chief, and James M. Darley, Chief Cartgrapher, *National Geographic Atlas of the World*, reviewed, XXIII, 288
Groton, grain elevator *(1883)*, XXXVIII, 141
"Grounding in the Bahamas in 1851, A," by Frank B. Evans, III, XLIX, 123–125
Grouse, U.S. Minesweeper (1943), XXV, 233

Grove, Eric J., *Vanguard to Trident: British Naval Policy Since World War Two*, reviewed, XLIX, 133
Grover, David H., "The *Panay* revisited: A Maritime Perspective, L, 260–269
Groves, Donald G., and Lee M. Hunt, *The Ocean World Encyclopedia*, reviewed, XL, 146
Groves, Freeborn, XXX, 96 n.
Growler, schooner *(1813)*, XLIV, 172
Growth of the Seaport Cities, 1790–1825, The, David T. Gilchrist, Editor, reviewed, XXVIII, 149–150
Grubb, W. J., comment by, VII, 78
Gruz, steamship (1892), XXIV, plate 16
Gt. Britain. See Great Britain
Guadalcanal, escort carrier *(1944)*, XXXVIII, 272
Guadaloupe, Mexican warship *(1843)*, XXI, 222 ff.
Guadaloupienne, French ship *(1800)*, XXXI, 175
Guadalupe, Mexican steam frigate *(1845)*, XXX, 47 ff.
Guadalupe, ship *(1757)*, XXIII, 280, 281
Guadeloupe, steamship (ex-*Tampico*, ex-*Imperador*) *(1870)*, XXVI, 194
"Guadeloupe, The Insular Campaign of 1759," by Marshall Smelser, VII, 21–34, plate 3
Guam, History, 20th century, XXIV, 272. See also Pacific, Islands of the
Guam, Ladrone Islands, Western Pacific, XXV, 184, plate 17
"Guano," query by G. Evelyn Hutchinson, VI, 233
Guano Act, XXVI, 172, 175
Guano trade, XXIV, 25
Guano trade, I, 108–110; VIII, 179; IX, 63
Guarland, H.M.S. *(1677)*, XXV, 279
Guatamozin (1801), XXIII, 217
Guatemala, steamship *(1864)*, XXXII, 198, 202; *(1872)*, X, 132, 134
Guayas, Ecuadorian war steamship *(1840)*, XXXV, 264
Gubbins, Thomas, VIII, 303–304
Gudin, Théodore, XLVI, 255
Guedes, Max Justo, editor, *Historical Naval Brasileira*, reviewed, XLIV, 276–277
Guernsey, H.M.S. *(1740)*, XXVI, 38
Guerra, Francisco Argilagos, XXXVI, 13
Guerre, French ship *(1801)*, XXXI, 175
Guerriere, H.M.S., XXVI, plate 19; XXVII, 29; *(1812)*, VII, 167; XXII, 156; XXV, 33; XLVI, 162; XLVII, 15 ff. Pictorial Supplement, XXXII, plates XXI-XXIV
Guerriere, U.S. frigate (1814), VII, 316; XXIII, 58; *(1815)*, XL, 39 ff.
Guerriere, U.S. razee *(1818)*, X, 41
Guerriere, warship *(1814)*, XLII, 112, 284; XLIII, 264; XLIV, 171; XLV, 175
Guerrière, British warship *(1830)*, XXXVIII, 114
Guest, Lieutenant John, XXX, 159, 162 n.
Guia de Orinoco, schooner *(1846)*, XXX, 261
Guide, schooner, XXI, 96, 101; *(1861)*, VIII, 217, 225
Guideboat, Adirondack, XXVI, plate 4
Guide to Key West, A, by Writers' Program Work Projects Administration, reviewed, I, 403–404

Guide to Naval Strategy, A, by Bernard Brodie, reviewed, V, 93
Guide to the Material in The National Archives, reviewed, I, 98–99
Guide to the Soviet Navy, by Norman Polmar, reviewed, XLIV, 133
Guiding Star, steamship *(1866),* IV, 146 ff., 152 ff.
Guillen, Capitan Julio F., XV, 57, 58
Guillou, Surgeon Charles, XLIX, 154
Guilmartin, John, XLVI, 84 ff.
Guion Line, I, 80
Guion Steamship Co., ship of, Pictorial Supplement, XXXIV, plate XVII
Guitar, woodboat *(1853),* XVII, 12
Guittar, Louis, XXX, 133, 134
Gulflight, American ship *(1915),* XLV, 201
Gulf Oil Co., XXIV, 34
Gulf Ranger, schooner, XXI, 101. *(1861),* XI, 283
Gulf Refining Co., Inc., XXXVIII, 181 ff.
Gulf Stream, dragger *(1961),* XLI, 50
Gulf Stream, I, 149.
Gull, sloop *(1861),* XI, 283
Gulnare, yacht *(1877),* XIII, 274
Gulnare, yawl, XXII, 185
Gummersell, C. G., XI, 4
"Gunboat Diplomacy: Operations of the North American and West Indies Squadron 1875–1915," by Colonel Roger Willock, USMCR; [Part I] XXVIII, 5–30; [Part II] XXVIII, 85–112
Gunboat Frontier: British Maritime Authority and the Northwest Coast Indians, 1846–1890, by Barry Gough, XLIV, 207
Gunboat No. 1, U.S.S. *(1803),* XXI, 134
Gunboat No. 2, U.S.S. *(1803),* XXI, 134
Gunboat No. 3, U.S.S. *(1803),* XXI, 131, 134 ff.
Gunboat No. 4, U.S.S. *(1803),* XXI, 134
Gunboat No. 5, U.S.S. *(1803),* XXI, 134
Gunboat No. 6, U.S.S. *(1803),* XXI, 134
Gunboats, XLII, 101; XLIII, 135, 245
"Gunboats and Diplomats," by Dwight R. Messimer, XL, 85–99
"Gunboats Down the Mississippi," by John D. Milligan, reviewed, XXVI, 224
"Gun Carriages," query by Horatio C. Flagg, VII, 77–78; answers by M. V. Brewington and Frank A. Taylor, VII, 171; by the Editors, VII, 319–321
Gundalow (boat), II, 127, 209; X, 249
"Gundalow *Fanny M.,* The," by D. Foster Taylor, II, 209–222
"Gundalow of Captain Edward H. Adams, now under construction," II, plates 29, 31, 32
Gundalows: of Merrimac River, X, 249–263, plates 25–26; of Piscataqua River, I, 68; II, 127–139, 209–222
"Gun Drill in the Sailing Navy, 1797 to 1840," by Charles R. Fisher, XLI, 85–92
Gunnery. *See* Naval gunnery

"Gunnery Practice, 1807," by M. V. Brewington, IV, 324
Gunnison, Nathaniel, XIX, 58–61
Gunpowder, attempted capture at Nassau, XXV, 194 ff.
Gun Rock, schooner (1855), XXIV, 45, 59
Guns. *See* Naval gunnery; Naval ordnance
Guns, naval, XXXVI, 276–295
Guns, Sails and Empires: Technological Innovation and the Early Phases of European Expansion 1400–1700, by Carlo M. Cipolla, reviewed, XXVI, 225
"Gun Salute with Echoes," document contributed by Captain Edgar K. Thompson, U.S.N. (ret.), XXII, 105
"Gun Shot," query by Eugene S. Ferguson, VII, 322
Guptill, Captain Robert, X, 218
Gurkha, motorboat (1915), XXIX, 74
Gurney, Francis, XXXII, 249; XXXVI, 56
Gustaf III, ship (1779), VI, 166
Guthenburg, ship (1854), V, 154, 242
Guthorn, Peter J., "Captain Paul Pinkham, Nantucket Hydrographer," XLIII, 51–55; *The Sea Bright Skiff and Other New Jersey Shore Boats,* reviewed, XXXIV, 147–148
Guthrie, Captain Archibald, XXI, 105
Guttridge, Leonard F., *The Commodores,* reviewed, XXX, 73; *Icebound: The Jeannette Expedition's Quest for the North Pole,* reviewed, XLIX, 305
Gutzlaff, Karl Friedrich, Prussian missionary, XLVIII, 278 ff.
Guy, Francis, II, 339
Guy C. Goss, bark (1879), II, 65–70, plates 13–16; II, 336
Guy C. Goss, ship, XXXIX, plate 5
Guyon, François, XXXV, 155
Guzza, motorboat (1924), IX, 24
Gwendolyn, sloop yacht (1904), XXXVI, 241, 242, 244–246
Gwendolyn II, yacht (1909), XXXVI, 245–246, 248
Gwenol, yacht (1904), XXXVI, 241
Gwers Shoal light-vessel (1788), IV, 265–266, plate 46
Gwinn, Captain Thomas, XXIII, 38
Gyfford, William, XIII, 19
Gypsey, schooner *(1861),* XI, 283; XII, 55, 157
Gypsey, whaler *(1865),* XXVII, 275
Gypsum, schooner (1846), XXIV, 44, 59
Gywn, Julian, "Shipbuilding for the Royal Navy in Colonial New England, XLVIII, 22–30.

H. and J. Nield, schooner *(1861),* VIII, 217
H. B. Hussey, hermaphrodite brig (1833), XXVIII, plate XXIII
H. B. Mildmay, ship (1856), III, 65
H. Baker (1862), XII, 55

H. Blackman, schooner *(1861),* XI, 283
H. C. Hansen, auxiliary schooner (1917), V, 140
H. C. Higginson, ship *(1888),* XXXVII, 85, wreck of, plate 2, 92–93
H. C. Sinclair, steamship *(1947),* VIII, 130
H. E. Boucher Manufacturing Co., XLII, 131
H. E. Spearing, barkentine *(1861),* XI, 283
H. E. Vincent, schooner *(1861),* VIII, 218, 225, 230
H. F. Alexander, ship (ex-*Great Northern,* ex-*Columbia*) XXVII, 150, 151; *(1922),* XLVII, 203
H. F. Dimock, steamship *(1884),* Pictorial Supplement, XXXIV, plate XIX
H. F. Morse, tug *(1889),* XXXVII, 89
H. F. Willing, schooner, XXI, 92; *(1861),* XV, 123
H. Hackfeld, ship (1865), IX, 298
H. J. Baker & Bros., XXIV, 32
H. K. Drake and Co., XXXIV, 47; XLIII, 207
H. K. Hall, schooner (1902), V, 137
H. L. Cook, steamship *(1847),* XLVII, 34
H. L. Hunley, Confederate submarine *(1864),* XLVII, 31; XLIX, 121
H. L. Richardson, ship (1865), IV, 244; V, 327
H. L. Tibbals, yacht *(1876),* XXXVI, 233
H. Louis Orcutt (1856), XLIV, 89
H. M. Hayes, ship *(1858),* XXXI, 191
"H.M.S. *Cormorant*: First Steam Warship in the North Pacific," by John Haskell Kemble, IX, 63–65, plate 5
H.M.S. Victory—*Building, Restoration & Repair,* by Arthur Bugler, O.B.E., reviewed, XXVII, 287–289
"H.M. Storeship *Porpoise,* 1780–83." by David Syrett, XLIX, 91–95
H. M. Williams, tug (1964), XXXVIII, 140
H. McGuin, bark *(1863),* XII, 157
H. P. Blaisdell, schooner *(1875),* XV, 226
H. P. Cushing, brig *(1855),* XXIV, 140
H. P. Etheridge, Inc., XXII, 167
H. P. Russell, schooner *(1861),* VIII, 218
H. P. Stoney, schooner, XXI, 87; *(1861),* VIII, 218; XI, 284
H. R. Mallory, American ship *(1943),* XLIV, 54 ff.
H. V. Baxter, ship (1860), II, 333
H. V. Moses, ship *(1861),* XI, 284
H. W. Brown, barkentine (1919), IV, 60, 68
Haag, Alfred H., XLI, 117
Haaheo o Hawaii. See *Cleopatra's Barge.*
Haardraada, steam whaler *(1898),* XLIV, 21 ff.
Haayen, Aelbert, L, 284
Habana, steamship *(1861),* XV, 288
Habanero, steamship *(1863),* XII, 157
Habanero, steamship, XXI, 100
Habenicht, Captain A., XXI, 92
Habenicht, Captain George F., XXI, 93
Habersham, John, XXXVI, 56
Habersham, Joseph, XXII, 55–64
Habert, Jacques, and Michel Mollat, Du Jourdin, *Giovanni et Girolamo Verrazano, navigateurs de François I*ᵉʳ, reviewed, XLIV, 281

Hackburn, schooner *(1861),* XV, 114, 123
Hacker, Captain Hoysted, XXXVI, 56
Hacker, Lieutenant Hoysteed, Continental Navy, XXV, 193, 198
Hackert, Jacob P., XXI, 143–144
Hackett, James, VIII, 13, 18
Hackett, William, VIII, 18, 19
Hackman, John and Basil Greenhill, *The Grain Races: the Baltic Background,* reviewed, XLVIII, 62
Hadassah, schooner *(1837),* XLIII, 54
Haddock, Sir Richard, XIII, 6 ff.
Haddon, A. C., XIII, 85 ff.
Haddon, Captain Richard, XXIII, 277 ff.
Hadley, John, XXXV, 114
Hadley Clark, ship *(1850),* XLV, 124
Hadley Quadrant (made by John Dupee), Pictorial Supplement, XXXV, plate IV
Hadley Quadrant (made by Thomas Ripley), Pictorial Supplement, XXXV, plate V
Hadley Quadrants: English (made by Spencer, Browning & Rust), Pictorial Supplement, XXXV, plate VI; French, Pictorial Supplement, XXXV, plate V
Hadlock, Wendell S., and Ernest S. Dodge, "A Canoe from the Penobscot River," VIII, 289–300
Haean, steamship *(1873),* XVI, 262; XVII, 39
Haesan, steamship *(1862),* XVI, 247; XVII, 39
Haeshin, steamship (1871), XVI, 261; XVII, 39
Haeting, steamship *(1873),* XVI, 262; XVII, 39
Hagan, Professor Kenneth J., editorial comment, XXXIX, 157
Hagan & Thurlow Shipyard, XXVII, plate XXVI
Hagar, John, XXXIII, 30
Hagarstown, ship (1874), II, 245
Hagerty, Reginald A., note by, XXVII, 279–280
Haggar, William G., XXI, 109
Hagger, William Guyse, XLVI, 258
Hague, Robert L., XLVII, 46
Hague, Robert Lyons, I, 314; II, 93
Hague Convention of 1907, XXXII, 106
Hah-Hah, yacht *(1898),* XI, 91
Hahn, Captain Edward E., XLV, 82
Hahn, Harold M., *Ships of the American Revolution,* reviewed, L, 229
Hahn, Captain Martin, XXI, 93
Haiching (ex-*Pootung*), gunboat *(1863),* XLIII, 99; *(1866),* XXXIV, 52
Haida, U.S. Coast Guard cutter (1921), XXXVII, 95 ff.; *(1928),* XVIII, 220
"*Haida's* Arctic Cruise," by Robert Erwin Johnson, XXXVII, 95–110
Haider, ship *(1860),* XXVII, 235
Hail Colombia! by Dana Story, reviewed, XXXI, 75–76
Haines, Charles, "Ship Preservation in the Old Navy," XLII, 276–294
"Hairy Ape Reconsidered: The American Merchant Seaman and the Transition from Sail to Steam in the

late Nineteenth Century, The," by Kenneth John Blume, XLIV, 33–47
"Haitian Harlequinade," by Captain Edgar K. Thompson, U.S.N. (ret.), XXVIII, 112
Hakluyt, Richard, VII, 83–85; XL, 280; L, 9; *The Principall Navigations, Voiages and Discoveries of the English Nation,* reviewed, XXVI, 73–74
Hakluyt Handbook, The, edited by D. B. Quinn, reviewed, XXXIX, 303
Hakluyt Society, XVI, 281
Hakluyt Society, London, VI, 308–309; VII, 81–86; XXV, 297
"Hakluyt Society," editorial from *The Times Literary Supplement,* VII, 83–85
Hakodadi Maru, steamship *(1865),* XVI, 246
Hakuno Maru, steamship (ex-*Contest*) *(1859),* XLIX, 26
Halbig, Captain F., XXI, 93
Halcyon, auxiliary yawl (1904), XXX, plate XX
Halcyon, brig *(1831),* XXXVIII, 267
Halcyon, schooner (1888), XXVI, plate II
Halcyon, ship (1793), X, 53; *(1794),* V, 89; *(1795),* XVIII, 106, 130
Haldane, Viscount, XXVIII, 100, 104
Haldane-Robertson, Langton, II, 252; "Some Philadelphia Ships Condemned at Jamaica during the Revolution," II, 203–208
Hale, E. J., XVI, 171, 248
Hale, Elwyn C., XXII, 171
Hale, Eugene, XXII, 187 ff.
Hale, Senator Eugene, XXIX, 30 ff.
Hale, George, XL, 44
Hale, George W., XVII, 119, 120
Hale, Horatio, XXX, 298
Hale, John P., XXX, 143, 144; XXXVI, 177
Hale, Richard W., I, 177; "Three Watercolors by Cornè," I, 163–164; query by, I, 171
Hale, Captain W. M., XXI, 93
Halewood, ship, XXXVI, 3
Haley, Nelson C., journal of, XXV, 104
Haley, Nelson Cole, *Whale Hunt,* reviewed, IX, 77
"Half Model of *America*," by Sydney A. Vincent, XII, 239–240
Halfmoon, ship *(1681),* XXIII, 112
Half Moon II, ship [replica] (1909), photo of, XIV, 111
Halifax, barge *(1829),* V, 301
Halifax, ship *(1756),* XLIX, 266 ff.
Halifax, steamship *(1872),* XXXVII, 237
Halifax Packet, brig *(1814),* I, 122
Hall, Arthur Cleveland, XXXIII, 135
Hall, C., VII, 66
Hall, Captain Christopher, XXII, 236, 244
Hall, Elton W., XXXIV, 219 n.; review by, XLV, 138; "Sailcloth For American Vessels," XXXI, 130–142; *Sperm Whaling from New Bedford: Clifford W. Ashley's Photographs of the Bark* Sunbeam *in 1904,* reviewed, XLIII, 56–58, 147–148
Hall, Gordon, XLVIII, 273

Hall, Henry, IV, 49–51; XV, 138; XLII, 135; XXIII, 12; XXV, 82 n.; query concerning, I, 90; answers by Harry W. Baehr, Jr., Vergil D. Reed, W. J. Lewis Parker and Richard S. Wormser, I, 173–174; notes on the Buckeye *Raven,* IV, 248; on Dickie Brothers of San Francisco, II, 74–76; on Hall Brothers Shipyard, V, 85–87; on Potomac long-boat, I, 159–163; on San Francisco lateen-rigged fishing boats, I, 306–308; on San Francisco Bay scow schooner, I, 87–88; on Virginia canoes, IV, 76; on Virginia canoes and bugeyes, III, 176
Hall, James Norman and Charles Nordhoff, *Botany Bay,* reviewed, II, 354
Hall, John, XXI, 115, 116, 119, 120
Hall, Captain John, XXXIV, 256
Hall, Captain Lott, XXXI, 28
Hall, Michael G., review by, XLVIII, 64
Hall, Phyllis, XXXVI, 11
Hall, Phyllis A., "The *Appam* and American Neutrality," XLVIII, 50–58; "Sinking of *William P. Frey,*" XLV, 199–203
Hall, S. Lyle, XXXII, 210 n.; XXXIII, 19
Hall, Samuel, XXII, 8
Hall, Captain Thomas Franklin, XXII, 236, 239, 240, 242, 243, 246, 247
"Hall Brothers' Shipyard in 1881," document contributed by John Lyman, V, 85–87
Halldin, Engineer Captain Gustaf, "Fredrik Henrik af Chapman," VI, 163–178, plates 21–28
Halleck, Fitz-Greene, VI, 6 ff., 84–85; VII, 181–182
Halleck, General Henry W., XXXI, 69
Hallet, Captain Augustus, XXV, 112, 114
Hallett, Abner, Davis and Elijah (shipbuilders), XXIV, 39, 43, 57–59
Hallett, Captain E. T. (shipbuilder), XXIV, 39
Hallett, Captain H. A., XVIII, 83
Halley, Edmond, VII, 269, 273–276; XXX, 205; XXXV, 114; XXXVIII, 42; L, 288
Hallie Jackson, brig, XXI, 88; *(1861),* XV, 123
Hallie Jackson, schooner *(1869),* XXXVIII, 83
Hallock, Captain William, Continental Navy, XXV, 193
Hallowell, Benjamin, XXV, 91
Hallowell, Benjamin, Sr., XL, 267
Hallowell, Briggs, XL, 277
Hallowell, Robert (Boston Tax Collector), XXXI, 201
Halsey, Helen, ed., *Incident on the bark* Columbia, *being Letters Received & sent by Captain McCorkle and the Crew of his Whaler, 1860–1862,* reviewed, I, 406–407
Halsey, James, XXI, 108; XLVI, 258
Halsey, James (instrument maker), Pictorial Supplement, XXXV, plate III
Halsey, John, XXXI, 87
Halsey, Joseph, XLVI, 258
Halsey, Thomas, XLVII, 164
Halsey, Thomas Lloyd, XL, 196
Halvorson, Captain C. A., IV, 201
Ham, James, Jr., XLVI, 258

Ham, Thomas, XII, 223
Hamar, Captain Joseph, XXVI, 44
Hamblin, William, "The Fatamid Navy During the Early Crusades: 1099–1124," XLVI, 77–83
Hamburg-America Co., XXXIII, 187
Hamburg American Line, XXIX, 233
Hamburgs Segelschiffe, by Jürgen Meyer, reviewed, XXXII, 288
Hamer, Philip M., I, 177; "Publication of Ship Registers and Enrollments," I, 165–166
Hamer, Dr. Philip M., VII, 67
Hamilton, brig (1830), Pictorial Supplement, XXXVIII, plate VII
Hamilton, ship *(1709),* XX, 11; *(1809),* XII, 105; *(1811),* V, 161
Hamilton, ship (1871), IV, 241; V, 327
Hamilton, steamship (1834), VII, 55; (1835), VII, 57
Hamilton, Alexander, XXII, 123; XXVI, 238, 245; XXVIII, 33; XXX, 119; XXXIII, 16; XXXVI, 55 ff.; XXXIX, 26 ff.
Hamilton, Georgia W., *Silent Pilots: Figureheads in Mystic Seaport Museum,* reviewed, XLV, 211
Hamilton, Harry D., answered query, VI, 232; query by, VII, 77
Hamilton, Jere, XXIV, 59
Hamilton, John, VII, 48, 56; XVIII, 284; XX, 83
Hamilton, Jonathan, XXXVI, 21
Hamilton, Mrs. Mary, XXXVI, 21
Hamilton, Paul, Secretary of the Navy, XLVII, 14
Hamilton, R. M., Consul, XLVI, 232
Hamilton, Robert, VII, 48
Hamilton, Dr. Thomas, XLIII, 14
Hamilton, William, XXIX, 277
Hamilton Gray, bark *(1861),* VIII, 217
Hamlet [model], XXXVII, 172
Hamlin, Cyrus, XXIX, 4
Hammer, Captain William C., XXI, 93
Hammers on Stone: A History of Cape Ann Granite, by Barbara H. Erkkila, reviewed, XLII, 221
Hammett, Captain H. W., XX, 238
Hammida, Admiral Rais, XL, 39 ff.
Hammitt, John K., XXX, 267
Hammond, schooner *(1861),* XV, 123
Hammond, Ebenezar, XX, 45
Hammond, George, British Minister, XXII, 84, 88
Hammond, John, XXXV, 297
Hammond, Pollipus, XXXV, 294
Hammond, William, XXXVI, 233 n.
Hamon, Thomas, XXXVII, 15
Hamond, Captain Andrew, XL, 10 ff.
Hampden, bark (1868), XII, plate 30
Hampden, brig *(1776),* XLVIII, 158
Hampden, ship *(1778),* VII, 201–212
Hampden, ship *(1778),* XLIII, 27
Hampden, sloop *(1779),* XXXVII, 293, 301
Hampden, John, Editor, *Francis Drake, Privateer,* reviewed, XXXIV, 284

Hampshire, ship *(1916),* L, 129
Hampton, galley (1709), XX, 11
Hampton, schooner, XXI, 92; *(1861),* XV, 114
Hampton, U.S.S. *(1777),* XIV, 52, 53
Hampton boat, III, 141
Hampton boat, I, 66–67, 173, 311–312; III, 141–147; VII, 3; XII, 128–130
"Hampton boat, The," by Phelps Soule, III, 141–147
"Hampton-Hamden Boat," query by Walter Muir Whitehill, I, 90; answer by Charles P. Emerson, I, 173; answers by Howard I. Chapelle, I, 311–312; II, 249–250
Hampton Roads, XXII, 253, 254, 256
Hanalei, steamship *(1903),* VIII, 192
Hanbury, Christopher, XXXVII, 20
Hancock, armed schooner *(1775),* XXVII, 222; XXX, 101 n., 107, 110–114
Hancock, brig *(1800),* XIX, 133–138
Hancock, frigate (1776), VI, 153; VIII, 11, 13, 15–17, 21–24, plates 3–4; IX, 165; *(1776),* XLII, 9 ff.; *(1777),* V, 187; XLVIII, 160; XLIX, 41 ff.; oil painting of, XLVIII, 161
Hancock, ship *(1799),* XXIII, 239
Hancock, sloop *(1780),* XXV, 109; XLI, 170; *(1862),* XXI, 103; *(1863),* XII, 157
Hancock, H., XVII, 60
Hancock, John, VIII, 11, 13, 20; XLII, 26
Hancock, Robert G., Jr., "Pestilence From the Sea and American Quarantine Policy," L, 94–106
Hancock, Thomas, XXXI, 21; XXXIII, 97 ff.; XL, 248; XLII, 25
Hancock County, steamship *(1923),* XXXII, 16
Hancock's Wharf, Boston, L, 270
Handmaid, ship *(1630),* XXIII, 63
Handy, Captain Samuel Clarke, IV, 164–165
Hanford, Frank, XXXVI, 233 n.
Hanford, William C., XXII, 286 n.
Hangchow, steamship (1863), XVI, 258; XVIII, 70
Hankow, steamship (1860), XVI, 171, 247, 253; XVIII, 70; (1861), XXXIV, 28 ff.; XLIX, 22; *(1864),* XLIII, 117 ff.
Hanley, Captain George W., XXV, 104
Hanlon, Ned, XXVII, 155
Hanna, sloop *(1717),* XXXVII, 270
Hanna, Jay S., *Marine Carving Handbook,* reviewed, XXXVIII, 148
Hanna, John G., review by, II, 181–182
Hanna, Senator Mark, XXXVII, 29
Hannah, armed schooner *(1775),* XXVII, 221–222; XXX, 86–116; (1797), III, 268
Hannah, schooner, XXII, 60 n.; XXVIII, 114; *(1760),* IX, 144; (1765), XXX, 97–116; (1771), XXX, 93–116; *(1785),* XXVIII, 31; (1797), XXX, plate 4
Hannah, ship (1823), XXV, plate 7
Hannah, sloop, XXII, 60 n.; *(1807),* XVI, 197; *(1864),* XV, 129
Hannah, transport schooner *(1775),* XXX, 115 f.

Hannah and Eliza, ship *(1805),* X, 54, 56, 57
Hannah and Elizabeth, schooner *(1776),* XX, 46; XXXIX, 198
Hannah and Molly, schooner *(1776),* XLII, 9 ff.
Hannah and Sally, ship *(1807),* X, 54
Hannah B. Boune, schooner *(1870),* XXXVIII, 83
Hannah Balch, brig (1852), XXIV, 40, 57
Hannah Balch, brigantine (1861), XV, 123; *(1868),* VIII, 218
Hannah Brewer, bark *(1855),* XLI, 295
Hannah M. Johnson, schooner *(1861),* XI, 283
Hannah Matilda, brig *(1861),* VIII, 218
Hannibal, H.M.S., XXVI, 195
Hannibal, ship *(1839),* XII, 36
Hannibal, whaler, XXV, 105
Hannibal, yacht *(1933),* XXXV, 132
Hanniel, steam yacht (1886), XXX, plate XXV
"Hannum, Caleb," query by William H. Hannum, III, 353
Hannum, Charles A., XXV, 103
Hanover, schooner *(1863),* XII, 157
Hanover, ship (1838), IV, 46–47, 50, 51, 52; XXVII, Plate III; *(1862),* XIX, 53
Hanover Sound, Nassau, Bahamas, XXV, 204–206, 212
Hanrahan, Private Dennis, U.S.M.C., VII, 111
Han River, Korea, XXV, 121
Hans, bark (1904), IV, 325–326; VI, 77; *(1927),* XVIII, 217
Hansa, steamship, XXI, 86, 98, 100, 105; *(1863),* VIII, 230, 234, 237
Hanscom, Charles R., III, 187–188
Hanscom, William (shipbuilder, of Elliot, Maine), XXV, 102
Hanseatic League, XXXVII, 157 ff.
Hansell, Victor, XXIX, 135
Hansen, Ann N., "Ships of the Puritan Migration to Massachusetts Bay," XXIII, 62–66
Hansen, Hans Jurgen, Editor, *Art and the Seafarer,* reviewed, XXIX, 68–69; *Schiffsmodelle: Die Geschichte der Shiffbaukunst im Spiegel Zeitgenossischer Modelle,* reviewed, XXXIII, 148–149
Hanson, Captain H., XXI, 93
Happy, H.M.S. *(1727),* XXI, 264 ff.
Happy Return, British ship *(1776),* XLVIII, 16
Haraden, Captain Jonathan, II, 286–287
Harbin, James W., Jr., V, 165
Harbinger, catboat *(1898),* XI, 93
Harbinger, steamship (1869), VI, 66
Harbor boat, Palermo, I, 371–373
Harbord, Major James G., XXXIV, 262
"Harbor Holiday," by Captain Edgar K. Thompson, U.S.N. (ret.), XXVIII, 223
Harbor improvements, Los Angeles, California, XXV, 262 ff.
Harbors:
   United States, XXV, 262
   —, **New Jersey,** XXXVII, 262

—, **North Carolina,** XXIX, 155
—, **Pennsylvania,** XXXII, 247
—, **South Carolina,** XLIV, 257
See also names of Rivers
Harbottle, John, XLVI, 47
Harbottle, Winshipa, XLVI, 47
Harbron, John D., *Trafalgar and the Spanish Navy,* reviewed, XLIX, 314
Harcort & Co., XLIII, 191 ff.
Hardee, Colonel William J., XL, 299
Hardenburg, Charles B., XXXIII, 57
Hardie, Captain James, XVIII, 83
Harding, Captain Henry F., VII, 66
Harding, Seth, XXXIX, 192
Harding, President Warren, XLI, 12
Harding, Senator Warren G., XXXV, 284
Hardrada, King Harald Sigurdson, XLIV, 96 ff.
Hardwicke, Lord, XXXI, 203
Hardy, Captain, XIII, 50; XXXVI, 239
Hardy, Admiral Sir Charles, R.N., VII, 99, 100; XL, 246
Hardy, Governor Sir Charles, XXII, 121, 122; XXIII, 279
Hardy, Captain F. H., VIII, 152
Hardy, Iza Duffus, quoted, VII, 156
Hardy, Captain Temple, XLV, 96
Hardy, Sir Thomas Masterman, XXIX, 189
Hare, Charles Willing, XLVIII, 247 ff.
Hargis, James (lighthouse keeper), XXXII, 252
Hariot, Thomas, XVII, 32; XXI, 107
Harkaway, schooner *(1862),* VIII, 225
Harker, Captain James B., XXI, 93
Harkness, Captain James, XXI, 93
Harlan, George H., *San Francisco Bay Ferryboats,* reviewed, XXVII, 289
Harlan and Hollingsworth, XXXII, 166
Harlan and Hollingsworth Co. (ship and engine builders), II, 225 ff.; XXII, 44
Harland, John and Mark Myers, *Seamanship in the Age of Sail,* reviewed, XLVIII, 187
Harland, Vice-Admiral Sir Robert, R.N., VII, 95
Harlequin, schooner *(1777),* XLII, 12 ff.
Harlequin, ship *(1756),* XLVIII, 38
Harlow, Captain Edward F., IV, 318–323
Harlow, Frederick Pease, VI, 92, 155, 307; VIII, 79–80; answered query, VI, 153–154; "Chanteying Aboard American Ships," VIII, 81–89; *Chanteying Aboard American Ships,* reviewed, XXII, 149–150; "'Twas the Night Before Christmas (An Old Tar's Dream)," VI, 275–276; "While I'm at the Wheel," VI, 108–111
Harlquin, schooner (1761), XXI, 8
Harmala, merchant ship *(1943),* XLIV, 54 ff.
Harman, F. Ward, *Ship Models Illustrated,* reviewed, III, 274
Harman, H. W., XXII, 44
Harman, Captain William, VII, 25
Harmless, British ship *(1776),* XLVIII, 18
Harmon, Captain Joseph, XVIII, 83

Harmon, Judd Scott, "Marriage of Convenience: The United States Navy in Africa, 1820–1843," XXXII, 264–276
Harmonia, ship (1875), III, 72
Harmonie, bark (1846), V, 149, 241
Harmonie, ship *(1837)*, XLI, 288
Harmony, brig *(1812)*, XXI, 18
Harmony, schooner *(1782)*, XI, 240 ff.; *(1861)*, VIII, 218
Harmony, ship *(1796)*, I, 393
Harnish, Seymour, XIII, 126 ff.
Harold G. Foss (ex-*T. N. Barnsdall*), schooner, XXIV, 25, plate 4
Harold Haarfager, bark (1850), V, 151
Haroldine, schooner (1884), XXIII, plate IX
Harp, H.M. frigate *(1674)*, XXV, 279
Harper, J. Russell, "St. Martin's Men Build a Ship," XXI, 279–291
Harper, Lawrence A., *The English Navigation Laws: A Seventeenth-Century Experiment in Social Engineering*, reviewed, I, 93
Harper, Robert Goodloe, XXXVI, 65, 66
Harper, General Robert Goodloe, XXXV, 83
Harpley, sailing vessel *(1854)*, XXII, 27
Harpoon, cutter (1891), XXX, plate XVIII
"Harpoon Smith, The," XXII, plate XIX
"Harpswell, The Dead Ship of," poem by John Greenleaf Whittier, VI, 233 ff.
Harpy, H.M.S. *(1845)*, XXXVI, 138–140
Harpy, privateer schooner *(1814)*, I, 116–122
Harrat, Charles (rigger), III, 280
Harriet, brig *(1851)*, XXVII, 61–65, plate 4
Harriet, schooner *(1807)*, X, 146; *(1828)*, XL, 42
Harriet and Sarah, schooner *(1862)*, VIII, 225
Harriet & Jessie, ship (1832), IV, 73
Harriet Lane, Confederate cutter *(1863)*, XLVIII, 92
Harriet Lane, steamship, XXI, 87
Harriet Lane, U.S. revenue cutter *(1857)*, XXXVI, 174 ff.; XXXVII, 279; XXXIX, 36
Harriet Lane, U.S.S. *(1861)*, XI, 271 ff.; XII, 230; XXVII, 242
Harriet Lowndes, schooner, XXI, 90; *(1861)*, VIII, 218, 225
Harriet Neal, schooner (1848), XXIV, 59
Harriet P. Ryan, schooner *(1861)*, VIII, 218
Harriet Pinckney, blockade runner *(1862)*, XXIV, plate 24
Harriet Ryan, schooner, XXI, 98
Harriett, bark *(1863)*, V, 154
Harriman, Averell, American Ambassador, XLI, 269; XLIII, 35 ff.
Harriman, Mrs. J. Borden, XXXII, 111
Harrington (1807), XXIII, 253 n.
Harrington, brig *(1804)*, XI, 146
Harrington, King, & Co., XV, 220–231
Harrington, Admiral P. E., XXXIX, 119
Harrington, Virginia, XXXVII, 50 ff.
Harriot, brig *(1796)*, XXXI, 191
Harriot, brigantine *(1791)*, XVIII, 132
Harriot, schooner *(1773)*, IX, 181–182
Harris, Benjamin, XXIV, 6
Harris, David, XLII, 42
Harris, Frank M., XXXII, 198
Harris, Captain Frank M., XXI, 93
Harris, Admiral Frederick R., XXXII, 161; XXXV, 281
Harris, Captain James, XXIII, 47 ff.
Harris, John, XII, 223; XXXI, 22
Harris, Captain John, XLIII, 22 ff.
Harris, Captain Samuel, XX, 173
Harris, Sheldon H., "Mutiny on *Junior*," XXI, 110–129; "Paul Cuffe's White Apprentice," XXIII, 192–196
Harris, Captain T. A., XXXVI, 48
Harris, Captain Thomas A., XVIII, 83
Harris, Townsend, XXXII, 123
Harris, Captain W. C., XXI, 93
Harris, General William Townsend, XXVII, 164
Harrisburg, steamship (ex-*City of Paris*), Pictorial Supplement, XXXIV, plate XX
Harrisburg Foundry & Machine Works, Harrisburg, Pa., XXXII, 31
Harrison, steamship *(1839)*, XVIII, 299
Harrison, Anna Symes, XXXVIII, 41
Harrison, President Benjamin, XXVII, 55, 56, 58
Harrison, Captain, XLVIII, 50 ff.
Harrison, Captain F. F., VII, 157–158
Harrison, George, XXXV, 234 ff.
Harrison, Captain John, XXI, 93
Harrison, John P., contributed document, XIV, 139–141
Harrison, Richard, XLIII, 22 ff.
Harrison, Captain W. H., VII, 150, 160, 165
Harrison, President William Henry, XXXVIII, 41
Harris Wharf, XXX, 58, 61
Harrold, D. C., XXV, 67
Harry F. Albaugh, bateau (1910), IV, 289
Harry Glynn, fishing vessel *(1964)*, XLI, 61
Harry Lewis, schooner (1899), XXVI, plate XV
Harry Luckenbach, steamship *(1905)*, XXXVIII, 188 ff.
Harry Morse, ship (1871), IV, 45, 52
Harry Warren, ship (1863), III, 71
Hart, Captain A., XX, 89 n.
Hart, Francis Russel, Nautical Museum, XXV, 219, 223
Hart, Colonel Hubbart L., VII, 119 ff.
Hart, Jane S. (Mrs. Parker T.), review by, L, 141–143
Hart, Kevin R., "Towards a Citizen Sailor: The History of the Naval Militia Movement, 1888–1898," XXXIII, 258–279
Hart, Captain R., XX, 89 n.
Hart, Robert A., *The Great White Fleet: Its Voyage Around the World, 1907–1909*, reviewed, XXVI, 145–146
Hart, Samuel, VIII, 134
Hart, William, XXI, 109; XLVI, 258
Hartage, Captain Ernest H., XIV, 108
Hartford, ship *(1861)*, XLIII, 276

Hartford, steam sloop *(1865),* XXXII, 124; XXXIII, 281; XXXIV, 119; XXXV, 29
Hartford, U.S.S. (1858), XX, 137–138, 214; *(1859),* XXVII, 173; *(1862),* XXXVI, 200; XXXVIII, 39
Hartford, U.S. steam frigate *(1868),* VII, 20
Hartlepool Iron Works, XXVI, 131, 207
Hartley, Condon & Co., XLVII, 104
Hartley, R. F. C., XLIV, 10
Hart Nautical Museum. *See* Francis Russel Hart Nautical Museum
Hartshore, Meyers and Salter, XXX, 21
Hartshorne, Richard T., XXX, 21
Hartshorne, Robert, XXV, 124
Hart Steamboat Line, Ocklawaha River, Florida, VII, 115–166, 224–239, plates 13–20, 29–32
Hartt's Naval Shipyard, Boston, XXV, 29
Harvard, ship, XXIV, 126
Harvard, steamship (1906), IX, 217–220; XXVII, 150; Pictorial Supplement, XXXIV, plate XXIX
Harvard, U.S.S., XXII, 276
Harvard University, Baker Library of, XIII, 118–124
Harvest, bark *(1861),* XV, 108 n.; XXI, 256
Harvest, schooner, XXI, 98; *(1863),* VIII, 230
Harvester, bark (1871), III, 71, 265
Harvest Home, yacht *(1876),* XXXVI, 233
Harvest of the Sea: The Mauritius Sea Story in Outline, by Auguste Toussaint, reviewed, XXVI, 285
Harvey, G., XXIV, plate XXXI
Harvey, Neal, XXXVI, 276, 277
Harvey A. Parks, two-sail bateau (1899), IV, 288, 293
Harvey Birch, ship (1854), XIX, Plate XXXII; XXV, 106; *(1861),* XXXIII, 59
Harvey Gamage Shipyard, XXIX, 153
Harwich Lights, XI, 5–34
Harwood Palmer, schooner (1904), V, 80
Hasbrouck, John L., XIV, 166
Haskell, Captain Andrew, XX, 236
Haskell, Captain Ellis E., XX, 238
Haskell, F. H., XVII, 46
Haskell, Captain William, XXV, 185
Haslach, Robert D., and Donald G. Shomette, *Raid on America: The Dutch Naval Campaign of 1672–1674,* reviewed, L, 228
Hassalo, U.S.S. *(1864),* XXVII, 36 n., 39 n., 44, 45
Hassan Pasha, steamship (1886), XI, 258 ff.
Hasse, Captain Charles, VII, 292
Hasselwood, Captain, XL, 115
Hassler, Ferdinand R., XXVIII, 47
Hassler, Frederick, XXXI, 253
Hastings, H.M.S. *(1840),* XXXVIII, 118
Hastings (Sussex), XXX, 154
Hastings, Battle of (1066), XLIV, 96
Hastings, Dana M., "Boston's Little-known Packet Lines," XV, 133–141
Hastings, E. Warren, sketches by, Pictorial Supplement, XXXVII, plates XXVII, XXVIII
Hastings, Captain John B., XXV, 172

Haswell, Robert, XV, 206 ff.
Hatch, Abigail (Mrs. Luther), XLV, 180
Hatch, Francis W., contributed document, XXV, 144–146; document by, XXVIII, 66–68; "Nautical Doodles," XXIII, 39–40; "Packet and 'Steam Cars' to Boston: A Sentimental journey in the 1840's," XXVI, 262–271
Hatch, Francis W., Sr., XLVI, 61
Hatch, Francis Whiting, contributed document, XXIV, 279; "From 'Leg of Mutton' to 'Brigantine,' Nautical ABC's for a Cruising Chaperone," XXII, 184–186; "Sea Going Bank Notes with Denominational Masts," XV, 213–216, plate 11
Hatch, John L., XLV, 186
Hatch, Marie Martel, edited "Letters of Captain Sir John Jervis to Sir Henry Clinton, 1774–1782," VI, 87–106
Hatch, Nathaniel, XL, 253 ff.
Hatch, Rufus, XXXI, 122
Hatcher, Captain, XIII, 50
Hatcher, Captain Michael, XLVII, 275
Hatfield, U.S. destroyer *(1921),* XLVI, 244 ff.
Hathaway, Felix, XXVIII, 135
Hathaway, Freeman R., X, 73
Hathaway, G. M., XXII, plate XXI
Hathaway, William, XXXIII, 53
Hathorne, Nathaniel (father of author Nathaniel Hawthorne), XVIII, 138–139
Hatrick, Captain James R., XXI, 93
Hattendorf, John B., "Sir Julian Corbett on the Significance of Naval History," XXXI, 275–285
Hattendorf, John B., B. Mitchell Sampson, III, and John R. Wadleigh, *Sailors and Scholars: The Centennial History of the U.S. Naval War College,* reviewed, XLVIII, 186
Hatteras, U.S. warship, XXIX, 167; *(1863),* XLV, 193
Hattie, schooner, XXI, 87; *(1863),* VIII, 230
Hattie, steamship *(1864),* XV, 129
Hattie A. Heckman, schooner (1895), XXVI, plate XIII
Hattie C., schooner *(1902),* XXIV, 49
Hattie C. Besse, 4–masted 'jackass' rig (ex-*Genesee*) *(1863),* XXV, 113
Hattie C. Bessie, bark (1862), IV, 238
Hattie E. Tapley, ship (1865), III, 66
Hattie H. Barbour, schooner *(1883),* XLIX, 29
Hattie L. M., Canadian schooner *(1902),* XLIX, 280
Hatton, Christopher, XIII, 11
Hatton, John, Collector at Salem, 1764, XXXVII, 273
Haudegan, German U-boat group, XLIV, 48 ff.
Haugen, Commander Lawrence T., XXXVIII, 281
Haugh, George F., contributed document, XI, 150–155
Haughty, H.M.S. *(1859),* XXVII, 168
Haughty, steam gunboat, XXII, 36
Havana, steamship *(1862),* XII, 55; (1863), IV, 142 ff.
"Havana Incident, The," by Captain John F. Campbell, XXII, 264–276
Havannah, frigate (1813), XLII, 110 ff.

Have at All, privateer *(1626)*, XLIX, 253
Havelock, H.M.S. *(1942)*, L, 44
Havelock, schooner *(1861)*, VIII, 218; *(1863)*, XV, 127
Havelock, steamship, XXI, 96; *(1863)*, VIII, 230; XV, 127
Haven, Captain E. J., XX, 106
Haven, Commander Hugh E., XXXVIII, 281
Havighurst, Walter, *The Long Ships Passing*, reviewed, II, 344–345
Havila, bark *(1896)*, XVIII, 9
Haviland, Dr. E. Kenneth, Reviews by: XXXII, 72–74; XXXIII, 218–221; XXXV, 222; XXXVII, 71, 74; XXXVIII, 201; XXXIX, 148; XL, 68, 140, 232; XLI, 149–151; XLII, 149, 223, 230; XLIII, 60, 227, 303–305; XLV, 204–206; XLVII, 59–62; XLVIII, 132, 193, 205; "American Steam Navigation in China, 1845–1878," XLIX, 21–28; "American Steam Navigation in China, 1845–1878," XVI, 157–179, 243–269; XVII, 38–64, 134–151, 212–230, 298–304; XVIII, 59–85; "Early Steam Navigation in China," XXII, 5–44; reviewed book, XXII, 225–227; "Early Steam Navigation in China: Hongkong and the Canton River, 1858–1867," XXXIV, 17–58; "Early Steam Navigation in China: Overseas Services to 1861," [Part I], XXVI, 5–32; [Part II], XXVI, 109–133; [Part III], XXVI, 189–209; "Early Steam Navigation in China: The Yangtsze River, 1861–1867, XLIII, 85–128 and 186–221; "Classification Society Registers from the Point of View of a Marine Historian," XXX, 9–39
Haviland, Jean, "American Concrete Steamers of the First and Second World Wars," XXII, 157–183; "Early American Tankers," XXXVIII, 175–202; "In the Twilight of Auxiliary Steam," XXXII, 5–33
Haviland, Thomas Heath, XXIX, 63
Havock, British ship *(1858)*, XLIII, 274 ff.
Havre, grain elevator *(1883)*, XXXVIII, 141
Havre, ship (1845), III, 262
Hawaii, boats of, XIII, 91 ff.
Hawaii (HI), History, to 1893, XLVI, 43. *See also* Shipping; Whaling
Hawaiian, steamship *(1940)*, IV, 62
Hawaiian Isles, bark *(1892)*, II, 290 ff.
Hawaiian petroglyphs, XXIII, plates 3, 4
"Hawaiian Whaling Days," by Edward Lee Dorsett, M.D., XIV, 42–46, plates 7, 8
Hawes, Captain C. A., XVIII, 83
Hawk, brig *(1778)*, X, 281–282
Hawk, British sloop-of-war *(1735)*, XXIII, 82; *(1742)*, XXVI, 44, 46, 47, 48
Hawk, schooner *(1775)*, XXX, 110; *(1776)*, XLII, 9 ff.
Hawk, steamship *(1864)*, VIII, 234, 237
Hawke, brig *(1777)*, V, 187
Hawke, H.M.S. *(1765)*, XXIII, 177, 179, 180
Hawke, schooner *(1776)*, XIII, 35; XIV, 47
Hawke, Admiral Sir Edward, XLVIII, 28
Hawker, Captain James, XXIII, 176

Hawkes, Isaac, XIV, 59
Hawkesworth, John, XXV, 297
Hawkeye State, steamship *(1921)*, X, 141
Hawkins, Alexander, VIII, 249
Hawkins, John, XXVII, 181–184
Hawkins, Vice Admiral John, XLIX, 5
Hawkins, Captain Richard, XXV, 254
Hawkins, Sir Richard, XXVII, 182
Hawkins, Captain Rufus, XVII, 93
Hawkins, William, XXVII, 179, 181
Haws, Duncan and Alex A. Hurst, *The Maritime History of the World*, reviewed, XLVII, 283
Hawthorne, steamship *(1892)*, XXIV, 237–239, plate 27
Hawthorne, Nathaniel, V, 266–285; XXV, 58, 63; XLVII, 169
Hay, John, XXXII, 257
Hay, Secretary John, XXXVII, 30
Hay, Robert, XXX, 299
Hayden, sailing packet, XXVIII, 121
Hayes, Adam, XLVI, 224
Hayes, Bully, IV, 112–113
Hayes, Frederic H., "John Adams and American Sea Power," XXV, 35–45
Hayes, I. I., XXXVIII, 45
Hayes, Rear Admiral John D., XXXII, 51
Hayes, Joseph, XIV, 59
Hayman, John, XXX, 57
Hayman, Nathan, XXX, 58
Hayman, Samuel, XXX, 58
Hayman Shipbuilding Co., XLI, 189
Haymon, Captain Daniel, XXI, 93
Haynen, W. J., XXXV, 282
Haynes, Andrew, XVII, 119
Hays, Moses M., XIII, 120
Hayti, brig *(1845)*, XVI, 64
Haywood, Charles F., *No Ship May Sail*, reviewed, II, 263
Hazard, brig *(1778)*, VII, 203, 205; X, 285–286; *(1779)*, XXXVII, 293
Hazard, ship (1798), II, 279; *(1798)*, XVIII, 121; (1799), Pictorial Supplement, XXXII, plates VII, VIII; *(1801)*, XXIII, 217; *(1808)*, XVI, 195
Hazard, sloop, XXVIII, 226
Hazard, Captain John, Continental Navy, XXV, 193
Hazard, Captain Morris, XX, 89 n., 92
Hazard, Lieutenant O. P., XXXV, 192
Hazard, Captain R. T., XXXV, 192
Haze, schooner *(1856)*, X, 231 ff.
Hazel-Leah, schooner (1903), XXIV, 60
Hazel M. Jackson, schooner *(1920)*, XLI, plate 1
Hazelwood, Nathaniel W., XXVI, 203
Hazen, Mildred McLean, XXXVII, 26
Hazen, General William B., XXXVI, 109 ff.
Heachow, steamship *(1867)*, XLIII, 299
Heade, Martin (artist), XXV, 59
Healey, Captain Frank, XLIX, 32

"Health Hazards of the West African Trader, 1840–1870," by E. Richmond Ware, M.D., XXVII, 81–97
Healy, Laurin Hall and Luis Kutner, *The Admiral,* reviewed, IV, 337
Healy, Captain Michael, XXXIX, 12
Healy, W. R., XXXVI, 248
Heard, Albert F., XVII, 47
Heard, Albert Farley, XXXIV, 44
Heard, Augustine, XVII, 42–64; XVIII, 66
Heard, Augustine, and Co., VI, 49; XVI, 254
Heard, George F., XVI, 175; XVII, 59, 63
Heard, J. (A. Heard and Co.), XXII, 13
Heard, J. (artist), XXIV, plate VII
Heard, Captain J. J., XLI, 298
Heard, John, XVII, 60, 61; XXXIV, 49 ff.
Heard and Co., XIII, 119, 122
Heard Island (Indian Ocean), Discovery and exploration, XLI, 280
Hearn, Lieutenant-Commander H. J., XXXV, 43
Hearne, Samuel, L, 35
Heart of Oak, British ship *(1778),* XLV, 248
Heath, John D., XXV, 295
Heath, Captain W. H., XVIII, 83
Heather, William, London, XXXIV, 202
Heaton, Alexander McGlashan, XXXIV, 54 fn.
Heavers, sailmaker's, IX, 286–288
Heavy Weather Cooking, by Jan Silver, reviewed, XL, 230
Hebble, steamship *(1891),* XXIV, plate XXV
Hebe, French frigate *(1782),* XXXVI, 288
Hebe, steamship, XXI, 105; *(1863),* XVIII, 144, 145; VIII, 230
Hébert, General P. O., XL, 302
Hebrus, frigate *(1814),* XLII, 113
Hecata, Bruna de, XIII, 212
Hecht, Arthur, "Government Owned and Operated Coastwise Mail Service of the Eighteenth Century," XXII, 55–64
Hector, bark *(1845),* XVI, 64
Hector, brig *(1805),* XXIV, 264, 266
Hector, schooner *(1864),* XII, 230
Hector, ship *(1804),* XXII, 200, 201, 202, 206; *(1807),* XIV, 91 ff.
Hedderwick & Rankin, XXVI, 207
Hedge, Captain Milton P., XXII, 234, 244
Hedges, James B., XXXVII, 50; "Disaster in the South Seas: The Wreck of the Brigantine *Eliza* and the Subsequent Adventures of Captain Corey," XXIII, 233–254
Hedgpeth, Joel W., V, 91; "The United States Fish Commission Steamer *Albatross,*" V, 5–15
Hedtoft, steamship (1959), XIX, 77
Heel-tapper, XXX, 88
Hefflin, Wilson L., query by, VIII, 154
Heffron, Paul T., "Secretary Moody and Naval Administrative Reform: 1902–1904," XXIX, 30–53
Heflin, Wilson L., note by, XXXVII, 143

Hegarty, Reginald B., photo from collection of, XXXIX, plate 4
Hegarty, Reginald B. and Philip F. Purrington, *Returns of Whaling Vessels from American Ports,* reviewed, XX, 71
Heian Maru, steamship (ex-*Scotland*) *(1862),* XLIII, 207; *(1865),* XLIX, 22
Heinrichs, Waldo H., Jr., "The Battle of Plattsburg, 1814—The Losers," XXI, 42–56
Heiress, ship *(1860),* IV, 72
Heitzmann, Wm. Ray, "The Ironclad *Weekawken* in the Civil War," XLII, 193–202; "In-Service Naval Officer Education in the Nineteenth Century: Voluntary Commitment to Reform," XXXIX, 109–125
Helen, bark, XXI, 103; *(1861),* VIII, 218; XV, 123; *(1864),* VIII, 234
Helen (ex-*Sea Bride*), bark *(1863),* XXVI, 103
Helen, schooner *(1863),* XII, 157; *(1899),* XXXVIII, 88
Helen, steamship, XXI, 99, 103, 105; *(1864),* VIII, 234; XVII, 253 n.
Helena, barge, XXI, 86; *(1861),* XI, 283
Helena, schooner, XXI, 88, 90; *(1863),* XII, 157; *(1940),* XXXIX, 180
Helena, ship *(1841),* VII, 5, 6; *(1899),* XXXV, 188
Helena, U.S.S. *(1915),* XLIV, 182
Helen B. Thomas, schooner *(1902),* XXX, 197
Helen Barnet Gring, schooner *(1940),* III, 163
Helen Brewer, ship *(1896),* XVI, 5
Helene, schooner *(1861),* VIII, 218
Helen Mar, bark *(1875),* XXII, plate XXI; *(1879),* XXXIX, 9; XLIV, 13
Helen Mar, ship *(1834),* XII, 179
Helen McGaw, bark *(1847),* V, 149
Helen McGregor, steamship (1843), XXIV, plate XX
Helen Peele, steam tug, XXXIV, 11 ff.
Helen Smith, steamship *(1870),* VI, 61; VII, 242
Helen Whittier, steamship *(1929),* IX, 226
Helga, steamship *(1895),* XI, 259 ff.
Hellenic International Lines, XXXVI, 31
Hellespont, steamship (1849), XVII, 213; XVIII, 70; XLIII, 97 ff.
Helm, Thomas, XLVI, 214
Helper, ship *(1807),* XVI, 192
Helvetia, schooner (1905), V, 292, plate 21; Pictorial Supplement, XXXVI, plate XXX
Helvetius, American whaler *(1830),* XXIX, 89
Hemingway, Ernest, XXV, 65; XLVI, 188
Henarie, S. K., XX, 119
Henderson, J. Welles, XXII, 79
Henderson, J. Welles and Harris B. Stewart, Jr., Editors, *B. Shephard's Sketchbook of the H.M.S.* Challenger *Expedition 1872–1874,* reviewed, XXXIII, 307
Henderson, Richard, *Choice Yacht Designs,* reviewed, XL, 147; commentator, *53 Boats You Can Build,* reviewed, XLVI, 130; *Philip L. Rhodes and his Yacht Designs,* reviewed, XLIV, 133
Hendrick, Burton J., XXXIII, 11

Hendrick Hudson, steamship, XVIII, 224
Henley, Captain John D., XXXI, 179
Henley, Commodore John D., XLVII, 27
Henly, Robert, XXXVI, 58
Henningsen, Henning, *Crossing The Equator: Sailors' Baptism and Other Initiation Rites,* reviewed, XXIII, 148–149; *Sømandens Tøj,* reviewed, XL, 230
Henrich, Joseph George, "Thomas Paine's Short Career as a Naval Architect, August-October 1807," XXXIV, 123–134
Henrietta, French ship *(1799),* XXXI, 175
Henrietta, schooner (1849), XXIV, 59; *(1861),* VIII, 218; *(1862),* XII, 55, 157
Henrietta, ship (1857), XV, 186
Henrietta, sloop, XXI, 102; *(1760),* IX, 144–145; *(1864),* XII, 230
Henrietta, whale ship, XXV, plate 8
Henrietta, yacht *(1908),* XXXVI, 245
Henrietta A. Whitney, schooner (1871), IX, 170–171
Henrietta Marcy, ship (1856), III, 67; *(1861),* XI, 283
Henri Le Chatelier, concrete ship (1944), XXII, 177
Henry, brig *(1812),* XXI, 18; *(1813),* XIII, 237; XXVI, 277
Henry, ship (1791), II, 281; V, 102
Henry, Captain G. F., XXVI, 28, 203
Henry, Captain John, IV, 77
Henry, Commander H., XLVI, 238
Henry, Joseph, XLVII, 176 ff.
Henry, Governor Patrick, XXXIII, 23
Henry A. Middleton, schooner *(1861),* VIII, 218
Henry A. Whitney, ship (1889), XXXVII, 84
Henry B. Hyde, ship (1884), quarter-deck scene, II, plate 28; VIII, 330; XXVII, plate XXI
Henry Buck, bark (1852), XXVIII, plate VII
Henry C. Chester, schooner *(1902),* XXIV, 49
Henry Chauncey, steamship (1864), X, 130
Henry Clay, packet ship (1845), XXIV, 135
Henry Clay, ship, XXVIII, 124
Henry Clay, steamship (1825), VI, 201, 203–205; VII, 45, 47, 64
Henry Clay, vessel (1851), XXXVI, 172
Henry Colthirst, schooner, XXI, 103
Henry Dodge, revenue cutter *(1861),* XL, 302; XLVIII, 87 ff.
Henry Eckford, bark *(1832),* VII, 193
"Henry Eckford (1775–1832), an American Shipbuilder," by Phyllis DeKay Wheelock, VII, 177–195, plates 21–24
"Henry Eckford's *United States* of 1831," by Cedric Ridgely-Nevitt, VIII, 7–10
Henry F. Colthrist, schooner *(1862),* XII, 55, 230
Henry F. Eaton, steamship, XXVIII, 125
Henry Fletcher, Son & Fearnall, XXVI, 207
Henry Ford, schooner, XXXVI, 77; (1922), XXV, 147
Henry Gildersleeve, steamship *(1840),* XX, 87, 89
Henry Grace a Dieu, ship, XV, 273; XXIV, 75
Henry H. Chamberlain, schooner (1891), III, 256

Henry Hughes & Son, XIII, 66–67
Henry Hughes Navigation Warehouse, XXXIV, 206
"Henry Hulton and the Greenwich Hospital Tax," by Joseph R. Frese, XXXI, 192–216
Henry J. Biddle, tug *(1918),* XVIII, 169
Henry Kneeland, ship *(1849),* XII, 106
Henry L. Richardson, ship (1865), V, 327
Henry Lewis, steamship, XXI, 104; *(1861),* XI, 283; XII, 157
Henry M. Stanley, schooner (1890), XXVI, plate X
Henry Nutt, schooner *(1861),* VIII, 218; XI, 154
Henry Travers, schooner, XXI, 97; *(1861),* VIII, 218; XI, 283; XII, 55
Henry Villard, ship *(1907),* XVIII, 16
Henry Warren, bark (1848), IV, 51
Henry Waters, schooner, XXI, 89; *(1861),* XI, 283
Hensel, Henry, XXXVI, 238, 239
Henshaw, David, XV, 138
Henshaw, Joshua, XL, 267
Henshaw, Walter (Instrument maker), ring dial by, Pictorial Supplement, XXXV, plate XVII
Henshawe, Captain John, XLIV, 26
Henson, Curtis T., Jr., *Commissioners and Commodores, The East India Squadron and American Diplomacy in China,* reviewed, XLIII, 145–146; "The U.S. Navy and the Taiping Rebellion," XXXVIII, 28–40
Henson, Matthew, XXXVIII, 51
Henwood, James N. J., "A Cruise on the *U.S.S. Sabine,*" XXIX, 102–105
Hepburn, Andrew H., Jr., XIII, 246; XV, 95
Herald, American merchant vessel *(1843),* XLVI, 232
Herald, bark (1855), II, 331
Herald, brig (1822), XIV, 40; *(1861),* VIII, 218
Herald, schooner *(1863),* VIII, 230
Herald, ship *(1798),* XLVI, 161; *(1800),* XXXI, 174; XXXIII, Pictorial Supplement, plates XX, XXI
Herald, ship *(1807),* II, 283; *(1807),* XVI, 195; *(1854),* XVIII, 321; *(1861),* XV, 108 n.; XXI, 256
Herald, steamship, XXI, 89, 91, 102; (1831), XXIV, Plate XIX; *(1862),* VIII, 203–204, 225, 230; *(1863),* XV, 111, 127
Herald, surveying vessel *(1845),* XXXII, 243
Herald, towboat *(1887),* XLII, 255
Herald, U.S.S. *(1799),* XXVII, 144, 145
Herald of the Morning, ship, XXII, 239; (1853), III, 68; *(1854),* XLI, 298
Heraldry, XVIII, 301
Herbert, Hilary A., XL, 101; XLI, 248
Herbert, Hilary A., Secretary of the Navy, XXXIV, 212
Herbert, J. C., XXXVI, 66
Herbert, Jacob, VI, 306
Herbert, John, XVIII, 188
Herbert, John R., III, 271; reviews by, XLIV, 137; XLV, 213; XLVI, 126; XLVIII, 205; XLIX, 134, 232, 306; query by, III, 353; "The *Polly* of Amesbury," IV, 164–171
Herbert, Captain T. K., XXI, 93

Herbert, William, XXI, 114 ff.
Herbert Fuller, barkentine *(1896),* XVI, 182–184
Herbert L. Rawding, schooner (1919), Pictorial Supplement, XXXVI, plate XXXII; *(1939),* XXIV, 25; *(1942),* III, 60, 166
Herbrandson, Dee, note by, XXXV, 139–141
Hercher, Gail P., "The Education Department at the Peabody Museum of Salem," XLV, 117–118
Hercules, brig, XXI, 86; *(1861),* XI, 283
Hercules, revenue cutter *(1863),* XXXV, 64
Hercules, ship *(1627),* XLIX, 254; *(1634),* XIX, 7, 8
Hercules, ship (1805), Pictorial Supplement, XXXII, plate IX; *(1807),* VIII, 164, 242–245, plate 20
Hercules, ship (1868), II, 334
Hercules, steamship, XXIV, 215; (1843), XVII, 101; XX, 261, 264; *(1846),* XII, 153
Hercules, tug *(1864),* XLIII, 297
Hereford, steamship (1890), 259 ff.
Herendeen, Edward Perry, XXXIX, 11
Heren Zeventien (or Gentlemen Seventeen), Dutch East India Co., XLVII, 241 ff.
Hereward, ship (1891), XVIII, 5
Hergesheimer, Joseph, XXV, 65
"Heritage, A Maritime," by Horace P. Beck, XXV, 51–67
Herman, steam barkentine *(1904),* XXXVIII, 89
Herman, steamship (1845), XLVIII, 114
Herman H. Hettler, steam barge (1890), I, 76
Herman Livingston, steamship, XVIII, 233
Herman Melville's Picture Gallery, by Stuart M. Frank, reviewed, XLIX, 60
Hermann, steamship, XXVII, 259; (1847), II, 25–26; (1869), X, 134
Herman Winter, steamship (1886), Pictorial Supplement, XXXIV, plate XIX
Hermes, carrier *(1942),* XLII, 203
Hermes, H.M.S., XXXI, Pictorial Supplement, plate I; *(1899),* XXVIII, 93, 96
Hermione, ship *(1808),* XVI, 201
Hermoine, H.M.S., XXVIII, 107
Hermon, ship (1868), II, 334
Hermosa, schooner *(1861),* XI, 283; XII, 55
Hernan Cortes, brig *(1861),* XI, 283
Herndon, Lieutenant William L., U.S.N., IV, 313; XXXI, 8
Hernia, steamship XXIV, 214
Hernia, warship *(1945),* XXXIX, 263
Hero, privateer (1762), VIII, 15, 16
Hero, schooner (1868), I, 73
Hero, ship, XIII, 121; *(1758),* IX, 144, 147
Hero, ship (1762), XXI, 76; *(1808),* X, 54; XI, 145–146
Hero, sloop, XXIV, 215; XXV, 54
Hero, steamship, XXI, 99; *(1862),* VIII, 225, 230; *(1863),* XII, 157
"Hero Against his Will or There Will Always Be an England, A," by Captain Edgar K. Thompson, U.S.N. (ret.), XXV, 45

Heroine, steamship *(1864),* XII, 230
Heroine (ex-*Aloha*), steam brig *(1912),* XLIV, 121
Herold, schooner *(1848),* XXXVIII, 60
Heron, yacht *(1900),* XXXVI, 240
Heron, Andrew, XX, 84
Heron, George, XIII, 11
Herquoit, Vancouver Island, IV, 318 ff.
Herrera, XXX, 252
Herreshoff, L. Francis, I, 102; document contributed by, XXXII, 67–68; *Captain Nat Herreshoff,* reviewed, XLVIII, 186; *An L. Francis Hereshoff Reader,* reviewed, XXXIX, 149
Herreshoff, Nathaniel, XIII, 246
Herreshoff, Nathaniel G., I, 400
Herrick, Walter R., Jr., *The American Naval Revolution,* reviewed, XXVII, 286–287
Herring, snow (1752), I, 297
Herrington, Dr. William C., XLV, 83
Hershing, Comander Otto, XXXVI, 33–44
Hertigennan Af Sodermanland, Swedish ship *(1780),* XLIX, 91 ff.
Hertiginnan af Södermanland, bark (1774), VI, 166
Herzog, Donald, XLIV, 33
Herzogin Cecilie, bark, XXX, 220
Hesper, schooner, XIII, 54
"*Hesperus,* Wreck of The," XXV, 64
Hessie, steamship, XXIII, 89
Hester, privateer *(1745),* XLII, 50
Hester, Captain Joseph G., XXI, 93
Hestia, steamship *(1902),* X, 193
Hetewan, schooner, XXI, 100; *(1862),* VIII, 225, 230
Hettie Bell, yacht *(1892),* XXXVI, 236–239
Hetty, brig *(1787),* XLIV, 6 ff.
Heureuse Rencontre, French ship *(1800),* XXXI, 174
Heureux, French ship *(1800),* XXXI, 174
Hewes, Captain C. B., XXII, 168
Hewes, Joseph, XXV, 194
Hewett, Captain William N. W., XXI, 93, 100
Hewitt, Henry, XXV, 172
Hewitt, Captain Henry Kent, U.S.N., XXV, 68
Heyerdahl, Thor, XXI, 159 ff.; XXIII, 114, 116
Heyl, Eric, note, XXXVII, 140
Heyman, Peter (Collector of Customs; d. 1700), XXX, 133, 134, 138
Heyman, Sir Peter, XXX, 133
Heyrman, Christine Leigh, *Commerce and Culture: The Maritime Communities of Colonial Massachusetts, 1690–1750,* reviewed, XLVI, 128
Heyward, Thomas, Jr., XIII, 30
Heyworth, James O., XXXV, 281
Hezekiah Williams, timber drogher *(1849),* XLVIII, 100
"Hiatus in Honors, A," document contributed by Captain E. K. Thompson, U.S.N. (ret.), XXII, 220–221
HI. *See* Hawaii
Hiawatha, barque, XXI, 86

Hiawatha, steamship (1880), XXV, 168; (1904), VII, 126, 143, 162, 230–232, 234–239, plates 29–30, stateroom plans, 142; XXIV, 241
Hiawatha, stern-wheel steamship (1898), I, 73
Hibbs, Captain James, XXI, 93
Hibernia, H.M.S., XXIII, 254
Hibernia, schooner, XXII, 60 n.; *(1776)*, XIII, 36
Hibernia, steamship, XXVI, 270; (1843), XLV, 180
Hickman, Dr. Money L., XLVI, 64
Hickman, Chief R. F., XXXIX, 43
Hicks, Albert W., XXVIII, 223
Hicks, Fred Cook, XXIX, 134, 138
Hicks, Frederick Charles, XXIX, 137
Hicks, Captain William A., XXI, 93
Hicks, William Cook, XXIX, 133 ff.
Hicks, William Francis, XXIX, 135
Hicks & Brothers of Saginaw, shipbuilders, XLII, 252
Higco, schooner *(1921)*, XLI, 42
Higginson, Captain Edward, XXXVIII, 266
Higginson, Francis Lee, Jr., Pictorial Supplements, XXIV, between 64–65, 140–141, 216–217, 292–293
Higginson, Henry, XXX, 289
Higginson, Stephen, XXX, 123, 292; XLII, 27
Higginson, Thatcher, XXXVIII, 104
Higginson, Thomas Wentworth, XXXVIII, 104
Higham, Robin D. S., "The Port of Boston and the Embargo of 1807–1809," XVI, 189–210; "The Russian Fleet on the Eastern Seaboard, 1863–1864," XX, 49–61
Highflyer, H.M.S., XXVIII, 108 n.
Highflyer, H.M. tender *(1813)*, XXXI, 286; XLVI, 167
Highlander, ship (1868), V, 149; (1869), figurehead of, Pictorial Supplement, XXXVII, plate X
Highlander, steamship (1835), XIV, 167, 168; *(1915)*, XIV, 290
"Highland Grace, A," contributed by Gilbert R. Payson, XXX, 186
High Priest, schooner *(1861)*, VIII, 218
Hight, William, XX, 190
Hildreth, Captain Jerome B., XVII, 55; XVIII, 83
Hildreth, Captain Richard, XLVI, 51
Hilgard, Captain Milosh R., XXXIV, 274
Hilhouse, George, XIV, 115
Hilhouse, Hill and Co., XIV, 115
Hilhouse, James, XIV, 115
Hilhouse, James M., XIV, 115
Hill, Arthur, XLII, 245 ff.
Hill, C. F., XLIII, 289
Hill, Charles, XIV, 115 ff.
Hill, Charles G., XIV, 116, 117, 126, 131
Hill, Charles L., XIV, 126, 131
Hill, Christopher, XL, 197
Hill, Edward B., XIV, 117
Hill, Edward S., XIV, 117, 126
Hill, Frederick Floyd, contributed document, I, 396–397
Hill, Frederic S., XXXVI, 202

Hill, H. O., and E. W. Paget-Tomlinson, *Instruments of Navigation*, reviewed, XIX, 146
Hill, Helen M., "It Was a Noble Calling...," XLV, 180–190
Hill, Howard C., XXXII, 258
Hill, Hugh, XXX, 110
Hill, Humphrey, XII, 225
Hill, James, VIII, 13, 18
Hill, James J., ship owner, III, 185–204
Hill, James J., XXXV, 167 ff.; XLVII, 193 ff.
Hill, Jim Dan, "Captain Joseph Fry, of S.S. *Virginius*," XXXVI, 88–100
Hill, Captain John, XXI, 105
Hill, Captain L. R., XXI, 93
Hill, Captain Norman, XLIII, 201
Hill, Captain Samuel, V, 158 ff.
Hill, Whitmill, XXXI, 239
Hillary, Sir William, XXXIV, 6 ff.
Hilliard, Captain L., VII, 50
Hillman, whaler *(1865)*, XXVII, 275
Hillman, Jethro (shipbuilder), XXV, 102
Hillman, Zachariah (shipbuilder), XXV, 102
Hillsborough, ship *(1798)*, XLI, 284
Hillyer, grain elevator *(1883)*, XXXVIII, 141
Hillyer, Admiral, U.S., XXXII, 244
Hilton, Captain Bradford, III, 106
Hilton, George W., *The Great Lakes Car Ferries*, reviewed, XXIII, 70–71; *The Night Boat*, XXIX, 144–145
Hilton, Joseph C., III, 106–130
Hilton, Nathaniel, XV, 155
Himalaya, ship (1863), VII, 288; VIII, 114–126, plates 9–12; X, 110
Hinchinbrook, H.M.S. *(1778)*, XIII, 46–50, 212
Hinckley, Captain Isaac, XLV, 154
Hinckley, William S., XXXII, 118 ff.
Hindman, William, XXXVI, 57
Hindoo, schooner (1819), XXIV, 45, 59
Hindostan, bark (1847), III, 265
Hindostan, steamship (1842), XXVI, 8, 9, 12, 30, 205, 209
Hinds, Owen B., XV, 179
Hinds, William, XV, 179
Hines, Mayor John L. (Birdie), XXXIV, 265 ff.
Hinks, J. & Son, XXX, 79
Hinman, Elisha, XXXIX, 192
Hinmers, Joseph, XIII, 20 n., 21, 22, 26
Hinnman, Captain Elisha, XIV, 49
Hinton, R. W. K., *The Eastland Trade and the Common Weal in the Seventeenth Century*, reviewed, XIX, 148
Hinton, William, XIV, 191
Hipper, Admiral, XL, 52 ff.
Hippisley, Sir John, XLIX, 251
Hippogriff, schooner *(1874)*, IX, 229
Hippogriffe, ship, XXII, 233, 238, 239, 245, 247, 248
Hippopotamus, dredge *(1780)*, XXXII, 251

Hirado, steamship (1863), XVI, 253; XVII, 39, 301; XVIII, 70; *(1865),* XXXIV, 49; XLIII, 121 ff.
Hiram, ship *(1800),* XV, 214; *(1812),* XLVI, 166; L, 104 ff.
Hiram Fogg & Co., XLIII, 111 ff.; XLIX, 26
Hiram Lowell, schooner (1892), XXVI, plate XII
Hirondelle, ship *(1864),* XXXVIII, 61
Hiroshige, XXX, 219
Hiroshima Maru, steamship *(1875),* XVII, 313, 314
Hiryu Maru, steamship (ex-*Promise*) *(1863),* XLIX, 27
Historians:
  Biography, XXXI, 275; XLIV, 61
  Criticism and interpretation, XLIX, 39
Historical Division of Marine Corp, The, XXXI, 4
Historical Naval Brasileira, edited by Max Justo Guedes, reviewed, XLIV, 276–277
"Historical Notes on the Gilbert and Marshall Islands," by Samuel Eliot Morison, IV, 87–118
Historical societies, VII, 83
Historical Society of Old Yarmouth, Massachusetts, XXV, 112
Historical Society of Pennsylvania, Philadelphia, VI, 253 ff.; VIII, 12 n. ff.
Historical Transactions, 1893–1943 (Society of Naval Architects and Marine Engineers), reviewed, VI, 86
"Historic American Merchant Marine Survey, The," by Frank A. Taylor, I, 63–79
Historic buildings, Massachusetts, IV, 5
Historic ships, I, 63, 333; XII, 7; XIII, 51; XXII, 99, 212; XXIX, 262; XLII, 276
  –, **Gt. Britain,** XXIX, 54
  –, **United States,** II, 289; VI, 112; X, 108; XIV, 5 105; XVII, 173
History, Methodology (Mathematical), XLVI, 179
History and Bibliography of The New American Practical Navigator *and* The American Coast Pilot, by John F. Campbell, Master Mariner, reviewed, XXIV, 221–223
"History and Growth of Boston Harbor," lecture by Sinclair Hitchings, Keeper of Prints, Boston Public Library; comment, Editorial, **The American Neptune,** XXXVIII, 3–4
History of American Marine Painting, A, by John Wilmerding, reviewed, XXIX, 139–141
History of American Steam Navigation, by J. H. Morrison, XXX, 15
"History of Flat Holm Lighthouse, The," by Captain W. R. Chaplin, XX, 5–43, plates 1–4
"History of Fluvial Navigation: The Example of the Meuse, A," by Marc Suttor, L, 165–177
"History of Harwich Lights and their Owners," by W. R. Chaplin, XI, 5–34
History of Nautical Astronomy, A, by Charles H. Cotter, reviewed, XXIX, 71–72
History of Naval Architecture, A, by John Fincham, reviewed, XLII, 309–10

History of Steamboating on the Upper Missouri, A, by William E. Lass, reviewed, XXIII, 285–286
History of Steam Navigation, by Rear Admiral G. H. Preble, XXX, 15
History of Steam Navigation between New York and Providence (1877), by Charles H. Dow, reviewed, II, 340
History of the American Sailing Navy, The, by Howard I. Chapelle, reviewed, X, 74–76
History of the Boston Marine Society, A, by William A. Baker, reviewed, XXIX, 141–142
History of the British Navy, The, by Michael Lewis, reviewed, XIX, 308
History of the Indian Ocean, by Auguste Toussaint, reviewed, XXVI, 285
"History of the Swordfishery of the Northwestern Atlantic," by Charles Dana Gibson, XLI, 36–65
History of the Tahitian Mission 1799–1830, written by John Davies, C. W. Newbury, Editor, reviewed, XXII, 74–75
History of the Town of Gloucester, Cape Ann including the Town of Rockport, by John J. Babson, reviewed, XXXIII, 224
History of Union Steam Ship Company of New Zealand, Limited (1875–1940), reviewed, I, 318–319
History Under the Sea, by Alexander McKee, reviewed, XXXI, 76
Hitchcock, E. A., XVII, 137, 140
Hitchcock, L. N., XVII, 134
Hitchcock, R. B., XXII, 284 n.
Hitchings, George H., XXV, 288
Hitchings, Sinclair, comment, Editorial, **The American Neptune,** XXXVIII, 3–4
Hitchman, James H., "The Origins of Yacht Racing in British Columbia and Washington, 1870–1914," XXXVI, 231–250
Hjalmar, hemmema (1799), VI, 165
Hjortsberg, Pilot Edward, U.S.N., letter quoted, VII, 109–110
Ho, Admiral Chêng, XLI, 126
Hoaxes, solemn, III, 57–59
Hobart, ship, XXVIII, 124
Hobart-Hampden, Captain Augustus Charles, XXI, 93
Hodge, Captain Isaac G., XXV, 184
Hodge, John, XXXVIII, 22
Hodges, Captain L. B., XVIII, 83
Hodgkins, D. D., XXIV, 60
Hodgkins, Philip, XLII, 22
Hodgkins, Timothy, XLVI, 217
Hodgson, James, VIII, 311
Hodgson, Captain Thomas, British Army, XXV, 208
Hodgson, William B., XXXVIII, 108
Hodshon, William, XL, 248
Hodson, Will, XXXVI, 241
Hoff, Rear Admiral C. B., XXXVIII, 236
Hoffman, Anne and E. Jeffrey Stann, editors, *Voyage to the Southern Ocean: The Letters of Lieutenant William*

Reynolds from the U.S. Exploring Expedition, 1838–1842, reviewed, L, 150
Hoffman, Charles, XXX, 241 ff.
Hofsommer, Don L., "The Maritime Enterprises of James J. Hill," XLVII, 193–205
Hof van Breda, Dutch East India vessel *(1675),* XLVI, 106
Hogan, Charles W., XLII, 246 ff.
Hogan, Timothy, XIV, 121
Hogarth, Donald D., "The *Emanuel* of Bridgwater and Discovery of Martin Frobisher's 'Black Ore' in Ireland," XLIX, 14–20
Hogdon, S., XXXVI, 279
Hogg, Thomas E., XXXII, 195, 198
Hogg Brothers, XLIII, 198 ff.
Hog Island, Nassau, Bahamas, XXV, 202 ff., 212, plates 21, 22
Holbrook, Francis X., "A Mosby or a Quantrill? The Civil War Career of John Clibbon Braine," XXXIII, 199–211; "To Strike a Blow at the California Trade," XXXII, 195–210
Holbrook, Francis X., and John Nikol, "The Chilean Crisis of 1891–1892," XXXVIII, 291–300; "Naval Operations in the Panama Revolution 1903," XXXVII, 253–261; "Reporting the Sicilian Revolution of 1848–1849," XLIII, 165–176
Holbrook, Josiah, XXXIX, 113
Holburne, Admiral Francis, XLVIII, 29
Holcomb, H. Sherman, carved billethead by, Pictorial Supplement, XXXVII, plate XXXII
Holcomb, Sherman, XLVII, 128
Holdcamper, Forrest R., I, 316; XXXII, 215; contributed document, XXIII, 225–227; "Biography of the *List* of Merchant Vessels of the United States," XXIV, 119–123; "Registers, Enrollments and Licenses in the National Archives," I, 275–294; "Thirty 'Easterns' and Others: Ships Built in Japan for the United States, 1919–1920," XXIII, 270–276
Holdcamper, Hope K., review by, XXVIII, 71–72
Holden, Theodore L., "The Songo River Steamboats," XXIV, 233–246
Holdfast, pinnace *(1628),* XLIX, 255
Hole, Henry, IX, 135 ff.
Hole-in-the-Wall, Great Abaco Island, Bahamas, XXV, 198, 200
Holgate, Captain Henry, XXI, 93
Holiday, Rollo, XXVI, 81 ff.
Holinger, 1st. Lieutenant Sebastián, XXX, 49
Holker, John, Jr., XLVI, 29
Holland, John, VII, 269
Holland, John P., XLVIII, 127
Holland, Stewart, XIV, 249
Holland, Stewart (cadet engineer), XXV, 79–80
Holland-American Line, VIII, 76
Hollandt [or Holland], Captain Samuel Jan, I, 144–145, 147–148, plate facing 143
Hollar, Wenceslaus, XXX, 219

Holling, Captain James T., XXXIV, 245
Hollingsworth, Jesse, VIII, 14; XII, 60–63
Hollingsworth, Levi, XXXII, 250. *See also* Hollinsworth, Levi.
Hollins, privateer *(1814),* XIX, 219
Hollins, George N., XL, 300
Hollins, Captain George N., XIX, 267, 268
Hollins, Commodore George N., XLVIII, 90
Hollinsworth, Levi, XXIX, 198
Hollond, John, Royal Navy Commissioner, XXV, 281–282
Holly, David C., *Steamboat on the Chesapeake: Emma Giles and the Tolchester Line,* reviewed, XLVIII, 209
Holly, H. H., review by, XXVI, 284–285; XXII, 290–291; "Comments on 'Boston's Little-Known Packet Lines,'" by Dana M. Hastings, in April 1955 Issue of *The American Neptune,*" XVI, 60–61; "More on *Sparrow-Hawk,*" XIV, 211–212; "*Sparrow-Hawk.* A Seventeenth-Century Vessel in Twentieth-Century America," XIII, 51–64, plates 4–8
Holly, H. Hobart, note contributed by, 143–144; "Wollaston of Mount Wollaston," XXXVII, 5–25
Holm, P. E., XXVII, plate X
Holm, Pieter (Instrument maker, Amsterdam), Pictorial Supplement, XXXV, plate XXII
Holman, Francis, oil paintings by, XLVIII, 161
Holman, Captain John, XXV, 184, plates 17, 19
Holmes, Captain A., XVIII, 83
Holmes, Alexander, XXV, 101
Holmes, Edward, XXV, 101
Holmes, Horace, XXV, 101
Holmes, James, XLII, 245 ff.
Holmes, Lieutenant John, XXIX, 211
Holmes, Jonathan, XXV, 102
Holmes, Joseph (shipbuilder), XXV, 101, 102
Holmes, Josiah, Jr., XXV, 102
Holmes, Josiah and Sons (shipbuilders), XXV, 102
Holmes, Nathaniel, XIII, 121
Holmes, Oliver Wendell, XXV, 63; XXXVII, 128
Holmes, Paraclete, XXV, 101
Holmes, R. C., XVI, 231–232; "Murder at Sea," XVI, 180–188; "Sailors and their clothing," XVII, 195–202; "The Sweet Swan on Salt Water," XI, 209–214
Holmes, Captain Robert P., XXVI, 21 n.
Holmes, Samuel, XLII, 245 ff.
Holmes, Captain William, XXI, 93
Holm-Petersen, F., *Windjammers under the Old Elephant Flag,* reviewed, XXXIX, 302; *Under Sejl i Fjernostlige Farvande* [Under Sail in Far East Waters], reviewed, XXXVI, 299
Holt, Alfred, and Co., XVI, 267
Holt, Captain John, XIX, 57
Holt, Judge, XXV, 67
Holyhead Light, 1835, XXIX, 198, plate XXIV
Holyoke, Edward, XIX, 139–140
Holyoke, Dr. Edward A., XLIX, 36

"Holy Smoke," contributed by Captain Edgar K. Thompson, U.S.N. (ret.), XXIII, 38
Home, schooner *(1861),* VIII, 218
Home, steamship *(1836),* XII, 149
Home, Captain William, XXI, 93
"Home is the Sailor," document contributed by Captain Edgar K. Thompson, U.S.N. (ret.), XXIII, 227
Home is the Sailor: the Sea Life of William Brown, Master Mariner and Penang Pilot, by William Blain, reviewed, I, 186–187
Homely Hippopotamus, scow *(1909),* XXXVIII, 91
Home Ports of Protected British Vessels, Table II, XLVIII, 8
Homer, brig *(1819),* XXIV, 271
Homer, Winslow (artist), XXV, 59
Homer and Homer, XXIII, 136
Homeric, liner *(1931),* XXXVI, 28
Homer Ramsdell, steamship, XVIII, 225
Honan, steamship *(1871),* XVI, 260; XVII, 39; XVIII, 70
Hondius, Jodocus, XVII, 34; XXXVII, 176; L, 284
Honduras, ship *(1863),* XXXI, 84
Honduras, steamship *(1872),* X, 132, 138
Hong Kong, Canton, and Macao Steamboat Co., XVI, 162, 171, 254; XVII, 39, 40, 43, 46, 142; XXXIV, 17 ff., plates 3, 4; XLIX, 24 ff.
Hong Kong, ship *(1858),* XXXIV, 17 ff.
Hong Kong, steamship *(1849),* XVII, 214; XVIII, 70; XXII, 13, 14, 15, 16, 20, 21, 25, 31, 35, 36, 40, 42, 43
Hong Kong, XXX, 294–296
Hong Kong, The Changing Scene, a Record in Art, by Laurence C. S. Tam, reviewed, XLI, 70
Hong Kong and Canton Steam Packet Co., XXII, 13, 16
Hong Que, steamship *(1868),* XVII, 135, 215
Hongsheng, Professor Cai. *See* Cai, Professor Hongsheng.
Honolulu, brig *(1841),* XIV, 44
Honolulu, topsail schooner (1825), X, 268
Honolulu, U.S.S. *(1913),* XXIX, 262
Honolulu, whaling at, XIV, 42–46
Honque, steamship (1868), XVIII, 70
Hood, Ronald Chalmers, III, *Royal Republicans: the French Naval Dynasties Between the World Wars,* reviewed, XLVIII, 131
Hood, Commodore Samuel, XXIII, 182
Hood, Ted, XXX, 80
Hood, William, XXV, 265
Hoogenboom, Ari, and W. Sachs, *The Enterprising Colonials,* reviewed, XXVI, 152
Hooke, Robert, VII, 268
Hooker, William, XXXIV, 210
Hooker, William (engraver), XXV, 46, 49
Hoole, W. Stanley, "Captain Richard H. Gayle of Alabama and the Voyage of the *Rodmond,* 1856," XI, 42–58; editor, "The Log of the Bark *Virginia* Sunk by C.S.S. *Alabama,* 1862," XXXIII, 52–62
Hooper, Calvin Leighton, XXXIX, 20

Hooper, Vice Admiral Edwin B., U.S.N. (ret.), XXXI, 5; XXXIII, 230; XXXIV, 281
Hooper, Edwin Bickford, *United States Naval Power in a Changing World,* reviewed, L, 150
Hooper, Captain R. H., XXI, 105
Hooper, Stephen, XXIX, 204
Hoosier State, steamship *(1921),* X, 141
Hooven, Owens, Rentschler Co., XXII, 182
Hoover, Karl D., "Commander Otto Hersing and the Dardanelles Cruise of S.M. U-21," XXXVI, 33–44
Hope (1802), XXIII, 217; *(1806),* XV, 153–154
Hope, brig (1808), VII, 317
Hope, brigantine *(1790),* XLI, 179; XLV, 104 ff.; *(1804),* XVIII, 133
Hope, schooner, XXI, 93; (1804), XXIV, 39, 59; (1808), VII, 317
Hope, schooner *(1861),* XI, 269, 283; XII, 231
Hope, ship *(1585),* XXXVII, 174
Hope, ship *(1776),* XXXIX, 198
Hope, ship (1791), XXXIII, 167 ff.; *(1792),* V, 89; X, 53; XIII, 213; *(1793),* XVIII, 106, 130
Hope, ship (1799), XV, 82–83; *(1800),* XIX, 133; *(1801),* X, 53; XVII, 66; *(1802),* IV, 98
Hope, ship (1805), II, 282; *(1807),* X, 54; *(1811),* XIV, 209, 210
Hope, ship (1841), XIV, 35, 37, 40, plate 5; XXII, 216; *(1843),* XXVII, 102
Hope, ship (1856), XX, 212
Hope, sloop, XXII, 85, 91, 95; *(1864),* XV, 113, 115, 129
Hope, steamship, XXI, 84, 93, plates VI, XII; (1811), XXIV, 161; XXVII, 19, 20, 24–26
Hope, steamship (1863), III, 136; *(1864),* VIII, 234
Hope, U.S.S. *(1810),* XXX, 292 n.
Hope, U.S privateer *(1782),* XXIX, 211, 223
Hope, Captain, XXXVI, 134 ff.
Hope, Admiral Sir James, XLIII, 105 ff.
Hope, Rear Admiral James, XXVII, 164–173
Hope, Vice Admiral Sir James, XXXIV, 103; XXVIII, 111
Hope, Linton, XX, 64
Hope Furnace Works, XLV, 36 ff.
Hope On, bark *(1883),* XXXIX, 11
Hopewell, British ship *(1776),* XLVIII, 16
Hopewell, flyboat *(1605),* XXXVII, 11
Hopewell, schooner *(1742),* XXVI, 43
Hopewell, ship *(1630),* XXIII, 63, 66
Hopkins, U.S.S. cruiser *(1921),* XLVI, 243 ff.
Hopkins, Christopher, XXX, 94
Hopkins, Major David, XXXVI, 63
Hopkins, Edward A., XXXVI, 180
Hopkins, Edward Augustus, XXXI, 7 ff.
Hopkins, Esek, XXXI, 250; XXXII, 174
Hopkins, Commodore Esek, I, 26, 37–38; V, 177 ff.; XIV, 47 ff.; XXV, 35, 192 ff.; XXX, 220; XLVIII, 157
Hopkins, Fred, "From Warship to School Ship: The History of U.S.S. *Ontario,* America's First Floating

School," XL, 38–45; "The Six *Baltimores,"* XXXIX, 29–44
Hopkins, Fred W., Jr., and Donald G. Shomette, "The Search for the Chesapeake Flotilla," XLIII, 5–19
Hopkins, Garland Evans, *The First Battle of Modern Naval History,* reviewed, VI, 87
Hopkins, Harry, XLII, 213
Hopkins, Captain J. C., XXXIV, 70
Hopkins, Captain James, XXI, 93
Hopkins, Captain John B., Continental Navy, XXV, 193
Hopkins, Vice-Admiral Sir John O., XXVIII, 112
Hopkins, Mark, XXXI, 123
Hopkins, Stephen, VIII, 13, 19; XXV, 194; XLII, 42
Hopkins, Timothy, XXXI, 124
Hopkins, Lieutenant Commander W. E., XXXII, 280
Hopkins, William Rogers, XXII, 287 n.
Hopkinson, Charles, XXIII, 39, plates 1, 2
Hopkinson, Francis, XXV, 64
Hopkinson, Mrs. George, XXXIII, 34
Hopkinson, Colonel H. S., XXXIII, 35
Hopkinson, Captain Joseph, XXI, 94
Hopper, Franklin F., XLI, 8
Hoppin, Captain Benjamin, XL, 196
Hopson, Major General Thomas Peregrine, VI, 291 ff.; VII, 21, 23, 24, 25, 31
Hoquang, steamship (1861), XVI, 174; XVIII, 70
Hora, Captain A., XXI, 94
Horace Luckenbach, steamship (ex-*Eastern Trader*), XXIII, 276
Horatio, bark *(1894),* XXXVIII, 85
Horatio Hall, steamship (1898), XXXIV, Pictorial Supplement, plate XXIII
Horicon, steamship (1877), III, plate 10
Horie, Kenichi, *Koduku: Sailing Alone Across the Pacific,* reviewed, XXX, 69
Horizon, bark (1862), V, 148
Horizontal Wheel, Hunter's, XXIV, 5–24
Hornby, Rear Admiral Sir Phipps, XXVIII, 112
Horne, Lieutenant Commander F. J., XXIII, 274
Hornell, James, *Fishing in Many Waters,* reviewed, XI, 295–296; XII, 306–308; XIII, 81 ff., 185 ff.; *Water Transport Origins and Early Evolution,* reviewed, VIII, 72
Horner, Frank, *The French Reconnaissance: Baudin in Australia, 1801–1803,* reviewed, L, 70
Hornet, brig *(1779),* XXXV, 141; *(1806),* XLIII, 250; XLIV, 171, 245 ff.
Hornet, carrier *(1944),* XXXIX, 43
Hornet, Continental Navy sloop *(1776),* XXV, 193, 198, 200; *(1777),* II, 207
Hornet, cutter sloop *(1805),* XXXIX, plate 9
Hornet, cutter yacht *(1892),* XXXVI, 236 ff.
Hornet, frigate *(1821),* XLVII, 28; L, 60
Hornet, gunboat *(1782),* XXXIX, 217
Hornet, H.M.S., XXII, 36
Hornet, privateer *(1870),* XXXVIII, 237
Hornet, schooner *(1861),* XI, 283
Hornet, schooner yacht (1819), I, 75
Hornet, ship *(1813),* XL, 28
Hornet, ship *(1855),* XXXI, 272; *(1866),* I, 100, 164–165, 185
Hornet, sloop *(1777),* XX, 46; *(1814),* XXIX, 195, 196; *(1820),* XXXII, 275
Hornet, torpedo launch *(1865),* XLII, 92 ff.
Hornet, U.S.S. *(1776),* XIII, 65; (1804), IV, 245–246; *(1813),* VII, 168; XI, 73; *(1814),* XIX, 219, 220
"*Hornet* Journals, The," by Alexander Crosby Brown, I, 164–165
Hornet's Longboat, The, by William Roos, reviewed, I, 85
Hornsburgh, James, *Directions for Sailing to and from the East Indies,* cited, XXV, 178, 183–186
Hornsby, Thomas, queries by, II, 81; III, 353; answered queries, II, 83; V, 246; "*Oregon* and *Peacemaker* — 12 inch Wrought Iron Guns," VI, 212–222, plates 31–32
"Horrid Murder of Captain Samuel Topliff, The," document contributed by Charles Knowles Bolton, IV, 245–246
Horsa, Danish steamship *(1910),* XXXV, 203
Horsa, steamship *(1863),* VIII, 230
Horsburgh, James, XXX, 215
Horse, schooner (1833), XXIII, 94
"Horse Biscuits for the Royal Navy," document contributed by Richard H. Dillon, XIV, 216–217
Horse head from unidentified vessel, Pictorial Supplement, XXXVII, plate XX
"Horseshoe Cove — A Correction," by Andrew Willis, XIII, 67
"Horse Soldiers in the Arctic: The Garlington Expedition of 1883," by Lawrence J. Fischer, XXXVI, 108–124
Horsey, Captain J., XXI, 94
Horsman, Reginald, *The War of 1812,* reviewed, XXIX, 288
Hortense, schooner, XXI, 91; *(1862),* XII, 55, 157
Hortensia, bark (1853), V, 150
Hortensia, schooner, XXIII, plate I
Horton, schooner *(1775),* XXX, 116
Hortwick, Lawrence, XXV, 125–126
Hosack, Dr., XXX, 62–67
Hoskins, Emmett A., "San Francisco to Balboa in the Schooner *Dauntless;* Memories of an A.B.," XII, 142–147
Hosmer, George, XLI, 20
Hospitals, naval and marine, XXXI, 192. *See also* Medicine
Hostages:
    Algiers, XLI, 208
    Morocco, XLI, 208
    See also prisoners
Hotchkiss, Mr., XXX, 62–67
Hotham, Captain Sir Charles, XXXVI, 128, 132–138, 140, 141
Hotham, Sir Henry, XXIX, 190

Hotspur, H.M.S. *(1899)*, XXVIII, 93
Houge, H.M. cruiser, XXXVI, 43
Hough, wooden steamship *(1917)*, XXXV, 279
Houghton, schooner *(1775)*, XXX, 115
Houghton, ship (1849), IV, 51; *(1861)*, XI, 284
Houghton, Alanson B., Ambassador to Great Britain, XXXIV, 162
Houghton Fleet, Bath (ME), IV, 45–52
Houghton Shipyard, XXVII, plate II
Houle, Professor Cyril O., XXXIX, 109
Hound, clipper ship *(1858)*, XXV, 105–106
Houqua, ship *(1833)*, XIV, plate 7
Houqua, ship (1844), VII, 5; XIX, plate XVIII
Houqua (Chinese merchant), XIII, 122; XXV, 156
Hourani, George F., *Arab Seafaring in the Indian Ocean*, reviewed, XI, 292–294
Hourihan, William J., "The Fleet That Never Was: Commodore John Crittenden Watson and the Eastern Squadron," XLI, 93–109
Housatonic, sloop of war (1861), XXXI, 263; XXXIV, 221
Housatonic, steam-sloop *(1864)*, XLVII, 31; XLIX, 121
Housatonic, U.S.S *(1863)*, XLIV, 266 ff.; *(1864)*, XXVII, 43
House, Colonel Edward M., XXXIV, 159; XLI, 275
House, T. W., XXXVI, 203
House Flags, I, 310; III, 205 ff., plate 27
"House Flags," query by C. L. Douglas, I, 310
House of Burgesses, XXX, 134
House of Conseequa, Chinese Merchant, photo of, XLVIII, 235
House of Hancock, The, by W. T. Baxter, reviewed, V, 249
Housman, Jacob, XXXIX, 267
Houston, cruiser *(1932)*, XXXVII, 186
Houston, C. S., XXVIII, 121
Hovey, John, XXXI, 22
Howard, bark (1883), view of stateroom, Pictorial Supplement, XXXI, plate XXIV. See also *Sam Scolfield.*
Howard, ship (1801), Pictorial Supplement, XXXII, plate IX; *(1840)*, XXV, 18 n.
Howard, Alan, XXVII, 155
Howard, Alice, XLI, 7
Howard, Captain C. W., VII, 150, 158, 165
Howard, Lord Admiral Charles, XLIX, 5
Howard, Dr. Frank, *Sailing Ships of War: 1400–1860*, reviewed, XLII, 141–143
Howard, Henry, XLI, 6
Howard, Captain Henry, XXI, 105
Howard, J. L., VII, 290
Howard, John Q., XIX, 55, 64
Howard, Lawrence W., XLI, 132
Howard, Peter, XXXIII, 163
Howard, Roland M., answered query, I, 312–313
Howard, Thomas, XVII, 212–214
Howard, Captain William A., XXIV, 14 ff.

Howard & Co., XLIII, 109 ff.
Howarth, David, XLIV, 25
Howarth, Herbert, XXV, 233
Howay, Frederic W., I, 100, 400; IV, 252; review by, II, 258–259; "First Use of the Sail by the Indians of the Northwest Coast, The," I, 374–380; editor, *The Journal of Captain James Colnett aboard the* Argonaut *from April 26, 1789 to Nov. 3, 1791,* reviewed, I, 97–98; "Some Lengthy Open-boat Voyages in the Pacific Ocean," IV, 53–57; *Voyage of the* Columbia *to the Northwest Coast, 1787–1790 and 1790–1793,* reviewed, II, 253–254
Howay, Judge F. W., XL, 48
Howe, Captain D., XX, 89 n.
Howe, Henry, VII, 177 ff.
Howe, Lord, XXX, 205, 207
Howe, Admiral Sir Richard, XXXIX, 198
Howe, Vice Admiral Richard Lord, XXXVI, 83; XL, 19 ff.
Howe, Thomas, XXX, 201
Howe, Sir William, VII, 87, 91 n., 92 n., 94, 97
Howe, General Sir William, XXXIX, 198
Howell, brig *(1837)*, XXXII, 65
Howell, hermaphrodite brig (1822), IX, 72
Howell, George, XLVIII, 252
Howell, Joshua, XXX, 100 n.
Howell, Susan P., *Practical Celestial Navigation,* reviewed, XL, 151
Howerton, Joseph B., contributed document, XVIII, 320–323
Howes, Captain Allison, XXII, 240
Howes, Captain Anthony, XXII, 238, 248
Howes, Daniel Willis, XXII, 239, 248
Howes, Captain Frederic, XLVII, 133
Howes, Levi, XXII, 236, 240, 244
Howes, Captain Osborn, XV, 221
Howes, Captain Thomas Prince, XXII, 243
Howes, Captain William Frederick, XXII, 240
Howes & Crowell, XV, 220, 221
Howes' Patent Topsail Rig, illustration of, XLVII, 134
Howland, ship (1845), XLV, 180
Howland, Abraham, XXXIX, 84
Howland, Captain Arthur, XIV, 30, 31
Howland, Captain, XXVII, 82, 95, 96
Howland, H. J., XXI, 94
Howland, J. H., and Co., XXXIX, 90
Howland, Llewellyn, contributed document, X, 231–234; "The Battle of Priest's Cove," X, 243–248; *The Middle Road,* reviewed, XXI, 291; "Neponset Estuary – 1898," XI, 83–94; "'Thar She Blows,'" XIII, 131–133
Howland, Weston, XXXIX, 10
Howland, Mrs. Weston, document by, XXVIII, 284–286
Howland and Aspinwall, XLVII, 43
Howland & Nelson, Beaumont, Texas, XXXII, 32
"How Many Ropes are There on a Ship?" document contributed by L. Francis Herreshoff, XXXII, 67–68

"How My Grandfather Nearly Lost the Civil War," by Porter R. Chandler, XXXIII, 5–15
Howquah, steamship (1863), XVIII, 70
Howse, Derek and Beresford Hutchinson, *The Clocks and Watches of Captain James Cook, 1769–1969,* reviewed, XXXI, 74–75
How To Make Ship Block Models, by Charles G. Davis, reviewed, VII, 172
"How to Tack a Schooner Single-Handed," by Fred Hunt, XV, 152–153
Hoyle, Charles, XXIX, 269
Hoyt, Edwin P., XXXVI, 266; *Submarines at War: The History of the American Silent Service,* reviewed, XLIV, 132
Hoyt, Frederick M., XXX, 195
Hoyt, William D., "Inventory of the Schooner *Friendship,* 1776," XI, 224; contributed document, XII, 60–63
Hoyt, Dr. William D., Sr., XLV, 83
Hoyt, William D., Jr., I, 316; V, 91, 165; VI, 155; contributed documents, I, 301–303; V, 83–84; VI, 302–304; "Articles of Agreement for the Galley *Conqueror,* 1779," VI, 101–107; "Letters Taken in Prizes," 1778–1780," V, 111–114
Hruby, Dr. Thomas, mention, XLIX, 38
Hsin-fou, auxiliary schooner (1918–1919), V, 141
Hsin-liang, auxiliary schooner (1918–1919), V, 141
Hsin-pao, auxiliary schooner (1918–1919), V, 141
Hsu Chi-yu, Chinese Governor, XLVI, 41
Hsü Nai-chao, XXX, 165
Huascar, Peruvian ironclad (1865), XXXIX, 274
Huasteca Petroleum Co., XLVII, 47
Hubbard, J. T. W., "'...En Otros Tiempos...' Did the Men of Bristol Discover Newfoundland in 1481?" XXXVII, 157–163; "John Cabot's Landfall: Cape Dégrat or Cape Bonavista? Some Observations," XXXIII, 174–177
Hubbard & Co., XXIII, 137
Hubbell, Henry W., XVII, 43, 47, 55; XVIII, 60
Hubbell, William S., XVII, 100
Hubble, Samuel, XLIX, 88
Hudgins, Captain Robert K., XL, 301; XLVIII, 87
Hudson, brig (1831), XXIII, 47 ff.
Hudson, grain elevator (1950), XXXVIII, 140
Hudson, ship (1855), XXIV, 142
Hudson, U.S.S., XXIII, 58 n.
Hudson, whaler, XXV, 105
Hudson, Alec, *Enemy Sighted,* reviewed, I, 410
Hudson, Captain Charles, R.N., VII, 98
Hudson, Dr. Daniel, XL, 36
Hudson, Henry, XXV, 239; XXVIII, 241
Hudson, Captain J. S., XXI, 94
Hudson, Lieutenant William L., XXX, 298
Hudson Bay Co. *see* Hudson's Bay Co.
Hudson River. *See* Steamboats, Steam navigation
Hudson River Day Line, XIV, 185, 186; XVIII, 223–234

Hudson River Day Line: The Story of a Great American Steamboat Company, by Donald C. Ringwald, reviewed, XXVI, 74
Hudson River Line, XXX, 72
Hudson River Sloop, XXIX, 4, 153
Hudson River Sloop Restoration, Inc., XXIX, 4, 154
"Hudson River Steamboat *Thomas Cornell,* 1863–1882, The," by Donald C. Ringwald, VI, 277–289, plates 33–34
Hudson River Steamboats, XXIV, 157 ff.
Hudson's Bay Co., XXXII, 153; XXVIII, 128, 132, 134, 136, 139; XXX, 79
Hueneme, schooner (1877), V, 86–87
Huff, Captain James, XXI, 69
Huffnung, cartel (1813), XXVIII, 177
Huggins, W. J., XXIV, plate XXIX
Huggins, William J., XXX, 219
Hughes, Captain Charles F., XL, 53 ff.
Hughes, Henry, & Son, XIII, 66–67
Hughes, J., XXVII, plates IV, XI; XXVIII, plate II
Hughes, Lieutenant Commander James J., L, 260 ff.
Hughes, Sir Richard, Lieutenant-governor, XLII, 18
Hughes, Lieutenant Commander Robert, XXXVIII, 273 ff.
Hughes, Ronald L., "Sierra," XXV, 288–294
Hughes, Samuel, XXXVI, 279; XXXIX, 30
Hugh Lindsay, steamship (1829), XL, 289
Hugh McDougal and Co., XXXIV, 34
Hugo, E. Harold, XXVIII, 238
Hugo, Harold, XXI, 3
Hulen, Captain Samuel, XXI, 94
Hull, Cordell, Secretary of State, XXXII, 104 ff.; XXXV, 135; XLI, 269; XLII, 39
Hull, Isaac, XXX, 74; XXXVII, 131; XXXVIII, 67
Hull, Captain Isaac, XLII, 105, 284 ff.; XLIII, 313–314
Hull, Commodore Isaac, U.S.N., VII, 167; XXI, 133, 135; XXII, 156; XXV, 29 ff.; XXXI, 139; XXXIII, 238; XXXIV, 190 ff.
Hull, Lieutenant Isaac, XLVI, 162; XLVII, 14 ff.
"Hull's First Victory—One Painting: Three Famous Men," by John Paul Russo, XXV, 29–34
Hulsart, Cornelius B., XXX, 218
Hulton, Henry, XXXI, 193
Humane Society Bronze Medal, XXXVII, plate 4, 92–93
Human Torpedoes, XXVII, 185–201
"Humbled in the Dust," by Captain Edgar K. Thompson, U.S.N. (ret.), XXVIII, 69
Humboldt, steam packet (1840), XLVIII, 114
Hume, schooner (1861), VIII, 218
Hummel, Arthur W., Jr., XLVI, 26
Humor, II, 79. *See also under* names of individual topics, e.g., Sailors, Humor
Humphrey, Lieutenant Colonel Charles F., XL, 174 ff.
Humphrey, James, XL, 37
Humphrey, William F., XXXV, 286
Humphreys, David, XXVI, 241, 243; XLI, 209; XLVI, 218

Humphreys, Joshua, I, 295–296; VII, 255–256; VIII, 14–17, 21–22; IX, 75, 161 ff.; X, 65–71; XXXV, 240; XXXVIII, 17; XXXIX, 159, 239 ff.; XLIX, 46
Humphreys, R. A., L, 26
Humphreys, Samuel, I, 80–81; III, 174–176; IX, 162 ff.; X, 70; XXXIV, 192 ff.; XXXV, 237
Humphreys & Tennant, XXVI, 207
Hunchback, gunboat *(1865),* XLII, 96 ff.
"Hundred Years of the Pacific Mail, A," by John Haskell Kemble, X, 123–143, plates 17–20
Hundred Years' War (1339–1453), Naval operations, XLVI, 84
Hunnewell, James, X, 265 ff.
Hunnewell and Co., XIII, 121
Hunt, Cecil, *The Gallant Little* Campeador, reviewed, II, 342–343
Hunt, Davis, XXVII, 16
Hunt, Captain Davis, XXXII, 217
Hunt, Fred, II, 252; III, 89; "Campeche Days," II, 229–242; referred to, II, 339
Hunt, Fred C., "How to Tack a Schooner Single-Handed," XV, 152–153
Hunt, Harvey W., XLVI, 262
Hunt, Henry, XXXVI, 177
Hunt, Hiram, XXIV, 58
Hunt, Lee M., and Donald G. Groves, *The Ocean World Encyclopedia,* reviewed, XL, 146
Hunt, Rear Admiral Livingston, XLII, 61
Hunt, Thomas F., & Co., XVI, 162 ff., 254; XVII, 46, 47, 144, 145
Hunt, Commander Timothy A., XXXIII, 45
Hunt, Commander William E., XXXIII, 42
Hunt, William H., XXII, 260
Hunt, William H., Secretary of the Navy, XXXIII, 262 ff.; XXXIX, 126
Hunt & Co., XXX, 296
Hunter, bark (ex-ship) (1851), Pictorial Supplement, XXXIII, plate XII
Hunter, schooner, XXI, 87, 92; *(1863),* VII, 19; XII, 157
Hunter, ship *(1778),* VII, 209–210; *(1810),* X, 54; *(1812),* XIII, 280
Hunter, steamship (1844), 8 ff.
Hunter, Alvah F., *A Year on a Monitor and the Destruction of Fort Sumter,* reviewed, XLIX, 311
Hunter, Lieutenant Charles G., XXXIX, 222
Hunter, Ensign James, XLVIII, 102
Hunter, Captain Joseph W., XLIV, 255
Hunter, Captain R. L., XXV, 260
Hunter, Lieutenant T. T., U.S.N., IV, 313
Hunter, W., XI, 155–156
Hunter, W. C., XVI, 160; XXII, 8, 30
Hunter, Wilbur Harvey, Jr., *Baltimore in World Trade, 1729–1947,* reviewed, IX, 78
Hunter, William C., XLVI, 36
Hunter, Commander William W., XLVIII, 92
Hunter, Lieutenant William W., U.S.N., XVII, 90–91; XXIV, 5–24, plate 1

Hunter Navigation Corp. of New York, XXXII, 25
Hunter's Horizontal Wheel, The Great Experiment, by Clark G. Reynolds, XXIV, 5–24
Hunter's River Steam Navigation Co., XXXIV, 19
Huntington, Benjamin, XXXI, 239; XXXIX, 194
Huntington, Collis Potter, XXV, 265–267
Huntington, Gale, editor, *Tom Tilton, Coaster and Fisherman,* reviewed, XLV, 135
Huntington, Hezekiah, XXXI, 133
Huntington, Jedediah, XXXVI, 56
Huntington, Joshua, XXXI, 134
Huntington, Samuel, XLII, 302
Huntington, W. V., XXXI, 124
Huntress, schooner *(1850),* XXIV, 45, 59
Huntress, steamship (1838), XIV, 192; *(1840),* XXVIII, 124; *(1863),* VIII, 230
Huntress, Keith, *A Checklist of Narratives of Shipwrecks and Disasters at Sea to 1860,* reviewed, XLIII, 142–143
Huntsville (1861), XV, 103 n.
Hupeh, steamship (1869), XVI, 260; XVII, 39; XVIII, 70
Huquang (1862), XXXIV, 32 ff.
Huquang, steamship *(1862),* XLIX, 23; *(1863),* XVI, 245, 248; XVIII, 70; *(1866),* XLIII, 117 ff.
Hurault, schooner *(1755),* XLIX, 264 ff.
Hurd, Abel, XXXV, 83
Hurd, Captain Jesse, XXXI, 141
Hurd, Captain Thomas, XXX, 213, 215
Hurlbut, Stephen A., XXXVIII, 246
Hurleston, Captain Nicholas, XXIII, 66
Hurley, E. N., XXII, 159
Hurley, Edward, XLI, 193
Hurley, Edward N., XXXII, 160, 169; XXXV, 278 ff.
Hurley Machine Co., XXXII, 160
Huron, bark *(1854),* XX, 183
Huron, ship *(1854),* XIV, 254, 255
Huron, steamship *(1839),* XVIII, 299; XX, 252, 256, 260, 264, 267
Huron, steamship (1852), I, 76; *(1896),* IX, 220–221
Huron, U.S. flagship *(1922),* XLIV, 180 ff.
Huron, whaler, XXV, 105
Hurricane, ketch yacht *(1940),* I, 189
Hurricane, ship (1851), XIX, plate III
Hurricanes, VI, 132
Hurricane's Wake, by Ray Kauffman, reviewed, I, 189
Hurst, Alex A. and Duncan Haws, *The Maritime History of the World,* reviewed, XLVII, 283
Hurt, R. Douglas, "The Settlement of Anglo-American Claims Resulting from World War I," XXXIV, 155–173
Hurtarte, Castillo, XXXVI, 22
Hurtarte, Mercedes, XXXVI, 22
Hussar, Revenue wherry, XXVIII, 196
Hussey, Captain Daniel, XXIII, 27
Hussey, George, XXXIX, 88
Hussey, Captain Nicholas, XXI, 9
Huston, Caleb, XV, 178 ff.

Hustwich, F., XXVII, plate III
Hutchings, John G. B., *The American Maritime Industries and Public Policy, 1789–1914*, reviewed, II, 260–261
Hutchins, Captain Thomas, I, 143
Hutchinson, Beresford and Derek Howse, *The Clocks and Watches of Captain James Cook, 1769–1969*, reviewed, XXXI, 74–75
Hutchinson, Captain Daniel H., XLVII, 121
Hutchinson, G. Evelyn, query by, VI, 233
Hutchinson, Israel, IV, 207 ff.
Hutchinson, Captain John, XXXVIII, 251
Hutchinson, Lieutenant Governor, XL, 271
Hutchinson, Captain Robert W., XVII, 140, 220; XVIII, 83
Hutchinson, Thomas, XL, 255
Hutoka, schooner *(1855)*, XXIV, 142
Hutton, James, III, 239 ff.
Hutton, Captain James S., XLI, 298
Huy, 1612, photo of, L, 175
Huycke, Harold, "Additional Notes on *Star of Lapland*, ex *Atlas*," XVII, 65; "Case-oil and Canned Salmon: *Star of Lapland*, ex *Atlas*," XVI, 2–27, 107–135, plates 1–8, 11–12; "From River Clyde to Unimak Pass: Ship *Star of Falkland*," XVIII, 5–24, 149–176, 201–222, plates 1–4
Huycke, Harold D., IV, 252; XV, 171; note by, XLIII, 300–301; query by, VII, 319; "The American Four-Mast Bark *Star of Poland*, ex-*Acme*," VIII, 279–288, plates 25–26; "Colonial Trader to Museum Ship: The Bark *Star of India*," X, 108–122; "Emigrant Ship to Copra Hulk: the Iron Bark *Bougainville*," VII, 114–126, plates 9–12; "The *Scottish Lady*," VII, 288–297, plates 33–36; "The Ship *Pacific Queen*," IV, 199–206; *To Santa Rosalia — Further and Back*, reviewed, XXXII, 142–143; "Voyages of *Star of Poland*," XIV, 210
Huzzar, British frigate *(1812)*, XLVI, 169
Hwaiyuen, steamship (1863), XVI, 254; XVII, 38
HX 224, Allied North Atlantic convoy, XLIV, 48 ff.
Hyades, schooner (1839), XXIV, 45, 59
Hyatt, Alpheus, XLV, 82
Hy Brasil, XXXVII, 157 ff.
Hydaspe, steamship *(1863)*, XLIII, 218
Hyde, E. C., XXXIX, 218
Hyder Alley, ship *(1833)*, XXXVIII, 268
Hyde Windlass Co. of Bath, XLVII, 132
Hydra, ship *(1785)*, XLVI, 9 ff.
Hydrographers, Biography, XXX, 200; XLIII, 51
Hydrographic Office, XXX, 206, 207, 210, 212–215
Hydrographic Office, U.S. Naval, XXV, 69
Hydrographic Office of the Admiralty, XXX, 210 f.
Hydrography, History, XXX, 200
Hyperion, bark *(1794)*, L, 103
Hyson, steamship *(1861)*, XVI, 172, 261; *(1862)*, XLIII, 123 ff.
Hythe, ship, XIV, 102

I

I. D. Coleman, steamship (1862), VI, 62
I. I. Borger Kiøbenhavn, Pictorial Supplement, XXXV, plate XIII
I. J. Merritt, wrecking steamship *(1897)*, XLII, 269 ff.
I. J. Merritt, Jr., schooner (1886), XXVI, plate VIII
I. L. Skolfield, ship (1879), IV, 239; VI, 76
Ibargoitia, Lieutenant Don Juan, XXXIV, 252
"I Build Men as Well as Ships," by H. Birchard Taylor, reviewed, I, 189
Iceacle, H.M.S. *(1814)*, XXI, 53
Icebound: The Jeanette *Expedition's Quest for the North Pole*, by Leonard F. Guttridge, reviewed, XLIX, 305
Ice Carrying Trade at Sea, edited by D. V. Proctor, reviewed, XLIV, 207
Iceland, ship (1877), XLVI, 63
Ice trade, XV, 249
Ice Trade, XIX, 40 ff.
Ida, schooner *(1861)*, VIII, 218; *(1863)*, XII, 157
Ida, ship *(1817)*, XLVI, 44
Ida, ship (1835), V, 149; *(1861)*, XV, 179
Ida, steamship, XVIII, 225; XXI, 99; *(1864)*, XV, 115, 129; *(1865)*, XXV, 67
Ida and Emma, ship (1875), VI, 83
Ida Della Torre, schooner *(1861)*, VIII, 218
Idaho, U.S.S. *(1864)*, XXVII, 43; *(1870)*, XLIII, 178; photo of, XLV, 239
Ida Lilly (1875), XXVII, 52
Ida M. Clark, Canadian schooner *(1902)*, XLIX, 280
Ida M. Clark, schooner, XXVIII, 288
Ida May, steamship (1897), VI, 228
Ida S. Dow, schooner *(1919)*, XXIII, plate XIX
Ida Schnauer, schooner (1875), V, 86
Idiona, brig *(1813)*, XIX, 217
Idlewild, schooner (1873), XXIV, 45, 59
Ile de France, steamship, XXXVII, 75
Illawarra, iron screw steamship (1853), XXXIV, 32; XLIII, 204 ff.
Illawarra Steam Navigation Co., XLIII, 204
Illinois, battleship *(1897)*, XXXVIII, 130
Illinois, steamship (1837), VI, 64; VIII, 46; (1838), XVIII, 282, 285–287, 291, 292, 298; XX, 89 n., 92, 101, 253, 254, 258; (1851), IV, 307, 310; *(1856)*, XI, 45 ff.
Illinois, U.S. battleship (1901), XXII, 211
"Ill-Timed Initiative: The Ship Purchase Bill Of 1915," by Lawrence C. Allin, XXXIII, 178–198
Illustrated London News, The, XXXII, plate 8
Illustration of schooners from Falconer's dictionary, XLIX, 199 ff.
Illustration of steam engines of *Tennessee* and *Cherokee*, XLVII, 38

Illustrious, H.M.S. *(1789),* XXII, 54; *(1807),* IX, 12–13
Illustrious, ship, XXI, 97; *(1861),* XI, 284
Illustrious President, ship (1798?), IX, 162, plate 18
Iltis, S.M.S. gunboat *(1906),* XL, 89
"Imaginary Mutiny on *Sabine,* The," document contributed by Charles J. Zibulka, XXV, 68
Imago Mundi, a Review of Early Cartogaphy, Vol. XVIII, reviewed, XXVII, 71–72; Vol. XX, reviewed, XXIX, 73–74
Imaum, bark (1850), Pictorial Supplement, XXXVIII, plate XVII
Imbrim, schooner (1847), XXIV, 59
Immigration, westward movement, VI, 58
Immore, Captain John, XXI, 94
Imogene, steamship, XXI, 86; *(1865),* XII, 234
Imp, yacht *(1896),* XXXVI, 239, 242
"Impact of French Privateering on New England, 1689–1713, The," by Donald F. Chard, XXXV, 153–165
Imperador, steamship (1854), XXVI, 192–194, 205, 209; XXIX, 234
Imperatriz, steamship (1854), XXVI, 192–194, 205, 209
Imperial, ship (1857), V, 147
Imperial Chinese Army, XXX, 155–166
"Imperial Defense of the Pacific Ocean in the Mid-Nineteenth Century: Ships and Bases, The," by John Bach, XXXII, 233–246
Imperial Hamilton, steamship (ex-*Sarnia*), XXVII, 156
Impey, Commander R. E., XXIII, 69
Importer, ship (1870), III, 71
Importing and Exporting Co. of South Carolina, IX, 36–40
Impressment, XXIII, 174
Imray, Laurie, Norie and Wilson, Ltd. (of St. Ives, Huntingdonshire), XXXIV, 202
Inaccessible Islands, XXV, 181
Inca, schooner (1896), V, 137
"*Inchcliffe Castle,* Melbourne for Los Angeles," by Jerry MacMullen, XX, 270–271
Inches, Henderson, XL, 267
"Incidental Intelligence—Harborside Semantics Division," document contributed by Alexander Crosby Brown, XXIV, 137
Incident on the bark Columbia, *being Letters Received & Sent by Captain McCorkle and the Crew of his Whalers, 1860–1862,* edited by Helen Halsey, I, 406–407
In Commemoration (Matsonews), reviewed, IV, 256
Indefatigable, H.M.S. *(1897),* XXVIII, 89, 93, 96–98, 105; *(1907),* XXIX, 129
Independance/Independence, sloop *(1777),* XLIII, 24, 44
Independence (1855), II, 331
Independence, privateer *(1776),* XXII, 268
Independence, receiving ship *(1861),* XXXIII, 47
Independence, schooner, XXI, 90, 102; *(1804),* XVII, 68; *(1804),* X, 54; *(1861),* XI, 284; XII, 55, 229

Independence, ship, XXI, 103; *(1809),* II, 283; *(1821),* IV, 99; *(1822),* XVII, 66; *(1830),* XXXVIII, 65 ff.; (1861), XI, 284
Independence, sloop *(1779),* XXXV, 141
Independence, steamship (1843), XVII, 101; XX, 261, 268; (1850), XIV, 192 ff.; *(1853),* XVI, 211
Independence, U.S. Razee (1814), XXI, 143; XXII, 186; XXIII, 55, 58; XXV, 159, 163, 217
Independence, U.S.S. (1837), XIX, 246; XX, 137 n.; *(1854),* XXVII, 161
Independence, U.S. warship (1814), XXIX, 197; *(1817),* XIII, 271; *(1820),* XXXI, 287; XLVI, 218; XLIX, 42
Independencia, Peruvian ironclad (1865), XXXIX, 274
Index, steamship, XXI, 93, 97; *(1864),* VIII, 234
India, ship *(1801),* XXIII, 217; *(1813),* XXXIX, 142 ff.
India, ship (1833), IV, 73; *(1861),* XXI, 258
India:
  Foreign relations
  —, **Gt. Britain,** XLVI, 18
  —, **United States,** XXXI, 38; XLVI, 18
  History
  —, **Mysore War (1790–1792),** XLVI, 18
  —, **Naval,** XL, 280
  See also Shipping, etc.
India, boats of, XIII, 85 ff.
India House, XXX, 208
India House, New York City, I, 196
Indian, H.M.S., XXVIII, 118
Indian, schooner *(1864),* VIII, 234; XII, 231
Indian, steamship *(1902),* XXIV, 52
Indiana, battleship *(1888),* XXXVIII, 27, 191 ff.; *(1898),* XLI, 103
Indiana, ship *(1855),* XXXVII, 169; *(1910),* XVI, 122; XVIII, 213
Indiana, steamship (1841), XX, 88, 253
Indiana, steamship (1873), XXIV, plate XII; *(1908),* X, 140
Indiana, U.S.S., XXVIII, 105; XXIX, 125
Indianapolis, U.S. Heavy Cruiser *(1936),* XXV, 68–69
Indian Chief, Confederate ship *(1861),* XLIV, 262
Indian Chief, ship (1877), figurehead of, Pictorial Supplement, XXXVII, plate VI
Indian-Chief, square-rigger *(1881),* XXXIV, 9
Indian Lands, purchase of by U.S. Federal Government, VI, 51
Indian Ocean. *See* British Indian Ocean Territory; Deslation Island; Heard Island; Kerguelen Island; Sealing; Shipping (Indian Ocean)
Indian Ocean, XXX, 207 ff.
Indian Princess figurehead, Pictorial Supplement, XXXVII, plate V
Indian River, steamship *(1884),* VI, 154
Indians of North America:
  Boats, VIII, 91; IX, 185; XXVIII, 53
  —, **Maine,** VIII, 289
  —, **Northwest Coast,** I, 374

Indians of South America:
   Boats:
     —, **Andes Region**, II, 107
     —, **Ecuador**, XV, 142
India Wharf Co., XIII, 120
Indo-China Steam Navigation Co., XVII, 40
Indomitable, carrier *(1941),* XLII, 203
Indonesia, boats of, XIII, 84 ff.
Indore, steamship (1862), XVII, 53; XXVI, 112 n.
Indra, auxiliary schooner (1900), XXX, plate XXVIII
Indra, ship *(1917),* XVIII, 162, 165, 210
Indrakuala, steamship *(1913),* XXXVIII, 188
Indus, bark *(1861),* VIII, 218
Indus, brig *(1824),* XXV, 183
Indus, ship (1815), XXXIII, 170
Industria, bark *(1861),* XI, 284
Industrie, French ship *(1800),* XXXI, 175
"Industries Allied to Shipbuilding in Newburyport," by Robert K. Cheney, XVII, 114–127, plates 9–12
Industrious Bee, brigantine (1777), X, 280 ff.
Industrious Bee, rig unknown (1764), X, 230
Industrious Union, British ship (1776), XLVIII, 19
Industry (1801), XXIII, 217
Industry, brigantine *(1802),* XVIII, 133
Industry, British ship *(1776),* XLIV, 158 ff.; XLVIII, 16
Industry, privateer, XXII, 92
Industry, schooner, XXVIII, 114; *(1775),* XXX, 109; *(1778),* XXXIX, 212
Industry, ship (1858), III, 69
Industry, sloop *(1748),* XX, 67; *(1787),* XLIX, 88; *(1808)* X, 149
Industry, victualer, XXII, 108
Inez, schooner *(1863),* XV, 127
"Infamous *Ningpo,* The," by Don H. Kennedy, XXIX, 262–274
Inflexible, H.M. warship *(1914),* XXXIII, 34 ff.
"Influence of Maritime Trade in Early American Development: 1750–1830," by J. Wade Caruthers, XXIX, 199–210
Ingall, Elisabeth, mention, XLIX, 226 ff.
Ingalls, Sarah P., review by, XXXIX, 303; XL, 146; XLIV, 278
Ingeneiro, armed tug *(1909),* XLIX, 284
Ingersoll, Charles Jared, XLVIII, 249
Ingersoll, H., XXVIII, 60–62
Ingersoll, Captain Jonathan, XLVI, 9 ff.
Ingham, U.S.C.G.C. *(1943),* XLIV, 52
Inglefield, Vice Admiral Sir Edward A., XXVIII, 112
Inglefield, Vice Admiral Sir F. S., XXXV, 43
Inglefield, Rear Admiral Frederick S., XXVIII, 103, 104, 112
Inglefield, Rear Admiral Samuel Hood, XXXVI, 128, 129, 133, 136, 137, 140, 141
Inglis, Captain A. C., XVIII, 15 ff.
Ingomar (1863), XII, 157
Ingraham, Captain, XIII, 213
Ingraham, Captain Duncan N., XLIV, 258
Ingraham, Joseph, XV, 206; XXXIII, 167
Ingram, U.S. revenue cutter *(1831),* VI, 18
Ingram, David, XI, 103
Inkster, Tom H., "Last Days of Sail on the North Pacific or Bound for Bering Sea," XXXIX, 184–189; "McDougall's Whalebacks," XXV, 168–175, plates 15, 16; "Orkney Marine Disasters Changed the Course of History," L, 127–131; "Voyage to Canada's Arctic Islands," L, 35–41
Inland Lloyd's, XXX, 25, 35
Inland Seas: Quarterly Bulletin of Great Lakes Historical Society, reviewed, V, 171–172
Inman, Henry, VII, 179 n., painting by, VII, plate 21
Inman Line, XXXVII, 233 ff.; ship of, Pictorial Supplement, XXXIV, plate X
Innes, James, Jr., VI, 269
Ino, schooner *(1888),* XXXIX, 8
Ino, sloop *(1808),* XVI, 202
Ino, U.S.S. *(1862),* XXVII, 36 n.
Ino-ooye (Japanese prince), XXVII, 164
"Inquiry into H. I. Chapelle's Research in Naval History, An," by W. M. P. Dunne, XLIX, 39–55
"Inquiry into the Conduct of Joshua Blake, An," by Linda and Christopher McKee, XXI, 130–141
"Inquiry into the Troop Strength of King Harald Hardrada's Invasion Fleet of 1066, An," by Miles W. Campbell, XLIV, 96–102
"In Search of Phebe," by Christopher Legge, XXV, 274–277, plates 29, 30
"In-Service Naval Officer Education in the Nineteenth Century: Voluntary Commitment to Reform," by Wm. Ray Heitzmann, XXXIX, 109–125
Inshore Craft of Britain: In the Days of Sail and Oar, by Edgar J. March, reviewed, XXXII, 139–140
Inshore Craft of Norway, by Bernhard and Øystein Færøyvik, reviewed, XLII, 308–309
"Inspection Comments on American Ships and Barks," by Robert Greenhalgh Albion, I, 42–50
Instrucion Nauthica, by Diego Garcia de Palacio [reprint], reviewed, VIII, 261
"*Instruction Nauthica* of 1587, The," reviewed by Vernon D. Tate, I, 191–195
"Instructions to Captain John Green, Commander of the *Empress of China,* for the First Voyage to China of a Ship Carrying the American Flag," document contributed by William Bell Clark, XIV, 298–299
Instruments (Nautical). See Nautical instruments; See also names of individual instruments
Instruments, early American scientific, XXV, 71–72
Instruments Nauticos En El Museo Naval, by Salvador G. Franco, reviewed, XX, 225
Instruments of Navigation, by H. O. Hill and E. W. Paget-Tomlinson, book reviewed by Marion V. Brewington, XIX, 146–147
"Insular Campaign of 1759: Guadeloupe, The," by Marshall Smelser, VII, 21–34, plate 3

"Insular Campaign of 1759: Martinique, The," by Marshall Smelser, VI, 290–300, plates 35–36
Insurance, marine, I, 42
Insurance Co. of North America, IV, 176–177
Insurgente, French frigate, XXXVI, 277; *(1798),* XXVII, 140, 142, 143; *(1799),* XXXI, 173; *(1800),* L, 245 ff.
Integridad, steamship *(1853),* XXX, 274
"Intelligence Reports of British Agents in the Long Island Sound Area, 1814–1815," by Richard K. Murdoch, XXIX, 187–198
Intemperance, allegorical ship wrecked on "Alcohol Rocks," XXV, plate V
Intended, brig *(1862),* VIII, 225
Intercoastal Lumber Co., XXX, 187
"Interior of a Midshipman's 'Birth,'" XXXI, Pictorial Supplement, plate V
"Interior of a Packet," Pictorial Supplement, XXXI, plate XVII
"Interior of the Saloon of a Sailing Packet Ship," Pictorial Supplement, XXXI, plate XXI
International, grain elevator *(1901),* XXXVIII, 134 ff.
International Board of Grain Measurers and Elevating Association, XXXVIII, 132 ff.
International Commission for Maritime History, XXXIII, 229
International Council on Archives, XXVI, 3–4
International Journal of Nautical Archaeology and Underwater Exploration, The, by Joan Du Plat Taylor, Editor, reviewed, XXXII, 293
International lifeboat racing team, illustration of, XLVII, 51
"International Line: A History of the Boston-Saint John Steamship Service, The," by Arthur L. Johnson, XXXIII, 79–94
International Mercantile Marine Co., XXIX, 231
International Migration Society, The, XXXV, 203
International Radio-Medical Centre, XXVI, 230
International Register of Historic Ships, by Norman J. Brouwer, reviewed, XLVII, 216
International relief, XIII, 252; XXIX, 118
International Steamship Co., XXVIII, 124; XXXIII, 84 ff.; XXXIV, 176; ship of, Pictorial Supplement, XXXIV, plate XVI; XXXVII, 235
International Trading Corp., Seattle, XXV, 293
Interstate Commerce Act of 1887, XXXI, 126
"In the Midst of a Great Excitement: The Argosy of the Revenue Cutter *C. W. Lawrence,*" by James P. Delgado, XLV, 119–131
"In the Twilight of Auxiliary Steam," by Jean Haviland, XXXII, 5–33
In the Wake of the Raiders and The Merchant Navy Fights, by A. D. Divine, reviewed, I, 101
Intimate Virginiana, edited by Anne Fontaine Maury, reviewed, II, 349
"Into the Ocean World," by William M. Fowler, Jr. and Jay R. Kaufman, XLIV, 110–113
Intrepid (1804), XXXVII, 131

Intrepid, barkentine-yacht (1930), XXXIII, 63
Intrepid, H.M.S. *(1897),* XXVIII, 89, 92, 105 n.
Intrepid, schooner yawl (1889), XXX, 196
Intrepid, ship, XXIX, 65–66; (1864), II, 334
Intrepid, U.S.S. (1903), XX, 143
Intrepid, yacht *(1906),* XXXVI, 242, 245
Intrepida, Venezuelan schooner *(1848),* XXX, 266
"Introduction to Fresh Perspectives on Qing Dynasty Maritime Relations," by Jonathan Goldstein, XLVIII, 221–224
"In Troubled Waters: The Elusive Schooner *Hannah,*" by Philip C. F. Smith and Russell W. Knight, XXX, 86–116
Invasion of England, 18th century plan for, IV, 193–198
Inveijado (ex-*Squirrel*), steamship *(1858),* XXXIV, 19; *(1862),* XLIII, 206 ff.
"Invented Too Late: The Introduction of Steam to the Arctic Whaling Fleet," by Robert Lloyd Webb, XLIV, 11–21
"Invention by Captain John Reynolds, An," by Neil R. Stout, XXII, 277–279
Inventory of Continental Frigate *Raleigh,* XXVI, 63–71
"Inventory of Sloop Tender *Edward,*" document contributed by William Bell Clark, VI, 301–302
Inventory of the Logbooks and Journals in the G. W. Blunt White Library, by Charles R. Schultz, reviewed, XXVI, 149–150
"Inventory of the Schooner *Friendship,* 1776," by William D. Hoyt, XI, 224
Inverarity, Robert Bruce, XXIV, 231–232; "The Adirondack Museum Boat Building," XXVI, plates 3–8
Invercoe, British ship *(1915),* XLV, 201
Inverland, bark *(1861),* XI, 284
"Investigating the Penobscot Fleet," note by Dean R. Mayhew, XXXV, 141
Investigator, schooner (1863), XIX, 57
Investigator, ship (1850), XXIX, 65
"Investment by Sea: The Civil War Blockade," by Robert Erwin Johnson, XXXII, 45–57
Invincible, French warship, XXII, 114
Invincible, H.M.S. *(1873),* L, 33; *(1904),* XXVIII, 101; *(1914),* XXXIII, 35 ff.
In With the Sea, by Gershom Bradford, reviewed, XXII, 291
In Yankee Windjammers, by Charles Nordhoff, reviewed, II, 92
Iola, yacht *(1908),* XXXVI, 245
Iona (I), steamship *(1862),* III, 138–139
Iona (II), steamship *(1863),* III, 138–139; *(1864),* XXI, plates IX, XIX
Ione, brigantine (1694), XIII, 139–140
Ionian, ship (1850), II, 246
Ionic, steamship *(1929),* XXIV, 206
Io Siera, schooner, XXI, 103; *(1861),* XI, 284; XII, 55
Iowa, battleship *(1896),* XXXVIII, 130; *(1898),* XLI, 97
Iowa, Spanish warship, XXIX, 74

Iphigenia, H.M.S., XXVIII, 105 n.
Iphigenia Nubiana (1788), XV, 206, 212
Ira, steamship *(1864),* XV, 113
Ireland, steamship (1856), XXVI, 131, 205, 209
Ireland. *See* Archaeology
Ireland, Captain David, XXI, 94
Ireland, John De Courcy, *Ireland's Sea Fisheries: A History,* reviewed, XLIX, 310
Ireland, Merritte W., XXXIV, 265
Irene, brig of war (1806), XXX, 301 f.
Irene, schooner, XXI, 102; *(1862),* VIII, 225
Irene, yacht *(1895),* XXXVI, 238
Irene and Jessie, schooner (1864), XV, 112, 129
Iris, brig *(1853),* XXX, 273
Iris, British ship *(1777),* XL, 20 ff.
Iris, gunboat *(1901),* XXXV, 195
Iris, schooner *(1861),* XXXVI, 188
Iris, ship (1797), Pictorial Supplement, XXXII, plate X; (1855), V, 153
Iris, steam tug, XXIII, 88
Iris, supply ship, XXXVII, 138 n.
Iris, U.S. Lighthouse steam tender *(1862),* V, 24
Irish, Captain James M., XXXVIII, 276
Irish Gimblet, ship *(1777),* XLII, 302
"Irish Pennant," by Captain Edgar K. Thompson, U.S.N. (ret.), XXII, 218
Irish Star fleet, VI, 292
Irma, decoy ship *(1917),* XXXVI, 267
Irolita, schooner (1906), XXX, plate XXII
Iron Afloat: The Story of the Confederate Ironclads, by William N. Still, Jr., reviewed, XXXII, 136–137
Iron and Steel Hull Steam Vessels of the United States 1825–1905, by John Harrison Morrison, reviewed, VI, 235–236
Ironclad frigates: see *No. (Number) 61*
Ironclads. *See* Armored vessels
"Ironclad *Weehawken* in the Civil War, The," by Wm. Ray Heitzmann, XLII, 193–202
Iron Cross, sail *(1859),* XLIII, 107 ff.
Iron Prince, ship *(1858),* XXXIV, 20 ff.
Iron Prince, steamship *(1845),* XXII, 26, 29, 31, 37, 42, 43; XLIII, 201
"Iron Sea Elephants, The," by Walter Millis, X, 15–32
Iron shipbuilding, IV, 183 ff.
Iron Ship: The Story of Brunel's SS Great Britain, *The,* by Ewan Corlett, reviewed, L, 230
Iron Ships. *See* Armored vessels; Foundries; Shipbuilding (Materials); Ships (Iron and Steel); Turret Ships
Ironsides, bark (1862), III, 65
Ironsides, ship *(1861),* XI, 284
Iron Steamboat Co., XLVII, 34
"Iron Steamer, The," by Herbert R. Spencer, IV, 183–192
Iron Witch, side-wheeler (1846), XLVIII, 118
Ironwork of Chesapeake Bay skipjacks, IV, 281–285

Iroquois, schooner *(1886),* XXX, Pictorial Supplement, plate III
Iroquois, steamship *(1832),* VI, 47; *(1861),* XXXVII, 282
Iroquois, steamship *(1931),* IX, 220
Iroquois, steam sloop *(1865),* XXXII, 125 ff.; XXXIII, 9 ff.; XXXV, 64
Iroquois, steam tug *(1942),* VI, 297
Iroquois, U.S.C.G. *(1952),* XIV, 24
Iroquois, U.S.S. (1858), XX, 136 n.; *(1861),* XV, 104, 300; *(1868),* XXV, 73; *(1900),* VIII, 191–192, 194
Iroquois elm-bark canoe, IX, 185–206
Irrestible, H.M.S., XXVIII, 19
Irtysh, 6, Russian transport *(1855),* XXXI, 272
Irving, A., & Co. (shipbuilders, of Mystic, CT), XXV, 102
Irving, Thomas, XXV, 214
Irving, Washington, XXV, 61; XXX, 250
Irwin, Lieutenant Commander John, XXXVI, 204
Irwin, Captain Noble Edward, XXXVII, 114
Isaac, bark (1580), sketch of, XXXIV, 235
Isaac Hicks, ship *(1856),* XLV, 110
Isaac Howland, ship, XXII, plate XVIII
Isaac Howland, whaler *(1865),* XXVII, 275
Isaac Hull, a Forgotten American Hero, by Helen Richmond, reviewed, XLIII, 313–314
"Isaac Hull's Victory Revisited," by Tyrone G. Martin, XLVII, 14–21
Isaack, Captain, XXXI, 97
Isaac M. North, steam tug *(1882),* VI, 288
Isaac Newton, ship, XIII, 121
Isaac P. Smith, steamship *(1863),* VIII, 230
Isaac Smith, ship *(1863),* XXXI, 84
Isaacson, Anthony, L, 21
Isaac Toucey, schooner, XXI, 93; *(1861),* XI, 284
Isaak Wright, ship *(1849),* XVIII, 313
Isabel, Mexican gunboat *(1846),* XXX, 55
Isabel, schooner, XXI, 94, 103; *(1862),* XII, 55, 157; *(1869),* I, plate facing 265
Isabel, ship *(1859),* XLI, 302; *(1863),* XXVI, 102; *(1864),* XXXVI, 204
Isabel, steamship, XXI, 87, 95, 100, 102, 106; *(1861),* VIII, 218, 225; *(1863),* XII, 157, 231
Isabella, brig (1845), Pictorial Supplement, XXXIII, plate VII; *(1861),* VIII, 218
Isabella, schooner *(1775),* XL, 7; *(1836),* XXXII, 120
Isabella, ship *(1811),* XXVII, 175
Isabella, ship (1859), III, 171
Isabella, sloop *(1863),* XII, 157
Isabella, steamship, XXI, 86; XXXVI, 182
Isabella, whaler *(1865),* XXVII, 275
Isabella Segunda, Spanish naval steamship (1831), IX, 260
Isabel May, Canadian schooner *(1902),* XLIX, 280
Isaiah Hart, schooner *(1889),* XXXV, 14
Isélèna, sloop, XXIV, plate 14
Isemonger, Thomas, XXII, 44
Isherwood, Benjamin F., XXII, 255

Isherwood, Benjamin Franklin, XXVI, 286; XLVIII, 119; XLIX, 117
Isis, grain elevator *(1898)*, XXXVIII, 134
Islamic Art, IX, 168
Island Belle, schooner, XII, 140; *(1861)*, VIII, 218
Island City, schooner (1871), XXIII, 9
Island Home, centerboard schooner (1885), I, 73
Island Home, steamship (1855), VI, 137
Island Queen (1861), XXXIV, 32; XLIII, 90 ff.; *(1863)*, XLVIII, 101
Island Queen, steamship (1843), XX, 262
Islands and Empires: Western Impact on the Pacific and Asia, Europe and the World in the Age of Expansion, by Ernest S. Dodge, reviewed, XXXVII, 223–224
Islands, Legends, XXIX, 275; XXX, 249
Islands of the Pacific. See Oceania; Pacific Islands
Isle of Man, 1837, XXIX, plate XXIX
Isle of Orleans, illustration of, XLVIII, 80
Isle of Wight, ship (1862), V, 152
Isles de Los (Sierra Leone?), XXX, 237
Isles of Scilly, *see* Scilly, Isles of.
Isles of Shoals Shay, XII, 130–133
Israel. *See* Palestine; Refugees, Jewish
Issac Allerton, ship *(1831)*, XXXVIII, 269
Isthmus, Pacific Mail steamship *(1850)*, XLV, 127
Italian, steamship (1855), XXVI, 110–112, 127, 205, 209
Italian Aeronautic Commission, XXXVII, 113
Italian Navy, XXVII, 185–201
Italie Conquise, French ship *(1799)*, XXXI, 173
Italy, History:
    13th century, XLVI, 84
    Revolution of 1848, XLIII, 165
    Navy, XXVII, 185
    See also Genoa; Shipping; Venice
Italy, boats of, XII, 240
Itasca, U.S.C.G. *(1906)*, XX, 143
Itasca, U.S.S. *(1861)*, XII, 271–276; *(1862)*, XXXVI, 194
Itata, Chilean ship *(1891)*, XXXVIII, 291 ff.
It's About Time, by Paul M. Chamberlain, reviewed, II, 354
Iturbide, Mexican ship *(1835)*, XXX, 47
"It Was A Noble Calling...," by Helen M. Hill, XLV, 180–190
Ivanhoe, steamship *(1847)*, XLVII, 34; *(1864)*, XII, 231
Ivanković, Captain Basi, XXIV, 124–126, plates 15, 16
Ivernia, troopship *(1915)*, XXXV, 52
Ives, Thomas Poynton, XVIII, 105
Ivy, C.S.S. (1862), XIX, 267
Ivy, Confederate ship *(1861)*, XLVIII, 90
Ivy, schooner *(1907)*, XXXVIII, 90
Iwa-say (Japanese prince), XXVII, 164
Izou, Prince of, VI, 14
Izumrud, Russian warship *(1863)*, XX, 51

J

J. A. Chanslor, tanker (1910), XXXVIII, 199 ff.
J. A. H., woodboat (1917), XVII, 12
J. A. Hazard, bark (1857), IV, 244; *(1861)*, VIII, 218
J. A. Thompson, ship (1869), II, 334
J. & C. G. Bolinders, Ltd., Stockholm, XXXII, 32
J. & G. Rennie, XXVI, 207
J. & G. Thomson, XXVI, 208
J. & W. Dudgeon, XXVI, 207
J. B. Newland, schooner (1870), II, plate 48; V, 145
J. B. Spafford, schooner (1864), XXXIII, 209
J. C. Acton, schooner *(1861)*, XI, 284; XII, 55
J. C. Cowper (Couper), Whampoa, XXXIV, 58
J. C. Guin, schooner *(1863)*, XII, 157, 231
J. C. Gwin, smack, XXI, 92
J. C. Gwinn, schooner *(1861)*, XI, 284
J. C. Kuhn, bark (1859), III, 72, 265
J. C. Manson, schooner *(1861)*, VIII, 218
J. C. Manson, sloop *(1863)*, VIII, 230
J. C. Marson, schooner, XXI, 102
J. C. Rahmn, bark (1845), I, 50
J. C. Reed, bark (1874), V, 153
J. C. Ritchie, steamship (1906), VI, plate 7
J. C. Roger, schooner *(1862)*, VIII, 225
J. C. Roker, schooner, XXI, 91
J. C. Wainwright, bugeye *(1881)*, III, 176
J. Chester Wood, schooner (1881), IX, 177–178
J. D. Swaim, steamship, XXI, 101; *(1861)*, XI, 268, 284
J. E. Bowley, schooner *(1855)*, XXIV, 141
J. E. DuBignon / Du Bignon, schooner (1890), VI, 132–134; XXIII, plate VI
J. Elder & Co., XXVI, 207
J. F. Bradford, schooner, XXI, 102; *(1861)*, XI, 284
J. F. Foster, ship (1870), III, 70, 265
J. G. McNeill, schooner, XXI, 88
J. G. Stille, schooner *(1861)*, VIII, 218
J. H. Bowers, bark *(1890)*, VIII, 70; *(1892)*, XXXV, 18
J. H. Scammel, schooner *(1861)*, VIII, 218
J. H. Wignall & Co., XLIII, 215 ff.
J. Henderson & Son, XXVI, 207
J. Hinks & Son, shipbuilders, XXX, 79
J. J. Crittenden, schooner *(1862)*, VIII, 225
J. J. McNeil, schooner *(1861)*, XI, 284; XII, 55
J. J. Spencer, schooner *(1861)*, XI, 284
J. Jones, ship (1854), XXVIII, plate VIII
J. L. Brower, grain elevator *(1883)*, XXXVIII, 141
J. L. Dimmock, ship *(1854)*, XLVII, 104
J. M. Guffey Petroleum Co., XXXVIII, 180 ff.
J. M. Todd, steamship (1875), XII, 289, 293
J. Mackey and Co., XXVI, 8, 9
J. Montgomery, ship (1861), XI, 284

J. Morton, ship (1856), II, 246

J. O. Webster, schooner (1919), V, 292–293

J. P. Wheeler, ship (1856), II, 332

J. S. Davis, schooner *(1861),* XI, 284

J. S. Parsons, ship *(1861),* XI, 284

J. T. Davis, schooner, XXI, 93; *(1863),* XII, 157

J. T. Sherman, steam tug (1903), VII, 221–222, plate 26; IX, 20, 25, 27

J. T. Wing, schooner (1919), V, 292–293

J. W. A. Lorentzen, ship (1850), XXIV, 56

J. W. Clise, schooner *(1940),* III, 163

J. W. Goodridge, schooner *(1861),* VIII, 219

J. W. Jackson, schooner *(1861),* XV, 114, 123

J. W. Mallory, lugger *(1861),* XI, 285

J. W. Mallory, schooner *(1862),* XII, 56

J. W. Marr, ship (1875), II, 335

J. W. McKee, schooner *(1861),* VIII, 219

J. W. Sommerville, schooner (1919), VI, 134

J. W. Townsend, schooner *(1862),* XII, 56

J. W. Wilder, schooner, XXI, 88, 100; *(1861),* XI, 279, 285; *(1862),* XII, 56

J. Welsh, brig *(1861),* XV, 114, 123

Jack, Andrew, XVI, 32

Jack, James R., XIV, 13, 14; *Some Historic Ships and their Models in the Francis Russell Hart Nautical Museum,* reviewed, I, 189

Jack Downing, steam ferry *(1833),* VII, 51

Jack-Hinton, Colin, "The Voyage of *Alliance*: American Contribution to the Rediscovery and Exploration of the Solomon Islands," XXV, 248–261, plates 27, 28

"Jack London in the Tradition of American Sea Fiction," by Bert Bender, XLVI, 188–199

Jackman, Eugene T., "Efforts Made Before 1825 to Ameliorate the Lot of the American Seaman: With Emphasis on his Moral Regeneration," XXIV, 109–118

Jackman, Moses, XVII, 123

Jackman, S. W., XXV, 140; contributed document, XXII, 143–144; XXV, 111; contributed note, XXIII, 67–68; reviews by, XXII, 147–148; XXIII, 71–72, 73–74, 75–76, 150–151, 288–289; XXIV, 223–225; XXV, 72–73, 148–149; XXVI, 147–148; XXVII, 224–226; XXVIII, 227–228; XXIX, 65–67; XXX, 68–69; XXXII, 138, 296; XXXVI, 301; XXXVII, 223; XXXVIII, 70; XL, 229; XLI, 142; XLII, 139, 145; XLIII, 58, 150, 224; XLIV, 208, 210; XLV, 211; XLVII, 55; XLVIII, 131, 186, 197, 201; "Admiral Wilkes Visits Bermuda during the Civil War," XXIV, 208–211; Editor, *At Sea and By Land: The Reminiscences of William Balfour Macdonald R. N.,* reviewed, XLIV, 278; "Captain Marryat Surveys the American Maritime Scene," XXIII, 56–61; "David Bates Douglass' Journal:...," XXIV, 280–293; *The Journal of William Sturgis,* reviewed, XXXIX, 145; "Rudolph Verner and the Battle of the Falkland Islands," XXXIII, 34–40; "Sir James Bland Burges Papers," XXIX, 244–261

"Jack of the Dust," by Captain Edgar K. Thompson, U.S.N. (ret.), XXV, 111

Jack Sabel, schooner, XXI, 101; (1861), XI, 284

Jackson, gunboat *(1862),* XXXVI, 196

Jackson, Andrew, XLII, 165 ff.

Jackson, President Andrew, XXV, 167; XL, 35

Jackson, Anne Martin, XXXVI, 21, 23

Jackson, Edward, XLVI, 47

Jackson, Jonathan, XXIX, 204

Jackson, Louise, XXXVI, 23

Jackson, Melvin H., XXV, 232; "The Consular Privateers; an account of French Privateering in American waters," XXII, 81–98; "The Philadelphia Steamboat of 1796," supplemented, edited and illustrated by Paul Forsythe Johnston, L, 201–218; *Privateers in Charleston, 1793–1796,* reviewed, XXX, 303

Jackson, Russell Leigh, XXI, 6–7

Jackson, Sheldon, XXXIX, 13

Jackson, Susan, XLVI, 47

Jackson, Willard B., XXX, Pictorial Supplement, plates XVII–XXXII

Jackson and Sharp Co., XXXVIII, 183 ff.

Jacksonville Ship Outfitting Co., XXII, 161

Jack Tars and Commodores: The American Navy, 1783–1815, by William M. Fowler, reviewed, XLV, 133

Jacmel, XXX, 127

Jacob Bell, clipper ship (1852), I, 46

Jacob Bell, ship (1852), XXIII, 264 ff.; *(1862),* XXXIX, 36

Jacob Bell, steamship *(1842),* XII, 288, 293

Jacob E. Ridgway, ship (1881), II, 335

Jacob H. Tremper, steamship, XVIII, 231

Jacob Leoy, bark (1851), III, 63, 264

Jacob Luckenbach, XXXIV, 171

"Jacob Petersen," by Lawrence Waters Jenkins, X, 230

Jacob S. Winslow, schooner (1889), XXIII, plate XV

Jacobs, Captain Solomon, XLIV, 115

Jacobs, W. W., XXXII, 81

Jacobsen, Alphonse T., "Antonio Nicolo Gasparo Jacobsen," III, 250–252

Jacobsen, Antonio, XXIV, plates XIV, XV, XXXII; XXVII, plates XXIII, XXVII; XXVIII, plate XXVI; painting by, XXXIX, plate 4

Jacobsen, Antonio Nicolo Gasparo (1850–1921), Steamship Paintings by, Pictorial Supplement, XXXIV: Part I, 48–49; Part II, 124–125; Part III, 182–183; Part IV, 258–259; XXXIII, plates 1, 2

"Jacobsen, Antonio Nicolo Gasparo," by Alphonse T. Johnson, III, 250–252

Jacobsen, Johan Adrian, XXXIX, 11

Jacobsen Affair, VIII, 184 ff.

"Jacob Spin, Ship Portraitist," by Charles H. D. Copeland, XV, 81

Jacobus, M. W., "Fine Forests for the Navy," XVIII, 315–316

Jaganda, raft, XXIII, 117
Jaguar, S.M.S. gunboat *(1906),* XL, 89 ff.
Jaguar, German U-boat group, XLIV, 48 ff.
Jahncke, Ernest Lee, XXXV, 131
Jahont, Russian warship *(1863),* XX, 51
Jaimdopi, Otirfai Man, XXVIII, plate XV
Jairus B. Lincoln, ship (1869), III, 66
"Jakey Boats, The," by Harold Peters, XIX, 73
Jaloux, French ship *(1798),* XXXI, 173
Jamaica, galley *(1708),* XX, 10
Jamaica, H.M.S. *(1763),* XXIII, 177
Jamaica, H.M. cruiser *(1949),* L, 291 ff.
Jamaica, Admiralty Courts, XX, 44–48
Jamaica, History, to 1962, XXIX, 118
Jamaica Vice-Admiralty Court, II, 203–208
James, galley *(1676),* XXIII, 108–112
James, schooner *(1800),* XLIX, 274
James, ship *(1777),* XLIII, 24
James I, King of England,, XXVIII, 245, 246, 250, 252–258
James II, King of England, XXV, 278
James, Ambrose, XXX, 97, 100
James, Charles, XXXVI, 293
James, Captain H. M. A., XVII, 251; XXI, 94
James, Henry R., XIV, 117
James, J. F., and Son, IX, 73–74
James, Captain Joshua (1826–1902), XXXVII, 83, 92–93, plate 1
James, Marquis, *Biography of a Business, 1792–1942,* reviewed, IV, 176–177
James, Osceola F., XXXVII, 87
James, Captain Richard, XXX, 93–102
James, Vice-Admiral Richard, XXVIII, 112
James, Captain Samuel (1824–1915), XXXVII, 83, 92–93, plate 1
James, William, XXXI, 277
James, William H., XXXIV, 91
James A. Garfield, tug *(1899),* VII, 290
James Adger, U.S.S. *(1863),* VIII, 203
James Allen, steamship (1836), XVIII, 275, 284
James and John Bard, by Harold S. Sniffen and Alexander C. Brown, reviewed, XI, 300
James and Mary, ship *(1686),* VII, 272
James Arnold, ship *(1852),* Pictorial Supplement, XXXIII, plates XI, XVIII, XXVI
James B. Duke, steamship (ex-*Eastern Cloud*), XXIII, 276
James Badger, U.S.S. *(1863),* XXV, 113
James Baines, ship *(1846–1857),* XLII, 121 ff.; *(1856),* XXVI, 158 n., 168, 170
James Baines and Co., XXXIV, 41
"James Bard," query by Harold S. Sniffen, II, 81
James Battle, steamship, XXI, 89; *(1863),* XII, 157
James Boyce, schooner *(1925),* IX, 172–173
James Burt, steamship *(1860),* VII, 120–124
"James Cook and the Origins of the Maritime Fur Trade," by Barry M. Gough, XXXVIII, 217–224

James Cook: The Opening of the Pacific, by Basil Greenhill, reviewed, XXXI, 74–75
James E. Newson, schooner *(1942),* III, 60, 163
James Foster, Jr., ship (1854), V, 154
James G. Pendleton, bark (1871), V, 152
James Grey, iron-hull tugboat *(1861),* XLIV, 258
James Grubbs, sloop *(1863),* XV, 112, 127
James H. Elmore, vessel *(1855),* XXXVI, 172
James H. Ladson, schooner *(1861),* VIII, 218
James Hartley, steamship (1856), XXVI, 131, 132, 205, 209
James Hodgson and Co., XXII, 44
James Howden & Co., XXVI, 207; XLIII, 297
Jamesina, ship *(1829),* XXVI, 5, 6
"James Keen's Journal of a Passage from Philadelphia to Blackbeard Island, Georgia for Live Oak Timber, 1817–1818," by Virginia Steele Wood, XXXV, 227–247
James L. Bogart, ship (1851), II, 330
James L. Day, steamship *(1862),* XII, 55
James M. Churchill, bark (1855), XXVIII, plate IX
James M. Vance, schooner, XXXVI, 256
James Madison, steamship (1837), VII, 63; (1839), XVIII, 285, 290, 298; XX, 89 n., 94, 95, 253
James Maury, bark (1826), III, 169
James Maury, whaler *(1865),* XXVII, 269, 275
Jas. McKee, steamship (1879), V, 86
James Montgomery, ship (1852), III, 67
James Munroe, steamship (1817), XVI, 36
"James Nicholson and the Continental Frigate *Virginia,*" by William M. Fowler, Jr., XXXIV, 135–141
James Norcon, schooner *(1862),* VIII, 225
James O'Donahue, schooner *(1883),* XLIX, 31 ff.
Jameson, J. Franklin, XXXVI, 84
Jameson, Niel, XXX, 136
Jameson, Captain R., XXI, 94
James P. Whidbee, schooner *(1861),* VIII, 218
Jas. R. Keeler, ship (1855), II, 246
Jas. R. Pringle, schooner *(1863),* VIII, 230
James R. Pringle, schooner, XXI, 102
James River, Kanawha Canal (VA), XVI, 41
James River steamboats: *Pocahontas* (1893), II, 223–228
James S. Lowell, schooner *(1888),* XXXV, 13
James S. Stone, bark (1868), III, 172
Jamestown, C.S.S. *(1862),* XX, 158, 159; *(1862),* XXXV, 27
Jamestown, sloop of war *(1860),* XXIX, 112
Jamestown, U.S.S. (1845), XX, 140, 141; *(1847),* XIII, 253–267; *(1863),* XXVII, 36 n., 174
Jamestown, U.S.S. (1885), photo of, XLIX, 294
Jamestown, U.S. sloop (1843), XXII, 220; XXIII, 264 ff.; XXIV, 70; (1847), XXVIII, 30
Jamestown, warship *(1849),* XLIII, 174 ff.
Jamestown Settlement (VA), X, 5; XVII, 173
Jamestown Voyages Under the First Charter 1606–1609, The, by Philip L. Barbour, Editor, reviewed, XXX, 302

James W. Baldwin, steamship, XVIII, 224, 225; (1860 or 1861), VI, 278 ff.; XIV, 164, 182
James W. Elwell, barkentine *(1892),* XXVII, plate XXVI
James W. Paul, Jr., schooner (1901), XXIII, plate XV
James Watt, steamship (1820), XXX, 10; XLVIII, 77; *(1822),* XXXII, 194
James Watt & Co., XXVI, 208
James Williams, schooner *(1863),* XII, 157, 231
Jamieson, A. J., editor, *A People of the Sea: The Maritime History of the Channel Islands,* reviewed, XLVII, 196
Jamieson, Alan, "The Tangier Galleys and the Wars Against the Mediterranean Corsairs," XXIII, 95–112
Jamieson, Alan G., "American Privateers in the Leeward Islands, 1776–1778," XLIII, 20–30
Jamieson, Thomas, XXVI, 203
Jane, brig *(1798),* XIX, 118; *(1812),* XXI, 18
Jane, knockabout (1892), XXX, 195, 196
Jane, schooner *(1807),* XVI, 196; *(1862),* XII, 55, 157
Jane, ship, XXII, 93; *(1800),* XXIII, 216; *(1820),* XXIX, 198
Jane, snow, XXII, 91
Jane Adele, schooner, XXI, 94; *(1861),* XI, 284; XII, 157
Jane and Margaret, sloop *(1811),* XLIV, 105
Jane Davis, schooner *(1861),* VIII, 218
Jane Fisher, schooner *(1861),* VIII, 218
Jane Godfey, sloop *(1863),* XV, 112, 127
Jane Gray, schooner *(1888),* XXXIX, 8
Jane Palmer, schooner (1904), V, 80, 138
Jane Parker, ship (1848), XXVIII, plate V
Janequeo, Chilean torpedo boat *(1880),* XXXIX, 286
Jane Rebecca, coaster *(1875),* XXXVIII, 63
Jan Mayen Island, Whaling off, XXII, plate II
Jan Melchers, ship (1886), III, 66
Jansen, Captain, XXV, 291
Jansen, Marin Henry, XLVIII, 45 ff.
Jansz, Willem, L, 288
Jantar, Polish tug, XXXVII, 75
Jan van Linschoten: The Dutch Marco Polo, by Charles McKew Parr, reviewed, XXV, 73–74
Janzen, Olaf Uwe, "The American Threat to the Newfoundland Fisheries, 1776–1777," XLVIII, 154–164
Japan, merchantman *(1863),* XLV, 191 ff.
Japan, paddle steamship *(1866),* XLIX, 26
Japan, steamship (1867–1868), II, 8, 37–38, 243, plate 5, plan facing 242; X, 130, 131, 134; *(1874),* XXV, 168
Japan. Foreign relations:
　United States, XX, 198; XXXII, 123; XXXVII, 185; XLI, 25
　History, XLVI, 55
　—, **Minamoto-Taira War (1180–1185),** XXVIII, 206
　—, **Restoration (1853–1870),** VII, 9
　—, **Sino-Japanese War (1894),** XXXIV, 211
　See also Shipping
Japan. Navy, XX, 198
Japan: 1807 voyage of ship *Mount Vernon* to, V, 255 ff.

"Japan, Commodore Perry's Landing in," contributed by John Goldsborough, VII, 9–20
Japan and the United States, 1790–1853, by Shunzo Sakamaki, reviewed, I, 319–320
"Japanese Anchors," by John Lyman, XI, 77–78
Japanese at Leyte Gulf, The, by James A. Field, Jr., reviewed, VII, 247–248
Japanese Compass, 1900, Pictorial Supplement, XXXV, plate XII
Japanese Naval and Merchant Shipping Losses During World War II, reviewed, VIII, 74–75
Japanese Ship Inspection Law, XXX, 31
Japonica, bark *(1851),* XLIX, 123
Jaques, Rupert W., III, 354
Jardine, steamship (1835), XXII, 7, 42, 43; *(1835),* XVI, 160
Jardine, Matheson and Co., XVII, 136, 139; XVIII, 60, 61; XXII, 6, 7, 91 12, 13, 29, 225; XXVI, 5, 118–124, 127–128, 201; XXXIV, 30 ff.; XLIII, 96 ff.; XLIX, 25
Jardine Matheson Archive, Cambridge, England, XLVIII, 254
Jarman, Colin, *Deck Seamanship,* reviewed, XL, 234
Jaruco, bark *(1861),* XI, 284
Jarvie, Thorburn & Co., XLIII, 212
Jarvis, Lieutenant David, XXXIX, 12
Jaseur, British sloop-of-war *(1815),* XXXIII, 247
Jason, Dutch warship *(1777),* XXXVI, 165 n.
Jason, French ship *(1800),* XXXI, 174
Jason, U.S. monitor (1862), X, 17, 31
Jason, U.S. privateer, XXX, 299
Jasper, bark *(1836),* XXVII, 98
Jasper, schooner *(1861),* VIII, 218
Jasseur, brig *(1814),* XLII, 111 ff.
Java, frigate *(1813),* XLII, 108 ff., 284; XLIV, 171; *(1834),* XXXVIII, 113
Java, H.M. frigate *(1812),* VII, 168; Pictorial Supplement, XXXII, plate XXVI; XLVII, 16
Java, ship (1868), I, 68
Java, U.S. frigate *(1832),* XXXII, 269
Java, U.S.S., XXIII, 58; *(1864),* XXVII, 36 n., 39 n., 44, 45
Java, boats of, XIII, 84 ff.
Jay, John, XXVI, 235
Jay, John, U.S. Minister of Foreign Affairs, XXXI, 177
Jay, John, U.S. Secretary of State, XXV, 7
Jayne, Captain Clement P., XVII, 49; XVIII, 83
Jay Treaty, XXV, 8, 11
Jean Domenique Cassini and his World Map of 1696, by Lloyd A. Brown, reviewed, II, 94
Jeanette, steam brigantine *(1893),* XXXVIII, 85
Jeanette, whaler *(1899),* XLIV, 12
Jeanie, steam schooner (1883), IX, 71; *(1897),* XXXVIII, 87
Jean Key, Belgian bark *(1841),* XXXVIII, 268
Jean L. Somerville, schooner (1919), VI, 133
Jeanne, French ship *(1800),* XXXI, 174
Jeanne d'Arc, French warship [model] (1930), XVI, 103

Jeannett, Captain James M., XXI, 94
Jeannette, exploration ship *(1882),* XXXIX, 11
Jeannette, ship *(1879),* XLIX, 305
Jeannette, steamship *(1864),* XII, 231, 234
Jearsey, William, XIII, 17–21, 27
Jebson, Captain Fred, XXXVIII, 177
Jed, H.M. frigate *(1943),* L, 220 ff.
Jeddo, screw steamship *(1859),* XLIII, 107 ff.; *(1866),* XXVI, 27
Jedo, bark (1848), I, 49
Jeff Davis, brig *(1861),* XI, 150 ff.
Jeff Davis, sloop *(1862),* VIII, 225; XII, 55
Jeffers, Lieutenant William N., XXXI, 14; XXXVI, 180
Jeffers, W. N., Jr., XXX, 43
Jefferson, brig *(1785),* XLI, 217
Jefferson, ship (1795), XXXIII, 162 ff.; *(1802),* XXIII, 217
Jefferson, sloop (1801), XIII, 236; *(1812),* XIV, 210
Jefferson, steamship *(1845),* XXXIX, 222
Jefferson, U.S. revenue cutter, XXIV, 14 n.; (1845), VIII, 146–147
Jefferson, Captain E. M., XXI, 94
Jefferson, Thomas, XI, 108 ff.; XXII, 84, 86, 88, 221; XXIII, 170; XXV, 10, 14, 35, 38; XXVI, 178, 181, 182, 185, 187, 232 ff.; XXVIII, 32, 115; XXX, 280; XXXVI, 63 ff.; XXXVIII, 101; XXXIX, 23
Jefferson, President Thomas, XXXIV, 125 ff.; XLI, 209; XLIII, 40 ff.
Jefferson Borden, schooner (1875), XXVII, 46 ff.
"*Jefferson Borden* Pirates and Samuel Gompers: Aftermath of a Mutiny, The," by Jay M. Pawa, XXVII, 46–60
Jefferson Davis, brig *(1861),* VIII, 196, 218
Jefferson Davis, schooner *(1862),* XII, 55
"Jeffersonian Gunboats in the War of 1812," by Dean R. Mayhew, XLII, 101–117
Jeffrey, Captain Samuel, IX, 228–229
Jeffreys & Darcy, XLVII, 93
Jehu, bark (1859), V, 151; VI, 82
Jellicoe, Admiral, XXXV, 102; XL, 52 ff.
Jemmy Twitcher, A Life of the Fourth Earl of Sandwich 1718–1792, by George Martelli, reviewed, XXIII, 150–151
Jenckes, Daniel, XLI, 175
Jencks, Captain Joseph, XL, 196
Jenings, Colonel Edmund, XXX, 134
Jenkins, Francis G., "The Saginaw Steel Steamship Company and Its Steamers," XLII, 245–275
Jenkins, James, XXXIX, 218
Jenkins, Captain John, XXXI, 29
Jenkins, Lawrence Waters, II, 252; V, 244, 267; XXI, 155; XXVIII, 237; contributed documents, VII, 72–76; XIII, 139–140; XX, 43, 67, 103, 111, 117, 145, 190, 216, 236, 242, 249, 269; XXI, 15, 41, 69; XXII, 142–143; queries by, I, 89; II, 339; answered queries, I, 312; II, 82–83; "Captain Thomas Petersen, Marine Artist," XV, 154; *"Europa's* misfortunes, The; Document from the Letter-Book of Captain Nathaniel Brown," VI, 19–50; "Jacob Petersen," X, 230; "A New Hampshireman Transports Spanish Troops to Oran – 1732," VI, 179–193; "Privateer Sloop *Jefferson,*" XIV, 210–211; "The Restoration of East India Marine Hall" (co-author with Walter Muir Whitehill), IV, 5–17
Jenkins, Lieutenant Thornton A., XXVIII, 47; XXIX, 177 ff,; XLVII, 175
Jenkins, Shadrach, VII, 43
Jenkins, W. S., VI, 4; "Wartime Canoe Building in the Marshall Islands," VI, 71–72, plates 9–12
Jenkins, William H., XLII, 254 ff.; portrait of, XLII, plate 8
Jenks, destroyer escort *(1944),* XXXVIII, 272 ff.
Jenks, Daniel, XLII, 42
Jennens (or Jennings), Abraham, XXXVII, 9
Jennie Cushman, bark, XXV, 107
Jennie Eastman, ship (1863), XXVIII, plate XI
Jennie Flood Kreger, schooner (1919), IV, 66, 68
Jennie Harkness, bark (1879), V, 153
Jennie Martin, schooner *(1872),* XV, 226
Jennie R. duBois, schooner (1901 or 1902), V, 138
Jennie S. Barker, ship (1869), IV, 241
Jennie S. Hall, schooner (1881), VI, 133
Jennie Walker, schooner (1880), V, 86
Jennifer, sloop *(1967),* XLV, 253
Jennings, Admiral Sir John, R.N., XXI, 263
Jennings, Captain John, XXI, 94
Jenny, schooner, XXI, 94; *(1777),* XLIII, 26; *(1792),* XIII, 212–213; *(1863),* XII, 157
Jenny, ship *(1778),* X, 281–282; *(1798),* XVIII, 119; *(1800),* XXIII, 216; *(1807),* X, 54, 55, 56, 63–64; XVI, 195; *(1808),* XXIII, 239 ff.
Jenny, sloop *(1748),* XLVIII, 34
Jenny, Captain Benjamin, XXIII, 27
Jenny Ford, barkentine (1854), VII, 315–316, plate 39
Jenny Lind, schooner *(1861),* VIII, 218
Jenny Sealing, ship *(1799),* XXXV, 208
Jensen, Arthur L., *The Maritime Commerce of Colonial Philadelphia,* reviewed, XXIII, 290
Jeremiah Thompson, ship (1854), I, plate facing 111, 113; *(1874),* XXV, 107
Jerman, Wilma, XLIV, 179 ff.
Jernegan, Laura, XXXVIII, 205 ff.
Jernigan, Consul General Thomas R., XL, 101
Jerry Fowler, brig, XXIV, 57
Jersey, British prison ship *(1781),* XXIV, 248; XXV, 110
Jersey, frigate, XXIII, 99
Jersey, gondola *(1776),* VIII, 256
Jersey Blue, steamship *(1861),* XXXIX, 94
Jersey City, steamship (1882), XIV, 117, 119, 124, 134; *(1888),* XXII, 219; *(1940),* XIV, 130
Jersey Standard, XLVII, 45
Jerusha, sloop *(1793),* XIV, 30, 31, 32, 36, 40; *(1800),* XXII, 216
Jervey, Captain J., XXI, 94

"Jervis, Captain Sir John, Letters of, to Sir Henry Clinton, 1774–1782," edited by Marie Martel Hatch, VII, 87–106

Jervis Bay, steamship *(1940),* I, 411; IV, 336; XIV, 130

Jervis Bay *Goes Down, The,* by Gene Fowler, reviewed, I, 411

Jesse H. Freeman, steam bark *(1894),* XXXVIII, 85

Jesse J. Cox, schooner, XXI, 92; *(1862),* XII, 55

Jesse Stevens, bark *(1854),* XXIV, plate IV

Jessie and Margaret, XXI, 105

Jessie Costa, schooner (1905), XXVI, plate XIX

Jessie McGregor, barkentine (1882), XXIV, 44, 57

Jessie Nickerson, schooner (1874), V, 86

Jessie Osborn, steamship (1877), II, 76

Jessie Richards, schooner *(1861),* XI, 284; XII, 55; XXI, 89, 98

Jessup, James, XXXVI, 252

Jetty, steamship (1895), XI, 289, 293

Jeune Creole, French ship *(1801),* XXXI, 175

Jeverland, bark *(1861),* XI, 284

Jewel, ship *(1630),* XXIII, 63, 65

Jewell, Captain George, XXV, 64

Jewel Line, XV, 133–141

Jewess, steamship (1840), VIII, 127

Jewett, Sarah Orne, XXV, 65

Jewitt, Louis, XXXVI, 242, 245

Jingo, yacht *(1898),* XI, 91

Jinkee, steamship *(1861),* XLIII, 106

Jireh Swift, ship *(1860),* XXII, plate XVII; *(1862),* XXVII, 263 ff.

"Jnº Gilbert Tower Hill London," Pictorial Supplement, XXXV, plate XIII

Joann, auxiliary schooner (1924), XXX, plate XXIII

Joanna Ward, schooner, XXI, 89; *(1861),* VIII, 218, 225; *(1862),* XXXVI, 194

Job, Captain Henry, XXVI, 215

Jobé, Joseph, Editor, *The Great Age of Sail,* reviewed, XXVIII, 233–234

Joe Flanner, schooner, XXI, 95; *(1862),* XII, 55, 157

Johanna Wilhelmine, ship *(1861),* XI, 284

Johanne Augusta, bark (1864), V, 154, 242

Johannes, ship (1862), III, 349

Johann Ludwig, bark (1870), II, 334; III, 264

Johansson, John W., XXXVI, 273

Johan Van Oldenbarnevelt, liner *(1930),* XXXVI, 7

John, brig *(1825),* XXXVIII, 55

John, brigantine *(1777),* XXXIX, 212

John, ketch (1795), II, 281; IV, 18–30, plate 5; *(1796),* XLI, 169

John, schooner, XXI, 90; XXII, 86; *(1861),* VIII, 218, 225; *(1863),* XII, 157, 231

John, ship (1795), Pictorial Supplement, XXXII, plate XI; *(1801),* XXIV, 262; *(1803),* XXV, plate 17; *(1804),* XLIII, 44

John, sloop, XXII, 60 n.

John, snow (1745), I, 297

John, whale ship, XXV, plate 8

John A. Hazard, schooner *(1864),* XII, 231

John A. Moore, steamship, XXI, 96; *(1861),* XV, 99, 123

John A. Robb, bark *(1861),* XII, 103

John A. Ross, whaleship *(1877),* L, 123

John A. Taylor, schooner *(1861),* XI, 284

John & Adam, ship *(1813),* XLVI, 165

John Adams, brig (1854), XXXV, 26

John Adams, corvette *(1838),* XXIX, 107, 176

John Adams, frigate (1799), XLVI, 151 ff., 232; XLVII, 22 ff.; XLIX, 41 ff.; L, 245 ff.; painting of vessel, XLVII, 23

John Adams, ship *(1825),* XLIV, 245

John Adams, U.S.S. *(1800),* XXXI, 138, 174, 183; XXXII, 271; XXXV, 238; *(1806),* XVIII, 183; *(1828),* XXXVIII, 39, 107; XL, 29; *(1832),* VII, 18, 189; *(1838),* XXI, 292, 298, 302; XXIII, 58, 291

John Adams, the Navy, and the Quasi-War with France, by William G. Anderson, XXX, 117–132

"John Adams and American Sea Power," by Frederic H. Hayes, XXV, 35–45

"John Adams and the Barbary Problem: The Myth and the Record," by James A. Carr, XXVI, 231–257

"John Adams of Pitcairn's Island," by Charles Knowles Bolton, I, 297–300

John Ammack, schooner *(1861),* VIII, 218; XI, 284

John & Fortune, ship *(1627),* XLIX, 254

John and James, ship *(1801),* XL, 47

John and Mary, sloop *(1723),* XXXVII, 265

John and Winthrop, bark *(1894),* XXXVIII, 85

John Arthur, schooner, XXI, 95, 97; *(1861),* XI, 284; XII, 55

John Arthur, ship *(1861),* XI, 284

John Atkinson, ship *(1806),* VII, 317

John B. Prescott, schooner (1899), XXIII, 14

John Balch, brig (1861), VIII, 218

John Barrow, bark *(1861),* XV, 114, 123

"John Barry to the Navy Board of the Eastern Department," document contributed by William Bell Clark, I, 168–170

John Bell, schooner *(1855),* XXIV, 141

John Bell, steamship (1854), XXVI, 132, 133, 205, 209

John Bertram, ship *(1850),* III, 169; XIX, plate XX

John Boulton, bark *(1858),* XVI, 241

John Bourne & Co., XXVI, 26, 207

"John Bradford to William Ellery," document contributed by William Bell Clark, II, 247

John Bright, steamship (1852), XXVI, 112 n.; (1862), XVII, 53

John Bunyan, barge (1889), XXXVII, 89

John Bunyan, ship, XII, 102, 104; (1850), XXVIII, plate VI

John By, steamship (1832), VII, 47–48

"John Cabot's Landfall: Cape Dégrat or Cape Bonavista? Some Observations," by Jake T. W. Hubbard, XXXIII, 174–177

John Carter Brown Library, Brown University, XXV, 299

John Carter Brown Library, Providence, Rhode Island. Report to the corporation of Brown University, July 1, 1940, reviewed, I, 99

John Carter Brown Libray: Annual Report 1949–1950, by Lawrence C. Wroth, reviewed, XI, 234

John Carver, bark (1842), XXVIII, plates III, IV

John Carver, ship *(1861),* XI, 151

John Cawte Beaglehole: A Bibliography, by Margery Walton, Julia Bergen, Janet Paul, reviewed, XXXIII, 222–223

John Constantine, bark [model], XXIV, 205

John Constantine, Liberty ship *(1943),* XXIV, 189

John Currier, ship (1882), I, plate facing 88; XVII, 118; *(1887),* XL, 108

John D. Archbold, ship *(1913),* XLVII, 45

John D. Colwell, schooner, XXIII, plate XXXI

John D. Long, mackerel schooner, cabin of, Pictorial Supplement, XXXI, plate XXVI

John D. Paige, schooner, XXIII, plate XV

John D'Aymer, pilot boat *(1835),* V, 163–164

John Douglass, schooner *(1863),* XII, 157, 231

John Dryden, schooner *(1864),* XII, 231

"John E. Ward and the Chinese Coolie Trade," by M. Foster Farly, XX, 209–216

John Ena, four-mast bark *(1911),* XXXIII, 146–147

John Endicott, steamship (1863), XII, 293

John Ericsson, whaleback steamship *(1913),* XXV, 174, plate 16

John F. Leavitt, schooner (1979), XL, 4

John Farnum, bark (1847), VII, 317

John Feeney, schooner (1885), XXVI, plate VII

John Forsyth, barge (1904), V, 139

John Fraser, ship, XXI, 93; (1854), II, 331; *(1861),* VIII, 218, 224

John G. Christopher, steamship (1892), I, 70

John Gilpin, schooner, XXI, 91; *(1862),* XII, 55

John Grant, concrete ship (1944), XXII, 178

John Greenwood in America 1745–1752, by Alan Burroughs, reviewed, II, 356

John Griffin, bark (1856), III, 65

John H. McManus, schooner (1885), XXVI, plate VIII

John H. Ryerson, ship (1854), III, 263

John Hale, schooner *(1865),* XII, 234

John Hancock, ship (1849), XVIII, 307–314

John Hancock, warship *(1854),* XXXVIII, 33

John Hathaway, brig *(1861),* VIII, 219

John Howland, schooner (1888), XXXIX, 9

John III, King, XXX, 255

John Jay, ship *(1794),* XLVI, 11 ff.; *(1795),* XVIII, 133; *(1800),* V, 90, 158; X, 53; *(1801),* XXIII, 216

John K. Hammitt (later, *Union*), steam packet *(1848),* XXX, 276

John L. Hasbrouck, steamship, XVIII, 225; *(1882),* VI, 286

John L. Stephens, steamship (1852), X, 130, plate 17; XX, 126, 132

John Laird, Son and Co., XXXIV, 38

John Law, ship *(1855),* XX, 130

John Ledyard's Journal of Captain Cook's Last Voyage, James Kenneth Munford, Editor, reviewed, XXIV, 225–226

John Leslie, ship (1860), VI, 82

John Marshall, steamship (1838), XVIII, 282

John Maxwell, schooner, XXIV, 27

John Noble, grain elevator *(1964),* XXXVIII, 140

"Johnny Woodboat," by George MacBeath, XVII, 5–16, plates 1–4

"Johnny" wood-boats, X, 204

"Johnny wood-bo't, A," Pictorial Supplement, XXXVI, plate XXIII

John Owen, steamship (1842), XX, 250

John P. Gray, destroyer escort (1944), XXXVIII, 284

John P. West, whaling bark (1857), XXV, 104

John Parker, ship, XXI, 87; *(1861),* XI, 284

John Paul, schooner, XXIV, 37

John Paul Jones, Fighter for Freedom and Glory, by Lincoln Lorenz, reviewed, III, 272–273

"John Paul Jones and His Ships: The Need for More Research," by William Salisbury, XXVIII, 195–205

John Paul Jones and the Battle of Flamborough Head: A Reconsideration, by Thomas J. Schaeper, reviewed, L, 143

John Pierce, brig, XXVIII, 148

John Porter, ship (1859), V, 151

"John Prichett Gillis," by Robert E. Owens, Jr., XXXVII, 276–287

John Quincy Adams and the Sloop "Restoration," by Theodore C. Blegen, reviewed, I, 324

John R. Manta, schooner (1904), IX, 27; *(1925),* XXXIII, 64

John R. Neal & Co., XLIV, 116

John R. Wilder, schooner *(1861),* XV, 123

John Randolph, steamship *(1847),* XLVII, 34; *(1861),* VIII, 219; XV, 99, 123

John Ravenel, ship, XXI, 94; *(1861),* VIII, 219, 225

John Roach, Maritime Entrepreneur: The Years as Naval Contractor, 1862–1886, by Leonard Alexander Swann, Jr., reviewed, XXVI, 286–287

"John Rodgers," query by Walter Muir Whitehill, VIII, 154

John S. Lee, schooner *(1861),* XI, 284

John S. McKim, steamship (1844), XXXVI, 253 ff.; XXXVII, 140

John S. Williams, steamship (1862), XVII, 45, 61; XVIII, 70

John Scott, schooner, XXI, 87, 106; *(1863),* XII, 157, 231

John Scott & Sons, Greenock, XXXIV, 58

John Scott Russell and Co., XXVI, 113, 196, 207

John Smeaton, concrete ship (1943), XXII, 177, 182

Johnson, schooner *(1777),* XLIII, 26

Johnson, Andrew, XXVI, 263

Johnson, Arthur L., "The Boston-Halifax Steamship Lines," XXXVII, 231–238; "From *Eastern State* to *Evangeline:* A History of the Boston-Yarmouth,

Nova Scotia Steamship Services," XXXIV, 174–187; "The International Line: A History of the Boston-Saint John Steamship Service," XXXIII, 79–94
Johnson, Captain B. R., XVII, 227; XVIII, 83; XLIX, 26
Johnson, Barbara E., review by, XXX, 70–71
Johnson, Captain Charles, XXI, 94
Johnson, Charles M., XXXVIII, 268
Johnson, Dean, XXXVI, 241
Johnson, Captain George C., XVI, 263; XVIII, 83
Johnson, Captain Henry, XXI, 94
Johnson, Captain Henry W., XVI, 252; XVII, 43, 302; XVIII, 83; XXXIV, 33 ff.; XLIII, 92 ff.
Johnson, J. H., XXXVI, 233
Johnson, Midshipman James L., U.S.N., XXV, 141
Johnson, John, XXXVI, 25
Johnson, Captain John, XXI, 94
Johnson, Lloyd, XXXVI, 241, 244, 245, 247 n.
Johnson, President Lyndon Baynes, XXV, 247
Johnson, Mary Louise, and David Klein, *They Took to the Sea,* reviewed, IX, 304
Johnson, Captain Nat., VII, 65
Johnson, Peter, VII, 46 n.
Johnson, Captain R., IV, 201
Johnson, Senator Richard M., XXXVIII, 43
Johnson, Captain Robert, XXI, 94
Johnson, Robert E., XXIX, 106
Johnson, Robert Erwin, "A Cruise in the U.S.S. *Lancaster,*" XXXIII, 280–293; "*Haida*'s Arctic Cruise," XXXVII, 95–110; "Investment by Sea: The Civil War Blockade," XXXII, 45–57; *Rear Admiral John Rodgers, 1812–1882,* reviewed, XXVIII, 294–295
Johnson, Captain Samuel, XIX, 10
Johnson, Stanley, XXXII, 29
Johnson, Captain Thomas, XXI, 94
Johnson, Turpin and Dunbar, XXXVIII, 62
Johnson, William, VII, 309–312; XXII, 118 ff.
Johnson, Captain William, XXI, 94
Johnson, Captain William O., XVIII, 83
Johnson's Coal Dock, XXX, 188
Johnson's Manual, XXX, 31
Johnstone, Commodore, R.N., V, 66 ff.
Johnston, Midshipman Frederick John, XVII, 203–211
Johnston, Major George, XII, 253, 258–268
Johnston, Henry Elliott, XXXVI, 178 n.
Johnston, James, XV, 64
Johnston, Lieutenant James D., XXVII, 162, 163, 166, 169, 171, 172
Johnston, Captain John, XXI, 94
Johnston, General Joseph, XXVII, 175; XXXIII, 14.; XXXIX, 37
Johnston, Paul Forsythe, reviews by, XLII, 228; XLIII, 142–143; XLV, 118; XLVI, 121; XLVII, 283; L, 63–65; editor, illustrator and supplementor of *The Philadelphia Steamboat of 1796,* by Melvin H. Jackson, L, 201–218; editor of *Proceedings of the Sixteenth Conference on Underwater Archaeology,* reviewed, XLVIII, 200; *Ship and Boat Models in Ancient Greece,* reviewed, XLVI, 120
Johnston, Robert, XLVI, 30
Johnston, Waldo C. M., editorial comment, XXXVII, 3–4; XXXVIII, 231
John Stroup, schooner (1861), XXIV, 59
John Swasey, bark (1850), VII, 318
John Swire and Sons, Ltd., XVIII, 61
John T. Wright, steamship (1860), XVII, 214; XVIII, 70; *(1860),* XLIII, 110 ff.
John Thompson, sloop *(1862),* VIII, 225; XII, 55
John W. Anderson, schooner, XXI, 87; *(1861),* XV, 123
John W. Haring, steamship (1872), VI, 62
John W. Wells, schooner (1918), V, 140
John Wade, ship (1851), XIX, Plate XXII
John Watts, American ship *(1863),* XLV, 197
John Welch, bark *(1861),* VIII, 219; XI, 150
"John Wentworth vs. Kennebeck Proprietors: The Formation of Royal Mast Policy 1769–1778," by Gordon E. Kershaw, XXXIII, 95–119
John Wesley, sloop *(1863),* XII, 157
John Williams, schooner, XXI, 91
John Wills, bark (1856), III, 70; VI, 82
Jolinck, Heyndrick, L, 284
Jolly, Israel, XXXI, 26
Jolly Robbins, schooner *(1800),* XXXIX, 35
Jolly Robin, privateer *(1757),* XXIII, 280, 281
Joly, XXX, 260
Jonah, ship (1809), XIV, 96 ff.
Jonas Smith, schooner *(1861),* VIII, 219
Jonathan Bourne, bark (1877), VI, 123
Jonathan Bourne Whaling Museum, XIV, 34
Jonathan Chase, ship *(1870),* XXXVIII, 237
"Jonathan Russell, *President Adams,* and Europe in 1810," by Norman E. Saul, XXX, 279–293
Jones, A. C., XL, 104
Jones, Alfred, XLVI, 105
Jones, Sir Alfred, XXIX, 122
Jones, Captain C. F., XLIII, 289
Jones, Consul Caleb, XXXVIII, 37
Jones, Commander Catesby, XXXVI, 202
Jones, Captain Christopher, XIV, 6, 16; XVII, 128–133; XVIII, 318
Jones, Fred, XXI, 200
Jones, George G., XV, 138
Jones, H. A., XXXVI, 247 n.
Jones, Henry, XXVI, 173–175, plate 18
Jones, Captain Henry, XLIII, 188 ff.
Jones, Commodore Jacob, XL, 41
Jones, Captain Jerome B., XXI, 94
Jones, Captain John, XLVIII, 35
Jones, John C., XLVI, 46
Jones, John Coffin, XIII, 122; XVIII, 324; XXXII, 119 ff.
Jones, John Coffin, Jr., XIII, 242
Jones, Senator John P., XXV, 266

Jones, Captain John Paul, U.S.N., XXV, 35, 202 n., 204, 211, 255
Jones, John Paul, III, 55–56, 272–273; XVIII, 301–305; XXVI, 179; XXVIII, 49, 51, 195–205; XXXVI, 162 ff.; XXXVIII, 232; XXXIX, 159 ff.; XLIII, 20 ff.; XLIV, 103 ff.; XLV, 246; XLVIII, 156
Jones, Jonathan, XXX, 94
Jones, Joseph, XXXIII, 32
Jones, Captain Richard, XIV, 124
Jones, Robert F., "The Naval Thought and Policy of Benjamin Stoddert, First Secretary of the Navy, 1798–1801," XXIV, 61–69
Jones, Russell K., and C. McKim Norton, *The Cruising Cookbook,* reviewed, IX, 306
Jones, Captain Samuel, XI, 23
Jones, Captain T., XXI, 105
Jones, Captain Thomas, XVII, 132
Jones, Captain Thomas ap Catesby, XLVI, 45
Jones, Commodore Thomas ap Catesby, XXIX, 174; XXX, 297
Jones, Lieutenant Thomas Ap Catesby, XLII, 115; XLIII, 140
Jones, Captain Thomas W., XXI, 94
Jones, Virginia Crowell, review by, XL, 230
Jones, W. & S., XLVI, 261
Jones, Captain W. C., XXI, 94
Jones, Wilbur D., XXIX, 10 n.
Jones, William, XIV, 215, 216; XV, 71; XXXI, 286; XXXV, 115
Jones, William (Secretary of the Navy, 1813), XXXIII, 231 ff.; XLIII, 6 ff.; XLVI, 158; XLVII, 20
Jones & Laughlin Steel Co., XXXIII, 155
Joppien, Rudiger, Andrew David and Bernard Smith, *The Charts and Coastal Views of Captain Cook's Voyages: The Voyage of the* Endeavor, *1768–1771* (The Hakluyt Society Extra Series No. 43), reviewed, XLIX, 318
Jordain, Silvester, XXIX, 276
Jordan, Captain John, XXI, 265
Jordan, Captain John W., IX, 171
Jordan, Captain Oliver, III, 92
Jordan, Thomas, XXXVIII, 234
Jörg, Christiaan J. A., XLVII, 275
Jorge Juan, H.C.M., steamship *(1860),* XXVI, 125
Jorgensen, Captain A. B., L, 260 ff.
Jorgenson, Captain J., XXI, 95
Jorgenson, Captain Lin, XXV, 293
Jorgenson Affair, VIII, 184 ff.
Jose Gaspar, schooner (1902), V, 293–294, plates 23, 24
Jose Olvaerri, schooner *(1885),* XXXII, 7
Joseph, brig *(1861),* VIII, 219
Joseph, schooner (1801), XXX, plate 4
Joseph, snow, XXII, 87
Joseph, Benjamin, XXVIII, 245, 246, 247, 248
Joseph, Captain W. F., XLIV, 18 ff.
Joseph and Robert, sloop *(1759),* IX, 144
Joseph and Ruth, brig (1810), VII, 317

Joseph Ann, schooner, *(1861),* VIII, 219
Joseph Aspdin, concrete ship (1943), XXII, 177
Joseph B. Thomas, ship *(1885),* IX, 68
Joseph Banks in Newfoundland and Labrador, 1776: His Diary, Manuscripts and Collections, by A. M. Lysaght, reviewed, XXXII, 137
Joseph Belknap, vessel *(1850),* XXXVI, 172
Joseph Buck, schooner (1872), XVII, 117
Joseph Cowperthaite, brig (1838), XXXVI, 225
Joseph Fish, ship (1866), IV, 244
Joseph H. Toone, schooner (1861), XI, 284
Joseph Howe, ship *(1860),* XLVII, 104
Josephine, barge *(1889),* XXXVII, 89
Josephine, bark (1877), II, 335; *(1877),* Pictorial Supplement, XXXIII, plate XIX (upper).
Josephine, brig, XXI, 89; *(1861),* XI, 284; XII, 55
Josephine, privateer corvette *(1807),* IX, 13
Josephine, schooner *(1865),* XII, 235
Josephine, schooner yacht *(1894),* XXXVI, 238
Josephine, ship *(1865),* XXII, plate XI
Josephine, sloop *(1864),* XII, 231
Josephine and Mary, fishing vessel *(1961),* XLI, 53
Josephine Rosa, schooner *(1862),* VIII, 225
Joseph L. Gerety, schooner *(1863),* XXXII, 195
Joseph Parke, brig *(1861),* XV, 289
Joseph Peabody, ship (1856), V, 149
Joseph T. Brenan, schooner, XXXVII, 165
Josephus, brig *(1861),* VIII, 219
Josephus, ship *(1790),* XLIV, 6 ff.
Josephus, ship (1876), cabin, II, plate 27; interior view of, Pictorial Supplement, XXXI, plate XXIII
Joseph W. Fordney, steamship (ex-*Beaumont*) (1901), Pictorial Supplement, XXXIV, plate XXVI
Joseph Walker, ship *(1853),* XVII, 21
Joseph Warner, auxiliary schooner, I, 65
Josepina Martine, bark (1868), III, 66, 265
Jose Ton, schooner *(1862),* XII, 56
Joshua Bates, ship (1831), XIV, 37, 38, 40; XV, 140
Josiah, Lieutenant James, XXX, 220
Josiah L. Hale, ship (1857), XXVIII, plate X
Josiah M. Reeve, sloop (1830), XXXVI, 255
Josie and Phebe, Boston schooner (1908), XLIV, 122
Josie Mildred, grain elevator *(1883),* XXXVIII, 141
Josie R. Burt, schooner (1882), XXIII, 10
Josselyn, John, XXV, 61; XLVI, 213
Jottings from a Cruise, by Captain Alfred J. Green, reviewed, V, 249–250
Jourdan, William P., XXX, 242
Journal aboard the Bark Ocean Bird *on a Whaling Voyage to Scammon's Lagoon, winter 1858–59,* by Charles Melville Scammon, reviewed, XXXIII, 212–213
Journal Aboard the Louise, by Otis Oldfield, reviewed, XXX, 304
Journal and Letters of Captain Charles Bishop on the North-West Coast of America, in the Pacific and in New South Wales 1794–1799, The, by Michael Roe, Editor, reviewed, XXVIII, 227–228

"Journal of a Passage Through the Straits of Magellan in 1829," by Captain Edgar K. Thompson, U.S.N. (ret.), XXIII, 186–191

"Journal of a Voyage from Boston to the Coast of California," by Richard Henry Dana, Jr., edited by James Allison, XII, 177–185

Journal of a Voyage with Bering, 1741–1742, by Georg W. Steller, reviewed, L, 141

Journal of Captain James Colnett aboard the Argonaut *from April 26, 1789 to Nov. 3, 1791, The,* edited by F. W. Howay, reviewed, I, 97–98

"Journal of Erasmus Darwin Rogers, the First Man on Heard Island, The," by Rhys Richards, XLI, 280–305

Journal of James Young, The, F. N. L. Poynter, Editor, reviewed, XXIV, 148

"Journal of Nathan Prince, The," by William L. Sachse, XVI, 81–97

Journal of Richard Henry Dana, Jr., The, by Robert F. Lucid, Editor, 3 volumes, reviewed, XXIX, 286

Journal of the Franklin Institute, XXX, 15

"Journal of the Ship *Empress of China,*" edited by William Bell Clark, X, 83–107, 220–229, 288–297; XI, 59–71, 134–144

"Journal of Voyages of the Brig *Venus* and the Schooner *Louisiana* in 1806, The," by George Barrell, edited by E. Lee Dorsett, III, 222–238

Journal of William Sturgis, The, S. W. Jackman, reviewed, XXXIX, 145

Journals and Letters of Sir Alexander Mackenzie, The, by W. Kaye Lamb, Editor, reviewed, XXXI, 291

Journals and Other Documents on the Life and Voyages of Christopher Columbus, translated and edited by Samuel Eliot Morison, reviewed, XXV, 75

Journals of Ashley Bowen (1728–1813) of Marblehead, The, by Philip Chadwick Foster Smith, Editor, reviewed, XXXIII, 305–307

Journals of Captain James Cook on His Voyages of Discovery, The, edited by J. C. Beaglehole, reviewed, XVI, 281–285

Journals of Captain James Cook on his Voyages of Discovery: III, The Voyage of the Resolution *and* Discovery, *1776–1780, The,* J. C. Beaglehole, Editor, reviewed, XXVIII, 146–148

Journals of Hezekiah Prince, Jr., reviewed, XXVI, 146

Journegan, Captain Leonard, XXXI, 288

Jovellar, Captain General, XXXVI, 94, 97

Joven Elvira, ship *(1861),* XI, 284

Joy, Captain George, XXXIV, 254

Joy, Reuben, XXXIII, 163

Joyner, Captain John, XXXIX, 168

Juana Teresa, brig *(1861),* XI, 284; XV, 116, 123

Juan F. Pearson, bark (1864), IV, 241

Juan Fernández Islands, XXX, 300

Juanita, schooner *(1864),* XII, 231

Juanita, yacht *(1906),* XXXVI, 242

Juan Rodriguez Cabrillo, Discoverer of the Coast of California, by Henry R. Wagner, reviewed, II, 258–259

Juan Sebastian de Elcano, Spanish training ship *(1927),* II, 327; *(1964),* XXIV, 79

Juarez, steamship *(1868),* XIV, 200 n.

Jubilee, bark *(1861),* XXI, 258

Jubilee, sloop (1893), XXX, Plate XV

Jubilee, yacht *(1897),* XXXVI, 239, 240

Judd, Bernice and Helen Yonge Lind, *Voyages to Hawaii Before 1860,* reviewed, XXXV, 217

Judeth, ship, XXII, 102

Judge, Mrs. Daisy Taylor, XXX, 22

Judkin, Lieutenant, British Army, XXV, 206–207

Judson, schooner, XXI, 102; *(1864),* XII, 231

Jugoslavenski Registrar Brodova, XXX, 31

Julia, bark *(1861),* XI, 284; XII, 56, 231

Julia, schooner, XXI, 92, 99; *(1861),* VIII, 219, 225

Julia, ship *(1861),* XI, 266, 284

Julia, sloop, XXI, 86; *(1854),* X, 231 ff.; *(1808),* XVI, 206; *(1861),* XI, 284; XII, 56; XV, 127, 129

Julia, steamship, XXI, 102, plate VIII; *(1864),* VIII, 234

Julia A. Hodges, schooner *(1864),* XII, 231

Julia A. Ward, schooner *(1888),* XXXV, 12

Julia Ann, brig (1826), XXIV, 57

Julia Dean, schooner *(1862),* VIII, 225

Julia E. Pratt, schooner (1861), XI, 284

Julia Farmer, ship (1854), II, 245; III, 264

Julia Frances, schooner (1889), XXIII, plate V

Julia Grace, schooner *(1861),* VIII, 219

Julia Luckenbach, steamship *(1905),* XXXVIII, 188 ff.

Julia Marshall, schooner *(1862),* 225

Julia Marshall, sloop, XXI, 87

Julian, ship (1828), XIV, 40; Pictorial Supplement, XXXVIII, plate VIII; *(1871),* XIV, 46

Juliana, lugger, XXI, 103; *(1861),* XI, 285

Julia Palmer, ship *(1839),* XVIII, 297; *(1840),* XX, 82 n., 90 n.

Julia Usher, steamship *(1862),* VIII, 225, 230

Julia Worden, schooner *(1861),* VIII, 219, 225

Julien, Gustave, XXXVI, 275

Juliet, schooner *(1813),* XLIV, 172

Juliet, schooner (1856), X, 231 ff.; *(1863),* XII, 157

Juliet Small, schooner (1856), XXIV, 59

Julie Usher, steamship, XXI, 98

Julién, schooner, XXI, 95

Julius, Charles, XXXVI, 271

Julius Caesar, ship (1804), XIV, 40

Julius Caesar, snow *(1747),* XX, 111

Julius Caesar, whaler (1852), XLI, 292

Julius Cammert, bark (1859), XV, 186

Julius Ceasar, ship (1837), XV, 185

Julius Cross, steamship *(1824),* XXXVII, 244

July, pinky *(1832),* XXXVII, 169

Jundo Maru, steamship *(1862),* XLIII, 106 ff.

Juniata, U.S. warship *(1873),* XXVIII, 23; *(1874),* XXXVI, 98; XXXVIII, 247

Junior, ship (1836), XXI, 110–129
Juniper, schooner *(1863),* XII, 157
Juniper, ship *(1853),* XXVIII, 122
Juniper Waterway: A History of the Albemarle and Chesapeake Canal, by Alexander Crosby Brown, reviewed, XLIII, 303–305
Junius Smith, pioneer promoter of Transatlantic Steam Navigation, by E. Le Roy Pond, reviewed, I, 318
Junkman Smiles, The, by G. R. G. Worcester, reviewed, XX, 147
Junks and Sampans of the Yangtze, The, by G. R. G. Worcester, reviewed, VIII, 257–258; reviewed, XI, 296–297; reviewed, XXXII, 226
Juno, brig *(1852),* XIV, 44
Juno, H.M.S. *(1799),* XLV, 93
Juno, packet *(1783),* XXXIX, 206; XL, 48
Juno, schooner *(1776),* XX, 45
Juno, ship *(1805),* XIX, 13
Juno, steamship, XXI, 81, 88, 99, 102, 105; *(1855),* XVII, 253 n.; *(1863),* XVII, 253 ff.; VIII, 230, 234
Junon, British frigate *(1813),* XXXI, 286; XL, 28; *(1814),* XLII, 108; XLIII, 140
Junsoku Maru, steamship (ex-*Meteor*) *(1858),* XLIX, 26
Jupiter, bark *(1861),* XXI, 258
Jupiter, collier, XXII, 142
Jupiter, French warship, XXII, 95
Jupiter, H.M.S. *(1826),* XXI, 57
Jurado, General Leon, XXIV, 27
"Jury Rudder for the Bark *Guy C. Goss,* A," by Lincoln Colcord, II, 65–70
Jury rudders, II, 65–70; VIII, 67
"'Just Ease Her When She Pitches,'" by William G. Saltonstall, XV, 249–258
Justice, auxiliary (1918), XXXII, 19, 30
Justin, supply ship, XXXVII, 138
Justina, schooner, XXI, 102
Justina, sloop *(1863),* XV, 128
Justina Randel, schooner *(1861),* VIII, 219
Jutland, Battle of, XXV, 277

Kaaterskill, steamship (1882), XVIII, 224, 230, plate 15
Kaga-no-kami, steamship (1861), XVIII, 70
Kagoshima Maru, steamship (ex-*Banri Maru,* ex-*Banri,* ex-*Cosmopolite*), XXVI, 113
Kahler, Captain Henry, XXI, 95
Kahn, A.D., XXII 180
Kahre, George, *Den Alandske Segelsjöfartens Historia,* reviewed, II, 351–352
Kaikioulaie, schooner (1880), V, 86
Kaimon Maru, steamship (ex-*Viola*) *(1864),* XLIX, 25
Kaiser, S.M S. *(1890),* XXV, 65

Kaiserin Augusta Victoria, Hamburg American liner (1905), XXXVIII, 10
Kaiser Wilhelm der Grosse, German ship, XXVIII, 108 n.; *(1915),* XLV, 199 ff.
Kaisha, Toyo Kisen, XXXV, 167
Kaiulani, 3-masted steel bark (1889), II, 172; VII, 294; VIII, 279, 284–285; XXV, 232; XXVII, plate XIII
Kakundy, XXX, 181, 185
Kalakaua, bark (1864), VII, 317
Kalamazoo, ship (1840), IV, 73
Kalamazoo, U.S. monitor (1862), X, 25, 32; *(1864),* XXVII, 42, 44; *(1867),* XXXIV, 61
Kaleta, yacht *(1899),* XXXVI, 240
Kalliopi, Greek merchant ship *(1943),* XLIV, 55
Kalm, Pehr, VIII, 91 ff.
Kalrola, schooner *(1861),* XI, 285
Kamehameha, King, XLI, 228 ff.
Kamschatka, steamship *(1841),* XXIV, 10
Kamtschatka, Russian frigate *(1840),* XLVIII, 110
Kan, David, XLIV, 110
Kanal, steamship *(1950),* XIV, 135
Kanawa, bark (1864), IV, 72
Kanawha, ship *(1863),* XLV, 238
Kanawha, steamship *(1920),* XXXV, 205
Kane, Dr. Elisha, XX, 105–111
Kane, Elisha Kent, XXV, 51
Kane, Captain Henry C., XXIX, 270
Kane, Captain Newell, IX, 171
Kane, Robert, "Sailors and Whalers: Lakemen of Pultneyville," XXXIV, 243–248
Kang, Colonel, L, 291 ff.
Kankakee, wooden steamship (1863), XVII, 62, 63; XVIII, 70; *(1869),* XLIX, 25
Kanrin Maru, Japanese steam warship (1859), XX, 198–208; *(1860),* XXI, 142–143
Kansas, U.S. warship *(1864),* XXXII, 199; *(1873),* XXXVI, 90 f.; XXXVIII, 239 ff.
Kansas City, steamship (1893), XIV, 122, 123, 125, 134
Kanus, H.M.S. *(1859),* XXVII, 168
Kanyei Maru, steamship *(1865),* XLIII, 211
Kapingamarangi Island, XXXIV, 256; outrigger canoe of, X, 40–41, plate 9
Karlsruhe, German cruiser, XXVIII, 108; *(1915),* XLV, 199 ff.
Karlsson, Elis, XXX, 219
Karluk, steam brigantine *(1893),* XXXVIII, 85
Karnes, Thomas L., *Tropical Enterprise: The Standard Fruit and Steamship Company in Latin America,* reviewed, XL, 140
Karsten, Peter, XXXIX, 118; *The Naval Aristocracy: the Golden Age of Annapolis and the Emergence of Modern American Navalism,* reviewed, XXXIII, 67–68
Katahdin, steamship (1863), XII, plate 30; *(1864),* XXXVI, 204
Kate, bark *(1860),* XI, 285; XXXVI, 183
Kate, brig, XXI, 102

Kate, iron screw steamship, XXI, 92, 96, 99, 106; *(1861),* VIII, 219, 225; XV, 99, 115, 120, 123, 126; XLIII, 192 ff.
Kate, schooner, XXI, 94; *(1862),* VIII, 225; XII, 56, 157
Kate, sloop, XXI, 91, 101; *(1863),* VIII, 230; XII, 158; XV, 111, 128
Kate (II), steamship, XXI, 102; *(1863),* VIII, 230
Kate Cory, brig *(1863),* XV, 292
Kate Dale, schooner, XXI, 96
Kate Dale, sloop *(1863),* XII, 158, 231
Kate Dale, steamship *(1863),* XII, 158
Kate Davis, wrecking schooner *(1894),* XLII, 265
Kate G. Pederson, barkentine (1920), V, 82
Kate Gregg, steamship, XXI, 103; *(1864),* VIII, 234; IX, 46
Kate Hale, schooner, XXI, 87
Kate Harding, bark (1869), II, 246
Kate L. Bruce, schooner, XXI, 102; *(1861),* XI, 285
Kate M. Hilton, schooner, XV, 227
Kate Merril, bark (1863), III, 65
Kate Price, ship (1864), XV, 300, 301
Kate Smith, schooner *(1904),* XXXVIII, 89
Kate Swanton, ship (1852), IV, 51
Katharine, schooner (1887), I, 78
Katharine of Clermont. See *Katherine of Clermont* and *Clermont,* XXIV 167 n.
Katherine, ship (1887), IV, 325; IX, 297
Katherine Mackall, barkentine (1920), V, 82
Katherine May, brig (1919), XLIX, 31
Katherine May, schooner, XXIV, 34
Katherine of Clermont, steamship (1807), XVIII, 316–317. See also *Clermont.*
Kathleen, bark *(1844),* Pictorial Supplement, XXXIII, plate XXII; *(1881),* XIX, 232–234; *(1902),* I, 394
Kathleen, steamship *(1862),* XLIII, 207
Katie Thomas, yacht *(1895),* XXXVI, 238
Katsu, Rintaro, XX, 201 ff.
Kauffman, Ray, Hurricane's *Wake,* reviewed, I, 189
Kaufman, Jay R. and William M. Fowler, Jr., "Into the Ocean World," XLIV, 110–113
Kaufman, Les, XLIV, 112
Kayak, West Greenland, XXVI, plate 4
Kazbek, Bulgarian ship *(1944),* XLIII, 35 ff.
Kearney, Captain Lawrence, U.S.N., XXV, 111
Kearney, Captain Stephen, U.S.A., Corps of Engineers, XXV, 111
Kearney, General Stephen W., XLIX, 112
Kearny, U.S.S. *(1941),* XLV, 52
Kearny, Captain Lawrence, XXIX, 110
Kearny, Commodore Lawrence, XXXI, 184
Kearsage, battleship *(1900),* XXXVIII, 130
Kearsarge, ship (1864), III, 71
Kearsarge, sloop of war (bark-rigged) (1864), XLVII, 118; XLIX, 117
Kearsarge, U.S.S. *(1861),* XV, 290; *(1862),* XXXIII, 7 ff.; *(1863),* XII, 254; XIX, 126–128; XX, 62; *(1864),* XXVII, 36, 39 n., 43, 266–268; XXIX, 167–173; *(1889),* IX, 63
Keate, George, XII, 256–257
Keelboat Age on Western Waters, The, by Leland D. Baldwin, reviewed, II, 343–344
Keeler, Acting Paymaster William Frederick, U.S.N., XXIV, 219–221
"Keel-hauling," query by L. W. Jenkins, II, 339
Keen, James, XXXV, 227 ff.
Keen, Jarius, XV, 179, 187
Keene, Joshua, XI, 73
Keer, Captain Robert, XX, 87
Keigaka Maru, steamship (ex-*China*) *(1862),* XLIX, 26
Kell, Lieutenant John M., XXXIII, 53
Kelley, ship *(1945),* XXXIX, 259
Kelley, Hall J., XXVIII, 129
Kelley, Lieutenant J. D. J., XLIV, 39
Kelley, Captain William, XXXIX, 8
Kelley-Spear Shipyard, XXVII, plate XXV
Kellie, Captain, VII, 191
Kellock, Adam, XXVI, 203
Kellogg, Captain E. S., U.S.N. (ret.), IV, 4, 31
Kellogg, Frank B., Secretary of State, XXXIV, 162
Kellogg, J. Stewart, I, 102
Kelly, Celsus, O.F.M., *La Austrialia del Espíritu Santo,* revised, XXVI, 220–221
Kelly, Heman, XXII, 243
Kelly, Henry & Sons, VII, 72
Kelly, Admiral Sir Howard, XXXVII, 194
Kelly, J., XXXVI, 238
Kelly, Commander John, XXX, 159–162, 166
Kelly, John W., XXXIX, 14
Kelpie, cutter yacht, XXXVI, 237–239, plate 7
Keltridge, William, XV, 152
Kelverdale, barque *(1886),* XL, 115
Kelvin, Bottomley, and Baird, XIII, 66
Kemble, Captain Edmund, XVII, 221; XVIII, 83
Kemble, John H., XI, 4
Kemble, Professor John H., XXXVII, 81
Kemble, John Haskell, II, 84, 340; V, 165; queries by, II, 339; III, 353; reviews by, I, 318; reviews by, XLIV, 205–206; XLVI, 123; XLVII, 217; XLVIII, 131; XLIX, 63; L, 151, 152; "Amphibious Operations in the Gulf of California, 1847–1848: A Contemporary Account," Edited by, V, 121–136; "Cabin Plan of the Pacific Mail Steamer *Japan,"* II, 243; "A Century of Pacific Steamers," I, 83; *"Chrysopolis:* The Queen of the Golden River," II, 299–306; "H.M.S. *Cormorant:* First Steam Warship in the North Pacific," IX, 63–65, plate 5; "A Hundred years of the Pacific Mail," X, 123–143, plates 17–20; *The Panama Route 1848–1869,* reviewed, IV, 80–81; *Pioneer Hawaiian Steamers, 1852–1877,* reviewed, X, 158; "Side-Wheelers Across the Pacific," II, 5–38; "The *Victoria,"* I, 80, plate facing 79
Kemp, Captain Peter, XLI, 288
Kempenfelt, Admiral, XXX, 210

Kemperfeldt, Admiral, XXXI, 219
Kenbane Head, steamship *(1940),* XIV, 130
Kendall, Abraham, XVII, 33
Kendall, Captain George, XLI, 53
Kendall, Henry B., XVII, 3–4
Kendall, Mrs. Henry P., XXII, 16
Kendall Whaling Museum, Sharon (MA), XVII, 3; XXI, plates I ff.; XXII, 16; XXXV, 4; Annual Whaling Symposium, mentioned, XLII, 244; *Maritime Titles in Print,* XXXVIII, 155; XXXIX, 60
Kendall Whaling Museum Prints, by M. V. and Dorothy Brewington, reviewed, XXX, 218–219
Kendrick, Captain, XLVIII, 246
Kendrick, John, XIX, 133–134; XLVI, 51
Kendrick, Captain John, XV, 205–212; XLI, 26
Kenilworth, bark (1887), I, 333–334, plates facing 334, 335; III, 266
Kenilworth, ship (1853), VI, 81
Kenmore, ship (1861), III, 70
Kennebec, steamship (1889), XIV, 192
Kennebeck Purchase Co., XXXIII, 95 ff.
Kennebec River (ME), XXV, plate XVII; XXX, 114, 115
Kennebunk (ME), III, 355; V, 94, 172; ships built at, XXV, 18 n.
Kennebunkport customs records, XIII, 123
Kennedy, Alexander Lucet, XVI, 234, 239
Kennedy, Captain Archibald, XXIII, 175 ff.; XXVII, 216–218
Kennedy, Don H., note by, 107; "The Infamous *Ningpo,*" XXIX, 262–274
Kennedy, Captain E. P., XXXII, 269
Kennedy, Jeremiah (shipbuilder), XXIV, 39, 40, 57 ff.
Kennedy, John F., XXXVI, 160
Kennedy, John P., XX, 107
Kennedy, John P., Secretary of the Navy, XXXI, 8
Kennedy, Paul, *The Rise and Fall of Naval Mastery,* reviewed, XLIV, 208
Kennedy, Captain Samuel, XVIII, 83
Kenney, Captain G. W., XVIII, 83
Kennithorpe, Arthur, XXXI, 88
Kennithorpe, George, XLVII, 77
Kenny, Herbert A., *Cape Ann: Cape America,* reviewed, XXXI, 291
Kenny, Robert W., "The Maiden Voyage of *Ann and Hope,* of Providence to Botany Bay and Canton, 1798–1799," XVIII, 105–136, plates 5–10; "Yankee Whalers at the Bay of Islands," XII, 22–44
Kensett, John F. (engraver), XXV, 46, 47
Kensett, John Frederick, XXV, 47
Kensett, Thomas (engraver), XXV, 46, 47, 49
Kensington, British steamship *(1912),* XXXVIII, 195 ff.
Kensington, ship (1861), XV, 108 n.; XXI, 256
Kent, British ship *(1914),* XXXIII, 35 ff.
Kent, cruiser *(1936),* XXXVII, 194 ff.
Kent, ship (1806), XIV, 89, 90; *(1863),* VIII, 230
Kent, steamship (1841), XX, 88, 89

Kent, First Lieutenant Bartholomew, XLVII, 16
Kent, Chancellor, XLVIII, 255
Kent, Captain Thomas, XXI, 105
Kentucky, brig (1805), VII, 317
Kentucky, U.S. battleship (1898), XXII, 211; XXXIV, 221; *(1900),* XXXVIII, 130
Kentville, bark (1863), III, 65
Keoka, ship *(1850),* XLV, 128
Keokuk, armored vessel *(1861),* XLVIII, 120; *(1863),* XLII, 196 ff.; XLIV, 268 ff.
Keokuk, U.S. monitor (1862), X, 18, 24, 31
Keon, George, XXIX, 63
Keora, yawl, XXVIII, 58
Keough, Richard, XIII, 214
Keough, Robert, XIII, 214
Keough, William T., XIII, 214
Kephalos, steamship *(1928),* XIV, 134
Kepler, bark *(1861),* VIII, 219; (1877), II, 335
Keppel, Admiral, XXXI, 220
Keppel, Admiral Augustus, VII, 88, 95, 98–100, 101 n.
Kerans, Lieutenant Commander John Simon, L, 291 ff.
Kerchove, Baron R. de, queries by, I, 398; II, 81, 174, 252; answered queries, III, 269, 270; review by, II, 345–346
Kergeulen Island (Indian Ocean), Discovery and exploration, XLI, 280
Kerguelen Sealing & Whaling Co., XL, 125
Kerr, Captain D., XXI, 95
Kerr, Gifford, and Co., XVIII, 12
Kerr, Robert, XL, 43
Kershaw, Gordon E., "John Wentworth vs. Kennebeck Proprietors: The Formation of Royal Mast Policy 1769–1778," XXXIII, 95–119
Kesler, Commander William, Jr., XXXVI, 26
Kessler, Franz, VII, 266, 278
Kestrel, H.M.S. *(1859),* XXVII, 168, 172; *(1860),* XXXIV, 25
Keswick, Maggie, *The Thistle and the Jade,* reviewed, XLIII, 149–150
Ketcham, Captain John, XIV, 166
Ketch (boat), XXX, 81
Ketches: "*Adventure,* A Seventeenth-Century Ketch," by William A. Baker, XXX, 81–85; colonial, Pictorial Supplement, XXXVI, plate III
Ketch rigs: XIX, 286–306; colonial, XXV, 89, 91
Kettelhas, Abraham, XVII, 292
Kewanee, steamship (1861), XVIII, 70; *(1869),* XLIX, 25
Keweenaw, steamship (1890), XLII, 246 ff., plates 5, 6
Key, Vice Admiral Sir Ashley Cooper, XXVIII, 87, 111
Key, Lieutenant Astley Cooper, XXXVI, 131, 135, 136
Key, George S., XXVI, 174–175, plate 18
Keymis, Lawrence, XXXVII, 10
Keystone State (1861), XV, 103 n.
Keystone State, steamship (1864), XXXIII, 207
Keystone State, U.S.S. *(1904),* XX, 137 n.
Keystone State, U.S. sidewheel steamship *(1863),* XLIV, 265

Key West, Florida, I, 403
Key West, steamship *(1860),* XXIII, 285
Khersonese, steamship (1855), XXVI, 198, 199, 205, 209
Khlebnikov, Kirik T., XLI, 230
Khosew, Capudan Pasha (Turkish Admiral), XL, 214 ff.
Kiangchang, steamship (1875), XVI, 265; XVII, 39
Kiangching, steamship (1865), XVI, 254; XVII, 39
Kiangfoo, steamship (1873), XVII, 39; (1878), XVI, 262
Kiang Ling Liberation, L, 291 ff.
Kiang Loong, steamship (1862), XVI, 254; XVII, 47, 48, 144; XVIII, 70; *(1862),* XLIII, 94 ff.; *(1867),* XXXIV, 53
Kiangpiao, steamship (ex-*Nautilus,* ex-*Fychow*) (1866), XVII, 39
Kiangpiau, steamship *(1877),* XVI, 261
Kiangse, steamship (1862), XVI, 246, 247; XVII, 39; XVIII, 70; *(1862),* XLIII, 116 ff., plate 3; XLIX, 23
Kiang Soo or *Kiangsoo,* steamship (1862), XVI, 173; XVII, 147; XVIII, 70
Kiangteen, steamship (ex-*Moning*) (1869), XVI, 260; XVII, 39; *(1869),* XLIX, 23
Kiangtsi/Kiangtsze, steamship (1862), XVI, 246; XXXIV, 32
Kiangtung, steamship (1871), XVI, 261; XVII, 39
Kiangwae, steamship (1864), XVI, 252; XVII, 38
Kiangyen, steamship (1863), XVII, 38
Kiao-chiao, steamship *(1861),* XLIII, 289 ff.
Kiautschou, steamship (1900), IX, 223
Kiawah, schooner *(1861),* VIII, 219
Kichisaburo, Vice Admiral Nomura, XXXVII, 198
Kickapoo, U.S. monitor (1862), X, 18, 31
Kidd, Captain William, XXXVII, 40
Kidd, Captain William (pirate), song about, XXV, 57
Kidd, James P., XXX, 243
Kiehne, Captain, XLV, 199 ff.
Kilbourne, Ralph, XXVIII, 135
Kilby, bark *(1854),* XLV, 26
Kilby, Daniel, XXVIII, 124
Kilham, Captain Abraham, XXII, 199
Kilian, Bernhard, *The Voyage of the Schooner* Polar Bear, reviewed, XLIV, 137
Killaloo, yacht *(1892),* XXXVI, 235
Killam, Samuel, XXXIV, 179
Killarney, schooner (1917), XXVI, plate XXVII
"Killick, The," by E. Lee Dorsett, IX, 299–300, plate 30
Killick Martin & Co., XLIII, 113 ff.
"Killicks," by Dohn A. Cluff, XV, 150–151
Killman, Captain D., XXI, 95
Kilmarx, Robert A., *America's Maritime Legacy: A History of the U.S. Merchant Marine and Shipbuilding Industry Since Colonial Times,* reviewed, XL, 142
Kilty, Captain A. H., XXII, 259
Kilty, Captain, U.S.N., XXV, 139
Kimball, Edward, XXX, 245
Kimball, Edward D., Salem merchant, Pictorial Supplement, XXXVIII, plate VII
Kimball, Edward D., XXX, 229 ff.

Kimball, Lieutenant Colonel Amos S., XL, 172 ff.
Kimball, Sumner I., XXXVII, 84 ff.
Kimberly, Commander L. A., U.S.N., VII, 111, 113, plate 9
Kimura, Lord, XX, 201 ff.
Kineo, schooner (1903), V, 138; XXIII, 10, 15, plate XIV
Kineo, U.S.S. *(1864),* XI, 275
King, Anna, XXXVIII, 208 ff.
King, Benjamin, XXI, 109; XLVI, 258
King, President Charles D. B., XXXIX, 179
King, Charles W., XLI, 26
King, Cyrus W., XXVII, plate XIV
King, Admiral Ernest J., XLII, 204; XLV, 60 ff.
King, Fay A. "U.S. Naval Expedition to the Dead Sea in 1848," IV, 71–72
King, Captain George J., VII, 62
King, Sir George St. Vincent, XXXII, 127
King, Gregory, XXV, 278
King, H. W., XXVI, 203
King, Henry, XXXVI, 93
King, Captain Irving, XLI, 42
King, Captain James, XXXVIII, 222
King, Lieutenant James, XXVIII, 146
King, John F. H., XXX, 21
King, Joseph, XXXIII, 166
King, Mary, L, 000
King, Captain N., XXI, 95
King, Captain Philip Parker, British Admiralty, L, 32
King, Pauline N., "Stephen Reynolds' Influence on Business and Culture in Hawaii, 1823–1855," XLVI, 43–49
King, R. H., III, 90
King, Rufus, XXXVI, 57
King, Samuel, XXXIV, 205
King, Captain T., XXI, 95
King, Thompson, *From the Potomac to the Thames, being the Progress of one James Rumsey (1743–1792),* reviewed, III, 357
King, Captain W. K., XXI, 105
King, W. W. (probably W. H.), XXII, 13
King, General William, XVI, 206
King, William F., XV, 220–231
King, William F., Jr., "The Sailmakers and Ship Chandlers of 79 Commercial Street, Boston," XV, 220–231
King, William H., XVI, 175
King, William R., XV, 220–231
King Boy Amain, XXXV, 79 ff.
King Cholric, ship (1875), I, 113
King-fa / King-Fa, steamship (1832), XVI, 160; XXII, 6, 7
Kingfisher (ex-*Marigram,* French trawler) *(1919),* XLIV, 125
King Forday Kulo, XXXV, 79 ff.
King George, British ship, XXIX, 247; (1787), XXXVIII, 223
"King George and the *Flying Dutchman,*" by Thomas Dunbabin, XVII, 156

King George's War (1744–1768). *See* United States (History)
King Jacket Mein, XXXV, 89
King Leopold, XXIX, 10
Kingmoor, steamship (1872), XXIV, plate XXV
King Philip, cutter (1884), XXX, plate IX
King Philip, figurehead sketch for, Pictorial Supplement, XXXVII, plates XXV, XXVII
King Philip, schooner (1845), XXIV, 45, 59
King Phillip, merchantman *(1874),* XXXIII, 286
King's Arms Tavern (Salem), XXXI, 198
Kingsford, schooner *(1811),* XXXIV, 245
Kingsley, steamship *(1900),* XIV, 124
Kingston, ship *(1783),* XXI, 213 n.; *(1805),* XLI, 286
Kingston, steamship (1833), VII, 51, 55; (1837), III, plate 14
Kingston Line, XVIII, 224
Kingston-upon-Hull Maritime Museum, XXX, 153
King v. Street, Thornton and Pastree, XXXI, 35
King William's War (1689–1697), XXXV, 153
Kinsatsu, steamship *(1871),* XLIX, 23
Kinsey, Comander William, XXXI, 22
Kinshan, steamship (1863), XVII, 45, 47, 144; XVIII, 70; XXXIV, 34 ff.
Kin Shan, steamship (1865), XXXIV, 55
Kinsman, Captain Nathaniel, XXV, 184
Kinyou, Reverend David, XIX, 53
Kinzie, Hunter & Co., agents, VII, 63
Kinzie, John H., XVIII, 274
Kipping, Robert, XXXI, 140
Kirby, Frank E., XXVII, 5
Kirby, H. S., XXXIX, 96
Kirby, John Henry, XXXV, 282
Kirk, H. F., XXXVI, 238
Kirkland, bark (1847), I, 45, 49
Kirkland, Edward Chase, *Men, Cities and Transportation, A Study in New England History,* reviewed, IX, 305–306
Kissinger, Frank, IV, 204–205
Kitagawa Utamaro, wood block print, XLVI, 54
Kit Carson, ship, XXII, 241
Kitchener, H.M.C.S. corvette *(1943),* L, 210 ff.
Kitchener Memorial, photo of, L, 130
Kitching, John B., XLVIII, 118
Kite, barkentine *(1891),* XXXVIII, 50
Kittredge, Henry C., "The Boston Packets," XXIV, 127–137
Kitty (1819), XV, 155
Kitty Sampson, ship *(1860),* XX, 215
Kiukiang, steamship (1861), XVI, 172; XVII, 134, 135; XVIII, 70; (1863), XXXIV, Plate 4, 40 ff.; *(1865),* XLIII, 195 ff.
Kiushiu, steamship (1862), XVI, 247; XVII, 138, 139 ff.; XVIII, 70
Kleber, French cruiser *(1907),* XXIX, 129
Klebingat, Fred, XXVIII, 224

Klein, Benjamin F. and Eleanor, *The Ohio River Handbook,* reviewed, X, 77–78
Klein, David, and Mary Louise Johnson, *They Took to the Sea,* reviewed, IX, 304
Klein, Eugene, *United States Waterway Packetmarks ... of Mail Carrying Steamboats ... 1832–1899,* reviewed, III, 94
Kleinschmidt, Captain James, XXV, 232; XXVIII, 163
Klep, Rolf, XXVI, 3
Klimm, Henry W., XLI, 51
Kline, M. S., and G. A. Bayless, *Ferryboats: A Legend on Puget Sound,* reviewed, XLIV, 205
Kling, Lieutenant, XXXVI, 272
Knap, Captain William, XXI, 12
Knap and Toten Foundry, XLV, 38
Knapp, B. R., XVII, 116
Knappenhof, Dutch ship *(1731),* XLVII, 245
Kneeland, Mrs. Thomas, XXXVI, 15
Knerr, Douglas, "Through the 'Golden Mist': A Brief Overview of Armada Historiography," XLIX, 5–13
Knickerbocker, steamship (1843), VI, 278
Knight, Charles, XXXV, 21
Knight, Captain E. D., XIX, 30–33
Knight, Ezra (shipbuilder), XXIV, 39, 57 ff.
Knight, Francis P., United States Consul, XXXII, 126
Knight, Nathaniel, XXX, 96 n.
Knight, R. J. B., "New England Forests and British Seapower: Albion Revised," XLVI, 221–229
Knight, Russell W., contributed document, XXIII, 143–145; XXIV, 72–73; XXV, 146; XXXII, 64–67; note by, XL, 226; reviews by, XX, 146, 224; XXIV, 233–246; XXV, 149–151; XXVI, 72–73, 146, 152; XXVII, 221–222; XXVIII, 149–150, 152, 232–233; XXIX, 70–71, 286; XXX, 303; XLIII, 310; XLVI, 120. "In Troubled Waters: The Elusive Schooner *Hannah,*" XXX, 86–116; "Letter from Captain Christopher Williams to Captain William D. Waters of Salem, dated 16 December 1833," XVII, 156; "Mr. Shaw 'Sees' *Portland* Sink," XXIX, 224–225
Knights, Captain John B., XII, 29, 40, 42
Knipe, William A., "The Mast Trade in New Hampshire," XXII, 65–70
Knives, sailmaker's, IX, 288
Knohr and Burchard Co., XVIII, 19, 151
Knorr, Viking vessel, XLV, 226
Knots, VIII, 154
Knowles, Admiral Charles, XLVIII, 25
Knowles, James A., query by, XLII, 220
Knowles, Josiah, XLIV, 20 ff.
Knowles, Josiah N., XXXIX, 7
Knowles, Captain Winslow L., XXXII, 3
Knowlton, Captain Harvey, XXVI, plate III
Knox, Dudley W., XI, 4
Knox, Captain Dudley W., U.S.N. (ret.), II, 269; IV, 181, 217, 261; V, 91; VI, 162; VIII, 157; IX, 237; XXXV, 4; editor, *Naval Documents Related to the United States Wars with the Barbary Powers,* Vol. III,

reviewed, II, 341; Vol. IV, reviewed, III, 180; editor, *Register of Officer Personnel United States Navy and Marine Corps and Ships' Data, 1801–1807,* reviewed, V, 248; "Yorktown, September-October, 1781," V, 240–241
Knox, Henry, XXX, 131
Knox, Henry, Secretary of War, XLIX, 47
Knox, Major General Henry, XLVI, 29
Knox, Captain Robert, XXIII, 176
Knox, Midshipman Samuel R., XLIX, 153
Knox, Thomas W., XXIV, 166 ff.
Knox, William, XXXVII, 290
Knudsen, Ruth, "Traces of Reed Boats in the Pacific," XXIII, 41–45
Kobbe, General William N., XXXV, 191
Kobell, H., XXII, plate XXXI
København, bark (1921), VI, 77, 135
Koch, Captain J., XVIII, 20–25, 149–152
Kochiss, John M., *The Deadeye: How it Was Made in Nova Scotia,* reviewed, XXXII, 74–75; *Oystering from New York to Boston,* reviewed, XXXVI, 147–148
Kock, J. J., XXIX, 209
Kodiak, Russian cutter *(1855),* XXXI, 272
Kodoku: Sailing Alone Across the Pacific, by Kenichi Horie, reviewed, XXX, 69
Koenig, Henry, XXXIX, 11
Kofuyo, steamship (ex-*Chusan*) *(1866),* XLIX, 26
Kohala, barkentine (1901), I, 77
Kohola, brig *(1862),* XXXVIII, 83
Kohola, ship *(1871),* XIV, 46
Koichi, Rear Admiral Shiozawa, XXXVII, 191
Koloa, brig (1853), VII, 316, plate 39
Komm, Captain John L., XXI, 95
Konigsberg, German raider *(1915),* XLV, 199 ff.
Kon Tiki, balsa raft, XXIII, 114
Kon-Tiki, raft (1947), XIII, 102 ff.; XV, 142, 143
Koopman, Captain James, XVI, 63
Koppel, Captain Herman, XXI, 95
Korea, steamship (1902), X, 137, 139, plate 20
Korea, Foreign relations, United States, VII, 107. See also Yalu River
Korea, Kingdom of, XXV, 117, 121
"Korea, The Navy in, 1871," by H. A. Gosnell, VII, 107–114, plates 9–12
Kortright, Lawrence, XXXVII, 61; XLVIII, 38
Kortum, Karl, XXXII, 29; note by, XXVIII, 224; "Star of India," XXII, 212–215
Koshi/Kinoyene, steamship (ex-*Carthage*) *(1864),* XXVI, 128
Kossak, brig (1866), XXVIII, plate XII
Kosugi, Jun, XIV, 19 ff., plate 4
Kosuku Maru, steamship (ex-*Fei Seen*) *(1867),* XXXIV, 51
Kotetsu. See C.S.S. *Stonewall.*
Kotzbue, Captain Otto Von, XXIII, 223–224
Kotzebue, Otto von, IV, 100–105, plates 21, 23
Kraken, cutter *(1651),* XV, 276

Krebs, German trawler *(1941),* XLV, 54
Kreger, Captain William R., XXXV, 12
Kremlin, bark (1890), II, 335, cabin of, plate 27
Krenkel, John H., "Development of the Port of Los Angeles," XXV, 262–273
Krieger, Martin L., Fleming MacLeish, *The Privateers, A Raiding Voyage to the Great South Sea,* reviewed, XXIII, 71–72
Kristsuden, Norwegian warship (A.D. 1262), XLIV, 100
Kronenshelt, Doctor John Kaspar Richter von, XIII, 235. See also Crowninshields of Salem.
Kronprins Gustaf, ship (1767), VI, 166
Kronprins Gustaf Adolph, ship (1782), VI, 169–170, plate 27
Kronprinzessin Cecelie, German ship, XXVIII, 108 n.
Kronprinz Wilhelm, German raider, XXVIII, 108 n.; *(1915),* XLIII, 270 ff.; XLV, 199 ff.; (1917), XLVIII, 53
Kru, XXX, 181, 231
Krueger, Hilmar C., "Genoese Shipowners and Their Ships in the Twelfth Century," XLVII, 229–239; *Navi e proprietá navale a Genove, seconda metá del sec. XII,* reviewed, XLVII, 216
Kruse, Admiral Gabriel, XXVIII, 257
Krusenstern, Adam Ivanovitch, IV, 100, plate 19
Kugler, Richard C., XXXIII, 4; review by, XXXIII, 212–213; editor, *New Bedford and Old Dartmouth: A Portrait of A Region's Past,* reviewed, XXXVI, 149
Kuhn, Gary G., "United States Maritime Influence in Central America, 1863–1865," XXXII, 277–286
Kumsing, steamship (1862), XVII, 143; XLIX, 25; (1863), XXXIV, 33 ff.
Kundhardt, C. P., XXX, 194; *Small Yachts: Their Design and Construction,* reviewed, XLIX, 232
Kungyi, steamship, XVI, 262
Kunhardt, Charles P., IV, 307
Kuniyoshi, XXII, plate XXXII; XXX, 219
Kuroda, steamship (1872), XVII, 306; XVIII, 70
Kuro Siwo Current (Japanese Gulf Stream), XXV, 95
Kurt, bark (1904), VI, 74–75, 77; *(1917),* XVIII, 165, 170
Kusaie, Caroline Islands, IV, 97–98
Kutner, Luis, and Laurin Hall Healy, *The Admiral,* reviewed, IV, 337
Kverndal, Ronald, note contributed by, XXXVIII, 142; *Seamen's Missions: Their Origin and Early Growth,* reviewed, XLIX, 309
Kvichak, steamship *(1924),* XVIII, 214
Kwangchow, steamship (1871), XVII, 138; XVIII, 70
Kwang Su, Chinese junk, XXIX, 270
Kwantung, steamship *(1863),* XLIII, 294 ff.
Kyamil Pasha, steamship *(1886),* XI, 258 ff.
Kylemore, bark *(1920),* XVIII, 208
Kyorin Maru, steamship *(1861),* XLIX, 23; *(1863),* XLIII, 93 ff.
Kyrenia, steamship *(1936),* XIV, 127, 135
Kyzikes, tanker *(1927),* XXXVIII, 180 ff.

L

L. A. Dunton, fishing schooner, XXIV, 79; (1921), XXXVI, 78; interior views of, Pictorial Supplement, XXXI, plates XXV, XXVIII
L. Anderson, schooner *(1874),* IX, 229
L. B. Stille, schooner *(1861),* VIII, 219
L. C. Eborn, schooner *(1861),* VIII, 219
L. C. Richmond, ship *(1861),* XV, 108 n.; XXI, 256
L. G. Barnard (1861), XI, 285
L. Gaynet, schooner *(1863),* XII, 158
L. J. Vicat, concrete ship (1944), XXII, 177, 178
L. L. Davis, schooner, XXI, 90, 91; *(1861),* XI, 285
L. L. Sturges, ship (1860), V, 148
L. Rebecca, sloop *(1862),* XII, 56
L. Walsh, schooner *(1855),* XXIV, 141
Laas, Virginia Jeans and Dudley Taylor Cornish, *Lincoln's Lee: The Life of Samuel Phillips Lee, United States Navy, 1812–1897,* reviewed, XLVIII, 192
La Australia del Espíritu Santo, by Celsus Kelly, O.F.M., reviewed, XXVI, 220–221
Labaree, Benjamin B., mentioned, XLIV, 110; "The Frank C. Munson Institute of American Maritime Studies," XLV, 41–45; *A Supplement (1971–1986) to Robert G. Albion's Naval and Maritime History: An Annotated Bibliography,* reviewed, XLIX, 136
Labaree, Benjamin W., Robert G. Albion, William A. Baker, Marion V. Brewington, *New England and The Sea,* reviewed, XXXIII, 63–64
Labaree, Benjamin Woods, *The Boston Tea Party,* reviewed, XXV, 149–151
Labels, sailmaker's, IX, 292–293
Labor, Genoese ship *(1915),* XLIII, 273
Labuan, steamship (1855), XXVI, 199, 205, 209; *(1862),* XII, 56
La Carolina, ship *(1834),* XII, 179
Lackawana, steamship (1900), Pictorial Supplement, XXXIV, plate XXIV
Lackawana, U.S.S. *(1864),* XI, 275
Lackawana Railroad, ship of, Pictorial Supplement, XXXIV, plate XXIV
Lackawanna, U.S.S. *(1867),* VIII, 180–181; *(1879),* XXXIII, 15
Lackawanna Railroad Dock, XXX, 188
Laconia, bark (1860), Pictorial Supplement, XXXIII, plate XIV
Laconia, Cunard liner *(1917),* XLVIII, 57
Laconia, steamship, XLII, 295 ff.
Laconic, bark *(1851),* XLVII, 99
La Cosa, Juan de (Spanish mariner), XLV, 249 ff.; map by, XXX, 259
La Criolla, schooner *(1862),* VIII, 225

La Croyable, French privateer *(1798),* L, 245 ff.
L'Actif, brigantine *(1777),* II, 204
L'Adele, brig *(1803),* XIII, 277
La Diligente, French corvette *(1799),* XXVII, 144 n., 145
La Divina Pastora, warship *(1810),* XLII, 115
Ladrone Islands, Western Pacific, XXV, 184, plate 17
Lady, steamship *(1841),* XX, 97, 254
Lady Adams of Nantucket, ship *(1802),* XLII, 4
Lady Blackwood, British ship *(1824),* XXXIV, 256
Lady Blessington, ship (1855), III, 64
Lady Davis, steamship, XXI, 106; *(1862),* VIII, 225, 230, 237
Lady Davis (ex-*James Grey*) *(1861),* XLIV, 258
Lady Eleanor, bateau (1915), IV, 289
Lady Franklin Bay Expedition, XXXVIII, 49
Lady Gower, yacht *(1771),* IX, 182
Lady Hurley, schooner *(1864),* XII, 231
Lady Josyan, steamship (1872), XXIV, plate XXIV
Lady Lou C., sloop, XXIV, plate 14
Lady Lycett, steamship (1872), XI, 255
Lady Maria, schooner, XXI, 103; *(1863),* XII, 158
Lady Mary Wood, steamship, XXII, 7; *(1842),* XXVI, 9–13, 17, 19, 114–116, 202, 203, 205, 209
Lady Milton, ship (1856), XV, 182
Lady Mine, pilot schooner (1880), V, 86
Lady Mine No. 9, pilot schooner (1880), XXIV, 196
Lady of Lyons, steamship *(1864),* VIII, 234, 237
Lady of the Lake, schooner, XXI, 98; (1814), VII, 180; *(1862),* XII, 56
Lady of the Lake, steamship (1833), VII, 52; (1842), XX, 250, 262
Lady of the Lake, steam canal boat (1830), VII, 66, 127 n.
"*Lady of the Lake* in Dismal Swamp, The," note by Alexander Crosby Brown, VII, 66
Lady's Choice, canoe *(1881),* IV, 76
Lady Sherbrooke, steamship *(1823),* XLVIII, 80 ff.
Lady Sterling, steamship, XXI, 89; (1864), VIII, 234; XVII, 252
Lady Van, yacht *(1930),* XXXVI, 249
Lady Washington, brig (1779), XII, 62, 63; *(1791),* XLI, 26
Lady Washington, galley *(1776),* XXXVIII, 25; XXXIX, 216
Lady Washington, ship *(1791),* XLVI, 51
Lady Washington, sloop *(1787).* See *Washington,* sloop.
Laeisz fleet, XXX, 219, 220
La Escocesa, ship (1868), VII, 288, 297; IX, plate 31
Lafayette, bark *(1863),* XV, 292
Lafayette, schooner *(1862),* XII, 56
Lafayette, steamship, XXVIII, 124
Lafayette, General, XXVI, 258–261
Lafayette, Marquis de, XXV, 7
"Lafayette in the Frigate *Brandywine,*" by Captain Edgar K. Thompson, U.S.N. (ret.), XXVI, 258–261
La Feber, Professor Walter, XLI, 246
La Felicite, brig *(1756),* XXIII, 279

Lafferty, Captain Edward, XXXV, 235
La Fine, barkalonga *(1756),* XXIII, 277, 278
La Follette, Senator Robert M., L, 59
Lafollette, Suzzanne, XXV, 54
La Follette Seamen's Act, XXXV, 167
La Fortune, French ship *(1777),* XXXI, 242
La Fortune, privateer *(1757),* XXIII, 279
La Gironde, schooner (1875), V, 86
La Gloire, French warship, XXIX, 10
Lagoda, bark (ex-ship) (1826), Pictorial Supplement, XXXIII, plate XII; *(1826),* XII, 180; XIII, 165; XIV, 33, 40
Lagoda, whaler *(1845),* XLI, 33; XLIV, 16
Lagos, gunboat *(1845),* XXXVI, 132
Lago Shipping Co., Ltd., XLVII, 47
La Grande Duchesse, steamship (ex-*Carolina*), Pictorial Supplement, XXXIV, plate XXII; *(1899),* XXXVII, 238
La Grande époque de la Marine á voile, by Martin Acerra and Jean Meyer, reviewed, XLVIII, 207
La Grange, bark (1835), Pictorial Supplement, XXXVIII, plate II
LaGrange, bark *(1849),* XLV, 121
La Guaira, XXX, 262
Laguna de Bay, ship *(1899),* XXXV, 190
"Laguna Madre Scow Sloop, The," NASOH paper by Professor Edwin Doran, XXXVII, 81
Lahaina, schooner (1873), XXIV, 45, 59
Lahainia, schooner (1874), XV, 183
Lahloo, ship *(1868),* XXXV, 32 ff.
L'Aigle, ship (1822), XXII, plate V
Laine, Captain George E., XVI, 175
Lainé, Admiral, XXXVI, 126
Laing, Alexander, *American Ships,* reviewed, XXXII, 294
Laing, E. A. M., "The Royal Navy on the River Parana During the Allied Intervention, 1845–1846," XXXVI, 125–143
Laing, James, XXVI, 110
Laing, Sir Maurice, Sir Hugh Forbes, Lieutenant Colonel James Myatt et al., *1979 Fastnet Race Inquiry,* reviewed, XL, 149
Laing, Captain Thomas, XXI, 73
Laird, John, XXVI, 28, 31, 192, 207
Laird, Magregor, XXXV, 81 ff.
Laird Rams, XXIX, 5
Lai Sung, XXVII, plate XVI
Lai Sung (Chinese artist), XLVII, 130
La Jolie, sloop (1777), II, 206–207
Lake, Captain G. W., XVIII, 83
Lake Borque, Louisiana, engagement on, 1814, III, plate 6
Lake Champlain, VIII, 256; Battle of (1776), III, plate 1
Lake Drummond Canal and Water Co., VI, 65 ff.
Lake Drummond Hotel, V, 211–212, plate 16; VII, 66
Lake Erie, Battle of, 1813, III, plate 3
Lake Gretna, steamship *(1919),* XXXII, 20, 30
Lake of Maracaibo, XXX, 260
"Laker's Log, A," by M. K. and C. Ritchie, XVII, 203–211
Lakes Register of the American Inland Lloyd's, XXX, 24
Lakonia, liner *(1960),* XXXVI, 7, 21
Lalla Rookh, steamship *(1864),* XLIII, 102 ff.
Lally's Expedition, XXXI, 109
Lamar, steamship *(1847),* XLVII, 34
Lamar, Gazaway Bugg, XV, 100 ff.
La Marianne, ship *(1756),* XXIII, 278
La Marie, brigantine *(1776),* XXI, 45
La Marquise de Vaudreuil, French ship *(1756),* XLIX, 266 ff.
Lamb, Anthony, XLVI, 258; XXI, 109
Lamb, John, XXVI, 234, 235; XLI, 218; XLII, 301 ff.
Lamb, Ursula, reviews by, XLIV, 276–277; XLVII, 64
Lamb, W. Kaye, III, 184, 271; query by, I, 171; reviews by, I, 318–319; II, 184–185, 259–260; Editor, *The Journals and Letters of Sir Alexander Mackenzie,* reviewed, XXXI, 291; "The Trans-Pacific Venture of James J. Hill," III, 185–204
Lambert, brig (1815), XLIV, 6
Lambert, Andrew, *Battleships in Transition: The Creation of the Steam Battlefleet, 1815–1860,* reviewed, XLVI, 129; *Warrior, The World's First Ironclad Then and Now,* reviewed, XLIX, 134
Lambert, S., XXV, 241
Lambert, Captain Samuel, charts by, XXV, 187
Lambert, Mrs. Sarah, XXXVI, 255
Lamm, Lloyd, XXXVI, 13
Lammergeir, ship (1857), XV, 185
Lamont, steamship *(1867),* XVI, 255
Lamont, XXII, 44
L'Amour de la Patrie, brig (1799), XXVII, 142
Lamplighter, bark (1854), VII, 316, plate 39
Lamps, lighthouse, Flat Holm, XX, 39–40
La Mutine, frigate *(1750),* XLIV, 187
Lanarkshire, bark *(1861),* XV, 114, 123
Lancaster, H.M.S., XXVIII, 107; *(1917),* XXXVI, 268 n.
Lancaster, ship *(1674),* XIII, 21; *(1799),* XLV, 89
Lancaster, U.S. 2nd rater *(1883),* XXV, 223
Lancaster, U.S.S. (1858), XX, 137; *(1861),* XXXI, 42 ff.; XXXII, 202; XXXIII, 280 ff.
Lancaster, U.S. steam frigate *(1885),* III, 85
Lancaster, John, XXVII, 267
Lancaster, William, XXXI, 87
Lancefield, steamship (1855), XVI, 176, 243; XXVI, 120–122, 124, 126, 205, 209
Lancer, bark (ex-ship) (1852), Pictorial Supplement, XXXIII, plate XIII
Lanchas (1958), XXVI, 32, plate 2
Lancha velera, XXVI, 33–36, plate 2
"Lancha Velera of Chiloé, The," by Clinton R. Edwards, XXVI, 33–36
Lanchester, F. W., XLVI, 185
Lancing, ship (1866), IX, 298
Lanckton, Sergeant Frank, XXXIV, 263

Land, Admiral Emory S., XLI, 268
Land, Admiral Jerry, XXIX, 235
Lander, John, XXXV, 77 ff.
Lander, Richard, XXXV, 77 ff.
"Landing at Fedhala, Morocco, November 8, 1942, The," by Samuel Eliot Morison, III, 99–105
Landing of the Pilgrims, oil by Cornè, Pictorial Supplement, XXXII, plate XXVII
Landouman, XXX, 179
Land's End, Cornwall, 1832, XXIX, 198, plate XXI
Landsknecht, German U-boat group, XLIV, 48 ff.
Landstein, William Rodolph, XXXIV, 41
Landstrom, Bjorn, *The Ship, An Illustrated History*, reviewed, XXIV, 148–149
Lane, Bruce M., and C. Gardner Lane, "New Information on Ships Built by Donald McKay," XLII, 118–137
Lane, C. Gardner, and Bruce M. Lane, "New Information on Ships Built by Donald McKay," XLII, 118–137
Lane, Captain George E., XVIII, 83; XLIII, 120 ff.
Lane, Carl D., *American Paddle Steamboats*, reviewed, IV, 175–176; *The Cruiser's Manual*, reviewed, IX, 306; and with John Montgomery, *Navigation the Easy Way*, reviewed, IX, 306
Lane, Fitz Hugh (artist, Gloucester, Massachusetts), XXIV, plate I; XXV, 59; Pictorial Supplement: plates I–XXXII; photo of painting by, XLIV, 63
Lane, Harriet, XXXVI, 178, 182, 184, 185
Lane, Preston W., XXXV, 231
Lane, Professor Frederick C., XXXVII, 81
Lang, Steven and Peter H. Spectre, *On the Hawser: A Tugboat Album*, reviewed, XLII, 138–139
Langbehn, Carl M., XXVII, plate I
Langdon, Henry Sherburne, VII, 169
Langdon, John, VII, 201; VIII, 13, 17–19; XXX, 89, 114; XXXI, 133
Langdon, Senator John, XXX, 143
Langdon, Judge Timothy, XLII, 16
Langdon, Tobias, XXI, 15
Langhorn, Sir William, XIII, 14, 18, plate 2
Langley, U.S. aircraft carrier (1913), XXII, 142, 146; *(1921),* XLVI, 250; L, 53
Langley, Harold D., mention, XXXVII, 81; reviews by, XXXII, 224; XLIX, 313; note by, XXXIV, 65–68; "Respect for Civilian Authority: The Tragic Career of Captain Angus," XL, 23–37
Langley, Samuel, XXXIX, 11
Langmaid, Samuel (shipbuilder), XXIV, 39
Langmaid, William, XXIV, 57 ff.
Langmaid & Co., XXV, 58
Langmaid and Mugford, XXIV, 58 ff.
Language, marine, IX, 5
   in literature, XI, 209
Lan-Hwa, wooden paddle steamship *(1861),* XLIII, 200 ff.
Lanier, Sidney, VII, 141; quoted, VII, 134, 135

La Ninfa, schooner *(1893),* XXXVIII, 85
Lansdale, Philip, U.S.N., XXXIX, 120
Lansing, steamship *(1902),* XXXVIII, 195 ff.
Lansing (ex-*British Queen*), freighter *(1902),* XLII, 247 ff.
Lansing, Robert, Secretary of State, XLIII, 273; XLVIII, 55
La Paix, pirate ship *(1700),* XXX, 134
La Paloma, yacht *(1894),* XXXVI, 237
La Perouse, hulk *(1946),* VIII, 126
LaPérouse, Comte de, XXI, 196–206; XXV, 259
La Petite Chance, French privateer *(1810),* XLII, 115
Lapham, Charles, XIX, 10, 11
Lapham, George Bryant, XIX, 9, 14–23, 25
Lapham, James., XIX, 23
Lapham, King, XIX, 10, 11
Lapham, Luther, XIX, 9
Lapham, Samuel, "Massachusetts Maritime Microcosm," XIX, 7–43
Lapham, Captain Samuel (II), XIX, 9
Lapham, Captain Samuel (III), XIX, 9, 12
Lapham, Samuel (IV), XIX, 23–39
Lapham, Samuel (V), XIX, 39 ff.
Lapham, Silas, XV, 139
Lapham, Thomas, XIX, 7
Lapland, bark (1880), IX, 68–70, plate 6
Lapland, steamship (1872), XI, 255
Laporte, XXX, 184
Lapraik, Douglas, XVII, 47; XXXIV, 19 ff.
Lapraik, John S., XVIII, 60
Lapraik, John Stewart, XXXIV, 56
Laprarie, steamship *(1823),* XLVIII, 80 ff.
Laptek, steamship (1872), XVIII, 70
Larchmont (ex-*Cumberland*), steamship (1885), XXXIII, 92; XXXIV, Pictorial Supplement, plates IX, XVIII
La Republicaine, French frigate *(1798),* XLIX, 272
Large, David, *The Port of Bristol, 1848–1884,* reviewed, XLV, 211
"Largest American-built Bark," by John Lyman, II, 336
Larimer, tanker (1903), XXXVIII, 193 ff.
Lark, catboat, *(1898),* XI, 92
Lark, schooner *(1848),* XXXVIII, 60
Lark, sloop *(1808),* X, 148; XVI, 202
Lark, steamship, XXI, 96, 101; (1865), XI, 277; XII, 235; *(1876),* XXXIX, 177
Larkin, Captain Jerome, XXI, 95
Larkin, Thomas, XXXII, 120
Larkin, Thomas O., XXIX, 88 n., 91, 92, 93, 96, 97, 98
Larkins, Thomas, XXII, 9
Larne, H.M.S. *(1823),* XXIII, 56 n.
Larned, H. S., XX, 89
Larned, Samuel, XXIII, 186–187
LaRochette, ship *(1855),* XLI, 298
La Rosa, ship *(1834),* XII, 180–182
La Royale, galeass [model], XXIII, 147
Larriston, steamship (1852), XXVI, 119, 120, 121, 205, 209

Larroche, José, XXX, 52
Larsen, Captain Jack, VIII, 287–288
Larson, Captain Adolv, XLVII, 51
La Savoie, steamship *(1900),* XXIV, plate XIV; Pictorial Supplement, XXXIV, plate XXV
Lasbek, ship *(1927),* XVIII, 216, 217
Lascar, brig *(1820),* XIII, 242
Las Casas, XXX, 253
Las Choapas, steamship *(1942),* XXXVIII, 179 ff.
La Seine, French brig *(1778),* XLIII, 26
"Lash and Carry," by Captain Edgar K. Thompson, U.S.N. (ret.), XXIX, 225–226
Lasker, Albert D., XXXV, 286
Laskey, James, XXII, 205
Laskier, Frank, *My Name is Frank,* reviewed, II, 354
La Sophia, schooner *(1811),* XLII, 115
Laspinasse, Albert, XXXVI, 275
Lass, William E., *A History of Steamboating on the Upper Missouri,* reviewed, XXIII, 285–286
"Last Days of Coasting on Union River Bay, The," by Ernest Stanley Dodge, IX, 169–179, plates 23–24
"Last Days of Sail on the North Pacific or Bound for Bering Sea," by Tom H. Inkster, XXXIX, 184–189
Last of the Logan: The True Adventures of Robert Coffin, Mariner in the Years 1854 to 1859, The, ed. by Harold W. Thompson, reviewed, II, 184
Last of the Steamboats: The Saga of the Wilson Line, by Richard V. Elliott, reviewed, XXXI, 76–77
Last Raft, The, by Joseph Dudley Tonkin, reviewed, I, 402–403
Last Resort, sloop, XXI, 90, 97; *(1864),* XV, 129
L'Astrolabe, French corvette *(1838),* XLIX, 154; photo of model, XLIX, 163; lithographs of, XLIX, 163
Last Sail Down East, The, by Giles M. S. Tod, reviewed, XXVI, 223
"Last Shall Be First, The," by Captain Edgar K. Thompson, U.S.N. (ret.), XXV, 175
Last Trial, sloop, XXI, 90, 97; *(1863),* XII, 158
Last Voyage of Drake and Hawkins, The, Kenneth R. Andrews, Editor, reviewed, XXXIV, 284
Last Voyage of the Schooner Rosamond, *The,* by Haakon Chevalier, reviewed, XXXII, 291
"Last Voyage of the Ship *Vigilant,* To Manila with Coal for Dewey in 1898, The," by Thomas A. Stevens, with an introductory note by Lincoln Colcord, II, 140–153
"Last Voyage of the *Star of Scotland,* The," by John Lyman, III, 266
Last Voyage of Thomas Cavendish, 1591–1592, The, by David Beers Quinn, ed., reviewed, XXXVI, 298
"Last Whale Ship *Charles W. Morgan,* The," by Carl C. Cutler, I, 391–393
"Last Years of the Sail Navy, The," by Commander Francis E. Clark, XX, 134–145
Latchem, J. W., XXXVI, 188
Lateen rig, XXXI, 49. *See also* Masts and Rigging
"Later History of American Sailing Ships 'Sold Foreign,' The," by Daniel R. Bolt [Parts 1–10]: II, 245–246, 330–335; III, 62–73, 169–173, 261–164, 349; IV, 72–73, 238–244, 326; V, 147–155
"Later History of Light-Vessel No. 50," by John Lyman, XI, 78
Latham, tanker *(1919),* XXII, 161, 165, 169, 170, 182
Lathley-Rich, ship *(1868),* III, 62
Latimer, Rear Admiral, XXXV, 128
Latimer, Rear Admiral Julian L., XXXVII, 116 ff.
Latitude, L, 5. *See also* Navigation
Latitude, from Polaris, I, 13–25
"Latitude Errors and the New England Voyages of Pring and Waymouth," by John H. Gilchrist, L, 5–17
Latooka, Canadian schooner *(1902),* XLIX, 280
La Traviata, schooner yacht *(1861),* XXVII, 248
Latrobe, coaster *(1840),* XXXVIII, 60
Latrobe, Benjamin, XLIII, 247 ff.
Latrobe, Benjamin H., XI, 109 ff.
Latrobe, Benjamin Henry, XVI, 31, 34; L, 209
Latta, Robert, *Mackerel Skies,* reviewed, XXXVII, 223–224
Lauenburg, German weather ship *(1941),* XLV, 54
Laughton, Sir John K., XXXI, 275; XLII, 180
Laughton, L. G. Carr, XXV, 81, 85 n., 91
Launceston, H.M.S. *(1721),* XXI, 262, 263
Launched from Prince Edward Island: A Pictorial Review of Sail, by Nicholas J. de Jong and Marven E. Moore, reviewed, XLII, 222
Launching a lifeboat, XXXIV, plates 1, 16
"Launching by Firelight, A," document contributed by Herbert T. Silsby, XXI, 304
"Launching Prosperity: Samuel Townsend and the Maritime Trade of Colonial Long Island, 1747–1773," by Geoffrey L. Rossano, XLVIII, 31–43
Laura, bark *(1861),* XI, 285; XV, 123
Laura, brig *(1825),* XXV, 184, plates 17, 19
Laura, schooner, XXI, 88, 93, 102; *(1817),* XLVI, 217; *(1861),* VIII, 219, 225; *(1864),* XII, 231
Laura, ship *(1807),* XVI, 192
Laura, sloop *(1863),* XII, 158
Laura, steamship, XXI, 99; XL, plate 6; *(1863),* XII, 158, 231, 235
Laura Annie Barnes, schooner *(1939),* IV, 172
Laurada, steamship *(1896),* XXXV, 203
Laura Dudley, sloop *(1862),* XII, 56, 158
Laura Virgin, schooner *(1849),* XLV, 124
Laurel, schooner, XXII, 60 n.; (1800), XXII, 216
Laurel, steamship, XXI, 99; (1863), III, 138; *(1864),* VIII, 234; IX, 33; *(1865),* XXVII, 274
Laurence, Frederick Sturgis, *Coasting Passage,* reviewed, X, 235
Laurence Hill & Co., XXVI, 130; XLIII, 297
Laurens, bark *(1855),* XLI, 300
Laurens, Henry, XIII, 35–37; XXXV, 291
Laurens Coster, ship (1857), VI, 82
Lauresitnus, gunboat *(1813),* XLII, 109 ff.
Lauretta, schooner, XXI, 94; *(1864),* XV, 129
Lauretta, ship *(1849),* XXX, 244

Lauriston, bark (1892), II, 290; IX, 298
Lautaro, bark *(1941),* VI, 113
La Vengeance, French frigate *(1800),* XL, 24
La Vengeance, ship *(1799),* XXX, 129
Lavery, Brian, *The Arming and Fitting of English Ships of War, 1600–1815,* reviewed, XLIX, 306; *Deane's Doctrine of Naval Architecture 1670,* reviewed, XLII, 66 and XLVIII, 198; *Nelson's Navy: The Ships, Men and Organization, 1793–1815,* reviewed, L, 148; *Ship of the Line, The,* Vol. I, reviewed, XLV, 208; Vol. II, reviewed, XLV, 209
Lavina, steamship *(1864),* XI, 271 ff.
Lavina (ex-*Harriet Lane*), XXXVI, 204
Lavinia (1801), XXIII, 217
Lavinia, H.M. frigate *(1812),* XLVI, 169
Lavinia, schooner *(1861),* VIII, 219, 225; XV, 115, 123
Lavinia Campbell, schooner (1883), XXIII, 18, 19, plates VII, VIII
Lavita, yacht *(1899),* XXXVI, 240, 241, 244, 245
Lavolta, schooner (1870), IX, 171–174, plate 23; XIV, 108
Law. See Claims; Commercial Law; Maritime Law
Law, Captain Andrew, British Army, XXV, 199
Law, commercial. See Commercial Law
Law, Governor Jonathan, XXXI, 133
Lawence, Francis W., XXV, 104
Lawhill, bark (1892), II, 290
Lawley, Fred, XXXVI, 242
Lawlor, Dennison J., XIII, 54 ff.
Lawrance, William, V, 83–84
Lawrence, flagship *(1815),* XLIV, 178
Lawrence, privateer schooner *(1814),* I, 301–303
Lawrence, ship *(1846),* XLI, 33
Lawrence, steamship (1838), XVIII, 282
Lawrence A., XXIII, 133
Lawrence, Amos, XV, 134, 138
Lawrence, Augustus, VIII, 14, 21; XXXVIII, 16
Lawrence, Colonel Charles, 1754, XXXI, 21
Lawrence, Edward Thomas, XXVI, 280–282
Lawrence, Captain Effingham, XLVIII, 37
Lawrence, Captain James, U.S.N., III, 90; IV, 252; VII, 168; XI, 73
Lawrence, Joseph, XXV, 104
Lawrence, Joseph J., XLIV, 8
Lawrence, The Reverend Lionel R., Sr., document contributed by, XXVI, 280–282
Lawrence, Mary Chipman, XXXVIII, 210; *The Captain's Best Mate, the Journal of Mary Chipman Lawrence on the whaler* Addison *1856–1860,* edited by Stanton Garner, reviewed, XXVII, 73–74
Lawrence, Minnie, XXXVIII, 207 ff.
Lawrence, Captain Reuben, XVII, 65
Lawrence, Captain Reuben J., VIII, 280–281
Lawrence, Sebastian D., XXV, 104
Lawrence, William, XV, 138
Lawrence Brown, ship (1863), XXXII, 256
Lawrence & Co., sealers, XXV, 104

Lawson, Captain Patrick, XXXI, 42
Lawson, Murray G., "The Boston Merchant Fleet of 1753," IX, 207–215
Lawton, A. R., XXVII, 237
Lawton, General Henry W., XXXV, 188 ff.
Lawton, Major General Henry W., XL, 175 ff.
Layman's Guide to Naval Strategy, A, by Bernard Brodie, reviewed, III, 92–93
Lays, whalemen's, IV, 74–76
Layton, Thomas B. L., XXXVI, 274
Lea, U.S. destroyer *(1918),* VII, 72
Lea, Lieutenant Edward, XXXVI, 198, 200
Lea, Captain John C., XXI, 105
Leach, Captain John, XIX, 10
Leach, Captain Joseph, XXI, 95
Leach, MacEdward, "Notes on American Shipping Based on Records of the Court of Vice Admiralty of Jamaica, 1776–1812," XX, 44–48
Leadbetter, Charles, L, 288
Leader, schooner *(1862),* XII, 56
Leading Edge, The, by Sandy Weld, reviewed, XXXII, 143
Leading Wind, ship (1874), II, 335
Leafountain, Captain R., XXI, 95
Leaf Upon the Sea: A Small Ship in the Mediterranean, 1941–1943, A, by Gordon W. Stead, reviewed, L, 140
Leahy, William D., XXXVI, 257 ff.; XXXVII, 123
Leahy, Admiral William D., Chairman Joint Chiefs of Staff, XLII, 212
Leaky, Alexander, XXXVII, 12
Leale, Captain John, II, 291–292
Lealtad, schooner, XXI, 91, 94, 98; *(1861),* XI, 285; XII, 158, 231
Leaming, E. B., XXXVI, 236–239
Leander, British warship *(1804),* XLIII, 40 ff.; XLIV, 171
Leander, cruiser (1883), XXXIX, 130
"*Leander* Affair, The," by Harvey Strum, XLIII, 40–50
Leaping Water, ship (1859), III, 171
"Leap Year That Wasn't, The," by Thomas Dunbabin, XIX, 133–138
Lear, Tobias, XXX, 74
Learmont, Captain James, XXVI, 157 ff.; XLI, 132
Leary, William M., Jr., "*Alabama* Versus *Kearsarge:* A Diplomatic View," XXIX, 167–173
Leather, John, *Gaff Rig,* reviewed, XXXII, 292; *Clinker Boatbuilding,* reviewed, XXXV, 216
Leaver, Captain William, XXXIV, 245
Leavitt, Frank M., XXXVII, 113
Leavitt, John, I, 102; V, 247
Leavitt, John F., introduction to "Coolies in the Ship *Rhine,*" by P. W. Robertson, XIX, 227–231; *Wake of the Coasters,* reviewed, XXXI, 73–74; *The Charles W. Morgan,* reviewed, XXXIV, 145
Leavitt, John Faunce, marine paintings of, see Pictorial Supplement, XXXVI
Leavitt, Reverend Joshua, XXXIX, 46 ff.
Lebanon, ship (1854), XIV, 255

Le Barri, French snow *(1745)*, XLII, 50
Lebby, Captain Henry Sterling, XXI, 95
Le Berceau, French corvette *(1800)*, XLVI, 151
LeBousquet, Captain John, XV, 134
LeBreton, Louis, XXVII, 3; XXX, 219; lithograph from drawing by, XLIX, 155–156
Le Brilliant Jeunesse, French privateer *(1800)*, XXXIX, 34
Lechmere, Thomas, XL, 246
L'Eclair, schooner *(1861)*, XI, 285
L'Eclaire, schooner, XXI, 90
LeCorre, Alexandre, XIII, 276
Leda, ship (1868), IV, 243
Leda P., schooner (1954), XXIV, 99, plate 13
Le Dauphin, schooner *(1750)*, XLIV, 191
Le Decade, French privateer *(1800)*, XLVII, 26
Leder, Lawrence H., "American Trade to China, 1800–1802," XXIII, 212–218
Le Duc de Montebello, French privateer (1810), XLII, 115
Ledwith, Thomas, XV, 116
Ledyard, John, XXXIII, 161; XLVI, 28
Lee, armed schooner *(1775)*, XXX, 104, 107, 110, 111, 114
Lee, gunboat, XXXIV, 112
Lee, H.M.S. *(1859)*, XXVII, 168, 172
Lee, ship (1830), XXII, plates IV, VI
Lee, Arthur, XXXI, 241; XXXVI, 161; XLI, 209
Lee, Charles, XXXIII, 26
Lee, General Charles, XXXIX, 195
Lee, Francis, XXII, 209
Lee, Captain Francis, XXI, 95
Lee, Francis D., XLIX, 121
Lee, Mr. Hardy, XI, 291
Lee, Henry, XXII, 209
Lee, Hugh J., XXXVIII, 51
Lee, Captain J. F., XXI, 95
Lee, James, *The Masting and Rigging of English Ships of War, 1625–1860*, reviewed, XLI, 71–73
Lee, Seaman James M., U.S.N., XXV, 161
Lee, Jeremiah, XXX, 116 n.
Lee, Joseph, XXII, 196; XLVI, 214
Lee, Captain Joseph, XXI, 95
Lee, Nathaniel, XXII, 196
Lee, Governor Richard Sim, XXXI, 244
Lee, Robert E., XXVII, 174.; XLII, 87 ff.
Lee, Rear Admiral S. P., U.S.N., XXII, 256, 257, 258
Lee, S. Phillips, XXXII, 51
Lee, Samuel P., XL, 212
Lee, Thomas, VIII, 30–31
Lee, Captain William, XXI, 105
Lee, William E., V, 165
Leeanaw, steamship (ex-*Earnwell*)(1886), XLII, 246 ff., plate 7 (lower).
Lee & Brinton, XXXVI, 247
Leech, Samuel, XXX, 299
Lee Cutter, sloop (1776), VII, 256

Leeds, William, XIV, 52, 56, 59
"Lee Lurch," Pictorial Supplement, XXXI, plate XVIII
Lee Min, XXXIV, 32
Leeson, Ida, IV, 336; "Captain Benjamin F. Simmons in Australia," IV, 324–325
Leeward Islands, West Indies, XXIV, 95–108
Leffingwell, Justice Christopher, XXXIX, 193
"Legacy of a Saxon King: Royal Prints of Whale Strandings in the Peabody Museum," by Klaus Barthelmess, XLIX, 226–229
Legare, U.S. Revenue cutter, XXIV, 14 n., 18
Legaspi, Miguel Lopez de, IV, 88
Legend on Puget Sound, A, by M. S. Kline and G. A. Bayless, reviewed, XLIV, 205
LeGendre, General Charles W., XXXII, 131
Legere, French ship *(1800)*, XXXI, 174
Legge, C. C., contributed document, XXIV, 70
Legge, Christopher, "In Search of Phebe," XXV, 274–277, plates 29, 30
Legge, Francis, Royal Governor, XLII, 11
Leghorn, Italy, View of the harbor, XXVIII, plate XVIII
"Legitimacy and Authority: A Case Study of Pirate Commanders in the Seventeenth and Eighteenth Centuries," by B. R. Burg, XXXVII, 40–49
Leg of mutton rig, XIX, 155, 274. *See also* Masts and Rigging
Le Grand, pirate ship *(1717)*, IX, 134
Le Guin, Charles A., "Sea Life in Seventeenth- Century England," XXVII, 111–134
Lehigh, U.S. monitor (1862), X, 17, 31; *(1864)*, XLVIII, 123.
Lehma, schooner (1863), XII, 158
Lehr, Nathan, XXXVI, 21
Lehto, Captain Johan, XXXVI, 18, 20
Leichhardt, Fredrich W. L., XXX, 304
Leif Erickson, Norwegian steamship *(1905)*, XXXVIII, 195 ff.
Leighton, barkentine (1856), I, 171; IV, 77
Leiner, Frederick C., reviews by, XLIX, 240; L, 145; "The Subscription of Warships of 1798," XLVI, 141–158; "The 'Whimsical Phylosophic President' and His Gunboats," XLIII, 245–265
Leipzig, German warship *(1914)*, XVIII, 160; XXXIII, 36 ff.
Leith, Scotland, 1835, XXX, plate XXVII
Leith Packet, sloop *(1813)*, XIX, 217
Le Jason, French privateer *(1800)*, XLVII, 26
Leland, Captain Frederick, XXI, 95
"Leland Stanford, President of the Occidental and Oriental Steamship Company: A Study in the Rhetoric and Reality of Competition," by Norman E. Tutorow, XXXI, 120–129
Lelia, steamship (1864), III, 137
Lelia Byrd, ship *(1803)*, XXIX, 85
Le Maire, Jakob, XXV, 251
LeMeme, Captain Francis, XXV, 103

Lemly, Lieutenant Samuel C., XL, 128
Lemon, Samuel, XXXI, 289
Lempriere, Clement, XIII, 29 ff.
Lemuel Dyer, ship *(1861),* XI, 285
Le Museé imaginaire de la marine antique, by Lucien Basch, reviewed, L, 63
Lena M., schooner, XII, 140
Lena Rose, two-sail bateau *(1943),* IV, 291, 302
L'Enfant d'Adele, brig *(1803),* XIII, 277.
Lenra, ketch (1855), XI, 291
L'Enterprise, schooner *(1802),* XIII, 276
Lenthall, John, X, 17; XXII, 255; XXXIX, 237; XLIX, 117
Leo, schooner (1908), XXVI, plate XXIII
Leo, Sam, L, 291 ff.
Leona, ship *(1861),* XI, 266, 285
Leona & Marion, schooner (1920), III, 256
Leonard, Charles F. and Eben F. Leonard, Pictorial Supplement, XXXIII, plate XXIII
Leonard, Ebenezer, Jr., Pictorial Supplement, XXXIII, plate XXIII
Leonard, Georgiana, XLIV, 24
Leonard, J. B., XXXVI, 238
Leonard, Jane Kate, "Geopolitical Reality and the Disappearance of the Maritime Frontier in Qing Times," XLVIII, 230–236
Leonard, Peter, XXXVII, 15
Leonard Chase Wason, concrete ship (1943), XXII, plate 7, 177
Leone, ship (1853), II, 245; III, 264
Leonidas, bark *(1861),* XV, 108 n.; XXI, 241, 256
Leonor, ship *(1831),* XXXII, 119
Leonora, schooner, XXI, 90; *(1861),* VIII, 219; XV, 124
Leonora, ship (1869), IV, 239
Leopard, XXII, 264
Leopard, brig *(1798),* IV, 27–28
Leopard, brigantine, XXIV, 248
Leopard, H.M.S. *(1807),* XXXVI, 209; XLIII, 41 ff.; XLIV, 172; L, 245 ff.; *(1825),* XXXI, 217
Leopard, schooner (1827), XXIV, 59
Leopard, steamship, XXI, 87, 91, 99; *(1824),* XXXVII, 243
Leopard, steamship *(1862),* VIII, 225, 230
Leopard, survey boat [model], photo of, XLIX, 162
Le Paix, French East Indiaman (1762), XXVIII, 201
Lepanto, ship (1860), III, 171
Lepanto, Spanish ship *(1898),* XLI, 100
Lepanto, steamship (1877), Pictorial Supplement, XXXIII, plate XIV
Le Plongeur, French submarine *(1863),* XLIX, 122
Le Roy, Edwin D., *The Delaware and Hudson Canal,* reviewed, XI, 230–231
LeRoy, Commander William E., XLIV, 265
Leroy C. Holmes, schooner *(1861),* VIII, 219
Les Amis, French ship *(1799),* XXXI, 173
Les Deux Amis, French ship *(1800),* XXXI, 175
Les Deux Anges, French ship *(1800),* XXXI, 174

Leslie, ship (1860), VI, 82
Leslie, Captain Charles, XXIII, 178
Leslie, Captain Robert, XL, 38
Leslie H., fishing vessel *(1963),* XLI, 55
Leslie L., Canadian schooner *(1902),* XLIX, 280
L'Esperance, French brig *(1799),* XXXIX, 34
Lessovsky, Admiral, XX, 50–61
Lester, Captain G. John, XXI, 95
Letcher, Governor John, XL, 303
Lethbridge, John, VII, 269, 271–272
Let Her B, steamship (1864), XI, 308–310
Let Her Be, steamship, XXI, 105, plate XIV; *(1864),* VIII, 234, 237
Let Her Rip, steamship, XXI, 93, 105; *(1864),* VIII, 234; XII, 309
L'Etoille, French warship, XVIII, 180
"Letter from Captain Christopher Williams to Captain William D. Waters of Salem, dated 16 December 1833," by Russell W. Knight, XVII, 156
"Letter of Marque. The Brig *Quantibaycook* of Boston, 1799," by E. Lee Dorsett, M.D., XI, 224–225
"Letters from J. D. Wilson to his Sister," document contributed by Francis W. Hatch, XXV, 144–146
"Letters of Captain Sir John Jervis to Sir Henry Clinton, 1774–1782," edited by Marie Martel Hatch, VII, 87–106
Letters of F. W. Ludwig Leichhardt, The, by M. Aurousseau, reviewed, XXX, 304
"'Letters Taken in Prizes,' 1778–1780," by William D. Hoyt, Jr., V, 111–114
"Letter to the Editors, A," by Clarkson A. Cranmer, X, 68–71
Letts, Malcolm, XVI, 281
Letty, schooner *(1861),* XI, 285
Leucothea, ship (1855), III, 69
Leuth, 1561, photo of, L, 174
Leutze, Emanuel, II, 167
Levant, brig (1825), XIV, 40
Levant, sailing sloop of war *(1861),* XXXIII, 42 ff.
Levant, ship *(1807),* XVI, 195; *(1815),* XLIV, 171.; *(1856),* XXXVIII, 36
Levant, U.S. sloop (1837), XXII, 33; XXIV, 212
Levant Co., XLVIII, 24
Levant Thompson, schooner *(1861),* XV, 123
Le Vengeance, warship *(1810),* XLII, 115
Leven Shipyard, XXXIX, 132
Lever, Darcy, XXX, 40, 41, 42, 43
Levermore, Charles H., XXXIV, 232
Leviathan, H.M.S., XXVIII, 107
Leviathan, ship *(1930),* XXXVII, 75
Leviathan, steamship *(1863),* XII, 158
Leviathan, U.S.S., XXIX, 234
Leviathan, 'The World's Greatest Ship,' Volume I, by Frank O. Braynard, reviewed, XXXIII, 218–221
Leviathan, 'The World's Greatest Ship,' Volume II, by Frank O. Braynard, reviewed, XXXVI, 299–300
Leviathan's Tonnage, The, note, XLIII, 302

Levi ben Gerson, XIV, 187
Levinge, Lieutenant, XXXVI, 136
Levi Rowe, schooner *(1862),* VIII, 225
Levi W. Ostrander, steam auxiliary (1917), V, 140
Levrette, French ship *(1800),* XXXI, 175
LeVri, French privateer *(1802),* XXV, 183
Levy, Captain Benjamin, XXXVII, 239
Levy, Captain Jonas Phillips, XXXVII, 239 ff.
Levy, Captain Morton, XXXVII, 239
Levy, Uriah P., XV, 83
Levy, Uriah Phillips, XXXVII, 239 ff.
Lewellyn J. Morse, ship *(1926),* XV, 95
Lewin, Ronald, "Ultra Goes to War," reviewed, XLI, 312–313
Lewinson, Victor A., "Duhamel du Monceau: *Savant* and Naval Architect," L, 132–137; "Sam Crocker, Boat Designer," XLVIII, 182–185
Lewis, ship *(1861),* XV, 108 n.; XXI, 239, 256
Lewis, Abraham, XXXVIII, 26
Lewis, Mrs. Albert B., XXV, 112, 115
Lewis, Archibald R., editorial comment by: XLI, 3, 83, 163, 243; XLII, 3, 83, 163, 243; XLIII, 3, 83, 163, 243; XLIV, 4, 76, 148, 220; XLV, 4, 80, 152; XLVI, XLVII, XLVIII, XLIX; reviews by: XLIII, 58; XLIV, 201; XLV, 206; XLVII, 216; XLVIII, 61, 206, 207, 210; XLIX, 136, 233–235, 319, 320; L, 66; "Byzantine and Moslem Shipping in the Mediterranean, 500–1250," XLVII, 157–160; "The Maritime Mediterranean, 500–1571 A.D.," review article, XLIX, 126–132; "The Medieval Background of European and American Oceanic History," XLV, 225–236; *Nomads and Crusaders, A.D. 1000–1368,* reviewed, XLIX, 310; *The Northern Seas,* reviewed, XIX, 147; "Robert G. Albion: 1893–1983, An Appreciation," XLIV, 61
Lewis, Archibald R. and Timothy J. Runyan, *European Naval and Maritime History, 300–1500,* reviewed, XLVI, 200
Lewis, Colonel, XXV, 82
Lewis, Francis, VIII, 14; XXXI, 237; XXXVIII, 15 ff.
Lewis, Fred, VII, 243
Lewis, Captain George W., XVI, 161; XVIII, 83
Lewis, Henry, XXVIII, 38
Lewis, Isaiah, I, 302–303
Lewis, Isaiah William Penn, XXVIII, 46
Lewis, J. W., XV, 135
Lewis, James, XXXV, 297
Lewis, Lieutenant John R. C., XL, 300
Lewis, Leonard, XVII, 292
Lewis, Michael, *The History of the British Navy,* reviewed, XIX, 308; *A Social History of the Navy, 1793–1815,* reviewed, XXII, 147–148
Lewis, Samuel W., contributed document, II, 79–80
Lewis, William, XLIV, 14
Lewis, Winslow, XXVIII, 31–48
Lewis, Captain Winslow, XV, 134; XXXI, 135
Lewis Cass, Confederate cutter (1855), XLVIII, 90

Lewis Cass, revenue schooner *(1861),* XL, 298
Lewis Chester, schooner, XXI, 102; *(1861),* XI, 285
Lewis McLean, lightship (1832), VII, 48, 307
Lewiston, steamship, XXVIII, 124, plate XXVII
Lewiston, U.S. steamship *(1856),* XXXIII, 87, 94
Lewis Whiteman, steamship, XXI, 96, 101; *(1861),* XI, 285; XII, 56
Lexington, brig *(1841),* XXXVIII, 269
Lexington, carrier *(1924),* XXXVII, 115
Lexington, sloop of war (1825), XXIII, 58 n.
Lexington, steamship (1838), XVIII, 282, 283
Lexington, U.S.S. (1830), XLVI, 230; L, 31; *(1839),* XXVIII, 69; *(1861),* XIX, 266
Leyden, U.S. gunboat *(1867),* XXVI, 283
Leyland, R. W., XXXVI, 3
Liais, Edouard, XXIX, 167
Liang Shih-yi, XXXV, 170
Libbey, Captain Henry, XV, 300
Libby-Burchell Fisheries, XLIV, 131
Liberdade, "canoe" (1887), XVIII, 192
Liberia, schooner *(1838),* XXXVIII, 57 ff.
Liberia, steamship (ex-*Curityba*) (1913), XXXV, 205
Liberia:
    Emigration and immigration, XXXV, 197
    History, Naval, XXXVIII, 52; XXXIX, 173
Liberia, XXX, 230
Liberian, The, Presidential yacht (1930), XXXIX, 181
Liberian Colonization Society, XXXV, 203
Liberian Development Association, XXXV, 204
Liberian Emigration Club, XXXV, 204
Liberian Exodus Joint Stock Steamship Co., XXXV, 202
"Liberian Sailing Navy, 1821–1892, The," by Dwight Nash Syfert, XXXVIII, 52–64; "Liberian Navy Since 1892, The," XXXIX, 173–183
Liberian Trading and Emigration Association of the United States of America, XXXV, 204
Libertad, launch *(1847),* V, 126–131
Libertad, Mexican schooner *(1843),* XXX, 53
Libertad, Peruvian corvette *(1830),* XXV, 143
Libertad, training ship *(1964),* XXIV, 79
Libertador, gunboat *(1848),* XXXIX, 223
Libertador (ex-*Augusta*), steamship *(1848),* XXX, 268 ff.
Libertador (II), three-masted steamship (1850), XXX, 272
Libertador Mexicano, Mexican ship *(1835),* XXX, 47
Liberté, auxiliary *(1919),* XXXII, 19, 30
Liberté, French warship [model] (1905), XVI, 103
Liberté, sloop *(1861),* XI, 285; XII, 56
Liberty, bark (1842), III, 261; (1857), IV, 326
Liberty, H.M.S. *(1769),* XX, 243–249; *(1776),* XLVIII, 16
Liberty, patrol boat *(1785),* XXXIII, 24
Liberty, schooner (1774), XXIX, 160; *(1779),* XXXV, 142
Liberty, schooner (1834), XXII, 216; *(1929),* XLI, 43
Liberty, ship *(1796),* XXXVIII, 254
Liberty, sloop *(1767),* XXVII, 219; *(1768),* XL, 277
Liberty, steamship *(1864),* XXXII, 200

Liberty, whaler *(1833),* XLI, 289
Liberty, 17th Century, XXVII, 132–134
Liberty Shipbuilding Co., XXII, 160, 161, 182; XLI, 190
Liberty Ships, by John Gorley Bunker, reviewed, XXXIII, 223–224
Liberty Ships, The, by L. A. Sawyer and W. H. Mitchell, reviewed, XXXI, 228
Libraries, Maritime collections, I, 149, 381; XLI, 5. *See also* Museums, libraries and maritime collections; and names of libraries:
  Baker Library, Harvard University (Cambridge, MA)
  Bodleian Library (Oxford University, England)
  Clements (William L.) Library, University of Michigan (Ann Arbor, MI)
  Detroit Public Library (Detroit, MI)
  John Carter Brown Library, Brown University (Providence, RI)
  Library of Congress (U.S.; Washington, DC)
  Maine State Library (Augusta, ME)
  Massachusetts Archives (Boston, MA)
  National Archives (Washington, DC)
  New Bedford Free Public Library (New Bedford, MA)
  New York Public Library (New York, NY)
  Phillips Library. *See* Peabody Museum of Salem
  Wadsworth Athenaeum (Hartford, CT)
  White (G.W. Blunt) Library. *See* Marine Historical Association (Mystic, CT); Mystic Seaport
Library of Congress (Washington, D C), VIII, 13 n. ff., 240, 258–259; IX, 78; XXXII, 29
Library resources. *See* names of individual libraries; Libraries, Maritime Collections; Museums, libraries and maritime collections
Licenses, XLVI, 165
Lida, schooner or sloop *(1861),* XV, 124
Lida Gretta, woodboat, XVII, 7
Liddell, Captain Charles, XXI, 95
Liddell, J. D., XXIV, plate XXIX
Lieb, Peter, XXXIX, 14
Lief Erickson, boat (1936), XIV, 111
Liége, photos of, L, 170, 173
Lien Ching, steamship *(1894),* XXIII, 69
Lieutenant Delorme, auxiliary (1917), XXXII, 20, 30
Lieutenant Granier, auxiliary (1918), XXXII, 20, 30
Lieutenant Pegoud, auxiliary (1918), XXXII, 21, 27, 30
"Lieutenant Silas Bent's Device to Eliminate Variation Correction in the Magnetic Compass, 1849," Edward L. Towle, XXV, 93–98, plate 4
"Lieutenant Silas Bent's Device to Eliminate Variation Correction in the Magnetic Compass, 1849," by Commander W. E. May, R.N., XXVI, 215
Life and Letters of Vasco Nunez de Balboa, by Charles L. G. Anderson, reviewed, I, 411
Life at sea. *See* Seafaring life; *see also* names of individual navies, e.g., United States, Navy
Lifeboat, rubber inflatable, proposed 1856, XXV, 69–70
Life-boat, The, journal, XXXIV, 8 ff.

Lifeboats, XV, 199; XXXVII, 83
Lifeboats, Cornish, XXVI, 75
Life in Feejee, or Five Years Among the Cannibals, by Mary Davis Wallis, reviewed, XXVIII, 292–293
"Life in the Forecastle," Pictorial Supplement, XXXI, plate XXX
"Life is Cheap," by Captain Edgar K. Thompson, U.S.N. (ret.), XXIX, 63
"Life Line," document contributed by Captain Edgar K. Thompson, U.S.N. (ret.), XXII, 193
Lifeline of the Confederacy: Blockade Running During the Civil War, by Stephen R. Wise, reviewed, L, 67
Life of Captain James Cook, The, by J. C. Beaglehole, reviewed, XXXV, 70–72
Life on Board American Clipper Ships, by Charles R. Schultz, XLIV, 138–139
"Life Preserving Dress," document contributed by Alexander Crosby Brown, VIII, 153
Life saving, XXVII, 61
  Gt. Britain, XXXIV, 3
  Massachusetts, XXXVII, 83
Light, schooner *(1861),* XI, 285
Lightfoot, clipper *(1854),* XLV, 20
Lighthorse, bark *(1784),* XXI, 214
Light Horse, ship (1784), XLVI, 10 ff.
Lighthouse Board, XXVIII, 34
Lighthouse Inspection Service, XXXVI, 89
Lighthouses, VIII, 26; XX, 5; XXVIII, 31
  Gt. Britain, XI, 5
  United States, XXXVI, 45; XLVII, 174
  —, **New York,** XXV, 123
Lighthouses, VI, 307; VII, 250; VIII, 26–36, plate 8; XI, 5–34; XXVIII, 31–48; Cape May, New Jersey, XXV, 49; Flat Holm, XX, 5–43; Navassa Island, XXVI, 176, plate 18; Sandy Hook, New Jersey, XXV, 123–127
Lighthouses and Lifeboats on the Redwood Coast, by Ralph C. Shanks, Jr. and Janetta T. Shanks, reviewed, XL, 145
Lighthouses and Other Aids to the Mariner, reviewed, VII, 250; exhibit mentioned, VI, 307
Lighthouse tender *Shubrick,* XXXVI, 45–53
Lighthouse tenders, XXXVI, 45
Lightning, ship, XXVI, 161, 164, 165, 168–170; *(1846–1857),* XLII, 121 ff.
Lightning, steamship (1855), XXVI, 123–127, 205, 209
"Lightning Rods," query by P. T. Wright, III, 177; answered by M. V. Brewington, Baron R. de Kerchove and B. Berenson, III, 269–270
Lightship No. 88, XXVI, 3
Lightships, V, 115; IX, 273
Lightships: *Columbia River,* IX, 273–277, plate 29; *Lewis McLean,* VII, 48, 307
"Light that Failed, The," document contributed by Captain Edgar K. Thompson, U.S.N. (ret.), XXII, 70
"Light-vessel of 1823 built by Henry Eckford, A.," by Cedric Ridgely-Nevitt, V, 115–120

"Light vessels," answers by M. V. Brewington and Thomas Hornsby, V, 245–246
Light-vessels, IV, 259, 265–268; V, 97–98, 115–120, 245–246; VII, 48, 307; IX, 159–160, 273–277
Ligonier, tanker *(1903),* XXXVIII, 193 ff.
Liholiho, schooner *(1878),* V, 86
Liholiho, XIII, 242 ff.
Lije Houghton, hermaphodite brig *(1865),* XXIV, 44, 58
Lilian, steamship, XXI, 96, 97, 105
Lilla, brig *(1861),* VIII, 219, 225
Lilley and Gillie, Ltd., London, XXXIV, 209
Lillian, steamship *(1863),* VIII, 205, 234
Lillian E. Kerr, schooner *(1920),* III, 60, 163; IV, 172–174, plate 28; VI, 134
Lillian Grace Agnes [model], XXXVII, 172
Lillian M. Warren, schooner, XXVIII, 148
Lillie, schooner *(1863),* XII, 158
Lillie Helen, schooner *(1875),* XXXVII, 171
Lilly, schooner, XXI, 87, 103; *(1861),* XI, 285; XII, 231; *(1935),* XVI, 137–138
Lilly, Captain Convers, XIX, 115
Lilly Rich, schooner *(1855),* XXIV, 141
Lily, H.M.S. *(1889),* XXVIII, 26
Lily, paddle steamship (1856), XXII, 30, 31, 33, 37, 38, 42, 43; *(1856),* XVI, 163; XVIII, 70
Lily, schooner, XXI, 89, 91; *(1862),* XII, 56, 158, 235; (1882), I, 78
Lily, ship *(1858),* XXXIV, 21
Limber, Jacob, XXVII, 49
Limeña, Peruvian ship *(1879),* XXXIX, 278
Limerick Lass, bark *(1883),* XLIX, 31 ff.
Limuria: The Lesser Dependencies of Mauritius, by Robert Scott, reviewed, XXIII, 74–75
Lina, tanker *(1928),* XXXVIII, 185
Lincluden Castle, ship *(1854),* XLI, 298
Lincoln, Abraham, XXVI, 263; XXIX, 5; 187; XXXVII, 276
Lincoln, President Abraham, XXII, 288; XXIII, 199; XXXII, 45; Abolishes grog in the U.S. Navy, XXV, 142
Lincoln, Benjamin, XXXIII, 16 ff.
Lincoln, General Benjamin, XXVI, 276
Lincoln, Joe, XXV, 65
Lincoln, Levi, XIII, 123
Lincoln, Robert T., Secretary of War, XXXIX, 132
Lincoln S.S. Co., XXII, 171
Lincoln's Blockade Proclamation, XXXI, 253 ff.
Lincoln's Lee: The Life of Samuel Phillips Lee, United States Navy, 1812–1897, by Dudley Taylor Cornish and Virginia Jeans Laas, reviewed, XLVIII, 192
L'Inconstant, French warship *(1830),* XXI, 146
Lind, Helen Yonge, and Bernice Judd, *Voyages to Hawaii Before 1860,* reviewed, XXXV, 217
Linda, schooner *(1864),* XV, 129
Linda, screw steamship *(1866),* XXXIII, 89; XXXIV, 176
Linda, yacht *(1904),* XXXVI, 241

Linda B., dragger *(1956),* XLV, 84
Linden, bark (1852), I, 50
Lindenborn, Martin, XXX, 30
L'Indien, frigate *(1780),* XXXIX, 159
L'Indien, ship *(1776),* XIII, 36
Lindsay, David, XXXV, 204
Lindsay, Lady Mary, XLVI, 19
Lindsay, W. S., XVII, 254, 256; XLVI, 104
Lindsay, William Schaw, XLIII, 106 ff.
Lindsay, William Shaw, M. P., XXVI, 129, 130, 131
Lindsay and Co., XVII, 302–304; XLIII, 201 ff.; ship of, XXXIV, plate 4, 49 ff.
"Lines of *Spray,*" by Howard I. Chapelle, XIX, 232
Link, Arthur S., XXXV, 276
Link, Edwin A., XIX, 79–113
Link, Marion C., XIX, 79–113
Link Belt Co., XXXV, 281 ff.
Linnard, Joseph H., XXXIX, 131
Linnell, Solomon, XIII, 55
Linnet, H.M.S. *(1813),* XXI, 47, 53, 54; *(1894),* XXIII, 68
Linnet, schooner *(1863),* XII, 158
Linnet, sloop *(1809),* XXII, 216; *(1814),* XXII, 216
L'Insurgente, XXX, 122, 129; French frigate *(1794),* XLV, 36; *(1799),* III, plate 2; *(1812),* XLVI, 114
Lintin, steamship (ex-*Rose*) *(1866),* XLIX, 25
Linton, Andy, XXXVI, 232
Linton, Hercules, XXX, 223–224
L'Intrepede, French warship *(1810),* XLII, 115
Lin-Tse-Hsü, Imperial Commissioner, XLVI, 37
L'Invention, ship (1801), IX, 297
Lion, brig *(1839),* XIV, 40
Lion, schooner *(1862),* VIII, 225; XII, 56
Lion, ship *(1828),* VI, 17; *(1831),* XIX, 27
Lion, Spanish steamship *(1838),* XLVIII, 112
Lion [*Lyon*], ship *(1630),* XXIII, 63, 64, 66
Lion Ferry, XXXIV, 186 ff.
Lipfert, Nathan, review by, XLII, 229; XLIII, 143–145, 146–147, 147–148
Lippitt, Captain Moses, XL, 196
Lipsey, yacht *(1908),* XXXVI, 245
Lipton, Sir Thomas, XXXVI, 247
Lissa, Battle of (1866). *See* Austro-Italian War
List of Maritime Meetings—1984–1985, XLIV, 198
Liston, Robert, XXII, 273
Litchfield, Mary Cressy, XLII, 134 ff.
Literature. *See* individual topics, e.g., Arctic regions; Cape Ann; Language, Marine; Navigation in literature; Sailors; Sea in literature; Sea poetry; Ships in literature; Shipwrecks in fiction; Whaling in literature
Literature, maritime, XXV, 60–65
Liting, steamship, XVI, 262
Littillar (1802), XXIII, 217
Little, Bertram K. and Nina F., Pictorial Supplement, XXXII, plates XII, XXVII
Little, David B., reviews by, XXV, 227–228; XXVI, 223, 287

Little, Nina Fletcher, reviewed books, XXIII, 72–73; XXVIII, 289–290
Little, Captain R., XVIII, 6
Little, Lieutenant William MacCarty, XXXII, 260
Little Ada, steamship, XXI, 95, 97; *(1863),* VIII, 205, 234
Little Belt, H.M. sloop-of-war *(1811),* III, plate 2
Little Carrie, schooner *(1864),* XII, 231
Little Cornelia, ship *(1804),* XLIII, 42 ff.
Little Cumbrae Light, 1824, XXIX, 124, plate XI
Little Dromo, schooner (1800), VII, 317
Little Erie, steamship *(1837),* VII, 305, 308; VIII, 47–48
Littlefield, Nahorn, Pictorial Supplement, XXXVII, plate VIII
Littlefield, Roger Sherman, XLVI, 48
Little Frank, brigantine (1802), XLIX, 86
Little George, sloop *(1732),* XII, 223–224
Little Hattie, steamship, XXI, 89, 95, 105; *(1864),* VIII, 234, 237; *(1865),* VIII, 237
Little James, ship *(1623),* XIII, 58
Little Juliana, steamship (1808), XII, 239, plate 20
Little Lila, steamship, XXI, 96; *(1863),* XII, 158, 231
"Little Man, The" (Little Admiral), XXXIV, 197 ff.
"Little Men." *See* American "Little Men," British "Little Men."
"Little Men: Carved Shop Signs of the Navigating Instrument Sellers, The," by Philip C. F. Smith, XXXIV, 197–210
Little Minnie, schooner (1872), XXIV, 60
Little Mystic River, Charlestown, XXXV, plate 1
"Little Night Music, A," document contributed by Captain Edgar K. Thompson, XX, 62
Little Orphan, steamship *(1863),* XVII, 45, 61, 143
Little Orphan (ex-*John S. Williams*), tug *(1862),* XLIII, 96 ff.; *(1865),* XXXIV, 38 ff.
Little Rebel, C.S. ironclad (1862), XIX, 268, 270 ff.; *(1862),* XXV, 138
Little Sarah, brig, XXII, 88
Little Scotia, steamship *(1864),* VIII, 234
Little Victory, H.M.S. *(1667),* XXV, 279
Little Western, steamship (1834), VII, 55
Liu, Kwang-Ching, *Anglo-American Steamship Rivalry in China: 1862–1874,* reviewed, XXII, 225–227
Lively, brig *(1799),* XLI, 289; XLV, 87
Lively, H.M.S. *(1775),* XXX, 88, 89
Lively, L. W., XXII, 171
Live Oak, ship *(1804),* XLIII, 43 ff.
Live oak, III, 239
   Georgia, XXXV, 227
   See also Shipbuilding materials (Wood)
Live Oaking: Southern Timber for Tall Ships, by Virginia Steele Wood, reviewed, XLII, 150–151
Livermore, Charles W., XIII, 53, 55
Livermore, Edward, XXVII, 136, 137
Livermore, Captain Joseph, XXVIII, 115
Livermore, Seward W., XXXII, 258
Liverpool, British man-of-war *(1776),* XL, 17 ff.
Liverpool, H.M.S. *(1743),* XLVIII, 23

Liverpool, grain elevator *(1883),* XXXVIII, 141
Liverpool, schooner *(1862),* VIII, 225
Liverpool, ship *(1828),* XV, 139; *(1889),* IX, 298; *(1896),* XVIII, 9
Liverpool, steamship (1837), IX, 266–267; (1839), XII, 149
Liverpool, 1825, XXIX, 124, plate XII
Liverpool and Charleston Steamship Co., IX, 33–34
Liverpool Packet, ship *(1834),* XII, 182
Liverpool Red Book, XXX, 13 ff.
Liverpool Register of Shipping, XXX, 13 ff.
"Liverpool Ships Built at Newburyport," by Arthur C. Wardle, I, 167; see also I, 297
Liverpool Transfer Designs on Anglo-American Pottery, by Robert M. McCauley, reviewed, II, 353
Living Age, ship (1855), XXVI, 21, 117
Livingston, C.S.S. (1862), XIX, 267
Livingston, Edward P., XVI, 33
Livingston, Felix, XV, 115
Livingston, John, XVI, 34
Livingston, Peter R., XXXVII, 62
Livingston, Robert F., answered query, II, 250
Livingston, Robert G., XLVIII, 40; L, 202
Livingston, Robert R., XXIV, 157–165; XXVII, 6, 9, 11, 15–20, 23–27; XXXII, 211 ff.; XXXVII, 62
Livingston, Chancellor Robert R., XVI, 28–40, 270–280
Livingston, Walter, XLVI, 29
Livingston, William, XV, 60, 69–71
Lizard, H.M. paddle steamship *(1845),* XXXVI, 138–140, 142
Lizzie, bark (1857), V, 150
Lizzie, barkentine (1875), IV, 241
Lizzie, sloop *(1862),* VIII, 225
Lizzie, steamship, XXI, 94, 96, plate XVII; *(1863),* VIII, 230; *(1865),* XII, 235
Lizzie A. Law, schooner (1875), I, 74, 163
Lizzie A. Tolles, schooner (1863), Pictorial Supplement, XXXVI, plate XXIX
Lizzie B. McNichol, schooner (1874), XXIV, 39, 44, 59
Lizzie B. Willey, schooner *(1896),* XXXV, 18
Lizzie Bell, schooner, XXVIII, 148
Lizzie Davis, steamship, XXI, 99; *(1863),* XII, 158
Lizzie Dewey, schooner (1872), XXIV, 44, 59
Lizzie Homans, bark (1855), IV, 242; V, 327
Lizzie J. Clark, schooner (1867), Pictorial Supplement, XXXVI, plate XI
Lizzie Mezick, schooner, XXI, 94
Lizzie Mezzick, schooner *(1861),* XI, 285; XII, 56
Lizzie Taylor, schooner *(1862),* VIII, 225
Lizzie Weston, schooner, XXI, 95; *(1861),* XI, 285, XII, 56
Lizzie Wyman, half brig (1868), XXXIV, 70
Llama, steamship, XXXIV, 171
Llandaff City, steamship (1882), XIV, 117, 120, 124, 134
Llanero, El Gran, XXX, 261
Llewellyn Iron Works, XXII, 182

Llewellyn J. Morse, ship *(1877),* XVI, 122, 128; XVIII, 213
Lloyd, Professor C. C., mentioned, XXXV, 151; editorial comment, XXXIX, 158; "Introduction" to *Sea Life in Nelson's Time,* by John Masefield, reviewed, XXXII, 289
Lloyd, Captain Charles V., XVIII, 83
Lloyd, Christopher, *William Dampier,* reviewed, XXVII, 227
Lloyd, Professor Christopher, XLII, 181
Lloyd, Christopher and R. C. Anderson, editors, *A Memoir of James Trevenen,* reviewed, XX, 276
Lloyd, Henry, XIII, 120, 122
Lloyd, William, XXVII, 51; XLVIII, 33
Lloyde, Johan, XXXVII, 160
Lloyd's, steamship, XXI, 101
Lloyds, steamship *(1862),* VIII, 225
Lloyds of London, XX, 36–37
Lloyd's Register, XXX, 12 ff.
Lloyd's Register of American Yachts, XXX, 194 ff.
Lloyd's Register of British and Foreign Shipping, XXX, 9, 11
Lloyd's Register of Shipping, XXX, 9, 90, 92
Lloyd's Register of Yachts, XXX, 21 ff.
Lloyd's Universal Register, XXX, 27, 34
Lloyd Triestino, Italian shipping line, XLVI, 108
Loa, Chilean transport *(1880),* XXXIX, 286
Loanda, ship *(1898),* IX, 69
Lobelia, British vessel *(1943),* XLIV, 49 ff.
Lobster fisheries, Maine, XIV, 203
"Lobster Fishing on the Maine Coast Past and Present," by Dohn A. Cluff, XIV, 203–208
Lochhead, John L., XIII, 216
Lochhead, John L. (Librarian, Mariners' Museum), XXXII, 29
Lochinvar, ship *(1835),* XLVII, 90 ff.
Loch Tyne, 1832, XXIX, 198, plate XXIII
Lockard, Charles, XXIX, 266, 267
Locke, Parson Mason, XLVI, 28
Locke, Captain V. G., XXI, 95
Locke, Vernon, XIX, 53 ff.
Locke, Captain Vernon G., XXXIII, 199
Lockery, F. B., XXVII, plate XXIV
Lockhart, James, VII, 64
Lockhart, John, XVIII, 273, 284
Lockhart, Paul D., "The Confederate Naval Squadron at Charleston and the Failure of Naval Harbor Defense," XLIV, 257–275
Lockhart-Ross, Captain Sir John, R.N., VII, 95
Lockwood, U.S.S. *(1862),* VI, 54
Lockwood, Surgeon John A., U.S.N., XXV, 141
Lockwood, Captain Robert W., XXI, 95, 105
Lockwood, Captain Thomas J., XXI, 81, 96, 105
Lodbrok, turuma type of vessel [model], VI, plate 24
Lodebar, brig *(1861),* XLVIII, 93
Lodestones and Instrument Makers' Magnets, Pictorial Supplement, XXXV, plate IX

Lodge, Henry Cabot, XIX, 27; XXXIV, 160
Lodge, Senator Henry Cabot, XXII, 190; XXXVII, 30 ff.; L, 55
Lodge, John E., XIX, 28, 33
Lodona, steamship *(1862),* XV, 126
Loe. *See* Low, Lowe.
Loestoft, H.M.S. *(1777),* XX, 46
Loewen, H. E., XXXVI, 232
Log, Deck, of U.S.S. *George Washington,* VII, 69–72
Log, patent, XIV, 214
Logan, ship *(1839),* XII, 35
Logan, Captain A. B., XXI, 96
Logan, James, XXXV, 112
Logan, W. John, query by, IX, 74
"Log-a-Rhythms," document contributed by Captain Edgar K. Thompson, U.S.N. (ret.), XXII, 289
Log Board, American, Instruments of Navigation, Pictorial Supplement, XXXV, plate XXXII
Logbook for Grace, by Robert Cushman Murphy, reviewed, X, 77
Logbooks, I, 154–158
Log Chip, Line and Reel, Pictorial Supplement, XXXV, plate XXIII
Log Chips, edited by John Lyman, reviewed, VIII, 261–262
Log Glasses: American, Pictorial Supplement, XXXV, plate XXI; French, Pictorial Supplement, XXXV, plate XXI
Logie, William, XXVI, 239
Log of a Sea Captain's Daughter, by Alice Rowe Snow, reviewed, IV, 338
Log of Christopher Columbus, The, by Robert H. Fuson, reviewed, XLVIII, 61
Log of H.M.S. Bounty, *1787–1789;* and *The Log of H.M.S.* Bounty *1791–1793,* by William Bligh, reviewed, XXXVIII, 71
Log of H.M.S. Mentor, *1780–1781,* reviewed, XLIV, 208
"Log of James Sutherland, The," by Frank MacShane, XVIII, 306–314
"Log of the Bark *Virginia* Sunk by C.S.S. *Alabama,* 1862, The," edited by W. Stanley Hoole, XXXIII, 52–62
"Log of the Brig *Tuskar* of Boston," document contributed by Gilbert R. Payson, XXXVII, 220–222
"Log of *Timoleon,*" query by Samuel B. Grant, II, 174
Log Slate, American, Instruments of Navigation, Pictorial Supplement, XXXV, plate XXXII
Log Timers: English, Pictorial Supplement, XXXV, plate XXII; Netherlands, Pictorial Supplement, XXXV, plate XXII
Loire, frigate *(1814),* XLII, 111 ff.
Loiterer, yacht *(1886),* XL, 111
Lokke, Carl L., contributed document, VII, 69–72
Lola Montez, sloop *(1861),* XI, 285
Lombard, ship *(1854),* II, 331
Lombard, William, XXXIII, 163
Lomen, Carl J., XXV, 292
Lomen Reindeer Co., XXV, 292

London, brig *(1756)*, XLIX, 266 ff.
London, grain elevator *(1883)*, XXXVIII, 141
London, H.M. cruiser *(1949)*, XLIX, 213; L, 291 ff.
London, H.M.S. *(1665)*, IV, 262
London, H.M.S. *(1874)*, XXXIII, 285
London, ship, XXV, 244 n.; *(1742)*, XXVI, 43; (1848), I, 44, 48
London, steamship *(1837)*, XLIII, 191 ff.; (1843), XVII, 102; XX, 262
London, vessel *(1761)*, XXX, 202
London, Jack, XXV, 62, 63, 65; XLVI, 188 ff.; photos of, XLVI, 194, 198
London and San Francisco Bank, Ltd., XXXI, 123
London City, steamship *(1951)*, XIV, 133, 135
Londoner, The (Massachusetts reef), XXV, 244–245
London Merchant (1735), XXIII, 82
London Missionary Society, XXIII, 134
London Packet, bark *(1840)*, XII, 103, 116
Lone, schooner, XXI, 89; *(1864)*, XII, 231
Lonely Lass, sloop *(1776)*, XX, 46
Lonely Midas, The Story of Stephen Girard, by Harry Emerson Wildes, reviewed, IV, 253–254
Lone Star, steamship *(1887)*, XIV, 121; XXXVIII, 184 ff.
Lone Star, yacht *(1880)*, XXXVI, 233
Long, Lieutenant Commander A. K., XII, 282–286
Long, Andrew K., XL, 43
Long, Captain I. C., XXIII, 55
Long, David F., "'Mad Jack' Percival in Vietnam: First American Hostilities, May 1845," XLVII, 169–173; *Nothing Too Daring: A Biography of Commodore David Porter, 1780–1843*, reviewed, XXXIII, 64–65; *Sailor-Diplomat: A Biography of Commodore James Biddle, 1783–1848*, reviewed, XLIV, 202
Long, John D., Secretary of the Navy, XXXVI, 257 ff.; XXXVII, 31; XL, 169 ff.; XLI, 94 ff.
Long, John Davis, XXIX, 31, 32
Long Beach, California, XXV, 269–271
"Longevity of Colonial Ships, The," by Marshall Smelser and William I. Davisson, XXXIII, 16–19
Longfellow, ship *(1860)*, III, 62
Longfellow, steamship (ex-*Louise*) *(1897)*, XXIV, 238, 241, plate 28
Longfellow, steam packet, XXIV, 135
Longfellow, Henry Wadsworth, XXV, 64, 65, 233
Longford, Elizabeth, XLVI, 23
"Long-Forgotten American Naval Cemetery, A," by James M. Maps, XXV, 157–167, plates 11–14
"Long-Forgotten American Naval Cemetery; A Postscript, A," by Captain Edgar K. Thompson, U.S.N. (ret.), XXVI, 218–219
Long Island, menhaden steamship *(1912)*, XLIV, 121
Long Island, New York, IV, 224–232
Long Island Historical Society, XXV, 126–127, plate 9
Longitude, L, 281; **Prime meridian**, XLIV, 77. *See also* Navigation

Longitude, tidskrift från de sju haven: A Magazine of the Seven Seas, reviewed, XXXV, 217
Longmore, ship *(1863)*, V, 151; VI, 82
Longridge, C. Nepean, *The "Cutty Sark"; The Ship and the Model*, reviewed, XLIV, 280
"Long Shadow of Benjamin Barons: The Politics of Illicit Trade at Boston, 1760–1762, The," by John W. Tyler, XL, 245–279
Long Ships Passing, The, by Walter Havighurst, reviewed, II, 344–345
Longwood, ship *(1863)*, I, 114
Loo, H.M.S. *(1744)*, XXVI, 42, 52, 57
Loochoo, ship *(1840)*, III, 320; *(1858)*, XXXIV, 21
"Look at the American Merchant Marine of the Last Fifty Years, A," by Jones F. Devlin, Jr., XXIX, 231–243
Loomis, Rear Admiral F. Kent, U.S.N. (ret.), XXIX, 80, 287
Loosestrife, H.M.S. *(1943)*, XIV, 130; L, 219 ff.
Lopez, Aaron, XIII, 120; XXV, 106
Lopez, Carlos Antonio, XXXVI, 180
Lopez, President Carlos Antonio, XXXI, 10 ff.
Lopez, David, Jr., XIII, 120
Lopez de Santa Anna, XXX, 54
Loray, Captain Charles Muggah, XXVIII, 288
Lord, Charles H., XXV, 26
Lord, Daniel, XIII, 121
Lord, George C., XIII, 121; XXV, 25, 26
Lord, Captain James, XXI, 96
Lord, Nathan, XIII, 121
Lord, Nelson T., XXI, 112, 115, 119, 124, 126
Lord, Simeon, XIII, 275 ff.
Lord, William, XXV, 18 n.
Lord Brassey, XXIX, 13 n.
Lord Charles, yacht *(1676)*, IX, 180
Lord Clive of India, XLVI, 29
Lord Clyde, steamship, XXI, 104, 106; *(1863)*, VIII, 230. 234
Lord Construction Co., XXII, 160
Lord Dartmouth, ship *(1774)*, IV, 207–216
Lord Elgin, bark *(1840)*, XLVII, 93
Lord Howe, brigantine *(1778)*, XXXIX, 212
Lord Nelson, brig *(1808)*, XVI, 197
Lord Rodney, snow *(1784)*, XXXI, 43
Lord Wenlock, bark *(1839)*, XXIX, 62
Lord Wolseley, ship *(1883)*, IV, 326; *(1884)*, IX, 298
Lorena, Guglielmo, VII, 263, 266, 267
Lorenz, Lincoln, *John Paul Jones, Fighter for Freedom, and Glory*, reviewed, III, 272–273
Lorenzo, ship *(1853)*, IV, 243
"Lorenzo Sabine's History of the Fisheries," by William L. Welch, XLVIII, 165–172
Lore of the Lakes, by Dana Thomas Bowen, reviewed, I, 187
Lore of the Wreckers, by Birse Shepard, reviewed, XXIII, 151–152
Loretto Fish, ship *(1869)*, II, 246

Loring, Augustus P. and Edwin B. Newman, "Some Notes on the Paper of the *Atlantic Neptune*," XLVI, 173–178

Loring, Augustus Peabody, Jr., I, 315; II, 252; IV, 5, 16, 230; X, 33–34, 37; XIII, 247; XXVIII, 237; "Mr. Joseph Peabody of Salem, Massachusetts and His Punch," II, 39–43

Loring, Lieutenant B. W., XLII, 193

Loring, Captain, XXII, 270, 272, 273

Loring, George B., XXXIX, 294

Loring, Captain John, XLV, 96

Loring, Rosamond Bowditch, XIII, 247

Loriotte, brig *(1834)*, XII, 180–181

Lorne, tug *(1902)*, XVIII, 12

Lorraine, Captain Sir Lambton, XXXVI, 97; XXXVIII, 245

Losa, sloop, XXI, 88, 96, 99; *(1861)*, XI, 285

Los Angeles and Wilmington Railroad, XXV. 265

"Los Angeles [Califorina], Development of the Port of," by John H. Krenkel, XXV, 262–273

Los Angeles Steamship Co., IX, 216–227; XXIX, 231

Losap Island, XXXIV, 254

"Loss of the Bark *Lapland*," by Charles S. Morgan, IX, 68–70, plate 6

"Loss of the *Malleville*," by Joanna C. Colcord, IV, 318–323

"Loss of the Schooner *Albert H. Willis*," by Robert H. I. Goddard, Jr., II, 243–245

"Loss of the Steamship *Independence*," by Captain Jason Collins, introduction by John Richards, XIV, 192–202

Losson, August, XLV, 203

Lothian, H. V., XIV, 127

Lothrop, Francis B., mention, XLIX, 226 ff.; reviews by: XXVI, 75–76, 149–150; XXVII, 75; XXIX, 143–144; XXX, 218–219; XXXI, 76, 149; XXXII, 140, 226; XXXIII, 66, 221, 308; XXXIV, 145; XXXVI, 144, 148, 149, 296, 299; XXXVII, 72, 224; XXXVIII, 301, 302, 304; XXXIX, 145, 153, 302; XL, 70, 231; XLI, 70, 79

Lott, Arnold S., *Brave Ship Brave Men*, reviewed, XXV, 227–228

Lottery, Sandy Hook Lighthouse, 1762, XXV, 124

Lottie Bell, bateau *(1910)*, IV, 289

Lottie Warren, ship (1863), III, 172

Lotus, ship *(1860)*, XXVII, 235

Lotus, steamship (1861), XVII, 48; XVIII, 70; XLIII, 198 ff.

Lot Whitcomb, steamship (1850), III, 160

Louis, French ship *(1799)*, XXXI, 173

Louis, schooner (1881), V, 137, 327

Louisa, bark *(1832)*, Pictorial Supplement, XXXIII, plates XX, XXI

Louisa, brig (1850), VII, 318

Louisa, schooner, XXI, 92, 103; *(1861)*, VIII, 219, 225; XI, 285; XII, 231, 235; *(1870)*, I, 73

Louisa, ship (1860), III, 171

Louisa, steamship (1862), XVII, 310

Louisa Agnes, schooner, XXI, 98; *(1861)*, VIII, 219

Louisa Ann Fanny, steamship (1865), III, 138

Louisa Hatch (1863), XV, 291

Louisa Mary, schooner *(1862)*, VIII, 226

Louisa Moore, steamship *(1866)*, XXXIX, 97

Louisa Morrison, oyster schooner (1868), I, 78

Louis Bucki, steam schooner (1881), IX, 71, plate 8

Louisbourg (Nova Scotia), Fortifications, XLIV, 186

Louise, schooner, XXI, 88; *(1931)*, XXX, 304

Louise, steamship, I, 65; *(1863)*, XLIII, 203 ff.; *(1897)*, XXIV, 238

Louise, transport *(1755)*, XLIX, 264 ff.

Louise, two-sail bateau (1943), IV, 289, 296

Louise Antoinette, schooner (1844), VII, 317

Louise Howard, schooner (1917), XXVI, plate XXVIII

Louisiana, schooner, XXI, 86; *(1806)*, III, 235–238

Louisiana, ship *(1863)*, XX, 53

Louisiana, ship (1873), IV, 51, 52; XXVII, plate IV

Louisiana, steamship, XXI, 95; *(1861)*, XI, 285

Louisiana, steamship *(1937)*, XXXVII, 191 ff.

Louisville, U.S. ironclad (1861), XIX, 266; *(1862)*, XXV, 134

Louis XV, French warship [model], XVI, 100

Louis XV's Navy, 1748–1762; A Study of Organization and Administration, by James Pritchard, reviewed, XLVIII, 195

Lounsbury, Peter, V, 28

Louredes, schooner *(1861)*, VIII, 219

L'Ouverture, General Pierre Francois Domingue Toussaint, XXX, 126, 127; XLVI, 159

Love, Dr. Robert William, Jr., editorial comment, XXXVII, 3–4

Love, Robert William, Jr. and Merrill Bartlett, "Anglo-American Naval Diplomacy and the British Pacific Fleet, 1942–1945," XLII, 203–216

"Love Afloat and Adrift," by Captain Edgar K. Thompson, U.S.N. (ret.), XXVIII, 65

"Love and Kisses in Wartime," document, II, 173.Lovejoy, E. D., query by, I, 398

Lovejoy, Owen, XXIX, 6

Lovelace, William, England, Pictorial Supplement, XXXV, plate XXII

Lovell, C.S. ram *(1862)*, XXV, 137

Lovell, Francis Cabot, XXIX, 205

Lovell, Brigadier General Solomon, XXXVII, 294

Lovell, General Solomon, VII, 203, 205, 209; XLII, 3 ff.

Lovely Lass (1801), XXIII, 216

Lovely Lass, brigantine, XXII, 90

Lovett, Captain Anson, XXI, 96

Lovett, Bessie and Nigel Wace, *Yankee Maritime Activities and the Early History of Australia*, reviewed, XXXIII, 308

Lovett, Captain C. J., XVIII, 83

Lovett, Henry Preston, XXVI, 203

Lovett, Robert W., "Maritime Manuscripts in the Baker Library," XIII, 118–124

Lovett Peacock, schooner *(1861),* XI, 285
Lovewell, Rominer, mention, XLI, 4
Low, Abiel Abbott, III, 162; V, 146; XVI, 163, 175
Low, Charles Rathbone, XL, 280
Low, Frederick F., VII, 108, 109
Low, Federick Ferdinand, U.S. Minister, XXV, 117, 119–121
Low, Garrett W., *Gold Rush by Sea,* reviewed, I, 406–407
Low, J. O., XVI, 164
Low, Lieutenant John, XXXIII, 53
Low, Seth, III, 162; V, 146
Lowe, Donald V., XXVII, 261, plate 12
Lowe [Loe], Captain John, XXIII, 65
Lowe, Joseph, X, 249–250
Lowe, Samuel L., Jr., XXXVII, 129
Lowell, bark *(1847),* XXIV, 57
Lowell, ship *(1832),* XV, 139, 140
Lowell, Captain A. C., XVIII, 83
Lowell, James Russell, XXXVIII, 104; XXXIX, 127, 197
Lowell, Ralph P., XIII, 79–80
"Lower Deck Metaphysics," document contributed by Captain Edgar K. Thompson, U.S.N. (ret.), XXIV, 60
Lowndes, Captain Charles, XXXIV, 119
Lowood, schooner *(1864),* XII, 231
Lowry, Lieutenant Commander, XXXVI, 202
Loyalist, steamship *(1827),* VI, 196
Loyal London, H.M.S. (1666), IV, 261–265, plates 41–44; V, 146
Loyalty, sail *(1924),* XXXII, 14
Loyasa, García de, IV, 88
Loyola, Dr. Juan Arias de, XXVIII, 254
LSM-201, medium landing ship (1944), XXXVIII, 286
LSM-207, medium landing ship (1944), XXXVIII, 287
LSM-446, medium landing ship (1945), XXXVIII, 288
LST-730, landing ship tank (1943), XXXVIII, 286
LST-748, landing ship tank (1944), XXXVIII, 287
LST-1059, landing ship tank (1945), XXXVIII, 288
Lubbock, Captain Henry S., XXXVI, 200
Lubec, brig (1826), XXIV, 57
Lubec, steamship (1891), XXIV, 54, 55
Lubec boat, XII, 126–128
Luburg, Frederick S., XXIX, 198
Lucas, Ed, XXXVI, 245
Lucas, George, VII, 158; XV, 118
Lucas, Captain J. Ed., VII, 163, 166
Lucas New Line, VII, 164, 166
Luce, Captain George A., XXI, 105
Luce, Captain James C., XIV, 237 ff.; XIX, 129; XX, 180, 181
Luce, Captain John A., XLIV, 23
Luce, Mary C. & Matthew, XXXIII, 54
Luce, Richard G., XXXIII, 54
Luce, Stephen B., XXIX, 31–53; XXX, 43, 44
Luce, Admiral Stephen B., XX, 135–136; XLI, 25
Luce, Commodore Stephen B., XXXIII, 262 ff.

Luce, Rear Admiral Stephen B., U.S.N., XXV, 175; XXXIX, 122; XL, 127, 168 ff.; photo of, XLIX, 301
Lucena, steamship *(1826),* XXXVII, 247
Lucerne, bark (1847), I, 43, 50; *(1862),* XII, 56
Lucet, Captain Alexander, XVI, 234
Luchs, S.M.S. gunboat *(1906),* XL, 89 ff.
Lucibelle, ship (1859), IV, 243
Lucid, Robert F., Editor, *The Journal of Richard Henry Dana, Jr.,* 3 volumes, reviewed, XXIX, 286
Lucilla, brig *(1838),* XXI, 296 ff.
Lucinda, yacht (1895), XXXVI, 239
Luckis, Oliver, shipwright, V, 328
Luckner, Count Felix von, XXX, 219
Lucretia, steam bark *(1888),* XXXIX, 9
Lucy (1801), XXIII, 217
Lucy, schooner, XXVIII, 123; *(1862),* XII, 56, 231
Lucy, ship *(1840),* XXXV, 261
Lucy, sloop *(1898),* XI, 92
Lucy, steamship, XXI, 86, 90; *(1863),* VIII, 231, 234
Lucy, tanker, XXV, 233
Lucy A. Nichols, ship *(1898),* XXXVII, 92
Lucy A. Nickels, bark (1855), XXVIII, plate IX
Lucy and Harriet, ship (1847), V, 241
Lucy C. Holmes, schooner, XXI, 89; *(1861),* VIII, 219, 226
Lucy Edwina, schooner (1922), XXVI, plate XXVIII
Lucy Evelyn, schooner (1917), II, 327–330, plate 46; IV, 236–237
Lucy Francis, schooner (1856), III, 65
Lucy Harriet, ship (1856), V, 147, 241
Lucy May, schooner (1888), Pictorial Supplement, XXXVI, plate XIX
Lucy Melville, ship (1864), II, 333
Lucy R. Waring, schooner, XXI, 101, 102; *(1861),* XV, 124
Lucy Ring, bark (1854), XXIV, 57
Lucy S. Wills, ship (1870), III, 137
Lucy Thompson, ship *(1854),* XLV, 29
Ludgate, W., O.S., U.S.N., XXV, 50
Ludin, John E. (United States Consul in Canton), XLVI, 26
Ludington, Brigadier General Marshall I., XL, 172 ff.
Ludlow, Captain C., XX, 89 n.
Ludlow, Charles, XLVII, 27
Ludwig, Anton, XXI, 117
Ludwig, Emil, *The Mediterranean, Saga of a Sea,* reviewed, II, 354
Ludwig, J. M., XLVI, 93
Luetić, Josip, "Captain Basi Ivanković, Painter of Mediterannean Sailing Vessels," XXIV, 124–126
Lugard, Lord, XLVI, 105
Lug rig, XIX, 155, 274. *See also* Masts and Rigging
Luis, Don J. G., XXX, 239
Luise Leonhardt, steamship (ex-*Niagara,* ex-*Eastern Breeze*), XXIII, 276
Luke, Thomas A. E., photographs by, plate facing I, 115
Lukenbach Steamship Line, XXIX, 231

Luku, schooner (1879), V, 86
Lullum, Midshipman David, XXI, 265
Lulu L., sloop (1901), XXIV, 60
Lulu W. Eppes, schooner (1895), Pictorial Supplement XXXVI, plate XXII
Lumber carriers, XXV, 288 ff.
Lumber rafts, Georgia, XXIII, 86–89
Lumber schooner, unidentified, XXV, plate XXIX
Lumber trade, IX, 169; XXI, 23; XXV, 288
Lumber, Transportation, XVII, 5; XXX, 187
Luna, steamship, XXI, 96, 100; *(1864),* XII, 231, 235
"Lunar Distances," query by J. M. Sheehan, VIII, 71
Lund, Benjamin, XX, 11–13, 16
Lund, Captain T. W., XXI, 96
Lund and Co., XXXI, 115
Lundeberg, Dr. Philip, XXXIX, 254
Lundeberg, Philip K., review by, XLVII, 211
Lundeberg, Philip K. and Dana M. Wegner, "'Not for Conquest But Discovery:' Rediscovering the Ships of the Wilkes Expedition," XLIX, 151–167
Lunderberg, Philip, XLI, 163
Lundy, Dan, XVIII, 199
Lune, ship *(1819),* XLI, 286
Lunéville, auxiliary (1918), XXXII, 21, 30
Lungley, C., XXVI, 125
Lunn, Captain C. A., XVIII, 167
Lunnette, schooner (1897), XXIV, 60
Lunt, Edwin, XVII, 116, 117
Lunt, Captain Micajah, Jr., XVII, 69–72
Lunt, Paul G., XVII, 123
Lunt, Richard, mention, XLI, 164
Lunt, Storer B., IX, 160; answered query, V, 245
Lurline, steamship *(1928),* XVI, 131
Lurline, yacht *(1888),* XXXVI, 232
Luscomb, William Henry, marine paintings by, Pictorial Supplement, XXXVIII, Part I, 40–41; Part II, 100–101; Part III, 216–217; Part IV, 300–301
Lusitania, british ship *(1915),* XLII, 295 ff.; XLV, 199; *(1917),* XLVIII, 56
Lusitania, steamship, XXXVI, 20; (1907) XXIV, plate XV; Pictorial Supplement, XXXIV, plate XXXII; XXXV, 36 ff.
Lusitania Disaster: An Episode in Modern Warfare and Diplomacy, The, by Thomas A. Bailey and Paul B. Ryan, reviewed, XXXVI, 300
Lutece, schooner *(1917),* XXXVI, 273–275
Lux and Bowly Shipbuilding, XLV, 244
Luxton, Norman, XXVIII, 53, 55–58, 64
Luzon, steamship (1864), XVIII, 70
Luzro, Giovanni, XXVIII, plate VII
L'Vengeance, warship, XLI, 85
Lyall, George, XXXIV, 30 ff.
Lyall, Still and Co., XXII, 16, 35; XXXIV, 18 ff.; XLIII, 195 ff.
Lyall, William, Shipbuilding Co., IX, 67–68
Lydia, American ship *(1816),* XXIX, 89
Lydia, bark *(1841),* XIX, 204–209
Lydia, boat *(1864),* XV, 129
Lydia, brig *(1805),* XIX, 13; *(1807),* XVI, 194
Lydia, ship *(1799),* XLV, 92
Lydia, sloop *(1746),* XLVIII, 33
Lydia Grant, schooner (1879), I, 71
Lydia M. Deering, schooner (1889), XII, plate 29
Lydon, James G., "*Castel del Rey,* an Early New York Privateer," XVII, 292–297; "The Cruise of *Charming Peggy,*" XXIII, 277–284; "North Shore Trade in the Early Eighteenth Century," XXVIII, 261–274
Lydon, Professor James G., XXXVII, 82
Ly-ee-moon, screw steamship *(1861),* XXXIV, 27; *(1874),* XLIX, 23
Lyford, Colonel Stephen C., XLVII, 180 ff.
Lykes Brothers, steamship owners, XXII, 176, 177, 178
Lyman, Chester S., IX, 64
Lyman, George H., VII, 8
Lyman, Dr. John, XXV, 112; XXXVII, 81
Lyman, John, I, 177, 400; II, 84; III, 184; V, 165, 247; VII, 77; XVII, 65; XV, 95; answered queries, I, 174–175, 311; II, 82, 83; III, 269; IV, 77; VII, 243, 322; contributed documents, I, 396–397; II, 74–76; III, 85; V, 85–87, 243; VIII, 152–153; editorial comment, *The American Neptune,* XXXVIII, 3–4; notes by, XXXIII, 51; XXIII, 141–142; XXXIV, 70; queries by, I, 171, 310; VII, 322; reviews by, I, 402; II, 183, 351–352; X, 74–76; XXXII, 71, 136, 146, 291; XXXV, 212, 217; XXXVIII, 70, 74. "Additional Notes on Later History of American Sailing-Ships 'Sold Foreign,'" III, 264–265; IV, 244; V, 241–242, 327; "American Ketches," XI, 291; "Average Sailing Vessel Passages to San Francisco," III, 56; "The Bark *Kaiulani,*" II, 172; "Bright Light on *Flying Cloud* vs. *Andrew Jackson,*" IX, 148–150; "The Changed Meaning of *Cargar,*" XIX, 234; "Charles Morris as a Commodore," XXVII, 29; "Double Gaff Rigs," VI, 73–77; "Early Barkentine Illustrations," VII, 315–316, plate 39; "Fifty Years of Sail: The Bark *Abraham Rydberg,*" II, 289–298; "First Four-masted Schooner," I, 163; "Five-masted Barkentines," V, 81–82; "The Five-masted Schooner *Elvira Ball,*" V, 327; "Five-masted Schooners," V, 137–141; "Five-masted Square-Riggers," VI, 135–136, plate 18; "Flying Cloud vs. *Andrew Jackson,*" VII, 318; "Four-masted Ships," IX, 297–298, plate 31; "Four-masted Topsail Schooners," II, 326–327; "Great General and Small General," XXV, 226; "Japanese Anchors," XI, 77–78; "The Last Voyage of the *Star of Scotland,*" III, 266; "Largest American-built Bark," II, 336; "Later History of Light-vessel No. 50," XI, 78; (editor of) *Log Chips,* reviewed, VIII, 261–262; "New Light on *Flying Cloud* vs. *Andrew Jackson,*" VIII, 326–328; "Pacific Codfishing Records," I, 296–297; "*Pitcairn,* Missionary Packet," XI, 203–208; "Register Tonnage and its Measurement," V, 223–234, 311–325; "Rigs of American Yachts in 1902," XXX, 194–199; "River-Built Ocean Going Vessels," VII,

317–318; "Rowing a Boat in Japan," IX, 65–67, plate 5; "Six-masted Rigs," IV, 325–326; "Some Misconceptions Concerning the Spinnaker," XXXII, 58–63; "Speed, Size amd Model," VIII, 151–152; "The *Star of Scotland, ex-Kenilworth*," I, 333–344; "Tonnage-Weight and Measurement," VIII, 99–113; "Two Masts Square-, Two Masts Schooner-Rigged," IV, 237–238; "Weight of Boats," XXVIII, 142–143; "When Did *Alice* Carry a Spinnaker?" XXX, 199
Lyman, Colonel Phineas, XXXIX, 191
Lyman, Theodore, XIX, 12–14
Lyman, W. P., VII, 8
Lyme, H.M.S. *(1740)*, XIII, 179
Lynam, Dr. Edward, VII, 82, 83; X, 82; *Richard Hakluyt and his Successors,* reviewed, VII, 85, 86
Lynch, Chilean ship *(1891)*, XXXVIII, 299
Lynch, schooner *(1776)*, XXIX, 288; XXX, 107
Lynch, Captain D. H., XVIII, 83
Lynch, James B., Jr., "Edmund Custis and His 'Wreck-Fishing' Invention," L, 18–25
Lynch, Commander W. F., C.S.N., VI, 51
Lynch, Lieutenant William F., U.S.N., IV, 71
Lynch, William F., explorer, XLVII, 29
Lynchburg, schooner, XXI, 93
Lynn, schooner *(1794)*, XIX, 114–119; *(1817)*, XXIV, 287
Lynn, J., XXIV, plates XVIII, XX
Lynnhaven, schooner *(1862)*, VIII, 226; XII, 56
Lynx, H.M.S. *(1796)*, XVIII, 140
Lynx, steamship, XXI, 100, 105, plate VII; *(1864)*, VIII, 234
Lynx, U.S. schooner (1814), III, 267, plate 36
Lyon, ship *(1630)*, XXIV, 212–213. *See also* Lion.
Lyon, Captain Thomas, XLVII, 37
Lyons, Vice Admiral Sir Algernon McL., XXVIII, 112
Lyons, Captain Thomas, XXI, 96
Lyons, Lord, XIX, 60 ff.; XXVII, 30–32; XXXVI, 189
Lyra, bark (1855), V, 151
Lysaght, A. M., *Joseph Banks in Newfoundland and Labrador, 1776: His Diary, Manuscripts and Collections,* reviewed, XXXII, 137
Lytham St. Anne's, Lancashire, XXXIV, 10

M., schooner (1829), XXIV, 45, 59
M. A. Baker, sloop *(1861)*, XV, 124
M. A. Starr, steamship *(1864)*, XXXVII, 235
M. A. Stevens, brig, XXI, 91
M. E. Foster, schooner (1877), V, 86
M. H. Le Chatelier, concrete ship (1944), XXII, 178
M.I.T. Sea Grant Program, XLIV, 110 ff.
M. J. Foley, bark *(1881)*, XIV, 119
M. L. Frank, bark (1855), III, 64
M. M. Hamilton, sloop (1869), Pictorial Supplement, XXXVI, plate XII
M. Martin, steamship *(1887),* XIV, 285
M. O'Neill, schooner *(1864),* VIII, 235
M. P. Burton, schooner *(1864),* XII, 232
M. P. Casselly, brig (1847), VII, 318
M. P. Howlett, schooner (ex-*Jennie and Agnes*) (1901), XXVI, plate XVII
M. R. Ludwig, ship (1856), III, 65
M. S. Dollar, tanker *(1900),* XXXVIII, 180 ff.
M. Vivian Pierce, schooner, XXIV, 25
MA. *See* Massachusetts
Maale, Lieutenant E., XXXV, 188
Mabel, schooner, XXI, 95; *(1861),* VIII, 219, 226; XI, 285; XV, 124
Mabel, yacht *(1892),* XXXVI, 225, 236
Mably, Abbé de, XXV, 41
Mabrey, yacht *(1875),* XXXVI, 233
Maby, Captain, XXX, 115
Macara, Sir Charles, XXXIV, 10 ff.
MacArthur, General Douglas, XXXV, 184 ff.; XXXIX, 43; XLII, 210
Macartney, Lord, XXXI, 44; XLIII, 23; XLVI, 8 ff.
Macarty, William, U.S. Consul, XXV, 11
MacBeath, George, "Johnny Woodboat," XVII, 5–16, plates 1–4
MacCallum More, ship *(1891),* XVIII, 5
MacConnell, Captain James B., XXI, 96
Macdonald, Allan, XXII, 159
MacDonald, Angus D., VI, 155
Macdonald, Ross H., XIII, 216
MacDonald Engineering Works, XXI, 172
MacDonough, Thomas, XXXIX, 111
MacDonough, Commodore Thomas, U.S.N. XXI, 42, 47 ff.; XXV, 159
Macebo, Captain Gervasio, XV, 297
Macebo, Commander Gervasio, XXII, 50, 51
Macedonia, bark (1845), II, 330
Macedonia, H.M. frigate (1812), III, plate 3; *(1914),* XXXIII, 35 ff.
Macedonian, H.M.S., XXXVI, 278; *(1812),* VII, 167; XXVIII, 30; XLVII, 12; *(1829),* XLIX, 41
Macedonian, ship *(1819),* XIII, 122; *(1823),* XLII, 284 ff.; XLIII, 264; XLIV, 171; *(1830),* XXXVIII, 66; XL, 39 ff.
Macedonian, sloop of war *(1862),* XLVII, 31
Macedonian, U.S. frigate (1812), XXIII, 58; *(1815),* XIX, 220, 221; *(1819),* XXIX, 281
Macedonian, U.S.S. (1835), XXVII, 41 n., 160, 175; (1847), XIII, 252–267, plate 13; (1863), XX, 135; (1874), XXVIII, 30
Macerata, barkentine (1919), IV, 68; V, 82
MacEwan, Captain H. C., XXI, 96
MacEwen and Co., XXII, 11
MacGowan, U.S. destroyer *(1944),* XXIII, 256
MacGregor, steamship *(1873),* II, 21

MacGregor, David R., *The China Bird,* reviewed, XXII, 71–72; *Fast Sailing Ships: Their Design and Construction, 1775–1875,* reviewed, XLIX, 315; *Merchant Sailing Ships, 1775–1875: Their Design and Construction,* reviewed, XLII, 68–69; *Merchant Sailing Ships 1815–1850: Supremacy of Sail,* reviewed, XLVI, 124; *Schooners in Four Centuries,* reviewed, XLVI, 201; *Square Rigged Sailing Ships,* reviewed, XXXIX, 304
Machias, gunboat *(1894),* XXXIV, 214
Machias, ship *(1895),* XL, 106
Macinaw, ship *(1862),* VIII, 226
Macintyre, Donald, *Sea Power in the Pacific: A History from the 16th Century to the present day,* reviewed, XXXIII, 224–225; *The Thunder of Guns,* reviewed, XX, 226
Macintyre, Captain Donald, *Admiral Rodney,* reviewed, XXIII, 288–289
MacIntyre, George, VI, 307
MacKay, Robert, "Wreck of the Ship *General Oglethorpe* – 1802" (edited by Charles F. Mills), II, 44–55; miniature, II, plate 10
MacKay, S. G., XXXVI, 237
Mackay-Smith, Bishop, XXV, 246
Mack Canfield, schooner *(1863),* XII, 158
Mackean, T. W. L., XXII, 13
Mackensen, General August von, XXXVIII, 13
Mackenzie, Alexander Slidell, L, 245 ff.
Mackenzie, Lieutenant Alexander Slidell, XL, 216
Mackenzie, William Lyon, VII, 300
Mackerel schooner, XXVI, plate VI
Mackerel Skm%s, by Robert Latta, reviewed, XXXVII, 223–224
Mackie, J. H., XVII, 139, 140, 215–216
Mackie, John M., XVI, 177
Mackinaw, ship, XXI, 81, 88, 93
Mackinnon, Lieutenant, XXXVI, 140
MacLeish, Fleming, and Martin L. Krieger, *The Privateers: A Raiding Voyage to the Great South Sea,* reviewed, XXIII, 71–72
MacLeod, D. Peter, "The French Siege of Oswego in 1756: Inland Naval Warfare in North America, XLIX, 262–271
MacLeod, Julia H., and Louis B. Wright, *The First Americans in North Africa,* reviewed, V, 329–330
MacMahon, bark [model] *(1898),* XVI, 103
MacMullen, Jerry, VI, 155; VII, 78; XXIX, 265; "*Inchcliffe Castle,* Melbourne to Los Angeles," XX, 270–271; (co-author with Jack McNairn) *Ships of the Redwood Coast,* reviewed, VI, 156–157; "Transpacific Voyages of *Pamir,* The," VI, 112–113
MacNeil, Daniel F., query by, VI, 232; answered by M. V. Brewington, VII, 170
MacNichol Packing Co., XXVIII, 126
Macoa, bark *(1861),* XI, 285
Macomb, steamship *(1837),* VII, 65
Macomb, General Alexander, XXI, 42

Macomber, Lieutenant Samuel P., XXXI, 288
Macon, Nathaniel, XLIII, 251
Macpherson Collection, XI, 297–298
MacQueen, Farquhar, XXVI, 203
MacShane, Frank, "The Log of James Sutherland," XVIII, 306–314
Macy, Captain Alexander, L, 213
Madagascar, ship *(1853),* XXXI, Pictorial Supplement, plate XVI
Madagascar, boats of, XIII, 85 ff.
Madawaska, barkentine *(1866),* V, 150
Madawaska, U.S.S. *(1867),* I, 53
Madden, Vice Admiral, XLIX, 208
Madeline, French ship *(1800),* XXXI, 174
Madeline, sloop yacht *(1900),* XXXVI, 240–242, 245
Ma del Pilar, schooner *(1864),* XII, 231
Madison, James, XXIII, 168 ff.; XXVI, 240, 241, 243, 251; XXVIII, 38; XXXI, 239; XXXVI, 65, 66, 209
Madison, James, Secretary of State, XXV, 8, 13
Madison, President James, XXV, 38; XLVII, 27
Madras, steamship *(1852),* XXVI, 17, 18, 20, 22–24, 27, 29, 30, 202, 203, 205, 209
Madras, XXX, 201, 202, 203, 207
Madrono, steamship *(1884),* XXXVI, 53
Madura, boats of, XIII, 97 ff.
Madurese, ship (1862), III, 72
Mae Dollar, ship *(1927),* XVIII, 217
Maffitt, Lieutenant John N., XV, 293
Maffitt, Captain John Newland, C.S.N., XXI, 96; XXV, 298
Maga, Timothy P., "Operation Rescue: The *Mefkure* Incident and the War Refugee Board," XLIII, 31–39
Magallanes, Chilean corvette (1874), XXXIX, 276
Magan, James E., XIV, 212–214
Magdalena, bark *(1850),* VII, 324
Magdalena, ship *(1856),* V, 152
Magdalene, ship *(1861),* XI, 285
Magee, James, XIII, 272
Magellan, Ferdinand, XIV, 187
Magellan, Straits of. See Straits of Magellan
Magenta, French ironclad, XXIX, 13 n.
Maggie, schooner *(1863),* XII, 158
Maggie Alice, woodboat (1897), XVII, 13
Maggie Blum, sloop *(1864),* XV, 129
Maggie Fulton, schooner, XXI, 100; *(1862),* VIII, 226; *(1863),* XV, 128
Maggie Harthan, schooner, XXIV, 44, 59
Maggie Lauder, steamship *(1863),* XVII, 309; XVIII, 71
Maggie Sullivan, schooner (1893), XXVI, plate XII
Magi, bark *(1858),* IV, 32
Magician, steamship *(1842),* plate XXI
Magicienne, French ship *(1799),* XXXI, 173
Magnanime, British frigate *(1801),* XXVII, 148
Magnet, brig *(1833),* XLI, 288
Magnet, cartel *(1814),* XXVIII, 190
Magnet, schooner, XIV, 40; *(1862),* XV, 116, 126
Magnet, ship *(1856),* XIX, 28, plate 2

Magnetic variation, compass, XXV, 93–98, plate 4
Magnifique, French warship *(1784),* XLII, 34
Magnolia, bark (1853), III, 68; (1855), III, 72
Magnolia, packet sloop *(1828),* XXV, 223
Magnolia, schooner, XXI, 98, 103; *(1833),* XXIII, 7; *(1862),* XII, 56; *(1863),* VIII, 231
Magnolia, ship *(1849),* XLV, 124; *(1863),* XII, 158
Magnolia, sloop, XXI, 95, 103
Magnolia, steamship, XXI, 89, 101; *(1852),* XXIII, 84; *(1861),* XI, 285; XII, 56
Magoun, David, XXV, 222
Magoun, David and Thomas (shipbuilders), II, 283
Magoun, Elias, XXV, 222
Magoun, F. Alexander, XIV, 13, 14
Magoun, Thatcher, XIII, 121; XV, 136, 139; XIX, 9, 15, 16, 20, 21, 23, 26
Magoun, Thatcher (shipbuilder), XLV, 154
Magruder, Captain G. A., XXXVII, 277
Magruder, Commander George, XXXV, 26 ff.
Magruder, Major General John Bankhead, XXXVI, 200 ff.
Maguire, James, XIII, 122
Magune, Captain Frank A., VIII, 70
Magune, Captain and Mrs. Frank A., XXXV, 13, plate 2
Magune, Frank L., "A Sea Yarn of the Nineties," VIII, 70
Magune, Captain James W., XVIII, 318–319
Mahan, U.S. destroyer *(1918),* VII, 72
Mahan, Rear Admiral A. T., U.S.N., IV, 129–130
Mahan, Admiral, XXVIII, 6
Mahan, Alfred T., XXXVII, 33; XXXIX, 24 ff.
Mahan, Captain Alfred T., XXXI, 275; XXXII, 55; XXXIV, 211 ff.; XXXV, 101
Mahan, Admiral Alfred Thayer, U.S.N., XXV, 37, 278; XXVI, 239; XLVIII, 10
Mahan, Captain Alfred Thayer, XLI, 95; XLII, 37, 180; XLIII, 135 ff.
Mahan, Captain Dennis H., XXIX, 125
Mahan, James, XXVI, 175
Mahee, Captain James, XIV, 44
Mahmoud, ship of the line *(1831),* VII, 190
Mahon, Captain James, XVIII, 9
Mahon, John K., "The Civil War Letters of Lieutenant Commander George Bacon," XII, 271–281
Mahon, Minorca, Balearic Islands, XXV, 157 ff.
Mahopac, U.S. monitor (1862), X, 19, 27, 32
Mahroussa, steamship (1865), XXIV, plate XXVI
Ma Huan Ying-yai Sheng-lan: "The Overall Survey of the Ocean's Shore," by J. V. G. Mills, reviewed, XXXII, 225–226
"Maiden Voyage of *Ann and Hope* of Providence to Botany Bay and Canton, 1798–1799, The," by Robert W. Kenny, XVIII, 105–136, plates 5–10
Maid of England, barkentine *(1920),* Pictorial Supplement, XXXVI, plate XXXII
Maid of Erin, British *(1846),* XXXIII, 85, 94

Maid of Orleans, bark (1839), Pictorial Supplement, XXXVIII, plate XVIII
Maid of Orleans, ship (1848), III, 262
Maidstone, British frigate *(1798),* XXXIX, 32; *(1814),* XXVIII, 118; XLII, 107 ff.; XLV, 96
Maidstone, H.M.S. *(1765),* XXIII, 181
Mail, schooner (1831), XLV, 189; *(1862),* XII, 56
Mail, sloop, XXIV, 131, 132, 135
Mail, steamship, XXI, 92, 96; *(1863),* XII, 158, 231
Mailand, John, rigger, III, 280
Mailliard, William, XXXVI, 29
Mail ships, XXII, 55
Mail steamers, XLI, 110
Mailu, boats of, XIII, 92 ff.
Maine, pinky schooner (1845), XXVI, plate II; Pictorial Supplement, XXXVI, plate IV
Maine, S.S. (1917), XXVII, plate XXX
Maine, ship *(1853),* XLVII, 101; *(1898),* XXXIII, 277
Maine, steamship *(1913),* VII, 217
Maine, U.S.S. *(1898),* XXXVI, 99 ff.; XXXIX, 40; XL, 167
Maine. History, XXIV, 38
 —, 19th century, XXII, 184
See also Bank notes; Boatbuilding; Canals; Eastport; Indians of North America; Lobster fisheries; Penobscot Expedition; Schooners; Shipbuilding; Shipping; Shipping Lines; Shipwrecks; Slave traders; Steamboats; Steam Navigation
"Maine Boy at Sea in the Eighties, A," by Albert E. Averill, X, 203–219
Maine historical manuscripts, I, 404–405
Maine Historical Society, Portland, IX, 133 n.
Maine Law, bark, XXIV, 45, 57
Maines, Captain Irving J., XXIV, 238 ff.
Maine salmon wherry, XXVI, 48, plate 4
Maine Seacoast Mission, I, 101
Maine State Library, query by, V, 164
Maine Steamship Co., ship of, Pictorial Supplement, XXXIV, plate XXIII
"Maine Transatlantic Salt Trade in the Nineteenth Century, The," by Wayne M. O'Leary, XLVII, 83–107
"Maine West India Trade, The," by William Hutchinson Rowe, VIII, 165–178
Mainwaring, Sir Henry, VIII, 306
Maipo, bark *(1861),* XI, 285
Maipu, schooner *(1845),* XXXVI, 127
Maitland, Ron, XXXVI, 245, 248
Majestic, bark *(1861),* XXI, 242, 258
Majestic, H.M.S. *(1915),* XXXVI, 41, 43
Majestic, ship *(1848),* XII, 106
Major, John, and Antony Preston, *Send a Gunboat!* reviewed, XXVII, 223–224
Major, Richard Henry, VII, 85
Major Barbour, schooner, XXI, 100; *(1861),* XI, 285; XII, 56
Major Barrett, steamship (1900), XXXVIII, 183 ff.

Major E. Willis, schooner, XXI, 93; (1863), VIII, 231
Major Pickands, schooner, XXXV, plate 2
Makee, James. *See* Mahee.
"Makers of Mariners' Compasses in Newburyport," by Martha G. Fales, XXVIII, 144–145
Makin, Captain John, XXI, 96
Mako II, charter boat *(1963),* XLI, 58
Malabar, H.M.S. *(1899),* XXVIII, 93, 93 n., 98
Malabar, ship (1856), XXXVII, 169; XLVI, 183
Malabar, steamship *(1858),* XXVI, 24–28, 203, 205, 209
Malachite, steamship *(1914),* XXXVI, 35
Malaga, brig (1827), XIV, 40
Malang, steamship (ex-*Eastern Leader*), XXIII, 276
Malay, ship (1852), XIX, plate XXVII
Malbone (furniture maker), XXV, 54
Malbone, Godfrey, XII, 222; XLII, 42 ff.
Malbone, William T., XIII, 271
Malcolm, schooner *(1840),* XX, 87
"Malcolm Storer Collection of Naval Medals, The," by Shepard Pond, II, 336–337
Malcom Baxter, Jr., schooner *(1900),* I, 396
Mallet, Captain Walter M., II, 65–70, 199, 293, plates 13–16, plate 26
Mallet, Mrs. Walter M., II, 66–67, 293
Malleville, bark (1866), IV, 318–323
Mallory, Charles, XXV, 105; XXXI, 137
Mallory, Charles H., XVI, 256
Mallory, Charles Henry, XXV, 105; XLVIII, 118
Mallory, Clifford Day, I, 205–208, 400; *Dilemma,* reviewed, II, 94
Mallory, S. R., XI, 273
Mallory, Honorable S. R., XXII, 286 n.
Mallory, Stephen, XXVII, 238
Mallory, Stephen B., XV, 287
Mallory, Stephen R., XXIX, 5–29
Mallory, Senator Stephen R. (Confederate Secretary of the Navy), XXXII, 198; XXXIII, 203; XL, 298; XLII, 90; XLVIII, 99; XLIX, 106; L, 108
Mallory Family papers, Mystic (CT), XXV, 102–103, 105
Malloy, Mary, review by, XLIV, 205; "*Storm Along: An American Sea Anthology,* a Manuscript by Joanna Carver Colcord in the Collection of the Peabody Museum of Salem," XLVI, 111–119
Malmberg, Captain and Mrs. Oscar, II, 297, plate 40
Maloja, steamship (1911), XXIV, plate XVI
Malolo, schooner (1879), V, 86
Malolo, steamship (1924), IX, 223–225
Malolo, U.S.S., XXIX, 234
Malone, Henry Dexter, XLIV, 117 ff.
Maloney, Linda M., *The Captain from Connecticut: The Life and Naval Times of Isaac Hull,* reviewed, XLIX, 238
Maloney, Linda McKee, "A Naval Experiment," XXXIV, 188–196
Maloney, Dr. Linda McKee, XXXVII, 143
Maloney, Paul R., contributed document, XXI, 222
Malster, grain elevator *(1883),* XXXVIII, 141

Malster, Robert, *Wherries and Waterways,* reviewed, XXXII, 290
Malta, schooner *(1865),* XII, 235
Malta, steamship *(1847),* XXVI, 13, 14, 15, 17, 19, 20, 22, 202, 203, 206, 209, plate 1; (1848), XXIV, plate IX
Malvern, U.S.S. *(1864),* XIV, 62, 63; *(1865),* XLII, 97; XLIII, 97 ff.
Malyar, Miguel, XXXV, 194
Mamaranack, ship, XXI, 89; *(1861),* XI, 285
Mameluke, ship (1855), V, 149
Mamie Mister, bateau (1910), IV, 289
"Management-Leadership in the United States Shipping Board 1917–1918," by William N. Thurston, XXXII, 155–170
Manassas, C.S.S. ironclad ram *(1861),* XXXI, 64; XLIX, 119
Manassas, steamship *(1861),* XV, 99, 106, 114, 124
Manassas (ex-*Minot*), schooner *(1861),* XLVIII, 95
Manatus, steamship (1864), XVI, 258
Manayunk, U.S. monitor (1862), X, 19, 32
Manby, Aaron, XIII, 157, 158
Manby, Charles, XIII, 157 ff.
Manby, Captain George, XXXIV, 6 ff.
Mancall, Mark, XLVIII, 261
Manchack, J., XXV, 125 n.
Manchester, ship *(1799),* XLV, 89
Manchester Merchant, S.S., XXXV, 4
Manchu, steamship (1866), XVI, 256; XVII, 217 ff.; XVIII, 71
Manchuria, steamship, XXIX, 231; (1904), X, 138, 139
Manco Capa, Peruvian ironclad (1866), XXXIX, 275
Mandarin, ship *(1807),* XVI, 192; *(1813),* XLVI, 170
Mandarin, steamship (1860), XVII, 61; *(1863),* XLIX, 25; *(1865),* XLIII, 95, 210 ff.
Mandell, Edward D., XXXIII, 53; XXXIX, 96
Mandella, Captain L., XXI, 96
Mandinka traders, XXX, 178 f.
Mandoline, schooner, XXI, 99; *(1864),* XII, 231
Mangareva, boats of, XIII, 97 ff.
Manger, Thomas, XVIII, 60
Manhasset, schooner (1902), XLIV, 117
Manhattan, American merchantman *(1805),* XLIII, 45
Manhattan, grain elevator *(1883),* XXXVIII, 141
Manhattan, Long Island steamship, XXVI, 74
Manhattan, packet ship (1849), I, 44, 48
Manhattan, steamship (1837), VII, 64; (1847), VI, 278
Manhattan, U.S. monitor (1862), X, 19, 32
Manhattan, U.S.S. (1934), XXIX, 235
Manhegan, ship (1876), IV, 240
Manhoudt, Hidde, Jr., *Zeilschepen en Hun Tuigage,* reviewed, VIII, 76
Manifest Destiny, XXXI, 8
Manihiki, boats of, XIII, 89 ff.
Manila, ship *(1899),* XXXV, 189; *(1901),* XXIX, 113
Manila, steamship (1873), XVI, 176
Manila, steamship (ex-*Yung Hai An,* ex-*Nimro/Jinju,* ex-*Lancefield*), XXVI, 122

Manila, XXX, 203
Manila Galleon, The, by William Lytle Schurz, reviewed, II, 85–86
Manila galleon, XXIII, 71–72
Manilla, schooner *(1917),* XXXVI, 268 ff.
Manilla, steamship (1853), XXVI, 24, 32, 111, 118, 203, 206, 209; XLIII, 103 ff.
Manitoba Museum, XXX, 79
Manitowoc Shipbuilding Co., XLIV, 123
Manjiro Nakahama, XX, 201 ff.
Manley, Captain John, V, 184 ff.; XXX, 86, 299; XLII, 12 ff.; XLVIII, 162
Manligheten, ship (1785), VI, 170
Manlius, ship *(1855),* XX, 124
Manly, H.M. Brig *(1813),* XXXI, 296
Manly, Captain John, U.S.N., XXV, 35
Mann, Captain Charles, XLIII, 191
Mann, Ebenezer (shipbuilder), II, 278 ff.
Mann, J. F., contributed note, XXIII, 140–141
Mann, Governor Thomas, XXXVIII, 101 ff.
Manners, Captain William, R.N., VII, 169
Manning, T. D., and C. F. Walker, *British Warship Names,* reviewed, XIX, 310
Manning, Thomas G., *U.S. Coast Survey vs. Naval Hydrographic Office: A 19th Century Rivalry in Science and Politics,* reviewed, XLIX, 317
Manning, William Montague, XLIII, 203
Manning Strait, XXV, 260
Manning's Yacht Register, XXX, 194 ff.
"Manning the Royal Navy in North America, 1763–1775," by Neil R. Stout, XXIII, 174–185
Mannix, Daniel P., XXXII, 267
Manshu Maru, steamship *(1872),* XLIII, 298
Mansilla, General, XXXVI, 132 ff.
Manson, Philip, XXXV, 172 ff.
Mantanden, George, XXV, 172
Manteo, ship (1843), XIV, 38, 40
Manter, Cyrus, XLIV, 14
Manton, Captain Benjamin D., XX, 214
Manucy, Captain J. E., VII, 119, 150
Manuel, brig *(1843),* XXXV, 255
Manuel de Rosas, General Juan, L, 31
Manuelita Planas, ship *(1863),* XXXII, 285
"Manuscript Collections of the Marine Historical Association, Inc. (Mystic Seaport)," by Charles R. Schultz, XXV, 99–111, plates 5–8
"Manuscript Maps in the William L. Clements Library," by Lloyd A. Brown, I, 141–148
Manuscripts, XIII, 118. *See also* names of individual libraries
Manx Museum, XXIX, 54, 56, 59
Many, bark *(1861),* XI, 285
Manzanares, Venezuelan brig *(1848),* XXX, 266
Manzanita, steamship *(1879),* XXXVI, 52
Maples, Henry, XIII, 21, 27
Maples, Captain Richard, XIII, 5–28, plate 1
Maples, Captain William, XIII, 8, 27

Map of the world, Dymaxion Projection by Richard Buckminster Fuller, IV, between 118–119
Map of Yorktown By Joachim du Perron, Comte de Revel, reviewed, III, 94
Map projection, IV, 119
Maps. *See also* Cartography; and under individual countries
Maps: A Historical Survey of Their Study and Collecting, by R. A. Skelton, reviewed, XXXIII, 221
Maps: I, 141–148, facing 214; II, 130, 148; III, 94; IV, 82, 119–136
  Acadia, Isle Royale, Isle St. Jean and Terre Neuve, XLIV, 188; Arabian sea, XLVIII, 150; China: coastline, L, 181; China: Grand Canal, 1793, XLVIII, 231; China: Yangtsze River in 1862–1874, XLIII, plate 1; English Channel: Battles of the Hundred Years' War, XLVI, 93; Genoese-Venetian War (first), XLVI, 87; India, XL, 282 ff.; Mahon, Port of, L, 135; Niger Delta, XXXV, plate 8; Route of *Lusitania* off Ireland, XXXV, 39; Sahara, western coast of, L, 120; Taku Forts Mouth of Pei-Ho, XXVII, 168; Trade routes ca. 1250, XLVI, 86; US: Charleston area, XLII, facing 194; L, 90
Maps and charts, VIII, 302–324
Maps and How to Understand Them, reviewed, IV, 82
Maps, James M., "A Long-Forgotten American Naval Cemetery," XXV, 157–167, plates 11–14
Maps, marine. *See* Nautical charts
Maracaibo, schooner *(1861),* VIII, 219
Maracaibo, Venezuelan bark *(1848),* XXX, 265
Marangoin (or *Little Mosketo*) *(1777),* XLIII, 23 ff.
Marañon, Peruvian ship *(1881),* XXXIX, 287
Marathon, bark (1833), V, 154; (1864), IV, 326
Marathon, ship (1849), I, 48; *(1861),* XI, 266, 285
Marathon, steamship *(1881),* XIV, 118
Marathon, transport *(1945),* XXXIX, 256
Marblehead, bark *(1837),* XXXII, 64
Marble Head, H.M.S., XIII, 179
Marblehead, ship *(1903),* XXXVII, 254
Marblehead, U.S.S. *(1894),* XXVIII, 92
Marblehead (MA), I, 320; XXX, 86 ff.; customs records, XIII, 123; trade, XXVIII, 261–274
"Marblehead Cartel in Ye Year 1731, A," document contributed by Russell W. Knight, XXIV, 72–73
Marblehead Historical Society, XXX, 93
Marbois, M. de, XXV, 7
Marcella, brig *(1831),* XXXVIII, 269 ff.
March, Edgar J., *British Destroyers: A History of Development, 1892–1953,* reviewed, XXVII, 281–284; *Inshore Craft of Britain: In the Days of Sail and Oar,* reviewed, XXXII, 139–140; *Spritsail Barges of Thames and Medway,* XXXII, 144–145
March, Major, XXXV, 190
March, General Peyton C., XXXIV, 269
Marchand, Captain John B., XXXVI, 203
Marchi, Francesco de", VII, 263
Marchi, John W., VII, 82, 254; IX, 238

Marcia, bark *(1861)*, XXI, 242, 258
Marcia, schooner *(1804)*, XIII, 278; *(1852)*, XXIV, 59
Marcia, ship *(1855)*, XLI, 299
Marcia Greenleaf, ship (1855), IV, 239
Marcia Reynolds, schooner (1871), XV, 183; XXIV, 45, 59
Marcil, Eileen Reid, "Ship-Rigged Rafts and the Export of Quebec Timber," XLVIII, 77–86
Marcus, brig *(1862)*, XX, 159
Marcus, coasting sloop (1899), XXXVII, 165
Marcus, Captain Fred, XLVII, 49
Marcy, Captain Samuel, XXI, 96
Marcy, William L., Secretary of State, XXXI, 14
Marcy, William L., Secretary of War, XXXVII, 250
Marder, Arthur J., *From the Dreadnought to Scapa Flow: The Royal Navy in the Fisher Era, 1904–1919* [Vol. I], *The Road to War, 1904–1914*, reviewed, XXII, 222–223
Marder, Arthur J., *From the Dreadnought to Scapa Flow: The Royal Navy in the Fisher Era, 1904–1919* [Vol. III], *Jutland and After: May 1916-December 1916*, reviewed, XXVII, 66–67
Marengo, schooner *(1834)*, VII, 53
"Marestier's *Mémoire sur les bateaux à vapeur des États-Unis d'Amérique*," by David B. Tyler, I, 412–416
Margaret, brig (1820), XIV, 40; *(1848)*, XXX, 241
Margaret, galley, XXIII, 103–108
Margaret, ketch (1697), XXV, 91
Margaret, Salem ship *(1801)*, XLVI, 53
Margaret, schooner *(1756)*, XXIII, 277, 278; *(1863)*, XII, 158
Margaret, ship *(1599)*, XXXVII, 174
Margaret, ship (1800), II, 279; *(1801)*, XXV, 184
Margaret, sloop, XXI, 103; *(1861)*, XI, 285; XII, 56
Margaret, steamship *(1920)*, XI, 78
Margaret A. Stevens, brig, XXI, 91; *(1861)*, XI, 285; XII, 56
Margaret and Jessie, steamship, XXI, 95, 104, 105, plate XXII; *(1863)*, III, 139; VIII, 204–205, 231; IX, 45; XI, 221, 223
Margaret [Margrett] and John, ship, XIV, 7; *(1630)*, XXIII, 64
Margaret Evans, ship (1846), III, 262
Margaret Kemble, steamship (1844), XXIV, 8 ff.
Margaret M., fishing vessel *(1963)*, XLI, 59
Margaret Mercer, schooner (1831), XXXVIII, 57
Margaret Quayle, ship (1855), III, 64
Margaret Scott, bark *(1861)*, XXI, 258
Margarett, schooner (1889), IX, 20, 29, plate 2
Margaretta, British schooner *(1775)*, XLII, 5
Margaret Throop, schooner (1918), XXVIII, plate XXVI
Margarita, gunboat, XXVIII, 99
Margarita, ship (1856), VI, 82
Margery, transport *(1781)*, XLVII, 11
Margie, schooner, XXVIII, 123
Margie Smith, schooner (1875), XXVI, plate III
Margrett and John. See *Margaret and John*.
Marguerita, schooner *(1864)*, XII, 231
Marguerite, schooner, XIII, 121; *(1888)*, XXX, Pictorial Supplement, plate V
Maria, brig *(1814)*, XLII, 114
Maria, schooner, XXI, 91, 92; XXII, 60 n., 93; *(1776)*, XIII, 42
Maria, schooner (1827), XVI, 211–213; *(1862)*, VIII, 226; XII, 56, 158
Maria, ship *(1785)*, XLI, 214
Maria, sloop, XXVII, 16; (1801), XIV, 40
Maria, steamship *(1818)*, VI, 195
Maria, steamship, XXI, 94; (1842), XVII, 215; *(1864)*, XII, 231
Maria (ex-*Ann*), steamship (1839), XLIII, 87 ff.
Maria, yacht *(1860)*, XXXVI, 185
Maria Alberta, schooner *(1863)*, XII, 158
Maria Alfred, schooner *(1864)*, XII, 232
Maria Bishop, schooner *(1863)*, VIII, 231
Maria Christiana, cartel, XXVIII, 176
Maria del Carmen, schooner *(1843)*, XXXV, 255
Maria Freeman, brig *(1854)*, XLV, 26
Maria Louise, sloop, XXI, 96; *(1864)*, XV, 129
Maria Lunt, schooner, XXVIII, 148
Maria Morton, bark *(1861)*, VIII, 219
Marian, steamship, XXI, 101; *(1864)*, XI, 276; XII, 232, 235
Mariana, ship *(1799)*, XLVII, 164 ff.
Mariana Islands, boats of, XIII, 99
Mariane, Swedish schooner *(1840)*, XXXV, 260
"Marianist Centennial," query by Brother Paul O'Brien, IX, 302
Marianna, schooner (1861), V, 154
Mariano, bark (1864), IV, 72
Marian Otis Chandler, steamship *(1929)*, IX, 226
Maria Rickmers, bark (1891), VI, 135
Maria Teresa, ship *(1861)*, XXI, 256
Maria Theresa, cruiser *(1850)*, XLI, 94 ff.
Maria Theresa, schooner (1847), Pictorial Supplement, XXXVIII, plate XXX
Maria Theresa, ship *(1861)*, XV, 108 n.
Marie, bark, figurehead of, Pictorial Supplement, XXXVII, plate VII
Marie, ship (1857), VI, 82
Marie Amelie, bark (1854), V, 153
Marie Antoine, sloop, XXI, 99
Marie & Antoinette, ship (1880), III, 62
Marie Antoinette, sloop *(1861)*, XI, 285
Mariechen, 3-masted bark *(1916)*, XXV, 277
Marie Coristie, schooner, XXI, 101; *(1861)*, XI, 285
Marie de Ronde, schooner (1918), IV, 62–63, plate 16
Marie Louise, sloop *(1863)*, XV, 112, 128, 129
Marie Palmer, schooner (1900), V, 80
Marietta, monitor *(1898)*, XXXVI, 258 ff.
Marietta, U.S.S. (1895), XX, 141; *(1899)*, XXVIII, 92
Marietta, yacht *(1904)*, XXXVI, 241
Mariette, schooner (1917), XIII, 246
Marin, Don Tomas, XXI, 222

Marin, 1st Lieutenant Juan Agustin, XXX, 52
Marina, ship *(1812),* XIV, 97
Marina, steamship *(1932),* XXXVIII, 184
Marine, brig *(1857),* IV, 315–316
Marine art, XXIII, 34; XXVII, 254; XXXVI, 170
Marine artists, XXIV, 124; L, 60
    Biography, XVI, 233; XXII, 184; XXXVI, 170
Marine biology, Study and teaching, XLV, 81; XLVII, 206; XLIX, 34
Marine Carving Handbook, by Jay S. Hanna, reviewed, XXXVIII, 148
Marine Engineers Beneficial Association, XXIX, 237
Marine Engines, by Robert Murray, XXX, 15
Marine Historical Association, Inc. (Mystic Seaport), Mystic, CT, I, 95, 102, 196–197, 207–208, 391–393; II, 340; III, 279 ff.; V, 247, 330; IX, 18, 77, 231–232; XV, 3; XVI, 3; XX, 63; XXV, 99–111, plates 5–8
Marine Industries of Eastern Arabia, by Richard LeBaron Bowen, Jr., reviewed, XI, 300
Marine Instruments, Ltd., XIII, 66
"Marine Intelligence from the *Panama Star* and *Star and Herald,*" by Captain John F. Campbell, XX, 118–133
Marine Museum of the City of New York, XXII, 232
Marine Museum of the Old State House, Boston, VII, 6, plate 2
Marine Museum of Upper Canada, XXVII, 155
Marine museums:
    France, XX, 231
    Italy, XX, 231
    Spain, XX, 231
    See also individual museums (listed under Museums, libraries and maritime collections)
"Marine Museums in Italy, Southern France and Spain, The," by Dorothy and Marion V. Brewington, XX, 231–236
"Marine Note of Protest, A," by John F. Campbell, XXIII, 46–55
Marine Paintings and Drawings in the Peabody Museum, The, by Dorothy and Marion V. Brewington, XXXVII, 79, 140 n.; mentioned, XXVIII, 83–84; reviewed, XXVIII, 289–290
Marine photography, China, XXXV, 32
Mariner, Gloucester trawler *(1919),* XLIV, 128
Mariner, sloop *(1812),* XLV, 8
Mariner, steamship *(1861),* VIII, 219, 226, 231
Marine Research Society, I, 197
Mariner's Astrolabe, Pictorial Supplement, XXXV, plate II
Mariner's Compasses: circa 1802, Pictorial Supplement, XXXV, plate IX; American, circa 1860, Pictorial Supplement, XXXV, plate X; American, circa 1920, Pictorial Supplement, XXXV, plate XI
Mariner's Dictionary, The, XXX, 40
Mariner's Mirror, The, journal, VIII, 4; XXIII, 155; XXXII, 58, XXXIV, 79, XXXV, 151; editorial comment, **The American Neptune,** XXXVIII, 3–4

Mariners' Museum, 1930–1950, The, by Alexander Crosby Brown, reviewed, XI, 226–228
Mariners' Museum, *American Merchant Sailing Vessels of the Nineteenth Century,* reviewed, XI, 234
Mariners' Museum, The (Newport News, VA), I, 176, 188, 197, 314, 400; II, 84, 93, 177, 225, 243, 252; III, 38, 88–89, 271, 354; IV, 81–82, 336; V, 165, 208, 247; VI, 137, 155, 307; VII, 249–250, plate 39; VIII, 75, 253, 265, plates 8, 16, 22, 23; IX, 78, 284, 291, 296; X, 9 n.; XI, 245 ff.; XV, 96; XVI, 3; XVII, 172, 174; XXV, 295, 302; XXVIII, 4, 238; XXX, 32; XXXI, 83; XXXII, 29; XXXIV, 10; *Maritime Titles in Print,* XXXIX, 61
Marines, Captain Archibald, XXI, 97
Marines, U.S., assault on Korean forts, XXV, 121; Continental, assault on Nassau, XXV, 202 ff.
Marine societies, XXVI, 272; **United States,** V, 266
Marine Society at Salem, XXVI, 272 ff.
Marino, General, XXX, 265
Marinship Corp., Sausalito, Cal. VIII, 76
Mario Croce, S.S. *(1942),* XXVII, 197
Marion, schooner *(1864),* XII, 232
Marion, ship *(1808),* X, 148; *(1850),* XXXVIII, 28
Marion, steamship (1871), VII, 134, 141, 142, 146 n., 150, 151, 153, 154, 157, 158, 160, plate 14
Marion, steamship, XXI, 91; *(1861),* VIII, 219; XV, 99, 115, 118, 124; XXI, 243
Marion, U.S.S. *(1862),* XX, 135, 136; XLVII, 31
Marion Chilcott, bark (1907), XVI, 111
Mariposa, steamship *(1905),* XLVI, 198
"Maritime Adventures of a Jewish Sea Captain, Jonas P. Levy, in Nineteenth-Century America, The," by Samuel Rezneck, XXXVII, 239–252
Maritime Belge (Belgian shipping line), XLVI, 108
Maritime Commerce of Colonial Philadelphia, The, by Arthur L. Jensen, reviewed, XXIII, 290
Maritime Commission, U.S., XXII, 174, 177
Maritime Enterprises of James J. Hill, The," by Don L. Hofsommer, XLVII, 193–205
"Maritime Excerpts from Rhode Island," document contributed by Eric Steinfeldt, XXIV, 70–72
"Maritime Heritage, A," by Horace P. Beck, XXV, 51–67
Maritime history:
    Ancient, XLV, 225; XLVII, 157
    Bibliography, XII, 64, 163, 241, 297; XIII, 68, 141, 215, 282; XIV, 66, 142, 218, 300; XV, 83, 157, 233, 311; XVI, 66, 139, 214, 286; XVII, 74, 157, 231, 315; XVIII, 86, 253, 325; XXXIX, 58
    Conferences, etc., XLVIII, 178
    Publishing, XLVIII, 178
    Study and teaching, XLV, 41.
    See also Navigation (History)
Maritime History [Vol. I, 1971], Editor, Robert Craig, reviewed, XXXIII, 216–218
Maritime History of Australia, A, by John Bach, reviewed, XLV, 204

Maritime History of Bath, Maine and the Kennebec River Region, A, by William Avery Baker, reviewed, XXXIV, 285–286

Maritime History of Maine, The, by William Hutchinson Rowe, reviewed, IX, 151–153; mentioned, VIII, 178 n.

Maritime History of Massachusetts, The, by Samuel Eliot Morison, reviewed, II, 262

Maritime History of Massachusetts: 1783–1860, The, by Samuel Eliot Morison, reviewed, XLII, 146

Maritime History of the World, The, by Duncan Haws and Alex A. Hurst, reviewed, XLVII, 283

"Maritime Industry of the St. Vincent Grenadines, West Indies," by John E. Adams, XXXII, 180–194

Maritime law, XXIII, 46; XXXI, 19

Maritime libraries. *See* Libraries

"Maritime Manuscripts in the Baker Library," by Robert W. Lovett, XIII, 118–124

"Maritime Material Discussed in the Printed Account of the American Crystal Palace Exhibition of 1853," note contributed by S. W. Jackman, XXIII, 67–68

"Maritime Mediterranean, 500–1571 A.D., The," review article by Archibald R. Lewis, XLIX, 126–132

Maritime Museum, Genoa, XX, 233

Maritime Museum of British Columbia, XXVIII, 53; *Maritime Titles in Print,* XXXIX, 62

Maritime Museum of Canada, *Occasional Papers,* reviewed, XIX, 310

Maritime Museum of the Zagreb Yugoslav Academy of Science and Arts at Dubrovnik, XXIV, 124–125

Maritime Research Society of San Diego, I, 100

"Maritime Studies at Sea Semester," by James Millinger, XLVII, 206–210

"Maritime Superstitions of the Arabs," by Richard LeBaron Bowen, Jr., XV, 5–48, plates 1, 2

Maritza, Bulgarian ship *(1944),* XLIII, 35 ff.

Marjoribanks, Sir John, XIV, 101 ff.

Marjoribanks, Stewart, XV, 102

Marjoribanks, Captain William, XIV, 102

Markell, Thomas, XXVII, 235, 236

Markell, William, XXVII, 235, 236

Markham, Clements, XL, 280

Markham, Sir Clements Robert, VII, 85

Markland, Canadian schooner *(1902),* XLIX, 280

Markland, William Thomas, XL, 44

Marks, Mrs. Josephine Peabody, XXXVIII, 7

"Mark Tiddeman's Chart of New York Harbor," by Coolie Verner, XIX, 44–50

Mark Twain, XXV, 57

Mark Well the Whale, Long Island Ships to Distant Seas, by Frederick P. Schmitt, reviewed, XXXII, 140–141

Marlbone, Rowland, XI, 35 ff.

Marline, Harry, XXXVIII, 108

Marlin spikes, IX, 283–284

Marlinspike Sailor, The, by Hervey Garrett Smith, reviewed, XXXII, 149

Marmion, ship, XXV, 184

Marmora, steamship (1844), XXXVII, 142 n.; *(1844),* XLVIII, 117; *(1845),* V, 163

Marooned, by Bertha S. Dodge, reviewed, XL, 143

Marquesas Islands, South Pacific, XXV, 184; boats of, XIII, 89 ff.

Marquet, schooner *(1838),* XXII, 216

Marquette and Bessemer No. 2, steamship, XXIII, 70

Marquis, Robert M., XXXIX, 106

"Marquis de Chabert and the Louisbourg Observatory in the 1750's, The," by Kenneth Donovan, XLIV, 186–197

Marquis de Lafayette, ship *(1781),* XLIV, 169

Marquis de Melauze, Le, reviewed, I, 101

Marquis de Somereulas, ship *(1805),* XXI, 292

Marquis de Somerulas, ship *(1800),* IX, 241–245

Marquis of Ely, cutter *(1809),* XLVIII, 240

Marr, O. K., XXVII, plate XXV

"Marriage of Convenience: The United States Navy in Africa, 1820–1843," by Judd Scott Harmon, XXXII, 264–276

Marriott, Joseph, XXXI, 24

Marryat, Captain Frederic, XXIII, 56 ff.

Marryat, Captain Frederick, R.N., III, 207 ff.

Mars (1802), XXIII, 217

Mars, brigantine (1794), Pictorial Supplement, XXXI, plate XII

Mars, Dutch frigate *(1781),* XXXVI, 167, 168

Mars, French ship *(1801),* XXXI, 175

Mars, gunboat *(1782),* XXXIX, 217

Mars, privateer, XXII, 268

Mars, schooner, XXI, 100; *(1795),* XXVIII, 32; *(1862),* XV, 126

Mars, ship *(1820),* XIV, 43

Mars (ex-*Indore*), steamship *(1862),* XLIX, 25

Mars, steamship (1862), XVIII, 71; *(1863),* XXI, 87, Plate XVIII; *(1864),* VIII, 234; (1868), XVII, 53, 56

Mars, whale ship, XXV, plate 8

Marsala, barkentine (1919), IV, 60–61, 68, plate 15; V, 82 n.

Marsden, Lieutenant Lawrence A., U.S.N.R., *Attack Transport,* reviewed, VI, 310

Marsden, Rev. Samuel, XII, 28

Marsh, Anne, editorial mention, XLIII, 243

Marsh, Philip M., VI, 155; "Philip Freneau, Our Sailor Poet," VI, 115–120

Marsh, Samuel, XXVI, 175

Marshall, Humphrey, XXX, 158; XXXIV, 104 ff.

Marshall, Commissioner Humphrey, XXXVIII, 29

Marshall, Jim, L, 260 ff.

Marshall, John, XV, 69; XXVI, 244, 248; XXXVI, 59, 62, 66

Marshall, Chief Justice John, L, 100

Marshall, Captain John, XXI, 105

Marshall, Captain John H., XXI, 97

Marshall, Josiah I., XVII, 92 ff.

Marshall, Captain P. S., XL, 43

Marshall, Samuel Chase, XXXVI, 63

Marshall, T. D., XXXIV, 36
Marshall, Thomas D., XXVI, 207
Marshall, Captain William, IV, 93–96, plate 18
Marshall Islands, IV, 87–118; boats of, XIII, 94 ff.; canoes of, VI, 71–72
Marshall J. Smith, schooner, XXI, 90, 99; *(1861)*, XI, 285; XII, 158
Marsilly Carriage, illustration, XLVII, 115
Marsouin, French ship *(1799)*, XXXI, 173
Marston, Levi, XXVII, 61–65
Martelli, George, *Jemmy Twitcher, A Life of the Fourth Earl of Sandwich, 1718–1792*, reviewed, XXIII, 150–151
Marten, Sir Henry, XLIX, 253
Martens, XXX, 219
Martha, cartel *(1813)*, XXVIII, 182
Martha, schooner *(1864)*, XV, 129
Martha, ship, XXIV, 260–262; (1796), II, 281; V, 43–63
Martha, whaler *(1865)*, XXVII, 276
Martha (II), bark, XXVII, 73
Martha A. McNeil, bark (1868), IV, 244
Martha Burgess, schooner *(1853)*, XLIV, 89
Martha Cobb, ship (1862), IV, 243
Martha Ellen, brig *(1858)*, XXI, 120
Martha Jane, schooner, XXI, 104; *(1863)*, XII, 158
Martha Jane, sloop *(1834)*, XXXVIII, 270
Martha Ogden, steamship (1824–1825), VI, 199–201, 206, plate 29; VII, 42, 48
Martha's Vineyard: A Camera Impression, by Samuel Chamberlain, reviewed, I, 403–404
Martha's Vineyard boat, XII, 135
Martha Whitmore, ship (1854), III, 264
Martin, brig *(1813)*, XLII, 108 ff.
Martin, British corvette *(1813)*, XL, 28
Martin, sloop *(1861)*, VIII, 219
Martin, Ann, "Young Tom Godfrey and His 'Sextant'," XXXV, 111–117
Martin, Christopher, XXII, 137, 139
Martin, Chryssee Perry and Esmond Bradley Martin, *Cargoes of the East*, reviewed, XL, 231
Martin, Captain D. A., XXI, 97
Martin, Daniel B., XI, 246
Martin, Esmond Bradley and Chryssee Perry Martin, *Cargoes of the East*, reviewed, XL, 231
Martin, Frank, *Rogues' River*, reviewed, XLV, 132
Martin, Captain Frank, XXI, 97
Martin, Captain John, XVI, 233; XXXVII, 12 ff.
Martin, John Stephen, XVI, 234
Martin, Kenneth, mention, XLIII, 83
Martin, Captain Matthew, XI, 23
Martin, S. W., XXXVI, 48
Martin, Captain Silas H., XXI, 97
Martin, Captain Stephen J., XLV, 81
Martin, Captain Thomas, XXI, 97
Martin, Tyrone G., mentioned, XLVII, 173; "Isaac Hull's Victory Revisited," XLVII, 14–21; "Underway Replenishment, 1799–1800," XLVI, 159–164

Martin, Commander Tyrone G., note by, XXXVIII, 65
Martin, Wallace E., *Sail & Steam on the Northern California Coast, 1850–1900*, reviewed, XLVII, 217
Martin, William Alexander Kennedy, XVI, 233–242
Martin, Colonel William F., XXXVII, 286
Martinez, Alfonzo, XXXVI, 12
Martinez, Captain Francisco, XXI, 97
Martinez, General, XXXV, 131
Martinez, Jose, XXXVI, 13
Martinez-Hidalgo, Jose Maria, *Columbus' Ships*, reviewed, XXVII, 67–71
Martinique, steamship (ex-*Vera Cruz*, ex-*Imperatriz*) *(1869)*, XXVI, 194
Martinique, VI, 290–300
Martins, Fernão, XXX, 254
Martin's Industry, light-vessel *(1862)*, V, 245
Martinson, Commander A. M., XLIV, 55
Martinson, Captain H., XXI, 97
Martin W. Brett, bark *(1847)*, XXX, 238; (1863), IV, 242
Martin White, steamship (1854), XVII, 147; XVIII, 71; *(1866)*, XLIX, 26
Martin White, tug *(1854)*, XLIII, 208 ff.
Maruin, Lieutenant Commander Joseph D., XXXIX, 120
Marvin, Judge William, XXXVIII, 265
Marvin, Winthrop L., XLI, 8
Marxen, Captain Charles, XXI, 97
Mary, armed merchant ship *(1799)*, L, 270 ff.
Mary, bark *(1806)*, XXIII, 132
Mary, brig, XXII, 95, 276; (1812), XXI, 18; *(1857)*, IV, 316
Mary, brigantine *(1861)*, VIII, 219
Mary, H.M. yacht *(1674)*, XXV, 279
Mary, Royal Yacht *(1740)*, XXVI, 38
Mary, schooner *(1762)*, XXI, 9, 10
Mary, schooner, XXI, 92, 102; XXIV, 257; (1812), VII, 317; (1815), XXIV, 59; (1831), XXIV, 59; *(1861)*, VIII, 219; XI, 285; XII, 56; XV, 131; *(1864)*, VIII, 235
Mary, ship *(1796)*, XXII, 196, 198, 199, 203, 204, 205, 206; *(1800)*, XXIII, 216; Pictorial Supplement, XXXII, plate XII; XLV, 98; *(1804)*, X, 53; *(1813)*, XIX, 219
Mary, sloop, XXI, 86, 90, 103; *(1725)*, XXXVII, 267; *(1736)*, XXXII, 172; *(1752)*, XLVIII, 36; *(1776)*, XX, 45
Mary, sloop *(1861)*, XV, 106, 124, 128, 129; *(1864)*, VIII, 235
Mary, steamship *(1864)*, VIII, 235; XII, 232
Mary, trawler *(1925)*, XLIV, 129
Mary A. Boardman, steamship (1862), XVII, 303; XVIII, 71
Mary A. Harmon, schooner (1869), XXIV, 45, 59
Mary A. Hood, ship (1894), XXXVII, 90
Mary A. Pender, schooner *(1861)*, VIII, 219
Mary A. Rowland, schooner (1861), VIII, 219

Mary Adelaide, schooner *(1861),* VIII, 219
Mary Adeline, schooner, XXI, 81, 88; *(1861),* VIII, 219
Mary Agnes, schooner *(1865),* XII, 235; XV, 113, 129
Mary Alice, bark (1864), V, 242
Mary Alice, schooner *(1861),* XI, 153
Mary and Catherine, bark *(1835),* XI, 183
Mary & Elsie, bark (1864), V, 151, 242
Mary & Helen, bark *(1855),* XLIV, 14 ff.
Mary & John, ship *(1630),* XXIII, 63
Mary and Susan, bark *(1888),* XXXIX, 8
Mary Ann, brig *(1824),* XXXVII, 245
Mary Ann, cartel, XXVIII, 176
Mary Ann, schooner, XXIV, 13; *(1861),* VIII, 219; *(1862),* XII, 56, 158
Mary Ann, ship *(1801),* XXIII, 234, 237, 243 n.
Mary Ann, sloop *(1861),* XI, 285; XII, 232
Mary Ann, steamship *(1863),* XII, 158
Mary Ann, U.S.S. *(1799),* XXXI, 175
Mary Anne, barge *(1906),* XXXVIII, 196 ff.
Mary Anne, steamship *(1863),* VIII, 231, 235
Mary Arnold, tugboat *(1931),* XXVIII, 126
Mary Atwell, ketch (1857), XI, 291
Mary Balch, schooner (1848), XXIV, 40
Mary Barry (ex-*Jessie McGregor*), barkentine *(1904),* XXIV, 44
Mary Bell, brig *(1862),* XXIX, 103
Mary Belle Roberts, bark (1864), VII, 317
Mary Block, ship *(1860),* XXVII, 235
Mary Bowers (or Bradford?), steamship, XXI, 94; (1854), III, 72, 265
Mary Bradford. See *Mary Bowers.*
Mary C. Harris, schooner, XXI, 97, 101; *(1862),* XII, 57
Mary C. Terbell, schooner *(1861),* XI, 286
Mary Campbell, schooner *(1863),* XII, 158
Mary-Caroline, brig *(1807),* XVII 194
Mary Celeste, brigantine (1872), I, 310; II, 250–251, 254–256; IV, 251; X, 191–202
Mary Celeste, hermaphrodite brig, XXVIII, 74
Mary Celeste, steamship, XXI, 105
"*Mary Celeste.* No, Not Again!" by Gershom Bradford, X, 191–202
"*Mary Celeste,* The," query by Charles Edey Fay, I, 310; answered by Charles Edey Fay, II, 250–251
Mary Celeste, *The Odyssey of an Abandoned Ship,* by Charles Edey Fay, reviewed, II, 254–256
Mary Celestia, steamship, XXI, 103; *(1864),* VIII, 235
Mary Clinton, schooner, XXI, 100; *(1861),* VIII, 219; XI, 285
Mary D. Hume, steam brigantine *(1890),* XXXVIII, 84
Mary D. Hume, steamship *(1905),* XLIV, 18 ff.
Mary Dollar, bark (1904), IV, 326; VI, 77; *(1927),* XVIII, 217
Mary Douglas, schooner *(1864),* XII, 232
Mary Dow, schooner (1834), XXIV, 59
Mary E. H. Dow I, schooner (1892), XXVII, plate XXIV
Mary E. Palmer, schooner (1895), V, 81; XX, 239–241
Mary E. Staples, schooner (1867), XXIV, 44, 59

Mary E. Thompson, brig *(1861),* XI, 151
Mary E. Whittier, bark (1851), IV, 326
Mary Elizabeth, schooner *(1862),* VIII, 226; *(1863),* XII, 158, 232; XV, 113, 129
Mary Ella, schooner, XXI, 97; *(1862),* XII, 57
Mary Ellen, schooner, XXI, 89, 98; *(1861),* XI, 286; XII, 57, 235
Mary Emma, ship (1864), III, 65
Mary F. Chisholm, schooner *(1891),* XLIV, 115
Mary F. Pike, schooner (1872), XV, 183; XXIV, 59
Mary Goodell, merchantman *(1874),* XXXIII, 285
Mary Goodwell, ship *(1861),* XI, 151
Mary Green, ship (1851), XV, 177
Mary Guilford, English ship *(1527),* XXVII, 179
Mary H. Case, schooner (1847), XXIV, 59
Mary H. Diebold, schooner (1920), IV, 66, 68; V, 138–139
Mary H. Lewis, schooner (1869), XXIV, 60
Mary Haley, schooner *(1861),* VIII, 219
Mary Hammond, ship (1855), V, 327
Mary Hasbrouck, bark (1877), XV, 188
Mary Jane, brig *(1808),* XVI, 206
Mary Jane, schooner, XXI, 91; *(1833),* XLV, 105 ff.; *(1863),* VIII, 231; XII, 158
Mary Jane, sloop, XXI, 90; *(1864),* XII, 232; XV, 113, 129; *(1903),* XXX, 195
Mary Jane Kennedy, schooner *(1861),* VIII, 220
Mary Kendall, bark *(1863),* XV, 295
Mary L. Brown, schooner, XXI, 90; *(1861),* XI, 286
Mary L. Cushing, ship (1883), XVII, 118
Maryland, auxiliary tanker (1903), V, 138
Maryland, frigate (1799), XLVI, 151 ff.; XLIX, 45 ff.
Maryland, U.S.S. *(1800),* XXXI, 175; *(1912),* VII, 35–38, plate 4
Maryland (MD). See Shipbuilding
Maryland Historical Society, Baltimore, V, 111; VI, 101, 302 ff.; XV, 4; XXVIII, 3; XXXVII, 164
Maryland Steamboat Co., XXX, 72
Mary Lewis, sloop *(1862),* XII, 57
Mary Lord, ship (1856), III, 62
Mary Louisa, schooner, XXI, 87
Mary Louisa, sloop *(1861),* VIII, 220; XV, 117, 124
Mary Lowell, brig *(1869),* XXXVIII, 233
Mary M. Lord, schooner (1903), XXIV, 60
Mary Magdelaine, schooner, XXI, 88; *(1861),* XI, 286
Mary Margaret, schooner *(1861),* XI, 286
Mary Nevis, sloop *(1862),* XII, 57
Mary Olivia, pilot boat *(1862),* XII, 57
Mary Otis, ketch *(1940),* VI, plate 8
Mary P. Burton, schooner *(1863),* XII, 158
Mary Parker, schooner, XXXVI, 256
Mary Powell, schooner *(1860),* XLI, 303; (1861), XIV, 161–186, 278–297, plates 17–20, 22
Mary Powell, steamship, XVIII, 225, 231
Mary Rose, ship (1623), XIV, 10, 11; *(1673),* XXIII, 97 n.
Mary Russell, bark (1864), II, 334
Marys, bark *(1861),* XI, 266, 286

Mary Scaife, brig, XXI, 87; *(1862)*, VII, 226
Mary Sorley, schooner, XXI, 90; *(1864)*, XII, 232
Mary Sorley (ex-*Henry Dodge*), revenue cutter (1863), XLVIII, 92
Mary Stewart, schooner, XXI, 90; *(1862)*, VIII, 226
Mary Stockton, barkentine (1853), VII, 315
Mary Stockton, schooner (1854), I, 74
Mary Storer, ship (1859), XV, 186
Mary Stuart, schooner (1846), XXIV, 42, 59
Marysville, woodboat (1869), XVII, 12
Mary Taylor, brig *(1855)*, XXIV, 143
Mary Taylor, pilot schooner (1849), I, 71; XI, 250; XII, 158
Mary Teresa, schooner, XXI, 101, 102; *(1862)*, VIII, 226
Mary Virginia, steamship *(1864)*, XII, 232
Mary Warren, ship (1862), III, 70
Mary Wood, schooner, XXI, 93; *(1861)*, VIII, 220
Mary Wright, brig, XXI, 95; *(1861)*, VIII, 220, 226
Marzala, steamship *(1915)*, XXXVI, 36, 37
Mascarene Islands. *See* British Indian Ocean Territory
Mascarene Group, Indian Ocean, XXV, 5–17
Mascolini, Captain Antonio, XXI, 97
Mascotte, steamship (1885), XII, 291, 293
Masefield, John, VIII, 330; *Sea Life in Nelson's Time*, reviewed, XXXII, 289; reviewed again, XLV, 207
Mashouda, Algerian frigate *(1815)*, III, plate 7, 89
Mashuda, Algerian flagship *(1815)*, XL, 39
Masick, Captain P., XXI, 97
Mason, Commissioner, XXIX, 15, 17, 18, 20, 21
Mason, Captain George, XXI, 97
Mason, George Carrington, "An Atlantic Crossing of the Seventeenth Century," XI, 35–41
Mason, H. W., XXVII, 280
Mason, Senator James, L, 113
Mason, Captain John, VII, 62
Mason, John B., VII, 298
Mason, John W., shipcarver, Pictorial Supplement, XXXVII, plates XXV, XXVI
Mason, John Y., XIII, 264
Mason, Senator, XXX, 144
Mason, Lieutenant Theodorus B. M., XXXIX, 126
Masonic, ship *(1861)*, XI, 286
Mass, Captain John, XXI, 97
Massachusetts, auxiliary steam packet (1845), I, 54–55, plate opposite 55
Massachusetts, battleship *(1898)*, XLI, 99
Massachusetts, brig *(1776)*, IV, 21
Massachusetts, ship *(1800)*, XLVI, 53; *(1890)*, XXXVIII, 124
Massachusetts, ship, stern drawings of, Pictorial Supplement, XXXVII, plate XXVIII
Massachusetts, steamship (1842), XXIV, 140, 143; XXV, plate VI; *(1845)*, XII, 151; *(1845)*, XXIII, 201
Massachusetts, steamship *(1817)*, Pictorial Supplement, XXXIV, plate XXX
Massachusetts, steamship (1907), Pictorial Supplement, XXXIV, plate XXX

Massachusetts II, revenue cutter *(1794)*, XLIX, 47
Massachusetts:
   Discovery and exploration, XXXIII, 131
   History, –, Colonial period (ca. 1600–1775), XXXVII, 5
   Social life and customs, VII, 213
   See also Boatbuilding; Boston; Cape Ann; Cartography; Customs Administration; Elizabeth Islands; Fisheries; Historic buildings; Life saving; Orleans; Quincy; Shipbuilding (United States); Ship chandlers; Shipping; Shipwrecks; Smuggling; Steamboats; Steam Navigation; Yachting
Massachusetts Archives, Boston, VII, 200 n. ff.
Massachusetts Bay Co., XXIII, 65
Massachusetts Bay Marine Studies Consortium, XLIV, 110
Massachusetts Bay Steamship Corp., XII, 291–292
Massachusetts Historical Society, I, 197; XXXVII, 129
Massachusetts Historical Society Collections, 1795, XXXIII, 162
Massachusetts Historical Society Proceedings, October 1932–May 1936, reviewed, I, 100
Massachusetts Hospital Life Insurance Co., V, 108
Massachusetts Humane Society, XIII, 236; XXXVII, 83 ff.; Lifeboat *Nantasket,* dimensions of, XXXVII, plate 2, 92–93; Silver Medal of, XXXVII, plate 4, 92–93
Massachusetts Institute of Techology, Cambridge, Mass., I, 68, 189, 410; IX, 81
"Massachusetts Maritime Microcosm," by Samuel Lapham, XIX, 7–43
Massachusetts Nautical Training School, XX, 138–139
Massasoit, gunboat *(1865)*, XLII, 93 ff.
Massasoit Historical Association, XXXVIII, 170
Massingham, Captain S. J., XXI, 97
Massman, Cornelius, XIII, 20
Mast and sail plan of a schooner, XLIX, 204
Mast cutting, XX, 216
Master, Captain N., XX, 90 n.
Master, Sir Streynsham, XIII, 14, 16, 22, 26, 27, plate 2
"Master B. finding things not exactly what he expected," XXXI, Pictorial Supplement, plate VI
Master Mariner of Maine, Being the Reminisences of Charles Everett Ranlett, 1816–1917, reviewed, III, 91–92
Master of the Mississippi: The Story of Henry Shreve, by Florence L. Dorsey, reviewed, II, 346–347
Master of the Moving Seas, by Gladys M. O. Gowlland, reviewed, XIX, 309
"Masters and Pilots who Tested the Blockade of Confederate Ports, 1861–1865," by Marcus W. Price, XXI, 81–107
Master's Cabin, 1825, XXXI, Pictorial Supplement, plate VIII
Masterson, Professor Daniel, U.S. Naval Academy, mentioned, XLII, 244

Masterson, Daniel M., *Naval History: The Sixth Symposium of the U.S. Naval Academy,* reviewed, XLIX, 313

Masting and Rigging of English Ships of War, 1625–1860, The, by James Lees, reviewed, XLI, 71–73

Masts and rigging, III, 279; V, 235; VI, 73; XIX, 155, 274; XXII, 65, 184; XXIV, 81; XXX, 194; XXXI,; 49; XXXIII, 95; XLVI, 221; XLIX, 198. *See also* Barkentine, Lateen, etc.; Sails; Shipbuilding

"Masts, A Schedule of, of 1703," document contributed by Lawrence Waters Jenkins, VII, 72–76

Masts: "New England Forests and British Seapower: Albion Revised," by R. J. B. Knight, XLVI, 221–229; Table 1, "What Diameters in the Rough State Will Make Masts, Yards and Bowspreets for a Ship of Each Class," XLVI, 222; Table 2, "Yards and Bowsprits: Average Annual Consumption, 1756–1782," XLVI, 226

"Mast trade in New Hampshire, The," by William A. Knipe, XXII, 65–70

Matador, ship *(1917),* XVIII, 165

Matagorda, barkentine (1847), I, 311

Matagorda, steamship, XXI, 101, 102; *(1861),* XI, 276, 286; XII, 57, 159, 232; *(1864),* XXXVI, 204

Matais Cousiño, Chilean transport *(1879),* XXXIX, 282

Matamoras, schooner *(1861),* XI, 286; XII, 159

Matanzas, screw-propeller (1859), XLVIII, 118

Matchless, schooner, XXVIII, 148

Mateer, C. W., XXXIV, 216

"Materials for Research in the Files of International Claims Commissions," by Marie Charlotte Stark, III, 48–54

"Materials of Maritime Interest in the New York Public Library," by Karl Brown, I, 381–390

Mathematical Practitioners of Hanoverian England, 1714–1840, The, by E. G. R. Taylor, reviewed, XXVIII, 290–292

Mathematicians, Biography, XX, 185; XXXVII, 174

Mather, Cotton, XXV, 61, 244; XXXVIII, 42

Mather, Frank J. III, XLI, 49

Mather, Increase, XXV, 61, 244

Mather, Richard, XXV, 61

Mathes, W. Michael, *Descriptions of Many Northern and Southern Lands and Seas in the Indies, Specifically of the Discovery of the Kingdom of California (1632). By Nicolas de Cardona,* reviewed, XXXV, 215

Matheson, Captain, XXXVI, 232

Matheson, Donald, XXII, 13

Matheson, James, XXVI, 5

Matheson, Captain John, L, 39

Matheson and Co., XXVI, 15 n.

"Mathew Carey, Advocate of American Naval Power, 1785–1814," by Edward C. Carter II, XXVI, 177–188

Mathew's Island, IV, 94–95, plate 17

Mathilda, ship (1860), III, 69

Mathilde, Danish brig (1864), XXXIII, 207

Matilda, bark, XXI, 87; (1848), VII, 318

Matilda, cartel *(1814),* XXVIII, 190

Matilda, schooner *(1813),* XV, 68; (1828), XXIV, 59; *(1862),* XII, 57, 159, 235

Matilda, ship *(1792),* XIII, 213

Matilda Barney, steamship (1833), VII, 50, 53

Matinicus Island, double-ender of, II, 321

Matron, brig *(1861),* VIII, 220

Matson, William, IV, 256

Matson Navigation Co. (San Francisco, CA), II, 294; IV, 256; VIII, 76

Matson Steamship Line, XXIX, 231

Matsushima, Japanese flagship *(1894),* XXXVIII, 166

Matsutoff, Prince, XXXVI, 50

Mattabesett, U.S.S. *(1862),* XXV, 72

Mattakees, steamship (1839), XXV 219

Mattakeesett, ship (1833), XIV, 40

Matteawan, freighter *(1899),* XLII, 246 ff.

"Matter of Definition: A New Jersey Navy, 1777–1783, A," by Robert L. Scheina, XXXIX, 209–217

Matteson, George, *Draggermen Fishing on Georges Bank,* reviewed, XXXIX, 303

Matthew, ship (1497), XXXIII, 174

Matthew Fontaine Maury, Scientist of the Sea, by Frances Leigh Williams, reviewed, XXIV, 223–225

"Matthew Fontaine Maury and the Introduction of Oceanography to the Netherlands in the Second Half of the Nineteenth Century," by William F. J. Mörzer Bruyns, XLVIII, 44–49

Matthew S. Greer, schooner *(1924),* IX, 29

Matthews, E. B., XV, 222

Matthews, G. F. (shipbuilder), XXV, 288, 291, 293

Matthews, George, & Co., XV, 220–231

Matthews, Dr. Leonard Harrison, F. R. S., Editor, *The Whale,* XXIX, 143–144

Matthewson, Captain George E., XXX, 45

"Matthew Walker Knot," query by W. S. Davenport, VIII, 154

Matthiessen, Peter, XLVI, 188

Mattice, Harold, A., *Perry and Japan,* reviewed, II, 352

Mattie, schooner *(1863),* XII, 159

Mattie J. Alles, schooner (1883), V, 294, plate 22; IX, 178

Mattie W. Atwood, schooner (1872), XXV, 148

Mattson, Captain William, XXIV, 3

Mattsson, A. A., VI, 155

Mattsson, A. Alfred, I, 315; II, 252; "Fur Seal Hunting in the South Atlantic," II, 154–166; "Sealing Boats," III, 327–332

Matt White, steamship *(1874),* XV, 227

Maude, H. E., *Slavers in Paradise: The Peruvian Slave Trade in Polynesia, 1862–1864,* reviewed, XLIII, 224–225

Maude Palmer, schooner (1900), V, 81

Maud Malloch, schooner (1868), XXIV, 44, 59

Maud S., schooner *(1895),* XLII, 261

Maudslay & Co., XXVI, 207

Maudsley, Joseph, XIII, 158

Maud Snare, schooner *(1883),* XLIX, 30

Mauduit, Jasper, XL, 276
Maumee, U.S. diesel oiler *(1913),* XXXVIII, 10 ff.
Maumee, U.S. warship *(1865),* XXXIII, 15
Maurelle, Francisco, XV, 53
Maurepas, C.S.S. (1862), XIX, 267
Mauretania, Cunard liner, XXVII, 155
Mauretania, steamship, XLII, 295 ff.
Maurice Guichard, schooner, XXI, 103; *(1861),* XI, 286
Mauripas, Conte Jean Frédéric, XVI, 98
Mauritius, steamship (1853), XXVI, 190–192, 206, 209
Mauritius, Island of, XXV, 5–17
Maury, Anne Fontaine, *Intimate Virginiana,* reviewed, II, 349
Maury, General Dabney, 1877, XXXIII, 261
Maury, James, II, 349
Maury, Matthew Fontaine, I, 149–158; IV, 130, 137; VIII, 147; XXVI, 279; XXX, 298; XXXI, 8; XLV, 191 ff.; XLVIII, 44 ff.; XLIX, 120
Maury, Lieutenant Matthew Fontaine, U.S.N., XIV, 139–141; XVIII, 320–323; XXIV, 223–225; XXV, 58, 69–70, 93–98, 187; XL, 43
Maury, Captain William L., XV, 293
Maury, Lieutenant William Lewis, XLV, 191 ff.
Maury River (VA). *See* Shipwrecks
Maverick, tanker *(1889),* XXXIII, 177 ff.; *(1910),* VIII, 283, plate 26
Maverick, Lewis A., "Yankee Doodle," XXII, 106–135
Maverick Navy, by Alexander W. Moffat, reviewed, XXXVII, 70
Maxtone-Graham, John, *The Only Way to Cross,* reviewed, XXXIII, 149
Maxwell, brig, XXII, 92
Maxwell, Hugh, VII, 185–186
Maxwell, James, XXXVIII, 170 ff.
May, brigantine *(1776),* XXXVI, 160
May, yacht *(1880),* XXXVI, 232
May, Arthur J., contributed document, IV, 327–329
May, Captain Robert, XXI, 97
May, Samuel, XV, 134
May, W. E., "Captain Frankland's *Rose,*" XXVI, 37–62
May, Commander W. E., "The Surveying Commission of *Alborough,* 1728–1734," XXI, 260–278
Maya, sloop (1898), XXX, 195
May Brown, schooner (1892), XIV, 108
Mayer, Dr. Alfred G., mentioned, XLIX, 37
Mayers, Colin, *Submarines, Admirals and Navies,* reviewed, I, 408
May Flower, American schooner *(1861),* XXXIV, 119
Mayflower, armed yacht *(1898),* XLI, 103
Mayflower, British ship *(1776),* XLVIII, 16
Mayflower, cutter rig *(1886),* XXX, Pictorial Supplement, plates III, VII
Mayflower, flagship *(1932),* XXXV, 131
Mayflower, packet sloop (1823), lines, XXV, 220
Mayflower, Presidential yacht and warship (1896), XXX, plate XXXI
Mayflower, [replica] Pilgrim ship, XXX, 79

Mayflower, schooner, XXXVI, 77; *(1777),* XLII, 13 ff.
Mayflower, schooner (1844), XXII, 216
Mayflower, ship (1620), XXII, 105, 136 ff.; *(1620),* XIV, 5, 17, 105, 262–277; XV, 262 ff.; XVII, 105–113, 128–133; XVIII, 318; *(1630),* XXIII, 63; XXIV, 213
Mayflower, ship *(1887),* XXXVII, 84 ff., 260
Mayflower, sloop *(1862),* XII, 57, 159
May Flower, sloop XXI, 89
Mayflower, steamship *(1864),* XII, 232
Mayflower, U.S.S. *(1863),* XII, 278
Mayflower, yacht *(1888),* XXXVI, 232; XXXVII, 37
Mayflower (II), ship, XXII, 99 ff.
"*Mayflower,* Another?" by William A. Baker, XXV 218–223
"*Mayflower* Problem, The," by William A. Baker, XIV, 5–17
"*Mayflower's* Jones, The," by Captain Edgar K. Thompson, XVIII, 318
"*Mayflower's* Jones, The," by Gershom Bradford, XVII, 128–133
Mayhew, Dean R., notes by, XXXV, 141–143; XL, 136; "Jeffersonian Gunboats in the War of 1812," XLII, 101–117
Mayhew, Captain William, XII, 44
Maynard, Lieutenant Robert, XXX, 137
Maynard Sumner, steam schooner (1881), IX, 71, plate 8
Mayo, Captain, XXVIII, 122
Mayo, Admiral H. T., XXXV, 103
Mayr, Dr. Otto, XXXVII, 167
Mazatlan, steamship *(1941),* XXXVIII, 179 ff.
Mazeppa, ship, XXI, 103; *(1861),* XI, 286
Mazeppa, steamship (1834), VII, 55
Mazière, Francis, *Mysteries of Easter Island,* reviewed, XXX, 73
Mazères, Lieutenant, XXXVI, 133
McAdam, Roger Williams, *Priscilla of Fall River,* reviewed, VIII, 73
McAdoo, William, XLI, 247
McAdoo, William G., Secretary of the Treasury, XXXII, 165; XXXIII, 179 ff.; XXXV, 169
McAlpine, Brigadier General, XXV, 142
McBride, John (shipbuilder), XXIV, 39, 40, 57 ff.
McCabe, Peter, XIV, 253 ff.
McCaldin Brothers, tug *(1899),* VII, 290
McCall, Captain James, XVII, 66; XIX, 133
McCall, Thomas, XXIX, 63
McCalla, Lieutenant Commander Bowman H., XXXIX, 126; XL, 127 ff.
McCalla, Captain, XXXV, 190
McCanfield, schooner *(1861),* XI, 286
McCann, John W., query by, V, 89
McCann, Admiral W. P., XLI, 249
McCann, Rear Admiral W. P., XXXVIII, 291 ff.
McCarthy, Captain Joseph, XXI, 96
McCartney, Daniel, XXXV, 83
McCartney, Lord, XLVIII, 237
McCaslin, Captain A. A., XVII, 55, 56, 59; XVIII, 83

McCaslin, Captain R. J., XVIII, 83
McCauley, Edward Yorke, Passed Midshipman, U.S.N., III, 179
McCauley, Robert H., *Liverpool Transfer Designs on Anglo-American Pottery,* reviewed, II, 353
McCauly, C. S., XXXI, 139
McClave, Edward F., review by, XLIII, 306
McClellan, General George B., U.S.A., XXV, 131–132, 139; XXXI, 62; XLII, 85 ff.
McClelland, wooden steamship *(1917),* XXXV, 279
McClintock, Vice Admiral Sir Francis Leopold, XXVIII, 87, 112
McCloskey and Co., XXII, 173, 174, 175
McClung, Gale and Robert McClung, "Captain Crowninshield Brings Home an Elephant," XVIII, 137–141
McClure, Robert, XXIX, 65–67
McColl, John Smith, XLIII, 96
McCollum, A. B., VII, 294
McComb, John, Jr., XXV, 125 n.
McCormick, Captain, XXXVI, 200
McCormick, Cyrus, XLVIII, 129
McCormick, Lieutenant Shepard, R.N., VII, 303
McCoy, Major General Frank, XXXV, 128
McCracken, John L. H., XXX, 236 ff.
McCrea, Commander Edward P., U.S.N., VII, 110, plate 9
McCrae, Captain Thomas, XVIII, 294
McCulloch, Hugh, XXXVI, 49
McCulloch, John, XXXIX, 105
McCullough, Hugh, XXXV, 184
McCusker, John, XXXVII, 50
McCusker, John J., "The Roosevelt Drawing of the Continental Ship *Alfred,*" XXVIII, 49–52
McCusker, John J., Jr., "The American Invasion of Nassau in the Bahamas," XXV, 188–217, plates 21, 22
McDermott, John, XXXI, 26
McDonald, David, and J. Barto Arnold, III, *Documentary Sources for the Wreck of the New Spain Fleet of 1554,* reviewed, XL, 139
McDonald, Gerald, XXXVI, 21
McDonald, John (shipbuilder), II, 324–325
McDonald, Captain P. A., V, 165, 247; VI, 77; "Mutton Spankers and Ringtail Topsails," V, 235–239; "Square Sails and Raffees," V, 142–145
McDonald (Chapman & Flint) Shipyard, XXVII, plate XXI
McDonnell, Lieutenant E. O., U.S.N., XXXVII, 113
McDonough, Captain Thomas, XXXVIII, 115
McDougal, Captain David, XXXIII, 46 ff.
McDougal, William, XXXVI, 241, 242, 245
McDougall, Captain Alexander, XXV, 168 ff.
McDougall, General Alexander, XXIX, 210
"McDougall's Whalebacks," by Tom H. Inkster, XXV, 168–175, plates 15, 16
McDowell, General, XXXII, 209

McEachern, Robert, XXVII, plate I
McElmon, Fred, XXXVI, 240 n.
McElroy, Captain J. W., "Disappearance of U.S.S. *Cyclops,*" XVI, 136–137
McElroy, Rear Admiral J. W., U.S.N.R., contributed note, XXIV, 214–215; XXV, 71
McElroy, Rear Admiral J. W., U.S.N.R. (ret.), XXVI, 80; "Do Right and Fear No Man Dont Write and Become a Naval Officer," XXVI, 217–218
McElroy, John W., I, 102, 316; IV, 164; XI, 4; contributed document, II, 173; "The Ocean Navigation of Columbus on his First Voyage," I, 209–240; "Reaction Report," XXXIX, 256–270
McElroy, Captain John W., U.S.N.R., VI, 161
McFadgen, Captain James, XX, 89 n.
McGeachy, A. V., XX, 122
McGiffin, Philo Norton, XXXVIII, 157 ff.
McGiffin, Captain Philo Norton, VIII, 267–278; IX, 301
McGilvery, bark *(1863),* III, 65
McGowan, Captain John N., IV, 310–311, 313
McGowan, Rear Admiral Samuel, L, 59
McGrail, Sean and John Coates, editors, *The Greek Trireme of the 5th Century B.C.: Discussion of a Projected Reconstruction,* reviewed, XLVI, 121
McGrath, W. H., XV, 289 ff.
McGregor, Duncan, XX, 89
McHenry, James, XXII, 265; XXX, 120; XXXVI, 55–57, 59, 61, 62, 64–67
McIlhenny, Edward Avery, XXXIX, 21
McIntire, Samuel: Pictorial Supplement, XXXVII, plate 1; carving attributed to, XXXVII, plate XXI (upper).
McIntosh, Charles and James, VII, 50
McIntyre, Captain George, XXXVIII, 268
McKanna, Clare V., "The *Water Witch* Incident," XXXI, 7–18
McKay, Captain Adelbert F., XVI, 5 ff.; XVII, 65
McKay, Albenia, XLII, 134 ff.
McKay, Cornelius, XLII, 134 ff.
McKay, Donald (Shipbuilder), XLII, 118
McKay, Donald (shipbuilder), I, 44, 58; letter to John Willis Griffiths, I, 85
McKay, Donald, XIX, plates IX–XVI; XV, 140, 141; XXII, 239; XXV, 231; XXVIII, plate XIII; XXX, 217 f.; XXXIX, 92
McKay, Captain F. E., XVIII, 164
McKay, Captain James M., XL, 175 ff.
McKay, John, *The Armed Transport* Bounty, reviewed, L, 72
McKay, Captain John, VII, 249
McKay, Captain Lauchlan, XVII, 20
McKay, Mungo, XLII, 27
McKay, Richard, XLII, 135 ff.
McKay, Captain William, XVII, 118
McKay & Dix, XXIII, plate XV
McKea, James, XXXIII, 31
McKee, steamship *(1862),* XII, 57

McKee, Alexander, *History Under the Sea,* reviewed, XXXI, 76

McKee, Alexander R., XXXII, 204

McKee, Christopher, contributed document, XVIII, 183; reviews by, XXIX, 67–68, 284, 289; XXX, 73–75; XXXIII, 67–68; Editor, "*Constitution* in the Quasi-War with France: The Letters of John Roche, Jr., 1798–1801," XXVII, 135–149

McKee, Christopher and Linda, "An Inquiry into the Conduct of Joshua Blake," XXI, 130–141

McKee, Eric, *Clenched Lap or Clinker: An Appreciation of a Boatbuilding Technique,* reviewed, XXXIII, 147–148

McKee, Lieutenant H. W., U.S.N., VII, 111, 114, plate 12

McKeever, Captain Isaac, XXXI, 187

McKeithen, Captain George, XXI, 106

McKelvey, William J., Jr., *The Delaware & Raritan Canal, A Pictorial History,* reviewed, XXXVII, 71–72

McKenna, Captain James, XXXIX, 12

McKenney, Commander W. E., XL, 42

McKenzie, Lieutenant Commander Alexander S., XXXII, 131

McKenzie, Captain Daniel, XIV, 139, 141; XVII, 17, 25

McKenzie, Captain John, XXI, 96

McKenzie, Captain Kenneth, XXI, 96

McKenzie, Murdoch, XXX, 206, 211

McKeon, John, XXXVI, 176

McKeon, Owen F., *The Railroads and Steamers of Lake Tahoe,* reviewed, X, 158

McKim, steamship (1844), XXXVII, 142 n.

McKim, Captain J. F., XXI, 96

McKinley, President William, XXII, 189; XXVII, 58; XXXV, 183; XXXVII, 28 ff.; XL, 167; XLI, 100

McKinney, Sam, *Reach of Tide, Ring of History: A Columbia River Voyage,* reviewed, L, 149

McKinney, Captain Thomas, XVII, 116

McKinsey, Captain John, XXI, 106

McKinstry, Lieutenant, U.S.N., IV, 313

McKittrick, concrete tanker (1921), XXII, 172, 182

McKown, Captain Robert, XX, 67

McLane, U.S. revenue cutter (1843), XXIV, 8 ff.

McLane, Captain Allen, XX, 127–128

McLane, Robert M., XXX, 158, 164, 166; XXXIV, 104 ff.; XXXVIII, 31

McLaren, yacht *(1892),* XXXVI, 237

McLaughlan, Captain John, XVIII, 8–13

McLaughlin, Captain Dan, XXVIII, 121

McLaughlin, Captain Daniel, XV, 178

McLaughlin, Lieutenant John P., XXIV, 16

McLaughlin, Philip K., "Blockading the New England Coast: The Journal of Lt. Henry Napier," XLV, 5–9

McLean, Duncan, XLII, 122

McLean, Brigadier General Francis, VII, 200, 205; XXXVII, 291

McLean, John, XXXIX, 47

McLeod, D., XXX, 24

McManaway, James G., review by, I, 321–323

McMillan, Robert, IV, 199

McMullen, Jerry, sketch of 1941 rig of *Star of Scotland,* I, 334; *Paddle Wheel days in Calfornia,* reviewed, V, 169–170

McMullen, John T., XXXVI, 31

McMullin, Fayette, XXXVI, 176

McMurray, Captain F. S., VIII, 61–62

McNab. *See also* M'Nab

McNab, Colonel Allan, VII, 300–306

McNairn, Jack (co-author with Jerry MacMullen), *Ships of the Redwood Coast,* reviewed, VI, 156–157

McNamara, C. (ship rigger), XXI, 288

McNamara, P. T., XXXVI, 48

McNarry, Donald, note by, XXVII, 262

McNiel, Captain Daniel, XXI, 212, 213

McNeil, Jim, *Charleston's Navy Yard: a picture history,* reviewed, XLVIII, 206

McNeill, C. B., XXXVI, 245, 246

McNeill, Daniel, XXX, 75

McNeill, Captain Hector, V, 184 ff.; XLVIII, 162.; XVIII, 302

McNitt, Rear Admiral R. W., XXXIX, 123

McPherson and Co., VII, 50

McQueen, Captain Archibald, XV, 294

McQueen, Captain, XLIII, 88 ff.

McQueen, Robert, V, 28

McRae, C.S.S. (1862), XIX, 267

McVay, Admiral Charles, Jr., L, 260 ff.

McVay, Charles B., Jr., XXXVII, 116 ff.

MD. *See* Maryland

M'Dermott, Benjamin, XXVI, 203

ME. *See* Maine

Mead, Sidney M., review by, XXVIII, 292–293

Meade, Richard, XXXVIII, 113

Meade, Richard K., XV, 287

Meadows, Martin, "Eugene Hale and the American Navy," XXII, 187–193

Meadows Marine Railway of New Bern, XLI, 189

Meaher, Captain Tim, XXI, 97

Means, Dennis R., "The Surfboat-Lifeboat *Nantasket,* Hull (MA): The boat that 'would not succeed'," XXXVII, 83–94

Means, Philip Ainsworth, "Pre-Spanish Navigation Off the Andean Coast," II, 107–126; *Newport Tower,* reviewed, II, 353

Meares, Captain John, XV, 206

Mears, G., XXIV, plates XIII, XXI, XXII, XXIV

"Measure for Measure," by Captain Edgar K. Thompson, U.S.N. (ret.), XXVIII, 30

Measurement of ship tonnage, XIV, 5–17

Mecca, steamship (1872), XVII, 138; XVIII, 71

Mecca (or *Vimy*), five-masted schooner, XXXIII, 51

Mechanic, ship *(1861),* XXI, 258

Mechanic, whaler *(1855),* XLI, 299

Mechanical Deep Sea Sounder, American, Pictorial Supplement, XXXV, plate XXIX (lower). *See also* Mechanical Sounders.
Mechanical Logs: American, Pictorial Supplement, XXXV, plates XXIII, XXIV; English, Pictorial Supplement, XXXV, plate XXIV
Mechanical Sounders: English, Pictorial Supplement, XXXV, plates XXVIII (upper), XXIX (upper). *See also* Mechanical Deep Sea Sounder.
Mechanic's Own, ship (1849), III, 319
Mechlin, Joseph, XXXVIII, 57
Mecktoub (ex-*Esquimalt*) *(1923),* XXXII, 32
Medal struck in 1687, II, plate 24
Mediator, H.M.S. *(1742),* XIII, 177–184
Medicine, naval, XXVII, 81, 111. *See also* Epidemics; Hospitals; Merchant mariners; Quarantines; Sailors; Scurvy
"Medieval Background of European and American Oceanic History, The," by Archibald R. Lewis, XLV, 225–236
Medieval Expansion of Europe, The, by J. R. S. Phillips, reviewed, XLIX, 233
"Medieval Ships," query by George M. Cunha, VII, 319; answered by C. A. Myers, VIII, 71
Medina, H.M.S. *(1897),* XXVIII, 89, 98
Medina, Pedro de, XV, 54; XXX, 251
Mediterranean, boats of, I, 352–373; II, 56–64; XIII, 85 ff., 185 ff.
Mediterranean region, History, naval, XLIX, 126
Mediterranean, Saga of a Sea, The, by Emil Ludwig, reviewed, II, 354
Mediterranean Squadron, U.S. Navy, XXV, 158 ff.
Medon, steamship *(1942),* XXVI, 148
Medora, schooner, XXI, 97, 101; *(1863),* XII, 159, 232
Medows, Sir William, XLVI, 20
Medusa, H.M.S. *(1842),* XXVI, 6 n.
Medusa of Nants, privateer *(1745),* XLII, 49
Medway, H.M.S. *(1897),* XXVIII, 89, 98
Medway, ship *(1814),* XLIV, 171
Meek, Joseph L., XXVIII, 129–133
Mee-lee, steamship (1869), XVI, 259; XVII, 310
MeeLee or *Good Profit* (later *Cricket*), steamship (1859), XXXIV, 24 ff.
"Meeting of the Ships *Dauntless* and *Thomas Dana* off Cape Horn," by Dr. William Allen Wilbur, VII, 39–41
Mefkure, Turkish motorcaique *(1944),* XLIII, 31 ff.
Megunticook, bark (1842), III, 264
Meherrin, barge (1829), V, 301
Mehrtens, Judge William O., XXXVI, 23
Mei An, merchant ship *(1937),* L, 260 ff.
Meiberna, brig *(1807),* IX, 12
Mei Foo, flagship *(1912),* L, 260 ff.
Meigs, Montgomery C., Quartermaster General of the Army, XXXI, 69
Mei Hing, merchant ship *(1938),* L, 260 ff.
Mei Hsia, merchant ship *(1937),* L, 260 ff.
Mei Hung, merchant ship *(1937),* L, 260 ff.
Meijenburg, Dutch ship (1713), XLVII, 248
Meiklejohn, George D., Asst. Secretary of War, XL, 173 ff.
Meili, steamship *(1877),* XVI, 259
Meinwen, bark *(1896),* XVIII, 9
Mei Ping, merchant ship *(1937),* L, 260 ff.
Meister, Leila von, XXXVIII, 12
Mei Tan, merchant ship *(1929),* L, 260 ff.
Meitz & Weiss (Newark, New Jersey), XXXII, 31
Mei Yi, motor tanker *(1937),* L, 260 ff.
Mei Ying, motor tanker *(1927),* L, 260 ff.
Mei Yung, merchant ship *(1938),* L, 260 ff.
Melakori River, XXX, 178 ff.
"'Melancholy Affair' — James Otis and the Pirates," by Hugh F. Bell, XXXI, 19–37
Melanesia. *See* Oceania
Melanesia, boats of, XIII, 87 ff.
"Melanesian Outrigger, A," by Richard LeBaron Bowen, Jr., XXIII, 255–260
Melbourne, ship *(1913),* XLI, 128
Melbourne, steamship (ex-H.M.S. *Greenock*) (1849), XXVI, 194, 195, 197, 206, 209
Melbourne, William T., XLVI, 218
Meli, steamship (1869), XVI, 259; XVII, 39
Melinda, brig (1807), VII, 317
Melissa, yacht (1900), XXXVI, 240
Mellen, Captain Archibald, Jr., XXI, 112, 113, 114, 115, 116
Mellen, Captain Thomas, XLIV, 177
Mellis, Mr., XXX, 62–67
Mellish, H.M.S. *(1776),* XXVIII, 49–52; *(1777),* XIV, 49
Mellus, Captain Edward, XVI, 167; XVIII, 83
Meloria, tanker (1926), XXXVIII, 81 ff.
Melpomene, H.M.S. (ex-*Indefatigable*) *(1910),* XXVIII, 89 n., 105, 107
Melrose, schooner, XXVIII, 224
Melville, H.M.S. *(1813),* XVII, 210
Melville, George Washington, XXXIX, 11
Melville, Herman, XII, 113; XXV, 61, 62, 63; XXXVI, 278; XLII, 57–65
Melville, John H., *The Great White Fleet,* reviewed, XLII, 149–150
Melville, General Robert, XXXVI, 286
Melvin, Captain, XIII, 50
Melvin R. Nawman, U.S. destroyer, XXIV, 126
Memminger, Christopher G., XL, 298–304
Memnon, steamship *(1941),* XXVI, 148
Memoir of James Trevenen, A, Lloyd and R. C. Anderson, editors, reviewed, XX, 276
"Memorandum Referente al R.O.U. *18 de Julio,*" by Oscar Tagle, II, 170–171
"Memories of Steamboat Days on the Hudson, 1884 to 1907," by A. Fred Saunders, XVIII, 223–234
Memphis, cruiser *(1930),* XXXV, 131
Memphis, steamship *(1862),* VIII, 226; XXI, 89, 105; XXVI, 135–137

Memphis, TN, XXV, 128, 135
Men, Cities and Transportation, A Study in New England History, by Edward Chase Kirkland, reviewed, IX, 305–306
"Men, Monotony, and Mouldy Beans – Life on Board Civil War Blockaders," by James M. Merrill, XVI, 49–59
Men Against the Rule, by Charles Lane Poor, reviewed, I, 408–409
Mendaña, Alvaro de, XXV, 248–250, 255
Mender, Peter G. A., L, 260 ff.
Mendonca, Salvador de, XLI, 253
Mendota, bark (1869), XXVIII, plate XIV
Mendota, gunboat *(1865),* XLII, 95 ff.
Mendoza, bark *(1880),* XIV, 117
Menegatos, Pentagiotis, XXXVI, 15
Menemon Sanford, vessel *(1855),* XXXVI, 172
Menevian, steamship *(1933),* XIV, 126, 135
Men of Marque: A History of Private Armed Vessels out of Baltimore during the War of 1812, by John Philips Cranwell and William Bowers Crane, reviewed, I, 94–95
Men of the Merchant Service, The, by Frank T. Bullen, reviewed, XLI, 145–146
Men O'War, reviewed, III, 274
Mentor, ship *(1800),* XLVII, 165; *(1820),* XIII, 242
Menzies, Alexander, XVII, 66
Menzies, Archibald, XVI, 62
Mercantile Dock, Mazagon, Bombay, XXII, 44
Mercantile Navy List, XXX, 31
Mercator's projection, XVII, 32–37
Mercedita, U.S. screw steamship *(1863),* XLIV, 264
Mercer, Charles F., XXXII, 264
Mercer, Captain Samuel, XXXVI, 190; XXXVII, 279
Mercer, Commander Samuel, XLIII, 174 ff.
Merchandise List from ship *Minerva,* XXXIII, plate 12
Merchant, commercial iron steamship (1861), XLVIII, 125; *(1862),* XXII, 157
Merchant, ship *(1804),* XLIII, 43 ff.
Merchant, ship (1864), III, 172
"Merchant Captain of the Pacific," by W. Wilfried Schuhmacher, XLI, 224–230
Merchant Fleet in War, 1939–1945, A, by Captain S. W. Roskill, R.N. (ret.), reviewed, XXVI, 148
Merchant Fleets, by Critchell Rimington, reviewed, IV, 340
Merchant marine, United States, History, XXIX, 231
Merchant Marine, U.S.: *Sail On: The Story of the American Merchant Marine,* by Allan Nevins, reviewed, VI, 236
Merchant Marine Act of 1920, The, XXXV, 287
Merchant Marine Act of 1936, XXIX, 234
Merchant Marine and Fisheries Committee, The, XXXIII, 181
Merchant Marine and World Frontiers, The, by Robert Earle Anderson, reviewed, VI, 157

Merchant Marine Distingished Service Medal, proposed award to Stewart Holland, XXV, 80
Merchant mariners:
Note: Here are entered works on sailors employed on commercial vessels. For general works on sailors and works on sailors enlisted in a navy, see **Sailors.**
   Accommodation on shipboard, XXVII, 111
   Medical care, XXVII, 81, 111; L, 89
   Missions and charities, XXXVII, 179; XXXIX, 45
   Salaries, etc., XXXVII, 179
   Social conditions, XXIV, 109
   Wages, etc., XLI, 165; XLIV, 33
   See also Medicine; Scurvy.
Merchant Sailing Ships, 1775–1875: Their Design and Construction, by David R. MacGregor, reviewed, XLII, 68–69
Merchants:
   Biography, I, 205; XXIV, 247
   China, XLVIII, 243
   United States, XXIX, 199
Merchant Sailing Ships, 1815–1850: Supremacy of Sail, by David R. MacGregor, reviewed, XLVI, 124
Merchant seamen. *See* Merchant mariners; Sailors
"Merchants in the Forecastle: The Private Ventures of New England Mariners," by Allan A. Arnold, XLI, 165–187
Merchant's Perspective: Captain Jacobus Boelen's Narrative of his Visit to Hawai'i in 1828, A, by Jacobus Boelen, reviewed, XLIX, 135
Merchant Vessels of the United States, XXX, 31
Merchant Vessels of the United States (1946), reviewed, VIII, 75
Mercier, Captain, XIII, 44
Mercury, brig *(1794),* V, 90; *(1807),* IX, 11 ff.
Mercury, packet *(1780),* XXXI, 242
Mercury, privateer *(1744),* XLII, 49; XLIII, 24
Mercury, ship *(1794),* X, 53; *(1809),* XLVIII, 240
Mercury, sloop *(1863),* VIII, 231
Mercury, steamship (1863), XXXIV, 34 ff.
Meredith J. C., *The Tattooed Man,* reviewed, XIX, 307
Merida, steamship *(1955),* XVII, 199
Meriden Gravure Co., XXVIII, 238
Meridian, pinky *(1832),* XXXVII, 169
Merill, James M., "Midshipman DuPont and the Cruise of *North Carolina,* 1825–1827," XL, 211–225
Merli, Frank J. (with Peter Payne), "A Blockade-Running Charter: Spring 1862," XXVI, 134–137; "A British View of the Union Navy, 1864: A Report Addressed to Her Majesty's Minister at Washington," XXVII, 30–45; "The South's Scottish Sea Monster," XXIX, 5–29
Merlin, bark *(1862),* XII, 104
Merlin, brig (1857), XVII, 17
Merlin, H.M.S. *(1775),* XXX, 97, 107; *(1920),* XXI, 264
Merlin, schooner *(1889),* XXX, Pictorial Supplement, plates V, VI
Merlin, ship *(1870),* XXXVIII, 215 ff.

Merlin, steamship *(1854),* XIV, 256
Mermaid, bark (1855), Pictorial Supplement, XXXIII, plates XIV, XIX; (1828), Pictorial Supplement, XXXVIII, plate III, IX
Mermaid, H.M.S. *(1722),* XXI, 262
Mermaid, raised deck Snipe, XXX, 69
Mermaid, ship (1755), IX, 147; *(1777),* XIV, 53, 54
Merrill, James M., "The Asiatic Squadron: 1835–1907," XXIX, 106–117; "Men, Monotony, and Mouldy Beans—Life on Board Civil War Blockaders," XVI, 49–59; "A Short History of the Los Angeles Steamship Co.: 1920–1930," IX, 216–227
Merrill, Professor James M., XXXII, 55
Merrill, Robert D., XXI, 121
Merrimac, blockade runner *(1862),* XXIV, plate 24
Merrimac, C.S.S., XXII, 288; XXIII, 197 ff.; XXIV, 219–221; XXV, 131; XXVII, 174; *(1862),* XLII, 193 ff.
Merrimac, ship, XXXIX, 120
Merrimac, steamship, XXI, 99
Merrimac, steamship *(1863),* VIII, 231
Merrimac, U.S.S. *(1859),* XVIII, 320–323; *(1864),* XXVII, 43
Merrimac (II), C.S.S. [replica] (1951), XIV, 107
Merrimack, ironclad *(1877),* XXXV, 61
Merrimack, screw frigate *(1862),* XLVI, 151; XLVIII, 125; XLIX, 114 ff.
Merrimack, steamship (1859), IV, 151, plate 25; *(1887),* XXXVII, 236
Merrimack, U.S.S. *(1799),* XXXI, 173
Merrimack, U.S. steam frigate (1855), XXII, 252, 253, 254; *(1862),* XXXI, 65
Merrimack (C.S.S. *Virginia*), ram *(1862),* XLII, 85 ff.
Merrimac River (MA and NH). See Shipping, US
Merrimac River Gundalow and Gundalowmen, The," by Wallace B. Ordway, X, 249–263, plates 25–26
Merritt, tug *(1906),* XXXVIII, 183 ff.
Merritt, Chapman and Scott, VII, 290; VIII, 62 ff.
Merritt, Israel J. (wrecker), XXV, 108
Merritt, Major General Wesley, XXXV, 183; XL, 172 ff.
Merritt & Chapman Derrick & Wrecking Co., XXV, 108–109
Merritt-Chapman & Scott Corp., XXV, 108
Merrivales, ship *(1899),* XXXV, 191
Merryman, Captain J. H., U.S. Revenue Cutter Service, XXXIV, 10
Mersey, cruiser *(1883),* XXXIX, 131
Mersey, schooner, XXI, 102; *(1862),* VIII, 226
Mersey, steamship (ex-*Adelaide*) *(1863),* XXVI, 196
Mersey or Brooklyn Navy Yard gun, VI, plate 32
Mertie B. Crowley, schooner (1907), IV, 325, plate 51
Mertola, bark (1866), XXIII, 11
Mervine, William, XXVII, 161
Mervine, Lieutenant William, XXXIV, 191 ff.; XXXV, 26

Meshouda, Tripolitan cruiser (former American ship *Betsey* of Boston; built 1795, converted 1796) *(1802),* XLVII, 26
Meshuda, Tripolitanian gunboat *(1803),* XLVI, 156
Messageries Imperiales, XXXI, 116
Messageries Line, The, XXXI, 118
Messenger, bark *(1861),* XXI, 258
Messenger, brig (1816), XIV, 40
Messenger, ship (1805), II, 282; *(1860),* XX, 213; *(1894),* XLVII, 127
Messenger, U.S. *(1842),* XXIX, 110
Messimer, Dwight R., "Gunboats and Diplomats," XL, 85–99
Messina, Sicily, VII, 249
Messsenger, brig (1834), XIV, 40
Mesurado, schooner (1829), XXXVIII, 56 ff.
Mesurado, steam launch *(1920),* XXXIX, 179
Meta, S.S. *(1942),* XXVII, 190
Meta, topsail schooner, I, 72
Metamora, schooner (1902), XXVI, plate XVIII
Metamora, ship *(1836),* XXX, 62–67
Metamora, steamship (1893), VII, 164–166, 225–226, 228–230, plates 17, 19, 31
Metamora, steamship *(1849),* XLVII, 42
Metcalf, Joel, XL, 196
Metcalfe, Senator Thomas, XXX, 144 n.
Meteor, gunboat *(1814),* XLII, 116
Meteor, schooner *(1863),* XII, 159
Meteor, ship *(1853),* XIV, 198; *(1861),* XV, 108 n.; XXI, 239, 256
Meteor, steamship (1850), XVII, 59; XVIII, 59; *(1850),* XLIX, 24; *(1862),* XLIII, 207 ff.; (1864), XVI, 173; XVIII, 71; (1882), XXIV, plate XXVI
Meteor, whaleback tanker (1896), XXV, 174, plate 15
Meteor (ex-*Chester W. Chapin*), steamship (1929), XXXIX, 107
Meteoro, Peruvian ship *(1881),* XXXIX, 287
Metha Nelson, schooner *(1923),* XVIII, 213, 214
Methodist Mission, XXVIII, 134, 139
Methuen, John, XXVII, 224–226
Methuen, Paul XXVII, 224–226
Methuen Castle, steamship (1883), XXXVIII, 194 ff.
Methuens and Portugal, The, by A. D. Francis, reviewed, XXVII, 224–226
Methven, Robert, XXVI, 204
Metis, bark (1868), V, 152
Metropolis, paddle-wheeler (1854), XLVIII, 114
Metropolis, steamship (1848), III, plate 14
Metropolitan, grain elevator *(1883),* XXXVIII, 141
Metropolitan Museum of Art, I, 176, 314, 324
Metropolitan Steamship Co., ship of, Pictorial Supplement, XXXIV, plates X, XIX, XXIX
Mettacomet, schooner *(1903),* XLI, plate 2
Metzelaar, A. C., Europa *Ahoy!,* reviewed, VII, 324
Meulen, Van der, XXX, 219
Meurer, Rear Admiral, XL, 60 ff.
Meuse, Ben V., XXX, 187

Meuse River, L, 165 ff.
Mexican gunboats, XXX, 54
Mexican Navy, XXX, 46–55
Mexicano, Mexican brigantine *(1845),* XXX, 47 ff.
Mexican War (1846–1848), Naval operations, XXX, 46
Mexican War, XXVII, 160
Mexico, barque *(1886),* XXXIV, 10
Mexico, ship, XXXVI, 176
Mexico, steamship, XXI, 102; *(1861),* XI, 286; *(1881),* II, 75
Meyer, Charles R., *Whaling and the Art of Scrimshaw,* reviewed, XXXVIII, 304
Meyer, H. B., XLI, 8
Meyer, Jean and Martin Acerra, *La Grande époque de la Marina á voile,* reviewed, XLVIII, 207
Meyer, Dr. Jürgen, *Hamburgs Segelschiffe,* reviewed, XXXII, 288; *150 Yahre Blankeneser Schiffahrt 1785–1935* [150 Years of Blankeneser Shipping 1785–1935], reviewed, XXX, 70–71
Meyers, Captain Henry, XXI, 97
MI. *See* Michigan
Miami, U.S.S. *(1863),* XIX, 68; XX, 160
Miantonomoh, U.S. monitor (1862), X, 18, 28, 31; *(1863),* XLVIII, 125; XLIX, 116; *(1864),* XXVII, 37 n.; *(1886),* XXXIX, 137
"Micajah Lunt, Jr.," document contributed by Katherine M. Dodge, XVII, 69–72
Micco, ketch *(1896),* XXX, 197, 198
Michaelmas Term of the Supreme Court of Judicature, 1754, XXXI, 19
Michaels, brig *(1801),* XXIV, 262
Michelson, Albert, XXXVIII, 125
Michigan, steamship (1833), VII, 49, 57, 58; *(1840),* XX, 86; (1881), XXXVIII, 187 ff.
Michigan, U.S. battleship (1909), XXII, 260
Michigan, U.S. gunboat (1843), II, 335, plate 47; IV, 181, 183–192, plates 29–32; V, 165, 172, 247; VIII, 135 ff., 141 ff., plate 16; XX, 261; XLVII, 96 ff.; photos of, XLVII, 97, 98; *(1864),* XXVII, 44; *(1865),* XXXII, 208
Michigan (MI). *See* Shipbuilding
Michigan Steamship Co., XXXVIII, 185; XLII, 249
Michlin, Joseph, XXXII, 269
Micmac canoes, VIII, 293
Microfilm, *The American Neptune,* XX, 3–4
Micronesia. *See* Cemeteries; Oceania
Micronesia, boats of, XIII, 93 ff., 190 ff.
Midas, steamship (1844), I, 52–53, plate facing 57, 167; XVI, 160; XVIII, 71; XXXVII, 142 n.; *(1844),* XXII, 8, 9, 11, 24, 42; XLVIII, 117
Middendorf, J. William, II, XXXIX, 29 ff.
Middle Church, Scotland, XXIX, 48, plate V
Middleham, snow (1742), I, 167
Middle Road, The, by Llewellyn Howland, reviewed, XXII, 291
Middleton, Arthur Pierce, reviews by, XXVI, 222; XXIII, 286–287; XXIV, 147–148; "New Light on the Evolution of the Chesapeake Clipper-Schooner," IX, 142–147; "The Struggle for the Cape Henry Lighthouse, 1721–1791," VIII, 26–36, plate 8; "Yachting in Chesapeake Bay, 1676–1783," IX, 180–184
Middleton, Charles, XLVI, 224
Middleton, Francis, XXXVI, 22
Middleton, Lewis, XX, 120
Middleton, Thomas, XXV, 286
Midnight, schooner *(1910),* XLI, 41
"Midshipman DuPont and the Cruise of *North Carolina,* 1825–1827," by James M. Merrill, XL, 211–225
Midshipman's "Birth," XXXI, Pictorial Supplement, plate V
Midshipmen's Berth, XXXI, Pictorial Supplement, plate III
Midshipmen, Biography, XXXVIII, 101
Midway Islands, VIII, 179–195
Miertsching, Johann, XXIX, 65–67
Mifflin, gunboat *(1782),* XXXIX, 217
Mignonette, H.M. corvette *(1943),* XLIV, 54
Mignonette, yacht *(1884),* XVI, 180–182
Migration, XXIII, 113
Mikuni Maru (ex-*Gerard*) *(1865),* XLIII, 212 ff.
Milan, ship (1847), IV, 51, 52
Milan Decree, 1807, XXX, 280
Milbanke, steamship (1868), XVII, 54; XVIII, 71
Milborne, Captain Peter, XXIII, 65
Mildred, brig (1806), VII, 317
Mildred, steamship *(1902),* XII, 290, 293
Mildred Bennett, coasting sloop (1899), XXXVII, 165
Miles, Vice Admiral Milton E., XLIV, 179 ff.
Miles, General Nelson A., XLI, 104
Miles, Major General Nelson A., XL, 169 ff.
Miles, Wilma Sinton, XLIV, 179 ff.
Milford, H.M.S., XXVI, 60
Milicete, cutter (1889), XXX, plate XIII
Military transportation. *See* Transportation, Military
Militia. *See* Naval Militia
Milka, Bulgarian ship *(1944),* XLIII, 35 ff.
Millar, Archibald, VII, 270
Millar, Robert Douglas, XXVI, 204
Millard, Captain Martin Van Buren, XXXIX, 8
Mill Dam Co., XXIV, 60
Miller, Adolph G., XXXVI, 271, 272
Miller, Bull & Knowlton, XXXVIII, 181 ff.
Miller, Chester C., XXV, 294
Miller, Captain Christopher, XXIII, 277 ff.
Miller, George, XXVII, 46 ff.
Miller, George L., "The Second Destruction of the *Geldermalsen,*" XLVII, 275–281
Miller, Lieutenant Jacob W., XXXIII, 265 ff.
Miller, John, XXXV, 299
Miller, Leatitia, XXXVI, 252 n.
Miller, Lewis, X, 161–162, 173, plates 21–22
Miller, Brigadier General Marcus P., XXXV, 185

Miller, Mary Emily, "Substantiation of Campbell's Study of a Blunt Chart," XXVI, 216–217
Miller, Pamela A., *And the Whale is Ours*, reviewed, XL, 70
Miller, Pedro, XXXVI, 273
Miller, Prince, XXXV, 299
Miller, Ravenhill & Co., XXXV, 251
Miller, Ravenhill and Salkeld, XXVI, 21, 207
Miller, Stuart Creighton, XLVIII, 271
Miller, Thomas, XVII, 152–155
Miller, William, XXXI, 288
Millet, steamship (1869), XVI, 259; XVII, 39; XVIII, 71
Millet, Captain George, XXI, 97
Millett, Richard, "The State Department's Navy: A History of the Special Service Squadron, 1920–1940," XXXV, 118–138; reviews by, XXXII, 147; XXXIII, 64
Millidge, Captain L. H., XIV, 127, 128
Millie G. Bowne, schooner *(1889)*, XXXV, 12
Milligan, Captain James F., XL, 301
Milligan, John D., "Charles Ellet, Naval Architect: A Study in Nineteenth-Century Professionalism," XXXI, 52–72; *Gunboats Down the Mississippi*, reviewed, XXVI, 224
Milligan, Robert W., XXXVI, 257 ff.
Milliken, Harry (of The Anthoensen Press), mentioned, XXXI, 3; XXXVII, 156; XXXIX, 234; XL, 3; XLIII, 243
Milliken, Captain John F., XLVII, 51
Milliken, Captain Joseph, XLVII, 33
Milliken, Moses J., XXV, 26
Millinger, James, "Maritime Studies at Sea Semester," XLVII, 206–210
Millis, Walter, "The Iron Sea Elephants," X, 15–32
Mills, dredge (1900), XXXVIII, 200 ff.
Mills, Hazel Emery, I, 316; "The Arizona Fleet," I, 255–274; review by, I, 405–406
Mills, Captain James, VII, 55
Mills, J. V. G., *Ma Huan Ying-yai Sheng-lan: The Overall Survey of the Ocean's Shores*, reviewed, XXXII, 225–226
Mills, John M., *Canadian Coastal and Inland Steam Vessels, 1809–1930*, reviewed, XL, 145
Mills, Randall V., III, 178; "A Note on Steamboat Decoration," III, 159–161; *Railoads Down the Valley*, reviewed, XI, 232; *Stern-Wheelers up Columbia*, reviewed, VIII, 158–159
Mills, Thomas B., XL, 299
Millwood, ship (1811), X, 54
Milne, Admiral Sir Alexander, XIX, 63
Milne, Rear Admiral Sir Alexander, XXVIII, 110–111
Milne, Captain, XXXII, 238
Milne, William, XLVIII, 275
Milne, William M., XXIX, 263
Milnes, Monckton, VII, 84
Milo, steamship *(1824)*, XXXVII, 244
Milo, whaler *(1865)*, XXVII, 269, 272, 273, 276

Milton B. Medary, steamship, XXIII, 52
Milton Martin, steamship, XVIII, 231
Milverton, ship, XXXVI, 3
Milwaukee, steamship (1837), VII, 65; VIII, 37; *(1838)*, XVIII, 283; XX, 80, 85, 92–94, 256, 260
Milwaukee, U.S. monitor (1862), X, 18, 28, 31
Milwood (1812), XIII, 280
Min, steamship (1856), XVI, 168; XVIII, 71
Mina, British ship *(1814)*, XLII, 106
Minas Prince, schooner *(1940)*, III, 163
Minatitlan, brig *(1861)*, XI, 286
Minchinton, Walter E., "The Canaries as Ports of Call," XLVI, 100–110
Mindanao, XXX, 202
Minden, H.B.M. (1914), XXXVII, 137
Minden, naval storeship, XXII, 37
Mindoro, bark (1856), V, 194, 242
Mindoro, clipper ship *(1877)*, XLVI, 63; XLVII, 120
Mindte, Commander R. W., "Another Navy Rodgers," XIX, 213–226
Mineola, schooner (1911), XXVI, plate XXV
Miner, Captain Sanford S., XI, 115–133
Miner, Sidney, XXV, 104
Minerva, brig *(1774)*, XXXIII, 303; *(1775)*, XXXIX, 194
Minerva, cutter (1888), XXX, plates XI, XII
Minerva, frigate (1782), VI, 170
Minerva, schooner *(1807)*, XVI, 194
Minerva, schooner (1896), XXVI, plate XIII
Minerva, ship, XXII, 94; XXVII, 73; *(1794)*, XVIII, 132; *(1799)*, XXXIII, 160 ff.; *(1801)*, XXIII, 217
Minerva, ship (1808), XIV, 40; (1834), XIV, 40; *(1844)*, journal of, XXV, plate 5
Minerva, yacht *(1906)*, XXXVI, 242 ff., plate 8
Minerva Reef, by Olaf Ruben, reviewed, XXIV, 226–227
Mines, XLIX, 114
Minho, steamship, XXI, 98; *(1862)*, VIII, 226; XXIV, plate 24
Minion of London, ship (1580), XXVII, 182
Minister Wedel, tanker *(1942)*, L, 46
Minna, brig *(1863)*, VIII, 231
Minna, steamship *(1863)*, VIII, 231
Minneapolis, steamship *(1890)*, XXXVIII, 130; (1900), Pictorial Supplement, XXXIV, plate XXV
Minneapolis, U.S. cruiser *(1906)*, XXV, 188
Minnehaha, barge, XXV, 168
Minnehaha, bugeye *(1881)*, III, 176
Minnehaha, schooner *(1861)*, VIII, 220
Minnehaha, steamship, XXIV, 241
Minnesetung, steamship (1834), VII, 54
Minnesota, frigate *(1861)*, XXXVI, 190; XXXVII, 283; XXXVIII, 37
Minnesota, ship (1848), I, 48; VII, 318; (1861), XI, 286; (1890), XXXIII, 270
Minnesota, ship (1903), XLVII, 199; (1915), XXXV, 167
Minnesota, steamship (1940), III, 187 ff., plate 25
Minnesota, steamship (ex-*Northland*, ex-*Zeeland*) (1901), Pictorial Supplement, XXXIV, plate XXVII

Minnesota, U.S.S. *(1858),* XXVII, 163; XXIX, 108; *(1863),* XVIII, 145; XX, 158, 160; *(1877),* XX, 135
Minnesota, U.S. training ship *(1875),* XLIX, 293
Minnesota, U.S. steam frigate (1855), XXII, 252, 253, 257; XXIV, 143, 220
Minnetonka, steamship *(1902),* XXXVIII, 196 ff.
Minnewaska, steamship *(1902),* XXXVIII, 197 ff.
Minnie, brig, XXI, 97; *(1863),* VIII, 231
Minnie, schooner *(1864),* XV, 129
Minnie, sloop, XXI, 88; *(1863),* XII, 159
Minnie, steamship, XXI, 92; *(1864),* VIII, 235
Minnie Hunter, barkentine (1874), XXIV, 39, 44, 57
Minorca, ship *(1802),* XXXIV, 251
Minorca, Balearic Islands, XXV, 157 ff.
Minos, H.M.S. (1840), VIII, 55–56, 132; XX, 84
Minot, lighthouse tender *(1861),* XLVIII, 87
Minot's Light, The Story of, by Edward Rowe Snow, reviewed, I, 189
Minott, Charles V., XIII, 121
Minott Shipyard, XXVII, plate XVIII
Minto, Lord (British, 1844), XXXII, 235
Minto, Captain Thomas and Eric Stevens, *The Search for the Kobenhaven,* reviewed, XLVII, 143
Minuse, John M., answered query, VII, 243
Mirage, ship *(1858),* XXXIV, 18 ff.
Mirage, steamship (1855), XXII, 30, 32, 40, 42, 43
Mirboha, Moroccan cruiser, XXX, 75
Miriam, schooner *(1746),* XX, 103; *(1863),* XII, 159, 232
Mirrielees, Alexander, XXIII, 138, 139
Mirror, schooner (1834), XIV, 40
Mirror for Americans, Likeness of the Eastern Seaboard, 1810, by Ralph H. Brown, reviewed, III, 355
"Misadventures of a Maine Slaver," by George A. Billias, XIX, 114–119
"Miscellaneous Disasters from Pirates, Privateers and Indians," document contributed by J. W. Snyder, Jr., V, 157–162
"Miscellaneous Manavelins," by Gilbert R. Payson, XXXI, 191
Mischief, schooner *(1863),* XII, 158
Mischief, steamship *(1872),* XII, 289, 293
Mispelkamp, Peter K. H., reviews by: L, 148; L, 231
Misroon, Commander J. S., XXI, 239
Missionaries:
 China, XLVI, 34; XLVIII, 271
 Oceania, XI, 203
 Pacific Islands, X, 264
 United States, 18th century, XX, 112
Missionaries in Pacific, IV, 111–113
Missionary Packet, topsail schooner (1825), X, 265–268, plate 27
Missionary ships, X, 264; XI, 203
Missionary Whaleship, The, by Thomas French, reviewed, XXII, 151
Missions, Fiji Islands, South Pacific, XXV, 274 ff.
"Mission to Peking, 1870: Captain McLane Tilton's Letter Describing his Trip with the Seward Party to Peking," by Truman R. Strobridge and Bernard C. Nalty, XXV, 116–122
Mission Transfer Co., XXXVIII, 176 ff.
Mississippi, frigate *(1839),* XLIX, 100; *(1853),* XLVI, 58; *(1920),* L, 54
Mississippi, paddle-wheel warship *(1841),* XXXIV, 221
Mississippi, schooner, XXI, 89
Mississippi, steamship (1856), XVIII, 71; (1859), IV, 151, plate 25; *(1862),* XXXVI, 195; XXXVII, 169; XXXVIII, 37
Mississippi, steamship (ex-*Memphis*) (1863), Pictorial Supplement, XXXIV, plate V
Mississippi, transport *(1862),* XXXI, 262
Mississippi, U.S.S. *(1852),* XXVII, 44, 161, 163; *(1857),* XII, 271
Mississippi, U.S. frigate, XXX, 50
Mississippi, U.S. steamship *(1853),* VII, 9, 12, 14, 16, 17
Mississippi, U.S. war steamship, XXIII, 55; XXIV, 6, 22
Mississippian, schooner *(1863),* XII, 159
Mississippi Colonization Society, XXXVIII, 59
Mississippi Packet, sloop *(1776),* XXV, 203, 210
Mississippi Panorama, reviewed, X, 77–78
Mississippi River. *See* Steamboats, Steam Navigation
Mississippi River Steamers, XVI, 28–40
Missouri, Confederate ironclad *(1863),* XLVIII, 92
Missouri, ship *(1801),* X, 53; *(1802),* XXIII, 217
Missouri, ship (1834), IV, 51; *(1857),* XXXVII, 169
Missouri, side-wheel frigate *(1839),* XLIX, 100
Missouri, steamship (1840), XX, 84, 86, 89 n., 92, 258, 266, 268; *(1843),* XXXI, 185; XXXIV, 95
Missouri, U.S.S., XXVIII, 104; XXIX, 125
Missouri, U.S. war steamship (1839), XXIV, 6
Mister. *See* Mr.
Mistico, gunboat *(1845),* XXXVI, 132
Mitchell, Alexander, XXXVIII, 44
Mitchell, Alonzo L., XXXVII, 87
Mitchell, Lieutenant B. J., XXXV, 192
Mitchell, Benjamin F., XLIII, 267
Mitchell, C. Bradford, X, 71–72; "Paddle-Wheel Inboard, some of the History of the Ocklawaha River Steamboating and of the Hart Line," VII, 115–166, 224–239, plates 13–20, 29–32
Mitchell, Christopher, XLIV, 22 ff.
Mitchell, Dr., XXXV, 235 ff.
Mitchell, Donald W., "A Forgotten Naval War in the Pacific: 1854–1856," XXXI, 268–274
Mitchell, Edward and Randall R. Reeves, "Right Whales, Not Humpbacks, Taken in Cintra Bay," L, 119–126
Mitchell, Edwin Valentine, *Anchor to Windward,* reviewed, I, 101
Mitchell, Eugene, XXXVII, 87
Mitchell, John K., XXII, 282 n., 286 n.
Mitchell, John L., XXXVII, 87
Mitchell, Captain Josiah Angier, I, 100, 164–165, 185
Mitchell, Obediah, XLV, 8
Mitchell, Reginald H., V, 165

Mitchell, Samuel L., XLVII, 36
Mitchell, Stephen, XLI, 219
Mitchell, W. F., XXII, plate VIII
Mitchell, W. H., and L. A. Sawyer, *The Liberty Ships,* reviewed, XXXI, 228
Mitchell, Walter, XLVI, 112
Mitchell, Brigadier General William, L, 52 ff.; photo of, L, 57
Mitchell, William B., XXXVII, 87
Mitchill, Samuel L., VI, 258, 263, 269 ff.
Mitman, Carl W., contributed documents, III, 350–352; IV, 74–76; V, 87
Mitsubishi Mail Steamship Co., II, 18; XVI, 256; XVII, 313, 314
Mitter, Radha, Kissen, Calcutta, picture of between, XLVI, 15–16
Mix, Elijah, XXXVI, 216–218
Mjelde, Michael Jay, *Glory of the Seas,* reviewed, XXX, 217–218
M'Nab & Clark, XXVI, 207
Mobile, schooner *(1861),* XI, 286
Mobile, steamship, XXI, 102; *(1861),* XI, 286
Mobile, steamship (1893), IX, 223
"*Moby-Dick:* The Two 'Missing' Prints by 'H. Durand,'" by Stuart M. Frank, XLVI, 252–257
Moctezuma, Mexican steam frigate *(1845),* XXX, 47 ff.
Model for the figurehead of the ship *Charles H. Lunt,* Pictorial Supplement, XXXVII, plate XX
Modelling The Brig-of-War "Irene," A Handbook for the Building of Historical Ship-Models, by E. W. Petrejus, reviewed, XXX, 301–302
Model of Nautical Instrument Seller's Shop, XXXIV, plate 9
Models. *See* Ship models
Models: XVI, 98–106; Rogers Collection, XVIII, 181–182
  Albatross, U.S. Fish Commission steamship (1882), V, plate 2; *Brynhilda,* pojama, VI, plate 23; *Cohota,* ship (1843), VII, plate 2; *Commonwealth,* steamship (1854), VIII, plate 22; French naval gun, III, plate 17; *Great Western,* steamship (1837), IX, plate 27; *Kronprins Gustaf Adolph,* ship (1782), VI, plate 27; Lighthouse tower, illustration of, XLVII, 188; *Lodbrok,* turuma, VI, plate 24; *Loyal London,* H.M.S. (1666), IV, plates 41–44; *Michigan,* U.S. gunboat (1843), VIII, plate 16; *Midas,* steam topsail schooner (1844), I, plate facing 57; Oklawaha River steamship (1893), VII, 162, plate 18; *Sirius,* steamship (1837), IX, plate 26; steamship, by Desblancs in 1802, photo of, L, 205; *Styrbjörn,* hemmema, VI, plate 23; *Thorborg,* udema, VI, plate 24; Trinity House models of light-vessels, IV, plates 45–48
Model Shipwright, Vol. I, No. 1, Editor, Arthur L. Tucker, reviewed, XXXIII, 68–69
Modern Greece, steamship *(1862),* III, 265; VIII, 226
Modern inshore lifeboat, XXXIV, plates 2, 17

Modoc, U.S. Coast Guard cutter, XXXVII, 95 n.
Moewe, German raider *(1915),* XLV, 199 ff.
Moffat, Alexander W., *Maverick Navy,* reviewed, XXXVII, 70
Moffatt, A. E., O.S., U.S.N., XXV, 50
Moffett, Rear Admiral William Adger, XXXVII, 115 ff.; photo of, L, 53
Moffitt, tanker (1920), XXII, 162, 171, 172, 182
Moger, Newton, IV, 225 ff.
Mogul, ship (1859), III, 69
Mohammed Pasha, XXXVI, 179
Mohave, steamship (1863), I, 261–262, 269
Mohave (II), steamship (1876), I, 261–262, plate between 272–273
Mohawk, British brig *(1813),* XLII, 110 ff.
Mohawk, H.M.S. (1843), VIII, 140, 144; XX, 262; *(1893),* XXVIII, 92
Mohawk, schooner *(1807),* IX, 13; XVI, 193
Mohawk, ship *(1756),* XLIX, 266 ff.
Mohawk, sloop (1836), XXXVI, 255
Mohawk, U.S.S. *(1861),* XI, 270
Mohawk Oil Co., XXXVIII, 186
Mohican, ship (1898), XXXIX, 41
Mohican, sloop (1862), XXIX, 104
Mohican, steam sloop (1864), XLIII, 179 ff.; XLV, 192
Mohican, U.S.S. (1861), XXI, 240; (1862), XXVII, 36 n. 43, 44; (1863), XV, 295
Mohinkis, steamship (1920), XVI, 131
Mohongo, schooner *(1861),* XI, 267, 286
Mohongo, U.S.S. *(1864),* XXVII, 43, 44
Mohrmann, A., XXXVI, 235
Mohrmann, J. H., XXIV, plate XIV
Mohum, Richard, XIII, 12, 15, 22, 26
Moira, H.M.S. *(1813),* XVII, 210
Mojave, U.S. Coast Guard cutter, XXXVII, 95 n.
Molasses Act, XXVII, 214
Moleta, I, 353–356
Molineux, William, XL, 248
Mollat, Professor Michel, XXXIV, 229
Molley Cn Aspire (1785), XXXI, 46
Molly, sloop *(1721),* IX, 136
Momus, steamship (1906), XXIV, plate XV
Mona, steamship (1863), XVII, 52; XVIII, 71; XLIII, 211 ff.
Monadnock, monitor, XLI, 95; (1862), X, 18, 27, 28, 31; *(1866),* XLIX, 116; *(1899),* XXXV, 185 ff.
Monadnock, ship, XXXVII, 140 n.
Monadnock, U.S.S. *(1864),* XXVII, 37 n., 42, 44; XXVIII, 69
Monagas, José Gregorio, XXX, 272 ff.
Monagas, General José Tadéo, XXX, 261 ff.
Monarch, H.M.S. *(1781),* XXXVI, 167, 168
Monarch, schooner (1900), XXVI, plate XV
Monarch, U.S. ironclad *(1862),* XXV, 136, 137, 138
Moncada, General, XXXV, 129
Monceau, Duhamel de, XVI, 98
Monckton, Lieutenant Colonel, XXXI, 36

Moneka, steamship (1865), XVI, 176
Monet, auxiliary schooner (1910), I, 79
Money. *See* Bank notes
Monfalcone, barkentine (1919), V, 82
Mongol, steamship (1873), XVII, 62; XVIII, 71
Mongolia, steamship, XXIX, 231; *(1904),* X, 138, 139
Monhegan, steamship (1901), XII, 291
Monitor, barkentine (1920), V, 82
Monitor, C.S.S. *(1862),* XXXI, 66; XXXV, 59 ff.
Monitor, ironclad *(1861),* XLVIII, 106 ff.; XLIX, 114 ff.; *(1862),* XLII, 85, 192 ff.; XLIII, 207; XLIV, 14
Monitor, U.S. ironclad (1862), XX, 159–162; XXII, 254, 261, 262; XXIII, 197 ff.; XXIV, 219–221
Monitor, U.S. monitor (1861), III, 161–162; VI, 87; X, 15–17, 19–21, 31,
Monitor, U.S.S., XXVII, 174
Monitor, U.S.S. [replica] (1951), XIV, 107
Monitor, warship *(1850),* XXXVIII, 121; XXXIX, 37, 120
"Monitor Companies: A Study of the Major Firms That Built the USS *Monitor,*" by William N. Still, XLVIII, 106–130
Monitors. *See* Armored vessels; Turret ships
Monitors, X, 15–32
Monk, George, XXXIX, 124
Monkey, log canoe (about 1880), IV, 249
Monkeydena, steam freighter, XXIV, 235 n.
"Monkey Sail," query by John Lyman, VII, 322
Monks, Leslie, XVI, 183–184
Monleon, Rafael, XV, 52
Monmouth, frigate, XXIII, 100
Monmouth, H.M.S. *(1713),* XXI, 262
Monmouth, ship *(1819),* XLI, 286
Monmouth, snow (1744), I, 167
Monmouth, steamship (1890), XI, 259 ff.
Monneraye, Jean de la, XXXIV, 230
Monnow, schooner (1918), vi 83
Monocacy, paddle steamship (1863), XXXII, 127; XXXIV, 212
Monocacy, U.S. gunboat (1865), VII, 107–110, 112–113, plate 10; VIII, 275
Monocacy, U.S.S. *(1894),* XXIII, 69; *(1896),* XXXVIII, 167; XL, 104; XXVIII, 143
Monohansett, steamship (1862), III, plates 15, 16
Monohasset, steamship *(1862),* ornament from, Pictorial Supplement, XXXVII, plate XXIV
Monongahela, bark *(1918),* XVIII, 170
Monongahela, screw-sloop *(1874),* XXXIII, 284
Monongahela, U.S.S. (1862), XX, 141
Monongahela Farmer, schooner, later ship (1800), VII, 317
Monongahela River (WV/PA). *See* Steamboats
Monopolists and Freebooters: The Pacific since Magellan, Vol. II, by Oskar H. K. Spate, reviewed, XLV, 206
Monroe, steamship *(1836),* VII, 62; *(1840),* XX, 82 n.
Monroe, James, XXVIII, 33; XLIII, 47

Monroe, President James, XXIII, 162, 168; XXIV, 16; XXXII, 265; XL, 31, 214
Monroe Doctrine, XXVIII, 87–88
Monserrate, ship *(1861),* XI, 266, 286
Monson, ship *(1813),* XLVI, 166
Monson, Sir William, XXVIII, 260
Monsoon, bark (1851), II, 331
Monsoon, ship, XXI, 93; *(1861),* XI, 286
Montagu, Admiral John, XXIII, 184
Montagu, Captain John, XXVI, 61
Montague, brigantine *(1778),* X, 282–283
Montague, H.M.S., XXVI, 54
Montana, steamship (1865), X, 130; *(1871),* I, 258; *(1872),* X, 132
Montana, U.S.S., XXVIII, 107
Montano, ship *(1845),* I, 393
Montauk, U.S. monitor (1862), X, 17, 31; *(1862),* XLVIII, 122; *(1863),* XLII, 196 ff.; XLIV, 268; *(1865),* XXV, 67
Montcalm, cruiser (1914), XXIV, 275
Montebello, ship (1859), II, 246
Monte Christo, sloop *(1862),* XII, 57
Montejo, Francisco de, VI, 243 ff.
Monterey, bark (1846), V, 241
Monterey, gasoline-auxiliary schooner *(1906),* XLIV, 21 ff.
Monterey, monitor *(1892),* XXXVIII, 298
Monterey, schooner, XXI, 90; *(1861),* XI, 286
Monterey, schooner, later barkentine (1878), I, 397; V, 82
Monterey, ship *(1861),* XV, 124; *(1898),* XXXV, 184 ff.
Monterey (ex-*Adrien Badin*) *(1925),* XXXII, 32
Montezuma, Mexican warship *(1843),* XXI, 221 ff.
Montezuma, ship *(1861),* XXI, 242, 258
Montezuma, U.S.S. *(1799),* XXXI, 173
Montgomery, *(1861),* XV, 103 n.
Montgomery, frigate (1776), VIII, 11, 14, 21, 24; *(1779),* XXXV, 141
Montgomery, ship (1776), XXXVIII, 24
Montgomery, steamship, XXI, 100; *(1863),* XII, 159; *(1877),* VII, 136
Montgomery, Commodore J. E., C.S.N., XXV, 129–131, 135, 139
Montgomery, John, and Carl D. Lane, *Navigation the Easy Way,* reviewed, IX, 306
Montgomery, John B., XXXIII, 42 ff.
Montgomery, Brigadier General Richard, XXXVIII, 24
Month at Goodspeed's, The, VI, 239
Monticello, gunboat *(1861),* XXXVI, 190; XXXVII, 282
Monticello, ship *(1871),* XIV, 46
Montmorenci, ship *(1854),* XXXVII, 169
Montour, yacht *(1890),* XXXVII, 170
Montreal, ship *(1852),* XII, 33
Montreal, steamship *(1861),* XXXIII, 87
Montreal City, steamship *(1933),* XIV, 127, 129, 135; *(1946),* XIV, 131, 135
Montresor, Captain John, I, plate facing 146

Montserrat, steamship *(1894),* XLII, 261
Montt, Captain Jorge, XXXIX, 39
Moody, Paul, XXIX, 205
Moody, Robert E., VIII, 164
Moody, Russell, XXXVI, 22
Moody, William H., XXIX, 31–53
Moonbeam, bark (*circa* 1886), I, 58–59
Mooney, Captain H., XXI, 97
Mooney, Captain J., XVIII, 83
Moore, Captain Andrew J., XXI, 97
Moore, Captain Edwin Ward, XXI, 221 ff.
Moore, Enoch, XXXVI, 256
Moore, Captain George, VII, 66
Moore, Henderson, XIV, 255
Moore, J. J., XXX, 40
Moore, J. J., and Co., IV, 200; VII, 294
Moore, James, XXXI, 45
Moore, James and James Dodds, *Building the Wooden Fighting Ship,* reviewed, XLVI, 202
Moore, Captain John, R.N., VI, 21, 23, 25, 26, 28–32, 34
Moore, John Hamilton, XXX, 207
Moore, Sir Jonas, XXXVII, 176
Moore, Marven E. and Nicholas J. de Jong, *Launched from Prince Edward Island: A Pictorial Review of Sail,* reviewed, XLII, 222
Moore, Captain Thomas J., XXI, 97
Moore Drydock Co., San Francisco, XXV, 292
Moore-McCormack Lines, XXIX, 233
Moores, Captain Menander, XXIII, 27
Moose, hermaphrodite brig (1851), XXIV, 58
Moosmie, bark *(1864),* XVII, 43; XLIII, 95
Mooy, J., XXII, plate XXXI
Mora, 4-masted barkentine (ex-U.S.S. *Agawam,* 1863).
Moralee, W. H. (nautical instrument maker), XXXIV, 209
Moran, Captain B., XXI, 97
Moran, Edward (Congressman), XLI, 119
Moran, James, XXI, 279–291
Mordaunt, Oswald, XXXVI, 3
Morea, ship (1828), II, 271 ff.
"More American-built Liverpool vessels," by Arthur C. Wardle, I, 297
Moredecai, John B., *A Brief History of Richmond, Fredericksburg, and Potomac Railroad,* reviewed, II, 91–92
"More Foreign Mud," document contributed by Marion V. Brewington, XIV, 215–216
More Good Boats, by Roger C. Taylor, reviewed, XL, 147
Morehead City Shipbuilding Corp., XLVII, 273
Morelos, Mexican pilot boat *(1843),* XXX, 53
More Marine Paintings and Drawings in the Peabody Museum, by Philip Chadwick Foster Smith, reviewed, 143
"More on Puritan Migration Ships," note contributed by Gershom Bradford, XXIV, 212–213

"More on *Sparrow-Hawk,*" by Hobart H. Holly, XIV, 211–212
Morgan, C.S.S. *(1864),* XXXVI, 89
Morgan (ex-*Lewis Cass,* built 1855), U.S./Confederate revenue cutter, XLVIII, 90, 91; XL, 298
Morgan, Charles S., V, 327; XXIII, 4; XXVII, 226; XXXI, 139; document contributed by, XXXI, 288; reviews by, XLVII, 143, 146; XLVIII, 65; XLIX, 238, 307; L, 151; mentioned, XLI, 164; XLIV, 137, 138, 139; XLV, 212; "Loss of the Bark *Lapland,*" IX, 68–70, plate 6; "New England Coasting Schooners," XXIII, 5–21
Morgan, Captain Charles W., XXI, 75
Morgan, Charles Waln, XXV, 103
Morgan, Captain David, XXI, 97
Morgan, Edward Delmar, VII, 85
Morgan, Governor Edwin D., XXXI, 64
Morgan, George D., XXI, 235, 237, 242
Morgan, Henry, XXXVII, 40
Morgan, J. P., XLIII, 3 ff.
Morgan, J. Pierpont, XXXIII, 269
Morgan, James Morris, XLV, 191 ff.
Morgan, Captain Jeremiah, XXIII, 176
Morgan, John T., Senator, XXV, 264
Morgan, Captain L. J., XXI, 97
Morgan, Captain Thomas, XLV, 86 ff.
Morgan, Captain William, XLII, 47
Morgan, William J., *Captains to the Northward: The New England Captains in the Continental Navy,* reviewed, XX, 148
Morgan, William James, mentioned, XXXVII, 81; XXXIX, 190; "American Privateering in America's War for Independence, 1775–1783," XXXVI, 79–87; Editor, *Naval Documents of the American Revolution* [Vol. V], reviewed, XXXI, 228–229; Editor, *Naval Documents of the American Revolution* [Vol. VI], reviewed, XXXIV, 145–146; Editor, *Naval Documents of the American Revolution* [Vol. VII?], reviewed, XXXVIII, 147; Editor, *Naval Documents of the American Revolution* [Vol. VIII], reviewed, XLII, 71
Morgan, Dr. William James, XXIX, 80, 287; XXX, 80; XLII, 6, 189 ff.; XLV, 248
Morgan, William Stuart, III, reviews by, XLVII, 282; L, 65, 67; "The Commerce of a Southern Port: New Bern, North Carolina, 1783 to 1789," XLIX, 77–90
Morgan's International Mercantile Marine Co., XXXIII, 183
Morgan Steamship Line, XXIX, 231
Morgenthau, Henry J., Secretary of the Treasury, XLII, 214
Moriarity, Captain Thomas, XXV, 183–184
Morina, Bulgarian ship *(1944),* XLIII, 35 ff.
Morison, Elting E., *Admiral Sims and the Modern American Navy,* reviewed, III, 93
Morison, Samuel Eliot, I, 177, 315; III, 97, 178; IV, 168; V, 98, 110, 214, 247; VI, 92, 153; VII, 81; VIII, 6; XI,

4; XLVIII, 181; XLIX, 111; editorial mention, XLIII, 164; XLV, 45; queries by, I, 89; answered query, II, 82; reviews by, II, 85–86, 253–254, 342–343; V, 166–169
Admiral of the Ocean Sea: A Life of Christopher Columbus, reviewed, II, 178–181; "The Arms and Seals of John Paul Jones," XVIII, 301–305; *The Battle of the Atlantic, 1939–1943,* reviewed, VIII, 155–157; "Captain Codman on the Mutiny in Dorchester Church, and the Seamanship of Saint Paul," II, 99–106; "Columbus and Polaris," I, 6–25, 123–137; *Coral Sea, Midway and Submarine Actions, May 1942–August 1942,* reviewed, X, 76–77; "The Dry Salvages and the Thacher Shipwreck," XXV, 233–247, plates 23–26; *The European Discovery of America: The Northern Voyages A.D. 500–1600,* reviewed, XXXI, 226–227; *The European Discovery of America: The Southern Voyages A.D. 1492–1616,* reviewed, XXXV, 211; mentioned, XXXIII, 174; "Historical Notes on the Gilbert and Marshall Islands," IV, 87–118; translator and editor, *Journals and Other Documents on the Life and Voyages of Christopher Columbus,* reviewed, XXV, 75; "The Landing at Fedhala, Morocco, November 8, 1942," III, 99–105; *The Maritime History of Massachusetts, 1783–1860,* reviewed, II, 262; re-reviewed, XLII, 146; "Notes on Writing Naval (*not* Navy) English," IX, 5–10; *Operations in North African Waters, October 1942–June 1943,* reviewed, VII, 244–247; "Oviedo on Navigation," I, 391; "A Review of the Hakluyt Society's Centenary Volume," VII, 85–86; *The Rising Sun in the Pacific, 1931–April 1942,* reviewed, IX, 76; *The Struggle for Guadalcanal, August 1942–February 1943,* reviewed, X, 76–77
Morison, Rear Admiral Samuel E., U.S.N.R. (ret.), XXVIII, 50, 51 n., note by, 283; XXX, 42, 199, 278
Morison, Rear Admiral Samuel Eliot, XXXVI, 153 ff.; XXXIX, 159
Morning, steamship (1869), XVI, 259
Morning Light, ship (1853), III, 67
Morning Star, auxiliary schooner (1947), X, 278–279, plate 28
Morning Star, bark (1913), VII, 221
Morning Star, barkentine (1883), X, 275–276, plate 27
Morning Star, Danish bark, XXIII, 268
Morning Star, hermaphrodite brig (1856), X, 269–272, plate 27; (1866), X, 272–273, plate 27; (1871), X, 273–275
Morning Star, schooner (1825), L, 217; (1855), XXIV, 141; (1862), VIII, 226
Morning Star, ship (1855), III, 69
Morningstar, sloop (1746), XLVIII, 33
Morning Star, sloop, XXI, 98
Morning Star, steamship (1862), XXXIII, 203, Pictorial Supplement, plate XXXII; (1866), IV, 146 ff., 152; (1904), X, 277, plate 28
Morocco, History, 17th century, XXIII, 95

Morpain, Pierre de, XXXV, 159
Morrell, Captain Benjamin, XII, 40 ff.; XXXIV, 255
Morris, merchantman (1779), XXXV, 141
Morris, revenue cutter (1832), XXXVIII, 58
Morris, schooner (1864), XII, 232
Morris, Lieutenant C. M., XXII, 45–54
Morris, Captain Charles, XXVI, 258–261; XXVII, 29
Morris, Captain Charles, C.S.N., XXV, 298
Morris, Lieutenant Charles, XLVII, 16, 30
Morris, Charles F., *Origins, Orient and Oriana,* reviewed, XLI, 149–151
Morris, Lieutenant Charles M., XV, 296
Morris, Edward P., XXV, 82, 87
Morris, Gerald E., XLVIII, 178
Morris, Judge Lewis, XXIII, 277, 280–284
Morris, Paul C., *Schooners and Schooner Barges,* reviewed, XLVII, 146
Morris, Commodore Richard V., L, 245 ff.
Morris, Robert, VIII, 12, 15; XXV, 7; XXXI, 39, 111; XXXII, 247; XXXVI, 81; XXXIX, 167; XLIII, 21
Morris, Robert, Superintendant of Finance, U.S.A., XLVI, 29; XLIX, 47
Morris, Robert G., XXV, 255
Morris-Davies, Mrs. F. M., XXIX, 244
Morrison, ship (1837), XLI, 26
Morrison, steamship (1861), VIII, 220, 226
Morrison, Captain George D., II, 140–153
Morrison, Captain Henry, XVIII, 83
Morrison, Captain J. J., XXI, 97
Morrison, J. S., *Greek Oared Ships, 900–322 B.C.,* reviewed, XXIX, 72–73
Morrison, Captain James J., XLVIII, 90
Morrison, Commander James J., XL, 298 ff.
Morrison, Captain John, L, 270 ff.
Morrison, John Harrison, XXIV, 168 ff.; *Iron and Steel Hull Steam Vessels of the United States — 1825–1905,* reviewed, VI, 235–236
Morrison, Robert, XLVI, 36; XLVIII, 274
Morrison, William, XX, 47
Morro Castle, liner (1934), XXXVI, 7 ff.; XXXVII, 75
Morrone, Father Joseph, XXV, 185
Morse, ship, XXXVII, 89
Morse, Captain A. H., XVIII, 83
Morse, Captain C. C., XXI, 106
Morse, Charles Wyman, XXXIV, 182
Morse, Edward S., mentioned, XXX, 3; XLVI, 55 ff.; XLIX, 35
Morse, Hosea Ballou, XLVIII, 221
Morse, J. G., XXIV, 60
Morse, Samuel F. B., XIII, 247
Morse, Professor Sidney, XXXVI, 84, 86
Morse, Sydney G., IV, 252; V, 247; "'The Fleet,'" V, 177–193; "Ship *Lord Dartmouth:* American-built Merchantman of Revolutionary Days, The," IV, 207–216
Morse, W. H., XVII, 125

"Morse in Japan and His Impact There," by John E. Thayer, XLVI, 55–65

Morse Shipyard, XXVII, plate VI

Morsier, Pierre, XLIV, 54

Mortimer, William George, XXIX, 135

Mortlock Island, XXXIV, 249

Morton, Harry, *The Wind Commands,* reviewed, XXXVI, 301–302

Morton, Nathaniel, XVII, 129

Morton, Thomas, XXXVII, 23

Moryson, Sir Richard, XXXI, 103

Mosbacher, Emil, Jr., editorial comment, XXXVII, 3–4

"Mosby or a Quantrill? The Civil War Career of John Clibbon Braine, A," by Francis X. Holbrook, XXXIII, 199–211

Moses Taylor, steamship *(1873),* X, 132

Moses Wheeler, ship (1850), III, 169

Moshulu, bark, XXX, 219; (1904), VI, 74–75, 77; *(1918),* XVIII, 170, 172

Mosiman, Captain W. E., XXI, 97

Mosketo, privateer *(1777),* XLIII, 22 ff.

Mosquito, brig *(1779),* XXXV, 141

Mosquito, launch *(1861),* XLVIII, 95

Mosquito, schooner *(1810),* XXIII, 252

Mosquito Fleet, XXVII, 160, 176

Moss, H. C., XXXVI, 248

Mostert, Noël, *Supership,* reviewed, XXXV, 214

Mottey, Joseph, XXX, 96 n.

Mottistone, Lord, XXXIV, 15

Moulton, Daniel, notarial records, XX, 43, 67, 103, 111, 117, 145, 190, 216, 236, 242, 249, 269; XXI, 15, 41, 69

Moultrie, Colonel William, XIII, 31 ff.

Mound City, U.S.S. (1861), XIX, 266, 269 ff.; (1862), XXV, 131, 139

Mount, Fisher, VIII, 311–313

Mount, Richard, VIII, 303, 307–309, 311–313; XVII, 153; XXIII, 219

Mount, William, VIII, 315–316, 321; XIX, 44

Mountaine, William, VIII, 317; XVI, 87 ff.; XX, 185–190; L, 288

Mountain Spring, whaleship *(1856),* L, 125

Mount and Davidson, VIII, 303 ff.

Mount and Page, VIII, 302, 310–311, 315–317

Mountbatten, 1st Earl Louis, XLVI, 24

Mt. Desert, steamship *(1884),* XI, 218 ff.

Mt. Desert Island, Maine, XXV, plate XI

Mount Pleasant, steamship *(1873),* XXIV, 237

Mount Vernon, bark *(1861),* XI, 266, 286

Mount Vernon, S.S., XXIX, 233

Mount Vernon, ship (1796), V, 255–265; (1798), I, 163; II, 279; V, 43; *(1799),* XXXII, 4; Pictorial Supplement, XXXII, plates XIII–XVI

Mount Vernon, U.S.S. (ex-*Kronprinzessin Cecelie*), XXVIII, 108 n.

Mt. Vernon (1801), XXIII, 217

"*Mount Vernon's* Voyage from Batavia to Nagasaki in 1807, The," by Allan B. Cole, V, 255–265

Mount Washington, ship (circa 1840), I, 65

Mount Washington ... *for Lake Winnipesaukee, The New S. S.,* by Paul H. Blaisdell, reviewed, I, 411

Mount Wollaston, bark *(1879),* XXXIX, 9

Mt. Wollaston, whaler *(1863),* XXVII, 268

Mourelle (Explorer), XXV, 253–254

Mouser, Bruce L., "The Voyage of the Good Sloop *Dolphin* to Africa 1795–1796," XXXVIII, 249–261; note by, XL, 63

Moussion, Captain, XLV, 201

Mouzon, Harold A., "*Defence,* A Vessel of the Navy of South Carolina," XIII, 29–50; "The Unlucky *General Armstrong,*" XV, 59–80

Mowat, Captain Henry, R.N., XXXVII, 291

Mowatt, Captain, XXXI, 215

Mowatt, Captain Henry, VII, 200, 204

Möwe (Seagull), German ex-fruit steamship *Ponga* (1916), XLVIII, 50 ff.; photo of, XLVIII, 52

Mower, C. D., XXX, 194

Mower, Charles D., XIX, 232

Mower, Captain George, XVIII, 233

Mowtan, steamship (1869), XVIII, 71

Moyen, Captain, XXXII, 14

Moylan, Stephen, XXX, 108

Moyune, steamship (1863), XVI, 251; XVII, 304; XVIII, 71; *(1863),* XLIII, 120 ff.; *(1865),* XXXIV, 49

M'Pherson, Charles, XXX, 299

M'Quhae, Captain Peter, XIII, 272

"Mr. Hardy Lee," by Alexander C. Brown, XI, 291

"Mr. Hardy Lee," query by Alexander Crosby Brown, VII, 321–322

"Mr. Jefferson's Dry Docks," by Eugene S. Ferguson, XI, 108–114

"Mr. Jefferson's Gunboat Navy," by Spencer C. Tucker, XLIII, 135–141

"Mr. Joseph Peabody of Salem, Massachusetts, and his Punch," by Augustus Peabody Loring, Jr., II, 39–43

"Mr. Shaw 'Sees' *Portland* Sink," by Russell W. Knight, XXIX, 224–225

Mrantz, Maxine, *Whaling Days in Old Hawaii,* reviewed XXXVII, 224–225

Mruck, Armin, and Arnold Blumberg, "An Austrian View of the United States Navy: 1867," XXXIV, 59–64

"Much Ado about Nothing," document contributed by Captain Edgar K. Thompson, U.S.N. (ret.), XXIV, 185

Muckleroy, Keith, *Discovering a Historic Wreck,* reviewed, XLII, 227

Mudge, Benjamin, XLIX, 36

Mufti, merchantman, XXXII, 97

Mugford, Robert (shipbuilder), XXIV, 39, 58

Mugford, Captain William, XLVI, 17

Muhammad, Sidi, Emperor of Morocco, XLI, 208

Muir, Thomas, XIX, 133–134

Muir, Captain William, XXI, 98

Muise, Captain John A., XXV, 243

Mukilteo, steam schooner *(1927),* VII, 293
Mulcahy, A., XXXVI, 232
Mullany, Captain J. R., XXI, 98
Mullen, A. T. E., XXXVI, 200
Muller, John, XLVII, 108
Muller, Norman E., "Beyond Cape Horn: The Voyage of the Ship *Minerva* October 1799-September 1802," XXXIII, 160–173
Mullings, Captain H. A., XXI, 98
Mullins, William, XIV, 6
Mullowney, Second Lieutenant John, L, 245 ff.
Mumford, William, XLII, 45
München, German weather ship *(1941),* XLV, 54
Mundy, Vice-Admiral Sir George R., XXVIII, 111
Munger, James F., *Two Years in the Pacific and Arctic Oceans and China, Being a Journal of .. a Whaling Voyage,* reviewed, XXVIII, 74
Munk, George, XV, 211
Munro, Daniel George, XXVI, 204
Munro, George C., VIII, 186–191
Munro, R. M., XXX, 198
Munroe, James, XIII, 239
Munson, Cora Mallory, XLV, 41 ff.
Munson, Drs. Eneas and Elijah, L, 98
Munson, Frank C. *See* Frank C. Munson Institute of Maritime Studies
Munson, Frank C., Institute of American Maritime History, Mystic (CT), XXV, 100
Munson, Frank C., XLV, 41 ff.
Munson Institute. *See* Frank C. Munson Institute of Maritime Studies
Munson Steamship Lines, XLV, 41 ff.
Muravyev, Count Nikolai N., XXXI, 268
Murchison, Sir Roderick, VII, 84
Murdaugh, Lieutenant, XXXI, 13
Murdaugh, Lieutenant William H., XLVIII, 99
Murden, Captain E. O., XXI, 98
Murder at sea, XVI, 180
"Murder at Sea," by R. C. Holmes, XVI, 180–188
Murders at Sea, VIII, 173–174
Murdoch, Richard K., "The Battle of Orleans, Massachusetts (1814) and Associated Events," XXIV, 172–182; "Intelligence Reports of British Agents in the Long Island Sound Area, 1814–1815," XXIX, 187–198
Murdock, John, XXXIX, 11
Murdock, William, XIII, 158
Murello, bark (1847), III, 68, 265
Murfett, Malcolm H., "An Old Fashioned Form of Protectionism: The Role Played by British Naval Power in China from 1860–1941," L, 178–191; "'Splice the mainbrace': The Story of a Naval Epic," L, 291–301; "What a Difference a Day Makes: The Royal Navy and the Yangtse Incident of 20–21 April 1949," XLIX, 208–225
Muriel M. Young, schooner (1906), XXVI, plate XXI
Murillo, bark *(1855),* XXIV, 142

Murilo Island, XXXIV, 254
Murion, French warship [model] (1798), XVI, 102
Murphy, Captain John, XXI, 98
Murphy, John McLeod, XXX, 43
Murphy, Robert C., XXX, 158, 160, 163–166
Murphy, Consul Robert C., XXXIV, 105 ff.
Murphy, Robert Cushman, *A Dead Whale or a Stove Boat,* reviewed, XXVIII, 72–73; *Logbook for Grace,* reviewed, X, 77
Murray, Commodore Alexander, XLVI, 163; L, 270 ff.
Murray, Dian, "Commerce, Crisis, Coercion: The Role of Piracy in Late Eighteenth and Early Nineteenth Century Sino-Western Relations," XLVIII, 237–242
Murray, James D., U.S.N., XXXIX, 120
Murray, Captain James M., XXI, 106
Murray, John, VII, 66; XLVI, 155
Murray, Captain John, XXI, 106
Murray, Captain L. M., XXI, 98
Murray, William Vans, XXXVI, 60
Murrow, Stephenson and Co., XXXIV, 19
Mursa, steamship *(1929),* IX, 226
Muscogee, steamship (1848), XLVII, 36
Muscoota, bark *(1918),* XVIII, 170; *(1921),* I, 397
Muscoota, iron side-wheeler *(1864),* XLVIII, 124
Muscovy Co., XXVII, 180; XXVIII, 241–247, 255, 257
"Musée de la Marine, Le," by R. C. Anderson, XVII, 65–66
Musée de la Marine (Paris, France), XIV, 188
"Musée de la Marine, Paris, Le," by H. Philip Spratt, XVI, 98–106, plates 9, 10
Musée Naval de Toulon (Toulon, France), XX, 234
Museo Correr (Venice, Italy), XX, 233
Museo della Scienza e della Tecnia (Milan, Italy), XX, 233
Museo di Storia della Scienza (Florence, Italy), XX, 232
Museo Naval de Madrid (Madrid, Spain), XV, 49–58, plates 3–8; XX, 235
"Museo Naval de Madrid, El," by H. Philip Spratt, XV, 49–58, plates 3–8
Museo Storico Navale (Venice, Italy), XX, 232–233
Museum and Art Gallery, Sunderland, XXX, 153
Museum of Fine Arts (Boston, MA), XVII, 87
Museum of Science and Engineering (Newcastle-upon-Tyne, UK), XXX, 153
Museum of the American China Trade. *See* China Trade Museum
Museums. *See also* Marine museums; names of individual museums
Museums, libraries, and maritime collections:
   Addison Gallery (Andover, MA)
   Adirondack Museum (Blue Mountain Lake, NY)
   American Museum of Natural History (NYC)
   Art Gallery & Museum (Glasgow, Scotland)
   Barnum Museum (Bridgeport, CT)
   Bath (ME) Marine Museum
   Bishop Museum (Honolulu, HI)
   Boston Athenæum (Boston, MA)

Bostonian Society (Boston, MA)
Bourne Whaling Museum (New Bedford, MA)
Brady Collection, National Archives (Washington, DC)
Brick Store Museum (Kennebunk, ME)
Brixham Museum
Broughty Castle Museum
Buckler's Hard Maritime Museum (Gt. Britain)
Calvert Marine Museum (Solomons, MD)
Chesapeake Bay Maritime Museum (St. Michaels, MD)
China Trade Museum (Milton, MA)
Columbia River Maritime Museum (Astoria, OR)
Erie Canal Museum (Syracuse, NY)
Essex Institute, Salem (MA)
Exeter Maritime Museum
Fogg Museum of Art (Cambridge, MA)
Forbes (Captain R. B.) House, Milton (MA)
Francis Russel Hart Nautical Museum (M.I.T., Cambridge, MA)
Jonathan Bourne Whaling Museum. *See* Bourne Whaling Museum
Kendall Whaling Museum (Sharon, MA)
Kingston-upon-Hull Maritime Museum (Gt. Britain)
Manitoba Museum (Canada)
Manx Museum
Marine Historical Association / Mystic Seaport (Mystic, CT)
Marine Museum of the City of New York (New York, NY)
Marine Museum of the Old State House (Boston, MA)
Marine Museum of Upper Canada (Canada)
Mariners' Museum, The (Newport News, VA)
Maritime Museum (Genoa, Italy)
Maritime Museum of British Columbia (Canada)
Maritime Museum of Canada (Canada)
Maritime Museum of the Zagreb Yugoslav Academy of Science and Arts at Dubrovnik (Yugoslavia)
Maryland Historical Society (MD)
Massachusetts Archives (Boston, MA)
Massachusetts Institute of Technology (Cambridge, MA)
Metropolitan Museum of Art (New York, NY)
Musée de la Marine (Paris, France)
Musée Naval de Toulon (Toulon, France)
Museo Correr (Venice, Italy)
Museo della Scienza e della Tecnia (Milan, Italy)
Museo di Storia della Scienza (Florence, Italy)
Museo Naval de Madrid (Madrid, Spain)
Museo Storico Navale (Venice, Italy)
Museum and Art Gallery, Sunderland
Museum of Fine Arts (Boston, Massachusetts)
Museum of Science and Engineering (Newcastle upon-Tyne, Gt. Britain)
Museum of the American China Trade. *See* China Trade Museum

Mystic Seaport Museum. *See also* Frank C. Munson Institute of Maritime Studies
Nantucket Whaling Museum (Nantucket, MA). *See* Nantucket Historical Association and Whaling Museum
National Archives (Washington, DC)
National Maritime Museum (Greenwich, England)
Naval Historical Foundation (Washington, DC)
Naval Museum of Venice
Nemi Museum
New Bedford Whaling Museum (New Bedford, MA)
New Brunswick Museum
New York Historical Society (New York, NY)
Norsk Sjofartsmuseum (Oslo, Norway)
Old Dartmouth Historical Society (New Bedford, MA)
Parc Borély Museum (Marseilles, France)
Peabody Essex Museum (Salem, MA)
Peabody Museum of Salem (Salem, MA)
Peale Museum (Baltimore, MD)
Penobscot Marine Museum (Searsport, ME)
Philadelphia Maritime Museum (Philadelphia, PA)
Pilgrim Hall Museum (Plymouth, MA)
Pilot House Museum, The
Plimouth Plantation (Plymouth, MA)
Portsmouth (VA) Naval Shipyard Museum
Prins Hendrick Museum
Radcliffe Maritime Museum of the Maryland Historical Society
Reales Atarazanas (Barcelona, Spain)
Rijksmuseum (Amsterdam, Holland)
Rothesay Museum, Bournemouth (Gt. Britain)
Royal Scottish Museum (Scotland)
San Francisco Maritime Museum (CA)
San Francisco Museum of Science and Industry (CA)
San Martino Museum (Naples, Italy)
Scheepvaart Museum (Netherlands)
Science Musem (Boston, MA)
Science Museum (London, England)
Scottish Fisheries Museum (Anstruther, Scotland)
Shelburne Museum
Shipyard Museum of Norfolk Naval Shipyard (Norfolk, VA)
Smithsonian Institution (Washington, DC)
South Street Seaport Museum (New York, NY)
Statens Sjöhistoriska Museum (Stockholm, Sweden)
Truxton-Decatur House, naval museum
Tudor House Museum (Southampton, Gt. Britain)
U.S. Coast Guard Museum (New London, CT)
U.S. National Museum (Washington, DC)
U.S. Naval Academy Museum (Annapolis, MD)
U.S. Navy Department, Office of Naval Records and Library
U.S. Navy Memorial Museum
Victory Museum
Wadsworth Athenaeum (Hartford, CT)

Webb Institute of Naval Architecture
Whitby Museum
Wool House Museum (Southampton, Gt. Britain)
Museums, marine. *See* Marine museums; Museums, libraries, and maritime collections; and names of individual museums
Museums, naval. *See* Marine museums; Museums, libraries, and maritime collections; and names of individual museums
Musgrove, H. E. (edited by Philip G. Rose), *U.S. Naval Ships Data Arranged by Hull Classification,* Vol. I, reviewed, XXXVIII, 149 (review reprinted, L, 71–72)
Musham, H. A., III, 354; V, 91; "The Battle of the Windmill and Afterward, 1838–1842," VIII, 37–60; "The *Caroline* Affair, 1837–1838," VII, 298–314, plates 37–38; "Early Great Lakes Steamboats" series: [Part I] "The Chicago Line, 1838–1839," XVIII, 273–300; [Part II] "Hard Times and the Erie Disaster, 1840–1841," XX, 79–103; [Part III] "The Last Years of the Hard Times, 1842–1843," XX, 250–269; [Part IV] "The First Propellers, 1841–1845," XVII, 89–104; "Early Great Lakes Steamboats 1816 to 1830," VI, 194–211, plates 29–30; "Early Great Lakes Steamboats: The *Ontario* and the *Frontenac,*" III, 333–344; "Early Great Lakes Steamboats: The *Walk-in-the-Water,*" V, 27–42; "Warships and Iron Hulls, 1841–1846," VIII, 132–149, plates 15–16; "Westward Ho! and Flush Times, 1831–1837," VII, 42–65, plates 5–6
Music. *See* Sea Songs
Musk, George, *Canadian Pacific: The Story of a Famous Shipping Line,* reviewed, XLII, 223
Musketoe, brig *(1777),* XLIII, 24
Muskingon, bark (1845), VII, 317
Muskingum, bark (1845), I, 50
Muskoka, bark *(1907),* XVIII, 16
Musley, vessel, XXVI, 59
Musquash Cove, XXXI, 24
Mustang, sloop *(1862),* XII, 57
Mute, submarine (1815), VI, 267–268
Mutine, French ship *(1800),* XXXI, 174
Mutine, H.M.S., XXVIII, 107
Mutiny, XV, 59; XXI, 110; XXVII, 46, 98
"Mutiny, The Imaginary, on *Sabine,*" document contributed by Charles J. Zibulka, XXV, 68
Mutiny and Romance in the South Seas: A Companion to the Bounty *Adventure,* by Sven Wahlroos, reviewed, L, 72
Mutiny in bark *B. Hilton,* III, 124–127
"Mutiny on *Junior,*" by Sheldon H. Harris, XXI, 110–129
"Mutton Spankers and Ringtail Topsails," by Captain P. A. McDonald, V, 235–239
Mutual, bark (1861), II, 246
Mutual Marine Insurance Co., XXXIII, 60
Myatt, Captain Edward, XXI, 98

Myatt, Lieutenant Colonel James, Sir Hugh Forbes, Sir Maurice Laing *et al., 1979 Fastnet Race Inquiry,* reviewed, XL, 149
Myddelton, Hugh, XXXVII, 177
My Dear Husband, by Genevieve M. Darden, reviewed, XLI, 70
Myers, Captain A. L., XXI, 98
Myers, C. A., answered query, VIII, 71
Myers, Captain Harry, XIII, 128 ff.
Myers, Mark and John Harland, *Seamanship in the Age of Sail,* XLVII, 187
Myers, Moses, XXX, 136
Myers, Ramon, XLVIII, 262
"My Last Voyage on the Coast of Peru," by Captain Ambrose H. Burrows, VII, 282–287
My Name is Frank, by Frank Laskier, reviewed, II, 354
"My One Trip Playing Boatswain," by John C. Bower, Jr., XXXVI, 101–107
Myra D. Spear, schooner (1888), XXVII, plate XXV
Myrtle, ship *(1804),* XLI, 229
Myrtle (II), steamship (1910), XII, 292, 293
Mysteries of Easter Island, by Francis Mazière, reviewed, XXX, 73
"Mystery of Banks's Baton," by Thomas Dunbabin, XVI, 62
Mystery Ship: The Mary Celeste *in Fancy and Fact,* by George S. Bryan, reviewed, II, 256
Mystic, sloop, XXV, 108
Mystic, steamship (1852), XII, 288, 293, plate 26
Mystic Seaport (Mystic, CT), XV, 4; XXIV, 4; XXV, 99–111, plates 5–8; XVI, 3; XIX, 138–139. *See also* Marine Historical Association, Inc.
Mystic Seaport Museum (Mystic, CT), XLV, 41; **Library collections,** XXV, 99. See also Frank C. Munson Institute of Maritime Studies; Marine Historical Association, Inc.
Mystic Seaport Museum, *Maritime Titles in Print,* XXXIX, 62
Mystic Seaport Museum Watercraft, by Maynard Bray, reviewed, XL, 66–67
Myth, yacht *(1893),* XXXVI, 237–239

N

N. A., sloop, XXIV, 100, plate 14
N. B. Palmer, ship (1850), III, 262; (1851), XIX, plate XXIII
N. D. Chase, whaleship *(1854),* L, 123
N. M. Haven, bark (1862), IV, 242
N. S. & G. Griswold, XXXI, 141
N. V. Scheepsbouwerft de Merwede vorheen van Vliet & Co., XXXII, 9
Nabby, brig, XXII, 93

Nabby, sloop *(1784)*, XLI, 168
Nabob, brig (1830), XIX, 26–28, 38; *(1833)*, V, 194–202
Nagasaki Maru, steamship *(1864)*, XLIII, 106 ff.
Nagle, Richard, XXXI, 98
Nagle Journal: A Diary of the Life of Jacob Nagle, Sailor, from the Year 1775 to 1841, The, edited by John C. Dann, reviewed, L, 65
Nagoya Maru, steamship *(1875)*, XVII, 313, 314
Nahant, gunboat *(1863)*, XLII, 196 ff.; XLIV, 268 ff.
Nahant, steamship (1878), Pictorial Supplement, XXXIV, plate XV
Nahant, U.S. monitor (1862), X, 17, 23, 24, 30, 31
Nahant (MA), ca. 1830, XXIX, 198, plate XVIII
"Nahant Canoe," query by G. B. Porter, III, 177; answered by H. I. Chapelle, III, 353
Nahant Steamboat Co., ship of, Pictorial Supplement, XXXIV, plate XV
Nahum Chapin, schooner (1882), XXXV, 6
Nahum Stetson, brig, XXI, 98; *(1861)*, XI, 286
Naiad, British warship *(1847)*, L, 33
Nairn, schooner *(1861)*, VIII, 220
Nalou, XXX, 179
Naltose, yacht, XXXVI, 248
Nalty, Bernard C., Dennis L. Noble, and Truman R. Strobridge, editors, *Wrecks, Rescues & Investigations: Selected Documents of the U.S. Coast Guard and its Predecessors*, reviewed, XLIII, 143–145
Nalty, Bernard C., and Truman R. Strobridge, "Mission to Peking, 1870: Captain McLane Tilton's Letter Describing his Trip with the Seward Party to Peking," XXV, 116–122
Nama island, XXXIV, 254
Namaqualand, steamship *(1919)*, XIV, 135
Names. *See also* Language
Names, geographic, IX, 83
"Names and Numbers: Statistical Notes on Some Port Records of Colonial North Carolina," by Joseph Goldenberg, XXIX, 155–166
Names of Ships, *See* Ship names
"Naming a Generation of Cunarders," by R. Wayne Anderson, XLII, 295–300
Namsenfjord, motor ship, XXII, 157, 158
Namur, 1838, photo of, L, 172
Nancy, auxiliary (1918), XXXII, plates 4, 21, 30
Nancy, bark (1867), V, 149
Nancy, brig, XXII, 93; *(1775)*, XXXIX, 193; *(1778)*, X, 282
Nancy, British privateer *(1798)*, XLV, 94 ff.
Nancy, knockabout (1892), XXX, 195, 196
Nancy, Salem sloop *(1794)*, XLI, 173; XLV, 171
Nancy, schooner (1819), XXXIV, 243; *(1879)*, XXVIII, 32
Nancy, ship, XIII, 121; *(1804)*, IV, 97–98
Nancy, sloop, XXIV, 135; *(1799)*, XXXV, 208; *(1807)*, X, 147, 148
Nancy, yacht *(1900)*, XXXVI, 240
Nancy and Sally, sloop (1752), XXXI, 22
Nancy Ann, brig (1809), Pictorial Supplement, XXXII, plate XVII
Nancy Hanks, schooner (1917), XXVII, plate XXVI
Nancy L. Wasson, fishing schooner *(1853)*, XLIV, 83
Nandi, steamship (1943), XIV, 135
Nanepashemet, harbor ferry, XXX, 195 f.
Nanina, brig (1802), VII, 317
Naniwa-Kan, Japanese cruiser *(1886)*, XXXIX, 137
Nankin (1861), XXXIV, 32
Nankin, H.M.S., XXII, 33, 34, 36
Nankin, steamship *(1861)*, XLIII, 186 ff.
Nanking, steamship (1873), XVI, 262; XVII, 39; XVIII, 71; *(1880)*, XLVIII, 127
Nan Nan, steamship *(1863)*, XII, 159, 232
Nan-Nan, steamship, XXI, 96, 99
Nannie May, bugeye schooner, XXXVII, 166
Nantasket, steamship (1857), XII, 288, 293
Nantasket, surfboat *(1887)*, XXXVII, 83 ff.; in The Mariners Museum, XXXVII, plate 3, 83 ff.
Nantucket, gunboat *(1863)*, XLII, 196 ff.; XLIV, 268 ff.
Nantucket, light-vessel *(1862)*, V, 245
Nantucket, ship *(1839)*, XII, 35
Nantucket, U.S. monitor (1862), X, 17, 23, 24, 31
Nantucket, U.S.S. *(1918)*, XX, 139
Nantucket Island (MA). See Steamboats
Nantucket Historical Association and Whaling Museum, Nantucket (MA), VI, 137, 234, 235, plate 19
Nantucket Island (MA), I, 409–410
Nantucket Steamboat Co., XXIV, 140
Nanzing, steamship *(1862)*, XLIII, 193 ff.
Naparima, steamship (1890), XII, plate 31
Napier, brig *(1862)*, VIII, 226
Napier, schooner *(1861)*, VIII, 220
Napier, Admiral Sir Charles, XIII, 157 ff.
Napier, David, XXII, 44; XXXVII, 231
Napier, Lieutenant Henry, XLV, 5–9
Napier, John, XXXVII, 178
Napier, Lord, XLVIII, 280 ff.
Napier, Rob, "The Ship *Sooloo* (II) of Salem 1861–1887: History and Research for Building a Model," XLVII, 119–137
Napier, Robert, XXVI, 28
Napier's Bones, English, Pictorial Supplement, XXXV, plate XXXI
Napolean, brig *(1854)*, XLV, 25
Napoleon, bark (1871), V, 150
Napoleon, schooner *(1861)*, XV, 115; *(1862)*, VIII, 226
Napoleon, ship *(1861)*, XV, 124
Napoleon III, Emperor of France, XXXIII, 11
Napoleon Bonaparte, XXV, 5, 11, 15, 158; XXX, 293
Napoletano (ex-*City of Chester*), Pictorial Supplement, XXXIV, plate X
Napoléon, French warship [model] (1850), XVI, 103
Naptha launch, XXVI, 48, plate 6
Narcissus, frigate *(1814)*, XLII, 111 ff.; XLIV, 171
Narragansett, U.S.S. *(1861)*, XXVII, 43, 44
Narragansett, U.S. warship *(1961)*, XXXIII, 42 ff.

Narrative of Joshua Gee of Boston, Mass., While he was Captive in Algeria of the Barbary Pirates, 1680–1687, reviewed, IV, 79
Narwhal, steam bark *(1892),* XXXVIII, 84
Narwhal, whaler *(1891),* XLIV, 16 ff.
Nascopie, ship, XXV, 175; *(1933),* L, 35 ff.
Nash, Captain Charles I., XVI, 182–184
Nash, Howard P., Jr., "A Civil War Legend Examined," XXIII, 197–203; *The Forgotten Wars,* reviewed, XXIX, 70–71
Nash, Lonson, XIII, 269 ff.
Nash, Hon. Lonson, XLVI, 213
Nashville, C.S.S. warship *(1861),* XXXIII, 59
Nashville, ship *(1899),* XXXV, 191; *(1903),* XXXVII, 254
Nashville, steamship, XXI, 86, 92, 98; *(1853),* XLVIII, 114; *(1861),* VIII, 220, 226; XXXVI, 187; *(1862),* XV, 110, 126
Nashville International Migration Steamship Co., The, XXXV, 203
NASOH (North American Society for Oceanic History); comments, XXXVII, 80; XXXIX, 157
Nassau, ship *(1836),* L, 32; *(1875),* XXXIII, 61
Nassau, steamship, XXI, 95, 96; *(1861),* VIII, 220, 226; XI, 154
Nassau, whaler *(1865),* XXVII, 276
"Nassau, in the Bahamas; The American Invasion of," by John J. McCusker, Jr., XXV, 188–217, plates 21, 22
Nastyface, Jack, XXX, 299
Natal, British shipping line, XLVI, 108
Natchez, schooner *(1833),* XXXIV, 194; XXXV, 208; *(1838),* XXXVIII, 59
Natchez, ship *(1850),* XII, 107
Natchez, steamship *(1814),* VI, 266
Natchez, U.S. ship *(1836),* VII, 18
"Nathaniel Bowditch," by Harold Bowditch, V, 99–110
"Nathaniel Hawthorne and the Museum of the East India Marine Society," by Charles E. Goodspeed, V, 266–285
"Nathaniel Hilton's Indenture," document contributed by Ernest S. Dodge, XV, 155
Nathaniel P. Banks, steamship *(1863),* XII, 288, 293, plate 27
Nathaniel T. Palmer, schooner *(1898),* XX, 239–241; XXIII, 13; *(1899),* V, 79 ff., 138
"Nathaniel T. Palmer's Fleet of Great Schooners," by George A. Billias, XX, 237–242
Nathaniel Taylor, schooner, *(1862),* VIII, 226
Nath'l Winsor and Co., XLVII, 121
National, ship *(1858),* II, 332
National Academy of Sciences, Announcement, XXVI, 95
National Archives (Washington, DC), III, 48
National Archives, Washington, D. C., I, 98–99, 149–158, 165–166, 188, 275–294; III, 239, plates 23, 34; V, 7, plates 1, 2; VI, 138–139, 254–255, plate 20; VII, 66, 67–69, 318, plate 7; VIII, 16, 239–241, plates 7, 17, 18; IX, plates 17–20
National Bulk Lines, XXXII, 193
National College at Margarita, XXX, 275
National Fisheries Co., The, XLIV, 119
National Geographic Atlas of the World, by Melville Bell Grosvenor, Editor-in-Chief and James M. Darley, Chief Cartographer, reviewed, XXIII, 288
National Guard, The, XXXIII, 261 ff.
National Historic Landmarks: Sandy Hook Lighthouse, dedication as, XXV, 79
National Maritime Historical Society, Washington, D. C., XXV, 232
National Maritime Museum (Greenwich, England), VIII, 15, plates 1–6; XIII, 177; XIX, 146–147; XXVIII, 3; XXX, 153; XXXIII, 229; XXXV, 75; Admiralty Collection, VIII, 15, plates 1–6
National Maritime Museum (Greenwich, England), *The Opening of the Pacific – Image and Reality,* reviewed, XXXII, 146–147, 229
National Maritime Museum Catalogue of Ship Models, Part I: Ships of the Western Tradition to 1815, by A. H. Waite, reviewed, XLI, 148–149
National Observatory, U.S., Washington, XXV, 93 ff.
National Trust for Historic Preservation, editorial comment, XXXVII, 3–4; *Maritime Titles in Print,* XXXIX, 65
National Watercraft Collection, The, Washington, D. C., XXV, 91
National Watercraft Collection, Second Edition, The, by Howard I. Chapelle, reviewed, XXXVII, 73–74
National Waterway: A History of the Chesapeake and Delaware Canal, 1769–1985, The, by Ralph D. Gray, reviewed, L, 147
Nation of Nantucket, The, by Edward Byers, XLVIII, 188
Native, bark *(1853),* XLV, 189
Natuna Islands, XXX, 201
Nau, Lambert, IX, 229–230
Naugatuck, gunboat *(1862),* X, 21
Naugatuck, steamship *(1861),* XX, 155–166
Naul, Arthur P. S., XLI, 191
Naum Keag, bark *(1855),* XX, 130
Naushon Island Quadrangle, U.S.C. & G.S. map of, XXXIII, plate 6; photos of, XXXIII, plates 7 and 8
Nautical ABC's from Wasson's sketch book, XXII, plates 10, 11, 12
Nautical charts, I, 149; XXI, 260; XLVI, 173
  History, XVII, 28
  New York, XIX, 44
"Nautical Doodles," by Francis W. Hatch, XXIII, 39–40
"Nautical Grave, A," document contributed by Captain Edgar K. Thompson, U.S.N. (ret.), XXII, 186
Nautical instruments, I, 6, 123, 209; XIV, 161; XXI, 107; XXXIV, 197; XXXV, 111; XLVI, 258
Nautical instruments: nocturnal, I, 8; quadrant of 1527, I, 21

"Nautical Knowledge," note by Captain Edgar K. Thompson, U.S.N (ret.), XXIX, 173

Nautical Research Guild, XXVIII, 4

Nautical Research Journal, Vol. I, No. I, reviewed, IX, 155

Nautical terms. *See* Language, marine

Nautilus, bark (1858), V, 150

Nautilus, brig *(1803),* XIII, 277; *(1814),* XL, 288; *(1815),* XLIV, 171

Nautilus, H.M. Brig *(1852),* XXVI, 215

Nautilus, H.M. Sloop *(1775),* XXX, 89, 90, 110; *(1778),* VII, 204, 209

Nautilus, H.M. warship *(1775),* XXXVII, 292; XL, 11

Nautilus, river boat (1815), XXXIV, 188 ff.

Nautilus, ship *(1815),* XIX, 223, 224

Nautilus, ship (1856), IV, 240; V, 327; *(1870),* XXXVIII, 211 ff.

Nautilus, steamship (1864), XVI, 258, 259, 261

Nautilus, U.S.S. *(1958),* XX, 174

Navahoe, tank barge (1908), IV, 325

Navahoe (ex-*Thuringer*), steamship (1880), Pictorial Supplement, XXXIV, plate XVI

Naval Academy at Maracaibo, XXX, 275

"Naval Action on Lake Champlain, 1776," document contributed by Stephen H. P. Pell, VIII, 255–256

Naval apprentices at Coasters Harbor Island, 1885, photo of, XLIX, 299

Naval architects:
  Biography, XXXI, 52
  Library resources, XLVIII, 182

Naval architecture, IX, 161; XXVI, 157; XXXVIII, 170; XXXIX, 235; XLIV, 82
  17th century, XIII, 51
  History, XXX, 81

Naval Aristocracy: the Golden Age of Annapolis and the Emergence of Modern American Navalism, The, by Peter Karsten, reviewed, XXXIII, 67–68

Naval art and science, XLIX, 114
  History, Sources, L, 132
  Study and teaching, XXX, 40

Naval attachés, XXXIX, 126

"Naval Ballad of the War of 1812, A," edited by Kenneth Scott, VII, 167–169

Naval biography. *See under* titles or professions; e.g., Admirals; Commodores, Midshipmen, Ship captains, Shipowners

Naval convoys, XLIV, 48; L 42, 219

Naval Documents of the American Revolution, edited by William Bell Clark, reviewed: [Vol. I], XXVI, 72–73; [Vol. II], XXVII, 221–222; [Vol. III], XXIX, 287; [Vol. IV], XXX, 220–221

Naval Documents of the American Revolution, edited by William James Morgan; [Vol. V], reviewed, XXXI, 228–229; [Vol. VI], reviewed, XXXIV, 145–146; [Vol. VIII], reviewed, XLII, 71

Naval Documents Related to the United States Wars with the Barbary Powers, edited by Captain Dudley W. Knox; [Vol. III], reviewed, II, 341; [Vol. IV], reviewed, III, 180

Naval engagements, views of: Algiers (1815), III, plate 6; *Constellation* and *L'Insurgente* (1799), III, plate 2; Decatur's squadron and *Mashouda* (1815), III, plate 7; Fort McHenry bombardment (1814), III, plate 4; Lake Borgne, Louisiana (1814), III, plate 6; Lake Champlain (1776), III, plate 1; Lake Erie (1813), III, plate 3; *Phoenix* and *Rose* (1776), III, plate 1; *President* and *Endymion* (1815), III, plate 5; *President* and *Little Belt* (1811), III, plate 2; *United States* and *Macedonian* (1812), III, plate 3

Naval engagements: Battle of the Yalu (1894), VIII, 267–275; Defence of *Raleigh* (1778), I, 168–170; Fedhala, French Morocco (1942), III, 99–105; Guadeloupe Campaign (1759), VII, 21–34, plate 3; Lake Champlain (1776), VIII, 255–256; Penobscot Expedition (1779), VII, 200–212; Porto Praya (1781), V, 64–78; Yorktown (1781), V, 240–241

"Naval Experiment, A," by Linda McKee Maloney, XXXIV, 188–196

Naval gunnery, III, 11, 148; VI, 212; XXII, 280; XLI, 85

Naval guns: III, 11–18, 148–158; 1797–1843, XXXVI, 276–295

Naval Historical Foundation, Washington, D. C., IV, 78, 181, 217, 336; V, 91, 240, 244; VI, 153; VIII, 157–158; IX, 160, 237–238; XXVI, 79–80

Naval history, XLVII, 157

Naval history conferences, XLVIII, 178

Naval History Division, Department of the Navy, *The American Revolution 1775–1783; An Atlas of 18th Century Maps and Charts,* reviewed, XXXIV, 281

Naval hospitals. *See* Hospitals, naval and marine

"Naval Innovation in Crisis: War in the Chesapeake, 1813," by William L. Calderhead, XXXVI, 206–221

Naval language, IX, 5–10

Naval medals, II, 336–337

Naval Militia, XXXIII, 258

Naval Monument, The, Pictorial Supplement, XXXII, plate XXV

Naval Observatory, Washington, I, 150–152

Naval Museum of Venice, XV, 199

Naval museums. *See* Marine museums

"Naval Office in Virginia, 1776–1789, The," by Edmund Berkeley, Jr., XXXIII, 20–33

"Naval Operations in the Panama Revolution 1903," by John Nikol and Francis X. Holbrook, XXXVII, 253–261

"Naval Operations of the United States Pacific Squadron in 1861," by Mitchell S. Goldberg, XXXIII, 41–51

Naval ordnance, XXII, 280; XXXVI, 276; XLVII, 108; XLIX, 96. *See also* Ordnance

Naval Ordnance Instruction, 1852, illustration, XLVII, 113

Naval policy. *See* Sea control

Naval Policy, American: *1775–1776:* I, 26–41; *1777:* V, 177–193

Naval policy during Quasi-War, XXX, 117–132

"Naval Portrait," query by John Haskell Kemble, III, 177

Naval prints, III, 5–10, 93

"Naval Punishments after the Abolition of Flogging," document contributed by M. V. Brewington, V, 243–244

Naval Reserve Association, XXXIII, 269 ff.

Naval sabotage, XXVII, 185–201

Naval School, Fort Severn, Annapolis, Maryland, XXV, 140–141

"Naval Self Help," by Captain Edgar K. Thompson, U.S.N. (ret.), XXV, 143

"Naval Strategy in the First Genoese-Venetian War, 1257–1270," by John E. Dotson, XLVI, 84–90

Naval Surgeon: Blockading the South, 1862–1866; Naval Surgeon: Revolt in Japan 1868–1869, by Samuel P. Boyer, Elenor & James A. Barnes, editors, reviewed, XXV, 72–73

Naval tactics, XIX, 265; XLIV, 171

"Naval Technology During the American Civil War," by Dean C. Allard, XLIX, 114–122

"Naval Thought and Policy of Benjamin Stoddert, First Secretary of the Navy, 1798–1801, The," by Robert F. Jones, XXIV, 61–69

Naval timber, III, 239–249

Naval Training Station, Coasters Harbor Island, Newport, circa 1887, photo of, XLIX, 292

Naval War College, XXXII, 259 ff.; XXXIII, 262 ff.

Naval War of 1812: A Documentary History, The [Vol. I], edited by William S. Dudley, reviewed, XLVII, 214

Navassa Island. *See* West Indies

"Navarassa: A Forgotten Acquisition," by Captain Edgar K. Thompson, U.S.N. (ret.), XXVI, 171–176

Navarch, steam bark (1892), Pictorial Supplement, XXXIII, plate XVI; *(1894),* XXXVIII, 85

Navarino, steamship (1870), I, 76

Navarino, Battle of, XXX, 299

Navarrete, Martin Fernandez de, XV, 50

Navarro, Jose F., IV, 141 ff.

Navassa Island, IX, 63; XXVI, plate 17; Lighthouse, plate 18

Navassa Phosphate Co., XXVI, 172 ff.

"Navassa The First," by Edgar K. Thompson, IX, 63

Navesink, Highlands of, New Jersey, XXV, 123

Navicello, Mediterranean, I, 367–369

Navi e proprietá navale a Genova, seconda metá del sec. XII, by Hilmar C. Krueger, reviewed, XLVII, 216

Navies, Deterrence & American Independence: Britain and Seapower in the 1760s and 1770s, by Nicholas Tracy, reviewed, L, 143

Navigating Britain's Coastline, by Adrienne and Peter Oldale, reviewed, XLI, 234

Navigating instruments. *See* Nautical instruments. *See also* names of individual instruments, e.g., cross staff, sextant

Navigation:
  Andes Region, II, 107
  France, History, L, 165
  History, II, 107; VIII, 302; XVII, 28; XXV, 93, 176; XXVI, 157; XXXIV, 197; XXXV, 111; XLIV, 77, 186
  –, **15th century,** I, 6, 123, 209; XIX, 79, 123
  –, **16th century,** XXXVII, 174
  –, **17th century,** L, 5
  –, **18th century,** XX, 185; XXI, 5
  –, **19th century,** I, 149
  Instruction and teaching, XVI, 81
  Pacific Ocean, XXIII, 113
  Study and teaching, XX, 185.
  See also Latitude, Longitude

Navigation: XVII, 28–37; Columbus' celestial, I, 6–25, 123–137; Columbus' dead reckoning, I, 209–240; Oviedo on practical navigation, I, 391

Navigation in literature, XX, 174

Navigation Instruments: Back Staff, XXI, 107–109; Cross-staff, XIV, 187–191, plates 23, 24; patent log, XIV, 214; XI, 147–148

Navigation Acts of 1696, XXXVII, 263

Navigational Instruments, XXVIII, 144–145

Navigation Paquet (French shipping line), XLVI, 108

Navigation the Easy Way, by Carl D. Lane and John Montgomery, reviewed, IX, 306

Navigator, XXX, 41

Navigators, Biography, V, 99; XX, 185; XXI, 5

Navoni, Nicholas, VII, 191

Navy, Great Britain, XXVIII, 85–112; First American War, XI, 239–244; XIII, 212; Second American War, 1813, XVII, 203–211

Navy, Italy, XV, 199–204

Navy, Russia: 1863, XX, 49–61

Navy, Sweden, VI, 163–178

Navy, U.S.: Revolution, XIII, 29–50, XIV, 47–60, XV, 59–80; War of 1812, XI, 73–77; 1806, XVIII, 183; War of 1812, XVII, 203–211; XIX, 213–226; 1835, XX, 167–173; 1860, XX, 198–208; Civil War, XVI, 49–59; XVII, 249–261; XIX, 51–72, 126–128, 265–273; Confederate States, XV, 287–302; Civil War, XI, 262–290, XII, 52–59, 154–161, 229–238, 271–281, XV, 97–132, 287–302; Training Vessels, XX, 134–145

Navy, Uruguay, II, 170–171

"Navy Allowance Tables," by M. V. Brewington, V, 326–327

"Navy Blues," note contributed by Captain Edgar K. Thompson, U.S.N. (ret.), XXXVII, 144

"Navy Board and Merchant Shipowners, During the American War, 1776–1783, The," by David Syrett, XLVII, 5–13

Navy Board Contracts 1660–1832: Contract Administration under the Navy Board, by Bernard Pool, reviewed, XXVIII, 229–232
"Navy Board's Report to the Admiralty on the First Coppering Experiment," document contributed by Dorothy R. Brewington, I, 304–306
Navy Department, Bureau of Yards and Docks, VII, 67
Navy Department Communiques 601–624, reviewed, VIII, 74–75
Navy in Boston, The," lecture by Bettina A. Norton, Essex Institute; comment, Editorial, *The American Neptune,* XXXVIII, 3–4
"Navy in Korea, 1871, The," by H. A. Gosnell, VII, 107–114, plates 9–12
"Navy Justice in the Pacific, 1830–1870: a Pattern of Precedents," by E. Mowbray Tate, XXXV, 20–31
Navy League, XXXVII, 33
Navy Regulations, Continental Navy, XXV, 142
"Navy's Battle Doctrine in the War of 1812, The," by James E. Valle, XLIV, 171–178
"Navy's Campaign against the Licensed Trade in the War of 1812, The," by Michael J. Crawford, XLVI, 165–172
"Navy's Last Yardarm Hanging, The," note contributed by Captain Edgar K. Thompson, U.S.N. (ret.), XXIV, 212
Navy Yard, Brooklyn, N.Y., VI, plate 32
Navy Yard, Charlestown (MA), VII, 67–69
Nazareth, William, XVII, 294
NC. *See* North Carolina
NC-1, photos of: crew with plane at Rockaway Beach, XLVII, 251; in water before rescue, XLVII, 254; on Rockaway, November 1919, XLVII, 250; towed by destroyer *Gridley,* XLVII, 254
NC aircraft personnel for May 1919 flight, photo of, XLVII, 249
NC flight track chart, May 1919, XLVII, 252
Neafie and Levy, XXX, 277
Neagle, John, XVI, 234
Neagle, Pickens, XXXVII, 120
Nea-Kah-nie Mountain, XLI, plate 5
Neal, David A., XIII, 122
Neal, Captain E. M., XVIII, 84
Neal, Frank L., XIII, 121
Neal, James G., "The American Merchant Marine Library Association: The First Decade of Its Development, 1921–1930," XLI, 5–24
Neal, John, XXXI, 34
Neal, Captain William, XXV, 184
Nearchus, ship (1873), III, 71
Neatby, L. H., Editor, *Frozen Ships, The Arctic Diary of Johann Miertsching 1850–1854,* reviewed, XXIX, 65–67
Neath, ship (1906), VI, 135
Neave, T. D., XXII, 13

Neblett, Thomas R., "The Yacht *America:* A New Account Pertaining to Her Confederate Operations," XXVII, 233–253
Nebraska, steamship *(1873),* X, 132
"Necklace," query by Edwin Newell Rich, I, 171
Nederlandische Handel-Maatschappij, XXX, 30
Nederlandsche Vereenigimg van Assuradeuren, XXX, 29
Needham, Joseph, *Science and Civilisation in China:* Vol. 4, *Physics and Physical Technology;* Part III, *Civil Engineering and Nautics,* reviewed, XXXII, 148
Needles, sailmaker's, IX, 278–280
Negro pilots, Hart Line, VII, 146
Negus, Thomas S. and John D., Pictorial Supplement, XXXV, plate XXIV
Nehls, Captain J. F., XXI, 98
Neil, William, XXVII, 61–65
Neilson, Anthony B., XVII, 134
Neilson, Jon M., "Penobscot: From the Jaws of Victory—Our Navy's Worst Defeat," XXXVII, 288–305
Neilson, William, XVII, 47; XXXIV, 44
Nelia Covert, schooner, XXI, 88; *(1862),* VIII, 226
Nellie, schooner (1857), XXI, 304; *(1862),* XV, 126
Nellie, sloop, XXI, 88; *(1863),* VIII, 231
Nellie, yacht *(1891),* XXXVI, 235 ff.
Nellie Blair, schooner *(1863),* XII, 159
Nellie Grant, schooner (1873), IX, 171
Nellie J. Dinsmore, hermaphrodite brig (1872), XXIV, 43, 58
Nellie L. Byrd, bateau (1911), IV, 289
Nellie Mowe, brig (1860), XV, 186
Nellie Staples, hermaphrodite brig (1870), XXIV, 44, 58
Nellie Tarbox, schooner (1862), XV, 186
Nellie Troop, steel bark, XXXV, plate 3
Nelly, steamship, XXI, 97; *(1862),* VIII, 226
Nelly Ogilvie, British ship *(1776),* XLVIII, 19
Nelms, gunboat *(1862),* XLVIII, 94
Nelson, H.M.S. *(1942),* XXVII, 199
Nelson, ship, XXI, 1–3; *(1861),* XI, 286
Nelson, Captain Andrew, XXI, 98
Nelson, Captain Andrews, II, 291
Nelson, Chief Officer, VII, 40, 41
Nelson, George A., I, 177; "First Cruise of the Privateer *Harpy,* The," I, 116–122; answered query, I, 313; contributed document, II, 338
Nelson, Admiral Horatio, XXVI, 249
Nelson, Captain Horatio, XI, 239 ff.
Nelson, J. G., "Drift Voyages in the Pacific," XXIII, 113–130; contributed note, XXIII, 221–222; "The Geography of the Balsa," XXI, 157–195
Nelson, J. P., XXXVI, 235
Nelson, John, XXXV, 156
Nelson, Stewart B., *Oceonographic Ships and Aft,* reviewed, XXXII, 145–146
Nelson, William, XXXVI, 48
"Nelson in Boston Bay," by Gershom Bradford, XI, 239–244

Nelson Lumber Yard, XXX, 187
Nelson's Dear Lord: A Portrait of St. Vincent, by Evelyn Berckman, reviewed, XXIII, 73–74
Nelson's Last Diary, by Oliver Warner, reviewed, XXXII, 289
Nelson's Navy: The Ships, Men and Organization, 1793–1815, by Brian Lavery, reviewed, L, 148
Nemesis, side-wheel steamship *(1839),* XLVI, 58
Nemesis, steamship (1857), XVII, 142
Nemi Museum, XX, 231–232
Nepean, Sir Evan, XII, 255–256
"Neponset Estuary – 1898," by Llewellyn Howland, XI, 83–94
Neptun, bark (1864), III, 65
Neptune (1801), XXIII, 216
Neptune, bark (1870), III, 68; VI, 73
Neptune, brig *(1790),* XLIV, 6; *(1813),* XVII, 70; (1829), XIV, 40
Neptune, British ship *(1776),* XLVIII, 16
Neptune, C.S.A. *(1861),* XI, 272
Neptune, French warship, XXVI, 55
Neptune, gunboat *(1862),* XXXVI, 200
Neptune, S.S. *(1882),* XXXVI, 109
Neptune, schooner (1789), XXIX, 55; *(1864),* XII, 232
Neptune, sloop, XXI, 91; *(1863),* VIII, 231; *(1864),* XII, 232
Neptune, steamship, XXI, 96; (1836), XII, 148–153, plates 13–15; *(1863),* XII, 159
Neptune, vessel *(1763),* XXX, 203
Neptune, Father, ceremonies, XXXVI, 258
Neptune, King, XXV, 69
"Neptune's Court in Court," note by Captain Edgar K. Thompson, U.S.N. (ret.), XXX, 45
Neptune's Favorite, ship (1854), V, 149
Nequassett, steamship *(1851),* XV, 177
Nereus, steamship *(1871),* XXXVII, 235
Nereus, storeship *(1843),* L, 33
"'Nerves' of the New Navy, The," by Paolo E. Coletta, XXXVIII, 122–130
Nesbitt, William, XXXI, 32
Nesdall, Andrew J., reviews by, XLVIII, 62; XLIX, 310
Nesmith, Senator J. W., XXVIII, 134, 138
Nesselrode, Count (Russian Chancellor), XXXI, 56
Nestor, steamship (1868), XXIV, plate XI
Nesutan, ship (1863), III, 69
Netherlands. *See* Oceanography
Netherlands Trading Co., XXX, 30
Netherlands Trading Society, XXXIV, 51
Netherlands West Indies, XXXVI, 155–169
Nettie, schooner *(1864),* XII, 232
Nettie, sharpie *(1867),* III, 167–168, plate 23
Nettie, tug (1872), VI, 66
Nettie Dobbins, XXIV, 49
"Nettie, The," by Vernon D. Tate, III, 167–168
Netto, Captain Francisco, XXI, 98
Neudigate, ship *(1945),* XXXIX, 259
Neutrality, brig *(1807),* IX, 13

"Neutral Trade and the Order in Council of 7 January 1807," by Earle Field, XXIII, 157–173
Nevada, steamship *(1853),* XIV, 200; (1865), XVII, 312, 313; XVIII, 71; (1865–1867), II, 18; *(1873),* X, 132; (1890), XIV, 134
Nevers, Father Ephraim de, XIII, 11
Never Tell, schooner, XXI, 94; *(1862),* XII, 57
Neville, Christopher, XLIV, 26
Neville, L. C., XXXVI, 247
Nevins, Allan, *Sail On: The Story of the American Merchant Marine,* reviewed, VI, 236
Nevitt, Cedric Ridgely-. *See* Ridgeley-Nevitt, Cedric.
New American Practical Navigator, XXV, 48, 187
Newark, cruiser *(1888),* XXXIX, 136; *(1898),* XLI, 98
New Bedford (MA), X, 231–234, 243–248; XXII, plates X, XXIII; XXV, Plate VI. Ship registers of, I, 188
New Bedford, Vineyard, and Nantucket Steamboat Co., XIII, 120
New Bedford and New York Steam Propeller Co., XXXIX, 96 ff.
New Bedford and Old Dartmouth; a Portrait of a Region's Past, edited by Richard C. Kugler, reviewed, XXXVI, 149
New Bedford Free Public Library (New Bedford, MA), photo courtesy of, XXXIX, plates 1, 2
New Bedford Line, XXXIV, 258. *See also* Steamship lines
New Bedford Line, VII, 217; XXXIV, 259
New Bedford Whaling Museum, *Maritime Titles in Print,* XXXIX, 66. *See also* Bourne Whaling Museum
Newbern, steamship *(1871),* I, 258–259
Newbern, U.S.S. *(1862),* XXV, 72
Newberry, Oliver, VII, 49
Newberry, Truman, XXII, 191
Newberry, Walter L., XVIII, 274, 292
Newberryport, steamship (1829), VII, 47. *See also Newburyport.*
New Britain, XXX, 214
New Bunswick, U.S. steamship XXVIII, 124; (1860), XII, plate 29; (1861), XXXIII, 88, 94; XXXIV, 177
New Brunswick, shipbuilding in, XVII, 5–16
New Brunswick Museum, *Maritime Titles in Print,* XXXIX, 66
Newburgh, steamship, XVIII, 225
Newburgh Line, XVIII, 225
Newbury, C. W., Editor, *The History of the Tahitian Mission 1799–1830,* written by John Davies, reviewed, XXII, 74–75
Newburyport, ship *(1861),* XXI, 242, 258
Newburyport (MA), XVII, 114–127; XXV, 46, 47
Newburyport (MA) Marine Society, XXI, 12, 13
Newburyport Woolen Manufactory, XLVI, 143
New Caledonia, boats of, XIII, 97 ff.
Newcastle, bark *(1831),* XXIX, 91
Newcastle, British cruiser *(1915),* XXXVIII, 177
Newcastle, H.M.S. *(1717),* XXI, 262; *(1814),* XXIV, 172 ff.

Newcastle, schooner *(1862),* XII, 57
Newcastle (NH), XXX, 94, 98
Newce, Captain Thomas, XV, 96
Newce, Sir William, XV, 96
Newcomb, Henry K., XXXVIII, 267
Newcomb, Captain W. E., XVI, 168; XVIII, 84
Newcomen Society, III, 357
Newcomer, Lee Nathaniel, "The Battle of the Rams," XXV, 128–139
Newcomer, Professor Lee Nathaniel, XXXI, 52
New Eagle, sloop, XXI, 94; *(1862),* XII, 57
Newell, Gordon, *Paddlewheel Pirate: The Life and Adventures of Captain Ned Wakeman,* reviewed, XX, 72
Newell, Gordon R., *Ships of the Inland Sea,* reviewed, XI, 298–299
Newell, Dr. Robert, XXVIII, 129, 133
Newell, Robert R., "Capture and Burning of the Ship *Anna F. Schmidt* by *Alabama,* XXV, 18–28
Newell, Samuel, XLVIII, 273
Newell, Thomas Moore, XXXV, 233
New England, barkentine (ex-steamship *Cornubia,* ex-U.S.S. *Cornubia*) (1858), XXV, 112–115
New England, ship *(1834),* XII, 180; XV, 138, 139; *(1861),* XXI, 258
New England, steamship (1833), XIV, 192; (1837), VII, 63, 64, 65, 307; *(1838),* XVIII, 283, 290, 296, 298; XX, 89 n., 92, 103; *(1862),* XXXIII, 88, 94; *(1863),* XIX, 54; *(1872),* XXVIII, 125
New England, Discovery and exploration, XI, 95; XXV, 233. *See also* Boatbuilding; Connecticut; Ice trade; Maine; Massachusetts; New Hampshire; Privateering; Rhode Island; Shipping (United States); Steamboats; United States History; Yachting
New England & Nova Scotia Steamship Co., Pictorial Supplement, XXXIV, plate VIII
New England and The Sea, by Robert G. Albion, William A. Baker, Benjamin W. Labaree, Marion V. Brewington, reviewed, XXXIII, 63–64
New England and the South Seas, by Ernest S. Dodge, reviewed, XXVI, 147–148
New England Co. (shipyard), XXVII, plate XXIII
"New England Coasting Schooners," by Charles S. Morgan, XXIII, 5–21
"New England Double Enders, The," by David Cabot, XII, 123–141
New England Fish Co., XLIV, 116
New England fishing industry, XXVIII, 261–274
"New England Forests and British Seapower: Albion Revised," by R. J. B. Knight, XLVI, 221–229
New England Navigation Co., XXXVIII, 107; ship of, XXXIV, plate XXXII
"New England Seafaring Family, A," by Dohn A. Cluff, XIX, 140
New England's Fishing Industry, by Edward A. Ackerman, reviewed, II, 261

New England Steamship Co., XXXIX, 107
New Era, ship, XXXVI, 176
Newfield, bark *(1893),* VI, 77
New Found Land, The: The English Contribution to the Discovery of North America, by David Beers Quinn, reviewed, XXV, 299
Newfoundland, Discovery and exploration, XXXIII, 174; XXXVII, 157. *See also* Canada
Newfoundland trade, XXVIII, 262, 272, 275–283
"Newfoundland Trade: The Decline and Demise of the Port of Poole, 1815–1894, The," by Peter Perry, XXVIII, 275–283
New France. *See* Canada
New Galen, ship *(1807),* XVI, 193
New Granada, iron paddle steamship *(1847),* XXXV, 272; *(1856),* XI, 52
New Guinea, XXX, 214; boats of, XIII, 87
Newhall, Beaumont, review by, I, 320–321; "Fishing Craft of Manfredonia," XII, 240, plates 23, 24
New Hampshire, steamship *(1913),* VII, 217–221, plate 25; *(1914),* XXXIII, 279
New Hampshire, U.S. flagship (1885), photo of, XLIX, 292; *(1900),* XX, 137
New Hampshire (NH). *See* Merrimac River; Piscataqua River
New Hampshire Historical Society, VII, 167–169, 201 n. ff.
"New Hampshireman Transports Spanish Troops to Oran — 1732, A," by Lawrence Waters Jenkins, VI, 179–193
"New Hampshire's Part in the Penobscot Expedition," by Kenneth Scott, VII, 200–212
Newhaven, gondola *(1776),* VIII, 256
New Haven, gondola *(1779),* XXXV, 142
New Haven Colony Historical Society, Pictorial Supplement, XXXII, plates XXI-XIV
New Hazard, ship *(1810),* XLVI, 44
New Hebrides, boats of, XIII, 89
New Idea, sloop (1954), XXIV, 99, plate 13
"New Information on Ships Built by Donald McKay," by Bruce M. Lane and C. Gardner Lane, XLII, 118–137
New Ironsides, U.S. frigate (1861), X, 16, 22, 24, 27, 29, 31; (1862), XXII, 255, 260, 262; *(1863),* XXXI, 264; XXXV, 61; XLVIII, 31; XLIX, 117; *(1864),* XXVII, 43, 44; *(1865),* XLII, 94 ff., 196 ff.; XLIV, 268 ff.
New Island, schooner *(1862),* XII, 57
New Jersey (1800), XXIII, 216
New Jersey, gunboat *(1782),* XXXIX, 217
New Jersey, ship *(1805),* XVII, 72
New Jersey, steam tug *(1839),* XII, 149
New Jersey (NJ):
  History, Colonial period (ca. 1600–1775), XXXVII, 262;
  —, **Revolution (1775–1788),** XXXIX, 209
  See also Customs administration; Harbors; Shipbuilding; Steamboats

New Jersey, saw millers and shipbuilders of, XXXVI, 251–256
"New Light on Ancient Rigging and Boatbuilding," by Lionel Casson, XXIV, 81–94
"New Light on *Flying Cloud* versus *Andrew Jackson*," by John Lyman, VIII, 326–328
"New Light on the Earliest American Voyages to Australia," by Thomas Dunbabin, X, 52–64
"New Light on the Evolution of the Chesapeake Clipper-Schooner," by Arthur Pierce Middleton, IX, 142–147
New Liverpool, brig *(1812)*, XXI, 20
New London, steamship *(1865)*, XXXIX, 96
New London, U.S.S. *(1864)*, XI, 275
New London, vessel *(1862)*, XXXVI, 202
New London Ship and Engine Co., XLIV, 129
Newman, Edwin B. and Augustus P. Loring, "Some Notes on the Paper of the *Atlantic Neptune*," XLVI, 173–178
Newman, Harry Shaw, VII, 249; IX, 150
Newman, John, VII, 64
Newman, Commandant Timothy, L, 245 ff.
New Mayflower, The, by William A. Baker, reviewed, XIX, 149
New Mexico, U.S. battleship (1918), XXIV, 205
Newnham, Captain William, XXVI, 54
New Orleans, cruiser *(1898)*, XLI, 105
New Orleans, ship *(1861)*, XI, 286
New Orleans, sloop, XXI, 88; *(1861)*, XI, 286
New Orleans, steamship (1811), XIV, 114; XVI, 31 ff.; *(1814)*, VI, 266
New Orleans, steamship (1848), XVII, 300; *(1902)*, XXXVIII, 183 ff.
New Orleans, U.S.S. *(1918)*, VII, 72
New Orleans, U.S. ship of the line (1814), VIII, 56
New Orleans II, steamship (1815), XVI, 34
Newport, centerboard schooner (1885), I, 73
Newport, steam barkentine *(1892)*, XXXVIII, 84
Newport, steamship (1875), XXIV, 197; *(1886)*, X, 137, 142
Newport, transport *(1899)*, XXXV, 185
Newport, U.S.S. (1897), XX, 142
Newport, whaler *(1891)*, XLIV, 16 ff.
Newport, Captain Christopher, XV, 96; XVII, 173
Newport (RI), ship registers, I, 410
Newport Naval Training Station (RI), XLIX, 291
Newport News, steamship *(1925)*, XVI, 130; XVIII, 214
Newport News (VA), XXV, 224
Newport News Shipbuilding and Dry Dock Co., I, 188, 325, 396; II, 94; III, 274; VIII, 68, 76; XVII, 174; XXIX, 233; XXXVIII, 187 ff.; XLI, 193; XLII, 249
Newport News Shipbuilding and Dry Dock Co., *For National Defense*, reviewed, II, 94
Newport Shipbuilding Co., Wilmington, North Carolina, XXII, 172
Newport Tower, by Philip Ainsworth Means, reviewed, II, 353

New Practical Navigator, XXX, 207
New Providence Island, Bahamas, XXV, 190 ff., plates 21, 22
Newsboy, bark (1882), I, 77
News Boy, brigantine, XIII, 54
New Sestos (Port, Africa), XXX, 239
New Shoreham, steamship (1901), XII, 292, 293
New South Wales (Australia), XXX, 10
Newspapers, Panama, XX, 118
Newton, Captain Alexander, XXI, 98
Newton, Captain H. W., XXXV, 193
Newton, Sir Isaac, XIV, 214
Newton, Captain Richard, XLIX, 14
Newton, Captain Samuel, XVI, 171; XVIII, 84
Newton, Thomas, Jr., VIII, 33
Newton, Captain Thomas W., XXI, 106
Newton, Captain W., XIV, 125
Newton Ash, merchant ship *(1943)*, XLIV, 57 ff.
New World, ship (1846), V, 147
New World, steamship (1848), XIV, 282
New Year, schooner *(1861)*, XI, 286
New York, cruiser *(1898)*, XLI, 99
New York, frigate *(1800)*, XLVI, 151; XLVII, 26; L, 245 ff.; *(1803)*, XL, 24; *(1812)*, XLII, 278 ff.
New York, gondola *(1776)*, VIII, 256
New York, grain elevator *(1950)*, XXXVIII, 140
New York, S.S., XXVIII, 114, 124
New York, ship *(1901)*, XXXV, 195
New York, steamship, XVIII, 224, 226, 231; XXIV, 126; XXIX, 231; *(1831)*, XLVIII, 109; *(1834)*, VII, 55, 65; (1840), XX, 82 n.; (1843), XVII, 103; XX, 262; (1865), XVII, 311, 313; XVIII, 71; (1864), X, 131; *(1864)*, II, 18, plate 4
New York, steamship (ex-*Mersey*, ex-*Adelaide*), XXVI, 196
New York, U.S. flagship *(1917)*, XL, 50 ff.
New York, U.S. Great Lakes steamship *(1852)*, XXXIII, 88, 94
New York, U.S.S. *(1802)*, XIV, 209; *(1806)*, XVIII, 183
New York (NY). *See* Pultneyville; Steamboats; Shipbuilding; Shipowners; Shipping, Steam navigation
New York, London and China Steamship Co., XVII, 61, 62
New York, New Brunswick & Bangor Steamship Co., XXXIX, 143 ff.
New York and Liberia Steamship Co., XXXV, 204
New York and Liverpool United States Mail Steamship Co., XXVI, 82
New York and Liverpool United States Steamship Co., XIV, 239
New York and Porto Rico Steamship Co., XIV, 123; XXII, 167
New York and San Francisco Steamship Line, X, 127
New York and Savannah Steam Navigation Co., XLVII, 33 ff.
New York & Texas Steamship Co., XXV, 105

New York and Yucatan Steamship Co., XIV, 121
New York Bay harbor craft, I, 399; III, plate 24
New York Bethel Union, XXIV, 111, 116
New York Board of Weighers and Measurers of Grain & Floating Elevator Co., XXXVIII, 133
New York City, steamship (1879), XIV, 116, 117, 134; (1907), XIV, 124, 132, 134; (1917), XIV, 125, 130, 135; *(1950),* XIV, 133, 135
New York City in 1911, VII, plate 25
"New York City Shipowning Community, 1715–1764, The," by Bruce M. Wilkenfeld, XXXVII, 50–65
New York Corn Exchange Elevator Co., XXXVIII, 137
New York Cuban Mail Line, XXIX, 231
New York Floating Elevator Co., XXXVIII, 133 ff.
"New York Frigates, The," by William M. Fowler, Jr., XXXVIII, 15–27
New York Harbor, XXV, plate XIII; chart of, XIX, 44–50
New York Historical Society, I, 314–316; IV, 252; VII, plate 39; VIII, plate 21
New York Marine Bible Society, XXIV, 110, 114
New York Marine Missionary Society, XXIV, 110, 115
New York Marine Register, XXX, 21
New York Maritime Exchange, XXXII, 29
New York Maritime Register, XXV, 101, 114
"New York Pilot Boat," query by Arthur C. Wardle, V, 163–164
New York Provincial Congress, The, XXXVIII, 16 ff.
New York Public Library, I, 381. *See also* Libraries
New York Shipbuilding Co., XXII, 161; XXXVIII, 198 ff.
New York Yacht Club Fleet, XXX, Pictorial Supplement, plates VIII, XII
New York Yacht Club Regatta, 1854, XXV, plate XXII
New Zealand, H.M.S., XXVIII, 107 n.
New Zealand, XII, 22–44; boats of, XIII, 88 ff.
NH. *See* New Hampshire
Niagara, screw frigate *(1850),* XLIX, 112
Niagara, ship, XXI, 95; XXV, 186; *(1861),* XI, 286
Niagara, steamship, XVIII, 230; *(1824),* VI, 199, 201; (1826), VI, 208; *(1837),* VII, 65; (1839), XVIII, 284; *(1850),* XXXVII, 233
Niagara, steamship (ex-*Eastern Breeze*), XXIII, 276
Niagara, U.S.S. *(1861),* XXXVI, 183 ff.; *(1864),* XXVII, 43
Niagara, U.S. steam frigate (1856), XXII, 252; XXIII, 265; XXIV, 211
Niagara, warship *(1863),* XLV, 192
Niagara, yacht *(1921),* XXXV, 121
Niagara Harbor and Dock Co., XX, 83, 89
Niagara Steam Forge Works, XLVIII, 109 ff.
Niantic, whaler *(1849),* XXXIII, 127
Niblack, U.S.S. *(1941),* XLV, 52
Niblack, Rear Admiral Albert P., XXXIII, 272 ff.; XXXV, 106, 186
Nicaragua, steamship (1891), X, 137, 138
Nicaragua Transit Co., X, 127

Nicholas, John, XXXVIII, 107; XXXIX, 25 ff.
Nicholas, Captain Samuel, Continental Marines, XXV, 206, 208, 209, 211, 212, 213
Nicholas, Wilson Cary, XXXVIII, 101
Nichol Latimer & Co., XLIII, 217
Nicholls, Sir John, XXIII, 163
Nicholls, Nicholas, VII, 269
Nichols, Captain Alexander, XLIV, 151; XXVIII, plate XVIII
Nichols, Captain E. D. P., I, 108–115
Nichols, Captain E. P., XXVIII, plate XV
Nichols, Captain Edward Payson, II, 199, 257
Nichols, Captain Edward T., U.S.N., VII, plate 9
Nichols, Captain George, XXV, 181
Nichols, Richard C., XXXIII, 54 ff.
Nichols, Lieutenant S. F., XIX, 57, 58
Nichols, Captain William, XVII, 69
Nichols, Captain William R., XXXVIII, 281
Nicholson, Sir Francis, XXX, 134
Nicholson, Ian Hawkins, *Shipping Arrivals and Departures, Sydney* [Vol. II, 1826–1840], XXXVIII, 302
Nicholson, Captain James, VI, 101 ff.; XXXI, 245; XXXIV, 135 ff.; XLVI, 30
Nicholson, John, XIII, 27
Nicholson, Captain John B., XXI, 144
Nicholson, Lieutenant Joseph, XLVI, 168
Nicholson, Philip Y., "Admiral George Dewey after Manila Bay: Years of Ambition, Accomplishment, and Public Obscurity," XXXVII, 26–39
Nicholson, R. H., G.M. 2nd class, U.S.N., XXV, 50
Nicholson, Captain Robert, XXI, 98
Nicholson, Captain Samuel, XXII, 269, 270; XXVII, 136, 139, 140 n., 143; XLV, 95; XLVI, 161
Nicholson, Captain Samuel, U.S.N., XXV, 29
Nicholson, Commodore Samuel, XXXVII, 136
Nicholson, Captain Somerville, XXXIII, 280
Nicholson, William Alleyne, XXX, 304
Nicholson, Captain William C., XXI, 304
"Nickel a Bucket: A History of the North Carolina Shrimping Industry, A," by William N. Still, Jr., XLVII, 257–274
Nickels, Captain J. C., I, 108–112
Nickerson & Co. of Boston (Vol. XXXI-XXXV), Pictorial Supplement, plate IV
Nickerson, Roy, *Brother Whale, A Pacific Whalewatchers Log,* reviewed, XXXVIII, 301
Nicks, John, XIII, 20 n.
Nicol, Captain Alexander, XXI, 98
Nicol, John, XXX, 299
Nicola, Lewis, XL, 12
Nicolai I, steamship *(1863),* VIII, 231
Nicolas, schooner *(1836),* XXXII, 120
Nicolas, Captain Toup, XXXII, 243
Nicoline, schooner *(1889),* XXXIII, 84
Nicolle, David, "Shipping in Islamic Art: Seventh Through Sixteenth Century AD," XLIX, 168–197

Nicolo, Pre Theodoro de, XIV, 265
Nicolosi, Anthony S., "The Founding of the Newport Naval Training Station, 1878–1883; An Exercise in Naval Politics," XLIX, 291–304
Nicolson, Commandant J. B., XL, 41
Nictheroy, gunboat *(1898),* XXXVI, 262
Niebergall, Captain V. C., XXXVI, 20, 25
Nielsen, Christian, *Danske Bådtyper* (*Wooden Boat Designs*), reviewed, XLII, 307-308
Nielsen, K. Aage, V, 91
Niels Iuel, Danish ship, XXIX, 27
Niemen, steamship *(1859),* XLIII, 111 ff.
Nietero, frigate *(1827),* VI, 18
Niger, brig *(1827),* VI, 17
Niger, H.M.S., XXII, 33
Niger, ship *(1798),* XXVII, 139 n.
Niger, ship (1844), Pictorial Supplement, XXXIII, plates X, XVII; XXXIV, 21; *(1905),* XXII, plate XX
Nigerian, steamship (1925), XIV, 135
Niger River (West Africa), Discovery and exploration, XXXV, 77
Night Boat, The, by George W. Hilton, reviewed, XXIX, 144–145
Night Hawk, steamship, XXI, 97; (1864), III, 135; *(1864),* VIII, 235
Nightingale, bark (1857), III, 67
Nightingale, H.M. gunboat *(1907),* XL, 90 ff.
Nightingale, ship (1851), XIX, plate III; *(1866),* view of First Officer's Cabin, Pictorial Supplement, XXXI, plate XXII
Nightingale, sloop *(1758),* XXI, 8
Nightingale, whaling sloop *(1768),* XXIII, 22 ff.
Nightingale, Joseph, XXXI, 250
Nightingale, Samuel A., quoted, VII, 151
Nikol, John, and Francis X. Holbrook, "The Chilean Crisis of 1891–1892," XXXVIII, 291–300; "Naval Operations in the Panama Revolution 1903," XXXVII, 253–261; "Reporting the Sicilian Revolution of 1848–1849," XLIII, 165–176
Nile, H.M.S. *(1863),* XX, 54
Nile, ship *(1802),* XXXIV, 251
Nile, steamship (1843), XX, 261; *(1911),* X, 138
Nile, whaler *(1851),* XLIV, 15; *(1865),* XXVII, 276
Nile boats, XII, 45–51
Nile River (Egypt), Commerce, XII, 45. *See also* Boats
Niles, John, XXX, 143; XXXIX, 190 ff.
Niles, Nathaniel, XXXIX, 190 ff.
Niles, Captain Robert, XXXIX, 190 ff.
Nimble, H.M.S. *(1863),* XX, 54
Nimbo, steamship (ex-*Yung Hai*) *(1862),* XLIX, 22
Nimbus, schooner *(1874),* XXXV, 7, plate 4
Nimitz, Baron von, XXXVIII, 10
Nimitz, Catherine Freeman, XXXVIII, 5 ff.
Nimitz, Charles Henry, XXXVIII, 10 ff.
Nimitz, Admiral Chester, XXXIX, 43; XLII, 209
Nimitz, Lieutenant Chester W., XXXVIII, 6 ff.
Nimrod, bark *(1862),* XXXIII, 56

Nimrod, British brig *(1812),* XLII, 106 ff.
Nimrod, H.M.S. *(1859),* XXVII, 168
Nimrod, schooner (1891), I, 65
Nimrod, ship *(1861),* XI, 286
Nimrod, whaler *(1865),* XXVII, 276
Nimro/Jinju, steamship (ex-*Lancefield*) *(1862),* XXVI, 122
Nina, schooner *(1863),* XII, 159
Nina, sloop, XXI, 104; *(1864),* XV, 129
Nina, steamship, XXI, 88; (1861), VIII, 220, 226
Nina (II), ship [replica] (1892), XIV, 109, 110
Nina Fravega, sailing vessel (ex-*Diamant,* ex-*St. Patrick,* ex-*John Bell*) *(1894),* XXVI, 133
Ninagawa, Dr. Chikumasa, XLVI, 56
Nina Tilden, steamship (1864), I, 261
(Nine) 9 de Julio, schooner *(1845),* XXXVI, 127; XXIX, 179
"1957 Jamestown Fleet, The," by Robert G. C. Fee, XVII, 173–180, plates 15–18, plans.
Ningpo, Chinese junk *(1913),* XXIX, 262 ff., plates IX, X, XI, XII
Ningpo Steam Navigation Co., XVI, 178
Niobe, bark (1847), V, 150; VI, 80; *(1867),* IV, 73
Niobe, H.M.S. *(1873),* XXVIII, 23, 24, 26, 107; XXXVI, 97; XXXVIII, 245
Niobe, XXXII, 61 ff.
Nip and Tuck, yacht *(1880),* XXXVI, 233
Niphon, steamship (1862), XVI, 174; XVIII, 71; *(1863),* XIV, 62
Niphon, U.S.S. *(1863),* XVIII, 144; XXV, 113
Nippon Kaigi Kyokai, XXX, 31
Nippon Maru, steamship (1878), XLIII, 91 ff.
Nipsic, S.S. *(1866),* XV, 301, 302
Nipsic, U.S.S. *(1864),* XXVII, 43; (1873), XX, 136 n.
Nisbet, Captain John, XXIX, 278
Nisbet, Clara, contributed document, XXX, 62–67
Nita, steamship, XXI, 87; *(1863),* XII, 159
Nitrate trade, XVIII, 5, 149, 201, 235
Nitze, Paul H., Foreword to *Dictionary of American Fighting Ships,* Vol. III, reviewed, XXIX, 75–75
Niven, John, *The American President Lines and its Forebears, 1848–1984,* reviewed, XLVIII, 201; "Gideon Welles and Naval Administration During the Civil War," XXXV, 53–66
Nixon, John W., XL, 303
Nixon, Captain William, XXI, 98
NJ. *See* New Jersey
No. 61. See (Number) 61.
Noa, U.S. destroyer *(1927),* L, 187
Noah, XXV, 261
Noah, M. M., XXXVII, 239 ff.
Noall, Cyril, and Grahame Farr, *Wreck and Rescue Round the Cornish Coast* [Vol. I], reviewed, XXVI, 75
Noank, schooner *(1861),* VIII, 220
Noble, bark *(1861),* XXI, 258
Noble, brig (1845), III, 349

Noble, hermaphrodite brig (1822), IX, 72
Noble, schooner (1846), XXIV, 45, 59
Noble, Dennis L., Bernard C. Nalty, and Truman R. Strobridge, editors, *Wrecks, Rescues & Investigations: Selected Documents of the U.S. Coast Guard and Its Predecessors,* reviewed, XLIII, 143–145
Noble, Admiral Sir Percy, XLII, 209
Noble, Richard B., XXVIII, plate XXIII
"Noblesse Oblige," document contributed by Captain Edgar K. Thompson, U.S.N. (ret.), XXIII, 291
Nocturnal, English, Pictorial Supplement, XXXV, plate XVII
"Nocturnal Gun Salute, 1839 Style," document by Captain Edgar K. Thompson, U.S.N. (ret.), XXIII, 269
Noer, Thomas J., "Commodore Robert W. Shufeldt and America's South African Strategy," XXXIV, 81–88
Nolam, E. H., XXXI, 269
Nolan, Major Dennis E., XXXIV, 262 ff.
Nolen, John E., VII, 66
Nomads and Crusaders, A.D. 1000–1368, by Archibald R. Lewis, reviewed, XLIX, 310
Noman's Land boat, XII, 135–137
"No Mistake About It: A Response to Jonathan R. Dull," by William S. Dudley and Michael A. Palmer, XLV, 244–248
Nomwin Island, XXXIV, 254
Nonaggression Pact of August 1939, XXXII, 105
Nonantum, bark (1861), IV, 241
Nonesuch, schooner *(1834),* XXXVIII, 115; XL, 216
Nonesuch, sloop *(1746),* XLVIII, 33
Nonpareil, ship (1853), III, 64, 265
Nonsuch, cutter (1813), XXXIV, 188 ff.
Nonsuch, ketch (1968), XXX, 79
Nonsuch, schooner *(1819),* XLVII, 28
"Non–Union Seamen," document contributed by E. Lee Dorsett, M.D., XVI, 211–213
Nootka Connection: Europe and the Northwest Coast 1790–1795, The, by Derek Pathick, reviewed, XLII, 144–145
Nootka Sound (British Columbia), XV, 205
"Nootka Sound: Winter, 1788–89," by Francis E. Cross, XV, 205–212
Nora, schooner *(1862),* VIII, 226
Nora, yacht, XXII, 91; *(1863),* VIII, 231
Nora Creina, (1849), XXXIV, 32
Nora Creina, steamship *(1861),* XLIII, 186 ff.
Norah E. Lawson, bugeye (1906), IV, 250
Nord Alexis, Haitian ship *(1907),* XXIX, 129
Nordberg Manufacturing Co., XXII, 182
Nordhoff, Charles, XXXIV, 248; Editor, *In Yankee Windjammers,* reviewed, II, 92
Nordhoff, Charles, and James Norman Hall, *Botany Bay,* reviewed, II, 354
Nordic, oyster schooner (1926), I, 70
Nore light-vessel (1732), IV, 265 ff.
Norfolk, brig (1765), XXV, 219; *(1799),* XLVI, 160; L, 245 ff.
Norfolk, H.M.S. (1706), XXI, 262
Norfolk, ship *(1798),* XXXIX, 32
Norfolk, steamship (1817), VIII, 153
Norfolk, U.S.S. *(1799),* XXVII, 144; XXXI, 173
Norfolk, vessel, XXVI, 47
"Norfolk Pilot Boats," query by R. C. Newbold, III, 177; answer by H. I. Chapelle, III, 353
Norie, John William, VIII, 319
Norie & Co., London, instrument by, Pictorial Supplement, XXXV, plate VI
Norma, bark *(1889),* VIII, 185
Norman, steam yacht (1895), XXX, plate XXVI
Norman, John, XLIII, 53
Normandie, steamship [model] (1932), XVI, 104
Normandie: Her Life and Times, by Harvey Ardman, reviewed, XLVII, 141
Normandy, bark (1877), IV, 240
Normandy, yacht *(1906),* II, 171
Norn, yacht, XXXVI, 248
Norna, steamship (1853), XXVI, 19, 21–23, 25, 27, 202, 203, 206, 209
Nørregård, Georg, *Danish Settlements in West Africa, 1658–1850,* reviewed, XXVIII, 70–71
Norris, Frank, XXV, 65
Norris, Captain Howes, XXVII, 98 ff.
Norris, John, XXXII, plate I
Norris, Sir John, XLVI, 226
Norris Stanley, brig *(1847),* XVI, 237
Norseman, class R. knockabout (1924), XXX, plate XXIV
Norsemen, XI, 95–107
Norske Veritas, XXX, 28, 29, 38
Norsk Sjofartsmuseum, Bygdoynesveien, Oslo, XXXV, 75
Norsman, steamship, XXI, 86; *(1863),* VIII, 231
North, H.M. sloop *(1778),* VII, 204, 209; *(1779),* XXXVII, 292
North, James H., XXVII, 238–243, 247, 249–252; XXIX, 6–29
North, Lieutenant, XXIX, 8, plate 1
North, Lord, XXX, 204, 206
North, Lord (Prime Minister), XLV, 247
Northam, ship (1858), IX, 298
Northam, steamship (1858), XXVI, 28–30, 203, 206, 209, plate 16
North America, British sidewheeler (1839), XXXIII, 94
North America, ship *(1824),* III, 74–85; (1852), IV, 242
North America, steamship (1833), VII, 52; *(1838),* XVIII, 277, 291; XX, 83 n., 89 n.; *(1843),* XXXVII, 233; *(1862),* IV, 143 ff.
North America from Earliest Discovery to First Settlements: The Norse Voyages to 1612, by David Beers Quinn, reviewed, XXXVIII, 68
North American, ship *(1860),* XVII, 18

North American Mail Steamship Co. of Tacoma, XXXVIII, 194
North American Panorama 1900–1976, P. Ransome-Wallis, reviewed, XXXIX, 148–149
North American Royal Mail Packet Co., XXXVII, 231 ff.
North American Society for Oceanic History, editorial, XLI, 163; mentioned, XLVIII, 180; XXXV, 3. *See also* NASOH.
Northampton, H.M.S. *(1879),* XXVIII, 87
Northampton, ship *(1852),* IV, 48, 51, 52; XXVII, plate IV
North Atlantic, by Adlard Coles, reviewed, XI, 296
North Atlantic and Gulf S.S. Co., XXII, 177, 178
North Atlantic Patrol, by Griffith Baily Coale, reviewed, II, 343
North Atlantic Steamship Co., XIV, 121
Northaven, steamship (ex-*Eastern Gale*), XXIII, 276
North Carolina, ark (1853), III, 349
North Carolina, flagship (1820), XL, 211 ff.
North Carolina, frigate (1818), XXXV, 64, 240
North Carolina, receiving ship *(1862),* XLVII, 114; XLVIII, 118
North Carolina, brigantine (1743), I, 167
North Carolina, schooner *(1832),* XXXVIII, 268; *(1861),* VIII, 220
North Carolina, ship *(1827),* XXIX, 176; *(1829),* XLII, 288 ff.
North Carolina, ship of the line *(1821),* XLVII, 28
North Carolina, steamship, XXI, 98; *(1862),* VIII, 226, 231
North Carolina, U.S.S. *(1824),* VII, 18; *(1826),* XXI, 75, 304
North Carolina (NC):
    History, Colonial period (ca. 1600–1775), XXIX, 155
    — , **Revolution (1775–1788),** XLIX, 77
    See also Harbors; Shipbuilding; Shipping; Shrimp fisheries
North Carolina Shipbuilding Co., Wilmington, N. C., VIII, 76; XLI, 191
North Carolina Transportation Co., VII, 66
North China Steamer Co., XVIII, 63; XXII, 226
Northeastern, steamship *(1901),* XXXVIII, 190 ff.
Northerner, steamship (1847), X, 131, 134; *(1847),* XLVII, 35
Northern King, ship *(1890),* XLVII, 194; *(1894),* XXXVIII, 85, 205 ff.
Northern Light, schooner, XIII, 126; XXIV, 135, 136
Northern Light, clipper ship (1851), XXII, 239
Northern Light, schooner yacht *(1845),* XXV, plate VII
Northern Light, ship *(1867),* XXVII, 110; (1872), VI, 123; (1873), III, 72; *(1888),* XLVII, 193; *(1917),* XVIII, 164–167
Northern Light, whaling bark *(1851),* XXV, 103
Northern Pacific, ship (1914), XLVII, 202
Northern Pacific, steamship *(1913),* III, 186
Northern Pacific Railroad, XXXV, 167 ff.

Northern Pacific Steamship Co., I, 80
Northern Queen, ship *(1980),* XLVII, 194
North River (MA). *See* Shipbuilding, US
Northern Seas, The, by Archibald R. Lewis, reviewed, XIX, 147
Northern Spray, H.M. trawler *(1943),* L, 219 ff.
Northern Star, ship *(1890),* XLVII, 194
Northern Steamship Co., XLVII, 193 ff.
"Northern Theater in the Civil War — the USS *Michigan* and Confederate Intrigue on the Great Lakes, The," by Bradley A. Rodgers, XLVIII, 96–105
Northern Wave, ship *(1890),* XLVII, 194
Northern Whale Fishery, XXII, plate V
Northey, Abijah, XXV, 185
Northey, William, E., I, 102; III, 89
North German Lloyd Line, XXIX, 233
North Haven, steamship *(1935),* VIII, 195
North Heath, steamship, XXI, 88, 105; *(1864),* VIII, 235
North Land, ship *(1894),* XLVII, 195 ff.
North Land, steamship *(1919),* XXXIV, 182 ff.
Northland, steamship (ex-*Zeeland*) (1901), Pictorial Supplement, XXXIV, plate XXVII
Northman, steamship *(1901),* XXXVIII, 190 ff.
North of England Shipbuilding Co., XXXVIII, 184
North Pacific Exploring Expedition, XXXVIII, 33
North Pacific Transportation Co., X, 132
North Pole, schooner (1754), I, 297
North River. See North River Steam Boat, XXIV, 161
North River Boat. See North River Steam Boat, XXIV, 161
North River of Clermont, steamship (1807), XVIII, 317
North River (Plymouth County (Massachusetts), shipbuilding on, XXV, 218–219, 222
North River Steam Boat, steamship, XXIV, 158 ff.; XXVII, 19, 20; (1807), XXVI, 74; XXVII, 16, 24, 27, 28; XXXII, 211 ff. See also: *Clermont.*
Northrop, Captain J. M., XXI, 98
Northrup, Mary, XXXIX, 191
North Shore, XXVIII, 261–274
"North Shore Trade in the Early Eighteenth Century," by James G. Lydon, XXVIII, 261–274
North Star, S.S., XXVII, 259
North Star, ship (1871), II, 334
North Star, steamship *(1854),* IV, 312; *(1880),* XLIV, 15 ff.; *(1881),* XXII, plate XV; *(1907),* XXXIV, 182 ff.
North Star, steam whaler *(1882),* XXXIX, 6 ff.
North State Lumber Co., XXX, 187
Northtown, steamship *(1901),* XXXVIII, 190 ff.
Northumberland, brig (1839), XXXVIII, Pictorial Supplement, Plate XXVI; *(1841),* XXVII, 83; XXX, 229 ff.
North West, bark (1846), V, 153
North West, ship *(1894),* XLVII, 195 ff.
Northwest, steamship (1861), I, 76
Northwest America, schooner *(1788),* XV, 206

Northwest Coast of America, I, 97–98, 374–380; V, 160–162; Indian Canoes, I, plates facing 376, 377; XI, 155–156; XV, 205–212; XXVIII, 53–65

Northwest Coast of North America. *See* America (Discovery and exploration); Fur trade; Indians of North America (Boats)

Northwestern, cargo steamship *(1901),* XXXVIII, 190 ff.

Northwestern, merchant steamship *(1941),* XXXVII, 100

Northwestern Livestock Corp. (of Juneau, Alaska), XXV, 292

Northwestern Steamship Co., XXXVIII, 190 ff.

"Northwest Passage," query by M. V. Brewington, I, 89

Northwest Territories, Discovery and exploration, XLIX, 14

North Wind, ship *(1890),* XLVII, 194

Norton, Bettina A., comment, Editorial, *The American Neptune,* XXXVIII, 3–4

Norton, C. McKim, and Russell K. Jones, *The Cruising Cookbook,* reviewed, IX, 306

Norton, Carlisle and Co., VII, 63, 64

Norton, Francis, XIII, 120

Norton, Susan Colt, XXXVII, 203

"Norumbega: New England Xanadu," by Sigmund Diamond, XI, 95–107

Norval, Captain William, XXI, 106

Norvik, tanker *(1942),* L, 44

Norville, Edward J., XXXII, 200, 204

Norville, Captain Edward J., XXI, 98

Norway, ship *(1859),* XX, 215

Norwegian, bark (1861), IV, 241

"Norwegian Ship Identification Signals, 1829–1867, The," by Laritz Petersen, XXI, 70–72

Nor'wester, ship (1854), XIX, 27, 37

Norwich, H.M.S., XXVI, 61; *(1754),* VII, 249

Norwich, steamship (1836), XVIII, 230, 231

Norwich, towboat *(1867),* VI, 281

Norwich, U.S.S. *(1863),* XXI, plate XXX

Norwich and New London Steamboat Co., VIII, 247, ff.

Norwich Packet, brig *(1767),* XXXIX, 192

Norwood, Captain Gustavus, XX, 242

Norwood, Richard, VIII, 305

Norzagaray, French ship *(1859),* XXVII, 165

No Ship May Sail, by Charles F. Haywood, reviewed, II, 263

Nostra Senora de Guadalupe, ship (1757), XXIII, 281

(Nostra) Noftra Signiora Delcarmel, Spanish ship (1795), XXIV, 70, 71

"Notarial Records of Daniel Moulton of York, Maine," contributed by Lawrence W. Jenkins, XX, 43, 67, 103, 111, 117, 145, 190, 216, 236, 242, 249, 269

"Notebook of Captain John Stanton, Master of the Black Ball Line Packet Ship *Amity,* The," document contributed by Eric Steinfeldt, XV, 306–310

"Note on American Small Craft," by Eric Steinfeldt, XIV, 61

"Note on Banks Baton, A," by Bern Anderson, XVII, 67

"Note on *DNB* and the Evacuation of Martinique, 1759," by Marshall Smelser, III, 168–169

"Note on Steamboat Decoration, A," by Randall V. Mills, III, 159–161

"Note on the Longevity of Colonial Ships, A," note by Daniel Scott Smith, XXXIV, 68–69

"Notes from Baltimore Customs Records," by M. V. Brewington, IX, 72

"Notes on American Shipping Based on Records of the Court of Vice Admiralty of Jamaica, 1776–1812," by MacEdward Leach, XX, 44–48

"Notes on a shallop," by William A. Baker, XVII, 105–113

"Notes on Chapman and Flint," by Lincoln Colcord, II, 324–326

"Notes on Chesapeake Bay Skipjacks," by Howard I. Chapelle, IV, 269–292

"Notes on Marine Disasters off Cape Horn, 1907," by Frank W. Thober, XVIII, 177–180

"Notes on Some New England Three-Masters," by Robert H. I. Goddard, Jr., V, 286–296

"Notes on the Action between *Hornet* and *Peacock,*" by Hardin Craig, Jr., XI, 73–77

"Notes on the Cross-Staff," by Marion V. Brewington, XIV, 187–191, plates 23, 24

"Notes on the Death of a Ship and the End of a World: The Grounding of the British Bark *Glenesslin* at Mount Neahkahnie on 1 October 1913," by William Appleman Williams, XLI, 122–138

"Notes on the First Fleet Engagement in the Civil War," by Robert S. Burpo, Jr., XIX, 265–273

"Notes on the Maritime History of Lubec, Maine," by Frank P. Adams, Sr., XXIV, 38–60

"Notes on the Palmer Schooners," by Robert B. Applebee, V, 79–81

"Notes on Writing Naval (*not* Navy) English," by Samuel Eliot Morrison, IX, 5–10

Notes: XXI, 70–72, 142–146; XXII, 216–218; XXIII, 67–69, 140–142, 219–224; XXIV, 212–216; XXXIV, 65–70, 219–221; XXXV, 139–143; XXVI, 215–219; XXVII, 279–280; XXVIII, 142–145, 223–224; XXIX, 224–226; XXXVII, 138–144; XXXVIII, 142–143; XXXIX, 65–67, 142–143; XLI, 66, 139; XLIII, 222, 301

"'Not for Conquest But Discovery:' Rediscovering the Ships of the Wilkes Expedition," by Dana M. Wegner and Philip K. Lundeberg, XLIX, 151–167

Nothing Too Daring: A Biography of Commodore David Porter, 1780–1843, by David F. Long, reviewed, XXXIII, 64–65

"Notice to Mariners," by Captain Edgar K. Thompson, U.S.N. (ret.), XXV, 273

Notre Dame, brigantine *(1776),* XIII, 39

Nott, Charles C., XIX, 128–132

Nottingham, H.M.S. *(1728),* XXI, 260

Nottoway, barge *(1829),* V, 301

Novara, Austrian frigate *(1864),* XXXIV, 59

Nova Scotia, British schooner *(1777),* XLII, 14 ff.
Nova Scotia, steamship *(1842),* XXXIII, 83
Nova Scotia. *See* Canada; Fishers; Fishing; Louisbourg; Shipping; Steam navigation
Nova Scotia, XIII, 125–130
Novascotiaman, by Clement W. Crowell, reviewed, XL, 150
Nova Scotia Steamship Co., XXXVII, 235
Nove, John, review by, XL, 234
Novelty, Kennebunkport steamship *(1885),* XLIV, 116
Novelty, steamship *(1830),* XLVIII, 111; *(1864),* XVII, 310
Novelty Iron Works (NY), II, 9–11; XVII, 43; XLVIII, 111 ff.
Novelty Iron Works of Stillman, Allen & Co., XLVII, 40
Noyes, Benjamin F., XXV, 106–107
Noyes, Captain William, XXI, 12
Noyon, auxiliary *(1918),* XXXII, 22, 30
Nuestra Señora de la Consolacion, Spanish ship (1773), XXXIV, 250
(Nueve) 9 de Julio. See under 9 (Nine) de Julio.
Nueve Lista Documentada de los Tribulantes de Colón en 1492, by Alicia B. Gould, reviewed, XLVI, 126
No. (Number) 61, ironclad frigate, the "Scottish Sea Monster," XXIX, Plates 1–4. *See also Danmark.*
Nunez, XXX, 230 ff.
Nunez River, XXX, 178 ff.
Nuremberg, ship *(1861),* XI, 286
Nurnberg, ship *(1914),* XXXIII, 36 ff.
"Nursury (*sic*) of seamen," XXV, 44
Nushagak, steamship *(1914),* X, 119
Nutfield, steamship *(1864),* VIII, 235
Nutt, J. B., XXIV, 59
Nutting, John, XXXVII, 290
NY. *See* New York
Nyack, U.S.S. *(1869),* XX, 62
Nye, bark *(1863),* XV, 292
Nye, Captain Ezra, XV, 140
Nye, Gideon, Jr., XVI, 164; XVII, 142; XX, 213
Nymph, brig, XXII, 85; *(1799),* XLVI, 162
Nymph, schooner *(1863),* XII, 159
Nymphe, French frigate *(1778),* XLII, 29 ff.
Nymphe, H.M. frigate *(1812),* XLV, 5
Nymphe, H.M.S. *(1903),* XLIX, 282

O. C. Williams, tug *(1894),* XLII, 267 ff.
O. K., schooner, XXI, 87; *(1864),* XII, 232. *See also OK.*
O. K., sloop *(1862),* XII, 57
Oahu Packet, topsail schooner (1825), X, 268
Oakland, ferry *(1860),* II, 299–306
Oakley C. Curtis, schooner (1901), IV, 61, 66, 68

Oak, Live. *See* Live Oak
Oaknoll, steamship (ex-*William Campion,* ex-*Eastern Exporter*), XXIII, 276
Oakville, steamship (1834), VII, 55
Oared Fighting Ships, From Classical Times to the Coming of Steam, by R. C. Anderson, reviewed, XXIII, 146–147
"Oars," document contributed by M. V. Brewington, II, 247
Obregon-Boulton, XXX, 275
O'Brien, Captain, XXV, 173
O'Brien, Brother Paul, query by, IX, 302
O'Brien, Richard, XXVI, 239, 241, 246, 248
O'Brien, Captain Richard, XLI, 216
O'Brien, Timothy, XLI, 175
Observatories, XLIV, 186
O'Cain, Captain James, XVII, 66
O'Callaghan, Captain, XXX, 160
Occacock, illustration of actual survey map, 1795, XLIX, 79
Occidental and Oriental Steamship Co., XXXI, 120 ff.; Pictorial Supplement, XXXIV, plate VII
Ocean, French ship *(1799),* XXXI, 173
Ocean, sloop *(1863),* XII, 159
Ocean, schooner, XIV, 40
Ocean, ship *(1860),* XIV, 45, 46
Ocean, steamship *(1850),* XXXVI, 171; *(1853),* XIV, 202
Ocean and Marine Dictionary, by David F. Tver, reviewed, XL, 234
Ocean Bird, bark *(1858),* XXXIII, 212
Ocean Bird, schooner *(1863),* XV, 128
Ocean Bride, ship *(1860),* XLVII, 104
"Ocean Chronicle, *Published by Captain E. P. Nichols on Board the Bark* Clara *and Ship* Frank Pendleton, *1878–1891, The,*" reviewed, II, 257
Ocean Chronicle, The, XXVIII, plate XV
Ocean currents, XXIII, 113. *See also* Gulf Stream
Ocean Express, ship (1854), III, 69; (1855), XIX, Plate VIII
Ocean Favorite, bark (1854), IV, 73, 244
Oceania:
  Note: Here are entered works on the islands of the Pacific Ocean belonging to the groups of Melanesia, Micronesia and Polynesia. Works on all islands of the Pacific Ocean, including the North Pacific Ocean, are entered under **Pacific, Islands of the.**
  Description and travel, XXIII, 113
  Discovery and exploration, XXI, 196
  See also Missionaries; Shipping; Shipwrecks; Solomon Islands
Oceanic, liner *(1965),* XXXVI, 5, 28
Oceanic, steamship (1870), XXXI, 126; Pictorial Supplement, XXXIV, plate VIII
Oceanic Steam Navigation Co., XXXI, 126
"Ocean Mail Controversy of 1934, The," by Thomas T. Spencer, XLI, 110–121
Ocean Mail Service Act, 1928, XXIX, 232

Ocean Monarch, ship *(1848),* XV, 140, 141
"Ocean Navigation of Columbus on his First Voyage, The," by John W. McElroy, I, 209–240
Oceanographic Ships and Aft, by Stewart B. Nelson, reviewed, XXXII, 145–146
Oceanography:
   Netherlands, History, XLVIII, 44
   Study and teaching, XLIV, 110; XLVII, 206
Oceanography, V, 9 ff.
Ocean Queen, steamship *(1861),* XXI, 241
Ocean Rover, bark *(1862),* XXVII, 264, 265
Ocean Star, ship *(1848),* XXV, 18 n.
Ocean Steed, bark *(1870),* XXII, plate XII
Ocean travel, III, 292; IV, 53; XI, 35
Ocean View, steamship (1894), VI, 66
Ocean Wave, schooner *(1861),* VIII, 220
Ochterlony, David, XLVI, 6 ff.
Ocilla, schooner *(1862),* XII, 57
Ocklahoma, steamship *(1895),* XVIII, 8
Ocklawaha, steamship (1867), VII, 126, 128, 132, 133, 134 n., 136, 137, 139, 141, 142, 147, 162, plate 14
Ocklawaha River, Florida, map, VII, 117; steamboating, VII, 115–166, 224–239
Ocmulgee, ship *(1862),* XXV, 21; XXVII, 265
Oconce, steamship *(1863),* XV, 128
O'Connell, F. E., XXXVI, 248
Oconto, steamship (1872), I, 76
Ocracoke Inlet, XXX, 137
Octavia, bark (1857), III, 349
Octavia, sloop *(1862),* XII, 57
Octorara, S.S. ship *(1863),* VI, 153
Octorara, U.S.S. (1864), XXVII, 43
Octorona, gunboat *(1862),* XXXVI, 197
Octorora, U.S.S. *(1862),* XX, 159, 160
Oculi, XV, 5, 191; XVII, 262; XVIII, 25. *See also* Ship decoration
Oculi, XVIII, 235–252
Odd Fellow, schooner, XXI, 100; *(1861),* VIII, 220, 231
Oddfellow, steamship *(1841),* XX, 103
Odell, schooner *(1873),* Pictorial Supplement, XXXVI, plate XIV
Odell, John, XLVI, 261
Odenwald, German blockade runner *(1941),* XLV, 52
Odenwald, steamship, XVI, 130
"Ode to Spiritus Frumenti," contributed by Captain Edgar K. Thompson, U.S.N. (ret.), XXXV, 288
Odin, John, VIII, 13
"Odyssey of *City of Flint,*" by John Garry Clifford, XXXII, 100–116
Offey, bark *(1858),* XLI, 302
"Officer and Gentleman," document contributed by Captain Edgar K. Thompson, U.S.N. (ret.), XXIV, 118
Office of Naval Intelligence. *See* United States. Office of Naval Intelligence
"Officers of the Revenue Marine Service in the Confederacy," by Ralph W. Donnelly, XL, 298–304

"Officers who served under John Paul Jones, The," by William Bell Clark, III, 55–56
Offley, David W., XL, 221
Of Yachts and Men, by William Atkin, reviewed, X, 157
Ogden, Aaron, XVI, 274–280
Ogden, Jonathan, XXIX, 198
Ogg, David, XXV, 278
Ogle, Rear Admiral Sir Chaloner, XXVI, 48, 55
Oglebay, Norton and Co., XXV, 169
O'Hara, Clifford B., XXVII, 260
O'Hara, John F., XLIV, 119
O'Hara, Oliver, XXXVIII, 268
O'Higgins, Chilean ship *(1867),* XXXIX, 276
O'Higgins, Bernardo, XXX, 300
Ohio, American whaler *(1862),* XXIX, 104
Ohio, bark (1840), III, 261; *(1857),* L, 125; *(1870),* XXXVIII, 206 ff.; *(1875),* XII, 101, 108, 119
Ohio, brig (1847), Pictorial Supplement, XXXVIII, plate X
Ohio, schooner (1810), VII, 317; *(1814),* XLIV, 172
Ohio, ship *(1830),* XLII, 282 ff.
Ohio, steamship *(1831),* VII, 43, 44; (1848), IV, 307
Ohio, U.S.S. *(1817),* XXI, 65; XXIII, 58, 269
Ohio, U.S. ship of the line (1820), VII, 182–185, plates 22–23
Ohio, whaling bark (1830), XXV, 104
Ohio River Handbook, The, edited by Benjamin F. and Eleanor Klein, reviewed, X, 77–78
Ohio Steamboat Navigation Co., XVI, 33
"Oh Pshaw!" note by Captain Edgar K. Thompson, U.S.N. (ret.), XXIX, 261
Oil trade, VIII, 279
   Pacific Ocean, XVI, 5, 107
Oil, Transportation, XXXVIII, 175
Oiseau, H.M.S. *(1782),* XXIX, 212
OK, yacht *(1894),* XXXVI, 238. See also *O.K.*
Okahumkee, steamship (1873). See *Okeehumkee.*
Okahumkee, stern-wheel steamship (1870), I, 73
Okeehumkee, steamship (1873), VII, 116 n., 126, 129 n., 138–144, 146 n., 150–152, 154, 157, 160, 162, 164–166, 225, 226, 236–239; stateroom plans, VII, 143, plates 15, 16, 17, 29–32
Oklahoma, tanker *(1908),* XXVIII, 198 ff., plate 8
Oklahoma, U.S.S., XXII, 146
Okumiya, Lieutenant Masatake (Japanese commander), L, 260 ff.
Olaf Tryggvason, minelayer *(1939),* XXXII, 111
Ola M. Balcom, Canadian schooner *(1902),* XLIX, 280
Olata, schooner *(1855),* XXIV, 142
Olcott, A. Van Santvoord, Jr., review by, L, 70
Oldale, Adrienne and Peter, *Navigating Britain's Coastline,* reviewed, XLI, 234
Old Bay Line, The, by Alexander Crosby Brown, reviewed, I, 96
Old Bay Line, XXII, 150, 231; XXX, 71
Old Butch, S. Crocker yacht (ex-*Seacrest*) *(1949–1961),* XLVIII, 185

Old Colony Steamboat Co., XXXIX, 103; ship of, Pictorial Supplement, XXXIV, plate XXVIII
Old Colony Wharf, XXXIX, plate 3
Old Dartmouth Historical Society, New Bedford (MA), I, 198; IX, 19
Old Dominion, steamship *(1864),* VIII, 235; XVII, 259 ff.; (1872), Pictorial Supplement, XXXIV, plates IX, XIX
Old Dominion (ex-*Alfred*), steamship, XXI, 88, 98, 105
Old Dominion Line, II, 228
Oldendorf, Admiral, XL, 52 ff.
Old Family Portraits of Kennebunk, reviewed, V, 94, 172
Old Fashioned Form of Protectionism: The Role Played by British Naval Power in China from 1860–1941, An," by Malcolm H. Murfett, L, 178–191
Oldfield, Otis, *Journal Aboard the Louise,* reviewed, XXX, 304
Oldfield, Dr. R. A. K., XXXV, 86
Oldham, John, XIII, 158
Olding, J. A., XXVI, 12, 14
"Old Light on the New Light," by Carl C. Cutler, VIII, 328–330
Old Marblehead: A Camera Impression, by Samuel Chamberlain, reviewed, I, 320–321
"Old Navy, The," by Captain Edgar K. Thompson, U.S.N. (ret.), XXIX, 64
"Old Navy, The," contributed by Captain Edgar K. Thompson, U.S.N. (ret.), XXIII, 196
Old Noll, ship (1743), I, 297
Old North State, concrete steamship (1919), XXII, 161, Plate 5
Old North State, steamship *(1862),* VIII, 226
Old Point Comfort, XXX, 136
Old Print Ship, New York, VII, 249; IX, 150
Olds, Robert E., XXXIV, 164
Old Ship Portraits of Kennebunk, reviewed, III, 355–356
Old South Association, comment in Editorial, *The American Neptune,* XXXVIII, 3–4
Old South Meeting House, lecture series at, comment in Editorial, *The American Neptune,* XXXVIII, 3–4
Old State House, Boston, XVII, 3
"Old Steam Shed, The," by Harold C. Roberts, VII, 196–199
Old Time Molasses Co., XXII, 170
Old Wrecks of the Baltic Sea: Archaeological Recording of the Wrecks of Carvel-built Ships, The, by Carl Olof Cederlund, reviewed, XLIV, 210
O'Leary, Arthur, XLI, 58
O'Leary, Wayne M., review by, XLVII, 284; "The Antebellum Maine Fishing Schooner and the Factors Influencing its Design and Construction," XLIV, 82–95; "The Maine Transatlantic Salt Trade in the Nineteenth Century," XLVII, 83–107
Oleum, tanker (1910), XXXVIII, 200 ff.
Olga, schooner (1901), XXXVIII, 88
Olimpia, bark *(1861),* VIII, 220
Olive, brig (1815), XVII, 69

Olive, hermaphrodite brig (1850), XXIV, 58
Olive, privateer, XXVIII, 117
Olive, schooner, XXI, 94, 102; *(1861),* XI, 286
Olivebank, bark (1892), II, 290
Olive Branch (I), schooner (1819), XXIV, 45, 59
Olive Branch (II), schooner (1854), XXIV, 59; *(1861),* XI, 267, 286; XII, 57
Olive Branch, horse ferry *(1831),* VII, 43
Olive Branch, schooner, XXI, 102
Olive Branch, ship *(1798),* XVIII, 133
Olive Branch, steamship *(1825),* XXXVII, 244
Olive E., sloop (1906), XLI, plate 2
Olive Pecker, schooner *(1897),* XXXV, 12
Oliver, Captain J., XX, 89 n., 103
Oliver, Captain John S., XV, 67
Oliver, Peter, XL, 255; "Travel by Water, To, From, Between and Within the United States in 1800," III, 292–313; contributed document, II, 77–79
Oliver, Robert, XLVI, 142
Oliver, Thomas E., XIII, 119
Oliver Cromwell, ship *(1777),* XLIII, 24; *(1778),* XXXIX, 206
Oliver Hazard Perry, schooner (1919), V, 292–293
Oliver Newberry, steamship (1833), VII, 52; *(1839),* XVIII, 299
Oliver S. Breeze, schooner *(1863),* XII, 159
Olive S. Southard, ship (1871), II, 245
Olivette, steamship, XXVIII, 124
Olivier, 2nd Lieutenant Carlos, XXX, 54
Olivier, Sir Sidney, XXIX, 130
Olivutzu, Russian corvette *(1855),* XXXI, 272
Olney, Captain James, XIV, 57
Olney, Captain Oliver, XXI, 98
Olney, Attorney General Richard, XLI, 254
Olnie, schooner *(1861),* XI, 286
Olsen, James, XXV, 188
Olsen, Captain Olaf C., VII, 290
Olshausen, Dr. Gustav, XXXVI, 36
Olson, Oliver J., XXII, 171
Oltenia, tanker (1942), L, 46
Olterra, S.S. *(1942),* XXVII, 188–201, plates 6–8
Olympia, cruiser *(1888),* XXXIX, 136
Olympia, flagship (1899), XXXVII, 26 ff., 140 n., 260
Olympia, ship (1898), XXXV, 184
Olympia, steamship *(1870),* XXXVI, 232; *(1893),* XIV, 120
Olympia, U.S. cruiser (1896), XXIX, 116
Olympia, yawl (1900), XXXVI, 240
Olympia (WA), XXXVI, 231 ff.
Olympian, steamship (1880), III, 160
Olympic, 4–masted jackass rig, XXV, 113
Olympic, bark (1892), I, 77; IV, 238, plates 39, 40
Olympic, ship *(1917),* XXXIV, 275
Olyphant, D. W. C., XVII, 134
Olyphant, David W. C., XXXIX, 54; XLI, 26; XLVI, 35; XLVIII, 275
Olyphant, Robert W., XVII, 134

Olyphant and Co., XVII, 55, 56, 134–142; XXXIV, 40; XLIII, 92 ff.
Omaha, U.S.S. (1867), XX, 136 n.; *(1941),* XLV, 52
Omega, bark (1836), V, 149; (1887), IX, 298
Omega, ship, XXVII, 73; *(1832),* XIX, 26, 27; *(1853),* XIV, 198; XVI, 211
Omeo, bark (1858), IV, 238, plate 40
Omer, Captain James, XXI, 265
Ömheten, ship (1783), VI, 170
"On a Lee Shore," by Gershom Bradford, XII, 282–287
Onaway, yacht *(1906),* XXXVI, 242
"On Crossing the Line," note contributed by Captain Edgar K. Thompson, U.S.N. (ret.), XXIV, 215–216
Ondine, M. V. *(1961),* XXIV, 187 n.
Oneca, ship (1829), XIV, 40
Oneco, ship (1829), XXII, 216
"One Hundred and Fiftieth Anniversary of the Peabody Museum of Salem, The," by Walter Muir Whitehill, X, 33–42
150 Yahre Blankeneser Schiffahrt, 1785–1935 [150 Years of Blankeneser Shipping, 1785–1935], by Dr. Jürgen Meyer, reviewed, XXX, 70–71
138, gunboat (1813), XXXVI, 211 ff.
Oneida (1801), XXIII, 216
Oneida, gunboat *(1867),* XXXII, 132
Oneida, ship (1866), XXVIII, plate XII
Oneida, steamship (1836), VII, 61, 310, 311; (1842), VIII, 133
Oneida, steam sloop *(1862),* XXXVII, 130
Oneida, U.S.S. *(1869),* XXX, 296
Oneida, yacht *(1905),* XXXVI, 241
Oneida Iron and Glass Mfg. Co., XLV, 38
O'Neill, Eugene, XXV, 65
Oneonta, U.S. monitor (1862), X, 19, 29, 32
Oneoto, warship (1866), XXXVIII, 233; XXXIX, 275
Only Way to Cross, The, by John Maxton Graham, reviewed, XXXIII, 149
Onodaga, ship (1865), XXXIX, 38
Onondaga, double-turret monitor *(1854),* XLII, 88 ff.; *(1864),* XLVIII, 123
Onondaga, U.S. Coast Guard *(1915),* XLV, 200
Onondaga, U.S. monitor (1864), X, 26, 29, 31; *(1864),* XXVII, 42, 44
Onslaught, H.M.S., XXXVI, 124
Onslow, John James, R. N., L, 31
Onslow, Captain R. G., L, 49
Ontario, ship *(1798),* XVIII, 121
Ontario, sloop *(1775),* XLIX, 264 ff.; *(1828),* XXXII, 275
Ontario, steamship, XVIII, 230; (1816), III, 333–344, plate 41; V, 28; VI, 196, 200; VII, 42, 43 n.; (1839), XVIII, 283, 284; XX, 86; (1867), IV, 158–159, plate 26
Ontario, U.S.S. (1813), XXII, 105; *(1833),* VII, 18
Ontario, warship (1813), XXXVIII, 107 ff.; XL, 38 ff., 216
Ontario and St. Lawrence Steamboat Co., VII, 42, 44
Ontario Boat Co., XXVI, 48, plate 6

Onteora, steamship, XVIII, 224
On the Hawser: A Tugboat Album, by Steven Land and Peter H. Spectre, reviewed, XLII, 138–139
On the Northwest: Commercial Whaling in the Pacific Northwest, 1790–1967, by Robert Lloyd Webb, reviewed, L, 152
Onward, bark (1859), II, 332
Onward, gunboat *(1867),* XXXII, 132
Onward, schooner *(1861),* XI, 286; XII, 159
Onward, U.S.S. *(1863),* XV, 295, 300; *(1864),* XXVII, 36
Onze Vendemiaire, French ship *(1799),* XXXI, 173
Ooragawa Village, Japan; Governor of, VII, 11–14, 16–17
Opdyke, Mayor George, XXV, 256
Opening of the Pacific — Image and Reality, The, National Maritime Museum, reviewed, XXXII, 146–147
"Opening the Yangtze Door," by George E. Paulsen, XXXIV, 103–122
"Operation Rescue: The *Mefkure* Incident and the War Refugee Board," by Timothy P. Maga, XLIII, 31–39
"Operation Sail 1976," XXXV, 75–76
Operations in North African Waters, October 1942–June 1943, by Samuel Eliot Morison, reviewed, VII, 244–247
Ophell, Captain Richard, XXIII, 66
Opium Trade, XIV, 215
Opium war, XXXI, 177. *See also* China
Opium War, XXVI, 6, 8; XXXI, 183 ff., 274
Oppert & Co., XLIII, 99 ff.
Opposum, H.M.S. (1859), XXVII, 168
OpSail 1976, editorial comment, XXXVII, 3–4
Oracle, ship (1853), IV, 244; (1863), IV, 244
Orahaa, steamship (ex-*Eastern Cross*), XXIII, 276
Oramoneta, schooner *(1864),* XV, 129
Oran, Africa, VI, 179–193
Orange Harbor, XXX, 298
Orangetree, Algerine ship *(1678),* XXIII, 109
Ora Peake, schooner *(1861),* VIII, 220
Orbit, sloop *(1821),* XLIII, 54
Orbita, H.M.S. *(1917),* XXXVI, 268 n.
Orca, ship *(1886),* XII, 106
Orca, steam bark (1882), XLIV, 16 ff.; Pictorial Supplement, XXXIII, plate XV
Ord, Captain George, XLIII, 22
Ord, Ralph, XIII, 27
Ordnance, XLV, 35. *See also* Naval ordnance
Ordnance, naval, III, 11–18, 148–158; VI, 212–222; VII, 240–241, 316, 319–321, plate 40; XXXVI, 276–295
Ordnance, Pre-Revolutionary, XI, 145
Ordway, Wallace B., X, 241–242; "The Merrimac River Gundalow and Gundalowmen," X, 249–263, plates 25–26
Oregon, 12 inch gun, VI, 212–222, plate 32
Oregon, battleship *(1898),* XLI, 97
Oregon, brig *(1838),* XLIX, 155
Oregon, gunboat *(1899),* XXXV, 190 ff.
Oregon, schooner *(1864),* XII, 232

Oregon, steamship, XXI, 87, 93; *(1848),* X, 125–126, 130; *(1856),* XI, 42 ff.;*(1861),* XI, 267, 286; *(1883),* Pictorial Supplement, XXXIV, plate XVII
Oregon, U.S. exploration vessel *(1841),* XXX, 298
Oregon, U.S.S., XXIX, 29 n.; *(1898),* XXXVI, 257 ff.; XXXVII, 138 ff.; XXXVIII, 127 ff.
Oregon Fir, schooner *(1920),* IV, 325, plate 52; V, 142
"Oregon" gun, photo of, XLIX, 103
Oregonian, steamship (1866), II, 18; XVIII, 71
"*Oregon* and *Peacemaker* — 12 inch Wrought Iron Guns," by Thomas Hornsby, VI, 212–222, plates 31–32
Oregon Pine, schooner (1920), IV, 325
Oreoma, steam ship *(1924),* XXIV, 203
Orestes, ship *(1814),* XIV, 99; *(1853),* XXXVII, 163
Oresti, Don Jose, XXX, 239
Oreta, cruiser *(1862),* XXXVII, 130
Oreto. See *Florida,* S.S.
Oriana, bark (1864), V, 154
Oribe, Manuel, XXIX, 174 ff.
Orient, brig *(1814),* XVIII, 118
Oriental, bark *(1853),* XLI, 295
Oriental, ship, XXII, 242; (1854), V, 147
Oriental, steamship (1840), XXVI, 9, 12, 29, 203, 206, 209; *(1864),* XXXVII, 234; *(1869),* XXIV, 237
Oriental, Venezuelan man-of-war *(1870),* XXXVIII, 241
Oriental Limited (passenger train), illustration, XLVII, 200
Oriental Screw Collier Co., XVII, 54
Orient Steam Navigation Co., XXXI, 115
Orifice, Captain Joseph, XXI, 98
Oriflamme, steamship (1863), XVI, 174; XVIII, 71; *(1863),* XLIII, 119 ff.; XLIX, 22
Original, English ship *(1790),* XXXIV, 7
Original American Lloyd's Register, XXX, 34
"Original Cost of an Antoine Roux, Sr., Water Color, The," document contributed by Marion V. Brewington, XVII, 72
Original Lloyd's Register of American and Foreign Shipping, XXX, 21
"Origin and Diffusion of Oculi," by Richard LeBaron Bowen, Jr., XVII, 262–291; XVIII, 235–245
"Origin and Diffusion of Oculi: A Rejoinder, The," by Carroll Quigley, XVIII, 25–58, 245–252
"Origin of the Lateen, The," by Lionel Casson, XXXI, 49–51
"Origin of the Marconi Rig, The," by Howard I. Chapelle, XX, 64–66
"Origin of the Marconi Rig, The," by R. C. Anderson, XX, 64
Origins, Orient and Oriana, by Charles F. Morris, reviewed, XLI, 149–151
"Origins of Fore–and–Aft Rigs, The," by Richard LeBaron Bowen, Jr., XIX, 155–199, 274–306
Origins of Sea Terms, by John G. Rogers, reviewed, XLV, 212
Orinoco, schooner-rigged steamship (1855), XXX, 276

Orinoco Steam Navigation Co. of New York, XXX, 269
Oriole, rig (1837), XIV, 40
Oriole, schooner (1852), XXIV, 44, 45, 59
Oriole, steamship (ex-*Eastern Glen*), XXIII, 276
Oriole, U.S.S. *(1904),* XX, 137
Orion, collier *(1887),* XLII, 255
Orion, H.M.S., XXII, 92
Orion, schooner, XXI, 97; *(1862),* XII, 57
Orion, steamship *(1863),* VIII, 231, 235; (1866), I, 76
Orissa, ship, XXII, 242
Orizaba, steamship, XXI, 89, 99; *(1861),* XI, 286; *(1872),* X, 132
Orizimba, ship *(1861),* XXXI, 257
Orkney Islands (Great Britain), History, L, 127
Orkney, Captain John, XLIII, 190 ff.
"Orkney Marine Disasters Changed the Course of History," by Tom H. Inkster, L, 127–131
Orlando, ship (1810), VII, 317
Orleans, schooner *(1914),* XXIII, plate XVIII
Orleans (MA), Battle of (1814), XXIV, 172. *See also* United States History (War of 1812)
Orleans Packet, schooner (1804), VII, 317
Orloff, steamship *(1869),* XVII, 57, 58
Orme, Robert, XXX, 200
Ormsbee's Peak, n.w. Bonin Islands, Pacific Ocean, XXV, plate 20
Orne, Edward, XXV, 183
Orne, Captain Joseph, XXV, 181–182, plate 18
Orne, Timothy, XLI, 176
Ørnen, ship (ex-*Josiah L. Hale*) (1857), XXVIII, plate X
Oroya, Peruvian ship *(1879),* XXXIX, 278
Orozimbo, ship *(1861),* XI, 286
Orpheus, H.M.S. *(1778),* VII, 98; *(1814),* XLIV, 175
Orr, Richard, I, 102; XIX, 153
Ortelius map, XXX, 259
Osado, torpedo boat *(1850),* XLI, 95
Osage, steamship *(1860),* VII, 127 n.
Osage, U.S.S. *(1864),* XXVII, 38 n., 42, 44
Osaka, steamship (ex-*Shanghai*) *(1827),* XLIX, 27
Osberg ships, ca. AD 800, XLIV, 98 ff.
Osborn, Captain Davis, XX, 129 n.
Osborn, Fairfield, Editor, *The Pacific World,* eviewed, V, 93
Osborn, Captain Sherard, XLIII, 294 ff.
Oscar, bark, XXX, 219
Oscar, sloop, XXI, 103; *(1863),* XII, 159, 232
Osceola, bark *(1862),* XXVII, 266; *(1881),* XIX, 232–234
Osceola, S.S. *(1865),* XI, 58
Osceola, schooner, XXI, 95; *(1861),* XI, 286
Osceola, sloop *(1862),* XXI, 92
Osceola, sloop (Boston packet), XXIV, 135
Osceola, steamship (1838), XVIII, 282, 298; (1874), VII, 139–144, 146 n., 150–151, 165, plates 15, 17, 19; (1913), VII, 237
Osceola, U.S. gunboat (1863), XXV, 113
Osgood, Charles, XXVIII, plate XXX
Osgood, Captain Nathaniel S., XXI, 12

Osliaba, Russian warship *(1863)*, XX, 51–53
Osmund, ship *(1922)*, XVIII, 211
"Osnaburg cloth," query by A. T. Dill, Jr., II, 174; answer by M. V. Brewington, III, 86
Osprey, rig *(1841)*, XIV, 44
Osprey, sloop, XXIV, 60
Ossipee, U.S.S. *(1864)*, XXVII, 43; *(1874)*, XXXVIII, 247
"Ostend Packet in a Squall," Pictorial Supplement, XXXI, plate XVII
Osterhaus, Lieutenant Hugo, XL, 128
Oswego, grain elevator *(1883)*, XXXVIII, 141
Oswego, sloop *(1755)*, XLIX, 264 ff.
Oswego, steamship (1833), VII, 52, 54; (1843), XVII, 100; XX, 262; (1848), XVIII, 230
Othello, brig *(1765)*, XXXV, 295 ff.
Othello, ship (1857), IV, 73
Otis, Amos, XIII, 54
Otis, Major General Elwell S., XXXVII, 27; XL, 173 ff.; XXXV, 185 ff.
Otis, James, Jr., XXXI, 19 ff.; XL, 255 ff.
Otis, Lemuel, XXXVIII, 268
Otis Norcross, ship (1862), V, 153
Otori | Taiho Maru (ex-*Columbia*) *(1862)*, XLIII, 197 ff.
d'Otrange Mastai, Boleslaw and Marie-Louise, XXXVII, 133
Otseonthe, ship (1852), II, 331
Otsucho Maru, steamship (ex-*Union*) *(1865)*, XLIX, 26
Ottawa, bark *(1917)*, XVIII, 162, 165, 170
Ottawa, steamship *(1836)*, VII, 62
Ottawa, U.S.S. *(1861)*, XXI, 240; *(1862)*, XV, 118
Ottawa and Rideau Canal Forwarding Co., VII, 62
Otter, brig *(1796)*, XLI, 226; (1811), V, 161
Otter, H.M. sloop *(1778)*, VII, 207
Otter, schooner *(1795)*, XIX, 133, 134
Otter, ship *(1796)*, X, 53
Otter, S.M.S. gunboat *(1910)*, XL, 88 ff.
"Otter Trawling Comes to America: The Bay State Fishing Company, 1905–1938," by Andrew W. German, XLIV, 114–131
Ottowa, steamship (1854), XXVI, 23–25, 29, 203, 206, 209
Ouachita, steamship *(1862)*, VIII, 226
Oudemans, A. C., XLVI, 214
Oudemans, Doctor A. C., XIII, 269
Ouless, P. J., XXIV, plate XXIII
Ouquang, steamship (1862), XVI, 248
Our Lady of Good Faith, Spanish ship *(1629)*, XLIX, 259
Outlook, racing scow (1902), XXX, plate XIX
Outrigger (boat), XXIII, 255
Outrigger canoe, Humboldt Bay, New Guinea, XXIII, 256
Overend, W. H. (artist), XXII, plate XII
Overland China Mail, XXXIV, 34
"Oviedo on Navigation," by Samuel Eliot Morison, I, 391
Owashenonk, steamship (1838), XVIII, 282

Owchita, steamship *(1862)*, XXIV, plate 24
Owen, E. F., X, 112
Owen, Captain Leander, XLIV, 14
Owen, Lewes, XXXI, 87
Owen, Russell, *The Antarctic Ocean*, reviewed, II, 185–187
Owen, W. E., XXVIII, 151
Owens, Dr. Clarence J., XXXV, 172
Owens, Hamilton, *Baltimore on the Chesapeake*, eviewed, II, 89–90
Owens, Robert E., Jr., "John Prichett Gillis," XXXVII, 276–287
Owl, steamship, XXI, 88, 90, 96, 105; *(1864)*, VIII, 235; IX, 33; *(1865)*, XII, 235
Owl's Head, Penobscot Bay, Maine, XXV, plates XX, XXVIII
Owsley, Frank Lawrence, Jr., "The Capture of the C.S.S. *Florida*," XXII, 45–54; *The C.S.S. Florida: Her Building and Operations*, reviewed, XXV, 298–299; re-reviewed, XLIX, 236
Oxford, freighter *(1894)*, XLII, 265 ff.
Oxford, H.M.S., XXVI, 37; *(1667)*, XXV, 279
Oxford, ship *(1855)*, XLI, 298; XLV, 112
Oxford, steamship (1887), XI, 259 ff.; XXXVIII, 185
Oxnard, Captain John H., XVI, 63–65
Oyster Bay, tug *(1879)*, V, 146
Oyster schooners, South Jersey, I, 70
Oyster wars, XXX, 137
Ozanne, Pierre (artist), drawing by, XXV, 126, plate 10

P

P. A. Sanders, schooner *(1862)*, VIII, 226
P. C. Ferguson, schooner *(1861)*, VIII, 220
P. C. Wallis, steamship, XXI, 86; *(1862)*, XII, 57
P. G. Blanchard, ship (1862), V, 154
P. J. Brooks, sloop *(1861)*, VIII, 220
P. J. Nevins, brigantine *(1861)*, VIII, 220
P. M. Anderson, concrete ship (1944), XXII, 179
P. S. Brooks, sloop *(1862)*, VIII, 227
PA. *See* Pennsylvania
Pacha, steamship (1843), XXVI, 115, 117, 203, 206, 209
Pacheco, Rodrigo, XXXVII, 56
Pacific, Collins liner, XXVI, 81 ff., plate 14
Pacific, schooner *(1863)*, XL, 121
Pacific, ship *(1816)*, XV, 306–310; *(1819)*, XV, 155–156
Pacific, steamship, Collins Line (1850), XIV, 239; XXIII, 264; XXIV, plate IV; *(1872)*, X, 132
Pacific, steamship (blockader) *(1863)*, XXI, plate XX
Pacific American, wooden steamship *(1917)*, XXXV, 279
Pacific and Orient Co., XXII, 11–13, 15–17
Pacific Basin: A History of its Geographical Exploration, The, Herman R. Friis, Editor, reviewed, XXVIII, 72

Pacific Coast Steamship Co., XXXVIII, 175 ff.
"Pacific Codfishing Records," by John Lyman, I, 296–297
Pacific Commerical Cable Co., VIII, 191–194
Pacific & Eastern Steamship Co., XXXV, 166 ff.
Pacific Graveyard, by James A. Gibbs, Jr., reviewed, XI, 231
Pacific Improvement Co., XXXI, 128
Pacific, Islands of the, Discovery and exploration, IV, 87; XXXV, 20; XLIX, 151
Note: Here are entered works on the islands of the Pacific Ocean, including the North Pacific Ocean. See also **Oceania;** Guam; Shipwrecks; Whaling
Pacific Mail Line, XXIX, 231
Pacific Mail Steamship Co., II, 5–38, 243; VIII, 180, 191; X, 123–143; XVII, 44, 61, 311–314; XX, 122, 124–129, 132–133; XXXI, 121; XXXII, 197; XXXIII, 47; XXXV, 167 ff.; XLV, 20 ff.; XLVII, 43; XLVIII, 114 ff.
Pacific Marine Construction Co., XXII, 162
Pacific Ocean, The, by Felix Risenberg, reviewed, V, 182–183
Pacific Ocean area, IV, 53–57, 87–118
Pacific Queen, ship *(1886),* IV, 199–206, plates 33–36; X, 121
Pacific Queen, ship *(1935),* XVI, 137–138; *(1936),* XV, 171
Pacific Ranger, freighter *(1930),* XXVIII, 62
Pacific Slope, bark *(1876),* V, 155, 242
Pacific Steam Navigation Co., I, 83; XXXV, 248
Pacific Steam Whaling Co. (of San Francisco), XXXIX, 6 ff.; XLIV, 16 ff.
Pacific Steel Barge Co., XXV, 172
Pacific Trader (1801), XXIII, 216
Pacific Trader, snow *(1792),* XLI, 171; *(1799),* XXXV, 207
Pacific Trading and Transportation Co., XXXV, 181
Pacific, War of the (1879–1884), XXXIX, 271
Pacific World, The, edited by Fairfield Osborn, reviewed, V, 93
Packard, Aubigne L., *A Town That Went to Sea,* reviewed, XI, 298
Packenham, Admiral, XL, 55 ff.
Packet, ship *(1799),* XLI, 174; *(1805),* XV, 133; *(1810),* XXX, 285
Packet, sloop *(1800),* XXVIII, 115; *(1807),* X, 146
"Packet and 'Steam Cars' to Boston: A Sentimental Journey in the 1840's," by Francis W. Hatch, XXVI, 262–271
Packet Lines, XV, 133–141, 306–310; XVI, 60–61; XVII, 25–27
Packets, XV, 133; XVIII, 306; XXIV, 127
Packets, Boston (MA), XXIV, 127–137
Packet ships, I, 44, 47–48, 85–87, 95, 109, plates facing 110–111, 113, 115, 171; II, 81, 176; V, 163–164
Packet ships, Western Ocean, XXII, 73–74
Pactolus, bark (1891), II, 336; VI, 76

Paddle Box Decorations, VI, 136
"Paddle Box Decorations of American Sound Steamboats," by Alexander Crosby Brown, III, 35–47; mentioned, III, 159
Paddle wheel days in California, by Jerry MacMullen, V, 169–170
"Paddle-Wheel Inboard, Some of the History of the Ocklawaha River Steamboating and of the Hart Line," by C. Bradford Mitchell, VII, 115–166, 224–239, plates 13–20, 29–32
Paddlewheel Pirate: The Life and Adventures of Captain Ned Wakeman, by Gordon Newell, reviewed, XX, 72
Paddle wheels, VI, 152
Padelford, Edward, XLVII, 34
Padelford, Fay & Co. (shippers and merchants), XLVII, 35
Padfield, Peter, XXIX, 67–68; *Tides of Empires: Vol. I, Decisive Naval Campaigns in the West, 1481–1654,* reviewed, XLII, 139–140; *Tides of Empires: Vol. II, Decisive Naval Campaigns in the Rise of the West, 1654–1763,* reviewed, XLIV, 279
Padget, Frank, XVI, 41–48
Padtbrugee, Robert, L, 285
Paez, bark *(1848),* XXX, 264
Páez, José Antonio, XXX, 260 ff.
Páez, Ramon, XXX, 265
Pagan's Patent, XXXVIII, 132
Page, Captain Benjamin, XVIII, 105 ff., 129–130
Page, Captain, XLVIII, 239 ff.
Page, Harriet Ware, XXX, 173
Page, Captain John, XXI, 98
Page, Captain Robert, XXI, 98
Page, Thomas, VIII, 310, 314–318; XIX, 44; XXIII, 219
Page, Lieutenant Thomas Jefferson, XXXI, 8, 16
Page, Ambassador Walter H., XXXIV, 157
Page and Mount, VIII, 303, 314
Pageant of the Sea, by M. S. Robinson, reviewed, XI, 297–298
Page & Ropes, XXIII, 131, 132
Paget-Tomlinson, E. W., and H. O. Hill, *Instruments of Navigation,* reviewed, XIX, 146
Paiea, ship *(1871),* XIV, 46
Paige, George W., XXI, 73
Paine, Alfred W., IV, 86, 182; review by, I, 95
Paine, Thomas, XXXIV, 123 ff.; XLVIII, 30
Painted decorations on boats, XXIV, plates 17–20
Paintings and Drawings by Fitz Hugh Lane at the Cape Ann Historical Association (Foreword by Edward Hyde Cox), reviewed, XXXIV, 283
Pak Yun, side-wheel steamship (ex-*White Cloud*) (1859), XVI, 170; XXXIV, 22 ff.
Palacio, Diego Garcia de. *See* Garcia de Palacio.
Palatine Ship, The, XXIII, 38
Palawan, XXX, 201, 202
Palestine, Emigration and immigration, VIII, 127. *See also* Refugees, Jewish
Palfrey, John G., XII, 54

Palgrave, ship (1884), IX, 298
Pallace, brig *(1778)*, VII, 205
Palladium, whale ship *(1821)*, L, 213 ff.
Pallas, bark (1825), XIV, 40; *(1834)*, XXV, 186
Pallas, frigate *(1854)*, XXXI, 268 ff.
Pallas, H.M.S. *(1897)*, XXVIII, 89, 98
Pallas, ship, XXVIII, 200; *(1784)*, XLVI, 32; *(1801)*, XXIV, 262
Pallas, snow *(1807)*, XVI, 196
Palliser, Vice-Admiral Sir High, R.N., VII, 95
Palma, schooner (1862), VIII, 226
Palmer, brig, XIX, 24; *(1824)*, L, 216
Palmer, Aaron Haight, XLI, 27
Palmer, Captain Burrows, XXI, 98
Palmer, Frederick, XXXIV, 270
Palmer, General, Continental Army, XXV, 36
Palmer, H. C., VII, 316; query by, I, 398
Palmer, Surgeon James, XLIX, 153
Palmer, Rear Admiral James S., XXXIV, 62
Palmer, John, VIII, 33, plate 8; XXV, 109; XXXVII, 211
Palmer, Major John McCauley, XXXIV, 262
Palmer, Michael A., L, 270 ff.; "The Dismission of Captain Isaac Phillips," XLV, 94–104
Palmer, Michael A. and William S. Dudley, "No Mistake About It: A Response to Jonathan R. Dull," XLV, 244
Palmer, N. T., XXIII, plate XI
Palmer, Captain Nathaniel, XXV, 54
Palmer, Nathaniel Brown, X, 231 ff.; XXIV, 215
Palmer, Nathaniel T., XX, 237–242
Palmer, William Spencer, document by, XXXV, 207
Palmer fleet, V, 79–81
Palmers' Shipbuilding & Iron Co., Ltd., XXXVIII, 195 ff.
Palmerston, Lord, British Prime Minister, XXXI, 57; XXXIII, 11
Palmette, bark *(1881)*, XII, 105
Palmetto, bark *(1861)*, XVI, 172; XLIII, 290
Palmetto Exporting and Importing Co., IX, 44, 47
Palmetto State, Confederate ironclad (1862), XLIV, 259
Palms, sailmaker's, IX, 281–282
Palmyra, brig (1822), XXIX, 64
Palmyra, ship *(1861)*, XXXIV, 175
Palmyra, ship (1876), XXVII, plate XIX
Palmyra, steamship (1866), XXIV, plate VI; *(1881)*, XIV, 119
Palo Alto, tanker (1920), XXII, 162, 171, 182
Paloma, 1st Lieutenant Ramón, XXX, 50
Palos, schooner, XXVIII, 123
Palos, U.S. gunboat (1866), VII, 108–111, 113, plates 10, 12; *(1867)*, XXVI, 282–283; *(1869)*, XXVII, 176; *(1927)*, L, 260 ff.
"*Palos* Experiments, The," by Captain Edgar K. Thompson, U.S.N. (ret.), XXVII, 176
"*Palos* Experiments, The," document contributed by Charles J. Zibulka, XXVI, 282–283

Paluka, Frank, *The Three Voyages of Captain Cook*, reviewed, XXXIV, 281
Pamelia, brig (1825), Pictorial Supplement, XXXVIII, plate IV
Pam Flush, bark (1855), IV, 239
Pamir, bark (1905), VI, 112–114, plates 13–16; VII, 78
Pampanga, U.S. gunboat *(1925)*, XLIV, 180
Pampero, steamship *(1861)*, XI, 286
Panama, bark (1868), V, 154
Panama, steamship (1848), XIV, 200; X, 125–126, 130; *(1850)*, XLV, 126
Panama Canal, I, 411; V, 231, 311 ff.; XXIV, 186 ff.; XXV, 3
Panama Canal Act, XXXV, 167
Panama, History, Revolution (1903), XXXVII, 253. *See also* Newspapers
Panama Railroad, X, 135–136
Panama Railroad Co., XXXII, 197, 204 ff.; XLVIII, 113
Panama Route, The, by John Haskell Kemble, reviewed, IV, 80–81
Panama Star, XX, 118–133
Panama Transit Steamship Co., X, 136
Pan American Airways, VIII, 195
Panay, gunboat *(1937)*, XXXII, 109; L, 260 ff.
Panay, Salem East Indiamen *(1877)*, XLVI, 63; XLVIII, 120
Panay, ship, XXXVII, 202
"*Panay* Revisited: A Maritime Perspective, The," by David H. Grover, L, 260–268
Pancha Larispa, schooner *(1864)*, XII, 232
P'an Chang-yao. *See* Consequa Pan Zhangyao.
Pangassett, schooner *(1861)*, VIII, 220; XV, 114, 124
Panope, schooner (1820), XIV, 40; XXII, 216
Panorama of San Francisco, XLV, 122–123
Pansoffkee, steamship (1868), VII, 126, 130–135, 138, 140, plate 13
Pantagoet, steamship, XXVIII, 124
Pantaleon, barque, XXI, 91
Pantheon, bark *(1841)*, XX, 184
Panther, bark *(1841)*, XX, 184
Panther, snow *(1800)*, XIX, 12
Panthot, M., VII, 267
Panting, Gerald E. and Lewis R. Fischer, *Change and Adaptation in Maritime History: The North Atlantic Fleets in the Nineteenth Century*, reviewed, XLVII, 64
Pantoleon, ship *(1861)*, XI, 287
Pantooset, steam yacht (1902), XXX, plate XXXII
Panzarbeiter, Captain Charles, XXI, 98
Pan Zhangyao (P'an Chang-yao). *See* Consequa Pan Zhangyao.
Paokong, steamship (1875), XVII, 229; XVIII, 71
Paou Shun, steamship (1851), XXVI, 118, 119, 206, 209
Paouting, steamship (1873), XVI, 262; XVII, 39; XVIII, 71
Papen, Franz von. *See* Von Papen, Franz.
Paper (used in nautical charts), XLVI, 173

Papers of Robert Morris, 1781–1784, The, by E. James Ferguson *et al.,* reviewed, XLVII, 54
Papin, Denis, III, 345 ff.; VII, 271
Papin, Priscilla, XV, 248
Papin, Mrs. Priscilla W., XXXVII, 156
Paradise Lost and Found: The Pacific Since Magellan [Vol. III], by O. H. K. Spate, reviewed, XLIX, 319
Paraense, steamship, XXII, 51
Paragon, steamship (1811), XXIV, 163 n.; XVIII, 317; XXVII, 20, 22, 25, 27
Paraguay:
  Discovery and exploration, XXXI, 7
  Foreign relations, United States, XXXI, 7
  See also Parana River; Plata River System
Paramour Pink, vessel *(1699),* XXX, 205
Parana River (Paraguay), XXXI, 7. *See also* Plata River System
Parc Borély Museum, Marseilles, XX, 234
Parchin, ship *(1911),* XVIII, 150
Pardee, schooner *(1839),* VIII, 49
Pares, Richard, XLI, 181
Paris, steamship (ex-*City of Paris*), XXIV, 126; Pictorial Supplement, XXXIV, plate XX
Paris, Admiral, XIV, 13
Paris, Vice-Admiral Edmond, XVI, 99, 104
Pariser, E. R., XLIV, 110
Paris Peace Conference, XXXIV, 159
Park, Captain John F. N., XXXV, 11
Park, Captain Weare, L, 213
Parke, Captain F. T., XXI, 98
Parke, Captain John P., M.B.E., *Cape Breton Ships and Men,* reviewed, XXVIII, 287–289
Parker, schooner, XXI, 101; *(1861),* XV, 115, 124
Parker, Captain Alden, XXXIX, 220
Parker, C. H., XVII, 47, 50
Parker, Captain Charles, XXXI, 271
Parker, Daniel, XIV, 298–299; XXXI, 39
Parker, Elisha, XXXVII, 270
Parker, Commodore Foxhall A., XXXI, 185; XXXIX, 118; XLI, 29
Parker, Frances D., review by, XLIII, 145–146
Parker, Franklin, "George Peabody and the Search for Sir John Franklin," XX, 104–111
Parker, Captain H., XXI, 99
Parker, Admiral Sir Hyde, R.N., XXII, 270
Parker, Captain Hyde, XXXVIII, 21; XLVI, 165
Parker, Sir Hyde, V, 156–157
Parker, J. C. VII, 51
Parker, John, XXXIII, 201; *Books to Build an Empire: A Bibliographical History of English Overseas Interests to 1620,* reviewed, XXVII, 75; reviews by, XXVII, 71–72; XXIX, 73–74
Parker, John R., III, 213 ff.
Parker, Josiah, XXIV, 66; XXX, 142; XXXIII, 24
Parker, Keith A., "The Bombay Marine," XL, 280–292
Parker, Peter, XXXIV, 105 ff.; XLIV, 9
Parker, Admiral Sir Peter, III, 266

Parker, Dr. Peter, XXXVIII, 28; XLVI, 37
Parker, Sir Peter, XL, 10 ff.
Parker, Robert, XIII, 23
Parker, W. J. Lewis, VI, 307; answered query, I, 174; V, plate 18; reviews by, XXVIII, 287–289; XXXIV, 142–144; XLIII, 311–313; *The Great Coal Schooners of New England, 1870–1909,* reviewed, IX, 231–232; "To 'The River', An Offshore Schooner Trade," XXXV, 5–19
Parker, Captain W. J. Lewis, U.S.C.G., review by, XXV, 147–148
Parker, Admiral Sir William, XLIII, 169 ff.
Parker, Commander William A., XLII, 88 ff.
Parker & Co., Daniel, XLVI, 29
Parker Cook, bark *(1850),* I, 394
Parkes, Oscar, XXII, 252; *British Battleships "Warrior" 1860 to "Vanguard" 1950,* review, XXVII, 281–284
Parkin, William, XVII, 134
Parkins, Captain Curtis F., XXXIV, 14
Parkinson, Charles, XXVI, 215
Parkman, Ebenezer, XXI, 303
Parkman, Francis, XXXV, 159; review by, XXXVII, 70–71
Parkman, John, XXI, 303
Parliament, schooner, XXI, 92; *(1861),* XV, 108, 124
Parliament, ship *(1850),* XV, 140
Parr, Charles McKew, *Jan van Linschoten: The Dutch Marco Polo,* reviewed, XXV, 73–74
Parr, Henry A., XXXIII, 203
Parr, John H., XIX, 53 ff.
Parris, Alexander, VII, 67
Parritt, William, XXIV, 58
Parrott, destroyer *(1932),* XXXVII, 197
Parrott, Commander E. G., XXI, 243
Parrott, Robert, XLIX, 111
Parrott, Robert P., XLV, 39
Parry, Edward, XLVI, 13
Parry, Captain W. E., L, 49
Parry, William E., XXVIII, 151
Parson, General Samuel, XLII, 302
Parsons, Albert E., query by, II, 248; "Government Publications Useful to Model Builders," XI, 215–218
Parsons, Sir Charles, XXX, 153
Parsons, El, XXIV, 58
Parsons, Captain Ernest, XLIV, 122
Parsons, Joshua, XXX, 96 n.
Parsons, Theophilus, XXIX, 204
Parthia, ship (1891), IV, 46, 48, 51, 52, plate 10; XXVII, plate V
Parthia, steamship (1870), I, plate facing 79
Parthina, ship (1852), III, 70, 265
Parthion, ship *(1821),* XXV, 106
Partridge, H.M.S., XXVIII, 18, 89
Partridge, James, XXXII, 279
Pascagoula, schooner, XXI, 91; *(1861),* XI, 287
Pasque Island (MA), VII, 213–223, plates 27–28; IX, 17, 21–24, plate 2; X, 71–73

Pasque Island Fishing Club, VII, 214 ff.
Pasquotank, barge *(1829)*, V, 301
Passaconaway, U.S. monitor (1862), X, 25, 32
Passage from Sail to Steam, by L. R. W. Beavis, reviewed, XLIX, 63
Passage Makers, The, by Michael K. Stammers, reviewed, XLII, 146–147
Passaic, U.S. armored vessel (1862), X, 17, 22–23, 24, 31; *(1862)*, XLVIII, 122; *(1863)*, XLII, 196 ff.; XLIV, 268 ff.; *(1864)*, XXVII, 42, 44
Passaic Mills Cotton, XXXI, 136
Passamaquoddy, schooner (1826), XXIV, 41, 45, 59
Passamaquoddy Ferry Co., XXIV, 53–56
Passenger, Captain W., XXI, 262
"Passenger Ships in the Coastwise Trade: American Public Policy Since 1789," by Mark D. Aspinwall, XLVIII, 173–177
"Passing of the Five Masters, The," by Robert H. I. Goddard, Jr., IV, 58–67
Passow, Captain Frederick M., XX, 193 ff.
Passport, steam tug (1874) XXIII, 88
Passsenger Ships of the World—Past and Present, by Eugene W. Smith, reviewed, XXIII, 228
Patapsco, schooner *(1850)*, XLII, 196 ff.; XLIV, 91, 268 ff.
Patapsco, ship-sloop (1799), XLVI, 151; XLIX, 45
Patapsco, U.S. monitor (1862), X, 17, 23, 24, 27, 31; *(1864)*, XLVIII, 123
Patapsco, U.S.S. *(1800)*, XXXI, 174
"Pat Bellinger and the May 1919 Transatlantic Flight," by Paolo E. Coletta, XLVII, 249–256
Patello, Captain, XXIX, 259
Patent, motor ship *(1917)*, XXII, 158
Patent, steamship, XXVIII, 124
"Patent Devices," query by Thomas Hornsby, III, 353
Pater, Alan F., Compiler and Editor, *United States Battleships: The History of America's Greatest Fighting Fleet*, reviewed, XXIX, 147–148
Paterson, Captain George, XXI, 99
Paterson, John, XXVI, 204
Pathfinder, schooner *(1911)*, XLIX, 278
"Pathway Out of Debt: The Privateering Activities of Sir John Hippisley During the Early Stuart Wars with Spain and France, 1625–30, A," by John Appleby, XLIX, 252–261
Patience, sloop (1739), XII, 226
Pato, schooner *(1877)*, XVIII, 193, 195
Patoka, U.S.S. cruiser *(1921)*, XLVI, 250
Patras, steamship, XXI, 90; *(1862)*, VIII, 226
Patrick Henry, ship (1839), V, 154; *(1844)*, XXXVII, 219
Patrick J. O'Hara (ex-*Spray*), trawler *(1929)*, XLIV, 129
Patridge, Captain Dan, XLIX, 25
Patriot, patrol boat *(1785)*, XXXIII, 24
Patriot, schooner, XXI, 103; *(1833)*, XXIV, 132; *(1861)*, VIII, 220, 226
Patriot, ship *(1804)*, XLI, 285
Patriota, cruiser (ex-*Columbia*) *(1850)*, XLI, 94

"Patriots' Pride, The," poem, VI, plate facing 16
Patron, schooner *(1861)*, VIII, 220
Patroon, ship *(1863)*, XXXI, 84
Patten, Captain F. W., XXIII, 10
Patten, Richard, XLVI, 262
Patten Shipyard, XXVII, plate XIV
Patterson, ship *(1800)*, XVIII, 133; *(1803)*, X, 53
Patterson, U.S.S. *(1810)*, XXX, 292 n.
Patterson, Charles, XXVII, 47, 48, 50
Patterson, Charles R., XIX, 154
Patterson, Charles Robert, II, 291–292; III, 88
Patterson, Corydon Trask, XXVII, 46, 47, 48, 51
Patterson, Emma, XXVII, 47, 48, 50, 54
Patterson, Captain Howard, XLIX, 206
Patterson, John, L, 202 ff.
Patterson, John F., XXXVIII, 241
Patterson, Midshipman John Smith, U.S.N., XXV, 160–161
Patterson, Captain M. F., XVIII, 84
Patterson, General Robert, XXXI, 62
Patterson, Samuel, XXIII, 240, 241, 243
Patterson, Captain William, XXVII, 46 ff.
Pattie, James O., XXIX, 93
Pattison, George C., XXII, 280 n.
Patton, George S., Jr., XXXIV, 265
Patty, sloop *(1778)*, XXXIX, 212
Patuxent River (MD), XLIII, 5
Paul, schooner, XXI, 100; *(1863)*, XII, 159
Paul, ship, XXVII, 182
Paul, Janet, Margery Walton, Julia Bergen, *John Cawte Beaglehole: A Bibliography*, reviewed, XXXIII, 222–223
Paul, Captain Josiah, XVI, 171; XVIII, 84
Paul, Saint, seamanship of, II, 102–106
Paul, Stephen, VIII, 13; XX, 190
"Paul Cuffe's White Apprentice," by Sheldon H. Harris, XXIII, 192–196
Paulding, Hiram, XLI, 29
Paulding, Rear Admiral Hiram, U.S.N., XXII, 259
Paulding, James K., Secretary of the Navy, XXXV, 23; XXXVIII, 119; XLII, 290
Paulet, Lord George, XXXII, 243
Paul F. Albert, schooner, XXXV, 4
Paul H. Harwood, tanker *(1940)*, XLVII, 52
Pauli, John Joachim, XIII, 23
Paulina, brig (1826), XIV, 40
Pauline, bark (1831), V, 150, 242; (1864), IV, 244
Pauline, French ship *(1800)*, XXXI, 175
Paul Jones, tug *(1906)*, XXXVIII, 183 ff.
Paullin, Charles O., XXXIX, 23; XXXV, 63
Paullin, Charles Oscar, *Commodore John Rodgers, Captain, Commodore, and Senior Officer of the American Navy, 1773–1838*, reviewed, XXVIII, 294–295; XXIX, 107 n.
Paul Palmer, schooner (1902), V, 81
Paul Pry, steamship (1830), VI, 210–211; VIII, 43, 44; *(1839)*, XVIII, 284

Paulsen, George E., "Opening the Yangtze Door," XXXIV, 103–122; "*Petrel* Shows the Flag," XL, 100–107; "Under the Starry Banner on Muddy Flat, Shanghai: 1854," XXX, 155–166

Paulsen, Captain Thomas, XXI, 99

Paulson, Captain Richard, XLI, 51

Pawa, Jay M., "The *Jefferson Borden* Pirates and Samuel Gompers: Aftermath of a Mutiny," XXVII, 46–60

Pawnee, U.S. steamship *(1850)*, XXXVII, 279; *(1860)*, XXI, 240

Pawtucket, schooner *(1855)*, XXIV, 141

Pawtuxet, steamship (1864), XVII, 63; XVIII, 71

Payne, Judge John Barton, XLI, 267

Payne, Peter, and Frank J. Merli, "A Blockade-Running Charter: Spring 1862," XXVI, 134–137

Paynter, Captain Charles, VII, 48

Paysan, steamship (1856), XVIII, 71; *(1856)*, XLI, 206 ff.; *(1861)*, XXXIV, 26

Payson, Gilbert R., XXXVII, 156; document contributed by, XXXVII, 220–222; notes by, XXXII, 256; XXXIV, 122; review by, XXXIII, 215; "A Highland Grace," XXX, 186; "Miscellaneous Manavelins," XXXI, 191; "Observations on a Passage in the Ship *Louvre*, 1839," XXXI, 252

PC-490, patrol ship *(1941)*, XXXVIII, 273

PC-595, patrol ship *(1943)*, XXXVIII, 274

Peabody, Captain E., XXV, 169

Peabody, George, XX, 104–111; XXIII, 138; XXV, 188; XXX, 3; XLVI, 60

Peabody, Henry G., Yachting Photographs, Pictorial Supplement, XXX, Plates I-XVI

Peabody, Joseph, II, 39–43, 281–282; XIII, 247

Peabody, Nathaniel, VII, 206–207, 211

Peabody, Robert E., II, 84, 252

Peabody Academy of Science, XLVI, 60

Peabody & Co., Henry W., XLVI, 63

Peabody Essex Museum:
　Art collections, XLIX, 226
　Educational Activities, XLV, 117
　Library resources, XLVIII, 182; XLIX, 230
　See also Essex Institute; Peabody Museum of Salem

Peabody Institute (Baltimore, MD), Editor, *Warner and Hanna's Plan of the City and Environs of Baltimore ... 1801*, reviewed, VIII, 160

Peabody Museum (Salem, Massachusetts) (now part of Peabody Essex Museum). Accreditation of, XXXI, 234; mentioned, XXXII, 29; XXVI, 4, 63, 147, 201, 216, 229; XXX, 3, 32, 91; XXXIV, plate I, 48, 202; XXV, 225; references to, I, 52, 68, 82–83, 198, 315; II, 84, 177, 252, 340; III, 89, 90, 178, 271, 354; IV, 5–17, 78, 87, 107, 252, 336; V, 91, 104, 247, 266–285; VI, 155, 162, 307; VII, 81; VIII, 3, 71, 289 ff., plates 27–28; IX, 82, 166, 185 ff., 296, 299, plates 21–22; X, 33–42, plates 9–12; XI, 3, 81; XIII, 156, 245, 279, 280; XIV, 188, 190; XVI, 3; XVII, 3, 152, 248; XIX, 138–140; XXI, 108, 155; XXIII, 255; XXV, 3, 4, 46, 58, 88, 187 n., 241–242, 277, plates 17–20

Peabody Museum Marine Associates, I, 102, 176, 315, 400; II, 39, 84, 177, 252, 340; III, 89, 178, 271, 354; IV, 78, 252, 336; V, 91, 247; VI, 155, 307; VIII, 3–4; XI, 81; XV, 247

Peabody Museum Collection of Navigating Instruments with Notes on Their Makers, The, by M. V. Brewington, reviewed, XXIV, 217–219

Peabody Museum of Salem. After 1992, *See* Peabody Essex Museum

Peabody Museum of Salem, Report of the Director, 1950, by Ernest S. Dodge, reviewed, XI, 234

Peabody Museum, *Maritime Titles in Print*, XXXIX, 67

Peabody Negative No. 860, XXXV, plate 6

"Peabody Negative No. 864," by John Crosse, XXXV, 32–35

Peace Establishment Act of 1801, The, XXXIV, 27

Peacemaker, 12 inch gun, VI, 212–222

Peaco, Dr. John W., XXXII, 272

Peacock, H.M.S. *(1813)*, VII, 168; XI, 73

Peacock, ship *(1812)*, XLIV, 171

Peacock, sloop *(1814)*, XXIX, 195; XL, 288; *(1815)*, XXXI, 139, 179 ff.; XXXV, 24

Peacock, tug *(1928)*, VIII, 62–65

Peacock, U.S.S. *(1813)*, XIX, 213–226; *(1835)*, XLV, 239; *(1838)*, IV, 105 ff.; XXX, 298; XLVI, 45

Peacock, U.S. sloop of war, XLIX, 152; photo of model, XLIX, 158; (1828), XXI, 303–304; XXV, 187

Peacock, Captain, XXXV, 256 ff.

Peacock, George, XIII, 20

Peale, Titian R., XXX, 298

Peale Museum (Baltimore, MD), IX, 78

Pearce, David, XV, 60

Pearce, Dr. George F., "William Bainbridge, A Journal from City of Washington to Pensacola on USS *Hornet*: Return on USS *John Adams* and by Stagecoach from Savannah, Georgia to Petersburg, Virginia, October-December 1825," XLIV, 245–256

Pearce, Samuel, insurance inspector, I, 43

Pearl, H.M.S. *(1667)*, XXV, 279; *(1717)*, XXX, 136, 137; *(1777)*, XL, 21 ff.

Pearl, H.M.S. *(1897)*, XXVIII, 89

Pearl, schooner, XXI, 87; *(1861)*, VIII, 220, 226

Pearl, ship, XXII, 108

Pearl, steamship *(1863)*, VIII, 231

Pearl, warship *(1776)*, XLIV, 158 ff.

Pearl, Captain Rufus, XXI, 99

Pearl Fisheries of the Persian Gulf, by Richard LeBaron Bowen, Jr., reviewed, XI, 300

Pearse, Elias, IX, 138 ff.

Pearse, Captain Vincent, XIX, 45

Pearson, Alonzo, XVII, 115

Pearson, Ariel, XVII, 123

Pearson, Captain C. P., XXI, 99

Pearson, Captain, XXX, 162

Pearson, Captain F., XVIII, 84

Pearson, George, XVII, 115, 123

Pearson, Captain George F., XXI, 142–143

Pearson, Rear Admiral George F., XXXII, 205
Pearson, Haydn S., *Sea Flavor,* reviewed, IX, 77–78
Pearson, W. Everett, XVII, 115
Pearson, William B., XIII, 270
Peary, Robert E., XXXVIII, 41 ff.
Peasely, A. M. (engraver), XXV, 48, 49
Peat, Captain James, XXI, 99
Peavey, W. S., XXIV, 58
"Peche de la Baleine, Baie de St. Georges, Cap Horn," XXII, plate II
"Peche de la Baleine, Whale Fishery," XXII, plate III
"Peche du Chacalot, Cachalot Fishery," XXII, plate III
Pechiney, auxiliary schooner (1917), XXXII, 32
Peck, Captain Ferdinand, XXI, 99
Peck, Professor W. D., XLVI, 217
Peden, James A., United States Minister to Argentina, XXXI, 16
Pedler of Boston, brig *(1814),* XLII, 4
Pedro Varela, schooner (former U.S. Revenue Cutter *Campbell*) (1853), Pictorial Supplement, XXXIII, plates II, XXXII
Pedro Varella, schooner *(1960),* XXII, plate XXV
Peele, Captain Robert, Pictorial Supplement, XXXII, plate V
Peele, Captain William H., XVII, 44, 47, 50; XLIII, 93
Peele, Hubbell and Co., XVII, 52; XVIII, 59, 60
Peep o'Day, boat *(1864),* XV, 129
Peep O'Day, brig *(1848),* VI, 80; VIII, 226
Peep o" Day, brig, XXI, 90
Pégase, French Navy ship *(1782),* VII, 88
Peggy, French ship *(1800),* XXXI, 174
Peggy, schooner, views of, XXIX, 56, plates 5–8
Peggy, ship *(1774),* VII, 276–277; *(1775),* XXXIX, 195
Peggy (I), schooner *(1791),* XXIX, 55–61
Peggy (II), schooner (1793), XXIX, 55–61
Peggy & Jane, sloop *(1813),* XIX, 217
Pegram, John C., XXII, 284 n.
Pehle, John W., XLIII, 32 ff.
Peiho, ship *(1911),* XVIII, 150
Peiho, steamship (1858), XVI, 170; XVII, 135, 226; XVIII, 71; *(1860),* XXVI, 29; (1866), XVIII, 71
Peirce, Waldo, VIII, 6; XXVIII, plate III
Peixoto, President Floriano, XLI, 245
Pejepscot, steamship (1907), I, 65
Pekin, steamship (1847), XXVI, 11, 12, 14–16, 20, 22–27, 29, 30, 115–117, 202, 203, 206, 209; *(1863),* XLIII, 294 ff.
Peking, ship *(1984),* XLVI, 25
Peking, Mission to, 1870, XXV, 116–122
Pelayo, Spanish warship *(1850),* XLI, 94
Pelican, H.M.S., XXVIII, 18, 26, 89; *(1814),* XLIV, 174 ff.
Pelican, schooner, XXI, 90, 98; *(1861),* XI, 287; XII, 57
Pelican, steamship *(1863),* XII, 159, 235
Pelican State, ship (1851), IV, 51; XXVII, plate III; *(1852),* XLVII, 86
Pell, Captain Jabez J., XX, 184
Pell, Stephen H. P., contributed document, VIII, 255–256
Pellegrin, Honoré, XXVIII, plate VIII
Pellegrin (artist), XXIII, plate III
Pelleport, Gabrielle Josephine de la Fite de, XL, 211
Pelly, Commander F. R., XL, 102
Pelly, Sir John, XIV, 103
Pelteere, Abraham, XXXVII, 14
Pelzer, John D., "Armed Merchantmen and Privateers: Another Perspective On America's Quasi-War with France," L, 270–280
Pemaquid, steamship, XXVI, 262
Pemberton, ship (1748), I, 167
Pemberton, Benjamin, IX, 207
Pemberton, Charles, XXX, 299
Pemberton, Israel, XXV, 106
Pembroke, H.M.S. *(1759),* XXIII, 143
Pembroke, schooner *(1845),* XXXIX, 221
Pembroke, steamship (1860), XVI, 172, 246, 247, 251; XVII, 216; XVIII, 7; *(1860),* XLIII, 116 ff.
Pembroke (MA), XXV, 218–219
Pembroke, Shipping at, ca. 1836, XXIX, plate XXVII
Penang, bark (1864), XXVII, plate XVI
Penang, Malay States, I, 186–187
Pendergrast, Commander C. J., XLVI, 231
Pendergrast, Garrett J., XXXII, 46; XXXVII, 277
Pendergrast, Commander Garrett J., U.S.N., XXIV, 21
Pendleton, Captain Andrew S., II, 199
Pendleton, Captain Barney, XXI, 84, 99
Pendleton, Captain J. O., XVIII, 84
Pendleton, Captain Joseph, XIII, 278
Pendleton, Captain Phineas, II, 327, plate 28
Pendleton Shipyard, XXVII, plate XXIX
Penelope, brigantine (1744), I, 297
Penelope, schooner (1849), XXV, 110; *(1900),* XXXVIII, 88
Penetanguishene, steamship (1836), VII, 62
Penguin, H.M.S. *(1815),* XIX, 220, 221
Penguin, ship *(1815),* XLIV, 171
Penhallow, John, VII, 210
Penhallow, Samuel, XXXV, 158
Peniche, First Lieutenant José Tomas, XXX, 274
Peninsula, wooden steamship *(1917),* XXXV, 279
Peninsular and Occidental Steamship Co., XXXIII, 92; XXXIV, 181
Peninsular and Oriental Steam Navigation Co., XXVI, 5–32; XXXIV, 36 ff.; XLIII, 103 ff.
Peninsula Shipbuilding Co., Portland, Oregon, XXXII, 32
Peniston, Captain Thomas, XVII, 294
Pennanen, Gary, "The Fortune Bay Affair, 1878–1881: Massachusetts Fishermen Versus The British Crown," XXXIX, 289–301
Penneager, William, XXXV, 294
Pennington, Captain John, XXXVII, 10
Pennington, Captain William T., XXI, 99
Pennoyer, Captain James, XII, 149–150

Pennsalt Chemicals Corp., XXII, 180
Pennsylvania, receiving ship *(1846)*, XXX, 144
Pennsylvania, steamship *(1831)*, XLVIII, 109; (1832), VII, 48, 65; *(1836)*, XVIII, 275; XX, 83 n.; *(1910)*, X, 140, 142
Pennsylvania, transport *(1899)*, XXXV, 185
Pennsylvania, U.S. armored cruiser (1905), XXII, 146
Pennsylvania, U.S. battleship *(1918)*, VII, 72
Pennsylvania, U.S.S. (1822), XXI, 62; XXIII, 58 n.; *(1831)*, VII, 190
Pennsylvania, warship *(1844)*, XL, 43; *(1921)*, XXXV, 122
Pennsylvania Committee of Safety, XL, 12
Pennsylvania Packet, ship *(1805)*, XLVIII, 250 ff.
Pennsylvania (PA). *See* Harbors, Philadelphia, Steamboats
Penobscot, bark (1878), XXVIII, plate XX
Penobscot, steamship (1882), XII, plate 29; *(1906)*, XXIV, 53
Penobscot, U.S. gunboat *(1862)*, VIII, 199
Penobscot, U.S. sidewheeler (1882), XXXIII, 94, 130
Penobscot, Sailing Days on the, by George S. Wasson, reviewed, IX, 232–233
Penobscot Bay (ME), XXV, plate XXVIII
Penobscot expedition (1779), VII, 200; XXXVII, 288. *See also* Maine; United States History (Revolution)
"Penobscot: From the Jaws of Victory—Our Navy's Worst Defeat," by Jon M. Nielson, XXXVII, 288–305
Penobscot Indian canoe, VIII, 289–300
Penobscot Marine Museum (Searsport, Maine), XLII, 121; I, 65, 68, 87, 198; III, 91–92; IV, 167; Pictorial Supplement, XXVIII, Part I, 32; Part II, 112; Part III, 192; Part IV, 250
Penobscot Marine Museum, *Maritime Titles in Print*, XXXIX, 73
Penrose, James, VIII, 15
Pensacola, ship *(1867)*, XXXIII, 281
Pensacola, U.S.S. *(1891)* XXXVIII, 291
Pensacola fishing fleet, II, 229–242
Pensacola (FL) Navy Yard, XLIV, 245
Pensecola, U.S.S. *(1900)*, XX, 136
People of the Sea: The Maritime History of the Channel Islands, A, by A. J. Jamieson, reviewed, XLVIII, 196
Peoples Liberation Army (PLA), L, 291 ff.
People's Line, XVIII, 224
"Pepper, Pirates and Grapeshot," by Captain John Campbell, XXI, 292–302
Pepperell, William, XLV, 42 ff.
Pepperrell, Colonel William, IX, 134 ff.
Pepperrell, Sir William, XLVIII, 25
Pepper trade, IX, 239; XXI, 292
Pepys, Samuel, XI, 6 ff.; XIV, 266, 270; XXV, 279–281, 283–286; L, 19 ff.
Pequod, ship, XLVI, 197
Peralta, tanker (1920), XXII, 162, plate 7, 171, 182
Perceval, Spencer, XXIII, 160, 163, 172

Percival, Captain John, XLVII, 169 ff.
Percy & Small, V, 138; XXIII, 14, plates XVI, XXIII, XXV
Percy and Small Shipyard, editorial comment, XXXIX, 158; XXVII, plate XXVII
Peregrine Galley (1700), XXVIII, 225
Pereira, John, XIII, 11
Pereira, Paulo, XIII, 11
Pere Marquette 21, steamship, XXIII, 71
Pere Marquette Line, XXIII, 70
Peresvet, Russian warship *(1863)*, XX, 52, 53, 56, 57
Pérez Embid, Florencio, *El Almirantazgo de Castilla*, reviewed, VII, 250
Peri, bark *(1861)*, XXI, 258
Pericles, ship (1860), V, 148
Periere, steamship (1866), IX, 298; (1869), XX, 184
"Perils of Invention: Bradley A. Fiske and the Torpedo Plane, The," by Paolo E. Coletta, XXXVII, 111–127
"Perils of the Sea," by Captain Edgar K. Thompson, U.S.N. (ret.), XXVII, 97
Periplus Maris Erythraei ("Sailing Guide to the Red Sea"), XLVIII, 149
Periwinkle, periagua (1879), XXX, 198 f.
Perkins, Captain Andrew, XXXIX, 207
Perkins, Captain Clement, VIII, 173
Perkins, Dexter, XXXII, 258
Perkins, Lieutenant Commander George W., XLVIII, 93
Perkins, Captain J. A., XVIII, 84
Perkins, Richard, XXVIII, 4
Perkins, S. G., XLVI, 213
Perkins, Thomas H., XIII, 269 ff.
Perkins, Colonel Thomas H., XLVI, 213; XLVIII, 246
Perkins, Thomas H., Jr., XVI, 161
Perkins, William, VII, 269
Perkins and Co., XIII, 122
Pero Mascarenhas, XXXI, 105
Peronne, auxiliary schooner (1918), XXXII, 32
Perry, brig *(1844)*, XXXI, 185; XXXIV, 82
Perry, U.S. brig *(1863)*, L, 93
Perry, Alonzo W., XXXVII, 238
Perry, Catharine A., drawings for "The Sailmaker's Gear," IX, 278–296
Perry, George D., XXXV, 286
Perry, Hamilton Darby, L, 260 ff.
Perry, Commodore M. C., XIII, 233
Perry, Lieutenant Commander Matthew C., XXXII, 126, 268; XXXIII, 269
Perry, Matthew Calbraith, XLI, 33; XLIV, 9
Perry, Commodore Mathew Calbraith, VI, 234; VII, 9–17; XXI, 33–35; XXV, 94–95, 159; XXVII, 160, 161, 162; XXIX, 108, 109, 111; XXX, 155, 158, 159; XLVI, 50; XLVII, 30. 174 ff.; L, 107
Perry, Oliver H., XX, 214
Perry, Oliver H. (boatbuilder), XLII, 105, 166
Perry, Commodore Oliver H., XXXVIII, 263 ff.; XLIV, 105; XLVII, 27

Perry, Captain Oliver Hazard, XXXV, 118
Perry, Peter, "The Newfoundland Trade: The Decline and Demise of the Port of Poole, 1815–1894," XXVIII, 275–283
Perry, Captain Samuel, XXIII, 28
Perry, Captain William, XXI, 99
Perry and Japan, by Harold A. Mattice, reviewed, II, 352
Persano, Admiral Pellion di, XV, 200 ff.
Perserverance, ship (1794), Pictorial Supplement, XXXII, plate XVII; *(1801),* XXIII, 216; *(1802),* XXIII, 217
Perseverance, auxiliary schooner (1922), V, 141
Perseverance, brig *(1819),* XL, 41
Perseverance, schooner, XXII, 60 n.
Perseverance, ship, XXV, 61; (1791), XXVIII, 178–180, 184; *(1804),* X, 54; (1809), II, 282; (1886), IX, 298
Perseverance, steamship *(1811),* XXVII, 19, 24–26; *(1831),* VII, 44
Pershing, Major General John J., XXXIV, 262 ff.
"Pershing Goes 'Over There': The Baltic Trip," by Donald Smythe, XXXIV, 262–277
Persia, brig *(1822),* XXV, 183
Persia, ship (1860), IV, 47, 51, 52
Persia, steamship *(1906),* X, 138
Persis, sloop, XXI, 102, 106; *(1864),* XV, 129
Persus, H.M.S. *(1777),* XIII, 46 ff.
Perth, cruiser *(1942),* XLII, 203
Perth Amboy Dry Dock Co., XXX, 188
Perthshire, ship *(1861),* XI, 264, 287
Peru, bark, XXV, 186
Peru, steamship (1840), XXXV, 248 ff.; (1892), X, 137
Peru, boats of, XIII, 89 ff.
Perusia, steamship *(1857),* XVII, 142; XVIII, 71
Peruvian, whaler *(1851),* XLI, 292
Peruvian navigation, II, 107–126
Pervenetz, Russian warship *(1863),* XX, 51, 56
Perves, Hugh, VII, 112
Peso, Captain Piento, XXI, 99
"Pestilence From the Sea and American Quarantine Policy," by Robert G. Hancock, Jr., L, 94–106
Pet, sloop *(1865),* XII, 235
Pet, steamship, XXI, 89, 105; (1861), XVII, 310; XLIII, 196 ff.; *(1863),* VIII, 231, 235; IX, 34–35
Pete Culler's Boats, by John Burke, reviewed, XLV, 212
Petee, sloop, XXI, 87
Peter, bark (1852), V, 147; *(1861),* VIII, 220
Peter C. Warwick. bark (1858), VI, 82
Peter Demill, bark *(1861),* XV, 108 n.; XXI, 239, 256
Peter Dickson, schooner *(1861),* VIII, 220
"Peter Funk Ticket," XX, 123
Peterhof, steamship *(1862),* VIII, 227
Peterhoff, steamship *(1863),* XXI, plate XXIV
Peter Kerr, steamship (ex-*Eastern Sailor*), XXIII, 276
Peter Marcy, ship, XXI, 97; *(1861),* XI, 287
Peter Rickmers, ship (1889), IX, 298
Peters, Captain Arthur B., XIV, 117
Peters, Chester, XXXIV, 243 ff.
Peters, Harold, XXV, 234, 246–247; "The Jakey Boats," XIX, 73
Peters, Lieutenant Commander J. H., U.S.N.R.F., VII, 72
Peters, James, XX, 36–38
Peters, Captain Osmond, XL, 300
Peters, Robeson, review by, XLII, 147–148
Petersburg, steamship (1819), V, 301–302
Petersen, Jacob, X, 230
Petersen, Lauritz, "The Norwegian Ship Identification Signals, 1829–1867," XXI, 70–72
Petersen, Captain Thomas, XV, 154
Peterson, Captain Charles, VII, 292
Peterson, Captain Frank H., IX, 70
Peterson, H., XXVII, plate X, XV
Peterson, Captain John, XXI, 99
Peterson, Captain Pet, IX, 229–230
Peter Stuyvesant, steamship *(1956),* XVIII, 234
Pethick, Derek, *The Nootka Connection: Europe and the Northwest Coast 1790–1795,* reviewed, XLII, 144–145
Petie, sloop *(1863),* XV, 111, 128
Petigru, Commander Thomas, XXXV, 26 ff.
Petite Clementine, schooner, XXI, 91; *(1861),* XI, 287; XII, 159
Petite Democrate, brig *(1793),* XXII, 81, 92–95
Petley-Jones, Evan W., reviews by, XXIX, 68–69, 145–147; XXX, 221–222
Petral, ship *(1898),* XXXIX, 41
Petral (ex-*William Aiken*), privateer *(1861),* XLVIII, 93
Petrejus, E. W., XV, 81; *Modelling The Brig-of-War "Irene;" A Handbook for the Building of Historical Ship-Models,* reviewed, XXX, 301–302
Petrel, Confederate privateer (ex-*William Aiken*) *(1861),* XLIV, 258
Petrel, gunboat *(1863),* XXXIV, 212
Petrel, Mexican gunboat *(1846),* XXX, 55
Petrel, schooner, XXI, 93, 99; (1840), Pictorial Supplement, XXXIII, plates XX, XXI; 209; *(1861),* VIII, 220
Petrel, ship *(1895),* XXXVII, 140 n.; XXXVIII, 124; XL, 100 ff., plate 2; *(1898),* XXXV, 184 ff.
Petrel, steamship *(1864),* VIII, 235
Petrel, U.S. gunboat *(1896),* XXIX, 116
"*Petrel* Shows the Flag," by George E. Paulsen, XL, 100–107
Pett, Peter, XXV, 284
Pettersen, Captain Harald, XVIII, 178–180
Pettigrew, Mark, XVII, 114
Pettit, Edward, XVII, 47; XXXIV, 44
Pettitt, Henry G., "'They Were a Class Apart:' The Story of Life Aboard One of the Four-Stack Flush Deck Destroyers in the Years Between the Two World Wars," XLVI, 240–251
Petty, Lord Henry, XXIII, 165
Petty, Lieutenant, XIII, 50
Pevensey, steamship *(1864),* VIII, 235
Peyster, Abraham. *See* dePeyster, Abraham.

Pfeil, German U-boat group, XLIV, 48 ff.
Phaeton, British ship *(1738),* XLVIII, 23
Phantom, schooner *(1908),* Pictorial Supplement, XXXIV, plate XVII
Phantom, ship, XXVIII, 152
Phantom, sloop, XXI, 90, 99; *(1864),* XII, 232, 235
Phantom, steamship, XXI, 88, 99; *(1863),* VIII, 231
Pharos, ship (1868), III, 172; (1877), III, 63
Phebe Chapman, schooner *(1888),* XI, 204
Phebe (Fijian child), XXV, 274 ff.
Phelomina Manter, schooner (1884), XXVI, plate V
Phelps, Anson G., XXXIX, 47
Phelps, Edward J., XXXIX, 127
Phenix, whaler, XXV, 105
Phenix, Spencer, XXXIV, 165 ff.
Phenix Manufacturing Co., XXXI, 136
Phenix Mill Cotton, XXXI, 136
Philadelphia, brigantine *(1792),* V, 89
Philadelphia, Continental gundalow *(1935),* XLIX, 39
Philadelphia, Continental Navy gondola *(1776),* VIII, 256; XLVII, 109
Philadelphia, cruiser *(1888),* XXXIX, 136
Philadelphia, schooner *(1855),* XXIV, 143
Philadelphia, ship *(1792),* X, 53, 55; *(1799),* XLI, 28; XLIII, 137 ff.; *(1803),* XXXVII, 131 ff.; XXXIX, 111; *(1892),* XXXVIII, 298
Philadelphia, U.S. steamship, XXIX, 231; *(1860),* XXI, 142–143, 240; *(1864),* XXII, 284 n.; *(1865),* VIII, 237
Philadelphia, steamship (ex-*City of Paris*), Pictorial Supplement, XXXIV, plate XX
Philadelphia, tow boat (1883), I, 72
Philadelphia, U.S. cruiser (1890), XXIV, 214; XXV, 50
Philadelphia, U.S.S. (1799), XXV, 159; XLVI, 151 ff.; XLVII, 14 ff.; photo of the building, XLVI, 153; (1800), XXXI, 175; XXXIII, 64; XXXIV, 128; (1860), XXXVII, 281
Philadelphia (PA):
  History (1703–1789), XXXII, 247
  Centennial Exhibition, (1876), XLVII, 174
Philadelphia, Market Street Bridge (1805), II, plate 22
Philadelphia arrivals (1800), III, 302–305
Philadelphia Centennial Exposition, XXXVIII, 123
Philadelphia customs record, XIII, 123
Philadelphia Maritime Museum, XXII, 79
Philadelphia Maritime Museum, *Maritime Titles in Print,* XXXIX, 73
Philadelphia on the River, by Philip Chadwick Foster Smith, reviewed, XLIX, 313
"Philadelphia Shipbuilding Contract of 1746, A," document contributed by John Lyman, V, 243
"Philadelphia Shipwrights," query by M. V. Brewington, II, 248
"Philadelphia Steamboat? An Early," document, III, 268
"Philadelphia Steamboat of 1796, The," by Melvin H. Jackson (supplemented, edited and illustrated by Paul Forsythe Johnston), L, 201–218

Philadelphia vessels condemned at Jamaica, II, 203–208
Philbrick, Richard B., contributed document, XXIII, 145
Philena, bark (1856), XXIV, 57
Philip III, King of Spain, XXVIII, 250, 258
Philip, Cynthia Owen, *Robert Fulton, A Biography,* reviewed, XLIX, 238
Philip, Lieutenant Commander John W., XXXII, 126
"Philip Freneau, Our Sailor Poet," by Philip Marsh, VI, 115–120
Philip L. Rhodes and his Yacht Designs, by Richard Henderson, reviewed, XLIV, 133
Philip P. Manta, schooner *(1932),* XXXIII, 64
Philippine Islands, boats of, XIX, 257–264
Philippines, History, –, Insurrection (1899–1900), XXXV, 183
Phillip, schooner (1848), XXIV, 59
Phillip Allen, Confederate cutter *(1860),* XLVIII, 90
Phillips, Benjamin Hammell, XLV, 98
Phillips, Miss Della, XXIX, 263 ff.
Phillips, Elisha, XXV, 222
Phillips, George, XXXI, 24
Phillips, Captain Isaac, XLV, 94 ff.; XXII, 264 ff.
Phillips, J. R. S., *The Medieval Expansion of Europe,* reviewed, XLIX, 233
Phillips, James Duncan, I, 400; II, 252, 340; V, 91; "The Adventures of the Ketch *John,*" IV, 18–30; "The Attack on the Marquis," IX, 239–248; "Routine trade of Salem under the Confederation Congress, The, May 1783–October 1789," I, 345–351; *Salem and the Indies,* reviewed, VII, 323; "The Salem Shipbuilding Industry before 1812," II, 278–288; "The Ship *Martha's* Shopping Trip in the Mediterranean in 1801," V, 43–63; review by, II, 348
Phillips, John, XXX, 58
Phillips, Captain John, VII, 66
Phillips, John C., XIII, 122
Phillips, Owen, XLVI, 105
Phillips, Captain S. J., XIV, 125
Phillips, Stephen, XLII, 121
Phillips, Captain Stephen, IV, 18, 28 ff.
Phillips, Stephen C., whaling fleet of, Pictorial Supplement, XXXVIII, plate VIII
Phillips, Stephen W., VI, 307
Phillips, Stephen Willard, I, 87, 176, 315; II, 252; III, 178; IV, 5
Phillips, Captain Thomas, XXI, 99
Phillips, William, XL, 267; XLI, 184
Phillips Academy (Andover, Massachusetts), XLII, 131
Phillipse, Adolph, XXXVII, 57
Phillipse, Frederick, XXXVII, 57
Philo-Parsons, steamship *(1863),* XLVIII, 101
Phineas Pendleton, ship (1866), XXVIII, plate XIII
Phineas W. Sprague, schooner (1887), VI, 133; XXXV, 16
Phipps-Hornby, Rear Admiral R. S., XXVIII, 108
Phips, Sir William, II, 171–172; VII, 272
Phlegathon, H.C.S.S. *(1842),* XXVI, 6 n.

Phoebe, British man-of-war *(1814)*, XLIV, 174 ff.
Phoebe, steamship *(1862)*, XXIV, plate 24
Phoenician war vessel, photo of bas relief, L, 196
Phoenix, American schooner *(1780)*, XXXI, 249
Phoenix, French ship *(1800)*, XXXI, 175
Phoenix, H.M. frigate *(1776)*, III, plate 1; XXXVIII, 21; *(1882)*, XXVIII, 26
Phoenix, H.M.S., XXVI, 40, 41
Phoenix, privateer *(1745)*, XLII, 50
Phoenix, schooner, XXI, 95; *(1794)*, XIV, 40; *(1861)*, XI, 287; XII, 57
Phoenix, ship *(1569)*, XLIV, 26 ff.; (1612), XIV, 10, 11; *(1861)*, XV, 108 n.; XXI, 239, 256
Phoenix, steamship (1807), XVI, 271; (1808), XII, 239, Plates 21, 22
Photographic Portraits of American Ocean Steamships, 1850–1970, reviewed, L, 69
"Photographs," query by M. V. Brewington, III, 353
Photography. *See* Marine photography
Phrenologist, steamship *(1864)*, XLIII, 111 ff.
Phyllis Comyn, barkentine (1920), V, 82
Pickens (ex-*Robert McCelland*), Confederate revenue cutter *(1861)*, XLVIII, 89 ff.; (1862), XL, 300
Pickering, U.S.S. *(1799)*, XXXI, 173
Pickering, Charles, XXX, 298
Pickering, Thomas, XXII, 273
Pickering, Captain Thomas, XIII, 39 ff.
Pickering, Lieutenant Thomas, XXXII, 135
Pickering, Timothy, Secretary of State, XLV, 37, 97; L, 270 ff.
Pickering, Timothy, VII, 255–256; XXVI, 244–246, 248; XXIX, 204; XXX, 126; XXXI, 112; XXXIV, 140
Pickernal, Samuel, XXI, 15
Pickett, General George, XLII, 90 ff.
Picking, Commander Henry F., XLI, 247
Picking, Lieutenant Commander Henry F., U.S.N., VII, 107, 110; diary quoted, VII, 112; VII, plate 9
Picking, Captain Sherwood, U.S.N., VII, 107
Pickman, Benjamin, XXII, 196
Pickman, Colonel Benjamin, XXIII, 132
Pickman, Dudley Earl, XXV, 180–181, 183
Pickman, Dudley Leavitt, XLVII, 119 ff.
Pickman, William D., XLVII, 120
Pickman-Derby-Brook House, cupola from, Pictorial Supplement, XXXII, plate XXVIII
Pickney, sloop *(1862)*, XII, 57
Pickwick, sloop *(1864)*, XII, 232
Pictorial Supplements: XIX, 64, 106, 198, 266; XX, 48, 122, 198, 242; XXI, 48, 124, 216, 268; XXII, 16, 108, 200, 292; XXIII, 16, 140, 184, 284; XXIV, 64, 140, 216, 292; XXV, 64, 140, 216, 292; XXVI, 64, 140, 200, 242; XXVII, 48, 124, 216, 276; XXVIII, 32, 112, 192, 250; XXIX, 48, 124, 198, 274; XXX, 64, 124, 198, 272; XXXVI, Marine Paintings of John Faunce Leavitt, Part I, between 32–33, Part II, between 138–139, Part III, between 198–199, Part IV, between 250–251; XXXVII, The Art of the Shipcarver at the Peabody Museum of Salem, Part I, between 32–33, Part II, between 124–125, Part III, between 184–185, Part IV, between 242–243; XXXVIII, Marine Paintings of William Henry Luscomb and Benjamin Franklin West of Salem, Part I, between 40–41, Part II, between 100–101, Part III, between 216–217, Part IV, between 300–301

Pictou-Quebec Line, XXXVII, 232 ff.
Piege, French ship *(1800)*, XXXI, 174
Pierce, A., XIV, 44
Pierce, Captain C. L., XXI, 99
Pierce, Daniel, XXVIII, 118
Pierce, Captain Ebenezer, XXVII, 279
Pierce, Captain Elijah L., XXXV, 83
Pierce, President Franklin, XXXI, 59
Pierce, Jerathmiel, XIII, 275
Pierce, Waldo, XXVIII, plate III
Pierpont, Francis, XXXI, 62
Pierrepont, Constable, XLVIII, 265
Piez, Charles A., XXXII, 162; XXXV, 281
Pigeon, Navy Tug *(1937)*, L, 260 ff.
"Piggin Stick," query by John R. Herbert, III, 353
Pigot, British galley *(1780)*, XXXI, 249; XXXV, 141
Pigot, Governor, XXX, 201–203, 207
Pigot, Admiral Sir Hugh, XIII, 254
Pike, Elias, XVII, 120
Pike, George, XVII, 120, 121
Pike, Nicholas, XXXI, 114
Pike, William, XVII, 120
Pilcomayo, Peruvian corvette *(1864)*, XXXIX, 275
Pile, William Jr. (shipbuilder), XLIII, 91 ff.
Pilgrim, brig, XXII, 94; *(1763)*, XLIV, 5; (1825), XII, 178–183; XIII, 164–171; XIV, 34; *(1835)*, XXIX, 87, 88; XXX, 300
Pilgrim, ship *(1804)*, X, 54; *(1861)*, XI, 287; *(1864)*, XLVII, 121
"Pilgrimage of Lt. Alexander Pinkham, U.S.N.—A Mariner's Adventure Ashore, The," by Edouard A. Stackpole, XLIV, 103–109
Pilgrim Hall Museum (Plymouth, MA), XIV, 14
Pilgrim Society, XIII, 58 ff.
Pillars of Gold, by Lucile Selk Edgerton, reviewed, I, 405–406
Pillsbury, Captain Hiram, X, 214
Pillsbury, Master John E., U.S.N., VII, plate 9
Pilot, schooner *(1823)*, VI, 100
Pilot Boat No. 8, XXXVII, 89
Pilot House Museum, The, XXVII, 156
Pilot's Bride, centerboard sloop (1886), I, 73
Pilot's Bride, schooner *(1880)*, XLV, 114
Pimer, John, XXXI, 136
Pimpernel, H.M.S. *(1942)*, L, 44
Piñango, General Judas Tadéo, XXX, 263
Pinar del Rio, steamship *(1933)*, XIV, 127, 135
Pinckney, Attorney General William, XLVI, 170
Pinckney, Charles Cotesworth, XXIV, 61

Pinckney, Major General Charles Cotesworth, XLVI, 141; XLVII, 22; L, 270 ff.
Pinckney, Pauline A., *American Figureheads and their Carvers,* reviewed, I, 178–181
Pinckney, Midshipman Richard S., XXIX, 281
Pinckney, Thomas, XXIII, 162
Pindar, British schooner *(1814),* XLII, 112 ff.
Pinder, Captain J. F., XXI, 99
Pine, Captain Ben, IX, 73
Pinedo, Captain José, L, 31
Pingon, steamship (1865), XVI, 166, 176–179; XVII, 51, 138, 140, 215 ff.; XVIII, 60, 71
Pingree, David, XXX, 229 ff.
Pingree, Thomas P., house flag, Pictorial Supplement, XXXVIII, plate XXIII
Pinhorn, Captain Thomas, XXXV, 262
Pink, H.M. corvette *(1943),* L, 219 ff.
Pinkham, Lieutenant Alexander, U.S.N., XLIV, 103 ff.
Pinkham, Captain Andrew, XLIV, 104 ff.
Pinkham, David Coffin, XXXVIII, 267
Pinkham, Captain Paul, XLIII, 51–55
Pinkie, XII, 133–135, plate 11
Pinkney, William, XLIII, 47
"Pinkys," query by W. B. Yarnall, VI, 153; answer by Harry D. Hamilton, VI, 232
Pinola, U.S.S. *(1861),* XII, 271–276
Pinta, schooner (1865), XXIV, 45, 46, 59
Pinta, Spanish ship, XXX, 257
Pinta II, ship [replica] (1892), XIV, 109, 110
Pinto, cruiser *(1891),* XXXVIII, 298
Pinzón, Martín Alonso, XXX, 257
Pio Benito, barkentine (1874), V, 86
Pio del Pilar, General, XXXV, 189
Pioneer, brig (1824), XIV, 40
Pioneer, derrick scow *(1865),* VII, 128
Pioneer, schooner, XXI, 100; (1826), XXIV, 45, 59; *(1861),* XI, 287; XII, 57, 159
Pioneer, ship *(1860),* XX, 215
Pioneer, sloop, XXI, 91; *(1862),* XII, 57
Pioneer, steamship (1825), VI, 199, 201, 206; X, 176; *(1834),* VII, 53, 55; *(1841),* V, 302; *(1851),* XXXIV, 97; (1854), XXVI, 112, 113, 206, 209; *(1856),* XLIII, 201 ff.; XLIV, 14
Pioneer, U.S. exploring vessel, Continental Navy, XXIII, 58 n.
"Pioneer Transatlantic Paddle Steamers," by H. Philip Spratt, IX, 249–272, plates 25–28
Piper, Robert, XVII, 122
Pique, H.M.S., XXII, 31
Piracy. *See* Pirates
Piracy and pirates: V, 157–159; VI, 93–100; VIII, 173–174; IX, 134, 239–248; XXX, 133–138; Chinese, XXX, 295, 296; Malay, XIX, 232–234; list of pirates, XXXVII, 44–45
Pirate, sharpie *(1902),* XXX, 198, 199
Pirates, XXXVII, 40
    Africa, XXIII, 95
    Atlantic Ocean, IX, 11
    China, XLVIII, 237
    South America, VII, 282
    Sumatra, XXI, 292
    United States, XXVII, 46; XXXII, 195
    West Indies, XLII, 165
    —, **19th century,** VI, 93
    See also Privateering; Privateers
"Pirates and Perfidy," Document contributed by Philip C. F. Smith, XXX, 294–296
Pires, Tomé, VI, 308–309
Piscataqua, Ports of, by William G. Saltonstall, reviewed, II, 91
Piscataqua, screw frigate *(1867),* XLIII, 179 ff.; XLV, 239; XXXII, 135
Piscataqua, ship *(1853),* XXV, 108
Piscataqua River gundalow, I, 68; II, 127–139, 209–222
"Piscataqua River Gundalow, The," by D. Foster Taylor, II, 127–139
"Pistols and Honor: The James Barron – Stephen Decatur Conflict, 1798–1807," by William M. P. Dunne, L, 245 ff.
Pitcairn, brig (1889), XI, 203–208, plate 24
Pitcairn, Major John, XXIII, 176
Pitcairn, Joseph, XXX, 286
"*Pitcairn,* Missionary Packet," by John Lyman, XI, 203–208
Pitcairn Island, XXXVII, 66–69
Pitcairn's Island, I, 297–300
Pitcher, William, XXII, 44
Pitt, brig *(1769),* IX, 9, 144
Pitt, British merchantman *(1804),* XLIII, 43
Pitt, ship (1809), XXIX, 48, plate II
Pitt, Maria Harriet, XLVI, 47
Pitt, Signor Martin, XIII, 23
Pitt, Thomas, XIII, 8, 12, 21, 22
Pitt, Thomas J., XL, 43
Pitt, William, VII, 21, 23, 29–34; XXVII, 213; XXIX, 244; XLVI, 24
Pittee, Charles Rodney, "The Gloucester Steamboats," XII, 288–293, plates 26–28
Pittman, Lieutenant Philip, I, 143
Pitt Packet, brig, XXIII, 144
Pittsburg, U.S.S. (1861), XIX, 266
Pittsburgh, ship (1801), VII, 317
Pittsburgh, steamship *(1923),* X, 193
Pittsburgh, U.S. destroyer *(1921),* XLVI, 249 ff.
Pittsburgh Cannon Foundry, XLV, 38
"Pittsburgh's Dravo Corporation and Naval Shipbuilding in World War II," by William F. Trimble, XXXVIII, 272–290
Pity, James, XXII, 269
Pitz, Herbert, II, 335–336
"Pitz Papers in the Burton Historical Collection, Detroit Public Library," by H. W. Potter, II, 335–336
Pixley, Captain William, XIV, 83–104
Pizarro, Spanish warship *(1871),* XXXVIII, 241

Pizarro, steamship, XXI, 100; *(1861),* XI, 287
Pizigani, XXX, 251
Planet, pinky *(1832),* XXXVII, 169
Planet, steamship (1855), I, 76
Planicus, Petrus, L, 281
Planking, steaming of, VII, 196–199
Plan of 8-incher and carriage carried on *Princeton* (1846), XLIX, 110
Plans, Light-Vessels: No. 50 *Columbia River,* IX, between 274–275; built by Henry Eckford (1823), V, 118
Plans, Local types (U.S.):
  Bugeye *Nora E. Lawson* (1906), lines, IV, 250
  Double-ender, Ash Point, ME; lines, II, 314, 315, 317
  Double-ender, Matinicus Island, ME; lines, II, 321
  Durham Boat, lines, II, 169
  Gundalow, *Fanny M.* (1886), lines, body plan and outboard profile, II, 212; sail plan, II, 215
  Log canoe *Monkey* (1880), lines, IV, 249
  Penobscot Indian canoe, lines, VIII, 292
  Potomac long-boat, sketches by Henry Hall and lines, I, 159–162
  San Francisco lateen-rigged fishing boats, sketches by Henry Hall, I, 306–307
  San Francisco bay scow schooners, sketches by Henry Hall, I, 87, 88
  Scooters, Great South Bay, Long Island, lines, deck plan and sail plan, IV, 226–227
  Sealing boats (*circa* 1900), deck and sail plans, III, 328–330
  Skipjacks, Chesapeake Bay, lines, IV, 292–305, V, 88
  Wherry, rowing and sailing, Ash Point, ME, lines and sail plan, II, 311 ff.
Plans, Local types (non-U.S.):
  Dhows of eastern Arabia, IX, 90, 91, 97, 98, 103, 104, 110
  Nile boats, XII, 47–48
Plans, Naval Vessels:
  Continental frigate *Hancock* (1776), lines, VIII, plate 3, deck plans, VIII, plate 4
  Continental frigate *Raleigh* (1776), lines VIII, plate 5, deck plans, VIII, plate 6
  Continental frigate *Randolph* (1776), lines VIII, plate 7
  Continental frigate *Virginia* (1776), lines VIII, plate 1, deck plans, VIII, plate 2
  Corvette *United States* (1831), lines VIII, 8–9
  44-gun frigate *Terrible,* IX, plate 19
  74-gun ship by Joshua Humphreys, IX, plate 17
  Swedish flat bottomed vessel, VI, plate 22
  Swedish small frigate, VI, plate 26
  U.S. brig *Prometheus* (1814), sail plan, V, plate 7
  U.S. brig *Spark* (1814), sail plan, V, plate 6
  U.S. frigate *Constitution* (1797), guns, VII, 241
  U.S.S. *Columbus'* boats, sail plan, III, plate 44
  U.S.S. *General Pike* (1813), sail plan, III, plate 35
  U.S. schooner *Lynx* (1814), sail plan, III, plate 36
Plans, Revenue cutter: designed by Samuel Humphreys (1829), lines, I, 81
Plans, Schooners and sloops:
  America, schooner yacht, XI, 248
  Anna M. Frome, oyster schooner (1904), inboard profile and deck plan, I, 69
  Ash Point, ME, sloops, lines and sail plan, II, 316, 318, 322
  Biloxi shrimp fishing schooner (before 1924), lines, I, 72
  Elsie, scow sloop (1874), profile, section and deck plan, I, 78
  Gjøa, sloop, XII, 14–18
  Hampton boats, sail plan, I, 66; lines and sail plan, III, 142–146
  Hornet, schooner yacht (1819), lines, I, 75
  Mediator, sloop, XIII, 178, 160
  Richard R. Higgins, fishing schooner (1858), lines and sail plan, I, facing 308
Plans, Ships, barks and ketches:
  Cohota, ship (1843), lines, deck plan, inboard profile, sail plan, facing VII, 8
  Eliza, ketch (1794), lines, IV, plate 6
  Emily F. Whitney, ship (1879), cabin plan, II, 196
  Illustrious President, ship, IX, plate 18
  Kenilworth, bark (1887), sail and deck plan, I, facing 340
  La Escocesa, ship (1868), rigging plan, VII, 295
  Mary Stockton, barkentine (1853), sail plan, VII, 315
  Spanish ship of 150 tons (1587), sheer plan and body sections, I, 194–195
  Spanish ship of 400 tons (1587), topsail plan, I, 193
Plans, Steamships and steamboats:
  Antelope, auxiliary steam packet (1855), lines, sail and deck plans, I, facing 52
  China, steamship (1866–1867), lines, II, facing 8
  Commonwealth, steamship (1854), bow elevation and midship section, VIII, 250
  George Law, steamship (1853), lines, sail and deck plans, IV, 304, facing 312
  Hiawatha, steamship (1904), stateroom plan, VII, 142
  Japan, steamship (1867–1868), cabin plan, II, facing 242
  Okeehumkee, steamship (1873), stateroom plan, VII, 143
  Pocahontas, steamship (1893), outboard profile and deck plans, II, plates 35, 36
Plans (Other types):
  Cutter, American 26', XV, 202
  Discovery II, pinnace, XVII, 176
  Godspeed II, ship, XVII, 176
  Mayflower, ship, XIV, 276
  Mayflower's shallop, XVII, 111–112
  Philippine Banca, XIX, 258
  Sakonnet River boat, XVI, 61–62, plate
  Sparrow-Hawk, ship, XIII, plates 5 and 6 (following

page 52)
Susan Constant II, XVII, 176
Plans of Buildings and Machinery ... Navy Yard, Boston ... 1830 to 1840, by Alex' Parris, document, VII, 67–69, plates 7–8
Plant, Henry B., XXXVII, 237
Plantagenet, H.M. warship (1813), XXIX, 188; XLII, 107 ff.
Planter, ship *(1862),* XVII, 18
Planter, steamship, XXI, 95; *(1861),* VIII, 220; *(1863),* XII, 159
Planters Line, II, 293
Plantina, bark, Pictorial Supplement, XXXIII, plate XXXII
Plata River System:
  (Paraguay), Discovery and exploration, XXXI, 7
  (Argentina and Uruguay), XLVII, 162
  See also Parana River; Smuggling
Platina, bark *(1890),* XXII, plate XXI
Plato, schooner (1816), Pictorial Supplement, XXXVIII, plate XXXI
Platt, Senator, XXV, 264
Platt, Virginia Bever, "Triangles and Tramping: Captain Zebediah Story of Newport, 1769–1776," XXXIII, 294–303
Plattsburgh (NY), Battle of (1814), XXI, 42. *See also* United States History (War of 1812)
Pleasants, J. Hall, query by, II, 339
Pleasonton, Stephen, XXVIII, 33, 41, 43–46; XLVII, 174 ff.
Pleasure, ship (1631), XXIII, 64
Pleiades, ship (1864), II, 334
Plimouth Plantation, XIV, 16
Plimsoll Line, XLIV, 39
Plimsoll mark, VIII, 102
Ploughboy, ship (1806), XIV, 215–216; *(1830),* XXI, 222
Plover, British sloop of war *(1795),* XLIX, 45
Plover, gunboat *(1899),* XXXV, 191
Plover, H.M.S. *(1859),* XXVII, 167, 168, 172
Plover, steam gunboat, XXII, 36
Plowden, David, *Farewell to Steam,* reviewed, XXVII, 151
Plum, Leverett, VII, 50
Plumber, Captain Joe, XIX, 12
Plumer, Cyrus, XXI, 113–129
Plumer, Senator William, XLIII, 247
Plummer, John F., XL, 43
Plumper, British brig *(1814),* XXVIII, 118
Plunger, submarine *(1908),* XXXVIII, 8
Pluto, H.M.S. *(1842),* XXVI, 6 n.
Pluto, steamship (1863), XVII, 303; XVIII, 72; XXXIV, plate 4, 38
Pluto (ex-*Fire Flash*), steamship *(1863),* XLIII, 202
Plymouth, ship (1833), XV, 139, 140; *(1846),* XLVI, 238; *(1848),* XXXI, 188
Plymouth, steamship, XXXIV, 259
Plymouth, U.S. sloop (1843), XXV, 225; *(1853),* VII, 9, 14, 16; XXVI, 119; XXXVIII, 30 ff.; *(1854),* XXX, 159, 160, 162 n., 166
Plymouth Rock, ship (1849), V, 147
Plymouth Rock, steamship *(1858),* XXXIX, 89; (1863), XVI, 171, 252; XVII, 38; XVIII, 72; XXXIV, plate 3; *(1863),* XLII, 121 ff.; XLIII, 120 ff.
Plymouth Sound, England, 1837, XXIX, plate XXIX
Poblana, Mexican gunboat *(1845),* XXX, 54
Pocahontas, blockade runner *(1864),* XLVII, 31
Pocahontas, schooner, XXI, 93; (1827), XXIII, 7; *(1864),* VIII, 235
Pocahontas, ship *(1833),* XIV, plate 7; *(1850),* I, 394; (1856), II, 332; IV, 46, 51
Pocahontas, steamship (1893), II, 223–228, plates 33–36
Pocohontas, ship *(1861),* XLIII, 130 ff.
Pocahontas, U.S.S. *(1850),* XXXVII, 277
Pocahontas, U.S. steam sloop *(1861),* XXI, 240, 242, 243
Pocotaligo, schooner, XXI, 97; *(1861),* VIII, 220, 227, 235
"Pod of Sperm Whales, A," XXII, plate XIII
Poe, Edgar Allan, XXV, 62
Poelet, brig, later ship (1808), VII, 317
Poertner, Rudolph, *The Vikings: Rise and Fall of the Norse Sea Kings,* reviewed, XXXVIII, 147
Poetry. *See* Sea Poetry
Poh, Admiral, XXX, 160, 164
Pohl, Frederick J., *Amerigo Vespucci, Pilot Major,* reviewed, VI, 87
Poictiers, gunboat *(1813),* XLII, 108 ff.
Poillon, C. & R., VII, 322
"Poillon's Rig," query by John Lyman, III, 177
"Poillon's Rig," answer by John Lyman, VII, 322, plate 40
Point Adams, steamship *(1919),* X, 141
"Point Barrow Refuge Station, The," by John Bockstoce, XXXIX, 5–21
Point Bonita, steamship *(1919),* X, 141
Point Judith steamship *(1919),* X, 141
Point Lobos, steamship *(1919),* X, 141
Polaanyi, Karl, XLVIII, 261
Polanyi, Karl, in collaboration with Abraham Rotstein, *Dahomey and the Slave Trade, An Analysis of an Archaic Economy,* reviewed, XXVIII, 70–71
Polar, brig *(1861),* XI, 287
Polar Bear, schooner, Pictorial Supplement, XXXIII, plate XXIX
Polar Sea, U.S. Coast Guard icebreaker *(1985),* L, 35 ff.
Polar Star, ship (1852), III, 68
Pole, W., XXX, 215
Polias, concrete ship *(1918),* XXII, 160, 164, 167, 168, 175, 182
Polk, U.S. revenue cutter, XXIV, 14 n.; *(1850),* XLV, 125
Polk, James K., XXXIII, 266; XLVI, 239
Polk, President James K., XXV, 141; XLI, 28
Polk's Directory, XXX, 31

Polland, Leon D., XLIX, 43
Polland, Leon D., and Howard I. Chapelle, *The Constellation Question*, reviewed, XXXII, 71–72
Pollard, Sidney and Paul Robertson, *The British Shipbuilding Industry, 1870–1914*, reviewed, XLII, 67–68
Polley, schooner, XXII, 143
Pollitt, Ronald, "Contingency Planning and the Defeat of the Spanish Armada," XLIV, 25–32; review by, XLIV, 137
Pollock Rip Light Vessel, XXIV, 139
Polly, brig *(1773)*, XXXV, 301; *(1816)*, XXII, 234
Polly, British sloop, XXII, 94
Polly, privateer *(1745)*, XLII, 47
Polly, schooner *(1778)*, X, 282; *(1789)*, XLI, 213; *(1805)*, IV, 164–171, plate 27
Polly, ship *(1759)*, XLVII, 12; XLVIII, 39; XLIX, 89; *(1801)*, XXIII, 217; *(1812)*, XLV, 7
Polly, sloop, XXII, 60 n.; *(1775)*, V, 99; *(1807)*, X, 146
Polly and Betsy, schooner *(1820)*, XXIV, 131
Polly Lewis, bark *(1869)*, III, 66
"*Polly* of Amesbury, The," by John R. Herbert, IV, 164–171
Polmar, Norman, *Guide to the Soviet Navy*, reviewed, XLIV, 133; mention, XLI, 163
Polski Rejstr Statkow, XXX, 31
Polyktor, merchant ship *(1943)*, XLIV, 52
Polynesia. *See* Oceania
Polynesia, boats of, XIII, 88 ff.
Polynesian Explorers of the Pacific, by J. E. Weckler, Jr., reviewed, III, 180
Pommern, bark *(1911)*, XVIII, 150
Pomona, eighteen-gun sloop *(1776)*, XLIII, 23 ff.
Pomona, schooner (1827), XIV, 40
Pomona, ship *(1861)*, XV, 124
Pomona, sloop (1800), XXII, 216
Pomona College, I, 83
Pomone, frigate *(1815)*, XLIV, 174
Pompeii, brigantine *(1802)*, XXV, 182
Ponape, boats of, XIII, 93 ff.
Pond, E. Le Roy, *Junius Smith, pioneer promoter of transatlantic steam navigation*, reviewed, I, 318
Pond, Shepard, "Sir William Phips' Treasure," II, 171–172; "The Malcolm Storer Collection of Naval Medals," II, 336–337
Pongo, XXX, 230
Pongo River, XXX, 178 ff.
Ponko, Vincent, Jr., *Ships, Seas, and Scientists: U.S. Naval Exploration and Discovery in the Nineteenth Century*, reviewed, XXXV, 67–68
Pons, Midshipman Jorge, XXX, 53
Pontiac, trawler *(1906)*, XLIV, 122
Poody, sloop, XXI, 89; *(1862)*, XII, 57
Pook, S. H., I, 55
Pook, Samuel Hartt, XXII, 239

Pool, Bernard, *Navy Board Contracts 1600–1832: Contract Administration under the Navy Board*, reviewed, XXVIII, 229–232
Pool, Eugene H., III, 3–4, 90; IV, 252
Pool, Captain Henry Child, XIII, 139–140
Poole, Bruce M., XLIX, 35
Poole (England), XXVIII, 275–283, plate 9; Custom House, XXVIII, plate 12
Poole, Captain Jonas, XXVIII, 241, 242, 243, 244, 245
Poor, Charles Lane, *Men Against the Rule*, reviewed, I, 408–409
Poor, Captain William, XVI, 161; XVIII, 84
Pootung, steamship *(1861)*, XLIII, 99 ff.
Pope, Dudley, *The Devil Himself: The Mutiny of 1800*, reviewed, XLIX, 235
Pope, Eben T., XXXVII, 87; medals given to, plate 4, 92–93
Pope, George F., XXXVII, 87
Pope, Jennie Barnes and Robert Greenhalgh Albion, *Sea Lanes in Wartime: the American Experience, 1775–1942*, reviewed, III, 91
Pope, Captain John, XXXVIII, 35
Pope, Joshua L., XXXIX, 90
Pope and Talbot, IV, 200
Pope Urban, XXX, 251
Pope Urban VI, XXX, 251
Popham, Captain Charles W., XXXVII, 219 ff.
Popham, Captain Sir Home, XXX, 213
Popham, Commodore Sir Home Riggs, R.N., L, 30
Popham, Sir John, XXXI, 86
Porcelain. *See* China trade porcelain
Porcher, Captain Philip, XVII, 253 n; XXI, 84, 99
Porcupine, British steamship *(1849)*, XLIII, 169 ff.
Pordeyan, John, XXXV, 87
Porpoise, brig, XXII, 183; *(1837)*, XLIII, 54
Porpoise, H.M. Storeship (ex-*Hertigennan Af Sodermanland*) *(1780)*, XLIX, 91 ff.
Porpoise, schooner *(1826)*, XL, 224; *(1860)*, XXIV, 45, 59
Porpoise, ship *(1824)*, XXXII, 273
Porpoise, ship *(1895)*, XL, 103
Porpoise, survey brig *(1838)*, XXX, 298; XLIX, 152 ff.; photo of model, XLIX, 160
Porpoise, U.S.S. (1838), IV, 105 ff.
Porpoise, U.S. schooner *(1822)*, XXIX, 64
Porras, Bellisario, XXIV, 187
Port Angeles, steamship *(1927)*, VII, 293
Port Anna Maria, Nukuhiva Island, XXXIII, plate 10
Port Brunswick, XXIX, 155
Port Elizabeth, Bequia, XXXII, plate 11, 188 ff.
Porter, steamship *(1843)*, XVII, 102, 103
Porter, U.S. destroyer (1929), VIII, 67
Porter, David D., XXIX, 178 ff.
Porter, Commodore David, U.S.N., VI, 239, 265; VII, 176, 187–194
Porter, Admiral David Dixon, U.S.N., XXXIII, 264 ff.; XXXIV, 63, 127, 189; XXXV, 63; XXXVIII, 108;

XXXIX, 116; XL, 131; XLVI, 156; XLVII, 28, 112; XLVIII, 96
Porter, Rear Admiral David Dixon, U.S.N., XXII, 259, 262, 286 n.; XXV, 142, 162; XLII, 87 ff., 165 ff.
Porter, George M., XV, 179
Porter, James, XV, 179
Porter, James Otis, answered query, II, 82
Porter, John L., design of ironclad bow, XXIX, 8, plate 3
Porter, Joseph, XV, 179
Porter, Captain Lemuel, XII, 105
Porter, Captain Seward, XXI, 99
Porter, Lieutenant T. K., XXII, 48, 49
Porter, Thomas K., XV, 297
Porter, William, XV, 179
Porter, Commander William D., XXXIII, 45
Port Essington, XXX, 304
Portia, steamship *(1824),* XXXVII, 245
Port Kingston, S.S. *(1907),* XXIX, 121, 122
Portland, brig, XXII, 87
Portland, coastwise steamship *(1898),* XXIV, 139; XXV, 222
Portland, ship *(1802),* X, 53
Portland, steamship, XXVIII, 125, plate XXI; *(1889),* XXVII, plate XXIII; *(1898),* XI, 86; XIV, 192
Portland, U.S. steamship *(1835),* XXXIII, 85, 94; *(1898),* XXIX, 224–225
Portland Cement Co., XXII, 171
Portland Harbor, XXIII, plate XX
Portland Lloyds, ship (1876), III, 66
Portland Steam Packet Co., ship of, Pictorial Supplement, XXXIII, 84; XXXIV, plate XXIV
Portlaw, ship (1864), V, 152
Portlock, Nathaniel, XXXVIII, 223
Port Louis, Mauritius, XXV, 6, 8, 9, 11, 12, 15
Port Mahon, H.M.S. *(1740),* XXVI, 38; *(1741),* XLVIII, 26
Portman, Reverend Richard, XIII, 22
"Port of Boston and the Embargo of 1807–1809, The," by Robin D. S. Higham, XVI, 189–210
Port of Bristol 1848–1884, The, by David Large, reviewed, XLV, 211
Port of Honolulu, The, by Clifford Gessler, reviewed, II, 350
Port of New York Society for Promoting the Gospel Among Seamen, XXIV, 110, 115
Port of Philadelphia, XXXII, Table I, Table II, 254, 255
Port of Quebec, map of, XLVIII, 78
Portolan charts, XLV, 226
Porto Plata, San Domingo, XXV, 30, 31, plate 1
Porto Praya, Battle of (1781), V, 64–78
Port Ponce, Puerto Rico, XL, plate 7
Portrait of a Port – Boston, 1852–1914, by W. H. Bunting, reviewed, XXXIII, 215–216
Port Roanoke, XXIX, 155
Port Royal, U.S.S. *(1862),* XX, 161–163
Port Royall, ship *(1670),* XXX, 82
Ports. *See* Harbors

Portsea, collier *(1840),* XXXV, 259
Portsmouth (1967), XXVIII, 3
Portsmouth, H.M.S. *(1727),* XXI, 263
Portsmouth, ship *(1777),* V, 187; *(1856),* XXXVIII, 36
Portsmouth, sloop-of-war *(1862),* XXXII, 46 ff., 124; XXXIII, 282
Portsmouth, U.S.S. *(1799),* XXXI, 173; *(1843),* XX, 135, 140, 141; XXII, 33
Portsmouth, whaler *(1850),* XXXIII, 127
Portsmouth (VA) Naval Shipyard Museum, XXII, 232
Portsmouth Whaling Co., XIII, 121
Ports of Piscataqua, by William G. Saltonstall, reviewed, II, 91
Port Sonachon, barque, XXVIII, 56
Port Stanley, ship, XLI, 129
"Port Stateroom of the bark *Howard,*" Pictorial Supplement, XXXI, plate XXIV
Port Tampa, expedition to Santiago, XL, plate 5
Port Texaco V, steamship *(1937),* XXXVIII, 191 ff.
Portugese voyages, VI, 308–309; voyages in Pacific, IV, 88–93
Poss, Victor, XXII, 159
Post, James A., XVII, 120
Post, Robert C., *The Tancook Whalers: Origins, Rediscovery, and Revival,* reviewed, XLVII, 284
Postal service, United States, 18th century, XXII, 55
Postboy, packet, XXIV, 134
Post Boy, schooner *(1875),* XLIX, 32
Post Boy, steamship (1836), VII, 61; *(1862),* VIII, 227
Postell, Captain W. Ross, XXI, 99
Postell, Captain William, XXI, 99
Postern Row, Tower Hill, VIII, 303, plate 31
"Postman Always Rings Twice, The," by Captain Edgar K. Thompson, U.S.N. (ret.), XXV, 287
"Postscripts to *The Search for Captain Slocum,*" by Walter Magnes Teller, XVIII, 189–200, plates 13, 14
"Postscript to the Voyages of LaPérouse," by Pierre Anthonioz, XXI, 196–206
Potemkin, V. P., XXXII, 106 ff.
Potomac, ship (1855), IV, 51; *(1861),* XV, 108 n.; XXI, 256
Potomac, U.S. frigate (1819), XXI, 61, 292–295; XXIII, 58 n., 261; *(1831),* XXXI, 182; XXXII, 275; XXXV, 20; *(1832),* XLVI, 114
Potomac, U.S.S. *(1939),* XXVI, 214
Potomack, ship *(1810),* L, 103
"Potomac Long-Boat, The," by M. V. Brewington, I, 159–163
Potomska, steamship *(1853),* XXXIX, 86, plate 2
Potomska, U.S.S. *(1863),* L, 93
Potosi, bark (1895), VI, 135, plate 18
Potosi, ship, XXVI, 157 n., 158 n.
Potter, Captain Edward E., U.S.N., III, 85
Potter, G. B., XXIV, 59
Potter, H. W., "Pitz Papers in the Burton Historical Collection, Detroit Public Library," II, 335–336
Potter, Captain J. W., XXI, 106

Potter, Captain John R., XVIII, 84
Potter, Simeon, XXXII, 173
Potter Brothers, XVIII, 5 ff.
Pottinger, steamship (1846), XXVI, 11, 12, 17, 19, 21, 22, 24, 28, 116, 202, 203, 206, plate 15
Potts, Captain Henry H., XXVI, 13, 204
Poughkeepsie Line, XVIII, 225
Poulson, XXVIII, plate I
Pound, Admiral Sir Dudley, First Sea Lord, XXVI, 279; XLII, 205
Pound, Ezra, XXV, 65
Pousland, William, XXX, 96 n.
Poutiatine, Count, XXXIV, 107 ff.
Powars, Captain W. Frank, XLVII, 125
Powell, John, XIII, 120; XXXI, 131
Powell, Mary L., XIV, 164
Powell, Pearsall B., V, 28
Powell, William, XIII, 120
Powell River Co., Ltd., XXII, 177, 178, 179, 180
Powelul, steamship (1855), XXVI, 197, 198, 206, 209
Power, Sir Manley, XXI, 51
Power, Peter, XXXI, 24
Power, Thomas B., XIX, 53
Power, Captain Thomas B., XXI, 99
Powerful, steamship *(1863),* XII, 159
Powerful, tug *(1864),* XLIII, 299
Powers, William, XXXVII, 168
Powhatan, paddle sloop, XXXII, 49
Powhatan, ship, XIV, 192
Powhatan, U.S.S. *(1850),* XXXVII, 278; XXXVIII, 33; *(1859),* XXVII, 157, 162–164, 171, 172, 223, plate 2; *(1861),* XI, 265 ff.; *(1862),* XVI, 57; XX, 199 ff.; *(1864),* XXVII, 44
Powhatan, U.S. steamship (1853), XXI, 142–143; XXII, 25
Pownall, Thomas, XL, 250
Powney, Captain John, XIII, 11
Poyang, steamship (1861), XVI, 171; XVII, 134, 135; XVIII, 72; XXXIV, 32 ff.; *(1862),* XLIII, 194 ff.; *(1895),* 102 ff.
Poyser, Captain Fred C., XXVIII, 4
Poytier, Captain Richard, XXI, 106
Pozen, Walter I., XXV, 79
Practical Celestial Navigation, by Susan P. Howell, reviewed, XL, 151
Prager, Frank D., "A Screw Propeller Drawing of the Fitch Period," XXIII, 204–211
Prairie, auxiliary cruiser *(1898),* XXXIII, 277
Pratas Shoals, XXX, 294
Pratt, Captain A., XX, 90 n.
Pratt, Captain, XXXV, 109
Pratt, Dana J., contributed document, XIII, 134–139
Pratt, Captain Frank, IX, 179
Pratt, Sir John, XXXVII, 192
Pratt, Taylor & Co., VII, 57
Pratt, William V., XXXVII, 114 ff.

Pratt, Winthrop, Jr., queries by, IX, 74–75; "Pre-Revolutionary Gun-Founding in America," XI, 145
Pray, B. S., XIII, 122
Pray, Samuel, XXI, 15
Preble, U.S. sloop of war (1839), XXI, 36; XXV, 93 ff.; (1848), XXXI, 188; XXXII, 48; *(1849),* XLI, 32
Preble, Captain A. P., XVIII, 84
Preble, Captain, XLVI, 151 ff.
Preble, Edward, XXX, 75
Preble, Commodore Edward, U.S.N., XVIII, 183; XXI, 130; XXV, 33, 159; XXXVII, 129; XXXIX, 112; XLIII, 136 ff.
Preble, Rear Admiral George Henry, U.S.N., XXIV, 165 ff.
Preble, Vice Admiral George Henry, XXXVII, 130
Preble, Captain Isaac, XVIII, 84
Preble, Brigadier General Jedidiah, XXXVII, 130
Preble, Mrs. Mary (Deering), XXX, 75
Precursor, steamship (1841), XXVI, 9, 115, 116, 203, 206, 209
Predpriatie, sloop *(1825),* XXIII, 223
Premier, schooner (1876), V, 86
Premier, ship (1853), IV, 238; (1875), IV, 244; VI, 83
Prentice, John, XII, 225–226
"Pre-Revolutionary Gun-Founding in America," by Winthrop Pratt, Jr., XI, 145
Prescott, Captain Charles D., XIV, 136–139, plate 16
Prescott, Mary J. R., XIV, 136–139, plate 16
Prescott, Worrall D., contributed document, XIV, 136–139, plate 16
Prescott Machinery Co., XXII, 183
Prescott Palmer, schooner (1902), V, 81
"Present-Day Craft and Rigs of the Mediterranean," by T. C. Gillmer, I, 352–373; II, 56–64
Present Succession, British ship *(1776),* XLVIII, 18
President, British flagship *(1840),* XXXV, 256
President, frigate, XXVII, 9; (1798), XLVI, 152 ff.; *(1803),* XL, 24 ff.; *(1815),* XLIV, 171; XLVII, 14; XLIX, 41
President, H.M.S., XXII, 215
President, schooner, XXI, 92, 99; *(1861),* XI, 287; XII, 57
President, ship (1860), V, 153, 242
President, steamship (1839), IX, 269–270, plate 28; (1841), XX, 88
President, U.S. frigate (1799), XXI, 131, 132, 133; XXII, 143, 215; XXIII, 261; XXV, 110, plate XIV; (1800), VII, 253; *(1806),* XVIII, 183; XIX, 219–221; *(1811),* III, plates 2, 5; *(1813),* XXXI, 286
President Adams, brig *(1809),* XXX, 282 ff.
"*President* and *Endymion,*" document contributed by S. W. Jackman, XXII, 143–144
President Arthur, steamship (1900), IX, 223
President Benson, ketch (1857), XI, 291
President Cleveland, steamship (1921), X, 141, plate 20; *(1925),* XLIV, 180
President Coolidge, S.S. *(1931),* XXIX, 234
Presidente, Venezuelan brig *(1848),* XXX, 266

President Fillmore, schooner, XXI, 95; *(1861),* XI, 287
President Grant, steamship, XXIX, 233; (1902), IV, 325
President Harrison, steamship *(1922),* IX, 222; X, 141
President Hayes, steamship *(1921),* X, 141
President Hoover, S.S. *(1931),* XXIX, 234
President Howard, schooner *(1913),* XXXIX, 178
President Lincoln, steamship *(1918),* IV, 325; *(1921),* X, 141
President Pierce, steamship *(1921),* X, 141
President Polk, steamship *(1921),* X, 141
President Taft, steamship *(1921),* X, 141
President Warfield, steamship, XXXVII, 75; (1928), VIII, 127–131, plates 13–14; IX, 300–301; (1928), XXII, 150. See *Exodus 1947.*
President Washington, schooner *(1847),* XXIV, 133
President Washington, ship *(1792),* XLVI, 11 ff.
President Wilson, steamship *(1921),* X, 141
"President Wilson's Departure for the Peace Conference," document contributed by Carl L. Lokke, VII, 69–72
"Pre-Spanish Navigation Off the Andean Coast," by Philip Ainsworth Means, II, 107–126
Pressing, naval seamen, XXV, 280
Presson, William, note by, XLIII, 222–223
Presto, bark (1847), V, 147
Presto, steamship *(1863),* XXI, plate I; *(1864),* VIII, 235
Preston, U.S. destroyer *(1927),* L, 187
Preston, warship *(1776),* XL, 14
Preston, Antony, and John Major, *Send a Gunboat!* reviewed, XXVII, 223–224
Preussen, ship, XXVI, 157, 158 n., 160, 163–165; (1902), VI, 135–136, plate 18; IX, 298
Prevost, Sir George, XXI, 42 ff.
Prevost, J. B., XXIX, 93
Preyoyante, French frigate *(1798),* L, 270 ff.
Price, Marcus W., "Additional Notes on *Ella and Annie,*" XIV, 61–63; "Additional Notes on *Margaret and Jessie,*" XI, 221–223; "Blockade Running as a Business in South Carolina during the War between the States," IX, 31–62; "*Chicora (Let Her B),*" XII, 308–310; "Four from Bristol," XVII, 249–261; "Masters and Pilots who Tested the Blockade of the Confederate Ports, 1861–1865," XXI, 81–107; "Ships that tested the Blockade of the Carolina Ports, 1861–1865," VIII, 196–241, plates 17–19; "Ships that Tested the Blockade of the Georgia and East Florida Ports, 1861–1865," XV, 97–132; "Ships that Tested the Blockade of the Gulf Ports, 1861–1865," XI, 262–290; XII, 52–59, 154–161, 229–238
Price, Rear Admiral David, XXXI, 269; XXXII, 244
Pride, schooner, XXI, 87, 99; (1852), XXIV, 45, 59; *(1862),* VIII, 227, 231
Pride of America, ship (1853), III, 264
Pride of Hawaii. See *Cleopatra's Barge.*
Pride of the Ocean, ship (1853), III, 72
Pride of the Port, ship (1866), IV, 244
Pridix, Thomas, IX, 138 ff.

Prima Dona, sloop *(1863),* XII, 159
Prima Donna, bark (1888), III, 66
Prima Donna, schooner *(1863),* XII, 159
"Primitive Watercraft of Arabia," by Richard LeBaron Bowen, Jr., XII, 186–221, plates 17–19
Primrose and Company, XVII, 60
Prince, Lieutenant Charles, XIII, 46
Prince, George Henry, XXIII, 138, 139
Prince, Henry, XXIII, 136
Prince, Captain Henry, XXV, 180, 182
Prince, James, XIII, 272
Prince, Captain John, Jr., V, 44 ff.
Prince, Nathan, XVI, 81–97; XX, 187
Prince 98, ship *(1798),* XLV, 97
Prince Albert, H.M.S. (1852), XXXIV, 32; *(1862),* XXII, 254, 261, 263
Prince Albert, steamship, XXI, 89, 105, 106; *(1864),* VIII, 235
Prince Alfred, schooner, XXI, 97; *(1862),* VIII, 227, 235
Prince Arthur, steamship *(1897),* XXXIII, 92; XXXIV, 180
Prince Edward, H.M. Brig *(1782),* XXIX, 211 ff.
Prince Edward, steamship (1841), XX, 88, 89; *(1897),* XXXIV, 180
Prince Edward Island Steam Navigation Co., XXXIV, 176
Prince Frederick, privateer *(1744),* XLII, 45
Prince Frederick, steamship (1823), XXIV, plate XVIII
Prince George, H.M.S., XXVI, 60
Prince George, ocean liner *(1911),* XXXIII, 92
Prince George, steamship (1898), Pictorial Supplement, XXXIV, plate XXIII, 180 ff.
Prince Imperial, ship (1862), V, 151
Prince Kung, steamship *(1863),* XXXIV, 48
Prince Leopold, schooner, XXI, 103
Prince of Denmark, schooner *(1860),* XLI, 296
Prince of Fundy, ferry *(1970),* XXXIV, 186
Prince of Orange, H.M.S., XXVI, 54
Prince of Wales, American ship *(1863),* XLV, 197
Prince of Wales, British battleship *(1941),* XLII, 203 ff.
Prince of Wales, British ship, XXIX, 248
Prince of Wales, privateer *(1744),* XLII, 46
Prince of Wales, schooner, XXI, 86, 102; *(1861),* VIII, 220, 227; *(1861),* XV, 116, 124
Prince of Wales, ship, XVI, 62; (1860), II, 333
Prince of Wales, Siamese sailing vessel *(1871),* XXVI, 133
Prince of Wales, steamship (1841), XX, 88, 259; (1842), VIII, 134
Prince Regent, H.M.S. *(1813),* XVII, 208, 210
Princesa, brig (1827), VI, 10–11
Princess, ship (1858), V, 148
Princess, steamship (1881), VII, 159
Princess, yacht *(1875),* XIII, 273
Princess Alexander, bark (1857), IV, 73, 244
Princess Alice, steamship (1865), XXIV, plate XXIV; (1900), IX, 223

Princess Carolina, ship *(1716),* XLIV, 230
Princess Charlotte, ship *(1828),* XIV, 100
Princess Charlotte, steamship (1855), XXVI, 196, 197, 206, 209
Princess Elizabeth, British P. O. packet *(1814),* I, 121; Pictorial Supplement, XXXVIII, plate XIII
Princess Gambia, ship *(1760),* IX, 144
Princess Matoika, steamship (1900), IX, 223
Princess Royal, blockade runner *(1863),* XLIV, 268 ff.
Princess Royal, British flagship, XXXII, 127
Princess Royal, British sloop, XXIX, 248
Princess Royal, ship *(1776),* XX, 45
Princess Royal, ship (1857), III, 171
Princess Royal, steamship, XXI, 95, plate XXXII; *(1840),* XX, 88, plate 4; *(1863),* VIII, 231
Princeton, bark (1842), IV, 51
Princeton, schooner, XXI, 86; *(1862),* XII, 57
Princeton, screw-propelled warship *(1842),* XLVIII, 117
Princeton, screw steamship (1843), XXXIV, 221; XXXV, 188 ff.
Princeton, steam cutter *(1845),* XXXIX, 219
Princeton, steamship *(1849),* XLIII, 165 ff.
Princeton, U.S. frigate, XXX, 48
Princeton, U.S.S. (1895), XX, 142
Princeton, U.S. steam frigate (1844), VI, 215–222
Princeton, U.S. war steamship (1842), XXIII, 199; XXIV, 18
Princeton II, screw frigate *(1851),* XLIX, 112
Princeton: sail plan of, XLIX, 99; photo of, XLIX, 101
Prince William, ship, XXVI, 59, 60; *(1730),* XXI, 267
Prince William Henry, brig, XXII, 89, 90 n.
Principall Navigations, Voiages and Discoveries of the English Nation, The, by Richard Hakluyt, reviewed, XXVI, 73–74
Pring, Captain Daniel, XXI, 47 ff.
Pring, Martin, XXV, 238; XXXIV, 233 ff.; L, 6 ff.
Pringle, Robert, XLII, 48 ff.
Prins Hendrick Museum, XIV, 187, 188
Prins van Oranje, Netherlands frigate *(1851),* XLVIII, 45 ff.
Prints, III, 5
Prinz Eitel Friedrich, German raider, XXVIII, 108; *(1914),* XXIV, 274; *(1915),* XLV, 199 ff.; (1917), XLVIII, 53
Prinz Eitel Friedrich, steamship *(1904),* XXXVII, 75
Prinzessen Victoria Luise, German ship *(1907),* XXIX, 126
Prinz Leopold, steamship (1882), XII, plate 30
Prinz Waldemar, German ship *(1907),* XXIX, 126
Priscilla, bark (1865), III, 66
Priscilla, schooner *(1861),* XI, 154
Priscilla of Fall River, by Roger Williams McAdam, reviewed, VIII, 73
Prisoners, XXXI, 159; XLI, 208
   in France, XX, 112
   Transportation of, XXVIII, 165
See also Hostages

Prissy, schooner (1789), XIV, 40
Pritchard, Captain, XLI, 128
Pritchard, Hugh, XVII, 52
Pritchard, James, *Louis XV's Navy, 1748–1762: A Study of Organization and Administration,* reviewed, XLVIII, 195
Pritchard, L. A., XIV, 14
Pritchard, Paul (Master Builder), XLVII, 24
Pritchard, William, XVII, 122
Privateering, XV, 59; XXIII, 277
   18th century, XVII, 292
   Confederate States of America, XXIII, 264
   France, XX, 112, XXII, 81; L, 270
   Gt. Britain, 17th century, XLIX, 251
   United States, I, 26, 116; VI, 101; X, 43; XXI, 16; XXXVI, 79; XLVIII, 87, 154; L, 270
   —, **18th century,** XLII, 5
   —, **Revolution (1773–1788),** X, 280
   —, **New England, 17th century,** XXXV, 153
      —, **18th century,** XXXV, 153
See also Pirates; Privateers
Privateering, VII, 283–287; X, 43–51; XXII, 81–97, 216 Confederacy, XI, 150–155; Elizabethan, XXV, 148; Quasi-War, 1799, V, 159–160; XI, 224–225; XXV, 112; Revolutionary War, I, 26–41; V, 111 ff., 177–193; XXV, 43, 44; War of 1812, I, 94–95, 116–122, 301–303; XV, 59–80; XXI, 16–22. "Pathway Out of Debt: The Privateering Activities of Sir John Hippisley During the Early Stuart Wars with Spain and France, 1625–30, A," by John Appleby, XLIX, 252–261; Table of prizes taken in 1625, XLIX, 259
Privateers, IV, 164
   Biography, XLII, 5
   Gt. Britain, —, **18th century,** XLII, 36
   United States, XLIII, 20
Privateers: A Raiding Voyage to the Great South Sea, The, by Fleming MacLeish and Martin L. Krieger, reviewed, XXIII, 71–72
Privateers in Charleston, 1793–1796, by Melvin H. Jackson, reviewed, XXX, 303
"Privateer Sloop *Jefferson,*" by Lawrence W. Jenkins, XIV, 210–211
Privateer wash, query, XVII, 156
"Privateer *Yankee* in the War of 1812, The," by Kenneth Scott, XXI, 16–22
Private Journal of John Glendy Sproston, U.S.N., A, edited by Shio Sakanishi, reviewed, I, 185–186
Priwall, bark *(1941),* VI, 113
Prize law, XLII, 5
Prizes, XXXII, 100. *See also* United States, History (Revolution)
Prizes, Confederate, XXVI, 96 ff.
"Prize to Privateer *Yankee,* 1812," by Grahame Farr, XXII, 216–217
Proceedings of the Sixteenth Conference on Underwater Archaeology, by Paul Forsythe Johnston, editor, reviewed, XLVIII, 200

Process for driving piles, by James A. Whipple, XXXIV, plate 8
Proctor, D. V., editor, *Ice Carrying Trade at Sea*, XLIV, 207
Proctor, Mrs. Eliza, XXX, 184, 185, 232
Proctor, Senator Redfield, XXXVII, 29
Proctor, Samuel, XXXI, 195
Procyon, U.S.S. *(1931)*, XX, 142
Productive Monopoly, A: The Effect of Railroad Control on New England Coastal Steamship Lines, 1870–1916, by William Leonhard Taylor, reviewed, XXXI, 148–149
"Profitability of Privateering: Reflections on British Colonial Privateers During the War of 1739–1748, The," by Carl E. Swanson, XLII, 36–56
Progreso, steamship (1885), XIV, 121, 134; *(1888)*, XXXVIII, 184 ff.
Progreso Steamship Co., XXXVIII, 184
Progress of Marine Engineering, by T. Main, XXX, 15
Projections of maps. See Map projection
Prometheus, ship *(1861)*, XXXIV, 175
Prometheus, steamship (1850), XIV, 201
Prometheus, U.S. Brig (1814), V, 79, plate 7
Promise, steamship (1863), XVII, 304; XVIII, 72
"Prompt Punishment," by Captain Edgar K. Thompson, U.S.N. (ret.), XXVII, 60
Propellers, XXIII, 204
Propeller Wharf, XXXIX, plate 3
Propontis, ship (1833), Pictorial Supplement, XXXVIII, plate XIV
Proserpina, torpedo boat *(1850)*, XLI, 95
Proserpine, H.C.S.S. *(1842)*, XXVI, 6 n.
Proserpine, H.M.S. *(1897)*, XXVIII, 89, 96
Prosper, schooner *(1923)*, XVIII, 213
Prosper, ship *(1775)*, XIII, 33 ff.
Prosperity, British ship *(1747)*, XLVIII, 33
Prosperous Fanny, British ship *(1776)*, XLVIII, 18
Protecteur, French warship [model] (1760), XVI, 102
Protector, schooner *(1861)*, XI, 154
Protector, ship, XXVIII, 120
"Protest: The Wreck of the Schooner *Charles W. Waterbury*," document contributed by E. Lee Dorsett, M.D., XV, 232
Proteus, bark (1867), IV, 326
Proteus, steamship *(1871)*, XXXVII, 235
Protheroe, Lorena Reed, XXXVIII, 207
Protractor, American, Pictorial Supplement, XXXV, plate XXVI (lower).
Proudfoot, Commander F. B., R.N., XLIV, 49 ff.
Providence, barge (1905), XXXVIII, 190 ff.
Providence, barque (1850), XLV, 125
Providence, brigantine (1783), XVIII, 130
Providence, Continental Navy sloop (1775), XXV, 193, 211, 213, 216 n.; *(1779)*, II, 247
Providence, frigate (1776), VIII, 11, 13, 14, 19, 24; X, 46; *(1776)*, XLVIII, 16, 158; *(1779)*, XLII, 30 ff.
Providence, gondola *(1776)*, VIII, 256; *(1779)*, XXXV, 142
Providence, H.M.S. *(1791)*, XII, 253; XIII, 213; *(1795)*, L, 28
Providence, schooner *(1839)*, XXXVIII, 58; *(1862)*, VIII, 227
Providence, ship *(1631)*, XXIII, 64
Providence, sloop *(1775)*, XXXVII, 293; XXXIX, 254; *(1778)*, VII, 203, 205; X, 284
Providence, steamship (1867), III, 44; (1905), Pictorial Supplement, XXXIV, plate XXVIII
Providence, U.S.S. *(1778)*, XVIII, 129
Providence Channel, Bahamas, XXV, plate 21
Providence Exploring and Trading Co., XXXV, 77
"Providence Exploring and Trading Company's Expedition to the Niger River in 1832–1833, The," by George E. Brooks and Frances K. Talbot, XXXV, 77–96
Providence Island. See New Providence.
Province Galley, ship *(1714)*, VIII, 164
Provoost, David, XVII, 292
Provost, Nelson, XXI, 112 ff.
Prows of a *mignole*, photo of, L, 169
Prudence, ship (1582), XIV, 10, 11
Prudent, schooner *(1861)*, XI, 287
Prussia, ship (1868), IV, 51, 52
Pryor, John A., *Geography, Technology and War: Studies in Maritime History of the Mediterranean, 649–1571*, reviewed, XLIX, 126–132
Ptarmigan, steamship *(1864)*, XXI, plate XI; *(1865)*, XII, 235
Ptolemy, XXX, 251
Publican, Captain, XXXII, 26
"Publication of Ship Registers and Enrollments," by Philip M. Hamer, I, 165–166
Publicover, Captain Archibald S., XXXIII, 51
Publicover, Captain James L., IV, 172–174
Public Record Office, London, England, XXXIV, 57; XXXVII, 9
"Publishing in Naval and Maritime History: A Report," by Timothy J. Runyan, XLVIII, 178–181
Puckle, Major William, XIII, 18
Puerto Cabello, XXX, 260
Puffer, George D., XXXVIII, 133
Pugach, Noel H., "American Shipping Promoters and the Shipping Crisis of 1914–1916: The Pacific & Eastern Steamship Company," XXXV, 166–182
Pulaski, steamship *(1838)*, XII, 149; XLVIII, 174
Pulaski, U.S.S. *(1864)*, XXVII, 44
Puleston, Captain W. D., U.S.N., *Annapolis — Gangway to the Quarter-deck*, reviewed, II, 263
Pullen, Hugh F., *The Sea Road to Halifax*, reviewed, XLI, 234
Pulsifer and Blackledge, XXXI, 141
Pultneyville (NY), XXXIV, 243.
Puluwat island, XXXIV, 252 ff.
Pumpelly, Raphael, XVI, 246

Punch (beverage), II, 39
Punch recipes, II, 42–43
Pungy, Chesapeake Bay, query on, by Naomi Yarnall, VII, 171; answer by Robert H. Burgess, VII, 243
Punishment, I, 116; XLII, 57
Punitive expedition, U.S. Navy against Korea, 1871, VII, 107–114
Purcell, H. G., query by, IV, 251
Purchas, Samuel, VII, 84, 85
Purchase, Captain J. W., XXVI, 15, 204
Purington, Philip F., and Reginald B. Hegarty, *Returns of Whaling Vessels Sailing from American Ports,* reviewed, XX, 71
Puritan, schooner (1922), IX, 73–74; XXVI, plate XXIX
Puritan, ship *(1887),* XXXVII, 84 ff.
Puritan, U.S. monitor (1862), X, 19, 29, 32; *(1864),* XLVIII, 123; *(1875),* XXII, 260, plate 15
Puritan, U.S.S. *(1864),* XXVII, 37, 42, 44
Purlieu, Jean Baptiste, XXXI, 25
Purrington, Philip F., "Anatomy of a Mutiny," XXVII, 98–110; *4 Years A-whaling: Charles S. Raleigh, Illustrator,* reviewed, XXXIII, 307
Purroy, Juan Bautista, XXX, 262
Purse, schooner *(1861),* VIII, 220
Pursey, sloop *(1864),* XV, 112, 129
Pursue, sloop *(1760),* XL, 263
Pursuit, bark, XXXII, 48
Purveyor, bark (1859), III, 72
Purviance, Hugh, XL, 43
Purviance, Samuel, Jr., VIII, 14
Pusey and Jones, V, 5
Pushbach, Lieutenant Hans, XXXII, 101 ff.
Pushee, Lyman, XXIV, 60
Pushmataha, schooner *(1863),* XII, 159
Putiatin, Vice Admiral E. V., XXXI, 268
Putnam, ship (1802), IX, 239–240; *(1802–1805),* V, 102, 104–105, 158; *(1805),* XXI, 292; XXV, 181, plate 18
Putnam, steamship (1883), VII, 228
Putnam, F. W., XLV, 81
Putnam, George R., XXVIII, 48
Putnam, Captain George W., V, 194–202
Putnam, Robert, *Early Sea Charts,* reviewed, XLV, 132
Putnam, Captain T., XXI, 106
Pycroft, Rev. James, VII, 84
Pye, Commodore Sir Thomas, XXVI, 62
Pylades, H.M.S., XXVIII, 17
Pyremon, steam frigate (1814), VI, 253, 259
Pyroscaphe, French steamship *(1783),* L, 205; photo, L, 206

Quadrant made by Nathaniel Bowditch, XXXV, Pictorial Supplement, plate I

Quail, H.M.S. *(1897),* XXVIII, 89, 98
Quail, schooner *(1859),* XXXVIII, 62
Quaker, H.M. ketch *(1684),* XXX, 133
Quaker, schooner *(1820),* XXXI, 288
Quaker City, U.S.S. *(1863),* XLIV, 265 ff.; *(1870),* XXXVIII, 237
Qualla Battoo, Sumatra, XXI, 293–295
Quantibaycook, brig (1799), XI, 224 ff.
"Quarantine Quandary: Ship Fever and Yellow Fever in Providence, Rhode Island, 1797, A," by Robert O. Tatge, XL, 192–210
Quarantines, XL, 192; L, 89, 94. *See also* Medicine, Naval
Quartermain, L. B., *South to the Pole: The Early History of the Ross Sea Sector, Antarctica,* reviewed, XXVIII, 73
"Quarter Wagener," by Charles E. Goodspeed, VI, 78–79
"Quarter Wagener," by W. Voorbeijtel Cannenburg, VII, 316–317
"'Quarter Wagener' of Captains Warner and DeAngelis," by Thomas A. Stevens, VI, 136
Quary, Colonel Robert, XXXV, 161
Quasi-War with France. *See* United States, History
Quasi-War with France (1797–1801), XXV, 12; XXX, 117–132
Quayle Family of Castletown, XXIX, 54–61
Quebec, British frigate *(1782),* XXXIX, 169
Quebec, ship *(1837),* XXIII, 56; *(1861),* XV, 214
Quebec (Canada). *See* Shipbuilding
Quebec, environs of, map of 1762, I, plate facing 143
Quebec, march to, XXX, 114 ff.
Queen, schooner *(1815),* XXI, 284
Queen, ship *(1860),* XLVII, 104
Queen, steamship, XXIV, plate XXII; *(1853),* XXII, 18, 31, 32, 33, 38, 42, 43; *(1952),* XIV, 24
Queen 98, British ship *(1798),* XXXIX, 32; XLV, 96
Queen, Midshipman Walter W., U.S.N., XXV, 141
Queen Anne's War (1702–1713). *See* United States, History
Queen Anne's War (1702–1713), XXXV, 153
Queen Charlotte, British ship, XXIX, 247; *(1787),* XXXVIII, 223; *(1800),* XIV, 216–217; *(1812),* XLIV, 178
Queen Charlotte, steamship (1818), VI, 194–196
Queen City, steamship *(1860),* II, 302
Queen Elizabeth, ship *(1917),* XL, 55 ff.
Queen Elizabeth, steamship (1940), XXIV, plate XVII
Queen Mab, schooner (1910), XXX, plate XXIII
Queen Mary, liner, XXVIII, 3; *(1967),* XXIX, 289
Queen of France, French frigate *(1778),* XLII, 30 ff.; XLIV, 169; *(1779),* XXXV, 141
Queen of Hungary, privateer sloop *(1740),* XLII, 42 ff.
Queen of Sheba, figurehead sketch for, Pictorial Supplement, XXXVII, plate XXVI
Queen of St. Johns, steamship (1883), IX, 298–299, plate 32

"Queen of the Hudson," by Donald C. Ringwald, XIV, 161–186, 278–297, plates 17–22
Queen of the Lakes, British ship *(1858),* XLVII, 102
Queen of the Pacific, ship *(1852),* XXVIII, 122
Queen of the Wave, steamship *(1863),* VIII, 231
Queen of the West, ship (1843), III, 261
Queen of the West, U.S. ironclad *(1862),* XXV, 136–139
Queensborough, H.M. yacht *(1676),* XXV, 279
Queens of the Western Ocean, by Carl C. Cutler, reviewed, XXII, 73–74
Queenston, steamship (1824), VI, 199, 202, 208, plate 30
Queenstown, ship (1876), IV, 243
Queen Victoria, steamship (1838), VIII, 37, 44, 46, 53; XVIII, 273, 280–281, 284; (1855), XXVI, 128, 206, 209
Queretana, Mexican gunboat *(1845),* XXX, 54
Querin, Captain Dominique, XXI, 99
"Query," by Rupert Furneaux, XXIX, 132
Quesada, Manuel, XXXVIII, 241
Quesnel, ship (1861), III, 69
Quest, S. Crocker yacht (1929), XLVIII, 184
Quevilly, ship [model] (1897), XVI, 104
Quickstep, barkentine (1876), V, 86
Quickstep, schooner *(1892),* XXX, Pictorial Supplement, plate VIII
Quickstep, steamship *(1852),* XXXV, 273
"Quid Pro Quo," document by Captain Edgar K. Thompson, U.S.N. (ret.), XXIV, 211
Quigley, Carroll, XVII, 262–291; "Certain Considerations on the Origin and Diffusion of Oculi," XV, 191–198; "The Origin and Diffusion of Oculi; A Rejoinder," XVIII, 25–58, 245–252
Quill, brig *(1834),* XXV, 186
Quincy (MA), History, XXXVII, 5
Quincy, Edmund, XLII, 29
Quincy, Josiah, XLIII, 251
Quincy, William S., *The Three-Masted Schooner,* reviewed, XLVIII, 65
Quincy Fore River Shipbuilding Co., XLIV, 116 ff.
Quindaro, schooner (1857), XXI, 304
Quinn, Alison M. and David B. Quinn, editors, *The English New England Voyages, 1602–1608,* reviewed, XLIV, 137–138
Quinn, David B., VII, 86; review by, XXIV, 144–145; *England and the Discovery of America 1481–1620,* reviewed, XXXIV, 280; Editor, *The Hakluyt Handbook,* reviewed, XXXIX, 303; *The New Found Land: The English Contribution to the Discovery of North America,* reviewed, XXV, 299; *North America from Earliest Discovery to First Settlements: The Norse Voyages to 1612,* reviewed, XXXVIII, 68; mentioned, XXXVII, 159; "The Voyage of *Triall,* 1606–1607: An Abortive Virginia Venture," XXXI, 85–103
Quinn, David B. and Alison M. Quinn, editors, *The English New England Voyages, 1602–1608,* reviewed, XLIV, 137–138
Quinnebaug, U.S.S. (1883), XXVII, 149

Quinolla, French ship *(1800),* XXXI, 175
Quinsay, China, XXX, 254
Quinsigamond, U.S. monitor (1862), X, 25, 32
Quintanilla, brig *(1823),* VII, 283–287
Quiros, Pedro Fernandes de, XXV, 250–252
Quiros, Pedro Fernandez de, IV, 88–90
Quistconk, freighter *(1918),* XXXII, 167
Quittance, ship (1590), XIV, 10, 11
Quoddy, schooner (1869), XXIV, 45, 59
Quoddy Belle, brigantine (1847), XXIV, 42, 43, 45, 57
Quoddy Boat, XII, 126–128
Quong Se, steamship *(1873),* II, 21
Quorra, side-wheel steamship *(1831),* XXXV, 81
Quyne, John, XXXI, 98

R

R. B. Clark, brig (1852), XXIV, 57
R. B. Coleman, schooner *(1857),* XLV, 111
R. B. Forbes, steam towboat, XXVII, 72
R. B. Hilton, schooner, XXI, 95
R. Burroughs, sloop *(1862),* XII, 57
R. Burrows, sloop, XXI, 101
R. C. Bishop, steamship (1880), V, 86
R. C. Files, schooner, XXI, 91, 93; *(1861),* XI, 287; XII, 57
R. C. Rickmers, ship (1906), VI, 135
R. D. Rice, ship (1883), VIII, 330
R. D. Shepherd, ship *(1861),* XI, 266, 287
R. E. Hopkins, American tanker *(1943),* XLIV, 51 ff.
R. E. Lee, steamship XXI, 90, 103, 104, 105; *(1862),* VIII, 203, 206, 227, 231; *(1863),* XIV, 62
R. H. Boughton, steamship *(1829),* VI, 210
R. H. Gamble, bark *(1861),* XI, 287
R. H. Tucker, ship *(1861),* VIII, 220
R. H. Vermilyea, schooner *(1865),* XII, 235
R. Hickson and Co., XXVI, 198, 207
R. Hilda, Canadian schooner *(1902),* XLIX, 280
R. J. Austin, steamship (ex-*San Lucas,* ex-*Eastern Knight*), XXIII, 276
R. K. Hawley, schooner *(1861),* VIII, 221
R. L. Hague International Lifeboat Racing Trophy, XLVII, 51
R. L. Mabey, tug *(1879),* V, 146
R. L. Myers, schooner *(1854),* XVII, 24
R. Napier & Sons, XXVI, 207
R. Pulsford, ship *(1849),* XLV, 124
R. R. Govin, schooner *(1939),* III, 163
R. W. Sherman, steamship (1851), III, plate 10
Rabateuse, French ship *(1799),* XXXI, 173
Raccoon, steamship, XXI, 93
Racehorse, brig *(1779),* XXXV, 141
Racer, schooner *(1862),* VIII, 227

Racer, ship (1851), XIX, plate IV
Racer, sloop *(1864),* VIII, 235; XV, 129
Rachael & Ebeneazer, ship *(1852),* XXXI, 289–290
Rachel, ship (1856), IV, 239
Rachel Coney, brig *(1883),* XLIX, 31 ff.
Racine, schooner *(1890),* XXIV, 44, 59
Racine, steamship (1843), XVII, 103; XX, 262
Racoon, steamship *(1863),* VIII, 231
Radcliffe Maritime Museum of the Maryland Historical Society, XXXVII, 172; *Maritime Titles in Print,* XXXIX, 74
Radford, Commander William, XXXII, 119; XLII, 94 ff.
Radford, Lieutenant William, XL, 42
Radiant, schooner *(1861),* VIII, 220
Radiant, ship, XXIV, 132
Raduga, bark (1848), V, 151, 242
Rae, Gideon, XXII, 207
Rae, William, XXII, 207
Raeder, Grand Admiral Erich, German Commander, XLV, 51
Raffees, V, 142–145
Raffles, Thomas Stamford, XLVI, 50
Raft Book, The, by H. Gatty, reviewed, IV, 253
Rafts, XLVIII, 77. *See also* Balsa
Rafts: I, 402–403
 Arabia, XXI, 180–183
 Central America, XXI, 170–171, 172–175
 China, XXI, 161–167
 Ecuador, XV, 142–149
 Formosa, XXI, 175–177
 India, XXI, 177–180
 Japan, XXI, 161–167, 175–177
 North America, XXI, 171–175
 Polynesia, XXI, 183–195
 South America, XXI, 158–161, 167–170, 172–175
Raftsman, steamship (1841), XX, 88, 89
Raggio, Captain David, XXI, 99
Rahder, Captain H., XXI, 99
Raiden Maru, whaler (ex-*Raiden*) *(1888),* XLIX, 26
Railroads, United States, XXXI, 120
Railroads and Steamers of Lake Tahoe, The, by Owen F. McKeon, reviewed, X, 158
Railroads Down the Valley, by Randall V. Mills, reviewed, XI, 232
Railway, marine, XIV, 215
Rainbow, gunboat *(1782),* XXXIX, 217
Rainbow, H.M.S. *(1765),* XXIII, 177; *(1777),* XLII, 12 ff.
Rainbow, H.M. frigate *(1748),* XLVIII, 34; painting of, XLVIII, 161
Rainbow, ship (1845), VII, 5
Rainbow, sloop *(1787),* XLIX, 88
Rainsford's Island, Boston Harbor, ca. 1840, XXIX, plate XXXI
Rainsonable, frigate *(1779),* XXXVII, 300
Raisbeck, Captain William, XXI, 99
Raison, Captain J., XXI, 99
Raisonable, H.M.S. *(1778),* VII, 207

Rajah, bark, XXVII, 98
Rajah, schooner *(1799),* XXI, 292
Rajah, steamship (1853), XVI, 246; XVII, 49; XXVI, 23, 32, 118, 203, 206, 209; XLIII, 100 ff.
Rajah Walla, steamship (1850), XIX, 27
"Rake of Bugeye Masts, The," by Frederic A. Fenger, XX, 66
Raleigh, C.S.S. *(1862),* XX, 158, 159
Raleigh, Continental frigate *(1778),* XXVI, 63–71, 138–140; XXVIII, 196
Raleigh, frigate *(1766),* XXXI, 134; (1776), VIII, 11, 13, 16–19, 24, plates 5–6; IX, 166, 283, 284; *(1777),* XLVIII, 160; XLIX, 41; *(1778),* I, 168–170
Raleigh, ship *(1778),* XLIII, 29; *(1898),* XXXIX, 41; XXXV, 184
Raleigh, U.S.S. *(1777),* XIII, 65
Raleigh, C. F., painting by, XLIV, 15
Raleigh, C. S., XVII, 4
Raleigh, C. S. (artist), XXII, plates XIV, XV, XVI; Pictorial Supplement, XXXI, plate XXIX
Raleigh, Sir Walter, XXXIV, 232; L, 9
Rambler, bark (1844), V, 150
Rambler, schooner *(1862),* XII, 57
Ramilies, ship *(1824),* XLVIII, 82
Ramillies, H.M. warship *(1813),* XXIX, 188
Ramognini, Antonio, XXVII, 186–191
Ramona, schooner *(1871),* XXX, Pictorial Supplement, plate VI
Ramsay, Commander Francis M., XXXIX, 126; XL, 130
Ramsden, Jesse, XLVI, 260
Ram (warship), XIX, 265; XXV, 128; XXIX, 5; XLIX, 114
Randall, sloop *(1864),* XII, 232
Randall, Captain F. G., XXXII, 102, plate 8
Randall, Captain H., XX, 89 n.
Randall, James, IX, 68
Randall, Mr., XXX, 62–67
Randall, Robert W., "Captains and Diplomats in the Río de la Plata, 1843–1846," XLVI, 230–239
Randall, Sarah, XLII, 23 ff.
Randall, Thomas, XIV, 298
Randall, Captain Thomas, XLVI, 29
Randall and Wendell, XIII, 121
Randall & Brent, VI, 228–230
Randier, Jean, *Grands Voiliers Français 1880–1930,* reviewed, XXXV, 212
Randolph, frigate (1776), VIII, 11, 12, 16, 21, 22, 24, plate 7; IX, 161 ff.; X, 70; *(1776),* XXXIV, 137; *(1790),* XLIX, 41
Randolph, ship *(1778),* XLIII, 27
Randolph, Captain Asher Fitz, XXXIX, 214
Randolph, Lieutenant Governor Beverley, XXXIII, 31
Randolph, Governor Edmund, XXXIII, 28
Randolph, Ellen Wayles, XXXVIII, 102
Randolph, Evan, "Roux Painting Mystery Solved," L, 60–62; "U.S.S. *Constellation,* 1797 to 1979," XXXIX, 235–255

Randolph, George Wythe, XXXVIII, 101
Randolph, Jefferson, XXXVIII, 105
Randolph, Margaret Smith, XXXVIII, 112
Randolph, Martha Jefferson, XXXVIII, 101 ff.
Randolph, Thomas Jefferson, XXXVIII, 102
Ranger, brigantine *(1776),* XX, 45
Ranger, H.M.S., XXVI, 46, 47
Ranger, schooner (1834), XIV, 40
Ranger, ship, XXVIII, 196
Ranger, sloop, XXVI, 59; *(1749),* XX, 117; *(1779),* XLII, 30; *(1863),* XII, 150; *(1903),* XXX, 195
Ranger, steamship *(1861),* XI, 287; XII, 57; *(1864),* VIII, 235
Ranger, U.S.S. *(1777),* XVIII, 304; XXVII, 136; (1873), XX, 139
Rankin, Hugh F., XVIII, 303
Rankin, Professor John, XXXI, 103
Ranking, Captain, XIII, 47
Ranlet, Philip, "The Two John Lambs of the Revolutionary Generation," XLII, 301–305
Ranlett, Captain Charles A., XXXII, 64
Ranlett, Captain Charles Everett, III, 91–92
Ransom B. Fuller, U.S. steamship *(1902),* XXXIII, 92, 94
Ransome-Wallis, P., *North Atlantic Panorama, 1900–1976,* reviewed, XXXIX, 148–149
Rapid, catamaran steamship (1834), VII, 54, 55
Rapid, schooner *(1863),* XII, 159
Rapido, cruiser (ex-*Normannia*) *(1850),* XLI, 94
Rappahannock, Confederate cruiser *(1864),* XXIX, 168; XLV, 198
Rappahannock, ship *(1848),* XVII, 17, 18
Rappahannock, ship (ex-*Nicholas*) *(1861),* XLIII, 131 ff.
Rappahannock, steamship *(1830),* XII, 63
Rappleyea, Captain George W., XIV, 108
Raritan, flagship *(1844),* XXIX, 183
Raritan, frigate *(1843),* XXXIV, 221
Rariton, steamship, XXVII, 9, 22, 27
Rarotonga, boats of, XIII, 108
Rasmussen, Nils, XLI, 52
Rasmussen, Captain P. C., XVI, 123, 124
Rassdall, Mr., XXXVII, 5 ff.
Rastall, Humphrey, XXXVII, 11 ff.
Rastall, James, XXXVII, 11
Rat, British ship *(1776),* XLVIII, 18
Ratcliffe, Captain John, XVII, 173
Rathbone, Captain, XXXI, 137
Rathbun, Captain John Peck, II, 247; XLII, 30
Rathjen, Warren F., XLV, 84
Raton del Nilo, schooner *(1863),* XII, 159
Ratsey, Ernest A., and W. H. DeFontaine, *Yacht Sails,* reviewed, VIII, 260
Rattler, H.M.S. *(1798),* XXIX, 144; *(1814),* XXVIII, 118
Rattler, ship (1852), III, 63
Rattler, sloop *(1862),* XII, 57
Rattlesnake, brig *(1814),* XLIV, 171
Rattlesnake, H.M.S. *(1779),* XXXIX, 204
Rattlesnake, privateer *(1777),* XLIII, 22 ff.; XLIV, 263

Rattlesnake, steamship *(1861),* VIII, 220, 227
Rättvisan, ship (1783), VI, 170
Raven, bugeye *(1881),* IV, 248
Raven, schooner *(1861),* VIII, 220
Raven, Captain W., XXXIV, 250
Ravena, steamship *(1895),* XX, 191
Ravens Point, S.S. *(1942),* XXVII, 197, 198
Ravenswood, bark (1877), VI, 73
Rawdon, Lord Francis, XLVI, 20
Rawleigh Warner, tanker *(1936),* XXX, 191
Rawson, Lieutenant Commander Geoffrey, "Tromelin Island," XVIII, 180
Ray, schooner *(1862),* XII, 57, 159
Ray, sloop *(1856),* X, 231 ff.
Ray, Dr. Isaac, XLVIII, 167
Ray, Captain Nathaniel, XV, 82–83
Raymenton, H. K, XXIX, 269
Raymond, ship *(1850),* XLV, 128
Raynard, Captain William H., XII, 103
Raynes, George, XV, 251
Raynor, James A., IV, 141 ff.
RCN in Retrospect, 1910–1968, edited by James A. Boutilier, reviewed, XLIII, 150–151
Rea, George Bronson, XXXV, 176
Rea, Robert R. and James A. Servies, *The Log of H.M.S. Mentor, 1780–1781,* reviewed, XLIV, 208
Reach of Tide, Ring of History: A Columbia River Voyage, by Sam McKinney, reviewed, L, 149
"Reaction Report," by John W. McElroy, XXXIX, 256–270
Read, Charles, XXXVII, 267 ff.
Read, Lieutenant Charles W., XV, 293
Read, Commodore George C., XXIX, 107; XXXI, 183; XLVII, 29, 172
Read, James, XV, 134
Read, James, Jr., XLVIII, 250
Read, Doctor John K., XVIII, 303
Read, Major Richard, XXXIV, 201
Read, Captain Thomas, XXXIX, 29
Reade, Lawrence, XXXVII, 62
Reader, Mr. Thomas, XXX, 235
Ready, H.M.S., XXVIII, 18, 108 n.
Ready Rhino, schooner *(1808),* XVI, 205
Reales Atarazanas, Barcelona, XX, 235
Reaney, Neafie & Co., XXX, 276
Reaper, brig *(1799),* XLI, 174; XLIV, 7; XLV, 153
Rear Admiral John Rodgers, 1812–1882, by Robert Erwin Johnson, reviewed, XXVIII, 294–295
Reardon, Captain Joseph, XVIII, 162
Rebecca, schooner *(1862),* VIII, 227; XII, 57, 159
Rebecca, ship *(1791),* XII, 100; *(1798),* XLV, 171; *(1799),* X, 53; *(1801),* XLVI, 53
Rebecca Edwards, schooner (1819), V, 217
Rebecca Hertz, sloop *(1864),* XV, 113, 129
Rebecca Palmer, schooner (1901), V, 81
Rebecca R. Douglas, schooner (1894), III, 255–258, plates 33, 43

Rebecca Sims, ship *(1861),* XV, 100 n.
Rebel, schooner *(1864),* XV, 129
Rebel, sloop *(1861),* XI, 187
Rebelledo, Juan Williams, XXXIX, 278
"Rebellion Roads," by Captain Edgar K. Thompson, U.S.N. (ret.), XXVII, 210
Rebow, Sir Isaac, XI, 14 ff.
"Recently Processed Manuscript Collections in the Phillips Library at the Peabody Museum of Salem," by Gregor Trinkaus-Randall and Robert P. Spindler, XLIX, 230–231
"Recent Problem in Ship Handling, A," by Robert H. I. Goddard, Jr., IV, 236–237
"Recent Writings in Maritime History," by Robert G. Albion, XII, 64–94, 163–172, 241–248, 297–304; XIII, 68–76, 141–152, 215–230, 282–301; XIV, 66–78, 142–156, 218–232, 300–317; XV, 83–92, 157–168, 233–244, 311–320; XVI, 66–76, 139–152, 214–228, 286–296; XVII, 74–84, 157–168, 231–243, 315–325; XVIII, 86–99, 253–267, 325–332
Rechten, J. P., XXVII, 280
Record of American and Foreign Shipping, XXX, 23 ff.
Recovery, brig (1805), VII, 317
Recovery, ship (1679), XIII, 8, 21
Recovery, ship (1794), I, 164; II, 279; *(1799),* XLI, 169
Red Book or Shipowners' Register, XXX, 11 ff.
Red Cloud, ship (1878), V, 152
Red Cross (ex-*Hamburg*), ship, XXXIII, 187
Red D Line, XXX, 261 ff.
Redfield, Secretary William C., XXXV, 173
Redford, U.S. destroyer *(1918),* VII, 72
Red Fox, schooner *(1861),* XI, 287
Red Gauntlet, ship (1853), XV, 178; *(1853),* XVII, 21; *(1863),* XXVIII, 122
Red Gauntlet, steamship *(1864),* XII, 232
Rediker, Marcus, *Between the Devil and the Deep Blue Sea,* reviewed, XLVIII, 61
Re d'Italia, Italian warship, XVI, 61; (1864), XV, 199 ff.
Red Jacket, bark *(1917),* XVIII, 165, 170
Red Jacket, dragnet boat (1900), I, 69
Red Jacket, ship (1854), XIX, plate VI; *(1854),* XXVI, 167, 169
Red Jacket, steamship (1838), XVIII, 282; XX, 82 n.; *(1838),* VII, 313; *(1860),* XXVIII, 223
Redkey, Edwin S., XXXV, 203
Redland, steamship (1880), XI, 257 ff.
Redmond, Robert A., "The Revenue Steamer *E. A. Stevens* in the Civil War," XX, 155–166
Red Rover, sailing vessel *(1845),* XXVI, 8
Red Rover, ship (1852), III, 67
Red Sea, XXX, 207, 211
Red Star Line, ship of, Pictorial Supplement, XXXIV, plates XI, XXVII
Redwing, fishing schooner *(1853),* XLIV, 83
Redwood, Abraham, XII, 227
Redwood, Jonas, XXXV, 294
Reed, Abner, XV, 215, 216

Reed, C. M., XX, 97
Reed, Captain Charles, XVII, 45; XVIII, 84
Reed, Colonel Charles M., VII, 48
Reed, Edwardo, XXX, 49
Reed, Captain Freeman K., XXXV, 13
Reed, George Washington (Master Commandant), XLIV, 175 ff.
Reed, Lieutenant Commander J. H., XXXII, 133
Reed, Colonel Joseph, XXX, 109, 115
Reed, Seth O., "The Trade between Providence, Rhode Island, and the Caribbean and South America, in 1796," XLV, 166–174
Reed, Vergil D., answered query, I, 174
Reed, William, XXXI, 286, 287; XXXIV, 105 ff.
Reed, William B., XXVII, 163, 164
Reed, William B. (American diplomat), XXXVIII, 37
Reed boats, XXIII, 41
Reed Line, XX, 84
Reefer, Mexican gunboat *(1846),* XXX, 55
Reese, Captain D. N., XIV, 127
Reeve, Richard, XX, 246
Reeves, Captain, XXX, 299
Reference List of Manuscripts Relating to the History of Maine, edited by Elizabeth Ring, Louis T. Ibbotson, Rising Lake Morrow, reviewed, I, 404–405
Reform, sloop (1830), XIV, 40
"Reform in the United States Navy: The 'Plucking' of Officers in the Latter 1850's," by Howard C. Westwood, L, 107–118
Refugees, Jewish, XLIII, 31
"Regatta at New Bedford, Massachusetts, 8 August 1856," document contributed by Llewellyn Howland, X, 231–234
Regeneración, schooner *(1859),* XXX, 276
Regent, brig *(1814),* XLII, 107 ff.
Regent, ship (1860), V, 149
Regina, steamship *(1892),* XIV, 120
Regiomontanus, XXX, 256
Register Book, XXX, 12 ff.
Register Book of British and Foreign Shipping, The, XXX, 11 ff.
Register of American and Canadian Yachts, XXX, 21
Register of Officer Personnel United States Navy and Marine Corps and Ships' Data 1801–1807, edited by Captain Dudley W. Knox, U.S.N. (ret.), reviewed, V, 248
Register of Shipping of the U.S.S.R, XXX, 31
"Registers, Enrollments and Licenses in National Archives," by Forrest R. Holdcamper, I, 275–294
Registers of ships. *See* Ship registers
"Register Tonnage and its Measurement," by John Lyman, V, 223–234, 311–325
Registrar General of Shipping and Seamen, XXX, 14
Registration of ships, XV, 303–306
Registre da la Navigation Intérieure, XXX, 26
Registre Maritime, XXX, 26, 27
Registro Aeronautico Italiano, XXX, 27

Registro Italiano Navali ed Aernautico per la Visita e la Classificazione delle Navi e degli Aeromobili Commerciali, XXX, 27
Registro Italiano Navali per la Classificazione delle Navi Mercantili, XXX, 27
Registro Italiano [Per la Classificazione dei Bastimenti], XXX, 27, 28, 29, 38
Registro Navale Italiano, XXX, 27
Registry General of Shipping and Seamen, Cardiff, XXXIV, 57
Regulator, steamship (1864), XII, 288, 293
Regulus, ship *(1844),* XXXVIII, 59
Reid, Ogden, XXVI, plate 8
Reid, Captain William, XX, 243–249
Reid & Co., XLIII, 196 ff.
Reilly, John C., Jr., *United States Navy Destroyers of World War II,* reviewed, XLVII, 144
Reilly, John C., Jr. and Robert L. Scheina, *American Battleships 1886–1923,* reviewed, XLI, 231–233
Reims, auxiliary (1918), XXXII, 22, 30
Reina Mercedes, U.S.S. *(1912),* XX, 138
Reina Regente, Spanish cruiser *(1886),* XXXIX, 134
Reinbek, ship *(1927),* XVIII, 217
Reindeer, H.M.S. *(1812),* VII, 169
Reindeer, schooner *(1861),* XI, 287; XII, 57; *(1888),* XXXIX, 9
Reine Marie Stewart, schooner *(1942),* II, 163
Reinemuth, Rolf, *Segel aus Downeast: die unerschrockener Männer von der Weser und ihre prächtigen Schiffe aus Neu-England,* reviewed, XXXII, 136
Reinsch, Paul S., XXXV, 170 ff.
Release, ship *(1859),* XLV, 237
Relempago, sloop *(1863),* XII, 159
Reliance, revenue cutter *(1863),* XXXIV, 122; XXXV, 64
Reliance, ship (ex-*Egalité*) *(1923),* XXXII, 15 ff.
Reliance, steamship *(1862),* XV, 110, 114, 126; *(1877),* VII, 136
Reliance Machine Co., XLVIII, 118
Relief, light-vessel *(1862),* V, 245
Relief, S.S. (ex-*Shanghai*), XXVI, plate 15
Relief, schooner *(1861),* XI, 269, 287; XII, 58, 159
Relief, steamship (1872), XVII, 311, 312; XVIII, 72; *(1873),* X, 134
Relief, storeship *(1838),* XXX, 298; XLIX, 152 ff.; photo of model, XLIX, 159; *(1865),* XXXII, 125
Relief, tug *(1882),* VI, 288
Relief, U.S.S. *(1838),* IV, 105 ff.; *(1839),* XII, 282–286, plate 25; *(1861),* XXXIV, 47, 175
Relief (aid). *See* International relief; Food relief
Relief carving attributed to Simeon Skillin, Pictorial Supplement, XXXVII, plate XXIV
Religious disputations, II, 79
"Religious Instruction," by Captain Edgar K. Thompson, U.S.N. (ret.), XXIX, 132

Remaking of the English Navy by Admiral St. Vincent: Key to the Victory Over Napoleon, The, by Charles B. Arthur, reviewed, XLVIII, 190
"Remarks on Seventeenth-Century Ship Design," by R. C. Anderson, XV, 151–152
Rembrandt, ship (1876), figurehead of, Pictorial Supplement, XXXVII, plate VIII
Remedy, H.M.S. *(1807),* IX, 13
"Remembering Days in Old China: A Navy Bride Recalls Life on the Asiatic Station in the 1920's," by Evelyn M. Cherpak, XLIV, 179–185
Remey, Commodore George C., XL, 176 ff.
Remey, Rear Admiral George C., XXVIII, 48
"Reminiscences of a Voyage in the Bark *William H. Besse,* including the Java Earthquake of 1883," by Mrs. B. C. Baker, edited by Harold Bowditch, VI, 121–131
"Reminiscences of Isle au Haut," by Stanton M. Smith, XI, 218–220
"Reminiscences of the Last Voyage of the Bark *Wanderer,*" by Alexander Crosby Brown, IX, 14–30, plates 1–4
Renault, L., XXVIII, plates IX, XI
Rengold Bros., bateau (1911), IV, 289
Rennie, Sir John, VII, 280–281
Rennie, Chief Justice Sir R. T., XL, 115
Rennoldson (Reynoldson), David, XXVI, 204
Renomee, French ship *(1800),* XXXI, 174
Renommée, French privateer *(1800),* XLV, 98
Renovator, grain elevator *(1870),* XXXVIII, 134 ff.
Renown, H.M.S., XXVIII, 87, 88, 89, 91, 92; *(1942),* XXVII, 99; L, 49
Renown, ship (1830), XIV, 40
Renshaw, schooner *(1863),* VIII, 231
Renshaw, Commodore James, U.S.N., VII, 18; XL, 42
Renshaw, Master Commandant James, XLIV, 177
Rensselaer Iron Works, XLVIII, 107 ff.
Rentone, Captain James, XXVI, 53
Renwick, Edward and Henry, I, 139–140
Renwick, James, VII, 186; XXXII, 220
Repeal, brig (1766), XXIX, 160
"Repel Boarders," by Captain Edgar K. Thompson, XIX, 232–234
Répertoire Général, XXX, 26, 27, 37
"Reply to Mr. Ferguson's Comments," by Howard I. Chapelle, X, 66–68
Reporter, schooner (1876), V, 86
Reporter, ship *(1854),* VIII, 71
"Reporting the Sicilian Revolution of 1848–1849," by Francis X. Holbrook and John Nikol, XLIII, 165–176
Reposo, Ascenso, XIII, 11
Reprisal, brig *(1776),* XLIII, 21 ff.
Republic, grain elevator *(1883),* XXXVIII, 141
Republic, sloop *(1853),* XXXIX, 86
Republican, boat *(1794),* XIV, 61
Republicano, Buenos Aires brig, XXIX, 179 ff.
Republica Peruana, barkentine (1920), V, 82

Republic of Venezuela, XXX, 260
République, auxiliary (1918), XXXII, 23, 27, 30
Repulse, battleship *(1941),* XLII, 203 ff.
Repulse, galley *(1779),* XXXV, 141
"Requiem," by Captain Edgar K. Thompson, U.S.N. (ret.), XXVI, 271
Rescue, ship *(1850),* XX, 106
Rescue, steamship *(1870),* XXXIX, 174 ff.
Rescues. *See* Life saving
Research vessels, V, 5
Reserve, schooner *(1863),* XII, 159
Resistance, brigantine *(1777),* XIV, 47–60; *(1778),* X, 284
Resoluda, Spanish bark *(1874),* XXXIII, 286
Resolute, beam trawler *(1891),* XLIV, 115
Resolute, ship *(1855),* XVII, 17, 25; (1857), I, 109–112, plate facing I, 110
Resolute, sloop *(1864),* XV, 129
Resolution, H.M. schooner (1864), XXXIII, 204
Resolution, H.M.S. (Captain Cook's ship) *(1780),* L, 128
Resolution, H.M.S. *(1773),* VII, 89 n.; *(1778),* XXXVI, 167; XXXVIII, 217 ff.
Resolution, schooner *(1862),* XII, 58
Resolution, ship *(1775),* XXXV, 71; *(1776),* XXVIII, 146–148; *(1796),* XVIII, 140; *(1806),* XIV, 91
Resource, ship *(1799),* V, 90; X, 53; XXXIV, 253; *(1817),* IV, 56–57
"Respect for Civilian Authority: The Tragic Career of Captain Angus," by Harold D. Langley, XL, 23–37
Restauración, schooner *(1848),* XXX, 264
Restaurador, gunboat, XXVIII, 99; *(1845),* XXXVI, 132
Restless, bark, XXXII, 48
Restoration, sloop *(1825),* I, 324
"Restoration of East India Marine Hall, The," by Lawrence Waters Jenkins and Walter Muir Whitehill, IV, 5–17
"Restoration of the Port of Philadelphia, 1783–1789, The," by George W. Geib, XXXII, 247–256
Restoration of the Smack Emma C. Berry *at Mystic Seaport, 1969–1971,* by Willits D. Ansel, reviewed, XXXIV, 148–149
"Resurrection," by Captain Edgar K. Thompson, U.S.N. (ret.), XXIX, 53 n.
Retribution, C.S.S. (1862), XXXIII, 199 ff.; *(1862),* XIX, 53
Retribution, H.M.S. (1902), XXVIII, 98
Retribution, schooner *(1862),* VIII, 227; XII, 58
Retriever, schooner *(1863),* XII, 159, 232
"Return of *Oregon* or How She Really 'Got Home', The," document by E. Mowbray Tate, XXXVII, 138–140
Returns of Whaling Vessels Sailing from American Ports, Reginald B. Hegarty and Philip F. Purrington, reviewed, XX, 71
Return to the Sea, by William Albert Robinson, reviewed, XXXIII, 214–215
Reuben Jones, U.S.S. *(1941),* XLV, 52
Revenge, H.M.S., XXVIII, 6

Revenge, privateer *(1813),* XXXVI, 211 ff.; XXXIX, 200
Revenge, privateer sloop *(1744),* XLII, 41 ff.
Revenge, schooner *(1776),* VIII, 256; *(1779),* XXXV, 142; *(1863),* XII, 159
Revenge, ship *(1577),* XLIV, 27; *(1627),* XLIX, 254
Revenge, sloop *(1777),* V, 187
Revenue, schooner *(1925),* IX, 178–179
"Revenue Cutter designed by Samuel Humphreys, A," by Howard I. Chapelle, I, 80–81; document contributed by Clarkson A. Cranmer, III, 174–176
Revenue Marine Service: The Nucleus of the Confederate Navy," by Ralph W. Donnelly, XLVIII, 87–95
Revenue ships, XX, 155, 243; XXXVI, 174; XL, 298; XLV, 119; XLVIII, 87
"Revenue Steamer *E. A. Stevens* in the Civil War, The," by Robert A. Redmond, XX, 155–166
Revere, schooner *(1861),* VIII, 220, 227
Revere, Paul, II, 348; III, 269–270; VII, 203, 210; XXXVII, 128, 294
Revere, Paul, and the World He Lived In, by Esther Forbes, reviewed, II, 348
Revolutionary War, VII, 87 ff., 200–212; XXVII, 220, 221–222; American vessels captured during, II, 203–208
Revolution of 1848–1849, The, XXX, 262
Rex (ex-*Kenilworth*), I, 340–342
Rey de los Araguatos (ex-*Iris*), brig *(1853),* XXX, 273
Reynard, French ship *(1799),* XXXI, 173
Reynard, Captain William, XXXVIII, 210
Reynolds, Clark G., XXXV, 3; reviews by, XLVIII, 206; XLIX, 314; "Yankee Supership? Sortie of *Spuyten Duyvil,*" XLII, 85–100
Reynolds, Clark G. (Secretary-Treasurer of NASOH), XXXVII, 81
Reynolds, E. A., XLIII, 200 ff.
Reynolds, Enos and Sarah, XLVI, 43
Reynolds, George H., XLIV, 14
Reynolds, James Joshua, XLI, 222
Reynolds, Jeremiah N., XXX, 297; XXXVII, 44
Reynolds, Stephen, XLVI, 43 ff.; portrait of, XLVI, 45
Reynolds, Captain William, U.S.N., VIII, 180–181; IX, 63
Rezneck, Samuel, "The Maritime Adventures of a Jewish Sea Captain, Jonas P. Levy, in Ninteenth-Century America," XXXVII, 239–252
Rhadamanthus, steamship (1832), IX, 261–262
Rhea, John, XXXIX, 23
Rheingold, steamship *(1935),* XIV, 132, 135
Rhenish Westphalia Co., XXXIX, 131
Rhind, Charles, VII, 187–188
Rhine, bark (1850), III, 262
Rhine, ship (1808), XIV, 95 ff.; *(1899),* XIX, 227–231
Rhoades, Samuel, XV, 220–222
Rhoades & Matthews, XV, 220
Rhode Burroughs, sloop *(1861),* XI, 287; XII, 57
Rhode Island, side-wheeler *(1864),* XXXII, 54

Rhode Island, steamship (1882), III, plate 11; VII, 77
Rhode Island (RI). *See* Slave trade, Triangle trade
Rhode Island Historical Society, XXXVIII, 250
Rhodes, Captain James, XLI, 173
Rhodes, William, XXXV, 83 ff.
Rhodes' Steamship Guide, XXX, 31
Rhondda, steamship *(1885),* XIV, 119
RI. *See* Rhode Island
Riachuelo, ironclad *(1883),* XXXIX, 131
Ribero, Diego, XI, 97, Plate 11
Rice, Captain A. L., VII, 132, 139, 150
Rich, Benjamin, XIX, 23
Rich, Edwin Newell, queries by, I, 171; II, 174
Rich, Captain Richard, XLVI, 217
Rich, Robert, XXXVII, 8
Richard, bark (1826), Pictorial Supplement, XXXVIII, plate VIII
Richard, schooner (1907), XXVI, plate XXI
Richard, ship *(1606),* XXXI, 95
Richard, sloop *(1804),* XLIII, 40 ff.; *(1862),* XII, 58, 160
Richard Cobden, ship (1847), V, 242
Richard E. Kraus, U.S.S. *(1961),* XXXVI, 159
Richard Hakluyt and his Successors, A Volume Issued to Commemorate the Centenary of the Hakluyt Society, edited by Edward Lynam, reviewed, VII, 85–86
Richard Morse, ship (1851), XXVII, plate VII
Richard O'Bryan, schooner *(1862),* XII, 58
Richard P. Buck, ship (1882), XXVIII, plate XXII
Richard R. Higgins, schooner (1858), I, 308
Richards, sloop *(1863),* XII, 159
Richards, John, introduction to "Loss of the Steamship *Independence,*" by Captain Jason Collins, XIV, 192–202
Richards, Michael, XX, 17
Richards, Rhys, *American Whaling on the Chathams Grounds, viewed from an antipodean perspective,* reviewed, XXXII, 226; "The Journal of Erasmus Darwin Rogers, the First Man on Heard Island," XLI, 280–305; *Whaling and Sealing at the Chatham Islands,* reviewed, XLIV, 204
Richardson, Alfred, III, 276–277
Richardson, Captain, VII, 56, 57
Richardson, Charles, XLVI, 59
Richardson, Duck and Co., XIV, 116
Richardson, Ebenezer, XL, 262 ff.
Richardson, Francis, XL, 8 ff.
Richardson, George Atwell, query by, V, 246
Richardson, Captain Hugh, XVIII, 284
Richardson, James B., XXX, 79, 81
Richardson, Jeffery, XIII, 122
Richardson, John, shipwright, V, 328
Richardson, John, VII, 153
Richardson, John M., I, 400; XIX, 121; *Steamboat Lore of the Penobscot,* reviewed, II, 262
Richardson, John R., "Captain Leroy Dow and *Clarissa B. Carver,*" XL, 108–116
Richardson, Lieutenant M. T., XLVI, 243

Richardson, Captain William, XIII, 275 ff.
Richard William, Canadian schooner, XLIX, 283
Richelieu, French warship [model] (1939), XVI, 103
Richmond, ironclad ram *(1862),* XLII, 85 ff.; XLIII, 130
Richmond, ship *(1799),* XXXIX, 33; *(1839),* XII, 37
Richmond, sloop *(1856),* X, 231 ff.
Richmond, steamship *(1814),* XXVII, 26, 27
Richmond, tanker *(1915–1916),* V, 139
Richmond, U.S.S. *(1799),* XXXI, 173; (1885), photo of, XLIX, 292
Richmond, U.S. steam sloop *(1861),* XXXI, 64; XXXIII, 281
Richmond, warship *(1798),* XLVI, 151 ff.; *(1857),* L, 122; *(1872),* XXXVIII, 238
Richmond, Fredericksburg, and Potomac Railroad, II, 91–92
Richmond, Helen, *Isaac Hull, a Forgotten American Hero,* reviewed, XLIII, 313–314
Richmond, Admiral Sir Herbert, XXXI, 278
Richmond, Sir Herbert W., XLII, 184
Rickard, L. S., *The Whaling Trade in Old New Zealand,* reviewed, XXVII, 75
Rickenbacker, Eddie, XXXIV, 265
Ricketson, Daniel, X, 73; XXXIX, 99
Ricketts, E. F., and John Steinbeck, *Sea of Cortez,* reviewed, II, 183
Ridderkerk, Dutch ship *(1783),* XLVII, 245
Riddle, Captain Thomas, III, 74–79
Rideau Canal, VII, 62
Rideout, Oliver B., XV, 181
Ridgely, Commodore Charles G., XXXIX, 115
Ridgely-Nevitt, Cedric, IV, 260, 336; V, 165; VII, 3; *American Steamships on the Atlantic,* reviewed, XLIII, 227–231; "Auxiliary Steamships and R. B. Forbes," I, 51–57; "Henry Eckford's *United States* of 1831," VIII, 7–10; "Light-vessel of 1823 built by Henry Eckford, A.," V, 115–120; "The *Steam Boat,* 1807–1814," XXVII, 5–29; "United States Mail Steamer *George Law,* The," IV, 304–317
Ridley, Mark, XXXVII, 176
Riedemann, Heinrich, XXXVIII, 175
Ries, Alfred, XXXV, 177
Riesenberg, Felix, Jr., *Golden Gate, The Story of San Francisco Harbor,* reviewed, I, 402; *Pacific Ocean, The,* reviewed, I, 182–183
Riesenberg, Captain Felix, XX, 142
Rigaud, General, XXX, 126, 127
Rigger's Apprentice, The, by Brian Toss, reviewed, XLVII, 56
Rigging, by Harold Augustin Calahan, reviewed, I, 189
Rigging of ships. *See* Masts and Rigging; names of rig types
Rigging: III, 279–291, plates 37–40
    Balsa, XV, 142–149
    Dolphin striker, XIII, 65–66
    Fore and aft sails, XIII, 213
    Roman ships, XV, 217–219, plate 12

Ship, XV, 306–310
Spritsail, XIII, 85–117, 185–211; XV, 217–219, plate 12
"Rigging of Schooners," query by Albert E. Parsons, II, 248
Rigging of Ships in the Days of the Spritsail Topmast, 1600–1720, The, by R. C. Anderson, reviewed, XLIII, 146–147
Rigging plan, Sweden, VI, plate 28
Rigging plan of ship *La Escocesa,* VII, 295–296
Riggs, William H. C. (Watchmaker), XXXIV, 206
Right Arm, steam tug *(1894),* XLII, 266 ff.
Rigs. *See* Masts and Rigging; names of rig types
Rigs, II, 326–327; III, 261; IV, 237–238, 325–326; V, 81–82, 137–141, 142–145, 235–239; of sailing vessels in 1892, II, 289–290
Rigs: barkentine, VII, 315–316, plate 39; dhow, IX, 87–132; double gaff, VI, 73–77; five masted square, VI, 135–136; four masted ships, IX, 297–298; schooner, IX, 72
Rigs:
　diffusion, XIX, 155–199, 274–306
　bugeye, XX, 64–66
　Marconi, XX, 66
"Rigs of American Yachts in 1902," by John Lyman, XXX, 194–199
Rihakuri Maru, steamship *(1865),* XLIII, 91 ff.
Rijksmuseum (Amsterdam, Holland), XIV, 187, 188
Rimac, Chilean transport *(1879),* XXXIX, 282
Rimac, topsail schooner *(1896),* II, 326–327
Rimington, Critchell, *Fighting Fleets,* reviewed, II, 352; *Fighting Fleets; Merchant Fleets,* reviewed, IV, 340; Editor, *The Sea Chest,* reviewed, VIII, 160
Rinaldo, H.M.S. *(1862),* XX, 158, 159
Ring Dials: English, Pictorial Supplement, XXXV, plate XVII; French, Pictorial Supplement, XXXV, plate XVII
Ring Dove, schooner *(1863),* XV, 128
Ringgold, Cadwalader, explorer, XLVII, 29
Ringgold, Commander Cadwalader, XXXVIII, 33
Ringgold, Commodore Cadwalader, XXIX, 102 ff.; XXX, 298
Ringtail Topsails, V, 235–239
Ringwald, Donald C., VI, 307; *Hudson River Day Line: The Story of a Great American Steamboat Company,* reviewed, XXVI, 74; "The Hudson River Steamboat *Thomas Cornell,* 1863–1882," VI, 277–289, plates 33–34; "Queen of the Hudson," XIV, 161–186, 278–297, Plates 17–22; *Steamboats for Rondout: Passenger Service Between New York and Rondout Creek, 1829 through 1863,* reviewed, XLII, 229
Rio de la Plata. *See* Plata River System
Ripley, Thomas (instrument maker), Pictorial Supplement, XXXV, plate V
Ripple, schooner *(1863),* XII, 160
Ripple, whaleback bow trawler *(1910),* XLIV, 119
Ripple, yacht *(1892),* XXXVI, 236, 237

Rippon, H.M.S., XXVI, 37, 53, 54
Rise and Fall of Naval Mastery, The, reviewed, XLIV, 208
Risenberg, Saul H., "Six Pacific Island Discoveries," XXXIV, 249–257
Rising Dawn, schooner *(1863),* VIII, 231
Rising Empire, steamship *(1822),* XXXV, 250
Rising Star, steamship (1821), IX, 253–255
Rising Star, steam warship (1818), XXXII, 194; XXXV, 249
Rising States, schooner (1798), XIV, 40
Rising States, ship *(1796),* XLV, 169
Rising Sun, brigantine (1796), XIV, 40
Rising Sun, sloop *(1795),* XXXVIII, 252; *(1861),* VIII, 220, 227
Rising Sun in the Pacific, The, by Samuel Eliot Morison, reviewed, IX, 76
Rita, schooner *(1861),* XI, 287
Ritchey, John, XL, 7 ff.
Ritchie, Carson I. A., review by, XXVIII, 73–74
Ritchie, Carson J. A., "A Laker's Log," XVII, 203–211
Ritchie, Elliott, XXXVI, 205
Ritchie, G. S., *The Admiralty Chart: British Naval Hydrography in the Nineteenth Century,* reviewed, XXVIII, 151
Ritchie, J. W., XIX, 65, 66
Ritchie, Margaret K. and Carson I. A. Ritchie, "American Prisoners of the French Privateers, 1707," XX, 112–117
Ritchie, Captain Robert, XXXIII, 43
Ritchie, Robert C., *Captain Kidd and the War against the Pirates,* reviewed, XLVII, 282
Riva Adriatica, tanker *(1926),* XXXVIII, 185 ff.
Rivadavia, bark (1856), IV, 239
Rival, schooner *(1811),* XXXIV, 245
Rival, yacht *(1908),* XXXVI, 245, 248
Rival Empires of Trade in the Orient 1600–1800: Europe and the World in the Age of Expansion, by Holden Furber, reviewed, XXXVII, 223–224
River Bird, steamship (1854), XVI, 164; XVIII, 72
River boats, France, L, 165
"River-Built Ocean-Going Vessels," by John Lyman, VII, 317–318
"River Craft of the Lower Nile," by Richard LeBaron Bowen, Jr., XII, 45–51
River Forth, steamship *(1914),* XVIII, 161
River Orinoco, XXX, 261
Riveros, Rear Admiral Galvarino, XXXIX, 283
River Queen, steamship (1864), VI, 137
Rivers. *See* names of individual rivers
Riverside, ship (1868), II, 334
River Tyne, 1832, XXIX, 198, plate XXII
Riviera Prima (1964) (renamed *Viking Princess*), XXXVI, 29
Rivière, Lieutenant de la, XXXVI, 131
Rivoli, French warship [model] (1812), XVI, 102
Rålamb, Åke Classon, XXX, 83
Roach, John, XXVI, 286–287; XXXIX, 129; XLVI, 62

Roald Amundsen, boat (1939), XIV, 111
Roane, Christopher, XXXIII, 39
Roanna, schooner *(1861),* XI, 287
Roanoke, 4-masted bark (1892), XXV, 156
Roanoke, armored vessel *(1864),* XLVIII, 125; XLIX, 112
Roanoke, barge (1828), V, 301
Roanoke, bark *(1901),* XVI, 11
Roanoke, U.S. steam frigate (1855), XXI, 142–143; XXII, 252 ff., plates 13, 14; *(1862),* X, 17–18, 25, 31; *(1864),* XXVII, 43; XXXII, 200; XXXIII, 14, 203
Roaring Bessie, schooner, XII, 140
Roaring Bessie, yacht, XXXVII, 225
Robarts, Edward, XXXIII, 168
Robarts, J. T., XXII, 5
Robb Engine Works, Ltd., Nova Scotia, XXXII, 31
Robbertsz, Robbert, L, 284
Robbins, steamship (1825), VI, 199, 203
Robbins, Chandler, XVII, 47
Robbins, Sarah Fraser, XLV, 117; mentioned, XLIX, 37; review by, XXXI, 291; XXXVI, 147–148
Robbins, Professor Stanley L., L, 95
Robbinston (ME), XV, 173–190
Robert, barge (1883), VI, 289
Robert, bark (1848), V, 150
Robert, brig *(1807),* XVI, 193; *(1839),* XXX, 174, 180, 181, 183–186; *(1843),* XXX, 230; *(1844),* XXVII, 85
Robert, William C. H., *The Explorations, 1696–1697, of Australia by Willem de Vlamingh,* reviewed, XXXIII, 218
Robert Browne, ship *(1832),* XLIV, 9
Robert Bruce, brig, XXI, 98; *(1861),* VIII, 199, 221, 227, plate 19
Robert Burns, cartel *(1813),* XXVIII, 191
Robert Burns, ship *(1806),* XVIII, 135
Robert Dixon, ship (1873), III, 62
Robert Dollar Co., XXIX, 234
Robert Dollar Line, XXXV, 175
Robert E. Lee, blockade runner *(1863),* XLVIII, 99
Robert F. Stockton, screw steamship *(1838),* XLIX, 96; *(1839),* XII, 149
Robert Fulton, steamship (1819), VII, 183; (1820), XXIV, 116; *(1820),* XXXV, 248
Robert Fulton, steamship (1835), VII, 56; *(1838),* VII, 307; *(1840),* XX, 86, 89 n.
Robert Fulton: A Biography, by Cynthia Owen Philip, reviewed, XLIX, 238
"Robert Fulton and the beginning of Modern Marine Transportation, 1808–1958," by Vincent Short, XVIII, 316–317
"Robert Fulton's *North River Steam Boat,*" document contributed by David Whittet-Thomson, XXXII, 211–221
"Robert G. Albion 1896–1983, An Appreciation," by Archibald R. Lewis, XLIV, 61–62
Robert G. Shaw, ship *(1887),* XXXVII, 84
Robert Granger & Co., XXVI, 102
Robert Hale, U.S.S. (1807), VII, 317; *(1810),* XXX, 292 n.
Robert Harding, ship *(1861),* XI, 266, 287
Robert Healey, schooner *(1861),* VIII, 221
Robert L. Lane (1853), III, 263
Robert L. Linton, schooner (1917), V, 139
Robert L. Stevens, steamship *(1853),* XIV, 163
Robert L. Webster, bateau (1915), IV, 289–290
Robert Lowe, steamship *(1863),* XLIII, 107 ff.
Robert Luckenbach, steamship (ex-*Eastern Merchant*), XXIII, 276
Robert McClelland, Confederate cutter *(1861),* XLVIII, 87; *(1861),* XL, 298
Robert Mills, bark (1852), V, 154
Robert Mowe, brig, XXVIII, 123
Robert Napier, steamship, XXIV, plate XXI
Roberto, Luigi, XXIV, plate VI
Robert Porter, bark (1866), IV, 243
Robert R. Kirkland, brig *(1861),* XI, 153
Robert Rankin, British freighter *(1845),* XXXIII, 84, 94
Roberts, Captain Bartholomew, XXXVII, 43
Roberts, Harold C., VII, 176; "The Old Steam Shed," VII, 196–199
Roberts, J. J., XXXVIII, 58
Roberts, Captain James, XXI, 100
Roberts, Captain James P., XVI, 248; XVIII, 84
Roberts, John, XXXVII, 11
Roberts, Captain John T., XXI, 100
Roberts, Captain Josiah, XXXIII, 162 ff.
Roberts, Kenneth, VIII, 255; XIV, 217; XXV, 65
Roberts, Kenneth G., and Philip Shackleton, *The Canoe,* reviewed, XLV, 137
Roberts, Captain Samuel, XXV, 91
Roberts, Stephen S., "The Decline of the Overseas Station Fleets: The United States Asiatic Fleet and the Shanghai Crisis, 1932," XXXVII, 185–202
Roberts, William H., XXVI, 204
Robert Salmon, Painter of Ship and Shore, by John Wilmerding, reviewed, XXXII, 69
Robertson, Captain Alexander, XXI, 100
Robertson, George, VII, 86
Robertson, Master George, XXV, 297
Robertson, Captain, J. W., VII, 128
Robertson, Lieutenant James, XXI, 54
Robertson, John, VII, 319; XLVII, 109
Robertson, Sir John, XIII, 157
Robertson, Captain P. W., "Coolies in the Ship *Rhine,*" XIX, 227–231
Robertson, Paul and Sidney Pollard, *The British Shipbuilding Industry, 1870–1914,* reviewed, XLII, 67–68
Robertson, Captain R. L., XX, 90 n.
Robertson, R. S., VII, 56
Robert Steele and Co., XXVI, 13, 119, 192, 208
Robert W. Cole, bateau (1911), IV, 290
Robert Watt, bark (1834), XV, 185
Robert Whitman Lesley, concrete ship (1944), XXII, 178

Robeson, George M., XXII, 259
Robinet, Captain W. R., XVIII, 84
Robinet and Co., XXXIV, 20 ff.
Robin Hood, sail (ex-*Vailly*) *(1923),* XXXII, 25, 30
Robin Hood, ship *(1846),* XIV, 45; *(1861),* XV, 108 n.; XXI, 241, 256
Robinson, U.S. destroyer *(1918),* VII, 72
Robinson, Captain Andrew, XXV, 82
Robinson, Beverley R., Collection, III, 93
Robinson, Dwight E., "Secret of British Power in the Age of Sail: Admiralty Records of the Coasting Fleet," XLVIII, 5–21
Robinson, Ebenezer, XL, 12
Robinson, Edward M., XXXIII, 54
Robinson, Captain F. G., XLIV, 120
Robinson, Sir Frederick, XXI, 51
Robinson, Isaiah, XXXVI, 158
Robinson, John, XIX, 123–125
Robinson, M. S., *A Pageant of the Sea,* reviewed, XI, 297–298; *Van de Velde Drawings,* reviewed, XIX, 146
Robinson, Michael, editorial mention, XLII, 83
Robinson, Nathan, IV, 22 ff.
Robinson, Robert, XXVIII, 68–69
Robinson, Rear Admiral Samuel M., XXXVIII, 275
Robinson, Wendy A., *First Aid for Marine Finds,* reviewed, XLIIm 227
Robinson, William Albert, *Return to the Sea,* reviewed, XXXIII, 214–215
Robinson Crusoe's Island: A History of the Juan Fernández Islands, by Ralph Lee Woodward, Jr., reviewed, XXX, 300–301
Roboreus, bark *(1806),* XXV, 183
Robotti, Frances D., *Whaling and Old Salem,* reviewed, XI, 233
Robottom, Lieutenant Commander Percy K., XXXVII, 123
Rob Parker, ship *(1861),* XV, 124
Rob Roy, schooner *(1863),* XII, 160, 232, 235
Rob Roy, yacht *(1905),* XXXVI, 241
Roccafortis, large nef *(1264),* XLVI, 89
Rochambeau, French ram (ex-*Dunderberg*) (1862), X, 29; *(1865),* XXXIV, 61; XLIX, 117
Rochambeau, French warship [model] (1865), XVI, 103
Roche, John, Jr., XXVII, 135 ff.
Roche, John, Sr., XXVII, 136 ff.
Roche, Lieutenant William G., XL, 300 ff.
Roche Harbor Lime and Cement Co., VII, 293 ff.
Roche Harbor Lime Transport, barge (1868), VII, 293–294, plates 34, 36
Rochelle, Captain J. H., XXI, 100
Rochester, heavy cruiser *(1923),* XXXV, 125, 131
Rochester, ship (1837), IV, 51; *(1844),* XIII, 139; (1856), II, 332; IV, 51
Rochester, steamship (1837), VII, 65; *(1838),* XVIII, 283, 298; XX, 83 n., 86, 89 n., 92, 103; (1843), XX, 262, 268

Rock, Rear Admiral George H. (CC), U.S.N. (Ret.), Chairman, *Historical Transactions 1893–1943,* reviewed, VI, 86
Rockaway, schooner *(1883),* XIX, 140
Rockendorff, Captain, XXXIII, 6 ff.
Rocket, H.M.S. *(1897),* XXVIII, 89, 96, 98
Rocket, steamship (1869), XVII, 308, 309; XVIII, 72
Rockets' Red Glare: The Maritime Defense of Baltimore in 1814, The, by Scott S. Sheads, reviewed, XLIX, 59
Rockland (ME), X, 203 ff.
Rocklands, ship *(1878),* XV, 186
Rockledge Line, VII, 152–154
Rock Light, ship (1855), II, 331
Rockport, U.S.S. *(1917),* XX, 139
Rocktown, revenue vessel *(1892),* XXXVIII, 64; XXXIX, 174
"Rocky Mountain Sea Captain," by Martin I. Seeger, III, XXVIII, 128–141
Rocky Neck, Gloucester (MA), XXV, plates III, V
Roddin, Captain Barney, XXI, 100
Roderick Random, U.S. brig, XXIX, 160
Rodger, N. A. M., *The Wooden World: An Anatomy of the Georgian Navy,* reviewed, XLVIII, 208
Rodgers, ship *(1882),* XXXIX, 11 ff.
Rodgers (ex-*Mary & Helen*) *(1880),* XLIV, 14
Rodgers, Bradley A., "The Northern Theater in the Civil War: The USS *Michigan* and the Confederate Intrigue on the Great Lakes," XLVIII, 96–105
Rodgers, Rear Admiral Frederick, XXXV, 195
Rodgers, Commandant George W., XXXVI, 187; XL, 33
Rodgers, John, XXX, 41, 73; XXXI, 287
Rodgers, Admiral John, XXIX, 107 n., 108, 114; XXXIV, 212 ff.
Rodgers, Captain John, XXXVI, 216; XL, 32 ff., 213
Rodgers, Commodore John, U.S.N., VII, 18, 183, 184; VIII, 154; XX, 161; XXI, 130, 131; XXII, 262; XXVIII, 294–295; XLVII, 14; L, 89
Rodgers, Rear Admiral John, U.S.N., VII, 108, 109, 113, plate 9; general order quoted, VII, 113–114; XXVIII, 294–295
Rodgers, Lieutenant William T., XIX, 213–226
Rodin, Abraham, XXIII, 193 ff.
Rodman, Admiral, XL, 51 ff.
Rodman, Admiral Hugh, XXXV, 102
Rodman, Samuel, XXXIX, 84
Rodman, Thomas, XLIX, 111
Rodmond, bark *(1856),* XI, 42 ff.
Rodney, by David Spinney, reviewed, XXXII, 296
Rodney, Sir George, VII, 102
Rodney, Admiral Sir George Brydges, XXXVI, 167, 168
Rodney, Admiral Lord, IV, 193–198
Rodrigues, Francisco, VI, 308–309
Roe, U.S. torpedo boat destroyer (1910) XXII, 142
Roe, Commander Francis A., XLVII, 103
Roe, Captain Francis Asbury, XXXIII, 280 ff.

Roe, Michael, Editor, *The Journal and Letters of Captain Charles Bishop on the North-West Coast of America, in the Pacific and in New South Wales, 1794-1799,* reviewed, XXVIII, 227-228
Roebuck, H.M.S. *(1776),* XL, 14 ff.; *(1777),* XIII, 46
Roebuck, schooner *(1863),* XII, 160
Roebuck, U.S.S. *(1798),* XXXI, 175
Roger Drury, schooner, XV, 227
Rogers, Alan, "'A Dangerous Sport:' A Boston Boy's Life at Sea, 1820-1837," L, 211-218
Rogers, Alfred, XIII, 55
Rogers, Augustus D., XIX, 209-212
Rogers, Bryant K., query by, I, 172
Rogers, Lieutenant C. C., XLI, 258
Rogers, Edward S., XXV, 296
Rogers, Captain Erasmus Darwin, XL, 120; XLI, 280 ff.
Rogers, Henry J., III, 215 ff.
Rogers, Captain Henry, XLI, 302
Rogers, J. W., XIV, 244; XIX, 129 n.
Rogers, Rear Admiral John, XXV, 116
Rogers, John G., *Origins of Sea Terms,* reviewed, XLV, 212
Rogers, John M., XXVI, 204
Rogers, Moses, XII, 239
Rogers, N. W., XXV, 185
Rogers, Nathaniel L., XIX, 200-212
Rogers, Captain R. M., XXI, 100
Rogers, Richard, XXXII, 131
Rogers, Commodore Robert, U.S.N., XXV, 161
Rogers, Lieutenant Robert M., XL, 298 ff.
Rogers, Stephen, XXV, 222
Rogers, Thomas, XXXV, 289 ff.
Rogers, William L., XIX, 200-212
"Rogers Collection of Ship Models, Annapolis, The," by William Salisbury, XVIII, 181-182
Rogers Shipyard, XXVII, plate XVII
Rogge, Captain William, XXI, 100
Roggeveen, Jacob, XXX, 73
Rogues' River, by Frank Martin, reviewed, XLV, 132
Rohilla, hospital ship *(1914),* XXXIV, 11
Rohilla, steamship (1880), XXIV, plate XII
Rohlf boatworks, XXXVI, 245
Roland, ship *(1861),* XI, 287
Roland, sloop *(1793),* XXII, 81, 95 ff.
"Role of the United States Navy in the Suppression of the African Slave Trade, The," by George M. Brooke, Jr., XXI, 28-41
Rolla, brig (1831), Pictorial Supplement, XXXVIII, plate V
Rolling Sea, brig (1833), XXIV, 45, 57
Rollins, Captain William, XII, 150-153
"Rollo On The Atlantic, by Jacob Abbott," Edited with Commentary by Alexander C. Brown, XXVI, 81-95
"Rollo on the Atlantic," illustrations from, XXVI, plates 9, 13, 14
Roma, steamship (1889), XXXVIII, 184 ff.
Roman, bark *(1874),* XLV, 109
Roman, clipper ship (1850), XXV, 110
Roman, ship *(1829),* XLVI, 36
Roman, ship *(1969),* XXXVIII, 205 ff.
Romance, brig *(1889),* XXVI, 174
Romania, ship *(1864),* XLVII, 123
Romans, Bernard, XXI, 11
Roman vessels, XV, 217-219, plate 12
Romanzoff, Count, XXXVIII, 44
Rome, Watertown & Ogdensburg Railroad, VII, 44
Romeo, ship *(1805),* XV, 133
Romer, William F., XIV, 163
Romer and Tremper, XIV, 164
"Rome's Maritime Trade with the Far East," by Lionel Casson, XLVIII, 149-153
Romney, H.M.S. *(1763),* XXIII, 175; *(1767),* XXVII, 219; *(1770),* XXII, 144
Romp, schooner *(1846),* XLIV, 88
Romp, ship (1809), II, 283
Rona, steamship (1862), XVII, 136, 137; XVIII, 72; *(1863),* XLIII, 98 ff.
Rondout, NY, VII, 277 ff.
Ronnberg, Erik A. R., Jr., XXX, 82; reviews by, XXX, 301-302; XXXII, 74, 139, 144, 149, 187, 292, 294; XXXIII, 147, 148, 149, 213; XXXIV, 146, 147, 148, 149, 286; XXXV, 68, 216; XLI, 71-73, 148-149; XXXVII, 74; XXXVIII, 144, 148, XXXIX, 146, 147, 149, 151, 304; XL, 230, 232; XLIV, 210, 280; XLII, 221-222
Rood, Mrs. Paul, document by, XXIX, 133-138
Roorbach, Captain, XXVII, 25
Roos, William, *The* Hornet's *Longboat,* reviewed, I, 185
Roosevelt, steam schooner (1905), I, plate facing 78, 79
Roosevelt, Clinton, XX, 167-173
Roosevelt, Franklin D., XXVIII, 50; XXXVI, 159; XXXVII, 113 ff.; XXXIX, 246
Roosevelt, President Franklin Delano, IV, 5; XXV, 69; XXXII, 104; XLI, 267; XLIII, 31 ff.
Roosevelt, Nicholas, L, 201
Roosevelt, Nicholas J., XVI, 29 ff., 271, 275
Roosevelt, Theodore, XXXVI, 264; XXXVII, 31
Roosevelt, President Theodore, XXII, 187 ff.; XXVII, 47 n., 59; XXIX, 30, 31, 33, 53; XXXII, 257 ff.
"Roosevelt, the Navy, and the Venezuela Controversy: 1902-1903," by Ronald Spector, XXXII, 257-263
"Roosevelt Drawing of the Continental Ship *Alfred,* The," by John J. McCusker, XXVIII, 49-52
Root, R. C., Anthony & Co., XXX, 21
Ropes, Ernest Edward, XXIII, 139
Ropes, G., painting of Crowninshield Wharf (1806) by, XLVI, 18
Ropes, George, XIII, 247
Ropes, Captain George, XXV, 181-182, plate 20
Ropes, Hardy, XXIII, 131
Ropes, John Codman, XXIII, 138
Ropes, Joseph, XXIII, 132
Ropes, Joseph Samuel, XXIII, 136, 138, 139
Ropes, Mary Tyler, XXIII, 135, 137

Ropes, Samuel, XXIII, 131
Ropes, William, XXIII, 131 ff.
Ropes, William Hooper, XXIII, 131, 133, 136, 138, 139
Ropes & Pickman, XXIII, 132
Rope walks, Salem (MA), II, 285–287
Rorqual, research vessel *(1962)*, XLI, 54
Rory Brown, bark (1852), VI, 80
Rosa, brig, XXI, 89; *(1861)*, XI, 287
Rosa, sloop *(1861)*, XV, 124
Rosabella, bark (1835), Pictorial Supplement, XXXVIII, plate XIX
Rosalba, American merchant vessel *(1844)*, XXIX, 177; XLVI, 233
Rosalie, sloop, XXI, 99; *(1862)*, VIII, 227, 231
Rosalind, bark *(1862)*, VIII, 227, 231
Rosalind, barkentine, XXI, 91
Rosamond, schooner (1900), XXXII, 291
Rosario, bark *(1861)*, XI, 266, 287
Rosario, schooner (1878), Pictorial Supplement, XXXIII, plate IV; *(1888)*, XXXVIII, 8, 45
Rosas, General, XXX, 264
Rosas, Juan Manuel, XXIX, 175
Rosas, General Juan Manuel, XXXVI, 125 ff., 142, 143
Roscoe, ship *(1860)*, XXXVIII, 209; *(1861)*, XI, 266, 287
Rose (1812), XIII, 280
Rose, British sloop-of-war *(1810)*, XXX, 286
Rose, H.M. frigate *(1776)*, III, plate 1; *(1776)*, XXXVIII, 21
Rose, H.M.S., XXIII, 144, 182, 184; (1740), XXVI, 37–62
Rose, H.M.S. [replica] (1970), XXX, 80
Rose, postal steamship *(1959)*, XXXIV, 21
Rose, schooner *(1862)*, XII, 58
Rose, ship *(1804)*, X, 54; *(1858)*, XXXIV, 18 ff.
Rose, steamship (1855), XXII, 21, 28, 29, 42, 43; *(1864)*, VIII, 235; *(1855)*, XLIII, 94 ff.; *(1865)*, XVII, 61, 142 ff.; XLIX, 24
Rose, David S., XXXV, 175
Rose, Philip G., Editor, *U.S. Naval Ships Data Arranged by Hull Classification,* Vol. I (by H. E. Musgrove), reviewed: XXXVIII, 149; review reprinted, XL, 71–72
Rose, Roger G., reviewed book, XXIX, 148–149
Rose, William J., XXXV, 84
Rosecrans, steamship (1883), XXXVIII, 194 ff.
Rosedale, steamship (1887), III, plate 12
Rose Medallion pattern: plate, initials U.S.G., XLIII, plate 6; plate, initial A., XLIII, plate 8; dinner service, photo, XLV, 240
Rosenbach, Dr. A. S. W., XXI, 6
Rosencrantz, Captain Peter, XXI, 100
Rose Standish, ship *(1854)*, XXX, 162
Rose Standish, steamship, XXVIII, 124, 125; (1912), XXIV, Plate XXXI
Roseway, pilot schooner, XXXIII, 64
Roseway, steamship (1918), XII, 291, 293
Rosie H., schooner *(1908)*, XXXVIII, 91
Rosier, James, XXXI, 85; XLVII, 77

Rosina, schooner (1849), XXIV, 59
Rosina, sloop *(1864)*, XII, 232
Rosinski, Herbert and Werner B. Ellinger, *Sea Power in the Pacific 1936–1941, A Bibliography,* reviewed, II, 352
Rosita, steamship, XXI, 98; *(1863)*, XII, 160, 232
Rosita-y-nene, steamship *(1872)*, XVII, 53
Roskell, N., XXVI, 204
Roskill, Captain S. W., R.N., *The Strategy of Sea Power: Its Development and Application,* reviewed, XXV, 75
Roskill, Captain S. W., R.N. (ret.), *A Merchant Fleet in War, 1939–1945,* reviewed, XXVI, 148
Rosner, Charles, XXVIII, plate XXVIII
Ross, First Lieutenant David, L, 245 ff.
Ross, Captain James Clark, XLI, 284
Ross, John H., XXV, 294
Ross, Thorvald S., "Seven Ropes," XXI, 145
Ross, W. Gillies, *Arctic Whalers, Icy Seas,* reviewed, XLVII, 62; Editor, *An Arctic Whaling Diary: The Journal of Captain George Comer in Hudson Bay 1903–1905,* reviewed, XLV, 210; "The Travels of Tilikum," XXVIII, 53–65; *Whaling and Eskimos: Hudson Bay, 1860–1915,* reviewed, XXXVII, 72
Ross, William, XXII, 44
Rossam, James, XX, 186
Rossano, Geoffrey L., "Launching Prosperity: Samuel Townsend and the Maritime Trade of Colonial Long Island, 1747–1773," XLVIII, 31–43
Rossie, privateer schooner *(1812)*, XLIII, 5 ff.
Rossindale, snow (1741), I, 297
Rosswell King, schooner *(1867)*, XLV, 111
"Roster of American Steam Vessels Equipped with the Hunter Wheel, A," by Alexander Crosby Brown, XXIV, 8–9
Rotary Steam Navigation Co., XXXIX, 89
Rotch, Benjamin, XVII, 66
Rotch, William J., XXXIX, 88
Rothesay Castle, steamship, XXI, 96, 106, plate XVI; *(1864)*, VIII, 235
Rothesay Museum, Bournemouth, XXX, 154
Rothley, Thomas, XX, 16 ff., 29–31
Rotterdam, Dutch warship *(1777)*, XXXVI, 165 n.
Rotterdam, steamship (1872), Pictorial Supplement, XXXIV, plate IX
Rouen, steamship [model] (1912), XVI, 104
Rouen, steamship *(1864)*, VIII, 235
Rough And Ready, sloop *(1855)*, XXIV, 142
Roukema, Captain E., "Columbus Landed on Watlings Island," XIX, 79–113
Roulette, schooner (1884), XXXIV, 144
"Round Tops in America," query by Winthrop Pratt, Jr., IX, 74–75; answer by R. C. Anderson, IX, 302
Rourke, Captain F. Thomas, XXI, 100
Rouse, Parke, Jr., "Early Shipping Between England and Chesapeake Bay," XXX, 133–138
Rousseau, Commodore Laurence, XLVI, 238

Route des Iles, La, by Auguste Toussaint, reviewed, XXVIII, 150–151

"Routine Trade of Salem under the Confederation Congress, May 1793–October 1789," by James Duncan Phillips, I, 345–351

Roux, Antoine, sketches, I, plates facing 360, 361, 370, 371; II, plates 11, 12; XIII, 3

Roux, Antoine, Sr., XVII, 72

Roux, Francois, XIX, 28

Roux, Frédéric, I, 82, plates facing 83, 100; XIX, 29, 30

Roux, Louis, XXVIII, plate XIV

"Roux Painting Mystery Solved," by Evan Randolph, L, 60–62

Rover, American bark *(1866),* XXXII, 130; XXXV, 29

Rover, brig *(1820),* L, 211 ff.

Rover, schooner, XXI, 99; *(1863),* VIII, 231, 235

Rover, steamship *(1863),* XVII, 220; XVIII, 72

Rowan, Captain, XXXVI, 190

Rowan, Commodore S. C., XLVII, 31

Rowan, Rear Admiral Stephen Clegg, XXXIV, 61; XLIII, 179 ff.

Rowe, Edward, XXIX, 134 ff.

Rowe, Jacob, VII, 269

Rowe, John, XIII, 122; XL, 252

Rowe, Joshua N., III, 314–326; IV, 31–44, 339, plate 8

Rowe, Stephen J., IX, 68

Rowe, William, XLVIII, 264

Rowe, William Hutchinson, VIII, 178 n.; "The Maine West India Trade," VIII, 165–178; *The Maritime History of Maine,* reviewed, IX, 151–153

Rowena, bark *(1861),* VIII, 221; XI, 153

Rowena, brig *(1848),* XXX, 263

Rowena, schooner *(1862),* VIII, 227

"Rowing a Boat in Japan," by John Lyman, IX, 65–67, plate 5

Rowland, Thomas Fitch, XLVIII, 119

Rowland & Marwoods Steamship Co., XXXVIII, 184

Rowlandson, Thomas, sketch by, XXXII, plate 5

Rowse, Captain Joseph, XVII, 62; XVIII, 84

Roy, John B., VII, 66

Royal Admiral, XXII, 75

Royal Alice, steamship *(1847),* XIII, 259

Royal Arch, bark (1854), III, 64; VI, 81

Royal Arch, ship, XXIV, 132

Royal Arthur, British man-of-war, XXIV, 126

Royal Bounty, ship *(1812),* XXI, 18, 19

Royal Britain, transport *(1781),* XLVII, 11

Royal Carolina, Royal Yacht *(1737),* XXVI, 37, 38

Royal Carriage Department, XXXVIII, 95

Royal Catherine, ship *(1683),* XI, 14

Royale, galley [model], XVI, 101

Royal Escape, Royal Yacht *(1740),* XXVI, 38

Royal George, H.M.S. *(1813),* XVII, 210

Royal Hester, ship *(1756),* XLVIII, 38

Royal Humane Society, XXVI, 20

Royal Katherine, ship *(1665),* XV, 152

Royall, Joseph, XXXVII, 59

Royal Louis, French warship [model] (1757), XVI, 102

Royal Mail, British shipping line, XLVI, 108

Royal Mail Steam Packet Co., XXXV, 254

Royal Merchaunt, British ship, XLIV, 29 ff.

"Royal National Life-Boat Institution, 1824–1974, The," by Oliver Warner, XXXIV, 5–16

Royal Navy, state of, in 1783, VII, 106

Royal Navy, XXVII, 66–67, 74–75, 211–220, 223, 224, 281–284, 287; XXVIII, 85–112

Royal Navy and the Northwest Coast of North America, 1810–1914: A Study of British Maritime Ascendancy, The, by Barry M. Gough, reviewed, XXXII, 141–142

Royal Navy and the Slavers, The, by W. E. F. Ward, reviewed, XXX, 68–69

"Royal Navy on the River Parana During the Allied Intervention, 1845–1846, The," by E. A. M. Laing, XXXVI, 125–143

Royal Oak, ship (1690), XV, 152

Royal Oak, ship *(1939),* L, 131

Royal Republicans: the French Naval Dynasties Between the World Wars, by Ronald Chalmers Hood, III, reviewed, XLVIII, 131

Royal Savage, schooner *(1776),* VIII, 256; *(1779),* XXXV, 142

Royal Scottish Museum, XXX, 153

Royal Society, XXX, 204, 205

Royal Sovereign, British man-of-war, XXIV, 126

Royal Sovereign, ship, XXXIII, 9

Royalston, brig (1855), IV, 239

Royal Tar, British steamship (1836), XXXIII, 80 ff.

Royal Victoria, ship *(1861),* VIII, 221

Royal Victoria Yacht Club, Ryde, XXXII, 61

Royal William, steamship (1831), IX, 259–261; *(1833),* XXXVII, 232; (1837), IX, 265–266

Royal Yacht, schooner *(1862),* XXXVI, 202; XLVIII, 92; *(1863),* XII, 160

Royce, Captain Thomas W., XXVII, 280

Royden, Thomas, XLI, 125

Roye, auxiliary (1918), XXXII, 23 ff.

Roye, E. F., XXXVIII, 63

Roys, John, XXXIV, 246 ff.

Roys, Captain Samuel W., XXXIV, 247 ff.

Roys, Captain Thomas, XXXIV, 246

Roys, Thomas Welcome, XLIV, 12

Roys, Captain Thomas Welcome, XXXIX, 5 ff.

Roy Somers, schooner *(1916),* XVI, 126

Rubbers, sailmaker's, IX, 288–289

Rubin, Norman N., "Cliometrics: Its Application to Nautical Research," XLVI, 179–187; "Variances in Dimensions of Half-Models," XXXVII, 164–168

Rubinstein, Murray A., "The Wars They Wanted: American Missionaries' Use of *The Chinese Repository* Before the Opium War," XLVIII, 271–282

Ruby (1795), XIII, 213

Ruby, brigantine *(1729),* XXI, 265

Ruby, ship, XXVIII, 227–228

Ruby, steamship, XXI, 81, 88, 92, 99; *(1863),* VIII, 231; XII, 160, 235; (1879) XXIII, 86
Rudd, Arthur M., "Correction on *Pacific Queen,*" XVI, 137–138
Rudd, Captain John, XXXIII, 45
Rudder, jury, II, 65–70
"Rudolph Verner and the Battle of the Falkland Islands," by S. W. Jackman, XXXIIl, 34–40
Ruffin, Edmund, V, 304
Rufus King, ship (1806), VII, 317
Rugg, C. B., XXXVII, 126
Rules and Regulations of the Navy of the United Colonies of North America (1775), cited, XXV, 36
Rules for Steel Lake and River Vessels, XXX, 24
Rules for the Regulation of the Navy of the United Colonies, reviewed, IV, 336
Rum, VIII, 175–176; Rum punch recipes, II, 42–43
Rumley, Captain John W., XXI, 100
Rum running, XIX, 73–74
Rumsey, James, III, 357; L, 201
Runyan, Timothy J., "Publishing in Naval and Maritime History: A Report," XLVIII, 178–181; "Ships and Fleets in Anglo-French Warfare, 1337–1360," XLVI, 91–99; *Ships, Seafaring and Society: Essays in Maritime History,* reviewed, XLVIII, 210
Runyan, Timothy J. and Archibald R. Lewis, *European Naval and Maritime History, 300–1500,* reviewed, XLVI, 200
Ruparell, ship *(1858),* XXXIV, 17 ff.
Rupert, ship (1666), XIV, 273
Rupert, Prince, XXV, 286
Rurik, brig *(1815),* IV, 100–104
Rush, fishing vessel *(1963),* XLI, 60
Rush, schooner *(1840),* XXXVI, 46
Rush, Benjamin, L, 97
Rush, Dr. Benjamin, XXVI, 183, 184, 188 n.; XL, 194 ff.
Rush, Richard, XXXI, 217; XXXIII, 254 ff.; L, 245 ff.
Rush, William, VII, 254–260; XXV, 54
Rushton, Gerald A., *Whistle Up the Inlet,* reviewed, XL, 68–70
Rushton, Ontario Boat Co., XXVI, plate 6
Rushton sailing craft, XXVI, plate 5
Rusk, Henry, I, 79; mentioned, XL, 244
Russel, Barnabas, XX, 45
Russel, Edgar, XXXIV, 265
Russell, bark *(1882–1886),* IV, 43
Russell, brig *(1808),* XVI, 202; (1835), Pictorial Supplement, XXXVIII, plate XXVII
Russell, whaleship *(1851),* XLIV, 15
Russell, Albert, XVII, 115
Russell, Benjamin, XVII, 4; XXVII, 269; XXX, 218
Russell, Captain Benjamin, XXII, plates X–XII; XXIII, 27
Russell, Captain C. A., XXI, 100
Russell, Judge Chambers, XL, 254
Russell, George, XXIV, 57 ff.
Russell, H. S., XVI, 243, 257
Russell, James, XXX, 58, 60
Russell, Captain James A., XXI, 100
Russell, Lord John, XXVII, 31, 32; XXXIII, 11, 12
Russell, John W., XXXIX, 83
Russell, Jonathan, XXX, 279; XLVII, 27; XL, 29
Russell, Joseph (Gun Captain), XLIV, 172 ff.
Russell, Joseph B., document contributed by, XXXI, 286–288
Russell, Captain Lewis, XXIII, 133
Russell, Lillian, XXXVIII, 7
Russell, Lord, XV, 104 ff.
Russell, Mr., XXX, 296
Russell, Nathaniel P., XV, 138
Russell, Norman S., VIII, 248–249
Russell, Osborne, XXVIII, 130–132
Russell, Captain Reuben, XXIII, 26
Russell, Captain Samuel, XXIII, 28
Russell, Sturgis and Co., XVII, 54, 56; XVIII, 59, 60; XLIII, 128 ff.
Russell, Captain Sylvanus, XXIII, 27
Russell, Thomas H., XXI, 16
Russell, Thomas S., XXVI, 204
Russell, Captain W., XXX, 110
Russell, William Howard, XXVII, 237, 238; XXXV, 55
Russell and Co., XIII, 122;, XVI, 160 ff., 243 ff.; XVIII, 60, 66; XXII, 8, 13, 15, 17, 40, 225; XXVI, 129; XXX, 296; XXXI, 183; XXXIV, 17 ff.
Russell Galley, ship, XXVIII, 68–69
"*Russell Galley* in a Hurricane," by Edmund Berkeley, Jr., XXVIII, 68–69
Russell Haviside, barkentine (1920), V, 82
Russia, grain elevator *(1883),* XXXVIII, 141
Russia, steamship *(1871)* (ex-*Mauritius*), XXVI, 191
Russia Co., XLVIII, 24
Russia, Foreign relations, United States, XX, 49; XXI, 207. *See also* St. Petersburg
Russian-American Fur Co., XXXI, 268
"Russian Fleet on the Eastern Seaboard, 1863–1864; A Maritime Chronology, The," by Robin D. S. Higham, XX, 49–61
Russian trade, XXI, 207–215
Russian voyages in Pacific, IV, 100–105
Russo, John Paul, "Hull's First Victory—One Painting: Three Famous Men," XXV, 29–34
Russwurm, Governor J. B., XXXVIII, 60
Rustomjee Dhunjeeshaw, XXXIV, 33 ff.
Rut, Captain John, XXVII, 179
Ruth, schooner (1930), XXIV, 99, plate 13
Ruth, ship *(1742),* XXVI, 43
Ruth E. Merrill, schooner, XXIII, 17; (1904), IV, 325
Ruth E. Pember, schooner (1901), XXVI, plate XVI
Ruther A. Thomas, bateau (1914), IV, 290
Rutherford, schooner, XXI, 92; *(1862),* VIII, 227
Ruth Jones, gundalow (1826), X, 251
Rutland, ship (1859), III, 171
Rutledge, Governor Edward, XLVII, 22
Rutledge, John, XIII, 38, 39; XXXIX, 167 ff.

Rutters of the Sea: The Sailing Directions of Pierre Garcie, The, by D. W. Waters, reviewed, XXVIII, 75
Ruyter, Admiral Michael A. de, XXV, 285
Ruzicka, Rudolph, I, 203; II, 84
Ryan, Allie, XXX, 32
Ryan, Brigadier General George Washington, XXXVI, 91
Ryan, John, XXVI, 10
Ryan, Captain Matthew, XXVIII, 288
Ryan, Captain Patrick Henry, XXI, 100
Ryan, Paul B., review by, XXXIV, 278; "The Great *Lusitania* Whitewash," XXXV, 36–52; "A Yankee Bride in the Old Navy: Catherine Freeman Nimitz Looks Back to the Days Before World War I," XXXVIII, 5–14
Ryan, Paul B., and Thomas A. Bailey, *The Lusitania Disaster,* reviewed, XXXVI, 300
Ryan, General W. A., XXXVIII, 244
Ryan, Captain William F., XXI, 100
Ryan, Captain William W., XXI, 101
Rydberg, Abraham, II, 295–296
Rydbergska Stiftelse, Stockholm, II, 295–296
Ryder, Albert Pinkham (artist), XXV, 59
Ryder & Hardy, XV, 221
Rye, H.M.S., XXVI, 41–44, 46, 47

S

S. B. Wheeler, schooner, XXVIII, 148
S. B. Wheeler, steamship *(1850),* XV, 181
S. C. Hart, steam tug *(1896),* VII, 222
S. D. Warren and Co., XL, 115
S. F. Abbott (1861), XV, 103 n.
S. F. Hersey, ship *(1865),* IV, 243; *(1897),* XLIV, 154
S. I. Allard, auxiliary schooner (1917), V, 140
S. L. Crowell, bark (1847), XXIV, 57
S. M. Williams, schooner *(1862),* XII, 58
S. Morris Waln, schooner *(1850),* XXX, 245
S. O. Co. No. 93, barge *(1904),* XXXVIII, 179 ff.
S. O. Co. No. 94, tank barge (1903), V, 139
S. O. Co. No. 95, tank barge (1903), V, 139, plate 9
S. O. Co. of N.Y. No. 56, schooner barge *(1892),* XXXVIII, 176
S. P. Brooks, sloop *(1861),* VIII, 221
S. P. Carter & Co., XLIV, 88
"S.S. *Bangor*: Harbinger of Destiny," by Lawrence C. Allin, XXXIX, 218–224
"S.S. *Great Western* — A Correction," by Grahame E. Farr, XII, 310
S.S. *Savannah: The Elegant Steam Ship,* by Frank O. Braynard, reviewed, XXIV, 74–75
S. Schmidt & Co., XLIII, 299
S. W. Pike, bark (1860), II, 333

S. W. Seaver, bark *(1863),* XLV, 195
Sabin, Captain Jonathan, XLIV, 6
Sabine, U.S. frigate (1855), XXIII, 261 ff., plates 14–16; XXV, 68, 110; *(1860),* XLI, 98; *(1861),* XI, 264; XVI, 57; *(1862),* XXVII, 36 n.; XXIX, 102–105
Sabine, Captain Edward, XXXII, 217
Sabine, Rev. Elijah and Hannah (Clark), XLVIII, 165
Sabine, Lorenzo, XLIV, 83
Sabino, ship *(1862),* II, 333
Sabiston, Captain D. O., XXI, 101
Saboah, schooner *(1862),* XX, 159
Sabotage, Naval, XXVII, 185–201
Sabotawan, steamship *(1925),* VI, 134
Sabrina, yacht, XXXVI, 248
"Saccarap," answers by Philip H. Cook and Storer B. Lunt, V, 245
Sachem, American ship *(1822),* XXIX, 86, 89
Sachem, brig *(1779),* XXXV, 141
Sachem, sloop *(1777),* VI, 301
Sachem, vessel *(1862),* XXXVI, 199
Sachs, W., and Ari Hoogenboom, *The Enterprising Colonials,* reviewed, XXVI, 152
Sachse, William L., "The Journal of Nathan Prince," XVI, 81–97
Sacramento, patrol gunboat *(1921),* XXXV, 121
Sacramento, steamship (1863), X, 130, 134, plate 18; *(1864),* XXXII, 202
Sadler, John, XXXV, 294
"Safe and Timely Arrival of Convoy SC 130, 15–25 May 1943, The," by David Syrett, L, 219–227
Saffin, John, XXXV, 161
Safford, Jeffrey J., "Anglo-American Maritime Relations during the Two World Wars: A Comparative Analysis," XLI, 262–279
Sagadahoc, steamship (1866), XIV, 192 n.
Sagadahock, ship (1812), XV, 173
Sagami, Prince of, VII, 13
Sagamore, steamship *(1850),* XLV, 124
"Saga of the Side-Wheel Steamer *Shubrick*: Pioneer Lighthouse Tender of the Pacific Coast," by Richard D. White, Jr., XXXVI, 45–53
Sager, Eric W., *Seafaring Labour: The Merchant Marine of Atlantic Canada, 1820–1914,* reviewed, L, 231
Saginaw, U.S.S. *(1860),* XXXVIII, 39; *(1861),* XXIX, 109; XLIII, 276; *(1863),* XXXII, 130, 280; XXXIV, 119; *(1864),* XXVII, 44; *(1869),* VIII, 183
"Saginaw Steel Steamship Company and Its Steamers, The," by Francis G. Jenkins, XLII, 245–275
Sagres, bark *(1964),* XXIV, 79
Saigon, steamship (1860), XVI, 170
Saigon (ex-*Peiho*), French warship *(1858),* XLIX, 22
Saikio Maru, steamship *(1877),* XVII, 313, 314
"Sailcloth For American Vessels," by Elton W. Hall, XXXI, 130–142
Sail hooks, IX, 289–290
Sailing Barges, by Frank G. G. Carr, reviewed, XXXII, 144–145

Sailing Days on the Penobscot, by George S. Wasson, reviewed, IX, 232–233

Sailing into the Past, by Ole Crumlin-Pedersen and Max Vinner, reviewed, XLVIII, 205

Sailing ships, VII, 288; VIII, 279; XXVI, 157; XLIX, 29
  17th century, XXII, 136
  18th century, XXIX, 54
  Design and construction, XXXVIII, 170
  —, **17th century,** XXX, 81; XXXIV, 231
  History, VIII, 114
  Maintenance and repair, XLII, 276
  United States, II, 65, 289; VI, 112
  See also Ships

Sailing Ships of War: 1400–1860, by Dr. Frank Howard, reviewed, XLII, 141–143

Sailing Vessels in The San Diego Trade, reviewed, I, 100

Sailmaker, Isaac, XXX, 83

Sailmakers, Salem, II, 285

"Sailmakers and Ship Chandlers Of 79 Commercial Street, Boston, The," by William F. King. Jr., XV, 220–231

"Sailmaker's Gear, The," by M. V. Brewington, IX, 278–296, plate 30

Sailmaking, IX, 278. *See also* Sails

Sailmaking Simplified, by Alan Gray, reviewed, I, 101

Sail On: The Story of the American Merchant Marine, by Allan Nevins, reviewed, VI, 236

Sailor-Diplomat: A Biography of Commodore James Biddle, 1783–1848, by David F. Long, reviewed, XLIV, 202

Sailor of Fortune, The Life and Adventures of Joshua Barney, by Hulbert Footner, reviewed, I, 317

"Sailors' Alphabet," query by Joanna C. Colcord, IX, 302

Sailors, XXIII, 174
  Note: *Here are entered general works on sailors and works on sailors enlisted in a navy. Works on sailors employed on commercial vessels are entered under* **Merchant mariners.**
  Biography, XIX, 7; XXVII, 157
  Diaries, XVII, 17
  Humor, XXXII, 58
  in literature, XXXII, 81
  Medical care, XLIV, 155
  Provisioning (food, etc.), XLIV, 155
  Spiritual life, XXIV, 109
  Wages, XXV, 278
  See also Merchant Mariners

Sailors and Scholars: the Centennial History of the U.S. Naval War College, by John B. Hattendorf, B. Mitchell Sampson, III, and John R. Wadleigh, reviewed, XLVIII, 186

"Sailors and Their Clothing," by R. C. Holmes, XVII, 195–202

"Sailors and Whalers: Lakemen of Pultneyville," by Robert Kane, XXXIV, 243–248

"Sailor's Epitaph, A," document contributed by Captain Edgar K. Thompson, U.S.N. (ret.), XXIII, 260

Sailors' Home, illustrations of, Boston, Portland, Maine, New York, XXXVII, 181 ff.

"Sailors' Home, The," by George Duncan Campbell, XXXVII, 179–184

"Sailor's Life, A," document contributed by Edward L. Towle, XXIV, 94

"Sailors on Horseback," document contributed by E. Lee Dorsett, M.D., XVI, 213

Sailors on Horseback, XXXII, plate 5

Sailors Taking a Land Cruise, XXXII, plate 6

"Sailor's Yarn, A," by Francis W. Hatch, XXVIII, 66–68

Sail plans by Charles Ware, III, 267–268, plates 35, 36, 44; V, 79, plates 6, 7

Sails, I, 374; V, 142; XIII, 81, 185; XV, 220; XXXI, 130; XXXII, 58. *See also* Masts and Rigging; Sailmaking; Spinnaker

Sails, specifications for schooner's, VI, 138

Sail & Steam on the Northern California Coast, 1850–1900, by Wallace E. Martin, reviewed, XLVII, 217

Sails, yacht, VIII, 260

Sails used by Northwest Coast Indians, I, 374–380

Sail & Sweep in China, by G. R. G. Worcester, reviewed, XXVII, 284

Sail training ships. *See* Training ships

St. Albans, H.M.S., XXVI, 54

St. Andrew, privateer *(1740),* XLII, 41 ff.

St. Andrews, steamship (ex-*Henry F. Eaton*), XXVIII, 125

St. Andrews, New Brunswick, XV, 173–190

St. Ann, schooner *(1736),* XXV, 83–86; Sail plan of, XXV, 86; Model of, XXV, plate 3; XXVIII, 226; photo of model, XLIX, 198

St. Anne, French ship *(1745),* XLII, 50

St. Anne, ship *(1629),* XLIX, 259

Saint Brandon's Island, XXX, 250

St. Canute, tug, XXX, 153

Saint Charles, ship *(1861),* XI, 287

St. Charles, ship (1883), XXVII, plate XVIII

Saint Clair, vessel, XXVI, 59, 60

St. Clair, brig *(1800),* VII, 317

St. Clair, steamship *(1836),* VII, 62

St. Claire, Canadian schooner *(1902),* XLIX, 280

St. Croix, steamship (1895), XXXIII, plate 2, 84, 94; XXXIV, Pictorial Supplement, plate XXII; *(1901),* XXIV, 49

St. Croix River. *See* **Shipbuilding, Canada**

St. Croix River (ME), XV, 173–190

St. David, steamship (1842), XX, 259

Saint Domingue (now Santo Domingo), XXX, 126 f.

Sainte Anne, schooner *(1777),* II, 205

St. Elmo's Fire, XXIII, 29–38; XXIV, 213–214

St. Eustatius and the Dutch West Indies, XXXVI, 155–169

Saint George, ship *(1844),* XIII, 139; *(1860),* XIV, 45

Saint George, whaleship *(1850),* XXVIII, 74
St. George, brigantine (1736), I, 297
St. George, schooner, XXI, 91; *(1863),* VIII, 232
St. George, ship *(1759),* IX, 144; *(1777),* XLIII, 25
St. George, steamship *(1840),* XX, 86, 89
St. George, Captain William, XXI, 106
St. Germain, Earl, XXXVI, 184
St. Helena, South Atlantic, XXV, 275
St. Iago, Cape Verde Islands, South Atlantic, XXV, 181–182
Saint James, ship *(1776),* XIII, 38
St. James, privateer, XXII, 268
St. James, ship (1856), II, 332; *(1875),* XXVII, 52
St. Jan, steamship *(1904),* XVI, 131
Saint John, automobile-carrying liner (1932), XXXIII, 93 ff.; XXXIV, 184 ff.
St. John, H.M. schooner *(1776),* XXV, 201
St. John, ship *(1659),* XL, 293–297
St. John, steamship, XVIII, 224, 225; *(1863),* III, 43, plate 11
St. John, J. Hector, XLIII, 51
St. John Baptist, vessel, XXVI, 47
St. John's, steamship *(1859),* VII, 119
St. Johns, steamship, XXI, 95; *(1861),* XV, 98, 111, 114, 115, 117, 118, 124, 128
St. Johns N. F., schooner (1918), V, 139
St. Johns, Newfoundland, XXVIII, plate 10
St. Johns, Porto Rico, XXV, plate XVI
St. John's River, Florida, VII, 118
St. Joseph, ship (1865), II, 334
Saint Lawrence, ship (1833), XIV, 40
St. Laurence, schooner *(1814),* XLII, 111 ff.
St. Lawrence, frigate *(1861),* XLVIII, 93
St. Lawrence, U.S. frigate (1844), XXIII, 261; XXIV, 24
St. Lawrence, U.S.S. *(1861),* XV, 104; XXXII, 48; XXXIII, 87; XXXVI, 190; XLIV, 258
St. Lawrence, steamship (1839), XVIII, 283, 288, 289, 291; XX, 83
St. Lawrence Boat Co., XXVI, plate 8
St. Leon, ship (1835), XXVIII, plate II; XLVII, 90; painting of, XLVII, 91
St. Lo, Captain Edward, XXI, 260
St. Louis, cruiser *(1888),* XXXIX, 136
St. Louis, sloop *(1843),* XXXI, 185
St. Louis, steamship, XXIX, 231; (1854), X, 130; *(1858),* XVII, 219
St. Louis, steamship (1895), XXIV, 214
St. Louis, U.S. ironclad (1861), XXV, 128, 134
St. Louis, U.S.S. (1828), XX, 137 n.
St. Louis, U.S.S. (1862), XIX, 267; *(1864),* XXVII, 36
St. Louis, U.S. sloop of war (1827), XXIII, 58 n.
Saint Louis, Senegal, XXX, 229
"St. Lucia Dug-Outs," by Philip P. Chase, II, 71–73
St. Mark, ship (1877), XXVIII, plate XVIII
"St. Martin's Men Build a Ship in 1814," by J. Russell Harper, XXI, 279–291
Saint Mary, bark, XXVIII, 123

St. Mary's, schooner, XXI, 93; *(1864),* XXXII, 202; XXXIII, 208 ff.
St. Mary's, sloop of war *(1861),* XXXIII, 42 ff.; XXXV, 26
St. Mary's, steamship, XXI, 91; *(1859),* VII, 119
St. Marys, steamship *(1861),* XV, 99, 100, 114, 115, 117, 118, 124, 130
St. Mary's, U.S.S. (1844), XX, 141; *(1856),* XI, 50; XII, 152
St. Mary's Steamboat Co., VII, 123
Saint Michael, schooner (1817), XIV, 40
St. Michael, French ship *(1800),* XXXI, 175
St. Patrick, sailing vessel (ex-*John Bell*) *(1875),* XXVI, 133
St. Paul, ship (1833), XXXVII, 124; figurehead of, Pictorial Supplement, plates XV, XXVII; XXXVIII, 54 ff.
St. Paul, steamship (1895), XXIV, 214; *(1908),* XX, 192–197, plate 11; *(1913),* XXVI, 280–282; XXIX, 231
"*St. Paul-Gladiator* Collision; A Personal Narrative, The," by Francis E. Cross, XX, 191–197, plates 10, 11
St. Paul, Minneapolis & Manitoba Railway, XLVII, 193 ff.
St. Paul Island, Indian Ocean, XXV, 181, 183–184, plate 19
Saint Paul's seamanship, II, 102–106
Saint Peter, whaler *(1847),* XXXII, 41, 42
St. Peter, French ship *(1626),* XLIX, 256
St. Peter, ship *(1778),* XLIII, 27
St. Petersburg, ship, XXIII, 139
St. Regis Yacht Club, XXVI, plate 8
St. Petersburg (Russia), XXIII, 131
St. Roch, Arctic patrol schooner *(1942),* L, 35
St. Simon's Island, Georgia, XXIII, plates 7–10
St. Theodosius, Russian steamship *(1861),* XXXIV, 119
St. Theodosius, steamship *(1858),* XLIII, 91 ff.; *(1862),* XVII, 44
St. Thomas, schooner *(1888),* XXXV, 10
St. Thomas, West Indies, XXV, 19, 26
St. Vallier, steamship *(1905),* I, 273
St. Vincent, Lord, XLVI, 221
St. Vincent, Nelson's Dear Lord, A Portrait of, by Evelyn Berckman, reviewed, XXIII, 73–74
St. Vincent Grenadines, Map II, XXXII, 182
Sakamaki, Shunzo, *Japan and the United States, 1790–1853,* reviewed, I, 319–320
Sakanishi, Shio, ed., *A Private Journal of John Glendy Sproston, U.S.N.,* reviewed, I, 185–186
"Sakonnet River Boat, The," by Robert H. Baker, XVI, 61–62, plate.
Salacia, bark (1857), V, 147
Salamander, H.M.S., XXVI, 61
Salamander, ship (1676), XIII, 140
Salatiga, steamship, XVI, 131; XVIII, 215

"Sale and Registration of British Vessels in the Late Eighteenth Century," document contributed by W. R. Chaplin, XV, 303–306
Salem, bark (1851), VII, 318
Salem, tug (1896), XXXV, 11
Salem (MA), XXV, 7, 146, 176 ff., 274–277, plate XXI
"*Salem* and *Marblehead,* An Act to prevent Damage by Fire in," document contributed by Russell W. Knight, XXV, 146
Salem and the Indies, by James Duncan Phillips, reviewed, VII, 323
"Salem-Bilbao Fish Trade, The," NASOH paper by Professor James G. Lydon, XXXVII, 82
Salem County, N. J., XXXVI, 251 ff.
Salem Custom House records, XXX, 91 ff.
Salem East India Marine Society, IV, 5–14; V, 266–285; VIII, 289; IX, 185; X, 33–42; XVII, 152; XXVI, 273; XXIX, 141–142
"Salem East India Marine Society, The Contributions to Exploration of the," by Ernest S. Dodge, XXV, 176–188, plates 17–20
Salem Gazette, XXX, 7
Salem Gazette and Newbury and Marblehead Advertiser, The, XXX, 96, 101
Salem Harbor, 1803, Pictorial Supplement, XXXII, plate XXVII
"Salem Marine Society, 1766–1966, The," by Philip C. F. Smith, XXVI, 272–279
Salem Marine Society, reconstruction of Ship's Cabin, XXVI, 274, plate 23
Salem Marine Society, XXVI, 229, 272–279, plates 23, 24. Certificate of the, 1797, XXVI, 274, plate 23
Salem Marine Society beacon, XXVI, 274, plate 24
Salem Maritime National Historic Site, reviewed, I, 190
Salem Mill-Dam Corporation, XXIX, 206
Salem Naval Office records, XXX, 91 ff.
"Salem Shipbuilding Industry before 1812, The," by James Duncan Phillips, II, 278–288
Salem Trade: XXVIII, 261–274. *1783–1789:* I, 345–351; *1795–1799:* IV, 18–30; *1801:* V, 43–63
"Salem Trading Voyages to Japan During the Early Nineteenth Century," by Peter J. Fetchko, XLVI, 50–54
Salisbury (MA), XXX, 98 ff.
Salisbury, W., "Admiral Wilkes at the Bermudas," XXV, 140; answered query, II, 82
Salisbury, William, XIII, 182; "John Paul Jones and His Ships: The Need for More Research," XXVIII, 195–205; "The Rogers Collection of Ship Models, Annapolis," XVIII, 181–182
Salisbury Furnace Works, XLV, 36 ff.
Salistan, Captain D. O., XXI, 101
Sallee River, Korea, VII, 108 ff., plate 12
Sallie, schooner, XXI, 105; (1863), VIII, 231
Sallie C. Marvil, schooner (1911), XXIV, 26–33, plate 3
Sallie Rose, schooner, XXI, 91; (1862), VIII, 227

Sally, brig (1764), XXXII, 173 ff.; XLVIII, 40 ff.; (1809), VI, 83
Sally, schooner, XXII, 60 n.; XXVIII, 114
Sally, ship (1779), XXXVII, 297; XXXVIII, 251; (1798), XXIV, 257, 258, 262
Sally, ship (1803), Pictorial Supplement, XXXII, plate XVII; (1805), XV, 133; (XXVIII, 32; (1807), XVI, 197; (1811), X, 54; XXIII, 253 n.; (1888), II, 334
Sally, sloop, XXII, 88; (1769), XX, 244–246; (1796), XLI, 173; XLII, 9 ff.; XLIII, 25; XLIV, 6 ff.; XLV, 92; (1799), XLVI, 162; (1800), XXV, 30–32, plate 1
Sally and Mary, brig (1807), XVI, 194
Sally Ann, brig (1807), XVI, 194
Sally Ann, schooner (1861), VIII, 221
Sally I'on, schooner (1884), I, 396
Sally Magee, barque, XXI, 102
Sailmaking, III, 112–114, 267–268
Salmon, Robert, II, 44, plate 9
Salmon, Robert (artist), XXIV, plate XXVIII; XXV, 29, 32, 33, 59, plate 1; XXIX, plates I-XXXII
Salmon canning industry, I, 333; XXXIX, 184
Salmon fishery, Bering Sea, XXXIX, 184
Salmon fishing, XXXIX, plates 5, 7
Salmon P. Chase, U.S.C.G. (1878), XX, 143 n.
Salmon River, woodboat (1814), XVII, 12
Salter, Commodore William D., XXXI, 15
Salter, Titus, VII, 202 ff., 208, 209
Salting vessels, IV, 50
Salt Island, Gloucester (MA), XXV, plate III
Saltonstall, Charles, XIV, 190
Saltonstall, Commodore, XXXVII, 296
Saltonstall, Dudley, VII, 203, 205–209, 212; XXXVII, 299
Saltonstall, Captain Dudley, Continental Navy, XXV, 193
Saltonstall, Commodore Dudley, XLII, 32 ff.
Saltonstall, Leverett, IV, 5
Saltonstall, William G., I, 102; "'Just Ease Her When She Pitches,'" XV, 249–258; *Port of Piscataqua,* reviewed, II, 91
Saltonstall, Winthrop, XXXI, 134
Salt trade, XLVII, 83
Salt Trade, analysis of: (Table I) Salt Ships Arriving at Maine Ports, XLVII, 93; (Table II) Departures of Liverpool Salt Ships for Maine Ports, XLVII, 95; (Table III) Subsequent Destinations of Vessels in Salt Trade, XLVII, 96; (Table IV) Comparative Triangular Routes for Vessels in Salt Trade, XLVII, 97; (Table V) Home Ports of Salt Trade Vessels, XLVII, 98; (Table VI) Characteristics of Vessels in Salt Trade, XLVII, 99
Saluda, ship (1839), XXXV, 199
Salumith, schooner (1805), XIV, 40
Salutation, ship (1632), XI, 6
"Salute on the Stocks," document contributed by Captain Edgar K. Thompson, U.S.N. (ret.), XXII, 54
"Salutes, Thomas Truxton on," document, V, 156–157

Salvador, steamship *(1864),* XXXII, 202
Salvador, steamship *(1872),* X, 132, 138
Salvage, VIII, 61; XLII, 5; XLIII, 5
   United States, XXXIV, 89; L, 18
   —, **Florida,** XXXVIII, 262
Salvages, The Dry (MA), XXV, 233 ff., plates 23–26
"Salving the Ship *Crystal Palace:* The Private Journals (1857–1858) of Captain Benjamin F. Simmons and Second Officer Joshua N. Rowe," edited by Joanna C. Colcord, III, 314–326; IV, 31–44
Salvor, steamship *(1861),* XI, 287
"Salvors versus Sea," by Philip H. Cook, VIII, 61–69
Samar, gunboat *(1899),* XXXV, 189 ff.
Samaria, ship *(1876),* IV, 48, 51, 52
Samaritan, ship *(1854),* XXVII, plate X; *(1901),* XVI, 11
Sambrooke, Samuel, XIII, 24
"Sam Crocker, Boat Designer," by Victor A. Lewinson, XLVIII, 182–185
Sam Houston, schooner, XXI, 89; *(1861),* XI, 287
Sammons, Captain Jacob, XXI, 101
Sammy Cornell, tug *(1867),* VI, 281
Sammy Ford, schooner (1872), XXIV, 41, 44, 59
Samoa, Foreign relations, United States, XXXV, 20
Samoa, boats of, XIII, 89 ff.
Sampa, Captain J. C., XXI, 106
Sample books of sailcloth, Brinckerhoff, Turner & Co., XXXI, plate 1
Sampson, Abigail, XXX, 168
Sampson, B. Mitchell, III, John B. Hattendorf and John R. Wadleigh, *The Centennial History of the U.S. Naval War College,* reviewed, XLVIII, 186
Sampson, C. A. L., Pictorial Supplement, XXXVII, plates IV, V
Sampson, Chandler, XXV, 222
Sampson, Captain John, XII, 103
Sampson, William, XXI, 120, 123
Sampson, Rear Admiral William T., XL, 127, 169 ff.; XLI, 97
Sam Salvador, Portugese nao *(1583),* XXV, 74
Sam Scolfield, bark *(1883),* XXXI, plate XXIV. *See* bark *Howard.*
Sam Slick, sloop *(1862),* XII, 58, 160
Samson, steamship *(1842),* XVII, 100; XX, 250, 264, 266; *(1864),* XVII, 308
Samson, tugboat *(1864),* XLIII, 298
Sam T. Christian, steamship *(1874),* XV, 227
Samuel, bark *(1866),* I, 110, 114
Samuel, schooner *(1758),* XXI, 8
Samuel Adams, schooner *(1861),* VIII, 221
Samuel Chuchman, brig, XXXVI, 256
Sam'l F. Martin, brig, XXI, 94
Samuel H. Pook Co., The (shipbuilders), XLII, 85
Samuel Huntington, merchant ship *(1943),* XLIV, 57
Samuel Lawrence, ship *(1851),* XXV, plate XXXI
Samuel Martin, sloop, XXI, 88, 103; *(1861),* VIII, 221
Samuel Robertson, ship *(1856),* XLV, 111

Samuel Russell, clipper ship *(1847),* I, 46; *(1851),* XXIII, 264
Samuel S. Sneeden Shipyard, XLVIII, 114
Samuel Smith, ship *(1803),* XLVI, 53
Samuel Watts, ship *(1870),* II, 246
San Andres, steamship *(1967),* XXXVI, 31
San Blas, steamship *(1882),* X, 137
Sanborn, Percy, XXVIII, plates XIII, XIX
Sancala, Montevidean schooner *(1844),* XXIX, 177 ff.
Sancala, schooner *(1844),* XLVI, 233
"*Sancala* Affair: Captain Voorhees Seizes an Argentine Squadron, The," by K. Jack Bauer, XXIX, 174–186
San Carlos, bark *(1856),* VI, 82
San Carlos, hermaphrodite brig *(1847),* XXIV, 44, 58
Sanches, Antonio, chart by, XXV, plate 27
Sancho Panza, ship *(1855),* III, 69; XIX, 27, 38
San Cosme, steamship *(1909),* XI, 78
Sand, Captain B. F., XXII, 256
Sandale, I, 366
San Demetrio, steamship *(1940),* XIV, 130
Sander, Fred, XXXVI, 233, 237
Sanderson, James, XX, 80
Sand Fly, launch *(1861),* XLVIII, 95
Sandford, Captain E. T., XVIII, 84
Sandford, Captain John L., XVIII, 84
Sand glass, I, 211
San Diego Marine Research Society, X, 121
San Diego Maritime Research Society, I, 100
San Diego Zoological Society, X, 120–121
Sandino, General Augusto Cesar, XXXV, 128
Sandler, Stanley, *The Emergence of the Modern Capital Ship,* reviewed, XL, 71
San Domingo, H.M.S. *(1813),* XXVIII, 186
San Domingos, H.M.S. *(1813),* XXXI, 286
Sands, Captain George U., XVI, 164, 170, 175; XVIII, 84; XXXIV, 42
Sands, Captain John, I, 90
Sands, John O., XXXIV, 187 n.; review by, XLIX, 317; "The U.S. Light-House Board: Progress through Process," XLVII, 174–192; *Yorktown's Captive Fleet,* reviewed, XLV, 133
Sandusky, steamship *(1834),* VII, 55; *(1839),* XVIII, 297; XX, 82 n.
Sandusky, U.S.S. *(1864),* XXVII, 38 n., 43
Sandwich, corvette *(1800),* XXV, 30–33, plate 1
Sandwich, French ship *(1800),* XXXI, 174
Sandwich, H.M.S. *(1726),* XXI, 263
Sandwich, privateer schooner *(1799),* XLVI, 162
Sandwich, John Montague, Fourth Earl of, XXV, 190, 286
Sandy, towboat *(1882),* VI, 288
Sandy Hook, bark *(1863),* IV, 240
Sandy Hook Lighthouse, New Jersey, XXV, 79, 123–127, plates 9, 10
"Sandy Hook Lighthouse, The," by Kenneth Scott, XXV, 123–127, plates 9, 10
Sandys, George, XXXVII, 13

San Fermin, Spanish man-of-war *(1746)*, XXII, 217
Sanford, Captain F. C., XII, 35
Sanford, Henry S., XXIX, 10
Sanford, Menemon, XII, 288
Sanford, Captain Thomas, XXV, 30
San Francisco, Manila Galleon, XXIII, 124
San Francisco, ship *(1891)*, XXXVIII, 291
San Francisco, steamship (1856), XX, 126 n.; (1853), X, 130, 133, 134; *(1853)*, XLV, 20 ff.
San Francisco, U.S. cruiser (1890), XXII, 145; *(1904)*, XLI, 251
San Francisco Bay Ferryboats, by George H. Harlan, reviewed, XXVII, 289
San Francisco Maritime Museum, XXX, 32; XXXII, 29
San Francisco Maritime Museum Association, *Maritime Titles in Print*, XXXIX, 74; editorial comment, XXXIX, 81
San Francisco Museum of Science and Industry, I, 102, 203–204, 315–316
San Francisco Shipbuilding Co., XXII, 159, 162, 166, 182
"San Francisco to Balboa in the Schooner *Dauntless;* Memories of an A.B." by Emmett A. Hoskins, XII, 142–147
Sangammon, monitor *(1864)*, XXXIII, 14 ff.
Sangamon, U.S. monitor (1862), X, 17, 31; *(1864)*, XLVIII, 123
San Jacinto, ship *(1857)*, XXXVIII, 36 ff.
San Jacinto, U.S.S. *(1862)*, XX, 161; *(1862)*, XXVII, 36 n., 43, 162–164; *(1863)*, XXXII, 123; XXXIII, 5 ff.
San Jacinto, U.S. steam sloop (1850), XXII, 33
San Jose, steamship (1882), X, 137, 142
San Jose Indiano, ship *(1812)*, XXI, 22
San Juan, schooner *(1861)*, VIII, 221
San Juan, steamship (1882), X, 137, 142, 143; *(1927)*, XXVII, 151
Sankaty, steamship, XXXIV, 261; *(1924)*, IX, 18
San Lucas, steamship (ex-*Eastern Knight*), XXIII, 276
San Luciano, steamship *(1940)*, XXXVIII, 187 ff.
San Martin, brig *(1845)*, XXXVI, 127, 129, 131, 133, 134, 137, 140
San Martino Museum (Naples,Italy), XX, 231
"San Martino Museum, The," by Aldo Caselli, XXI, 143–144
San Miguel, galleon *(1551)*, VI, 244 ff.
San Pablo, ferryboat, XXVII, 289
San Pablo, steamship *(1884)*, XXXI, 126
San Pasqual, tanker (1920), XXII, 162, plate 8, 170, 182
San Pedro, ferryboat *(1912)*, XXVII, 289
San Pedro, California, XXV, 262, 264–268, 271
San Pedo Alcantara, Man-of-War *(1854)*, XXXIV, plate 6
San Roman, ship (1854), II, 246
San Salvador, Federal screw steamship *(1864)*, XXXII, 198
Sans Culottes, privateer *(1793)*, XXII, 81 ff.
Sans Pareil, French ship *(1798)*, XXXI, 173
Sans Pareil, French warship [model] *(1760)*, XVI, 102
Sans Pareil, steamship *(1842)*, XX, 250
Santa Ana, Manila galleon, XXIII, 124
Santa Ana, ship, XV, 273
Santa Anna, Mexican brigantine *(1843)*, XXX, 51
Santa Anna, XXVII, 159
Santa Anna, Lopez de, XXX, 54
Santa Christo de Lezo, Spanish privateer shallop, XXVI, 38
Santacilia, J. Juan y, XV, 53
Santa Clara, brig *(1861)*, XV, 110, 114, 124
Santa Clara, ship (1876), XVI, 122; XVIII, 213; *(1926)*, XV, 95
Santa Clara Steamship Co., XIV, 127
Santa Cruz, steamship (1856), XVII, 212; XVIII, 72; *(1856)*, XLIII, 109 ff.; *(1917)*, X, 140
Santa Cruz, wooden steamship *(1868)*, XXXVIII, 176 ff.
Santa Cruz, boats of, XIII, 92
Santa Fe Railroad, XXV, 264, 267
Santa Gertrudis, ship, XXIII, 249
Santa Ina, steamship *(1946)*, XIV, 132, 135
Santa Margarita, British frigate *(1799)*, XXVII, 143
Santa Maria, schooner *(1811)*, XLII, 115
Santa Maria, Spanish ship *(1507)*, XLV, 250
Santa Maria, steamship *(1906)*, XXXVIII, 197 ff.
Santa Maria (Columbus' ship), XLVI, 182 ff.
Santa Maria II, ship [replica] (1892), XIV, 109, 110
Santa Maria Steamship Co., XXXVIII, 197 ff.
Santa Marta, Colombia, XXX, 261
Santa Monica, California, XXV, 265–268
Santa Rita (ex-*Minnewaska*), steamship *(1902)*, XXXVIII, plate 7
Santa Rosa, ship, XXIII, 249
Santee, bark *(1862)*, XII, 58
Santee, brig *(1878)*, XXXVIII, 158; XXXIX, 100
Santee, schooner *(1861)*, VIII, 221
Santee, U.S. escort carrier *(1943)*, XLV, 63
Santee, U.S. frigate (1820), XXIII, 261; (1855), XXVII, 41 n.
Santee, U.S. warship, XXXII, 48
Santiago, ship *(1792)*, XIII, 212
Santiago de Cuba, merchant steamship, XXXII, 48
Sao Joao, ship, XV, 273
Sapona, concrete steamship, XXII, 161, 165, 168, 182, plate 5
Sapor, ship *(1813)*, XV, 60
Sapphire, H.M. frigate *(1681)*, XXIII, 112
Sapphire, H.M.S. *(1830)*, XXV, 143
Sapphire, pink *(1679)*, XIII, 26
Sapphire, ship *(1823)*, XV, 136–137; (1864), V, 152, 242
Sappho, bark (1870), IV, 72
Sappho, steamship *(1883)*, XVII, 54
Saracen, auxiliary schooner (1924), XXX, plate XXIV
Sarah, brig, XXII, 95
Sarah, brigantine *(1760)*, XL, 248 ff.
Sarah, hermaphrodite brig (1847), XXIV, 44, 58
Sarah, packet (ex-*Expedition*), XXVIII, 118, 121

Sarah, schooner, XXI, 100, 101; *(1861),* VIII, 221, 227; XI, 287; XII, 58, 160; XV, 116, 124, 126
Sarah, ship *(1749),* XLVIII, 34
Sarah, sloop *(1749),* XX, 173
Sarah, sloop *(1862),* XII, 58
Sarah, sloop, XXI, 99; XXIV, 135
Sarah, steamship *(1862),* XII, 58
Sarah, vessel, XXVI, 60
Sarah [1st], schooner (1825), XXIV, 59
Sarah [2nd], schooner (1857), XXIV, 59
Sarah and Caroline, American ship *(1836),* XXIX, 90
Sarah and Caroline, schooner, XXI, 87; *(1861),* XV, 117, 124
Sarah and Catherine, schooner *(1861),* XV, 124
Sarah and Mary, schooner, XXI, 86
Sarah Anna, schooner *(1855),* XXIV, 143
Sarah Barry, whaler *(1833),* XLI, 289
Sarah Bentley, brig (1844), XVI, 63–65
Sarah Bladen, schooner, XXI, 88; *(1861),* XI, 287
Sarah Burr, schooner, XXI, 103; *(1861),* XI, 267, 287
Sarah C. Ropes, schooner *(1897),* X, 235; XXIII, 19
Sarah Cole, schooner *(1861),* XI, 264, 287
Sarah D. Sparks, schooner *(1853),* XLIV, 83
Sarah E. Palmer, schooner (1894), V, 79 ff.; XX, 238, 241
Sarah E. Pettigrew, ship *(1861),* XI, 287
Sarah Eaton, schooner (1874), Pictorial Supplement, XXXVI, plate XV
Sarah Elizabeth, schooner (1847), Pictorial Supplement, XXXVI, plate VI
Sarah Franklin, schooner (1846), Pictorial Supplement, XXXVI, plate V
Sarah G. Hyde, ship (1851), II, 331
Sarah H. Falconer, schooner *(1862),* VIII, 227
Sarah Hignett, ship (1869), III, 173
Sarah Hooper, schooner *(1851),* XLV, 128
Sarah Isabella, sloop *(1832),* XXXVIII, 267
Sarah J. Boyd, ship *(1853),* XVII, 17
Sarah Jordan, schooner *(1862),* XII, 58, 160
Sarah L. Bryant, bark *(1847),* XLIV, 94
Sarah L. Harding, schooner (1866), XXVI, plate II
Sarah MacFarlane, brig *(1857),* XX, 129 n.
Sarah Mary, sloop *(1864),* XV, 130
Sarah Matilda, schooner (1846), XXIV, 59
Sarah Newman, bark (1857), V, 151
Sarah (or Sarrah), King of Landouman people, W. Africa, XXX, 184
Sarah S. Ridgeway, bark (1877), I, 70
Sarah Starr, schooner *(1861),* VIII, 221
Sarah W. Hunt, schooner *(1883),* XI, 115–133
Saranac, sidewheel steamship *(1861),* XXXIII, 42 ff.
Saranac, U.S.S. *(1864),* XXVII, 44, 161
Saranak, bark (1844), III, 264
Sarandí, Argentine schooner *(1820),* L, 31
Saratoga, American sloop-of-war *(1777),* XXXI, 244
Saratoga, carrier *(1924),* XXXVII, 115
Saratoga, ship *(1845),* XXII, plate I; *(1853),* XVII, 17, 25–27

Saratoga, ship (1874), III, 173
Saratoga, steamship, XVIII, 224, 225; (1878), XXIV, plate XXXII
Saratoga, U.S. aircraft carrier (1927), XXII, 146
Saratoga, U.S. corvette (1814), XXI, 48, 53, 55
Saratoga, U.S.S. *(1842),* XX, 135, 141; *(1842),* XXI, 40, 72; *(1853),* VII, 9, 14, 19; *(1858),* XXXIV, 66 ff.; *(1864),* XXVII, 36 n., 160, 176; *(1885),* photo of, XLIX, 294; *(1917),* XLIV, 180 ff.
Sardoine, H.M.S. *(1764),* XXVII, 217; XXIII, 177
Sargent, Captain C. L., XLVI, 215
Sargent, Epes (fisherman of Gloucester), XXXI, 198
Sargent, Commander Nathan, U.S.N., *Admiral Dewey and the Manila Campaign,* reviewed, VIII, 157–158
Sargent, William, XLVI, 217
Sargent Co., XIII, 120
Sarnia, S.S., XXVII, 156
Sarratt, Commander Robert C., XXXVII, 95 ff.
Sarrazin, Captain J. E., XXI, 101
Sarstoon, steamship (1925), XIV, 135
Sartorius, Sir George, XXXI, 60
"*Sartor Resartus,*" by Captain Edgar K. Thompson, U.S.N. (ret.), XXVI, 170
Sassacus, U.S.S. *(1864),* XXVII, 43, 44; *(1865),* XLVIII, 104
Satellite, schooner (1860), XXIV, 60
Saterlee, Doctor, XLV, 21 ff.
Satire. *See* Humor; and under names of individual topics, e.g., Sailors
Satisfaction, sloop *(1777),* V, 187
Satsuma, Japanese battleship (1914), XXIV, 276
Satterlee, Herbert L., XXXIII, 276 ff.
Satterwhite, Purser Edwin T., XLIV, 175 ff.
"Saturday Night at Sea," XXXI, Pictorial Supplement, plate IV
Saturn, tug *(1892),* XLVII, 127
Saucy Jack, schooner *(1812),* XV, 59
Saugerties, steamship, XVIII, 225
Saugerties Line, XVIII, 225, 228
Saugus, U.S. monitor (1862), X, 19, 26, 27, 29, 32
Saul, Norman E., "Jonathan Russell, *President Adams,* and Europe in 1810," XXX, 279–293
Saumarez, Henry de, XIV, 214
Saumerez, Admiral, XXX, 212, 287
Saunders, A. Fred, introduction to "Extracts from the diary of William Saunders, Mariner, 1848–1863," XVII, 17–27, plate 5; "Memories of Steamboat Days on the Hudson," XVIII, 223–234
Saunders, Daniel, Jr., XIX, 10, 11
Saunders, E. E. and Co., II, 229 ff.
Saunders, Captain J. C., XVIII, 84
Saunders, Jonathan P., journal of, XXV, 184
Saunders, Captain Robert, XXI, 101
Saunders, William, XVII, 17–27, plate 5
Sauvage, Captain Pierre, XXIII, 277
Savage, H.M. sloop of war *(1776),* XXV, 200
Savage, schooner (1833), XXIII, 7

Savage, Captain Edward, XLVIII, 36
Savage, Captain John, XXI, 106
Savage, Samuel Phillips, XL, 267
Savage, Thomas, XXXVI, 204; XXXII, 204
Savageau, David Le Pere, "The United States Navy and its 'Half War' Prisoners, 1798–1801," XXXI, 159–176
Savannah, nuclear merchant ship (1959), XXIII, 231
Savannah, schooner, XXI, 86; *(1861)*, VIII, 221
Savannah, steamship (1818), Pictorial Supplement, XXXIV, plate II; XXXV, 248; (1818) (Vol. ?), 249–253; (1819), XXIV, 74–75;*(1819)*, XXXVII, 140 n.; XLVII, 33 ff.; (1824), I, 414
Savannah, U.S.S. *(1851)*, XX, 124; *(1861)*, XXXII, 48, 55; *(1917)*, XVIII, 163
Savannah, U.S. sloop *(1847)*, XXIII, 260, 261
Savannah Engineering & Construction Co. (Savannah, Georgia), XXXII, 32
Savannah National Wildlife Refuge, XXXV, 231
Savannah Steam Ship Co., IX, 250–251; XLVII, 33
Savary, P., XXXVI, 237
Saville, William, XLVI, 215
Savoia, steamship (ex-*Cristobal Colon*, ex-*Bahiana*) *(1891)*, XXVI, 194
Sawa Maru (ex-*Mackinaw*), Japanese *(1916)*, XLII, 258
Saw Mill, Boston Navy Yard, VII, plate 8
Sawyer, Carroll Ray, V, 247
Sawyer, Captain Horace B., L, 116
Sawyer, L. A., and W. H. Mitchell, *The Liberty Ships*, reviewed, XXXI, 228
Sawyer, Philip, I, 71
Sawyer Brothers, schooner (1906) XXIII, plate VI
Sawyer Brothers Co., XIII, 120
Saxifrage, H.M.S. *(1942)*, L, 44
Saxon (ex-*Lucy Johnson*), vessel *(1863)*, XXVI, 104–106
Saxonia, steamship *(1915)*, XVIII, 159–162, plate 2
Sayer, Robert, VIII, 319
Sayon, Vincent, XIII, 20, 22, 26, 27
Sayre, Clifford L., review by, I, 183–184
SC. *See* South Carolina
Scallop fishery, X, 243
SC 118, Allied North Atlantic convoy, 1941, XLIV, 48 ff.; XLV, 55
Scammel, U.S.S. *(1800)*, XXXI, 174; *(1801)*, XXVII, 148
Scammon, Captain C. M., XXXVI, 50, 51
Scammon, Charles Melville, *Journal aboard the Bark* Ocean Bird *on a Whaling Voyage to Scammon's Lagoon, winter 1858–59*, reviewed, XXXIII, 212–213
Scammon, George, XL, 117
Scandanavian, steamship *(1884)*, XIV, 120
Scandinavian Airways System, XXXV, 75
Scandinavian East Africa Line, XXXI, 118
Scarborough, frigate *(1724)*, XXII, 107
Scarborough, H.M.S. *(1732)*, XXVI, 37; *(1741)*, XLVIII, 26
Scarborough, ship *(1787–1788)*, IV, 93–96
Scarcies River, XXX, 178 ff.

Scarr, Deryck, *A Cruize in a Queensland Labour Vessel to the South Seas,* reviewed, XXIX, 290
"Scene of the Main Deck of a Line of Battle Ship in Harbour," XXXI, Pictorial Supplement, plate III
Schaefer, Rudolph J., *J. E. Buttersworth: 19th Century Marine Painter,* reviewed, XXXVI, 146–147; *John Paul Jones and the Battle of Flamborough Head: A Reconsideration,* reviewed, L, 143
Schakamaroon, ship *(1867)*, XXXIV, 61
Schalka, Dr. Eldon, XXVIII, 84
Scharnhorst, flagship *(1914)*, XXXIII, 36 ff.
Scharnhorst, German Cruiser, XXVIII, 108
Schaw, Magree, XXXI, 18
Schawn, coaster *(1875)*, XXXVIII, 63
"Schedule of Masts of 1703, A," document contributed by Lawrence Waters Jenkins, VII, 72–76
Scheel, Henry A., *15 Modern Yacht Designs,* reviewed, XLIV, 201
Scheepvaart Museum, XIV, 187, 188
Scheina, Robert L., "Benjamin Stoddert, Politics, and the Navy," XXXVI, 54–68; "Forgotten Fleet: The Mexican Navy on the Eve of War, 1845, The," XXX, 46–55; "A Matter of Definition: A New Jersey Navy, 1777–1783," XXXIX, 209–217
Scheina, Robert L. and John C. Reilly, Jr., *American Battleships, 1886–1923,* reviewed, XLI, 231–233
Schell, Augustus, XXXVI, 178, 180, 184
Schenck, U.S. destroyer *(1943)*, XLIV, 52
Schenck, Commander James F., XXXIV, 120
Schene, Michael G., "The Early Florida Salvage Industry," XXXVIII, 262–271
Schevill, William E., "Weight of a Whaleboat," XX, 63–64
Schiffsmodelle: Die Geschichte der Schiffbaukunst im Spiegel Zeitgenossischer Modelle, by Hans Jurgen Hansen, reviewed, XXXIII, 148–149
Schiller (1875), XXIX, 137
Schley, Admiral William T., XXXVII, 37
Schley, Commodore Winfield S., XXXIX, 39, 131; XL, 174 ff.
Schmitt, Frederick P., *Mark Well the Whale; Long Island Ships to Distant Seas,* reviewed, XXXII, 140–141; *The Whale's Tale as told on postage stamps,* reviewed, XXXVI, 148–149
Schmitt, Frederick P., Cornelis de Jong and Frank H. Winter, *Thomas Welcome Roys: America's Pioneer of Modern Whaling,* reviewed, XLI, 144–145
Schmitt, Lou A., *All Hands Aloft! An Account of the Voyage of the Square-Rigger* Arapahoe *to Manila in 1918,* reviewed, XXVI, 224–225
Schmitt, Vice Consul, XXXVI, 96
Schmitt, Waldo L., V, 91; Appendix to "The United States Fish Commission Steamer *Albatross,*" V, 15–26
Schock, E. B., XXXVI, 248
Schoenfeld, Maxwell P., "The Restoration Seaman and His Wages," XXV, 278–287

Schöffer, I. and J. R. Bruijn, *Dutch Asiatic Shipping in the 17th and 18th Centuries*, reviewed, XLVIII, 206
Schofield, John McAllister, Commanding General U.S. Army, XXXIII, 268
Schofield, Samuel, XXI, 284
Schonfeld, Moses, XLI, 58
Schooner (clipper schooner), IX, 142
Schooner, IV, 58; IX, 169; XX, 237; XXI, 23; XXIII, 5; XXV, 81; XXX, 187; XXXV, 5; XLIV, 82; XLIX, 198
  Maine, XIX, 120; (3 masted), V, 286; (5 masted), V, 137
Schooner, topsail, of 1820, Pictorial Supplement, XXXVI, plate IV
"Schooner *Albert F. Paul*, The," by Robert H. I. Goddard, Jr., III, 163–166
"Schooner *Bohemia*," by Robert H. Burgess, X, 155, 230
"Schooner Building in Wisconsin, 1874," document contributed by Henry N. Barkhausen, IX, 229–230
"Schooner *Columbia*," query by W. B. Yarnall, VII, 171; answers by John M. Minuse, VII, 243; by John M. Clayton, IX, 73–74
Schooner construction, Bequia, XXXII, plate 9
"Schooner *Doris Hamlin*," query by Robert H. I. Goddard, Jr., II, 174; answer by Robert H. Burgess, II, 251
"Schooner *Dovrefjeld*," query by Robert H. Burgess, VII, 77
"Schooner Experiment: More Like a Crab Than a Duck, The," note contributed by Wilson L. Heflin, XXXVII, 143
Schooner from Windward, by Mifflin Thomas, reviewed, XLVII, 59
"Schooner *Golden West*," document contributed by Charles R. Schultz, XXVI, 283
"Schooner *Lillian E. Kerr*, The," by Robert H. I. Goddard, Jr., IV, 172–174
"Schooner *Lucy Evelyn*, The," by Robert H. I. Goddard, Jr., II, 327–330
"Schooner *Peggy*: An Eighteenth-Century Survival, The," by Basil Greenhill, XXIX, 54–61
"Schooner *Rebecca R. Douglas*, The," by Robert H. I. Goddard, Jr., III, 255–258
"Schooner *Richard R. Higgins* of Wellfleet," I, 308
"Schooner Rig; A Hypothesis, The," by Merritt A. Edson, Jr., XXV, 81–92, plate 3
"Schooner Rig: Its First Appearance and Development, The," by Merritt A. Edson, Jr., XLIX, 198–207
Schooners, by Basil Greenhill, reviewed, XL, 232
Schooners, coastal, XX, 237–242
Schooners, I, 69 ff., 90, 174–175, 181–182, 308, 312–313, 334, 341–342, 396–397, plate facing 396; II, 174, 175, 229–231, 243–245, 251, 326–330, 335; III, 163–166, 255–258, 266, plate 43; IV, 58–67, 164–171, 172–174, 236–237, 325–326; V, 79–81, 85–87, 137–141, 286–296, 327; VII, 317–318; VIII, 171; IX, 67–68, 70–72, 142–147, 169–179, 229–230; X, 155, 203 ff., 230
"Schooners, Three-Masted," query by V. M. W., I, 90; answer by John Lyman, I, 174–175; answers by Roland M. Howard and George A. Nelson, I, 312–313
Schooners and Schooner Barges, by Paul C. Morris, reviewed, XLVII, 146
Schooners in Four Centuries, by David MacGregor, reviewed, XLVI, 201
"Schooner *Speedwell*," query by Captain H. A. Baldridge, U.S.N. (ret.), IV, 335
"Schooner *William Jewell*, 1853–1947," by Philip P. Chase, XIX, 120–122, plate 5
Schooner Yacht, details of, XLIX, 206
Schoonmaker, Frank, answered query, I, 173
Schöpf, Dr. Johann David, XXV, 200, 202
Schott, Gaspar, VII, 266–267
Schouten, Captain Willem Cornelis, XXV, 251
Schroeder, John H., *Shaping a Maritime Empire: The Commercial and Diplomatic Role of the American Navy*, reviewed, XLIX, 237
Schrymger, Captain William, XXI, 101
Schuhmacher, W. Wilfried, "South African Light on American Fur Trade Vessels," XL, 46–49, note by, 135
Schultz, Charles R., document contributed by, 283; *Inventory of the Logbooks and Journals in the G. W. Blunt White Library*, reviewed, XXVI, 149–150; *Life on Board American Clipper Ships*, reviewed, XLIV, 138–139; "Manuscript Collections of the Marine Historical Association, Inc. (Mystic Seaport)," XXV, 99–111, plates 5–8
Schultz, Mark Roman, "Acting Master Samuel B. Gregory: The Trials of An Unexperienced Captain on the South Atlantic Blockading Squadron," L, 89–93
Schumacher, W. Wilfried, note by, XLI, 66–69; "Merchant Captain of the Pacific," XLI, 224–230
Schurman, Jacob, XXXVII, 28
Schurz, William Lytle, *The Manila Galleon*, reviewed, II, 85–86
Schuykill Navigation Co., XXXVI, 253, 256
Schuyler, Captain Philip, XXII, 122, 123, 124
Schuyler, Major General Philip, XXXVIII, 18
Schwab, Charles M., XXXII, 165 ff.; XXXV, 281
Schwab, Lawrence, query by, VI, 153
Schwaben, German merchant ship *(1939)*, XXXII, 112
Schwarzwald, steamship (1922), XIV, 132, 135
Schwatka, Frederick, XXXIX, 11
Schweighauser, John, XXXIX, 203
Schwerin, R. P., XXXV, 171
Schwieger, Kapitän-leutnant Walther, XXXV, 41
Science, bark *(1863)*, XII, 160
Science, sloop *(1861)*, XV, 124
Science, U.S.S. *(1817)*, XIII, 271

Science and Civilisation in China: Vol. 4, *Physics and Physical Technology;* Part III, *Civil Engineering and Nautics,* by Joseph Needham, reviewed, XXXII, 148
Science from Shipboard, reviewed, IV, 177
Science Museum (Boston, MA), XIV, 13
Science Museum (London, Gt. Britain), IX, plates 26–27; XIV, 187; XXX, 153
Scientists, Archives, L, 132
Scilly Isles, XXXI, 288 f.
Scindia, supply ship, XXXVII, 138 n.
Scindian, steamship (1854), XXVI, 109, 206, 209
Sciota, U.S. gunboat *(1864),* XLVIII, 93
Scire, submarine *(1942),* XXVII, 185
Scollay, John, XL, 267
Scollay Square, Boston (MA), XXV, 80
Scooter (boat), IV, 224
"Scooters, Great South Bay," by David B. Tyler, IV, 224 ff.
Scoresby, Thomas, M.D., XXII, plate VII
Scoresby, Captain Thomas, XXV, 104, plates 7, 8
Scoresby, William, XXX, 153
Scoresby, Captain William, XXII, plate VII; XXV, 104
Scoresby, William, Jr., XXV, 104
Scorpion, block-sloop *(1814),* XLII, 110; XLIII, 5 ff.; XLIV, 172
Scorpion, H.M.S., XXVIII, 19, 98
Scorpion, torpedo launch *(1864),* XLII, 91
Scorpion, U.S. cutter *(1813),* XXXVI, 221
Scotia, blockade steamship *(1861),* XXI, 90, 95, 105, plates III, XV
Scotia, ship, (1847), III, 133; *(1861),* XXXIV, 175; (1865), IV, 51, 52, plate 11
Scotia, steamship (1857), XXVI, 190, 192, 198; *(1862),* VIII, 227, 231, 235
Scotia, U.S. vessel *(1862),* XXXVI, 202
Scotland, ship (1855), V, 153
Scotland, steamship (1856), XVI, 178; XVIII, 72; XXVI, 129, 130; *(1865),* XLIX, 22; *(1876),* XLIII, 106 ff.
Scotland, Description and travel, XLIV, 103
Scott, Captain Bur, XVI, 64
Scott, Christopher, XV, 176
Scott, Edward, XII, 225
Scott, Rear Admiral G. H., XXXVIII, 256
Scott, George, XII, 222–228
Scott, Mrs. Hugh L., XXXIV, 263
Scott, J., XXIV, plates II, XXV
Scott, Joseph, XXX, 96 n.
Scott, Kenneth, VI, 155; XXV, 79; "Bonaparte Toscan and the Cuban Pirates," VI, 93–100; "The Cruise of the Whaler *Nightingale* in 1768," XXIII, 22–28; "George Scott, Slave Trader of Newport" XII, 222–228; "Naval Ballad of the War of 1812, A," VII, 167–169; "New Hampshire's Part in the Penobscot Expedition," VII, 200–212; "The Privateer *Yankee* in the War of 1812," XXI, 16–22; "The Sandy Hook Lighthouse," XXV, 123–127; "Source of Whittier's 'The Dead Ship of Harpswell,' The," VI, 223–227;

The Voyages and Travels of Francis Goelet, 1746–1758, reviewed, XXXI, 227–228
Scott, Robert, *Limuria: The Lesser Dependencies of Mauritius,* reviewed, XXIII, 74–75
Scott, Robert, Sailing Master, XLVII, 16
Scott, Sinclair & Co., XXVI, 195, 208
Scott, T. A., Co., Inc. (New London), XXV, 108
Scott, Captain William, XIII, 31 ff.
Scott, General Winfield, XXXVII, 279; XLII, 33 ff.
Scott, Major General Winfield, VII, 45, 46, 305–307
Scottish-American Steamship Co., Ltd., XXXVIII, 194
Scottish Chief, steamship *(1863),* XII, 160
Scottish Coast, 1824, XXIX, 124, plate X
Scottish Fisheries Museum, Anstruther, XXX, 153
Scottish Lady, schooner (1868), VII, 288–297, plates 34–36
"*Scottish Lady,* The," by Harold D. Huycke, VII, 288–297, plates 33–36; mentioned, IX, plate 31
Scourge, three-masted iron steamship *(1848),* XXX, 269
Scourge, warship (ex-*Bangor*) *(1846),* XXXIX, 222 ff.
Scow schooners, I, 75–76, 87–88
Screw propeller, XVII, 92 n.
"Screw Propeller Drawing of the Fitch Period, A," by Frank D. Prager, XXIII, 204–211
Scribed Board, James Maxwell House, drawing of, XXXVIII, 170
Scribner, Captain David A., II, 199
Scrimgeour, Captain William, XXI, 101
Scrimshaw, XII, 99
Scrimshaw, XXVIII, plate XXVIII
Scrimshaw and Scrimshanders, Whales, and Whalemen, by E. Noman Flayderman, reviewed, XXXIII, 66–67
Scud, yacht *(1888),* XXXVI, 232, 235
Scuppernong, steamship *(1862),* VIII, 227
Scurvy, XLIV, 155. *See also* Medicine
"Scurvy and Anson's Voyage Round the World, 1740–1744: An Analysis of the Royal Navy's Worst Outbreak," by Eleanora C. Gordon, M.D., XLIV, 155–166
Scuttling. *See* Ships, scuttling of
Scylla, H.M.S. *(1870),* XXXVI, 232
Sea, bark (1862), XV, 185
Sea, trawler *(1919),* XLIV, 125
"Sea Battle of Dannoura, The," by Captain W. R. Wilson, U.S.N. (Ret), XXVIII, 206–221
Sea Bird, C.S. steamship *(1862),* VI, 51; VIII, 227
Sea Bird, schooner, XXI, 86; *(1843),* XXXVII, 249; *(1861),* XI, 287; XII, 160
Sea Bird, woodboat (1868), XVII, 12
Seaboard, steamship (1874), XXXIV, plate IX
Seaborn, auxiliary schooner (1916), V, 140
Seaborn, Captain Adam, XXXVIII, 44
"Seaborne Frontier to California 1796–1850, The," by J. Wade Caruthers, XXIX, 81–101
Sea Breezes, American edition, Vol. VII, No. I, reviewed, IX, 154
Sea Bride, bark *(1863),* XXVI, 88, 89, 101–103, 106

Sea Bright Skiff and Other New Jersey Shore Boats, The, by Fancis E. Bowker, reviewed, XXXIV, 146–147
Seaburn, Captain H., XXI, 101
Seabury, Humphrey W., XXXIX, 106
Seabury, Otis, XXXIX, 96
Seabury, Captain William B., XVIII, 84
Sea chanties (chanteys). See Sea Songs
Sea Chaplains: A History of the Chaplains of the Royal Navy, The, by Gordon Taylor, reviewed, XXXIX, 302
"Sea Chart and the English Colonization of America, The," by D. W. Waters, XVII, 28–37
Sea Chest, The, edited by Critchell Rimington, reviewed, VIII, 160
"Sea Chests," query by Henry Darnell, Jr., I, 171–172; answers by L. W. Jenkins and Count Pehr Sparre, I, 312
Sea control, V, 177; XXIII, 157; XXVI, 177; XXVII, 5; XXIX, 244; XXX, 117; XXXI, 7; XLI, 262
Note: Here are entered works on the strategic and tactical employment of land or sea-based forces of a country at the time its maritime interests are threatened, so as to gain or exploit control of the sea or deny its use to the enemy. Works on long-term questions of naval strength, including weapons, installations, national resources, etc., allowing a country to maintain control of the sea and the air space above, are entered under **Sea power.**
Gt. Britain, VI, 290; VII, XXI
United States, I, 26
Seafaring life, II, 193; VII, 39; IX, 5
17th century, XI, 35; XIV, 83; XXVII, 111; XXXII, 81
18th century, XXIII, 22; XXXII, 81; XXXVIII, 249
19th century, I, 58, 116; II, 271; III, 106, 222; V, 194; VI, 121; VII, 282; VIII, 242; X, 203; XI, 42, 115; XII, 142, 177; XIII, 162; XVII, 17; XVIII, 306; XIX, 200; XXI, 110; XXIII, 186, 264; XXIV, 109; XXVI, 81, 262; XXXII, 34; XXXVII, 203; XXXVIII, 203; XLIV, 33; XLV, 86; L, 211
20th century, XIV, 18; XIX, 227; XXXIV, 258; XXXVI, 101; XXXVIII, 203; XXXIX, 184; XLV, 253
Middle East, XI, 161
See also Gt. Britain. Navy (Sea life); United States. Navy (Sea life)
Sea Crest, ship *(1863),* XV, 185
"Sea Drama in Stone," by Lionel Casson, XV, 217–219, plate 12
Seadrift, schooner *(1832),* XIV, 40
Sea Drift, schooner, XXI, 99; *(1856),* X, 231 ff.; XI, 267, 287
Seadrift, schooner *(1863),* XII, 160
Sea Eagle, ship *(1851),* XXV, 18 n.
Sea Eagle, tug *(1921),* VIII, 124
Sea Education Association (S.E.A.), The, XLVII, 206 ff.

Seafaring Labour: The Merchant Marine of Atlantic Canada, 1820–1914, by Eric W. Sager, reviewed, L, 231
Sea Flavor, by Haydn S. Pearson, reviewed, IX, 77–78
Seaflower, schooner *(1754),* XXI, 69
Sea Flower, schooner *(1800),* XXXIX, 35
Sea Flower, ship (1853), III, 68
Sea Flower, sloop *(1763),* XLIV, 6 ff.
Seaford, frigate *(1778),* XLIII, 29
"Seagoing Bank Notes with Denominational Masts," by Francis Whiting Hatch, XV, 232–216, plate 11
"Seagoing Hack," by Captain Edgar K. Thompson, U.S.N. (ret.), XXV, 167
Sea Gull, pilot boat *(1838),* IV, 105 ff.; XXX, 298; XLIX, 152 ff.; photo of model, XLIX, 161
Sea Gull, U.S.S. *(1839),* XII, 282
Seagull, yacht *(1906),* XXXVI, 242
Seahorse, H.M.S., XXVI, 54
Sea Horse, schooner, XXI, 91; *(1815),* XLII, 105 ff.; XLIV, 172; *(1861),* XI, 287
Sea Horse, steamship (1812), XXIV, 163 n.
Sea in literature, XII, 177; XIII, 131, 162; XLVI, 188. *See also* individual topics, e.g., Arctic regions; Cape Ann; Language, Marine; Navigation in literature; Sailors; Sea poetry; Ships in literature; Shipwrecks in fiction; Whaling in literature
Sea King, steamship *(1863),* XLIII, 124 ff.; *(1864),* XXVII, 274
Sea King, tug (1901), XVI, 7
Seal, S.S. (ex-*Scindian*), XXVI, 110
Seal, wooden trawler *(1917),* XLIV, 124
Sea Lanes in Wartime; the American Experience, 1775–1942, by Robert Greenhalgh Albion and Jennie Barnes Pope, reviewed, III, 91
Sea language, IX, 3–4, 5–10
"Sea Language," answer by Frederick Pease Harlow, VI, 153–154
Sea Lark, schooner (1871), XXIV, 44, 45, 59
"Sea Lawyer," by Captain Edgar K. Thompson, U.S.N. (ret.), XXVIII, 127; XXX, 132
Sealby, Inman, answered query, II, 175–176
Sealers, Cape Verde Islands, XLV, 104
Sea life, XXX, 222
Sea Life in Nelson's Time, by John Masefield, reviewed, XXXII, 289; re-reviewed, XLV, 207
"Sea Life In Seventeenth-Century England," by Charles A. Le Guin, XXVII, 111–134
Sealing, XI, 115; XXXIII, 160
Indian Ocean, XL, 117; XLI, 280
South Atlantic Ocean, II, 154; III, 327; XLIX, 278
Sealing, XV, 205–212
"Sealing Boats," by A. Alfred Mattsson, III, 327–332
Sea Lion, schooner, XXI, 98; *(1861),* XI, 287; XII, 160; *(1863),* VII, 19
Seaman, schooner (1830), XXII, 216
Seaman's Bride, ship (1859), IV, 256

"Seaman's clothing," document contributed by Marion V. Brewington, XX, 62
Seamanship, Handbooks, manuals, etc., XXX, 40
Seamanship in the Age of Sail, by John Harland and Mark Myers, reviewed, XLVIII, 187
Seamanship in Theory and Practice, XXX, 41
"Seaman's Offensive Letter to Thomas Jefferson, A," document contributed by Walter Muir Whitehill, XXII, 221
Seamen. *See* Merchant mariners; Merchant seamen; Sailors
Seamen, British, Restoration period, XXV, 278–287
Seamen's Act, 1915, XXIX, 232
Seamen's Bethel, The, XXVI, plate 24
Seamen's homes. *See* Merchant mariners (Missions and charities); Seamen's missions
Seamen's missions, XXIV, 109. *See also* Merchant mariners (Missions and charities)
Seam gauge, sailmaker's, IX, 289–290
Sea monsters, XIII, 268; XLVI, 213
Seams, sailmaker's, IX, 294–295
Sea Nymph, schooner *(1861),* VIII, 221
Sea Nymph, steamship *(1826),* XXXVII, 246
Sea of Cortez, by John Steinbeck and E. F. Ricketts, reviewed, II, 183
"Sea of Troubles: The Voyage of *Bonetta,* 1718," by Byron Fairchild, IX, 133–141
"Sea Otters, North and South," by Thomas Dunbabin, XVII, 66
Sea poetry, American, VI, 108, 115, 275; VII, 167; VIII, 165; XLVI, 111. *See also* Sea in literature
Seaports south of Sahara, by Robert G. Albion, reviewed, XIX, 309
Sea power, XXIV, 61; XXV, 35; XXVI, 177; XXXIX, 22; L, 178
Note: Here are entered works on long term questions of naval strength, including weapons, installations, national resources, etc., allowing a country to maintain control of the sea and the air space above. Works on the strategic and tactical employment of land or sea-based forces of a country at the time of its maritime interests are threatened, so as to gain or exploit control of the sea or deny its use to the enemy, are entered under **Sea control.**
Sea power, U.S., XXV, 35 ff.
Sea Power and British North America, 1783–1820: A Study in British Colonial Policy, by Gerald S. Graham, reviewed, II, 259–260
"Sea Power and South America: The 'Brazils' or South American Station of the Royal Navy, 1808–1837," by Barry M. Gough, L, 26–34
Sea Power in the Pacific 1936–1941, A Bibliography, by Werner B. Ellinger and Herbert Rosinski, reviewed, II, 352
Sea Power in the Pacific: A History from the 16th Century to the present day, by Donald Macintyre, reviewed, XXXIII, 224–225

Sea Princess, British cruise ship *(1980),* XLVI, 109
Sea Queen, bark (1864), V, 242
Sea Queen, steamship *(1862),* VIII, 227
Sea Ranger (1861), XV, 103 n.
Search for Speed Under Sail, 1700–1855, The, by Howard I. Chapelle, reviewed, XXVIII, 225–227
"Search for the Chesapeake Flotilla, The," by Donald G. Shomette and Fred W. Hopkins, Jr., XLIII, 5–19
Search for the Kobenhaven, The, by Captain Thomas Minto and Eric Stevens, reviewed, XLVII, 143
"Searching for Stowaways," XXXI, Pictorial Supplement, plate XIII
Searchlight, 'light wood' brazier, VII, 145, 146
Searchlight, steamship *(1905),* I, 273; III, plate 34
"Sea Rescue," by Captain Edgar K. Thompson, U.S.N. (ret.), XXV, 188
Searle, Joseph, XXX, 89
Sea Road to Halifax, The, by Hugh F. Pullen, reviewed, XLI, 234
Sears, David, XXVIII, plate XXX
Sears, Captain David Seabury, XXII, 237, 238, 247
Sears, Ezra, XXII, 238
Sears, Frederic, XXVIII, plate XXX
Sears, Heman (blacksmith), XXII, 236
Sears, Captain Joseph Henry, XXII, 245
Sears, Joshua, XXII, 233, 242, 243
Sears, Seleck, XXII, 238
"Searsport 'Thirty-six': Seafaring Wives of a Maine Community in 1880, The," by John F. Battick, XLIV, 149–154
Searsville, schooner *(1837),* XXII, 235
Seas, Charles A., U.S. Consul, XXXII, 196
Sea Serpent, ship (1850), IV, 73; *(1854),* XXXI, 83; XXXV, 213
Sea Serpent Journal: Hugh McCulloch Gregory's Voyage around the World in a Clipper Ship, 1854–55, The, Robert H. Burgess, editor, reviewed, XXXV, 213
Sea serpents. *See* Sea monsters
"Sea Serpents? No or Maybe," by Gershom Bradford, XIII, 268–274, plates 15, 16
Sea shanties (shanteys). *See* Sea Songs
"Sea Solace," by Captain Edgar K. Thompson, U.S.N. (ret.), XXV, 115
Sea songs, I, 58; VIII, 81; XXII, 106; XLV, 175
Seaton, Fred, XXXVI, 245
Seattle, U.S. destroyer *(1921),* XLVI, 249 ff.
Seattle, wooden steamship *(1917),* XXXV, 279
Seattle or *Geary,* wooden steamship *(1917),* XXXV, 279
Seattle, Washington, XXXVI, 231 ff.
Seattle Far North Fleet, XXV, 292
Seattle Port of Embarcation, World War II, XXV, 293
Seaver, Benjamin F., XXIX, 208
Seavy, J. H.,, XXIV, 57 ff.
Seaward, Lieutenant William, XIII, 43
Sea Witch, clipper ship (1846), I, 69; VII, 5, 6; XIX, plate XIX; XX, 212; XXII, 237
Sea Witch, schooner *(1861),* XI, 154; XII, 232

"Sea Yarn of the Nineties, A," by Frank L. Magune, VIII, 70
Sebago, steamship *(1870)*, XXII, 237
Sebago Lake, Songo River and Bay of Naples Steamboat Co., XXIV, 238
Sebago Lake & Long Pond Steam Navigation Co., The, XXIV, 235, 236
Sebastian, ship *(1784)*, XXI, 214 n.
Sebasticook, ship *(1861)*, XV, 124
Secesh, ship, XXI, 97
Secesh, sloop *(1863)*, VIII, 231
"Second *Chesapeake* Affair, The," by Robin W. Winks, XIX, 51–72
"Second Destruction of the *Geldermalsen*, The," by George L. Miller, XLVII, 275–281
"Second Great Western Steamship Company, of Bristol, England, The," by Grahame E. Farr, XI, 251–261
Second International Congress of Maritime Museums, XXXV, 75
Second of July, brig (1827), VI, 17
"Secretary Moody and Naval Administrative Reform: 1902–1904," by Paul T. Heffron, XXIX, 30–53
"Secret of British Power in the Age of Sail: Admiralty Records of the Coasting Fleet," by Dwight E. Robinson, XLVIII, 5–21
Secret of Mary Celeste, The, by Gershom Bradford, reviewed, XXVIII, 74–75
Seddon, James A., Confederate Secretary of War, XLVIII, 99
Sedgewick (ex-*City of Chester*), Pictorial Supplement, XXXIV, plate X
Sedgley, Captain C. P., XLIV, 9
Seeadler, German raider *(1917)*, XXXVI, 266–275. See also *Seedaler*.
Seeandbee, steamship (1912), IV, 192
Seedaler, German raider *(1915)*, XLV, 199 ff. See also *Seeadler*.
Seeger, Martin L., III, "Rocky Mountain Sea Captain," XXVIII, 128–141
Seeley, J. H., XXXVI, 232
Segel aus Downeast: die unerschrockener Männer von der Weser und ihre prächtigen Schiffe aus Neu-England, by Rolf Reinemuth, reviewed, XXXII, 136
Selby, Galloway, XLIII, 12 ff.
Selfridge, Thomas O., XL, 212; XLII, 58
Selfridge, Thomas O., Jr., *What Finer Tradition: The Memoirs of Thomas O. Selfridge, Jr., Rear Admiral, U.S.N.*, reviewed, XLIX, 133
Selkirk, Alexander, XXX, 300
Sellers, Rear Admiral David, XXXV, 128
Sellars, Captain John, XIX, 44
Sellars, Captain R., XXI, 106
Seller, John (author, d. 1697). See **English Pilot, The**
Seller, John, VIII, 306–307; XIV, 189
Selma, brig *(1849)*, XXV, 110
Selma, brig (1855), XIV, 212–214
Selma, tanker (1919), XXII, 161, 165, 169, 170, 182

Selman, Archibald, XXX, 102, 110, 111
Selman, Captain Archibald, Pictorial Supplement, XXXII, plate IV
Selman, Captain John, XXX, 110, 111
Selwood, Archie, XXXVI, 247 n.
Seminole, sloop of war *(1861)*, XXXVII, 287
Seminole, steamship *(1896)*, I, 394; *(1917)*, XII, 293,
Semiramis, ship *(1798)*, V, 90; *(1798)*, X, 53; XVIII, 121
Semiramis, ship (1863), III, 68
Semiramis, steamship (1858), XXVI, 24
Semmes, Captain, XXVII, 265
Semmes, Captain Raphael, XIX, 126–128; XV, 288 ff.; XXVI, 98 ff.; XXIX, 167 ff.
Semmes, Captain Raphael, C.S.N., XXV, 18 ff.; XXXII, 198; XXXIII, 7 ff., 52 ff., 210
Semmes, Rear Admiral Raphael, XLII, 98
Senator, American steamship (1848), X, plate 18; *(1848)*, XXXIII, 85, 94; *(1849)*, XXXVI, 171; *(1872)*, X, 132
Senator Jken, ship *(1861)*, XI, 266, 287
Senator Sullivan, schooner (1890), XXVIII, plate XXIV
Senator Weber, ship (ex-*Wellfleet*), XXVIII, plate VII
Send a Gunboat! A study of the Gunboat and its Role in British Policy, 1854–1904, by Antony Preston and John Major, reviewed, XXVII, 223–224
Seneca, U.S. steam gunboat (1861), XXI, 240
Senegal River, XXX, 177 ff.
Sennen, H.M.S. (ex-U.S. Coast Guard cutter) *(1943)*, L, 220 ff.
Senning, Calvin F., "Anglo-Spanish Rivalry in the Spitsbergen Whale Fishery, 1612–1616," XXVIII, 239–260
Señora Isabel, schooner *(1861)*, VIII, 221
Sento Maru, steamship *(1864)*, XLIII, 201
Senyavin, Russian ship (1828), XXXIV, 250
Sequine, brigantine (1845), III, 262
Serapis, frigate *(1775)*, XLIV, 169
Serapis, H.M.S. *(1778)*, XIII, 65
Serapis, ship, XXVIII, 197–205
Serçe Liman, medieval ship, mentioned, XLVI, 76
Serçe Liman, Greek shipwreck at, XLV, 10 ff.
Sereta, schooner, *(1862)*, VIII, 227
Serica, ship *(1868)*, XXXV, 32 ff.
Seringapatam, ship *(1805)*, XLI, 285
Seripano, brig *(1863)*, XV, 292
Serle, Ambrose, XXXVI, 83
Serrano, José, XXX, 265
Servia, ship (1883), IV, 48–49, 51, 52, plate 12; XXVII, plate V
Servies, James A., and Robert R. Rea, *The Log of H.M.S. Mentor 1780–1781*, reviewed, XLIV, 208
Serving tools, IX, 286 ff.
Sesostris, H.C.S.S. *(1842)*, XXVI, 6 n.
Sete Cidades Island, XXX, 259
Seth Grosvenor, steamship *(1859)*, XXXVIII, 62
Seth Low, steam tug (1861), III, 161–163, plate 22; V, 146–147, plate 12; IX, plate 20; XXIV, 220
Seth Sprague, bark (1847), IV, 242

Setsu Maru, steamship (ex-*Cuyahoga*) *(1868),* XLIX, 25
"Settlement of Anglo-American Claims Resulting from World War I, The," by Douglas Hurt, XXXIV, 155–173
"Seven Cities: The Role of a Myth on the Exploration of the Atlantic, The," by Commander George E. Buker, U.S.N. (ret.), XXX, 249–259
"Seven Ropes," by Thorvald S. Ross, XXI, 145
"Seven Sisters," XXXI, 107
"Seventeenth Century Chart Publisher, A," by Captain W. R. Chaplin, VIII, 302–324, plates 29–32
"Seventeenth-Century German Submarine, A," by David Whittet Thompson, III, 345–349
Seven Years' War (1756–1763), Naval operations, XLIX, 262
Severijn & Haesebroeck, XXX, 286
Severin, Tim, *The Brendan Voyage,* reviewed, XXXVIII, 303
Severn (1800), XXIII, 216
Severn, frigate *(1814),* XLII, 114 ff.; XLIV, 158 ff.
Severn, H.M.S *(1740),* XXII, 108, 112
Severn, H.M.S. [model] (1885), XVI, 103
Severn, ship, XXXII, 98
Severn, U.S.S. *(1907),* XX, 143
Sewall, Arthur, VIII, 279
Sewall, Arthur and Co., I, 335–336; V, 81; XVI, 5
Sewall, Arthur & Co. (shipbuilders), XXV, 231
Sewall, Samuel, XXII, 68; XXXV, 157
Sewall Fleet, Chart of Signal Flags, XXVII, plate XIV
Sewall Shipyard, XXVII, plate IX
Seward, George F., XVI, 157–179
Seward, George F. (consul general), XXV, 117
Seward, Professor Herbert, XLV, 43
Seward, Professor J. L., XXXVI, 29
Seward, William, XXVII, 31; XXXVI, 51, 177, 189
Seward, William, Secretary of State, XXXI, 64
Seward, William H., XIX, 60 ff.; XXII, 45, 50, 52, 53, 289 n.; XXV, 25–27, 116–122; XXIX, 168; XXXV, 53
Seward, William Henry, Secretary of State, XLVIII, 120. Mission to Peking, 1870, XXV, 116–122
Sewell, Samuel, XXV, 61
Sextant, XXXV, 111
Sextants: English, made by Owens, Liverpool, Pictorial Supplement, XXXV, plate VI; made by Heath & Co., Ltd., London, Pictorial Supplement, XXXV, plate VII
Sexton, Captain John G., XXI, 106
Sexton, Markham W. (Peabody Museum Staff Photographer) photographs by: in Pictorial Supplement "Instruments of Navigation," XXXV, plates I-XXXII
Seybolt, T. E., XXII, 288, 289 n.
Seychelles (British Indian Ocean Territory), History, XXXI, 104
Seydlitz, German ship (1917), XL, 59
Seymour, XXX, 241
Seymour, Admiral, XXXII, 243

Seymour, G. N., VII, 61
Seymour, Sir Michael, XXVII, 163
Seymour, Rear Admiral Sir Michael, XXII, 32, 35, 36, 37, 39; XXXVIII, 36
Shackamaxon, ship (1851), IV, 73
Shackamaxon, U.S. monitor (1862), X, 25, 32
Shackelford, George Green, "George Wythe Randolph, Midshipman, United States Navy," XXXVIII, 101–121
Shackford, Jacob, XV, 187; XXVIII, 114
Shackford, Captain John, XXVIII, 114, 115, 118
Shackford, Samuel, XXVIII, 118
Shackford, William, XXVIII, 118
Shackleton, Sir Ernest, XXVIII, 3, 59
Shackleton, Sir Ernest Henry, XXIII, 117, 118
Shackleton, Philip, and Kenneth G. Roberts, *The Canoe,* reviewed, XLV, 137
Shadow, sloop yacht, XXXIII, 63
Shadyside, steamship *(1920),* XXXV, 205
Shaffner, Colonel Taliaferro P., XLV, 187
Shafter, Major General, XL, 172 ff.
Shaftesbury, steamship (1862), XVII, 56, 138, 140; XVIII, 72; XXIV, plate VIII
Shah, H.M.S. *(1873),* XXIX, 261
Shakespeare, bark (1854), II, 245; (1856), III, 72
Shakespeare, William, XI, 209–214; XXV, 236
Shaler, William, XXIX, 85, 86, 88
Shall, Captain W. B., XLV, 175 ff.
Shallop (boat), XVII, 105; XXXIV, 231
Shallop, XVII, 105–113; plans 111–112
Shallop, colonial, Pictorial Supplement, XXXVI, plate II
Shallop-rigged lobster fishing boat, XXIX, 56, plate 6
"Shallops and Pinnaces," query by Harry D. Hamilton, VII, 77; answer by Howard I. Chapelle, VII, 170–171
Shamrock, ship (1853), II, 331; IV, 46, 51
Shamrock, sloop *(1861),* VIII, 221
Shamrock, steamship *(1841),* XXXIV, 19 ff.; *(1842),* XX, 259
Shamrock, steamship (1856), XXII, 21, 28, 31, 34, 39, 42, 43
Shamrock (I), yacht, XXXVI, 244 n.
Shamrock (III), yacht, XXXVI, 244 n.
Shanabrook, Paul E., *The Boston (A History of the Boston Yacht Club) 1866–1979,* reviewed, XLIV, 199
Shandon, steamship *(1863),* XLIII, 125 ff.
Shanghai, steamship (1851), XXVI, 16, 21, 23, 116, 117, 203, 206, 209, plate 15
Shanghai. *See* China
Shanghai, Battle of Muddy Flat, XXX, 155–166
Shanghai Line, XXII, 17
Shanghai Steam Navigation Co., XVI, 164 ff., 244–269; XVII, 38–42, 46; XVIII, 60, 62–64, 66, 67; XXII, 225; XXV, 118, 120; XXXIV, 17 ff.; XLIII, 86 ff.
Shanghai-Tientsin Line, XXII, 226
Shanghai Tug Boat and Lighter Co., XVII, 308
Shanghai Tug & Lighter Co., XLIII, 298

Shank, Captain, XXIX, 55, 56, 61
Shanks, Ralph C., Jr., and Janetta T., *Lighthouses and Lifeboats on the Redwood Coast,* reviewed, XL, 145
Shannon, British brig
Shannon, H.M.S., XXXVI, 213, 293; *(1812),* XLVI, 168; XXVIII, 30; XXIX, 67–68; *(1813),* XXXI, 286; XLIV, 171
Shannon, steamship (1826), XXIV, plate XX; *(1836),* VII, 62
Shanse, steamship (1862), XVI, 248; XVII, 39; XVIII, 72; *(1863),* XLIII, 118 ff.
Shantung, steamship (1861), XVII, 44; XVIII, 72; *(1861),* XLIII, 93 ff.; *(1861),* XLIX, 23; (1870), XVI, 260; XVII, 39; XVIII, 72; *(1870),* XXV, 118
Shanyuan, steamship *(1871),* XLIII, 299
Shaping a Maritime Empire: The Commercial and Diplomatic Role of the American Navy, by John H. Schroeder, reviewed, XLIX, 237
Shark, British sloop *(1776),* XLIII, 21 ff.
Shark, schooner, XXI, 99; *(1821),* XXXII, 272 ff.; *(1861),* XI, 288
Sharon, whaleship *(1841),* XXVII, 98 ff.
Sharp, Andrew, XXIII, 114
Sharp, Mr., XXX, 296
Sharpie *Nettie* on Trukee River, Nevada, III, plate 23
Shatemuc, bark (1859), III, 65
Shatswell, John H., XLVII, 124
Shattuck, Carl, XLI, 16
Shaum, John H., Jr. and William H. Flayhart, III, *Majesty at Sea — The Four Stackers,* reviewed, XLIII, 303
Shaw, ship *(1795),* XXV, 182
Shaw, Henry I., Jr., and Rowland P. Gill, *American Marines in the Revolutionary War,* XXXI, 4
Shaw, James, XIV, 49
Shaw, John, XXIV, 58; XLVII, 27
Shaw, Captain John, XXX, 74
Shaw, John W., XXXIX, 85
Shaw, Linus, XXIX, 224–225
Shaw, Nathaniel, Jr., XIV, 47 ff.; XXXIX, 192
Shaw, Captain Nathaniel, Jr., XX, 246
Shaw, Samuel, XI, 59–71; XIV, 54, 298
Shaw, Major Samuel, XLVI, 25; XXXI, 39, 177
Shaw, Thomas, XXXI, 134
Shaw Brothers & Co., XLIII, 90 ff.
Shawmut, bark (1853), V, 149
Shawmut, ship *(1902),* XLVII, 200
Shawmut, steamship (1902), III, 195–196
Shaw Perkins, tender *(1843),* XLI, 289
Shaw Savill (British shipping line), XLVI, 108
Shay (boat), XII, 123
Shay, Frank, *American Sea Songs and Chanteys,* reviewed, IX, 77
Shay and Merritt, VII, 50
Sheads, Scott S., *The Rockets' Red Glare: The Maritime Defense of Baltimore in 1814,* reviewed, XLIX, 59
Sheaffe, William, XL, 249

Shearwood, James, XXXV, 233
Sheboygan, steamship (1869), I, 76
Sheehan, Harry R., XVI, 14 ff.
Sheehan, J. M., query by, VIII, 71
Sheep Wish, British ship *(1776),* XLVIII, 19
Sheer, Admiral, XL, 52 ff.
Sheet Anchor, schooner *(1861),* VIII, 221
"Sheet Iron Steamboat *Codorus,* The," by Alexander Crosby Brown, X, 163–190, plates 21–24
Sheets, Captain George, XXXVI, 255
Sheffield, bark *(1861),* XI, 288
Shelburne Museum, XIX, plates I–VIII
Shelburne Papers, Clements Library, VII, 88
Sheldon Thompson, steamship (1830), VI, 209, 210; VII, 44, 45, 62
Shelmidine, Lyle S., "The Early History of Midway Islands," VIII, 179–195
Shelton & Kensett (engravers), Cheshire, XXV, 47
Shenandoah, C.S. cruiser (ex-*Sea Knight*) (1864), XXIII, 268; *(1864),* XIV, 46; XV, 300; XLIII, 125 ff.; (1865), XXVII, 267–278; XXIX, 5; (1865), L, 35
Shenandoah, schooner *(1902),* XXX, 196
Shenandoah, ship *(1883),* XL, 123
Shenandoah, steam sloop (1867), XXXII, 130; XXXIII, 60, 128
Shenandoah, U.S.S. *(1864),* XXVII, 43; *(1865),* VII, 19
Shepard, Birse, *Lore of the Wreckers,* reviewed, XXIII, 151–152
Shepard, Captain Stephen, XXVI, 105
Shepardess, bark, XXXVII, 217; *(1840),* XIX, 200–204, 207
Shepheard, Rear Admiral H. C., XXXVI, 29
Shepherd, James, XXXVII, 50
Shepherdess, brig *(1810),* XXX, 62–67
Shepherdess, schooner, XXI, 89; *(1861),* XI, 288
Sheppard, F. E., XXII, 282 n.
Sheppard, Matthew, XIII, 20
Sherbro, German ship *(1893),* XXXIX, 175
Sherburn, John, VI, 180 ff.
Sheridan, transport *(1899),* XXXV, 189
Sherman, steamship (1893), IX, 223
Sherman, Captain Albert C., XXXIX, 18
Sherman, Asa, Jr., XXV, 222
Sherman, Captain Asa, XXV, 222–223
Sherman, Constance D., "An Account of the Scuttling of His Majesty's Armed Sloop *Liberty*," XX, 243–249
Sherman, Doctor, XIII, 22
Sherman, Captain Jireh, XII, 108
Sherman, John, XXIX, 6
Sherman, Stuart C., XXXVIII, 155; *The Voice of the Whaleman with an Account of the Nicholson Whaling Collection,* reviewed, XXVI, 149–150
Sherman, William T., XXXVIII, 234
Sherman, General William T., XXXIV, 62
Sherman, General William Tecumseh, XXVII, 175
Sherman, Captain W. W., VII, 54
Sherriff, Captain William H., XLII, 109

Sherron, A. W., XXXVI, 255
Sherwood, Captain Joseph, XX, 80
Shields, Benjamin G., XXX, 262
Shields, Harbor of, ca. 1833, XXIX, 198, plate XXIII
Shields, Leighton, Jr., "Recent Writings in Maritime History," XVII, 74–84
"Shifting Ensigns," query by J. H. Kemble, III, 353
Shih-yi, Liang, *see* Liang Shih-yi.
Shi-k'ai, Yuan, *see* Yuan Shi-k'ai.
Shiloh, schooner *(1862)*, XII, 58
Shineberg, Dorothy, *They Came for Sandalwood: A Study of the Sandalwood Trade in South-West Pacific, 1830–1865*, reviewed, XXIX, 145
Shingking, steamship (1873), XVI, 261; XVII, 39; XVIII, 72
Shinpu Maru, steamship (ex-*Martin White*) *(1859)*, XLIII, 208 ff.;*(1866)*, XLIX, 26
Shinryu (ex-*City of Nantes*), steamship *(1867)*, XLIII, 190 ff.
Ship and Boat Models in Ancient Greece, by Paul Forsythe Johnston, reviewed, XLVI, 120
Ship: An Illustrated History, The, by Bjorn Landstrom, reviewed, XXII, 148–149
"Shipboard Life on Brig *Shepherdess*," document contributed by Clara Nisbet, XXX, 62–67
Shipbuilders, Biography, VI, 163; VII, 177; XIX, 7. *See also* names of individual shipbuilders
Shipbuilders of the Thames and Medway, by Philip Banbury, reviewed, XXXII, 72–74
Shipbuilding, VII, 196
    Ancient (Mediterranean area), XLV, 10
    Equipment and supplies, III, 239
    Materials:
    —, **concrete**, XXII, 157
    —, **Iron**, IV, 183; X, 163, XIII, 157
    —, **Wood**, III, 239; XXXV, 227, 275
    See below for shipbuilding by country; *see also* Ships
Shipbuilding: Canada
    New Brunswick, XXI, 279
    —, **St. Croix River;** XV, 173
    Quebec (province), XLVIII, 77
Shipbuilding: Great Britain, 17th century, XIV, 262; XVII, 152
Shipbuilding: Japan, XXIII, 270
Shipbuilding: Scotland, XXIX, 5
Shipbuilding: Sweden, VI, 163
Shipbuilding: United States, I, 51; III, XXXI; XXXVIII, 170; XXXVIII, 272; XLVIII, 22
    20th century, XXXV, 275
    Chesapeake Bay, IX, 142
    Maine, IV, 45; XX, 237; XLIV, 82; XLIX, XXIX
    Maryland, III, XIX
    Massachusetts, II, 278; XVII, 114; XLII, 118
    —, **18th century**, IV, 207
    —, **19th century**, XIX, 7
    —, **Cape Cod**, XXII, 233
    —, **Duxbury**, XIV, XXIX
    —, **Newburyport**, XVII, 114
    —, **North River**, XXV, 218
    Michigan, XLII, 245
    New Jersey, XXXVI, 251
    New York, VII, 177; VIII, 7; XXI, 57
    —, **19th century**, IV, 305
    North Carolina, 20th century, XLI, 188
    South Carolina, XLIV, 221
    Virginia, 18th century, XIII, 177
Shipbuilding: West Indies, XXXII, 180
Shipbuilding, General: XXII, 65–70, 99–105; XI, 204–207; in 1892, II, 289–290; in New England, XIV, 29–41, 217, 262–277; XV, 173–190; XXI, 15; XLVIII, 22–30; Great Lakes, XVII, 89–104
Shipbuilding (CA): I, 77–79
    Bernicia, Mathew Turner, I, 77
    San Francisco, V, 155
    Dickie Brothers, I, 78; II, 74–76
    James Dickie, I, 78
Shipbuilding, Canada: XV, 173–190
    New Brunswick, XVII, 5–16; XXI, 279–291
    British Columbia: Vancouver, IX, 67–68
Shipbuilding (CT):
    East Haddam, I, 48
    Mystic, IV, 72
    Williams, I, 45
    New Haven, IV, 72
    Stonington, IV, 72
Shipbuilding (DL):
    Wilmington, Jackson and Sharp, I, 69–70
Shipbuilding, FL: I, 72–73
    Tarpon Springs, I, plate facing 73
Shipbuilding (GA): St. Mary's, II, 44
Shipbuilding, Gt. Britain:
    17th century, XIII, 60–64; XV, 259–286
Shipbuilding (IN): VII, 317
Shipbuilding (KY): VII, 317–318
Shipbuilding (ME): I, 44–45; VII, 196–199; XX, 190, 237–242, 249, 269
    Addison, IV, 326
    Alna, IV, 326
    Ash Point, II, 302–323
    Bangor, IV, 238
    Bath, II, 324 ff., 330–335; IV, 45–52; V, 79–81, 138; VIII, 279–280; XXVII, plates I–VIII, 48; plates IX–XVI, 124; plates XVII–XXIV, 216; plates XXV–XXXII, 276; G. G. Deering and Sons, VII, plate 24; Goss, Sawyer and Packard, VIII, 152–153
    Portland Railway and Shipbuilding Co., I, 65
    Richardson and Stubbs, I, 65
    Belfast, IV, 238–239
    Bowdoinham, IV, 239
    Brewer, IV, 239
    Bristol, I, 50
    Brunswick, IV, 239
    Bucksport, IV, 326
    Calais, IV, 239–240

Camden, IV, 240; V, 138
Castine, IV, 326
Columbia Falls, IV, 326
Crotch Island, III, 144
Cumberland, IV, 326
Damariscotta, I, 49; II, 234; III, 62; IV, 240
Dresden, I, 49
East Machias, VII, 315
Ellsworth, IX, 170 ff
Eastport, IV, 240
Falmouth, IV, 240
Franklin, IV, 326
Frankport, IV, 240
Freeport, I, 100; IV, 241
Georgetown, IV, 326
Great Island, III, 146
Hallowell, V, 153
Harpswell, IV, 241
Harrington, V, 153
Kennebunk, III, 62–63; IV, 241–242
Machias, V, 153
Millbridge, IV, 242
Newcastle, I, 47; IV, 242
Pembroke, IV, 242
Phippsburg, V, 153
Portland, I, 49; IV, 242–243
Prospect, V, 153
Richmond, II, 245–246; IV, 243
Rockport, V, 153
Searsport, IV, 243–244
Stockton, V, 153
Thomaston, I, 50; II, 79–80, 246, 324; IV, 244
Waldoboro, I, 49; V, 138, 153
Warren, I, 50
Woolwich, V, 153
Yarmouth, III, 63; V, 153
Shipbuilding, Marshall Islands: Aomon Island, VI, 72–73
Shipbuilding (MD): IV, 249–250, 269–292
Annapolis, VI, 302–304
Baltimore, I, 49; III, 26–34, 73, 349
Bodkin Creek, I, plate facing 72
Shipbuilding (MA): XVII, 114–127
Boston, I, 47, 297; III, 169–173; V, 147–149, 328; Campbell and Brooks, I, 58; Samuel Hall, I, 46, 52, 53; D. D. Kelley, I, 58; Donald McKay, I, 44, 46, 58, 308; Smith and Townsend, I, 58
Chelsea, V, 149
Cohasset, Hall Brothers, V, 85
Danvers, IV, 207–212
Essex, VII, 243; IX, 73–74; Tarr and James, I, 68
Haverhill, I, 49
Medford, III, 68–70; V, 149–150; Thatcher Magoun, I, 82
New Bedford, V, 150
Newbury, I, 48
Newburyport, I, 167; III, 70–72; V, 150–152; VIII, 22–23; Currier & Townsend, I, 47
Quincy, V, 152
Salem, II, 278–288; IV, 18; V, 153
Swansea, V, 153
Shipbuilding (MI):
Newport, I, 76
Port Huron, I, 74
Saugatuck, I, 74
Spoonville, I, plate facing 72
West Bay City, I, 74
Shipbuilding (MO), VII, 318
Shipbuilding (NH), II, 338:
Durham, II, 209–222
Hampton, III, 145–146
Portsmouth, I, 47, 48, 315; III, 66–68; IV, 73
Shipbuilding (NJ): I, 70; XXXVI, 251 ff.
Shipbuilding, New York City (NY): III, 261–264; V, 154
Bell, I, 46
Brown and Bell, I, 46
Henry Eckford, I, 51; V, 115–120
S. and F. Fickett, I, 82
Smith and Dimon, I, 42
William H. Webb, I, 44, 45, 47, 48, 109; IV, 305 ff.; J. A. Westervelt, I, 46, 47
Westervelt and MacKay, I, 48
Shipbuilding (NC): XLI, 188–207
Shipbuilding (OH): VII, 317–318
Cincinnati, I, 48
Huron, J. Keating, I, 74
Marietta, I, 50
Toledo, V, 137
Shipbuilding (OR):
Coos Bay, I, 78
North Bend, V, 137
Portland, V, 139–140
Shipbuilding (PA): VII, 317
Kensington, I, 48
Philadelphia, III, 264; IV, 73; V, 243
Pittsburgh, IV, 183–187
Shipbuilding (RI):
Bonnysville, I, 49
Newport, IV, 72–73
Warren, IV, 73
Shipbuilding, Sweden, VI, 163–177, plates 21–28
Shipbuilding (TN): Chattanooga, VI, 139–140, plate 20
Shipbuilding, Turkey: Constantinople, VII, 190, 194
Shipbuilding, U.S. Gulf States: IV, 59–61; V, 81–82
Shipbuilding (VA):
Alexandria, I, 159–163
Newport News, III, 271
Norfolk, I, 297
Shipbuilding (WA):
Port Blakely, V, 137
Seattle, Hall Brothers, I, 78; V, 85–87
Tacoma, V, 139–140
Shipbuilding (WV): VII, 317

Shipbuilding (WI), II, 253–255: VII, 315
   Green Bay, IX, 229–230
   Greenfield, S. Rand, I, 76
   Manitowoc, I, plate facing 73
   S. Bates and Son, I, 74
   W. W. and S. Bates, I, 76
"Shipbuilding," query by M. V. Brewington, I, 172
"Shipbuilding and Clipper Ships," lecture by William Avery Baker; Francis Russell Hart Nautical Museum, M.I.T.; comment in Editorial, *The American Neptune,* XXXVIII, 3–4
Shipbuilding and Iron Ships, XXX, 15
Shipbuilding and Shipping Record, XXXII, 29
Shipbuilding and Steam Ships, by Andrew and Robert Murray, XXX, 14
Shipbuilding contracts, II, 338; IV, 207–212; V, 115–120, 243, 328; VIII, 22–23, 152–153; query by Adrian Block, I, 172
"Shipbuilding for the Royal Navy in Colonial New England," by Julian Gwyn, XLVIII, 22–30
"Shipbuilding in Bath, Maine," XXVII, plates I–VIII, 48; plates IX-XVI, 124; plates XVII–XXIV, 216; plates XXV-XXXII, 276
"Shipbuilding in North Carolina: The World War I Experience," by William N. Still, Jr., XLI, 188–207
"Shipbuilding on the St. Croix," by Harold Davis, XV, 173–190
Ship captains, Biography, XXIV, 247; XXVII, 157; XXVIII, 128; XXX, 167, 229; XXXVI, 88; XXXVII, 239, 276; XXXVIII, 157; XXXIX, 159, 190; XL, 23, 108; XLI, 224; XLV, 94, 180; XLVII, 169
Ship carpenters, Biography, XVII, 128
Shipcarvers Of North America, by M. V. Brewington, reviewed, XXIII, 72–73
Ship carving. *See* Carving; Ship decoration
Ship carving, XXVIII, plate XXXII
Ship chandlers, Massachusetts (Boston), XV, 220
"Ship *Crescent,*" query by George Atwell Richardson, V, 246
"Ship *Crusoe,* The," by H. W. Belknap, IV, 235–236
Ship decoration, III, 35; XV, 5, 191; XVII, 262; XVIII, 25; XXIV, 172. *See also* Carving; Oculi
Ship Design, XIV, 262–277
"Ship *Goddess,*" answer by Walter Muir Whitehill, VI, 153
"Ship *Goddess,*" query by W. H. Watson, II, 174
Ship handling, XV, 217
"Ship in the Medieval Economy, 600–1600, The," by Richard W. Unger, reviewed, XLI, 306–312
Ship Licenses issued to vessels under twenty tons and Ship Licenses on Enrollments issued out of the Port of Newport, Rhode Island 1790–1939 [Vol. II], reviewed, II, 93
"Ship *Lord Dartmouth:* American-built Merchantman of Revolutionary Days," by Sydney G. Morse, IV, 207–216

"Ship *Martha's* Shopping Trip in the Mediterranean, The," by James Duncan Phillips, V, 43–63
Ship model building, VII, 172
Ship models, XI, 245; XVI, 98; XXXVII, 164; XLVII, 119
   Gt. Britain, IV, 261
Ship Models:
   at Addison Gallery, XVII, 87
   at Museum of Fine Arts, XVII, 87
"Ship Models," by Donald McNarry, XXVII, 262
Ship Models Illustrated, by F. Ward Harman, reviewed, III, 274
Ship Model Society, NY, I, 103
Ship Model Society, Washington, III, 178; V, 165
Ship Model Society, XXII, 232
Ship names, XLII, 295
"Ship Names," document contributed by Captain Edgar K. Thompson, U.S.N. (ret.), XXII, 276
Ship of Destiny, by Greville Bathe, reviewed, XI, 233
Ship of the Line, The, by Brian Lavery: Vol. I, reviewed, XLV, 208; Vol. II, reviewed, XLV, 209–210
Shipowners. Biography, I, 205; XXXI, 120; XXXV, 197; XLVIII, 31
   New York, XXXVII, 50
   South Carolina, XLIV, 221
"Shipowning and Shipbuilding in Colonial South Carolina: An Overview," by Converse D. Clowse, XLIV, 221–244
Shipp, William, XI, 36
"Ship *Pacific Queen,* The," by Harold D. Huycke, IV, 199–206
Shippen, Captain W. W., XX, 156–161
Shipping (By country / Body of water):
Shipping: Africa, III, 222; XXXV, 197
   West, XXVII, 81; XXX, 167; XXX, 229; XXXV, 77; XXXVIII, 249
Shipping: Asia, XVI, 5, 107; XLVII, 193
Shipping: Atlantic Ocean, XIV, 115
   North Atlantic, XI, 251; XV, 133
Shipping: Australia, VIII, 114; X, 52; XIII, 275
   18th century, XVIII, 105
Shipping: Canada,
   New Brunswick, XXXIII, 79
   Newfoundland, XXVIII, 275
   Nova Scotia, XXXI, 19; XXXIV, 174; XXXVII, 231
Shipping: Canary Islands, XLVI, 91; XLV, 166
Shipping: China, II, 140; III, 314; IV, XXXI; VI, XIX; VII, 5; X, 83, 220, 288; XI, 59, 134; XVI, 157; 243; XVII, 38, 134, 212, 298; XVIII, 59; XXII, 5; XXIII, 212; XXV, 116; XXVI, 109, 189; XXVI, 5; XXXIII, 160; XXXIV, 17; XXXV, 166; XLI, 224; XLVI, XXV; XLVIII, 237; XLVIII, 243, 261; XLIX, XXI
   18th century, XVIII, 105
Shipping: Cuba, XI, 42
Shipping: East Indies, II, 271; V, 194; XIII, 5
Shipping: Europe, XX, 237; XXXIII, 294
Shipping: Fiji, XIII, 275

Shipping: Gibraltar, III, 222
Shipping: Germany, XXVII, 254
Shipping: Gt. Britain, XXIV, 127; XXX, 133; XLVIII, 5
Shipping: India, IV, 18; XV, 249; XVIII, 137; XXII, 194; XXXI, 38; XLV, 153; XLVI, 6; XLVII, 119
Shipping: Indian Ocean, XI, 161
    Chagos Islands, XXXI, 104
    Mascarene Islands, XXXI, 104
    Seychelles, XXXI, 104
    See also British Indian Ocean Territory; Mauritius
Shipping: Italy, 12th century, L, 229
Shipping: Japan, V, 255; XLVI, L
Shipping: Java, XLV, 86
Shipping: Marquesas Islands (French Polynesia), XXXIII, 160
Shipping: Mauritius, XXV, 5
Shipping: Mediterranean area, V, 43; XLVII, 157
Shipping: Middle East, XI, 161
Shipping: New Zealand, VIII, 114
Shipping: Oceania, XIX, 200
Shipping: Pacific Area, VI, 112; VII, 288
Shipping: Philippines, II, 140
Shipping: Russia, XXI, 207; XXIII, 131; XXX, 279
Shipping: South America, IV, 137; XI, XLII
    Argentina, XXXV, 5
    Panama, XI, 42; XX, 118
    Peru, VII, 282
    Plata River System (Argentina and Uruguay), XLIX, 272
    Surinam, XLV, 166
    Venezuela, XXIV, XXV
Shipping: Spain, IV, XVIII
Shipping: Sumatra, VI, 19; IX, 239
Shipping: United States, I, 205, 333; XXIX, 199; XXX, 187
    California, IV, 193; XXIX, 81
    Chesapeake Bay Region (Md. & Va.), XXX, 133
    Connecticut, XLIV, 5
    East Coast, IV, 58; XXI, 23; XXIII, 5; XLVIII, 173
    Georgia, 47, XXXIII
    Great Lakes, XX, 79, 250; XXXIV, 243; XLVII, 193
    —, **19th century,** V, XXVII; VI, 194; VII, 42, 298; VIII, 37, 132
    Hawaii, IX, 216; XLVI, 43
    Maine, IV, 45; VIII, 165; IX, 169; XXIV, 38; XXXIX, 218
    Massachusetts, IX, 207; XXVIII, 261
    —, **18th century,** I, 345
    —, **Boston,** XVI, 189
    —, **Merrimac River (MA and NH),** X, 249
    New York, XXXVII, 50; XXXIX, 83; XLVII, 33; XLVIII, 31
    North Carolina, III, XIV; XXIX, 155; XLIX, 77
    Pacific Coast of North America, IV, 193
    West Coast, IV, 199; XLII, 245
Shipping: West Indies, II, 203; VIII, 165; IX, 133; XIV, 83; XX, 44; XXIV, 95; XXXII, 180; XXXIII, 294

—, **18th century,** XXXVI, 155
Shipping, Accidents, III, 314; IV, XXXI
Shipping Act of 1916, XXXII, 155; XXXV, 287
Shipping Arrivals and Departures, Sydney [Vol. II, 1826–1840], by Ian Hawkins Nicholson, XXXVIII, 302
"Shipping a Sea in the Gunroom," XXXI, Pictorial Supplement, plate VIII
"Shipping in Islamic Art: Seventh Through Sixteenth Century AD," by David Nicolle, XLIX, 168–197
Shipping on the Mersey, 1812, XXIX, 48, plates IV, VI
Ship plans. *See* Ships (Design and construction); Naval architecture
Ship Plans, A select List from the Collection at The National Maritime Museum, by A. H. Waite and A. L. Tucker, reviewed, XIX, 309
"Ship Preservation in the Old Navy," by Charles Haines, XLII, 276–294
Ship Purchase Bill, The, XXXIII, 178 ff.
"Ship *Rachael & Ebeneazer,*" document contributed by William A. Baker, XXXI, 289–290
Ship registers, V, 223, 311; VIII, 99; XXIV, 109; XXX, 9
    United States, I, 275
Ship Registers and Enrollments of New Orleans, Louisiana [Vol. I, 1804–1820], reviewed, II, 93
Ship Registers and Enrollments of Newport, Rhode Island, 1790–1939 [Vol. I], reviewed, I, 410
Ship Registers and Enrollments of Providence, Rhode Island, 1773–1939 [Vol. I, Parts 1 and 2], reviewed, II, 93
Ship Registers of New Bedford, Massachusetts [Vol. II, 1851–1865], reviewed, I, 188; [Vol. III, 1866–1939], reviewed, II, 93
Ship Registry Act, XXXIII, 183
"Ship *Reporter,*" query by Addie Cushing Colman, VIII, 71
"Ship-Rigged Rafts and the Export of Quebec Timber," by Eileen Reid Marcil, XLVIII, 77–86
Ship rigging. *See* Masts and Rigging
Ships:
    Accidents, II, 65; XII, 282; III, 314; IV, XXXI
    —, **Collisions,** XIV, 237
    Ancient, XV, 217; XXIII, 41, 113; XXIV, 81; XXXI, 49; XLV, 10; XLVI, 77; XLVIII, 149; XLIX, 168; L, 192
    Conservation and restoration, I, 63; XII, 7
    Design and construction, I, 63; XXXI, 52; XXXIII, 16; XXXIV, 188
    —, **17th century,** XIV, 262; XV, 259; XXII, 99
    Economic aspects, XXXIII, 178
    Equipment and supplies, XLV, 153
    Fires, II, 140; XIV, 192
    Health regulations, XL, 192
    Historic. *See* Historic Ships
    Inspection, I, XLII
    Insurance. *See* Insurance, Marine
    Iron, XIII, 157; XXII, 212

—, **Iron and steel,** IV, 183
Library resources, XIII, 118
Maintenance and repair, XXX, 56
Manuscripts, XIII, 118
Pictorial works, XXII, 184
Propulsion, XXII, 277; XXIII, 204; XXIV, 5; XXVI, 157; XXXI, 5
Repairing, I, 138; II, 65; XI, 108
Replicas, XIV, 5, 105
Scuttling of, XLV, 199
Statistics, XXXIII, 16
Steel, XVIII, 5, 149, 201, 235. *See also* Ships (Iron)
Transportation (of passengers), III, 292
See also Naval Architecture; Steam; Shipbuilding (Materials); Shipping; and types of ships, i.e., Packets, Sailing ships
Ships and boats, Asiatic types of:
   Baghlas, IX, 96, 99, 105, plate 9
   Ballams, IX, 104, 106, plate 11
   Bhums, IX, 96, 99–101, 105, 109, 111
   Dhows, IX, 87–132
   Ganjas, IX, 96, 100
   Houris, IX, 104
   Jalbhuts, IX, 90, 102–104, 106, 109–119, plates 9, 11–14
   Japanese row boats, IX, 65–67
   Nuggars, IX, 89, 91–92
   Sambuks, IX, 99–101
   Shewes, IX, 104, plate 10
Ships and boats, European types of:
   Alijador del lago, Lake Albufera (Valencia), I, 357–359
   Beach boat, Riviera, I, 369–371
   Bragozzi, II, 56–57
   Catalonian fishing boat, I, 359–360
   Harbor boat, Palermo, I, 371–373
   Moleta, I, 353–356
   Navicello, I, 367–369
   Sandale, I, 366
   Straits boat, I, 356–357
   Taffarel, II, 59–60
   Tagus River barges, Portugal, I, 353
   Tartane, I, 361, 365; II, 62–63
   Topo, II, 57–58
   Trabacola, I, plate facing 371; II, 58–59
   Tunisian fishing lateener, II, 61–62
   Tuscan coaster, I, 365–366
Ships and boats, North American types of:
   Barge, Dismal Swamp Canal, V, 305–306; Middlesex Canal, II, 134 ff
   Bermuda sloop, IX, 143, 145–147
   Beetle whale boats, III, 350–352
   Biloxi shrimp fishing schooner, I, 71–72
   Bugeyes, II, 86–88
   Chesapeake clipper schooner, IX, 142–147
   Crotch Island Pinkies, III, 141–142
   Dories, II, 310 ff
   Double-enders, II, 311 ff
   Dragnet boats, Connecticut River, I, 69
   Dugout canoe, Dismal Swamp, V, plate 14
   Dugout, St. Lucia, II, 71–73
   Durham boat, II, 167–170; III, 253–255
   Felucca, I, 79, 306–308
   Gundalows, I, 68; II, 127–139, 209–222
   Hampton boat, I, 66, 90, 173, 311–312; II, 249–250; III, 141–147, plate 18
   Indian birch bark canoes, VIII, 91–98, 289–300
   Indian elm bark canoes, IX, 185–206
   Jamaica sloop, IX, 143
   "Johnny" wood-boats, X, 204
   Log canoes, IV, 249
   Merrimac River gundalows, X, 249–263
   Nahant Pilot Canoe, III, 177, 353
   New York harbor lighter, III, plate 24
   Oyster schooner, South Jersey, I, 70
   Potomac longboat, I, 159–163
   Rafts, I, 402–403
   San Francisco Bay lateen-rigged fishing boat (felucca), I, 306–308, plates facing 297, 312, 313
   Scooters, Great South Bay, IV, 224–232
   Scow schooners, I, 75–76, 79, 87–88
   Sealing boats, III, 327–332
   Sharpies, III, 167–168, plate 23
   Skipjacks, IV, 269–292
   Virginia canoes and bugeyes, III, 176; IV, 76
   Wherries, II, 311 ff.
Ships and boats, Pacific types of:
   Carolina Islands canoes, X, 40–41
   Marshall Islands canoes, VI, 71–72
Ships and boats, South American types of:
   Balsa, II, 112 ff
   Inflated sealskin boats, II, 115 ff
   Reed boats, II, 115 ff.
"Ships and Fleets in Anglo-French Warfare, 1337–1360," by Timothy J. Runyan, XLVI, 91–99
Ships and Sailing, reviewed, XI, 300
Ships and Seamanship in the Ancient World, by Lionel Casson, reviewed, XLVIII, 63
Ships in art, XV, 217; XLIX, 168
Ships in a Storm, 1840, XXIX, Pictorial Supplement, Part IV, plate XXXII
Ships in literature, XII, 177; XIII, 162
"Ship's Log," query by Henry W. Belknap, III, 353
Ship's Logbook, A, by Frank R. Farrar, reviewed, XLIX, 306
Ships of the American Revolution, by Harold M. Hahn, L, 229
Ships of the Esso Fleet in World War II, reviewed, VIII, 75
Ships of the Inland Sea, by Gordon R. Newell, reviewed, XI, 298–299
"Ships of the Puritan Migration to Massachusetts Bay," by Ann N. Hansen, XXIII, 62–66
Ships of the Royal Navy; Statement of Losses, 1939–1945, reviewed, VIII, 74–75

"Ship *Sooloo* (II) of Salem, 1861–1887: History and Research for Building a Model, The," by Rob Napier, XLVII, 119–137

Ships, Seafaring and Society: Essays in Maritime History, by Timothy J. Runyan, reviewed, XLVIII, 210

"Ships' Sails," document contributed by William Bunting, XXXVII, 219–220

Ships That Sail No More: Marine Transportation from San Diego to Puget Sound, 1910–1940, by Giles T. Brown, reviewed, XXVII, 150–151

"Ships that tested the Blockade of the Carolina Ports, 1861–1865," by Marcus W. Price, VIII, 196–241, plates 17–19

"Ships that Tested the Blockade of the Georgia and East Florida Ports, 1861–1865," by Marcus W. Price, XV, 97–132

"Ships that Tested the Blockade of the Gulf Ports, 1861–1865," by Marcus W. Price, XI, 262–290; XII, 52–59, 154–161, 229–238

Ship stores, XIX, 251–253

Shipworm, XXVII, 177–184

Shipwreck, A, 1838, XXIX, Pictorial Supplement, Part IV, Plate XXX

Shipwreck, on Thachers Island, XXV, 233–247

Shipwrecks:
  Atlantic Ocean, XIV, 237; XXVII, 61
  —, **South Atlantic,** XVI, 180
  Bahamas, II, 44; XLIX, 124
  Chile, I, 108
  Fiji, XXIII, 233
  Mitchell Islands (Ellice group, Southwestern Pacific), VIII, 61
  Newfoundland, XX, 177
  Orkney Islands, L, 127
  Society Islands (French Polynesia), XXXVI, 266
  South China Sea, L, 275
  United States, I, 138; IV, 305; X, 191; XLV, 20
  —, **Maine,** IV, 318
  —, **Massachusetts,** XXIV, 138; XLV, 180; XLVII, 119
  —, **Oregon,** XLI, 122
  —, **Virginia, James & Maury Rivers,** XVI, XLI
  Venezuela (Margarita Island), XIV, 192
  Virgin Islands (Santa Domingo), VI, 241
  See also individual subjects, e.g., Collisions at sea; Fire at sea; Life saving; Ships (Accidents; Collisions; Fires)

Shipwreck, unidentified (1852), XXV, plate XIX

Shipwreck Anthropology, edited by Richard A. Gould, reviewed, XLIV, 134

Shipwrecked Fishermen and Mariners Royal Benevolent Society, XXXIV, 8 ff.

"Shipwreck in the Mountains: The Loss of the Canal Boat *Clinton* and the Heroism of Boatman Frank Padget," by Alexander Crosby Brown, XVI, 41–48

Shipwrecks, XII, 60–62; XIII, 52, 134–139; XIV, 237–261; XV, 155, 232

Shipwrecks in fiction, XXV, 233

Shipwrecks on the Chesapeake: Maritime Disasters on Chesapeake Bay and Its Tributaries, 1608–1978, by Donald G. Shomette, reviewed, XLIV, 203

Shipwrights Corp., XIII, 123

Shipwright's Trade, The, by Sir Westcott Abell, reviewed, IX, 232

Shipyard, Chattanooga, Tennessee, VI, 139, plate 20

Shipyard Museum of Norfolk Naval Shipyard, Virginia, XXII, 232

Shipyards, views of, Bath, Maine, VII, plate 24

"Ship *Zouave*," query by Edward G. Curtis, V, 246

Shirley Gut, Boston Harbor, XXIX, Pictorial Supplement, Part IV, Plate XXV

Shish, Jonas, IV, 261 ff.

Shiverick, Asa, Jr., XXII, 235, 246

Shiverick, Asa, Sr., XXII, 234, 236

Shiverick, David, XXII, 235

Shiverick, Paul, XXII, 235, 237, 246

Shiverick, Reverend Samuel, XXII, 234

Shiverick Shipyard, XXII, 233–251

Shizume, Moriharu, XIV, 19 ff., plate 4

Shna Yak, tanker *(1911),* XXXVIII, 180

Shoalhaven, H.M.A.S., British destroyer *(1949),* XLIX, 209 ff.

Shoalhaven Steam Navigation Co., XLIII, 204

Shoemaker, Lieutenant Benjamin D., Jr., XXXVII, 97 ff.

Shoemaker, Lieutenant Charles, XLVIII, 90

Shoho Maru, steamship (ex-*Lotus*) *(1868),* XLIX, 23; *(1864),* XLIII, 199 ff.

Shokaku Maru, steamship (ex-*Yangtsze*) *(1857),* XLIX, 27

Shokokon, U.S.S. *(1863),* XVIII, 142–148

Shoko Maru, steamship *(1863),* XLIII, 187 ff.

Shomette, Chief Dale, XLIII, 11 ff.

Shomette, Donald, Director of Nautical Archaeological Associates, XLIII, 9 ff.

Shomette, Donald G., *Shipwrecks on the Chesapeake: Maritime Disasters on Chesapeake Bay and Its Tributaries, 1608–1978,* reviewed, XLIV, 203

Shomette, Donald G. and Robert D. Haslach, *Raid on America: The Dutch Naval Campaign of 1672–1674,* reviewed, L, 228

Shooey-leen, steamship *(1864),* XLIII, 190 ff.

Shooks, Captain J., XX, 90 n.

Shooting Star, ship (1851), XIX, plate XXI; *(1861),* XI, 288

Shoreham, H.M.S., XXVI, 48; *(1700),* XXX, 133

Short, Charles, XV, 181 ff.

Short, George, XXVIII, 144–145

Short, John, XV, 181 ff.

Short, Joseph, XXVIII, 144

Short, Vincent, "Robert Fulton and the beginning of Modern Marine Transportation, 1808–1958," XVIII, 316–317

Short Brothers, XXIV, 58

Short History of Navigation, A, by W. J. V. Branch and E. Brook-Williams, reviewed, IV, 177
"Short History of the Los Angeles Steamship Co.: 1920–1930, A," by James M. Merrill, IX, 216–227
Shortland, Captain John, R.N., XXV, 254–255, 259–260
Short Staple, brig *(1808),* XVI, 202–203
Shoshone, steamship *(1913),* XXIX, 266
Shot, schooner *(1863),* XII, 160
"Shot into the Blue, A," by Captain Edgar K. Thompson, U.S.N. (ret.), XXV, 140–141
Shovell, Sir Cloudesley, British admiral, XLVIII, 14
Show Boat, schooner *(1929),* IV, 67, 68, plate 16
Shreve, Henry M., XVI, 35 ff.
Shreve, Henry Miller, II, 346–347
Shrimp fisheries, North Carolina,, L, 257
Shrimpton, William, XIII, 17
Shubrick, lighthouse steamship (tender), XXXVI, 45–53; *(1861),* XXXIII, 47
Shubrick, Captain Irvine, XXI, 72
Shubrick, Captain W. Branford, XXIV, 7
Shubrick, Commodore William, L, 110
Shubrick, Commodore William B., XXXVI, 46, 180 ff.; XL, 42
Shuckburgh, Dr. Richard, XXII, 106, 115, 116, 117 ff.
Shufeldt, Commander R. W., XXXII, 125; XXXIV, 81 ff.
Shufeldt, Commodore Robert W., XXIX, 116
Shuldham, Vice Admiral Molyneux, XL, 16
Shuma, S.S. *(1942),* XXVII, 190
Shunlee, iron screw steamship *(1862),* XLIII, 193 ff.
Sibbald, Captain John, XLII, 49
Siberia, steamship, XXIX, 231; (1902), X, 138, 139
Sicard, Rear Admiral Montgomery, XLI, 95
Sicily, decorated boats, XXIV, 183–185, plates 17–20
Sickles, Dan, XXXVIII, 235 ff.
Sickel's Patent Cut-Off Valves, IV, 191
"Side-Wheelers Across the Pacific," by John Haskell Kemble, II, 5–38, 243
Siebrand, Carl, XXXVI, 237
Sierra, German ship *(1917),* XLIV, 180
"Sierra," [Motorship, 1916], by Ronald L. Hughes, XXV, 228–294
Sierra Leone, XXX, 230 ff.
Sierra Nevada, ship (1854), III, 67; (1861), IV, 255
Sieur de Monts, steamship, XXVI, 262
"Sight-Seeing Ship," by Captain Edgar K. Thompson, U.S.N. (ret.), XXV, 277
"Signal Books," query by M. V. Brewington, III, 177; answer by R. de Kerchove, III, 269; answer, IV, 251
"Signal Event, A," by Captain Edgar K. Thompson, U.S.N. (ret.), XXVI, 214
Signal flags, XXI, 70–72
Signals and signaling, III, 205
"Signal Systems and Ship Identification" by M. V. Brewington, III, 205–221
Sign of the Quadrant, XXX, 41
Sigsbee, Captain C. D., U.S.N., V, 7, 8

Sigsbee, Captain Charles D., XXXII, 262 ff.
Sigsbee, Rear Admiral Charles D., XXXVIII, 27
Silas E. Burrows, ship *(1939),* XXXVII, 248
Silas Henry, sloop *(1862),* XII, 58, 160
Silas O. Pierce, steamship, XVIII, 230
Silas Wright, ship *(1853),* XVII, 21
Silent Pilots: Figureheads in Mystic Seaport Museum, by Georgia W. Hamilton, reviewed, XLV, 211
Silent Traveller in Boston, The, by Chiang Yee, XX, 3–4
Sill, Edward Rowland, *Around the Horn,* reviewed, IV, 255
Sill, John M. B., XXXIV, 213
Silliman, Benjamin, XXXIX, 113
Silliman, Professor Benjamin, XLVI, 219
Silliman, Benjamin D., XXXIII, 210
Silliman, Captain Joseph A., XXI, 101
Silloway, Thomas, XVII, 116
Silsbee, Benjamin H., XLVII, 120
Silsbee, Captain, XLVI, 11
Silsbee, John H., XLVII, 120
Silsbee, Nathaniel, XLVII, 119 ff.
Silsbee, Pickman and Stone, VI, 19 ff.
Silsby, Enoch, XXV, 106
Silsby, Herbert T., contributed document, XXI, 304
Silva, Francisco, XXVII, 236
Silvanus, schooner *(1864),* XV, 130
Silver, Jan, *Heavy Weather Cooking,* reviewed, XL, 230
Silver, Captain Peter, XXI, 302
Silver, Captain William, XXI, 296 ff.
Silver Cloud, schooner *(1853),* XLIV, 83; XLV, 110
Silvermaple, steamship (1927), VIII, 66–67
Silver Spray, yacht *(1906),* XXXVI, 244
Silver Spring, steamship (1860), VII, 120–123, 125–126, 128, 129 n., 166
Silver Springs, Florida, VII, 115 ff.
Silver Springs Co., VII, 234
Silver Wave, refrigerator ship *(1927),* XXV, 292
Silver Wave, schooner *(1890),* XXXVIII, 84; XXXIX, 13
Simison, Barbara D., co-editor with Stanley T. Williams of *Around the Horn: A Journal; December 10, 1861 to March 25, 1862* by Edward Rowland Sill, reviewed, IV, 255
Simister, Adele, XXXVI, 22
Simmonds, Lieutenant Richard, XXIX, 211 ff.
Simmons, Captain Benjamin F., III, 314–326; IV, 31–44, 324–325, plate 8
Simmons, Captain C. E., XVIII, 84
Simmons, J. W., XXXVI, 48
Simmons, Sylvester, XVIII, 107
Simmons, Captain Thomas, VIII, 67
Simon, Sir John, XXXVII, 194
Simond, Captain D. D., XXI, 101
Simonds, W. A., I, plate facing 114
Simon's Bay, XXX, 207
Simoon, ship (1852), III, 262
Simper, Robert, *East Coast Sail: Working Sail 1850–1970,* reviewed, XXXIII, 213–214

Simpson, B. Mitchell, III, *Admiral Harold R. Stark, Architect of Victory 1939–1949*, reviewed, L, 146
Simpson, Charles, XXXVI, 237 ff.
Simpson, Colin, XXXV, 37
Simpson, Edward, XL, 127
Simpson, Captain Edward, XXXIII, 280
Simpson, George, XXXVI, 236 ff.
Simpson, James, XLI, 214
Simpson, Captain John, XX, 43
Simpson, Mark, XXIX, 135
Simpson, Captain Thomas, XLII, 30
Sims, Admiral William S., XXXV, 97 ff.
Sims, Commander William S., L, 52
Sims, Lieutenant William S., XLI, 96
Sims, Lieutenant Commander William S., XXII, 191
Sims, Admiral William Sowden, U.S.N., III, 93
Sinclair, Arthur, XXXIX, 31
Sinclair, Commander Arthur, XXXV, 26
Sinclair, Lieutenant Arthur, XV, 293
Sinclair, George, VII, 269–270
Sinclair, George Tarry, XXXVIII, 118
Sinclair, John, XXX, 136
Sinclair, Captain John, XV, 59–80
Sinclair, Robert A., *Winds Over Lake Huron*, reviewed, XXXVIII, 74
Sinclair, T. L., Jr., "You can't beat the Banca," XIX, 257–264
Sinclair Navigation Co., XXXVIII, 185
Sindren, Adrian Van, XXXIX, 46
Singapore, steamship (1850), XXVI, 15, 17, 18, 19, 21, 23, 25, 27, 30–32, 202, 203, 206, 209
Singer, Isaac, XLVIII, 130
Single-handed Passage, by Edward C. Allcard, reviewed, X, 235–236
Singleton Palmer, schooner (1904), V, 81
"Sinking of *William P. Frey*," by Phyllis A. Hall, XLV, 199–203
Sino-Japanese War (1894–1895), VIII, 267
Sintram, schooner (1920), V, 139
Siple, Paul A., review by, II, 185–187
Sir Allan McNab, ship (1861), VIII, 221
Sir Charles Forbes, ship (1858), XXXIV, 18 ff.
Sir Charles Forbes, steamship (1846), XXII, 16–18, 21, 23, 31, 34–36, 38, 42, 43; *(1846)*, XLIII, 105 ff.;*(1851)*, XXVI, 14, 109, 202
Sir Edward Hawke (1767), XXVIII, 226
Siren, Government steam yacht, Bermuda (1862), XXIV, plate 24
Siren, sandbagger cutter *(1891)*, XXXVI, 235
Sireno, schooner *(1861)*, XI, 288
Siren Queen, whaler (1853), XXXIV, 248
Siren Vase, photo of, L, 194 ff.
Sir George Gray, steamship *(1859)*, XVII, 48; XVIII, 72; XLIX, 23
Sir Harry Parkes, steamship *(1878)*, XLIII, 91 ff.
"Sir Isaac Newton on Saumarez Patent Log," by Herbert R. Spencer, XIV, 214

Sirius, H.M.S., XXVIII, 105 n., 107
Sirius, S. Crocker yacht *(1957)*, XLVIII, 185
Sirius, ship (1858), III, 73
Sirius, steamship, XXI, 90, 106; (1837), IX, 262–264, plate 26.; *(1839)*, XII, 149; *(1863)*, VIII, 231, 235
"Sir James Bland Burges Papers," by S. W. Jackman, XXIX, 244–261
Sir James Brooke, steamship (1856), XXVI, 199, 200, 209
Sir James Kempt, steamship (1829), VI, 209
Sir James Kempt, steamship (1841), XX, 88
Sir Jamsetjee Jeejeebhoy, paddle steamship (1849), XXII, 23, 38, 42, 43; *(1855)*, XXVI, 22, 24, 202
Sir Jamsetjee Jeejeebhoy, transport *(1858)*, XXXIV, 20 ff.
Sir John Brown and Co., XXXIX, 130
Sir John Harvey, steamship *(1841)*, XXXVII, 233
Sir John Lawrence, bark (1864), I, 113
"Sir Julian Corbett on the Significance of Naval History," by John B. Hattendorf, XXXI, 275–285
Sir Lancelot, ship *(1868)*, XXXV, 32 ff.
Siroc, sailing wherry (1902), II, 319–320
Sir Robert Peel, schooner, XXI, 92; *(1861)*, XV, 117, 124; *(1862)*, VIII, 227
Sir Robert Peel, steamship (1837), VII, 64, 310–312; *(1838)*, XVIII, 273
"Sir Samuel Argall, Kt., of East Sutton, County Kent, an Elder Bother of Trinity House and Sometime Governor of Virgina," by W. R. Chaplin, XIV, 64–65
Sir Sidney, H.M.S. *(1813)*, XVII, 209, 210
Sir Tom, yacht *(1914)*, XXXVI, 247–249, plate 6
Sirus, British ship *(1878)*, XXXIX, 291
Sirus, steamship *(1840)*, XXXV, 254
Sir William Armstrong Co., XXXIX, 130
Sir William Peel, steamship (1854), XXVI, 197, 206, 209
Sir Wm. Peel, steamship *(1863)*, XII, 160
"Sir William Phips' Treasure," by Shepard Pond, II, 171–172
Sir William Wallace, brig (1824), XV, 185
Sisson, Charles C., XXV, 106–107
Sisson, Mrs. Charles, XXXVII, 205
Sissy, yacht (1861), XXVII, 250
Sister Kate, Jr., schooner, XXI, 91; *(1861)*, XI, 288
Sister Kate, schooner, XXI, 91; *(1861)*, XI, 288
Sisters, brig *(1801)*, VI, 83
Sitka, bark *(1834)*, XII, 182
Sitka, Russian transport *(1854)*, XXXI, 271
Sivoutch, H.I.M.S. *(1894)*, XXIII, 69
"Six *Baltimores*, The," by Fred Hopkins, XXXIX, 29–44
"Six Pacific Island Discoveries," by Saul H. Riesenberg, XXXIV, 249–257
"Sixteenth-Century English Seamen Meet a New Enemy—The Shipworm," by Tom Glasgow, Jr., XXVII, 177–184
"Sixth Battle Squadron, A Reminiscence, The," by Vice Admiral Allan E. Smith, U.S.N. (ret.), XL, 50–62
Sixth International Conference on the History of Cartography, XXXIV, 230

Sixth Naval History Symposium, United States Naval Academy, mentioned, XLII, 244
Skandia Pacific Oil Engine Co., Oakland, California, XXXII, 31
Skara Brae (in the Bay of Skaill), photo of, L, 127
Skate, U.S.S. *(1959),* XX, 174
"Skeets," long-handled dippers, XXXI, plate 4
Skelton, R. A., VII, 85; XVI, 282–284; XXVI, 230; *Captain James Cook—After Two Hundred Years: A commemorative address delivered before the Hakluyt Society,* reviewed, XXX, 222; *Explorer's Maps,* reviewed, XIX, 307; *Maps: A Historical Survey of Their Study and Collecting,* reviewed, XXXIII, 221
Skene, Captain Alexander, XLIII, 44
Skeps Byggerij, by Åke Classon Rålamb (1691), XXX, 83
Skerrett, Rear Admiral Joseph S., XXXIV, 212 ff.
Skerrett, R. G., VIII, 68
Sketch of Berry Islands, Bahamas, XLIX, 124
Skiff, St. Lawrence, XXVI, plate 7
Skillin, Simeon, relief carving attributed to, Pictorial Supplement, XXXVII, plate XXIV
Skillings, Warren F., XXVIII, 238; XXX, 228; XXXI, 3; XXXVII, 156
Skin boats, North American, XXV, 295–297
Skinner, A. H., review by, XLIV, 133–134
Skinner, John S., XXVIII, 192–194
Skinner, Lieutenant Commander, XLIX, 209
Skinner, Robert P., Consul General, XXXIV, 157 ff.
Skinner, Thomas, C., III, 271; VI, 155; lithograph of S. S. *America,* reviewed, I, 188
Skipjack, schooner *(1779),* XXXIX, 213
Skipjack (boat), IV, 269
Skjold, bark (1858), VI, 82
Skomvaer, bark *(1890),* VI, 77
Skottoe, Nicholas Joseph, XXVI, 204
"Skysail Yard on Ship *Torrens,*" document contributed by A. D. Edwardes, XXIII, 284
Slacke, Benjamin, V, 68 ff.
Slacum, William A., XXIX, 93, 94
Slade, R. and J., XXVIII, 279, 282
Slade, W. J., and Basil Greenhill, *Westcountry Coasting Ketches,* reviewed, XXXVI, 145–146
Slafter, Edmund F., L, 5
Slater, Commander W. D., XL, 42
Slater, John, XXIX, 236
Slater, Samuel, XXIX, 205
Slaven, Anthony and Fred M. Walker, editors, *European Shipbuilding: One Hundred Years of Change,* reviewed, XLIV, 136–137
Slavers in Paradise: The Peruvian Slave Trade in Polynesia, 1862–1864, by H. E. Maude, reviewed, XLIII, 224–226
Slavery, Insurrections, etc., XII, 222; XXXII, 171
Slavery, Negro, introduction into Mascarenes, XXV, 6
Slave ships, XL, 293
Slave trade:
    17th century, XL, 293
    Rhode Island, XII, 222; XXXV, 289; XIX, 114; XXI, 28; XXXII, 171
    See also Slave ships; Slave traders; Triangle trade
Slave trade, I, 348, 389; XII, 222–228; XIX, 114–119; XXI, 28–41; XXX, 178 f.; Slave irons, slave decks, XXX, 239; Slave Trade Act of 1819, XXXII, 264
Slave traders:
    Biography, XXXV, 289
    United States, XII, 222
    —, **Maine,** XIX, 114
    See also Slave trade, Triangle trade
Slaving center, XXX, 230
Slayton, Captain William, VI, 180–181 ff.
Sleeper, Sylvester B., XIII, 54 ff.
Sleigh, William B., Jr., review by, XLVIII, 186
Slentz, S. D., XXXVI, 241
Slessor, Sir John, RAF Coastal Commander, XLV, 57
Slidell, schooner, XXI, 97; *(1863),* VIII, 231
Slidell, John, XXIX, 11, 20 n., 96, 97
Slidell, William J., XXI, 75
Sliney, Patrick, XXXIV, 13
Sloan, Edward William, III, *Benjamin Franklin Isherwood, Naval Engineer: The Years as Engineer in Chief, 1861–1869,* reviewed, XXVI, 286–287
Sloan, Captain William, XII, 37
Sloan Shipbuilding Corp., XXXII, 163
Sloat, Commodore J. D., XXIX, 99
Slocum, James Garfield, XVIII, 191, 198
Slocum, Joshua, XXVIII, 55; XXXVI, 263
Slocum, Captain Joshua, XVIII, 189–200, plates 13, 14; XIX, 232
Slocum, Victor, *Captain Joshua Slocum,* reviewed, X, 156–157
Sloops, XIII, 177
Sloops, II, 311 ff.; VI, 166
Sloops and Shallops, by William A. Baker, reviewed, XXVI, 284–285
Smale, Captain Rudolph, *There Go the Ships,* reviewed, III, 92
Small, Benjamin, XXXI, 130
Small, Edwin W., I, 102; query by, III, 177
"Small-boat whaling in the Azores," by Mrs. Weston Howland, XXVIII, 284–286
Smalley, Anthony, XXV, 106–107
Smalley, James A., XXII, 236
Small Sword Society, XXX, 155
Small Yachts: Their Design and Construction, by C. P. Kundhart, reviewed, XLIX, 232
Smeaton, John, VII, 278–280
Smedley, Samuel, XXXI, 134
Smelser, Marshall, VI, 307; XXXI, 217; "Admiral Sir Peter Parker's First Ship of the Line," III, 266; "Clinton Roosevelt's Invulnerable Steam Battery, 1835," XX, 167–173, plate 5; *The Congress Founds the Navy,* reviewed, XX, 149; "The Insular Campaign of 1759: Martinique," VI, 290–300, plates 35–36; "The Insular Campaign of 1759: Guadeloupe," VII,

21–34, plate 3; "Note on DNB and the Evacuation of Martinique, 1759," III, 168–169
Smelser, Marshall, and William L. Davisson, "The Longevity of Colonial Ships," XXXIII, 16–19
Smerwick Harbour, map of, XLIX, 17
Smidt, Burgermeister Johann, XXVII, 256, 262
Smith, Captain Alex, XXI, 101
Smith, Vice Admiral Allan E., U.S.N. (ret), "The Sixth Battle Squadron, A Reminiscence," XL, 50–62
Smith, Captain A., VII, 61
Smith, Captain Angus, XXI, 101
Smith, Bernard, Andrew David and Rudiger Joppien, *The Charts and Coastal Views of Captain Cook's Voyages: The Voyage of the* Endeavor, *1768–1771* (The Hakluyt Society Extra Series No. 43), reviewed, XLIX, 318
Smith, Captain C. F., XXI, 101
Smith, Captain C. G., XXI, 106
Smith, Captain Charles, XXXVI, 90 ff.; XXXVIII, 242
Smith, D. E. Huger, XXXIX, 163
Smith, Daniel Scott, XXXIV, 68–69 n.
Smith, Captain David C., XXI, 101
Smith, David John, VII, 47
Smith, Dorrien, XXIX, 138
Smith, Edward, XXVI, 175, plate 18
Smith, Eugene W., *Passenger Ships of the World—Past and Present,* reviewed, XXIII, 228; *Trans-Atlantic Passenger Ships, Past and Present,* reviewed, VIII, 74
Smith, Freddie, XXXVIII, 215
Smith, Captain Frederick, XXV, 104
Smith, Sir Frederick, XXXV, 43
Smith, Gaddis, "Agricultural Roots of Maritime History," XLIV, 5–10
Smith, George F., XXXIX, 14
Smith, George Girdlin, XXII, 197
Smith, Captain Gilbert L. XXV, 103
Smith, H. Armour and A. Day Bradley, "George Watson's *Diagram of Navigation,*" XI, 147–149
Smith, Captain Haldor, XXXVI, 273
Smith, Captain Henry, XLI, 302
Smith, Hervey Garrett, *The Marlinspike Sailor,* reviewed, XXXII, 149
Smith, Captain J., XXVIII, 116
Smith, Captain J. A., XVIII, 84
Smith, Jabez, XIV, 52, 59
Smith, Captain Jacob, XVIII, 121
Smith, James, XIV, 252
Smith, Captain James E., XXI, 101
Smith, Jay D., *The Commodores,* reviewed, XXX, 73–75
Smith, Jedediah, XXIX, 93
Smith, Job, XXIV, 59
Smith, John, XXI, 16, 21, 112–117
Smith, Captain John, XIV, 7, 189; XXI, 101, 133, 136; XXV, 61, 236, 239; XXVI, 11; XXVIII, 259; XXX, 40, 302; XXXVII, 9; L, 11
Smith, Captain John P., XXI, 101
Smith, Joseph, XXX, 96 n.

Smith, Admiral Joseph, XXXV, 58
Smith, Joseph B., XXVII, 271
Smith, Captain Joseph H., VII, 128, 130, 136 n., 148, 150, 152–156, 163, 165
Smith, Captain Joshua B., XXXVIII, 268
Smith, Josias, XXV, 124, 126
Smith, Junius, I, 318
Smith, Kelley & Co., XXIV, 27
Smith, Kennedy and Co., XVI, 252; XXII, 13; XLIII, 211 ff.
Smith, Leah, XLIV, 110
Smith, Leon, XXXVI, 200
Smith, Lorenzo, XXXIII, 54
Smith, Lucy, XXXVIII, 211
Smith, Mary Lou, editor, *Woods Hole Reflections,* reviewed, XLV, 136
Smith, Captain Moses, XLVII, 16
Smith, Nathan Skiff, XXVII, 98, 106, 107
Smith, Captain O. F., XVII, 68
Smith, Philip Chadwick Foster, XXIV, 75; XLVI, 154; XXVIII, 237–238; XXX, 199; XXXVII, 81; XL, 84; editorial mention, XLIII, 244
Editorials by, XXIX, 3–4, 79–80, 141–142, 229–230; XXX, 3–8, 79–80, 153–154, 227–228; XXXI, 3, 83, 157, 233; XXXII, 3, 79, 153, 229; XXXIII, 3, 77, 153, 229; XXXIV, 3, 79, 153, 229; XXXV, 3, 75, 151, 225; XXXVI, 3, 77, 153, 229; XXXVII, 3, 79, 155, 229; XXXVIII, 3, 79, 155, 231; XXXIX, 3, 81, 157, 233; reviews by, XXVI, 75, 222–223; XXVII, 72, 74–75, 287–289; XXVIII, 70–71, 225–227, 233–234; XXIX, 141–142, 283, 288; XXX, 220–221, 222–223, 299; XXXI, 75, 227, 228; XXXII, 289, 293; XXXIII, 68; XXXIV, 145, 281, 283, 285; XXXV, 213, 215; (Volume XXXVI-XL), 147
Document contributed by, XXX, 294–296; research notice, XLI, 69; **The American Neptune,** list of Maritime Titles in Print by Member Organizations of the Council of American Maritime Museums, XXXIX, 58–77; *The Artful Roux, Marine Painters of Marseilles,* reviewed, XXXIX, 144, mention, XXXIX, 254; *Captain Samuel Tucker (1747–1833), Continental Navy,* reviewed, XXXVII, 72; *The Empress of China,* reviewed, XLIV, 205; "The *Empress of China's* voyage, 1784–1785," XLVI, 25–33; *Fired by Manley Zeal: A Naval Fiasco of the American Revolution,* reviewed, XXXVIII, 70; *The Frigate* Essex *Papers: Building the Salem Frigate, 1798–1799,* reviewed, XXXV, 68–70; "In Troubled Waters: The Elusive Schooner *Hannah,*" XXX, 86–116; Editor, *The Journals of Ashley Bowen (1728–1813) of Marblehead,* reviewed, XXXIII, 305–307; "The Little Men: Carved Shop Signs of the Navigating Instrument Sellers," XXXIV, 197–210; *More Marine Paintings and Drawings in the Peabody Museum,* reviewed, XL, 143; *Philadelphia on the River,* reviewed, XLIX, 313; "The Salem Marine Society, 1766–1966," XXVI, 272–279

Smith, Philip Chadwick Foster and Frederick S. Allis, Jr., Editors, *Seafaring in Colonial Massachusetts,* reviewed, XLII, 69-71, 150–151, 310–311
Smith, R. Lawrence, XLI, 191
Smith, Captain Robert, XXI, 101
Smith, Robert, Secretary of the Navy, XLIII, 138; XXXIV, 127 ff.
Smith, Robert, Jr., XXV, 26
Smith, Captain Robert Nelson, XXI, 101
Smith, S., and Co., VIII, 303, 322
Smith, S. and F., VIII, 303, 322
Smith, Captain S. G., XIV, 130
Smith, Captain S. S., XXI, 101
Smith, S. W., VII, 281
Smith, Sallie (Mrs. Frederick Smith), XXV, 104
Smith, Samuel, VIII, 303 ff.; XXXVI, 63
Smith, Captain Samuel, XXI, 101
Smith, Samuel H., XXVIII, 37, 39, 40, 43
Smith, Stanton M., "Colonel John Stevens," XII, 239, plates 20–22; "Reminiscences of Isle au Haut," XI, 218–220
Smith, Susan Adelaide, XXX, 294
Smith, Thomas, XXXI, 207, 211
Smith, Sir Thomas, XXXI, 86
Smith, Thomas H., XXVII, 98, 103, 104, 106–109
Smith, Captain W., XVIII, 84
Smith, W. H., XVII, 47
Smith, Captain W. H., XXI, 106; XXXV, 16
Smith, Dr. Whitney, "*Constitution's* Not So Tattered Ensign," XXXVII, 128–137
Smith, William, XXVII, 46 ff.; XXXIX, 30
Smith, Captain William, XXI, 101
Smith, William P., XXVIII, 179, 180 n.–184 n.
Smith, Rear Admiral Sir William Sidney, L, 29
Smith and Dimon (shipbuilders), I, 42
Smith and Ebbs, Ltd., VIII, 302–324
Smith and Rodger, XXVI, 18, 208
Smith and Venner, VIII, 303 ff.
Smith K. Martin, schooner (1899), I, 70
Smith & Rhuland, Ltd., XXX, 80
Smith's Dock Co., Ltd., XLV, 49
Smithsonian, schooner *(1861),* VIII, 221
Smithsonian Institution, Washington, D. C., VII, 162; XIV, 13, 14; XXV, 232, 295–296
Smith Townsend, schooner, XXI, 90; *(1862),* XII, 58
"Smoking Lamp, The," by Captain Edgar K. Thompson, U.S.N. (ret.), XXV, 34
"Smollett's Sailors," by Nathan Comfort Starr, XXXII, 81–99
Smuggling, XXXI, 19
   California, XXXII, 117
   Massachusetts (Boston), X, 144
   Plata River system (Argentina and Uruguay), XLVII, 162
   See also Contraband trade
"Smuggling, Boston, 1807–1815," by John D. Forbes, X, 143–154

Smull, Thomas, XXX, 229 ff.
Smull, Thomas and Co., XXX, 174, 180, 181
Smyrna, brig (1825), XIV, 34, 41; (1839), XIV, 41; XXII, 216; XLV, 181
Smyth, Brigadier General Alexander, XL, 25
Smyth, Admiral Sir Jeremy, R.N., IV, 261–162
Smythe, Donald, "Pershing Goes 'Over There': The Baltic Trip," XXXIV, 262–277
Smythe, Sir Thomas, XXXVII, 178
Snapper, British brig *(1820),* XXXII, 271; XLVII, 28
Snare, Captain Elisha W., XLIX, 30
Snark, ship *(1907),* XLVI, 194
Sneed, James R., XV, 112 ff.
Sneider, Christopher, XL, 277
Snell, Captain Thomas, L, 270 ff.
Sniffen, Harold S., VII, 315; query by, II, 81
Sniffen, Harold S. and Alexander Crosby Brown, *James and John Bard,* reviewed, XI, 300
Snipe, American ship *(1822),* XXIX, 89
Snow, Alice Rowe, IV, 42; *Log of a Sea Captain's Daughter,* reviewed, IV, 338
Snow, Edward Rowe, IV, 336; *Great Storms and Famous Shipwrecks of the New England Coast,* reviewed, IV, 337–338; *Story of Minot's Light, The,* reviewed, I, 189
Snow, Captain Israel, XVI, 211–213
Snow, James M., shop of, Pictorial Supplement, XXXIII, plate XXIII
Snow, Loum, XXXIX, 96
Snow, P. C., American Consul, XXXI, 183
Snow, Samuel, XXIII, 212; XVIII, 133–134
Snow & Burgess, ship (1878), V, 139
Snowdon, bark (1869), III, 263
Snowflake, H.M. corvette *(1943),* L, 219 ff.
Snyder, J. W., Jr., contributed document, V, 157–162
Soames, William, XXVI, 204
Soames, Captain William, XXII, 9
Soc. d'Armement Van Hemelryck & Cie., Paris, XXXII, 33
Social History of the Navy, A, by Michael Lewis, reviewed, XXII, 147–148
Societies. *See* type of society, e.g. Historical societies
Societies, historical and others, associations, etc.:
   Buffalo Historical Society, VII, 303, plate 37
   Chicago Historical Society, VI, 194 n., plates 29–30; VII, 43 n., 298 n., plates 5–6; VIII, 134 n., plate 15
   Hakluyt Society, VI, 308–309; VII, 81–86
   Historical Society of Pennsylvania, VI, 253 ff.; VIII, 12 n. ff
   Maine Historical Society, IX, 133 n
   Maryland Historical Society, VI, 101, 302 ff
   Nantucket Historical Association, VI, 137, 234–235, plate 19
   Naval Historical Foundation, IX, 160, 237–238
   New Hampshire Historical Society, VII, 167–169, 201 n. ff
   New York Historical Society, VII, plate 39; VIII, plate 21

Old Dartmouth Historical Society, IX, 19
Peabody Museum Marine Associates, VI, 155, 307; VIII, 3–4
San Diego Marine Research Society, X, 121
San Diego Zoological Society, X, 120–121
Society of Naval Architects and Marine Engineers, VI, 86, 157
Steamship Historical Society of America, VI, 235, 236, 307; IX, 233–234
Washington County (Penna.) Historical Society, VIII, 278
Society for Nautical Rearch, The, XXXV, 3, 151
Society for the Establishment of Useful Manufactures, XXXI, 136
Society for the History of Discoveries, XXVIII, 4
Society Islands, boats of, XIII, 93 ff.
Society of Merchant Adventurers of Bristol, XX, 6–9
Society of Naval Architects and Marine Engineers, IV, 78
Society of Naval Architects and Marine Engineers, NY, VI, 86, 157
Socony, tanker *(1892),* XXXVIII, 176
Socony-Vacuum Oil Co., L, 260 ff.
Soestdyk, steamship (1909), XIV, 112
Sofia, brig *(1861),* XI, 288
Soissons, auxiliary (1918), XXXII, 23, 30
Sojun Maru (ex-*Emperor*) *(1866),* XLIII, 214
Sokokis, steamship (1894), XXIV, 241
Sokoloff, Jules, XXXVI, 9, 10, 24, 28, 29
Sol, General Jesue del, XXXVI, 91, 95
Solana, steamship (1921), X, 142
Soledad Cos, schooner *(1861),* XI, 288
Soleil Royal, French warship [model] (1690), XVI, 102
Soler, steamship *(1863),* XII, 160
Soleta, schooner *(1861),* VIII, 221, 227
Soley, James Russell, XXIX, 6 n.
Soley, John Codman, XXXIII, 264 ff.
Solferino, French ironclad, XXIX, 13 n.
Solferino, French warship [model] (1861), XVI, 103
Solicitor General, sloop, XXII, 86
Solid, bark (1864), IV, 240
"Solitary Grave of Diego Ramirez Islands, The," by Captain Edgar K. Thompson, XVIII, 177
Solomon, armed sloop *(1749),* XLVIII, 36 ff.
Solomon Islands, Discovery and exploration, XXV, 248. *See also* Oceania
Solomon Islands, Western Pacific: VI, 91–92, 139–152; XXX, 205, 215
  exploration of during voyage of *Alliance,* 1787, XXV, 248–261, plates 17, 27, 28
  maps, Mendaña's expedition of 1568, XXV, 249
  maps, eighteenth-century navigators, XXV, 253, plates 27–28
Solomon Piper, bark (1845), figurehead of, Pictorial Supplement, XXXVII, plate XVI
Solon, brig *(1835),* XII, 184

Sømandens Tøj, by Henning Henningsen, reviewed, XL, 230
"Some Blockade-Runners of the Civil War," by Arthur C. Wardle, III, 131–140
Some Historic Ships and their Models in the Francis Russell Hart Nautical Museum, by James R. Jack, reviewed, I, 189
"Some Lengthy Open-boat Voyages in the Pacific Ocean," by F. W. Howay, IV, 53–57
"Some Misconceptions Concerning the Spinnaker," by John Lyman, XXXII, 58–63
"Some Missionary Ships in the Pacific," by Philip H. Cook, X, 264–279
"Some Notes Concerning the Dutch West Indies During the American Revolutionary War," by F. C. van Oosten, XXXVI, 155–169
"Some Notes on the Paper of the *Atlantic Neptune,*" by Edwin B. Newman and Augustus P. Loring, XLVI, 173–178
"Some Notes on the Penobscot Photographs," by Andrew Willis, XII, 305, plates 29–32
"Some Philadelphia Ships Condemned at Jamaica during the Revolution," by Langton Haldane-Robertson, II, 203–208
Somerby, Frederic, XXV, 48
Somer, Richard, L, 245 ff.
Somerby, Horatio, XXV, 48
Somerby, J. F. (engraver), XXV, 48
Somerby, Joseph, XXV, 48
Somerby, Lorenzo, XXV, 48
"Some Replicas of Historic Ships," by Alexander Crosby Brown, XIV, 105–114, plates 11, 12
Somers, schooner *(1814),* XLIV, 172
Somers, ship *(1842),* XL, 131
Somers, ship *(1941),* XLV, 52
Somers, U.S. brig (1842), XXV, 68
Somers, Colonel Richard, XXXIX, 212
Somersby, Captain, XXX, 115
Somerset, grain elevator *(1883),* XXXVIII, 141
Somerset, steamship, XXII, 219; *(1871),* XXXVII, 235
Somerset, steamship (1875), XI, 255 ff.; XII, 310; Pictorial Supplement, XXXIV, plate XIII
Somerville, schooner (1915), XXVI, plate XXVII
Somerville, J. W., XXIII, plate VI; "Tug *Seth Low,*" V, 146
Somerville Primrose & Co., XLIII, 216
Somes Sound, Maine, XXV, plate XXIV
"Something About a Buoy," by Captain Edgar K. Thompson, U.S.N. (ret.), XXVIII, 205
Somme, schooner *(1919),* XXIII, 11
Sommers, Captain Richard, XXI, 130 ff.
Sommerville, Admiral Sir James, XLII, 203 ff.
Sommerville, J. W., "East Coast Steam Schooners," IX, 71, plate 8; "The Steamer *Queen of St. Johns,* IX, 298–299, plate 32; "West India Hurricanes," VI, 132–134
Soncino, Raimondo di, XXX, 258

Sonderklasse boats *(1906),* XXX, plate XXII
Songo, steamship (1901), XXIV, 241, plate 28
Song of the Clyde, by Fred M. Walker, reviewed, XLVII, 57
Songo River Line, XXIV, 240 ff., plate 25
"Songo River Steamboats, The," by Theodore L. Holden and Russell W. Knight, XXIV, 233–246
Songs, sailors', XXV, 57
Songs of American Sailormen, by Joanna C. Colcord, reviewed, III, 356–357
Sonneck, Dr. O. G. T., XXII, 106, 107, 115, 117, 118, 120, 126, 129
Sonoma, U.S. frigate *(1864),* XLVII, 31
Sonoma, U.S. steamship *(1862),* XXIV, 208 ff., plate 24
Sonora, ship (1854), XVII, 116
Sonora, steamship (1853), X, 130; *(1865),* XII, 235
Sonorense, Mexican schooner *(1845),* XXX, 46
Sons of the Thames, steamship (1844), XXIV, plate XVIII
Soochow, steamship (1858), XVII, 44; XVIII, 72; (1865), XVIII, 72
Soochow, steamship (ex-*St. Theodosius*) *(1858),* XLIX, 23; *(1864),* XLIII, 92 ff.
Soochow Creek, Shanghai, XXX, 157 ff.
Sooghoodlee, steamship *(1886),* XI, 258 ff.
Sooloo, clipper ship *(1877),* XLVI, 63
Sooloo (II), ship *(1861),* XLVII, 119 ff.; line drawings of, XLVII, 120, 126, 132, 134; at Union Wharf, Boston, XLVII, 129; color scheme chart, XLVII, 135; author's model of, XLVII, 136
Sophia, bark, XXI, 102; *(1862),* VIII, 227
Sophia, boat [model], XVI, 101
Sophia, brig *(1814),* XLII, 116
Sophia, schooner (1787), XIV, 41; *(1864),* XV, 130
Sophia, steamship (1818), VI, 195–196; *(1853),* XIV, 200
Sophia Jane, steamship *(1831),* XXXV, 248
Sophia M., brig (1833), XXIV, 57
Sophia R. Luhrs, bark (1874), IV, 242
Sophia Sutherland, schooner, XLVI, 190 ff.; *(1900),* XXXVIII, 88
Sophia Thornton, whaler *(1865),* XXVII, 269, 272, 273, 276
Sophie, ship *(1922),* XVIII, 211
Sophronia, schooner *(1802),* IV, 45
Sorenson, Captain William, XVIII, 204–213
Sorrento, steamship (ex-*Guadeloupe,* ex-*Tampico,* ex-*Imperador*) *(1889),* XXVI, 194
Sort, schooner *(1864),* XII, 232, 235
Sotero, steamship (1882), XIV, 134
Soublette, General Carlos, XXX, 261, 263
Souchez, auxiliary (1918), XXXII, 24, 30
Souchon, Admiral Wilhelm, XXXVI, 34, 44
Soule, Captain Alexander, XXI, 102
Soule, Captain, XXV, 290–291
Soule, Captain Freeman, XIV, 37; XIX, 41
Soule, Phelps, "The Hampton Boat," III, 141–147
Soule, Whitney and Co., XXX, 245

Sounders, American, Pictorial Supplement, XXXV, plate XXVIII (lower).
"Sound Off," by Captain Edgar K. Thompson, U.S.N. (ret.), XXIX, 63
"Source of Whittier's 'The Dead Ship of Harpswell,' The," by Kenneth Scott, VI, 223–227
South, steamship *(1860),* VII, 127 n.
Southack, Captain Cyprian, XXV, 240; XXXV, 154
South Africa. Foreign relations:
  Confederate States of America, XXVI, 96
  United States, XXVI, 96; XXXIV, 81
"South African Light on American Fur Trade Vessels," by W. Wilfried Schuhmacher, XL, 46–49
South America, bark *(1861),* XXI, 239, 256
South America, steamship (1860), IV, 143 ff.
South America, whaler *(1850),* XXXIII, 127
South America. *See* names of countries and rivers; Harbors; Shipping; Steam navigation
South America, boats of, XIII, 89 ff.
South America, steamship lines to, IV, 137–163
South America, watercraft of, XXVI, 33–36
South American, bark *(1861),* XV, 108 n.
South American and General Steam Navigation Co., XXVI, 192
Southampton, frigate *(1812),* XLIV, 175 ff.
Southampton, ship (1851), III, 62
Southampton, Earl of, XIV, 7
Southard, Captain Fred XXXVI, 269, 270
Southard, S. H., XXX, 297
Southard, Samuel L., Secretary of the Navy, XXXII, 272; XL, 31, 216; XLII, 165 ff.
South Boston Iron Works, XLV, 39
Southbourne, steamship (1881), XI, 255
South Carolina, battleship *(1910),* XLVII, 249
South Carolina, frigate (1776), XXXIX, 160 ff.
South Carolina, merchant ship *(1798),* XLVII, 25
South-Carolina, revenue cutter (1798), XLVII, 24
South Carolina, ship *(1776),* XIII, 36
South Carolina, ship (1851), V, 154, 242
South Carolina, U.S.S., XXVIII, 107; *(1861),* XI, 269
South Carolina (SC):
  Charts, XXI, 260
  History, Revolution (1775–1788), XIII, 29
  See also Charleston; Shipbuilding; Shipowners
"South Carolina Frigate: A History of the Ship *John Adams,* The," by W. M. P. Dunne, XLVII, 22–32
South Carolina Tricentennial Commission, XXX, 79, 81 ff.
"'*South Carolina* We've Lost': The Bizarre Saga of Alexander Gillon and His Frigate, The," by Richard G. Stone, Jr., XXXIX, 159–172
Southeast Caribbean, Map I, XXXII, 181
South Eastern Sail: From the Medway to the Solent, 1840–1940, by Michael Bouquet, reviewed, XXXIII, 213–214
Southern, schooner, XXI, 95; (1832), XXIV, 59; *(1861),* XI, 288

Southern Chief, bark *(1894)*, XLII, 262
Southern Cross, ship (1868), III, 172–173; *(1875)*, XXXIII, 61
Southerner, schooner *(1861)*, XI, 288
Southerner, ship (1861), VIII, 221
Southerner, steamship (1846), XLVII, 35; XLVIII, 114
Southerner, vessel *(1846)*, XXXVI, 170
Southerner [The], steamship (1863), III, 140
"Southern Hemisphere Fur Sealing from Atlantic Canada," by A. B. Dickinson, XLIX, 278–290
Southern Importing and Exporting Co., IX, 44, 47, 48
Southern Independence, schooner, XXI, 88, 102; *(1861)*, XI, 266, 288; XII, 58
Southern New England Maritime History Symposium, Mystic Seaport Museum, mentioned, XLII, 244
Southern Pacific Railroad, XXV, 264–267
Southern Pride, whale catcher *(1939)*, XLV, 49
Southern Republic, sloop, XXI, 98; *(1862)*, XII, 58
Southern Rights, schooner, XXI, 86; *(1863)*, XII, 160
"Southern Sea Otters and the Ship *Hope*," by Thomas Dunbabin, XV, 81–82
Southern Star, sloop *(1863)*, XII, 160
Southey, Robert, XXV, 233
Southgate, ship, XXXVI, 3
South Kingston, vessel, XXVI, 47
South Park, whaleback barge (1896), XXV, 174
Southron, schooner, XXI, 93; *(1861)*, XI, 288
South Sea Castle, H.M.S., XXVI, 47
South Sea Vagabonds, by John W. Wray, reviewed, I, 409
South Sea Whale Fishing, 1835, XXIX, plate XXVI
"South's Scottish Sea Monster, The," by William E. Geoghegan, Thomas W. Green, Captain R. Steen Steensen, R.D.N., Frank F. Merli, XXIX, 5–29
South Stack Lighthouse and Signal Station, ca. 1832, XXIX, 198, plate XX
South Street Seaport Museum, Friends of, XXVII, 156
South Street Seaport Museum, *Maritime Titles in Print*, XXXIX, 75
South to the Pole: The Early History of the Ross Sea Sector, Antarctia, by L. B. Quartermain, reviewed, XXVIII, 73
Sovereign, C.S. transport *(1862)*, XXV, 135
Sovereign, steamship *(1843)*, XX, 262
Sovereign, yacht *(1964)*, XXIV, 231
Sovereign of the Seas, ship *(1846–1857*, XLII, 121 ff.; (1852), VII, 324; XIX, plate V; *(1853)*, XXVI, 165, 167 n., 168; XXX, 218; (1868), III, 173
Sowle, Captain Cornelius, IV, 56–57
Soya, yacht *(1907)*, XXXVI, 247
Spain, Navy. VI, 179. *See also* Armada
Spadille, sloop *(1748)*, IX, 144
Spalding, Charles, VII, 277–278
Spalding, Thomas, XXXV, 236
Spangler, Henry, XXXVI, 48
Spanish-American War (1898), XXXVI, 257; XL, 167; XLI, 93

"Spanish-American War and United States Army Shipping, The," by William Joe Webb, XL, 167–191
Spanish Caribbean: Trade and Plunder, 1530–1630, The, by Kenneth R. Andrews, reviewed, XXXIX, 150–151
"Spanish Expedition to Chesapeake Bay in 1609, A," by Victor M. Tyler, XVII, 181–194
Spanish Lake, The, by O. H. K. Spate, reviewed, XL, 229
Spanish Lake: The Pacific since Magellan, The, Vol. I, by Oskar H. K. Spate, reviewed, XLV, 206
Spanish Scientists in the New World: The Eighteenth-Century Expeditions, by Iris H. W. Engstrand, reviewed, XLIV, 278
"Spanish Treasure Fleet of 1551, The," by Robert S. Chamberlain, VI, 241–252
Spanish voyages in Pacific, IV, 88–93
Sparhawk, Nathaniel, XX, 269
Sparitiate, ship of the line *(1833)*, L, 32
Spark, schooner, XXIX, 197
Spark, ship *(1815)*, XL, 39 ff.; *(1858)*, XXXIV, 18 ff.
Spark, steamship, XXII, 15, 16, 17, 18, 21, 22, 24, 31, 32, 38, 39, 42; *(1849)*, XVI, 161; XVIII, 72
Spark, U.S. brig (1814), V, 79, plate 6; *(1824)*, XLIV, 166
Spark, Alexander Brodie, XLIII, 203
Sparkes, George Crabbe, XXVI, 204
Sparling, Fred, XXXVI, 233 n.
Sparr, Captain John, XVI, 131
Sparre, Count Pehr, I, 203–204; III, 19, 89, 279; VIII, 265; photographs by, II, plates 38–42; answered query, I, 312; letter to the Editors, I, 326–327
Sparrow, schooner *(1813)*, XLII, 107 ff.
Sparrow, James L., XIII, 54
Sparrow, Captain Thomas, XLVIII, 95
Sparrowhawk, H.M.S. *(1870)*, XXXVI, 232
Sparrow-Hawk, sloop *(1626)*, XIII, 51–64; XIV, 211–212; XV, 277 ff.; Pictorial Supplement, XXXVI, plate II
"*Sparrow-Hawk*, A Seventeenth-Century Vessel in Twentieth-Century America," by H. H. Holly, XIII, 51–64, plates 4–8
Spartan, schooner (1830), XXIV, 45, 59
Spartan, ship *(1825)*, XXXIV, 256
Sparton, British frigate *(1814)*, XXVIII, 118
Spate, Oskar H. K., *Monopolists and Freebooters: The Pacific since Magellan,* Vol. II, reviewed, XLV, 206; *Paradise Lost and Found: The Pacific Since Magellan* [Vol. III], reviewed, XLIX, 319; *The Spanish Lake,* reviewed, XL, 229; *The Spanish Lake: The Pacific since Magellan,* Vol. I; reviewed, XLV, 206
Spaulding, steamship, XXI, 95; *(1863)*, VIII, 231
Spaulding, Captain James, X, 218
Speake, Josias, XXII, 266, 274
Speake, Lieutenant Josias, XXXIX, 31
Spear, Nathan, XXXII, 120
Spears, John R., XXXII, 267
Spearwater's Sea Foam House, XXXVII, 92
Spec, steamship (1862), XVI, 162, 163; XVIII, 72
Special Exhibits by other museums, XLIV, 63; XLV, 65
Specie, schooner *(1861)*, XV, 124

"Specifications for a Schooner's Sails," document contributed by M. V. Brewington, VI, 138
Specifications for four vessels, VI, 228–231, 304–306
Spector, Ronald, "Roosevelt, the Navy, and the Venezuela Controversy: 1902–1903," XXXII, 257–263
Spectre, oyster sloop (1883), I, 71
Spectre, Peter H. and Steven Lang, *On the Hawser: A Tugboat Album,* reviewed, XLII, 138–139
Spedding, D. R., XVII, 216; XVIII, 84
Spedding, Captain John, XXXV, 43
Spee, Admiral Graf von, XXVIII, 106 n., 108
"Speed, Size and Model," by John Lyman, VIII, 151–152
Speed records, clipper ship, VIII, 325–330
Speedwell, centerboard schooner (1896), I, 73
Speedwell, schooner *(1775),* XXX, 110; *(1777),* V, 187; (1817), IV, 335
Speedwell, ship *(1602),* L, 9; *(1604),* XXII, 136 ff.; XXV, 238; *(1620),* XIV, 6
Speedwell, ship *(1776),* XLVIII, 16; *(1828),* XLIX, 254; *(1861),* XIV, 46
Speedwell, sloop *(1725),* XXXVII, 267; *(1758),* XXI, 8
Speedwell, steamship *(1877),* XLV, 81, 187
"*Speedwell*—Another Look, The" by Gershom Bradford, XXII, 136–141
Speedwell Iron Works, IX, 250
Spence, H.M.S. *(1740),* XXVI, 38
Spence, Captain R. T., XXXVIII, 53
Spence, Captain Robert T., L, 245 ff.
Spence, Graeme, XXX, 206, 211
Spence, Isaac, XXXVIII, 60
Spence, James, XXIX, 15, 16
Spence, Robert T., XXI, 139
Spencer, H.M.S. *(1814),* XXIV, 179 n.
Spencer, ship (1799), XXVII, 142
Spencer, U.S. revenue cutter (1843), XXIV, 8 ff.; *(1845),* XXXIX, 219
"Spencer, Browning, and Rust: Nautical Opticians," by W. R. Chaplin, XIII, 66–67
Spencer, Browning & Rust; instruments by, Pictorial Supplement, XXXV, plate VI
Spencer, Henry, IV, 233
Spencer, Herbert R., IV, 252; V, 165; "'The Iron Steamer,'" IV, 183–192; "Sir Isaac Newton on Saumarez Patent Log," XIV, 214
Spencer, John C., XXIV, 13, 14
Spencer, Lord, XXX, 210
Spencer, R. B., XXIV, plate V
Spencer, Dr. Thomas, XL, 36
Spencer, Thomas T., "The Ocean Mail Controversy of 1934," XLI, 110–121
Spencer, Warren F., *The Confederate Navy in Europe,* reviewed, XLIV, 206
Spencer, William, XXXI, 204 ff.
Spencer Fullerton Baird and the U.S. Fish Commission: A Study in the History of American Science, by Dean Conrad Allard, Jr., reviewed, XLII, 306–307

Sperm whales stranded ashore, photos of, XLIX, 227–228
Sperm Whaling from New Bedford: Clifford W. Ashley's Photographs of the Bark Sunbeam *in 1904,* by Elton W. Hall, reviewed, XLIII, 56–58, 147–148
Sperry, Captain C. S., XXXV, 187
Sperry, Elmer A., XXXVIII, 125
Spey, H.M. frigate *(1943),* L, 220 ff.
Sphinx, French warship [model] (1829), XVI, 103
Sphinx, XXXII, 61 ff.
Sphinx, yacht *(1866),* XXX, 199
Spicer, Elihu, papers of, XXV, 105
Spicer, Levi (merchant of Noank, CT), XXV, 110
Spiller, Captain John W., U.S.N., VI, 307
Spiller, Roger J., editor, and Edward G. Dawson, associate editor, *Dictionary of American Military Biography* [Vol. I–III], reviewed, XLV, 257
Spin, Jacob, XV, 81
Spindler, Robert P. and Gregor Trinkaus-Randall, "Recently Processed Manuscript Collections in the Phillips Library at the Peabody Museum of Salem, XLIX, 230–231
Spindrift, ship *(1868),* XXXV, 32 ff.
Spiniks. See *Sphinx.*
Spinnaker, XXXII, 58. *See also* Sails
Spinnaker, origin of the term, XXX, 199
Spinney, David, *Rodney,* reviewed, XXXII, 296
Spirit, yacht *(1907),* XXXVI, 243, 244, 246, plate 6
Spirit II, yacht (1909), XXXVI, 245, 246
Spirit of the Wind, XXI, 90
Spirit room, on naval vessels, XXV, 142
Spiteful, H.M.S. *(1842),* XXVI, 6 n.
Spitfire, gondola *(1776),* VIII, 256; *(1779),* XXXV, 142
Spitfire, gunboat *(1814),* XLII, 107 ff.
Spitfire, schooner, XXIX, 197; *(1862),* XII, 58
Spitfire, ship *(1815),* XL, 39 ff.
Spitfire, U.S.S. *(1846),* XII, 152; XXVII, 160
Spitfire, U.S. tug *(1862),* XXV, 135
Spitsbergen whale fishery, XXVIII, 239–260
Splendid, pinky *(1832),* XXXVII, 169
Splendid, sailing packet, XXVIII, 121
Splendid, sloop *(1861),* VIII, 221; XV, 124
"'Splice the mainbrace:' The Story of a Naval Epic," by Malcolm H. Murfett, L, 291 ff.
Spofford, Tileston and Co., XLVII, 35
Spoilers of The Sea: Wartime Raiders in the Age of Steam, by John Philips Cranwell, reviewed, I, 401
Spooner, John, XXXIII, 134
Spotswood, Alexander, XXX, 137
Spotswood, Governor Alexander, VIII, 26 ff.
Spotswood, George W., XXXVI, 58
Sprague, Horatio J., XLI, 96
Sprague, Laura F., *Agreeable Situations: Society, Commerce and Art in South Maine, 1780–1830,* reviewed, XLIX, 62
Sprague, Peleg, XXI, 124
Sprague, Captain Seth, XIV, 35

Sprague, Stuart Seely, "The Whaling Ports: A Study of Ninety Years of Rivalry, 1784–1875," XXXIII, 120–130
Spratt, H. Philip, *The Birth of the Steamboat*, reviewed, XIX, 148; "El Museo Naval de Madrid," XV, 49–58, plates 3–8; "The First Iron Steamer," XIII, 157–161; "Le Musée de la Marine," XVI, 98–106, plates 9, 10; "Pioneer Transatlantic Paddle Steamers," IX, 249–272, plates 25–28; *Transatlantic Paddle Steamers*, reviewed, XI, 294; re-reviewed, XXVIII, 296
Spray, first American otter trawler, XLIV, 117
Spray, sloop *(1895)*, XVIII, 189–200, plates 13, 14; XIX, 232; *(1898)*, XXXVI, 263
Spray, steamship *(1866)*, XXIV, 53, 54, 55
Spray, yacht, XXXVI, 247 ff.
Spray, yawl *(1898)*, XXVIII, 55
Spray, W. A., "Alexander Dalrymple, Hydrographer," XXX, 200–216
Spreewald, German cruiser, XXVIII, 108 n.
Sprightly, ship *(1825)*, XLI, 289
Springer, Captain Cornelius, XXXIX, 100
Springer, Captain Joseph, XXI, 106
Springfield, ship *(1868)*, III, 70
Sprit rig, II, plate 11
Spritsail rig, XIX, 155, 274. *See also* Masts and Rigging
Spritsail, XIX, 155–199
Spritsail Barges of Thames and Medway, by Edgar J. March, reviewed, XXXII, 144–145
Sproston, John Glendy, I, 185–186
Sprout, Harold and Margaret, XXXIX, 23
Spry, sloop *(1793)*, XXII, 86
Spunkie, steamship *(1863)*, VIII, 232, 235; *(1865)*, XLIII, 299
Spunky, schooner *(1864)*, XV, 130
Spy, brig, XXV, 186; *(1833)*, XII, 29, 40
Spy, H.M.S., XXVI, 48, 51, 52, 54
Spy, schooner (ex-*Britannia*) *(1775)*, XXXIX, 194
Spy, sloop *(1887)*, XXXVIII, 83, 84
"Squaeling," query by Harold Bowditch, V, 89
Squando, ship *(1856)*, IV, 243
Square Rigged Sailing Ships, by David R. McGregor, reviewed, XXXIX, 304
Square-Rigger Round the Horn: The Making of a Sailor, by C. Ray Wilmore, reviewed, XXXIII, 146–147
"Square Sails and Fore-and-aft Sails," by R. C. Anderson, XIII, 213–214
"Square Sails and Raffees," by Captain P. A. McDonald, V, 142–145
Squier, Captain A., XX, 89 n.
Squirrel, ship *(1858)* (later *Inveijado*), XXXIV, 19
Squirrel, steamship *(1856)*, XXII, 30, 31, 37, 42, 43
St. *See* Saint.
"Stability of the Ark, The," by J. Frederick Douty, XXV, 261
Stackpole, Edouard A., XV, 3; XX, 63; XXV, 100, 101; review by, XLVIII, 190; XLIX, 61; *The Charles W. Morgan, the Last Wooden Whaleship*, reviewed, XXVII, 226–227; — A Mariner's Adventure Ashore," XLIV, 103–109; XLV, 41 ff.; "The Pilgrimage of Lt. Alexander Pinkham, U.S.N.; *Whales & Destiny, The Rivalry between America, France, and Britain for Control of the Southern Whale Fishery, 1785–1825*, reviewed, XXXIII, 221–222
Stackpole, Joshua, VII, 202
Stafford, Judge William P., XXXVII, 123
Staffordshire, ship *(1846–1857,* XLII, 121 ff.; *(1853)*, XV, 141
Stag, H.M. warship *(1761)*, XXXII, 98; *(1778)*, XLV, 248
Stag, steamship, XXI, 88, 92, 103; *(1864)*, VIII, 235, 237; IX, 33; XI, 58
Stag Hound, ship *(1850)*, I, 46; *(1846–1857)*, XLII, 121 ff.; *(1858)*, XV, 221
Stalwart, ship *(1854)*, XV, 186
Stamford, steamship *(1863)*, XIV, 288, 293
Stammers, Michael K., *The Passage Makers*, reviewed, XLII, 146–147
Stamp Act, XXVII, 218, 220
Stancliffe, Benjamin, XLVI, 261
Standard, brigantine *(1862)*, XV, 109, 114, 126
Standard, steamship *(1875)*, XXXVIII, 176, plate 5
Standard Oil Co., The, XXXVIII, 175 ff.; XVI, 107 ff.; XVIII, 10; XXXIII, 183; XLVII, 45 ff.; L, 260 ff.
Standard Oil Co. of California, XXIV
Standard Oil Co. of N. J., VIII, 75–76
Standard Oil Co. of N. Y., VIII, 279–281
Standard Pneumatic Tube Co., XXXII, 160
Standard S.S. Co., XXII, 168
"Stand by the Pic.," by Captain Edgar K. Thompson, U.S.N. (ret.), XXIX, 29
"Standing Lug, The," by John C. Bower, Jr., XX, 271–272
Stanford, Leland, XXV, 264–265; XXXI, 122 ff.
Stanford and Co., XXXI, 122
Stanley, schooner *(1864)*, XII, 233
Stanley, Charles, XXI, 120, 123, 125, 126
Stanley, Commander Fabius, XXXV, 27
Stanley, John Mix, XLVI, 49
Stanley, Samuel G. (carpenter), journal of, XXV, 110
Stann, E. Jeffrey and Anne Hoffman, editors, *Voyage to the Southern Ocean: The Letters of Lieutenant William Reynolds from the U.S. Exploring Expedition, 1838–1842,"* reviewed, L, 150
Stanton, Captain John, XV, 306–310
Stanton, Edwin M., Secretary of War, XXV, 131–132; XXXI, 66; XXXIII, 260; XLVIII, 98
Stanton, Admiral Oscar F., XLI, 247
Stanton, Samuel Ward, VII, 162; "Steam Navigation on the Carolina Sounds and the Chesapeake in 1892," *Steamship Historical Society Reprint No. 4*, reviewed, IX, 233–234
Stanton, William, *The Great United States Exploring Expedition of 1838–1842*, reviewed, XXXVIII, 148
Stanworth, Commander Charles S., XLIII, 267

Stapleton, Darwin H., "Assistant Charles O. Boutelle, of the United States Coast Survey, with the South Atlantic Blockading Squadron, 1861–1863," XXXI, 253–267

Stapleton, John, VII, 269

Star, bark (1838), painting of, Pictorial Supplement, XXXVIII, plate XX

Star, brig *(1806),* XIII, 276; *(1807),* XVI, 195

Star, schooner, XXI, 87, 91, 97, 100; (1820), XXII, 216; (1839), XXIV, 59; *(1861),* XI, 288; XII, 58, 160

Star, sloop, XXII, 236

Star, steamship (1837), VII, 65; *(1863),* XXI, plate XVI

Star, yacht *(1894),* XXXVI, 237

Starbuck, steamship *(1896),* X, 137, 138

Stark, Admiral Harold, XLII, 207

Stark, Marie Charlotte, III, 89, "Materials for Research in the Files of International Claims Commissions," III, 48–54

Stark, Suzanne J., "The Adventures of Two Women Whalers," XLIV, 22–24

Starke, Bolling, XXXIII, 32

Starkotter, hemmema (1790), VI, 165

Starlight, schooner *(1862),* XXVII, 265, 266

Starlight, ship, XXII, 240

Starling, H.M.S. *(1859),* XXVII, 168

Starling, steam gunboat *(1857),* XXII, 36

Star of Alaska, ship (1886), IV, 199–206; X, 121; XXII, 231; *(1906),* XV, 171; *(1927),* XVI, 133; XVIII, 216

Star of Bengal, ship *(1906),* VII, 292; X, 114, 118; *(1907),* XVI, 124

Star of Chile, ship (1868), VII, 292–293, plate 33; *(1910),* XVI, 122; XVIII, 213

Star of Empire, ship *(1850),* XV, 141; (1854), XX, 132; *(1846–1857,* XLII, 121 ff.

Star of England, bark *(1927),* XVI, 133; *(1928),* IV, 202–203

Star of Erin, ship *(1863),* XXIV, 23, 24, 26

Star of Falkland, ship *(1923),* XVIII, 213–222

Star of Finland, bark (1899), VII, 294; VIII, 285; *(1910),* II, 172; XVI, 122, 134; XVIII, 216

Star of France, ship, XXII, 213; *(1906),* VII, 292; X, 114, 118; *(1910),* XVI, 122; XVIII, 216

Star of Greenland, bark *(1909),* II, 294–295; *(1934),* XVI, 133; XVIII, 215

Star of Holland, ship *(1915),* XIV, 210; *(1927),* XVI, 132–134; XVIII, 216

Star of Hope, ship (1855), III, 284–286; (1868), III, 173

Star of India, bark *(1863),* VII, 288; X, 108–122, plates 15–16; *(1910),* XVI, 122; XXII, 212 ff.

"Star of India," by Karl Kortum, XXII, 212–215

Star of Italy, ship *(1906),* VII, 292; X, 114, 118; *(1910),* XVI, 122; *(1927),* XVIII, 215

Star of Lapland, bark (1901), VIII, 283; *(1910),* XVI, 5–27, 107–136; XVII, 65; XVIII, 215, 216

Star of Oregon, schooner *(1842),* XXVIII, 128, 134, 136, 138

Star of Peru, bark (1863), VII, 288; VIII, 122–126, plates 9–12; *(1910),* XVI, 122

Star of Poland, bark (1901), VIII, 279–288, plates 25–26; *(1913),* XVI, 123, 124; XVIII, 202; *(1915),* XIV, 210

Star of Russia, ship *(1906),* VII, 292; VIII, 126; X, 114, 115; *(1910),* XVI, 122

Star of Scotland, bark (1887), I, 333–344, plates facing 338–339; III, 266; IV, 325

Star of Scotland, schooner (1887–1941), I, 334, 341–342; III, 266; IV, 325; *(1942),* VII, 294, 296

Star of Scotland, ship *(1927),* XVIII, 217

"*Star of Scotland,* ex-*Kenilworth,* The," by John Lyman, I, 333–334

Star of Shetland, bark *(1924),* XVI, 131, 134; XVIII, 213, 215

Star of the East, steamship (1866), XIV, 193

Star of the South (1861), XXXVI, 188

Star of the West, ship *(1851),* XXVII, 64

Star of the West, steamship *(1861),* XLIV, 258; *(1857),* IV, 312

Star of Zealand, bark (1900), VIII, 283; *(1912),* XVI, 123, 132, 134; XVIII, 216

Starr, Major C. T., XXXV, 188

Starr, Nathan, "Smollett's Sailors," XXXII, 81–99

Starratt, Herbert Risteen, XXXIV, 201

Starrett, Captain H. A., II, 199

Stars and Stripes, ship (1862), III, 62

Stasia (ex-*Beatrice Castle*) *(1917),* XXXII, 33

"State Department's Navy: A History of the Special Service Squadron, 1920–1940, The," by Richard Millett, XXXV, 118–138

Stateliest, Ship: Queen Mary, "The, reviewed, XXIX, 289

Staten Island (near Cape Horn, South Atlantic), XXV, 184, plate 19

Staten Island Shipbuilding Co., Port Richmond, NY, XXXII, 31

Statens Sjöhistoriska Museum (Stockholm, Sweden), VI, 163 n.; XXV, 86

State of Georgia (1861), XV, 103 n.

State of Maine, ship *(1861),* XI, 288; (1878), II, plate 25

State of Maine, steamship, XXVIII, 124, 125; (1881), XXXI, plate 3; XXXIII, 90, 94; XXXIV, Pictorial Supplement, plate XVI

State of Ohio, canal boat *(1827),* VI, 204

Statesman, schooner *(1863),* XII, 160

State Street Trust Co. of Boston, *A Brief Account of the Yacht* America, reviewed, XI, 300

Station Pointer, Pictorial Supplement, XXXV, plate XXVII (lower).

Statistical Tables, XXX, 19

Staunton, barge (1828), V, 301

Staunton, Sir George, XLVIII, 256

Stavorinus, Johan Splinter, L, 287

Stayon, Lieutenant William H., XL, 132

"Staysails," query by Baron R. de Kerchove, I, 398; answered by John Lyman, III, 269

Stayton, Lieutenant Commander W. H., XXXIII, 274

Stead, Gordon W., *A Leaf Upon the Sea: A Small Ship in the Mediterranean, 1941–1943,* reviewed, L, 140
Stead, Captain John, XIII, 13, 21, 22
Stead, Joseph Rosedon, XXVI, 204
"Steam bark *Clarion,* The," note contributed by Cedric Ridgely-Nevitt, XXXVII, 140–142
Steam battery (warship), XX, 167
Steam Boat, steamship (1807), XXVII, 5–29
"*Steam Boat,* 1807–1814, The," by Cedric Ridgely-Nevitt, XXVII, 5–29
Steamboat Association, Great Lakes, VII, 53, 55, 63
Steamboat Bill of Facts [Vol. I], reviewed, I, 101; reviewed, III, 357
Steam Boat Co. of Georgia, XLVII, 34
Steam-Boat Comes to Norfolk Harbor, The, by John C. Emmerson, Jr., reviewed, IX, 78, 234
"Steamboat Decoration, A Note on," by Randall V. Mills, III, 159–161
"Steamboat Engines," query by E. W. Small, III, 177; query by John W. McCann, V, 89; answer by George W. Dyson, IV, 77; answer by H. Allen Gosnell, V, 163
Steamboat Lore of the Penobscot, by John M. Richardson, reviewed, II, 262
Steamboat on the Chesapeake: Emma Giles and the Tolchester Line, by David C. Holly, reviewed, XLVIII, 209
"Steamboat *Pocahontas,* The, 1893–1939, Typical East Coast Side-Wheeler of the 1890's," by Alexander Crosby Brown, II, 223–228
Steamboats:
  China, XLIII, 85, 186, 274
  Design and construction, X, 163; XIII, 157; XXIV, 5; XXVII, 5; L, 201
  History, VI, 253; XXVII, 254; L, 201
  United States, II, 223; XII, 148; XLIX, 114
  —, 19th century, IX, 249; XIV, 161; XIV, 278; XLIX, 96
  —, **Design and construction,** II, 5; III, XXXV
  —, **Arizona Territory,** I, 255
  —, **California,** II, 299; IX, 216
  —, **East Coast,** VIII, 246
  —, **Florida,** 19th century, VII, 115, 224
  —, **Great Lakes,** III, 333; XVIII, 273
    —, 19th century, V, XXVII; VI, 194; VII, 42, 298; VIII, 37, 132; XVII, 89; XX, 79, 250
  —, **Hudson River,** VI, 277; XVIII, 223; XXVII, 5
    —, 19th century, XXIV, 157
  —, **Maine,** XXIV, 233
  —, **Massachusetts,** XII, 288
    —, **Nantucket,** XXXIV, 258
  —, **Mississippi River,** 19th century, XVI, 28, 270
  —, **Monongahela River (W. Va. and Pa.),** XXXIII, 155
  —, **New England,** XXXIV, 258
  —, **New Jersey,** XXXVI, 251
  —, **Pennsylvania,** L, 201
  Wooden, 20th century, XXXV, 275
  See also Shipbuilding (Materials); Steam battery; Steam navigation; Steamships
Steamboats, I, 101; III, 35–47, 94, 131–140, 159–161, 161–163, 333–344, 357; IV, 77, 175–176, 327–329; V, 27–42, 169–170; VI, 136–137, 151–152, 194–211, 277–289; VII, 66, 240, 248, 249; VIII, 73–74, 158–160, 246–254; IX, 78, 298–299; X, 163–190; XI, 42–58, 251–261; XII, 148–153, 288–293, 308–310; XIII, 157–161, 214; XIV, 61–63, 115–135, 161–186, 192–202, 237–261, 278–297. *See also* Steamers, Steamships.
  219–220, 225–227, 231–232
  American, before 1824, I, 412–416
  Chesapeake Bay, I, 96
  China, XVI, 157–179, 243–269; XVII, 38–64, 134–151, 212–230, 298–314; XVIII, 59–87
  Colorado River, I, 255–274, 405–406; III, plate 34
  Florida, VII, 115–166, 224–239
  Great Lakes, I, 76–77, plate facing 73; III, 333–334; IV, 183–192; V, 27–42; VII, 42–65, 298–314; VIII, 37–60, 132–149; XVII, 89–104; XVIII, 273–300; XX, 79–103, 250–269
  Hudson River, XVI, 28–40; XVIII, 223–234
  James River, II, 223–228
  Lake Winnipesaukee, I, 411
  Stern wheel steamboats, recessed, VII, 120, 126
  Transatlantic, XIX, 128–132
Steamboats Come True, by James Thomas Flexner, reviewed, V, 92–93, 217; re-reviewed, XL, 232
Steamboats for Rondout: Passenger Service Between New York and Rondout Creed, 1829 through 1863, reviewed, XLII, 229
Steamboats out of Baltimore, by Robert H. Burgess and H. Graham Wood, reviewed, XXX, 71–72
"Steamer *Marmora,*" query by Arthur C. Wardle, V, 163
"Steamer *Queen of St. Johns,* The," by J. W. Somerville, IX, 298–299, plate 32
Steamers. *See also* Steamers, Steamboats, ??
Steam navigation:
  —, **19th century,** V, XXVII; VI, 194; VII, 42, 298, 132; VIII, 37; XVII, 89; XX, 79, 250
  Atlantic Ocean, IX, 249
  Canada:
    —, **New Brunswick,** XXXIII, 79
    —, **Nova Scotia,** XXXIV, 174
  China, XVI, 157, 243; XVII, 38, 134, 212, 298; XVIII, 59; XXII, 5; XXVI, 109, 189; XXVI, 5; XXXIV, 17; XLIII, 186; XLIII, 274; XLIII, 85; XLIX, 21
  Hong Kong, XXXIV, XVII
  Pacific Ocean, II, 5; III, 185, XXXI, 120
  South America, IV, 137; XXXV, 248
  United States
    —, **Arizona Territory,** I, 255
    —, **California,** II, 299
    —, **East Coast,** VII, 213; VIII, 127; XLVII, 33

—, Florida, Ocklawah River, VII, 115, 224
—, Great Lakes, III, 333; XVIII, 273
—, Maine, XXIV, 233
—, Massachusetts, XII, 288
—, Mississippi River, 19th century, XVI, 270; XVI, XXVIII
—, New England, XXXIV, 174
—, New York, Hudson River, VI, 277; XIV, 161; XIV, 278; XVIII, 223
—, 19th century, XXIV, 157
Steamships. ???
Steamers, Schooners, Cutters & Sloops: Marine Photographs of N. L. Stebbins Taken 1884 to 1907, by W. H. Bunting, reviewed, XXXV, 215
Steamers *Ly-ee-moon* and *Yangtsze (1862),* XLIII, plate 2
"Steamers to Savannah: The Origins and Establishment of the New-York and Savannah Steam Navigation Co.," by James P. Delgado, XLVII, 33–44
"Steamers to the Whalemen's Port: The New Bedford-New York Lines, 1853–1880," by Martin J. Butler, XXXIX, 83–108
"Steamer *Vesta*, Neglected Partner in a Fatal Collision, The," by Alexander Crosby Brown, XX, 177–184, plates 5, 6
Steam Navigation in Virginia and Northeastern North Carolina Waters, 1826–1836, by John C. Emmerson, Jr., reviewed, X, 157–158
"Steam Navigation on the Carolina Sounds and the Chesapeake in 1892," *Steamship Historical Society Reprint No. 4,* by Samuel Ward Stanton, reviewed, IX, 233–234
Steam Packets on the Chesapeake: A History of the Old Bay Line Since 1840, by Alexander Crosby Brown, reviewed, XXII, 150
Steam schooners, lumber-carrying, U.S. Pacific coast, XXV, 288
Steam sheds, VII, 196–199
Steamship Great Britain, The, by Grahame Farr, reviewed, XXV, 228
Steamship Great Western, the First Atlantic Liner, The, by Grahame Farr, reviewed, XXIV, 149
Steamship Historical Society of America, I, 103, 176, 316, 400; II, 340; V, 91; VI, 235, 236, 307, IX, 233–234; XXVII, 257, 259
Steamship Historical Society of America Reprint Series No. 3, reviewed, VI, 235–236
Steamship Historical Society Reprint Series No. 4, reviewed, IX, 233–234
Steamships, I, 138–140; IV, 69–71, 137–163, 305–317: IX, 216–227; X, 123–143; XXII, 5–44, 150, 157–183. *See also* Steamboats, Steamers
auxiliary, I, 51–57
trans-Pacific, II, 5–38, 243; III, 185–204
warships, IX, 63–65; Turkish warship, I, plate facing 89
Steamship lines:
United States, XXXV, 197
—, New Bedford (MA), XXXIX, 83
See also Steamboats; Steam navigation
Steamships, Fires, XIV, 192
Steamships, United States:
Design and construction, I, 51
20th century, XXII, 157
See also Steamboats; Steam navigation; Steamship lines
"Steam Turbine Bibliography," Note by John C. Bower, Jr., XXXIV, 69–70
Steanes, Captain Levi, XXI, 102
Stedman, Dr. Charles Ellery, XI, 291
Stedman, Captain Giles, XIV, 127
Steel, David, XXV, 82; XXX, 41
Steele, Ian K., *The English Atlantic, 1675–1740,* reviewed, XLVIII, 64
Steele, Captain Jonathan W., XXI, 102
Steele, Richard, XXX, 300
Steelmaker, steamship (1920), VIII, 61–66
Steel ships. *See* Shipbuilding (Materials); Ships (Iron and Steel; Steel)
Steenes, Captain Levi, XXI, 102
Steensen, Captain R. Steen, "The South's Scottish Sea Monster," XXIX, 5–29
"Steering Wheels," query by Walter Muir Whitehill, I, 90
Steers, George, XI, 245; XIII, 54; XXXVI, 172
Steers, J. A, *The Coast of England and Wales in Pictures,* reviewed, XX, 277
Stefansson, Vilhjalmur, *Ultima Thule: Further Mysteries of the Arctic,* reviewed, I, 322–324
Stegg, Norwegian destroyer *(1939),* XXXII, 110 ff.
Steiglitz & Co., XXIII, 133, 134, 136
Stein, Captain John F., XXI, 102
Steinbeck, John, and E. F. Ricketts, *Sea of Cortez,* reviewed, II, 183
Steinbek, ship *(1909),* XVIII, 19–24, 149–167, plate 2
Steinfeldt, Eric, contributed documents, XV, 306–310; XXIV, 70–72; query by, II, 248; "Note on American Small Craft," XIV, 61
Steinhardt, Lawrence, American Ambassador, XXXII, 104 ff.; XLIII, 32 ff.
Steinlein, Eric J., I, 63
Steinmuller, Captain A. C., XLVII, 49
Steller, Georg W., *Journal of a Voyage with Bering, 1741–1742,* reviewed, L, 140
Steller, Georg Wilhelm, XXXIX, 186
Stellwagen, Captain Henry S., XLIV, 264
Stellwagen, Commander Henry S., U.S.N., XXI, 234
Stembel, Captain Roger N., U.S.N., XXV, 130, 139
Stephen, James, XXIII, 158
Stephen Baldwin, brig (1839), XXXVI, 255
Stephen Girard, schooner *(1839),* VIII, 49
"Stephen Girard's Instructions to the Master and Supercargo of his Ship *North America,*" documents contributed by Dorothy E. R. Brewington, III, 74–85

Stephen Hart, schooner, XXI, 90; *(1862),* XII, 58
Stephen Olney, schooner (1832), XXIV, 59
"Stephen Reynolds' Influence on Business and Culture in Hawaii, 1823–1855," by Pauline N. King, XLVI, 43–49
Stephens, Captain Tristram, XLIX, 255
Stephens, W. P., XXX, 196
Stephens, William P., II, 177; *Traditions and Memories of American Yachting,* reviewed, II, 352
Stephen Whitney, ship *(1845),* XXXVII, 219
Stephen Young, bark *(1861),* XXI, 258
Sterett, J., XXXVI, 56
Sterett, Samuel, XXXVI, 56
Sterling, bark (1864), III, 172
Sterling, supply ship, XXXVII, 138 n.
Sterling Castle, British warship *(1760),* XLVIII, 39 ff.
Stern carving, VI, plate 21
Sterns, Mrs. Hannah, XXXVIII, 103
Stern wheel steamboats. *See* Steamboats, Steamers, Steamships.
Stern-Wheelers up Columbia, by Randall V. Mills, reviewed, VIII, 158–159
Sterrett, Lieutenant Andrew, XL, 24
Stetson, Caleb, XV, 176
Stetson, Jonathan, XXV, 222
Stettin, steamship, XXI, 90; *(1862),* VIII, 227
Stevens, Bryan W., XIV, 19 ff., plates 2–4
Stevens, Edward, XXX, 126, 127
Stevens, Consul Edward, XLVI, 160 ff.
Stevens, Edwin, XX, 155–166; XLVIII, 274 ff.
Stevens, Enock, XXI, 15
Stevens, Eric and Captain Thomas Minto, *The Search for the Kobenhaven,* reviewed, XLVII, 143
Stevens, Hawley, review by, XLVII, 143; "C.S.S. *Georgia:* Memory and History," XLV, 191–198
Stevens, Captain Isaac, XLI, 214
Stevens, J. W., XXXVI, 232 n.
Stevens, Captain J. W., XXI, 102
Stevens, John, XXIII, 209–211; XXXVII, 269; L, 201
Stevens, Colonel John, XVI, 271
Stevens, John R., query by, VII, 77; *An Account of the Construction, and Embellishment of Old Time Ships,* reviewed, X, 236
Stevens, Joseph Lowe (Doctor), XXI, 22
Stevens, M. B., XXIV, 59
Stevens, Perry, XIII, 128
Stevens, Raymond B., XXXII, 157
Stevens, Robert, XX, 155
Stevens, Robert Livingston, XII, 239
Stevens, Commandant T. H., XL, 42
Stevens, Lieutenant T. H., XV, 118
Stevens, Thomas, XXX, 109, 110
Stevens, Thomas A., I, 102; VII, 316; "Last Voyage of the ship *Vigilant* to Manila with Coal for Dewey in 1898, The," II, 140–153; "'Quarter Wagener' of Captains Warner and DeAngelis," VI, 136
Stevens, Wallace, XXV, 65

Stevenson, Midshipman Byrd W., U.S.N., XXV, 141
Stevenson, D. Alan, *The World's Lighthouses before 1820,* reviewed, XX, 68
Stevenson, Captain John, XXI, 102
Stevenson, Leander, XXXIX, 16
Stevenson, Sir Ralph, XLIX, 211
Stevenson, Robert Louis, IV, 113–118; XXVIII, 84
Stevenson, Captain William, L, 211
Stewart, Reverend C. S., XXXIX, 115
Stewart, Captain Charles, XXXVI, 219; XXXVII, 131; XXXVIII, 106; XL, 215
Stewart, Commodore Charles, XXXI, 218; L, 117
Stewart, Charles A., VII, 240–242
Stewart, Charles S., XIX, 246–247
Stewart, Delia, XXXVIII, 106
Stewart, Harris B., Jr., and J. Welles Henderson, Editors, *B. Shephard's Sketchbook of the H.M.S.* Challenger *Expedition, 1872–1874,* reviewed, XXXIII, 307
Stewart, Captain Keith, XXII, 33
Stewart, Robert (son of King James V), L, 127 ff.
Stewart, Captain William R., XI, 291
Stewart, Captain William Robert, XLVI, 50
Stewart at Cardigan, XXXIV, 41
Stickney, Caleb, XVII, 120, 121
Stieper, Captain C. H., XXI, 102
Stier, motor ship *(1917),* XXII, 158
Stiles, Copeland, XXXI, 211
Stiles, Captain G., XLVI, 53
Stiles, Lieutenant Colonel H. R., I, 66–67
Stiles, Richard, XXX, 96 n., 101, 102, 108
Stiletto, schooner (1910), XXVI, plate XXIII
Still, Charles Frederick, XXII, 16
Still, William N., Jr., review by, XLVI, 129; *Iron Afloat: The Story of the Confederate Ironclads,* reviewed, XXXII, 136–137; "A Nickel a Bucket: A History of the North Carolina Shrimping Industry," XLVII, 257–274; "Monitor Companies: A Study of the Major Firms That Built the USS *Monitor,*" XLVIII, 106–130; "Shipbuilding in North Carolina: The World War I Experience," XLI, 188–207
Stilphen, N., II, 79–80
Stimers, Alban, XXXV, 59
Stimers, Captain Albin C., XLVIII, 123
Stimpson, J. H., XXXII, 125
Stimson, Charles, XXXVI, 240
Stimson, Fred S., XXXVI, 240
Stimson, Henry, XLI, 279
Stimson, Herbert L., Secretary of State, XXXVII, 186
Stinchcomb, Captain, XXXVII, 104 ff.
Stingaree, schooner, XXI, 104; *(1863),* XII, 160, 233
Stingray, schooner, XXI, 101; *(1863),* XII, 160, 233
Stinson, Thomas, XIV, 247
Stirling, Admiral Sir James, XXXVIII, 34
Stirling, Rear Admiral Sir James, XXXI, 269; XXXII, 244
Stirling Castle, British ship *(1780),* XXXVIII, 94

Stocker, David (marine optician, Scotland), XXXIV, 208
Stockfleth, J., XXVIII, plate XII
Stockman, Henry, XVII, 120
Stockman, Moses, XVII, 120
Stockton, Frank, XXXII, 81
Stockton, Frank R., XX, 174–176
Stockton, Captain Robert F., U.S.N., VI, 212 ff.
Stockton, Commodore Robert F., XXXII, 46
Stockton, Lieutenant Robert F., XLVIII, 116; XLIX, 96
Stockton gun, or *Oregon,* VI, 212–222
Stoddard, Daniel, XLVII, 128
Stoddard, Captain E. M., XXI, 102
Stoddard, L. H., XVII, 137
Stoddard, Captain Mark, XXI, 102
Stoddard, Captain Robert, XXXV, 296
Stoddard, William, XLVIII, 33
Stodder, David, Constructor, XXXIX, 235 ff.
Stoddert, Benjamin, XXII, 264 ff.; XXIV, 61–69; XXV, 31; XXVI, 244, 247, 250; XXX, 120–132
Stoddert, Benjamin, First Secretary of the Navy, XXXIII, 77; XXXIX, 31; XLIII, 135; XLVI, 147; XLVII, 23; L, 270 ff.
Stokely, Captain George, XX, 45
Stokes, Samuel, XXX, 299
Stommel, Henry, *Science of the Seven Seas,* reviewed, VI, 157–158
Stone, Captain A. O., XXI, 102
Stone, Captain Albert, XXI, 102
Stone, Captain David, XXI, 102
Stone, Captain Edward E., U.S.N., XXV, 67
Stone, Herbert, XLIII, 270
Stone, Richard G., Jr., "'The *South Carolina* We've Lost'; The Bizarre Saga of Alexander Gillon and His Frigate," XXXIX, 159–172
Stone, Robert, XLVII, 119 ff.
Stone fleet, XXI, 233
Stone, Silsbee and Pickman, XLVII, 119 ff.
Stone, Silsbee, Pickman & Allen, XLVI, 63
Stone, Captain William, Continental Navy, XXV, 193
"Stone Fleet, The," by John Woodman, Jr., XXI, 233–259
Stonegate, British merchantman *(1939),* XXXII, 101 ff., plate 8
Stone sloop, Pictorial Supplement, XXXVI, plate XXV
Stones of Atlantis, The, by David Zink, reviewed, XXXVIII, 301
Stonewall, C.S. ironclad ram (1864), I, 241–254, plate facing 248; XXII, 259; XXIII, 202 n.; XXXIII, 210
Stonewall, schooner *(1863),* XII, 160
Stonewall, twin-screw *(1865),* XLIX, 119
Stonewall, XXIX, 5
Stonewall Jackson, steamship, XXI, 99; *(1862),* VIII, 227, 232
Stono, steamship, XXI, 100; *(1863),* VIII, 232
Storck (Artist, Dutch), XXII, plate XXVII
Storer, Dr. D. Humphreys, XLIX, 34
Storer, Captain George W., XXIV, 21
Storer, Captain John, XXXIX, 213
Storer, Dr. Malcom, II, 336
Store Yard on the Thames, XXXIV, plates 1, 16
Stork, sloop *(1807),* XVI, 192
"Storm Along: An American Sea Anthology, A Manuscript by Joanna Carver Colcord in the Collection of the Peabody Museum of Salem," by Mary Malloy, XLVI, 111–119
Storm at Sea, 1840, XXIX, plate XXXII
"Storm at Sea, A," document contributed by E. Lee Dorsett, IV, 245–246
Storm King, schooner barge *(1892),* XLVII, 127
Storm King, ship *(1860),* XXI, 40
Storm Petrel, schooner (1870), IX, 171–172, plate 24
Stormy Petrel, steamship, XXI, 90; *(1864),* VIII, 235
Storms at sea, XLV, 20. *See also* Weather
"Stormy Voyage, A," document contributed by Lawrence W. Jenkins, XXI, 41
Story, Arthur D., XXV, 147; XXXVI, 77, 78
Story, Arthur Dana (shipbuilder), VII, 171; IX, 73–74
Story, Captain, XXX, 235
Story, Charles, VII, 73, 75
Story, Dana, XXXVI, 77; *Building the Blackfish,* reviewed, L, 151; *Frame Up! The Story of Essex, Its Shipyards and Its People,* reviewed, XXV, 147–148; *Hail Columbia!,* reviewed, XXXI, 75–76
Story, Dana A., and John M. Clayton, *The Building of a Wooden Ship,* reviewed, XXXII, 70–71
Story, William, XL, 253
Story, Captain William, IX, 241–244; XXI, 292
Story of Maps, The, by Lloyd A. Brown, reviewed, IX, 305
Story of Minot's Light, The, by Edward Rowe Snow, reviewed, I, 189
Stoudinger, steamship, XXIV, 163 n.; *(1817),* XVI, 278
Stouffer, Captain John, XLV, 253
Stout, Neil R., "Goals and Enforcement of British Colonial Policy, 1763–1775," XXVII, 211–220; "An Invention by Captain John Reynolds," XXII, 277–279; "Manning the Royal Navy in North America, 1763–1775," XXIII, 174–185
Stout Engine Laboratories, XXXVII, 115 ff.
Stove, Charlotte W., XVIII, 191, 199
Stover, Captain, XXX, 62–67
Stover, Maria C., XXXVII, 203
Stoveren, ship *(1922),* XVIII, 211
Stow, Honorable Alexander, verses by, quoted, VII, 60–61
Stowe, Harriet Beecher, VII, 161; XXV, 65; quoted, VII, 127
Stradley, John, XXXVIII, 92
Strain, Lieutenant Commander George, L, 291 ff.
Straits boat, I, 356–357
Straits of Malacca, XXX, 208, 209
Stran, T. P., XXXIV, 210
Strandberg, Captain F. A., XVIII, 84

Stranger, ship *(1814)*, XXIX, 197
Straits of Magellan, XXIII, 186
Strategy of Sea Power: Its Development and Application, The, by Captain S. W. Roskill, R.N., reviewed, XXV, 75
"Stratford Canning on Shipping in America," document contributed by Arthur J. May, IV, 327–329
Strathairly, steamship *(1914)*, XVIII, 158, 160, 161
Strathleven, steamship *(1884)*, XIV, 120
Stratton, Captain William, XXIII, 27
Straub, Mabel, XXXVI, 22
Strauss, Rear Admiral Joseph, XXXV, 106
Strauss, Nathan, XXXVII, 35
Street, Benjamin, XXXI, 23
Stribling, Commodore C. K., XXIX, 109
Stribling, C. O., Flag Officer, XXXII, 130
Stribling, Commodore Charles, XX, 214
Stribling, Commodore Cornelius, XXXVIII, 38
Stribling, Commodore Cornelius K., XXXIV, 116
Strichert, Charles, XI, 115–133
Strickland, William, II, plate 21
Stringham, U.S. torpedo boat (1905), XXII, 142
Stringham, Captain Silas, XXXV, 55
Stringham, Silas H., XXXVI, 189 ff.; XXXVII, 283
Stringham, Commander Silas K., XLVII, 29
Strobridge, Truman R., and Bernard C. Nalty, "Mission to Peking, 1870: Captain McLane Tilton's Letter Describing his Trip with the Seward Party to Peking," XXV, 116–122
Strobridge, Truman R., Bernard C. Nalty, and Dennis L. Noble, *Wrecks, Rescues & Investigations: Selected Documents of the U.S. Coast Guard and Its Predecessors*, reviewed, XLIII, 143–145
Strobridge, William and Lois, note by, XXXIX, 142–143
Strobridge, William F., "Book Smuggling in Mexican California," XXXII, 117–122
Stromboli, ironclad *(1864)*, XLII, 85 ff.
Stromness, Orkney Island: photo of, L, 128
Strong's Island, IV, 97–98
Strother, David Hunter, V, 305 ff.
Struggle for Guadalcanal, August 1942-February 1943, The, by Samuel Eliot Morison, reviewed, X, 76–77
"Struggle for the Cape Henry Lighthouse, The, 1721–1791," by Arthur Pierce Middleton, VIII, 26–36, plate 8
Strum, Harvey, "The *Leander* Affair," XLIII, 40–50
Stuart, Alexander, VI, 153
Stuart, Captain Charles, U.S.N., XXV, 159
Stuart, Charles B., U.S. Navy, XLIX, 104
Stuart, Captain John, XVIII, 285
Stuart, John. See Bute, Earl of.
Stuart, Mary, XLIV, 25 ff.
Stuart, Vivian, *The Beloved Little Admiral: Admiral of the Fleet the Hon. Sir Henry Keppel, G.C.B., O. M.*, reviewed, XXVIII, 73–74
Stubbs, W. P., XXVII, plates VIII, XX, XXII; XXVIII, plates XVI, XXIII-XXV

"Stubbs, W. P.," query by J. M. Burdell, I, 398; answered by Thomas Hornsby and Frank A. Taylor, II, 83
Studdert, William P., XXV, 293
Studies in Maritime Economics, by R. O. Goss, reviewed, XXIX, 145–147
Stumminger, Captain William, XXI, 102
Sturdy Beggar, schooner *(1776)*, XX, 45
Sturdy Begger, brig *(1777)*, XLIII, 24
Sturges, Michael D., XXXVIII, 231
Sturgis, H. P., XVIII, 59
Sturgis, James, XVII, 47
Sturgis, Vice-Consul Robert, XXXVIII, 34
Sturgis, Robert S., XVI, 164, 170, 175
Sturgis, Russell, XVI, 163; XVIII, 59
Sturgis, Samuel, XIII, 121
Sturgis, William, XIII, 242
Sturmy, Samuel, XIV, 191
Sturtevant, U.S. destroyer *(1921)*, XLVI, 247 ff.
Sturtevant, W. B., VI, 73 ff.
Sturtevant, William, XLIV, 41
Sturtevant, William B., I, 102: "Boy's First Day at Sea in the Bark *Belle of Oregon – 1886*, A," I, 58–62; "The Up-to-date Method of Getting a Ship Under Way," I, 83–84
Styles, Rutherford, XLVIII, 50 ff.
Styrbjörn, hemmema type of vessel [model] (1790), VI, 165, plate 23
Styria, steamship *(1902)*, XXXVIII, 188 ff.
Suazo, 2nd Lieutenant C. Ramón, XXX, 54
Subercase, Daniel d'Auger de, XXXV, 153 ff.
Sublime, brig (1823), IV, 50, 51
Submarine Boat Co., XXXII, 163
Submarines, XX, 174; XXXVI, 33
Submarines, Admirals and Navies, reviewed, I, 408
Submarines, early, II, 345–349
Submarines at War: The History of the American Silent Service, by Edwin P. Hoyt, reviewed, XLIV, 132
Submarine trumpet, by James A. Whipple, XXXIV, plate 7
"Subscription Warships of 1798, The," by Frederick C. Leiner, XLVI, 141–158
Subsidios para a História Maritima do Brasil, edited by Didio Iratim Alphonso da Costa, reviewed, I, 325
"Substantiation of Campbell's Study of a Blunt Chart," by Mary Emily Miller, XXVI, 216–217
Success, brig *(1760)*, IX, 144
Success, H.M.S., XXVI, 46, 47; *(1754)*, VII, 249; *(1776)*, XLVIII, 16
Success, Newport sloop *(1774)*, XLII, 41 ff.
Success, schooner *(1760)*, XL, 253; *(1801)*, XXIII, 7
Success, ship *(1630)*, XXIII, 63
Success, ship, XXXII, 92
Sucré, schooner *(1853)*, XXX, 273
Sue, schooner, XXI, 90, 101; *(1862)*, VIII, 227, 232
Suenson, Captain Otto F., XXIX, 26
Suez Canal turret ships, XXV, 170–171
Suffolk, H.M.S., XXVIII, 107, 108

Suffolk, schooner *(1861),* XI, 288
Suffren, Bailli de, V, 65 ff.
Sugar Act, XXVII, 216–220
"Suit Against Jonathan Woodman of Newbury, 1694, A," contributed by Lawrence W. Jenkins, XIII, 139–140
Sukeforth, Captain G. E., XXIV, 187
Sukey, brig *(1796),* XLV, 168; *(1803),* XXV, 181
Suleiman, steamship (ex-*Willboro,* ex-*Eastern Light*), XXIII, 276
Sullivan, brig (1866), Pictorial Supplement, XXXIII, plate VIII
Sullivan, Commander, XXXVI, 131 ff.
Sullivan, Frank, XLIV, 110
Sullivan, Captain George L., XXXIX, 291
Sullivan, J. W. (NY City builder), XXXII, 31
Sullivan, Captain P. A., XXI, 102
Sullivan, Captain Thomas, XLIV, 22 ff.
Sullivan, Captain Timothy, XLIII, 192
Sultan, ship *(1819),* I, 298–299
Sultan, steamship *(1847),* XVIII, 72; XXVI, 206, 209
Sultana, schooner *(1768),* XXV, 91–92; sail plan, XXV, 90
Sultana, steam barkentine (1909), XXX, plate XXVII
"Sultan of Swat, The," by Captain Edgar K. Thompson, U.S.N. (ret.), XXVII, 149
Sulu Archipelago, XXX, 201, 202, 203
Suma Oriental of Tomé Pires and the Book of Francisco Rodriques, edited by Armando Cortesão, reviewed, VI, 308–309
Sumatra. *See* Pirates
Sumatra, boats of, XIII, 83 ff.
Sumatra: pepper trade, IX, 239–248
Suminoye Maru, steamship *(1877),* XVII, 54
Summer Cruise on the Coast of New England, A, by Robert Carter, reviewed, XXXI, 77
Summerlee, ship *(1861),* XI, 288
Summers, Day and Baldock, XXII, 44
Summers, Day and Co., XXII, 44; XXVI, 23, 26, 28, 208
Summersell, Charles Grayson, *The Cruise of C.S.S. Sumter,* reviewed, XXVI, 221
Summerville, Walter, XXV, 69–70
Sumner, sloop, XXVIII, 120
Sumner, Senator Charles, XXXIII, 60; L, 113
Sumner, General Edwin V., XXXIII, 46
Sumner, Commander G. W., U.S.N., XXVI, 173
Sumner, Thomas H., XXIII, 47, 51
Sumner, Captain Thomas H., XXIX, 71
Sumter, C.S.S. ship, XXVI, 98 n., 100 n.; XXXIII, 9 ff.; *(1861),* XXII, plate VIII; XXV, 21; XV, 288 ff.
Sun, tanker *(1907),* XXXVIII, 198 ff.
Sunapee, fishing vessel *(1961),* XLI, 53
Sunbeam, bark *(1845),* III, 68
Sunbeam, schooner *(1904),* XXVIII, 59
Sunbeam, steamship *(1862),* VIII, 227
Sun Chief, turret motor ship (ex-*Turret Cape*) (1895), XXV, 171

Sun Co. of Philadelphia, XLII, 249
Sunda Straits, XXX, 208, 209
Sunday naval recruit parade, Coasters Harbor Island, 1914, photo of, XLIX, 297
Sunderland, British ship *(1776),* XLVIII, 18
Sunderland, Bridge at, XXIX, 124, plate XV
Sunflower, H.M. corvette *(1943),* L, 219 ff.
Sunfoo, steamship *(1870),* XVII, 54, 58, 59; XVIII, 72
Sunny South, schooner *(1861),* VIII, 221
Sunol [model], XXXVII, 172
Sunrise, bark *(1861),* XI, 288
Sunrise, schooner *(1864),* XV, 113, 130
Superb, schooner, XXII, 60 n.
Superb, ship, XXII, 137
Supercargo, duties of, XXX, 176
Superior, ship *(1841),* XX, 103, 268; *(1849),* XLIV, 12 ff.
Superior, steamship *(1818),* VI, 196–198, 201, 204, 205; *(1832),* VII, 45, 46, 54, 57
Superior Trading & Transportation Co., XXIV, 25
Supership, by Noel Mostert, reviewed, XXXV, 214
Supple, wooden steamship *(1917),* XXXV, 279
Supply, R.N. tug, XXVIII, 89
Supply, ship *(1661),* XIII, 7
Supply, U.S. Storeship *(1847),* IV, 71–72; *(1867),* XXXII, 135
Surat Merchant, ship *(1677),* XIII, 13
Surf, trawler *(1910),* XLIV, 120
"Surfboat-Lifeboat *Nantasket,* Hull, Massachusetts: The boat that 'would not succeed,' The," by Dennis R. Means, XXXVII, 83–94
Surfboats and Horse Marines: U.S. Naval Operations in the Mexican War, 1846-48, by K. Jack Bauer, reviewed, XXXII, 147–148
"Surgery and Shipbuilding," by Philip H. Cook, VII, 318
Surinam, brig *(1804),* XXIV, 265
Surpass, schooner *(1861),* VIII, 221
Surprise, H.M.S., XXX, 299; *(1885),* XXXIX, 136
Surprise, English frigate, XXII, 275
Surprise, H.M.S. *(1958),* XXV, 166
Surprise, schooner, XXI, 99, 102
Surprise, ship *(1850),* XXII, 239
Surprise, steamship *(1824),* XLIII, 114 ff.; *(1853),* XVI, 245, 247, 248; XVIII, 72
Surprize, pinkie *(1937),* XII, 135
Surprize, schooner *(1802),* XIII, 276; *(1863),* XII, 160
Surrey, steamship *(1888),* XXXVIII, 187 ff.
Survey boats, XXI, 260
Surveying, marine, XXX, 200–216
"Surveying Commission of *Alborough,* 1728–1734, The," by Commander W. E. May, XXI, 260–278
Surveyor (ex-*Colonel Abert*), steamship *(1844),* XXIV, 8
Surveyor's Compass: American, circa 1730, Pictorial Supplement, XXXV, plate XVI; American, circa 1810, Pictorial Supplement, XXXV, plate XVI
Surville (Navigator, French), XXV, 253–254, 258, 260
Susan, schooner, XXI, 99; *(1864),* XV, 130
Susan, ship *(1795),* XVIII, 132; *(1796),* X, 53

Susan, sloop, XXII, 58, 63, 64
Susana, steamship, XXI, 86, 92, 96; *(1864)*, XI, 276; XII, 233
Susan Abigail, brig *(1865)*, XXVII, 269, 273, 276
Susan Ann Howard, schooner *(1861)*, VIII, 221, 227
Susan Catharine, schooner *(1861)*, VIII, 221
Susan Constant, ship, XXX, 302; (1603), XXXIV, 233; *(1607)*, X, 5–14, plates 1–8; XIV, 106; XVII, 173–180, plan 176
Susan Constant II, ship [replica] (1956), XVII, 175 ff., plates 15, 16; plans, XVII, 176
Susan Fearing, ship (1861), V, 148
Susan G. Owens, ship *(1861)*, VIII, 221
Susan Hincks, ship (1861), V, 150
Susan Jane, schooner *(1861)*, VIII, 221
Susan McPherson, sloop *(1861)*, VIII, 221, 227
Susanna, sloop *(1745)*, XX, 145; *(1799)*, XLV, 93
Susanna, yacht *(1689)*, IX, 180
Susannah, schooner *(1760)*, IX, 144
Susannah, ship (1794), VI, 83
Susan Sturgis, schooner (1848), XXIV, 59
Susie D., water boat, XXIV, 52
Susie P. Oliver, schooner (1882), XXIII, 11
Susquehanna, bark (1833), IV, 73
Susquehanna, flagship *(1851)*, XLI, 34; *(1861)*, XXXVII, 284; XXXVIII, 32; XXXIX, 38; XL, 100 ff.
Susquehanna, steamship (1825), X, 176–177; (1835), VII, 57
Susquehanna, transport *(1861)*, XXXI, 259; XXXIV, 62
Susquehanna, U.S. frigate *(1826)*, XXI, 61
Susquehanna, U.S.S. *(1862)*, XX, 161; *(1864)*, XXVII, 44
Susquehanna, U.S. steamship *(1853)*, VII, 9, 11, 13, 14, 16, 17; XLVI, 58
Sussex, British ship *(1916)*, XLVIII, 56
Susu, XXX, 181
Sutcliffe, Alice Crary, XXVII, 13
Sutcliffe, Thomas, XXX, 300
Suter, Captain John, XIII, 242
Sutherland, James, XVIII, 306–314
Sutherland, Captain James, VII, 56
Sutherland, William, XXX, 83
Sutlej, frigate *(1863)*, XXXII, 283 ff.
Sutro Library Notes, reviewed, XI, 300
Sutton, Dr. Manners, XXXIV, 5 ff.
Suttor, Marc, "A History of Fluvial Navigation: The Example of the Meuse," L, 166–177
Suwanee, steamship *(1861)*, XI, 288
Suwonada, steamship (1864), XVII, 49 ff., 53, 54, 58; XVIII, 72; *(1864)*, XLIX, 23
Suzanne, schooner (1918), VI, 83
Suzie M. Jones, ship (1863), III, 349
Svedel Line, XXXI, 118
Sveriges Lycka, bark (1774), VI, 166
Swain, Edward A., XXXII, 198 ff.
Swain, John, XIII, 120
Swain, Micajah, XXXIII, 163
Swaine, Charles, VI, 232, 233, 310

Swallow, brig *(1850)*, XXXVIII, 83
Swallow, British Admiralty's survey ship *(1866)*, XXII, 248
Swallow, British post office packet *(1812)*, XLVI, 168
Swallow, H.M.S. *(1766)*, XXV, 297–298
Swallow, schooner *(1756)*, XXIII, 143; *(1775)*, XXX, 115, 116
Swallow, ship *(1761)*, XL, 259; *(1856)*, Pictorial Supplement, XXXIII, plates XX, XXI
Swallow, sloop, XXI, 92; *(1777)*, XLIII, 24; *(1864)*, VIII, 235
Swallow, yacht *(1893)*, XXXVI, 237
Swan, bark *(1624)*, XXXVII, 22
Swan, schooner *(1861)*, VIII, 221
Swan, ship *(1690)*, XXXV, 154
Swan, sloop *(1862)*, XII, 58
Swan, steamship, XXI, 94; *(1862)*, XII, 58
Swan, Captain E. W., XXIX, 270
Swan, Captain Henry, XXI, 102
Swan, James, XLII, 27
Swan, R. A., *Australia in the Antarctic: Interest, Activity and Endeavour*, reviewed, XXIII, 150
Swan, Captain Samuel, XXVII, 82
Swan, William U., I, 102; II, 177
Swann, Commander F. R. H., XXXIV, 14
Swann, Leonard Alexander, Jr., *John Roach, Maritime Entrepreneur: The Years as Naval Contractor, 1862–1886*, reviewed, XXVI, 286–287
Swan's Island (ME), XXX, 115
Swanson, Carl E., "The Profitability of Privateering: Reflection on British Colonial Privateers During the War of 1739–1748, XLII, 36–56
Swartwout, Commander Samuel, XXXII, 52
Swasey, Captain Alexander G., XXI, 102
Swasey, Samuel, XXX, 96 n.
Sweden, ship, XXV, 110
Swedish Navy, VI, 163–178
Sweeney, Captain John, XVIII, 84; XLIII, 207
Sweepstake, ship *(1626)*, XLIX, 255
Sweepstakes, ship (1853), XIX, plate VII
Sweet, Captain Benjamin, XXV, 180
Sweet, Dick, mentioned, XLVII, 281
Sweet, Manley, XXI, 16
Sweeting, Captain William H., XXI, 102
Sweetingham, Walter, XXVII, 236
Sweetser, J. P., XXVIII, plate XXI
Sweetser, Captain Joseph P., II, 199
"Sweet Swan on Salt Water, The," by R. C. Holmes, XI, 209–214
Swell, trawler *(1911)*, XLIV, 120
Swem, E. G., *Views of Yorktown and Gloucester Town, 1755*, reviewed, VII, 249–250
Swendon, Captain, XXXI, 97
Swettenham, Sir James Alexander, K.C.M.G., XXIX, 121, 127, 129, 130
"Swettenham Incident," XXIX, 119
Swift, Clement (artist), XXII, plate XXIV

Swift, H.M.S., XXVI, 42, 46, 47, 51
Swift, schooner *(1863)*, XV, 111, 128, 130; *(1864)*, VIII, 235
Swift, ship *(1798)*, XVIII, 121
Swiftsure, H.M.S. *(1915)*, XXXVI, 40
Swiftsure, schooner, XXIV, 45, 59
Swiftsure, ship *(1625)*, XIV, 65
Swiftsure, steamship *(1823)*, XLVIII, 80 ff.
Swineburne, Commander W. T., XXXV, 192
Swipe, yacht *(1906)*, XXXVI, 242, 245
Swire, John, XVIII, 61, 64
Sword Fish, ship (1851), I, 44, 47
Swordfish, ship *(1856)*, XX, 212
Swordfish, sloop (1888), XXX, plate XI
Swordfishery, XLI, 36
Swordfishing: XLI, plates 1–4; landings, 1909–1959 (map), XLI, 46; tonnage graph, XLI, 62
Swords, Colonel Thomas R., XLV, 20 ff.
Sword Steamship Line, Inc., XXXVIII, 199 ff.
Sybil, H.M.S. *(1781)*, XXXVI, 167
Sybilla, ship *(1855)*, XXXI, 272
Sybille, H.M.S., XXII, 36
Sydney, Australian cruiser *(1915)*, XLIII, 273
Sydney, steamship (1852), XXVII, 194, 196, 206, 209
Syfert, Dwight Nash, "The Liberian Sailing Navy, 1821–1892," XXXVIII, 52–64; "The Liberian Navy Since 1892," XXXIX, 173–183
Sylph, brig *(1827)*, VI, 9, 15
Sylph, sailing vessel, XXII, 14
Sylph, schooner *(1865)*, XLIV, 114
Sylphide, schooner *(1861)*, XI, 288; XII, 233
"Sylvan Steamboats on the East River—New York To Harlem," *Steamship Historical Society of America Reprint Series No. I*, reviewed, II, 94
Sylvester, Admiral E. W., XV, 96; XVI, 3
Sylvester Gildersleeve, ship *(ca. 1862)*, XXV, 106
Sylvia, bark (1855), V, 327
Sylvia, brig (1800), XXII, 216
Sylvia, Louis, XXII, plate XXV
Symington, William, photos by: model steamship, L, 208; model marine steam engine of 1788, L, 209
Symmes, Americus Vespucius, XXXVIII, 41 ff.
Symmes, Elmore, XXXVIII, 45
Symmes, Judge John Cleves, XXXVIII, 41
Symond (1735), XXIII, 82
Symonds, Craig, "The Antinavalists: The Opponents of Naval Expansion in the Early National Period, XXXIX, 22–28; mention, 82
Symonds, Commander Frederick M., XXXVI, 258, 261
Symons, G. J., XXVI, 215
Synesius, Bishop, XII, 294–296
Syracuse, steamship, XVIII, 230
Syren (1800), XXIII, 216
Syren, brig *(1814)*, XLIV, 171; *(1861)*, XV, 124
Syren, French ship *(1799)*, XXXI, 173
Syren, H.M.S., XXVI, 61; (1776), XIII, 35
Syren, ship (1851), XIX, Plate XIII
Syren, steamship, XXI, 94, 100, 105, 106; *(1863)*, VIII, 232, 235, 237; IX, 45
Syrene, French privateer *(1799)*, XXXIX, 34
Syren Queen, ship, XXVII, 73
Syrett, David (Professor), XXXVII, 81; review by, XLIX, 133; "American and British Naval Historians and the American Revolutionary War, 1875–1980," XLII, 179–192; "The Battle for Convoy TM 1, January 1943," L, 42–50; "The Battle of the Atlantic: 1943, The Year of Decision," XLV, 46–64; "German U-Boat attacks on Convoy SC 118: 4 February to 14 February, 1943," XLIV, 48–60; "H.M. Storeship *Porpoise*, 1780–83," XLVII, 91–95; "The Navy Board and Merchant Shipowners During the American War, 1776–1783," XLVII, 5–131; "The Safe and Timely Arrival of Convoy SC 130, 15–25 May 1943," L, 219–227
Szechuen, steamship (1862), XVI, 248; XVII, 39; XVIII, 72; *(1867)*, XLIII, 103 ff.; (1875), XVI, 265; XVIII, 72

T

T. D. Wagner, steamship, XXI, 93, 98; *(1862)*, VIII, 227, 232
T. H. Perkins, supercargo *(1789)*, XLI, 173
T. J. Chambers, schooner *(1861)*, XI, 288
T. J. Potter, steamship (1888), III, 160–161, plate 21
T. N. Barnsdall, schooner, XXIV, 25
T. R. Huglett, schooner *(1861)*, VIII, 221
T. Wingate & Co., XLIII, 187 ff.
Tabor, ship (1869), II, 334; III, 264
Tackerbury, Thomas, XXVIII, 68–69
Tacoma, cruiser *(1921)*, XXXV, 121
Tacoma, ship *(1918)*, XVIII, 204
Taconi, Captain F., XXI, 102
Tacony (1864), XXXII, 55; XXXIII, 60
Tacony, C.S. prize *(1863)*, XXII, 45; XXV, 298
Tactics, naval. *See* Naval tactics
Taeping, ship *(1866)*, XXXV, 32 ff.
Taffarel, II, 59–60, plate 12
Tafola, schooner (1889), XII, plate 29
Taft, President William Howard, XXXV, 97 ff.
Tagle, Oscar, "Memorandum Reference al R.O.U. *18 de Julio*," II, 170–171
Tagus River barges, Portugal, I, 353
Tahiti, boats of, XIII, 108
Tahiti, Memoirs of Arii Taimai, by Henry Brooks Adams, reviewed, XXIX, 148–149
Tahiti, The Discovery of, edited by Hugh Carrington, reviewed, IX, 154
Tahn Wan, steamship *(1860)*, XXXIV, 25
Tah Wah, steamship *(1862)*, XLIII, 121 ff.

Tah-Wah, steamship (1862), XVI, 255; XVIII, 72
Tah-yue-fong, steamship (1872), XVII, 229
Taian Maru, steamship *(1891)*, XIV, 134
Taihei Maru, steamship (ex-*Yugao Maru*) *(1865)*, XLIII, 191 ff.
Taiko|Ooe Maru, steamship (ex-*Takiang*) *(1862)*, XLIII, 195 ff.
Taisnier, Johannes, VII, 263–265
Tait, Thomas, XXX, 299
Tai-Wan, steamship *(1867)*, XLIX, 22
Taiwan, Foreign relations, United States, XXXV, 20
Takao Maru, steamship (ex-*Ashuelot*) *(1869)*, XLIX, 25
"Take the Jackass Out of the Manger," note by Captain Edgar K. Thompson, U.S.N. (ret.), XXIX, 223
Takiang, screw steamship (1861 or 1862), XVII, 134, 135; XVIII, 72; XXXIV, 32; *(1862)*, XLIII, 194 ff.
Taku Forts Mouth of Pei-Ho, Map of, XXVII, 168
Talbot (1927), XXV, 292
Talbot, H.M.S. *(1897)*, XXVIII, 89
Talbot, ship (1630), XXIII, 63, 65; XXIV, 213
Talbot, U.S. torpedo boat (1896), VI, 66
Talbot, Master Commandant Cyrus, L, 245 ff.
Talbot, Frances K., and George E. Brooks, "The Providence Exploring and Trading Company's Expedition to the Niger River in 1832–1833," XXXV, 77–96
Talbot, Captain Joseph Napoleon, XXI, 102
Talbot, Silas, XXVII, 143, 144; XXX, 124–127; XXXI, 249
Talbot, Captain Silas, XLVI, 159
Talbot, Commodore Silas, U.S.N., XXV, 29–32, 109–110
Talbot, Captain W. H., XXI, 102
"Tale of a Tow," contributed by Captain Edgar K. Thompson, U.S.N. (ret.), XXIII, 55
"Tale of Two Flags, A," Captain Edgar K. Thompson, U.S.N. (ret.), XXI, 145–146
"Tale of Two Pictures, A," by Frank O. Braynard, XXVII, 254–262
"Tales of Banks Fishermen," by Horace P. Beck, XIII, 125–130
Talisman, bark (1860), III, 349
Talisman, Peruvian ship *(1881)*, XXXIX, 287
Talisman, steamship, XXI, 95, 105; *(1864)*, VIII, 235
Tallahassee, ship *(1874)*, XXXIII, 60
Tallman, Benjamin, XVIII, 132–133
Tallman, Captain, XXXIII, 134
Tall Ships: editorial comment, XXXVII, 3–4
Tall Ships on Puget Sound: The Marine Photographs of Wilhelm Hester, Robert A. Weinstein, reviewed, XXXIX, 145
Tally Ho, schooner (1827), VI, 80
Talma, ship (1825), I, 82, plate facing 83; IX, 72; (1827), I, 82–83; IX, 72
Talma, figurehead of, Pictorial Supplement, XXXVII, plate III
Talma, Francois Joseph, Pictorial Supplement, XXXVII, plate III

Talman, Benjamin, VIII, 13
Talon, Jean, XXX, 221
Tam, Laurence C. S., *Hong Kong:The Changing Scene, a Record in Art*, reviewed, XLI, 70
Tamaha, merchant ship *(1943)*, L, 219 ff.
Tamar, British steamship *(1864)*, XXXII, 201; *(1878)*, XVII, 61
Tamar, H.M.S. *(1775)*, XIII, 29 ff.
Tamarin, Alfred, and Shirley Glubok, *Voyaging to Cathay: Amerians in the China Trade*, reviewed, XXXVI, 296–297
Tamaulipas, schooner, XXI, 86; *(1861)*, XI, 288. See also *Temaulipas*.
Tamerlane, ship (1854), III, 64
Tamesi, tanker *(1915)*, XXXVIII, 185 ff.
Tam O'Shanter, ship *(1884)*, XIV, 136–139
Tampa, U.S. Coast Guard cutter, XXXVII, 95 n.
Tampen, Norwegian ship *(1961)*, XLI, 50
Tampico, schooner, XXI, 99; *(1862)*, XII, 58, 160
Tampico, steamship (ex-*Imperador*) *(1862)*, XXVI, 194
Tanaka, Yoshio, XIV, 19 ff.
Tancook, bark (1873), VI, 124
Tancook Whaler, XII, 124–126, plate 11
Tancook Whalers: Origins, Rediscovery, and Revival, The, by Robert C. Post, reviewed, XLVII, 284
Taney, Roger Brooke, XXXVI, 66
Tangier, bark (1851), III, 264
"Tangier Galleys and the Wars Against the Mediterranean Corsairs, The," by Alan Jamieson, XXIII, 95–112
Tango, bark (1904), IV, 326; VI, 77
Tanjore, bark (1862), III, 69
Tanker No. 1, concrete tanker (1921), XXII, 172, 182
Tankers, XXXVI, 101; XXXVIII, 175; XLVII, 45
"Tankers in the Patuxent: The ESSO Fleet Lay-Up Site in the 1930's," by Merle T. Cole, XLVII, 45–53
Tank-Nielsen, Rear Admiral Carsten, XXXII, 113
Tanner, Lieutenant Commander Z. L., U.S.N., V, 5 ff.
Tantamount, schooner (1812), XXIV, 45, 60
Taoutai, steamship (1862), XVII, 227; *(1862)*, XLIII, 207
Ta Pang Nyo, steamship *(1865)*, XVII, 49, 222
Tapley, John, XXI, 15
Tappan, John, XXXIV, 100
Tappan, Lewis, XV, 134
Tapperheten, ship (1785), VI, 170
Taques, Benvenuto Augusto de Magalhaes, XV, 287
Tarapaca, ship (1886), IX, 298
Taratara, bark *(1855)*, XXX, 275
Tarawa, Gilbert Islands, IV, 89, 94–95, plate 17
Tarbay, Captain Antonio, XXXIX?, 192
Tarbell, U.S. destroyer *(1918)*, VII, 72
Tarbell, Joseph, XLVII, 27
Tarbox, schooner, XXVIII, 123
Tardy, schooner, XXI, 92; *(1862)*, XII, 58
Targat, Morris, XXXVII, 159
Tarleton, Brigadier General Banastre, XLVI, 19 ff.

Tarn, ship *(1812)*, XXI, 17
Tarquin, ship *(1862)*, scene aboard, Pictorial Supplement, XXXI, plate XXI
Tars, Turks, and Tankers, by Thomas A. Bryson, reviewed, XLI, 73
Tartane, I, 361–365, plate facing 361; II, 62–63
Tartar, bark (1831), V, 149
Tartar, brig *(1813)*, XV, 61
Tartar, frigate *(1859)*, XXXIV, 66
Tartar, H.M.S. *(1724)*, XIX, 45; *(1741)*, XXVI, 40, 53, 54, 60
Tartar, privateer *(1777)*, XIII, 212
Tartar, ship *(1820)*, XIII, 242
Tartar, steamship *(1854)*, XXII, 18, 21, 23, 36, 42, 43; XXVI, 20, 203; (1874), XVII, 62; XVIII, 73
Tartufe, French ship *(1799)*, XXXI, 173
Tasman, Abel Janszoon, and the Discovery of New Zealand, reviewed, III, 358
Tasman, Captain Abel Janszoon, XXV, 251
Tasmania, ship *(1914)*, XVIII, 161
Tasson, ship *(1841)*, XXXVIII, 59
Tate, E. Mowbray, note contributed by, XXXVII, 138–140; "American Merchant and Naval Contacts with China, 1784–1850," XXXI, 177–191; "Admiral Bell and the New Asiatic Squadron 1865–1868," XXXII, 123–135; "Navy Justice in the Pacific, 1830–1870: A Pattern of Precedents," XXXV, 20–31; *Transpacific Steam,* reviewed, XLVIII, 132
Tate, Vernon D., I, 177; VI, 307; VIII, 4; XII, 4; contributed document, VI, 138–139, plate 20; query by, I, 309; reviews by, I, 185–187. "Boston Navy Yard, 1840," document contributed by, VII, 67–69, plates 7–8; "The Complete Modelist of Thomas Miller, 1667," XVII, 152–155; "Dr. Willem Voorbeijtel Cannenburg," V, 240; "The *Instrucion Nauthica* of 1587," I, 191–195; "The *Nettie,*" III, 167–168
Tate Island, Moluccas, XXV, 182
Tatge, Robert O. A., "A Quarantine Quandary: Ship Fever and Yellow Fever in Providence, Rhode Island, 1797," XL, 192–210
Tatnall, Commodore Josiah, XX, 159–161, 198–200
Tatoosh, tug *(1917)*, XVIII, 166–168
Tattler, schooner *(1901)*, XXVI, plate XVIII
Tattnall, Josiah, XXVII, 157 ff., 223–224, 237, plate I; XXIX, 112
Tattnall, Captain Josiah, XXXVIII, 37; XXXIX, 37
Tattnall, Commodore Josiah, C.S.N., XXI, 142–143
Tattnall, Governor Josiah, Jr., XXVII, 158
Tattnall, Paulding, XXVII, 164
Tattooed Man, The, by J. C. Meredith, reviewed, XIX, 307
Tatumo, gunboat, XXVIII, 99
Taunt, Emory S., XXX, 44
Taurus, towboat *(1887)*, XLII, 255
Tavenner, Thomas W., review by, XXVIII, 74–75
Tawes, Captain Leonard S., XXVIII, 148–149
Taxation, XXXI, 192

Tay, H.M. Postal Packet ship (1817), XXIX, 48, plate VII
Tay, H.M. frigate *(1943)*, L, 219 ff.
Tay, ship *(1806)*, XLVIII, 239
Tay, John J., XI, 204–207
Tayler, Captain Bushrod B., U.S.N., XXV, 118
Tayler, R. W., XLVII, 184
Taylor, U.S.S. *(1861)*, XIX, 266
Taylor, Commander Bushrod Bennett, XLIII, 184 ff.; photograph of, XLV, 238
Taylor, D. Foster, I, 67, 102; VIII, 292–293; XXIX, 154; "The Gundalow *Fanny M.,*" II, 209–222; "The Piscataqua River Gundalow," II, 127–139
Taylor, David W., XXXIX, 131
Taylor, Captain Charles, XVIII, 233
Taylor, Charles H., II, 177; XIII, 118
Taylor, E. G. R., *The Mathematical Practitioners of Hanoverian England 1714–1840,* reviewed, XXVIII, 290–292; editor, *The Troublesome Voyage of Captain Fenton, 1582–1583,* reviewed, XX, 275
Taylor, F. R. Forbes, XXXVII, 158 ff.
Taylor, Father, XIII, 257
Taylor, Chaplain Fitch W., XXXI, 184
Taylor, Frank, III, 178; "Historic American Merchant Marine Survey, The," I, 63–79; contributed document, I, 85; review by, I, 96; answered query, II, 83
Taylor, Frank A., XXXII, 213; answered query, VII, 171
Taylor, Gordon, *The Sea Chaplains: A History of the Royal Navy,* reviewed, XXXIX, 302
Taylor, H. Birchard, *"I Build Men as well as Ships,"* reviewed, I, 189
Taylor, Captain H. C., XXXIII, 272 ff.
Taylor, Harry, XXXIV, 265
Taylor, Henry Clay, XXIX, 31–53
Taylor, Captain Henry Clay, XXXVII, 31; XL, 175 ff.
Taylor, James A., XIV, 162
Taylor, Joan Du Plat, Editor, *The International Journal of Nautical Archaeology and Underwater Exploration* [Vol. I], reviewed, XXXII, 293
Taylor, Joel F., VII, 56
Taylor, John, XLVII, 119 ff.
Taylor, Captain John, IV, 262
Taylor, Captain John D., XVII, 254, 256
Taylor, Captain John Davis, XXI, 102
Taylor, Captain John E., XXX, 241, 246
Taylor, Justin E., XLVI, 63; XLVII, 119
Taylor, Admiral Montgomery Meigs, XXXVII, 186 ff.
Taylor, Dr. Nathaniel, XLI, 293
Taylor, Robert, XII, 226
Taylor, Roger C., *The Elements of Seamanship,* reviewed, XLIII, 224; *Good Boats,* reviewed, XXXVII, 225; *More Good Boats,* reviewed, XL, 147
Taylor, Captain S. N., XVII, 135; XVIII, 84
Taylor, Thomas, XXX, 59
Taylor, Thomas D., XXX, 21
Taylor, Captain Thomas De Hart, XXX, 22

Taylor, Thomas Teakle, XXXV, 294
Taylor, W. L., XXII, plate XIX
Taylor, Walter W., VII, 295
Taylor, William H., XIV, 117; XXXIII, 57
Taylor, William Leonhard, *A Productive Monopoly: The Effect of Railroad Control on New England Coastal Steamship Lines, 1870–1916*, reviewed, XXXI, 148–149
Taylor, Zachary, XXXVII, 35
Taylor, General Zachary, XXV, 175
Taylors Island bateau, IV, 290, 298
Ta Yung, steamship (1858), XVI, 179; XVIII, 72; *(1858)*, XLIII, 90 ff.
Ta Yung, tug *(1865)*, XXXIV, 38 ff.
Tea Act, XXVII, 220
Teal, H.M. frigate *(1930)*, L, 188
Teamster, yacht *(1892)*, XXXVI, 236
Tea packing for purchase, photo of, XLVIII, 251
Teasdale, Major H. R., C.S.A., VII, 122
Teaser, C.S.S. *(1862)*, XX, 158
Teaser, ship *(1776)*, XIII, 128
Teaser, U.S.S. *(1798)*, XXXI, 175
Teast, Sidenham, XIII, 213
Tea trade, XLVIII, 261. See also China
Teazer, steamship *(1863)*, XXI, plate XXIII. See also *Teaser*.
Tecklenburg, Captain Peter, XXI, 102
Tecumseh, U.S. monitor (1862), X, 19, 26–27, 32; (1866), III, 172
Teddy Bear, schooner *(1909)*, XXXVIII, 91
Tedesco, bark *(1856–1857)*, I, 100
"*Te Deum*," by Captain Edgar K. Thompson, U.S.N. (ret.), XXI, 28
Teenstra, Anno, *De Clippers*, reviewed, VII, 324
Tefft, Nelson, IX, 228–229
Teghettoff, Admiral Wilhelm von, XV, 201 ff.
Tejuca, steamship *(1865)*, XVI, 174
Telegraph, bark (1854), XV, 186
Telegraph, clipper ship *(1851)*, XLV, 128
Telegraph, grain elevator *(1883)*, XXXVIII, 141
Telegraph, schooner *(1855)*, XXIV, 143; *(1861)*, VIII, 221; *(1864)*, XII, 233, 235
Telegraph, ship, XXII, 239; *(1815)*, XIX, 222
Telegraph, steamship (1836), VII, 61, 62, 311; *(1838)*, VIII, 38, 43, 52, 53, 133; *(1840)*, XX, 86; XXVIII, 124
Telegraph, vessel *(1837)*, XXXVI, 170
Telegraph, marine, III, 211 ff.
Telemachus, snow (1747), I, 167
Telemacus, ship, XXV, 181
Telemaque, schooner, XXI, 103; *(1861)*, XI, 288
Telemico, sloop *(1865)*, XII, 235
Teles, Fernão (or Fernam Tellez) XXX, 251, 253, 254
Telescopes: XI, 220–221; English, Pictorial Supplement, XXXV, plate XXX
Telica, steamship *(1825)*, XXXV, 249
Teller, Captain, XXV, 12, 13
Teller, Walter, XXV, 61

Teller, Walter Magnes, "Postscripts to *The Search for Captain Slocum*," XVIII, 189–200, plates 13, 14
Telles, G. (artist), XXII, plate IX
Tellez, Ferman. See Teles, Fernão.
Tell-Tale Compass: Danish, circa 1760, Pictorial Supplement, XXXV, plate XIII; English, circa 1790, Pictorial Supplement, XXXV, plate XIII
Telos, brig (1883), XLIX, 29 ff.
"*Telos*, the Last American Brig and Bangor River's 'Class of '83,'" by Lawrence Carroll Allin, XLIX, 29–33
Temarario, Spanish torpedo boat *(1898)*, XXXVI, 260, 262
Temaulipas, schooner, XXI, 90. See also *Tamaulipas*.
Tembinoka, King of Apemama, IV, 116–117
Temperance, schooner, XXI, 96; *(1863)*, XII, 160
Temperance, ship (1804), VII, 317
Templar, bark (1862), IV, 239
Temple, Robert, XL, 263
Temple of the Muses, showboat (1817), VIII, 153
Templeton, William, XXXVI, 245
Tempête, French warship [model] (1876), XVI, 103
"Ten Cent War: Naval Phase, The," by Martin L. Seeger, XXXIX, 271–288
Ten (Diez) de Junio, Venezuelan schooner (1848), XXX, 265
Tenedos, bark (1861), XV, 108 n.; XXI, 241, 256
Tenedos, H.M. frigate *(1813)*, XLVI, 165; *(1814)*, XLII, 105 ff.; XLIV, 174
Tenerif, woodboat (1881), XVII, 16
Tenerife Coaling Co., XLVI, 105
Teneriffe, brig *(1854)*, XLV, 189
Tennent, Thomas, XXXIV, 210
Tennessee, C.S.S. ram, XLI, 98; (1862), XIX, 267; (1864), X, 26
Tennessee, ironclad *(1863)*, XLIX, 119
Tennessee, steamship *(1861)*, XI, 288
Tennessee, steamship (ex-*Muscogee*) (1848), IV, 306; XLVII, 38 ff.; lithograph of, XLVII, 39; line drawings of, XLVII, 40, 41
Tennessee, steamship (1853), XXIV, plate XXXII; *(1853)*, X, 134
Tennyson, ship (1864), II, 334
Ten Pound Island, Gloucester (MA), XXV, plates IV, XII
Tenshin Maru, steamship *(1895)*, XI, 259 ff.
Tenyu Maru, steamship (ex-*England*) *(1861)*, XXVI, 130
Teredos, XXVII, 177–184, plate 3
Teresa, schooner *(1863)*, XII, 160
Teresita, bark, XXI, 90; *(1861)*, XI, 266, 267, 288; XII, 58, 160
Termagant, British sloop of war (1795), XLIX, 45
Terminal Island, California (former Rattlesnake Island), XXV, 262–263, 265, 270–272
Terminal Railroad, California, XXV, 265
Terra Australis, XXX, 205, 206
Terra Brass, schooner *(1864)*, XII, 233

Terrapin, schooner, XXI, 89; *(1864),* XV, 130
Terrible, frigate (1798?), IX, 163, plate 19; X, 66, 70
Terrible, steamship *(1849),* XLIII, 169
Terror, H.M.S., XXVIII, 19, 93, 96, 98, 107; *(1845),* XX, 104; L, 128
Terror, U.S. monitor (1862), X, 18, 31
Terry, U.S. torpedo boat, XXII, 142
Terry, Lieutenant Commander Edward, XXXIX, 120
Tessier, Captain Eugene, XXI, 102
Tetautua, schooner *(1898),* IV, 53
Tetis, frigate (1784), VI, 170
Teupken, D. A., XXVIII, plate II
Tevis, Lloyd, XXXI, 124
Texas, battleship *(1850),* XLI, 94; *(1895),* XXXVIII, 137; XXXIX, 127 ff.; XL, 50 ff.
Texas, ship *(1866),* XXXII, 126
Texas, steamship, XXI, 91; *(1861),* XI, 288
Texas, tanker (1908), XXXVIII, 199 ff.
Texas, U.S.S. *(1941),* XLV, 52
Texas (TX), History, Republic (1836–1846), XXI, 216
Texas Co. Shipyard, XXVII, plate XXX
Texas Navy, XXI, 216–221
Texas Ranger, steamship, XXI, 96; *(1861),* XI, 269, 288; XII, 58
Thacher, Anthony, XXV, 234, 244–247
Thacher, Oxenbridge, XXXI, 28
Thacher, Peter, XXV, 244
"Thacher Shipwreck, The Dry Salvages and the," by Samuel Eliot Morison, XXV, 233–247, plates 23–26
Thachers Island (MA), XXV, 233 ff., 244 ff.
Thaddeus, brig, XXII, 151; *(1819),* X, 265
Thaddeus Merriman, concrete ship (1944), XXII, 177, 180
Thales, steamship (1864), XVII, 138; XVIII, 73
Thalia, schooner (1892), XXVI, plate XI
Thames, H.M.S. *(1778),* XXXIV, 139
Thames, ship *(1812),* XXI, 22
Thames, steamship (1835), VII, 57, 313; *(1838),* VIII, 47; (1862), XVIII, 60, 73; (1883), XII, 293
Thames, whaler, XXII, 151
Thames, wooden screw (ex-*Viborg*) *(1847),* XLIX, 26
Thames Sailing Barge, Her Gear and Rigging, The, by Dennis J. Davis, reviewed, XXXII, 144–145
Thann, auxiliary (1918), XXXII, plate 3, 24, 30
Thann Navigation Corp. of New York, XXXII, 24
"'Thar She Blows,'" by Llewellyn Howland, XIII, 131–133
Thatcher, Captain Frederick, XVI, 64
Thatcher, Rear Admiral H. K., U.S.N., VIII, 180–181
Thatcher Magoun, ship (1856), III, 69; *(1866),* XX, 62
"That Prodigal Son: Philo McGiffin and the Chinese Navy," by Richard H. Bradford, XXXVIII, 157–169
Thaxter, Celia, XXV, 65
Thaxter, Samuel, XXXIV, 201; XLVI, 260
Thayer, Gideon, XL, 263
Thayer, John E., "Morse in Japan and His Impact There," XLVI, 55–65

Thayer, Rear Admiral Louis M., XXXVI, 25
Thayer, Captain Robert B., XXI, 102
Thayer, William R., XXXII, 257
Thayer & Lincoln, Boston, XXV, 107
Thebaud, Captain E., XVII, 55; XVIII, 84
Thebes, steamship (1857), XXVI, 111 n., 126, 127, 206, 209
Thebout, Johannus, XVII, 292
The Dare. See *Dare, The.*
Thelma Roberts, three-sail bateau *(1943),* IV, 290–291, 300
Themis, grain elevator *(1959),* XXXVIII, 140
Thence Round Cape Horn, by Robert Erwin Johnson, reviewed, XXIV, 149
Thennett, ship *(1703),* VII, 74, 76
Theobald, ship (1861), I, 110, 113
Theobald, Rear Admiral R. A., U.S.N., VI, 307
Theodora, sloop *(1864),* XII, 233
Theodora, steamship, XXI, 95, 96; *(1861),* VIII, 197, 221, 227; XI, 154; XV, 124
Theodore, brig *(1834),* XXXVIII, 270
Theodore E. Goodhue, schooner (1867), XXXVIII, 63
Theodore Roosevelt, schooner (1901), XXVI, plate XVI
Theodore Stoney, schooner *(1861),* VIII, 221
Theoline, schooner, XXIII, plate XXVIII; *(1942),* III, 60, 163
Thera, lugger (1874), XXX, 198
There Go the Ships, by Captain Rudolph Smale, reviewed, III, 92
Theresa, schooner *(1862),* XII, 58
Thermopylae, ship, XLI, 130; *(1866),* XXXV, plate 5
Theseus, H.M.S., XXXVI, 290
Thetis, cartel schooner *(1814),* XXVIII, 176
Thetis, H.M.S. *(1778),* XLV, 248; *(1824),* XXXV, 31
Thetis, schooner *(1861),* XI, 288; XII, 58
Thetis, ship *(1757),* IX, 144; *(1828),* XIV, 101; *(1861),* XI, 288
Thetis, U.S. cutter *(1906),* XLIV, 19 ff.
Thetis, U.S. Revenue Cutter *(1888),* XXXIX, 9
Thevet, Andre, XI, 101
"They Built Clipper Ships in Their Back Yard," by Admont G. Clark, XXII, 233–251
They Came for Sandalwood: A Study of the Sandalwood Trade in South-West Pacific, 1830–1865, by Dorothy Shineberg, reviewed, XXIX, 145
They followed the Sea — Captain Oliver Jordan of Thomaston, Maine, 1789–1879 — his Sons and his Daughters and the Ships they built, sailed, and commanded, reviewed, III, 92
They Took to the Sea, by David Klein and Mary Louise Johnson, reviewed, IX, 304
"'They Were a Class Apart,' The Story of Life Aboard One of the Four-Stack Flush Deck Destroyers in the Years Between the Two World Wars," by Henry G. Pettitt, XLVI, 240–251
Thibault, Carrow, X, 82, 85; XIV, 298–299
Thicke, Walt, XXXVI, 242, 245

"Thick Night, A," Pictorial Supplement, XXXI, plate XX
Thielbeck, ship *(1927),* XVIII, 216
Thierichens, Captain, XLV, 200
Thinkers and Tinkers: Early American Men of Science, by Silvio A. Bedini, reviewed, XXXVIII, 69
Third International Congress of Maritime Museums, XXXVIII, 231
30 (Trece) de Diciembre, schooner *(1855),* XXX, 275
"Thirty 'Easterns' and Others: Ships Built in Japan for the United States, 1919–1920," by Forrest R. Holdcamper, XXIII, 270–276
"30-Gun Salute, A," document contributed by Captain Edgar K. Thompson, U.S.N. (ret.), XXII, 183
"Thirty Years of *The American Neptune,*" by former Managing Editor, Ernest S. Dodge, XXXII, 231
"'This Bargain Shall Be Kept a Secret,'" document contributed by E. Lee Dorsett, M.D., XV, 155–156
"'This Day Comes in Fine': The Log of the Brig *Selma,*" by E. L. Dorsett, M.D., XIV, 212–214
Thistle, schooner *(1864),* XII, 233; *(1901),* XXX, 196
Thistle, schooner (1918), V, 140
Thistle, steamship, XXI, 94, 98, plate IX; *(1855),* XXII, 21, 28, 29, 31, 34, 39, 42, 43; *(1863),* VIII, 232, 235; *(1864),* VIII, 235
Thistle, yacht *(1888),* XXXVI, 232
Thistle and the Jade, The, by Maggie Keswick, reviewed, XLIII, 149–150
This was Chesapeake Bay, by Robert H. Burgess, reviewed, XXIV, 147–148
Thober, Frank W., "Notes on Marine Disasters off Cape Horn," XVIII, 177–180
Thomas, bark (1837), IV, 73
Thomas, brig *(1778),* X, 281–282
Thomas, dredge (1900), XXXVIII, 200 ff.
Thomas, ship *(1816),* XXX, 45
Thomas, Cephas L., journal of, XXV, plate 5
Thomas, Edward B., I, 102
Thomas, George, XXXVIII, 234.*Thomas A. Cromwell,* schooner (1905), XXVI, plate XX
Thomas, Ichabod (shipbuilder), XXV, 218–219
Thomas, John, XIII, 17
Thomas, Lowell, XXXVI, 266
Thomas, Mifflin, *Schooner from Windward,* reviewed, XLVII, 59
Thomas, Pascoe, XXII, 113
Thomas, Phillip Drennon, XXXIV, 65 n.
Thomas, Captain S. Joseph, XXXIV, 41
Thomas, Sylvanus, XXXIX, 95
Thomas A. Edison, steamship (1901), I, 71, 77, plate facing 78
Thos. A. Metcalf, steamship *(1847),* XLVII, 34
Thomas Bennett, ship *(1850),* XLV, 124
Thomas C. Acton, schooner, XXI, 99; *(1862),* XII, 58
Thomas C. Arthur, schooner *(1861),* XI, 288
Thomas Clyde, bateau (1911), IV, 290

Thomas Cornell, steamship (1863), VI, 277–289, plates 33–34; *(1865),* XIV, 176 ff.
Thomas Coutts, ship (1817), XIV, 102, 103
Thomas Dana, ship (1873), III, 71; *(1874),* VII, 39–41; *(1877),* XXV, 107; *(1889),* XL, 108
Thomas Gordon, ship, XIII, 121
Thomas H. Lawrence, schooner (1891), V, 294–295, plate 20
Thomas H. Perkins, ship (1842), XIX, 27, 38, plate 2; (1845), V, 149
Thomas Hallett, schooner (1926), XXVI, plate XXXI
Thomas Hart, ship *(1850),* XLV, 125
Thomas Harvard, ship (1859), II, 333
Thomas Holcombe, bark (1855), III, 263
Thomas Hunt and Co., XVII, 46, 47, 144, 145; XXII, 15, 32, plate 2; XXXIV, 18 ff.; XLIII, 94 ff.; XLIX, 25
Thomas J. Stewart, barkentine (1890), XII, 305
Thomas Jefferson, steamship (1834), VII, 55; (1839), XVIII, 285, 290; XX, 83 n., 266; (1867), VI, 61; VII, 240, 242
Thomas Kemp Boatyard, XL, 38
Thomas L. Randall, ship *(1832),* XXXVIII, 62
Thomas L. ('S') Gorton, sail-schooner *(1932),* XXXIII, 64
Thos. L. Wragg, steamship *(1861),* VIII, 221, 227
Thomas Mcmanus, steamship, XVIII, 229
Thomas Newton, steamship (1881), VI, 62, plate 4; VII, 242
Thomas Nye, bark (1851), III, 72
"Thomas Paine's Short Career as a Naval Architect, August-October 1807," by Joseph George Henrich, XXXIV, 123–134
Thomas Patten, side-wheel tug *(1917),* XXXIV, 264
Thomas Penrose, ship (1806), VII, 317
Thomas Powell, steamship (1879), VI, 284; (1846), XIV, 163 ff.
Thomas R. Foster, ship *(1885),* V, 327
Thomas Richardson & Sons, XXVI, 207
"Thomas Rogers and the Rhode Island Slave Trade," by Darold D. Wax, XXXV, 289–301
Thomas Russell (1801), XXIII, 217
Thomas Smull and Co., XXX, 174, 180, 181
"Thomas Truxtun on Salutes," document, V, 156–157
Thomas W. Lawson, 7-masted schooner (1902), I, 396; XXIII, 15, plate XXVII; Pictorial Supplement, XXXVI, plate XXVIII
Thomas W. Lawson, American sailing ship *(1907),* XXIX, 133–138
Thomas Watson, steamship, XXI, 96
Thos. Watson, ship *(1861),* VIII, 221
Thomas Welcome Roys: America's Pioneer of Modern Whaling, by Frederick P. Schmitt, Cornelis de Jong, and Frank H. Winter, reviewed, XLI, 144–145
Thomas White and Sons, XXII, 44
Thomes, Ansel L., XVIII, 177
Thompson, Captain Albert A., XII, 104
Thompson, Alexander, XXXI, 204 ff.

Thompson, Benjamin, XXXVI, 255
Thompson, Captain, XXXI, 97
Thompson, Charles, XXXVI, 273
Thompson, Captain Charles, XXI, 102
Thompson, David Whittet, III, 354; "A Seventeenth-Century German Submarine," III, 345–349. *See also* Thomson, David Whittet.
Thompson, Ebenezer, XIII, 120
Thompson, Captain Edgar, "*Cleopatra's Barge,* Navy Style," XV, 83
Thompson, Captain Edgar K., contributed documents, XX, 62; XXI, 303–304; XXII, 142, 220, 220–221; XXIII, 227; XXV, 68–69
  notes by, XXI, 70, 72, 142–143, 144–145, 145–146, 255, 278, 291; XXII, 54, 70, 105, 183, 186, 193, 211, 215, 218, 276, 289; XXIII, 38, 55, 68–69, 196, 222–224, 254, 260, 269, 292; XXIV, 37, 60, 108, 118, 143, 185, 211, 212, 213–214, 215–216, 246; XXV, 28, 34, 45, 50, 67, 111, 115, 122, 127, 140–141, 141–143, 143, 167, 175, 188, 217, 223, 224–226, 273, 277, 287;
  notes and documents by: XXVI, 62, 170, 176, 214–216, 218–219, 257, 271; XXVII, 45, 60, 97, 110, 149, 176, 210; XXVIII, 30, 65, 69, 112, 127, 143–144, 205, 223–224, 286; XXIX, 29, 53, 63–64, 132, 173, 186, 198, 223, 225–226, 261, 281; XXX, 45, 132, 138, 216; XXXI, 18, 37, 51, 146; XXXII, 135; XXXIII, 130; XXXIV, 102, 134, 196, 218, 220, 221; XXXV, 19, 31, 35, 96, 110, 117, 206, 288; XXXVI, 68, 87, 124, 250; XXXVII, 25, 127, 137, 144, 163, 173, 202; XXXVIII, 14, 27, 174; XXXIX, 28, 57, 108, 183, 208, 217. "Journal of a Passage Through the Straits of Magellan in 1829," XXIII, 86–191; "Lafayette in the Frigate *Brandywine,*" XXVI, 258–261; "The *Mayflower's* Jones," XVIII, 318; "Navassa: A Forgotten Acquisition," XXVI, 171–176; "Navassa the First," IX, 63; "Repel Boarders," XIX, 232–234; "The Solitary Grave of Diego Ramirez Islands," XVIII, 177; "The Trojan Horse of Gibraltar, From the Book *Decima Flottiglia M.A.S.,* by Commander Valerio Borghese," XXVII, 185–201
Thompson, Harold W., ed., *The Last of the Logan: The True Adventures of Robert Coffin, Mariner in the Years 1854 to 1859,* reviewed, II, 184
Thompson, Jeremiah, I, 85–87
Thompson, Captain John, XXI, 102
Thompson, Rev. John Bodine, XXXVI, 251
Thompson, Jonathan, V, 115 ff.
Thompson, Captain L. H., XXI, 102
Thompson, General M. Jeff, C.S.A., XXV, 130, 136, 139
Thompson, P. N., XXXVI, 245 ff.
Thompson, P. W., VII, 238–239
Thompson, R. H., VII, 224 ff.; VII, 231
Thompson, R. W., XXII, 260
Thompson, Ralph Newell, V, 247; "Voyage of the Brig *Nabob* from Boston to Batavia, Java in 1833," V, 194–202

Thompson, Richard W., Secretary of the Navy, XLIX, 293
Thompson, Captain Samuel L., XXI, 102
Thompson, Smith, XXXIX, 46; XL, 31
Thompson, Smith, Secretary of the Navy, XLII, 166 ff.
Thompson, Thomas, VIII, 13, 17
Thompson, Captain Thomas, XXVI, 63–71; XLIX, 49
Thompson, Thomas L., XLI, 256
Thompson, Waddy, XXIX, 95, 96
Thompson, William, I, 85–87; XXXVIII, 56
Thompson, Captain William, XXI, 102, 106
Thompson's Island, Boston Harbor, ca. 1840, XXIX, plate XXXI
Thomsen, Captain T. A., XVI, 120; XVIII, 213–215
Thomson, David Whittet, "The Great Steamboat Monopolies" series: Part I: 'The Mississippi,' XVI, 28–40; Part II: 'The Hudson,' XVI, 270–280; "Two Thousand Years Under Sea; The Story of the Diving Bell," VII, 261–281. *See also* Thompson, David W.
Thomson, Captain George, XXI, 102
Thomson, George and James, XXXIX, 134
Thomson, J. and G. H., XXII, 44
Thomson, J & G, XXIX, 5 n.
Thorborg, udema type of vessel [model], VI, plate 24
Thoreau, Henry David, XXV, 63
Thorn, ship *(1864),* XXXIX, 96
Thornborough, Captain, XIII, 29 ff.
Thorndike, Israel, XIII, 122; XXIX, 204
Thorndike, Captain Israel, XXII, 195 ff.; XXIV, 247
Thorndike, Captain Nicholas, XXII, 194 ff.; XXIV, 247–271
Thorne, Robert, XVIII, 271
Thornton, Edward, XXVI, 253
Thornton, Sir Edward, XXXIX, 290
Thornton, John, XIX, 44; XXV, 240
Thornton, R. H., *British Shipping,* reviewed, XX, 225
Thornton, Samuel, XXXI, 25
Thornton, Solomon, XXXIV, 251
Thornton, William, XVI, 28
Thornton, Dr. William, XXVII, 19, 23
Thorsen, Lars, V, 247
Thos. *See* Thomas.
Thrasher, schooner *(1812),* note, XLIII, 222
Thrasher, steam bark *(1894),* XXXVIII, 85; XXXIX, 19
Three Bells, Glasgow *(1854),* XLV, 27
Three Bricks and Three Brothers, by Will Gardner, reviewed, VI, 234–235
Three Brothers, schooner *(1794),* XXIV, 253; *(1809),* X, 150; *(1861),* XI, 288; XII, 58, 160, 233
Three Brothers, ship *(1651),* XIII, 24; (1857), III, 129–130, 263; *(1920),* XVIII, 207
Three Brothers, sloop *(1746),* XLVIII, 33
Three Brothers, steamship *(1872),* XII, 289, 293
Three Centuries of Freeport, Maine, by Florence G. Thurston and Harmon S. Cross, reviewed, I, 100
Three Friends, ship (1741), I, 297; *(1751),* XX, 43
Three Friends, steam tug *(1895),* I, 73; V, 146–147

Three Marys, steamship, XXI, 92, 104; *(1865),* XII, 235
Three-Masted Schooner, The, by William S. Quincy, reviewed, XLVIII, 65
"Three-Masted Schooners," query by V. M. W., I, 90; answers by M. V. Brewington, III, 86; by John Kyman, II, 175; III, 269
Three Sisters, brig *(1784),* XLVI, 10 ff.
Three Sisters, schooner, XXI, 94; *(1812),* XLV, 6; *(1861),* XI, 288; XII, 58
Three Sisters, ship *(1800),* XL, 48; (1811), VII, 317
Three Sisters, sloop (1788), XLIX, 86
Three Sisters, supercargo *(1763),* XLI, 177
Three Voyages of Captain Cook, The, by Frank Paluka, reviewed, XXXIV, 281–282
"Three Watercolors by Cornè," by Richard W. Hale, I, 163–164
Throop, Captain Horatio N., XXXIV, 245
Throop, Samuel and Ruth, XXXIV, 243
"Through the 'Golden Mist:' A Brief Overview of Armada Historiography," by Douglas Knerr, XLIX, 5–13
Thrower, Norman J. W., *Captain James Cook and His Voyages of Discovery in the Pacific,* reviewed, XXXI, 74–75
Thrush, H.M.S., XXVIII, 18
Thule, steamship *(1863),* XLIII, 294 ff.
Thunder, 74, British ship *(1798),* XXXIX, 32
Thunder, H.M.S., XXVI, 54; XXXII, 85
Thunder, steamship (1859), XXVI, 125, 126, 206, 209
Thunderbum, frigate *(1831),* XXXVIII, 109
Thunderer 74, ship *(1798),* XLV, 96
Thunderer, British ship *(1780),* XXXVIII, 94
Thunder of the Guns, The, by Donald MacIntyre, reviewed, XX, 226
Thurloe, snow (1742), I, 297
Thurlow, A., XXXVI, 233
Thurston, Florence G., and Harmon S. Cross, *Three Centuries of Freeport, Maine,* reviewed, I, 100
Thurston, Robert H., XXIV, 167 ff.
Thurston, William N., "Management-Leadership in the United States Shipping Board, 1917–1918," XXXII, 155–170
"Thus," document contributed by Captain Edgar K. Thompson, U.S.N. (ret.), XXIII, 254
Thynne, A. G., XXXVI, 245
Thynne, Sir Henry, XXXI, 91 ff.; XLVII, 77
Tiara, ship *(1850),* XLV, 125
Tiara Toporo, schooner, XXXVI, 275
Tiare, French warship *(1956),* XXI, 200
Tiber, ship (1864), III, 172
Tice, John, IV, 313 ff.
Tickler, tender *(1814),* XLII, 105
Ticonderoga, U.S.S. (1813), XXI, 48, 53, 54; *(1814),* XXXI, 287; *(1863),* XLV, 237; *(1878),* XXXIV, 83
Tidalwave, schooner yacht *(1891),* VII, 223
Tidal Wave, sloop, XXXVII, 225
Tidal wave, I, 108

"Tidal Wave at Huanillos, Chile, in 1877, A," by Lincoln Colcord, I, 108–115
Tiddeman, Captain Mark, XIX, 44–50
Tides of Empires: Vol. I, Decisive Naval Campaigns in the West, 1481–1654, by Peter Padfield, reviewed, XLII, 139–140
Tides of Empires: Vol. II, Decisive Naval Campaigns in the Rise of the West, 1654–1763, by Peter Padfield, reviewed, XLIV, 279–280
Tidewater Shipbuilding Co., XLI, 193
Tiebout, Cornelius (engraver), XXV, 126, plate 9
Tientsin, steamship *(1863),* XLIII, 294
Tiger, flagship *(1613),* XXVIII, 245, 246, 247, 248
Tiger, ship *(1845),* XII, 102, 106
Tiger, S.M.S. gunboat *(1906),* XL, 89 ff.
Tiger, whale ship, XXV, 104
Tigre, H.M.S. *(1799),* XXXVI, 290
Tigress, schooner *(1814),* XLIV, 172
Tiira, Ensio, XXIII, 114–116
Tilbury, British ship *(1757),* XLVIII, 29
Tilden, Bryant P., V, 194 ff.
Tilden, Nathaniel, XIX, 8
Tilikum, dugout canoe *(1901),* XXVIII, 53–65, plates 3–8
Tilley, A. F., "Warships of the Ancient Mediterranean," L, 192–200
Tilley, John A., reviews by, XLVI, 122; XLVII, 55, 59; XLIX, 61; *The British Navy and the American Revolution,* reviewed, XLIX, 315
Tillicum, yacht *(1905),* XXXVI, 241, 245
Tillie, steamship (1862), XXIV, plate XXX
Tillinghast, Daniel, VIII, 13; XIV, 51; XXXI, 133
Tillinghast, Jonathan, XLII, 41 ff.
Tillinghast, Mr., XXX, 296
Tillman, Senator Ben ("Pitchfork"), XLI, 194
Tilly Baker, bark (1876), XXVIII, plate XVII
Tilton, Lieutenant E. G., XXXI, 186
Tilton, Captain Henry W., XXI, 103
Tilton, Captain McLane, U.S.M.C., XXV, 116–122; XXXIX, 120
Tilton, Captain Shadrack, XXV, 23
Tilton, Captain Shadrack R., XXXIII, 52 ff.
Tilton, John Gibson, XXV, 117
Tilton, Nan (Mrs. McLane Tilton), XXV, 116–122
Timber, III, 239; XLVI, 221
Transportation, XLVIII, 77
Timbotta, Giorgio, XIV, 264
Timbuctoo, schooner *(1838),* XXXVIII, 57
Time, bark (1855), IV, 241
Time, schooner *(1861),* VIII, 232; XV, 124
"'Time and Waste Books' of James Wilson, builder of the *Ann McKim,*" by David B. Tyler, III, 26–34
Times Literary Supplement, The, VII, 81; editorial quoted, VII, 83–85
Timewell, H. C., "*Exodus 1947* Takes on her Cargo," IX, 300–301
Timmings, E. K., XXIX, 5 n.

Timor, ship *(1861)*, XV, 108 n.; XXI, 238, 256
Timothy Field, brig *(1883)*, XLIX, 31 ff.
Tinchenborn, Judge, XXXVI, 91
Tingey, Thomas, XXXIX, 34
Tingey, Captain Thomas, XXII, 275; XLIII, 137
Ting Ju-cu'ang, Admiral, XXXVIII, 162
Tingqua, ship (1852), XVII, 17, 19–25
Ting Yuen, Chinese battleship (1881), VIII, 268 ff.; IX, 301; *(1894)*, XXXVIII, 165 ff.
Tinker, Governor John, of Nassau, XXV, 203; XXVI, 38, 40, 59
Tinklepaugh, Captain, IV, 144 ff.
Tioga, U.S. steamship (1861), XXIV, 208 ff.
Tippecanoe, U.S. monitor (1862), X, 19, 32
Tippoo Sahib, ship *(1853)*, XV, 252
Tip Top, schooner *(1864)*, XII, 233, 235
Tiranicide, brig *(1777)*, XLIII, 24
Tirona, General Daniel, XXXV, 190
Titan, steamship *(1865)*, XVII, 43, 308; XLIII, 95 ff.; XLV, 29
Titana, steamship *(1868)*, XVII, 57
Titanic, liner *(1912)*, XXXV, 43 ff.; XXXVI, 7, 9, 20, 32
Titanic, White Star liner (1914), XXII, 80
Titanic: End of a Dream, The, by Wyn Craig Wade, reviewed, XL, 65
Titt Bitt, sloop *(1756)*, XXXV, 294 ff.
Titus, Captain T. J., XX, 89 n., 95–99
TN. *See* Tennessee
Toadfish, brig *(1812)*, XXI, 21
Tobacco Trade, XXI, 207–215
Tobin, Austin J., XXVII, 261, 262, plate 12
Tobin, Daniel, Jr., mention, XL, 163
Tobin, Patrick, XIV, 250, 258
Tobin, William, XV, 95
Toby, Charles B., XLII, 4
"To California in '49," document contributed by F. Sheldon Drew, IV, 329–334
Tod, Giles, M. S., I, 102; II, 84; VI, 307; reviews by: XXVIII, 148–149; XXX, 217–218, 219–220; XXXI, 73; XXXII, 142; XXXIII, 63, 146; XLV, 133; XLVII, 142; XLVIII, 188; *The Last Sail Down East*, reviewed, XXVI, 223
Tod and McGregor, XXVI, 11, 15, 18, 19, 22, 115, 118, 208. *See also* Todd and MacGregor.
Tod & MacGregor (shipbuilders), XLIII, 90 ff. *See also* Todd and MacGregor.
Todd, Captain E. H., XXXIV, 245
Todd, Elias, XVII, 120
Todd, J. C., XVIII, 13
Todd, Mallory, XXX, 136
Todd and MacGregor, XXII, 44. *See also* Tod and McGregor (MacGregor).
Toey-wan, British steamship *(1859)*, XXVII, 157, 166–170, 223–224
Toeywan, steamship *(1858)*, XXXIV, 21
Toft, Captain Yes (or James S.), XXIX, 263

Tokei Maru, steamship (1852), XVII, 57; XVIII, 73; *(1874)*, XVII, 313
Toledo, steamship (1902), XXXVIII, 183 ff.
Toledo Shipbuilding Co., XXII, 183
Tolle, Captain J. R., XXI, 103
Tolles, Frederick B., query by, I, 171
Tolley, Kemp, *Cruise of the* Lanikai: *Incitement to War*, reviewed, XXXIV, 278
Tolman, Elisha, XXV, 222
Tolten, Chilean ship *(1867)*, XXXIX, 276
Tom, Krouman, XXX, 184
Tomba della Nave ship, XXIV, plate 9
Tomblin, Barbara B., "United States Navy and the Philippine Insurrection," XXXV, 183–196
Tom Bowline, U.S.S. *(1815)*, XIX, 219, 220
Tom Cod, English brig (1825), XXXVIII, 55
Tom Hicks, schooner (1861), XI, 288
Tomkinson, Captain S. D., XXXIV, 245
Tomlinson, George, XXIV, 21
Tompkins, John, VII, 153
Tom Sugg, schooner *(1863)*, XII, 160
Tom Thumb, steamship, XXVIII, 124
Tom Tilton, Coaster and Fisherman, edited by Gale Huntington, reviewed, XLV, 135
Tonawanda, ship *(1920)*, XVIII, 210
Tonawanda, U.S. monitor (1862), X, 18, 31
Tonga, boats of, XIII, 95 ff.
Tonkin, Joseph Dudley, *The Last Raft*, reviewed, I, 402–403
Tonnage: VIII, 99–113; measurement of, XIV, 5–17
Tonnage, Measurement, V, 223, 311; VIII, 99
Tonnage, register, V, 223–234, 311–325
"Tonnage Rules in 1799," by M. V. Brewington, I, 295–296
"Tonnage — Weight and Measurement," by John Lyman, VIII, 99–113
Tonnere, sloop *(1861)*, XI, 298
"To No Avail" by Captain Edgar K. Thompson, U.S.N. (ret.), XXVI, 257
Tonquin, ship *(1811)*, V, 160–161; (1845), XXXII, 210; XXXIV, 256
Tonyn, Governor Patrick, of East Florida, XXV, 211
Toombs, Senator Robert, L, 113
Topaz, ship *(1807)*, X, 54, 56, 59–61; (1822), XV, 136–137
Topliff, Captain Samuel, I, 298; IV, 245–346
Topo, II, 57–58
Topping, Morgan, V, 327
"Topping Lifts and Dipping the Spanker Gaff, also West Coast *vs.* East Coast Schooner Style," by Karl Kortum, XXVIII, 224
"Topsail Schooner *Americana*, The," by Nicholas Wagner, III, 261
Topsail schooners, Colonial, XXV, 87 ff.
Topuios, Ataunasiosk Satama, XXXVI, 17
Torbay, steamship, XXII, 219
Torch, ship *(1815)*, XL, 39 ff.

Torche, schooner, XXIX, 197
Tornado, ship (1852), III, 264
Tornado, Spanish vessel *(1864),* XXXVI, 93 ff.; XXXVIII, 244
Toronto, H.M.S. *(1841),* VIII, 38, 56, 132
Toronto, steamship (1824), VI, 199, 202, 206; *(1843),* XVII, 102
Toronto City, steamship *(1936),* XIV, 127, 129, 135
Torpedo boats, XLII, 85; XLIX, 114
Torpedo bombers, XXXVII, 111
Torpedoes, XXVII, 185
Torpedoes, human, XXVII, 185–201
Torpedo Launch No. 4 (1864), XLII, 89 ff.
Torrens, clipper ship, XXIII, 140–141, 284
Torres, Captain Luis Vaez de, XXV, 251
Torres Strait, XXX, 205
Torrey Canyon, tanker *(1967),* XXXVI, 10; XXXVIII, 175 ff.
Torr Head, steamship *(1933),* XIV, 127, 129, 135
To Santa Rosalia — Further and Back, by Harold D. Huycke, Jr., reviewed, XXXII, 142–143
Toscan, Bonaparte, VI, 93–100
Toscan, Elizabeth Parrott, VII, 168
Toscan, Frank, VII, 168, 169
Toscan, Jean, VII, 168
Toscanelli, Paulo, XXX, 254, 255, 256
Toscan Papers, New Hampshire Historical Society, VII, 167–169
Toss, Brian, *The Rigger's Apprentice,* reviewed, XLVII, 56
Tostig, Earl, XLIV, 96 ff.
"To Strike a Blow at the California Trade," by Francis X. Holbrook, XXXII, 195–210
"To the Faraway Island: Philadelphia to Nantucket Half a Century Ago," by William A. Wiedersheim, XXXIV, 258–261
To the Rescue; a true Story, by Phillips N. Case, reviewed, II, 263
"To 'The River', An Offshore Schooner Trade," by W. J. Lewis Parker, XXXV, 5–19
Totten, Lieutenant B. J., U.S.N., XXX, 43
Totten, Brigadier General Joseph, XXXI, 70
Toucey, Isaac, XXVII, 157, 165, 172–174; XXXI, 60; XXXVI, 180; XXXVIII, 37
Toucey, Isaac, Secretary of the Navy, XXV, 224–225
Touitia, steamship (1862), XVIII, 73
Toul, auxiliary (1918), XXXII, 24, 30
Toulon, ship *(1861),* XI, 288
Toulon Fleet, *1778,* XXV, 189, 191
Toulza, J. Etienne (artist), mention in editorial comment, XLII, 3
Tourmaline, H.M.S., XXVIII, 16, 17, 24, 88
Tourtourelle, French ship *(1800),* XXXI, 175
Toussaint, Auguste, "Franconesia, A Little Known Quarter of the Indian Ocean," XXXI, 104–119; *Harvest of the Sea: The Mauritius Sea Story in Outline,* reviewed, XXVI, 285; *History of the Indian Ocean,* reviewed, XXVI, 285; *La Route des Iles,* reviewed, XXVIII, 150–151
Toussaint L'Ouverture, François Dominique, XXV, 30
Tovarich, ship (1892), IX, 298
Tovarisch, bark (1892), II, 290
Tovarisch, training vessel *(1964),* XXIV, 80
Toward, ship *(1943),* XLIV, 49 ff.
"Towards a Citizen Sailor: The History of the Naval Militia Movement, 1888–1898," by Kevin R. Hart, XXXIII, 258–279
Towboats and Tugs, edited by Elizabeth Stanton Anderson, L, 139
"Tow-boat *Seth Low,* The: An Unsung Hero," by Alexander Crosby Brown, III, 161–163
Towel, Lamina, XXX, 184, 185
Tower, Walter T., Jr., review by, XLI, 234–235
Tower Galley, privateer, XXVI, 40
Towle, A. M., XXXVI, 237
Towle, Edward L., XXV, 111; "Lieutenant Silas Bent's Device to Eliminate Variation Correction in the Magnetic Compass, 1849," XXV, 93–98, plate 4; contributed documents, XXIV, 94; XXV, 69–70
Towle, Hamilton E., IV, 69–71
Towne, Captain Solomon, XLVI, 26
Townes, John D., VII, 66
Townsend, steamship (1840), XX, 82 n.
Townsend, Charles Haskell, XLIX, 38; L, 119
Townsend, Chauncey, XLVIII, 26
Townsend, Coit and Co., VII, 57
Townsend, Dr. James, XLVIII, 37
Townsend, John, XVII, 125; XXIV, 58; XXVI, 204
Townsend, Captain Josiah, XVII, 68
Townsend, Robert, XLVIII, 42
Townsend, Commander Robert, XXXII, 125 ff.
Townsend, Samuel, XLVIII, 31 ff.
Townsend, Captain Samuel L., XXI, 102
Townsend, Solomon, XLII, 41 ff.
Townsend, Captain Solomon, XLVIII, 43
Townshend, Captain Charles Hervey, I, 95
Townshend, Honorable George, XXVI, 40
Townshend, Rt. Hon. Lord J., L, 32
Townshend Act, XXVII, 218–220
Town that Went to Sea, A, by Aubigne L. Packard, reviewed, XI, 298
Trabacolas, I, plate facing 371; II, 58, 59
"Traces of Reed Boats in the Pacific," by Ruth Knudsen, XXIII, 41–45
Track of the Bear, by William Bixby, reviewed, XXVIII, 71–72
Tracy, Benjamin, Secretary of the Navy, XXXVIII, 291; XXXIX, 141; XL, 130, 168
Tracy, Ira, XLVIII, 274
Tracy, Nathaniel, XXX, 114, 115
Tracy, Nicholas, *Navies, Deterrence & American Independence: Britain and Seapower in the 1760s and 1770s,* reviewed, L, 143
Tracy, Robert C., query by, II, 81

Trade acts. *See* Acts of Trade and Navigation
"Trade between Providence, Rhode Island, and the Caribbean and South America, in 1796, The," by Seth O. Reed, XLV, 166–174
Trade Designations of Protected British Vessels, Table III, XLVIII, 9
Trade Makers, The, by P. N. Davies, reviewed, XXXV, 218
Trader, schooner *(1861),* VIII, 221
"Tradition of St. Elmo's Fire, The: A Postscript," note contributed by Captain Edgar K. Thompson, U.S.N. (ret.), XXIV, 213–214
"Tradition of the St. Elmo's Fire, The," by George G. Carey, XXIII, 29–38
Traditions and Memories of American Yachting, by W. P. Stephens, reviewed, II, 352
Trafalgar, Battle of, XXV, 45
Trafalgar, H.M.S. *(1896),* XXV, 163
Trafalgar, schooner *(1812),* XXI, 17
Trafalgar, steamship (1871), XVII, 54; XVIII, 73; *(1871),* XLIX, 24
Trafalgar and the Spanish Navy, by John D. Harbron, reviewed, XLIX, 314
Tragic History of the Sea, The, C. R. Boxer, editor, reviewed, XX, 275
"Tragic Slaving Voyage of *St. John,* The," by James M. Bellarosa, XL, 293–297
Train, Enoch, XV, 140, 141; XLV, 181
Train, Samuel, XV, 178
Training ships, XX, 134
  United States, XL, 38
Training Squadron off Coasters Harbor island, Newport, circa 1885, photo of, XLIX, 294
Training vessels, Swedish, II, 295–298
Training vessels, United States Navy, XX, 134–145
Traite de l'Hélice Propulsive, by Admiral E. Paris, XXX, 15
Tramontana, ship *(1606),* XXXI, 85 ff.
Tranquebar, ship (1868), II, 245
Transatlantic flights, L, 249
Transatlantic Paddle Steamers, by H. Philip Spratt, reviewed, XI, 294
Trans-Atlantic Passenger Ships, Past and Present, by Eugene W. Smith, reviewed, VIII, 74
"Transfer of Grain by Elevators," illustration, XXXVIII, 138
Transit, steamship *(1835),* VII, 57; *(1840),* VIII, 53
Transit of Venus, 1768, XXX, 205
Transmediterránea (Spanish shipping line), XLVI, 108
Transpacific Steam, by E. Mowbray Tate, reviewed, XLVIII, 132
"Trans-Pacific Venture of James J. Hill, The; A History of the Great Northern Steamship Company," by W. Kaye Lamb, III, 185–204
"Transpacific Voyages of *Pamir,* The," by Jerry MacMullen, VI, 112–114, plates 13–16
Transportation, military, VI, 179
Transports, XXVI, 192–199
Transylvania, Rumanian flag vessel *(1944),* XLIII, 33 ff.
Trantmann and Co., XVIII, 63
Trask, Captain Benjamin, XVII, 17, 25–27
Trask, Charles Hooper, XXIII, 139
Travel. *See* Ocean travel
"Travel by Water, To, From, Between and Within the United States in 1800," by Peter Oliver, III, 292–313
Traveller, brig *(1806),* XXIII, 194–195; *(1816),* XXXV, 198
Traveller, H.M.S. *(1838),* VIII, 49 ff.
Traveller, steamship (1835), VII, 56, 308–309
Traveller, yacht *(1908),* XXXVI, 247
Travels and Controversies of Friar Domingo Navarrete 1618–1686, The, J. S. Cummins, Editor, reviewed, XXIII, 290
"Travels of *Tilikum,* The," by W. Gillies Ross, XXVIII, 53–65
Traverse Boards: American (left), French (right), Pictorial Supplement, XXXV, plate XXV (upper).
Trawlers, XLIV, 114
Treadwell, Daniel, VII, 69
Treadwell, Captain Jonathan, XL, 196
Treandrea, schooner (1918), I, plate facing 73
Treasure fleet (Spanish—1551), VI, 241
Treaty, steamship *(1861),* VIII, 221
Treaty of 1853, XXXI, 13
Treaty of Aigun, 1858, XXXI, 274
Treaty of Aix-la-Chapelle, 1748, XXXI, 20
Treaty of Amity, Commerce and Navigation, XXIII, 162
Treaty of Ghent, XXVIII, 119
Treaty of Münster, XXX, 203
Treaty of Nanking, XXXI, 187
Treaty of Paris, 1783, XXXIII, 246
Treaty of Tientsin, XXXIV, 52, 103 ff.
Treaty of Wanghia, XXXIV, 105
Treaty of Wang-Hsia, XXXI, 185
Trece de Diciembre, see *30 (thirty) de Diciembre.*
Trecothick, Barlow, XXXIII, 96
Tredegar Iron Works (Richmond, VA), XXII, 252; XLIV, 261; XLV, 40; XLVIII, 110
Tredwell, American Consul Roger, XLIV, 181
Tregantle, British steamship *(1916),* XLVIII, 50
Tregear, William James, XXVI, 204
Trelawny, Edward John, XL, 218
Tremont, ship, XXVIII, 124; (1902), III, 195–196; *(1902),* XLVII, 200
Tremontana, ship (1586), XIV, 10, 11
Trenholm, George A., IX, 32 ff.; XV, 100 ff.
Trent, British mail steamship *(1861),* XXXIII, 6
Trent, steamship *(1878),* XVII, 61
Trent Affair, 1861, XXVII, 30; XXV, 140
Trenton, American flagship *(1889),* XLVI, 115
Trenton, brig (1836), XIV, 41
Trenton, cruiser *(1882),* XXXVIII, 124; XXXIX, 128
Trenton, ship (1832), XV, 139; (1840), XXVII, plate XV
Trenton, U.S. cruiser *(1926),* XLVI, 240 ff.

Trescot, Captain George F., XXI, 103
Trescot, William Henry, XXXIX, 292
Trescott, Lemuel, XXVIII, 119
Tres de Mayo, brig *(1861),* XI, 288
Trevenen, Midshipman James, XXXVIII, 218 ff.
Trevett, Lieutenant John, Continental Marines, XXV, 208, 213, 216 n.
Tréhouart, Captain, XXXVI, 131 ff.
Trial, boat (1787), XIII, 157
Trial, ship *(1630),* XXIII, 63, 65
Trial, sloop *(1750),* XLVIII, 28
Triall, freighter *(1606),* XXXI, 87 ff.; XLVII, 77 ff.
"Trials of an Unarmed Brig, The," by Gershom Bradford, IX, 11–16
"Trials of a Yankee Sailor: Robert Gray in the Río de la Plata, 1798–1802," by Jerry W. Cooney, XLIX, 272–277
"Triangles and Tramping: Captain Zebediah Story of Newport, 1769–1776," by Virginia Bever Platt, XXXIII, 294–303
Triangle trade, XXXIII, 294. See also Slave trade; Slave traders
Trias, Rolando A. Laguarda, *Nueva Lista Documentada de los Tribulantes de Colon en 1492,* reviewed, XLVI, 126
Tribune, H.M.S. *(1830),* XXV, 143; *(1899),* XXVIII, 93, 98
"Tribute, Defensiveness, and Dependency: Uses and Limits of Some Basic Ideas About Mid-Qing Dynasty Foreign Relations," by John E. Wills, Jr., XLVIII, 225–229
Trident Fisheries Co., XLIV, 121
Trier, schooner *(1862),* XV, 126
Triewald, Martin, VII, 276
Trigonometer, American, Pictorial Supplement, XXXV, plate XXVI (upper).
Trimble, South, Jr., XLI, 117
Trimble, William F., "Pittsburgh's Dravo Corporation and Naval Shipbuilding in World War II," XXXVIII, 272–290
Trimmer, schooner *(1814),* XLII, 114 ff.
Trinidad Island, South Atlantic, XXV, 180–181
Trinity, balinger *(1481),* XXXVII, 161
Trinity, bark *(1880),* XL, 121
Trinity House, XI, 5 ff.; XIII, 5–28; XIV, 64–65; XV, 303–306; XVI, 87–97; XX, 6–9, 28, 32, 35–39, 185–190
"Trinity House Ship Models, The," by Captain W. R. Chaplin, IV, 261–286; note by R. C. Anderson, V, 146
"Trinity House Yachts," documents contributed by Captain W. R. Chaplin, VI, 228–231, 304–306
Trinkaus-Randall, Gregor, review by, XLV, 136
Trinkaus-Randall, Gregor and Robert P. Spindler, "Recently Processed Manuscript Collections in the Phillips Library at the Peabody Museum of Salem," XLIX, 230–231

"Triple National Salute, A," document contributed by Captain Edgar K. Thompson, U.S.N. (ret.), XXI, 70
Triplicaine, ship *(1678),* XIII, 13 ff.
Tripoli, Pictorial Supplement, XXXII, plate XX
Tripolitain War (1801–1805). See United States History
Tripp, William H., I, 400; IX, 19, 29, plates 2–3
Trippe, Captain Edward, XXX, 72
Trippe, Lieutenant, XXI, 134–135, 136
Trist, Nicholas P., XXXVIII, 104
Tristan de Cunha, South Atlantic, XXV, 181, plate 18
Tristram Shandy, steamship *(1864),* VIII, 235; XXI, plate XIII; XXXII, 199
Triton, bark *(1894),* XXXVIII, 85; XXXIX, 8
Triton, brig *(1813),* XIX, 218
Triton, privateer *(1745),* XLII, 50
Triton, schooner (1815), XIV, 41; (1825), XXII, 216; *(1832),* XXXV, 83
Triton, ship *(1784),* XI, 61 ff., 134; *(1823),* VI, 99
Triton, steamship, XXI, 87; *(1864),* XII, 233
Triton, tug *(1894),* XLII, 267 ff.; *(1901),* XVI, 7
Triumph, H.M.S. *(1915),* XXXVI, 40, 41, 43; L, 185
Triumph, schooner *(1865),* VIII, 237
Triumph, ship *(1570),* XLIV, 28
Trobriand Islands, boats of, XIII, 111
Trois Frères or *Freres,* schooner, XXI, 99; (1861), XI, 289
Trojan, ship (1875), IV, 241
"Trojan Horse of Gibraltar, From the Book *Decima Flottiglia* M.A.S. by Comander Junio Valerio Borghese, The," translated by Captain Edgar K. Thompson, U.S.N. (ret.). XXVII, 185–201
"Tromelin Island," by Lieutenant Commander Geoffrey Rawson, XVIII, 180
Tronson, Thomas Harold, XXVI, 204
Troop transport. See Transportation
Tropic, brig *(1807),* XVI, 195
Tropic, steamship, XXI, 87; (1863), VIII, 232
Tropical Diseases, XXVII, 81–97
Tropical Enterprise: The Standard Fruit and Steamship Company in Latin America, by Thomas L. Karnes, reviewed, XL, 140
Tropic Bird, bark (1851), Pictorial Supplement, XXXIII, plate XIII
Trott, Raymond H., "Down East Merchant Fleet, A," IV, 45–52
Troubled Waters, schooner *(1775),* XXX, 111
Troublesome Voyage of Captain Fenton, 1582–1585, The, edited by E. G. R. Taylor, reviewed, XX, 275
Troutman, Commodore, XXXVIII, 240
Trowbridge, Edmund, XL, 256
Trowbridge, Captain Elias, VII, 44
Troy, schooner *(1862),* XII, 59
Troy & Erie and United States Lines, VII, 56
Truair, Rev. John, XXXVII, 182; XXXIX, 46
True, Nathaniel, XLVI, 60
True American, schooner *(1777),* V, 187
True Blood, schooner *(1777),* XXI, 10
True Blue, picaroon *(1728),* XLII, 23 ff.

True Blue, sloop *(1777),* V, 187
Truelove, bark (1764), III, 264
Truelove, ship *(1729),* XXI, 265
Trueman, Captain James, XXI, 18
Trueworthy, Captain Thomas E., XLIII, 110 ff.
Truite, schooner *(1780),* XXXV, 141
Trumble, row galley *(1776),* VIII, 256
Trumbull, Continental frigate *(1781),* XLIV, 169
Trumbull, frigate (1776), VIII, 11, 14, 20, 21, 24; *(1776),* XXXI, 134, 174, 244; XXXIV, 141; XXXV, 142
Trumbull, ship *(1779),* XXXVII, 293
Trumbull, U.S.S. *(1777),* XIV, 49
Trumbull, Governor, XXXI, 134
Trumbull, Governor Jonathan, XXXIX, 193
Trumpeter, steamship *(1860),* XXXVI, 185
Trussell, Richard, XXII, 288 n.
Trusty, ship, XXII, 90
Truxton, Captain Thomas, VII, 257; XIII, 65; XXX, 121, 124, 128, 129; XXXVI, 58, 276 ff.; XXXIX, 131, 235; XL, 23 ff.
Truxton, Commodore Thomas, XLV, 94 ff.; XLVI, 159; XLVII, 25; XLIX, 44
Truxton-Decatur House, naval museum, IX, 238
Truxtun, Thomas, V, 156–157
Truxtun, Captain Thomas, U.S.N., XXII, 267, 268, 269, 270, 273, 274
Tryal, schooner *(1807),* XVI, 194
Tryal, ship, XXII, 108, 109, 111; XXV, 61
Tryal, sloop *(1776),* XLIV, 158 ff.
Tryall, H.M.S. *(1727),* XXI, 263
Tryckare, Tre and W. A. Baker, *The Engine-Powered Vessel; From Paddle-Wheeler to Nuclear Ship,* reviewed, XXVI, 150–151
Tryton, ship *(1757),* IX, 144
Tsatlee, steamship *(1862),* XVI, 249; XVIII, 73; *(1862),* XLIII, 123 ff.
Tsing-Tau or *Tsingtau,* German gunboat *(1900),* XL, plate 1; *(1910),* 88 ff.
Tuaikaepau, cutter, XXIV, 226
Tuamotu Archipelago, XXX, 298; boats of, XIII, 89 ff.
Tubal Cain, steamship, XXI, 102; *(1862),* VIII, 228
Tubman, President William V. S., XXXIX, 180 ff.
Tucker, A. L., and A. H. Waite, *Ship Plans,* reviewed, XIX, 309
Tucker, Arthur L., *Model Shipwright,* Vol. 1, No. 1, reviewed XXXIII, 68–69
Tucker, Captain John, XII, 37
Tucker, J. S., VII, 88
Tucker, R. D., XXIII, 136
Tucker, Spencer C., "Arming the Fleet: Early Cannon Founders to the United States Navy," XLV, 35–40; *Arming the Fleet: U.S. Navy Ordnance in the Muzzle-Loading Era,* reviewed, L, 45; "Mr. Jefferson's Gunboat Navy," XLIII, 135–141; "U.S. Navy Gun Carriages from the Revolution through the Civil War," XLVIII, 108–118; "U.S. Navy Steam Sloop *Princeton,*" XLIX, 96–113

Tuckerman, Edward, XV, 134
Tudor, Frederick, XIII, 122; XV, 249
Tudor, Henry, XXXVII, 162
Tudor, Samuel, VIII, 14, 21; XXXVIII, 16
Tudor, William, Jr., XXXI, 19
Tudor House Museum, Southampton, XXX, 154
Tudor Ice Co., XLVI, 63
Tufts, Cotton, XXV, 82
Tufts, Otis, I, 55
Tufts, Captain Simon, XIII, 31 ff.
"Tug *Seth Low,*" by J. W. Somerville, V, 146
Tulloch & Denny, XXVI, 208
Tulsa, cruiser *(1923),* XXXV, 127
"'Tumble-Home' Gun Carriages," query by Winthrop Pratt, Jr., IX, 75
Tungting, steamship *(1872),* XVII, 216
Tunisian fishing lateener, II, 61–62
Tunsin, steamship *(1863),* XVII, 136, 137; XVIII, 73; *(1863),* XLIII, 219 ff., plate 4
Tunxis, ship, XXXV, 60
Tupper, Charles, XIX, 58, 59
Turan, Captain Kazim, XLIII, 36 ff.
Turbinia, steam yacht *(1894),* XXX, 153
Turenga, yacht *(1914),* XXXVI, 248
Turkey, Foreign relations, United States, XL, 241
Turkey Mill (Paper mill in Kent, England), XLVI, 175
"Turkish Steam Warship," query by L. W. Jenkins, I, 89
Turnbull, Alexander, XLI, 280
Turnbull, Marmie & Co., Philadelphia, XLVI, 30
Turner, Captain A., XXI, 103
Turner, Captain Benjamin, XXV, 219
Turner, Christopher, XIII, 236
Turner, Christopher (shipbuilder), II, 282
Turner, Commander Daniel, XLVI, 231
Turner, Lieutenant Daniel, XLIV, 176
Turner, Frederick J., Frontier Thesis, XXV, 52
Turner, Bishop H. McNeal, XXXV, 204
Turner, J. M., Chief Officer, XLVIII, 239
Turner, Captain John, XLI, 185
Turner, Obadiah, XLVI, 213
Turner, Thomas, I, 295–296
Turner, Commander Thomas, XXXIV, 66 ff.
Turner, Captain William T., XXXV, 36 ff.
Turner and (&) Co., XXII, 13; XLIII, 107 ff.
"Turning In," Pictorial Supplement, XXXI, plate XVIII
Turpie, Senator, XXV, 264
Turpin, Captain, XIII, 37
Turret Cape, turret steamship *(1895),* XXV, 171
Turret Chief, turret steamship *(1896),* XXV, 171
Turret ships, XXIII, 197; XXXI, 52; XLIX, 114
    Design and construction, XLVIII, 106
    United States, X, 15
Turret ships, English, XXV, 170–171, plate 16
Turtle, sidewheel yacht *(1889),* XXX, plate XXVI
Turtle, submarine *(1776),* XXXIV, 146
Turtle Shell Wreck, XLIII, 13 ff.
Tuscaloosa, C.S.S. *(1863),* XLVIII, 95

Tuscaloosa, ship *(1873),* XXXIII, 60; XXXIV, 82 ff.
Tuscaloosa, whale ship *(1885),* XXII, plate XXII
Tuscaloosa (ex-*Conrad*), clipper ship, XXVI, 98, 100, 102–104, 106–108
Tuscan Coaster, I, 365–366, plate facing 366
Tuscany, ship *(1836),* XV, 250
Tuscarora, ship *(1806),* VII, 317
Tuscarora, ship *(1868),* XL, 127
Tuscarora, U.S.S. *(1860),* XXXV, 27; *(1861),* XV, 290; *(1862),* XVIII, 250; *(1864),* XXVII, 36
Tuscarora, U.S. steam sloop (1861), XXII, 289
Tusitala: The Story of a Voyage in the Last of America's Square Riggers, by Roland Barker, reviewed, XX, 70
Tuskar, brig *(1841),* XXXVII, 220 ff.
Tuskawilla, steamship (1875), VII, 140, 141, 144, 164, plate 14
Tusker, brig (1831), XIX, 26, 27
Tutorow, Norman E., "Leland Stanford, President of the Occidental and Oriental Steamship Company: A Study in the Rhetoric and Reality of Competition," XXXI, 120–129
Tuttle, Morton C., XXXV, 282
Tuxberry Lumber Co., XXX, 187
Tver, David F., *Ocean and Marine Dictionary,* reviewed, XL, 234
Twabras, schooner *(1864),* XII, 233
Twain, Mark, XIV, 44; XXV, 57
Twambly, Captain Henry B., XXV, 18 ff.
"'Twas the Night Before Christmas (An Old Tar's Dream)," poem by F. P. Harlow, VI, 275–276
"Twelve-inch Wrought-iron Gun and Carriage," design of, XLIX, 107
"Twentieth-Century Parallelisms of the Double Canoe and the Double Outrigger," by Richard LeBaron Bowen, Jr., XII, 306–308
28 (Veintiocho) de Julio, Venezuelan schooner *(1843),* XXX, 261 ff.
25 de Mayo, corvette *(1845),* XXXVI, 127, 128
25 (Veinticinco de) Mayo, Argentine flagship, XXIX, 178 ff.; *(1828),* VI, 18
"26-foot American Cutter in the Naval Museum of Venice, A," by G. B. Rubin de Cervin, XV, 199–204, plates 9, 10, plan.
Twenty-two-foot-class yachts (1905), XXX, plate XXI
Twiggs, Colonel, U.S.A., VII, 45
Twiggs, Major General David E., XLVIII, 91; XL, 300
Twilight, schooner (1842), XXIV, 60; *(1856),* X, 231 ff.; *(1862),* XII, 59, 160; (1874), V, 86; *(1906),* XXV, 188
Twilight, steamship (1883), VII, 159
Twins, schooner *(1817),* XXXV, 232
Twin screw propellers, I, 53, 57
Twin Sisters, British ship *(1776),* XLVIII, 19
Twisden, John, XXX, 110
Twitcher, Jemmy: A Life of the Fourth Earl of Sandwich, 1718–1792, by George Martelli, reviewed, XXIII, 150–151

"Two American Vessels Wrecked on the Irish Coast," by Joanna C. Colcord, IX, 68
Two brigs engaging during War of 1812, XXVIII, plate I
Two Brothers, bark (1862), III, 62
Two Brothers, brig *(1785),* XLIX, 88
Two Brothers, schooner *(1775),* XXX, 110
Two Brothers, sloop, XXI, 95; *(1864),* XV, 130
"Two Drawings by Bligh of *Bounty,*" by Richard H. Dillon, XI, 146–147
Two Early Works on Arctic Exploration, by Howard N. Eavenson, reviewed, VI, 310
Two Friends, brig *(1795),* XIV, 32; *(1808),* XVI, 201; (1819), XIV, 41
Two Friends, schooner *(1789),* XXIV, 248, 250, 251, 254; *(1795),* XXII, 195
"Two John Lambs of the Revolutionary Generation, The," by Philip Ranlet, XLII, 301–305
Two Johns, brigantine *(1776),* XX, 45
"Two Marine Articles in Anthropological Journals," by E. S. Dodge, XI, 223–224
"Two Masts Square-, Two Masts Schooner-Rigged," by John Lyman, IV, 237–238
"'Two men at the Wheel,' The bark *Carlotta,* Magune, Master," by E. Lee Dorsett, M.D., XVIII, 318–319
"Two Photographs of American Naval Vessels," by Ernest S. Dodge, XV, 81, plate 8
"Two Prize Masters from the Baltimore Privateer *Lawrence,* 1814," document contributed by William D. Hoyt, Jr., I, 301–303
"Two Revolutionary Naval Inventories," by M. V. Brewington, XXVI, 63–71, 138–144, 210–214
Two Sisters, schooner, XXI, 89, 94; *(1862),* XII, 59
Two Step, yacht *(1905),* XXXVI, 241, 242, 244, 245
"Two Thousand Years Under Sea: The Story of the Diving Bell," by David Whittet Thomson, VII, 261–281
Two Years Before the Mast (by Richard Henry Dana), XII, 177; XIII, 162
Two Years in the Pacific and Arctic Oceans and China, Being a Journal of . . . a Whaling Voyage, by James F. Munger, reviewed, XXVIII, 74
TX. *See* Texas (History)
Tybee, brig *(1849),* XLVII, 42
Tyler, A. H., XXX, 244
Tyler, David B., I, 177; III, 89; IV, 252; VI, 307; "Fulton's Steam Frigate," VI, 253–274; "Great Eastern in Long Island Sound, The," I, 138–140; "Great South Bay Scooters," IV, 224–232; "Marestier's *Mémoire sur les bateaux à vapeur des États-Unis d'Amérique,*" I, 412–416; "'Time and Waste Books' of James Williamson, builder of the *Ann McKim,*" III, 26–34; *The Wilkes Expedition: The First United States Exploring Expedition (1838–1842),* reviewed, XXX, 297–298
Tyler, Doctor David B., XIV, 4
Tyler, John, XLVII, 172 ff.
Tyler, John E., query by, I, 310

Tyler, John W., "The Long Shadow of Benjamin Barons: The Politics of Illicit Trade at Boston, 1760–1762," XL, 245–279
Tyler, Royall, XL, 258 ff.
Tyler, Victor M., "A Spanish Expedition to Chesapeake Bay in 1609," XVII, 181–194
Tyler, William, XXXVIII, 164
Tyndall, Professor John, XLVII, 178
Tyne, brig *(1861),* VIII, 221
Tyne, H.M.S., XXV, 166
Tynemouth, auxiliary steamship (1854), XXVI, 129, 206, 209
Tynemouth Castle, XXIX, plate XXV
Tyrannicide, brig *(1778),* VII, 203–204; *(1779),* XXXVII, 293
Tyrant, schooner (1845), VII, 318
Tyro, schooner (1841), XXIV, 60
Tyron, William, Royal Governor, XL, 14 ff.
Tyrwhitt, Captain, R.N., XXV, 282
Tyrwhitt, Lieutenant Reginald, XXVIII, 92, 93, 97, 111
Tyson, George, XVII, 46
Tyson, Levering, XLI, 18
Tyssen, Francis, VII, 269

U-21, German submarine, XXXVI, 33–44
U-69, German sub *(1941),* XLV, 52
U-110, German sub *(1941),* XLV, 55
U-129, submarine *(1942),* XXXVIII, 179 ff.
U-154, submarine *(1918),* XXXIX, 179
U-187, German sub *(1941),* XLV, 55
U-402, German sub *(1941),* XLV, 55
U-505, German sub *(1944),* XXXVIII, 272 ff.
U-568, German sub *(1941),* XLV, 52
U-570, German sub *(1941),* XLV, 54
U-652, German sub *(1941),* XLV, 52
Underwater archaeology. *See* Archaeology
U.S. Army at Manila Bay, XL, plate 8
"U.S. Brig of War *Argus,*" query by John Haskell Kemble, II, 339
U.S. Coast Guard Museum (New London, CT), XXVIII, 3
U.S. Coast Pilot, Atlantic Coast, Section A, quoted, XXV, 233
U.S. Coast Survey vs. Naval Hydrographic Office: A 19th Century Rivalry in Science and Politics, by Thomas G. Manning, reviewed, XLIX, 317
"U.S. Frigate *Constitution,* in Borneo, 1845," IV, 217–223
U. S. Grant, steam tug *(1880),* XLIV, 115
U.S. Light-House Board display, illustration of, XLVII, 186
"U.S. Light-Vessel No. 50 *Columbia River,*" by William A. Baker, IX, 273–277, plate 29, folding plans between 274–275
U.S. National Museum, Washington, D. C., IX, 282, 296; XXV, 232, 295
U.S. Naval Academy Museum, Annapolis, Maryland, VI, 158, 222, Plate 32
U.S. Naval Base, Los Angeles, California, XXV, 272–273
"U.S. Naval Expedition to the Dead Sea in 1848," by Fay A. King, IV, 71–72
U.S. Naval Ship Data Arranged by Hull Classification, Vol. I, by H. E. Musgrove, edited by Philip G. Rose, reviewed, XL, 71–72
"U.S. Navy and the Taiping Rebellion, The," by Curtis T. Henson, Jr., XXXVIII, 28–40
U.S. Navy Duck, XXXI, 136
"U.S. Navy Gun Carriages from the Revolution through the Civil War," by Spencer C. Tucker, XLVII, 108–118
U.S. Navy Memorial Museum, *Maritime Titles in Print,* XXXIX, 76
"U.S. Navy Steam Sloop *Princeton,*" by Spencer C. Tucker, XLIX, 96–113
U.S. Navy: XXII, 3–4, 45–54, 70, 105, 142, 143–144, 145–147, 155–156, 183, 187–193, 211, 220–221, 252–263; creation of, XXV, 35 ff.; XXVI, 210–214, 217–219; XXVII, 30–45, 135–149, 157–176, 221–224, 242, 286–287; XXVIII, 116, 143–144; XXIX, 30–53, 106–117; XXX, 117–132, 139–146
U.S. & Porto Rico Navigation Co., ship of, Pictorial Supplement, XXXIV, plate XXII
"U.S.S. *Constellation,* 1797 to 1979," by Evan Randolph, XXXIX, 235–355
"U.S.S. *Monocacy* at Tientsin," note contributed by Captain Edgar K. Thompson, U.S.N. (ret.), XXIII, 68–69
"U.S.S. *Sabine,*" by Henry P. Bakewell, Jr., XXIII, 261–263
Udall, William, XXXI, 94
Ugashik Cannery (Alaska), VII, 291–292
Uhrland, John L., XXXV, 171
Ukraine, bark (1865), II, 334
Ulloa, Gonsalo, XXX, 47
Ulmo, Fernando de, XXX, 250
Ulrica, English schooner *(1896),* XXXVII, 91
Ulster, steamship, XVIII, 225
Ultima Thule: Further Mysteries of the Arctic, by Vilhjalmur Stefansson, reviewed, I, 322–324
Ultima Vela – The Last Sail, by Tomaso Gropallo, reviewed, XXX, 219–220
"Ultra Goes to War," by Ronald Lewin, reviewed, XLI, 312–313
Ulysses, ship (1794), Pictorial Supplement, XXXII, plate XVIII; *(1799),* XLV, 92; *(1801),* XXIV, 262; *(1804),* XLVI, 15–16
Ulysses, steamship (1867), XXVI, 283

Umbria, Italian cruiser *(1895),* XL, 102 ff.
Una, sloop *(1856),* X, 231 ff.
Unadilla, U.S.S. *(1864),* XXVII, 43, 44; *(1867),* XXXII, 132
Unalga, U.S.C.G. *(1928),* XVIII, 220
Uncatena, steamship, XXXIV, 261
Uncle Bill, schooner, XXI, 98; *(1864),* XII, 233
Uncle Mose, schooner *(1862),* XII, 59
Uncle Sam, bark *(1861),* XI, 289
Uncle Sam, schooner *(1863),* XV, 128
Uncle Sam, steamship *(1832),* VII, 48, 62; (1852), I, 257, 260; *(1852),* XVII, 56, 57; *(1868),* XLIX, 27; (1871), XXXIV, 51
Uncle Tobey, ship (1866), IV, 241; V, 327
Undaunted, schooner (1921), V, 140
Undaunted, ship (1853), II, 331
Undaunted, tug (1926), X, 121
Underhill, Robert, L, 203
Under Sejl i Fjerøstlige Farvande, by F. Holm-Petersen, reviewed, XXXVI, 299
"Under the Starry Banner on Muddy Flat, Shanghai: 1854," by George E. Paulsen, XXX, 155–166
"Under Two Flags," document contributed by Captain Edgar K. Thompson, U.S.N. (ret.), XXII, 215
"Underway Replenishment, 1799–1800," by Tyrone G. Martin, XLVI, 159–164
Underwood, First Lieutenant John A., XLVIII, 93
Underwood, Senator Joseph Rogers, XXX, 144 n.
Underwood, Oscar W., XXXIII, 183
Underwriter, ship (1850), I, 48
Underwriter, steamship (1854), XVII, 307; XVIII, 73; (1854), XXII, 28, 29, 42; *(1892),* XLVII, 127
Underwriter, U.S.S. *(1862),* VI, 52
Underwriters' Register, XXX, 10 ff.
Underwriters' Register for Iron Vessels, XXX, 13 ff.
Undine, paddle steamship *(1859),* XXXIV, 21 ff.
Undine, screw steamship (1861), XLIII, 108 ff.
Undine, ship (1831), XIV 41
Undine, yacht *(1884),* XII, 61
"Unexpected End to *Seeadler,* The," by Robert Clifford, XXXVI, 266–275
Unger, Richard W., review by, XXXIV, 282; "The Ship in the Medieval Economy, 600–1600," reviewed, XLI, 306–312; XLV, 212
Unicorn, H.M.S. (1778), I, 168–170; *(1801),* XLI, 227
Unicorn, ship *(1851),* XXVII, 61–65, Plate 4
Unicorn, steamship (1836), IX, 268–269; XVII, 144 ff.; XVIII, 73; *(1840),* XXXVII, 232
Unidentified Vessels: in *(1860),* Pictorial Supplement, XXXIII, plate XVII (upper); Bark: Pictorial Supplement, XXXIII, plates XX, XXI; XXXVIII, plate XII; Schooner: Pictorial Supplement, XXXIII, plate XXXI (lower); Sloop: Pictorial Supplement, XXXII, plate XIX; Stern drawings of, Pictorial Supplement, XXXVII, plate XXVIII
Uniforms, XVII, 195–201

Uniforms of the Sea Services, by Robert H. Rankin, reviewed, XXIV, 145–146
Union, bark (1865), IV, 240; *(1872),* XXXVIII, 238
Union, brig *(1804),* X, 54, 62; XIII, 278; XVII, 68; *(1807),* XVI, 194
Union, cartel *(1814),* XXVIII, 190
Union, French ship *(1799),* XXXI, 173, 175
Union, grain elevator *(1883),* XXXVIII, 141
Union, H.M.S. *(1726),* XXI, 263
Union, Mexican gunboat *(1845),* XXX, 54
Union, Peruvian corvette *(1864),* XXXIX, 275
Union, schooner, XXI, 95; (1803), XIV, 41; *(1807),* XVI, 193; (1826), VI, 208; *(1861),* XI, 289; XII, 160
Union, schooner-rigged steam packet (ex-*John K. Hammett*) *(1858),* XXX, 276
Union, ship *(1799),* XLV, 88; *(1807),* I, 393; *(1809),* XXX, 284; *(1815),* XIX, 222; (1850), XIX, 27; (1857), II, 332; (1882), IX, 298
Union, sloop *(1796),* XXV, 8; (1842), XXII, 216
Union, steamship (1834), VII, 55; (1843), XX, 261; (1854), XVIII, 73; (1861), I, 76; *(1862),* XII, 59, 161, 233
Union, U.S.S. *(1861),* XV, 102
Union, U.S. steamship *(1861),* VII, 19
Union, U.S. steam sloop (1842), XXIV, 8 ff.
Union, whaler *(1826),* XLI, 289
Union and Central Pacific Railroad Companies, XXXI, 123
Union-Castle (British shipping line), XLVI, 108
Union Dock Co., Hongkong, XXXIV, 37 ff.
Union Flag, schooner *(1880),* XIV, 118
Union Iron Works, XXXII, 166
Union Mutual Marine Insurance Co., XXXIII, 60
Union Oil Co. of California, XLII, 249
Union River Bay, Maine, IX, 169–179
Union Star, wooden propeller steamship (1861), XVII, 149 ff.; XVIII, 73; *(1861),* XLIII, 206; *(1862),* XLIX, 24
Union Steam Navigation Co., XVI, 177, 266; XVII, 136, 137; XVIII, 63, 80; XXII, 225; XLIII, 99 ff.
Union Steamship Co., XXXVIII, 185 ff.; XLII, 249
Union Steamship Co. of New Zealand, I, 318
Union Steam Tug Co., Ltd., XXVI, 9
Unique, schooner (1887), XXVI, plate IX
Unite, French ship *(1800),* XXXI, 174
United, steam ferry (1836), VII, 61
United Fruit Co., XXXIII, 183
United Kingdom, steamship (1832), VII, 48
United Service, steamship (1857), XVII, 136, 137; XVIII, 73; XXVI, 110, 112, 209
"United States Revenue Cutter *Harriet Lane,* 1857–1884, The," by Philip E. Yanaway, XXXVI, 174–205
United States (1784), XXXI, 40
United States, cartel, XXVIII, 174 n.
United States, corvette *(1831),* VII, 175, 189 ff.; VIII, 7–10

United States, express liner, XXXIII, 150
United States, frigate *(1798)*, XXXVI, 62, 278; XXXVII, 144; XXXIX, 30; XL, 301; XLVI, 8 ff., 147; L, 245 ff.; *(1812)*, XXVIII, 30; XLII, 57, 285; XLIII, 264; XLIV, 171
United States, packet ship (1817), XXIX, 48, plate VII
United States, passenger liner, XXVII, 256, 257
United States, schooner (1929), XXXVIII, 56
United States, ship, XXXII, 42; *(1784)*, XLV, 153 ff.; *(1807)*, XVI, 193; *(1823)*, XVI, 234
United States, steamship *(1823)*, XXXVII, 243; XXXIX, 100; *(1831)*, VII, 44, 49, 55, 56, 60, 62, plate 5; (1835), VII, 57, 58; *(1838)*, VII, 312; VIII, 39 ff.; *(1839)*, XVIII, 283, 284, 290, 291, 296, 299; XX, 83, 101, 262, 265, 267; (1851), XX, 132; (1854), Pictorial Supplement, XXXIV, plate IV; (1857), XVII, 54; (1874), IV, 306; (1952), XXIV, 137; XXV, 224; (1953), XV, 96
United States, U.S.S., XXIX, 243; U.S.S. (1797), VII, 167, 253; XXIII, 58; XXV, 29; *(1798)*, XXXI, 173; *(1799)*, XXVII, 143; *(1806)*, XVIII, 183; *(1812)*, III, plate 3
United States (General subjects):
  Cartography, XXXI, 253
  Description and travel, XXI, 57; XXIII, 46
  Emigration and immigration:
  —, California, XXIX, 81
  —, Gt. Britain, XXIII, 62
  Maritime influences, XXV, 51; XXV, 51; XXIX, 199United States and Brazil Mail Steamship Co., IV, 141 ff.
"United States and British North American Fisheries, The," by V. Dennis Golladay, XXXIII, 246–257
United States and Congo National Emigration Steamship Co., The, XXXV, 203
United States Battleships: The History of America's Greatest Fighting Fleet, by Alan F. Pater, reviewed, XXIX, 147–148
United States Coast Guard: Always Ready! The Story of the, by Kensil Bell, reviewed, IV, 176
United States Coast Guard, XXXVII, 95 ff.
United States Coast Guard Bibliography, reviewed, XI, 234
United States Department of the Navy, XXXII, 232
United States Exploring Expedition (1838–1842), XLIX, 151. See also Wilkes, Charles
United States Exploring Expedition, 1838–1842, IV, 105–111; XXXI, 7
United States, Foreign relations:
  Argentina, XXIX, 174; XLVI, 230
  Brazil, XIX, 239; XXII, 45; XLI, 245
  Central America, XXXII, 277
  Chile, XXXVIII, 291
  China, XX, 209; XXV, 116; XXXI, 177; XXXIV, 103; XXXV, 166; XXXVII, 185
  Fiji, XXXV, 20
  France, XXIV, 61; XXIX, 167
  Germany, XXXII, 257; XLVIII, 50
  Gt. Britain, XXIII, 157XXIV, 61; XXXIX, 289; XLI, 262
  India, XXXI, 38; XLVI, XVIII
  Japan, VII, 9; XX, 198; XXXII, 123; XXXVII, 185; XLI, XXV
  Korea, VII, 107
  Paraguay, XXXI, 7
  Russia, XX, 49; XXI, 207
  Samoa, XXXV, XX
  South Africa, XXVI, 96; XXXIV, 81
  Taiwan, XXXV, XX
  Turkey, XL, 241
  Venezuela, XXXII, 257
  Vietnam, 47, 169
  See also Diplomats, U.S
"United States Fish Commission Steamer *Albatross,* The," by Joel W. Hedgpeth, V, 5–15; Appendix by Waldo L. Schmitt, V, 15–26
United States Frigate Constitution, *A Sesquicentennial Exhibition,* by Alexander Crosby Brown, reviewed, VIII, 75
United States, History (chronological):
  Colonial period, (ca. 1600–1775), XXIII, 62
  Queen Anne's War (1702–1713), XVII, 292
  King George's War (1744–1748), XXIII, 277
  Revolution (1775–1788), VIII, 9
    Campaigns, XXXVII, 288
    Historiography, XLII, 179
    Naval operations, I, XXVI; IV, 193; V, 177; V, 64; VII, 200; X, 280; XI, 239; XIII, XXIX; XIV, 47; XXIX, 211; XXXIII, 20; XXXVI, 81; XXXIX, 160; XXXIX, 209; XLII, 25; XLV, 244
    —, **American,** XXV, 189; XXX, 86; XXXIV, 135
    —, **British,** VII, 87; XI, 239; XXIII, 174; XL, 7
    Pictorial works, III, 5
    Privateering, XLIII, 20; XLVIII, 154
    Prizes, etc., II, 203; V, 111
    Pictorial works, III, 5
  Quasi-War with France (1797–1801), IV, 18; XXII, 81; XXV, 29; XXXI, 159; L, 270
    Naval operations, XXX, 117; XLV, 94; XLVI, 141
    —, **American,** XXVII, 135
  Tripolitain War (1801–1805), IX, 11; XXVI, 231
    Naval operations, XXI, 130
  1809–1817, XXX, 279
  War of 1812, I, 116; IV, 164; XXII, 264
    Causes, XLIII, 42
    Intelligence, British, XXIX, 187
    Naval operations, XXI, 42; XXIV, 172; XXXVI, 206; XL, 23; XLII, 101; XLIII, 245; XLIII, 5; XLVII, 14
    —, **American,** XIX, 213; XLVI, 165
    —, **British,** XVII, 203; XLV, 5
    Privateering, XXI, 16
    Prizes, etc., XV, 59
    Transportation, XXVIII, 165

Mexican War (1846–1848), V, 121
Civil War (1861–1864):
    Blockade, III, 131; VIII, 196; IX, 31; XI, 262; XII, 52, 154, 229 XV, 97; XVII, 249; XVIII, 142; XXI, 233; XXI, 81; XXVI, 134; XXIX, 5; XXXII, 45; L, 89
        Economic aspects, XX, 155
        Foreign public opinion, XIX, 51
        —, **France,** XXIX, 167
    Naval operations, I, 241; X, 15; XI, 262; XII, 154, 229; XII, 52, 271; XV, 287; XVI, 49; XIX, 265; XX, 155; XXII, 252; XXII, 45; XXV, 128; XXV, 18; XXIX, 102; XXIX, 167; XXIX, 5; XXXI, 52; XXXII, 195; XXXII, 277; XXXIII, 41; XXXIII, 5; XXXV, 53; XXXVI, 174; XXXVII, 276; XLII, 193; XLII, 85; XLIV, 257; XLV, 191
        —, **British (Great Lakes),** XLVIII, 96
    Personal narratives, XXXIII, 199
See also America; names of states; New England; Penobscot Expedition (Revolution); World War (1914–1918); World War (1939–1945)
United States History, Naval, XXII, 186; XXX, 86; XXXIII, 20; XXXIV, 188; XXXV, 20; XXXV, 53; XXXIX, 22; XLI, 25; XLV, 244
—, **to 1900,** XIX, 239; XXVII, 135; XXXIV, 123; XXXIV, 59
United States Life Saving Service, XXXVII, 93 ff.
United States Lines Co., XXIX, 234
"United States Mail Steamer *George Law*, The," by Cedric Ridgely-Nevitt, IV, 304–317
United States Mail Steamship Co., X, 127; XXXVI, 253
United States Mail Steamship Co. (NY-Panama), IV, 306 ff.
United States Marine Mammal Commission, XXXVIII, 155
United States Marine Service, XXXVI, 49, 175 ff.
United States Maritime Commission, XXII, 180; XXXII, 102
United States Maritime Commission publications, reviewed, I, 190
"United States Maritime Influence in Central America, 1863–1865," by Gary G. Kuhn, XXXII, 277–286
United States Merchant Marine, The, by Clinton H. Whitehurst, *et al.,* reviewed, XLIV, 209
United States National Museum, Watercraft Collection, I, 63–79
United States Naval Academy, Annapolis, Maryland, XXV, 224–226; editorial comment, XXXIX, 3, 82, 158
United States Naval Academy Museum, Annapolis, Maryland: The Beverley R. Robinson Collection of Naval Battle Prints, reviewed, III, 93
United States Naval Academy Museum, Annapolis, Md., I, 176–177; III, 93; IV, 308, 335; Pictorial Supplement, XXXII, plate XX
United States Naval Astronomical Expedition to the South Hemisphere, 1849–1852, XXXI, 8
United States Naval Lyceum, The, XXXIX, 110 ff.

United States Naval Power in a Changing World, by Edwin Bickford Hooper, reviewed, L, 150
United States Navy, XXXIII, 258 ff.; XXXVII, 95 ff.; Korean expedition (1871), VII, 107–114
"United States Navy and its 'Half War' Prisoners, 1798–1801, The," by David LePere Savageau, XXXI, 159–176
United States Navy and Marine Corps Bases: Domestic, by Paolo E. Coletta and K. Jack Bauer, reviewed, XLIX, 59
United States Navy and Marine Corps Bases: Foreign, by Paolo E. Coletta and K. Jack Bauer, reviewed, XLIX, 59
"United States Navy and the Philippine Insurrection, The," by Barbara B. Tomblin, XXXV, 183–196
"United States Navy and the Sino-Japanese War of 1894–1895, The," by Jeffery M. Dorwart, XXXIV, 211–218
United States Navy Destroyers of World War II, by John C. Reilly, Jr., reviewed, XLVII, 144
United States Navy in the Pacific, 1909–1922, The, by William Reynolds Braisted, reviewed, XXXII, 224–225
"United States Navy's 'Two Fannies,' The," note contributed by Alexander C. Brown, XXIII, 141
"United States Policy during the Brazilian Naval Revolt, 1893–94: The Case for American Neutrality," by James F. Vivian, XLI, 245–261
United States Revenue Marine, XXIV, 5–24
United States Revenue Marine Service, XXXIV, 10
United States Shipping Board, XXIII, 270; XLI, 264
United States Shipping Board Emergency Fleet Corp., XXXV, 276 ff.
United States Standard Register, XXX, 24, 35
United States Standard Steamship Owners, Builders, and Underwriters' Association, Ltd., XXX, 24
United States Steel Corp., XXXII, 165; XXXIII, 183
United States Tank Ship Corp., XXXVIII, 183
United States Waterway Packetmarks ... of Mail Carrying steamboats ... 1832–1899, by Eugene Klein, reviewed, III, 94
"United States Wooden Steamship Program During World War I, The," by William Joe Webb, XXXV, 275–288
United States. Armed Forces: Registers, XLV, 257
United States. Army:
    Biography, Dictionaries, XLV, 20
    Transportation, XXXIV, 262
United States. Customs Service (San Francisco, CA), XLV, 119. *See also* California
United States. Navy:
    Administration, XXXI, 235; XXXIII, 20; XXXIII, 233; XXXV, 53; XXXVI, 54; XXXVII, 26; XLV, 94
    —, **Reform,** XXIX, 30
    Asiatic Squadron, XXXII, 123; XLV, 237
    Aviation, XXXVII, 111; L, 51
    Biography, XXXVI, 54

Brazil Squadron, XXIX, 174; XLVI, 230
Chesapeake Flotilla, XLIII, 5
Communications, XXXVIII, 122
Description, 19th century, XXXI, 217
Eastern Squadron, XLI, 93
Equipment and supplies, XXXVIII, 122
Family life, XXXVIII, 5
Far Eastern Squadron, XL, 100
Foreign opinion, XXXIV, 59
History.
—, 19th century, IV, 217
—, Civil War (1861–1864), XXIV, 208
—, Korean expedition, VII, 107
—, Revolution (1775–1788), V, 177
Lighting, XXXVIII, 122
Navy Board, XXXI, 235
Newport (RI) Naval Training Station, XLIX, 278
Office of Naval Intelligence, XXXIX, 126
Officers, L, 107
—, Training of, XXXIX, 109
Pacific Squadron, XXXIII, XLI
Personnel management, L, 107
Political aspects, XXII, 186; XXX, 139
Provisioning, XLVI, 159
Regulations, XXX, 139
Sea life, XII, 271; XVI, 49; XIX, 213; XXIX, 102; XXXIII, 280; XXXVII, 95; XXXVIII, 101; XXXVIII, 5; XLII, 57; XLIV, 245; L, 89
Secretary of the Navy, XXXVI, 54
6th Battle Squadron, XL, L
Ships, IV, 183; VIII, 11; VIII, 7; X, 15; XX, 134; XXII, 252; XXIII, 197, 261; XXVI, 258; XXVIII, 195; XXVIII, 49; XXX, 86; XXXI, 7; XXXIV, 135, 188; XXXIX, 218; XXXIX, 29; XL, 211; XLIII, 135; XLIII, 245; XLVI, 141; XLVII, 22; XLIX, 96
—, steam, XX, 167.]
Special Services Squadron, XXXV, 118
West Indies Squadron, XLII, 165
United States. Navy Department, *Dictionary of American Naval Fighting Vessels*, reviewed, XX, 147
United States. Navy Department, Office of Naval Records and Library, I, 198; II, 341; III, 180, 267–268; V, 91, 122, 245, 246, 248, 326; VI, 151–153, 162; "Summary of Service of John Rodgers Goldsborough, U.S.N.," VII, 18–20
United States. Revenue Marine Service, XXXVI, 174
United States. Shipping Board, XXXII, 155
United States. War Refugee Board, XLIII, XXXI
United Steamship Co., XLII, 249
United States Naval Academy, XXXVIII, 157
United States Naval Operations. *See* United States Navy; United States, History
Unity, British ship *(1776)*, XLVIII, 16
Unity, gunboat *(1782)*, XXXIX, 217
Unity, ship *(1624)*, XXXVII, 15; *(1775)*, XXX, 89, 114
Universal Dictionary of the Marine, XXX, 40
Universal Negro Improvement Association, XXXV, 197

Universal Register, XXX, 18, 26
Unloading salmon, XXXIX, plate 7
"Unlucky *General Armstrong*, The," by Harold A. Mouzon, XV, 59–80
Unpathed Waters: Studies in the Influence of the Voyagers on Elizabethan Literature, by Robert Ralston Cawley, reviewed, I, 321–322
Unsen, steamship (ex-*Whampoa*) *(1866)*, XLIII, 102 ff.
"Unusual photographs of schooners and barkentines," document contributed by Frederick F. Hill, John Lyman and Alexander Crosby Brown, I, 396–397, plates facing I, 396–397
Update on Americana, note, XLIII, 300–301
Updike, Daniel, XII, 226
Updike, Richard W., "Winslow Lewis and the Lighthouses," XXVIII, 31–48
Upham, Charles W., XLVIII, 170
Upham, Edward E., XXXIX, 218
"Upholders," note contributed by D. L. Dennis, XXIV, 212
Upland, coal barge *(1873)*, XXXVIII, 240
Upshur, A. P., XVII, 91
Upshur, Abel, Secretary of State, XLIX, 109
Upshur, Abel Parker, XXIV, 15
Upshur, Captain George Parker, U.S.N., XXV, 140–141, 175
Upshur, Secretary of the Navy, XXXIX, 109
"Up to date Method of Getting a Ship Under Way," by William B. Sturtevant, I, 83–84
Upton, Clotworthy, XXXI, 286
Upton, Captain Jeduthan, IV, 164, 166
Upton, Robert, Pictorial Supplement, XXXVIII, plate XVIII
Uradaneta, warship *(1899)*, XXXV, 191
Urania, schooner yacht *(1861)*, XXVII, 248
Uranus, Bucksport banker *(1845)*, XLIV, 83
Urda, bark (1850), V, 147
Urgent, H.M.S., XXVIII, 19, 98
Urquhart, Captain Walter, XXI, 103
Urquiza, President Justo José, XXXI, 9
Ursulita, schooner *(1861)*, XI, 289
Uruguay, navy of, II, 170–171
"Use of Cartel Vessels During the War of 1812, The," by Anthony G. Dietz, XXVIII, 163–194
Usher, James, XXI, 16
Usque Ad Mare, by Thomas E. Appleton, reviewed, XXX, 221–222
Usrow Angelica, French sloop *(1744)*, XLII, 49
Ussher, Admiral Sir Thomas, XIII, 259
Usuma, cruiser, XXXVI, 274
Utilis, sharpie *(1898)*, XXX, 198
Utopia, steamship *(1894)*, XX, 191
Utrecht, R.N.S. *(1909)*, XIV, 112
Utting, Midshipman Ashby, R.N., XXI, 264, 265

V. Barkelew, schooner, XXI, 88; *(1861),* XI, 289
V. H. Ivy, schooner, XXI, 86
V. Olyphant & Co., XLIX, 25
VA. *See* Virginia
Vaderland, steamship (1872), Pictorial Supplement, XXXIV, plate XI
Vail, David C., XVII, 134
Vail, Stephen, IX, 250
Vailly, auxiliary (1918), XXXII, 25, 30
Vainqueur, French ship *(1799),* XXXI, 173
Vainqueur de la Bastille, privateer, XXII, 90 n.
Valacia, steamship *(1946),* XIV, 133, 135
Valdes, Antonio, XV, 49
Valentina, bark *(1861),* XI, 266, 289
Valentine, ship *(1794),* XLI, 174
Valentine, René, XXX, 229
Valentiner, W. R., *Five Centuries of Marine Painting,* reviewed, II, 353
Valetta, steamship (1883), XXIV, plate X
Valiant, British gunboat *(1814),* XLII, 107 ff.
Valkyrie, cutter (1893), XXX, plate XV
Valle, James E., reviews by: XLV, 134, 208, 209, 210; XLVI, 202; XLVII, 142, 145, 213; XLVIII, 190, 193, 197, 208, 209; XLIX, 59, 236, 306; L, 141, 146, 148; "The Navy's Battle Doctrine in the War of 1812," XLIV, 171–178
Vallejo, Mariano Guadalupe, XXXII, 119
Valley Forge, steamship (1839), IV, 184
Vallone, John, XLI, 58
Valmy, French warship [model] (1847), XVI, 102
Valorous, H.M.S. (1863), III, 172; XXVI, 101; *(1864),* XVII, 258
Valparaiso, Chile, XXV, 50
Valparaiso, English ship *(1849),* XLV, 124
Valparaiso, ship *(1861),* XI, 288; XXI, 258; (1863), III, 71
Van Berckel, P. J., XXXVI, 168
Van Bibber, Abraham, XXXVI, 157
Van Bleiswijk, P., XXXVI, 161
van Boylen, Jules, XXIX, 69
Vanbrugh, Captain Philip, XXVI, 37
Van Brunt, Captain, XLVII, 115
Van Brunt Carronade Carriage, 1843, drawings of, XLIX, 105
Van Buren, Martin, VII, 188–189
Van Buren, President Martin, XXIII, 186–187; XXV, 167
Van Bylandt, Captain Count F.S., XXXVI, 67
Van Bylandt, Rear Admiral Count Lodewijk, XXXVI, 165–167
Vance, steamship (1838), XVIII, 282

Vance, Solomon, XVII, 115
Van Cleve, Captain James, III, 333 ff.; V, 29 ff., plate 4; VI, 194 n.; VII, 43 n., 56, 60, 61, 298; VIII, 39 ff., 134; painting by, VI, plates 29–30; VII, plates 5–6; VIII, plate 15; XVII, 92 ff.
Van Cortlandt, Annie, XXX, 172
Van Cortlandt, Stephanus, XXX, 172
Vancouver, bark (1862), II, 333
Vancouver, steamship (1874), XVII, 61; XVIII, 73
Vancouver, British Columbia, XXXVI, 231 ff.
Vancouver, George, XXVIII, 151; XXX, 206, 211
Vancouver, Captain George, XIII, 212–213; XLI, 225
Vandalia, ship *(1799),* XLIX, 42; (1835), XIV, 41; *(1833),* XXXVIII, 33, 112
Vandalia, sloop of war *(1842),* XXXII, 273; XXXIII, 5 ff.; XXXV, 26
Vandalia, steamship (1841), XVII, 95 ff., plates 7, 8; XX, 88, 250, 264
Vandalia, U.S.S. *(1838),* XV, 83; *(1851),* V, 243–244; *(1861),* VIII, 196–197; *(1889),* XXVIII, 16
Vandalia, U.S. sloop (1825), XXI, 145–146; XXIII, 58 n.
van den Velde, Esaias (Dutch artist), XLIX, 227
Vanderbell, Adolph, XXVIII, 68–69
Vanderbilt, steamship (1857), III, 129, 263
Vanderbilt, transport *(1866),* XXXII, 129
Vanderbilt, U.S.S. *(1863),* XLIV, 274; XLV, 191 ff.; XXVI, 103–105; *(1864),* XVI, 53, 56; XX, 161; XXVII, 36
Vanderbilt, Aaron, XXXIII, 268
Vanderbilt, Cornelius, X, 127; XVI, 278, 280; XXV, 55
Vanderbilt, Commodore Cornelius, XIV, 192; XXX, 172; XXXIX, 89
Vanderford, Captain Benjamin, XXV, 187
Van der Vat, Dan, *The Grand Scuttle: The Sinking of the German Fleet at Scapa Flow in 1919,* reviewed, XLIV, 132
van der Vinne, Vincent (Dutch artist), XLIX, 227
Van de Velde Drawings, by M. S. Robinson, reviewed by Marion V. Brewington, XIX, 146–147
Van de Veldes, catalog of, mention, XLII, 83
Van de Water, Captain D. J., VII, 56
Van Diemen's Land, XXX, 10
Vandiver, Frank E., editor, *Confederate Blockade Running Through Bermuda,* reviewed, VIII, 259–260
Van Dorn, C.S. gunboat *(1862),* XXV, 138
Van Dorn, Colonel Earl, XXXIII, 47
van Doornick, F. H., Jr., review by, XLVI, 200.
van Doornick, Frederick E., and George F. Bass, *et al., Yassi Ada, Vol. 1: A Seventh Century Byzantine Shipwreck,* reviewed, XLIII, 58–59
Van Dusen, Albert, XLV, 42 ff.
Van Dusen, Joseph B., XXXIX, 101
Van Dyke, J. R., XXXVI, 247
Vanessa, H.M. destroyer *(1943),* XLIV, 49 ff.
van Gerrevinck, Abram, XLVI, 174
van Gerrevinck, Isaac, XLVI, 174
van Gerrevinck, Lubertus, XLVI, 174

Vanguard, schooner *(1863),* XII, 161
Vanguard, ship (1586), XIV, 266, 271
Vanguard to Trident: British Naval Policy Since World War Two, by Eric J. Grove, reviewed, XLIX, 133
van Heemskerck, Jacob, L, 284
Van Imhoff, Governor-General, XLVII, 243 ff.
Van Ingen, James, XVI, 271 ff.
Vanishing Frenchman: The Mysterious Disappearance of LaPérouse, by Edward W. Allen, reviewed, XX, 71
Vanja, tanker *(1942),* L, 44
Van Keppel, Augustus, XXII, 113
van Linschoten, Jan Huyghen, XXV, 73–74; L, 282
Van Name, A. L., Jr., "*Bohemia,* Last of the Chesapeake Schooners," IX, 70–71, plate 7
van Nassau, Prince Mauritius, XXXI, 108
Van Oosten, F. C., "Some Notes Concerning the Dutch West Indies During the American Revolutionary War," XXXVI, 155–169
van Oosten, Kltz F. C., L. M. Akveld, Ph. M. Bosscher, J. R. Bruijn, Editors, *Vier Eeuwen Varen — kapiteins, kapers, kooplieden en geleerden,* reviewed, XXXIV, 282–283
van Rensselaer, S.S. *(1943),* XLIV, 56
Van Renssalaer, Major General Solomon, XL, 25
Van Renssalaer, Stephen, XXXIX, 47
Van Rensselaer, Rensselaer, VII, 300, 307
Van Santvoord, Alfred, XIV, 177
Vansittart, ship *(1819),* XLI, 286
Van Slyke, Captain Charles, XVIII, 234
Vantage at Sea, by Thomas Woodrooffe, reviewed, XIX, 148
Van Valkenburgh, General R. B., XXXII, 128
Van Vlecq, Henry, XXXVII, 65
van Vlissingen, Paul, XXVI, 196, 208
Van Zandt, Jacobus, VIII, 14; XXXVIII, 17 ff.
Variag, Russian warship *(1863),* XX, 52, 55, 57, 58
"Variances in Dimensions of Half-Models," by Norman N. Rubin, XXXVII, 164–168
Variation Compass, English, circa 1770, Pictorial Supplement, XXXV, plate XV
Varick, Captain Richard, XXXVIII, 20
Varina, U.S. revenue cutter *(1861),* XXI, 238
Varnum, Joseph, L, 270 ff.
Varona, General Bernare, XXXVI, 91
Varuna, steamship (1863), XVI, 175, 243; XVIII, 73; *(1863),* XLIX, 22
Vary, Captain Sam, VII, 44
Vasa, Swedish warship, XXI, 231–232; XXX, 154
Vasa, Viking ship (1628), XXIII, 155; XIX, 237
Vasaorden, barge (1775), VI, 165
Vasco da Gama, schooner (1921), V, 141
Vasco da Gama, ship (1849), III, 169, 265
Vasco de Gama, steamship (1873), XVII, 61; XVIII, 73; (1875), X, 132
Vassall, William, XXXIII, 97 ff.
Vatan, rescue ship *(1944),* XLIII, 34 ff.

Vaterland, S.M.S. (German) gunboat, XXIX, 234; *(1910),* XL, 88 ff.
Vaughan, Daniel, XXI, 280, 283, 286
Vaughan, George, XXXV, 161
Vaugn, Captain Robert, XXI, 103
Vaughn, Captain William, VII, 48, 49
Vauquois (originally *Général Gallieni*), auxiliary (1918), XXXII, 25, 30
Vautier, George, XXXVI, 235
Vazeos, George, XXXVI, 13, 17
Veinticinco (de) Mayo. See *25 (twenty-five) (de) Mayo.*
Veintiocho de Julio. See *28 (twenty-eight) de Julio.*
Velasco, schooner *(1861),* VIII, 221; XI, 289
Velasco, Pedro de, XXX, 253
Velasco-Simancas Map, ca. 1610. L, 14
Velocity, schooner *(1862),* XII, 59
Vencedor, brig *(1861),* VIII, 221
Vencedor del Alamo, Mexican ship *(1835),* XXX, 47
Venelia, schooner *(1801),* XVIII, 133
Venetia, steamship (1864), XXIV, plate VIII
Venezolano, schooner *(1859),* XXX, 276
Venezuela, steamship *(1916),* X, 140, 142, 143
Venezuela (ex-*William Foulks*), steamship *(1860),* XXX, 277
Venezuela:
 Foreign relations, United States, XXXII, 257
 History, naval, XXX, 260
Venezuelan Claims Controversy, 1902, XXXII, 257
Vengeance, French ship *(1800),* XXXI, 174
Vengeance, H.M.S. *(1915),* XXXVI, 40
Venice, schooner, XXI, 93; *(1861),* XI, 289; XII, 59
Venice (Italy), History, Naval, XLVI, 84
Venture, sloop *(1862),* XII, 59
Ventures (merchant seamen), XLI, 165
Venturesome Voyages of Captain Voss, The, by John C. Voss, reviewed, II, 184–185
Venus, brig *(1772),* XXXIII, 297; *(1806),* III, 222–235; XXV, plate 20; *(1813),* XIX, 217
Venus, frigate (1783), VI, 170
Venus, schooner, XXI, 98; *(1861),* XI, 289
Venus, ship, XXI, 29; *(1761),* XL, 268; *(1815),* XIX, 222, 223; *(1899),* XXXV, 191
Venus, sloop, XXII, 93
Venus, steamship, XXI, 92, 98, 106; (1831), XXIV, plate XXIX; *(1862),* XVII, 53, 58; XVIII, 73; *(1863),* VIII, 232
Vera Cruz, steamship (ex-*Imperatriz*) *(1862),* XXVI, 194
Veracruzano Libre, Mexican brigantine *(1845),* XXX, 47 ff.
Veranzio, Fausto, VII, 265
Verdun, auxiliary schooner (1918), XXXII, 32
Verena, cutter (1889), XXX, plate XI
Verenigde Provincien, Dutch East Indiaman (1652), XLVI, 109
Vergennes, Charles Gravier, Comte de, XXV, 191
Verhoog, Captain P., XIX, 79–113
Verill, Addison E., XLV, 81

Verité, auxiliary (1918), XXXII, plate 4, pp. 26, 30
Veritas Adriatico, XXX, 27
Veritas Austro-Ungarico, XXX, 27
Veritas Ellenico, XXX, 29
Vermillion, steamship (1838), XVIII, 288; XX, 82 n., 86, 89 n., 97, 102, 251, 254, 263
Vermilyea, Louis H., XVIII, 320–323
Vermont, schooner (1853), I, 74
Vermont, U.S.S. (1818), XXI, 67, plate XXVII; XXII, 211; XXIII, 58 n., 262; *(1862)*, XII, 276; L, 91; *(1900)*, XX, 137; *(1907)*, XLVII, 249; *(1910)*, XXXVIII, 7 ff.
Vermudian, brig *(1760)*, IX, 144
Verner, Coolie, "Mark Tiddeman's Chart of New York Harbor," XIX, 44–50
Verner, Commander Rudolf H. C., R.N., XXXIII, 34 ff.
Verner, Lieutenant Colonel Willoughby, XXXIII, 34 ff.
Vernet, Claude Joseph, XVI, 102
Vernon, bark (1839), VII, 249; IX, 150
Vernon, Vice Admiral Edward, XXVI, 48
Vernon, Samuel, XXXV, 296
Vernon, William, XXXI, 235; XXXV, 294 ff.; XXXVII, 300; XLII, 28
Vernon Daniel, bateau (1910), IV, 290
Verona, yacht *(1906)*, XXXVI, 242
Ver Steeg, Clarence L., XLVI, 27
Vesta, French iron steamship *(1854)*, XXV, 79
Vesta, schooner *(1852)*, XLIV, 88
Vesta, steamship *(1854)*, XIV, 244 ff., plate 29; XIX, 129; XX, 177–184, plates 5, 6; *(1864)*, VIII, 236
Vestal, schooner *(1831)*, VII, 191
Vesuvious, steamship *(1814)*, VI, 266
Vesuvius, British ship *(1783)*, XLVIII, 23
Vesuvius, gunboat *(1814)*, XLII, 107 ff.
Vesuvius, steamship (1814), XVI, 33 ff.
Vetch, Samuel, XXXV, 162 ff.
Veto, Revenue cutter (1836), XXXIII, 82
Viall, Nathaniel, nocturnal by, Pictorial Supplement, XXXV, plate XVII
Vichot, Capitaine Jacques, XVI, 100
Vickery, Admiral Howard, XLI, 276
Vicksburg, gunboat *(1901)*, XXXV, 193 ff.
Vicksburg, U.S.S. (1897), XX, 142
Victoire, French ship *(1800)*, XXXI, 174
Victor, Gloucester schooner *(1870)*, XLIV, 89
Victor, transport *(1755)*, XLIX, 264 ff.
Victor, Alexander O., XIX, 138
Victoria (1851), XXXIV, 32; XXXV, 27
Victoria, brig, XXI, 91, 102
Victoria, Mexican pilot boat *(1844)*, XXX, 54
Victoria, schooner, XXI, 103; *(1861)*, VIII, 222; *(1862)*, VIII, 228, 232; XII, 59, 161, 233; XV, 106, 109, 110, 117, 125, 126
Victoria, ship *(1832)*, XIV, 44; *(1861)*, XI, 266, 289; *(1871)*, XIV, 46
Victoria, sloop *(1863)*, XII, 161
Victoria, steamship, XXI, 91, 95; *(1862)*, XII, 59; *(1864)*, VIII, 236; (1870), I, plate facing 79, 80; (1879), II, 76

Victoria, Queen of England, XXVII, 31
Victorian and Edwardian Sailing Ships from Old Photographs, by Basil Greenhill and Ann Giffard, reviewed, XXXIX, 304
Victoria's Navy: The Heyday of Steam, by Colin White, reviewed, XLIV, 209
"Victoria, The," by John Haskell Kemble, I, 80, plate facing 79
Victorious, carrier *(1943)*, XLII, 207
Victory, H.M.S. (1765), XXII, 212; *(1797)*, XLIX, 42
Victory, H.M.S. *(1941)*, XXVII, 287–289; *(1973)*, XXXIII, 78
Victory, H.M.S., XXVIII, 6; XXX, 299; XXXI, Pictorial Supplement, plates IV, VII
Victory, privateer *(1739)*, XLII, 46
Victory, schooner *(1862)*, VIII, 228, 232
Victory, ship (1670), XIII, 8; (1857), III, 70
Victory, steamship, XXI, 93, 98; (1834), VII, 55
Victory Museum, XXX, 154
Victory Sword, tanker *(1941)*, XXXVIII, 199 ff.
Vidette, H.M. destroyer *(1943)*, L, 219 ff.
Viedma, Sancho de, VI, 241 ff.
Vier Eeuwen Varen — kapiteins, kapers, kooplieden en geleerden, Editors, L. M. Akveld, Ph. M. Bosscher, J. R. Bruijn, and Kltz F. C. van Oosten, reviewed, XXXIV, 282
Vietnam, Foreign relations, United States, XLVII, 169
Vietor, Alexander O., mention, editorial comment, XLII, 3–4
"View from Below Deck: The British Navy, 1777–1781, The," by Richard C. Barnett, XXXVIII, 92–100
View of Canton, about 1760, XLVI, 25
View of Louisbourg, 1731, XLIV, 192
Views of Yorktown and Gloucester Town, 1755, by E. G. Swem, reviewed, VII, 249–250
View south, Ocean Beach, San Francisco, XLV, 130
Vigilant, barge *(1813)*, XLIII, 6 ff.
Vigilant, bark *(1879)*, XXXIX, 9
Vigilant, cutter, XXXVII, 97; (1893), XXX, plate XVI
Vigilant, H.M.S. *(1745)*, XVI, 82; *(1777)*, XL, 20 ff.
Vigilant, schooner, XXI, 95; *(1755)*, XLIX, 264 ff.; *(1861)*, XI, 289; (1920), V, 141
Vigilant, ship, XXI, 87; *(1861)*, XI, 289; (1877), II, 140–153; V, 175
Vigilant, steamship (1894), VI, 66
Vigilante, man-of-war *(1873)*, XXXVIII, 243
Vigilate, ship (1866), IV, 239
"Vignette of the Naval Career of William Boden, A" (of Marblehead, MA), document contributed by Joseph B. Russell, XXXI, 286–288
Viking, bark (1892), XVI, 115; XVIII, 177–180; (1908), X, 200
Viking, boat (1893), XIV, 110
Viking, steam schooner *(1926)*, VIII, 125
Viking, steam yacht (1883), XXX, plate XXV
Viking Princess, liner *(1950)*, XXXVI, 28, 29

Vikings: Rise and Fall of the Norse Sea Kings, The, by Rudolph Poertner, reviewed, XXXVIII, 147
Vila, bark (1883), XXIV, plate 16
Vilar, 2nd Lieutenant Domingo, XXX, 54
Vila y Hermano, schooner (1891), XV, 173, 189
Villa, Colonel Simon, XXXV, 194
Villa Franca, ship (1859), II, 333
Village Belle, bark (1859), III, 65
Village Belle, Canadian schooner *(1902)*, XLIX, 280
Village Girl, British brig *(1864)*, XXXIII, 206
Village of Woods Hole (MA), photograph of, XLVII, 208
Village Pride, schooner *(1873)*, XXXVIII, 243
Villard, Henry, *The early History of transportation in Oregon*, reviewed, V, 170–171
Villebon, Joseph Robineau de, XXXV, 154 ff.
Villedary, Jean, XLVI, 174
Ville de Paris, ship (1865), IX, 298
Villiers, Alan, XXVI, 157 ff.
Villiers, Sir George, XLIX, 252
Vimy, auxiliary (1918), XXXII, 26, 30
Vimy, H.M. destroyer *(1943)*, XLIV, 49 ff.
Vinal Haven, steamship (1892), XXVIII, plate XXVII
Vincennes, sloop *(1835)*, XXXV, 22
Vincennes, sloop of war *(1812)*, XLI, 29; *(1829)*, XXXI, 181 ff.; XXXII, 48
Vincennes, U.S.S. *(1838)*, IV, 105 ff.; *(1849)*, XIII, 123
Vincennes, U.S. sloop of war (1825), XXII, 151; XXIV, 223; XXV, 94; *(1838)*, XXX, 298; (Vol. XLVI-L?), 152 ff.; photo of model, XLIX, 157
Vincent, Captain B., XXI, 106
Vincent, Captain D. B., XXI, 103
Vincent, Joseph, II, 286
Vincent, Lucy P., XXXVII, 205
Vincent, Matthias, XIII, 21
Vincent, Sydney A., "Half Model of *America*," XII, 239–240
Vine, G. L., Lieutenant of Marines, XXXI, 286
Vineland, XI, 95–107
Vinner, Max and Ole Crumlin-Pedersen, *Sailing into the Past*, reviewed. XLVIII, 205
Vinnie Small, steamship, XXIV, 60
Viola, brig (1910), Pictorial Supplement, XXXIII, plates VIII, XXXII
Viola, steamship (1862), XVII, 139 ff.; *(1862)*, XLIX, 25
Violet, U.S. steam lighthouse tender *(1862)*, V, 245
Viper, H.M.S., XXVIII, 19
Virent, steamship *(1890)*, XIV, 120
Virgil G. Dean, three-sail bateau *(1943)*, IV, 290, 299
Virgin, steamship, XXI, 84, 99, 105; (1864), XXXVI, 89; *(1864)*, XII, 233
Virginia, bark *(1862)*, XXVII, 265, 266
Virginia (ex-*Merrimac*), C.S. Ironclad (1862), III, 161; V, 146; XX, 157, 158–162, 164; XXII, 253, 254, 255, 263, 286 n.; XXIV, 219–221; *(1862)*, XXVII, 174–175; XXXI, 65; XLVIII, 99, 122; XXXVIII, 121; XXXIX, 37; XLIV, 260. *See also* U.S.S. *Merrimack*.
Virginia, C. S. ram (1861), VI, 87
Virginia, cutter *(1798)*, XLV, 95 ff.
Virginia, frigate (1776), VIII, 11, 14, 15, 19, 22, 25, plates 1–2; *(1776)*, XXXI, 173; XXXIV, 135 ff.; *(1790)*, XLIX, 41 ff.
Virginia, H.M. frigate *(1778)*, VII, 207
Virginia, pinnace (1607), XXV, 52, 156; Pictorial Supplement, XXVII, plate I; XXXVI, plate I
Virginia, schooner, XXI, 87; XXII, 60 n.; XXVIII, 224; (1834), XIV, 41; (1865), I, 72; (1868), XXIV, 44, 60; (1910), II, 230
Virginia, ship (1863), IV, 51; *(1930)*, XXXIX, 181
Virginia, sloop *(1861)*, XV, 125
Virginia, steamship, XXI, 97, 106; (1817), VIII, 153; *(1864)*, VIII, 236, 237
Virginia, U.S.S. (1818), XXI, 67
Virginia, whaling bark *(1862)*, XXXIII, 52 ff.; *(1863)*, XXV, 23
Virginia (II), C.S.S. [replica] *(1951)*, XIV, 107
Virginia: History, Colonial period (1600–1775), X, 5; XVII, 173; XXXI, 85; XLVII, 77
Virginia Antonieta, schooner, XXI, 101; *(1861)*, XI, 289
Virginia-Carolina Chemical Co., XXIV, 28
Virginia Co., XIV, 7
Virginia Dare, ship (1860), III, 73
Virginia Gazette, Williamsburg, XXV, 82
Virginia Gazette Index, by Lester J. Cappon and Stella F. Duffy, reviewed, XI, 229–230
Virginia Historical Magazine, XXXVII, 193
Virginia John, schooner *(1861)*, XI, 267, 289
Virginia Navigation Co., II, 226 ff.
Virginius, blockade runner *(1870)*, XXXVI, 88 ff.; XXXVIII, 241 ff.
Virmond, Henry, XXXII, 119
Viscount Canning, steamship (1857), XXVI, 133, 206, 209
Visger, Alfred H. S. S., XIV, 117
Visintini, Lieutenant Commander Licio, XXVII, 188–201
Visurgis, ship (1858), II, 332
Vitiaz, Russian wsrship *(1863)*, XX, 52, 55, 56
Vitoria, ironclad *(1898)*, XLI, 100
Vitruvius, concrete ship (1943), XXII, 175, 176, 177
Vitula, ship (1855), V, 148
Vivian, James F., "United States Policy during the Brazilian Naval Revolt, 1893–1894: The Case for American Neutrality," XLI, 245–261
Vixen, brig *(1812)*, XLIV, 175
Vixen, H.M.S., XXVIII, 19; *(1843)*, XXII, 7; XXVI, 6
Vixen, schooner *(1806)*, XL, 25
Vixen, ship *(1861)*, XXXI, 257, 259
Vixen, steamship *(1864)*, VIII, 236
Vixen, warship *(1846)*, XXXIX, 223
Vocabulary, nautical, XXV, 56
Vogel, Joseph P., XXXVII, 140 n.
Vogle, Arnold, XLI, 49

Voice of the Whaleman with an Account of the Nicholson Whaling Collection, The, by Stuart C. Sherman, reviewed, XXVI, 149–150
Volage, yacht *(1895),* XXXVI, 238
Volant, bark (1853), V, 151
Volant, brig *(1807),* XVI, 194; *(1832),* XXIII, 51
Volant, schooner *(1742),* XLI, 179; *(1798),* XIV, 41
Volant, ship (1853), VI, 81
Volante, brig *(1863),* XII, 161
Volante, British blockage runner *(1862),* L, 93
Volante, schooner *(1861),* VIII, 222, 227; *(1863),* XV, 128
Volckamer, Tobias, XV, 54
Volkmer, Chief Engineer Eldon, XLIII, 13 ff.
Vollmers, Harry, XXVIII, 55
Volpey, Captain John, XV, 178
Voltigeuse, French ship *(1799),* XXXI, 173
Volunteer, American bark *(1830),* XXXII, 118
Volunteer, cutter (1887), XXX, plate X
Volunteer, schooner (1833), XIV, 37, 41; *(1887),* XXX, Pictorial Supplement, plate IV
Volunteer, ship *(1811),* XIV, 209, 210; (1861), XXXIV, 32; (1863), III, 172; *(1887),* XXXVII, 84 ff.
Volunteer, steamship *(1863),* XLIII, 106 ff.
Volunteer, yacht *(1892),* XXXVI, 235
Volusia, ship (1801), Pictorial Supplement, XXXII, plate XIX
Von Bunsen, Captain Lieutenant Karl, XXV, 165
von Forstner, Baron, German commander, XLIV, 58
von Heine-Geldern, Robert, XXIII, 128
von Holleben, Theodore, German Ambassador, XXXII, 258
Von Kotzebue, Captain Otto, XXIII, 223
Von Krohn, Captain Hans, XXXVI, 36, 37
Von Luckner, Lieutenant Commander Felix Count, XXXVI, 266 ff.
Von Sanders, Liman, XXXVI, 43, 44
VonSteuben, U.S.S. (ex-*Kronprinz Wilhelm*), XXVIII, 108 n.
von Tegetthoff, Vice Admiral Baron Wilhelm, XXXIV, 59
Von Usedom, Vice Admiral Guido, XXXVI, 42
Voorhees, Captain Philip F., XXIX, 174–186; XLVI, 231
Vorhees, Commodore Philip F., XXXVIII, 28
Vorwärts, SMS gunboat *(1910),* XL, 88 ff.
Vose, Peter T., XV, 77
Vose, S. Morton, II, review by, XL, 143
Vose, Thomas, XV, 176
Voss, John C., *The Venturesome Voyages of Captain Voss,* reviewed, II, 184–185
Voss, Captain J. C., XXVIII, 53–58, 64, 65
Voutsinas, Captain Byron, XXXVI, 11 ff.
Voyage, ship *(1787),* XXXVIII, 224
"Voyage for Health, A," by Captain John F. Campbell, XIX, 200–212

"Voyage in the Half Brig *Lizzie Wyman,* A," Note by John Lyman, XXXIV, 70
"Voyage of *Alliance:* American Contribution to the Rediscovery and Exploration of the Solomon Islands," by Colin Jack-Hinton, XXV, 248–261, plates 27, 28
Voyage of Discovery to the Southern Parts of Norumbega, A, by Rev. Warner F. Gookin, reviewed, X, 236
"Voyage of *Experiment:* A Letter of W. Hunter, The," document contributed by Richard H. Dillon, XI, 155–156
"Voyage of *Jenny* of Bristol," by Thomas Dunbabin, XIII, 212–213
"Voyage of the Brig *Nabob* from Boston to Batavia, Java in 1833," by Ralph Newell Thompson, V, 194–202
"Voyage of the Good Sloop *Dolphin* to Africa 1795–1796, The," by Bruce L. Mouser, XXXVIII, 249–261
"Voyage of the *Kanrin Maru,* 1860; an Episode in American Naval Diplomacy, The," by George M. Brooke, Jr., XX, 198–208
"Voyage of the *Kanrin Maru,* 1860, The, A Postscript," by Captain Edgar K. Thompson, U.S.N. (ret.), XXI, 142–143
Voyage of the Schooner Polar Bear, *The,* by Bernhard Kilian, reviewed, XLIV, 137
"Voyage of *Triall,* The, 1606–1607: An Abortive Virginia Venture," by David B. Quinn, XXXI, 85–103
Voyages and travels, IV, 53; XII, 294; XIV, 18; XXX, 249; XXXI, 85; XXXII, 100; XLVII, 77
Voyages and Travel [Vol. 1], XXIX, 71
Voyages and Travels of Francis Goelet, 1746–1758, The, by Kenneth Scott, reviewed, XXXI, 227–228
Voyages around the world, XVIII, 189; XLIV, 155
"Voyages of *Star of Poland,*" by Harold D. Huycke, XIV, 210
Voyages of the Columbia *to the Northwest Coast, 1787–1790 and 1790–1793,* edited by Frederic W. Howay, reviewed, II, 253–254
Voyages to Hawaii Before 1860, by Bernice Judd and Helen Yonge Lind, reviewed, XXXV, 217
"Voyage to Canada's Arctic Islands," by Tom H. Inkster, L, 35–41
"Voyage to Java in 1799–1800, A," by Frank B. Evans, III, XLV, 86–93
Voyage to the Southern Ocean: The Letters of Lieutenant William Reynolds from the U.S. Exploring Expedition, edited by Anne Hoffman and E. Jeffrey Stann, L, 150
Voyaging to Cathay: Americans in the China Trade, by Alfred Tamarin and Shirley Glubok, reviewed, XXXVI, 296–297
Vulcan, boat (1818), XIII, 157
Vulcan, British ship *(1738),* XLVIII, 23.
Vulcan, steamship (1818), VIII, 133; *(1841),* XX, 88; (1863), XVII, 303; XVIII, 73; *(1863),* XLIII, 202 ff.; *(1864),* XXXIV, 38 ff.

Vulcan Co., Troy, NY, XLVIII, 108 ff.
Vulture, brig, XIV, 41
Vulture, H.M. sloop of war (1754), XXXI, 22
Vulture, steamship, XXI, 92, 105; *(1864),* VIII, 236

W. E. Meyer & Co., XXXII, 16
W. F. Babcock, ship (1882), XXVII, plate XII
W. H. D. C. Wright, ship *(1853),* XLVIII, 46
W. H. Wardley and Co., XXXIV, 19
W. J. Alt & Co., XLIII, 105 ff.
W. L. Hardison, tanker *(1888),* XXXVIII, 176 ff.
W. M. Goodspeed, trawler *(1908),* XLIV, 122
W. M. Robinet & Co., XLIX, 26
W. R. Adamson & Co., XLIII, 210 ff.
W. R. Grace & Co., XXXV, 180
W. S. Porter, tanker *(1906),* XXXVIII, 197 ff.
WA. *See* Washington (State)
Wabash, David, XXVII, 50, 51
Wabash, flagship *(1861),* XXXI, 258
Wabash, screw frigate *(1850),* XLIX, 112
Wabash, ship *(1890),* XXXIII, 270 ff.
Wabash, U.S.S. (1859), XXVIII, 286; *(1861),* XXXVI, 46, 190, XXXVII, 283; XL, 127
Wace, Nigel, and Bessie Lovett, *Yankee Maritime Activities and the Early History of Australia,* reviewed, XXXIII, 308
Wachusett, steam sloop *(1865),* XXXII, 125; XXXIII, 10; XXXIX, 38; XL, 127
Wacrete Shipbuilding Co., XLI, 196
Waddell, Captain James I., XXVII, 272, 273, 274
Waddill, Judge Edmund, Jr., XLVIII, 56
Wade, Thomas F., XXX, 161
Wade, Sir Thomas, L, 179
Wade, Wyn Craig, *The Titanic: End of a Dream,* reviewed, XL, 65
Wadenaar, Heer (Dutch factory manager in Nagasaki), XLVI, 53
Wadleigh, John R., John B. Hattendorf and B. Mitchell Sampson III, *Sailors and Scholars: The Centennial History of the U.S. Naval War College,* reviewed, XLVIII, 186
Wadsworth, Colonel Decius, XLIII, 7 ff.
Wadsworth, James, XXXI, 133
Wadsworth, General Peleg, XXXVII, 294
Wager, Sir Charles, XXXVII, 272
Wager, warship *(1776),* XLIV, 158 ff.
Wagner, Captain Claude, XLI, 43
Wahlroos, Sven, *Mutiny and Romance in the South Seas: A Companion to the* Bounty *Adventure,* reviewed, L, 72
Wailua, brig *(1859),* XXXVIII, 83

Wainwright, Commander Jonathan M., XXXVI, 193, 198, 200, 201
Wainwright, Rear Admiral Richard, XXXVII, 112 ff.
Waite, A. H., *National Maritime Museum Catalogue of Ship Models, Part I: Ships of the Western Tradition to 1815,* reviewed, XLI, 148–149
Wakamuraskai, steamship (ex-*Nancai*) *(1871),* XLIX, 26
Wakeman, Frederic, Jr., "China's New Historical Archives," XLVIII, 283–285
Wake of the Coasters, by John F. Leavitt, reviewed, XXXI, 73–74
Wakulla, schooner, XXVI, 271
Walcott, Captain Henry G., XXXIV, 18
Waldo, Francis, XXXI, 214
Waldock, Captain, XXIX, 266
Waldron, C. J., XXVIII, plate XIII
Wales, Prince of: Edward VIII, Prince of Wales, XXXIV, 11 ff.; Edward Albert, Prince of Wales, XXXVI, 183 ff.
Walker, Rear Admiral B. W., XXVI, 100
Walker, Borradaile and Co., XXXIV, 26
Walker, David, *Champion of Sail: R. W. Leyland and his Shipping Line,* XLVII, 213
Walker, Fred M., *Song of the Clyde,* reviewed, XLVII, 57
Walker, Fred M. and Anthony Slaven, editors, *European Shipbuilding: One Hundred Years of Change,* reviewed, XLIV, 136–137
Walker, James, XLVIII, 77 ff.
Walker, Commodore James G., XXIII, 263 ff.
Walker, John, XXX, 214
Walker, John E., XL, 129 ff.
Walker, Rear Admiral John Grimes, XXXIX, 126; XXXVIII, 297; XL, 128
Walker, Captain Matthew, XLVIII, 84
Walker, Ralph, London, Pictorial Supplement, XXXV, plate XIV
Walker, William, XXXIII, 168
Walkers [Thomas], Pictorial Supplement, XXXV, plate XXIV
Wallace, R. L., and Son Shipyard, Thomaston, Maine, XL, 4
Wallace Shipyards, Ltd., Vancouver, XXXII, 33
Wallace Triumph, schooner *(1971),* XXXII, 187
Waller, Captain D. D. Porter, XXXV, 195
Wallis, Captain Benjamin, XXVIII, 292–293
Wallis, Mary Davis, *Life in Feejee, or Five Years Among the Cannibals,* reviewed, XXVIII, 292–293
Walrus, wooden trawler *(1917),* XLIV, 124
Walsh, Hall & Co., XLIX, 26
Walsh, Captain Matt, XXIX, 266
Walter Forward, revenue cutter *(1841),* XLV, 120
Walter Irving, ship *(1855),* L, 122
Walton, Gary, XXXVII, 50
Walton, Margery, Julia Bergen, Janet Paul, *John Cawte Beaglehole: A Bibliography,* reviewed, XXXIII, 222–223

Wampanoag, screw steamship *(1863),* XLVIII, 125; XLIX, 118
Wamsutta, ship *(1853),* XXXIX, 86, plate 2
Wanda, yacht *(1892),* XXXVI, 236, 237
Wanderer, bark (1878), photo c. 1920 in Pictorial Supplement, XXXIII, 63, plate XXV; *(1894),* XXXVIII, 86
Wan Loong Fei, steamship *(1863),* XLIII, 220
Wanton, Joseph, XXXII, 173
Wantung, merchant ship *(1937),* L, 260 ff.
War against the seals: A history of the North American seal fishery, The, by Briton Cooper Busch, reviewed, XLVIII, 131
Waratah, steamship *(1863),* XLIII, 125 ff.
"War between Pacific Mail and the Pacific Railroads, The," XXXI, 125
Ward, Commander J. H., XLVII, 112
Ward, Vice-Admiral J. Ross, XXXIV, 9 ff.
Ward, John E., XXVII, 157, 164, 165, 169, 172, 173, 223; XXXIV, 14 ff.; XXXVIII, 38
Ward, R. Gerard, Editor, *American Activities in the Central Pacific,* reviewed; [Vol. 1], XXVII, 285–286; [Vol. 2], XXVIII, 293–294; [Vols. 3 and 4], XXIX, 69–70; [Vols. 5, 6, and 7], XXIX, 291
Ward, Governor Richard, XXXV, 292
Ward, Stillman & Co., XLVIII, 112
Ward, W. E. F., *The Royal Navy and the Slavers,* reviewed, XXX, 68–69
Ward Steamship Line, XXXIII, 268
Ware, E. Richmond, XXX, 174
Ware, Edward James, XXX, 168
Ware, Edward Richmond, M.D., "Enoch Richmond Ware: Impressions by His Grandson," XXX, 167–173; "Health Hazards of the West African Trader, 1840–1870," XXVII, 81–97
Ware, Emma Forbes, XXX, 168
Ware, Enoch Richmond, XXVII, 81 ff.; XXX, 167–186, 229–248; portrait, XXX, plate 5
Ware, Gertrude Talbot, XXX, 172
Ware, Mary Coutant (Peck), XXX, 168, 169, 237
Ware, Robert, XXX, 168
Ware, William, XXX, 237 ff.
Ware, William Barlow, XXX, 167
Ware, William Bayliss, XXX, 175
Ware, William Richmond, XXX, 168
Waring, C. M., XXXVIII, 63
Waring, Thomas, XXXI, 236
Warner, David T., XLVII, 46
Warner, Deborah Jean, "At the Sign of the Quadrant: The Navigational Instrument Business in America to the Civil War," XLVI, 258–263
Warner, Captain Elisha, XXXIX, 211
Warner, Oliver, *Nelson's Last Diary,* reviewed, XXXII, 289; "The Royal National Life-Boat Institution, 1824–1974," XXXIV, 5–16
Warner, William W., *Distant Water: The Fate of the North Atlantic Fisherman,* reviewed, XLIV, 139–140

War of 1812: XXVI, 178, 183, 184; XXVII, 26, 158–159; XXVIII, 117, 165–194; XXX, 73
War of 1812, The, by Reginald Horsman, reviewed, XXIX, 288
War of Jenkins' Ear, XXVI, 37–62
War of the Pacific (1879–1884). *See* Pacific, War of the
Warren, armed schooner *(1775),* XXX, 104, 107, 110, 111, 114
Warren, frigate *(1776),* XLVIII, 158; L, 245 ff.; *(1779),* XXXV, 142; XXXVII, 293
Warren, receiving ship *(1861),* XXXIII, 42 ff.
Warren, U.S.S. *(1829),* VII, 18
Warren, James, XXXVII, 300
Warren, Admiral John, XXXVI, 207, 208, 214, 217
Warren, Sir John, XXVIII, 116
Warren, Captain Peter, XLVIII, 22 ff.
Warren Fisher, bark (1851), XLIX, 123
Warriner, Francis, XXXI, 182
Warrington, Captain Arthur A., XIV, 290
Warrington, Commodore, XXXI, 138
Warrington, Lewis, XLVII, 28
Warrington, Captain Lewis, XIX, 214–226
Warrington, Commodore Lewis, XLIV, 245
Warrior, sloop, XXI, 103; *(1861),* XI, 289
Warrior, steamship, XXI, 104; *(1863),* XVI, 257; *(1863),* XII, 161
Warrior, XXIX, 13 n., 14
Warrior: The World's First Ironclad Then and Now, by Andrew Lambert, reviewed, XLIX, 134
War Risk Insurance Bureau, XXXIII, 184
Wars:
  Austro-Italian War (1866)
  Barbary War (1801–1805). *See* United States History (Tripolitan War)
  Chinese-Japanese War (1894–1895). *See* China; Japan (Sino-Japanese War)
  Civil War (China) (1945–1949). *See* China
  Civil War (U.S.) (1861–1864). *See* United States History; United States. Navy
  Crimean War (1853–1856)
  Crusades, First (1090–1099)
  Hundred Years' War (1339–1453)
  King George's War (1744–1748). *See* United States, History
  Mexican War (1846–1848)
  Minamoto-Taira War (1180–1185). *See* Japan
  Mysore War (1790–1792). *See* India
  Opium War. *See also* China
  Quasi-War with France (1797–1801). *See* United States, History
  Queen Anne's War (1702–1713). *See* United States, History
  Revolution (U.S.) (1775–1788). *See* United States History; United States. Navy
  Seven Years' War (1756–1763)
  Sino-Japanese War (1894–1895). *See also* China; Japan

Spanish-American War (1898). *See also* United States History

Taiping Rebellion (1850–1864). *See* China

Tripolitan War (1801–1805). *See* United States History

War of the Pacific (1879–1884). *See* Pacific, War of the

World War: 1914–1918

World War: 1939–1945

Warships, Mediterranean area, L, 192. *See also* Armored vessels, etc.

"Warships of the Ancient Mediterranean," by A. F. Tilley, L, 192–200

Warspite, cruiser *(1882),* XXXIX, 130

"Wars They Wanted: American Missionaries' Use of *The Chinese Repository* Before the Opium War, The," by Murray A. Rubinstein, XLVIII, 271–282

"Wartime Canoe Building in the Marshall Islands," by W. S. Jenkins, VI, 71–72, plates 9–12

Warwick, steamship, XXII, 219; (1882), XI, 257 ff.

Washakie, schooner (1908), XXVI, plate XXII

Washburn, Wilcomb E., XXXVII, 81; review by, XLV, 132; "The Canary Islands and the Question of the Prime Meridian: The Search for Precision in the Measurement of the Earth," XLIV, 77–81

Washburn Marine Railway Co., XXIV, 58

Washington, brig *(1777),* V, 187; *(1807),* XVI, 195

Washington, Confederate revenue schooner (1837), XLVIII, 87 ff.

Washington, frigate (1776), VIII, 11, 12, 21, 24; *(1776),* XXXIV, 137; *(1777),* XXXIX, 29; XL, 32

Washington, galley *(1779),* XXXV, 141

Washington, passenger liner *(1947),* XXVII, 254

Washington, row galley *(1776),* VIII, 256

Washington, ship *(1807),* XVI, 192; *(1810),* XXIV, 267, 270; *(1850),* XII, 107

Washington, sloop *(1787),* XV, 205–212; *(1814),* XXIV, 177, 179

Washington, steamship (1815), I, plate facing 414; II, 92; (1816), XVI, 36

Washington, steamship (1844), XVII, 60; XVIII, 73; *(1845),* XLVIII, 114, 174; *(1847),* XXVII, 254 ff., plates 9–12; (1854), XVIII, 73; *(1864),* XX, 184; *(1934),* XXIX, 234

Washington, tug *(1844),* XLIII, 296 ff.

Washington, U.S. battle ship *(1910),* XXII, 142

Washington, U.S.S. (1814), XXI, 65

Washington (DC). *See* National Archives

Washington, DC, XXV, plate VI; yacht racing in, XXXVI, 231–250

Washington (WA). *See* Yacht racing

Washington, George (President): XXV, 189 n., 191, 194; XXVI, 237–239, 242–245, 255; XXX, 86 ff., 109; XXXVI, 55, 80; XXXVII, 304; XXXVIII, 21 Dismal Swamp Canal, V, 205–207; naval effort, I, 29–31; Potomac River, V, 207, 219

Washington, Captain John, XXXII, 245

Washington, Brigadier General William, XLVII, 22

Washington B. Thomas, schooner, XXIII, plate XIII

Washington County Historical Society, PA, VIII, 278

Washington Ditch, V, 207–208, 216, 219, plate 14

Washingtonian, steamship (ex-*Willzipo,* ex-*Eastern Mariner*), XXIII, 276

Washington Irving, ship (1845), XV, 140

Washington Navy Yard, XXIV, 11

Washington Rediva, sloop (1787), XXXIII, 161 ff.

"Washington's Boat at the Delaware Crossing," by M. V. Brewington, II, 167–170

Washington Ship Model Society, III, 178; V, 165

Washtenaw, steamship *(1887),* XXXVIII, 185 ff.; *(1895),* XI, 259 ff.

Wasp, brigantine *(1783),* XXI, 212 n.

Wasp, Continental Navy schooner *(1776),* XXV, 193, 206, 211, 212, 213

Wasp, frigate *(1811),* XL, 25; *(1812),* XLI, 28; XLIV, 171

Wasp, H.M.S., XXVI, 195

Wasp, privateer *(1813),* XXXVI, 211 ff.

Wasp, schooner *(1779),* XXXV, 141; *(1864),* XII, 233

Wasp, U.S.S. *(1808),* XXVIII, 116

Wasp, U.S.S. (former British sidewheel) *(1874),* XXXIII, 287

Wasp, U.S. sloop *(1812),* VII, 167–169

Wasp, yacht *(1892),* XXXVI, 236 ff.

Wasson, George, XVII, 7, 8; XXII, 184, plate 9, 185, 186

Wasson, George S., IX, 3–4; XII, 305; XIII, 274; XV, 213; *Sailing Days on the Penobscot,* reviewed, IX, 232–233

"Was the Continental Navy a Mistake?" by Jonathan R. Dull, XLIV, 167–170

Wataga, ship *(1843),* XXXVI, 253 ff.

Wataridori, ketch (1952), XIV, 18–28, plates 1–4

Watchful, schooner *(1864),* XII, 233

Watch House Point, Gloucester (MA), XXV, plate XXXII

Watchman, schooner *(1837),* XXII, 235

Watercraft. *See also* Boats.

Watercraft, Great Lakes, XXVII, 155–156

Watercraft, South American, XXVI, 33–36, 224, plates 3–8

Wateree, U.S.S. *(1864),* XXVII, 43, 44; *(1865),* XXXII, 285

Waterford, schooner (1787), VI, 136

Waterford Commercial Steam Navigation Co., XLIII, 204

Waterhouse, Captain Samuel, XX, 111

Waterlily, schooner *(1843),* IV, 324–325

Waterloo, schooner *(1855),* I, 394; *(1863),* XII, 161

Waterloo, ship *(1815),* XXI, 291; *(1878),* IX, plate 31

Waterloo, steamship (1840), XX, 84

Waterman, H.M. water boat *(1860),* XLIII, 105 ff.

Waterman, H.M.S. (ex-*Sir Charles Forbes*), XXXIV, 25

Waterman, Asa, XXXI, 134

Waterman, C. C., XXIX, 224–225

Waterman Steamship Corp., XLI, 114

Waters, D. W., *The Art of Navigation in England in Elizabethan and Early Stuart Times*, reviewed, XX, 274; "Comments on the Coale Painting," XI, 220–221; *The Rutters of the Sea: The Sailing Directions of Pierre Garcie*, reviewed, XXVIII, 75; "The Sea Chart and the English Colonization of America," XVII, 28–37
Waters, Captain Daniel, XIV, 57
Waters, Captain Samuel, XXI, 103
Waters, Captain William D., XVII, 156
Water Transport Origins and Early Evolution, by James Hornell, reviewed, VIII, 72
Water Witch, brig *(1875)*, XXVIII, 148
Water Witch, Idem Class Sloop, XXVI, plate 8
Water Witch, schooner, XXI, 103; (1847), Pictorial Supplement, XXXVIII, plate XXXII; *(1861)*, XI, 284; XII, 59
Water Witch, ship (1853), XIX, plate XXIX; *(1855)*, XXXVI, 180
Water Witch, sloop (1832), XXXVI, 255
Water Witch, U.S.S. (1855), XXXI, 7 ff.; (1858), XIX, 241
Waterwitch, U.S.S. *(1863)*, XXI, plate XXVIII; *(1864)*, XXVII, 44
Water Witch, Union steamship *(1861)*, XLVIII, 90
Water Witch (I), U.S. tender (1843), XXIV, 8 ff.
"*Water Witch* Incident, The," by Clare V. McKanna, XXXI, 7–18
Watkins, C. H., XXII, plate VIII
Watkins, Captain, XLV, 22
Watkins, Captain J. T., XX, 126–129
Watkins, Lieutenant Robert, XXXII, 98
Watkinson, James, XXXI, 144
Watson, George, XI, 147–148; XXX, 299
Watson, Vice-Admiral George W., XXVIII, 14, 16, 19, 20, 23, 25, 27, 112
Watson, Captain J. S., XVI, 173; XVIII, 84
Watson, Lieutenant James M., XXXIII, 45
Watson, Captain James R., XXI, 103
Watson, Commodore John Crittenden, XLI, 93 ff.
Watson, Jonas, XIV, 117
Watson, R. C., XI, 87
Watson, W. H., query by, II, 174
Watt, James, XXIII, 205; steam engine, drawing of, L, 204
Watts, Billy, XXXVI, 235
Watts, Captain S., II, 79–80, 246
Watts, Samuel, XLIV, 10
Watts, Thomas, XXIV, 59
Waugh, Captain, XXIX, 251, 259
Waugh, F. W., XXV, 296
Waunita, steamship (1882), VII, 153–156, 165
Wave, schooner, XXI, 100; *(1861)*, XI, 289; XII, 59, 161; *(1862)*, VIII, 228
Wave, sloop *(1862)*, XII, 59
Wave, steamship (1864), XII, 233, 235
Wave, trawler *(1913)*, XLIV, 121

Wavecrest, sloop, XXII, 186
Wave Queen, steamship *(1863)*, VIII, 232
Waverley, bark (1857), IV, 243; *(1859)*, XLV, 176; (1860), IV, 326; (1863), IV, 240
Waverly, brig *(1832)*, XIV, 44
Waverly, whaler *(1865)*, XXVII, 276
Wavertree, iron vessel (1885), mention, XXXVI, 3; XL, 164
Wavertree, ship *(1907)*, XXIX, 282
Wawona, schooner (1897), I, 296–297; *(1963)*, XXV, 294
Wax, Darold D., "The Browns of Providence and the Slaving Voyage of the Brig *Sally*, 1764–1765," XXXII, 171–179; "Thomas Rogers and the Rhode Island Slave Trade," XXXV, 289–301
Way, Frederick, Jr., *Way's Directory of Western Rivers Packets*, reviewed, XI, 299
Waymouth, George, XXXI, 85; XLVII, 77; L, 6 ff.
Wayne Lawrence, fishing vessel *(1964)*, XLI, 61
"Way of a Book, The," by J. M. Edelstein, XIX, 123–125
Way's Directoy of Western Rivers Packets, by Frederick Way, Jr., reviewed, XI, 299
Wealthy, schooner (1808), XVI, 206
Wealthy Pendleton, bark *(1880)*, XLIV, 151
Wear, H.M. frigate *(1943)*, L, 220 ff.
Weare, Meshech, VII, 200–203, 207–208, 210–211
Wearin, Otha, Congresssman, XLI, 119
Weather, VI, 132; VII, 35. See also types of weather, e.g., Hurricanes, Storms at sea
Weather Gage, schooner *(1862)*, XXVII, 265
Weatherly, America's Cup Defender sloop (1958), XXII, 232
Weaver, Second Lieutenant Thomas, Continental Marines, XXV, 204–206, 208
Webb, Captain A. L., XIV, 129
Webb, George Randolph and Jane Carter Webb, *The Best on the Bay: Fifty Years of Racing*, reviewed, XLV, 135
Webb, Isaac, VII, 184–185
Webb, J. Watson, XXII, 52
Webb, Mrs. J. Watson, XIX, plate I
Webb, General James W., XV, 287 ff.
Webb, Jane Carter and George Randolph Webb, *The Best on the Bay: Fifty Years of Racing*, reviewed, XLV, 135
Webb, Joseph, XXXI, 27
Webb, Captain Stephen, Pictorial Supplement, XXXII, plate IV
Webb, Robert Lloyd, reviews by, XLVII, 64; XLIX, 308; L, 152; "Invented Too Late: The Introduction of Steam to the Arctic Whaling Fleet," XLIV, 11–21; *On the Northwest: Commercial Whaling in the Pacific Northwest, 1790–1967*, reviewed, L, 152
Webb, William H., VII, 3–7; X, 19; XV, 203; XVIII, 192; XX, 53; XXXVI, 177–179; XLV, 20 ff.
Webb, William H. (shipbuilder), I, 44; IV, 305 ff.
Webb, William Joe, "The Spanish-American War and United States Army Shipping," XL, 167–191; "The

United States Wooden Steamship Program During World War I," XXXV, 275–288
Webber, Augustin M., XIII, 269
Webber, J., XXXVI, 235
Webber, Captain Seth, XV, 134
Webb Institute of Naval Architecture, V, 115 ff.; VII, 4, 6, plates 22–23; VIII, 7; XLVII, 37
Webfoot, ship, XXII, 234, 244, 246; *(1856),* III, 72
Webster, Daniel, XLVI, 213
Webster, E. M., XXXVI, 30
Webster, John A., XVI, 213
Webster, Captain Levi, XXI, 103
Webster-Ashhburton Treaty of 1842, XXXII, 274
Weckler, J. E., Jr., *Polynesian Explorers of the Pacific,* reviewed, III, 180
"Wedding on a Warship, A," Note by Harold D. Langley, XXXIV, 65–68
Wedgewood, Captain, XLV, 201
Weehawken, U.S. monitor *(1862),* X, 17, 23, 24, 27, 31; XLIV, 268 ff. and plate 1; *(1863),* XLIX, 116
Weehawken, U.S. steam launch *(1871),* VII, 110, 112
Weeks, Captain Ambrose, XX, 46
Weeks, Commander John W., XXXIII, 276
Weems Line, XXX, 72
Weetamoe, sloop *(1903),* XXX, 195
Wegner, Dana M. and Philip K. Lundeberg, "'Not for Conquest But Discovery:' Rediscovering the Ships of the Wilkes Expedition," XLIX, 151–167
Wehmann, Howard H., document by, XXXV, 208
"Weight of a Whaleboat," by William E. Schevill, XX, 63–64
"Weights of Boats," by John Lyman, XXVIII, 142–143
Weinstein, Robert A., *Tall Ships on Puget Sound: The Marine Photographs of Wilhelm Hester,* reviewed, XXXIX, 145
Weir, Robert, journal of, XXV, 104
Weiss, Captain Thomas L., XIV, 118, 119, 121, 122
Welaka, steamship *(1859),* VII, 119
Welch, William L., "Lorenzo Sabine's History of the Fisheries," XLVIII, 165–172
Welch and Co., II, 292–293
Welcome, coal transport *(1840),* XXXV, 260
Weld, Dr. Charles Goddard, VII, 6 n.; XXX, 3; XL, 111
Weld, Mrs. Charles Goddard, I, 67
Weld, Philip, mention, XLIV, 199; review by, XLIV, 201
Weld, Sandy, *The Leading Edge,* reviewed, XXXII, 143
Weld, William F., & Co., I, 67–68
Weld and Baker, I, 67
Weldon, George, XLIV, 23 ff.
Welland, steamship (1842), XX, 250
Welland Canal, VII, 43, 44; VIII, 56–57
Welles, Gideon, Secretary of the Navy, XXXI, 63; XXXII, 45, 124 ff.; XXXIII, 44; XXXIV, 63; XXXV, 53 ff.; XXXVI, 196, 280; XXXIX, 38; XLVII, 31; XLVIII, 120

Welles, Gideon, XV, 102, 298; XXII, 54, 236, 256, 257, 258, 283, 284, 287 n.; XXIII, 197 ff.; XXVII, 34 n., 35 n., 37, 243
Welles, Samuel, XL, 258
Wellesley, Vice-Admiral Sir George G., XXVIII, 111
Wellfleet, pinky schooner *(1829),* XXVI, plate I
Wellfleet, ship (1853), III, 170; XXVIII, plate VII
Wellings (explorer, 1840's), XXV, 260
Wellington, George, XVII, 122
Wells, Captain C. H., XVIII, 84
Wells, Captain Daniel, XXI, 103
Wells, George, XXXIV, 135
Wells, Captain George, VII, 14
Wells, Gideon, IV, 254–255
Wells, Sumner, Ambassador to Cuba, XXXV, 133
Wells, Commander Tom Henderson, "The Battle of Campache," XXI, 216–221
Wells, William, VII, 298, 301 ff.; XXXVIII, 104
Wells City, steamship (1885), XXXVIII, 184 ff.; *(1885),* XIV, 121, 126, 134; *(1951),* XIV, 132, 135
Welsh, Charles W., XXXI, 58
Welsh, Frank, XL, 7 ff.
Welsh, Captain John, XXXVII, 298
Welt, G. L., V, 138
Welt, George, XXIII, plate XVII
Welwyn, William, XXXVII, 11
Wendell, George B., XXV, 106–108
Wendell, Jacob, XIII, 121
Wendell, John, XVIII, 301
Wendell and Co., XIII, 121
Wendover, Peter, XXXVII, 133
Wenona, schooner, XXI, 95; *(1863),* XII, 161
Wentworth, Benning, XXXIII, 96 ff.
Wentworth, Governor Benning, XXII, 66, 68
Wentworth, General, XXVI, 48
Wentworth, George, VII, 211
Wentworth, Governor John, XXII, 66, 67, 69; XXXIII, 95 ff.
Wentworth, Joshua, VII, 210–211
Wentworth, Samuel, XXX, 136
Werden, Lieutenant Reed, XXI, 234, 235
Werner Vinnen, auxiliary schooner (1922), V, 141, plate 10
Wertha Ann, ship *(1803),* XII, 162; XIII, 278
Wesley, Charles, XXIII, 82
Wesley, John, XXIII, 82
Wesphal, Lieutenant G., XXXI, 286
West, Benjamin Franklin, marine paintings by, Pictorial Supplement, XXXVIII, Part I, 40–41; Part II, 100–101; Part III, 216–217; Part IV, 300–301
West, Captain Ebenezer, XXV, 7
West, Captain Edward, Pictorial Supplement, XXXII, plate IX
West, Ellsworth Luce, *Captain's Papers, a Log of Whaling and Other Sea Experiences,* reviewed, XXVI, 149
West, Captain Frank, XXXVI, 48, 49
West, Gertrude Eager, XXXVII, 213

West, James (shipbuilder), V, 243
West, Job, XXXVI, 211
West, Nathaniel, XXII, 195, 196, 208, 209; XXVI, 277
West, Nathaniel, (1799), XXXIII, 162 ff.
West, Captain Nehemiah, XII, 104
West, Richard S., Jr., *Gideon Wells — Lincoln's Navy Department,* reviewed, IV, 254–255
West, Captain W. A., XVII, 48; XVIII, 84; XLIII, 92 ff.
West African trade, XXX, 174–186, 230–248
West Coast Shipbuilding Co., XLI, 197
Westcountry Coasting Ketches, by W. J. Slade and Basil Greenhill, reviewed, XXXVI, 145–146
Westcountry Sail: Merchant Shipping 1840–1960, by Michael Bouquet, reviewed, XXXIII, 213–214
West Coyote, steamship *(1918),* XVIII, 204
West Cumberland, British tramp steamship *(1889),* XXXV, 12
Westendorff, Captain G. W., XXI, 103
Westerlund, Captain Charles F., XXI, 103
Western, steamship *(1839),* XVIII, 294
Western, John R., XXXVIII, 267
Western Belle, bark (1876); XXVII, plate XX; figurehead of, XXXVII, Pictorial Supplement, plate IV
Western Continent, ship *(1864),* XXVIII, 122
Western Cooperage Co., XXV, 293
Western Development Co. XXXI, 121
Westernland, steamship (1884), Pictorial Supplement, XXXIV, plate XVIII
Western Marine and Salvage Co., The, XXXV, 286
"Western Ocean Engineering in the 1880s," document contributed by Grahame Farr, XXII, 219–220
Western Seamen's Friends Society, XXXIX, 47
Western Trader, ship (1805), VII, 317
Western World, steamship *(1862),* XXXIX, 143; *(1922),* VIII, 67–68
Western World, U.S.S. *(1862),* L, 90 ff.
West Erral, steamship *(1927),* IX, 224
West Falkland, map of, XLIX, 282
West Faralon, steamship *(1922),* IX, 222
Westfield, gunboat *(1862),* XXXVI, 198, 201
West Florida, schooner, XXI, 88; *(1861),* XI, 289; XII, 59
West Haven, steamship *(1929),* IX, 226
West Hosokie, steamship *(1929),* IX, 226
West India Co., XLVII, 6 ff.
"West India Hurricanes," by J. W. Somerville, VI, 132–134, plate 17
West Indian, brig *(1861),* VIII, 222
"West Indian Droghers," query by Baron R. de Kerchove, II, 174
West Indian sailing vessels, XXIV, 95–108
West Indian trade, XIX, 115, 116
"West Indian Trader, A," by Captain W. R. Chaplin, XIV, 83–104, plates 9, 10
West India Packet Co., Ltd., XXX, 80
West India trade, VIII, 165–178
West Indies, XXVI, 171. *See also* Pirates; Shipbuilding; Shipping

West Kasson, steamship *(1920),* X, 141
West Lianga, steamship *(1929),* IX, 226
Westoe, bark *(1863),* XXIX, 104
Weston, Alden, XIV, 38
Weston, Ezra, XIV, 29–41
Weston, First Lieutenant G. L., XLIX, 209
Weston, Captain Gershom B., XIV, 37, 38
Weston, Henry, Esq., XXX, 235
Weston, John, XX, 186
Weston, Nathaniel, XIV, 210
Weston, R. W., XVII, 47, 50
Weston, Thomas, XX, 186; XXXVII, 13
Weston Meritt, ship (1860), V, 242
West Point, ship (1847), III, 262; *(1849),* XVIII, 314
West Point, U.S. transport (ex-*America,* 1940), XXV, 224
West Point, XXX, 140
West Point Foundry Assoc., XLV, 39
West Portal, merchant ship *(1943),* XLIV, 52
Westward, schooner, XLV, 44
Westward, ship *(1971),* XLVII, 206 ff.; illustration of, XLVII, 209
Westward, staysail schooner (1961), XXXIV, 80
Westward Crossing, by Humphrey Burton, reviewed, XI, 231–232
West Wind, schooner *(1861),* XI, 289
Westwood, David, *Anatomy of the Ship: The Type VII U-Boat,* reviewed, XLVII, 55
Westwood, Howard C., "Reform in the United States Navy: The 'Plucking' of Officers in the Latter 1850s," L, 107–118
Wetherbee, J., U.S.N., XXV, 50
Wetling, Thos. (artist), XXII, plate XVII
Wetmore, Cryder & Co., XVII, 224; XLIII, 215
Wetmore, William S., XX, 107
Wexler, Mrs. Minerva Crowell, XXII, 233, 248
Weybosset, steamship, later schooner (1863–1879), I, 163; *(1880),* XXIII, 12, plate IX
Weymouth, H.M.S. (1713), XXI, 262
Weymouth, sloop *(1746),* XLVIII, 33
Weymouth, Lord, XXX, 204
Weyts, P., XXVII, plate II; XXVIII, plates IV, VI
Whale, ship *(1630),* XXIII, 63
Whale, The, by Dr. Leonard Harrison Matthews, F.R.S., Editor, reviewed, XXIX, 143–144
Whaleback (ship), XXV, 168
"Whalebacks, McDougall's," by Tom H. Inkster, XXV, 168–175, plates 15, 16
Whaleboat: A Study of Design, Construction, and Use from 1850 to 1970, The, Willits D. Ansel, reviewed, XXXIX, 151–153
Whaleboat being crushed by a Sperm Whale's Jaws, XXII, plate XIV
Whaleboat Caught by a Whale's Flukes, XXII, plate XIV
Whaleboat on wagon, Pictorial Supplement, XXXIII, plate XXIV (upper).
Whaleboats, III, 350–352; XX, 63–64

Whale Fishing, 1831, XXIX, 198, plate XIX
Whale Hunt, by Nelson Cole Haley, reviewed, IX, 77; cited, XXV, 104
"Whale Hunt," XXII, plate XXXII
"Whale Hunt, The," XXII, plate XXVIII
"Whale Hunters, The," XXII, plate VII
Whale is Ours, And the, by Pamela A. Miller, reviewed, XL, 70
"Whalemen's Lays," document contributed by Carl W. Mitman, IV, 74–76
Whalemen's Shipping List and Merchants' Transcript, XXV, 105
Whale Oil: an Economic Analysis, by Karl Brandt, reviewed, I, 101
"Whaler in the Ice," XXII, plate XVI
"Whaler *Ploughboy*," document contributed by Paul R. Maloney, XXI, 222
Whalers. Biography, XLIV, 22
Cape Verde Islands, XLV, 104
Whale ships, XLIV, 11
United States, IX, 17
"Whalers and a Shore Try-works," XXII, plate XXVIII
"Whalers at New Bedford," XXII, plate XXIV
"Whaler's Letter, A," document contributed by Joseph B. Howerton, XVIII, 320–323
"Whalers near Wanganui, New Zealand ... (1875)," XXII, plate VIII
Whales & Destiny: The Rivalry between America, France, and Britain for Control of the Southern Whale Fishery, 1785–1825, by Edouard A. Stackpole, reviewed, XXXIII, 221–222
Whales in art, XLIX, 226
"Whale Ship *Benjamin Tucker* of New Bedford, The," document contributed by E. Lee Dorsett, X, 298–300
Whale Ships and Whaling: A Pictorial History, by George Francis Dow, reviewed, L, 138
Whale's Tale as told on postage stamps, The, by Frederic P. Schmitt, reviewed, XXXVI, 148–149
Whaling, XXXII, 34
Africa (Northwest), Statistics, L, 119
Arctic regions, XXXVIII, 81; XXXIX, 5; XLIV, 11
Cintra Bay Ground, Statistics, L, 119
Hawaii, XIV, 42
Pacific Ocean, XII, 22; L, 211
Spitzbergen, XXVIII, 239
United States, XXI, 110; XXIII, 22; XXVII, 98, 263; XXXIII, 120; XLV, 104
Whaling: I, 391–394, 410; IX, 17–30, 77, 228–229; X, 298–300; XII, 22–44, 99–122; XIII, 131–133; XIV, 42–46, 139–141; XIX, 78; XX, 129; XXVII, 73, 75, 98–110, 226, 263–278, 279–280; XXI, 110–129; XXII, 16–17, 108–109, 151, 200–201, 292–293; XXIII, 22–28
"Whaling, Naval and Merchant Vessels," query by Bryant K. Rogers, I, 172; answered by W. Salisbury, II, 82

Whaling and Eskimos: Hudson Bay 1860–1915, by W. Gillies Ross, reviewed, XXXVII, 72
Whaling and Old Salem, by Frances D. Robotti, reviewed, XI, 233
Whaling and Sealing at the Chatham Islands, by Rhys Richards, reviewed, XLIV, 204
Whaling and the Art of Scrimshaw, by Charles R. Meyer, reviewed, XXXVIII, 304
Whaling Days in Old Hawaii, by Maxine Mrantz, reviewed, XXXVII, 224–225
"Whaling Fleet, A," XXII, plate XXX
Whaling industry, XXVIII, 239–260, 284–286, plates XXVIII, XXIX
Whaling Industry of New London, by Robert Owen Decker, reviewed, XXXVI, 144
Whaling in literature, XLVI, 252
"Whaling in the South Seas" *(1865),* XXII, plate XX
"Whaling Logs," query by Wilson L. Hefflin, VIII, 154
"Whaling Ports: A Study of Ninety Years of Rivalry, 1784–1875, The," by Stuart Seely Sprague, XXXIII, 120–130
"Whaling Scene," XXII, plate XXVII
Whaling scenes: *Clara Bell* journal, XXV, plate 6; *Elizabeth* journal, XXV, 184
Whaling Trade in Old New Zealand, The, by L. S. Rickard, reviewed, XXVII, 75
Whampoa, river steamship *(1862),* XXXIV, 32, 57; XLIII, 101 ff.
Whampoa Dock Co., XXXIV, 36 ff.
Whampoa Reach, XXVIII, plate V
Whangpu River, XXX, 157 ff.
Wharton, Goodwin, VII, 269
Wharton, John, VIII, 14–15; XXXI, 239; XLIX, 47
Wharton, Rear Admiral Sir William J. L., XXVIII, 151
Wharton, Texas warship *(1843),* XXI, 221 ff.
Wharton and Humphreys, VIII, 12, 22
"What a Difference a Day Makes: The Royal Navy and the Yangtse Incident of 20–21 April 1949," by Malcolm H. Murfett, XLIX, 208–225
"What a Fool a Man is To Go To Sea," document contributed by Russell W. Knight, XXXII, 64–67
What Finer Tradition: The Memoirs of Thomas O. Selfridge, Jr., Rear Admiral, U.S.N., reviewed, XLIX, 133
"What's in a Name?" by Captain Edgar K. Thompson, U.S.N. (ret.), XXVIII, 144; XXXVI, 124
Wheatland, David P., reviewed book, XXVIII, 290–292
Wheatland, David Pingree, reviewed book, XXIV, 217–219
Wheatland, Dr. Henry, XLIX, 34
Wheaton, Dr. Levi, XL, 193 ff.
Wheaton, Brigadier General Lloyd V., XXXV, 186
Wheeler, Captain Guy C., VII, 66
Wheeler, Captain John, XXIII, 64
Wheeler, John H., New York, Pictorial Supplement, XXXV, plate XV; XLVI, 263
Wheeler, L. A., XXXVI, 235

Wheeler, Samuel, XXVIII, 118
Wheeler, Susan, L, 245 ff.
Wheeler, Lieutenant William K., U.S.N., VII, plate 9
Wheeler Line, XXX, 72
Wheeling, ship, XXXVII, 140 n.; *(1899)*, XXXV, 188
Wheeling, U.S.S. (1895), XX, 141
Wheelock, J. A., XVII, 60, 149, 150
Wheelock, J. Andrews, XLIII, 206
Wheelock, Marden & Co., XLIII, 207
Wheelock, Phyllis DeKay, VII, 176; VIII, 7; contributed document, VI, 84–85. "An American Commodore in the Argentine Navy," VI, 5–18, plates 1–2; "Commodore George DeKay and the Voyage of *Macedonian* to Ireland," XIII, 252–267, plates 13, 14; "Edmund Fanning and Henry Eckford," XIV, 209–210; "Henry Eckford (1775–1832), an American Shipbuilder," VII, 177–195, plates 21–23
Wheel of Fortune, schooner *(1759),* XXXII, 172
Wheelright, Andrew C., XVII, 68
Wheelwright, Captain A., XXI, 12
Wheelwright, Lot, XXII, 235
Wheelwright, Mary C., answered query, II, 82
Wheelwright, Timothy, I, 167
Wheelwright, William, XXXV, 248 ff.
Wheland, James, XXXI, 34
Wheldon, James, XXIV, plate XXIV
"When did *Alice* Carry a Spinnaker?" by John Lyman, XXX, 199
"When Happiness Was a Good Cook," note contributed by H. H. Holly, XXXVII, 143–144
Wherries, II, 311 ff.
Wherries and Waterways, by Robert Malster, reviewed, XXXII, 290
Whiddington, R., and J. G. Crowther, *Science at War,* reviewed, IX, 156
"While I'm at the Wheel," poem by F. P. Harlow, VI, 108–111
"'Whimsical Phylosophic President' and His Gunboats, The," by Frederick C. Leiner, XLIII, 245–265
Whipple, Captain Abraham, Continental Navy, XXV, 193
Whipple, Commodore Abraham, XLV, 246
Whipple, Captain James Aldrich, portrait of, XXXIV, plate 5, 89 ff.
Whipple, John T., XVI, 161
Whipple, Joseph, XXXIII, 16 ff.
Whipple, U.S.S., XXVIII, 105; *(1907),* XXIX, 125
Whipple, William, IX, 161; XIV, 51; XXXI, 236; XLVIII, 159
Whirlwind, ship, XXVI, 169
Whisper, steamship, XXI, 103; *(1863),* VIII, 232
Whistler, schooner *(1917),* XXXII, 190
Whistle Up the Inlet, by Gerald A. Rushton, reviewed, XL, 68–70
Whitaker, Captain Charles, XXI, 103
Whitby, Captain Henry, XLIII, 40 ff.
Whitby Museum, XXX, 153

Whitcomb, Haynes and Whitney Lumber Co., IX, 169 ff.
White, Andrew, XXVII, 101
White, Captain Arthur Fenner, XXI, 103
White, Captain, XXVI, 99, 101
White, Colin, *Victoria's Navy: The Heyday of Steam,* reviewed, XLIV, 209
White, Cornelius, XIX, 56
White, Captain Frederick, XXI, 103
White, Captain H. L., VII, 148
White, Henry, XXXVI, 50
White, James B., XXXII, 157
White, James P., XIII, 121
White, Captain John, IX, 245–247; XXV, 184
White, Rev. John, VII, 270–271; XXXVII, 9
White, John H., Jr., L, 201
White, Joseph, XXX, 96 n.
White, Richard D., "Saga of the Side-Wheel Steamer *Shubrick*: Pioneer Lighthouse Tender of the Pacific Coast," XXXVI, 45–53
White, Robert, XL, 12
White, Senator, XXV, 267
White, Stephen, XXV, 185
White, Thomas, VI, 228, 305–306; XXXVII, 46
White, Tobias, XXXVII, 15
White, Captain W. M., VII, 147
White, Captain William, XX, 45
White, Captain William J., III, 279 ff.
White, William P., XXIX, 208
White Cap, schooner yawl (1878), XXX, 196
White Cloud, schooner *(1855),* XXIV, 142
White Cloud, ship *(1865),* XLIX, 22
White Cloud, U.S. side-wheel steamship (1859), XVI, 170, 171; XVIII, 73; *(1859),* XXXIV, 22 f.; XLIII, 92
White Diamond Line, XV, 140, 141
Whitehaven (?) Harbor, ca. 1824, XXIX, 124, plate X
Whitehead, Captain John C., XXI, 103
Whitehead, Captain William, XXXVIII, 266
White Heather, steam bark (1890), XXX, plate XXVIII
Whitehill, Walter, XLIX, 35; XXVIII, 237–238; XL, 83; mentioned, XLVIII, 180; XXXVII, 3, 79
Whitehill, Walter M., XI, 3 ff., 81; XII, 3; XV, 83, 247; XX, 3–4; "Cunard Cocktails in 1847," XVII, 68; "George Crowinshield's Yacht *Cleopatra's Barge,*" XIII, 235–251, plates 9–12
Whitehill, Walter Muir, I, 102, 314, 400; II, 252, 340; III, 89, 178; IV, 252; V, 16, 267; VI, 155, 162; VII, 82, 86; IX, 232–233; XXI, 3–4; XXII, 3–4; XXV, 177 n., 187 n.; editorial, X, 239–242; editorial by, XXIII, 79–80; editorial tribute to Lincoln Colcord, VIII, 3–6; queries by, I, 90; II, 248; V, 89–90; VI, 153; VIII, 154; contributed document, XXII, 221; reviews by, I, 97–99, 181–182, 188, 406–407; II, 257, 257–258, 343, 349; XXII, 149–150
"A Figurehead of Talma," I, 82–83; introduction to *Forty-Four Ship Portraits at The Penobscot Marine Museum,* reviewed, XXIII, 289–290; "The One Hundred and Fiftieth Anniversary of the Peabody

Museum of Salem," X, 33–42; "The Restoration of East India Marine Hall," (co-author with Lawrence Waters Jenkins), IV, 5–17
"White House 'Rose Medallion': Daniel Ammen and the Ulysses S. Grant Porcelain, The," by John Quentin Feller, XLIII, 177–185
Whitehurst, Clinton H., Jr. et al., *The United States Merchant Marine,* reviewed, XLIV, 209
White Mountain, ship (1861), II, 333
Whiteoak, sloop *(1748),* XXXI, 28
White Pine Act of 1711, The, XXXIII, 97
White Squall, ship *(1853),* XVII, 20–21
White Star, yacht *(1895),* XXXVI, 238, 239
White Star Line, ship of, Pictorial Supplement, XXXI, 126; XXXIV, plate XII
White Wing, bark (1852), XVI, 241
White Wing, sloop, XXX, plate XIII
Whiting, Captain, XXXV, 184
Whiting, Charles, XXV, 144 ff.
Whiting, Captain Comfort, XVI, 175; XVIII, 84
Whiting, Mary Jane Green Wilson (Mrs. Samuel Kidder Whiting), XXV, 144–146
Whiting, Colonel Nathan, XXXIX, 191
Whiting, Nathaniel B., XXXV, 301
Whiting, Samuel Kidder, XXV, 144 ff.
Whitman, John W., XXXV, 12
Whitman, Walt, XXV, 64
Whitmore, Captain Jacob D., XVII, 17, 19–25
Whitmore, Captain John S., IX, 172
Whitney, U.S.S. *(1926),* XLVI, 240 ff.
Whitney, Jared, XXX, 62–67
Whitney, Captain Joseph, VII, 42
Whitney, Samuel, XIII, 244
Whitney, Captain Samuel A., XV, 214
Whitridge, John C., XXXIX, 85
Whittaker, Captain M. M., IX, 172
Whittall, James, XXXIV, 30
Whittet-Thomson, David, document by, XXXII, 211–221
Whitthorne, Senator Washington Curran, XXXIII, 266
Whittier, tanker (1903), XXXVIII, 193 ff.
Whittier, John Greenleaf, VI, 223 ff.; XXV, 64, 244
Whitwall, Mark, XI, 255
Whitwill & Son, ship of, Pictorial Supplement, XXXIV, plate XIII
Whitworth, Sir Joseph, XXXIX, 131
Whitworth, William Armstrong, XXXVIII, 127
"Who Built the *Enterprise?*" by M. V. Brewington, IV, 233–235
Whormby, John, XX, 6, 13
"Who Was *Ann Parry*'s Jonah?" by David D. Zink, XXXII, 34–44
Whydah, sloop *(1762),* XXXV, 295
Wibird, Richard, VII, 72, 73, 75
Wickes, Captain I. C., XIV, 182, 185
Wickes, Captain Lambert, XLV, 246
Wickham, Thomas, XII, 227

Wickham, Walker & Co., VII, 60
Wickwire, Franklin B., reviews by, XLVII, 54; XLVIII, 62; "Cornwallis in India and the American Experience," XLVI, 18–24
Wide Awake, schooner, XXI, 91, 97, 100; *(1861),* XI, 280; XII, 59, 161
Wideawake, sloop yacht *(1900),* XXXVI, 240–242, 244, 245, plate 5
Widerstrom, Captain John, XVIII, 215–222
Widgeon, brig *(1848),* XXX, 267 ff.
Widgeon, H.M. frigate *(1926),* L, 187
Widgeon, sloop *(1856),* X, 231 ff.
Wiedersheim, A., "To the Faraway Island: Philadelphia to Nantucket Half a Century Ago," XXXIV, 258–261
Wier, Benjamin, XIX, 65, 66
Wier, Robert, journal of, XXV, plate 6
Wig, R. J., XXII, 158, 165
Wiggins, Captain Louis, XXI, 103
Wigglesworth, Captain E., XXI, 12
Wight, Captain J. F., VII, 53
Wignall, Sidney, XLVI, 185
Wilber, Amelia Adeline: photo of, XLV, 238
Wilberforce, ship (1855), III, 170
Wilbur, Curtis D., XXXVII, 121
Wilbur, Curtis D., Secretary of the Navy, XXXIV, 167
Wilbur, Captain John P., VII, 39, 41
Wilbur, Captain Robert P., VII, 40, 41
Wilbur, Dr. William Allen, "The Meeting of the Ships *Dauntless* and *Thomas Dana* off Cape Horn," VII, 39–41
Wilcocks, Benjamin, XXIX, 209
Wilcocks, Benjamin C., XXXI, 179
Wilcocks, Benjamin Chew, XLVIII, 245 ff.
Wilcox, Captain T. D., XXXII, 217
Wilcox, schooner *(1861),* XI, 289
Wild Dayrell, steamship (1863), III, 134; *(1864),* VIII, 236
Wilde, Captain, XXXV, 186
Wilde, Thomas, XIV, 245
Wilder, J. A., XXIV, 58
Wilder, Joseph A., Jr., XXIV, 58
Wildes, Captain Frank, XXXVI, 112, 114, 115, 120–122, 124
Wildes, Harry Emerson, *Lonely Midas, The Story of Stephen Girard,* reviewed, IV, 253–254.
Wild Hunter, ship (1855), XXII, 242, 243, 244
Wildmore, ship *(1861),* XI, 289
Wild Pigeon, British schooner (1864), XXXIII, 205; *(1864),* XII, 233
Wild Pigeon, ship (1851), III, 67
Wild Rover, steamship, XXI, 102, plate VI; *(1864),* VIII, 236, 237
Wiley, H. W., XXXVI, 245
Wilhelmina, ship *(1861),* XI, 289
Wilhelmina, ship (1915), XXXIII, 193; *(1919),* XXV, 289–291
Wilhelmsen, Captain Hans, XVIII, 169, 202, 203

Wilkenfeld, Bruce M., "The New York City Shipowning Community, 1715–1764," XXXVII, 50–65
Wilkes, U.S. destroyer *(1918)*, VII, 72
Wilkes, Admiral Charles, U.S.N., XXIV, 208 ff.; XXV, 140, 186–187
Wilkes, Captain Charles, XII, 23 ff., 282–286
Wilkes, Commander Charles, XXVIII, 128, 134–139; XXX, 297–298
Wilkes, Lieutenant Charles, U.S.N., IV, 105–111; XXXI, 7; XXXV, 23 ff.; XLIII, 54; XLIV, 109; XLVII, 172; XLIX, 151; L, 107
Wilkes Expedition. *See* United States Exploring Expedition (1838–1842); Wilkes, Charles
Wilkes Expedition: The First United States Exploring Expedition (1838–1842), The, by David B. Tyler, reviewed, XXX, 297–298
Wilkes Land, XXX, 298
Wilkins, Captain Charles F., XXI, 296 ff.
Wilkinson, Captain, XXXI, 138
Wilkinson, Ernest, XXXVII, 118 ff.
Wilkinson, Captain J., XXI, 103
Wilkinson, General James, XLIII, 137
Wilkinson, John, XIII, 157; XLVII, 5
Wilkinson (explorer?), XXV, 260
Wilks, John, XIII, 17
Wilks, Timothy, XIII, 6, 21, 22
Will, William, XXXI, 250
Willamette, paddle steamship *(1849),* XVI, 168–171; XVIII, 73; *(1849),* XLIX, 21; *(1855),* XXII, 25, 26, 31, 33, 38, 39, 40, 42, 43
Willamette, ship *(1858),* XXXIV, 17 ff.
Willamette, steamship *(1824),* XLIII, 114 ff.
Willamette Landings, by Howard McKinley Corning, reviewed, VIII, 159–160
Willard, bark (1864), V, 154
Willard, Enoch G., XLVII, 106
Willard A. Pollard, concrete ship (1944), XXII, 179
Willboro, steamship (ex-*Eastern Light*), XXIII, 276
Willcock, Roger, *Bulwark of Empire, Bermuda's Fortified Naval Base, 1860–1920,* reviewed, XXIII, 75–76
Willcox, William B., IV, 252; V, 91; "Admiral Rodney Warns of Invasion, 1776–1777," IV, 193–198; "The Battle of Porto Praya, 1781," V, 64–78
Willem I, King, XXX, 30
Willerby, ship *(1915),* XLV, 201
Willett, Captain E. W., XVI, 168
Willett, Captain Isaac, XXXIII, 201
Willett, Captain Isaiah, XIX, 55
Willewa, schooner *(1863),* XII, 161
William, bark *(1813),* XIX, 217
William, brig *(1784),* II, 278; *(1798),* VI, 83; *(1826),* XXXVII, 245
William, brigantine *(1765),* XXV, 126
William, schooner *(1795),* XXXVIII, 260; *(1807),* XXIV, 266; *(1818),* XVI, 233; *(1861),* XI, 289; XII, 59, 233
William, ship *(1631),* XXIII, 64; *(1793),* XXII, 84, 87, 88, 92; *(1817),* XXII, plate XVII

William (the) IV, steamship *(1832),* VII, 47, 48, 50, 52, plate 6; XXXIV, 32; *(1866),* XLIII, 197 ff. See also *William the Fourth.*
William A. Cooper, ship *(1855),* XXIV, 140
"William A. K. Martin: Philadelphia Marine Artist," by Francis James Dallett, Jr., XVI, 233–242
William A. Kain, schooner *(1862),* XII, 59, 161, 233
William Abbott, schooner *(1861),* XI, 289
William Aiken (ex-*Eclipse*), revenue cutter *(1860),* XLVIII, 93; *(1861),* XLIV, 257 ff.
William & Eliza, ship *(1822),* XXII, plate XVIII
William & Francis, ship *(1630),* XXIII, 63
William and Jane, schooner *(1804),* XXXI, 288–289
William and John, schooner *(1861),* VIII, 222
William and Martha, brig *(1812),* XXI, 18
William & Mary, Royal Yacht *(1740),* XXVI, 38
William & Mary, ship *(1701),* XLVIII, 14
William & Mary, sloop *(1813),* XIX, 217
William and Mary, brigantine *(1690),* XXXV, 154
William and Ralph, ship *(1631),* XXIII, 65
William and Sally, schooner, XXVI, 264–268
William Avery, steamship *(1831),* VII, 43
William B. Anderson (1862), XXXVI, 202
William B. Palmer, schooner *(1896),* V, 81; *(1896),* XX, 239, 241
William B. Rogers, steamship *(1880),* VI, 62; VII, 242
William Bagaley, steamship, XXI, 91, 101
Wm. Bagaley, steamship *(1861),* XI, 289; XII, 161
"William Bainbridge: A Journal from City of Washington to Pensacola on USS *Hornet*: Return on USS *John Adams* and by Stagecoach from Savannah, Georgia, to Petersburg, Virginia, October-December 1825," by Dr. George F. Pearce, XLIV, 245–256
William Batty, sloop *(1863),* XII, 161
William Baylies, bark *(1886),* XXII, plate XV; *(1894),* XXXVIII, 86; *(1906),* XLIV, 19 ff.
William Beardmore and Co., XXXIX, 181
William Bisbee, schooner *(1902),* I, 71; V, 293–294, plates 23, 24
William Bond & Son, astronomical clock made by, Pictorial Supplement, XXXV, plate XVIII
Wm. C. Atwater, schooner, XXI, 95
William C. Clark, brig *(1856),* XXXV, 129
William C. Nye, whaler *(1865),* XXVII, 276
William C. Redfield, steamship *(1899),* XVIII, 229
William Campion, steamship (ex-*Eastern Exporter*), XXXIII, 276
William Cramp and Sons, XXVII, 37 n.
William Cramp and Sons Ship and Engine Building Co., XXXIX, 39 ff.
William Cummings, bark *(1856),* II, 332
William Dampier, by Christopher Lloyd, reviewed, XXVII, 227
William Denny and Bros., XXVI, 110, 126, 207
William Denny and Brothers Shipbuilders, XXXIX, 132
William Dodge, ship *(1857),* XXXIV, 101
William Doran, schooner *(1811),* XXXIV, 245

William Douglass, schooner *(1864)*, XII, 233
Wm. E. Chester, sloop, XXI, 90
William E. Chester, sloop *(1862)*, XII, 59
Wm. Ebbitt, schooner, XXI, 96; *(1861)*, XI, 289
"William Ellery: An American Lord of Admiralty," by William M. Fowler, Jr., XXXI, 235–252
William F. Romer, steamship, XVIII, 224
William F. Weld and Co., XL, 111
William Fairbairn and Sons, XXVI, 11, 207
William Foster Cowham, concrete ship (1944), XXII, 179, 180
William Foulks, steamship (1859), XXX, 277
William Frederick, British bark *(1858)*, XXVI, 131
William Frothingham, ship (1851), III, 63
William G. Hewes, steamship *(1860)*, XIV, 61–63
Wm. G. Hewes, steamship, XXI, 101; *(1862)*, XII, 59
William Gates, steamship *(1880)*, VII, 242
William Gray, bark, XXIV, 267
William H. Besse, bark (1873), VI, 121–131
William H. Clarke, tug *(1889)*, XXXVII, 85
William H. Conner, ship (1877), quarter-deck scene, II, plate 28; XXVIII, plate XIX
William H. Connor, ship (1877), interior view of, Pictorial Supplement, XXXI, plate XXIV
William H. Jewell, schooner (1853), Pictorial Supplement, XXXVI, plate VII
William H. Knight, schooner *(1879)*, XXVIII, 148
William H. Middleton, sloop *(1862)*, XII, 59
William H. Northrop, schooner *(1861)*, VIII, 222
William H. Northrup, schooner, XXI, 101
William H. Smith, ship (1883), V, 139
William H. Webb, steamship *(1862)*, XII, 59
William Hamilton, ship *(1839)*, XII, 37
William Hayes, schooner (1912), XXVI, plate XXVI
Wm. Henly, sloop, XXI, 98
William Henry, bark (1849), I, 50
William Henry, brigantine (1854), VI, 81
William Henry, sloop *(1861)*, XI, 289; XII, 59
William Jarvis, ship (1848), XLVII, 92
William Jewell, schooner (1853), XIX, 120–122
Wm. L. Beebe, schooner (1875), V, 85–86
William L. Clements Library (Ann Arbor, MI). *See* Clements (William L.) Library
William L. Douglas, schooner (1902), XXIII, 15; (1903), IV, 325
William L. White, schooner (1880), I, 163; XXIII, 12
"William Lawrance's 'Dreadfull Adventure,' 1777," document contributed by William D. Hoyt, Jr., V, 83–84
William Leavitt, ship (1863), I, 110–112, 114
William Lee, ship *(1861)*, XXI, 242, 258
William Lewis, steamship, XXII, plate XVI; *(1891)*, XLIV, 21
William M. Reed, ship (1867), II, 334
Wm. M. Riggs, half brig *(1861)*, XI, 282
William Mallory, schooner *(1861)*, XI, 289; XII, 59
Wm. Mallory, schooner, XXI, 88, 97

William McGilvery, brig *(1861)*, XI, 154
William Miller, steamship (1869), XVII, 54; XVIII, 73
William Mitchell, ship, XVI, 185
William Money, British ship *(1851)*, XLV, 128
"William Mountaine, F.R.S., Mathematician," by Captain W. R. Chaplin, XX, 185–190, plates 8, 9
William Mudgett, bark *(1904)*, XLIV, 151
William of Orange, XXXI, 192
William P. Benson, schooner *(1862)*, XII, 59
William P. Frye, American ship *(1799)*, XLVIII, 55
William P. Frye, four-mast bark (1901), XXVII, plate XIII; *(1915)*, XLV, 199 ff.
William P. Frye, ship, XXXIII, 146
William Patten, bark (1848), IV, 243
William Patterson, Bristol, XXXIV, 58
William Peacock, steamship (1829), VI, 209, 210; VII, 43, 44, 57
William Penn, ship *(1835)*, XXXV, 22
William Penn, steamship (1826), VI, 201, 203, 205, 206; *(1832)*, VII, 45, 46, 62; *(1846)*, XXIV, 17
William Pustau and Co., XXII, 32; XLIII, 299
William Roach, ship *(1833)*, XIV, plate 7
William Rockefeller, ship *(1913)*, XLVII, 45
William Ropes & Co., XXIII, 131 ff.
William Ross, bark (1869), III, 68
William Ross, sloop *(1841)*, XXXVIII, 269
William Rotch, ship. See *William Roach*, ship.
Williams, Abigail Lord, XXV, 18 n.
Williams, Captain Albert N., XXV, 18 n.
Williams, Anthon and Co., XXII, 32; XXXIV, 120
Williams, Captain, XXX, 296
Williams, Captain Charles, XXV, 18, 24–28
Williams, Charles P., XXXI, 137 ff.
Williams, Captain Charles W., XXV, 18 n.
Williams, Captain Christopher, XVII, 156
Williams, Clarence C., XXXIV, 265
Williams, Admiral Clarence S., XLIV, 182
Williams, E. T., XXXV, 179
Williams, Mrs. Eleanor Belknap, XXV, 24, 25
Williams, Elijah, Jason and John, XXXIX, 35
Williams, Eliza, XXXVII, 212 ff.
Williams, Captain Frank, XVIII, 84
Williams, Frederick Wells, XLVIII, 274
Williams, Fred J., XXXVI, 272, 273
Williams, Guy R., *The World of Model Ships and Boats*, reviewed, XXXII, 287
Williams, Harold, "Yankee Whaling Fleets Raided by Confederate Cruisers: The Story of the Bark *Jireh Swift*, Captain Thomas W. Williams," XXVII, 263–278
Williams, I. H., XIX, 201
Williams, Captain Israel, XXV, 181, plate 19
Williams, J. Stanley, V, 165
Williams, Captain James L., XXXVIII, 242
Williams, Captain Jerome Wheeler, VIII, 251–254, plate 23
Williams, John, XXXIX, 25 ff.; XXXV, 25

Williams, John B., XII, 39
Williams, John Foster, XLIX, 47
Williams, Jonathan, XXXI, 134
Williams, Captain Joseph, XXI, 103
Williams, Leonard, L, 291 ff.
Williams, Lydia (Pickering), 1799, XXXIII, 162
Williams, Osgood, review by, XXVI, 148; XXIV, 149–150; XXV, 228
Williams, Captain Owen, XLI, 124 ff.
Williams, Q. H., XXXVI, 247, 248
Williams, R. Lancaster, XXXV, 173
Williams, R. T., *Greek Oared Ships 900–322 B.C.*, reviewed, XXIX, 72–73
Williams, S. Wells, XX, 215
Williams, Samuel Wells, XLVI, 42; XLVIII, 274
Williams, Stanley T., co-editor with Barbara D. Simison of *Around the Horn, A Journal: December 10, 1861 to March 25, 1862* by Edward Rowland Sill, reviewed, IV, 255
Williams, Timothy, 1799, XXXIII, 162 ff.
Williams, Reverend Thomas, XXV, 276
Williams, Captain Thomas W., XXVII, 263 ff.
Williams, Captain W. G., XX, 102
Williams, William, XXI, 109; XXXIV, 200; XLVI, 258
Williams, William Appleman, "Notes on the Death of a Ship and the End of a World: The Grounding of the British Bark *Glenesslin* at Mount Neahkahnie on 1 October 1913," XLI, 122–138
Williamsburgh, horse boat *(1814),* VI, 264
William Schroder, bark (1840), Pictorial Supplement, XXXVIII, plate XXI
William Seabrook, Confederate steamship *(1861),* XLIV, 258
William Seabrook, steamship *(1848),* XLVII, 37; *(1861),* VIII, 222, 228
Wm. Seabrook, steamship, XXI, 92, 103; *(1861),* XV, 99, 115, 125
Williamsen, Thomas, VII, 66
William Simons and Co., XXVI, 30, 208
Williamson, U.S. destroyer *(1921),* XLVI, 246 ff.
Williamson, Daniel, XXV, 103
Williamson, James (shipbuilder), III, 26–34
Williamson, Dr. James A., VII, 84, 85; *The Cabot Voyages and Bristol Discovery under Henry VII,* reviewed, XXIII, 148
Williamson, Commander John, XL, 42
Williamson, W. M., Editor, *Cornell's Sea Packet,* reviewed, II, 188
Wm. Sprague, tow boat *(1887),* XLVII, 130
William Sutton, schooner *(1873),* XI, 116
William the Fourth, steamship (1838), XVIII, 281; XX, 87; *(1838),* VIII, 46. See also *William IV.*
William Thompson, whaler *(1865),* XXVII, 265, 269, 276
William Tittamer, steamship *(1864),* IV, plate 25
Wm. Totten, schooner *(1861),* XV, 125
William W. Crapo, bark *(1810),* VIII, 152–153; *(1880),* II, 336

William Ward Burrows, U.S. transport (1929), XXIV, 126
William Wesley, sloop (1874), I, 70
William Wilberforce, merchant ship *(1942),* L, 48
William Wilcox, bark (1863), V, 150
William Wilson, schooner (1856), Pictorial Supplement, XXXIII, plate I
William Wirt, whaler *(1849),* XXXIII, 19
William Witherle, ship *(1850),* XLVII, 98
William Witherle & Co., XLVII, 93
Willie L. Bennett, sloop (1899), XXXVII, 165
Willie L. Bennett, two-sail bateau (1899), IV, 288
Willing Maid, schooner *(1789),* XLIX, 89
Willings & Francis, Canton firm, XLVIII, 250 ff.
Willis, Andrew, "Horseshoe Cove – A Correction," XIII, 67; "Some Notes on the Penobscot Photographs," XII, 305
Willis, Andrews, review by, XLVIII, 193
Willis, Captain, XXVII, 171, 172
Willis, Captain J. M., XXI, 237
Willis, J., XXVI, 215
Willis A. Slater, concrete ship (1943), XXII, 176, 182
Willis & Co., XLVII, 93
Willock, Alex, XXXV, 295
Willock, Colonel Roger, USMCR, reviews by: XLIV, 66; XLV, 257; XLVII, 214; "Caribbean Catastrophe: The Earthquake and Fire at Kingston, Jamaica, B.W.I., 17–19 January 1907," XXIX, 118–132; "Gunboat Diplomacy, Operations of the North America and West Indies Squadron 1875–1915;" [Part I], XXVIII, 5–30; [Part II], XXVIII, 85–112
Will o" the Wisp, British schooner, XXXII, 53
Will o" the Wisp, schooner *(1862),* XII, 59
Will O" (the) Wisp, steamship, XXI, 88, 92; *(1864),* VIII, 236; *(1865),* XII, 235
Willoughby, Captain, XXXVI, 233
Willoughby, Sir Hugh, XXVIII, 240
Willoughby, Robert, XXII, plate VI
Willow, schooner, XXIV, 60
Wills, Horace,, XVII, 116
Wills, J. N., XVII, 116
Wills, John E., Jr., "Tribute, Defensiveness, and Dependency: Uses and Limits of Some Basic Ideas About Mid-Qing Dynasty Foreign relations," XLVIII, 225–229
Wills, Thomas, XXVII, plate VII
Willsco, steamship (ex-*Eastern Admiral*), XXIII, 276
Willscott, bark *(1901),* X, 115
Willy Smith, ship *(1865),* XLI, 37
Willzipo, steamship (ex-*Eastern Mariner*), XXIII, 276
Wilmarth, Henry Dane, XLVI, 48
Wilmerding, John, *Fitz Hugh Lane,* reviewed, XXXII, 69; *Fitz Hugh Lane, American Marine Painter,* XXV, plates I-XXXII; *A History of American Marine Painting,* reviewed, XXIX, 139–141; *Robert Salmon, Painter of Ship and Shore,* reviewed, XXXII, 69
Wilmington, ship *(1834),* XII, 182

Wilmington, California, XXV, 262
Wilmington Marine Railway, XLI, 189
Wilmington Wooden Shipbuilding Co., XLI, 190
Wilmore, C. Ray, *Square Rigger Round the Horn: The Making of a Sailor,* reviewed, XXXIII, 146–147
Wilse, J. O., App., U.S.N., XXV, 50
Wilshaw, Captain Thomas, XI, 14
Wilson, steamship *(1862),* VIII, 228
Wilson, Sir Arthur K., XXVIII, 106 n.
Wilson, Colonel Belford Hilton, H.B.M., XXX, 264
Wilson, Benito, XXV, 262
Wilson, Charles E., XXXVIII, 287
Wilson, Captain Charles P., XXI, 103
Wilson, Captain David, VII, 50
Wilson, Edward, XV, 182
Wilson, Edward A., Book Illustrator, by Lawrence Oakley Cheever, reviewed, II, 353
Wilson, F. Downes, XXV, 145
Wilson, Gary E., "The First American Hostages in Moslem Nations, 1784–1789," XLI, 208–223
Wilson, Harold C., and William C. Carr, "Gosnold's Elizabeth's Isle: Cuttyhunk or Naushon?" XXXIII, 131–145
Wilson, Rear Admiral Henry B., XXXV, 106
"Wilson, J. D., Letters from, to his Sister," document contributed by Francis W. Hatch, XXV, 144–146
Wilson, Lieutenant J. Wall, XX, 163–166
Wilson, James, XVII, 121
Wilson, Captain James, XXV, 260
Wilson, John A., XLIII, 133
Wilson, John Q., XXVII, 15; XXXII, 219
Wilson, Joseph, purser, U.S.N., XXV, 144
Wilson, Captain Oliver, XXI, 16–22
Wilson, Peter, XLI, 54
Wilson, Thomas, XIII, 157; XXVI, 30, 208; XXXI, 100
Wilson, Thomas, M. P., XXXIV, 9 ff.
Wilson, Thomas F., XV, 294 ff.; XXII, 46–54
Wilson, Colonel W. E., XXXIV, 202
Wilson, Captain W. R., U.S.N. (ret.), "The Sea Battle of Dannoura," XXVIII, 206–221
Wilson, Captain William, XXI, 104
Wilson, Willis, XXXIII, 25
Wilson, President Woodrow, VII, 69–70; XXVII, 54; XXXVII, 113; XL, 60 ff.
Wilvers, Captain A. C., I, 397
Wimshurts, Henry (shipbuilder, Ratcliff Cross Dock), XLIII, 293
Winball, Samuel, VII, 269
Winchelsea, vessel *(1759),* XXX, 201
Winchester, H.M.S., XXVI, 62
Winchester, sailing vessel (ex-*Emeu*) *(1876),* XXVI, 28
Winchester, ship *(1854),* XXVII, 259, plate 10
Winchester, steamship *(1872),* X, 132
Wind Commands, The, by Harry Morton, reviewed, XXXVI, 301–302
Winder, William, XXXVI, 57
Windermere, bark *(1861),* XI, 289; (1870), XV, 188

Windjammers under the Old Elephant Flag, by F. Holm-Petersen, reviewed, XXXIX, 302
Windrim, James H., XLVII, 181
Windsor, steamship (1846), XXIV, plate VII
Windsor Castle, ship (1854), IV, 239; V, 327
Windsor Forest, ship (1854), V, 327; *(1861),* XI, 289
Winds Over Lake Huron, by Robert A. Sinclair, reviewed, XXXVIII, 74
Windward, schooner *(1861),* XI, 151
Windward Coast of Africa, XXX, 177 ff., 230 ff.
Windward Isles, St. Lucia dug-outs, II, 71–73
Wind Waves at Sea, Breakers and Surf, by Henry B. Bigelow and W. T. Edmondson, reviewed, IX, 304
Winfield Scott, ship (1851), IV, 242; *(1853),* X, 134
Wing, Joseph, XXXIII, 53
Wing, William G., "Escape from Internment on the Yacht *Eclipse:* 1915," XLIII, 267–273
Wing, William R., XXXIII, 53
Winged Arrow, ship *(1852),* XXV, Plate XIX
Winifred, barque, XXI, 94
Winifred, steamship *(1898),* XXXVIII, 181 ff.; XXXIX, 142 ff.
Winks, Robin W., "The Second *Chesapeake* Affair," XIX, 51–72
Winn, J. R. (artist), XXII, plate XIII
Winn, Commander Roger, RNVR, XLIV, 58
Winnebago, U.S. monitor (1862), X, 18, 29, 31; *(1864),* XXVII, 42, 44
Winnebago Chief, steamship (1829), VI, 210
Winnegance, schooner (1890), XXIV, 40, 60
Winnegance, ship (1842), XXVII, plate VI
Winnet, Captain, XXX, 270
Winniett, Alexander, XXXI, 32
Winona, gunboat *(1862),* XXXVI, 195
Winona, ship (1862), III, 71
Winona, yacht *(1906),* XXXVI, 244, 245
Winship, T. J., XXXVI, 48, 51, 52
Winslow, Albert, XXIII, 13
Winslow, Commander, XXVII, 267
Winslow, Captain H. C., XXI, 104
Winslow, J. S., & Co., XX, 241
Winslow, Captain John A., XIX, 126–128
Winslow, Captain Jonathan, XVII, 254
Winslow, Josiah, XXXIX, 193
Winslow Lewis & Co., XXVIII, 38
"Winslow Lewis and the Lighthouses," by Richard W. Updike, XXVIII, 31–48
Winsor, Captain Alexander, XVII, 57; XVIII, 84
Winsor, Captain George, XLV, 181
Winsor, Joshua, XIV, 29, 30
Winsor, Nathaniel, XIV, 29, 30
Winsor, Nathaniel & Co., Boston, XXV, 26
Winsor Map Collection, XLVI, 176
Winston S. Churchill: Finest Hour, 1939–1941, by Martin Gilbert, reviewed, XLVII, 143

Winter, Frank H., Frederick P. Schmitt, and Cornelis de Jong, *Thomas Welcome Roys: America's Pioneer of Modern Whaling,* reviewed, XLI, 144–145
Winter, William, XLIV, 29
Winterport, Maine, XXX, 168 ff.
Winters, Captain John, XXI, 104
Winters, Captain William Henry, XXI, 104
Winter Shrub, schooner *(1862),* VIII, 228
Winthrop, steamship, XXVIII, 124. *(1886),* XXXIX, 143
Winthrop, Governor John, XXIII, 66; XXV, 240, 245
Winthrop, John, Jr., XXX, 84
Winthrop, Robert C., XIII, 54, 58
Winthrop Fleet, XXIII, 62–66
Winyaw, schooner *(1861),* VIII, 222
Wire rigging, III, 288–289
"Wire Rigging," query by E. D. Lovejoy, I, 398; answers by Dorothy R. Brewington, I, 399; John Lyman, II, 82; L. W. Jenkins, II, 82–83
Wiscasset in Pownalborough, by Fannie S. Chase, reviewed, II, 262–263
Wisconsin, battleship *(1897),* XXXVIII, 130; *(1907),* XLVII, 249
Wisconsin, steamship (1837), VII, 64; *(1840),* XX, 80, 89 n., 252, 255, 259, 260
Wisconsin, U.S. battleship (1944), XXII, 211
Wise, George, XXV, 26
Wise, Henry A., XLVII, 169
Wise, Representative Henry A., XXIV, 12
Wise, Stephen R., *Lifeline of the Confederacy: Blockade Running During the Civil War,* reviewed, L, 67
Wiseman, destroyer escort (1944), XXXVIII, 284
Wishart, Admiral Sir James, R.N., XXI, 262
Wisterbottom, bark *(1861),* XV, 125
Wiswall, Captain, XXVII, 25
Witch, H.M.S. *(1943),* XLIV, 49 ff.
Witch of the Wave, clipper ship (1852), IV, 73
Witch of the Wave, ship (1851), XIX, plate XVII
Wither Away or Whither Away, XXX, 6
Witherle Co., XIII, 120
Witherly, Captain John, XIX, 7
Withers, George, XXV, 237
Withlacoochie and Lake Pansoffka Steamboat and Canal Co., VII, 130, 131
With Perry in Japan; the Diary of Edward Yorke McCauley, edited by Allan B. Cole, reviewed, III, 179
Wivenhoe, H.M. ketch *(1676),* XXV, 279
Wizard, ship (1853), III, 170
Woburn Abbey, ship (1855), IV, 72
Wodehouse, General, XXVI, 96 ff.
Wohlers, Captain Johannes, XVIII, 152–164
Wokee, iron screw steamship *(1867),* XLIII, 190 ff.
Wolcott, Oliver, XXXVI, 56, 59, 61, 62
Wolcott, Oliver, Secretary of the Treasury, L, 99
Wolderstone, Captain, XXXVII, 15 ff.
Wolf, German raider *(1915),* XLV, 199 ff.
Wolf, S.M.S. *(1894),* XXIII, 68
Wolfe, H.M.S. *(1813),* XVII, 207, 210

Wolga, Russian steamship (ex-*Fei Pang*) *(1868),* XXXIV, 47
Wollaston, Captain, XXXVII, 5 ff.
"Wollaston of Mount Wollaston," by H. Hobart Holly, XXXVII, 5–25
Wollett, William, engraving by, Pictorial Supplement, XXXII, plate XXVI
Wolstenholme, Sir John, XXXIX, 178
Wolverine, U.S. gunboat *(1843),* II, 335, plate 47; IV, 183–192, plates 29–32
Wolverine, U.S.S. (ex-*Michigan*) *(1905),* XLVIII, 105
Wolverine State, steamship *(1922),* IX, 222; X, 141, 142
"Women and Children First," (memorial plaque for Stewart Holland), XXV, 80
Women and Children Last, by Alexander Crosby Brown, reviewed, XXII, 72–73
"Women and Children Last: The Tragic Loss of the Steamship *Arctic,*" by Alexander Crosby Brown, XIV, 237–261, plates 25–30
Women and the sea, VI, 121; VIII, 242; XXXVII, 203; XLIV, 22, 149, 179. See also Seafaring life
Wonder, schooner *(1863),* VIII, 232
Wonderhow, yacht (1898), XI, 83–94, plate 10
Wood, Amos, XXI, 284
Wood, Cato, XXXIII, 31
Wood, Charles, XLVIII, 77 ff.
Wood, David, XXVIII, 145
Wood, E. K., Lumber Co., San Francisco, XXV, 288 ff.
Wood, Captain Edwin A., XLIII, 211
Wood, H. Graham, *Steamboats out of Baltimore,* reviewed, XXX, 71–72
Wood, John, XXII, 9, 44; XLVIII, 77 ff.
Wood, John Taylor, XXXII, 208
Wood, Captain Lemuel C., XXXIX, 89 ff.
Wood, Richard G., "Brazilian Students of Naval Construction," XII, 162
Wood, Captain S. C., XVIII, 84; XLIII, 196 ff.
Wood, Virginia Steele, "James Keen's Journal of a Passage from Philadelphia to Blackbeard Island, Georgia for Live Oak Timber, 1817–1818," XXXV, 227–247; XXXIX, 255 n.
Wood, Cadet W. C., XXXV, 192
Woodboat (boat), XVII, 5
Woodboats, New Brunswick, XVII, 5–16
Woodbury, Charles, XXI, 304
Woodbury, Charles L., XXI, 124
Woodbury, Levi, XXVIII, 45
Woodbury, Levi, Secretary of the Navy, XXXV, 21 ff.
Woodbury, Thomas, XXXI, 130
Woodcock, Nicholas, XXVIII, 244, 245, 250
Woodell, David T., XVII, 116
Wooden printing block for stamping sails, XXXI, plate 2
Wooden sails, I, 379–380, plate facing 377
Wooden World: An Anatomy of the Georgian Navy, The, by N. A. M. Rodger, reviewed, XLVIII, 208

Woodfine, Philip and Jeremy Black, *The British Navy and the Use of Naval Power in the Eighteenth Century*, reviewed, XLIX, 314
Woodford, steamship *(1818),* XXXII, 194
Woodford, Thomas, XXXI, 239
Woodhouse, Captain Samuel, XLIV, 247
Woodman, John, Jr., "The Stone Fleet," XXI, 233–259
Woodman, Jonathan, XIII, 139–140
Woodrooffe, Thomas, *Vantage at Sea,* reviewed, XIX, 148
Woodruff, British steamship *(1899),* XXXI, 146–147
Woodruff, Samuel M., XIV, 251
Woods, Henry, XXVIII, 135, 139
Woods, Lieutenant David L., U.S.N.R. (ret.), XXV, 139
Woods, Lieutenant Edward, XXIX, 125
Wood Ship Division, XXXV, 281
Woods Hole Reflections, edited by Mary Lou Smith, reviewed, XLV, 136
Woodward, C. Vann, *The Battle for Leyte Gulf,* reviewed, VII, 247–248
Woodward, E. A., XXXVI, 247 n.
Woodward, Captain John, XXI, 104
Woodward, John G., XXXV, 238
Woodward, Joseph H., XXXIX, 131
Woodward, Capt. M. L., XVII, 59; XVIII, 84
Woodward, Ralph Lee, Jr., *Robinson Crusoe's Island: A History of the Juan Fernández Islands,* reviewed, XXX, 300–301
Woodworth/Wigglesworth Geological Survey Chart, XXXIII, 137
Wool, Major General John E., U.S.A., XXII, 256
Woolfe, Henry D., XXXIX, 11
Wool House Museum, Southampton, XXX, 154
Woolsey, U.S. destroyer *(1918),* VII, 72
Woolsey, Commodore M. T., XL, 42
Woolwich, H.M.S. *(1813),* XVII, 203, 204
Woortman, Henry, XXXV, 301
Woosung, steamship (1864), XVII, 308; XVIII, 73
Worcester, steamship *(1863),* XII, 161; *(1871),* XXXVII, 235; (1887), XI, 259 ff.
Worcester, G. R. G., *The Junkman Smiles,* reviewed, XX, 147; *The Junks and Sampans of the Yangtze,* reviewed, VIII, 257–258; XI, 296–297; and XXXII, 226; *Sail & Sweep in China,* reviewed, XXVII, 284
Worcestre, William, XXXVII, 159
Worden, Lieutenant John L., U.S.N., XXIII, 202
Worden, Rear Admiral John L., XXXIX, 118
Work, Captain J., XXI, 104
Work, W. T., XVII, 122
Workman, Harry C., XXXVII, 124
Works of Ta'unga: Records of a Polynesian Traveller in the South Seas, 1833–1896, The, by R. G. and Marjorie Crocombe, reviewed, XXIX, 290
World of Model Ships and Boats, The, by Guy R. Williams, reviewed, XXXII, 287
World's Fair (Chicago, 1893), XXV, 170

World's Lighthouses Before 1820, The, by D. Alan Stevenson, reviewed, XX, 68
World War: 1914–1918, XLIII, 274
   Claims, XXXIV, 155
   Equipment and supplies
   —, Transportation, XXXV, 275
   Falkland Islands, Battle of, XXXIII, 34
   Naval operations, XLVIII, 50
   —, **Submarine,** XXXVI, 33
   —, **American,** XL, 50
   —, **British,** XXXIII, 34
   —, **German,** XXIV, 272; XXXVI, 266; XL, 85
      —, **Submarine,** XXXV, 36
   Transportation, XXXII, 155; XXXIII, 178; XLI, 188
   See also United States History
World War: 1939–1945
   Boat construction, Islands of the Pacific, VI, 71
   Campaigns:
   —, **Africa, North,** III, 99
   —, **Atlantic Ocean,** XLV, 46
   —, **Pacific Ocean,** XXXII, 100; XLII, 203
   Equipment and supplies, XXXIX, 258; L, 42, 219
   Fuel supplies, XXXVI, 101
   Naval operations, XLV, 46
   —, **Pacific Ocean,** L, 260
   —, **American,** XXXV, 97
   —, **German,** XLV, 199
   Pacific Ocean, XXXIX, 258
   Refugees, XLIII, 31
   Ship construction, XXXVIII, 272
   Submarine operations, XLIII, 31
   —, **German,** XLIV, 48
   See also United States History
World War I. *See* World War, 1914–1918
World War II. *See* World War, 1939–1945
World War II, I, 101, 410, 411; XXVII, 185–201
Wormser, Richard S., answered query, I, 174
Wormstead, Enoch, XVII, 123
Wormstead, Michael, XVII, 123
Worrambus, steamship *(1911),* XXIV, 241, plate 28
Worth, Captain William, XXI, 237
Worthington Pump and Machinery Co., XXII, 182
Wotherspoon, George H. (artist), XXII, plate XXIV
Wotje, IV, 102, plates 21, 22
Wouldhave, William, XXXIV, 7
Wray, Jacob, XXXIII, 23
Wray, John W., *South Sea Vagabonds,* reviewed, I, 409
"Wrecked and Taken by the French," document contributed by Lawrence W. Jenkins, XXII, 142–143
"Wrecked at York, Maine," document contributed by Lawrence W. Jenkins, XXI, 69
Wreckers, ship, XXV, 108
"Wreck of Bark *Cashmere* in Japan," document contributed by L. Carrrington Goodrich, XXIV, 72
"Wreck of *Kitty,*" document contributed by Grahame E. Farr, XV, 155

"Wreck of *San Francisco*, The," by Richard E. Crighton, XLV, 20–34
"Wreck of the Ship *General Oglethorpe* – 1802," by Robert MacKay (edited by Charles F. Mills), II, 44–55
"Wreck of *Thomas W. Lawson*," by Mrs. Paul Rood, XXIX, 133–138
"Wreck on Norman's Woe, A," document contributed by Francis G. Wallet, XXI, 303
Wreck Returns, XXX, 19
Wrecks, I, 108–112; II, 35–38, plate 8, 44–55; III, 163–166, 196 ff., plate 26, 265, 266, 324–326; IV, 47–48, 155–156, 158–159, 174, 236–237, 313–316, 318–323, 337–338; V, 286 ff.; VIII, 61–69, 184–190, 288; IX, 17–30, 68–70, plates 3, 4, 31; X, 134, 138, 142
Wrecks, Rescues & Investigations: Selected Documents of the U.S. Coast Guard and Its Predecessors, Bernard C. Nalty, Dennis L. Noble, and Truman R. Strobridge, editors, reviewed, XLIII, 143–145
"Wrecks of Civil War Blockade-runners," by Augustus H. Fiske, III, 265
Wren, steamship, XXI, 97, 98; *(1865),* XI, 277; XII, 235
Wrestler, barkentine (1880), V, 85–86
Wright, carrier *(1924),* XXXVII, 115
Wright, steam tug *(1865),* XXXVI, 50
Wright, U.S. aircraft tender (1920), XXII, 146
Wright, Charles M., II, 177, 252; IV, 86
Wright, Edward, XIV, 189; XVII, 28–37; XXXVII, 174 ff.
Wright, Mrs. Frank, XXXVI, 21
Wright, Captain George T., XXVI, 31, 204
Wright, Irene, VII, 86
Wright, Louis B., and Julia H. MacLeod, *The First Americans in North Africa,* reviewed, V, 329–330
Wright, Peter, XIII, 121
Wright, Robert (artist), Pictorial Supplement, XXXII, plate XXVI
Wright, Ruth, XXXVI, 16
Wright, Stephen, XXXVI, 21
Wright, Thomas, XXXVII, 174 ff.
Wright, William, XI, 35 ff.
Wrightson, Christopher, XIII, 17
Wrigley, Gladys M., answered query, III, 86–87
Writers' Program, Work Projects Administration, *A Guide to Key West,* reviewed, I, 403–404
Wroth, Lawrence C., XXI, 7; *The John Carter Brown Library: Annual Report 1949–1950,* reviewed, XI, 234
Wu Chien-chang, XXX, 158, 159, 164, 165
Wulff, Captain Henry, XXI, 104
WV. *See* West Virginia
Wyandotte, U.S. monitor (1862), X, 19, 32
Wycombe Marsh Paper Mills, Ltd., XLVI, 175 ff.
Wyer, Christopher, XXXIII, 163
Wyeth, Albert, XXXVIII, 236
Wyeth, Nathaniel, XV, 250; XXVIII, 130, 132
Wyfe, schooner *(1862),* XII, 59
Wyllie, Captain Joannes, XXI, 104

Wyman, bark (1845), XLV, 187
Wyman, Lieutenant Robert H., XXXVI, 193
Wyman, Commander Thomas W., XLVII, 29
Wyman, Captain W. T., XXI, 298–302
Wyndham, Thomas, XXVII, 179
Wynn, Captain R., XXI, 262
Wynstay, schooner (1742), I, 297
Wyoming, schooner (1909), IV, 325; V, 140; XXIII, 14, plate XXV; cabin plan, plate XXVI; XXV, 156, 231; XXVII, plate XXVIII
Wyoming, U.S. warship *(1861),* XXXII, 125; XXXIII, 42 ff.; XXXV, 29; *(1863),* XXVI, 122; *(1864),* XXVII, 36; *(1872),* XXXVI, 159; XXXVII, 238 ff., 254; XL, 51 ff.
Wyon, William (Royal Mint Engraver), XXXIV, 7
Wyse, Major, XLV, 31 ff.
Wythe, Chancellor George, XXXVIII, 101

Xara, cutter (1888), XXX, plate XVII
Xenia, bark (1870), III, 264
Xora, yacht *(1894),* XXXVI, 238, 239
XYZ Affair, XXX, 119
XYZ crisis, XXV, 37

Yacht, steamship *(1844),* XII, 288, 293, plate 26; *(1845),* XXV, plate III
"Yacht *America:* A New Account Pertaining to Her Confederate Operations, The," by Thomas R. Neblett, Ph.D., XXVII, 233–253
Yacht Designing and Planning for Yachtsmen, Students & Amateurs, by Howard I. Chapelle, reviewed, XXXIII, 65–66
Yachting:
   Chesapeake Bay, IX, 180
   Massachusetts, XI, 83
   New England, XLV, 253
"Yachting in Chesapeake Bay, 1676–1783," by Arthur Pierce Middleton, IX, 180–184
Yacht racing:
   British Columbia, XXXVI, 231
   Washington (State), XXXVI, 231
Yacht rigs, XXX, 194–199
Yachts:
   Library resources, XLVIII, 182
   United States, XXX, 194; XLIII, 267

Yachts and yachting:
  Great Britain, XXVII
  United States, XIII, 235
Yacht Sails, by Ernest A. Ratsey and W. H. DeFontaine, reviewed, VIII, 260
Yachtsman's Guide to Celestial Navigation, The, by Stafford Campbell, reviewed, XL, 139
Yachtsmen, Biography, I, 205
Yakima, schooner (1902), II, 230
Yakumo Maru, steamship (ex-*Taoutai*) *(1862),* XLIX, 26; *(1863),* XLIII, 207
Yale, steamship (ex-*City of Paris*), Pictorial Supplement, XXXIV, plate XX
Yale, steamship, XXVII, 150; XXVIII, 124; (1889), XXII, 276; XXIV, 126; (1906), IX, 217–219
Yale, Elihu, XIII, 6, 21, 22, plate 1; XXXI, 38; XLVI, 6 ff.
Yalu, Battle of the, VIII, 267–275
Yalu River (China and Korea), VIII, 267; XXXVIII, 157
Yamacraw, cutter (1936), XXX, 191
Yamagi, Admiral Kazuyoshi, XXXVI, 274
Yamoyden, bark (1863), III, 349
Yanaway, Philip E., "The United States Revenue Cutter *Harriet Lane,* 1857–1884," XXXVI, 174–205
Yanch, ship *(1801),* XLVII, 166
Yangkingpang Creek, Shanghai, XXX, 158, 161, 162, 165
Yangtsze, steamship (1857), XVI, 170; XVII, 298 ff.; XVIII, 73; *(1857),* XLIII, 87 ff.; photo in 1862, XLIII, plate 2; (1868), XVII, 225; XVIII, 73
Yangtze Rapid Steamship Co., L, 261 ff.
Yangtze River, XXXIV, 103; XLIII, 85, 186, 274; XLIII, 85. *See also* China; Great Britain. Navy
Yankee, auxiliary cruiser *(1898),* XXXIII, 277; XLI, 98
Yankee, bark *(1860),* XIV, 46
Yankee, brigantine *(1812),* XXI, 16–22
Yankee, brigantine *(1971),* XLVII, 206
Yankee, privateer *(1812),* XXII, 216
Yankee, tug *(1861),* XXXVI, 187
Yankee Blade, bark (1849), III, 63
"Yankee Bride in the Old Navy: Catherine Freeman Nimitz Looks Back to the Days Before World War I, A," by Paul B. Ryan, XXXVIII, 5–14
"Yankee Clipper & the Cape Cod Boy, The," by Captain B. L. Fessenden, XXIII, 264–269
Yankee Doodle, sloop *(1864),* XII, 233
"Yankee Doodle," by Lewis A. Maverick, XXII, 106–135
Yankee Mariner & Sea Power, America's Challenge of Ocean Space, The, by Joyce C. Bartell, reviewed, XLIV, 66–68
Yankee Stargazer – The Life of Nathaniel Bowditch, by Robert Elton Berry, reviewed, II, 257–258
Yankee Surgeon: The Life and Times of Usher Parsons, 1788–1868, by Seebert J. Goldowsky, reviewed, L, 74
Yankee Surveyors in the Shogun's Seas, edited by Allan B. Cole, reviewed, VIII, 72–73

"Yankee Whalers at the Bay of Islands," by Robert W. Kenny, XII, 22–44
"Yankee Whaling Fleets Raided by Confederate Cruisers: The Story of the Bark *Jireh Swift,* Captain Thomas W. Williams," by Harold Williams, XXVII, 263–278
Yankton, U.S.S. *(1907),* XXIX, 125
Yantic, S.S. *(1883),* XXXVI, 112 ff.
Yantic, U.S.S. (1864), XX, 136
Yantic Iron Works, Norwich (CT), L, 202
"Yardarm Hanging, A," document contributed by Captain Edgar K. Thompson, U.S.N. (ret.), XXI, 303–304
Yardley, Francis, XIII, 17
Yarmouth, automobile-carrying liner (1927), XXXIII, 93 ff.; XXXIV, 183
Yarmouth, frigate *(1778),* XLIII, 28
Yarmouth, schooner *(1768),* XXV, 70; *(1807),* XVI, 195; *(1855),* XXIV, 141
Yarmouth, ship *(1920),* XXXV, 205
Yarmouth, steamship *(1885),* XXXIV, 179; (1927), XXXVI, 5, 9, 11, 28, 31
Yarmouth Castle, steamship (ex-*Evangeline*) (1965), XXXIV, 186; XXXVI, plates 1, 2; XXXVII, 75
"Yarmouth Castle Inferno, The," by Alexander Crosby Brown, XXXVI, 5–32
Yarmouth Cruise Lines, XXXVI, 10, 31
Yarmouth Steam Navigation Co., XXXIV, 174 ff.; XXXVII, 233 ff.
Yarmouth Steamship Line, XXXIV, 178
Yarnall, Naomi, query by, VII, 171
Yarnall, W. B., queries by, V, 164; VI, 153; VII, 171
Yarnell, Captain Harry E., L, 51
Yarnell, U.S. destroyer *(1918),* VII, 72
Yassi Ada, medieval ship, mention, XLVI, 76
Yassi Ada, Greek shipwreck at, XLV, 10 ff.
Yates, Leroy M., XXXIII, 54
Yates, R. W., XVII, 119
Yat Sen, nationalist ship *(1949),* XLIX, 209. (?*Sun Yat Sen?*)
Yawry Bay, XXX, 235
Yazoo, U.S. monitor (1863), X, 26, 32; *(1864),* XXVII, 37 n., 43–45
Y Bannes, Captain Philip, XXIII, 282–284
Yeatman, schooner (1796), XXII, 58, 61–63
Yeaton, Captain Samuel, XVII, 62; XVIII, 84
Yeddo, steamship *(1863),* XLIII, 211 ff.
Yeddo Bay, Japan, VII, 9–12, 15–17
Yee, Chiang, XX, 3–4
Yeiju Maru, schooner *(1903),* VIII, 192
Yellott, Jeremiah, XXII, 266, 276
Yellow Bird, U.S. sloop, XXIX, 160
Yellowstone, steamship *(1831),* XXIII, 285
Yemassee, schooner *(1861),* VIII, 222
Yentsch, Dr. Charles S., XLV, 84
Yentsch, Dr. Clarice, mention, XLIX, 37
Yeo, Sir James, XVII, 203

Yeo, Sir James Lucas, XXI, 46 ff.
Yeoward, British shipping line, XLVI, 108
Yesso, schooner *(1846)*, XXIV, 45, 60
Yesso, steamship *(1864)*, XVII, 51, 300 ff.; XVIII, 73
Yokohama Maru, steamship (ex-*Uncle Sam*) *(1868)*, XLIX, 27
Yolanda, Canadian schooner *(1902)*, XLIX, 280
Yonder is the Sea, by Gershom Bradford, reviewed, XIX, 308
Yonge, James, *Journal*, XXIV, 148
York, H.M.S. *(1731)*, XXVI, 37
York, schooner *(1861)*, VIII, 222
York, sloop *(1752)*, XX, 43
York, steamship, XXIII, 225
York, Duke of, XII, 259–261
York, William King, XLI, 183
Yorke, Sir Joseph, XXXVI, 157
Yorke, Sir Philip, XXXI, 203
Yorke, W. H., XXIV, plate XII; XXVII, plate XVIII
York Spit, light-vessel *(1862)*, V, 245
Yorkstown, C.S.S. *(1862)*, XXVII, 174
Yorktown, aircraft carrier *(1944)*, XLVI, 152; XXXIX, 43
Yorktown, C.S.S. *(1862)*, XX, 158
Yorktown, frigate *(1855)*, XLVII, 30
Yorktown, schooner, XXI, 101
Yorktown, ship (1878), XXVIII, plate XXI
Yorktown, sloop of war *(1849)*, XXXVIII, 61, 128, 296 ff.
Yorktown, steamship *(1862)*, XII, 59
Yorktown, U.S. gunboat *(1894/6)*, XXXIV, 214; XXXV, 187; XXIX, 116
"Yorktown, September – October 1781," by Captain Dudley W. Knox, U.S.N. (ret.), V, 240–241
Yorktown, Va., Surrender of Cornwallis at, VII, 105
Yorktown, Virginia, Battle of, 1781, XXV, 189, 217
Yorktown's Captive Fleet, by John O. Sands, reviewed, XLV, 133
Yosemite, auxiliary cruiser *(1898)*, XXXIII, 277; XLI, 98
Yosemite, steamship *(1863)*, II, 303
"You can't beat the Banca," by T. L. Sinclair, Jr., XIX, 257–264
Youell, George, XXVI, 79
Youell, John, XXVI, 79
Youell, T. H., XXVI, 79
Young, Captain E. S., XII, 289
Young, Ewing, XXVIII, 129, 130, 133, 134
Young, Captain George, XXXVII, 247
Young, Gideon, XL, 197
Young, Dr. Hugh H., XXXIV, 272
Young, Captain Israel, XXI, 12
Young, Vice-Admiral James, XLIII, 21 ff.
Young, John, XLI, 226
Young, Captain John, XXXI, 245
Young, John H., XXXVII, 140 n.
Young, Samuel B., XXXV, 189
Young, William, VII, 54

Young America, ship (1853), III, 263; (1853), XIX, plates VII, XI; (1855), XX, 131; *(1872)*, VII, 289
Young Brander, ship (1853), III, 64
Young Greek, bark (1855), V, 150
Young Phoenix, bark *(1888)*, XXXIX, 8; XLIV, 16
Young Racer, sloop *(1864)*, XV, 130
Young Republic, steamship, XXI, 93; *(1864)*, VIII, 236; XXXII, 198
Young Tom (Chinese man), XIV, 215–216
"Young Tom Godfrey and His 'Sextant'," by Ann Martin, XXXV, 111–117
Young William, British ship *(1795)*, XXXIV, 249
Ypres, auxiliary schooner (1918), XXXII, 32
Ysable, steamship *(1863)*, XII, 161
Ysches, Itron, XXX, 49
Yuan Shi-k'ai, President of Chinese Republic, XXXV, 170
Yucateco, Mexican warship *(1843)*, XXI, 222 ff.
Yuen-fa, steamship *(1863)*, XLIII, 289 ff.
Yuen-fah, steamship (1863), XVII, 305
Yugao Maru, steamship *(1865)*, XLIII, 191 ff.
Yulee, David, XXX, 143
Yungching, steamship (1872), XVII, 218; XVIII, 73
Yung Hai An, steamship (1855), XVI, 176, 244; XVIII, 73
Yungning, steamship (1854), XVII, 217
Yu Nuen, steamship *(1867)*, XVII, 215

Z

Zaandam, steamship *(1882)*, XXXVIII, 188 ff.
Zaccheus Sherman, schooner, XXIII, 11
Zachary, ship *(1777)*, XLIII, 24
Zack, Baron de, XIII, 239, 248
Zafiro, ship *(1901)*, XXXV, 195
Zafiro, steam tug *(1898)*, II, 152–153
Zaidee, schooner, XXI, 86; *(1862)*, VIII, 228
Zaine, brig (1840), Pictorial Supplement, XXXVIII, plate XI
Zamalek, rescue ship *(1943)*, L, 219 ff.
Zambesi, freighter *(1891)*, XXV, 172
Zamora, General, XXX, 263
Zanoguerra, Captain S., XXI, 104
Zapata, Elilio, VII, 35
Zavala, schooner *(1861)*, XI, 289
Zavalla, schooner, XXI, 86
Zavoyko, Rear Admiral Vassiliy S., XXXI, 270
Zealand, Edward, VII, 303
Zealandia, steamship *(1875)*, X, 133
Zealous, H.M.S. (1870), XXXVI, 232
Zealous, ironclad (1866), XXXII, 239
Zebedee and Ann, British ship *(1776)*, XLVIII, 18
Zebulon B. Vance, steamship, XXXVII, 75

Zebulon M. Pike, steamship (1813), XVI, 35
Zédé, Amédé–Pierre, XVI, 98
Zeeland, steamship (1901), Pictorial Supplement, XXXIV, plate XXVII
Zeilschepen en Hun Tuigage, by Hidde Manhoudt, Jr., reviewed, VIII, 76
Zelee, ship *(1837),* XXVII, 3
Zeleika, steamship *(1862),* VIII, 228
Zelia, schooner, XXVIII, 123
Zellisa, schooner (1829), XXIV, 45, 60
Zemchug, Russian warship *(1863),* XX, 51
Zemire, frigate (1785), VI, 170
Zempoalteca, Mexican brigantine *(1845),* XXX, 47 ff.
Zenith, schooner *(1861),* VIII, 222
Zenobia, ship *(1796),* XVIII, 131–133
Zeno Doty, yacht (1890), XXXVI, 235
Zephine, steamship, XXI, 101; *(1864),* XI, 276; XII, 235
Zephyr, barkentine (1894), III, 65
Zephyr, ship (1828), XXXIV, 220; (1854), V, 148
Zephyr, yacht *(1900),* XXXVI, 240
Zibulka, Charles J., contributed documents, XXV, 68; XXVI, 282–283
Zidon, bark (1846), XXIV, 45, 57
Zierikzee, East Indiaman *(1620),* L, 285
Zimmerman, Captain L. F., IV, 144 ff.; XVIII, 84

Zingara, sloop (1852), I, facing 72
Zingari, steamship *(1860),* XLIII, 293 ff.
Zink, David, *The Stones of Atlantis,* reviewed, XXXVIII, 301; "Who Was *Ann Parry*'s Jonah?" XXXII, 34–44
Zion, ship (1894), III, 62
Zodiac, steamship *(1866),* XXXIX, 97; *(1881),* XLIV, 114
Zoe, bark *(1862),* XXXVIII, 83
Zogbaum, Rufus Fairchild, Rear Admiral, U.S.N., *From Sail to Saratoga: A Naval Autobiography,* reviewed, XXII, 145–147
Zonda, schooner (1898), XXIV, 60
Zorro Colorado, schooner, XXI, 97; *(1861),* XI, 289
Zotoff, bark (1840), Pictorial Supplement, XXXVIII, plate XXII; XXVIII, 292; *(1844),* XXV, 274–277, plate 29
Zouave, ship (1862), V, 246
Zouche, Lord Edward, XXXI, 85
Zouche, Sir John, XXXI, 85; XLVII, 77
Zowthe Phenix, ship *(1623),* XXXVII, 16
Zuckschwerdt, Captain Adalbert, XXIV, 273 ff.
Zulime, schooner, XXI, 88; *(1861),* XI, 289
Zulueta, ship (1856), II, 332
Zurich, ship (1844), III, 262

The American Neptune 50-Year Index - APPENDIX

REVERSE LISTING OF COMPOUND NAMES OF SHIPS

From Index to *The American Neptune*

Ships with numbers in their names:

1 through 6, U.S. Gunboat No.
2, Marquette & Bessemer No.
4, Torpedo Launch No.
6, Ann Arbor No.
9, Lady Mine No.
8, Pilot Boat No.
21, Pere Marquette
32, City of Flint
56, S.O. Co. of N.Y.
61, No.
61, C.S.S. No.
74, Bellerophan
74, Thunderer
81, Barge No.
88, Lightship No.
94, S. O. Co. No.
95, S. O. Co. No.
98, Prince
98, Queen
1947, Exodus
XV, Louis
XII, Charles

A

A., Cora
A., Elisabeth
A., N.
Abbey, Furness
Abbey, Woburn
Abbott, Gertrude
Abbott, S. F.
Abbott, William
Abert, Colonel
Abigail, Susan
Ackerly, George C.
Actif, L'
Acton, J. C.
Acton, Thomas C.
Ada, Little
Ada, Yassi
Adams, Clara J.
Adams, Colonel
Adams, Eliza
Adams, Geo. M.
Adams, John
Adams, Lady
Adams, Point
Adams, President

Adams, Samuel
Adelaide, City of
Adelaide, Mary
Adele, Jane
Adele, L'
Adele, L'Enfant d'
Adeline, Mary
Adger, James
Adler, Der Grosse
Admiral, Eastern
Admiral, General-
Admiral, Great
Admiral, Royal
Adolph, Kronprins Gustaf
Adriatica, Riva
Adventurer, Felice
Age, Golden
Age, Living
Agnes, Lillian Grace
Agnes, Louisa
Agnes, Mary
Aigle, L'
Aiken, Governor
Aiken, William
Aimé, Bien
Aires, Buenos
Alamo, Vencedor del
Alaska, Star of
Albans, St.
Albaugh, Harry F.
Alberni, City of
Albert, Colonel
Albert, George
Albert, Paul F.
Albert, Prince
Alberta, Maria
Alcantara, San Pedro
Alexander, Ann
Alexander, Emma
Alexander, Great
Alexander, H. F.
Alexander, Princesa
Alexander, Princess
Alexander, W. E.
Alexis, Nord
Alfred, Maria
Alfred, Prince
Alice, Emma and
Alice, Maggie
Alice, Mary
Alice, Princess
Alice, Royal

All, Have at
Allard, S. I.
Allen, Alfred
Allen, Edith L.
Allen, Ethan
Allen, James
Allen, Philip
Allerton, Isaac
Alles, Mattie J.
Alley, Hyder
Allyn, Francis
Allyn, Franklin
Alto, Palo
Amadjuak, Fort
Amalia, Charlotte
Amelia, Emma
Amelie, Marie
America, Central
America, North
America, Northwest
America, Pride of
America, South
America, Young
American, Anglo-
American, Fair
American, North
American, Pacific
American, South
American, True
Ames, Betsey
Ames, Ezra
Ames, Governor
Amis, Les
Amis, Les Deux
Amitie, Bonne
Ammack, John
Amour de la Patrie, L'
Amundsen, Roald
Amy, Francis
An, Mei
An, Yung Hai
Ana, Santa
Anchor, Sheet
Anderson, Addie M.
Anderson, Bessie A.
Anderson, John W.
Anderson, L.
Anderson, P. M.
Anderson, William B.
Andres, San
Andrew, St.
Andrews, St.

353

Angeles, City of Los
Angeles, Port
Angelica, Usrow
Angell, Emma F.
Anges, Les Deux
Ann, Amelia
Ann, Bertha
Ann, Betsey
Ann, Cape
Ann, Charlotte
Ann, Clara
Ann, Clarissa
Ann, Eliza
Ann, Joseph
Ann, Julia
Ann, Mary
Ann, Nancy
Ann, Rebecca
Ann, Sally
Ann, St.
Ann, Wertha
Ann, Zebedee and
Anna, Glory
Anna, Santa
Anna, Sarah
Anne, Florence and
Anne, Mary
Anne, Sainte
Anne, St.
Annie, Ella and
Ant, E.
Antoine, Marie
Antoinette, Louise
Antoinette, Marie &
Antoinette, Marie
Antonieta, Virginia
Antonio, City of San
Apcar, Arratoon
Apcar, Catherine
Araguatos, Rey de los
Arc, Jeanne d'
Arch, Royal
Archbold, John D.
Argus, Eastern
Ariza, Colonel
Arm, Right
Armstrong, General
Arnold, James
Arnold, Mary
Arrow, Winged
Arthemus, Frances
Arthur, John
Arthur, President
Arthur, Prince
Arthur, Royal
Arthur, Thomas C.
Asche, F. D.

Ash, Newton
Aspdin, Joseph
Astrolabe, L'
Atkinson, John
Atlanta, City of
Atwater, Wm. C.
Atwell, Mary
Atwood, E. H.
Atwood, Mattie W.
Augusta, Emily
Augusta, Johanne
Augusta Victoria, Kaiserin
Austin, Calvin
Austin, City of
Austin, R. J.
Avery, William
Awake, Wide
Aymar, B.
Ayres, Buenos
Ayres, City of Buenos

B

B., A.
B., Annie
B., Linda
B, Let Her
Babcock, W. F.
Bacon, Granville R.
Badger, Ella E.
Badger, James
Badin, Adrien
Bagaley, William
Bagaley, Wm.
Bailey, General
Baines, James
Baker, Adelaide
Baker, C.
Baker, Calvin F.
Baker, Geo. G.
Baker, Grace E.
Baker, H.
Baker, M. A.
Baker, Tilly
Balano, Fred B.
Balch, Hannah
Balch, John
Balch, Mary
Balcom, Edith R.
Balcom, Ola M.
Baldwin, Arthur J.
Baldwin, James W.
Baldwin, Stephen
Ball, Alice
Ball, Elvira
Balmaha, Pass of
Baltimore, City of

Banbury, Clara W.
Bandel, A. A.
Bangs, Benjamin
Bank, Dartmstaedler
Banks, General
Banks, Nathaniel P.
Banles, General
Baptist, St. John
Baratier, Général
Barbour, Hattie H.
Barbour, Maj.
Barbour, Major
Barclay, Edwin
Barclay, George
Barge, Cleopatra's
Barkelew, V.
Barker, Jennie S.
Barnard, Ed.
Barnard, L. G.
Barnes, Daniel
Barnes, Laura Annie
Barnett, Br.
Barney, Matilda
Barnsdall, T. N.
Barrett, Major
Barri, Le
Barrie, Commodore
Barrow, John
Barry, Mary
Barry, Sarah
Barstow, Frances A.
Bartlett, Fannie J.
Barton, Agnes
Bastille, Vainqueur de la
Bates, Joshua
Bath, Belle of
Battle, James
Batty, William
Baxter, G. W.
Baxter, H. V.
Baxter, Malcolm, Jr.
Bay, Belle of the
Bay, Bristol
Bay, City of Green
Bay, Coos
Bay, Jervis
Bay, Laguna de
Bay, Oyster
Baylies, William
Bayne, Peter
Be, Let Her
Beach, A. F.
Bear, Polar
Bear, Teddy
Beauchamp, Capitaine de
Beaumont, City of
Beauregard, General

Beckwith, Elias
Beckwith, Eliot
Beckwith, Elisha
Bee, Industrious
Bee, W. C.
Beebe, Wm. L.
Beggar, Sturdy
Begger, Sturdy
Behm, G. W.
Belknap, Joseph
Bell, Anna
Bell, Blue
Bell, Clara
Bell, Daisy
Bell, Eva
Bell, Hettie
Bell, Jacob
Bell, John
Bell, Lizzie
Bell, Lottie
Bell, Mary
Belle, Anna
Belle, Eastern
Belle, Forest
Belle, Island
Belle, Quoddy
Belle, Village
Belle, Western
Bells, Three
Belt, Little
Benbury, Clara W.
Bengal, Star of
Benito, Pio
Benks, Arthur
Bennett, Freddie L.
Bennett, Mildred
Bennett, Thomas
Bennett, Willie L.
Benson, President
Benson, William P.
Bent, Felton
Bentley, Sarah
Bently, George
Berceau, Le
Berry, Emma C.
Berry, General
Bertram, John
Besse, Hattie C.
Besse, William H.
Bessemer No. 2, Marquette and
Bessie, Hattie C.
Bessie, Roaring
Betsey, Charming
Betsy, Charming
Betsy, Polly and
Betty, Charming
Bibb, George M.

Biddle, Henry J.
Bigelow, G. A.
Bill, Uncle
Bill III, Cap'n
Billings, George E.
Billow, Bounding
Birch, Harvey
Bird, Frigate
Bird, Green
Bird, Ocean
Bird, River
Bird, Sea
Bird, Tropic
Bird, Yellow
Birdsall, Emelie F.
Bisbee, William
Bischoff, J. D.
Bishop, Maria
Bishop, R. C.
Bitt, Titt
Blackman, H.
Blackwood, Lady
Blade, Yankee
Bladen, Sarah
Blair, Nellie
Blaisdell, H. P.
Blake, Admiral
Blake, Commodore
Blanchard, P. G.
Blas, San
Blaze, Cumberland
Blessington, Lady
Bligh, Governor
Bliss, Col.
Bliss, Colonel
Block, Mary
Blood, True
Blout, Frank
Blue, Jersey
Blue, True
Blum, E. H.
Blum, Maggie
Boardman, Mary A.
Boat, North River Steam
Boat, Show
Boat, Steam
Bogart, James L.
Bolivar, General
Bolster, George D.
Bonanza, Big
Bonaventure, Edward
Bonaventure, Elizabeth
Bonita, Point
Borden, Jefferson
Bordes, A. D.
Borja, Francisco de
Boston, City of

Boughton, R. H.
Boulogne, Bark of
Boult, Frank
Boulton, John
Boune, Hannah B.
Bounty, Royal
Bourne, Hannah B.
Bourne, Jonathan
Boves, General
Bowers, J. H.
Bowers, Mary
Bowley, J. E.
Bowline, Tom
Bowman, Captain A. H.
Bowne, Millie G.
Boy, News
Boy, Post
Boyce, G. J.
Boyce, James
Boyd, Sarah J.
Boynton, Daisy
Bradford, Abbie
Bradford, J. F.
Bradford, Mary
Bradley, Grace
Brady, E. S.
Brady, General
Braganza, Duc de
Bragg, General
Brainard, Frank
Brainard, G. M.
Brainerd, Frank
Bramble, Eva
Branch, Olive
Brander, Young
Brandzen, General
Branford, Addie
Brass, Fiery
Brass, Terra
Bravo, General
Breeze, Eastern
Breeze, Oliver S.
Brenan, Joseph T.
Brett, Martin W.
Brett, Walter
Brewer, Hannah
Brewer, Helen
Bride, Ocean
Bride, Pilot's
Bride, Sea
Briggs, Charles A.
Bright, John
Brilliant Jeunesse, Le
Britain, Great
Britain, Royal
Brockenborough, G. L.
Bronson, Cassie F.

Brook, Ellis and
Brooke, Sir James
Brooklyn, City of
Brooks, Arthur
Brooks, Governor
Brooks, P. J.
Brooks, P. S.
Brooks, S. P.
Bros., Rengold
Brothers, Brown
Brothers, Five
Brothers, Four
Brothers, McCaldin
Brothers, Sawyer
Brothers, Three
Brothers, Two
Brower, J. L.
Brown, Alice
Brown, Belle
Brown, David
Brown, Governor
Brown, H. W.
Brown, Lawrence
Brown, Mary L.
Brown, May
Brown, Rory
Browne, Millie G.
Browne, Robert
Bruce, Kate L.
Bruce, Robert
Brunswick, New
Brutus, Caroline
Bryant, C. D.
Bryant, Sarah L.
Buck, Fanny
Buck, Henry
Buck, Joseph
Buck, Richard P.
Bucki, Louis
Buckner, General
Buenos Ayres, City of
Bunting, Doctor
Bunyan, John
Burgess, Martha
Burgess, Snow &
Burkhart, George
Burns, Robert
Burr, Sarah
Burroughs, R.
Burroughs, Rhode
Burrows, General
Burrows, Rhode
Burrows, Silas E.
Burrows, William Ward
Burrrows, R.
Burt, James
Burt, Josie R.

Burton, M. P.
Burton, Mary P.
Butch, Old
Butler, General
Butts, Billy
By, John
Byrd, Lelia
Byrd, Nellie L.

C

C., Catherine
C., Elsa
C., Hattie
C., Hattie
C., Lady Lou
Caesar, Julius
Cain, Tubal
Caithness, County of
Calf, Fatted
Cammert, Julius
Camp, Anna
Camp, Empire
Campbell, Charles A.
Campbell, Eliza
Campbell, Lavinia
Campbell, Mary
Campion, William
Canada, Empress of
Canfield, Mack
Canning, Viscount
Canute, St.
Canyon, Torrey
Cap, White
Capa, Manco
Cape, Turret
Carlon, Frederick W.
Carlos, San
Carlos V., Emperator
Carlton, Rinnie J.
Carmen, Maria del
Carolina, La
Carolina, North
Carolina, Princess
Carolina, Royal
Carolina, South
Carolina, South-
Caroline, Mary-
Caroline, Sarah and
Carrie, Little
Carroll, Charles
Carson, Kit
Carver, Abbie
Carver, B. F.
Carver, Clarissa B.
Carver, John
Case, George M.

Case, Mary H.
Cass, Lewis
Casselly, M. P.
Castle, Beatrice
Castle, Bombay
Castle, Carisbrooke
Castle, Conway
Castle, Cumloden
Castle, Drummond
Castle, Galgorm
Castle, Inchcliffe
Castle, Lincluden
Castle, Methuen
Castle, Morro
Castle, Rothesay
Castle, South Sea
Castle, Sterling
Castle, Stirling
Castle, Windsor
Castle, Yarmouth
Catharine, Susan
Catherine, Eliza
Catherine, Eliza and
Catherine, Mary and
Catherine, Royal
Catherine, Sarah and
Catskill, City of
Cavanagh, D.
Ceasar, Julius
Cecelie, Kronprinzessin
Cecilie, Herzogin
Celeste, Mary
Celestia, Mary
Cement, Diamond
Chace, Adelia
Chaffee, George A.
Challes, Commandant
Chaman, Wm. E.
Chamberlain, Henry H.
Chambers, T. J.
Chance, By
Chance, La Petite
Chandler, Constance
Chandler, Marian Otis
Chanslor, J. A.
Chapin, Chester W.
Chapin, Nahum
Chapman, Af
Chapman, Allan A.
Chapman, Phebe
Charles, Lord
Charles, Saint
Charles, St.
Charlotte, Princess
Charlotte, Queen
Chase, Adelia
Chase, Jonathan

Chase, N. D.
Chase, Salmon P.
Chatelier, Henri Le
Chauncey, Henry
Chester, City of
Chester, Henry C.
Chester, Lewis
Chester, William E.
Chester, Wm. E.
Chiao, Kiao-
Chicago, City of
Chief, Indian
Chief, Indian-
Chief, Scottish
Chief, Sea
Chief, Southern
Chief, Sun
Chief, Turret
Chief, Winnebago
Chilcott, Marion
Child, A. J.
Childers, Flying
Childs, Annie
Chile, Star of
China, Empress of
Ching, Dai
Ching, Lien
Chisholm, Mary F.
Chisolm, Geo.
Choapas, Las
Choice, Lady's
Cholric, King
Christenson, Edna
Christian, Sam T.
Christiana, Maria
Christo, Monte
Christopher, John G.
Church, Elliott B.
Churchill, James M.
Churchman, Samuel
Cilento, Francesco
Cisneros, Cardinal
City, Baltimore
City, Bath
City, Bayou
City, Birmingham
City, Boston
City, Bristol
City, Brooklyn
City, Capital
City, Chicago
City, Clipper
City, Crescent
City, Eastern
City, Elizabeth
City, Empire
City, Exeter

City, Forest
City, Fresno
City, Gloucester
City, Golden
City, Granite
City, Island
City, Jersey
City, Kansas
City, Llandaff
City, London
City, Montreal
City, Mound
City, New York
City, Quaker
City, Queen
City, Toronto
City, Wells
Claiborne, Clarissa
Clair, Saint
Clair, St.
Claire, St.
Clapp, Annie
Clara, Santa
Clark, Carrie M.
Clark, Elezar W.
Clark, Freeman
Clark, Hadley
Clark, Ida M.
Clark, Lizzie J.
Clark, R. B.
Clark, William C.
Clarke, William H.
Clay, Henry
Clementine, Petite
Clerks, Bishop &
Clermont, Katherine of
Clermont, North River of
Cleveland, President
Clifton, Emma
Clinch, General
Clinton, DeWitt / De Witt
Clinton, George
Clinton, Mary
Clise, J. W.
Cloud, Black
Cloud, Eastern
Cloud, Flying
Cloud, Golden
Cloud, Red
Cloud, Silver
Cloud, White
Clyde, Falls of
Clyde, Lord
Clyde, Thomas
Cn Aspire, Molley
Coast, Eastern
Cobb, Amelia F.

Cobb, Governor
Cobb, Martha
Cobden, Richard
Coburn, Abner
Cochran, F. W.
Cochrane, Almirante
Cod, Tom
Coit, W. W.
Cole, Robert W.
Cole, Sarah
Coleman, I. D.
Coleman, R. B.
Colgate, Charles
Colita, Gloria
Collier, E. P.
Collins, George W.
Colon, Cristobal
Colorado, Gino
Colorado, Zorro
Colt, Caldwell H.
Colthirst, Henry
Colthirst, Henry F.
Colthrist, Henry F.
Columbus, Christopher
Colwell, John D.
Comyn, Anne
Comyn, Phyllis
Concordia, Car of
Coney, Rachel
Congress, American
Conner, William
Connor, William H.
Conquise, Egypt
Conquise, Italie
Considère, Armand
Consolacion, Nuestra Señora
Constant, Susan
Constantine, John
Continent, Western
Conwell, E. B.
Conwell, Eleanor B.
Cook, Captain
Cook, H. L.
Cook, Parker
Coolidge, President
Cooper, Alexander
Cooper, Alice D.
Cooper, Charles
Cooper, Elwood
Cooper, Fenimore
Cooper, William A.
Coristie, Marie
Corkum, Beatrice L.
Cornelia, Little
Cornell, Sammy
Cornell, Thomas
Cortes, Herman

Cory, Kate
Cos, General
Cos, Soledad
Cosme, San
Costa, Contra
Costa, Jessie
Coster, Laurens
Counce, Alice
County, Hancock
Cousiño, Matais
Coutts, Thomas
Cove, Glen
Covert, Nelia
Cowham, William Foster
Cowperthaite, Joseph
Cox, Jesse J.
Cox, Jessie J.
Coyote, West
Cracker, Fire
Crag, Eastern
Cramer, Corwith
Crandal, A.
Crapo, William W.
Cratzer, Bettie
Creighton, E.
Creina, Nora
Crenshaw, Fannie
Creole, Jeune
Crespo, General
Cressey, Cora F.
Cressy, Cora F.
Crest, Sea
Criolla, La
Crittenden, J. J.
Croce, Mario
Crocker, Charles F.
Crockett, David
Crockett, Davy
Croix, St.
Cromwell, Oliver
Cromwell, Thomas A.
Crosby, Alicia B.
Cross, Eastern
Cross, Fiery
Cross, Iron
Cross, Julius
Cross, Red
Cross, Southern
Crowell, S. L.
Crowley, Mertie B.
Crown, Eastern
Croyable, La
Cruz, Santa
Cruz, Vera
Cuba, Santiago de
Culottes, Sans
Cumberland, Duke of

Cumberland, West
Cumming, G. B.
Cummings, William
Currier, John
Curtis, Caleb
Curtis, Oakley C.
Cushing, Caleb
Cushing, H. P.
Cushing, Mary L.
Cushman, Jennie
Cutter, Lee

D

D., Cecelia
D., Ella
D., Gertrude
D., Susie
da Gama, Vasco
Dale, Anna
Dale, Kate
Dallas, City of
Dame, Notre
Dan, Christine and
Dana, Thomas
Daniel, Ezra and
Daniel, Vernon
D'Arc, Jeanne
Dare, Virginia
Dart, Fire
Dartmouth, Lord
Dauphin, Le
Davenport, Alice May
Davenport, Ann C.
Davenport, Charles
David, St.
Davis, Anna
Davis, C. M.
Davis, Governor
Davis, J. S.
Davis, J. T.
Davis, Jane
Davis, Jeff
Davis, Jefferson
Davis, Kate
Davis, L. L.
Davis, Lady
Davis, Lizzie
Dawn, Eastern
Dawn, Rising
Day, Break of
Day, Break O'/o'
Day, James L.
Day, Peep O'/o'
D'Aymer, John
Dayrell, Wild
Dean, Julia

Dean, Virgil G.
Deane, Bertha
Deans, Anna
Deas, Ann S.
DeBary, Fred'k
De Bary, Fred'k
de Bay, Laguna
de Beauchamp, Capitaine
Decade, Le
de Cuba, Santiago
de Elcano, Juan Sebastian
Deering, Carroll A.
Deering, Gardner G.
Deering, Lydia M.
Deford, Ben
de Gama, Vasco
de Graff, Governor
de Julio, Nueve
De Klerk, General
de la Consolacion, Nuestra Señora
de Lafayette, Marquis
del Alamo, Vencedor
de la Mer, Fleur
Delcarmel, Nostra (Noftra)
   Signiora
de Lezo, Santa Christo
Delius, Eberhard
Della Torre, Ida
Delorme, Lieutanant
del Rey, Castel
de Mayo, Veinticinco
Demetrio, San
Demill, Peter
Democrate, Petite
Denmark, Prince of
de Roca, Cabo
De Ronde, Marie
de Rose, Commandant
De Rosset, A. J.
Desert, Mt.
de Terlines, Aviateur
de Ulloa, Don Antonio
Deux Amis, Les
Deux Anges, Les
de Vaudreuil, La Marquise
Dewey, Admiral
Dewey, Lizzie
Diciembre, Trece de
Dickson, Peter
Diebold, Mary H.
Diligente, La
Dimmock, J. L.
Dimock, H. F.
Dingle, Coombe
Dingley, Governor
Dinsmore, Clara
Dinsmore, Nellie J.

The American Neptune 50-Year Index - APPENDIX

Divina Pastora, La
Dix, Catherine T.
Dixon, Robert
Dobbins, Nettie
Dodge, Eben
Dodge, Henry
Dodge, William
Dog, Black
Doggett, Charles
Dole, George W.
Dollar, Alice
Dollar, David
Dollar, M. S.
Dollar, Mae
Dollar, Mary
Domingo, San
Domingos, San
Dominion, British
Dominion, Old
Dona, Prima
Donahoe, Agnes G.
Donaldson, Fort
Donkin, Cwm
Donna, Prima
Donnell, Clara A.
Doodle, Yankee
Dorado, El
Doran, William
Doria, Andrea
Doria, Andrew
Dorme, Adjutant
Dorn, Van
Doty, Zeno
Douglas, Baron
Douglas, Mary
Douglas, Rebecca R.
Douglas, William L.
Douglass, John
Douglass, William
Douro, Foz Do
Douthwaite, George
Dove, Carrier
Dove, Ring
Dow, Ida S.
Dow, Mary
Dow, Mary E. H.
Downing, Jack
Dows, David
Dragon, Gilt
Drake, Colonel E. L.
Dream, Forest
Drew, Daniel
Driant, Colonel
Drift, Sea
Dromo, Little
Drummond, E.
Drury, Roger
Dryden, John
Du Bignon, J. E.
DuBignon, J. E.
duBois, Jennie R.
Duc de Montebello, Le
Duchesse, La Grande
Dudley, Governor
Dudley, Laura
Duke, James B.
Dunbar, Elisha
Duncan, Alexander
Dundas, Charlotte
Dundee, City of
Dunton, L. A.
DuPont, Admiral
Duras, Duc de
Dutard, Fanny
Dutchman, Flying
Dyer, Lemuel

E

E, Olive
Eager, Elvira
Eagle, Federal
Eagle, Golden
Eagle, Grey
Eagle, New
Eagle, Sea
Eagle, War
East, Far
East, Star of the
Eastern, Great
Eastman, Jennie
Eaton, Annie K.
Eaton, Henry F.
Eaton, Sarah
Ebbitt, Wm.
Ebeneazer, Rachael &
Eborn, L. C.
Eckel, Edwin Clarence
Eckford, Henry
Eclair, L'
Edinbugh, County of
Edison, Thomas A.
Edward, Albert
Edward, Prince
Edwards, Rebecca
Edwina, Lucy
Egar, Elvira
Eger, Emma
Eglington, Earl of
Egmont, Earl of
Elcano, Juan Sebastian de
Eldridge, Asa
Eldridge, D. W.
Eleanor, Lady
Elgin, Lord
Eliott, Daniel
Eliza, Ann
Eliza, Esther
Eliza, Hannah and
Eliza, William &
Elizabeth, Hannah and
Elizabeth, Mary
Elizabeth, Princess
Elizabeth, Queen
Elizabeth, Sarah
Ella, Mary
Ellen, Martha
Ellen, Mary
Elliott, Daniel
Ellsworth, Albert S.
Elmore, James H.
Elsie, Mary and / &
Elvira, Joven
Elwell, James W.
Ely, Marquis of
Emery, Dean
Emery, Edith
Emma, Friendly
Emma, Ida and
Emma, Mary
Empire, British
Empire, Rising
Empire, Star of
Ena, John
Encalada, Blanco
Endicott, Governor
Endicott, John
Enfant d'Adele, L'
England, Maid of
England, New
England, Star of
Enoch, Frederick
Enterprise, L'
Eppes, Lulu W.
Era, New
Erickson, Leif
Ericsson, John
Erie, Little
Erikson, Lief
Erin, Maid of
Erin, Star of
Erral, West
Escape, Royal
Escocesa, La
Esperance, L'
Estrees, d'
Etoille, L'
Ettrick, Falls of
Evans, Clarence L.
Evans, Margaret
Evelyn, Lucy

Everett, City of
Everett, Edward
Exeter, City of
Exporter, Eastern
Express, Ocean

F

F., Celia
Fá, Cum
fa, King-
Fa, Yuen-
Fah, Yuen-
Falcon, General
Falconer, Sarah H.
Falkland, Star of
Fame, Chariot of
Fanny, Louisa Ann
Fanny, Prosperous
Faralon, West
Farmer, Julia
Farmer, Monongahela
Farnum, Emily
Farnum, John
Farwell, Charles A.
Faust, David
Favorite, Neptune's
Favorite, Ocean
Fear, Cape
Fearing, Albert
Fearing, Susan
Feather, Grey
Feeney, John
Fei, Wan Loong
Felicite, La
Felitz, Gracie
Fellow, Odd
Ferdinand Maximillian, Erherzog
Ferguson, P. C.
Fermin, San
Fern, Fanny
Field, Timothy
Files, R. C.
Fillmore, President
Fine, La
Finisterre, Cap
Finland, Star of
Finnegan, General
Fir, Oregon
First, Fulton the
Fish, Annie
Fish, Black
Fish, Flying
Fish, Flying-
Fish, Joseph
Fish, Loretto

Fish, Sword
Fisher, Jane
Fisher, Warren
Fisk, Eliza M.
Fiske, Eliza
Fitchburg, City of
Flag, Union
Flanner, Joe
Flash, Fire
Fleece, Golden
Fleming, Ella
Flight, Eagle
Flint 32, City of
Flint, City of
Flint, Fanny
Flint, Frank
Flint, W. B.
Florida, West
Flower, May
Flower, Sea
Floyd, David G.
Flush, Pam
Fly, Fire
Fly, Sand
Fock, Gorch
Foley, M. J.
Fong, Tah-Yue-
Foo, Mei
Forbes, Charles
Forbes, Governor
Forbes, R. B.
Forbes, Sir Charles
Ford, Henry
Ford, Jennie
Ford, Sammy
Fordney, Joseph W.
Forest, Windsor
Forester, Donna
Forge, Valley
Forsyth, John
Forth, River
Fortune, Good
Fortune, John
Fortune, John and
Fortune, La
Fortune, Wheel of
Forward, Walter
Foss, Harold G.
Foster, Andrew
Foster, Frank
Foster, J. F.
Foster, James Jr.
Foster, M. E.
Foster, Thomas R.
Fou, Hsin-
Foulks, William
Fourth (IV), William the

Fowler, Emily
Fowler, Jerry
Fox, Red
Fox, Sea
Franca, Villa
France, Ile de
France, Queen Of
France, Star of
Frances, Eliza
Frances, Julia
Francis, Lucy
Francis, William &
Francisco, City of San
Francisco, San
Francois, Grand
Frank, Little
Frank, M. L.
Franklin, Ben
Franklin, Elma
Franklin, Sarah
Fraser, John
Fravega, Nina
Frederick, Prince
Frederick, William
Freeman, Jesse H.
Freeman, Maria
Fremont, Colonel
French, Bradford C.
Freres / Frères, Trois
Frey, Agnes C.
Friedrich, Prinz Eitel
Friend, Forest
Friends, Three
Friends, Two
Frome, Anna M.
Frost, E. L.
Frothingham, William
Fry, Agnes
Fry, Agnes E.
Frye, William P.
Fuller, A. J.
Fuller, Herbert
Fuller, Ransom B.
Fulton, Maggie
Fulton, Robert
Fundy, Prince of

G

G., Fannie
Gabain, E. F.
Gage, Weather
Galatin, Albert
Gale, Eastern
Galen, New
Gallatin, Albert
Galley, Bridgtown

Galley, Dursley
Galley, Peregine
Galley, Province
Galley, Russell
Galley, Tower
Gallieni, Général
Galveston, City of
Gama, Vasco da
Gama, Vasco de
Gambia, Princess
Gamble, R. H.
Garding, Cassader
Garfield, James A.
Garibaldi, G.
Gaspar, Jose
Gate, Golden
Gates, E. C.
Gates, General
Gates, William
Gauntlet, Red
Gaynet, L.
Geary, Seattle or
Gee, Annie
General, Governor
General, Solicitor
Genet, Citizen
George, Anti-
George, By
George, Federal
George, Fort
George, King
George, Little
George, Prince
George, Royal
George, Saint
George, St.
Georgia, State of
Gerety, Joseph L.
Gerrish, C. P.
Gertrude, Alice
Gertrude, Caroline
Gertrudis, Santa
Gibbs, Alfred
Gibson, Anna
Giddings, Ernestine
Gilcher, W. R.
Gildersleeve, Henry
Gildersleeve, Sylvester
Gillerson, Ann
Gillise, Annie
Gilpin, John
Gilroy, George
Gimblet, Irish
Girard, Stephen
Girl, American
Girl, Village
Gironde, La

Glade, Eastern
Glen, Eastern
Gloire, La
Gloucester, City of
Glover, C. B.
Glynn, Harry
Godfrey, Jane
Goethals, General G. W.
Goodell, Mary
Good Faith, Our Lady of
Goodhue, Theodore E.
Goodridge, J. W.
Goodspeed, Ellen
Goodspeed, W. M.
Goodwell, Mary
Good Will, Father's
Goodwill, Friends
Goose, Golden
Gordon, Charles F.
Gordon, Thomas
Gorges, Ferdinando
Gorton, Thomas L. ("S")
Goss, Guy C.
Govin, R. R.
Gower, Lady
Grace, Julia
Grace à Dieu, Henry
Granada, New
Grand, Le
Grande Duchesse, La
Grand Haven, City of
Grange, La
Granier, Lieutenant
Grant, Charles
Grant, Daniel
Grant, John
Grant, Lydia
Grant, Nellie
Grant, President
Grant, U.S.
Gratia, Dei
Gratiot, General
Gray, Hamilton
Gray, Jane
Gray, John P.
Gray, Sir George
Gray, William
Gray's, Capt.
Greece, Modern
Greek, Young
Greely, Eliphalet
Green, Cora
Green, Cox &
Green, E. H.
Green, Mary
Green Bay, City of
Greene, Captain

Greene, General
Greenland, Star of
Greenleaf, Marcia
Greer, Matthew S.
Gregg, Kate
Gretna, Lake
Gretta, Lida
Grey, Empire
Grey, James
Grey, Sir George
Grice, Daniel S.
Grice, George W.
Griffin, John
Griggs, Everett G.
Gring, Helen Barnet
Grinnell, Cornelius
Griswold, George
Grosse, Friedrich der
Grosse, Kaiser Wilhelm der
Grosse Adler, Der
Grosvenor, Seth
Grove, Golden
Grubbs, James
Guadalupe, Nostra Senora de
Guatamala, City of
Guichard, Maurice
Guide, Eastern
Guilford, Mary
Guin, J. C.
Gulfport, City of
Gull, Sea
Gus, Annie
Gustaf, Kronprins
Gustaf Adolf, Kronprins
Guynemer, Capitaine
Gwin, J. C.
Gwinn, J. C.

H

H., J. A.
H., Leslie
H., Rosie
Haarfager, Harold
Hackfeld, H.
Hai, Yung-
Hale, E. B.
Hale, Eugene
Hale, John
Hale, Josiah L.
Hale, Kate
Hale, Robert
Haley, Mary
Halifax Packet,
Hall, Brown
Hall, Christopher
Hall, D. M.

Hall, H. K.
Hall, Horatio
Hall, Jennie S.
Hallett, Thomas
Halstead, Admiral
Hamilton, Alexander
Hamilton, Elizabeth
Hamilton, General
Hamilton, Imperial
Hamilton, M. M.
Hamilton, William
Hamlin, Doris
Hammitt, John K.
Hammond, Mary
Hampshire, New
Hancock, General
Hancock, John
Hankow, City of
Hanks, Nancy
Hansen, H. C.
Hanson, Charles
Harbor, Grays
Harding, Kate
Harding, Robert
Harding, Sarah L.
Hardison, W. L.
Hare, George and
Haring, John W.
Harkness, Jennie
Harmon, Mary A.
Harnden, Florence A.
Harold, Childe
Harriet, Lucy
Harriet, Lucy and
Harris, Mary C.
Harrison, General
Harrison, President
Hart, Isaiah
Hart, S. C.
Hart, Stephen
Hart, Thomas
Harthan, Maggie
Hartley, James
Harvard, Thomas
Harvey, Sir John
Harwood, Paul H.
Hasbrouck, John L.
Hasbrouck, Mary
Hatch, Louisa
Hathaway, John
Hattie, L. M.
Hattie, Little
Haven, City of Grand
Haven, N. M.
Haven, New
Haven, North
Haven, Vinal

Haven, West
Haverhill, City of
Haviside, Alicia
Haviside, Russell
Hawaii, Haaheo o
Hawaii, Pride of
Hawk, Black
Hawk, Night
Hawk, Sparrow
Hawk, Sparrow-
Hawke, Sir Edwad
Hawley, R. K.
Haws, Calesta
Hayes, H. M.
Hayes, President
Hayes, William
Hayward, Cassie
Hazard, J. A.
Hazard, John A.
Hazard, New
Head, Diamond
Head, Gay
Head, Kenbane
Head, Marble
Head, Torr
Healy, Robert
Heath, North
Heather, White
Heckman, Hattie A.
Heckscher, C. A.
Heidritter, Anna R.
Helen, Anna
Helen, Lillie
Helen, Mary &
Helens, City of St.
Henderson, Annie L.
Henly, Wm.
Hennebique, François
Henrietta, Frances
Henry, Charles
Henry, Emma
Henry, Patrick
Henry, Prince William
Henry, Silas
Henry, William
Henry C. Chester,
Herald, Boston
Herbert, Frank
Hermano, Vila y
Hero, Baltimore
Hersey, S. F.
Hertz, Rebecca
Hester, Royal
Hettler, Herman H.
Hewes, William G.
Hewes, Wm. G.
Hicks, Andrew

Hicks, Isaac
Hicks, Tom
Higgins, Richard R.
Higginson, H. C.
Hignett, Sarah
Hilda, R.
Hill, Bunker
Hill, Edward
Hilligonda, Geziena
Hills, Adela S.
Hilton, B.
Hilton, Kate M.
Hilton, R. B.
Hincks, Susan
Hind, Golden
Hing, Mei
Hinkly, Evelyn W.
Hippopotamus, Homely
Ho, Tally
Ho, Westward
Hodge, A. J
Hodges, Julia A.
Hodgkins, Delia
Hogsdon, Alexander
Holcombe, Thomas
Holland, Star Of
Holmes, Leroy C.
Holmes, Lucy C.
Holt, Cassie
Homans, Lizzie
Home, Harvest
Home, Island
Honolulu, City of
Hood, Mary A.
Hood, Robin
Hook, Sandy
Hooper, Sarah
Hoover, President
Hope, Ann & / and
Hope, Good
Hope, Star of
Hopkins, R. E.
Horn, Cap
Horn, Golden
Horse, Flying
Horse, Light
Horse, Sea
Horse, White
Horton, Edward A.
Hosokie, West
Hoth, Carrie
Houck, Courtney C.
Houghton, Charles
Houghton, Lije
Hound, Stag
Houston, City of
Houston, Sam

Howard, Elizabeth
Howard, Louise
Howard, President
Howard, Susan Ann
Howard, W. H.
Howe, Joseph
Howe, Lord
Howland, Gideon
Howland, Isaac
Howland, John
Howlett, A. B.
Howlett, M. P.
Hoxie, Belle
Hoyle, Duncan
Hoyt, Colgate
Hoyt, Edna
Höpken, Baron And. von
Hsia, Mei
Hudson, City of
Hudson, Hendrick
Huglett, T. R.
Hull, Commodore
Hulse, D. C.
Humberton, Charles
Hume, Mary D.
Humphrey, Richard Lewis
Hung, Mei
Hungary, Queen of
Hunley, H. L.
Hunt, Augustus
Hunt, Sarah W.
Hunter, Bold
Hunter, Gold
Hunter, Minnie
Hunter, Wild
Huntington, Samuel
Hurley, Lady
Hussey, H. B.
Hwa, Lan-
Hyde, Henry B.
Hyde, Sarah G.

I

Ida, Alice
Idea, New
Imperial, Prince
Importer, Eastern
Ina, Santa
Inconstant, L'
Independence, Southern
India, Empress of
India, Star of
Indian, West
Indiano, San Jose
Indien, L'
Industry, Martin's

Ingalls, C. H.
Ingersoll, A. J.
Inkster, Walter
Insurgente, L'
Intent, Good
Intrepede, L'
Invention, L'
I'on, Sally
Ironsides, New
Irving, Walter
Irving, Washington
Isabel, Señora
Isabella, Sarah
Island, Deer
Island, Long
Island, New
Island, Rhode
Isles, British
Isles, Hawaiian
Italia, Belle
Italia, Re d'
Italy, Star of
Iuel, Niels
IV, William
Ivy, V. H.

J

Jacinto, San
Jack, Federal
Jack, Saucy
Jacket, Blue
Jacket, Grey
Jacket, Red
Jackson, Andrew
Jackson, City of
Jackson, Fort
Jackson, General
Jackson, Hallie
Jackson, Hazel M.
Jackson, J. W.
Jackson, Stonewall
Jacksonville, City of
Jacobs, Alice M.
Jamaica, Governor of
James, John and
James, Little
James, Reuben
James, Saint
James, St.
Jan, St.
Janauria, Doña
Jane, Annie and
Jane, Betsey
Jane, Charles &
Jane, Clara
Jane, Crazy

Jane, Martha
Jane, Mary
Jane, Peggy &
Jane, Sophia
Jane, Susan
Jane, William and
Janeiro, City of Rio de
Janes, E. S.
Januaria, Doña
Japan, Emperor of
Jarvis, William
Jason, Le
Jay, Blue
Jay, John
Jayne, C. E.
Jeejeebhoy, Sir Jamsetjee
Jeffers, Albert
Jefferson, Thomas
Jenkins, W. D.
Jenny, Fanny and
Jersey, New
Jessie, Emilie and
Jessie, Harriet &
Jessie, Irene and
Jessie, Margaret and
Jessup, General
Jesucristo, Asuncion de
Jeunesse, Brillante
Jeunesse, Le Brilliant
Jewell, William
Jewell, William H.
Jinju, Nimro
Jken, Senator
Jo-Ann, Debbie and
Joao, Sao
John, City of St.
John, Margaret and
John, Margrett and
John, Mary and
John, Saint
John, St.
John, Virginia
John, William and
John's, St.
Johns, St.
Johns, Two
Johnson, A. B.
Johnson, F. W.
Johnson, Hannah M.
Johnson, Lucy
Johnston, Edward
Joker, Black
Jolie, La
Joliff, Chatfield
Jonas, Elizabeth
Jonathan, Brother
Jones, Al

Jones, Alfred
Jones, B. F.
Jones, Bradford E.
Jones, Commodore
Jones, Deborah
Jones, E. S
Jones, E. Starr
Jones, Edna
Jones, F. B.
Jones, Frank
Jones, J.
Jones, Paul
Jones, Reuben
Jones, Ruth
Jones, Suzie M.
Jordan, George V.
Jordan, Sarah
Jordenskjold, Admiral P.
Jose, Don
Jose, San
Joseph, St.
Josyan, Lady
Juan, Jorge
Juan, San
Judah, W. H.
Judith, Point
Julia, Ana
Julia, Emma
Julia, Emma
Juliana, Little
Julio, 9 de
Julio, 9 de - see Nueve de Julio
Julio, 18 de - see Veintiocho de Julio
Julio, Nueve de
Julio, Veintiocho de
July, Second of
Junio, 10 de - see Diez de Junio
Junio, Diez de
Jurado, General Leon
Justo, Don

K

K., O.
Kahn, Albert
Kain, W. A.
Kain, William A.
Kalb, De
Kami, Kaga-no-
Kan, Naniwa-
Kaptan, Riza
Kasson, West
Kate, Dainty
Kate, Sister
Kate, Sister, Jr.
Katherine, Royal

Keag, Naum
Kee, Fah
Keeler, Jas. R.
Keeling, D. F.
Kelley, D. & E.
Kellie, Earl of Mar and
Kelly, Earl of Mar and
Kemble, Margaret
Kempt, Sir James
Kendall, Mary
Kennedy, Caroline H.
Kennedy, Elodia A.
Kennedy, Mary Jane
Kereem, Fazl
Kerr, Lillian E.
Kerr, Peter
Key, Jean
Kiang, Chi
Kidder, Edward
Kimball, Annie
Kimball, David
King, Erl
King, Forest
King, Northern
King, Roswell
King, Rufus
King, Sea
King, Storm
King, W. R.
Kingdom, United
Kingman, E. H.
Kingston, City of
Kingston, Port
Kingston, South
Kinoyene, Koshi
Kirkland, Robert R.
Klinck, Charles H.
Klinck, George E.
Knapp, C. P.
Kneeland, Henry
Knight, Eastern
Knight, Ellie
Knight, William H.
Knowles, Alice
Kobbe, Augustine
Kong, Hong
Koppisch, Edward
Kraus, Richard E.
Kreger, Jennie Flood
Kuhn, J. C.
Kung, Prince
Kurfurst, Grosser
Kyokai, Nippon Kaigi

L

L., Leslie

L., Lulu
L. M., Hattie
Ladson, James H.
Ladson, W. H.
Lady, Scottish
Lafayette, City of
Lafayette, Marquis de
Lagarto, El
Lake, Lady of the
Lakes, Queen of the
Lamar, C. A. L.
Lamar, G. B.
Lamb, Col.
Lamb, Colonel
Lance, Essex
Lancelot, Sir
Land, North
Lane, A. J.
Lane, Amy A.
Lane, Harriet
Lane, Robert L.
Langdon, Governor
Lapland, Star of
Laramie, Fort
Larder, Annie E.
Larispa, Pancha
Lark, Sea
Lass, Ayrshire
Lass, Limerick
Lass, Lovely
Latham, Emma C.
Lauder, Maggie
Laurence, St.
Laurie, Fannie
LaValley, Alexander
Law, George
Law, John
Law, Lizzie A.
Law, Maine
Lawrence, Abbott
Lawrence, Addie M.
Lawrence, Alice M.
Lawrence, Amos
Lawrence, C. W.
Lawrence, Edward J.
Lawrence, Saint
Lawrence, Samuel
Lawrence, Sir John
Lawrence, St.
Lawrence, Thomas H.
Lawrence, Wayne
Laws, George
Lawson, Norah E.
Lawson, Thomas W.
Lea, Alice
Lead, Golden
Leader, Eastern

Leah, Hazel-
Leavitt, General
Leavitt, John F.
Leavitt, William
Le Chatelier, Henri
Le Chatelier, M. H.
Lee, Alice
Lee, Ann F.
Lee, Fanny
Lee, John S.
Lee, Mee-
Lee, R. E.
Lee, Robert E.
Lee, William
Leen, Shooey-
Leicester, Gallion
Leitch, W. Y.
Leon, St.
Leonhardt, Luise
Leopold, Prince
Leopold, Prinz
Leoy, Jacob
Lesley, Robert Whitman
Leslie, General
Leslie, John
Leverett, Ann C.
Lewis, Charles R.
Lewis, Fanny
Lewis, Harry
Lewis, Henry
Lewis, Mary
Lewis, Mary H.
Lewis, Polly
Lewis, William
Lezo, Santa Christo de
Liang, Hsin-
Lianga, West
Liberian, The
Libre, Veracruzano
Light, Eastern
Light, Electric
Light, Morning
Light, Northern
Light, Rock
Lila, Little
Lilla, Little
Lilly, Ida
Lilly, Little
Lily, Little
Liman, Serçe
Lincoln, Jairus B.
Lincoln, President
Lind, Jenny
Lindsay, Hugh
Line, Air
Liner, Golden
Linlithgow, County of

Linton, Robert L.
Lion, Coeur de
Lion, Sea
Littlefield, Charlotte A.
Liverpool, Great
Liverpool, New
Livingston, Chancellor
Livingston, Herman
Lüling, Charles
Lloyds, Portland
Lobos, Point
London, Loyal
London, Minion of
London, New
Long, Colonel
Long, John D.
Loomis, George
Loong, Fe
Loong, Kiang
Loong, Wang
Lopez, Antonio
Lord, Anna G.
Lord, Anne
Lord, Annie
Lord, Charles H.
Lord, Mary
Lord, Mary M.
Lord, Walter
Lorentzen, J. W. A.
Los Angeles, City of
Lothrop, Carl D.
Louder, Emily B.
Louis, Royal
Louis, St.
Louisa, Agnes
Louisa, Ann
Louisa, Clara
Louisa, Mary
Louise, Clara
Louise, Florence
Louise, Maria
Louise, Marie
Lovell, Colonel
Low, Seth
Lowe, Robert
Lowell, City of
Lowell, Hiram
Lowell, James S.
Lowell, Mary
Lowery, Fanny
Lowndes, Harriet
Lucas, Captain A. F.
Lucas, San
Luciano, San
Luck, Good
Luckenbach, Harry
Luckenbach, Horace

Luckenbach, Jacob
Luckenbach, Julia
Luckenbach, Robert
Ludwig, Johann
Ludwig, M. R.
Luhrs, Sophia R.
Luigi, Don
Luigi Re di Portogallo, Don
Luise, Prinzessen Victoria
Lunt, Charles H.
Lunt, Maria
Lycett, Lady
Lycka, Sveriges
Lydia, Charming
Lyle, Annie
Lynwood, Grace
Lyon, Golden
Lyon, Goulden
Lyons, Lady of
Lytton, Empire

M

M., Fanny
M., Lena
M., Margaret
M., Sophia
Má, Fei
Mà, Fei
Má, Fei-
Mab, Queen
Mabey, R. L.
MacFarlane, Sarah
Machridachis, G.
Mackall, Katherine
Macomb, General
MacTavish, Clan
Madison, James
Madras, City of
Magdelaine, Mary
Magee, Sally
Magnus, Carolus
Magoun, Thatcher
Mahon, Port
Maid, Dairy
Maid, Willing
Mail, China
Mail, Eastern
Maine, State of
Malloch, Maud
Mallory, H. R.
Mallory, J. W.
Mallory, William
Manby, Aaron
Manchester, Duke of
Manley, Aaron
Manning, Agnes

Manoury, Général
Mansfield, Alexander
Manson, J. C.
Manta, John R.
Manta, Phillip P.
Manter, Phelomina
Mar, Helen
Mar and Kellie (Kelly), Earl of
March, Peter
Marcy, Daniel
Marcy, Governor
Marcy, Henrietta
Marcy, Peter
Margaret, Jane and
Margaret, Jessie and
Margaret, Mary
Margarita, Santa
Maria, Ann
Maria, Anna
Maria, Lady
Maria, Santa
Maria Domingo, Santa
Marianne, La
Marie, La
Mariner, Cracker State
Mariner, Eastern
Mariner, Empire
Marion, Frank
Marion, Leona &
Mark, St.
Marquette 21, Pere
Marquis, British
Marquise de Vaudreuil, La
Marr, J. W.
Marshall, Charles H.
Marshall, Emily
Marshall, John
Marshall, Julia
Marson, J. C.
Marston, W. H.
Martel, Charles
Martha, William and
Martin, B. F.
Martin, Grace A.
Martin, Jennie
Martin, M.
Martin, Milton
Martin, Sam'l F.
Martin, Samuel
Martin, San
Martin, Smith K.
Martine, Josepina
Maru, Banri
Maru, Banryu
Maru, Chiri
Maru, Eihei
Maru, Genkai

Maru, Genko
Maru, Hakodadi
Maru, Hakuno
Maru, Hakuno
Maru, Heian
Maru, Hiroshima
Maru, Hiryu
Maru, Hoan
Maru, Jundo
Maru, Junsoku
Maru, Kagoshima
Maru, Kaimon
Maru, Kakumo
Maru, Kanrin
Maru, Kanyei
Maru, Keigaka
Maru, Kosuku
Maru, Kyorin
Maru, Manshu
Maru, Mikuni
Maru, Nagasaki
Maru, Nagoya
Maru, Nippon
Maru, Ooe (see Taiko Maru)
Maru, Otsucho
Maru, Raiden
Maru, Rihakuri
Maru, Saikio
Maru, Sawa
Maru, Sento
Maru, Setsu
Maru, Shinpu
Maru, Shoho
Maru, Shokaku
Maru, Sojun
Maru, Suminoye
Maru, Taian
Maru, Taihei
Maru, Taiho
Maru, Taiko
Maru, Takao
Maru, Tenshin
Maru, Tenyu
Maru, Tokei
Maru, Tokio
Maru, Yakumo
Maru, Yeiju
Maru, Yokohama
Maru, Yugao
Marvil, Sallie C.
Marvin, E. B.
Mary, James and
Mary, John and
Mary, Josephine and
Mary, Louisa
Mary, Queen
Mary, Saint

Mary, Sally and
Mary, Sarah
Mary, Sarah and
Mary, William & / and
Mary's, St.
Marys, St.
Marys, Three
Marzo, 5 de
Mason, Fanny
Mason, Governor
Massena, General
Matilda, Hannah
Matilda, Sarah
Matoika, Princess
Matthews, C. G.
Maury, James
Maximilian, Erherzog Ferdinand
Maxwell, John
May, Cape
May, Geneva
May, Ida
May, Isabel
May, Katherine
May, Lucy
May, Nannie
Mayo, 25 de [under Tw]
Mayo, Tres de
Mayo, Veinte (25) (or 20??)
McCaw, Georgiana
McClelland, Robert
McDonald, General
McDonnough, Commodore
McGaw, Helen
McGilvery, Clara E.
McGilvery, William
McGregor, Helen
McGregor, Jessie
McGuin, H.
McHenry, Fanny
McKay, Donald
McKee, J. W.
McKee, Jas.
McKenzie, Ann
McKim, Ann
McKim, John S.
McKinnon, Ellen J.
McLean, Lewis
McManus, John H.
McManus, Thomas
McNab, Sir Allan
McNeel, J. J.
McNeil, Alexander
McNeil, Collin C.
McNeil, Eliza
McNeil, J. J.
McNeil, Martha A.
McNeill, J. G.

McNichol, Lizzie B.
McPherson, Susan
McRae, Fanny
McRea, Colonel
Meade, General
Meade, Richard Kidder
Means, F. S.
Mears, Carrie
Medary, Milton B.
Melchers, Jan
Melville, Lucy
Mer, Fleur de la
Mercedes, Reina
Mercer, Margaret
Merchant, American
Merchant, Argo
Merchant, Eastern
Merchant, London
Merchant, Manchester
Merchant, Surat
Merchaunt, Royal
Merck, Ernst
Merida, City of
Meritt, Weston
Merril, Kate
Merrill, Ruth E.
Merriman, Thaddeus
Merritt, I. J.
Merritt, I. J., Jr.
Metcalf, B. D.
Metcalf, Thos. A.
Mexicano, Libertador
Mexico, New
Mezick, Lizzie
Mezzick, Lizzie
Michael, Great
Michael, Saint
Mick, Big
Middleton, Henry A.
Middleton, William H.
Mifflin, General
Miguel, San
Mildmay, H. B.
Mildred, Josie
Miller, Daniels S.
Miller, William
Mills, Egypt
Mills, Robert
Milton, Lady
Min, Lee
Mine, Lady
Minnie, Little
Minstrel, Wandering
Miramon, General
Mister, Fulton T.
Mister, Mamie
Mitchell, Christopher

Mitchell, William
Molley, Charming
Mobile, City of
Moines, Des
Molly, Hannah and
Monarch, Ocean
Money, William
Monreale, Citta de
Montebello, Le Duc de
Montez, Lola
Montgomery, J.
Montgomery, James
Monts, Sieur de
Moon, Eastern
Moon, Half
Moon, Ly-ee-
Moore, Blanche
Moore, John A.
Moore, Louisa
Moran, Alice M.
More, MacCallum
Morey, Frank A.
Morgan, Charles
Morgan, Charles W.
Morgan, Chas.
Morgan, Fort
Morning, Herald of the
Morrison, Louisa
Morse, Anna J.
Morse, Belle
Morse, C. W.
Morse, Clara
Morse, Elizabeth
Morse, H. F.
Morse, Harry
Morse, Lewellyn J.
Morse, Llewellyn J.
Morse, Richard
Morton, Charlie
Morton, Governor
Morton, J.
Morton, Maria
Mose, Uncle
Moses, H. V.
Moses, W. J.
Moses, W. V.
Mosketo, Little
Moulton, Governor A.
Moultrie, General
Mountain, White
Mowe, Nellie
Mowe, Robert
Mudgett, William
Muir, Carrie
Munroe, James
Munsie, Florence M.
Murdoch, Edgar W.

Muses, Temple of the
Mutine, La
Myers, R. L.

N

N., Charry
Nag, Bobtail
Nantes, City of
Nants, Medusa of
Napier, Robert
Naples, Bay of
Natchez, City of
Navigator, China
Nawman, Melvin R.
Neal, Belle S.
Neal, Harriet
Nelson, Dora
Nelson, Lord
Nelson, Metha
Nene, Rosita-y-
Neptune, Car of
Nevada, Sierra
Nevins, P. J.
Nevis, Mary
Nevsky, Alexander
New Bedford, City of
Newberry, Oliver
Newcastle, Duke of
Newland, J. B.
Newman, Sarah
News, Newport
Newson, James E.
Newton, Isaac
Newton, Thomas
New York, City of
Nicholas, Eunice
Nicholas, St.
Nichols, Lucy A.
Nickels, Lucy A.
Nickerson, Bertha D.
Nickerson, E.
Nickerson, Jessie
Nield, H. and [&] J.
Nigel, Empire
Nilo, Raton del
Ninfa, La
Noble, John
Noll, Old
Norcon, James
Norcross, Otis
Nord, Cap
Norte, Del
North, Isaac M.
Northcote, Charles
Northern, Great
Northrop, William H.

Northrup, William H.
Northumberland, Duke of
Norton, Ella
Norzagarey, Fernando de
Noyes, A. B
Nubiana, Iphigenia
Nuen, Yu
Nulton, Admiral
Nutt, Henry
Nye, Thomas
Nye, William C.
Nymph, Sea
Nyo, Ta Pang

O

O., Dorothy
Oak, Charter
Oak, Forest
Oak, Heart of
Oak, Live
Oak, Royal
Oakley, E. and I.
O'Brien, Edward
Obrig, Adolph
O'Bryan, Richard
Ocala, City of
Ocean, Eastern
Ocean, Pride of the
Odell, Benjamin B.
O'Donahue, James
Ogden, Francis B.
Ogden, Martha
Ogilvie, Nelly
Oglethorpe, General
O'Hara, Patrick J.
Ohio, State of
Oldenbarnevelt, Johan Van
Oliver, Flora L.
Oliver, Susie P.
Olivia, Mary
Olney, Stephen
Olvaerri, Jose
On, Hope
O'Neill, M.
Orange, City of
Orange, Prince of
Oranje, Prins van
Orcutt, H. Louis
Oregon, Belle of
Oregon, Star of
Orinoco, Guia de
Orleans, City of
Orleans, Maid of
Orleans, New
Orphan, Little
Orr, Geo. W.

Orr, George W.
Osborn, Jessie
Ostrander, Levi W.
Oswego, Charlotte of
Otis, Mary
Oughtred, Gallion
Owen, Elvira
Owen, John
Owens, Susan G.
Own, Mechanic's

P

P., Leda
Pablo, San
Pacific, Northern
Pacific, Queen of the
Packard, Benjamin F.
Packet, Baghdad
Packet, Boston
Packet, Carolina
Packet, East India
Packet, Halifax
Packet, Leith
Packet, Liverpool
Packet, London
Packet, Missionary
Packet, Mississippi
Packet, Norwich
Packet, Oahu
Packet, Orleans
Packet, Pennsylvania
Packet, Pitt
Paige, John D.
Paine, C. B.
Paine, Fannie
Paine, Fanny
Paix, La
Paix, Le
Palace, Crystal
Palaces, City of
Palmella, Conde de
Palmer, Augustus
Palmer, Baker
Palmer, Davis
Palmer, Dorothy
Palmer, Elizabeth
Palmer, Fannie
Palmer, Frank A.
Palmer, Fuller
Palmer, Harwood
Palmer, Jane
Palmer, Julia
Palmer, Marie
Palmer, Mary E.
Palmer, Maude
Palmer, N. B.

Palmer, Nathaniel T.
Palmer, Paul
Palmer, Prescott
Palmer, Rebecca
Palmer, Sarah E.
Palmer, Singleton
Palmer, W. B.
Palmer, William B.
Paloma, La
Palos, Cap
Panama, City of
Pang, Fei
Panza, Sancho
Pao, Hsin-
Papeete, City of
Para, City of
Pardee, Annie J.
Pareil, Sans
Paris, City of
Paris, Commerce de
Paris, Ville de
Park, Fairmount
Park, South
Parke, Joseph
Parker, Frances M.
Parker, Jane
Parker, John
Parker, Mary
Parker, Rob
Parkes, Sir Harry
Parkhill, General
Parks, Harvey A.
Parry, Ann
Parsons, J. S.
Parsons, Philio-
Partridge, A. H.
Partridge, G. M.
Pascagoula, City of
Pasha, Ali Saib
Pasha, Hassam
Pasha, Hassan
Pasha, Kyamil
Pasley, C. W.
Pasqual, San
Pastora, La Divina
Patrick, St.
Patrie, Amour de la
Patrie, L'Amour de la
Patten, George F.
Patten, Thomas
Patten, William
Paul, Albert F.
Paul, James W., Jr.
Paul, John
Paul, St.
Pauline, George and
Peabody, George

Peabody, Joseph
Peacock, Lovett
Peacock, William
Peake, Ora
Pearson, Juan F.
Peavy, General
Pecker, Olive
Pederson, Kate G.
Pedro, San
Peebles, County of
Peel, Sir Robert
Peel, Sir William
Peele, Helen
Peep, Bo
Peggy, Charming
Pegoud, Lieutenant
Peirce, M. Vivian
Peking, City of
Pelican, Gourde du
Pember, Ruth E.
Pender, Mary A.
Pendleton, Anna
Pendleton, Frank
Pendleton, James G.
Pendleton, Phineas
Pendleton, Wealthy
Penn, William
Pennell, Charles S.
Penrose, Thomas
Percy, Eleanor A.
Pere, Bon
Pere, De
Perkins, Albert
Perkins, Shaw
Perkins, T. H.
Perkins, Thomas H.
Perouse, La
Perry, A. W.
Perry, Annie C.
Perry, Commodore
Perry, Oliver Hazard
Peru, Star of
Peruana, Republica
Pery, A. W.
Peter, Saint
Peter, St.
Petersburg, City of
Petersburg, St.
Peterson, Annie M.
Petite Chance, La
Petrel, Storm
Petrel, Stormy
Pettigrew, Sarah E.
Pettit, C. W.
Phebe, Josie and
Phenix, Zowthe
Philip, King

Philips, George A.
Phillip, King
Phillips, Carrie E.
Phoenix, Golden
Phoenix, Young
Pickands, Major
Pickering, Arthur
Pierce, General Frank
Pierce, John
Pierce, M. Vivian
Pierce, President
Pierce, Silas O.
Pigeon, Cape Horn
Pigeon, Wild
Pike, General
Pike, Mary F.
Pike, S. W.
Pike, Zebulon M.
Pilar, Ma del
Pilot, Alcoa
Pilot, East
Pilot, Eastern
Pinckney, Cotesworth-
Pinckney, General C. C.
Pinckney, Gen'l C. C.
Pinckney, Harriet
Pine, Oregon
Ping, Mei
Pink, Paramour
Piper, Solomon
Pitts, B. D.
Planas, Manuelita
Planet, Eastern
Plant, Cotton
Pleasant, Mount
Plongeur, Le
Point, City
Point, Ravens
Point, West
Poland, Star of
Pole, North
Polk, General
Polk, President
Pollard, Willard A.
Pollock, George
Polly, Betsey &
Polly, Charming
Port, Pride of the
Portal, West
Porter, David
Porter, General
Porter, John
Porter, Robert
Porter, W. S.
Portland, City of
Portland, Duke of
Portogallo, Don Luigi Re di

Post, Duff
Potter, T. J.
Powell, Baden-
Powell, Mary
Powell, Thomas
Power, George H.
Powney, Cecil
Prat, Captain
Pratt, Julia E.
Preble, Commodore
Preble, Edward
Prence, Governor
Prescott, John B.
President, Illustrious
Price, Flora A.
Price, G. W.
Price, General
Price, Kate
Pride, Forest
Pride, Southern
Pride, Village
Priest, High
Prim, General
Prima, Riviera
Prince, Asturian
Prince, Black
Prince, Cyprian
Prince, Iron
Prince, Minas
Princess, Sea
Princess, Viking
Prindel, E. F.
Pringle, James R.
Pringle, Jas. R.
Prior, C. H.
Prior, W. H.
Prize, Essex
Profit, Good
Progress, Century of
Provincien, Verenigde
Pry, Paul
Pulsford, R.
Putnam, General

Q

Quayle, Margaret
Que, Hong
Queen, British
Queen, Delta
Queen, Eastern
Queen, Fairy
Queen, Fire
Queen, Island
Queen, Northern
Queen, Ocean
Queen, Pacific

Queen, River
Queen, Sea
Queen, Siren
Queen, Syren
Queen, Virgin
Queen, Wave
Quijote, Don
Quixote, Don

R

Racer, Young
Radich, Christian
Rahmn, J. C.
Ralph, William and
Ramsdell, Homer
Randall, Thomas L.
Randel, Justina
Randolph, John
Random, Roderick
Ranger, Gulf
Ranger, Pacific
Ranger, Sea
Ranger, Texas
Rankin, Robert
Ravenel, John
Rawding, Herbert L.
Raynes, George
Read, Caroline
Read, Charlotte
Ready, Rough And
Rebecca, Jane
Rebecca, L.
Rebel, Little
Recontre, Heureuse
Redfield, William C.
Rediva, Washington
Reed. Elias
Reed, Carrie
Reed, Edwin
Reed, J. C.
Reed, William M.
Reefer, Chilean
Reeve, Josiah M.
Reeves, B. F.
Reeves, Dorothea
Regent, Prince
Regente, Reina
Reichert, Elsie M.
Reid, Aaron L.
Rencontre, Heureuse
Renfrew, Baron of
Rensselaer, Van
Republic, Great
Republic, Southern
Republic, Young
Republicaine, La

Reserve, Western
Resort, Last
Return, Happy
Reuben, Annie &
Revenge, Chesapeake's
Rey, Castel del
Reyes, Francisco
Reynolds, Marcia
Rhino, Ready
Rica, Costa
Rice, Charles G.
Rice, Emery
Rice, R. D.
Rich, Lathley-
Rich, Lilly
Richard, Bon Homme
Richard, Bonhomme
Richard, Dean
Richards, Jessie
Richardson, H. L.
Richardson, Henry L.
Richmond, City of
Richmond, Dean
Richmond, L. C.
Rickmers, Maria
Rickmers, Peter
Rickmers, R. C.
Ridgeway, Sarah S.
Ridgway, Jacob E.
Riggin, Addie S.
Riggs, Wm. M.
Rights, Southern
Ring, Andrew
Ring, Blanche
Ring, C. W.
Ring, Lucy
Rio, Pinar del
Rio de Janeiro, City of
Rip, Let Her
Ripley, General
Rita, Santa
Ritchie, Elliott
Ritchie, J. C.
Rivaux, Grandes
River, Black
River, Columbia
River, Indian
River, North
River, Salmon
Rivera, General
Rivers, D. H.
Rémy, Capitaine
Roach, William
Roan, Charles H.
Roanoke, Port
Robb, Arthur C.
Robb, John A.

Robbins, Jolly
Robert, Joseph and
Roberts, Mary Belle
Roberts, Thelma
Robertson, Samuel
Robin, Cock
Robin, Jolly
Robinson, Almira
Robinson, Chief Jusice
Roca, Cabo da
Roch, St.
Rock, Gun
Rock, Plymouth
Rockefeller, Frank
Rockefeller, William
Rocket, Fire
Rockland, City of
Rod, Golden
Rodney, Lord
Roger, J. C.
Rogers, William B.
Roison, Commandant
Roker, J. C.
Roman, San
Romer, William F.
Ronterean, C.
Rookh, Lalla
Roosevelt, Theodore
Ropes, A. G.
Ropes, Charles A.
Ropes, Sarah C.
Rosa, Josephine
Rosa, La
Rosa, Santa
Rose, Commandant de
Rose, Friendship
Rose, Lena
Rose, Mary
Rose, Sallie
Ross, Annie C.
Ross, Betsey
Ross, John A.
Ross, William
Rotch, William
Routereau, C.
Rover, Ocean
Rover, Red
Rover, Wild
Rowe, Levi
Rowland, Mary A.
Roy, Edward
Roy, Rob
Roya, Eusebia N.
Royal, Fort
Royal, Port
Royal, Princess
Royal, Soleil

Royale, La
Royall, Port
Royce, Alice
Roye, E. J.
Rozer, J. C.
Rule, Golden
Rush, General
Rusk, General
Russell, Albert
Russell, Benjamin
Russell, Charles
Russell, H. P.
Russell, Mary
Russell, Samuel
Russell, Thomas
Russia, Star of
Russie, Emma D.
Ruth, Joseph and
Rutter, Evelina
Ryan, Ann
Ryan, Harriet
Ryan, Harriet P.
Ryarson, Addie
Rydberg, Abraham
Ryerson, John H.

S

S., Cordie
S., Gracie
S., Maud
Sabel, Jack
Sachem, Grand
Sahib, Tippoo
Sailor, Eastern
Saint John, City of
Sally, Charming
Sally, Hannah and
Sally, Nancy and
Sally, William and
Salvador, Sam
Salvador, San
Sam, Uncle
Sampson, Kitty
Samuel, Edwin and
San Antonio, City of
Sanders, P. A.
Sanford, Carrie
Sanford, Menemon
San Francisco, City of
Santa Maria, Domingo
Santiago, City of
Sarah, Ann and
Sarah, Harriet and
Sarah, Little
Sargent, C. F.
Sargent, D.

Sark, Cutty
Sauvage, Belle
Savage, Royal
Savannah, City of
Savoia, Conte di
Savoie, La
Saxon, Anglo-
Saylor, David O.
Scaife, Mary
Scammel, J. H.
Scarborough, Countess of
Scheer, Admiral
Schmidt, Anna F.
Schnauer, Ida
Schroder, William
Schuyler, General
Scolfield, Sam
Scotia, Little
Scotia, Nova
Scotland, Star of
Scott, General
Scott, John
Scott, Margaret
Scott, Winfield
Scud, Flying
Södermanland, Hertiginnan af
Se, Quong
Sea, Gem of the
Sea, Polar
Sea, Rolling
Seabrook, William
Seabrook, Wm.
Sealing, Jenny
Sears, Charles E.
Sears, Ellen
Seas, Champion of the
Seas, Empress of the
Seas, Glory of the
Seas, Sovereign of the
Seattle, City of
Seaver, S. W.
Sebastian de Elcano, Juan
Second, Frederick the
Seen, Fei
Segunda, Isabella
Seine, La
Sen, Yat
Serpent, Flying
Serpent, Sea
Serret, Général / General
Service, United
Sewall, Benjamin
Sewall, Edward
Sewell, Arthur
Shan, Kin
Shandy, Tristram
Shannon, G. D. and R. F.

Shanter, Tam O'
Shattuck, George
Shaw, Robert G.
Sheba, Queen of
Shelton, A. C.
Shepard, Anna
Shepherd, R. D.
Sherbrooke, Lady
Sherman, Forrest
Sherman, General
Sherman, General H. M.
Sherman, J. T.
Sherman, R. W.
Sherman, Zaccheus
Shetland, Star of
Shore, Eastern
Shoreham, New
Shores, E. A., Jr.
Shrub, Winter
Shuey, Foong
Shuey, Fung
Shun, Paou
Sibley, Amory
Sidney, Sir
Siegel, General
Sierra, Io
Silsbee, Elizabeth
Simonds, General George S.
Sims, Rebecca
Sinclair, H. C.
Sisters, Three
Sisters, Twin
Sisters, Two
Skinner, Fanny
Skofield, I. L.
Skolfield, Fannie
Skolfield, I. L.
Slade, R. C.
Slater, Willis A.
Slick, Sam
Sloat, George W.
Slocum, General
Slope, Pacific
Small, Juliet
Small, Vinnie
Smalley, Emma K.
Smeaton, John
Smith, Alba
Smith, Anna
Smith, Annie H.
Smith, Edward R.
Smith, Eugenie
Smith, Florence M.
Smith, Helen
Smith, Isaac
Smith, Isaac P.
Smith, Jonas

Smith, Kate
Smith, Margie
Smith, Marshall J.
Smith, Samuel
Smith, William H.
Smith, Willy
Smoot, G. H.
Smull, Annie M.
Smyser, Cora
Smythe, Charles I.
Snake, Black
Snare, Maud
Snipe, Empire
Snow, Alfred D.
Snow, Augusta W.
Snow, Dorothy G.
Sol, El
Somereulas, Marquis de
Somers, Roy
Somerulas, Marquis de
Somerville, Gertrude A.
Somerville, J. W.
Somerville, Jean L.
Sommerville, J. W.
Sonachon, Port
Sons, Four
Sonyrk, A. E.
Soo, Kiang
Sophia, Anna
Sophia, Betsey and
Sophia, La
Sorley, Mary
Sorly, Mary
Soto, De
Souder, Emily B.
Soule, C. H.
South, Star of the
South, Sunny
Southard, Ellen
Southard, Olive S.
Southerner, The
Sovereign, Royal
Spafford, J. B.
Sparks, Sarah D.
Spear, Myra D.
Spearing, H. E.
Spears, Albert T.
Spedden, Captain / Capt.
Spee, Graf
Spencer, J. J.
Spit, York
Sprague, Phineas W.
Sprague, Seth
Sprague, Wm.
Spray, Northern
Spray, Silver
Spring, Mountain

Spring, Silver
Spur, Flying
Squall, Black
Squall, White
St. Helens, City of
St. Johns, Queen of
St. Pierre, Emily
Standish, Rose
Stanley, Edward D.
Stanley, Henry M.
Stanley, Norris
Stanley, Port
Staple, Short
Staples, Mary E.
Staples, Nellie
Star, Bahama
Star, Evening
Star, Guiding
Star, Lone
Star, Morning
Star, North
Star, Northern
Star, Ocean
Star, Panama
Star, Polar
Star, Rising
Star, Shooting
Star, Southen
Star, Union
Star, White
Starr, Emily C.
Starr, M. A.
Starr, Sarah
State, Bay
State, Buckeye
State, Creole
State, Eastern
State, Empire
State, Forest
State, Golden
State, Granite
State, Hawkeye
State, Hoosier
State, Keystone
State, Old North
State, Palmetto
State, Pelican
State, Wolverine
States, Confederate
States, Rising
States, United
Steam Boat, North River
Steed, Ocean
Step, Two
Stephens, John L.
Sterling, E. R.
Sterling, Lady

Stetson, Nahum
Steuben, Von
Stevens, E. A.
Stevens, Jesse
Stevens, M. A.
Stevens, Margaret A.
Stevens, Robert L.
Stewart, Edward
Stewart, Ellen
Stewart, Mary
Stewart, Reine Marie
Stewart, Thomas J.
Stille, J. G.
Stille, L. B.
Stockton, Mary
Stockton, Robert F.
Stone, James S.
Stoney, H. I.
Stoney, H. P.
Stoney, Theodore
Storer, Mary
Stratton, Charles C.
Stream, Gulf
Street, W. E.
Strickland, Genevieve
Stripes, Stars and
Strong, Governor
Stroup, John
Stuart, Mary
Stubbs, Abbie C.
Sturges, L. L.
Sturgis, Susan
Stuyvesant, Peter
Su, Kwang
Succession, Present
Sudden, Catherine
Suey, Foong
Sugg, Tom
Sullivan, Maggie
Sullivan, Senator
Sumner, Maynard
Sumpter, General
Sumter, General
Sun, Fei
Sun, Rising
Surprise, General
Susan, Ann and
Susan, Doris
Susan, Mary and
Sussex, Duke of
Sutherland, Sophia
Sutton, William
Swaim, J. D.
Swan, Black
Swan, Edward L.
Swanton, Kate
Swasey, John

Swift, Elizabeth
Swift, Ellen A.
Swift, Jireh
Sword, Eastern
Sword, Victory
Sydney, City of

T

T., Nellie
Taft, President
Talbot, Arthur Newell
Tan, Mei
Tapley, Hattie E.
Tar, Royal
Tarbox, Nellie
Tarr, Gardner W.
Tartar, American
T(asmania), Great
Tau, Tsing-
Taylor, Anna
Taylor, Annie
Taylor, Emily
Taylor, G.
Taylor, General
Taylor, John A.
Taylor, Lizzie
Taylor, Mary
Taylor, Moses
Taylor, Nathaniel
Taylor, W. F. P.
Taylor, W. & P.
Teagle, C. W.
Tell, Never
Tempest, Eastern
Temple, Eastern
Temple, Flora
Tenbrook, E.
Terbell, Mary C.
Teresa, Juana
Teresa, Maria
Teresa, Mary
Terlines, Aviator de
Texaco V., Port
Thacher, Edwin
Thames, Sons of the
Thayer, Bethiah / Bethia
Thayer, C. A.
Thayer, Frank N.
Thebaud, Gertrude L.
Theodosius, St.
Theresa, Maria
Theriault, E. P.
Thomas, Helen B.
Thomas, Joseph B.
Thomas, Katie
Thomas, Ruther A.

Thomas, St.
Thomas, Washington B.
Thompson, A. W.
Thompson, Anna
Thompson, Annie
Thompson, Benjamin
Thompson, Charles
Thompson, E. F.
Thompson, General Jeff
Thompson, J. A.
Thompson, Jeremiah
Thompson, John
Thompson, Levant
Thompson, Lucy
Thompson, Mary E.
Thompson, Sheldon
Thompson, William
Thornton, Sophia
Throop, Margaret
Thumb, Tom
Tibbals, H. L.
Tidings, Glad
Tiki, Kon
Tiki, Kon-
Tilden, Nina
Tilley, Governor
Tittamer, William
Tobey, Uncle
Todd, Georgia
Todd, J. M.
Tokio, City of
Tokyo, Esso
Tolles, Lizzie A.
Tom, Sir
Ton, Jose
Toone, Jos. H.
Toone, Joseph H.
Top, Tip
Topeka, City of
Toporo, Tiara
Toronto, Charlotte of
Toronto, City of
Torre, Ida Della
Torrey, Annie
Torrey, David
Totten, A. C.
Totten, Wm.
Toucey, Isaac
Townsend, Adeline
Townsend, Charles
Townsend, Daniel
Townsend, J. W.
Townsend, Smith
Trade, Free
Trader, Eastern
Trader, Eastern
Trader, Pacific

Trader, Western
Trafalgar, Cap
Train, Enoch
Transport, Roche Harbor Lime
Travers, Henry
Traviata, La
Treat, Florence
Tremper, Jacob H.
Trial, Last
Triplett, W. S.
Triumph, Wallace
Troop, Nellie
Trowbridge, C. C.
Troy, City of
Trufant, G. C.
Trundy, Gertrude L.
Tryggvason, Olaf
Tuck, Nip and
Tucker, Benjamin
Tucker, Genevie M.
Tucker, R. H.
Tudor, Frederick
Tuen, Chen
Turk, Grand
Tuttle, Emma

U

Ulloa, Don Antonio de
Union, American
Union, Industrious
Upton, George B.
Urrea, General
Usher, Julia
Usher, Julie
Utter, Emma

V

Vail, Walter
Valentine, A. B.
Valley, Assam
Vallier, St.
Valparaiso, City of
Van, Lady
van Breda, Hof
Vance, A. D.
Vance, Ad-
Vance, James M.
Vance, Zebulon B.
Vanderbilt, C.
Van Dorn, General Earl
van Oldenbarnevelt, Johan
Varela, Pedro
Varella, Pedro
Vaudreuil, La Marquise de
Vendemiaire, Onze

Vengeance, L'/ La / Le
Vera, Clarissa
Verdade, Flor da
Verden, Annie
Veritas, Norske
Vermilyea, R. H.
Vernon, Mount
Vernon, Mt.
Vert, Cap
Viage, El Virgin del Rosario y El Sancto Christo de Buen
Vibbard, Chauncey
Vicar's, Captain
Vicat, L. J.
Viceroy, British
Vickery, Charles
Vicksburg, City of
Victoria, Queen
Victoria, Royal
Victoria Luise, Prinzessen
Victory, Elko
Victory, Little
Vidal, Emile N.
View, A. J.
View, Ocean
Viglance, British
Villard, Henry
Vincent, Cap
Vincent, Edward
Vincent, H. E.
Vinnen, Adolf
Vinnen, Arnoldus
Vinner, Werner
Virgen del Rosario..., El
Virgin, Laura
Virginia, Caroline
Virginia, Mary
Visitor, Eastern
Vista, Buena
Vivian, Alice
Von Beer, G. F.
von Höpken, Baron And.

W

W., Carrie
W., Esther
Waco, City of
Wade, John
Wagner, T. D.
Wah, Tah
Wah, Tah-
Wainwright, J. C.
Waldemar, Prinz
Wales, Prince of
Walk, Cock of the
Walker, Abbie S.

Walker, Ann
Walker, Bertha A.
Walker, Elisha
Walker, Jennie
Walker, Joseph
Walla, Rajah
Wallace, Sir William
Wallis, P. C.
Walls, Berwick
Waln, S. Morris
Walnut, Black
Walsh, L.
Walter, Ellwood
Walters, E. B.
Wan, Fei-
Wan, Fi
Wan, Tahn
Wan, Tai-
Wan, Toey-
Wands, Gertrude
War, Fortune of
Ward, Aaron
Ward, Agnes H.
Ward, Flaurence E.
Ward, General
Ward, Joanna
Ward, Julia A.
Warfield, President
Waring, Lucy R.
Warley, Ella
Warner, D. B.
Warner, G. S.
Warner, Joseph
Warner, Rawleigh
Warren, Charles A.
Warren, Fred
Warren, General
Warren, George H.
Warren, Harry
Warren, Henry
Warren, Lillian M.
Warren, Lottie
Warren, Mary
Warrick, Eliza
Warrior, Black
Warwick, Constant
Warwick, Eliza
Warwick, Peter C.
Washington, General
Washington, Geo.
Washington, George
Washington, Lady
Washington, Mount
Washington, President
Wason, Leonard Chase
Wasson, Nancy L.
Water, Leaping

Water, Walk-in-the-
Waterbury, Charles W.
Waterman, E. J.
Waters, Henry
Waters, Toubled
Watson, Brook
Watson, Thomas
Watson, Thos.
Watt, James
Watt, Robert
Watts, John
Watts, Samuel
Wave, Dashing
Wave, Northern
Wave, Ocean
Wave, Queen of the
Wave, Silver
Wave, Tidal
Wave, Witch of the
Wayne, Clifford
Wayne, General
Webb, Eckford
Webb, W. H.
Webb, William H.
Weber, Senator
Webster, Daniel
Webster, J. O.
Webster, Robert L.
Wedel, Minister
Weeks, G. S.
Welch, Andrew
Welch, John
Wellesley, General
Wells, George W.
Wells, John W.
Welsh, J.
Wenlock, Lord
Wentworth, Alice C.
Wentworth, Alice S.
Wesley, John
Wesley, William
West, Belle of the
West, Edward R.
West, Far
West, Golden
West, John P.
West, Key
West, North
West, Northern
West, Queen of the
West, Star of the
Western, Great
Western, Little
Weston, Lizzie
Wetmore, C. W.
Wetmore, Charles W.
Wheeler, Dunham

Wheeler, J. P.
Wheeler, Moses
Wheeler, S. B.
Whidbee, James P.
Whitcomb, Lot
White, C. A.
White, Emma
White, Martin
White, Matt
White, William L.
Whiteman, Lewis
Whiting, General
Whitmore, A. J.
Whitmore, Colonel J.
Whitmore, Martha
Whitney, Emily F.
Whitney, General
Whitney, Henrietta A.
Whitney, Henry A.
Whitney, Stephen
Whittier, Helen
Whittier, Mary E.
Whitting, Catherine
Whiz, Gee
Wight, Isle of
Wilberforce, William
Wilbur, Charles E.
Wilcox, William
Wilder, J. W.
Wilder, John R.
Wilhelm, Kronprinz
Wilhelm der Grosse, Kaiser
Wilhelmine, Johanna
Will, Father's Good
Willey, Ella M.
Willey, Lizzie B.
William, Prince
William, Richard
William, Royal
William, Young
William Henry, Prince
Williams, C. E.
Williams, Daniel S., Jr.
Williams, General
Williams, H. M.
Williams, Hezekiah
Williams, James
Williams, John
Williams, John S.
Williams, O. C.
Williams, S. M.
Willing, H. F.
Willis, Albert H.
Willis, Ben
Willis, Major E.
Wills, John
Wills, Lucy S.
Wilson, Ann
Wilson, Charles R.
Wilson, G. Hunt
Wilson, President
Wilson, William
Wind, East
Wind, Fair
Wind, Leading
Wind, North
Wind, Northern
Wind, West
Wing, J. T.
Wing, White
Winslow, Edward B.
Winslow, Jacob S.
Winter, Herman
Winthrop, John and
Wirt, William
Wish, Sheep
Wisp, Will O' the
Wisp, Will o' (the)
Witch, Iron
Witch, Sea
Witch, Water
Witherle, William
Wollaston, Mount
Wollaston, Mt.
Wolseley, Lord
Wood, Belleau
Wood, Daniel
Wood, J. Chester
Wood, Lady Mary
Wood, Mary
Woodside, B. R.
Worcester, City of
Worden, Julia
World, New
World, Western
Worth, General
Wragg, Thomas L.
Wragg, Thos. L.
Wright, Isaak
Wright, John T.
Wright, Mary
Wright, Silas
Wright, W. H. D. C.
Wyman, Lizzie

X

Xmas, Fancy
XV, Louis

Y

Yacht, Royal
Yak, Shna
Yarnall, Francis C.
Yarrow, Flower of
Year, New
Yi, Mei
Ying, Mei
York, City of New
York, Duke of
York, New
Young, Mei
Young, Muriel M.
Young, Stephen
Youth, Blooming
Yuen, Chen
Yuen, Chih
Yuen, Ching
Yuen, Fee
Yuen, Ting
Yun, Mei
Yun, Pak
Yung, Ta

Z

Z., A.
Zane, Ethel
Zealand, New
Zealand, Star of
Zwicker, E. F.

VOLUME I   JANUARY 1941   NUMBER 1

THE AMERICAN NEPTUNE is a quarterly journal devoted to the many aspects of marine research. The field of action will include the Americas, North and South, and the journal, although published in the United States, will include, in so far as possible, studies of the maritime history of Canada and Hispanic America. It will combine many phases of activity and several related, although somewhat divergent fields of interest. These will include:

1. *Technical nautical and marine historical research.*
   Articles dealing with the design, construction, and operation of various types of vessels at different periods.

2. *General historical articles.*
   Articles dealing with the activities of merchants and shipping lines; histories of individual vessels and voyages; studies of ports; naval, privateering, steamship, and yachting history.

3. *History of scientific navigation.*
   Articles dealing with the development of the science of navigation, nautical instruments, charts, and maps.

4. *Sea lore.*
   Eye-witness accounts and memoirs dealing with marine activities in various regions; examples of sea lore, chanteys, etc. may be included from time to time.

5. *Biography.*
   Biographical sketches of shipmasters, merchants, and ship builders will be included where the subjects were of significance in the maritime history of their region. Genealogical accounts and works of local piety will be avoided.

6. *Marine art.*
   Articles on marine painting, prints, shipcarving, and the historic decoration of watercraft.

7. *Documents.*
   Significant unpublished manuscripts, reprints of very rare tracts, and reproductions of contemporary photographs of sailing vessels and early steamships.

8. *Ship models.*
   Accounts of collections of historical models. Data including plans for the construction of models. Sets of plans of highest possible historical and technical accuracy will be frequently included. The emphasis in this section will be upon *what* to build rather than *how* to built it.

9. *Marine museums.*
   Articles dealing with the collections and activities of various marine museums, and accounts of the marine possessions of institutions primarily devoted to other purposes.

10. *Bibliography.*
    Reviews, listings, and notes on old and new maritime books. Contributions toward an annual bibliography of significant articles appearing in serial publications.

11. *Notes and queries.*
    A section, containing notes of general interest, requests for information, and replies whenever possible, will be included in each issue. Subscribers are urged to forward notes and queries.

The conduct of the journal, the editorial policy in general, and the acceptance and rejection of articles submitted for publication rest in the hands of five Editors, assisted by an Editorial Advisory Board, which includes representatives of regions and institutions and specialists in various fields of maritime history. The Editors and members of the Advisory Board serve without compensation and undertake to divide the work among themselves to the best of their ability. The Editors of THE AMERICAN NEPTUNE hope to achieve a balance between accurate technical articles and readable general articles without undue emphasis upon either. They will endeavor to maintain the highest possible standards of accuracy and style, but will endeavor with equal purpose to keep the journal from becoming dull. Each number will contain articles in a number of the fields mentioned, and no number will become clogged with tables of figures. Care will be taken to insure against undue emphasis upon any particular region. While accepting editorial responsibility, the Editors do not necessarily accept or endorse the opinions expressed by the